*P*erspectives
Turning Reading
into Writing

*P*erspectives
Turning Reading into Writing

▶ ————————————————

Joseph J. Comprone

UNIVERSITY OF LOUISVILLE

Houghton Mifflin Company   *Boston*

DALLAS   GENEVA, ILLINOIS
LAWRENCEVILLE, NEW JERSEY   PALO ALTO

For Connie and J. Oliver,
who were always there when I needed them

Cover Illustration by Richard Anuszkiewicz. *Vol. I.* 1965. Synthetic polymer, 84″ × 84″. Hirshhorn Museum and Sculpture Garden, Smithsonian Institution.

Acknowledgments begin on page 937.

Printed in the U.S.A.

Library of Congress Catalog Card Number: 86-81508

ISBN: 0-395-34934-6

ABCDEFGHIJ-MP-89876

Contents

▶ ──────────────

In What Should We Believe?   183

What Do the Arts Tell Us About Ourselves?   *253*

How Does Language Define Our Identities?   *383*

What Does It Mean To Be a Woman?   *497*

In What Ways Must We Change?   *573*

How Should We Use Power?   *641*

What Does It Mean To Be Independent?   *743*

Is Education What It Should Be?   825

Preface

▶ ────────────────────

Learning to read and write well is not an end in itself, but part of a larger enterprise, the general education of students. More than simply a reader for freshman writing classes, *Perspectives* strives to make reading and writing the center of students' general education by promoting five particular kinds of interaction that will start them off on a lifetime habit of knowing and thinking through reading and writing.

Perspectives begins by promoting thematic interaction. Students need interesting and rich topics to encourage their writing. Each of the ten sections of this text includes six to eight essays that introduce students to selections by writers in a variety of fields, including the social sciences, the humanities, and the natural sciences. A small number of short stories and poems are also mixed in. But as important as the themes themselves is the method used to introduce them. Each section opens with questions that the apparatus and essays help students to explore. The approach is inductive, encouraging students to discover a theme and the issues that surround it as they read, write, and think about the section's thematic question. With this approach, theme becomes a way of introducing students to intellectual life and becomes an integral part of their general education.

This book also promotes the interaction of reading and writing. Professional writers write because they read, read because they write. Reading what others say about a theme is the writer's link with the audience. *Perspectives* encourages students to ask questions about their reading, to write as they read, and to read and reread as they write. Section introductions introduce themes, reading selections, and questions; headnotes to reading selections give students information about the background of authors and about writing strategies in relation to theme; questions on comprehension, rhetorical purpose and strategy, and theme, as well as the learning activities, help students connect each reading to others and to particular treatments of theme. Writing assignments at the end of sections guide students in bringing their thematic ideas together in essays of their own.

Perspectives further fosters active learning through apparatus that encourages students to make their own connections, find their own answers, and ask their own questions in response to what they read. It also provides essays that students can use to direct their own inquiry. Students learn to inquire by seeing how other learners and thinkers inquire, and by using those methods as they themselves inquire.

The organization of *Perspectives* also engages students in a cumulative learning experience. Students can read several or all of the essays represented in a section. The book's apparatus encourages them to build their responses to specific issues into more comprehensive thematic topics, culminating in the more general approaches to theme that are included in each writing assignment. Small questions get small answers, which turn into larger questions and more comprehensive answers.

Finally, *Perspectives* presents rhetorical principles in context, rather than in the abstract. Students learn to organize ideas by finding and using rhetorical strategies as they read and write, rather than by reading abstract definitions and applying them in artificial and mechanical ways. Thematic content, in other words, governs rhetorical choice, just as ideas will govern forms of writing in students' later writing.

In addition, *Perspectives* includes two appendices as further resources for students. A glossary provides functional definitions of rhetorical terms that appear in the book's apparatus. This glossary adds a rhetorical dimension to the book's thematic approach. ''Keeping a Journal'' explains the function and process of keeping a journal in a writing course. This appendix expands on the book's treatment of personal writing as a means for students to develop public writing skills by connecting their personal responses to readings to classroom discussions of theme and to other writers' treatments of those themes.

Books are collective efforts. Those who provided indispensable help to me as I wrote this book include Virginia Callan, who word-processed my drafts and gave me invaluable editorial help as well; Sharon Mitchell, who typed some of the supplementary materials and whose daily secretarial help is also invaluable; and Connie Comprone, whose encouragement and advice kept me going when I might have quit. Kate Ronald of the University of Nebraska gave me sound advice in numerous discussions of teaching and writing, some directly related to this book, some simply to our roles as fellow professionals. Most of my gratitude must go to my students—graduate students past and present who have joined with me in figuring out ways to teach and undergraduates who have tried to learn in my classes. These people made the cliché that teachers learn more from their students than students from their teachers into a reality for me.

I wish also to thank the following teachers at colleges and universities across the country who reviewed this book and helped me to see different perspectives when I was locked into my own ways of seeing: Katherine H. Adams, University of Tennessee; Martin L. Bond, Delta State University; Virginia Spencer Carr, Georgia State University; Dennis Gartner, Frostburg State College; Brooke Horvath, Purdue University; Elizabeth Kiszley, University of Wisconsin–Milwaukee; Nancy M. Lowe, Pennsylvania State University; Thomas E. Martinez, Villanova University; David Peck, California State University, Long Beach; James A. Preston, Jr., Miami–Dade University–South; Honora Rankine-Galloway, C. W. Post College, Long Island University; James C. Raymond, University of Alabama; John E. Ruden, Sacramento City College; Carol J. Singley, Brown University; John Trimbur, Boston University; Suzanne S. Webb, Texas Woman's University; Clifford Wood, University of Wisconsin–Oshkosh; William F. Woods, Wichita State University; Nancy T. Zuercher, University of South Dakota.

J.J.C.

General Introduction to Perspectives

▶ ────────────

Perspectives contains sixty-eight writings by accomplished writers in a variety of fields. Some of the writers are journalists and popular essayists who describe and explain their experiences and observations of events. Some are active workers in various fields who wish to change the attitudes of readers concerning their work. Others are critics and experts in a particular area who use their skills to interpret and evaluate current events or issues. And still others render their themes in poetry or fiction that enables readers to interpret a theme from within a complex, literary situation. Different purposes and styles aside, all these writers have in common an ability to use writing first to discover ideas and then to communicate them to readers.

Along with the reading selections, *Perspectives* contains useful directions for reading, analyzing, and writing about the selections. Each of the ten sections is organized around a theme question. The theme question will help you focus your reading around a common set of related ideas, and it will help you and your classmates develop common points of discussion.

As you read some or all of the selections in a particular section, you will also share with your teacher and classmates an introduction to the theme of the section, brief headnotes on each author and selection that you read, and a set of questions and activities that you and your class can work through after reading each selection. These materials will help you think about the section's theme as you read, and they will help you develop ideas for discussion and writing.

Each section closes with longer writing assignments. Each set of final assignments contains two options: the first asks you to respond in any form you choose to a particular aspect of the section's theme; the second option provides a fuller context for the assignment, defining some of the content for and definitions of the audience and purpose of the assignment. In every section, these final writing assignments encourage you to integrate your reading of and thinking about several of the selections into an essay that responds to the theme question of the section.

Writing, Reading, and the Idea of Community

By using reading and writing to develop themes, you will learn to turn effective reading into effective writing. Themes, as they are presented in this book, are important because they help you define a community of readers. The shared interests and conventions of a community of readers become the general context within which an individual writes. By working through a cluster of readings with a teacher and class you, like most professional writers, will define a community of readers and writers who will serve as your audience as you write final drafts of essays. This sense of audience will help you decide what readers need —how information should be arranged and expressed, when an idea needs to be illustrated by an example, or when one idea needs to be more directly related to another.

All writers belong to a variety of communities. Some are biologists who write for other biologists, for scientists in general, or for popular audiences. Others are sportswriters who write for fans or for a general audience interested in a broader, cultural interpretation of sports. As professional writers address one community or another, they must adapt their writing to meet the needs of different audiences. They must consider what they know or need to know about their subject and what their readers may or may not need to know about that subject. They must be able, in other words, to "read" the communities for whom they write, as well as being able to read the works of other writers. Learning to read communities begins with analyses of other writers' thinking and writing strategies as they address different communities. Your critical reading of the pieces in this book will help you to imagine your readers and will prepare you to translate that reading into strategies for writing.

Writing as Learning and Communication

Writing, along with reading, is a means of developing personal responses to general subjects. For most professional writers, writing serves a wide variety of purposes. A writer often writes business letters to solicit support for a project, to investigate a problem or subject, or to sell a manuscript. Many writers take notes as they explore a subject or as they attempt to learn a new skill or subject, or they keep a journal or diary of experiences that they may write about later. Many academic writers take notes while they observe, read about, and analyze the subject about which they are writing. In other words, experienced writers engage in many kinds of writing, only some of which is intended to be published and read by a critical audience. This book will encourage you to engage in similar kinds of practice writing as you develop your ideas.

Every reading selection in this book is followed by a set of four types of questions and activities. Each set guides you in examining different aspects of the selection it follows. The first set, "Comprehension Questions," will help you attend closely to the content and structure of the selection—to what was said and where, to how the writer has presented ideas, facts, examples, and illustrations. The second set, "Questions of Rhetorical Purpose and Strategy," will help you analyze the author's writing strategies—how he or she addresses and engages readers and develops a purpose or intention. The third set, "Theme Questions," will help you transform your reactions to a selection into a personal perspective on the theme of the section. The fourth set, "Learning Activities," consists of oral and written activities that will help you shape your responses to the selection and experiment with writing strategies; this material will often be useful when you do the longer writing assignments at the end of a section.

This book, then, is based on the idea that we all learn to write by first reading and then thinking and writing about what we have read. And it assumes as well that we learn to read and write by practicing those skills in a classroom, which is like the community faced by professional writers, in which ideas are read, written about, and reacted to by the members.

What Is the Place
of Recreation
in Our Lives?

▶ ————————————————

Introduction

▶ ──────────────

The readings in this section provide a variety of perspectives on the theme of recreation. Some of the writers examine very personal activities: Robert Finch, a naturalist, spends even his free time observing the natural world; May Sarton, a writer, finds dramatic feeling and pleasure in the seemingly everyday sights and activities of a visit to a friend; Ellen Goodman, a journalist, thinks about the different but necessary worlds of leisure and work. Roger Kahn and Red Smith, both eminent sports writers, look at the economic and political issues that exist in professional and international sports. Pauline Kael, a noted movie reviewer, examines a recent film and provides critical and social commentary on its entertainment value. Irwin Shaw tells the story of a man for whom a past "high point" of athletic glory has tragically dominated his emotional, psychological, and professional development.

We often associate leisure time with escape — freedom from the demands and pressures of our workaday lives. Ellen Goodman describes her vacation as "doing nothing . . . letting go, being at ease with time" and compares it to the "purpose and structure and struggle" of her work life. Enroute from her rural vacation, she examines the nature of her leisure time and the "duality" between relaxation and accomplishment and seeks to understand the necessary balance they create in her life and, by extension, in the lives of her readers. Each writer in this section, by describing his or her leisure time or by examining forms of recreation, explores the nature and value of such activities. Robert Finch and May Sarton, both lovers of the New England landscape, describe the pleasure and meaning they find in roaming in nature. In their descriptions of leisure time, neither Finch nor Sarton makes a sharp distinction between work and recreation; rather, they seem to maintain that one enhances and enriches the other.

Several of the writers remind us that what may be our spectator entertainment — going to the movies or watching sports — is others' work, whether as participants in or writers about such events. In reviewing the recent popular movie, *White Nights,* Pauline Kael assesses how the quality of certain actors and dancers struggles against the stagnant limitations of a "transparently opportunistic" Cold War plot. She obviously believes that entertainment need not exclude or insult "our intelligence," but rather can and should engage it. And Red Smith and Roger Kahn take their sports-fan readers out of the bleachers and show them the inside politics and economics of sports. Smith nowhere discusses the sports or athletes of the 1980 Olympic Games but calls on his readers to support an American boycott of this "carnival of nationalism." Kahn, however, looks at professional sports through the difficult and failed career of one athlete, the baseball player Carl Furillo. He explores how and why this "indomitable centurion" who "played with dedication and...played in pain and...was awesome in his strength and singleness" came to be fired and blacklisted. Kahn interviews Furillo at his hard-hat job, where he bitterly recounts his professional career in the business of sports. Irwin Shaw's character, thirty-five-year-old Christian Darling, comes to realize that he is pathetically trapped in his glorious days as a college football player and hero. The supposed recreation of sport has arrested his development.

The readings in this section present several kinds of leisure activities as well as different evaluations of the value of such activities. To appreciate these perspectives and form your own, you will need to think about your assumptions about and participation in recreation. You will also need to assess how your ideas connect with or disagree with those of the writers. You may want to begin this section by formulating some questions on the theme of recreation. Here are some general thematic questions that other students have found helpful for exploring the place of recreation in our lives:

1. How much importance does recreation have in your life and your friends' lives? Is recreation mainly an escape from work and its pressures? Does it ever become an end in itself?
2. Do you ever feel that others in this culture make some forms of recreation more important than they should be? Are sports, for example, given too much importance by some people?
3. Can you think of activities that are difficult to define as either work or leisure? For example, can a leisure-time approach to painting pictures become more like work than play?
4. Do you think that this society spends too much money on leisure and recreation? Are elaborate recreational vehicles, memberships in health spas, and luxury vacations signs of an overemphasis on recreation? Or do they represent the fulfillment of a healthy need to be free from the pressures of serious work?

5. As you plan your own future, do you assign more or less importance to what you will do in your career than to what your career will provide in the way of leisure and recreation? Might you, for example, consider becoming a doctor because a medical career would allow you to help others, or would you think first of the advantages being a doctor would provide for yourself — time on the golf course, trips in your boat or private plane, weekends in your pool?

6. What is your perception of an ideal blend of job and recreational activities? Why might it be difficult to achieve such a blend in everyday life?

7. How are your attitudes toward spending leisure time different from those of your classmates?

8. How are your perspectives on leisure different from those represented in the readings in this section?

9. How might you change your attitudes because of these different opinions and perspectives?

Tide Fingers: A Day in the Life of Cape Cod

ROBERT FINCH

Robert Finch is a natural scientist. He has lived for more than twelve years on Cape Cod, a popular seashore resort area southeast of Boston, Massachusetts. The Cape's extensive sand dunes and rural roadways combine with its traditional New England landscape and architecture to create a haven for nature lovers, many of whom bicycle, walk, or jog its beaches and paths, doing what Finch describes himself doing in this essay. When he isn't walking and observing nature, Finch spends his time as the director of publications for the Cape Cod Museum of Natural History, a writer of essays on one man's relation to nature, a carpenter, and a literature professor. This essay is taken from Finch's book of nature essays, *Common Ground,* published by David Godine in 1981.

Finch is an appreciative observer of nature. In this essay, he uses detailed description to show his readers what he sees during one of his nature walks. He also sounds like a person who cares deeply about what he is observing. Through his voice and eye, Finch gives his readers a sense of how they might develop a comparable appreciation of nature. As you read, take note of the places in this essay where Finch's purpose in writing seems clearest to you.

Finch asks us as readers to share two different experiences with him: that of imaginative responder to the natural world, and that of the objective recorder of its physical phenomena. In the first, we are poets trying to capture the deeper significance of the universe; in the second, we are fact gatherers, looking at nature with the practiced and precise eyes of professional observers. What is the value of taking on both these roles?

As you read, consider the following questions:

1. The northeastern sections of this country are often associated with large cities (New York and Boston), industrialization, and high population densities. Do you think that the general association of the Northeast with urbanization and industrialization might have had something to do with Finch's promotion of amateur nature observation as a form of leisure?
2. Does Finch's vocation as a natural scientist influence his attitude toward nature, even in this essay he has written for a generally educated rather than a specialized audience?

3. What else can you find out about *Common Ground,* the book from which this essay was taken?
4. Finch chooses to show and explain how the tides have affected him over the years rather than to persuade or to inform his readers using facts, reasons, or analysis. Does his background as a scientist and teacher suggest reasons for this choice?

▶ ————————————————

While walking along the inner edge of a salt marsh the other   *1*
day, I stopped to watch a finger of the incoming tide poking its way up one of the dry creek beds. It seemed like something alive, inching and probing forward, twisting and sliding among the interlaced ripple channels, veering off to one side and then the other, halting momentarily as though coiling and gathering strength, then striking out in a long, slow, sinuous glide for several feet.

Looking more closely, I saw that the lengthening, watery digit was   *2*
populated. A hermit crab was scuttling about near its tip, a small marsh shrimp clambered over the sand grains just behind the crab, and behind the shrimp some sort of long, thin marine worm weaved its way along—all encased, like the organelles in an amoebic cell, in this moving, transparent finger of water.

The tide, advancing across the flats and up creek channels, often does   *3*
this, creating numerous temporary marine aquariums, spreading out, for our approval and investigation, more organisms than we could assemble with a good deal of time and effort. Similarly, when it recedes, it often leaves its collections of shells, plants and dead animals in the channels between the ripple marks, laid out neatly in parallel rows as though on museum shelves.

I played with the hermit crab a little, prodding him with my own fin-   *4*
ger to the very limit of the advancing tidal probe. He appeared frustrated that he could not run ahead any faster than his medium of escape was progressing, and tried to retreat, only to be blocked by a dark swatch of seaweed. I tossed him a few inches ahead of the moving channel and he stood there, rocking indecisively, as though he did not know his way back to the water and had to wait for it to catch up with him.

As I stood watching these creatures trapped within the thin, probing   *5*
edge of the tide, the finger itself ceased to advance and stood there, marking tide, as it were. This was high tide, marked and underscored with a precision impossible on the rhythmic, oscillating shores of the

outer beach. It was as though the water itself pointed and said, "Here I stop—no further."

6   After no more than a minute, it began visibly to withdraw, leaving a narrow, winding, moist trail in its wake. I had that sense, as Emily Dickinson once did in the presence of the withdrawing tide, that we live, or survive, at the indulgence of some great global courtesy, a net of seemliness or manners thrown over the earth's blind and wrathful forces, a primitive lust of the sea for the land checked by some overriding decorum that we call the regularity of the tides.

7   And then I saw, for the first time graphically, that strange property of the tide born of planetary inertia. Even as the long finger of the tide withdrew back down the creek bed, innumerable bits of seaweed and other marsh debris continued to be carried *forward* inside it, like a separate flow of arterial blood. The tide has two separate components, one vertical—which we call the rise and fall—and the other, less obvious and horizontal—which is known as the ebb and flood, or current, of the tides.

8   The first of these two motions is caused by the bulge of the ocean's waters outward toward the moon (and to a lesser extent, the sun). The second motion is the apparent backward and forward movement of the water as the earth's ocean floors turn beneath it. The extremes of the rise and fall motions are called high water and low water, while the turning point between flooding and ebbing currents is known as slack water.

9   In the open sea, these two movements are indistinguishable. But in harbors, estuaries and flats there may be up to an hour's difference, or lag, between high or low water and slack water. Thus, on our shores, the tide actually begins to fall while it is still flooding, and to rise while it is still ebbing. Yet only in certain protected places, such as the upper reaches of tidal creeks, can the interaction of these two great natural forces be observed so distinctly, unconfused by the competing spectacles of waves and crashing surf.

10   If this double movement of the tides sounds complicated to us, it can deceive its inhabitants as well. Treacherously, silently, appearing to continue inland even as it withdrew, the finger of tide had moved out, stranding the creatures it had carried in with it. The hermit crab stood with a puzzled air, the shrimp began some ineffectual burrowing, and the worm writhed out its life on the wet sands.

11   Anthropocentrically, I chose to save the crab (it has "arms") and tossed it several yards downstream. But when I looked again at the "worm," I saw that it was actually a pipefish, a relative of the seahorse and a common inhabitant of eelgrass beds where its eellike body is invisible among the waving grass stands. I picked it up and tossed it along

with the crab, and then, just to be catholic, threw the prawn after as
well.

I am fascinated by all of the various ways the tides approach our
shores: the small, relatively inconsequential fluctuations of Vineyard
Sound, the strong, treacherous rips and channels around Monomoy and
Woods Hole, the greater height and heaving advance of the Outer
Beach, and the impressive sweeps and withdrawals across the wide flats
of Cape Cod Bay. Yet whenever I think of the tide it is always like this,
as a slow-moving finger of shallow water across grooved sands. I think it
must have something to do with the first time I saw the tide come in—I
mean the first time I *saw* it, and sensed in its inanimate force that our
shores were something alive.

It was in Provincetown Harbor, one summer night many years ago. I
was walking the dark shore with a friend, a large, affectionate man with
a child's passion for showing people things. We walked in half-lit shadows, behind the Crown and Anchor Inn, in the sallow naked glow of the
building's backlights, with the muted noise of whatever dance music
was in fashion that season blaring in the background. All at once my
friend stopped, pointing down at our feet, and said, "There it is."

I stopped, too, looked down, and jumped back in alarm, as though
a basket of snakes had been spilled out at my feet. It did look like
snakes—small, sliding serpents of black water, twisting and thrusting
and sidling across the dark sands, intertwining, separating and finally
coalescing to the rear as it ate up that beach under the piers in small,
advancing nibbles. I could not have been more startled and amazed than
if I had witnessed the famous tides of Southern France that come in over
the flats with the speed of a race horse, or the incredible Amazon tidal
bore, a moving waterfall 25 feet high and several miles long that moves
up the river at twelve knots for some 300 miles, with a roar that can be
heard inland for 15 miles.

There are times in our lives, decreasingly so as we get older, when we
seem peculiarly open to certain impressions. No one can predict these
times, nor can we always successfully analyze them afterwards, nor
does the force of the impression necessarily bear any proportionate relation to the object that made it. Just why the tide impressed me so that
night I do not know. But it has stayed with me ever since, so that when I
think of the tide—as I might think of God or Communist China or some
other large abstraction—it is not as some great lunar heave and splash of
the planetary bathtub, or as some massive, rising inundation, or as any
other of its more majestic and dramatic incarnations; but as an intimate
running and feeling of water snakes and water fingers across dark sands,
an intricate consumption of the land by water, a loving and almost passive tracing of the earth's contours by the advancing sea, taking on

those contours, flowing into her curves and edges, even as it obliterates them.

16   Somehow, in this gentle movement of the tide across the ripples and channels of the flats, I sense the advance of whole oceanic waters across the continental shelf, roaring silently through submerged canyons, across drowned plains and river valleys, taking bends and turns along our crenulated shorelines, funneling up into bays and estuaries, spilling through channels and sinking into holes.

17   Over the years I have watched these delicate fingers of tide push their way along, slowly and thickly, in and out, like summer and winter. So fragile do they seem that I can change their course or block their passage momentarily with my own fingers, as we easily melt the first snowflakes of winter on our palms.

18   Yet they have behind them the power and inevitability of suns and satellites in their orbits, the force of the world's oceans and the mass of the moon. The actual drops of water in their deft, searching tips may have come in [from] no more than a few hundred feet offshore, yet they have the knowledge of all drowned earth in them. This soft tidal probe is infused with the running of thousands of miles across unknown complexities of terrains, the visible resultant of an untraceable intercourse between sea-bed and sea-heave. It is the moving finger of universal forces that writes, here on these shallow summer sands—inspired, passionate holy water.

Questions and Activities

▶ *COMPREHENSION QUESTIONS*

1. How does Finch start his essay? What effect might this type of beginning have on his readers? Does it effectively draw them into his subject? Does it help define the audience of this piece?

2. In paragraphs 7, 8, and 9, Finch explains and elaborates on what scientists call high and low water and flooding and ebbing currents. Within the overall structure of the essay, these explanations serve as examples of how natural phenomena are often simply missed by the untrained person. The trained person sees things and connections between things that less trained people cannot see. Also, the amateur who links close observation with imagination can see connections between concrete and universal ideas that the unobservant person misses. Go back over the essay and explain (perhaps to

a classmate) Finch's distinctions between the trained and untrained eye and between the observant and unobservant amateur.

3. Why does Finch title his essay "Tide Fingers"? Only a few paragraphs of the essay are devoted to the actual observation of a tide finger. How does the title capture Finch's general intention?

4. Make a list of semitechnical terms in this essay—such as "slack water," "estuaries," and "flats" (paragraphs 8 and 9). Are their meanings clearly defined by the context, or do you need to look them up in a dictionary?

▶ *QUESTIONS OF RHETORICAL PURPOSE AND STRATEGY*

5. What type of person did Finch assume would be reading his essay? Is his assumed reader someone who already respects and loves nature, or is it someone who has never experienced the pleasure of a nature walk? How do you know that your answers to these questions are right? Are there words, phrases, or whole passages in this essay that are obviously aimed at a particular kind of reader?

6. Finch closes his essay by calling the tidewater that he has been observing "inspired, passionate holy water" (paragraph 18). This kind of language is not typical of exact scientists. However, technical words also appear in this essay. What does this implied comparison tell you about Finch's overall aims? Is he trying to convince his readers to develop a technical, scientific perspective on nature or a more imaginative, artistic one?

▶ *THEME QUESTIONS*

7. Compare the kind of recreation that Finch describes to watching television. What types of pleasure does a leisurely but observant walk bring that are different from the kinds of pleasure a television situation comedy affords? Is recreation always a form of escape from ways of making a living? Have you seen television shows that emphasize the kind of careful observation of nature that Finch has described in this essay?

8. Does this essay offer you a previously unthought of perspective on leisure and recreation? What is that perspective? Does it change your attitude toward recreation? If yes, what was your attitude and how has this article changed it? If no, how does Finch's article reflect or reinforce your attitude toward leisure and recreation?

▶ *LEARNING ACTIVITIES*

9. Try a version of Finch's sort of observation. First, choose a subject—a natural phenomenon, as Finch did, or a particular part of the city that you live in, or simply a place, such as a bus stop or res-

taurant, in which you frequently spend time. Then, take a notebook along and record your observations in note form. Be as specific in your wording as you can be. To finish this process, rewrite your notes in narrative form, as Finch did in writing about his tidewater walk.

10. Do you feel that Finch writes as a specialist to other specialists — perhaps biologists or naturalists — or as a specialist to nonspecialists? After you have thought about this question, write a one-page description of the audience Finch is addressing. What do members of that audience have in common? What do you think they learn from Finch's article? If they are specialists, describe what they specialize in and why you believe they are specialists of this type.

11. Work with another student on the following project. One of you should make a list of negative reactions to Finch's suggested way of spending leisure time. The other should then write a brief response to each item on the list, explaining from Finch's perspective why the reaction is not justified.

From *Recovering: A Journal 1978-1979*

MAY SARTON

May Sarton is a seventy-five-year-old writer who lives in York, Maine. She has published more than thirty-five books, mostly poetry, novels, and nonfiction. Much of her writing develops a highly individualized perspective on her natural surroundings, on her relations with friends and other writers, and on her solitary life with her animals in the old house by the sea in which she lives. Sarton's books usually do not record what many people would call important or highly dramatic events; rather, they explore her thoughts and feelings as she responds to the places and people that fill her life. Her readers, over the many years in which Sarton's books have been published, have come to expect and enjoy her introspective voice and to respect her insights about her private and social life.

As you read, it is important to hear Sarton's voice. Her word choice and her manner of expressing what she feels concerning other people and nature become Sarton's way of addressing her readers in a way that convinces them to take a similar stance. Perhaps it is Sarton's voice that brings her readers into her world and makes them susceptible to her way of seeing and evaluating it.

In this excerpt from her ongoing journals, Sarton turns the leisure and recreation of visiting a friend into work. Most of us just want to be kept busy during our free time, but she examines her leisure experiences to create a meaning out of them. As you read, consider the somewhat weightier value of everyday and leisure activities that Sarton reveals through her writing:

1. Do you feel that Sarton's way of turning leisure activities into material for her work as a writer is a good way to live? Or do you feel that her doing so represents an undesired intrusion of work into leisure?
2. What is her purpose? Do you think that Sarton wants to persuade others to do as she does, or is she simply interested in communicating her personal discoveries to others?

▶ ────────────────────────────

Wednesday, September 26th

1   I have been away for a few days in Center Sandwich, New Hampshire, at Huldah's, an uplifting taste of mountains and lakes, and those charming woodsy roads, still unpaved, that remind me of Nelson. Huldah invited Tamas, so he had a fine holiday with us and her two big collies.* All my feeling for New England returned as I drove along on my way there, though the season is not advanced and only a few swamp maples were scarlet. What I thought, not for the first time, was that there is nowhere, perhaps, in the world where one sees so many distinguished small houses, and this surely has something to do with the character of the people who built them. In the South there are magnificent "great houses," but small houses are apt to be shabby and architecturally nondescript. All along the road by Lake Winnipesaukee I passed small white houses with sparkling many-paned windows and beautifully designed doorways often with a huge barn attached or beside them, the shingles weathered dove gray—what dreams they evoke of another life, though it is a life I lived once for fifteen years in Nelson. However, the country around Center Sandwich is more beautiful, on a grander scale, than that in the Monadnock region. There are many ranges making a strong elegant profile against the sky wherever one turns, and many rich brooks tumbling over smooth granite stones, so the sound of water is never far away, an intimate sound, very different from that of the ocean.

2   When I reached Huldah's house I kept listening and was startled by the total silence, not a bird singing or a cricket chirping for the first hours I was there. And I realized finally that what made the silence so immense was the absence of the ocean, and how much I missed it, and also the constant cries of gulls and the wood pigeons cooing and the goldfinches' delightful running cheeps in flight.

3   How marvelous to live in a world where all this is within reach, gentle mountains, clear lakes, and the ocean! New England. Its essence is a fine mixture of grandeur—the natural scene—and intimacy, the small much lived-in house where one sits by the fire in a room lined with books.

4   In the four days there were two peak experiences as Maslow would name them.† One was late in the afternoon when the sun suddenly

*Tamas is Ms. Sarton's dog.
†Abraham Maslow, who died in 1970, was the father of motivational psychology. His most well-known contribution to this field is his concept of a hierarchy of human motivations, with the need to actualize the self at the top. Once free of physical constraints and needs, human beings are motivated by higher, more intellectual needs, such as the achievement of potential. It is the satisfying of this type of higher motivation that Sarton is alluding to in the reference to "peak experiences."

touched a bowl of lavender colchicum (they appear to be huge crocuses and bloom in the autumn) on the sill in Huldah's big room. In the slanting light they became transparent, lavender flames. They seemed to gather all the light into themselves, centering for a few moments the whole world so nothing else existed. A moment of ecstasy.

The other peak experience came after a splendid walk to Dog   5
Cove—a walk through great trees, moss underfoot and the leaves of many wildflowers to note, mushrooms, great lichen-covered rocks looming up, and the broken light through birch and ash leaves, and through white pine. Huldah's collies move about all this with great elegance in their white ruffs on their long legs. Tamas, more sedate, trundles ahead, like a small animated barrel of fur. The path leads finally to Squam Lake and a series of small white birches...lovely when one glimpses the shining blue through the trees. There we spread a blanket and had our picnic, fish chowder and a great salad of hard-boiled eggs, lettuce and blue cheese with French dressing, and a Bartlett pear.

And then the silence fell.   6

We simply sat there and drank in the dappled water, a couple of gulls   7
swimming around a big rock, and far away a pine-covered island and beyond that rising up in the distance the deep blue rounded peaks of the Sandwich range. How rare in our world to sit absolutely still for an hour, not thinking, not even feeling, simply being in the presence of great beauty! At first one notices the small things, the subtle changes as wind suddenly ruffles a small space in the water, the amber color of still water over sand, or the reflection of a single tree, but little by little, it is the whole unified scene that takes over. And it is the silence itself that unifies it. One slides down deep deep into contemplation. This is not ecstasy like the light on lavender petals. It is more like prayer. Beauty beyond our understanding and beyond our uniqueness as individuals. Presence that asks nothing of us except to be in its presence. And filled with that presence we walked back into our separate lives.

Questions and Activities

▶ COMPREHENSION QUESTIONS

1. Find the references to specific places, things, and scenes in Sarton's first paragraph. How do these references contribute to your sense of Sarton's authority about what she describes?

2. Why does Sarton refer to Maslow (paragraph 4) as she begins her narrative describing her trip? What are "peak experiences"?

▶ *QUESTIONS OF RHETORICAL PURPOSE AND STRATEGY*

3. What is the organizational strategy behind this essay? How does Sarton arrange her narrative-descriptive material? Do you find it easy to relate the parts of the essay to one another?
4. Reread Sarton's last paragraph. There are several sentence fragments in this final paragraph. Why does Sarton use them? Does her style in this paragraph suggest the purpose behind her essay? What effect does she want this last paragraph to have on her readers?
5. Both Robert Finch and May Sarton are careful observers of nature. What do you think are the essential differences between the ways Finch and Sarton describe what they see, smell, and hear? Which writer seems more like a natural scientist? In what ways does this more scientific writer use language differently from the other writer? How would you describe Sarton's style and perspective? How do they help Sarton develop her overall purpose?
6. How does this essay, written as part of a journal that Sarton knew would be published, differ from entries in a journal that a writer had no intention of publishing?

▶ *THEME QUESTIONS*

7. What advantages do you think the leisure activity Sarton describes has over other forms of recreation, particularly activities of a more organized kind? What might be the disadvantages of this type of leisure activity?
8. Do you think that you could be successful, as Sarton is, in making a leisure activity into a way of making a living? What activity or skill would you choose to exploit? Do you think the fun of the activity might be destroyed in the process?

▶ *LEARNING ACTIVITIES*

9. Rewrite one of Sarton's paragraphs in a different style, without changing its content. What words in the original are most difficult for you to find substitutes for?
10. Create a journal entry in which you describe being in the same place when you are in two different moods. What changes of language reflect the differences of mood?
11. Write a one-page description of the reader that is implied by Sarton's essay. What is this implied reader looking for as he or she reads? Are the answers to these questions supported by close analysis of the essay? What features of the text contribute most directly to your description of the implied reader?

The Commuter's Worlds

ELLEN GOODMAN

Ellen Goodman is a journalist who has written for the *Boston Globe* since 1961. Her daily column, which is nationally syndicated by the Washington Post Writers Group, has become one of the most popular sources of professional commentary on American social life during the past fifteen years. She has received many journalism awards, including the New England Press Columnist of the Year Award in 1975 and a Pulitzer Prize for commentary in 1980. Her writing has been collected and published in *Ellen Goodman at Large* (1981) and *Close to Home* (1979). She has been a radio commentator on the CBS network and a television commentator on NBC's *Today Show*. This article originally appeared in the *Boston Globe* in September, 1980; it is also included in *Ellen Goodman at Large*.

Goodman has developed a distinctive voice in her writing. Using short paragraphs and clipped journalistic sentences, she manages to create a definite personality—witty, intelligent, tough-minded, well-informed, and opinionated. Her ability to confront important issues directly or to find their manifestations in seemingly common occurrences combines with her willingness to take definite positions on these issues. Even in this seemingly personal column about commuting back to work after a vacation, she makes a statement about the nature and worth of human endeavors and creativity.

Goodman has come to be associated with moderately feminist causes; she is frequently invited to speak to women's groups, and she often devotes her column to issues that directly concern women.

1. Do you find any evidence of this concern in this piece?
2. Do you feel that Goodman would give up her "city clothes of purpose and structure" for what some might feel is the freer and more flexible life of a suburban housewife?

Another facet of Goodman's background is her work in television and radio. With this media experience in mind, consider the question of the audience of this piece.

1. Does Goodman seem to have a particular kind of reader in mind?
2. Do you feel that her experience as a social commentator on television and radio might have influenced her style and tone?
3. Television, many experts argue, is a relaxed, informal medium. The talk show is television's most natural form of expression. Does Goodman seem here to be writing as if she were addressing a friend

or someone who might be sitting across from her on a television talk show?

4. What is Goodman's purpose in this essay? Is she trying to open up new perspectives for her readers? Is she persuading them to accept her views or simply expressing her own opinion? (You might want to apply these questions to the essay's first paragraph and then keep them in mind as you finish reading the essay.)

▶ ————————————————————

1   Finally the dirt road in Maine was leading home. The tire touched the first profanity of pavement, and subtly my vacation began slipping away.

2   By the first tollbooth my state of mind had shifted from neutral to first gear. By the time I had passed all my favorite landmarks—the sign to Biddeford, the bridge labeled Cat Mousam Road—I had slowly and reluctantly begun to relocate my sense of place, my sense of values.

3   I was going back, to lists and alarm clocks and stockings and school lunches and all the external pressures of the life known as civilization. I was going back to things I had to do.

4   This time even the skies divided these two halves of my life. Along Route 95, a curtain of almost impenetrable rain separated one world from the other. The day before, this rain on the roof of the house would have been a comforting boundary to the day, a prediction of reading and fires. Now, the rain on the windshield of the car was a hassle, a challenge to overcome.

5   I turned up the radio, so I could hear the final installment of *Jane Eyre* over the pelting rain, and thought about these different rhythms that mark my own life, many of our lives. Left behind was a world in which I simply lived . . . according to its patterns. Ahead of me was the world of agendas and problems that I was expected to encounter and resolve.

6   Was it country versus city? Leisure versus work? Nature versus human environment? Both and neither. Vacation is a state of mind as much as a state of the union.

7   For two and a half weeks in Maine I watched the sky, the cove, the cormorants and a seagull with the gall to steal chicken off our barbecue. I am told that I became an accomplished mud watcher, sitting on the porch, watching the bottom of the cove at low tide for hours. I prided myself on developing a hobby rarely listed in *Who's Who:* I became a fine stick-in-the-mud.

8   To me, an urban woman who lives much of her life according to other people's deadlines and demands, this was a chance to literally vacate the world of schedules and struggles.

I did not, do not, use my vacation to climb mountains, shoot rapids   9
or fulfill itineraries of some travel agent. I preferred to drift along my inclination down through the circle of goals to the mud of acceptance.

I was content with the harmony we call doing nothing. There was a   10
sense of letting go, being at ease with time rather than at odds with it. I wallowed in the understanding that there was nothing that had to be done beyond watching the clothes dry and casting for mackerel.

But I was also returning. Returning to the energy, the structure, the   11
demands, the pressure. I also chose engagement.

There are, I suppose, these two sides to all of us. The side that   12
wallows like any other organism in the world, and the other side that seeks some purpose "above" that. The side that feels most content in nature, and the other side that feels more energized "on top of the world."

I am aware of this duality, the urge to watch the mud, the urge to   13
build something out of it. Our peculiar human creativity doesn't come from harmony but from wrestling with chaos as well. Every poem and every building was wrested out of raw material by people who refused to accept things as they were.

Too often we work by clocks instead of sunsets and become more   14
attuned to air conditioning than the condition of the air. But there is also in all this the challenge and energy and pleasure of accomplishment.

At one time, I thought these worlds were at odds, that we had to   15
choose engagement or disengagement, acceptance or accomplishment, watching the mud or building with it.

But traveling this kind of road again and again, I realized that they are   16
just two destinations, points along a path of dirt and pavement. Now it is the tension that intrigues me. The search for a balance between comfort and purposefulness, between accepting things and struggling with them.

Driving home, I was reluctant to leave one world for the other, reluc-   17
tant to put on my city clothes of purpose and structure and struggle. But I knew that I was lucky to be a commuter.

Questions and Activities

▶ COMPREHENSION QUESTIONS

1. What kind of vacation does the phrase "dirt road in Maine" (paragraph 1) suggest?
2. How do the things Goodman notices on her way back to Boston from Maine show you what she thinks about vacation and business frames of mind? Why, for example, does she make particular note of the toll-booth, the Cat Mousam sign, and the rain?
3. Paragraphs 12 through 17 in this essay all share a pattern of comparison. Put the two sides of this comparison into your own words. How does this comparison help to explain why Goodman feels "lucky to be a commuter"?

▶ QUESTIONS OF RHETORICAL PURPOSE AND STRATEGY

4. What kind of person would find Goodman's voice appealing? Does she ever seem to talk down to her audience? Does she ever seem too familiar or too formal? Why might her essay seem appropriate for a busy reader of a newspaper? Does her voice seem appropriate to her purpose?
5. Compare this piece with Robert Finch's or May Sarton's. Does Goodman seem to have a definite purpose she wishes to communicate to her readers? Do you think she has a main point she wants to get across in her essay? Where in the essay do you find this main point most explicitly expressed? What kind of person might find this essay important?

▶ THEME QUESTIONS

6. Goodman's experiences are in opposition to the position of social critics who believe that commuting—with its traffic jams, rushing, and people isolated in their automobiles—is a negative aspect of modern society. She finds that commuting provides time to reflect in an otherwise busy life. Do you agree? Are you able to make positive use of the time you spend driving or riding to and from work, school, or social events? Do we all need two separate, seemingly irreconcilable worlds? Should we separate work and leisure or combine them (like Robert Finch and May Sarton)?
7. In a paragraph, explain how you usually spend your leisure time and why. Have other students read your paragraph and question you about your perspective on leisure time. The class as a whole might develop a questionnaire to be used to interview students in general concerning their uses of leisure time.

▶ *LEARNING ACTIVITIES*

8. Think back over some trip you have often taken. Describe your usual frame of mind when you begin and compare it to your frame of mind when you arrive at your destination. Write a narrative about the trip, trying to include particular objects or places along the way that demonstrate how your mind works during the trip. Put your narrative in chronological order, with a clear beginning, middle, and end.

9. Write a brief essay in which you compare your preferences for spending leisure time to Goodman's. To help you write the essay, make a point-by-point list of the major aspects of your leisure preferences and another of Goodman's. Review these two lists, thinking about the points of comparison and contrast between you and Goodman. Then write down your reasons for preferring your way of spending leisure time to Goodman's. Now consider and describe how you will present the items in the lists in the essay. Will you alternate, first presenting one of your points and then one of Goodman's? Or will you present all her points first and all yours second? Why would you pick one strategy over the other? What would be the advantages of one over the other, as far as your readers are concerned?

On Playing in Ivan's Yard

RED SMITH

Walter Wellesley "Red" Smith was probably the best-known and most widely read American sportswriter of this century. He was able both to inform and to entertain his readers because he combined expert knowledge of sports with definite opinions on the broader social implications of his subject.

Smith began his career as a cub reporter for the *Milwaukee Sentinel* in 1927, served as a copyeditor, rewrite man, and sports reporter for the *St. Louis Star* from 1928 to 1936 and as a sports columnist and general sportswriter for the *Philadelphia Record* from 1936 to 1945. From 1945 to 1966, he worked along with Roger Kahn (an essay of his appears later in this section) and many other first-rate newswriters on the staff of the *New York Herald Tribune*. When the *Tribune* ceased publishing in 1966, Smith went to work for the *World-Journal Tribune*. Then, in 1967, he went to the *New York Times,* where he wrote sports columns until his death in 1983.

Red Smith was a career newspaperman, a popular sportswriter, and a respected commentator on American culture. His writings have been anthologized in many books; this article is taken from *The Red Smith Reader,* edited by Dave Anderson (Random House, 1982). It originally appeared in the *New York Times* in 1980.

In this column, Smith presents himself as an authoritative social and political commentator. He states facts with very little qualification; he gives reasons for his opinions that have very little example or detail to support them; he is consistently serious and moralistic in tone. This is not a customary role for sportswriters. Smith's purpose in writing this essay on boycotting the 1980 Olympics is different from that behind most sports columns. He considers, and wants his readers to consider, the Olympics to be a political and cultural event, as well as a sporting event. To create this emphasis and persuade his readers, he must be accepted as a sophisticated, worldly observer, not merely as someone knowledgeable about sports.

As you read this column, consider whether your views about politics and sports are influenced by Smith's:

1. Do you find Smith's voice convincing? Does he sound sufficiently knowledgeable to be making arguments on the social and political implications of the Olympic Games?
2. Do you feel that a sports columnist should be writing with this kind of broader purpose in mind? How might Smith's general reputation as a

journalist (this column was written toward the end of his long career) have influenced his readers to take seriously opinions they might have found offensive if expressed by less experienced or lesser-known sportswriters?

3. Would the fact that Smith was writing for the *New York Times* have influenced his readers' reactions to his opinions on the social implications of the Olympics?

▶ ─────────────────────────

President Carter has warned that the United States might with-   *1*
draw from the Moscow Olympics if the Soviet Union's aggression in Afghanistan continues. Some voices have seconded the motion, Saudi Arabia has already pulled out, and sentiment in favor of a boycott will spread as Soviet tanks and troops press on with their bloody work.

It is unthinkable that in the present circumstances we could go play   *2*
games with Ivan in Ivan's yard. The United States should lead a walk-out now, making it clear to the Russians that even if the shooting ends and the invading forces go home, the rape of a neighbor will not be quickly forgotten. With their parades and flags and anthems and the daily count of medals won, the Olympic Games are a carnival of nationalism. The festival is a showcase for the host nation to display its brightest face to the world. It is inconceivable that we should lend our presence to a pageant of Soviet might.

Dispatches from Moscow tell of an "Olympic purge" already under   *3*
way to present the Communist society as an ideal surpassing even the dazzled view that Lincoln Steffens got.* ("I have been over into the future, and it works.") To scrub up the capital for an anticipated 300,000 visitors, "undesirables" will be sent out of the city and contact with foreigners will be discouraged. Dissidents, drunkards, psychotics and Jews who have applied for emigration are undesirable. School children will be sent to summer camps. Kevin Klose, the *Washington Post* correspondent, reports that some teachers are telling their pupils that American tourists will offer them poisoned chewing gum.

Unofficial sources, Klose writes, "sardonically use the Russian word   *4*
chistka or 'cleaning' to describe what is going on. It is a word with dread connotations for Soviets because it is the term used in designating the Stalinist purges that swept millions to their death in slave labor camps beginning in the late 1930s."

*Lincoln Steffens was the most famous of the reform journalists of the early twentieth century. Always a political liberal, Steffens spent his later life reporting on communist and other revolutions in various parts of the world. To Red Smith, Steffens represents those Westerners who are misled by the superficial surface of communism.

5   All of this hints at how important the Olympics are to the government. Diminishing their vast propaganda show or possibly causing its cancelation would be a sterner measure than many might think. And the millions of tourist rubles involved are no small matter.

6   It was inevitable that as soon as the President mentioned the possibility of a boycott, the stuffed shirts in the Olympic movement would revive the threadbare argument that politics should not be injected into the Olympics—as if the games ever had been free of politics, as if the Olympic movement itself weren't shot with politics. Not that the playground directors have a monopoly on unrealistic thinking or fatuous speech. Consider the statement of Gerhart Baum, West Germany's Interior Minister:

7   "In the opinion of the government, sports cannot be used as a means for political ends. Sports cannot solve problems whose solution can only be achieved politically."

8   In 1956, Egypt, Lebanon, and Iraq withdrew from the Melbourne Olympics to protest an Israeli invasion of the Sinai and the Gaza strip. Spain, Switzerland and the Netherlands walked out to protest the Soviet march into Hungary. In 1976 the entire African continent boycotted the Montreal games because of the presence of New Zealand, which countenanced athletic relations with South Africa. The quadrennial quarrel over the two Chinas remains unresolved.

9   And still the Olympic brass clings to the fantasy that these are contests for individuals, not nations. Then after each contest they raise the winner's national flag and play his national anthem. Between games, Olympic fund raisers beg for contributions to help beat the Russians.

10   Aside from the garbage about politics, the only argument against withdrawal is that it would penalize American kids who have endured the drudgery of training for four years or more with their dreams fixed on this one opportunity for international competition.

11   It would, indeed, be a disappointment, perhaps not their first and surely not the last they will ever experience. But any measures taken against Soviet aggression will demand sacrifices from someone. As Mary McGrory observed in her *Washington Post* column, if we got into war, those kids are the ones who would do the fighting.

12   Chances are the savants who write editorials in *The New York Times* today weren't even reading that page in 1936, but the paper opposed American participation in the Nazi Olympics of that year. When the Nazis "deliberately and arrogantly offend against our common humanity," the *Times* said, "sport does not 'transcend all political and racial considerations.' "

13   "Deliberately and arrogantly" sound like the words Jimmy Carter used last week. Considering the provocation, they are mild. The Sovi-

ets invaded an independent nation—which happens, incidentally, to be
a member of the Olympic family—executed the leader of that nation's
government and then said the government had invited them in.

In ancient Greece, wars were suspended when the Olympics rolled   14
around. It says here the Olympics should be suspended when the caissons roll.

Questions and Activities

▶ *COMPREHENSION QUESTIONS*

1. Summarize Smith's argument in favor of a United States boycott of
   the Olympic games.
2. Examine the vocabulary of the first three paragraphs of this article.
   How does Smith's use of words such as "unthinkable," "rape,"
   "carnival," "bloody," "purge," "dazzled," and "poisoned," affect
   your response to what he is saying? Is he appealing, with these
   words, to your reason or your emotions? Does his appeal seem
   pushy, appropriate, or foolish?
3. Summarize the situation in Afghanistan in 1980, when the Olympic
   boycott occurred. You will need to check newspapers (such as the
   New York Times) and news magazines of the time to find facts for
   your summary. What else might the United States have done at that
   time, aside from boycotting the Olympics, to show a negative reaction to the Soviet invasion? Was the boycott ineffectual? Why?
4. State what you think would be Smith's definition of the purpose of
   the Olympics. Support your statement by referring to specific parts
   of this article.
5. Explain what Smith means by his last sentence: "It says here the
   Olympics should be suspended when the caissons roll."

▶ *QUESTIONS OF RHETORICAL PURPOSE AND STRATEGY*

6. Describe Smith's readers. What do they know? What are their general interests? What are their attitudes toward sports? Do they read
   extensively? Do they participate in sports? Are they assumed to be
   experts on sports? What, in the article, supports your answers to
   these questions?
7. What do you think is Smith's general aim in writing this article?
   Does he want his readers to change their minds, or does he just want
   them to be better informed? How would you support your answer to
   this question? Does the way Smith writes suggest an answer?

► *THEME QUESTIONS*

8. Do you agree with Smith about the 1980 Olympic boycott by the United States? Consider whether or not the boycott really did have an effect on world politics and on the Soviets in particular. Consider the arguments made by the "Olympic brass" that Smith summarily dismisses. Consider the historical instances involving the games that Smith cites. Consider also the damage you think the boycott might have done to the American athletes. Do you think such boycotts simply recognize the political nature of international sports, or do they in fact politicize them? You might wish to read a few other magazine and newspaper articles from 1980 for opinions other than Smith's.

9. What are the advantages and disadvantages of participating in highly organized activities during leisure time? What are the advantages and disadvantages of participating in more solitary leisure activities such as nature walks, fishing, or jogging? Does this article illustrate the advantages or disadvantages of highly organized leisure?

► *LEARNING ACTIVITIES*

10. Recall a time in your childhood when you engaged in some type of highly organized recreation, such as Girl Scouts, Little League baseball, or a museum club. Was it a positive or a negative experience? Record your memories in writing, including only important details and organizing them chronologically. Use these notes as you discuss your experience with your classmates.

11. Look up the Olympics in a good encyclopedia. Think about the similarities and differences between the encyclopedia's definition of the Olympics and Red Smith's implied definition of their purpose; write a list of the specific similarities and differences you see. Using your list as a basis, write a paper that defines the Olympics and addresses the questions of why the Olympics were started and why nations participate today. Your introduction should establish your thesis—your perspective—on the purpose of the Olympic games. Subsequent paragraphs should compare and contrast opposing views. Or you may want to establish one perspective in the first one or two paragraphs, and then the other, comparative perspective in the next paragraphs.

White Nights

PAULINE KAEL

Pauline Kael has been one of this country's leading movie critics since she began writing reviews for *The New Yorker* in 1968. Part of her appeal is her distinctive voice. Readers have become familiar with the sound of Kael's writing, which is never stuffy or rigid, but always precise in its detailed analyses of movies. As she analyzes specific aspects of a movie — actors, characters, plot, etc. — Kael also knowledgeably considers film technique and history and displays an understanding of how American themes and broad cultural and political patterns are reflected in the particular film. Kael is able to help her readers to understand how the strengths and weaknesses of films are related to the social conditions in which they were made. The review reprinted here demonstrates Kael's combination of a precise eye, knowledge about film, and insight into social and cultural conditions.

Kael's movie reviews have been collected and published in many books, including *I Lost It at the Movies* (1965), *Kiss Kiss Bang Bang* (1968), *Deeper into Movies* (1973), *Reeling* (1976), and *When the Lights Go Down* (1980). She has also published many articles on film in magazines and periodicals such as *Partisan Review, Vogue, The New Republic, McCall's, The Atlantic,* and *Harper's.*

Pauline Kael's reviews always seem to go beyond the surface of movies to explain their appeal and quality. In this review of *White Nights,* which stars the Russian defector and ballet star Mikhail Baryshnikov, Kael shows the conflict between the "transparently opportunistic" Cold War plot about dancers who defect and the quality of the acting and dancing, between the "freedom of movement" the movie purports to show and the "freedom of movement" achieved despite the movie. She helps us place our responses to the movie in larger social, political, artistic, and psychological contexts.

Consider Kael's strategies for achieving her purpose:

1. Note how she introduces the content of the movie. What does she emphasize? How does she get you interested in the film, whether or not you have seen it?
2. Note how Kael addresses her readers. What kind of personality does her writing create? Think of some adjectives that accurately describe the role she assumes as she writes. Why do you think she chooses this role as the one most apt to persuade her readers to respond as she does to the film she is reviewing?

▶ ────────────────────

1   At thirty-seven, the Mikhail Baryshnikov of "White Nights" isn't the lighthearted seducer that he played in his only other movie, "The Turning Point," in 1977. He has a tragic, melancholy dimension now, and more depth. If he can be said to embody the aesthetic of classical dance, he has also reached the point where he's fighting that aesthetic—fighting his body. You can't see the fighting in the dance sequences of "White Nights"; at least, I couldn't detect it—he leaps and soars as if it were effortless. But you know that it's happening, just as you know that it's not happening to the tap dancer Gregory Hines—his co-star here—who, belonging to a different tradition of dance, may be able to go on just about forever. You can sense it in the perfection of Baryshnikov's face: he's not boyish anymore. His face is drawn now and as expressively modelled as his muscular body—he has a man's awareness. Baryshnikov is magnificent in "White Nights." He might have been created for the movie camera, and he shames the movie he's in.

2   In "White Nights," a great star of the ballet world who defected from the Soviet Union in the seventies and became an American citizen is on his way to dance in Tokyo when his plane crash-lands in Siberia. The Soviet authorities apprehend him and put him in the care of a black American tap dancer, who defected from the United States during the Vietnam War, and the tap dancer's Russian wife. This may have seemed like a sharp idea—a gimmick with a built-in dialectic—but it's transparently opportunistic. The tap dancer is conceived as an embittered man who deserted from the U.S. Army because of American racism and the folly and horror of Vietnam. Except for the happiness he has found with his wife, he's miserable, yet he can't admit to himself that he's allowed to dance (in a moth-eaten provincial theatre in Siberia) only if he toadies to the bureaucrats and accepts humiliating tasks. And now a K.G.B. colonel tells him that he must persuade the ballet star to renounce the U.S. and perform in just a few days at a Kirov gala at the company's base in Leningrad's old Maryinsky Theatre. His own future depends on it: if he fails, he'll be sent to work in the mines.

3   This cheap plot is like a straitjacket that the director, Taylor Hackford, got into voluntarily and can't wriggle out of. The film opens with the credits on one side of the screen and Baryshnikov's face on the other side—he appears to be lying back on his bed and smoking a cigarette contemplatively; then he leaps up and dances in a garretlike studio, where he's joined by a ballerina. It's a minute or two before we recognize that they're performing Roland Petit's "Le Jeune Homme et la Mort," and that the garret is in fact the stage of a huge theatre crowded

with people, who break into applause. This sequence is superb. It has us watching a ballet before we know we are; even the closeup of Baryshnikov's face is part of the dance. Lighted by the cinematographer David Watkin, this ballet has an entrancing naturalistic formality. But once the plot begins, the dance numbers—solos by Baryshnikov and Hines, and a duet choreographed by Twyla Tharp to the fast rock rhythms of David Pack's "Prove Me Wrong"—aren't as exhilarating as we want them to be, because they're followed by so many scenes of the trapped Baryshnikov trying to figure out what to do and of Hines sitting around morosely.

"White Nights" is meant to be about freedom of movement—about two dancers who, each in his own way, have fled their countries in quest of it. But what we get is a movie about dancers in a funk. They go from the cramped quarters in the Siberian playhouse to the ballet star's luxurious old apartment in Leningrad and the rehearsal studios at the Kirov; the tap dancer is glum just about every step of the way, and the picture itself is stagnant. The script, credited to James Goldman and Eric Hughes, keeps going back over the same muddy ground, and when heroic climaxes are wanted it insults the dancers (and our intelligence) by relying on stunt work—on doubles climbing out windows and swinging from ropes. With its solemnly melodramatic mixed-twins premise, the picture certainly can't be accused of excessive artistic integrity, yet it doesn't gratify the audience by letting the performers do what the audience wants them to do. Baryshnikov, a *danseur noble* if ever there was one, is given no love partner; the movie does its best to unsex him. Hines, whose loose, casual style of tap suggests breezy comedy and joyous goofing around, is even more crushed and abject here than he was in "The Cotton Club." Instead of playing a dapper, debonair fellow who has an underlayer of suffering, he puts the suffering on top. And he's at a particular disadvantage because he doesn't have a dramatic presence as a dancer, while Baryshnikov's dance movements are large and spectacular. As Hines' Russian wife, Isabella Rossellini—the great beauty brought forth by Roberto Rossellini and Ingrid Bergman—evokes her mother around the time of "Casablanca," and her voice is low, like her mother's, but gentler, more caressing. She appears here in shabby clothes and a mousy schoolgirl haircut, and has almost nothing to do except act meek and soothe her husband's raw nerves. Hackford and David Watkin manage to enrich some of the compositions by working her profile in, and there's a lovely closeup of her at the end, but she's never allowed to blossom. (If Hackford directed "Cinderella," the poor girl would never get to go to the ball.)

Admittedly, Baryshnikov isn't easy to cast except as a great Russian ballet dancer who defects to the West. He could play other roles; though he's an erratic actor, his confident, quick inflections give his lines a comic snap. But, of course, we want to see him dance. The screenwriters' answer here—adding another defector—compounds the problem. The Cold War dialogue scenes, designed to advance the pesky plot, are never convincing. Even the supporting players are all working to push the unwieldy mechanism along. The Polish expatriate director Jerzy Skolimowski plays the K.G.B. colonel as a jokey turn; he acts with the smirk and relish of a cartoon predator. He has a sly, bemused nastiness (and a teasing resemblance to Zbigniew Brzezinski), but he stays in one key, and he may be entertaining himself more than he entertains the audience. Geraldine Page's role as the ballet dancer's manager is purely functional, and so is Helen Mirren's as the lover he left behind when he defected—she has become the director of the Kirov. Mirren makes her impact, though; probably no other actress can let you know as fast and economically as she can that she's playing a distinguished and important woman. The only supporting actor who offers much surprise is John Glover, in the tiny role of Wynn Scott, an official from the American Embassy; Glover has an off-center style—even when he plays a good guy, as he does here, he gives it an extra squirt of energy, a kinky originality. The film's title—but nothing else—is lifted from Dostoyevski. The action is set during the "white nights" phenomenon, yet that doesn't seem to serve a story point, and if it's a metaphor it passed me by. Maybe it merely served the purposes of the moviemakers: city streets could be photographed in daylight (the exteriors were mostly shot in Finland) without the expense of traffic or extras, because the scenes are said to be taking place in the middle of the night.

6   Unsatisfying as the movie is, you keep pulling for it. You want it to be good for Baryshnikov's sake. I remember feeling this same way at some of Garbo's feebler pictures, yet people still watch those pictures that didn't rise to the occasion of her presence. There's enough footage of Baryshnikov here to carry you past the embarrassments of the tacky script. And there are scenes where Hackford shows an instinct for what he should be doing. When the ballet dancer says goodbye to the director of the Kirov in her apartment at the theatre, she flips on her video machine to a tape of him twenty years earlier, and as the scene ends he sees himself as a youth leaping and suspended in the air. The blurred video image has a ghostly magic. The scene that follows—his farewell to the empty old Maryinsky—is trite, but it's almost as affecting as it's meant to be, because the theatre that is used (the Teatro de São Carlos, in Lisbon) is glorious: a theatre that lives up to a performer's dreams of appearing before princes and gods. The best reason to see "White Nights" is that Baryshnikov demonstrates that he found the freedom of movement he defected for.

Questions and Activities

1. What does Kael mean, at the end of paragraph 1, when she says that Baryshnikov "shames the movie he's in"?
2. Why does Kael say that the plot of *White Nights* is "cheap" (paragraph 3)?
3. Does Kael feel that the use of a videotape of the dancer as a younger man toward the end of this movie (paragraph 6) is effective? What makes this device effective or ineffective?
4. Who is Zbigniew Brzezinski (paragraph 5)? Why would an actor's "teasing resemblance" to Brzezinski be an interesting fact to a knowledgeable movie-goer?

5. Describe Kael's voice. How does she create that voice? What word choices and sentence structures contribute to your impression of her personality?
6. Does Kael seem to know the pertinent facts about this movie? Does she seem to have a strong general background knowledge of movies? What parts of this essay contribute most directly to your evaluation as to whether Kael is a film expert?
7. What type of reader did Kael have in mind for this review? Point to places in the review where a specific impression of the intended reader is created. How does the language of the review create this impression? Would you say that Kael is very casual, moderately informal, or formal?

8. Pauline Kael dislikes the plot of *White Nights*. What are the reasons behind her dislike? Why might the director of the film have thought that the film's plot would successfully appeal to a 1980s audience? Do you think that a plot involving Soviet and American defectors would appeal to some people simply because of its political implications? Can you think of other movies whose plots feature Soviet-American entanglements? How are those movies different from *White Nights*? Why, during a cold war, might many film-goers enjoy movies about espionage involving the United States and Russia?
9. Do you think that *White Nights* caters to movie-goers' appetites for explicit adventure and escape rather than intellectual and aesthetic pleasure? Or does the movie seem to stimulate critical thinking and intellectual involvement?

10. Use this review as the basis for an argument either that the popular arts distort reality or that they accurately represent it. How does this film distort reality? How does it reflect reality?
11. Explain why Taylor Hackford, the director of this film, chose to emphasize the political rather than the aesthetic aspects of the film's plot. Why would Hackford make such a choice? Do you think that Hackford emphasized Soviet-American politics over the dance aspects of the plot because he felt that American audiences would want it that way? Do you think the majority of American filmgoers would want the political intrigue emphasized?

▶ *LEARNING ACTIVITIES*

12. Interview other students about their reactions to *White Nights* as it is described by Kael. Do they make interpretations that differ from Kael's interpretations? Prepare a set of specific questions to direct your interviews.
13. After you have completed your interviews of other students, write an informal evaluation of Kael's review. What specific points in her review do you disagree with as a result of your discussions with other students? Did your interviews turn up any points that Kael should have included in her review?
14. Briefly describe another recent popular movie that you think gave plot more importance than theme. What underlies the overemphasis on plot in that movie? Might plot have been emphasized because the director thought the film's audience would prefer such an emphasis?

The Hard Hat Who Sued Baseball

ROGER KAHN

Born in Brooklyn in 1927, Roger Kahn has been a writer for some of the best newspapers in the world. After spending three years at New York University, Kahn left school to pursue a career as a journalist. From 1948 to 1954, he worked first as a reporter, then as a sportswriter, for one of the most respected newspapers in the world, the now defunct *New York Herald Tribune* . He followed this job with sportswriting and editing jobs with *Newsweek* (from 1956 to 1960), *The Saturday Evening Post* (from 1963 to 1968), *Esquire* (from 1970 to 1975), and *Time* (from 1976 to the present). He received the E. P. Dutton Award for the best sports article of the year in 1960, 1969, and 1970. His books include *The Boys of Summer* (1972), *The Battle for Morningside Heights: Why Students Rebel* (1970), *How the Weather Was* (1973), *But Not To Keep* (1979), and *The Seventh Game* (1983).

Kahn is not just a sportswriter. Like Red Smith, he also takes on the role of social commentator, as his book on the 1968 student riot and protest against the Vietnam War (*The Battle for Morningside Heights*) and his earlier book on American Jews (*The Passionate People,* 1968) attest. In fact, his sportswriting has attracted a broad range of readers precisely because Kahn asks probing questions and offers insightful commentary on the social issues that lie behind the game scores, sports personalities, and technical descriptions that usually fill sports articles. One of Kahn's most recent books, *The Seventh Game,* is a baseball novel; his journalistic tendency toward narrative has crossed the line into fiction.

In writing this essay, which first appeared in *The Boys of Summer,* Kahn contributed to the development of what has come to be called the "new journalism." This type of journalism uses literary methods — story forms, personal voices, dialogue, and characterizations of real people — to make magazine or newspaper articles read as though they were fiction. This type of writing was commonly found throughout the 1960s and 1970s in *Esquire* magazine and in works by Tom Wolfe, Hunter Thompson, and Joan Didion (whose essays are included later in this book).

In this essay, Kahn wants his readers to understand Carl Furillo from the inside out. Another writer doing a straight and objective feature on Furillo would probably have dwelled far more than Kahn does on physical facts, baseball statistics, and biographical information. Kahn, in contrast, seems far more interested in having his readers feel the way Furillo feels, in having them empathize with his anger and frustration. This purpose justifies Kahn's use of more subjective, literary techniques and a personal, familiar voice. He plays the role of baseball-lover talking casually to fellow baseball-lovers. Look for evidence of this voice as you read.

Kahn's writing career would seem to make him a supporter of the argument that no reporter, no matter how sincerely he or she tries, can really be totally objective. Look for Kahn's subjectivity and literary techniques as you read this essay:

1. What makes this article different from straight news reporting? Does Kahn seem to side with or against Carl Furillo? Or does he seem as objective as a newswriter is traditionally supposed to be? How are Kahn's methods of exploring and developing his subject different from those of most journalists?
2. If journalism can be only imperfectly objective, should a journalist acknowledge biases of emotion and perspective in his or her articles? Should a reporter write "news" articles that are based on personal values and emotions?
3. If this emphasis on a personal perspective became an adopted journalistic practice, how might it change readers' expectations when they read journalism?

▶ ────────────────────────

> *Disability directly resulting from injury . . . shall not impair the right of the Player to receive his full salary for the period of such disability or for the season in which the injury was sustained.*
> —Clause in the Official Player's Contract,
> cited in the original *Baseball Encyclopedia*

1   The wine has soured. There are not going to be any more hurrahs for Carl Furillo, and those that he remembers, if he truly remembers any, are walled from him by harsher, newer memories. His career ended in anger, lawsuits, frustration. He speaks of one prominent baseball official as "that prick." Another is "a lying bastard." One of his lawyers "ended up buddies with the guy I paid him five thousand bucks to sue."

2   When I found Carl Furillo, he was a laborer, installing Otis Elevator doors in one tower of the World Trade Center, rising bright, massive, inhuman, at the foot of Manhattan Island. We sat in a basement shack, beneath incalculable tons of metal and cement, and talked across ham

sandwiches at lunch. Furillo seemed to enjoy being interviewed. He wanted to hear about some of his teammates, Carl Erskine and Preacher Roe. But mostly he wanted to spit rage. He believes that he has been cheated. The Dodgers released him while he was injured. He fought back with litigation. "You can't beat them bastards," he says. "I won. I got my money. Then all of a sudden I was blacklisted. Nobody wanted me to coach, to pinch-hit, not even in the minors. You seen me. Could I play ball?"

Carl Anthony Furillo was pure ball player. In his prime he stood six   3 feet tall and weighed 190 pounds and there was a fluidity to his frame you seldom see, among such sinews. His black hair was thick, and tightly curled. His face was strong and smooth. He had the look of a young indomitable centurion. I can imagine Reese running a Chevrolet dealership and Andy Pafko coaching high school football and Duke Snider operating a dude ranch in Nevada. But I cannot imagine Carl Furillo in his prime as anything other than a ball player. Right field in Brooklyn was his destiny.

He was a solitary, private man, but not unhappy. He had stopped   4 school at the eighth grade, and on a team of facile, verbal athletes, he felt self-conscious. He thought that he and his wife, a Pennsylvania Dutch girl named Fern, were treated as outsiders. His locker stood diagonally across from the tumult of Reese, Robinson and Snider. "Where I dress," he said, "is where I am. They don't want me in the middle of things."

"Does that bother you?"   5

"Nah. I ain't got the mouth for that crap"—he said, nodding at the   6 others—"if you know what I mean."

He played with dedication and he played in pain and he was awesome   7 in his strength and singleness. People came early just to watch Furillo unlimber his arm. The throws whined homeward, hurtled off a bounce and exploded against Roy Campanella's glove—pom, pom, pom, pom—knee-high fast balls thrown from three hundred feet. Throws climaxed his most remarkable plays. With a man on first, someone stroked a hard, climbing line drive. It was going to hit the wall, then carom at one of five angles. Furillo glanced up and ran to a spot. The drive cracked into cement and bounced into his hands. He whirled and loosed a throw. The base runner had to stop at third. The batter had to settle for a single. The crowd gasped at the throw, and then Dodger fans, appreciating how Furillo had read the right-field wall, began to clap, not wildly but rather with respect. Throughout the grandstands men said to one another, "He's a master."

Off the field, Furillo sized up people slowly, then made intuitive,   8 unshakable decisions. He hated Leo Durocher. He disliked Jackie Robinson. He respected Campanella. He admired Dick Young. For reasons I never knew, he accepted me. He spoke with honesty rather than discretion and trusted you to keep him out of trouble. Once in a while, when something he said fired controversy, he stood by his remark. "Maybe I shouldn'ta said it, but I did." He was a man of uncomplicated virtues.

9   He was proud of the way he had learned to hit good righthanded pitching and of the way he played the wall, but his deepest pride was in his arm. After Willie Mays followed a remarkable catch by whirling and throwing out Billy Cox at home, Furillo said, "I'd like to see him do that again."

10   "Well," I said, "he did it once."

11   "I'd like to see him do it again, know what I mean?" Furillo said.

12   "He can't throw with you," I said, and Furillo nodded.

13   He seemed enduring as granite in Ebbets Field. It shocked me to see him playing in Los Angeles. Without the old wall, he had lost his native backdrop. He ranged an Antony without the Capitoline, a gladiator in a cardboard coliseum.

14   I had not kept close track of Furillo when *Newsweek* magazine dispatched me in 1959 to Los Angeles, where the Dodgers and White Sox thrashed through a World Series. In a crowded press row, I found myself beside the Hollywood columnist for the *Herald Tribune*, who had been ordered to cover the Dodger clubhouse and complained periodically, "I don't know what I'm doing here. I haven't seen any baseball since I was thirteen, and I never liked it."

15   Furillo was no longer starting, but that day he pinch-hit a single with the bases loaded. The ball scooted up the middle, hopping narrowly over the shortstop's glove. It was not an old-time Furillo hit, but it won the game. (And the Dodgers went on and won the Series.) Some ninety thousand people cheered, and I told the columnist, "If you think that's something, you should have seen the homer Furillo hit off Allie Reynolds."

16   The columnist frowned. Near dusk I saw him alone in the press row, crumpled yellow paper scattered about his typewriter. He seemed near tears. "I can't write *anything*," he said. "I don't know these people, so I thought I'd write down quotes and look at their backs and get the numbers and check the program later and see who it was who'd said what. But"—terror touched his face—"they take off their *clothes* in the dressing room. They weren't wearing shirts. Who is the black-haired, handsome guy who talks in short sentences?"

17   That is how I came to write three sports stories for an infirm *Herald Tribune* under the by-line of a gossip columnist. It was fun trying my hand again and the columnist provided obbligatos of Hollywood chatter, plus door-to-door transportation in the Mercedes-Benz he said had

been given to him by Lauren Bacall. But among the shine of walnut dashboards, the glitter of pool parties, I thought, what a hard way for stolid Carl to finish: pinch-hitting in a strange town and being interviewed by people who were surprised to discover that a baseball was stitched with red yarn.

That next spring the Dodgers fired Furillo. Newspapers told a fragmented story of lawsuits, and Furillo faded. Episodic publicity greeted his reappearance as part owner of a delicatessen in Queens, but then he sold his interest and no one seemed to know where he had moved. Several ball clubs offered me addresses, but Furillo no longer lived at any. The telephone company had no record of him in New York City. Someone said he had gone south. Someone said he was living out west. Someone else was certain he had remained in Queens, under another name. I looked for months and mailed half a dozen letters, but I had all but given up when the telephone rang at 9:30 of a Friday morning and a large voice boomed my name.

"Who's this?"

"Carl Furillo."

"Where in the world are you?"

"Downtown. The family's back where I come from, but I'm working in the city during the week."

"Nobody knows that."

"You want to be bothered a hundred times a week? But I got your letters and I been thinking and it's okay. But look, when you come down, do me one favor. Put it down right. I ain't greedy. I ain't nuts. I only wanted what I had coming. I read my fucking contract so many times I got that part memorized by heart." Then he recited the lines that precede this chapter.

By the time Furillo called, winter had come. One tower of the World Trade Center had been topped and sheathed. It stood 1,350 feet, the tallest building on earth, an aluminum hulk against the sky. The other tower still showed girders. Wind was slamming across the Hudson, blowing bits of debris from unfinished floors. Four thousand men had been working for two years, and the sprawling site had acquired the scarred desolation that comes with construction or with aerial bombardment. The sun gleamed chilly silver. It was 11 degrees and getting colder.

A broad stairway led below grade to a cement floor that was wet and patched with ice. Enough daylight entered the vast basement so that wall signs were clear. *"To hell with Goodell." "Vote Buckley." "Vote Conservative."* This was hard-hat country.

"Otis is over there," someone said, pointing toward a clutch of unpainted wood cabins. "Furillo? The ball player? He dresses in that one."

28   Inside, a workman standing under a bare bulb said Furillo would be down in a minute. "See that paper bag on that bench? You *know* he's gonna be here. That's his lunch."

29   The workman's name was Chester; Chester Yanoodi. "Carl stays with me out on the island," Chester said. "He's moved his family back to Pennsylvania. He's in good shape. Real good." Chester was a compact man, with leathery skin and eyeglasses. "I've played some ball myself. On the Grumman Aircraft softball team. I could hit a few."

30   Furillo entered. "Ho," he called for "hello." Then "Cold mother out there, huh?" He wore baggy brown pants and layers of clothing. His hair was still black, but he looked heavier. He peeled off a windbreaker and walked in front of an electric heater, beating his arms and blowing on his hands. "Ho," he said again. Then, "Hey, what do you think of the building? It's something, huh? I'm still learning about elevator doors, but I'm not bad. Do I look fatter? I go around 220. Preacher called me one time, and when I told him, he said he was ready to wrestle. Him, that skinny guy, Preacher weighs 223. How do you like that?"

31   According to a spokesman for the Port of New York Authority, each tower of the World Trade Center requires a thousand elevator doors. "What do you do, Carl," I said, "when all the doors are in and the job is through?"

32   "Then I'm through."

33   "Meaning?"

34   "Back to Pennsylvania. Hunt. Fish. You remember my boy, Butch? He's gonna be a trooper. We'll be all right where we came from. I like to hunt and fish."

35   "And clam," Chester Yanoodi said. "He's a helluva clam-digger."

36   "I'm bitter about baseball," Furillo said.

37   "He could break some necks," Yanoodi said.

38   "Lousy bastards," Furillo said.

39   He sat on a bench and opened a sandwich and offered me half. Chester handed me a Thermos cup full of coffee. Three other workmen ate silently along the opposite wall, under another naked bulb. Furillo was one of them in the work clothes, but an interview reminded them that he was set apart, too. They knew it. They sat respectful. Furillo began to tell what had happened.

40   He never won the batting championship again after 1953, but he had six more good years. In 1955 he hit 26 homers and batted .314. In 1958, when the Dodgers sank to seventh at Los Angeles, he was still the solid man, with a .290 average and 18 homers. By then he was fighting pain. Under the beating of fifteen thousand innings and five thousand sprints to first base, his legs began to cramp. He had to miss days and

later weeks. Professionalism and toughness drove him, but in 1959, the year of the World Series ground single, he played in the outfield only twenty-five times.

During the first week of the following season, Furillo was running *41* out a ground ball, hurrying across first base, when his left foot found a soft spot on the floor of the Los Angeles Coliseum. Something tore in the calf. Pain crippled him.

Buzzy Bavasi wanted change. The Dodgers of 1959 were ribbed by *42* Brooklyn veterans. Nineteen-sixty was a time to turn over personnel. A team must change constantly if it is to win. The calf injury convinced Bavasi that Furillo's glories were history. He summoned Furillo to his office at the Statler Hilton Hotel and asked, "What do you think of Frank Howard, Carl?"

"I don't think he hits the curve good." *43*

"But he has promise." *44*

"You don't hit the curve, you don't belong here." *45*

"How's your leg?" *46*

"Coming along, but slow." *47*

"That Howard's gonna be something," Bavasi said. *48*

Bavasi was bearing a message down Byzantine ways. He was suggest- *49* ing that Frank Howard had arrived, and that Furillo, like Carl Erskine, should make way gracefully to the judgment of years. Retire. Then, perhaps, the Dodgers would find him a job.

Fighting for his career and the last days of his youth, Furillo beat off *50* that conclusion. Three days later, as the Dodgers prepared to fly to San Francisco, an official telephoned and said, "Carl, don't bother to pack." Furillo decided that Bavasi was giving him more time to rest his leg. But after the series Bavasi himself called and said, "I'm sorry to have to inform you that you've been given an unconditional release."

Furillo cursed and hung up. Then he studied his contract. He drove *51* through thirty-two arid paragraphs until he found the clause he wanted. He was hurt, unable to play, and the Dodgers had released him. It didn't matter how slick Bavasi was or how much money O'Malley had. They *couldn't* release him when he was hurt. He took out a pencil and began to calculate.

His salary for 1960 was to be $33,000. He had drawn $12,000. That *52* meant the Dodgers were welshing on $21,000. "You know, Fern," he said, "I think I'm gonna do something. I got an idea."

Within an hour reporters came unannounced to the house he rented *53* in Long Beach. A Dodger official had tipped them to the story. "What do you think about being released?" one sportswriter said.

"I don't like it." *54*

55   "Are you hurt bad?"

56   "I can't play, and that means they can't release me." Furillo explained the official contract succinctly.

57   "What are you going to do?"

58   "You asked me so I got to tell you. I'm gonna talk to two guys I know."

59   "What two guys?"

60   "You asked me so I got to tell you. Two guys who're lawyers."

61   Furillo had not intended to reveal his scheme, but he felt that principle forced him to speak. When a man is released, he has to face reporters, and when he faces reporters, he has to answer what he is asked. He was surprised the next day to see his name and projected lawsuit in headlines.

62   Bavasi's secretary called and asked him to stop in again. "Soon as I take care of something," Furillo said.

63   He found Bavasi enraged. "Of all the dumb dago things to do. I was going to find a spot for you. Now I can't. You've made trouble for you and me and everybody. What a rock."

64   "Hey, Buzz," Furillo said. "I got a message for you. It's from the clubhouse man."

65   "What's that?"

66   "In my pocket here." Furillo reached into his jacket and withdrew a subpoena.

67   Bavasi maintains that he "would really have looked after the guy, but not at $33,000." He speaks of sending Furillo to Spokane and developing him into a coach. O'Malley shakes his head and says a man has to learn to accept things as they are. Both feel Furillo broke a code. In the extralegal world of baseball, a dissatisfied player may protest to the Commissioner, who is supposed to look upon club owners and their chattels without partiality, but is hired and fired by the owners. Turning to the courts is considered nihilistic. No one in baseball, or in the law, knows just when a judge will decide that the official player's contract is itself invalid. The people who run baseball regard anyone exposing them to such risk as indecent. "I'm not sure what would have happened with Furillo," Bavasi said, "but there were options." Hiring lawyers foreclosed every option but one. There would be battle.

68   While the legal proceedings dragged, one of Walter O'Malley's representatives asked if Carl would settle for a job as counselor in the Dodgertown Camp for Boys at Vero Beach. Furillo moved toward court and the following spring wrote letters to eighteen major league teams. He would pinch-hit or play; he had plenty left. Nobody hired him. "It's gotta be because I'm hurt," he said. "That damn injury is still messing me up." He wanted to sue for two years, instead of one.

In May of 1961, a year after the injury, Furillo met with Ford Frick, the Commissioner, and Paul Porter, Frick's attorney. According to Furillo, he collected the $21,000 due for 1960, and collected nothing for 1961.   69

If one thinks of blacklist in terms of the old McCarthyism when the three television networks in concert refused to employ writers or actors with a so-called radical past, then Carl Furillo was not blacklisted. As far as anyone can learn, the owners of the eighteen major league clubs operating in 1961 did *not* collectively refuse to hire him. What they did was react in a patterned way. Here was one more old star who wanted to pinch-hit and coach. He could have qualified marginally, but once he sued, people in baseball's conformist ambiance decided he was a "Bolshevik." Hiring him at thirty-nine was not worth the potential trouble. Walter O'Malley was no Borgia,* plotting to bar Furillo from the game. Only Furillo's decision to hire lawyers was at play. The existential result was identical.   70

Furillo returned to Reading, investigated several businesses and liked none. In 1963 he resettled in Queens. Then he bought a half interest in a small delicatessen and restaurant on Thirty-second Avenue under the shadow of a Consolidated Edison gas tank. At Furillo and Totto's cheeses hung from the ceiling. Neighborhood people bought prosciutto and Italian sausage. Children loitered and in the afternoon you could hear Furillo's voice booming. "Hey, kid. The candy's for buying not for touching." Late at night, in the restaurant, you could order hero sandwiches prepared by Furillo himself.   71

The trouble, said Fern, was the hours. Carl had to get up early and he had to work late. "You hardly see the family any more," Fern said.   72

"I got to make a living."   73

After seven years, Furillo sold his share in the store and moved his family back to Stony Creek Mills, on the north side of Reading, where he was born. Then he took his job with Otis. He wanted to think several years ahead. He would work hard until he was fifty, spending only weekends with the family. But then, with the money he made in construction and with his pension, he would be set. There would be nothing but time for hunting and fishing, for Fern and the boys. That was how, he explained, he had come to be wearing a yellow hard hat and these rough clothes in this barren workingman's shack.   74

"You've missed some damn nice years," I said.   75

---

*Cesare Borgia (1475–1507) was an Italian leader who used intrigue, cruelty, and bravery to gain control over the province of Romagna in early sixteenth-century Italy. Borgia has become a symbol of worldly power in a human-centered universe. Kahn uses Borgia's name here to imply rule by cunning and power rather than by honesty.

76   "They really screwed him," pronounced Chester Yanoodi.

77   "Aah," Furillo said. "It ain't been bad."

78   He reached back in memory beyond the bitter time. He could always play ball, he said. He could throw, and his brother Nick encouraged him to play and, hell, he said, when he got through with grade school what were the jobs? Picking in an apple orchard for $5 a week. Helping in a woolen mill for $15. But the family kept him close, and it wasn't till he was eighteen and his mother died that he could go off to be a professional. He spent a year at Pocomoke City on the Eastern Shore of Maryland and hit .315. A season after, he played at Reading under Fresco Thompson, who watched him throw, gasped and encouraged him to pitch. "The experiment," Fresco said, "ended within three games. He could certainly throw, but who knew where? He broke four ribs and two wrists before we decided as an act of public safety to make him spend all his time in the outfield."

79   He came to Brooklyn in 1946, the vanguard of Branch Rickey's youth movement, and moved into center field between Dixie Walker and Pete Reiser. Once he spoke to Reiser about a radio program he enjoyed. "Hey," Reiser shouted. "This guy thinks 'The Dorothy and Dick Show' is 'The Dorothy Dix Show.' What a rock. Hiya, Rock." With Furillo's hard body and deliberate ways, ball players thought the cruel nickname fit. Furillo felt like an outsider because in many ways he was made to feel that way.

80   "I started having trouble with Durocher the year after that," he said in the Otis shack. "A guy's no good, he's no good. He didn't want to play me against righthanders, and Mike Gaven asked how I liked being platooned. He asked. I had to tell. I didn't like it. He wrote the story. Durocher said, 'Hey, kid. You trying to run my team?' Why didn't he get on Gaven?"

81   "It's a good thing for Durocher Carl can't get his hands on him today," Chester said.

82   "Forget it," Furillo said.

83   In 1949 Durocher was managing the Giants, but before one game in Brooklyn he poked his head into the Dodger clubhouse. Furillo was sitting on a black equipment trunk. "Hey," Durocher shouted. "We had you skipping rope with the lefthander last night. Tonight we got the righthander. You'll be ducking."

84   "Go fuck yourself," Furillo said.

85   A minute later Herman Franks looked in. "In your ear," he cried. "Tonight we get you, dago."

86   Chester broke into the story. "*Dago?* They called *you* 'dago' to your face?"

87   "All the time," Furillo said. Then, kindly to the old Grumman sotfball player, "Things are different in the big leagues."

That night the righthander, Sheldon Jones, hit Furillo with a pitch. 88
The next afternoon, Jones visited the hospital where Furillo was recovering from a concussion. "I'm sorry, Carl," Jones said. "It was a curve."

"First fucking curve that never bent," Furillo said. 89

"I just threw what Durocher told me to," Jones said. 90

"I know," Furillo said. "I ain't blaming you." He promised himself 91 to get even. It was that 1949 promise that flared at the Polo Grounds when Furillo charged to tackle Durocher and the entire Giant ball club in 1953.

"Six times I got hit in the head," Furillo said. "Maybe I ducked slow, 92 but they was always gunning for me. So I had a right to gun for the guy that started it. Right?"

"You gunned 'em yourself," I said. "How many did you throw out 93 from right field?"

"They all the time write eight. They count seven I caught rounding 94 the bag. I threw behind them. There's only one guy I really threw out. A pitcher. Mel Queen. He hit a liner at me. I grabbed it on a hop and my throw beat him. Write the truth. I threw out *one* guy."

"About the right-field wall," I said. 95

"I knew you'd ask that." His dark face lit. 96

"Well, how did you get to play it like that?" 97

"I worked, that's fucking how. I'd be out early and study it. Preacher 98 and Billy Cox hit fungoes* for me. Now as the ball goes out you sight it, like you were sighting down a gun barrel. Except you got to imagine where it's going. Is it gonna hit above the cement? Then you run like hell toward the wall, because it's gonna drop dead. Is it gonna hit the cement? Then run like hell to the infield. It's gonna come shooting out. Now you're gonna ask me about where the scoreboard came out and the angles were crazy. I worked. I worked every angle in the fucking wall. I'd take that sight line and know just where it would go. I wasn't afraid to work."

"Do you still play ball?" I said. 99

"He don't even play catch," said Chester. 100

"Arm still hurt?" 101

"It ain't that. The Mets were after me when I had the store. Play in 102 old-timers' games. I figured, why? I got the store and I got to work at it, but once the Yankees was having one and Fern said, 'Go ahead. See the guys you played with.' I went. I put on spikes. I'd been off 'em ten years. I rocked. I thought I was gonna fall over. I couldn't walk on spikes. I made it to the outfield. Someone hit a little fly. I ain't caught a

---

*"Fungoes" is a baseball term for ground balls that are hit by one player so another can practice fielding them; the batter uses a small, light bat to hit balls in rapid succession so that the fielder can improve in coordination and agility.

fly in ten years. Son of a bitch, the ball looked as though it was six miles up. I said to myself, 'See the old guys if you want to, but for Christ's sakes, don't do this no more. Don't ever put on spikes again.'"

103   The three young workers across the shack sat wide-eyed. "You got to watch out for yourself," Furillo told them. "There was this guy on the team, Carl Erskine, and he was such a nice guy that when they ordered him to throw at a hitter, he'd throw ten feet over the man's head. And he had arm trouble and he quit young and they put out stories that they were really looking after him. He was through in 1959, the year before I got hurt. I said to him, 'Hey, is that right? The ball club treated you fair?' He didn't want no trouble, but I'll never forget what he told me. He said, 'Carl. Take care of Carl.' "

104   Furillo puffed air and offered me more coffee. "If I really wanted to hit 'em," he said, "I'd have another suit. Two back operations. The bad leg had me walking funny and I had to have two operations for a ruptured disc. That come on account of the injury, but I figure, fuck it, I got to take care of myself and I can do it." The young hard hats nodded vigorously.

105   "Hey," Furillo said, "what is it with the colored today? They got to get welfare? It's tough, but was it easy for the Italians? Five dollars a week in the apple orchard, was that easy? Why should the colored have it easier than anybody?"

106   More nods.

107   "It isn't the same," I said. "You were playing ball and Robinson couldn't."

108   "He wasn't the only guy got thrown at."

109   "Ah, you're talking like a hard hat."

110   "That's what I fucking am. But when this building gets through, it's in the barrel. I put the lid on this city, New York, where I had some good times, and Los Angeles, where I should never have gone, and back with Fern up around Reading and hunt and fish and take my pension. I'll be fifty. Hey, I like a lot of colored. Campy and Joe Black, he was a nice guy. I don't think they ought to have it easy, that's all."

111   He does talk like a hard hat and he was a baseball Bolshevik. He fits no label. He is too human, too large, too variable, too much the independent. In one voice he talks against welfare, like a Buckley, and in another voice, which is the same, he talks about ball players' rights and defies a system, like Bartolomeo Vanzetti.*

---

*Born in Italy, Bartolomeo Vanzetti (1888–1927) was convicted of murder in Massachusetts in 1921, along with Nicola Sacco. Both men remained in prison for six years while their conviction was appealed. Despite mass demonstrations in their favor, they were executed in 1927. Vanzetti's letters reveal an intelligent, sensitive man who may well have been the victim of political intolerance and prejudice. Kahn uses Vanzetti to symbolize anyone who fights for individual rights against a system.

"Hey," he shouted. "Who got a hammer? I need a hammer. Having   *112*
trouble with a door." He turned. "I got plenty tricks to learn," he said.
Someone found him the hammer and he began zipping into his winter
clothes, gruff, cheerful and defiant of pity.

"Come 'round in spring," Furillo said, slamming a yellow hard hat   *113*
on his head. "In spring we'll sit outside and you and me can take a little
sun."

Questions and Activities

▶ *COMPREHENSION QUESTIONS*

1. Is Carl Furillo, according to the rule cited at the beginning of the
   article, legally justified in making this suit against baseball? Why
   does Kahn suggest that Furillo may have been technically or legally
   right but still did the wrong thing in the opinion of many "baseball
   people"? What was the baseball code of ethics like in 1959,
   according to Kahn?
2. Describe briefly, in your own words, Carl Furillo the ball player.
   Then, as a contrast, summarize Kahn's description and evaluation
   of Furillo's life outside of baseball. Compare these two perspectives
   on Furillo and develop a statement that explains the course of his
   career and life.
3. What does "blacklisting" mean (paragraph 70)? Go to the library
   and find out about the phenomenon of McCarthyism in the early
   1950s. How does the term "blacklisting" apply to the McCarthy era?
   Report back to the class on your findings.

▶ *QUESTIONS OF RHETORICAL PURPOSE AND STRATEGY*

4. Now that you have read Kahn's article, why do you think he chose
   to begin it with a citation from the *Baseball Encyclopedia*? Does the
   citation help the reader see both the justice and the irony of Carl
   Furillo's suit against the Dodgers?
5. Why does Kahn go into such detail (paragraph 18) concerning his
   difficulties in finding Furillo in order to interview him for this
   article? Why is it important that the reader have this information?
   How does it fit in with Kahn's overall purpose in writing this essay?
6. Is Kahn trying to persuade you that Furillo was right and should be
   admired or that he was wrong and should be subject to criticism? Or
   is Kahn attempting to provide an objective description of Furillo's
   character? Can you find evidence in this essay to support your an-

swers to the preceding questions? Does Kahn like Furillo? How do you know? Does Kahn's language—"hard hats," "gladiators," and so on—demonstrate his attitude toward Furillo and baseball?

7. Consider the overall form of this essay. Kahn's interpretation of Furillo's role on the Brooklyn Dodger team—as the frustrated hard hat—controls the essay's form. Can you point to one place in the essay where it is obvious that Kahn has arranged his material to conform to and support his interpretation of Furillo's role?

▶ *THEME QUESTIONS*

8. Do you feel, particularly after reading this article, that it is accurate to call professional baseball—or any professional sport—a *sport*? For the players, baseball seems more a job than a sport. How does this look at the business aspect of sports affect your perception of sports as recreation?

9. How is the recreation described in this essay (professional baseball) different from the more solitary forms of recreation described in the selections by Robert Finch, May Sarton, and Ellen Goodman?

10. From what you have learned from this essay about Carl Furillo's life, when do you think baseball ceased being fun for him and became a job? Why did this change occur? Does this generally happen to professional athletes?

▶ *LEARNING ACTIVITIES*

11. Can you remember a movie star, athlete, politician, or television personality with whom you closely identified in your childhood? Look up some biographical information about that person (use the biographical indexes and dictionaries in the reference section of your school or local library). Then write a one-page report in which you combine facts about the person with reasons why you admired him or her.

12. In this essay, Kahn sympathetically explores the causes behind Carl Furillo's ouster from baseball and his continuing bitterness. Read the essay again, jotting down these causes and Kahn's evidence for their validity. Think about this list, and write a statement conveying your own perspective on Furillo's life and career. Using your thesis statement, write a paper explaining the causes of Furillo's failure and frustration.

13. Draw up a list of questions that you would have used to interview Carl Furillo. How are your questions different from the ones Kahn asked? Do they reflect a different purpose? If so, what is it? Would they have elicited different kinds of answers from Furillo?

The Eighty-Yard Run

IRWIN SHAW

Irwin Shaw died at the age of seventy-one in 1984. Born in New York City, he graduated from Brooklyn College and immediately embarked on a writing career. His early short stories, many of which were published in *The New Yorker*, were praised by critics for their realistic and vivid episodes and their memorable and representative characters. Many of his early stories dealt with American characters in wartime situations. His story "Walking Wounded" won the O. Henry Memorial Award in 1944. In the early 1940s, Shaw served as drama critic for *The New Republic*, and he also published essays of literary and social criticism in *The Yale Review*, *The New Republic*, and other magazines.

With the publication of *The Young Lions* in 1948, Shaw began a career as a popular novelist. Although his novels were never as widely praised by critics as his short stories were, Shaw nonetheless went on to publish nine best-selling novels. *The Young Lions*, a story about two Americans and an Austrian Nazi who meet on a World War II battlefield, was made into a popular film starring Marlon Brando, Dean Martin, and Montgomery Clift. Shaw's book *Rich Man, Poor Man* was about a German-American family and was made into a television miniseries. Two of his later novels — *Beggarman, Thief* and *Two Weeks in Another Town* — were also adapted as television productions in the 1970s. A few of Shaw's plays have met with success — notably *Bury the Dead*, his critically acclaimed antiwar play — but many of the plays he wrote remain unpublished. Shaw also wrote movie screenplays, biographical studies, and a travel book.

In "The Eighty-Yard Run," Shaw demonstrates his best fiction writing. He creates in Christian Darling a character who is never able to capture the glory and sense of identity he achieved one fall day on a football field. Shaw's ability to render Darling's character and to recreate the eighty-yard run that became the high point of Darling's life allows us to evaluate the relationship between recreation and vocation in the development of a man's character. This story, in other words, gives us an intimate look at the effects of sport on one average American man.

As you read, think about these questions:

1. Why does the story begin with a detailed description of Christian Darling's one moment of athletic glory?
2. Why is it important to remember that the rest of Darling's football career was an anticlimax to his eighty-yard run?

3. Who is telling this story? Where is the person who is telling this story? Why is it important to remember who the narrator is?
4. Why is Darling never able to find a job that gives him the same satisfaction he experienced as a football player? Is the fault in the jobs, or in Darling?
5. Why do you think Shaw named his character Christian Darling?

▶ ————————————————

1   The pass was high and wide and he jumped for it, feeling it slap flatly against his hands, as he shook his hips to throw off the halfback who was diving at him. The center floated by, his hands desperately brushing Darling's knee as Darling picked his feet up high and delicately ran over a blocker and an opposing linesman in a jumble on the ground near the scrimmage line. He had ten yards in the clear and picked up speed, breathing easily, feeling his thigh pads rising and falling against his legs, listening to the sound of cleats behind him, pulling away from them, watching the other backs heading him off toward the sideline, the whole picture, the men closing in on him, the blockers fighting for position, the ground he had to cross, all suddenly clear in his head, for the first time in his life not a meaningless confusion of men, sounds, speed. He smiled a little to himself as he ran, holding the ball lightly in front of him with his two hands, his knees pumping high, his hips twisting in the almost girlish run of a back in a broken field. The first halfback came at him and he fed him his leg, then swung at the last moment, took the shock of the man's shoulder without breaking stride, ran right through him, his cleats biting securely into the turf. There was only the safety man now, coming warily at him, his arms crooked, hands spread. Darling tucked the ball in, spurted at him, driving hard, hurling himself along, his legs pounding, knees high, all two hundred pounds bunched into controlled attack. He was sure he was going to get past the safety man. Without thought, his arms and legs working beautifully together, he headed right for the safety man, stiff-armed him, feeling blood spurt instantaneously from the man's nose onto his hand, seeing his face go awry, head turned, mouth pulled to one side. He pivoted away, keeping the arm locked, dropping the safety man as he ran easily toward the goal line, with the drumming of cleats diminishing behind him.

2   How long ago? It was autumn then, and the ground was getting hard because the nights were cold and leaves from the maples around the stadium blew across the practice fields in gusts of wind, and the girls were beginning to put polo coats over their sweaters when they came to

watch practice in the afternoons....Fifteen years. Darling walked slowly over the same ground in the spring twilight, in his neat shoes, a man of thirty-five dressed in a double-breasted suit, ten pounds heavier in the fifteen years, but not fat, with the years between 1925 and 1940 showing in his face.

The coach was smiling quietly to himself and the assistant coaches were looking at each other with pleasure the way they always did when one of the second stringers suddenly did something fine, bringing credit to them, making their $2,000 a year a tiny bit more secure.

Darling trotted back, smiling, breathing deeply but easily, feeling wonderful, not tired, though this was the tail end of practice and he'd run eighty yards. The sweat poured off his face and soaked his jersey and he liked the feeling, the warm moistness lubricating his skin like oil. Off in a corner of the field some players were punting and the smack of leather against the ball came pleasantly through the afternoon air. The freshmen were running signals on the next field and the quarterback's sharp voice, the pound of the eleven pairs of cleats, the "Dig, now *dig!*" of the coaches, the laughter of the players all somehow made him feel happy as he trotted back to midfield, listening to the applause and shouts of the students along the sidelines, knowing that after that run the coach would have to start him Saturday against Illinois.

Fifteen years, Darling thought, remembering the shower after the workout, the hot water steaming off his skin and the deep soapsuds and all the young voices singing with the water streaming down and towels going and managers running in and out and the sharp sweet smell of oil of wintergreen and everybody clapping him on the back as he dressed and Packard, the captain, who took being captain very seriously, coming over to him and shaking his hand and saying, "Darling, you're going to go places in the next two years."

The assistant manager fussed over him, wiping a cut on his leg with alcohol and iodine, the little sting making him realize suddenly how fresh and whole and solid his body felt. The manager slapped a piece of adhesive tape over the cut, and Darling noticed the sharp clean white of the tape against the ruddiness of the skin, fresh from the shower.

He dressed slowly, the softness of his shirt and the soft warmth of his wool socks and his flannel trousers a reward against his skin after the harsh pressure of the shoulder harness and thigh and hip pads. He drank three glasses of cold water, the liquid reaching down coldly inside of him, soothing the harsh dry places in his throat and belly left by the sweat and running and shouting of practice.

Fifteen years.

The sun had gone down and the sky was green behind the stadium and he laughed quietly to himself as he looked at the stadium, rearing above the trees, and knew that on Saturday when the 70,000 voices roared as the team came running out onto the field, part of that enormous salute would be for him. He walked slowly, listening to the gravel crunch satisfactorily under his shoes in the still twilight, feeling his clothes swing lightly against his skin, breathing the thin evening air, feeling the wind move softly in his damp hair, wonderfully cool behind his ears and at the nape of his neck.

10   Louise was waiting for him at the road, in her car. The top was down and he noticed all over again, as he always did when he saw her, how pretty she was, the rough blonde hair and the large, inquiring eyes and the bright mouth, smiling now.

11   She threw the door open. "Were you good today?" she asked.

12   "Pretty good," he said. He climbed in, sank luxuriously into the soft leather, stretched his legs far out. He smiled, thinking of the eighty yards. "Pretty damn good."

13   She looked at him seriously for a moment, then scrambled around, like a little girl, kneeling on the seat next to him, grabbed him, her hands along his ears, and kissed him as he sprawled, head back, on the seat cushion. She let go of him, but kept her head close to his, over his. Darling reached up slowly and rubbed the back of his hand against her cheek, lit softly by a street lamp a hundred feet away. They looked at each other, smiling.

14   Louise drove down to the lake and they sat there silently, watching the moon rise behind the hills on the other side. Finally he reached over, pulled her gently to him, kissed her. Her lips grew soft, her body sank into his, tears formed slowly in her eyes. He knew, for the first time, that he could do whatever he wanted with her.

15   "Tonight," he said. "I'll call for you at seven-thirty. Can you get out?"

16   She looked at him. She was smiling, but the tears were still full in her eyes. "All right," she said. "I'll get out. How about you? Won't the coach raise hell?"

17   Darling grinned. "I got the coach in the palm of my hand," he said. "Can you wait till seven-thirty?"

18   She grinned back at him. "No," she said.

19   They kissed and she started the car and they went back to town for dinner. He sang on the way home.

20   Christian Darling, thirty-five years old, sat on the frail spring grass, greener now than it ever would be again on the practice field, looked thoughtfully up at the stadium, a deserted ruin in the twilight. He had started on the first team that Saturday and every Saturday after that for the next two years, but it had never been as satisfactory as it should have been. He never had broken away, the longest run he'd ever made was thirty-five yards, and that in a game that was already won, and then

that kid had come up from the third team, Diederich, a blank-faced German kid from Wisconsin, who ran like a bull, ripping lines to pieces Saturday after Saturday, plowing through, never getting hurt, never changing his expression, scoring more points, gaining more ground than all the rest of the team put together, making everybody's All-American, carrying the ball three times out of four, keeping everybody else out of the headlines. Darling was a good blocker and he spent his Saturday afternoons working on the big Swedes and Polacks who played tackle and end for Michigan, Illinois, Purdue, hurling into huge pile-ups, bobbing his head wildly to elude the great raw hands swinging like meat-cleavers at him as he went charging in to open up holes for Diederich coming through like a locomotive behind him. Still, it wasn't so bad. Everybody liked him and he did his job and he was pointed out on the campus and boys always felt important when they introduced their girls to him at their proms, and Louise loved him and watched him faithfully in the games, even in the mud, when your own mother wouldn't know you, and drove him around in her car keeping the top down because she was proud of him and wanted to show everybody that she was Christian Darling's girl. She bought him crazy presents because her father was rich, watches, pipes, humidors, an icebox for beer for his room, curtains, wallets, a fifty-dollar dictionary.

"You'll spend every cent your old man owns," Darling protested   *21*
once when she showed up at his rooms with seven different packages in her arms and tossed them onto the couch.

"Kiss me," Louise said, "and shut up."   *22*

"Do you want to break your poor old man?"   *23*

"I don't mind. I want to buy you presents."   *24*

"Why?"   *25*

"It makes me feel good. Kiss me. I don't know why. Did you know   *26*
that you're an important figure?"

"Yes," Darling said gravely.   *27*

"When I was waiting for you at the library yesterday two girls saw   *28*
you coming and one of them said to the other, 'That's Christian Darling. He's an important figure.' "

"You're a liar."   *29*

"I'm in love with an important figure."   *30*

"Still, why the hell did you have to give me a forty-pound dictio-   *31*
nary?"

"I wanted to make sure," Louise said, "that you had a token of my   *32*
esteem. I want to smother you in tokens of my esteem."

Fifteen years ago.   *33*

They'd married when they got out of college. There'd been other   *34*
women for him, but all casual and secret, more for curiosity's sake, and vanity, women who'd thrown themselves at him and flattered him, a

pretty mother at a summer camp for boys, an old girl from his home town who'd suddenly blossomed into a coquette, a friend of Louise's who had dogged him grimly for six months and had taken advantage of the two weeks that Louise went home when her mother died. Perhaps Louise had known, but she'd kept quiet, loving him completely, filling his rooms with presents, religiously watching him battling with the big Swedes and Polacks on the line of scrimmage on Saturday afternoons, making plans for marrying him and living with him in New York and going with him there to the night clubs, the theaters, the good restaurants, being proud of him in advance, tall, white-teethed, smiling, large, yet moving lightly, with an athlete's grace, dressed in evening clothes, approvingly eyed by magnificently dressed and famous women in theater lobbies, with Louise adoringly at his side.

35   Her father, who manufactured inks, set up a New York office for Darling to manage and presented him with three hundred accounts, and they lived on Beekman Place with a view of the river with fifteen thousand dollars a year between them, because everybody was buying everything in those days, including ink. They saw all the shows and went to all the speakeasies and spent their fifteen thousand dollars a year and in the afternoons Louise went to the art galleries and the matinees of the more serious plays that Darling didn't like to sit through and Darling slept with a girl who danced in the chorus of *Rosalie* and with the wife of a man who owned three copper mines. Darling played squash three times a week and remained as solid as a stone barn and Louise never took her eyes off him when they were in the same room together, watching him with a secret, miser's smile, with a trick of coming over to him in the middle of a crowded room and saying gravely, in a low voice, "You're the handsomest man I've ever seen in my whole life. Want a drink?"

36   Nineteen twenty-nine came to Darling and to his wife and father-in-law, the maker of inks, just as it came to everyone else. The father-in-law waited until 1933 and then blew his brains out and when Darling went to Chicago to see what the books of the firm looked like he found out all that was left were debts and three or four gallons of unbought ink.

37   "Please, Christian," Louise said, sitting in their neat Beekman Place apartment, with a view of the river and prints of paintings by Dufy and Braque and Picasso on the wall, "please, why do you want to start drinking at two o'clock in the afternoon?"

38   "I have nothing else to do," Darling said, putting down his glass, emptied of its fourth drink. "Please pass the whisky."

39   Louise filled his glass. "Come take a walk with me," she said. "We'll walk along the river."

"I don't want to walk along the river," Darling said, squinting in-   40
tensely at the prints of paintings by Dufy, Braque and Picasso.

"We'll walk along Fifth Avenue."   41

"I don't want to walk along Fifth Avenue."   42

"Maybe," Louise said gently, "you'd like to come with me to some   43
art galleries. There's an exhibition by a man named Klee...."

"I don't want to go to any art galleries. I want to sit here and drink   44
Scotch whisky," Darling said. "Who the hell hung those goddam pictures up on the wall?"

"I did," Louise said.   45

"I hate them."   46

"I'll take them down," Louise said.   47

"Leave them there. It gives me something to do in the afternoon. I   48
can hate them." Darling took a long swallow. "Is that the way people
paint these days?"

"Yes, Christian. Please don't drink any more."   49

"Do you like painting like that?"   50

"Yes, dear."   51

"Really?"   52

"Really."   53

Darling looked carefully at the prints once more. "Little Louise   54
Tucker. The middle-western beauty. I like pictures with horses in
them. Why should you like pictures like that?"

"I just happen to have gone to a lot of galleries in the last few   55
years...."

"Is that what you do in the afternoon?"   56

"That's what I do in the afternoon," Louise said.   57

"I drink in the afternoon."   58

Louise kissed him lightly on the top of his head as he sat there   59
squinting at the pictures on the wall, the glass of whisky held firmly in
his hand. She put on her coat and went out without saying another
word. When she came back in the early evening, she had a job on a
woman's fashion magazine.

They moved downtown and Louise went out to work every morning   60
and Darling sat home and drank and Louise paid the bills as they came
up. She made believe she was going to quit work as soon as Darling
found a job, even though she was taking over more responsibility day by
day at the magazine, interviewing authors, picking painters for the illustrations and covers, getting actresses to pose for pictures, going out
for drinks with the right people, making a thousand new friends whom
she loyally introduced to Darling.

"I don't like your hat," Darling said, once, when she came in in the   61
evening and kissed him, her breath rich with Martinis.

62   ''What's the matter with my hat, Baby?'' she asked, running her fingers through his hair. ''Everybody says it's very smart.''

63   ''It's too damned smart,'' he said. ''It's not for you. It's for a rich, sophisticated woman of thirty-five with admirers.''

64   Louise laughed. ''I'm practicing to be a rich, sophisticated woman of thirty-five with admirers,'' she said. He stared soberly at her. ''Now, don't look so grim, Baby. It's still the same simple little wife under the hat.'' She took the hat off, threw it into a corner, sat on his lap. ''See? Homebody Number One.''

65   ''Your breath could run a train,'' Darling said, not wanting to be mean, but talking out of boredom, and sudden shock at seeing his wife curiously a stranger in a new hat, with a new expression in her eyes under the little brim, secret, confident, knowing.

66   Louise tucked her head under his chin so he couldn't smell her breath. ''I had to take an author out for cocktails,'' she said. ''He's a boy from the Ozark Mountains and he drinks like a fish. He's a Communist.''

67   ''What the hell is a Communist from the Ozarks doing writing for a woman's fashion magazine?''

68   Louise chuckled. ''The magazine business is getting all mixed up these days. The publishers want to have a foot in every camp. And anyway, you can't find an author under seventy these days who isn't a Communist.''

69   ''I don't think I like you to associate with all those people, Louise,'' Darling said. ''Drinking with them.''

70   ''He's a very nice, gentle boy,'' Louise said. ''He reads Ernest Dowson.''

71   ''Who's Ernest Dowson?''

72   Louise patted his arm, stood up, fixed her hair. ''He's an English poet.''

73   Darling felt that somehow he had disappointed her. ''Am I supposed to know who Ernest Dowson is?''

74   ''No, dear. I'd better go in and take a bath.''

75   After she had gone, Darling went over to the corner where the hat was lying and picked it up. It was nothing, a scrap of straw, a red flower, a veil, meaningless on his big hand, but on his wife's head a signal of something . . . big city, smart and knowing women drinking and dining with men other than their husbands, conversation about things a normal man wouldn't know much about, Frenchmen who painted as though they used their elbows instead of brushes, composers who wrote whole symphonies without a single melody in them, writers who knew all about politics and women who knew all about writers, the movement of the proletariat, Marx, somehow mixed up with five-dollar dinners and the best-looking women in America and fairies who made

them laugh and half-sentences immediately understood and secretly hilarious and wives who called their husbands "Baby." He put the hat down, a scrap of straw and a red flower, and a little veil. He drank some whisky straight and went into the bathroom where his wife was lying deep in her bath, singing to herself and smiling from time to time like a little girl, paddling the water gently with her hands, sending up a slight spicy fragrance from the bath salts she used.

He stood over her, looking down at her. She smiled up at him, her eyes half closed, her body pink and shimmering in the warm, scented water. All over again, with all the old suddenness, he was hit deep inside him with the knowledge of how beautiful she was, how much he needed her.   76

"I came in here," he said, "to tell you I wish you wouldn't call me 'Baby.' "   77

She looked up at him from the bath, her eyes quickly full of sorrow, half-understanding what he meant. He knelt and put his arms around her, his sleeves plunged heedlessly in the water, his shirt and jacket soaking wet as he clutched her wordlessly, holding her crazily tight, crushing her breath from her, kissing her desperately, searchingly, regretfully.   78

He got jobs after that, selling real estate and automobiles, but somehow, although he had a desk with his name on a wooden wedge on it, and he went to the office religiously at nine each morning, he never managed to sell anything and he never made any money.   79

Louise was made assistant editor, and the house was always full of strange men and women who talked fast and got angry on abstract subjects like mural painting, novelists, labor unions. Negro short-story writers drank Louise's liquor, and a lot of Jews, and big solemn men with scarred faces and knotted hands who talked slowly but clearly about picket lines and battles with guns and leadpipe at mine-shaftheads and in front of factory gates. And Louise moved among them all, confidently, knowing what they were talking about, with opinions that they listened to and argued about just as though she were a man. She knew everybody, condescended to no one, devoured books that Darling had never heard of, walked along the streets of the city, excited, at home, soaking in all the million tides of New York without fear, with constant wonder.   80

Her friends liked Darling and sometimes he found a man who wanted to get off in the corner and talk about the new boy who played fullback for Princeton, and the decline of the double wing-back, or even the state of the stock market, but for the most part he sat on the edge of things, solid and quiet in the high storm of words. "The dialectics of the situation...The theater has been given over to expert jugglers... Picasso? What man has a right to paint old bones and collect ten thou-   81 sand dollars for them?...I stand firmly behind Trotsky...Poe was the last American critic. When he died they put lilies on the grave of American criticism. I don't say this because they panned my last book, but..."

82   Once in a while he caught Louise looking soberly and consideringly at him through the cigarette smoke and the noise and he avoided her eyes and found an excuse to get up and go into the kitchen for more ice or to open another bottle.

83   "Come on," Cathal Flaherty was saying, standing at the door with a girl, "you've got to come down and see this. It's down on Fourteenth Street, in the old Civic Repertory, and you can only see it on Sunday nights and I guarantee you'll come out of the theater singing." Flaherty was a big young Irishman with a broken nose who was the lawyer for a longshoreman's union, and he had been hanging around the house for six months on and off, roaring and shutting everybody else up when he got in an argument. "It's a new play, *Waiting for Lefty;* it's about taxi-drivers."

84   "Odets," the girl with Flaherty said. "It's by a guy named Odets."
85   "I never heard of him," Darling said.
86   "He's a new one," the girl said.
87   "It's like watching a bombardment," Flaherty said. "I saw it last Sunday night. You've got to see it."
88   "Come on, Baby," Louise said to Darling, excitement in her eyes already. "We've been sitting in the Sunday *Times* all day, this'll be a great change."
89   "I see enough taxi-drivers every day," Darling said, not because he meant that, but because he didn't like to be around Flaherty, who said things that made Louise laugh a lot and whose judgment she accepted on almost every subject. "Let's go to the movies."
90   "You've never seen anything like this before," Flaherty said. "He wrote this play with a baseball bat."
91   "Come on," Louise coaxed, "I bet it's wonderful."
92   "He has long hair," the girl with Flaherty said. "Odets. I met him at a party. He's an actor. He didn't say a goddam thing all night."
93   "I don't feel like going down to Fourteenth Street," Darling said, wishing Flaherty and his girl would get out. "It's gloomy."
94   "Oh, hell!" Louise said loudly. She looked coolly at Darling, as though she'd just been introduced to him and was making up her mind about him, and not very favorably. He saw her looking at him, knowing there was something new and dangerous in her face and he wanted to say something, but Flaherty was there and his damned girl, and anyway, he didn't know what to say.
95   "I'm going," Louise said, getting her coat. "I don't think Fourteenth Street is gloomy."

"I'm telling you," Flaherty was saying, helping her on with her coat,   96
"it's the Battle of Gettysburg, in Brooklynese."

"Nobody could get a word out of him," Flaherty's girl was saying as   97
they went through the door. "He just sat there all night."

The door closed. Louise hadn't said good night to him. Darling   98
walked around the room four times, then sprawled out on the sofa, on
top of the Sunday *Times*. He lay there for five minutes looking at the
ceiling, thinking of Flaherty walking down the street talking in that
booming voice, between the girls, holding their arms.

Louise had looked wonderful. She'd washed her hair in the afternoon   99
and it had been very soft and light and clung close to her head as she
stood there angrily putting her coat on. Louise was getting prettier
every year, partly because she knew by now how pretty she was, and
made the most of it.

"Nuts," Darling said, standing up. "Oh, nuts."   100

He put on his coat and went down to the nearest bar and had five   101
drinks off by himself in a corner before his money ran out.

The years since then had been foggy and downhill. Louise had been   102
nice to him, and in a way, loving and kind, and they'd fought only once,
when he said he was going to vote for Landon. ("Oh, Christ," she'd
said, "doesn't *anything* happen inside your head? Don't you read the
papers? The penniless Republican!") She'd been sorry later and apologized for hurting him, but apologized as she might to a child. He'd tried
hard, had gone grimly to the art galleries, the concert halls, the
bookshops, trying to gain on the trail of his wife, but it was no use. He
was bored, and none of what he saw or heard or dutifully read made
much sense to him and finally he gave it up. He had thought, many
nights as he ate dinner alone, knowing that Louise would come home
late and drop silently into bed without explanation, of getting a divorce,
but he knew the loneliness, the hopelessness, of not seeing her again
would be too much to take. So he was good, completely devoted, ready
at all times to go any place with her, do anything she wanted. He even
got a small job, in a broker's office and paid his own way, bought his
own liquor.

Then he'd been offered the job of going from college to college as a   103
tailor's representative. "We want a man," Mr. Rosenberg had said,
"who as soon as you look at him, you say, 'There's a university man.' "
Rosenberg had looked approvingly at Darling's broad shoulders and
well-kept waist, at his carefully brushed hair and his honest, wrinkle-
less face. "Frankly, Mr. Darling, I am willing to make you a proposition. I have inquired about you, you are favorably known on your old
campus, I understand you were in the backfield with Alfred Diederich."

Darling nodded. "Whatever happened to him?"   104

105   "He is walking around in a cast for seven years now. An iron brace. He played professional football and they broke his neck for him."

106   Darling smiled. That, at least, had turned out well.

107   "Our suits are an easy product to sell, Mr. Darling," Rosenberg said. "We have a handsome, custom-made garment. What has Brooks Brothers got that we haven't got? A name. No more."

108   "I can make fifty, sixty dollars a week," Darling said to Louise that night. "And expenses. I can save some money and then come back to New York and really get started here."

109   "Yes, Baby," Louise said.

110   "As it is," Darling said carefully, "I can make it back here once a month, and holidays and the summer. We can see each other often."

111   "Yes, Baby." He looked at her face, lovelier now at thirty-five than it had ever been before, but fogged over now as it had been for five years with a kind of patient, kindly, remote boredom.

112   "What do you say?" he asked. "Should I take it?" Deep within him he hoped fiercely, longingly, for her to say, "No, Baby, you stay right here," but she said, as he knew she'd say, "I think you'd better take it."

113   He nodded. He had to get up and stand with his back to her, looking out the window, because there were things plain on his face that she had never seen in the fifteen years she'd known him. "Fifty dollars is a lot of money," he said. "I never thought I'd ever see fifty dollars again." He laughed. Louise laughed, too.

114   Christian Darling sat on the frail green grass of the practice field. The shadow of the stadium had reached out and covered him. In the distance the lights of the university shone a little mistily in the light haze of evening. Fifteen years. Flaherty even now was calling for his wife, buying her a drink, filling whatever bar they were in with that voice of his and that easy laugh. Darling half-closed his eyes, almost saw the boy fifteen years ago reach for the pass, slip the halfback, go skittering lightly down the field, his knees high and fast and graceful, smiling to himself because he knew he was going to get past the safety man. That was the high point, Darling thought, fifteen years ago, on an autumn afternoon, twenty years old and far from death, with the air coming easily into his lungs, and a deep feeling inside him that he could do anything, knock over anybody, outrun whatever had to be outrun. And the shower after and the three glasses of water and the cool night air on his damp head and Louise sitting hatless in the open car with a smile and the first kiss she ever really meant. The high point, an eighty-yard run in the practice, and a girl's kiss and everything after that a decline. Darling laughed. He had practiced the wrong thing, perhaps. He hadn't prac-

ticed for 1929 and New York City and a girl who would turn into a woman. Somewhere, he thought, there must have been a point where she moved up to me, was even with me for a moment, when I could have held her hand, if I'd known, held tight, gone with her. Well, he'd never known. Here he was on a playing field that was fifteen years away and his wife was in another city having dinner with another and better man, speaking with him a different, new language, a language nobody had ever taught him.

Darling stood up, smiled a little, because if he didn't smile he knew   *115* the tears would come. He looked around him. This was the spot. O'Connor's pass had come sliding out just to here...the high point. Darling put up his hands, felt all over again the flat slap of the ball. He shook his hips to throw off the halfback, cut back inside the center, picked his knees high as he ran gracefully over two men jumbled on the ground at the line of scrimmage, ran easily, gaining speed, for ten yards, holding the ball lightly in his two hands, swung away from the halfback diving at him, ran, swinging his hips in the almost girlish manner of a back in a broken field, tore into the safety man, his shoes drumming heavily on the turf, stiff-armed, elbow locked, pivoted, raced lightly and exultantly for the goal line.

It was only after he had sped over the goal line and slowed to a trot   *116* that he saw the boy and girl sitting together on the turf, looking at him wonderingly.

He stopped short, dropping his arms. "I..." he said, gasping a little,   *117* though his condition was fine and the run hadn't winded him. "I—once I played here."

The boy and the girl said nothing. Darling laughed embarrassedly,   *118* looked hard at them sitting there, close to each other, shrugged, turned and went toward his hotel, the sweat breaking out on his face and running down into his collar.

Questions and Activities

▶ COMPREHENSION QUESTIONS

1. Did Christian Darling move up to the starting team after his eighty-yard run?
2. Who called Darling "an important figure"?
3. Who were Dufy, Braque, and Picasso (paragraph 37)? Why do you think Darling disliked their work and his wife liked it?

4. What did Louise's hat signify to Darling (paragraph 75)?
5. What happened to Darling's teammate Alfred Diederich after he left college? What does Darling's reaction to Diederich's fate indicate about his feelings about Diederich?
6. Why does Darling ask his wife to stop calling him "Baby"? Does she stop?

▶ *QUESTIONS OF RHETORICAL PURPOSE AND STRATEGY*

7. What does the repetition of the phrase "fifteen years" in paragraphs 2, 5, and 8 tell you about the narration of this story? Who, for the most part, is telling the story? Is the narrator of this story looking back on his own past or on someone else's?
8. There is a significant amount of dialogue in this story. How does the dialogue reveal the characters of Darling and Louise? Which character is the more intelligent of the two? Which character is living in the past? What does the dialogue reveal about what these characters think of each other?

▶ *THEME QUESTIONS*

9. Christian Darling spends much of his young life pursuing excellence in a sport. Later in his life he plays sports simply as a leisure activity. Do you think Darling ever successfully adapts to this change in emphasis? Why does he have trouble adapting, when most other men don't?
10. Should exceptional athletes be pampered and taken care of, as Darling was? How might such pampering harm an athlete? Is it ever harmless?
11. Louise and her friends have many different kinds of interests — politics, the arts, social movements, and so on. Why isn't Darling able to develop such interests? Do you think his job as a tailor's representative on college campuses is the answer to his problems of adjustment to adult life?

▶ *LEARNING ACTIVITIES*

12. Find a newspaper or magazine article in which a current star athlete is interviewed or described. Analyze the article for evidence that it is suggesting that the athlete has qualities other than those required for his or her athletic career.
13. Recall an exceptional athlete from your high school days. Report to the class on the kind of treatment that person received from other students and teachers. Was that treatment different from the way other students were treated? How was it different?

14. Write a brief sketch describing an exceptional person in a field other than sports, for example, music, the arts, or science. Do you feel that exceptional persons in that other field are subjected to the same kind of treatment that exceptional athletes often receive from others?

Writing Assignments

The writing assignments that appear at the end of each section of this book give you an opportunity to develop a general response to each section's theme and to write a formal essay to be evaluated by your teacher. The assignments that follow will help you focus the responses you had to the views of recreation presented in the selections in this section and will ask you to look back over and develop your practice writings, as you produce a more formal response to this theme.

Each set of writing assignments includes a free-response option and a situational-response option. If you choose the free-response option, you will simply be asked to respond to the section's theme from a perspective that has been defined in the section's introduction, readings, headnotes, and study questions. If you choose the situational-response option, your assignment will be to follow a systematic sequence of steps in writing a formal essay. In each situational-response option, the audience and purpose of your writing will be partially defined.

On Recreation and Its Functions

Consider the following sets of terms. Each one pairs the word "recreation" with a word or phrase describing some advantage or disadvantage that people associate with recreation.

> recreation / release from pressure
> recreation / waste of time
> recreation / human achievement
> recreation / embarrassment
> recreation / waste of money
> recreation / social enhancement
> recreation / relaxation
> recreation / competition

Select one or two pairs of terms and explore them by writing freely about your ideas and associations. You may first want to look over and rethink your responses to the readings in this section and to class discussions. Your writing should develop your perspective on these terms by referring back to your responses to the readings as well as to other students' ideas. You should also carefully consider your purpose before you write. Will you be explaining, persuading, or simply expressing your perspective? Why would others in your class want to hear what you have to say?

VIDEO GAMES AS RECREATION

Imagine that you have been asked by your college newspaper to write a feature article on college students and leisure time. In addition to reading at least two of the selections in this section, you read the article on video games that appears with this writing exercise (pages 68–80). This article convinces you to restrict yours to the advantages and disadvantages of video games as a leisure activity for college students.

Your audience of college students, however, will want more than a simple reproduction of the statistics and expert testimony that appear in the magazine article. They will also want you to discuss the advantages and disadvantages of video games in the context of some general statement on the function of recreation in Americans' lives. You will need to draw on ideas from some of the readings in this section to develop that general idea.

Develop your essay in two general stages. First, go back over your notes on the selections you have read. Sift through the examples, issues, and perspectives in these notes and develop a generalization on the place of recreation in our lives. Then use the attitudes toward particular kinds of recreation that are expressed or implied by two or three of the readings from this section to support your generalization. At this stage, you should review the notes you have decided to use; then put them aside and simply write on the subject of recreation for twenty minutes. Then write your generalization below your free writing. Later you can look back at your free writing as you use your generalization to guide the writing of your first draft.

Second, use the generalization about recreation to read and analyze the video game article. Develop a second generalization that defines your attitude toward video games as a recreational activity. You might repeat the free-writing process as you develop this second generalization. This generalization combined with your earlier one on recreation should become the main thesis of your essay.

For example, you might begin the developmental sequence by writing down the following generalization: "Most recreation should include some activity that will make the person doing it a more effective person in the rest of his or her life." Then, as the second generalization, you might extend the first one to video games as recreation: "Video games are not desirable ways to spend recreational time because they have no long-term value for those who play them." These generalizations could become the main thrust of an essay in which you develop arguments concerning the possible positive or negative long-term effects of playing video games. The readings in this section would provide some pro and con arguments to use in writing this essay. A conclusion to such an essay might weigh the pros and cons of video games and make some general statement on the purpose of recreation in a person's life.

Remember the audience for whom you will be writing. They are similar to you — they share the same college experience with sports, games, and entertainment. But they are also different — they have not read the articles that you have read and they may not share your viewpoint on video games. You will need to know what they will recognize as familiar information. Then, you will need to give them some new information (from your reading and discussions) that builds on their knowledge.

Follow this step-by-step process as you compose:

1. Review the selections from this section that you will use.
2. Write freely on the subject of recreation for twenty minutes.
3. Write a generalization that you feel captures the attitude toward recreation that is expressed or implied in the readings you have chosen.
4. Read the following article on video games.
5. Write freely on video games as recreation for twenty minutes.
6. Write a generalization that you feel expresses your attitude toward recreation.
7. Combine both of your generalizations into a thesis statement.
8. Plan and write your essay around your combined generalization. Your plan might include three or four subpoints concerning each generalization.

Games That Play People
JOHN SKOW

1   Those beeping video invaders are dazzling fun—and even addictive.

2   Let us have no more lamentation that our microprocessed era lacks heroes (plinkety-plunk of Pete Seeger's banjo). The spirit of mighty John Henry, the steel-driving man who beat the steam drill (plunk-plunk-plunk), lives on in the indomitable courage and abused optic nerves of a Mount Prospect, Ill., high school boy named Steve Juraszek (Seeger whacks out several yards of fancy banjo work and begins a ballad):

> *Well, Steve Juraszek dropped in his quarter,*
> *Just half an hour before noon (plink-plunk).*

He would die in the end, when the blasters zapped his men,
But he vowed that wouldn't happen soon, poor boy.
He vowed that wouldn't happen soon.

At six that night they called his mother,
Said, "Ma'am, your boy's not comin home.
He's shootin fast and hot, at the mutants and the pods,
And the microchip is processing a groan, oh my.
The microchip is letting out a groan."

Oh they fed him on pizza and cola.
His fingers were cramping up and cold.
His eyeballs were raw, when a dum-dee-dum he saw,
And it something dum-de-dum foretold.

What nonsense is this? The answer is very nearly, but perhaps not   3
quite, in the increasingly crowded category labeled If You Have to Ask,
You Will Never Understand. What Juraszek, 15, recently did at an
Arlington Heights, Ill., arcade called One Step Beyond was play Defender, one of those beeping, flashing, quarter-eating arcade video games,
for 16 hours and 34 minutes on the same 25¢, ringing up a score of
15,963,100 before he finally made a mistake and lost his last ship. Anyone who knows arcade games, and especially Defender, which is one of
the most difficult, will agree that this is very close to being impossible.
It is definitely not one of those non-feats thought up by the untalented
to memorialize themselves in *The Guinness Book of World Records*,
such as eating seven miles of spaghetti, or riding an exercise bicycle for
a week and a half.

Defender is an attack-from-outer-space game. It is played on a large   4
color video screen where nullity bombs and destructo beams are hurled
at the player by the machine's computer. Increasingly rowdy sound effects suggest what James Joyce, under the influence of William Blake
(who would have loved these gadgets), called "the ruin of all space,
shattered glass and toppling masonry and time one livid final flame."
The Defender player controls a small cannon-firing jet plane that flies at
varying altitudes and speeds over a barren planetscape. He must shoot
down a bewildering variety of alien bad guys, each with his own pattern
of behavior, dodge an assortment of missiles, and rescue helpless space-
men, vulnerable to being kidnapped, who appear randomly on the
planet's surface. He must have reflexive control of a joystick that deter-
mines altitude and of five separate buttons that fire the cannon, change
forward thrust, reverse direction, make the ship skim off the screen
into hyperspace and fire a limited supply of smart bombs, which blow

up everything in sight. As is fiendishly true of all of the good new video games, as the game progresses Defender shifts to subtler strategies and sends out its alien waves with increasing speed. You play the machine and it plays you.

5   A neophyte has as much chance with Defender as he would if he were to take over the controls of an F-16. A reasonably good video-game athlete—that is how game junkies are beginning to describe themselves—will last it out for a few thousand points, or a couple of minutes. A superb player, the kind not seen in every arcade, may hit 500,000 on his best day. That is why when Juraszek began to close in on 1 million points toward the end of the first hour of his enchanted run, people began to notice. Darrell Schultz, one of the arcade's owners, asked Steve if he thought he could set a record.

6   ''I said, 'Yeah,''' Juraszek recalls, ''and he said, 'Go for it.' '' Juraszek is a gangly young man who began playing pinball when he was ten before video games had hit the scene. ''I could buy a car or something with the money I've put into games,'' he says, with no appearance of regret. He started playing Defender in June, and by August he was pretty good. On his record day he kept up his strength by snapping at pizza slices that people held in front of his face. He said later that he was so excited he never even thought about going to the bathroom. His mother, Joanne Juraszek, watched for a while, utterly unimpressed, and agreed reluctantly to let him play till he dropped ''I just wish,'' she said later, ''that he was this good about doing his homework.''

7   As the scornful cry ''So what?'' echoes from glen to glen, and as the unmoved Joanne Juraszek admits that she finds her son's new fame ''very strange,'' skeptical citizens might do well to pay attention to a peculiar clinking sound audible across the land. The noise is made by the estimated 20 billion quarters that poured last year into the arcade monsters. This is a figure that may be the public relations roar of a healthy young industry beating its chest, but one that investment analysts who specialize in the entertainment industry agree is not far wrong. While they spent this $5 billion, video-game addicts also were spending 75,000 man-years playing the machines.

8   These figures do not include an estimated $1 billion that consumers paid for video-game consoles that hook up to home television sets, and for the expensive cassettes that make them work. For comparison, $5 billion is exactly twice the reported take in the last fiscal year of all of the casinos in Nevada. It is almost twice the $2.8 billion gross of the U.S. movie industry. And it is three times more than the combined television revenues and gate receipts last year of major league baseball, basketball, and football.

From what vast aquifer of cash does this astonishing gush of money   9
flow? From the lunch money of school children, say angry parents who
are determined, so to speak, to give video games no quarter. The town
fathers of Irvington, N.Y. (pop. 6,000), rose up in wrath last July and
passed an ordinance designed "to protect the adolescents of the village
against the evils associated with gambling" (though video games offer
no cash payoff and indeed almost never click out a single free game);
they limited each establishment to three machines. Ralph Provenzano,
owner of a deli opposite the Irvington Middle School, resents the suggestion that he is corrupting the youth, but agreed to turn off his three
machines (Defender, Pac Man and Centipede) before the start of classes
each morning. With some justice, he says, "I baby-sat a bunch of kids
here all summer. It may have cost them money, but they were here,
they were safe, and they didn't get into trouble."

The fears that occasionally are voiced of drug-buzzed, beery teen-   10
agers hanging around video parlors in menacing packs seem absurdly
exaggerated, and the likelihood is that communities with troublemak-
ing youngsters had them before the arcades opened. But the video
games are enormously addictive, and they do eat a lot of quarters. Atari,
one of the leading video-game manufacturers, advertises a cheerful,
fast-moving and very popular arcade game called Centipede with the
words "Chomp. Chomp. Chomp. Chomp. Chomp" above a drawing of
a voracious-looking centipede gnawing a coin.

An adult observer in New London, N.H. (pop. 3,000), wanders into   11
Egan's, a pizza parlor with twelve video games, which has become the
town's teen hangout since it opened a few months ago. The place is
clean and friendly, with no smell of funny cigarettes (many arcades
sternly forbid smoking of any kind) and nothing in sight more menacing
than an anchovy pizza. But a conversation with a twelve-year-old boy
who is holding his own against Scramble, a Stern Electronics game in
which the player tries to fly a jet through what looks like Mammoth
Cave, produces unsettling information. "I usually bring $20," says the
boy, when asked how much money he spends. As the observer is
digesting this, the boy adds, "But today I brought $40." Proprietor Bob
Egan, an insurance broker in New Jersey before he moved to New
Hampshire last year, says that he too was surprised, but yes, the boy did
change $40.

In Orlando, Fla., the consensus of fifth-graders at Blankner Elemen-   12
tary School is that $3 is a "minimum satisfactory amount" to take to an
arcade, but several children talked of spending $10 or $20. "I used to
spend money on my bike," one boy said ruefully. Not all game players
throw huge sums into the coin chutes, but they agree that it takes an in-

vestment of between $20 to $50 to become proficient at any game challenging enough to be fun. There is no question that the money drain is one reason why such communities as Babylon, Long Island, Oakland, Calif., Pembroke Pines, Fla., and Durham, N.H., have passed ordinances restricting play by teen-agers of various ages. The New Hampshire Civil Liberties Union asked that enforcement be postponed till the U.S. Supreme Court rules on an ordinance passed in Mesquite, Texas, forbidding play by people under 17. Lower courts have twice struck down the ordinance.

13   The fact is, however, that teen-agers hoping to bankrupt themselves blissfully with a session of Asteroids or Missile Command may be frustrated not by a prejudicial ordinance but by a lunchtime crowd of adults monopolizing the machines. The Station Break Family Amuse-ment Center in Washington's L'Enfant Plaza opens at 7 a.m.; by 7:15 a dozen men in business suits are blasting away at the games while coffee in plastic cups grows cold. L'Enfant Plaza is within walking distance of at least five major Government agencies. "Office workers seem to need to blow it out" in their fantasies more than other people, says Tom McAuliffe, 33, vice president for operations of the 51-store chain that owns the arcade.

14   By lunchtime, with no teen-agers and not one pair of blue jeans in sight, the 47 machines are making a commotion like Mount St. Helens clearing its throat. Curt Myron, 37, is there, a mortage supervisor at HUD, who is one of the arcade's top guns. Years ago, pinball cowboys would tape notes to the sides of the machines boasting of their best scores. One of the cleverest come-ons of the video games is circuitry that congratulates hot-shooters with GREAT GAME! and the opportu-nity to record on-screen their initials and scores for a display that flashes periodically. It is the solid-state equivalent of "D. Boone Killed a Bar," and it means that Myron, who earned the four top scores on the arcade's Centipede machine, is held in awe by the other regulars. He skips lunch, he says, and plays every day, so proficiently that he rarely spends more than 75¢. "I also play in airports," he says, "much to my wife's chagrin."

15   Eric Mondres, 26, a Department of Agriculture staffer, is less cheer-ful about his addiction. "It's like a drug," he says. "You see the same people here week after week. I've tried to wean myself. I'd like to have back all the money I've spent." Near by, wearing a wet raincoat and steamy glasses, a middle-aged man jabs furiously at the thruster of a Star Castle game. He admits to being an attorney in private practice, but says, "I'd really rather you didn't use my name. This is my secret place. It would drive my wife crazy. I really don't come here very

often.'' Two hours later, he is still there battling the machine's alien psychology—and his own.

An onlooker watching such a scene and disposed to gloom would   *16*
have no trouble detecting the smell of society's burning insulation. Contrariwise, an optimist sees these lunchless loners as sensible adults wisely granting themselves a period of therapeutic play, avoiding the intake of cholesterol and booze, and emptying their minds of clutter by a method quite as effective as meditation. In Japan, where many of the games originate, a 29-year-old magazine executive named Shozo Kimura, who admits the games have hooked him, views the mass addiction moodily: ''Tokyo is a big town. You think you are not lonely, but it is the opposite. People have nothing to do. They don't care about anything. They can't buy houses. They can do nothing with their money except play the games.''

The video-game craze, more frenzied even than the universal lust for   *17*
designer jeans and Kalashnikov assault rifles, has spread across the globe. In West Germany, merchandisers are toting up astonishing Christmas season sales figures that may reach $88 million for home-video consoles and cartridges. In Australia, the quarter-eaters, actually 20¢-piece eaters, bring in $182 million a year. Fascination with the games, often accompanied by cosmic brooding about their presumed bad effect on faith, morals and school attendance, seems to be universal. The games have appeared in Arab settlements in Israel, and in Soweto, Johannnesburg's huge black township. Brazil's laws forbid the importing of video games, so they are manufactured locally, and are given the necessary touch of international chic with such English names as Aster Action and Munch Man. In Mexico City, the hot arcade is Chispas (''Sparks''). Video arcades are replacing pool halls as the traditional lounging places for young men in Madrid.

Homosexual cruising is a problem in Amsterdam's arcades. In   *18*
Stockholm, the games are associated in the public mind with teen-age hoodlumism involving drugs, prostitution and illegal hard liquor. Video addicts under 18 are banned from arcades in West Germany, although younger teen-agers manage to play on home sets in department stores.

In the Philippines, outcries against ''the ravages of a destructive so-   *19*
cial enemy, the electrical bandit,'' as one infuriated citizens' group called the video games, reached such a level of indignation that President Ferdinand Marcos banned the machines in November and gave owners two weeks to smash them. The Catholic Women's League of Caloocan City applauded the ban, asserting darkly that the games had lured young men into beer houses, where they saw burlesque dancers. A

wealthy businessman was reduced to public despair because the games had caused the ruin of one of his children, a 17-year-old son whose infatuation with gadgets was so complete, he refused to attend school or even see his friends. The distracted father thinks of sending the boy to school in the U.S., but has doubts about it, because "I fear the video games will catch up with him there." He says that "when it finally dawned on me what had hit me, my first impulse was to put up a video-machine parlor and let my son manage what he enjoys doing most. But then my wife prevailed on me, begging me not to, saying that if I went ahead with my plan, how many more young boys and girls would be ruined?" In the meantime the arcade owners, who, of course, merely hid their machines, are lobbying President Marcos to relax his ban. Not long ago, 50 disassembled video games, listed as "rectifying apparatus parts," were seized by Philippines customs agents.

20   In Hollywood, on the other hand, Producer Frank Marshall thinks the video games are "great if you want to take 15 minutes and block everything out. When you're shooting a movie, you're constantly on this high level of adrenaline, and these games use that level to completely absorb you." He kept an Asteroids machine in his office during preproduction work on *Raiders of the Lost Ark.* "It got out of hand," he confesses. "People actually got fired for spending too much time on it." Nevertheless, there are a Defender, a Missile Command and a Donkey Kong game in the offices he shares with Director Steven Spielberg and Producer Kathleen Kennedy. Not many citizens can afford video-arcade games that cost up to $3,500, but two Manhattan dentists, Phil Pierce and Jeanette Tejada, have a Space Invaders on order for their waiting room. There are also machines at other odd way-stops: a Y.M.C.A. in Grand Haven, Mich.; a Baptist church in Merritt Island, Fla,; the basement of Yale's freshman dorm. At Fort Eustis, Va., the Army employs a modified Battlezone as a weapons-training device. The Epilepsy Center at Johns Hopkins University Medical School uses three specially wired Atari sets to determine the effects of anticonvulsant drugs on learning and ability. The advantage of the games, according to Dr. Eileen Vining, associate director of the center, is that children are eager to make their best efforts in eye-hand coordination tests. The Capital Children's Museum in Washington uses video-game techniques, including wildly changing colors and fast interaction between machine and operator, to teach preschoolers about computers. Children learn measurement by playing with a hungry cartoon worm that eats centimeter segments of lines.

21   Last year Dun & Bradstreet held a conference for 120 of its managers at Bagatelle Place, a "VIP amusement complex" in the Rye Town,

N.Y., Hilton Hotel, which offers a library, a *cappuccino* bar and 33 video games. This classy arcade enforces a dress code after 6 p.m., and serves banquets at which the changemaking attendants, upon request, dress in dinner jackets.

Although Bagatelle staffers deny it, experience suggests that unless   22
these black-tie dinners are stag affairs, they are almost certain to be social disasters. The reasons are that male arcade players tend to outnumber females by about 20 to 1, and that women, especially if they are wives, generally resent the games, and quite often regard them with outright loathing. Ask men and women at random to explain this undeniable phenomenon, and you get chauvinistic patronizing or matronizing of the worst pop-psychological kind. The most temperate analyst is likely to mention that most women are not conditioned as children to be comfortable with complicated gadgets, or to play shooting games. Ear-weary males, their backs welted with wifely sarcasm, may grumble that women are afraid to look foolish in public, or that they simply do not know how to play (a glib reduction comparable to the feminist slur of a few years ago that men do not know how to cry). They say that women view the games as black holes, soaking up male attention, and that even liberated wives are made nervous when their male protectors act like little boys. Women say they are too sensitive to enjoy the bloodthirsty games, and men counter that, no, women are simply too literal-minded to see that the blood is not real and that the games are harmless fantasy. (Though it is hard to deny that some of the fantasies are fairly creepy. As Producer Frank Marshall admits, when you lose your last city—there goes Cleveland—in Missile Command, ''it's depressing.'')

The sunny and cheerful exception to the prevalent theme of electron   23
ic *Gotterdämmerung*, and one of the few games so far that women play in large numbers, is Bally's Pac Man. Pop psychologizers note that it is not a game of shooting, but—aha!—engulfing. It may also be the ultimate eating disorder; the player directs a happy-looking yellow disc around a maze, as it gobbles cookie-shaped dots, and tries to avoid some not-very-menacing monsters. It is by no means easy to play, though some men feel it is unworthy of serious attention because it has only one hand control. Linda Starkweather, 29, who runs a beauty salon in Union Park, Fla., got hooked on a Pac Man she discovered near by at Jake's Ice Cream shop. So did her two women employees. Then they found another Pac Man at a neighborhood sandwich shop and began straggling back late from lunch hour.

When Starkweather found herself struggling to limit herself at each   24
session to $3 or $4, the obvious next step was to install a Pac Man in her

shop. "We've spent all our tips already this morning," she said not long ago, laughing. Ann Williams, one of her former operators and now a Tupperware saleswoman, calls herself a "closet Pacperson." She admits to spending $15 on one session, and although for a while she didn't tell her husband, she feels no guilt: "It's my money; I earned it. There's not a lot of fun things in life. It's taken away my boredom. I've never been as serious about anything as Pac Man."

25   Serious? Listen to Los Angeles Screenwriter Jeffrey Alan Fiskin, who discovered Pac Man earlier this year during the Hollywood writers' strike: "Oh, pipe down, all you fans of Asteroids and Defenders," he wrote in *California* magazine. "Take your arrested adolescence elsewhere!...We want philosophical rigor, a metaphor for life..." The task of Pac Man, Fiskin notes solemnly, is to clear a labyrinth, and as he succeeds, he collects point-scoring rewards, all very symbolic: first food in the form of fruit, then keys—"the key to wisdom, the key to the next level; ah, the pure Jungian simplicity of it." Fiskin warns that "you will pay and pay to learn the intricacies of this labyrinth, these demons. The parallel to psychoanalysis has, perhaps, not escaped you..."

26   Like many of the best games, Pac Man is a Japanese design, and so far Bally's Midway division, the U.S. licensee, has produced 96,600 of the machines here (Asteroids is second, at 70,000; and third, at 60,000, is Space Invaders, the game that began the video craze three years ago). Counterfeit machines sell briskly, much to the displeasure of Bally's lawyers, who are kept busy fighting copyright infringements. Forging a Pac Man or Centipede game is not much more complicated than pirating a music cassette or videotape. A modern game may require six $20 ROM 32-K chips, each of which handles 32,000 bits of information. ROM means "read only memory," and refers to a permanently programmed chip, not one that can "learn" and "forget" information. Joel Gilgoff, owner of a four-store arcade games supply chain called G.A.M.E.S., in Van Nuys, Calif., says, "That amount of memory rented for $50,000 a month six years ago."

27   The waves of color, shape and sound that crash about the ears of the bedazzled player are really incredibly lavish waves of information. Home TV and such games as Space Invaders use a "raster" TV monitor that forms images made of tiny line segments; Asteroids, Space Fury and other games use an "x-y" monitor that employs unbroken lines. Each line on the TV screen is controlled by an instruction from the machine's microprocessor. So is each fragment of each sound. The player reacts to the images on the screen and the uproar in his ears, and waggles his controls, which flash impulses to the microchips. The machine depicts the player's maneuvers instantly, and takes its own countermeasures a microsecond later, all the while keeping score. In due

course the dreaded "Game Over" sign flashes, as the chips have ordained.

A desk-top machine called a EPROM programmer (for Erasable Programmable Read Only Memory) can steal the information on a programmed chip and transfer it to a blank chip in about one minute. EPROM units cost about $2,500, which is a great improvement over the $1 million or more it takes to develop a successful new game. Thus it is not hard for a counterfeiter to offer immediate delivery and a price several hundred dollars lower than list.   *28*

Ten minutes ago, let's say, Pac Man pirates—yo, ho, ho and a chip of ROM—did not exist. Now they are only one of the dangers in a fast-shifting market in which hot-shot operators whisper into the ears of kindly and greedy old candy-store proprietors that the right game in a good location can bring in $400 a week, or more than a strong man can earn selling used cars. Put in one and you've got a used-car salesman. Take ten and you have a tame orthodontist on a leash. A few store and arcade owners buy their own game machines, counterfeit or not, but most give floor space to machines owned by distributors who farm out and service hundreds of them. Store owners and distributors generally split the take equally. In either case a machine usually must earn back its cost in a few weeks, before local players "learn the board" and are no longer interested. The $400 figure turns out, most often, to be sucker bait, dangled to obscure the dreary truths that markets are becoming saturated and that dud games and obsolete good games bring in no money at all. The fads whirl by so fast that Bally does not even manufacture the historic game Space Invaders any more, although fans buy used machines for sentimental reasons, and many arcades keep one around as a gesture toward the old days.   *29*

Wait a minute. Old days? Historic Space Invaders? Just so. There is prehistory, and that is pinball. (And, of course, in Japan there were the jingly pachinko games.) Middle-aged arcade lurkers learned from pinball the cool, bent-kneed stances and the correct ominous angle at which to lip a toothpick. Pinball cost a nickel and had no-K intelligence. It used electromechanical kickers and—talk about primitive! —gravity for power. If you jostled too much it tilted. The very skillful pinball bandit would lift the entire 500-lb. front ends of pinball games off the floor and onto the toes of his Army boots, lessening the incline of the table and foxing gravity. If he won 50 free games, as he was likely to, the blood stopped flowing in his feet. Pinball is still around, although it is not very lively.   *30*

Pong, invented by Atari's founder, Nolan Bushnell, in the early 1970s, signaled the dawn of video-game history. Electronic paddles slapped a ball—really just a white blip—back and forth across a black-   *31* and-white TV screen. As Pong evolved, it permitted you to play another person, or, and this was the big excitement, the game would play you. Pong sold enormously for a few months in 1973. And then died. It was pushed into extinction not by a better game, but by its own lack of intelligence; it took a bit of time to master, but after that it was no challenge, and players became bored.

32   Nothing much happened in the arcades during the mid-'70s. Those were the Dark Ages: people picked up their pizzas and trudged home. Magnavox had marketed a console programmed so that some 20 games could be played on home television, but the games were not much more challenging than Pong. A line of Mattel hand-held, battery-powered computer games was cleverly engineered, but the games themselves were dull, and the firm almost lost its shirt. Milton Bradley sold a good hand-held computer game called Blockbuster, in which the player tried to break down a wall on a tiny video screen. The firm also did well with a simple but clever computer puzzler called Simon; and Texas Instruments made a supposedly educational game called Speak & Spell that used a voice simulator and talked to you. Chess Challenger 7 made a good seven-level chess computer and then complicated it unnecessarily with a voice simulator.

33   The industry seemed fogbound until 1979. Then, suddenly, airports, delicatessens, gas stations and Chinese restaurants started crawling with electronic columns of squiggly, glowing monsters that marched toward earthmen with a measured thump, thump, thump that changed, as the battle boiled faster, to a frenzied thumpthumpthump. The subtleties that make a game great, or fail to do so, are akin to the mumblings of metaphysics. Space Invaders, a Japanese import licensed to Bally, had an eerie capacity for seizing sane people by the imagination. A minor delight was that the forts behind which the shooter crouched crumbled as they took enemy fire. A major occasion for romantic fatalism occurred as each wave of attackers was expunged and another took its place, so that even the most valiant defender at last was overwhelmed: each teen-ager or corporation bluesuit was his own Beau Geste. But what gave the machine special fascination was its ability to increase the fury of the attack and, as the players improved, the mocking bombast of its splendid sound effects. It was not just a clanking coin-eater. It was, or seemed to be, a sentient alien.

34   Anyone who played Space Invaders even semiseriously in those days remembers that reports soon spread by jungle telegraph of stupendous scores racked up elsewhere, by ''a kid out in Chicago,'' ''a guy in Jersey.'' But by 1980 there was a new big video-game hit, Atari's Asteroids. This free-moving, doom-in-space melodrama, in which the

weightless, drifting shooter tries to blast his way through showers of astral garbage and an occasional scout ship, also had a measure of immortality programmed into it: it was among the first arcade games to invite heroic scorers to record their initials. No game manufacturer has bothered yet to program a system in which local high scores are fed into a national data bank, but there is nothing impossible about the idea, and it might even be profitable, as quarters continue to pour down the coin shoots.

Whither vid-mania? In a Walt Disney film called *Tron*, to be released 35 this summer, one designer goes berserk and enters the microchip world of video games. Just now, the games are everywhere, and trade publications are full of puff pieces by manufacturers and distributors assuring each other that the game phenomenon is not a fad. They may be right; the Brock Hotel Corp., whose stock registered a 130.2% increase last year, the third highest on the New York Exchange, owes its success to a chain of video-and-pizza parlors. Whatever the future holds, just now the game manufacturers require earth-moving equipment to clear away the coin. In 1981 Bally's sales jumped to an estimated $880 million from $693 million in 1980. Williams, which makes Defender, saw nine months' gross sales go from $83 million in 1980 to $126 million last year, and it has just opened a new plant in Gurnee, Ill., capable of producing 600 to 700 Defenders a day.

The other big manufacturer is Atari, whose sales are estimated to 36 have risen more than 120% from 1980 to 1981. Part of this sunny good fortune comes from its heavily promoted consoles and game cartridges for play on home TV. Mattel's Intellivision and Magnavox's Odyssey 2 are the primary competitors with Atari for the home market, and the odds are that all three will live or die less on the quality of their engineering than on the cleverness of their games. Until home video consoles evolve as programmable computers (at least two software firms, Broderbund and USE, are marketing programmable games for Apple home computers for less than $50), and until somebody makes a designing breakthrough on the order of Space Invaders to popularize them, it seems probable that the arcade coin-eaters will continue to be the flashiest, noisiest and most villainously intelligent of the video products.

Talking games are commonplace now; Sega/Gremlin's Space Fury 37 growls menacingly at prospective players, "So, a creature for my amusement." As might be expected, new mazes on the order of Pac Man were common at a recent trade exposition in Chicago. The hit of the show was a highly sophisticated space saga called Eliminator, made by Sega/Gremlin, an imaginative small manufacturer. Up to four players man the deluxe Eliminator and try to blast each other and the computer until only one player survives for the final combat with the computer. Sega/Gremlin has demonstrated its own three-dimensional game, and a company official says that it should be on the market in twelve to 20 months. Holographic 3-D is a distant possibility, and voice-activated games may come fairly soon. Only high costs block the manufacture of arcade space trainers, in which the player would sit inside a closed, movable cockpit and see nothing but void and space monsters through his windshield. Such a gadget may soon be feasible; computer costs are coming down, and exactions on players are rising to meet them. The 50¢ game is already a gruesome reality in some arcades, and the $1 game is surely speeding toward us by bankrupto-beam through hyperspace.

38   Mere earthlings, meanwhile, cope as best they can. As might be expected, with-it doctors have detected such video-related maladies as Space Invaders wrist and Pac Man elbow. And of course there are psychological swamps into which enthusiasts may sink. Julie Winecoff, 21, an unemployed truck driver from Charlotte, N.C., paid her way to an Atari tournament in Chicago recently, lost ignominiously to Ok-Soo Han, 25, a Korean immigrant from Los Angeles, and dolefully swore off the stuff. "I'm never going to play another game of Centipede as long as I live," she said. "I've been whupped bad. I've been sure 'nuff tore down."

39   And Steve Juraszek, hero of song and news story? His high school banned him from leaving the school grounds for a few days because he missed afternoon classes on the day he set his record. But his eye remains on distant peaks. "I'm going to pick a weekend," he says. "I'll work out before on those spring things to strengthen my wrists and fingers. Then I'm going to go to sleep right after school on that Thursday and Friday and I'll start on Saturday morning and go the whole weekend."

> . . .*A man ain't nothin' but a man (plink, plunk)*
> *But before I let that Defender beat me down,*
> *I'll die with my blaster in my hand (plink, plunk)*
> *Die with my blaster in my hand.*

Do We Define Ourselves by Our Work?

▶ ───────────────────────────────

Introduction

▶ ─────────────────────────────

The readings in this section address, from a variety of perspectives, the question of self-definition through work. They constitute pairs of related approaches to the question of how workers define themselves by their work. Benjamin Franklin saw endless possibilities for personal satisfaction and material gain in American business enterprise. Practicality and common sense, harnessed to personal initiative, Franklin believed, will result in successful enterprise over the long haul. Stephen Cruz, the subject of Studs Terkel's sketch, has found only disappointment in business, the activity that Franklin addressed with such optimism. These are two contrasting perspectives on American business, yet Cruz's negativism and Franklin's optimism may actually have the same idealistic belief in personal initiative at their roots.

Adrienne Rich and Toni Cade Bambara share a radical concern with changing social attitudes toward work as it affects women and blacks. Rich calls on women to maintain their sense of community with other women as they enter previously male-dominated professions and jobs. Bambara calls on blacks to support social change without sacrificing their basic optimism about the potential for achieving self-fulfillment in working for the cause of equality.

William Ouchi and Harvey Swados, writing in different decades, point to what they perceive as weaknesses in the work force of industrial and corporate America. American workers, Swados asserts, have come to place personal and material gain over the social good that might be accomplished through their jobs. Writing some twenty years later, Ouchi contrasts American and Japanese workers and finds the Japanese "collective sense of responsibility" better suited to an industrial society, in which workers must cooperate to produce products. Franklin's idea of the individual producing high-quality goods or running a small business on his or her own seems outdated to Ouchi.

Richard Selzer and Robert Penn Warren offer two variations on the theme of the individual who is both committed to and part of some form of work. Selzer, a surgeon who compares his professional role to that of a priest, finds the joy and gratification in his work that elude Stephen Cruz and seem lacking in American workers as they are described by Ouchi and Swados. Jeff York, the protagonist of Penn Warren's story, is totally committed to his life as a respectable small farmer, but he is unable to hold that sense of commitment when his situation changes radically.

Another way of thinking about the readings in this section is to use Franklin's essays as the focal point for a consideration of the work theme. Franklin describes what has come to be known as the classic American work ethic: success achieved through hard work, moral commitment, and consistency. The essay by Selzer and the short story by Penn Warren confirm this basic work ethic; however, Selzer's confirmation is positive and self-fulfilling, and Penn Warren presents, in Jeff York, a character whose hard work brings some degree of material success but spiritual tragedy. This American ethic is criticized for its over-emphasis on individualism in Ouchi's essay comparing American and Japanese business practices, and its death is reported in Harvey Swados's essay on how the American working classes have been spiritually destroyed by having to do work that often seems meaningless to them. Studs Terkel's account of the views of Stephen Cruz demonstrates in a more personal way this death of the American dream of hard work and happiness going hand in hand. Bambara's essay describes how her writing is dedicated to recapturing a positive attitude toward work, like Franklin's, but with a focus on collective rather than individual benefits.

Two categories of thematic questions will help you appreciate the ideas contained in these readings. The first category consists of some questions focused on individual relationships with jobs and careers:

1. How does a person's work provide him or her with satisfaction and a sense of well-being?
2. Are there social conditions that influence how a person finds satisfaction in work? Should workers receive more than material compensation for work? Should a person's work have a social dimension; should a worker, in other words, be able to perceive the worth of his or her work to others?
3. What has caused the unhappiness and sense of failure in some workers, for example, Stephen Cruz and Jeff York?
4. What do you want from the work you do? Should work be the center of one's life?

As you read through the section, a second category of questions focused on the social or public significance of work should arise to complement the first set of questions:

1. Why do so many people seem discontented in their jobs?
2. Does the American system seem to encourage competitiveness at the expense of cooperation?
3. Have some groups of people always been victimized by American business and industry? If so, how can their situations be improved?
4. Why are some people satisfied in their work? How can these individuals be used as models as we try to create a more fulfilled and satisfied work force?

Advice to a Young Tradesman and *The Way to Wealth*

BENJAMIN FRANKLIN

Benjamin Franklin has a secure place in the American cultural heritage. We think of Franklin as an early personification of the common American virtues of frugality, practicality, inventiveness, ambition, pragmatic intelligence, and boundless energy. He lived for eighty-four years (from 1706 to 1790), spanning the century of colonial development, revolution, independence, and rising American commercial interests. He lived happily for long periods in England, where he served as American ambassador and received degrees from Oxford and St. Andrews. He attempted for some time to negotiate a peace between England and its colonies before he finally reconciled himself to the inevitability of American independence. He was our first postmaster general, a successful small businessman (printer) in Philadelphia who was able to retire at the age of forty-two, and also one of the eighteenth century's best applied scientists. He invented the Pennsylvania fireplace in 1741, received worldwide recognition for research on electricity that he did in the years between 1748 and 1754, and became the consummate diplomat, politician, and man-of-the-world in later life.

"Advice to a Young Tradesman" was published by Franklin in 1748 using his own printing press. He was about to retire after twenty years of successful business life—as a printer, scientist, newspaper publisher, and amateur inventor. In this tract, he tries to pass on his business sense to all would-be entrepreneurs.

"The Way to Wealth" was first printed in 1758 as a preface to the first complete edition of *Poor Richard's Almanac*. Posing as Richard Saunders, a rags-to-riches character modeled on himself, Franklin composed entries for this almanac from approximately 1732 through the early 1750s. Into *Poor Richard's Almanac* Franklin crams all the practical wisdom he gathered while making his way in trade and business, from the time he started assisting his father as a candlemaker in 1716 until he retired to a life of science, statesmanship, and study in the early 1740s.

In these two brief pieces, Franklin speaks to others like himself, people who believe that industry and frugality can bring wealth and success. Franklin's words fulfilled the expectations of his original readers, who were eager to learn and believe in his practical recipes for material success. We find in his words early evidence of a belief in the relationship between hard work and success, which gradually became the essence of the American dream.

These essays by Franklin give us a base from which to interpret the other selections in this section. Franklin's positive analysis of what it takes to be successful — personal initiative, hard work, and moral integrity — has motivated individual workers through the centuries. Franklin believed firmly in the individual's responsibility for his or her own success. Opportunities must be seized and developed through patience and effort. But other selections in this section seem to question such a focus on the individual. Perhaps there is more social concern embodied in Franklin's individualism than his later readers have seen. Perhaps individuals who have defined success solely in material terms have been too quick to dismiss Franklin's social concerns.

Consider the following questions as you read these selections:

1. Are the values Franklin attempts to communicate still useful guides to success? Has our society changed so much that these guides now seem idealistic and simplistic?
2. Does Franklin address spiritual concerns as well as material ones?
3. Do you think a contemporary adolescent considering a career in business or trade would find Franklin's advice useful? What particular pieces of Franklin's advice seem most relevant to today's work environment?

▶ ─────────────────────

Advice to a Young Tradesman

To my Friend, A. B.

As you have desired it of me, I write the following hints, which have been of service to me, and may, if observed, be so to you.   *1*

Remember, that *time* is money. He that can earn ten shillings a day by his labor, and goes abroad, or sits idle, one half of that day, though he spends but sixpence during his diversion or idleness, ought not to reckon *that* the only expense; he has really spent, or rather thrown away, five shillings besides.   *2*

Remember, that *credit* is money. If a man lets his money lie in my hands after it is due, he gives me the interest, or so much as I can make of it during that time. This amounts to a considerable sum where a man has good and large credit, and makes good use of it.   *3*

Remember, that money is of the prolific, generating nature. Money can beget money, and its offspring can beget more, and so on. Five shillings turned is six, turned again it is seven and three-pence, and so on till it becomes an hundred pounds. The more there is of it, the more it   *4* produces every turning, so that the profits rise quicker and quicker. He that kills a breeding sow, destroys all her offspring to the thousandth generation. He that murders a crown, destroys all that it might have produced, even scores of pounds.

5   Remember, that six pounds a year is but a groat a day. For this little sum (which may be daily wasted either in time or expense unperceived) a man of credit may, on his own security, have the constant possession and use of an hundred pounds. So much in stock, briskly turned by an industrious man, produces great advantage.

6   Remember this saying, *The good paymaster is lord of another man's purse.* He that is known to pay punctually and exactly to the time he promises, may at any time, and on any occasion, raise all the money his friends can spare. This is sometimes of great use. After industry and frugality, nothing contributes more to the raising of a young man in the world than punctuality and justice in all his dealings; therefore never keep borrowed money an hour beyond the time you promised, lest a disappiontment shut up your friend's purse for ever.

7   The most trifling actions that affect a man's credit are to be regarded. The sound of your hammer at five in the morning, or nine at night, heard by a creditor, makes him easy six months longer; but, if he sees you at a billiard-table, or hears your voice at a tavern, when you should be at work, he sends for his money the next day; demands it, before he can receive it, in a lump.

8   It shows, besides, that you are mindful of what you owe; it makes you appear a careful as well as an honest man, and that still increases your credit.

9   Beware of thinking all your own that you possess, and of living accordingly. It is a mistake that many people who have credit fall into. To prevent this, keep an exact account for some time, both of your expenses and your income. If you take the pains at first to mention particulars, it will have this good effect; you will discover how wonderfully small, trifling expenses mount up to large sums, and will discern what might have been, and may for the future be saved, without occasioning any great inconvenience.

10   In short, the way to wealth, if you desire it, is as plain as the way to market. It depends chiefly on two words, *industry* and *frugality*; that is, waste neither *time* nor *money*, but make the best use of both. Without industry and frugality nothing will do, and with them every thing. He that gets all he can honestly, and saves all he gets (necessary expenses excepted), will certainly become *rich*, if that Being who governs the world, to whom all should look for a blessing on their honest endeavours, doth not, in his wise providence, otherwise determine.

An Old Tradesman.

The Way to Wealth

Courteous Reader,

I have heard, that nothing gives an author so great pleasure as to find 1 his works respectfully quoted by others. Judge, then, how much I must have been gratified by an incident I am going to relate to you. I stopped my horse lately, where a great number of people were collected at an auction of merchants' goods. The hour of the sale not being come, they were conversing on the badness of the times; and one of the company called to a plain, clean, old man, with white locks, "Pray, Father Abraham, what think you of the times? Will not these heavy taxes quite ruin the country? How shall we ever be able to pay them? What would you advise us to?" Father Abraham stood up, and replied, "If you would have my advice, I will give it you in short; for *A word to the wise is enough*, as Poor Richard says." They joined in desiring him to speak his mind, and gathering round him, he proceeded as follows.

"Friends," said he, "the taxes are indeed very heavy, and, if those 2 laid on by the government were the only ones we had to pay, we might more easily discharge them; but we have many others, and much more grievous to some of us. We are taxed twice as much by our idleness, three times as much by our pride, and four times as much by our folly; and from these taxes the commissioners cannot ease or deliver us, by allowing an abatement. However, let us hearken to good advice, and something may be done for us; *God helps them that help themselves*, as Poor Richard says.

"I. It would be thought a hard government, that should tax its people 3 one-tenth part of their time, to be employed in its service; but idleness taxes many of us much more; sloth, by bringing on diseases, absolutely shortens life. *Sloth, like rust, consumes faster than labor wears; while the used key is always bright*, as Poor Richard says. *But dost thou love life, then do not squander time, for that is the stuff life is made of*, as Poor Richard says. How much more than is necessary do we spend in sleep, forgetting, that *The sleeping fox catches no poultry*, and that *There will be sleeping enough in the grave*, as Poor Richard says.

"*If time be of all things the most precious, wasting time must be*, as 4 Poor Richard says, *the greatest prodigality*; since, as he elsewhere tells us, *Lost time is never found again; and what we call time enough, always proves little enough*. Let us then up and be doing, and doing to the purpose; so by diligence shall we do more with less perplexity. *Sloth makes all things difficult, but industry all easy; and He that riseth late must trot all day, and shall scarce overtake his business at night; while Laziness travels so slowly, that Poverty soon overtakes him. Drive thy* business, let not that drive thee; and *Early to bed, and early to rise, makes a man healthy, wealthy, and wise*, as Poor Richard says.

5   "So what signifies wishing and hoping for better times? We may make these times better, if we bestir ourselves. *Industry need not wish, and he that lives upon hopes will die fasting. There are no gains without pains; then help, hands, for I have no lands*; or, if I have, they are smartly taxed. *He that hath a trade hath an estate; and he that hath a calling, hath an office of profit and honor*, as Poor Richard says; but then the trade must be worked at, and the calling followed, or neither the estate nor the office will enable us to pay our taxes. If we are industrious, we shall never starve; for, *At the working man's house hunger looks in, but dares not enter*. Nor will the bailiff or the constable enter, for *Industry pays debts, while despair increaseth them*. What though you have found no treasure, nor has any rich relation left you a legacy, *Diligence is the mother of good luck, and God gives all things to industry. Then plough deep while sluggards sleep, and you shall have corn to sell and to keep*. Work while it is called to-day, for you know not how much you may be hindered to-morrow. *One to-day is worth two to-morrows*, as Poor Richard says; and further, *Never leave that till to-morrow, which you can do to-day*. If you were a servant, would you not be ashamed that a good master should catch you idle? Are you then your own master? Be ashamed to catch yourself idle, when there is so much to be done for yourself, your family, your country, and your king. Handle your tools without mittens; remember, that *The cat in gloves catches no mice*, as Poor Richard says. It is true there is much to be done, and perhaps you are weak-handed; but stick to it steadily, and you will see great effects; for *Constant dropping wears away stones; and By diligence and patience the mouse ate in two the cable; and Little strokes fell great oaks.*

6   "Methinks I hear some of you say, 'Must a man afford himself no leisure?' I will tell thee, my friend, what Poor Richard says, *Employ thy time well, if thou meanest to gain leisure; and, since thou art not sure of a minute, throw not away an hour*. Leisure is time for doing something useful; this leisure the diligent man will obtain, but the lazy man never; for *A life of leisure and a life of laziness are two things. Many, without labor, would live by their wits only, but they break for want of stock*; whereas industry gives comfort, and plenty, and respect. *Fly pleasures, and they will follow you. The diligent spinner has a large shift; and now I have a sheep and a cow, everybody bids me good morrow.*

7   "II. But with our industry we must likewise be steady, settled, and careful, and oversee our own affairs with our own eyes, and not trust too much to others; for, as Poor Richard says,

I never saw an oft-removed tree,
Nor yet an oft-removed family,
That throve so well as those that settled be.

And again, *Three removes are as bad as a fire;* and again, *Keep thy shop, and thy shop will keep thee;* and again, *If you would have your business done, go; if not, send.* And again,

He that by the plough would thrive,
Himself must either hold or drive.

And again, *The eye of a master will do more work than both his hands;* and again, *Want of care does us more damage than want of knowledge;* and again, *Not to oversee workmen, is to leave them your purse open.* Trusting too much to others' care is the ruin of many; for *In the affairs of this world men are saved, not by faith, but by the want of it;* but a man's own care is profitable; for, *If you would have a faithful servant, and one that you like, serve yourself. A little neglect may breed great mischief; for want of a nail the shoe was lost; for want of a shoe the horse was lost; and for want of a horse the rider was lost,* being overtaken and slain by the enemy; all for want of a little care about a horse-shoe nail.

"III. So much for industry, my friends, and attention to one's own business; but to these we must add frugality, if we would make our industry more certainly successful. A man may, if he knows not how to save as he gets, keep his nose all his life to the grindstone, and die not worth a groat at last. *A fat kitchen makes a lean will;* and

Many estates are spent in the getting,
Since women for tea forsook spinning and knitting,
And men for punch forsook hewing and splitting.

If you would be wealthy, think of saving as well as of getting. The Indies have not made Spain rich, because her outgoes are greater than her incomes.

"Away then with your expensive follies, and you will not then have so much cause to complain of hard times, heavy taxes, and chargeable families; for

Women and wine, game and deceit,
Make the wealth small and the want great.

And further, *What maintains one vice would bring up two children.* You may think, perhaps, that a little tea, or a little punch now and then, diet a little more costly, clothes a little finer, and a little entertainment now and then, can be no great matter; but remember, *Many a little makes a mickle.* Beware of little expenses; *A small leak will sink a great ship,* as Poor Richard says; and again, *Who dainties love, shall beggars prove;* and moreover, *Fools make feasts, and wise men eat them.*

10   "Here you are all got together at this sale of fineries and knick-knacks. You call them *goods;* but, if you do not take care, they will prove *evils* to some of you. You expect they will be sold cheap, and perhaps they may for less than they cost; but, if you have no occasion for them, they must be dear to you. Remember what Poor Richard says; *Buy what thou hast no need of, and ere long thou shalt sell thy necessaries.* And again, *At a great pennyworth pause a while.* He means, that perhaps the cheapness is apparent only, and not real; or the bargain, by straitening thee in thy business, may do thee more harm than good. For in another place he says, *Many have been ruined by buying good pennyworths.* Again, *It is foolish to lay out money in a purchase of repentance;* and yet this folly is practised every day at auctions, for want of minding the Almanac. Many a one, for the sake of finery on the back, have gone with a hungry belly and half-starved their families. *Silks and satins, scarlet and velvets, put out the kitchen fire,* as Poor Richard says.

11   "These are not the necessaries of life; they can scarcely be called the conveniences; and yet, only because they look pretty, how many want to have them! By these, and other extravagances, the genteel are reduced to poverty, and forced to borrow of those whom they formerly despised, but who, through industry and frugality, have maintained their standing; in which case it appears plainly, that *A ploughman on his legs is higher than a gentleman on his knees,* as Poor Richard says. Perhaps they have had a small estate left them, which they knew not the getting of; they think, *It is day, and will never be night;* that a little to be spent out of so much is not worth minding; but *Always taking out of the meal-tub, and never putting in, soon comes to the bottom,* as Poor Richard says; and then, *When the well is dry, they know the worth of water.* But this they might have known before, if they had taken his advice. *If you would know the value of money, go and try to borrow some; for he that goes a borrowing goes a sorrowing,* as Poor Richard says; and indeed so does he that lends to such people, when he goes to get it in again. Poor Dick further advises, and says,

> *Fond pride of dress is sure a very curse;*
> *Ere fancy you consult, consult your purse.*

And again, *Pride is as loud a beggar as Want, and a great deal more saucy.* When you have bought one fine thing, you must buy ten more, that your appearance may be all of a piece; but Poor Dick says, *It is easier to suppress the first desire, than to satisfy all that follow it.* And it is as truly folly for the poor to ape the rich, as for the frog to swell in order to equal the ox.

> *Vessels large may venture more,*
> *But little boats should keep near shore.*

It is, however, a folly soon punished; for, as Poor Richard says, *Pride that dines on vanity, sups on contempt. Pride breakfasted with Plenty, dined with Poverty, and supped with Infamy.* And, after all, of what use is this pride of appearance, for which so much is risked, so much is suffered? It cannot promote health, nor ease pain; it makes no increase of merit in the person; it creates envy; it hastens misfortune.

"But what madness must it be to *run in debt* for these superfluities? [12] We are offered by the terms of this sale, six months' credit; and that, perhaps, has induced some of us to attend it, because we cannot spare the ready money, and hope now to be fine without it. But, ah! think what you do when you run in debt; you give to another power over your liberty. If you cannot pay at the time, you will be ashamed to see your creditor; you will be in fear when you speak to him; you will make poor, pitiful, sneaking excuses, and, by degrees, come to lose your veracity, and sink into base, downright lying; for *The second vice is lying, the first is running in debt,* as Poor Richard says; and again, to the same purpose, *Lying rides upon Debt's back;* whereas a free-born Englishman ought not to be ashamed nor afraid to see or speak to any man living. But poverty often deprives a man of all spirit and virtue. *It is hard for an empty bag to stand upright.*

"What would you think of that prince, or of that government, who [13] should issue an edict forbidding you to dress like a gentleman or gentlewoman, on pain of imprisonment or servitude? Would you not say that you were free, have a right to dress as you please, and that such an edict would be a breach of your privileges, and such a government tyrannical? And yet you are about to put yourself under such tyranny, when you run in debt for such dress! Your creditor has authority, at his pleasure, to deprive you of your liberty, by confining you in gaol till you shall be able to pay him. When you have got your bargain, you may, perhaps, think little of payment; but, as Poor Richard says, *Creditors have better memories than debtors; creditors are a superstitious sect, great observers of set days and times.* The day comes round before you are aware, and the demand is made before you are prepared to satisfy it; or, if you bear your debt in mind, the term, which at first seemed so long, will, as it lessens, appear extremely short. Time will seem to have added wings to his heels as well as his shoulders. *Those have a short Lent, who owe money to be paid at Easter.* At present, perhaps, you may think yourselves in thriving circumstances, and that you can bear a little extravagance without injury; but

> *For age and want save while you may;*
> *No morning sun lasts a whole day.*

Gain may be temporary and uncertain, but ever, while you live, expense is constant and certain; and *It is easier to build two chimneys, than to keep one in fuel,* as Poor Richard says; so, *Rather go to bed supperless, than rise in debt.*

> *Get what you can, and what you get hold;*
> *'Tis the stone that will turn all your lead into gold.*

And, when you have got the Philosopher's stone,* sure you will no longer complain of bad times, or the difficulty of paying taxes.

14   "IV. This doctrine, my friends, is reason and wisdom; but after all, do not depend too much upon your own industry, and frugality, and prudence, though excellent things; for they may all be blasted, without the blessing of Heaven; and, therefore, ask that blessing humbly, and be not uncharitable to those that at present seem to want it, but comfort and help them. Remember, Job suffered, and was afterwards prosperous.

15   "And now, to conclude, *Experience keeps a dear school, but fools will learn in no other,* as Poor Richard says, and scarce in that; for, it is true, *We may give advice, but we cannot give conduct.* However, remember this, *They that will not be counselled, cannot be helped;* and further, that, *If you will not hear Reason, she will surely rap your knuckles,* as Poor Richard says."

16   Thus the old gentleman ended his harangue. The people heard it, and approved the doctrine; and immediately practised the contrary, just as if it had been a common sermon; for the auction opened, and they began to buy extravagantly. I found the good man had thoroughly studied my

*The term "Philosopher's stone" is usually used metaphorically to refer to the precious intellectual ore that philosophers attempt to mine through rigorous thinking. Finding the stone supposedly brought the finder wisdom and a life of freedom from physical care, but no real philosopher has ever achieved this goal. Franklin is implying here that wisdom provides greater wealth than material goods do.

Almanacs, and digested all I had dropped on these topics during the course of twenty-five years. The frequent mention he made of me must have tired any one else; but my vanity was wonderfully delighted with it, though I was conscious that not a tenth part of the wisdom was my own, which he ascribed to me, but rather the gleanings that I had made of the sense of all ages and nations. However, I resolved to be the better for the echo of it; and, though I had at first determined to buy stuff for a new coat, I went away resolved to wear my old one a little longer. Reader, if thou wilt do the same, thy profit will be as great as mine. I am, as ever, thine to serve thee,

Richard Saunders.

Questions and Activities

▶ *COMPREHENSION QUESTIONS*

1. What values does Franklin endorse as he discusses the relationship between an individual and his or her work? Does he seem to focus on material gain and prosperity, on security and peace of mind, or on more intangible benefits? Would you find a life lived according to Franklin's advice dull and mechanical or invigorating and enlightening?

2. In "The Way to Wealth," Franklin often strings together a whole series of maxims. Look up the word "maxim" in a dictionary and write a paragraph defining this term in your own words. Use your definition to help you explain the particular principle that you think lies behind all the maxims in paragraph 7 of "The Way to Wealth." Does, for example, "using time effectively," "working hard," or some other principle seem to serve as the generalization behind the maxims?

▶ *QUESTIONS OF RHETORICAL PURPOSE AND STRATEGY*

3. Choose one of Franklin's brief sayings and discuss its application to work and people in contemporary society. Does the saying apply—directly or indirectly, positively or negatively—to a friend or relative of yours? Do you find the saying too simplistic for or accurately reflective of today's conditions? Do you think Franklin aims to convince the reader to live according to his moral values, or is he simply offering general advice on how to succeed in business?

4. What kind of person do you feel the writer of these selections assumes the reader to be? What types of values does Franklin assume that the reader holds? Does he assume idealism or skepticism concerning the possibility of becoming a success? What kinds of daily activities do you think he would suggest as aids to success in the business world? Why would he think these activities useful? What types of skills do you think he would advocate learning before trying to succeed in business or trade? Are these types of skills likely to foster such success?

5. Does Franklin's style seem to support his message to would-be business and tradespeople? How would you characterize his style—simple, complex, sophisticated, honest, manipulative? Give reasons supporting your choice of descriptive terms. Does Franklin's style suggest that his primary aim in writing is to tell businesspeople how to be successful?

▶ *THEME QUESTIONS*

6. Interview someone you think is a successful businessperson. Think out your questions ahead of time; take notes. Then, write a comparison of this person's advice and Franklin's. Conclude by telling your reader whether you think the two sets of recommendations for success in business are similar or different.

7. Define the words "industry" and "frugality" as Franklin uses them in paragraph 10 of "Advice to a Young Tradesman." How can you apply those terms to someone you have known well as a fellow employee or student?

▶ *LEARNING ACTIVITIES*

8. Read some of a current how-to-succeed-in-business type of book. How is the book similar to or different from Benjamin Franklin's works? Does it consider more aspects of business than Franklin does? Is it more psychological in its orientation than Franklin is? Does it include a more complex set of ingredients when it describes success? Is the type of job or profession that is described in the book very different from the work Franklin wrote about?

9. Write one page of advice addressed to a person younger and less experienced than yourself who is considering going to college. Tell this person what he or she should do and how he or she should think in order to be successful in college.

10. Franklin was an avid journal keeper. His journals contain a record of his observations of the natural world. These observations contributed to Franklin's success as an empirical and applied scientist. His

journals also helped him keep track of his business career. He wrote his experiences down and drew commonsense principles of morality from them. Try Franklin's techniques as you read through this section. Record your responses to each selection in a journal. Date and define each entry. In this way, as you work your way through this section, you will create an ongoing account of your thinking on its overall theme.

Stephen Cruz
STUDS TERKEL

Studs Terkel has had a long career as a radio commentator in Chicago. Although he got a law degree from the University of Chicago in 1934, instead of pursuing a legal career during the hard times of the Great Depression, Terkel went to Washington, D.C., where he worked as a civil servant. He soon gave that up for jobs as a stage actor and movie house manager, and eventually turned to radio and television broadcasting. He returned to Chicago, where he was a fixture for many years as the moderator of the "Wax Museum" on radio station WFMT, an early version of the radio talk show. From 1950 to 1953, he hosted a television talk show called "Stud's Place." Later in his career he turned to writing as a complement to his radio and television work and has published a half-dozen books since 1957.

In the most well-known of his books, Terkel combines his radio and television interviewing skills with his writing skills to produce collections of firsthand reports on common American subjects, including those of hard times (the Depression), work, and the American dream. Whereas most twentieth-century journalism attempts to stress objectivity and almost scientifically precise methods of reporting, Terkel has committed himself to salvaging the personal element of journalism. He spends more time capturing the individual behind the event or issue than he does explicating the issue itself. Another writer said of Terkel that he practices "a new form of writing 'history,' a special extension of personal journalism in an ever increasingly impersonal world. It is putting the I back into a them society."*

The selection that follows was taken from *American Dreams: Lost and Found* (1980). It reveals the typical Terkel talent for interviewing subjects concerning a theme of his in such a way that elicits significant responses from them. It also demonstrates his ability to edit the spoken responses into coherent written monologues that manage to capture the diverse voices and personalities of the people he interviews.

Consider these questions as you read:

1. What do you feel readers find of value in a case study such as this one of Stephen Cruz? What can readers learn about themselves by hearing Cruz discuss his dreams of success, his renunciations and al-

---

*Cited in *Contemporary Authors*, vols. 57–60, p. 553.

terations of those expectations, and his explanations of the reasons behind these alterations?

2. Can you relate Cruz's disappointments with corporate life to Benjamin Franklin's writings on business? What was missing for Cruz in his search for meaningful work in business?

▶ ─────────────────────

He is thirty-nine.   1

"The family came in stages from Mexico. Your grandparents usually   2
came first, did a little work, found little roots, put together a few bucks,
and brought the family in, one at a time. Those were the days when con-
trols at the border didn't exist as they do now."

You just tried very hard to be whatever it is the system wanted of   3
you. I was a good student and, as small as I was, a pretty good athlete. I
was well liked, I thought. We were fairly affluent, but we lived down
where all the trashy whites were. It was the only housing we could get.
As kids, we never understood why. We did everything right. We didn't
have those Mexican accents, we were never on welfare. Dad wouldn't
be on welfare to save his soul. He woulda died first. He worked during
the depression. He carries that pride with him, even today.

Of the five children, I'm the only one who really got into the business   4
world. We learned quickly that you have to look for opportunities and
add things up very quickly. I was in liberal arts, but as soon as Sputnik
went up, well, golly, hell, we knew where the bucks were. I went right
over to the registrar's office and signed up for engineering. I got my degree in '62. If you had a master's in business as well, they were just paying all kinds of bucks. So that's what I did. Sure enough, the market was
super. I had fourteen job offers. I could have had a hundred if I wanted to
look around.

I never once associated these offers with my being a minority. I was   5
aware of the Civil Rights Act of 1964, but I was still self-confident
enough to feel they wanted me because of my abilities. Looking back,
the reason I got more offers than the other guys was because of the government edict. And I thought it was because I was so goddamned brilliant. (Laughs.) In 1962, I didn't get as many offers as those who were
less qualified. You have a tendency to blame the job market. You just
don't want to face the issue of discrimination.

I went to work with Procter & Gamble. After about two years, they   6
told me I was one of the best supervisors they ever had and they were

gonna promote me. Okay, I went into personnel. Again, I thought it was because I was such a brilliant guy. Now I started getting wise to the ways of the American Dream. My office was glass-enclosed, while all the other offices were enclosed so you couldn't see into them. I was the visible man.

7   They made sure I interviewed most of the people that came in. I just didn't really think there was anything wrong until we got a new plant manager, a southerner. I received instructions from him on how I should interviews blacks. Just check and see if they smell, okay? That was the beginning of my training program. I started asking: Why weren't we hiring more minorities? I realized I was the only one in a management position.

8   I guess as a Mexican I was more acceptable because I wasn't really black. I was a good compromise. I was visibly good. I hired a black secretary, which was *verboten*. When I came back from my vacation, she was gone. My boss fired her while I was away. I asked why and never got a good reason.

9   Until then, I never questioned the American Dream. I was convinced if you worked hard, you could make it. I never considered myself different. That was the trouble. We had been discriminated against a lot, but I never associated it with society. I considered it an individual matter. Bad people, my mother used to say. In '68 I began to question.

10   I was doing fine. My very first year out of college, I was making twelve thousand dollars. I left Procter & Gamble because I really saw no opportunity. They were content to leave me visible, but my thoughts were not really solicited. I may have overreacted a bit, with the plant manager's attitude, but I felt there's no way a Mexican could get ahead here.

11   I went to work for Blue Cross. It's 1969. The Great Society is in full swing. Those who never thought of being minorities before are being turned on. Consciousness raising is going on. Black programs are popping up in universities. Cultural identity and all that. But what about the one issue in this country: economics? There were very few management jobs for minorities, especially blacks.

12   The stereotypes popped up again. If you're Oriental, you're real good in mathematics. If you're Mexican, you're a happy guy to have around, pleasant but emotional. Mexicans are either sleeping or laughing all the time. Life is just one big happy kind of event. *Mañana.* Good to have as part of the management team, as long as you weren't allowed to make decisions.

13   I was thinking there were two possibilities why minorities were not making it in business. One was deep, ingrained racism. But there was still the possibility that they were simply a bunch of bad managers who just couldn't cut it. You see, until now I believed everything I was

taught about the dream: the American businessman is omnipotent and fair. If we could show these turkeys there's money to be made in hiring minorities, these businessmen—good managers, good decision makers—would respond. I naïvely thought American businessmen gave a damn about society, that given a choice they would do the right thing. I had that faith.

I was hungry for learning about decision-making criteria. I was still too far away from top management to see exactly how they were working. I needed to learn more. Hey, just learn more and you'll make it. That part of the dream hadn't left me yet. I was still clinging to the notion of work your ass off, learn more than anybody else, and you'll get in that sphere.

14

During my fifth year at Blue Cross, I discovered another flaw in the American Dream. Minorities are as bad to other minorities as whites are to minorities. The strongest weapon the white manager had is the old divide and conquer routine. My mistake was thinking we were all at the same level of consciousness.

15

I had attempted to bring together some blacks with the other minorities. There weren't too many of them anyway. The Orientals never really got involved. The blacks misunderstood what I was presenting, perhaps I said it badly. They were on the cultural kick: a manager should be crucified for saying "Negro" instead of "black." I said as long as the Negro or the black gets the job, it doesn't mean a damn what he's called. We got into a huge hassle. Management, of course, merely smiled. The whole struggle fell flat on its face. It crumpled from divisiveness. So I learned another lesson. People have their own agenda. It doesn't matter what group you're with, there is a tendency to put the other guy down regardless.

16

The American Dream began to look so damn complicated, I began to think: Hell, if I wanted, I could just back away and reap the harvest myself. By this time, I'm up to twenty-five thousand dollars a year. It's beginning to look good, and a lot of people are beginning to look good. And they're saying: "Hey, the American Dream, you got it. Why don't you lay off?" I wasn't falling in line.

17

My bosses were telling me I had all the "ingredients" for top management. All that was required was to "get to know our business." This term comes up all the time. If I could just warn all minorities and women whenever you hear "get to know our business," they're really saying "fall in line." Stay within that fence, and glory can be yours. I left Blue Cross disillusioned. They offered me a director's job at thirty thousand dollars before I quit.

18

All I had to do was behave myself. I had the "ingredients" of being the good Chicano, the equivalent of the good nigger. I was smart. I could articulate well. People didn't know by my speech patterns that I was of

19

Mexican heritage. Some tell me I don't look Mexican, that I have a certain amount of Italian, Lebanese, or who knows. (Laughs.)

20   One could easily say: "Hey, what's your bitch? The American Dream has treated you beautifully. So just knock it off and quit this crap you're spreading around." It was a real problem. Every time I turned around, America seemed to be treating me very well.

21   Hell, I even thought of dropping out, the hell with it. Maybe get a job in a factory. But what happened? Offers kept coming in. I just said to myself: God, isn't this silly? You might as well take the bucks and continue looking for the answer. So I did that. But each time I took the money, the conflict in me got more intense, not less.

22   Wow, I'm up to thirty-five thousand a year. This is a savings and loan business. I have faith in the executive director. He was the kind of guy I was looking for in top management: understanding, humane, also looking for the formula. Until he was up for consideration as executive v.p. of the entire organization. All of a sudden everything changed. It wasn't until I saw this guy flip-flop that I realized how powerful vested interests are. Suddenly he's saying: "Don't rock the boat. Keep a low profile. Get in line." Another disappointment.

23   Subsequently, I went to work for a consulting firm. I said to myself: Okay, I've got to get close to the executive mind. I need to know how they work. Wow, a consulting firm.

24   Consulting firms are saving a lot of American businessmen. They're doing it in ways that defy the whole notion of capitalism. They're not allowing these businesses to fail. Lockheed was successful in getting U.S. funding guarantees because of the efforts of consulting firms working on their behalf, helping them look better. In this kind of work, you don't find minorities. You're got to be a proven success in business before you get there.

25   The American Dream, I see now, is governed not by education, opportunity, and hard work, but by power and fear. The higher up in the organization you go, the more you have to lose. The dream is *not losing.* This is the notion pervading America today: Don't lose.

26   When I left the consulting business, I was making fifty-five thousand dollars a year. My last performance appraisal was: You can go a long way in this business, you can be a partner, but you gotta know our business. It came up again. At this point, I was incapable of being disillusioned any more. How easy it is to be swallowed up by the same set of values that governs the top guy. I was becoming that way. I was becoming concerned about losing that fifty grand or so a year. So I asked other minorities who had it made. I'd go up and ask 'em: "Look, do you owe anything to others?" The answer was: "We owe nothing to anybody." They drew from the civil rights movement but felt no debt. They've quickly forgotten how it happened. It's like I was when I first got out of

college. Hey, it's really me, I'm great. I'm as angry with these guys as I am with the top guys.

Right now, it's confused. I've had fifteen years in the business world   27
as "a success." Many Anglos would be envious of my progress. Fifty thousand dollars a year puts you in the one or two top percent of all Americans. Plus my wife making another thirty thousand. We had lots of money. When I gave it up, my cohorts looked at me not just as strange, but as something of a traitor. "You're screwing it up for all of us. You're part of our union, we're the elite, we should govern. What the hell are you doing?" So now I'm looked at suspiciously by my peer group as well.

I'm teaching at the University of Wisconsin at Platteville. It's nice.   28
My colleagues tell me what's on their minds. I got a farm next-door to Platteville. With farm prices being what they are (laughs), it's a losing proposition. But with university work and what money we've saved, we're gonna be all right.

The American Dream is getting more elusive. The dream is being   29
governed by a few people's notion of what the dream is. Sometimes I feel it's a small group of financiers that gets together once a year and decides all the world's issues.

It's getting so big. The small-business venture is not there any more.   30
Business has become too big to influence. It can't be changed internally. A counterpower is needed.

Questions and Activities

▶ *COMPREHENSION QUESTIONS*

1. Explain the function of the italicized headnote preceding Stephen Cruz's monologue. Does it help to define the context under which Cruz discusses his attitude toward work? What is the topic within which this monologue fits? What does Cruz say about that subject? How does it tie in with the general theme of this section?

2. Explain the meaning of this sentence from paragraph 4: "I was in liberal arts, but as soon as Sputnik went up, well, golly, hell, we knew where the bucks were." Where did Cruz, back then, think the bucks were? What was Sputnik, when did it go up, and why did it influence Cruz in his choice of career?

3. In paragraph 9, Cruz recounts how he reconsidered his dedication to the notion of "the American Dream." What caused this reconsideration? (This paragraph is a good example of how Terkel puts Cruz's responses together in a way that serves Terkel's purpose,

which is to offer his readers an interpretation of the way that Cruz's experiences influence his concept of the American dream.)

4. In paragraph 14, Cruz describes his desire to learn about "decision-making criteria." Why do you feel that Cruz ultimately loses this desire? What kills his drive to make decisions, to become a manager in the business sense of that term? Find several specific factors, then organize them into a general answer to the question. Does Cruz's emphasis on his desire and his ultimate rejection of it suggest a deeper aim in this monologue? Is Cruz explaining why the American business ethic is not the answer to the minority person's question of how to gain happiness?

▶ *QUESTIONS OF RHETORICAL PURPOSE AND STRATEGY*

5. Why do you think Terkel chooses to use the first-person point of view? What does Terkel gain by having Cruz speak to the reader directly, rather than through an intermediary, a professional interviewer? How does this help Terkel accomplish his overall purpose?

6. Terkel transcribed Stephen Cruz's responses into a monologue or personal essay form. Why do you think he uses this form instead of a question and answer format? What effect does this choice have on readers?

▶ *THEME QUESTIONS*

7. What knowledge does Studs Terkel assume that his readers share as they read about Stephen Cruz? Reconsider the essay's headnote here. What do you know—from films, books, or stories you have heard—about the experiences of immigrant, ethnic, and minority groups? Does your own experience agree or disagree with Cruz's experience? Does Cruz's early belief that "if you worked hard, you could make it" (paragraph 9) seem to you characteristic of most first- or second-generation members of ethnic groups?

8. Terkel's subject in this sketch is the American dream—the belief that hard work leads to success. Interview another member of your class concerning his or her reasons for going to college. Are these reasons similar to the reasons that motivate Cruz and others like him to pursue education and careers? How are they similar or different?

▶ *LEARNING ACTIVITIES*

9. Transcribe an interview with a person you know. Try to approach this interview as you imagine Studs Terkel might have approached his interview with Stephen Cruz. Ask your subject to explain what he or she hopes to accomplish through his or her work. Either tape-

record or take notes of his or her responses and write them up as a two- or three-page monologue in the first person. This interview should be aimed at getting at the causes of your subject's satisfaction or dissatisfaction with his or her work. Edit your material so that it builds up and clarifies your subject's attitude toward his or her job.

10. Work with two or three members of your class to devise a set of questions to be used to interview someone about his or her job. Organize these questions around a common theme and pick out a job that you believe has a direct connection with that theme. For example, if you agree with Cruz that many people who work in management positions are motivated by a need for power rather than by a desire to help others, you might devise a list of questions that will indirectly lead a management employee that you know to comment on the power theme. After interviewing the person you choose, you and your collaborators should work the transcribed answers into an analytical comment on your subject's response. Do your subject's answers surprise you? Do they confirm your original expectations? Remember to avoid asking obviously leading questions, but do lead your subject gradually to your point. Open your subject up with some friendly questions and comments before you begin the actual interview.

11. Write a narrative that describes your attitude toward a job you have held. Edit your material so as to reflect your purpose, which is to communicate the attitude you developed on the job, not to describe everything that happened to you while you held the job.

The Surgeon as Priest

RICHARD SELZER

Richard Selzer is a surgeon and professor of surgery at Yale University Medical School. His father was a family doctor in Troy, New York, and Selzer grew up under the influence of his father's dedication to medicine. Selzer has combined a medical career with a career as a writer. He has written many articles for popular magazines such as *Esquire, Redbook, Mademoiselle, American Review,* and *Antaeus.* His articles almost always focus on what it is like to be a doctor and surgeon and are addressed to a general audience that does not have any first-hand experience of performing surgery or practicing medicine. In 1975, Selzer received the National Magazine Award from the Columbia University School of Journalism for essays that were published in *Esquire.* Many of his essays on medicine have been collected in two books: *Letter to Young Doctors* (1982) and *Mortal Lessons* (1977), from which the autobiographical essay published here is taken. Selzer has also published a book of short stories whose theme is medicine, *Rituals of Surgery* (1974).

Behind almost every Selzer essay lies his firm belief in the significance and usefulness of his career as a surgeon. This conviction gives his prose style an energy and vividness that would be lacking in drier, more technical treatments of this subject. The conviction that energizes Selzer's prose style would also seem to be a natural part of his everyday practice of surgery. His language connects personal experience with religious belief and spiritual philosophy.

In this essay, Selzer narrates four different stories to establish his idea that being a surgeon is far more than holding membership in a profession. To him, it is a way of helping others that connects itself to ancient religious cults and mysteries, and it is very much influenced by the spiritual convictions of both surgeon and patient.

Selzer seems to be searching for the significance of his work as he writes. His readers may find themselves also searching.

1. To what degree can anyone's work provide the kind of satisfaction that Selzer's provides? What about less glamorous jobs and careers; do they contain a comparable level of significance and potential for fulfillment?

2. To what degree does Selzer's attitude *create* the significance that he attributes to his work as a surgeon? What creates the inner satisfac-

tion that Selzer gains from his work, as opposed to the dissatisfaction felt by Stephen Cruz as reported by Studs Terkel?
3. Is Selzer's commitment to his work different from that advocated by Franklin in "Advice to a Young Tradesman"?

▶ ────────────────────

In the foyer of a great medical school there hangs a painting of   *1*
Vesalius. Lean, ascetic, possessed, the anatomist stands before a dissecting table upon which lies the naked body of a man. The flesh of the two is silvery. A concentration of moonlight, like a strange rain of virus, washes them. The cadaver has dignity and reserve; it is distanced by its death. Vesalius reaches for his dissecting knife. As he does so, he glances over his shoulder at a crucifix on the wall. His face wears an expression of guilt and melancholy and fear. He knows that there is something wrong, forbidden in what he is about to do, but he cannot help himself, for he is a fanatic. He is driven by a dark desire. To see, to feel, to discover is all. His is a passion, not a romance.

I understand you, Vesalius. Even now, after so many voyages within,   *2*
so much exploration, I feel the same sense that one must not gaze into the body, the same irrational fear that it is an evil deed for which punishment awaits. Consider. The sight of our internal organs is denied us. To how many men is it given to look upon their own spleens, their hearts, and live? The hidden geography of the body is a Medusa's head* one glimpse of which would render blind the presumptuous eye. Still, rigid rules are broken by the smallest inadvertencies: I pause in the midst of an operation being performed under spinal anesthesia to observe the face of my patient, to speak a word or two of reassurance. I peer above the screen separating his head from his abdomen, in which I am most deeply employed. He is not asleep, but rather stares straight upward, his attention riveted, a look of terrible discovery, of wonder upon his face. Watch him. This man is violating a taboo. I follow his gaze upward, and see in the great operating lamp suspended above his belly the reflection of his viscera. There is the liver, dark and turgid above, there the loops of his bowel winding slow, there his blood runs extravagantly. It is that which he sees and studies with so much horror

─────────────────────────

*Medusa was one of three female monsters who were called Gorgons in Greek mythology. They had snakes for hair, and whoever looked into their eyes was turned to stone.

and fascination. Something primordial in him has been aroused—a fright, a longing. I feel it, too, and quickly bend above his open body to shield it from his view. How dare he look within the Ark! Cover his eyes! But it is too late; he has already *seen;* that which no man should; he has trespassed. And I am no longer a surgeon, but a hierophant* who must do magic to ward off the punishment of the angry gods.

3   I feel some hesitation to invite you to come with me into the body. It seems a reckless, defiant act. Yet there is more than dread reflected from these rosy coasts, these restless estuaries of pearl. And it is time to share it, the way the catbird shares the song which must be a joy to him and is a living truth to those who hear it. So shall I make of my fingers, words; of my scalpel, a sentence; of the body of my patient, a story.

4   One enters the body in surgery, as in love, as though one were an exile returning at last to his hearth, daring uncharted darkness in order to reach home. Turn sideways, if you will, and slip with me into the cleft I have made. Do not fear the yellow meadows of fat, the red that sweats and trickles where you step. Here, give me your hand. Lower between the beefy cliffs. Now rest a bit upon the peritoneum. All at once, gleaming, the membrane parts . . . and you are *in*.

5   It is the stillest place that ever was. As though suddenly you are struck deaf. Why, when the blood sluices fierce as Niagara, when the brain teems with electricity, and the numberless cells exchange their goods in ceaseless commerce—why is it so quiet? Has some priest in charge of these rites uttered the command "Silence"? This is no silence of the vacant stratosphere, but the awful quiet of ruins, of rainbows, full of expectation and holy dread. Soon you shall know surgery as a Mass served with Body and Blood, wherein disease is assailed as though it were sin.

6   Touch the great artery. Feel it bound like a deer in the might of its lightness, and know the thunderless boil of the blood. Lean for a bit against this bone. It is the only memento you will leave to the earth. Its tacitness is everlasting. In the hush of the tissue wait with me for the shaft of pronouncement. Press your ear against this body, the way you did as a child holding a seashell and heard faintly the half-remembered, longed-for sea. Now strain to listen *past* the silence. In the canals, cilia paddle quiet as an Iroquois canoe. Somewhere nearby a white whipslide of tendon bows across a joint. Fire burns here but does not crackle. Again, listen. Now there *is* sound—small splashings, tunneled currents of air, slow gaseous bubbles ascend through dark, unlit lakes. Across the diaphragm and into the chest . . . here at last it is all noise; the whisper of the lungs, the *lubdup, lubdup* of the garrulous heart.

*A hierophant is a priest or a teacher of any mystery that is related to religion.

But it is good you do not hear the machinery of your marrow lest it 7
madden like the buzzing of a thousand coppery bees. It is frightening to
lie with your ear in the pillow, and hear the beating of your heart. Not
that it beats . . . but that it might stop, even as you listen. For anything
that moves must come to rest; no rhythm is endless but must one day
lurch . . . then halt. Not that it is a disservice to a man to be made mindful of his death, but—at three o'clock in the morning it is less than philosophy. It is Fantasy, replete with dreadful images forming in the
smoke of alabaster crematoria. It is then that one thinks of the bris-
tlecone pines, and envies them for having lasted. It is their slowness, I
think. Slow down, heart, and drub on.

What is to one man a coincidence is to another a miracle. It was one 8
or the other of these that I saw last spring. While the rest of nature was
in flux, Joe Riker remained obstinate through the change of the seasons.
"No operation," said Joe. "I don't want no operation."

Joe Riker is a short-order cook in a diner where I sometimes drink cof- 9
fee. Each week for six months he had paid a visit to my office, carrying
his affliction like a pet mouse under his hat. Every Thursday at four
o'clock he would sit on my examining table, lift the fedora from his
head, and bend forward to show me the hole. Joe Riker's hole was as big
as his mouth. You could have dropped a plum in it. Gouged from the
tonsured top of his head was a mucky puddle whose meaty heaped edge
rose above the normal scalp about it. There was no mistaking the
announcement from this rampart.

The cancer had chewed through Joe's scalp, munched his skull, then 10
opened the membranes underneath—the dura mater, the pia mater, the
arachnoid—until it had laid bare this short-order cook's brain, pink and
gray, and pulsating so that with each beat a little pool of cerebral fluid
quivered. Now and then a drop would manage the rim to run across his
balding head, and Joe would reach one burry hand up to wipe it away,
with the heel of his thumb, the way such a man would wipe away a tear.

I would gaze then upon Joe Riker and marvel. How dignified he was, 11
as though that tumor, gnawing him, denuding his very brain, had given
him a grace that a lifetime of good health had not bestowed.

"Joe," I say, "let's get rid of it. Cut out the bad part, put in a metal 12
plate, and you're cured." And I wait.

"No operation," says Joe. I try again. 13

"What do you mean, 'no operation'? You're going to get meningitis. 14
Any day now. And die. That thing is going to get to your brain."

I think of it devouring the man's dreams and memories. I wonder 15
what they are. The surgeon knows all the parts of the brain, but he does
not know his patient's dreams and memories. And for a moment I am

tempted . . . to take the man's head in my hands, hold it to my ear, and listen. But his dreams are none of my business. It is his flesh that matters.

16   "No operation," says Joe.

17   "You give me a headache," I say. And we smile, not because the joke is funny anymore, but because we've got something between us, like a secret.

18   "Same time next week?" Joe asks. I wash out the wound with peroxide, and apply a dressing. He lowers the fedora over it.

19   "Yes," I say, "same time." And the next week he comes again.

20   There came the week when Joe Riker did not show up; nor did he the week after that, nor for a whole month. I drive over to his diner. He is behind the counter, shuffling back and forth between the grill and the sink. He is wearing the fedora. He sets a cup of coffee in front of me.

21   "I want to see your hole," I say.

22   "Which one?" he asks, and winks.

23   "Never mind that," I say. "I want to see it." I am all business.

24   "Not here," says Joe. He looks around, checking the counter, as though I have made an indecent suggestion.

25   "My office at four o'clock," I say.

26   "Yeah," says Joe, and turns away.

27   He is late. Everyone else has gone for the day. Joe is beginning to make me angry. At last he arrives.

28   "Take off your hat," I say, and he knows by my voice that I am not happy. He does, though, raise it straight up with both hands the way he always does, and I see . . . that the wound has healed. Where once there had been a bitten-out excavation, moist and shaggy, there is now a fragile bridge of shiny new skin.

29   "What happened?" I manage.

30   "You mean that?" He points to the top of his head. "Oh well," he says, "the wife's sister, she went to France, and brought me a bottle of water from Lourdes. I've been washing it out with that for a month."

31   "Holy water?" I say.

32   "Yeah," says Joe. "Holy water."

33   I see Joe now and then at the diner. He looks like anything but a fleshly garden of miracles. Rather, he has taken on a terrible ordinariness—Eden after the Fall, and minus its most beautiful creatures. There is a certain slovenliness, a dishevelment of the tissues. Did the disease ennoble him, and now that it is gone, is he somehow diminished? Perhaps I am wrong. Perhaps the only change is just the sly wink with which he greets me, as though to signal that we have shared something furtive. Could such a man, I think as I sip my coffee, could such a man have felt the brush of wings? How often it seems that the glory leaves as

soon as the wound is healed. But then it is only saints who bloom in martyrdom, becoming less and less the flesh that pains, more and more ghost-colored weightlessness.

It was many years between my first sight of the living human brain   34
and Joe Riker's windowing. I had thought then, long ago: Could this one-pound loaf of sourdough be the pelting brain? *This*, along whose busy circuitry run Reason and Madness in perpetual race—a race that most often ends in a tie? But the look deceives. What seems a fattish snail drowzing in its shell, in fact lives in quickness, where all is dart and stir and rapids of electricity.

Once again to the operating room . . .   35

How to cut a paste that is less solid than a cheese—Brie, perhaps?   36
And not waste any of it? For that would be a decade of remembrances and wishes lost there, wiped from the knife. Mostly it is done with cautery, burning the margins of the piece to be removed, coagulating with the fine electric current these blood vessels that course everywhere. First a spot is burned, then another alongside the first, and the cut is made between. One does not stitch—one cannot sew custard. Blood is blotted with little squares of absorbent gauze. These are called patties. Through each of these a long black thread has been sewn, lest a blood-soaked patty slip into some remote fissure, or flatten against a gyrus like a starfish against a coral reef, and go unnoticed come time to close the incision. A patty abandoned brainside does not benefit the health, or improve the climate of the intelligence. Like the bodies of slain warriors, they must be retrieved from the field, and carried home, so they do not bloat and mortify, poisoning forever the plain upon which the battle was fought. One pulls them out by their black thread and counts them.

Listen to the neurosurgeon: "Patty, buzz, suck, cut," he says. Then   37
"Suck, cut, patty, buzz." It is as simple as a nursery rhyme.

The surgeon knows the landscape of the brain, yet does not know   38
how a thought is made. Man has grown envious of this mystery. He would master and subdue it electronically. He would construct a computer to rival or surpass the brain. He would harness Europa's bull to a plow.* There are men who implant electrodes into the brain, that part where anger is kept—the rage center, they call it. They press a button, and a furious bull halts in mid-charge, and lopes amiably to nuzzle his

*In Greek mythology, Europa was a Phoenician princess who was kidnapped by Zeus and taken to Crete. In order to smuggle her into Crete, Zeus transformed her into a white bull. Here, Selzer is using "Europa's bull" to refer to the mystery of intellect and refinement harnessed to the "plow" of technology, or machinery.

matador. Anger has turned to sweet compliance. Others sever whole tracts of brain cells with their knives, to mollify the insane. Here is surgery grown violent as rape. These men cannot know the brain. They have not the heart for it.

39   I last saw the brain in the emergency room. I wiped it from the shoulder of a young girl to make her smashed body more presentable to her father. Now I stand with him by the stretcher. We are arm in arm, like brothers. All at once there is that terrible silence of discovery. I glance at him, follow his gaze and see that there is more brain upon her shoulder, newly slipped from the cracked skull. He bends forward a bit. He must make certain. It *is* her brain! I watch the knowledge expand upon his face, so like hers. I, too, stare at the fragment flung wetly, now drying beneath the bright lights of the emergency room, its cargo of thoughts evaporating from it, mingling for this little time with his, with mine, before dispersing in the air.

40   On the east coast of the Argolid, in the northern part of the Peloponnesus, lies Epidaurus. O bury my heart there, in that place I have never seen, but that I love as a farmer loves his home soil. In a valley nearby, in the fourth century B.C., there was built the temple of Asclepius, the god of medicine. To a great open colonnaded room, the abaton, came the sick from all over Greece. Here they lay down on pallets. As night fell, the priests, bearing fire for the lamps, walked among them, commanding them to sleep. They were told to dream of the god, and that he would come to them in their sleep in the form of a serpent, and that he would heal them. In the morning they arose cured. . . .

41   Walk the length of the abaton; the sick are in their places, each upon his pallet. Here is one that cannot sleep. See how his breath rises and falls against some burden that presses upon it. At last, he dozes, only to awaken minutes later, unrefreshed. It is toward dawn. The night lamps flicker low, casting snaky patterns across the colonnade. Already the chattering swallows swoop in and out among the pillars. All at once the fitful eyes of the man cease their roving, for he sees between the candle-lamp and the wall the shadow of an upraised serpent, a great yellow snake with topaz eyes. It slides closer. It is arched and godlike. It bends above him, swaying, the tongue and the lamplight flickering as one. Exultant, he raises himself upon one arm, and with the other, reaches out for the touch that heals.

42   On the bulletin board in the front hall of the hospital where I work, there appeared an announcement. "Yeshi Dhonden," it read, "will make rounds at six o'clock on the morning of June 10." The particulars were then given, followed by a notation: "Yeshi Dhonden is Personal

Physician to the Dalai Lama.''* I am not so leathery a skeptic that I would knowingly ignore an emissary from the gods. Not only might such sangfroid be inimical to one's earthly well-being, it could take care of eternity as well. Thus, on the morning of June 10, I join the clutch of whitecoats waiting in the small conference room adjacent to the ward selected for the rounds. The air in the room is heavy with ill-concealed dubiety and suspicion of bamboozlement. At precisely six o'clock, he materializes, a short, golden, barrelly man dressed in a sleeveless robe of saffron and maroon. His scalp is shaven, and the only visible hair is a scanty black line above each hooded eye.

He bows in greeting while his young interpreter makes the introduc-   43
tion. Yeshi Dhonden, we are told, will examine a patient selected by a member of the staff. The diagnosis is as unknown to Yeshi Dhonden as it is to us. The examination of the patient will take place in our presence, after which we will reconvene in the conference room where Yeshi Dhonden will discuss the case. We are further informed that for the past two hours Yeshi Dhonden has purified himself by bathing, fasting, and prayer. I, having breakfasted well, performed only the most desultory of ablutions, and given no thought at all to my soul, glance furtively at my fellows. Suddenly, we seem a soiled, uncouth lot.

The patient had been awakened early and told that she was to be   44
examined by a foreign doctor, and had been asked to produce a fresh specimen of urine, so when we enter her room, the woman shows no surprise. She has long ago taken on that mixture of compliance and resignation that is the facies of chronic illness. This was to be but another in an endless series of tests and examinations. Yeshi Dhonden steps to the bedside while the rest stand apart, watching. For a long time he gazes at the woman, favoring no part of her body with his eyes, but seeming to fix his glance at a place just above her supine form. I, too, study her. No physical sign nor obvious symptom gives a clue to the nature of her disease.

At last he takes her hand, raising it in both of his own. Now he bends   45
over the bed in a kind of crouching stance, his head drawn down into the collar of his robe. His eyes are closed as he feels for her pulse. In a moment he has found the spot, and for the next half hour he remains thus, suspended above the patient like some exotic golden bird with folded wings, holding the pulse of the woman beneath his fingers, cradling her hand in his. All the power of the man seems to have been drawn down into this one purpose. It is palpation of the pulse raised to the state of

*The Dalai Lama is the traditional ruler and high priest of the Buddhist religion in Tibet, an ancient kingdom in the Himalayan mountains, which is now a part of China. Unlike most world leaders of today, the Dalai Lama combines spiritual and secular leadership.

ritual. From the foot of the bed, where I stand, it is as though he and the patient have entered a special place of isolation, of apartness, about which a vacancy hovers, and across which no violation is possible. After a moment the woman rests back upon her pillow. From time to time, she raises her head to look at the strange figure above her, then sinks back once more. I cannot see their hands joined in a correspondence that is exclusive, intimate, his fingertips receiving the voice of her sick body through the rhythm and throb she offers at her wrist. All at once I am envious—not of him, not of Yeshi Dhonden for his gift of beauty and holiness, but of her. I want to be held like that, touched so, *received.* And I know that I, who have palpated a hundred thousand pulses, have not felt a single one.

46   At last Yeshi Dhonden straightens, gently places the woman's hand upon the bed, and steps back. The interpreter produces a small wooden bowl and two sticks. Yeshi Dhonden pours a portion of the urine specimen into the bowl, and proceeds to whip the liquid with the two sticks. This he does for several minutes until a foam is raised. Then, bowing above the bowl, he inhales the odor three times. He sets down the bowl and turns to leave. All this while, he has not uttered a single word. As he nears the door, the woman raises her head and calls out to him in a voice at once urgent and serene. "Thank you, doctor," she says, and touches with her other hand the place he had held on her wrist, as though to recapture something that had visited there. Yeshi Dhonden turns back for a moment to gaze at her, then steps into the corridor. Rounds are at an end.

47   We are seated once more in the conference room. Yeshi Dhonden speaks now for the first time, in soft Tibetan sounds that I have never heard before. He has barely begun when the young interpreter begins to translate, the two voices continuing in tandem—a bilingual fugue, the one chasing the other. It is like the chanting of monks. He speaks of winds coursing through the body of the woman, currents that break against barriers, eddying. These vortices are in her blood, he says. The last spendings of an imperfect heart. Between the chambers of her heart, long, long before she was born, a wind had come and blown open a deep gate that must never be opened. Through it charge the full waters of her river, as the mountain stream cascades in the springtime, battering, knocking loose the land, and flooding her breath. Thus he speaks, and is silent.

48   "May we now have the diagnosis?" a professor asks.

49   The host of these rounds, the man who knows, answers.

50   "Congenital heart disease," he says. "Interventricular septal defect, with resultant heart failure."

A gateway in the heart, I think. That must not be opened. Through it   *51*
charge the full waters that flood her breath. So! Here then is the doctor
listening to the sounds of the body to which the rest of us are deaf. He is
more than doctor. He is priest.

I know...I know...the doctor to the gods is pure knowledge, pure   *52*
healing. The doctor to man stumbles, must often wound; his patient
must die, as must he.

Now and then it happens, as I make my own rounds, that I hear the   *53*
sounds of his voice, like an ancient Buddhist prayer, its meaning long
since forgotten, only the music remaining. Then a jubilation possesses
me, and I feel myself touched by something divine.

Questions and Activities

▶ *COMPREHENSION QUESTIONS*

1. Look at Selzer's use of telling details. Reread the stories (about Riker,
   Yeshi Dhonden, and the girl with the cracked skull) that are used to
   support the general ideas in this essay. Each story is carefully told.
   Point out one arresting and pointed detail in each story. What is the
   effect of that detail on you, as the reader? Why does the detail stand
   out? What significance does the detail take on in the context of the
   whole essay? What is the point of these stories? What is Selzer trying
   to tell us about the surgeon's profession through these stories?

2. Two extended personal experiences support Selzer's connection
   between the surgeon and priest in their service to humankind. One involves Joe Riker and his cancerous skull (paragraphs 8 through 35);
   the other involves Yeshi Dhonden, the personal physician to the
   Dalai Lama (paragraphs 42 through 53). What writing skills does
   Selzer use to bring these two people alive for you? Consider his use of
   telling detail, his sense of narrative flow and action, and his ability to
   make every detail count.

▶ *QUESTIONS OF RHETORICAL PURPOSE AND STRATEGY*

3. Readers of "The Surgeon as Priest" must first be interested in Richard
   Selzer. Selzer's voice must attract us, must convince us of its
   uniqueness. Only if so attracted will we go along on his journey of
   discovery, will we take seriously his extremely subjective perspective
   on surgery and medicine. Reread Selzer's first paragraph. How are

you engaged by Selzer's voice? What in his style immediately makes you feel in the presence of a distinct personality—someone capable of providing a fresh look into the subjects he writes about? Why is Vesalius used to introduce Selzer's feelings about his profession? How would you describe Selzer's personality to another person?

4. Which of the following four statements do you think best describes Selzer's purpose in writing this essay?

   a. He wants to persuade the reader to become a surgeon.

   b. He wants the reader to gain a better understanding of what it is like to be a surgeon.

   c. He wants the reader to write a letter to the local newspaper praising the contributions surgeons make to society.

   d. He wants the reader to understand him and his life as a surgeon. Provide evidence from the essay to support your choice. Does the statement you have chosen suggest that Selzer's purpose is persuasive, informative, or expressive? If none of these statements suits you, write your own statement describing Selzer's purpose, and defend and characterize it.

   ▶ *THEME QUESTIONS*

5. Compare Selzer's testimony about work with that of Stephen Cruz (pages 99–103). Both offer very personal responses; both are professionals. Yet the messages in their testimonies are opposed. What is there in Selzer's work that gives him personal satisfaction? What is missing in Cruz's work that causes him to keep moving on to something else? Selzer feels connected to others through his work; Cruz feels alienated from others by his work. Why?

6. What is Selzer's point in this essay? What is he saying about being a surgeon? Through the story about Yeshi Dhonden, is Selzer establishing the superiority of Eastern over Western medicine, or is he simply suggesting that the two approaches should be combined and mutually respected? Or, perhaps, is he considering the possibility that religion and medicine have much in common, despite what modern science might say? Why might Selzer feel that religion and medicine should, once again, be brought together?

   ▶ *LEARNING ACTIVITIES*

7. Write several paragraphs describing a person you have observed doing a job well. Write the first draft quickly; then revise it, incorporating at least a few of the writing techniques Selzer employs. Try to use some of Selzer's descriptive techniques, such as metaphors, as you write. Tell a few brief stories that support your idea. To accomplish this, you will need to think creatively about the subject of your

description. Is there some general observation that led you to pick the subject? Does that general idea suggest some metaphors or descriptive phrases? Your classmates should read your description and produce a generalization that they believe captures the significance of your description. Do you think their generalization captures its significance?

8. Your class should divide into smaller workshop groups to carry out the analysis of question 4 above. Each group should choose one of the four statements and compile a list of reasons supporting that choice. The group members should conclude their work together by reporting to the rest of the class on why they chose that particular statement and by providing a written elaboration justifying their choice.

Japanese and American Workers: Two Casts of Mind

WILLIAM OUCHI

William Ouchi was born in Hawaii in 1943. He was educated at Williams College, Stanford University, and the University of Chicago. He has taught in the business schools at Stanford and the University of Chicago and is currently a professor in the graduate school of management at the University of California at Los Angeles. Ouchi has served as a consultant for many Fortune 500 companies and has worked as an associate study director for the National Opinion Research Center. In short, he has studied and participated in the business world from an enormous range of perspectives in a relatively short period of time.

The essay included here first appeared as a chapter in Ouchi's enormously popular book, *Theory Z: How American Business Can Meet the Japanese Challenge* (1981). In this book, Ouchi argued that the Japanese spirit of cooperation should be creatively combined with American competitiveness to achieve greater productivity. Thus this essay is aimed at American businesspeople who are concerned that we may be lagging behind Japan in industrial productivity and who are also feeling the effects of a tight economy. Do you share either or both of these concerns? Have any of your family or friends been directly affected by Japanese productivity? How are you affected by Japanese products, either positively (do you drive a Japanese car, for example) or negatively?

On a more general level, Ouchi speaks directly to our concern with the relationship between work and individual identity. As we observed while reading Benjamin Franklin, Americans have consistently seen work as an important means of defining the individual's difference from others. Personal initiative, creativity, and self-reliance were all part of the individualism characterizing both farmers and entrepreneurs. This type of individualism, Ouchi suggests, may well have become a problem once America began to move toward widespread industrialization and corporate business. The Japanese example may be suggesting that factories and corporations thrive on collective effort. Ouchi's comparison may imply that our myths have to be revised toward cooperation and away from individualism if we are to reach Japanese levels of production.

As you read, consider Ouchi's purpose:

1. At what points in the essay is his purpose to inform his readers of Japanese culture?

2. At what points in the essay does he want to persuade his readers that values held by the Japanese are ones that should be adopted by American business?

▶ ───────────────────────

Perhaps the most difficult aspect of the Japanese for Westerners   *1*
to comprehend is the strong orientation to collective values, particularly a collective sense of responsibility. Let me illustrate with an anecdote about a visit to a new factory in Japan owned and operated by an American electronics company. The American company, a particularly creative firm, frequently attracts attention within the business community for its novel approaches to planning, organizational design, and management systems. As a consequence of this corporate style, the parent company determined to make a thorough study of Japanese workers and to design a plant that would combine the best of East and West. In their study they discovered that Japanese firms almost never make use of individual work incentives, such as piecework or even individual performance appraisal tied to salary increases. They concluded that rewarding individual achievement and individual ability is always a good thing.

In the final assembly area of their new plant long lines of young   *2*
Japanese women wired together electronic products on a piece-rate system: the more you wired, the more you got paid. About two months after opening, the head foreladies approached the plant manager. "Honorable plant manager," they said humbly as they bowed, "we are embarrassed to be so forward, but we must speak to you because all of the girls have threatened to quit work this Friday." (To have this happen, of course, would be a great disaster for all concerned.) "Why," they wanted to know, "can't our plant have the same compensation system as other Japanese companies? When you hire a new girl, her starting wage should be fixed by her age. An eighteen-year-old should be paid more than a sixteen-year-old. Every year on her birthday, she should receive an automatic increase in pay. The idea that any one of us can be more productive than another must be wrong, because none of us in final assembly could make a thing unless all of the other people in the plant had done their jobs right first. To single one person out as being more productive is wrong and is also personally humiliating to us." The company changed its compensation system to the Japanese model.

Another American company in Japan had installed a suggestion sys-   *3*
tem much as we have in the United States. Individual workers were

encouraged to place suggestions to improve productivity into special boxes. For an accepted idea the individual received a bonus amounting to some fraction of the productivity savings realized from his or her suggestion. After a period of six months, not a single suggestion had been submitted. The American managers were puzzled. They had heard many stories of the inventiveness, the commitment, and the loyalty of Japanese workers, yet not one suggestion to improve productivity had appeared.

4   The managers approached some of the workers and asked why the suggestion system had not been used. The answer: "No one can come up with a work improvement idea alone. We work together, and any ideas that one of us may have are actually developed by watching others and talking to others. If one of us was singled out for being responsible for such an idea, it would embarrass all of us." The company changed to a group suggestion system, in which workers collectively submitted suggestions. Bonuses were paid to groups which would save bonus money until the end of the year for a party at a restaurant or, if there was enough money, for family vacations together. The suggestions and productivity improvements rained down on the plant.

5   One can interpret these examples in two quite different ways. Perhaps the Japanese commitment to collective values is an anachronism that does not fit with modern industrialism but brings economic success despite that collectivism. Collectivism seems to be inimical to the kind of maverick creativity exemplified in Benjamin Franklin, Thomas Edison, and John D. Rockefeller. Collectivism does not seem to provide the individual incentive to excel which has made a great success of American enterprise. Entirely apart from its economic effects, collectivism implies a loss of individuality, a loss of the freedom to be different, to hold fundamentally different values from others.

6   The second interpretation of the examples is that the Japanese collectivism is economically efficient. It causes people to work well together and to encourage one another to better efforts. Industrial life requires interdependence of one person on another. But a less obvious but far-reaching implication of the Japanese collectivism for economic performance has to do with accountability.

7   In the Japanese mind, collectivism is neither a corporate or individual goal to strive for nor a slogan to pursue. Rather, the nature of things operates so that nothing of consequence occurs as a result of individual effort. Everything important in life happens as a result of teamwork or collective effort. Therefore, to attempt to assign individual credit or blame to results is unfounded. A Japanese professor of accounting, a brilliant scholar trained at Carnegie-Mellon University who teaches now in Tokyo, remarked that the status of accounting systems in

Japanese industry is primitive compared to those in the United States. Profit centers, transfer prices, and computerized information systems are barely known even in the largest Japanese companies, whereas they are a commonplace in even small United States organizations. Though not at all surprised at the difference in accounting systems, I was not at all sure that the Japanese were primitive. In fact, I thought their system a good deal more efficient than ours.

Most American companies have basically two accounting systems.   8
One system summarizes the overall financial state to inform stockholders, bankers, and other outsiders. That system is not of interest here. The other system, called the managerial or cost accounting system, exists for an entirely different reason. It measures in detail all of the particulars of transactions between departments, divisions, and key individuals in the organization, for the purpose of untangling the interdependencies between people. When, for example, two departments share one truck for deliveries, the cost accounting system charges each department for part of the cost of maintaining the truck and driver, so that at the end of the year, the performance of each department can be individually assessed, and the better department's manager can receive a larger raise. Of course, all of this information processing costs money, and furthermore may lead to arguments between the departments over whether the costs charged to each are fair.

In a Japanese company a short-run assessment of individual perfor-   9
mance is not wanted, so the company can save the considerable expense of collecting and processing all of that information. Companies still keep track of which department uses a truck how often and for what purposes, but like-minded people can interpret some simple numbers for themselves and adjust their behavior accordingly. Those insisting upon clear and precise measurement for the purpose of advancing individual interests must have an elaborate information system. Industrial life, however, is essentially integrated and interdependent. No one builds an automobile alone, no one carries through a banking transaction alone. In a sense the Japanese value of collectivism fits naturally into an industrial setting, whereas the Western individualism provides constant conflicts. The image that comes to mind is of Chaplin's silent film "Modern Times" in which the apparently insignificant hero played by Chaplin successfully fights against the unfeeling machinery of industry. Modern industrial life can be aggravating, even hostile, or natural: all depends on the fit between our culture and our technology.

The *shinkansen* or "bullet train" speeds across the rural areas of   10
Japan giving a quick view of cluster after cluster of farmhouses surrounded by rice paddies. This particular pattern did not develop

purely by chance, but as a consequence of the technology peculiar to the growing of rice, the staple of the Japanese diet. The growing of rice requires construction and maintenance of an irrigation system, something that takes many hands to build. More importantly, the planting and the harvesting of rice can only be done efficiently with the cooperation of twenty or more people. The "bottom line" is that a single family working alone cannot produce enough rice to survive, but a dozen families working together can produce a surplus. Thus the Japanese have had to develop the capacity to work together in harmony, no matter what the forces of disagreement or social disintegration, in order to survive.

11   Japan is a nation built entirely on the tips of giant, suboceanic volcanoes. Little of the land is flat and suitable for agriculture. Terraced hillsides make use of every available square foot of arable land. Small homes built very close together further conserve the land. Japan also suffers from natural disasters such as earthquakes and hurricanes. Traditionally homes are made of light construction materials, so a house falling down during a disaster will not crush its occupants and also could be quickly and inexpensively rebuilt. During the feudal period until the Meiji restoration of 1868, each feudal lord sought to restrain his subjects from moving from one village to the next for fear that a neighboring lord might amass enough peasants with which to produce a large agricultural surplus, hire an army and pose a threat. Apparently bridges were not commonly built across rivers and streams until the late nineteenth century, since bridges increased mobility between villages.

12   Taken all together, this characteristic style of living paints the picture of a nation of people who are homogenous with respect to race, history, language, religion, and culture. For centuries and generations these people have lived in the same village next door to the same neighbors. Living in close proximity and in dwellings which gave very little privacy, the Japanese survived through their capacity to work together in harmony. In this situation, it was inevitable that the one most central social value which emerged, the one value without which the society could not continue, was that an individual does not matter.

13   To the Western soul this is a chilling picture of society. Subordinating individual tastes to the harmony of the group and knowing that individual needs can never take precedence over the interests of all is repellent to the Western citizen. But a frequent theme of Western philosophers and sociologists is that individual freedom exists only when people willingly subordinate their self-interests to the social interest. A society composed entirely of self-interested individuals is a society in which each person is at war with the other, a society which has

no freedom. This issue, constantly at the heart of understanding society, comes up in every century, and in every society, whether the writer be Plato, Hobbes, or B. F. Skinner. The question of understanding which contemporary institutions lie at the heart of the conflict between automatism and totalitarianism remains. In some ages, the kinship group, the central social institution, mediated between these opposing forces to preserve the balance in which freedom was realized; in other times the church or the government was most critical. Perhaps our present age puts the work organization as the central institution.

In order to complete the comparison of Japanese and American living situations, consider a flight over the United States. Looking out of the window high over the state of Kansas, we see a pattern of a single farmhouse surrounded by fields, followed by another single homestead surrounded by fields. In the early 1800s in the state of Kansas there were no automobiles. Your nearest neighbor was perhaps two miles distant; the winters were long, and the snow was deep. Inevitably, the central social values were self-reliance and independence. Those were the realities of that place and age that children had to learn to value. 14

The key to the industrial revolution was discovering that non-human forms of energy substituted for human forms could increase the wealth of a nation beyond anyone's wildest dreams. But there was a catch. To realize this great wealth, non-human energy needed huge complexes called factories with hundreds, even thousands of workers collected into one factory. Moreover, several factories in one central place made the generation of energy more efficient. Almost overnight, the Western world was transformed from a rural and agricultural country to an urban and industrial state. Our technological advance seems to no longer fit our social structure: in a sense, the Japanese can better cope with modern industrialism. While Americans still busily protect our rather extreme form of individualism, the Japanese hold their individualism in check and emphasize cooperation. 15

Questions and Activities

▶ *COMPREHENSION QUESTIONS*

1. What are "collective values" (paragraph 1)? Give both a general definition and some examples.
2. Why does Ouchi believe that the "cluster after cluster of farmhouses surrounded by rice paddies" that visitors would see from a speeding train's windows as it crosses Japan (paragraph 10) would contribute

to "a chilling picture of society" for "the Western soul" (paragraph 13)? What would be "chilling" to a Westerner? Why would it be so? Review paragraphs 10 through 13 before answering.

3. What might Japanese readers of this selection learn from it? Assuming that these Japanese readers wanted to "meet the American challenge," what might they do to adapt themselves to the American corporate style?

4. To which of the two interpretations in paragraphs 5 and 6 does Ouchi subscribe? How does the contrasting of Japanese and American corporate accounting systems in paragraphs 8 and 9 support this interpretation?

▶ *QUESTIONS OF RHETORICAL PURPOSE AND STRATEGY*

5. Ouchi organizes this essay inductively, working from anecdotes and illustrations to a general thesis concerning the contrast between Japanese and American attitudes toward productivity. Do you think this type of organization has a more persuasive effect on neutral readers than a deductive type might have had? In deductive organization, a writer weighs data or examples against a general truth, which has usually been introduced early in the piece. Might this selection by Ouchi have been more persuasive had it begun with generalizations that described Japanese and American companies and then illustrated these generalizations with examples, facts, and descriptions?

6. What goal is Ouchi pursuing in this essay? Does he wish to persuade readers to prefer the American or Japanese corporate model, or is he giving readers objective facts and ideas so they can decide for themselves?

▶ *THEME QUESTIONS*

7. What type of problems might you or a friend or family member have working in a Japanese corporation? What problems might you or your friend or relative have with Japanese workers, with Japanese management? Why would these problems occur?

8. Compare Franklin's emphasis on work as a means of developing individualism to Ouchi's account of the Japanese emphasis on collective responsibility and the sharing of material gains for work done. Does Richard Selzer emphasize individual or social aspects of work? How do these considerations affect Selzer's sense of pride and satisfaction in his work? Does Stephen Cruz, as portrayed by Studs Terkel in the sketch included in this section, seem affected by a similar tension between individualism and collectivism in his life in corporate America?

▶ *LEARNING ACTIVITIES*

9. Imagine that you are a Japanese worker in an automobile plant. Write a letter to your American boss explaining why you have not contributed to the company's suggestion box (paragraphs 3 and 4). As the basis of your letter, use Ouchi's explanation of the reasons behind Japanese workers' refusal to submit suggestions. But write the letter in an informal style.

10. Have you heard of or experienced or can you imagine a situation in an industry or corporation where individualism causes production or morale problems? If you have, describe the situation to the rest of the class and explain why a more collectively oriented attitude might help resolve the problems.

11. Do you think fast-food chains expect more collective cooperation and less individualism from their employees than do most other companies? The next time you eat at a fast-food restaurant, observe the employees carefully and use their behavior to support your answer. Observe their cooperation and interchange of tasks, and use these observations to make your point.

Conditions for Work: The Common World of Women

ADRIENNE RICH

Born in 1929, Adrienne Rich has become a well-known American poet. Her book of poems *Diving into the Wreck* won the National Book Award in 1973. She has published several other volumes of poetry, has translated Russian and Yiddish poems, and has written and edited a number of books of social criticism. She has also published many magazine and journal articles in *Poetry, The Nation, The New York Review of Books, Partisan Review, Paris Review,* and others. She is a graduate of Radcliffe College and has held teaching positions and residencies at many other colleges and universities.

The following essay is an example of the prose Rich has produced recently in support of the feminist movement. Her poetry had always been of a controlled and deeply introspective sort; in it, as a careful observer of her inner consciousness, she constructs intricate visions of her thoughts and feelings. In her later prose, however, Rich has taken that earlier, poetic focus on controlled self-revelation and transformed it into the voice of a sociologist and historian of woman's consciousness. In this essay, she argues that women must accept and value both the domestic work they have been given by our social context and the career activities that were previously assigned by our social context to men. Women must, she argues, create a new synthesis of roles, in which the domestic and the professional aspects are intertwined. The beginning of this synthesis, Rich suggests, will be found in and through women's attempts to establish a new, public sense of community. In this essay, addressed primarily to women, Rich attempts to begin to create such a sense of community. Rich's audience is more limited than those for other essays in this section; her purpose is also more explicitly persuasive than those of other essays in this section (except perhaps for Harvey Swados's essay, pages 140–148).

As you read Rich's work, think about these questions:

1. What are the broader thematic implications of this essay? Does it suggest that individuals need to belong to a community of workers who share values if they are to find satisfaction in their work? Consider William Ouchi's account of Japanese workers in this context.
2. Do too many American workers feel isolated from others as they work? Is this especially true of women?

▶ ───────────────────────────

> ...the common world is what we enter when we are born and what we
> leave behind when we die. It transcends our life-span into past and fu-
> ture alike; it was there before we came and will outlast our brief so-
> journ into it. It is what we have in common not only with those who
> live with us, but also with those who were here before and with those
> who will come after us. But such a common world can survive the
> coming and going of the generations only to the extent that it appears
> in public. It is the publicity of the public realm which can absorb and
> make shine through the centuries whatever men [sic] may want to
> save from the natural ruin of time.
> —Hannah Arendt, The Human Condition

Women both have and have not had a common world. The mere   1
sharing of oppression does not constitute a common world. Our
thought and action, insofar as they have taken the form of difference,
assertion, or rebellion, have repeatedly been obliterated, or subsumed
under "human" history, which means the "publicity of the public
realm" created and controlled by men. Our history is the history of a
majority of the species, yet the struggles of women for a "human" status have been relegated to footnotes, to the sidelines. Above all, wom-
en's relationships with women have been denied or neglected as a force
in history.[1]

The essays in this book are parts of a much larger work, which we are   2
still struggling to possess: the long process of making visible the experience of women.* The tentativeness, the anxiety, sometimes approaching paralysis, the confusions, described in many of these essays by intelligent, educated, "privileged" women, are themselves evidence of
the damage that can be done to creative energy by the lack of a sense of
continuity, historical validation, community. Most women, it seems,
have gone through their travails in a kind of spiritual isolation, alone
both in the present and in ignorance of their place in any female

---

[1]Joan Kelly suggests that a feminist view of history is not merely "compensatory history," a parallel to the accepted views of history as male. It means "to look at ages or
movements of great social change in terms of their liberation or repression of woman's potential, their import for the advancement of her humanity as well as 'his.' The moment
this is done—the moment one assumes that women are a part of humanity in the fullest
sense—the period or set of events with which we deal takes on a wholly different character or meaning from the normally accepted one. Indeed, what emerges is a fairly regular
pattern of relative loss of status for women in those periods of so-called progressive
change." "The Social Relation of the Sexes: Methodological Implications of Women's
History," in Signs, vol. 1, no. 4, summer 1976.
*This essay was first published as part of an anthology of feminist writing that included
essays by several professionals and academics.

tradition. The support of friends, of a women's group, may make survival possible; but it is not enough.

3   It is quite clear that the universities and the intellectual establishment intend to keep women's experience as far as possible invisible, and women's studies a barely subsidized, condescendingly tolerated ghetto. The majority of women who go through undergraduate and graduate school suffer an intellectual coercion of which they are not even consciously aware. In a world where language and naming are power, silence is oppression, is violence. Writing of the destruction of the civilization of Languedoc by the forces of the Church under Simon de Montfort, Simone Weil reminds us: "Nothing is more cruel to the past than the commonplace which asserts that spiritual values cannot be destroyed by force; on the strength of this belief, civilizations that have been destroyed by force of arms are denied the name of civilization; and there is no risk of our being refuted by the dead."[2]

4   For spiritual values and a creative tradition to continue unbroken we need concrete artifacts, the work of hands, written words to read, images to look at, a dialogue with brave and imaginative women who came before us. In the false names of love, motherhood, natural law—false because they have not been defined by us to whom they are applied—women in patriarchy have been withheld from building a common world, except in enclaves, or through coded messages.

> The protection and preservation of the world against natural processes are among the toils which need the monotonous performance of daily repeated chores....In old tales and mythological stories it has often assumed the grandeur of heroic fights against overwhelming odds, as in the account of Hercules, whose cleansing of the Augean stables is among the twelve heroic "labors." A similar connotation of heroic deeds requiring great strength and courage and performed in a fighting spirit is manifest in the mediaeval use of the word: labor, *travail, arbeit*. However, the daily fight in which the human body is engaged to keep the world clean and prevent its decay bears little resemblance to heroic deeds; the endurance it needs to repair every day anew the waste of yesterday is not courage, and what makes the effort painful is not danger but its relentless repetition.[3]

Hannah Arendt does not call this "woman's work." Yet it is this activity of world-protection, world-preservation, world-repair—the million tiny stitches, the friction of the scrubbing brush, the scouring cloth, the iron across the shirt, the rubbing of cloth against itself to exorcise the

---

[2]Simone Weil, *Selected Essays, 1934–1943*, Richard Rees, trans. (New York: Oxford, 1962), p. 43.
[3]Hannah Arendt, *The Human Condition* (Chicago: University of Chicago, 1958), p. 55.

stain, the renewal of the scorched pot, the rusted knifeblade, the invisible weaving of a frayed and threadbare family life, the cleaning up of soil and waste left behind by men and children—that we have been charged to do ''for love,'' not merely unpaid, but unacknowledged by the political philosophers. Women are not described as ''working'' when we create the essential conditions for the work of men; we are supposed to be acting out of love, instinct, or devotion to some higher cause than self.

Arendt tells us that the Greeks despised all labor of the body   5
necessitated by biological needs. It was to spare themselves such labor that men kept slaves—not as a means of cheaper production. ''Contempt for laboring, originally arising out of a passionate striving for freedom from necessity and a no less passionate impatience with every effort that left no trace, no monument, no great work worthy to remembrance, spread with the increasing demands of *polis* life upon the time of the citizens [i.e., males] and its insistence on their abstention from all but political activities.''[4]

And, in the aside of a footnote: ''Women and slaves belonged and   6
lived together...no woman, not even the wife of the household head, lived among her equals—other free women—so that rank depended much less on birth than on 'occupation' or function....'' According to the index, this footnote is the last reference to women, on page 73 of a volume of 325 pages on *The Human Condition*, written by a woman.

Every effort that left no trace...The efforts of women in labor, giv-   7
ing birth to stillborn children, children who must die of plague or by infanticide; the efforts of women to keep filth and decay at bay, children decently clothed, to produce the clean shirt in which the man walks out daily into the common world of men, the efforts to raise children against the attritions of racist and sexist schooling, drugs, sexual exploitation, the brutalization and killing of barely grown boys in war. There is still little but contempt and indifference for this kind of work, these efforts. (The phrase ''wages for housework'' has the power to shock today that the phrase ''free love'' possessed a century ago.)

II

There is a natural temptation to escape if we can, to close the   8
door behind us on this despised realm which threatens to engulf all women, whether as mothers, or in marriage, or as the invisible, ill-paid sustainers of the professionals and social institutions. There is a natural fear that if we do not enter the common world of men, as asexual beings

[4]Ibid., pp. 81–83.

or as "exceptional" women, do not enter it on its terms and obey its rules, we will be sucked back into the realm of servitude, whatever our temporary class status or privileges. This temptation and this fear compromise our powers, divert our energies, form a potent source of "blocks" and of acute anxiety about work.

9   For if, in trying to join the common world of men, the professions molded by a primarily masculine consciousness, we split ourselves off from the common life of women and deny our female heritage and identity in our work, we lose touch with our real powers and with the essential condition for all fully realized work: community.

10   Feminism begins but cannot end with the discovery by an individual of her self-consciousness as a woman. It is not, finally, even the recognition of her reasons for anger, or the decision to change her life, go back to school, leave a marriage (though in any individual life such decisions can be momentous and require great courage). Feminism means finally that we renounce our obedience to the fathers and recognize that the world they have described is not the whole world. Masculine ideologies are the creation of masculine subjectivity; they are neither objective, nor value-free, nor inclusively "human." Feminism implies that we recognize fully the inadequacy for us, the distortion, of male-created ideologies, and that we proceed to think, and act, out of that recognition.

11   In the common world of men, in the professions which the writers of these essays have come to grips with, it takes more than our *individual* talent and intelligence to think and act further. In denying the validity of women's experience, in pretending to stand for "the human," masculine subjectivity tries to force us to name our truths in an alien language, to dilute them; we are constantly told that the "real" problems, the ones worth working on, are those men have defined, that the problems we need to examine are trivial, unscholarly, nonexistent. We are urged to separate the "personal" (our entire existence as women) from the "scholarly" or "professional." Several of the women who contribute to this book have described the outright insults and intellectual sabotage they encountered as women in graduate school. But more insidious may be the sabotage which appears as paternal encouragement, approval granted for internalizing a masculine subjectivity. As Tillie Olsen puts it in this book, "Not to be able to come to one's own truth or not to use it in one's writing, even when telling the truth having to 'tell it slant,' robs one of drive, of conviction, limits potential stature...." Everywhere, women working in the common world of men are denied that integrity of work and life which can only be found in an emotional and intellectual connectedness with ourselves and other women.

More and more, however, women are creating community, sharing   *12*
work, and discovering that in the sharing of work our relationships
with each other become larger and more serious. In organizing a
women's self-help clinic or law collective or a writing workshop, in
editing a magazine or creating a center for women's work like the
Women's Building in Los Angeles, in running a press that publishes
"lost" books by women or contemporary work that may be threatening
or incomprehensible to male editors, in participating in a women's prison project or a crisis center, we come to understand at first hand not
only our unmet needs but the resources we can draw on for meeting
them even in the face of female poverty, the hostility of institutions,
the lack of documentation of our shared past. Susan Griffin has said
that, for a feminist, writing may be solitary but thinking is collective.
Any woman who has moved from the playing fields of male discourse
into the realm where women are developing our own descriptions of the
world knows the extraordinary sense of shedding, as it were, the en-
cumbrance of someone else's baggage, of ceasing to translate. It is not
that thinking becomes easy, but that the difficulties are intrinsic to the
work itself rather than to the environment. In the common world of
men, the struggle to make female experience visible at all—Will they
take seriously a thesis on women? Will they let me teach a course on
women? Can I speak bluntly of female experience without shattering
the male egos around me, or being labeled hysterical, castrating?—such
struggles assume the status of an intellectual problem, and the real intellectual problems may not be probed at all.

Working together as women, consciously creating our networks   *13*
even where patriarchal institutions are the ones in which we have to
survive, we can confront the problems of women's relationships, the
mothers we came from, the sisters with whom we were forced to divide
the world, the daughters we love and fear. We can challenge and inspirit
each other, throw light on one another's blind spots, stand by and give
courage at the birth throes of one another's insights. I think of the poet
H. D.'s account of the vision she had on the island of Corfu, in the *Tribute to Freud:*

> And there I sat and there is my friend Bryher who has brought me to Greece. I
> can turn now to her, though I do not budge an inch or break the sustained
> crystal-gazing at the wall before me. I say to Bryher, "There have been pic-
> tures here—I thought they were shadows at first, but they are light, not shad-
> ow. They are quite simple objects—but of course it's very strange. I can
> break away from them now, if I want—it's just a matter of concentrating
> —what do you think? Shall I stop? Shall I go on?" Bryher says without hesita-
> tion, "Go on."

> . . .I had known such extraordinarily gifted and charming people. They had made much of me or they had slighted me and yet neither praise nor neglect mattered in the face of the gravest issues—life, death. . . .And yet, so oddly, I knew that this experience, this writing-on-the-wall before me, could not be shared with anyone except the girl who stood so bravely there beside me. This girl had said without hesitation, "Go on." It was she really who had the detachment and integrity of the Pythoness of Delphi. But it was I, battered and dissociated. . .who was seeing the pictures, and who was reading the writing or granted the inner vision. Or perhaps, in some sense, we were "seeing" it together, for without her, admittedly, I could not have gone on.[5]

Even for those who would mistrust visionary experience, the episode is revealing as metaphor. The personal relationship helps create the conditions for work (out of her vision H. D. went on to create her great, late, long poems celebrating a matriarchal world and the quests of female heroes); no less does the fact of working together deepen and sustain a personal relationship. "If Chloe likes Olivia and they share a laboratory. . .this of itself will make their friendship more varied and lasting because it will be less personal."[6] By "like" I believe Virginia Woolf (still, in that book, writing more cautiously than later in *Three Guineas*) also meant "love"; for "a laboratory" we can read "the creation of a common world."

14   Many women have known the figure of the male "mentor" who guides and protects his female student or colleague, tenderly opening doors for her into the common world of men. He seems willing to share his power, to conspire with her in stealing what Celia Gilbert names in this book "the sacred fire" of work. Yet what can he really bestow but the *illusion* of power, a power stolen, in any case, from the mass of women, over centuries, by men? He can teach her to name her experience in language that may allow her to live, work, perhaps succeed in the common world of men. But he has no key to the powers she might share with other women.

15   There is also the illusion that if you make your emotional and erotic life with women, it does not matter that your intellectual work is a collaboration with silence and lying about female experience. At a panel of lesbian writers at the Modern Language Association in San Francisco in December 1975, Susan Griffin spoke of the damage we do to ourselves and our work in censoring our own truths:

> I feel that this whole idea of the Muse, of inspiration, is a kind of cop-out. There is something very fascinating going on with a writer's psyche when you are undergoing a silence, an inability to write. Each silence and each

[5]H. D., *Tribute to Freud* (Oxford: Carcanet Press, 1971), pp. 50–54.
[6]Virginia Woolf, *A Room of One's Own* (London: Hogarth Press, 1929), p. 126.

eruption into speech constitute a kind of struggle in the life of a writ-er.... The largest struggle around silence in my life has had to do with the fact that I am a woman and a lesbian. When I recognized my feelings as a woman, when I recognized my anger as a woman, suddenly my writing was transformed—suddenly I had a material, a subject-matter.... And then a few years later I found myself unhappy with my writing, unhappy with the way I expressed myself, unable to speak; I wrote in a poem, *Words do not come to my mouth anymore.* And I happened also...to be censoring the fact that I was a lesbian. I thought that I was doing this because of the issue of child cus-tody, and that was and still is a serious issue. But I wasn't acknowledging how important it was to me, both as a writer and as a human being, to be able to...write about my feelings as a lesbian.

In fact, I think that writers are always dealing with taboos of one sort or another; if they are not taboos general in society, you may just have a fear in your private life of perceiving some truth because of its implications, and that will stop you from writing.... But when we come to the taboo of lesbianism, this is one which is most loaded for everyone, even those who are not lesbians. Because the fact of love between women...is one which affects every event in this society, psychic and political and sociological. And for a writer, the most savage censor is oneself.[7]

The whole question of what it means or might mean to work as a lesbi-an might have occupied an entire essay in this book. Of past women whose thought and work have remained visible in history, an enormous number have been lesbians, yet because of the silence and denial that has enveloped lesbianism, we learn little from women's biographies about the relation of their work to their relationships with women or to the social taboos they lived among. One writer in this book mourns that "there was only one Alice B. Toklas." But in fact women's support to women *has* been there all along, lifetime or long-term comradeships. For many women, struggling for economic survival in the common world of men, these relationships have had to be dissimulated, at what cost to the work (let alone the relationships) we cannot begin to know. Every lesbian has been forced to walk past the distorting mirrors of homophobia before she could get down to the real problems of her work. Every lesbian artist knows that when she attempts to embody lesbian sexuality in her work she runs the risk of having it perceived pornographically, if it is not simply denied visibility. When a lesbian feels she may have to choose between writing or painting her truths and keeping her child, she is flung back on the most oppressive ground of maternal guilt in conflict with creative work. The question of econom-ic survival, of keeping one's job, is terribly real, but the more terrible questions lie deeper where a woman is forced, or permits herself, to lead a censored life.

[7]*Sinister Wisdom*, vol 1., no. 2, pp. 24–25.

III

16   In thinking about the issues of women and work raised in this book, I turned to Hannah Arendt's *The Human Condition* to see how a major political philosopher of our time, a woman greatly respected in the intellectual establishment, had spoken to the theme. I found her essay illuminating, not so much for what it says, but for what it is. The issue of women as the laborers in reproduction, of women as workers in production, of the relationship of women's unpaid labor in the home to the separation between "private" and "public" spheres, of the woman's body as commodity—these questions were not raised for the first time in the 1960s and 1970s; they had already been documented in the 1950s when *The Human Condition* was being written. Arendt barely alludes, usually in a footnote, to Marx and Engels's engagement with this theme; and she writes as if the work of Olive Schreiner, Charlotte Perkins Gilman, Emma Goldman, Jane Addams, to name only a few writers, had never existed. The withholding of women from participation in the *vita activa*, the "common world," and the connection of this with reproductivity, is something from which she does not so much turn her eyes as stare straight through unseeing. This "great work" is thus a kind of failure for which masculine ideology has no name, precisely because in terms of that ideology it is successful, at the expense of truths the ideology considers irrelevant. To read such a book, by a woman of large spirit and great erudition, can be painful, because it embodies the tragedy of a female mind nourished on male ideologies. In fact, the loss is ours, because Arendt's desire to grasp deep moral issues is the kind of concern we need to build a common world which will amount to more than "life-styles." The power of male ideology to possess such a female mind, to disconnect it as it were from the female body which encloses it and which it encloses, is nowhere more striking than in Arendt's lofty and crippled book.

17   Women's minds cannot grow to full stature, or touch the real springs of our power to alter reality, on a diet of masculine ideology. This is not the same thing as saying that we can use nothing of these ideologies, or their methods, or that we need not understand them. But the common world of men cannot give us what we need, and parts of it are poisoning us. Miriam Schapiro, in this book, describes the process through which she begins to work: filling sheets of paper with smeared paint, images created "freely, mindlessly," going back to that place in childhood where she simply painted and was happy. To her husband, this appeared as "deprofessionalizing" herself. Yet the very concept of "professionalism," tainted as it is with the separation between personal life and work, with a win-or-lose mentality and the gauging of suc-

cess by public honors and market prices, needs a thorough revaluation by women. Forty years back Virginia Woolf was asking:

> What is this "civilization" in which we find ourselves? What are these ceremonies and why should we take part in them? What are these professions and why should we make money out of them? Where in short is it leading, the procession of the sons of educated men?[8]

Her answer was that it is leading to war, to elitism, to exploitation and the greed for power; in our own time we can also add that it has clearly been leading to the ravagement of the nonhuman living world. Instead of the concept of "professionalism," we need, perhaps, a vision of work akin to that described by Simone Weil in her "Theoretical Picture of a Free Society":

> A clear view of what is possible and what impossible, what is easy and what difficult, of the labors that separate the project from its accomplishment —this alone does away with insatiable desires and vain fears; from this and not from anything else proceed moderation and courage, virtues without which life is nothing but a disgraceful frenzy. Besides, the source of any kind of virtue lies in the shock produced by the human intelligence being brought up against a matter devoid of lenience and of falsity.[9]

If we conceive of feminism as more than a frivolous label, if we conceive of it as an ethics, a methodology, a more complex way of thinking about, thus more responsibly acting upon, the conditions of human life, we need a self-knowledge which can only develop through a steady, passionate attention to *all* female experience. I cannot imagine a feminist evolution leading to radical change in the private/political realm of gender that is not rooted in the conviction that all women's lives are important; that the lives of men cannot be understood by burying the lives of women; and that to make visible the full meaning of women's experience, to reinterpret knowledge in terms of that experience, is now the most important task of thinking. *18*

If this is so, we cannot work alone. We had better face the fact that our hope of thinking at all, against the force of a maimed and maiming worldview, depends on seeking and giving our allegiance to a community of women co-workers. And beyond the exchange and criticism of work, we have to ask ourselves how we can make the conditions for work more possible, not just for ourselves but for each other. This is not a question of generosity. It is not generosity that makes women in com- *19*

[8]Virginia Woolf, *Three Guineas* (New York: Harcourt Brace, 1966), p. 63; first published 1938.
[9]Simone Weil, *Oppression and Liberty*, Arthur Wills and John Petrie, trans. (Amherst: University of Massachusetts, 1973), p. 87.

munity support and nourish each other. It is rather what Whitman called the "hunger for equals"—the desire for a context in which our own strivings will be amplified, quickened, lucidified, through those of our peers.

20   We also, of course, need community with our past. Women's art and thought and action will continue to be seen as deviant, its true meaning distorted or buried, as long as women's work can be dismissed as "exceptional," an interesting footnote to the major texts. Or, it will be encouraged for its timidities and punished for its daring. This is obvious to women who have tried to work along seriously feminist lines in the established professions. But even before the work exists, long before praise or attack, the very form it will assume, the courage on which it can draw, the sense of potential direction it may take, require—given the politics of our lives and of creation itself—more than the gifts of the individual woman or her immediate contemporaries. We need access to the female past.

21   The problem, finally, is not that of who does housework and child-care, whether or not one can find a life companion who will share in the sustenance and repair of daily life—crucial as these may be in the short run. It is a question of the community we are reaching for in our work and on which we can draw; whom we envision as our hearers, our co-creators, our challengers; who will urge us to take our work further, more seriously, than we had dared; on whose work we can build. Women *have* done these things for each other, sought each other in community, even if only in enclaves, often through correspondence, for centuries. Denied space in the universities, the scientific laboratories, the professions, we have devised our networks. We must not be tempted to trade the possibility of enlarging and strengthening those networks, and of extending them to more and more women, for the illusion of power and success as "exceptional" or "privileged" women in the professions.

Questions and Activities

▶ COMPREHENSION QUESTIONS

1. How does Rich define the modern woman's problem in her final paragraph? How does the idea of community fit into that definition? What does Rich say is *not* the modern woman's problem?

2. What is the point behind Rich's use of the long quotation from Susan Griffin in paragraph 15? Why does Griffin think it important

for writers to be able to write about their most private and perhaps even socially taboo experiences? How does Griffin's idea link up with Rich's earlier argument that we must expand our conceptions of work to include all kinds of useful activities, domestic as well as career-oriented?

▶ *QUESTIONS OF RHETORICAL PURPOSE AND STRATEGY*

3. Why does Rich use Hannah Arendt, a woman writer, to illustrate her view of what is wrong with the traditional male perspective on work (paragraphs 4, 5, and 6)? Assuming that women are the intended readers of this essay, why do you think Rich uses a woman writer as her example?

4. Throughout this essay, Rich emphasizes the sense of community that work creates for workers. Define the community that Rich is trying to persuade the women who read this essay to join. What does that community value? What is it trying to change? After you have considered these questions, gather specific evidence from the essay that supports your definition of this community.

5. Make a list of characteristics that define the intended audience of this essay. Is the essay addressed only to women? Is it addressed only to those women who might consider joining a community of liberated, working women? Are any men included in its audience?

6. What is Rich trying to get her readers to do? Does she want them to change their behavior, to take on a new attitude, to treat other people in a particular way?

7. This essay is primarily persuasive. Effective persuasive writing for an educated audience must be supported by sound facts. Does Rich provide sufficient supporting information for her persuasive arguments? Is that information drawn from objective sources?

▶ *THEME QUESTIONS*

8. In paragraph 4, Rich argues that the everyday, domestic, life-sustaining tasks have consistently been done by women. She goes on to argue that women must learn to respect this kind of work, because it is important and because it has been women's common experience. State what might be the central argument of a feminist who is on the opposite side of this argument. How might this attitude hinder a woman, for example, who wants to pursue a career in law or management?

9. Think about Benjamin Franklin's advice on how to succeed in a trade or business. All of Franklin's advice has as its premise the idea that financial gain and increased productivity are automatically good for all people. Do you feel that Franklin's perspective has contributed to the tendency in our culture to diminish the value of work

that does not produce more or better products? Why are the "products" of traditional woman's work, as Rich defines it, *not* valued highly in our culture?

▶ *LEARNING ACTIVITIES*

10. Interview a successful working woman. Transcribe the interview, keeping only the pertinent parts. Then discuss the interview with your class. Write up the interview in a narrative format, as a case study, organizing the subject's answers to your questions chronologically. Work in occasional interpretive comments, in your opening or closing paragraphs or in transitional paragraphs where you lead the reader from one main point to another.

11. Write a main idea or statement that concisely conveys your response to Rich's argument in this essay. Begin by stating Rich's main idea. Then make a list of what you believe to be significant qualifications of Rich's idea. Follow this listing by organizing your qualifications into a one-sentence statement that you can use to develop your response to Rich's argument. As a final step, you should combine Rich's main idea and your own counteridea into a generalization that you could use to write an essay whose purpose was to redefine Rich's perspective on working women and the women's movement.

    In carrying out this activity, you will go through the following four steps, which will prove useful when developing a main idea or generalization for any essay in which you plan to interpret something that you have read.

    a. Restate the author's main idea.
    b. Make a list of your qualifications of that idea.
    c. Organize the list of qualifications into an assertion about the author's main idea.
    d. Combine the author's main idea and your assertion into a generalization for an interpretive essay.

12. Tell a detailed story, organized chronologically, that describes you carrying out a mechanical, domestic chore—doing the laundry, shopping for food, or ironing a shirt, for example. When you have finished your first draft, reread it as a piece of personal writing in which your goal is to discover your attitude toward domestic work. Add a main idea that characterizes your attitude. Then rewrite your story so that it supports that main idea.

Work and the Professions

HARVEY SWADOS

Harvey Swados was an American novelist, short story writer, and essay-
ist who was born in 1920 and died in 1972. His social thinking was
shaped by the Depression of the 1930s; he was a socialist who
consistently, in both his fiction and his essays, looked critically at the
American working classes. Unlike other leftist critics, Swados focused
on the suffering and daily hardships of the American working and middle classes. He tried to search out the causes of their intellectual
impoverishment, rather than simply criticizing their weaknesses.

Swados's writings include five novels of social commentary: *Out
Went the Candle* (1955), *False Coin* (1960), *The Will* (1963), *Standing Fast*
(1970), and *Celebrations* (published posthumously in 1975). The main
character of his last novel, Sam Lumen, is a ninety-year-old radical educator who looks back over his life and at his current situation in order to
make judgments about American radical causes and the effects of the
industrial age on the working and middle classes. Among Swados's
respected writings are his short story collections *Nights in the Gardens
of Brooklyn* (1961) and *A Story for Teddy, and Others* (1965). Also well
regarded are the collections of essays *A Radical's America* (1962) and
The American Writers and the Great Depression (1966) and the social
commentary that he wrote for *The Nation, Saturday Review, Esquire,
The Saturday Evening Post,* and other magazines.

The following essay, published in *A Radical's America,* conveys
Swados's compassion for the masses of American workers he felt were
the victims of industrialization and administrative and corporate bureaucracy. Because of his compassion for his subjects, Swados's criticism of American society appealed to a broad range of educated
readers of diverse political persuasions.

In this essay, and in much of his published work, Swados advocated a
turning away from the commercialism of mass culture and a return to
the basic values of the traditional American work ethic. His purpose in
writing is persuasive; he hopes to convince readers that something is
radically wrong in that so many Americans lack a sense of commitment
to meaningful work.

This essay should help you address questions such as these:

1. How do we evaluate the benefit of our work to others? In the first
   place, is it necessary for our work to be of value to others? Can you
   think of types of work that have little social value yet seem worthwhile in themselves?

2. What are the differences between satisfaction and pleasure in work? Should professionals get more of a sense of service to others from their work than other types of workers do?
3. What has happened to the kind of pride in craftsmanship that Benjamin Franklin advocated in "Advice to a Young Tradesman"?

▶ ───────────────────

1   One of the great ironies of our time: The country that achieved pre-eminence in considerable part through an almost religious dedication to work has become the land where leisure and fun are enthroned as the new gods. We Americans were so fanatically devoted to work not only as the source but as the end of life that we became the butt of jokes to our own writers, from Sinclair Lewis to H. L. Mencken, as well as to European hotelkeepers and boulevardiers, who tagged our menfolk as people who didn't know how *not* to work. But in a few short years we have not only picked up the fallen flag of the aristocrats and fainéants*—we have emblazoned on it our current national motto, in the international neon language of the mass media: Work is for squares.

2   One day we awoke to the discovery that we had developed the capacity to produce more than we could consume with less expenditure of effort than is required in other nations simply to stave off hunger. More, we discovered that more and more people could get more and more by working less and less—or by not working at all. *Fortune* magazine was not kidding when it called "not working" the fastest-growing occupation in the United States. Consider: Between thirteen and fourteen billion dollars a year in personal income is now going to individuals in the form of stock dividends, three times the amount paid in dividends twenty years ago. Over twenty-five billion dollars a year is being paid as interest income, and over twelve billion as rental income. If you take into account the twenty-eight billions going to individuals as "transfer payments" (which means payments not resulting from current production—that is, mostly social-insurance benefits and veterans' payments), this boils down to the fact that, as Sylvia Porter, a syndicated financial columnist, puts it rather excitedly, "18 to 20 per cent of all the personal income being paid in this country today is going to Americans who are NOT WORKING for the income."

---

*The French word *fainéants* means idle, lazy, slothful, or sluggish; here it is used to refer to people who manifest these qualities.

Inevitably, the news of this spreading stream of gravy seeps through   3
even to those who aren't getting any of it. If the message is not plain
even to the dullest, the mass media are in there punching to drive it
home. What other conclusion can we draw from the unlamented quiz
shows, their wild proliferation checked only when its cancerous nature
became a national shame.* The sick fascination was not in any display
of brains (patent nincompoops and muttonheads shared in the swag)
but in the demonstration that absolutely anyone could lay his hands legally on enormous sums of money without lifting a finger or shedding
one drop of honest sweat. If the quiz shows are gone, "Queen for a Day"
remains, and in the supermarkets you can now enter contests without
so much as writing one jingle or completing one sentence in twenty-
five words or less. To jet to Paris for two on a detergent manufacturer or
retire with a lifetime tax-free income on a dog-food distributor, you
need labor no longer over rhyming dictionaries. In keeping with the
times, such intellectual trials are often dispensed with, and the loot is
passed out on a no-sweat straight lottery basis.

Why work? You don't have to be beat to be ruefully aware that, in-   4
creasingly, middle-class occupations are as phony as the title to an acre
of land on the moon. I believe that not one person in a hundred who
"works" in advertising, merchandising, public relations, radio, television, mass circulation magazines or movies is engaged in what was
once known as honorable, socially useful labor. A growing proportion of
the new middle class is being paid for putting in the hours between
amusements at tasks that cannot be justified by traditional standards in
terms of either public utility or personal satisfaction.

Those who are indignant at the irresponsibility of labeling practical-   5
ly all careers related to the mass media as non-work or fake-work jobs
might think about some of the implications of the following excerpt
from an undelivered speech by an advertising agency official, as reported in the *New York Times* of February 17, 1960: "As long as the object
of the mass communications industry is to deliver a maximum audience at a minimum cost, cultural factors must take a back seat. Entertainment, art, culture and enlightenment are only means toward fulfilling the economic objectives of the mass media.... Artistry, morality
and religion are permitted as part of the public relations of the field.
They provide a means of avoiding serious criticism and legal action.
..." I wish only that there were space to quote further from this confes-

---

*In the 1950s, several quiz shows gave out enormous cash prizes to contestants who suc-
cessfully answered difficult and obscure questions. Toward the end of the decade, it was
discovered that several of these shows were supplying contestants with answers. The
most famous quiz-show scandal occurred in relation to the show "The $64,000 Ques-
tion."

sion, about which the *Times* goes on to explain, "When the official learned to his horror on last Friday that his speech was not to be private, but was to be publicized, he telephoned the school and canceled the engagement."

6   There are others just as frank and apparently even more shameless about what the new middle class is perpetrating to earn its fun and games. In a paper in the *Harvard Business Review* entitled "The Dangers of Social Responsibility," Dr. Theodore Levitt, marketing and economic consultant and advisor to Standard Oil of Indiana, has opined that "If what is offered can be sold at a profit (not necessarily a long-run profit) then it's legitimate. The cultural, spiritual, social, et cetera, consequences of his [*the seller's*] actions are none of the businessman's business."

7   Significantly, the hucksters and their hired hands, the boating enthusiasts and barbecue experts, who should be the last to complain about the laziness or the dishonesty of others, are the very people who are most vociferous at their watering holes—coffee breaks, lunch dates and cocktail parties—in their annoyance that the lower orders are not putting out as they used to.

8   Certainly it is true that, as millions of toaster owners have discovered to their dismay and outrage, it is almost impossible to get a small appliance honestly and reasonably repaired. And it becomes less and less likely that the instinct of workmanship will have found vital expression either in the original construction or in the repair of such enormously expensive items as a Detroit automobile or a development house. No argument here. The real question is whether this decline in pride of craft and standards of honest dealing comes about as a result of union-enforced slackness and the unlikelihood of being fired simply for sloppiness or whether, as I believe, it reflects an economy increasingly dedicated to planned obsolescence (read: short-lived junk) and dominated by types who have no aim in life beyond making a bundle (ponder the case of the recently deposed president of one of our largest corporations, currently under stockholder suit for allegedly having knowingly purchased, on personally profitable kickback terms, inferior parts for his company's product).

9   In our understandable frustration at struggling with a national situation dominated by lack of respect for the "pro"—the man who cares enough about what he produces to work long and hard at making it both handsome and satisfying—we find it easier to refer our irritations with bad service, rudeness, sloppy workmanship, and inferior products to a few large, easily identifiable, malign bodies. But it simply will not answer to attribute all these maddening and shameful annoyances to Big Unionism on the one hand or Madison Avenue on the other.

The unions cannot be seen as either parent or midwife to these   *10*
iniquities; they are rather a mirror, reflecting a disturbed awareness on
the part of their members that as their tasks are made increasingly minute and differentiated, they themselves become separated from any
vital relationship to the finished product, and that in many cases the
finished product is hardly worth making anyway. Not only does the
same hold true for the advertising-agency employee (who is additional-
ly burdened psychologically with the manufacture of personal enthusiasm for products of dubious utility); *his* organization reflects the
enormous pressure in our society to move goods and consequently to
brainwash consumers into believing that they want or need these
goods—without real regard to their quality or indeed the very necessity
for their existence.

Given this dual deification of production and the continuous move-   *11*
ment of goods (no matter what kind), we should not be too surprised
that an increasingly uneasy public tends to blame unions, or any other
easily labeled entity, in preference to the harder task of analyzing the
impersonal forces that create our new national hypocrisy. Nor should
we be quite so unprepared for the personality deformations occurring as
a result of grown men being bribed to spend their waking hours at tasks
that mock the very possibility of a serious, professional achievement
with one's hands or brain.

Not least among these deformations, along with the blind, pot-and-   *12*
kettle, middle-class complaint about the falling-off of working-class
performance standards, has been a virtual disappearance of our concern
for those whose lives are not overmastered by the forty billion dollars
which *Life* magazine happily assures us are now spent annually on
"nonworking." Last year Albert Whitehouse, who runs the Industrial
Union Department of the AFL-CIO, described to a public-relations seminar of the Harvard Graduate School of Business Administration "a
gathering of polite people in an upper middle-income suburb. The lo-
cale could have been outside any large city in the U.S.A. The group was
all-professional, of middle age and upward—doctors, lawyers, government careerists, and their wives. To hear these good people, organized
labor is to blame for virtually everything from the Berlin crisis to na-
tionalist outbursts in Nyasaland. What bothered me most was that all
the disagreement was virtually as polite as the agreement. . . . These
professionals seemed to have forgotten the past. . . . A strange myopia
afflicted the crowd, or so it seemed to me. . . ."

Mr. Whitehouse went on, "Something seems to have gone out of   *13*
American life. It's a sense of sympathy for one's fellow man, a sense of
integrity, an understanding of the other fellow's right to human dignity. There was a day when the picket line of underpaid textile workers

commanded sympathy. There was a time when the plight of the farm worker was of national concern. There was a day even when the nation cared about its poor, and that wasn't so long ago.''

14   The nature of the complaint is already known. What is infinitely depressing is that, as Mr. Whitehouse indicates, the infection has spread from the much-pummeled admen to such presumably unassailable areas of selfless endeavor as the learned professions. I am particularly sensitive to the conduct of the new generation of medical men because my grandfather, my father and a number of uncles and cousins have acquitted themselves with a certain distinction in the field; and I fear that some of them would be hard put to justify the action—lack of action would describe it more accurately—of a number of their contemporary colleagues. Surely no one will begrudge a hard-working medico an undisturbed day off such as he used never to be able to enjoy—or two days off, for that matter. But now it becomes increasingly difficult to obtain the personal services of any physician after five o'clock on any afternoon, particularly if you need to have him come to you, and not vice versa.

15   We have all read hair-raising stories about silly women jabbering on a party line and refusing to get off so that a frantic father could reach his family doctor in an emergency. What we haven't been told is whether, when the idiots finally ran out of breath, the doctor finally condescended to come to the phone. There are doctors now who will speak to you, all right—and will subsequently bill you two dollars for having taken up a moment or two that might otherwise have been spent at the lake or on the putting green. The after-me-the-deluge attitude of some of these practitioners, together with the unrepudiated last-ditch Bourbonism* of their union, the A.M.A., may very likely serve to give impetus to the passage of a national medical insurance program; in the meantime, however, it helps to carve out one more stone in the monument to greed and laziness now arising in our midst. The same has to hold true for the lawyers who are so busy making money and having fun that they cannot spare a moment to restrain the American Bar Association from sniping at the Supreme Court of the United States, simply because that body has been taking seriously the upholding of constitutional liberties.

16   I would hold no group immune. The college teachers, of whom I have been one in recent years, have let it be known that they are overworked and underpaid. This is generally true, just as it is true that they are entitled to more time and money for travel and research. But the hot pursuit of the gravy train of grantsmanship and the chase after cushy

*Bourbonism, from the French royal family named Bourbon, refers to stubborn conservative thought or to people who are behind the times and unteachable.

overseas deals must arouse suspicion as to how much these selfless scholars actually intend to accomplish in the unsullied realm of free thought and to what lengths (or distances) they will go to escape from the American classrooms they claim to be so concerned about. The effect on graduate students of the antics of these goof-off artists of academe cannot be estimated here. What we can say is that college kids smarten up in a hurry, and that by the time they graduate they know as many angles as a five-percenter or an influence peddler. You still have to work in graduate or professional school, but more often than not you labor now not to extend the boundaries of human thought but to gain admission to the club or the club-car of the gravy train.

Now if these things are true, as I believe them to be, in such rarefied   *17*
areas as the learned professions, consider how much more depressing they are when we encounter them, swollen to ugly proportions, in the population at large. The counterman or waitress who cannot be troubled to remember that you asked for tea instead of coffee, the cook who cannot be bothered to drain the water from a plate of lukewarm spaghetti before dumping it in front of you, the optometrist who sells you harlequin glasses when in fact you do not need any glasses—all are demonstrating in their particular ways the deformations wrought on pride of performance and the integrity of a job well and honestly done by a culture that no longer puts any premium on such accomplishments, but glorifies instead the "instant," the "magic," the "ready mix," all euphemisms by and large for the quick, the sloppy, the careless buck.

The effects are perhaps most acutely painful in the field of popular   *18*
entertainment, partly because they are most pervasive and hence most unavoidable, and partly because they catch kids—future doctors, lawyers, professors, countermen, cooks, optometrists—at their most vulnerable, and inculcate them with values (whether they accept them or rebel against them) that must color their adult lives.

For quite a while one of the handsomer attributes of the American   *19*
public performer, the real pro, was grace under pressure, which might be more closely defined as a carefully developed faculty of making the difficult look easy and effortless. This kind of grace helped to endear Crosby, Sinatra, Joe DiMaggio, and Ted Williams to their fans.

But now we find many young athletes motivated less by an urgent de-   *20*
sire to do, with grace, what has never been done before, than by an expectation of doing what has already been done by many around them. The dream of the talented as well as the hopelessly untalented athlete is to clean up in a hurry.

As for the popular singers, we can in all truth regard a number of   *21*
them not as human beings aspiring to impart an air of effortlessness to their performances but, rather, quite simply, as manufactured objects, with neither more nor less relationship to the rest of the human race

than the juke boxes whose glassy insides they feed with an assortment of noises. One of the current favorite singers was found, by an ambitious agent, at age fifteen with his guitar on a tenement stoop. The agent gave him a name, a wardrobe, a hairdo, some recording tests and singing lessons. These were soon given up as hopeless because the boy was tone-deaf; but this made no difference—the agent had guessed correctly that the boy would be attractive, or could be rendered attractive, to young girls, no matter what sort of noises he made. As a result, this adolescent, who will not be of voting age for some years and who is more of a concoction than he is a developing human being, is already more "successful" than Szilard, Waksman or Salk.* And although he will be more quickly forgotten, his life story (such as it is) and its implicit moral is to be found not in the sociological journals but in the daily papers and the fan magazines, and is being digested by millions of youthful Americans.

22   Even the modest but at least honorable ambition of learning to sing popular tunes pleasingly, an ambition which implies the development of a professional attitude of respect for one's craft and for the people at whom it is aimed, now goes by the board in favor of a willingness to be shaped into a commodity that will sell phonograph records to fill empty hours and empty heads. The test is solely in the speed of the payoff, since neither the performer nor his handlers—nor, in the final analysis, his fans—have any image of him as a man building a career: they see him instead as an ambulatory bank account. Inevitably, this shambling dollar sign is taken by millions of the impressionable young, both here and abroad, to be the true Voice of America.

23   Are we all getting worse? Were Americans actually better human beings back in the Thirties, that decade which seems to grow more noble in our eyes as it recedes in time? I don't think so. As one who is grateful that he grew up in that exciting period, I believe that we ought to be cautious about overestimating the extent to which most young people were caught up by unselfish and idealistic movements. After all, even in the collegiate hotbeds of radicalism at the pitch of the depression, the great majority of the student body went about their single-minded business, ignoring public problems, studying commerce and accounting, trying to pass civil-service examinations.

---

*Leo Szilard was a Hungarian-born theoretical physicist who made significant contributions to the development and construction of the first atomic bomb. Selman Abraham Waksman was an American microbiologist who received a Nobel Prize for his work with soil microbiology and the discovery of the antibiotic streptomycin. Jonas Salk, an American immunologist, made major contributions to the development of the first poliomyelitis vaccine.

What differentiated the intellectually aspiring young people of the   24
Thirties from today's was, it seems to me, that the best of them found a
relationship between their private aspirations and the public needs.
The boy who wanted to go into electrical engineering knew that the
Rural Electrification Administration was in the process of bringing the
modern era to millions of farm homes; the young law student saw that
Washington needed him and wanted him; the youthful visionary felt
not only that the world could be remade but that he had a vital part to
play in that remaking, whether in the skill of his hands or in the exercise of his mind.

Today the best of our young people find no such relationship and in   25
consequence are so quickly corrupted that it is horrifying. Those who
do not turn their backs on the whole sell and go beat, refusing to work
except at odd jobs in odd moments, abdicate by settling for those values
embodied in the editorial columns and the advertising pages of the
upper middlebrow magazines: a blenderized liberalism, a deep cynicism about what they do for a living and about the entire possibility of
achievement through work and an intense desire for nothing more than
the trips to Europe, the little cars, the liqueurs, the collecting of paintings or other objects.

It does not follow that this is what the millennium must look like.   26
These are the people who spend about seven hundred thousand dollars
every single night of the year on tranquilizers to still uneasy consciences and to bring on the oblivion of sleep after days spent in
unwork. Every study that I am aware of indicates that man is a creature
who thrives best on work and (at least until now) has not found means
of deriving continuous personal satisfaction in a society from which
work has been outlawed.

This does not mean that we need ever go back to a social order built   27
on the backbreaking toil of millions of drudges; we are on the verge of an
era in which it will not be necessary or lawful for a single human being
to be so ill-used. But I would deny with all my strength the notion that
young people now are so rotten with soft living that they shun work as
they would the plague. From my own experience as a teacher and a writer whose work has brought him into correspondence with many young
people, I must assert that the flame of idealism burns as brightly as ever,
that the search for fruitful work to which one can dedicate one's life is
as strong as ever. It is just that it is choked off all too soon by the cynics
of a culture built on corporate profit and dedicated to the principle that
nothing counts but the fast buck.

This is not the place to spell out the kinds of work that could still   28
pick college kids up by the throat and instill them with that sense of
purpose we all recognize as having disappeared from the national scene.

I would only note my personal conviction that it will have to be found abroad, in friendly partnership with the new nations; and I will ask only what the effect would be if, instead of sitting around and making cheap jokes about revolutionary leaders, a few thousand trained young Americans were to pitch in and try to help these revolutions achieve their professed goals, to see if they really mean business about public health, housing, literacy, agricultural diversification, full electrification, full employment. The answer to our American dilemma, as to those different problems faced by less-developed countries, cannot be found in happy hobbies or even in the most high-flown leisure. It must still be sought in fruitful work, applied to the great and greatly challenging tasks that still confront the human race.

Questions and Activities

▶ *COMPREHENSION QUESTIONS*

1. Swados tells his readers that Sylvia Porter reported that "18 to 20 per cent of all the personal income" earned in 1961 went to people who were not working (paragraph 2). Find out what that percentage was in a recent year. Has there been any change in this percentage? If there has been, does the change add to or detract from the strength of Swados's argument concerning the diminished sense of worth in most workers?

2. Compare Swados's account of the family doctor in paragraph 15 to Richard Selzer's portrait of the surgeon as priest. Which example do you feel is most representative of doctors? How are the examples similar or different?

3. People, Swados argues, were no different in the 1930s than in 1961; but, he claims, the society within which people work did change. What, essentially, does Swados think are the differences between the society of the 1930s and that of the 1960s, and what effects do these differences have on the workers of the 1960s (paragraphs 24 and 25)?

▶ *QUESTIONS OF RHETORICAL PURPOSE AND STRATEGY*

4. Analyze the effect on readers of Swados's conclusion to this essay (paragraph 28). What is Swados asking for in this conclusion? What kind of work would "pick college kids up by the throat and instill them with that sense of purpose"? Do you feel that your generation needs that sense of purpose? Is this an effective way to close this piece—by spelling out some general directions that might be taken

to correct the ills that the rest of the essay has documented and discussed? Why might this type of conclusion make readers more receptive concerning the negative points that were made earlier in the essay? Does Swados's conclusion seem to make his essay persuasive or informative?

5. Swados maintains that making money without any physical or mental labor is bad for people (see paragraph 2, in particular). List at least five reasons why he holds this belief. Give an example of a person in our society who makes money without doing physical or mental work. What is that person being paid for—using money wisely, having been born into a wealthy family? Do you think such a person is better off or worse off for not having to do physical or mental work?

▶ *THEME QUESTIONS*

6. Some social critics have suggested that Swados's writings in the late 1950s and early 1960s led directly to John F. Kennedy's creation of the Peace Corps. Do some research on the origins of the Peace Corps (the government documents section of your library or any mass circulation news magazine of 1961 would be excellent sources). Write a report, to be read to your class, on why the Peace Corps was started. Are there connections between Swados's criticisms of the professions for their lack of satisfying work opportunities and the reasons that were given for starting the Peace Corps?

7. Does this essay provide further insight into the causes of Stephen Cruz's dissatisfaction with his management career, as reported in the Studs Terkel piece? Does Benjamin Franklin seem at all concerned with public service in his mid-eighteenth century formulas for success in business? In other words, has service to others been continually an important element of American professional or laboring life?

▶ *LEARNING ACTIVITIES*

8. Swados criticizes popular singers and athletes of 1961 because they seem to him to be motivated purely by the desire to make a lot of money (paragraphs 19, 20, and 21). They have no inner drive to attain excellence. Would you direct the same criticism at today's popular music and sports stars? Provide some concrete examples in a report to the class, and describe them in detail.

9. Work with other members of your class to produce a description of how people who do not have to labor mentally or physically for their money might put their free time to socially constructive use. Why might Swados argue that most people in this category, even if they might potentially do constructive things during their free time, would choose not to? What, according to Swados, would their lives be miss-

ing that is necessary to sustain individual productivity? These specific questions should be used as guides for your group discussion:

a. Can you describe at least three careers in which labor is not required?

b. Why is labor not a part of these careers?

c. What do the people in these laborless careers sacrifice by not having to work?

d. How can people gain social satisfaction from the benefits of these laborless careers?

What It Is I Think I'm Doing Anyhow

TONI CADE BAMBARA

Toni Cade Bambara graduated from Queens College of the City University of New York in 1959. She holds a master's degree, has studied in Italy and France, and has been a student of modern dance. At various times early in her career, she held jobs as a social investigator, a director of recreation in a psychiatry department, and a director of Head Start programs for preschool children. Since the 1960s, Bambara has been primarily a writer as well as a teacher at City College of the City University of New York, Rutgers University, and Spelman College in Atlanta, Georgia.

Bambara's first novel, *The Salt Eaters* (1980), was praised for its vitality, its realistic presentation of black language and experience, and its complex treatment of the dynamics of social change. Her short stories have been collected in *Gorilla My Love* (1973) and *The Seabirds Are Still Alive* (1977). Bambara's stories are peopled by contemporary black characters who learn through struggle how to face the challenges of prejudice and deprivation without losing their sense of optimism. Bambara's career as writer, teacher, and social worker has been consistently directed by her desire to work for social improvement.

In this essay, Bambara discusses her struggle as a writer to avoid the extremes of pessimistic cynicism and blind belief in the American dream. She speaks from her experiences talking with and reading the works of other writers—white and black, liberal and conservative—and from her "Pan-Africanist-socialist-feminist" philosophy. She writes straightforwardly about the problems she has had transforming her experiences into fiction that she believes is an honest and "upbeat" portrayal of contemporary life. Some qualities of her fiction show up in this essay—such as her ability to capture the voice of everyday people in dialogue, to express the significance of an idea in a brief phrase. Her control of her immediate and vital point of view, the bits of dialogue interspersed in descriptive passages, and her consistently developed theme of the balancing of extremes combine in this essay to capture the writer's ongoing struggle to synthesize experience and thought in her writing.

Think about how the following sentence from Bambara's essay links it up with other essays in this section: "A writer, like any other cultural worker, like any other member of the community, ought to try to put her/his skills in the service of the community.''

1. How does this sentence connect Bambara's thinking with Harvey Swados's criticism of the American working classes?
2. How might this conclusion be related to William Ouchi's comparison of Japanese and American workers?
3. Does Bambara's conclusion have anything in common with Adrienne Rich's call for a sense of community among women involved in the feminist movement?
4. Does Stephen Cruz, in Studs Terkel's piece, seem to sense a lack of community consciousness in his work?

▶ ——————————————

1   Winter 1979. We are now in the fourth year of the last quarter of the twentieth century. And the questions that face the millions of us on the earth are—in whose name will the twenty-first century be claimed? Can the planet be rescued from the psychopaths? Where are the evolved, poised-for-light adepts who will assume the task of administering power in a human interest, of redefining power as being not the privilege or class right to define, deform, and dominate but as the human responsibility to define, transform, and develop?

2   The previous quarter-century, from 1950 to 1975, was an era hallmarked by revolution, a period in which we experienced a radical shift in the political-power configurations of the globe. The current quarter, from 1976 to 2000, is also characterized by revolution, a period in which we are awakening to and experiencing a profound change in the psychic-power configurations of the globe.

3   There is a war going on and a transformation taking place. That war is not simply the contest between the socialist camp and the capitalist camp over which political/economic/social arrangement will enjoy hegemony in the world, nor is it simply the battle over turf and resources. Truth is one of the issues in this war. The truth, for example, about inherent human nature, about our potential, our agenda as earth people, our destiny.

4   Writing is one of the ways I participate in struggle—one of the ways I help to keep vibrant and resilient that vision that has kept the Family going on. Through writing I attempt to celebrate the tradition of resistance, attempt to tap Black potential, and try to join the chorus of voices that argues that exploitation and misery are neither inevitable

nor necessary. Writing is one of the ways I participate in the transformation—one of the ways I practice the commitment to explore bodies of knowledge for the usable wisdoms they yield. In writing, I hope to encourage the fusion of those disciplines whose split (material science versus metaphysics versus aesthetics versus politics versus . . .) predisposes us to accept fragmented truths and distortions as the whole. Writing is one of the ways I do my work in the world.

There are no career labels for that work, no facile terms to describe   5
the tasks of it. Suffice to say that I do not take lightly the fact that I am on the earth at this particular time in human history, and am here as a member of a particular soul group and of a particular sex, having this particular adventure as a Pan-Africanist-socialist-feminist in the United States.* I figure all that means something—about what I'm here to understand and to do.

Of all the mothers in the world I might have been born to, I was born   6
at a particular moment to mine and to no other. As a kid with an enormous appetite for knowledge and a gift for imagining myself anywhere in the universe, I always seemed to be drawn to the library or to some music spot or to 125th Street and Seventh Avenue, Speaker's Corner, to listen to Garveyites,† Father Diviners, Rastafarians, Muslims, trade unionists, communists, Pan-Africanists. And when I recall the host of teachers who have crossed my path and always right on time, so unfull of shit, so unlike the terrified and lost salaried teachers in the schools—and not only that, but having managed to survive Mather Academy boarding school's diet to come of age in the sixties—and all the while having some swamphag all up in my face asking me about my dreams (have I had a vision yet, have the voices given me instructions yet)—certainly it all means something. This is, after all, not a comic book. It's my life. So I pay attention. And I understand that I am being groomed to perform particular work in this world. Writing is one of the ways I try to do it.

The old folks say, "It's not how little we know that hurts so, but that   7
so much of what we know ain't so." As a mother, teacher, writer, community worker, neighbor, I am concerned about accurate information, verifiable facts, sound analyses, responsible research, principled study, and people's assessment of the meaning of their lives. I'm interested in usable truths. Which means rising above my training, thinking better

---

*Pan-Africanism was a movement made popular by the black leader Marcus Garvey in the 1920s and 1930s. It promoted a renewal of interest in African culture among black Americans.
†Garveyites were followers of Marcus Garvey.

than I've been taught, developing a listening habit, making the self available to intelligence, engaging in demystification, and seeking out teachers at every turn. In many respects the writings are notebooks I'm submitting to those teachers for examination. There have been a host of teachers. Once I thought anyone with enthusiasm about information was a good teacher. Then, anyone with an analysis of this country who could help illuminate the condition, status, and process of the Family, who could help me decide how to put my wrath and my skills to the service of folks who sustain me. Later, anyone who could throw open the path and lead me back to the ancient wisdoms was teacher. In more recent times, any true dialectician (material/spiritual) who could increase my understanding of all, I say all, the forces afoot in the universe was teacher. I'm entering my forties with more simplistic criteria—anyone with a greater capacity for love than I is a valuable teacher. And when I look back on the body of book reviews I've produced in the past fifteen years, for all their socioideolitero brilliant somethinorother, the underlying standard always seemed to be—Does this author here genuinely love his/her community?

8   The greatest challenge in writing, then, in the earlier stages was to strike a balance between candor, honesty, integrity, and truth—terms that are fairly synonymous for crossword puzzlers and thesaurus ramblers but hard to equate as living actions. Speaking one's mind, after all, does not necessarily mean one is in touch with the truth or even with the facts. Being honest and frank in terms of my own where—where I'm at at a given point in my political/spiritual/etc. development—is not necessarily in my/our interest to utter, not necessarily in the interest of health, wholesomeness. Certain kinds of poisons, for example—rage, bitterness, revenge—don't need to be in the atmosphere, not to mention in my mouth. I don't, for example, hack up racists and stuff them in metaphorical boxes. I do not wish to lend them energy, for one thing. Though certainly there are "heavies" that people my stories. But I don't, for example, conjure up characters for the express purpose of despising them, of breaking their humps in public. I used to be astounded at Henry James et al., so nice nasty about it too, soooo refined. Gothic is of no interest to me. I try not to lend energy to building grotesqueries, depicting morbid relationships, dramatizing perversity. Folks come up to me 'lowing as how since I am a writer I would certainly want to hear blah, blah, blah, blah. They dump shit all over me, tell me about every ugly overheard and lived-through nightmare imaginable. They've got the wrong writer. The kid can't use it. I straightaway refer them to the neighborhood healer, certain that anyone so intoxicated would surely welcome a cleansing. But they persist—"Hey, this is for real, square business. The truth." I don't doubt that the

horror tales are factual. I don't even doubt that ugly is a truth for somebody . . . somehow. But I'm not convinced that ugly is *the* truth that can
save us, redeem us. The old folks teach that. Be triflin' and ugly and
they say, "Deep down, gal, you know that ain't right," appealing to a
truth about our deep-down nature. Good enough for me. Besides, I can't
get happy writing ugly weird. If I'm not laughing while I work, I conclude that I am not communicating nourishment, since laughter is the
most sure-fire healant I know. I don't know all my readers, but I know
well for whom I write. And I want for them no less than I want for myself—wholesomeness.

It all sounds so la-di-da and tra-la-la. I can afford to be sunny. I'm but   9
one voice in the chorus. The literature(s) of our time are a collective effort, dependent on so many views, on so many people's productions. I
am frequently asked to name my favorite writer, or the one writer who
best captures the Black experience, or the one sister who is really doing
it. What can I do but crack up and stuff another carrot in the juicer? No
way in the world I can swing over to that frame of reference so dominated by solo-voice thinking. Given the range of experiences available
to a soul having the human adventure in this time and place, given that
we have just begun to tap the limitless reservoir of cultural, societal,
global, possibilities. Hell, there aren't even phrases in the languages for
half the things happening just on the block where I live, not yet anyhow. Who could possibly be this *one* writer that interviewers and reviewers are always harping about? I read everybody I can get to, and I appreciate the way "American literature" is being redefined now that the
Black community is dialoguing without defensive postures, now that
the Puerto Rican writers are coming through loud and clear, and the
Chicano and Chicana writers, and Native American and Asian-
American. . . . There's a lot of work to do, a lot of records to get straight,
a lot of living to share, a lot to plumb. This reader wants it all—the odd-
ball, the satiric, the grim, the ludicrous, what have you. As for my own
writing, I prefer the upbeat. It pleases me to blow three or four choruses
of just sheer energetic fun and optimism, even in the teeth of rats, racists, repressive cops, bomb lovers, irresponsibles, murderers. I am
convinced, I guess, that everything will be all right.

When I originally drafted the title story of my first story collection,   10
Gorilla, My Love, the tone was severe, grim. The confrontations between the kid and the adults who so nonchalantly lie to and de-spirit
little kids were raging red. Writing in a rage can produce some interesting pyrotechnics, but there are other ways to keep a fire ablaze, it seems
to me. Besides, I know that everything will be O.K. for that little girl, so
tough, so compassionate, so brave. Her encounter with the movie
manager who put a come-on title on the marquee and then screened an-

other movie altogether, and her encounter with her uncle who promised to marry her when she grew up and then turned right around and married some full-grown woman—those are rehearsals that will hold her in good stead in later encounters with more menacing and insidious people. That's second of all. First of all, while little kids' lives are most definitely characterized by intense anger over the injustices heaped upon them, it's not an anger that can sustain itself for twelve typewritten pages. Bunny rabbits and new socks and the neighbor kid's skates have a way of distracting kids. So clearly I had to solve a problem in pitch and voice. Once I could grin/cry through it, the writing felt right. Readers seem to laugh through it as well, as I've observed on subways, in laundromats, in libraries, and classrooms. And the lesson is not missed. So, as my classroom experience as a teacher has taught me, there are hipper ways to get to gut and brain than with hot pokers and pincers.

11   ''Broken-Field Running,'' in the 1977 collection *The Seabirds Are Still Alive*, was more of a challenge. It wasn't so much a problem in pitch as a problem in balancing the elements of mood. I'd been observing architectural changes in my community since the street rebellions. Schools, public housing, parks were being designed in such a way as to wreck community sovereignty, to render it impossible for neighbors to maintain surveillance and security of turf. I was enraged. I wrote a blazing essay on the subject, snarling, shooting from both hips. Hadn't a clue as to how to finish it or to whom to send it. Wrote a story instead. The first problem then was balancing the essay voice and the story voice; the second to keep the two dominant emotions of the narrator stabilized, in tension. The story is an odd sort of moody piece about a combatant, a teacher whose faith is slipping, whose belief in the capacity for transformation is splintering. I was trying to get at how difficult it is to maintain the fervent spirit at a time when the Movement is mute, when only a few enclaves exist. The teacher's work, her friend, her training, and most of all her responsibility to the children help to keep her centered, help to keep her in touch with the best of herself. But her task is rough.

12   Time out to say this—I often read in reviews that my stories are set in the sixties and are nostalgic and reminiscent of days when revolution was believed in. News to me. With the exception of ''The Long Night,'' all the stories in *Seabirds* are in the ''right now'' time they were drafted. I suppose for too many people the idea that struggle is neither new nor over is hard to grasp, that there is a radical tradition as old as the H.M.S. *Jesus* or whatever that ship was that hauled over the first boatload. Some weeks ago, I read from my new work at a workshop of novels-in-progress. It was an excerpt about an elderly woman recalling the days

when she worked for the Sleeping Car Porters and organized Ida B. Wells clubs in Harlem. Two out of three people at the reading assumed that the novel was set in the late sixties and that the woman was talking about the earlier sixties. Gives a person pause. Amnesia is a hellafying thing. The impulse to pronounce the Movement dead ain't no joke either.

Back to "Broken-Field Running." It was spring 1974 and I'd just   *13* returned from a rally at which I heard that genocide was a fact in the Colored World, that the struggle was all over cause nobody cared anymore and blah, blah, blah, blah, accompanied by statistics and all the evangelical zeal of the brimstone tent belters. So in that woe-is-us mood, I began work on the story. And before I knew it, my character Lacy had picked it up and run off with it. Even while she was slipping in the snow and so in need of all kinds of support now that the thousands of combatants of a few years ago were/are no longer very visible, she managed to horse around enough to keep the story from getting depressing—depression being, to my mind, a form of collaboration. The kids in her orbit after all, are proof, mandate, motive to keep on keeping on. I guess then, that the message is—and I am a brazenly "message" writer, which seems to unsettle many reviewers—that in periods of high consciousness, one has to build the network and the foundation to sustain one through periods of high conflict and low consciousness. What goes around, comes around, as folks say.

Of course it is difficult to maintain the faith and keep working to-   *14* ward the new time if you've had no *experience* of it, not *seen* ordinary people actually transform selves and societies. That is the back-and-forth of the story "The Apprentice" in *Seabirds*. The young sister who narrates the story underestimates her own ability to fashion a revolutionary outlook, for she's not seen what my other character, the organizer Naomi, has seen. We, however, know that she will grow. She's got fine spirit for all her caterwauling. And we suspect too, I imagine, that whatever moved her into the circle of community workers and made her an apprentice in the first place will continue to operate, to inform her choices. And too, Naomi is kinda fun to hang out with. And that is the way many join ranks, after all, through an attraction to a given person. It's like the gospel song instructs, "You never know who's watching you," who's taking you as a model. I seem to recall that I invited Naomi onto the scene as a way of answering the grim reapers at that 1974 rally. If you're trying to recruit people to a particular kind of work, the recruiter has to stand for something attractive. I'd be willing to follow Naomi anywhere. She has heart to spare.

I got a lot of mixed reactions about the story "The Organizer's Wife"   *15* in *Seabirds*. Feminist types didn't like the title; some said they refused to read the story because the title was such a putdown. Others liked the fact that Virginia, the lead character, kicked the preacher's ass for more reasons than for turning her husband in but, nonetheless, would have been happier had she left town or died in childbirth, by way of my protesting the system. Some letters and calls said I should have had Graham, the organizer, die some gruesome death in that southern jail to protest, etc. Kill Graham off and have Virginia go batty, or leave, or die in childbirth? What kind of message would that have been? How would I have explained that to my daughter? She's looking forward to growing up as a responsible change agent. I'm well aware that we are under siege, that the system kills, that the terms of race and class war have not altered very much. But death is not a truth that inspires, that pumps up the heart, that mobilizes. It's defeatist to dwell always on the consequences of risks. It's proracist to assume we can't take a chance. I am not interested in collaborating with the program of the forces that systematically underdevelop. So Graham lives and Virginia wakes up.

16   "The Organizer's Wife," written in 1975 and set in 1975, is a love story, layer after layer. Lovers and combatants are not defeated. That is the message of that story, the theme of the entire collection, the wisdom that gets me up in the morning, honored to be here. It is a usable truth.

17   I'm reminded of a rip-roaring visit to a couple, friends of mine, who invited me to dinner and began discussing Charles Johnson's wonderful book *Faith and the Good Thing.* Leaning across the table at each other, rattling dishes, knocking over the candlestick, they proceeded to debate with brandished forks whether or not the author's burning up of a baby on page such and such was metaphorical infanticide. I love literary dinner conversation, especially of the passionate kind. "It's a metaphor, an act of language," yelled Larry, tugging on his omnipresent cap lest he blow his wig. "I don't care about all such as that," Eleanor hollered, hiking up her gown to climb onto the table to come at him to make her point. "He burned up that baby." I thoroughly enjoyed the meal and the passion. And I'm thoroughly in Eleanor's camp if I understand her right. Words are to be taken seriously. I try to take seriously acts of language. Words set things in motion. I've seen them doing it. Words set up atmospheres, electrical fields, charges. I've felt them doing it. Words conjure. I try not to be careless about what I utter, write, sing. I'm careful about what I give voice to. To drive Virginia nuts or Graham to death is not a message I want to send to my heart, my lungs, my brain. My daughter. My readers. Or, to the Grahams and Virginias. But then I come from a particular tradition. I identify with the championship tradition.

18   Ali, in his autobiography, *I Am the Greatest*, defines a champion as one who takes the telling blow on the chin and hits the canvas hard,

can't possibly rally, arms shot, energy spent, the very weight of the body too heavy a burden for the legs to raise, can't possibly get up. So you do. And you keep getting up. *The Awakening* by Kate Chopin is not my classic. *Their Eyes Were Watching God* by Zora Neale Hurston is. Sylvia Plath and the other obligatory writers on women's studies lists—the writers who hawk despair, insanity, alienation, suicide, all in the name of protesting woman's oppression, are not my mentors. I was raised on stories of Harriet Tubman, Ida B. Wells, Paul Robeson, and my grandmother, Annie, whom folks in Atlanta still remember as an early Rosa Parks. So Virginia does not go batty and Graham does not die. Were I to do them in, my granny would no doubt visit me in the night to batter me gingerly about the head and shoulders with an ancestral bone pulled out of the Ethiopic Ocean called the Atlantic.

In the title story of *Seabirds*, I once again focus on resistance rather than despair and dramatize too, I think, the power of words, of utterances. The story is set in Southeast Asia aboard a boat transporting various people with various agenda to the city where the liberation forces, the royalist troops, and the foreign imperialists battle. The central characters are a little girl and her mother. Both are combatants. Both have been tortured. Both resist. When the mother closes her eyes and shivers, the girl fears she is remembering her torture and will begin to chant the words that enable her to come through her ordeal: ''Nothing, I'll tell you nothing. You'll never break our spirits. We cannot be defeated.'' I weave the chant into a flashback scene in which her mother, reliving the experience, thrashes about on the floor while the girl attempts to work a bit of wood between her teeth. I weave it again into the current scene: 19

> The little girl continued brushing and smoothing her mother's hair, wondering if the gentleman in shoes could be relied upon if her mother bolted. If she herself didn't panic, she would demand he jump to aid the minute the first words were blurted out. ''Nothing, I'll tell you nothing.'' It would take nimble timing, for often the upper folks would not touch the miserable shoeless. ''You'll never break our spirits.'' But then the engine was shut off and her mother relaxed, looking over the side, her face full in the wind. ''We cannot be defeated.'' So. It had been the vibrations of the boat, the little girl concluded, that had made her mother shiver. It had been the lurching of rough waters that had tipped the gentleman away from them.

I am currently working on a novel, though my druthers as writer, reader, and teacher is the short story. The short story makes a modest appeal for attention, slips up on your blind side and wrassles you to the mat before you know what's grabbed you. That appeals to my temperament. But of course it is not too shrewd to be exclusively a short story writer when the publishing industry, book reviewers, critics, and   20 teachers of literature are all geared up for the novel. I gave myself an assignment based on an observation: there is a split between the spiritual, psychic, and political forces in my community. Not since the maroon experience of Toussaint's era* have psychic technicians and spiritual folk (medicine people) and guerrillas (warriors) merged. It is a wasteful and dangerous split. The novel grew out of my attempt to fuse the seemingly separate frames of reference of the camps; it grew out of an interest in identifying bridges; it grew out of a compulsion to understand how the energies of this period will manifest themselves in the next decade.

21   I have three working titles to help me stay focused. "In the Last Quarter" is to remind myself of the period I'm "reading," to remind myself to script flashforwards as well as flashbacks, to remind myself that powerful events of the 1980s and 1990s (nuclear explosions, comet splashdowns, asteroid collisions) resonate in the present. Legionnaire's Disease, for example, may well be a backwash reverberation of the 1984 epidemics that many have predicted. The second title, "The Seven Sisters" (calling all numerologists, astrologists, astronomers, voodooists), helps me to stay within the law of As Above, So Below. In this case I'm trying to link the double helix of the Pleiades constellations (duplicated in the DNA molecule) with one of the central characters—a swamphag healer—and with a traveling troupe of seven women known as sisters of the yam, sisters of the plantain, sisters of the rice, sisters of the corn. These women from the ancient mother cultures perform multimedia shows at rallies and conferences and help me to argue the bridging of several camps: artists and activists, materialists and spiritualists, old and young, and of course the communities of color. The third working reminder is "The Salt Eaters." Salt is a partial antidote for snakebite. Bleeding the wound and applying the tourniquet, one also eats salt and applies a salt poultice to the wound. To struggle, to develop, one needs to master ways to neutralize poisons. "Salt" also keeps the parable of Lot's Wife to the fore. Without a belief in the capacity for transformation, one can become ossified. And what can we do with a saltlick in the middle of the projects, no cows there?

22   I'd never fully appreciated before the concern so many people express over women writers' work habits—how do you juggle the demands of motherhood, etc.? Do you find that friends, especially intimates, resent your need for privacy, etc.? Is it possible to wrench yourself away from active involvement for the lonely business of writing? Writing had

---

*Toussaint L'Ouverture (1743–1803) was the Haitian general who liberated Haiti from French rule. His era was marked by an integration of mystical religion, scientific thought, and guerrilla warfare.

never been so central an activity in my life before. Besides, a short story is fairly portable. I could narrate the basic outline while driving to the farmer's market, work out the dialogue while waiting for the airlines to answer the phone, draft a rough sketch of the central scene while overseeing my daughter's carrot cake, write the first version in the middle of the night, edit while the laundry takes a spin, and make copies while running off some rally flyers. But the novel has taken me out of action for frequent and lengthy periods. Other than readings and an occasional lecture, I seem unfit for any other kind of work. I cannot knock out a terse and pithy office memo any more. And my relationships, I'm sure, have suffered because I am so distracted, preoccupied, and distant. The short story is a piece of work. The novel is a way of life.

When I replay the tapes on file in my head, tapes of speeches I've given at writing conferences over the years, I invariably hear myself saying—"A writer, like any other cultural worker, like any other member of the community, ought to try to put her/his skills in the service of the community." Some years ago when I returned south, my picture in the paper prompted several neighbors to come visit. "You a writer? What all you write?" Before I could begin the catalogue, one old gent interrupted with—"Ya know Miz Mary down the block? She need a writer to help her send off a letter to her grandson overseas." So I began a career as the neighborhood scribe—letters to relatives, snarling letters to the traffic chief about the promised stop sign, nasty letters to the utilities, angry letters to the principal about that confederate flag hanging in front of the school, contracts to transfer a truck from seller to buyer, etc. While my efforts have been graciously appreciated in the form of sweet potato dumplings, herb teas, hair braiding, and the like, there is still much room for improvement—"For a writer, honey, you've got a mighty bad hand. Didn't they teach penmanship at that college?" Another example, I guess, of words setting things in motion. What goes around, comes around, as the elders say.

It will be a pleasure to get back to the shorts; they allow me to share. I much prefer to haul around story collections to prisons, schools, senior citizen centers, and rallies and then select from the "menu" something that suits the moment and is all of a piece. But the novel's pull is powerful. And since the breakthrough achieved in the sixties by the Neo-Black Arts Movement, the possibilities are stunning. Characters that have been waiting in the wings for generations, characters that did not fit into the roster of stereotypes, can now be brought down center stage. Now that I/we have located our audience, we are free to explore the limits of language. Now that American history, American literature, the American experience is being redefined by so many communities, the genre too will undergo changes. So I came to the novel with a sense that everything is possible. And I'm attempting to blueprint for myself the merger of these two camps; the political and the spiritual. The possibilities of healing that split are exciting. The implications of actually yoking those energies and of fusing that power quite take my breath away.

Questions and Activities

▶ *COMPREHENSION QUESTIONS*

1. Why does Bambara say that the era from 1950 to 1975 was "hallmarked by revolution" (paragraph 2)? What specific historical events might she be referring to?
2. Look again at the first sentence of paragraph 9. What does "la-di-da and tra-la-la" mean in this sentence? How does this phrase relate to Bambara's discussion in paragraph 8 of her optimism as contrasted with the more pessimistic outlook of people from her community?

▶ *QUESTIONS OF RHETORICAL PURPOSE AND STRATEGY*

3. Bambara addresses her audience using a casual, informal voice. What word choices, sentence structures, and punctuation marks does she employ to create this informality? Why do you think she feels this casual voice is appropriate to her audience and purpose?
4. Like Geneva Smitherman, whose essay appears later (pages 389–416), Toni Cade Bambara is a black writer who sometimes uses black spoken dialect in her writings. What do you think is the strategy behind Bambara's use of dialect in an essay that is otherwise written in standard English? What effect might this use of dialect have on black readers—or on white readers? Consider the title of this essay and paragraphs 7 and 9 as you answer these questions.

▶ *THEME QUESTIONS*

5. Consider Bambara's attitudes toward women and minorities and their work. How does work clarify an individual's sense of self if that person is not a member of a majority group of the society? Why does Bambara feel that a person's job is important to his or her sense of individual worth? Why does Bambara consider it important that women be the intellectual equals of men as they continue their involvement with domestic life—with cooking and serving food, for

example? Why might it be especially important for members of a minority group to be able to work?

6. Throughout this essay, Bambara makes clear her position that a professional writer must have a social purpose that justifies his or her work. What does this value judgment imply might be her attitude toward writers who are motivated by money to produce escapist or purely entertaining literature? How does Bambara's conviction that a writer's work must have social purpose tie in with Richard Selzer's attitude toward his work as a surgeon? Does Selzer emphasize the same sense of social commitment, or is he more interested in tying together the social and religious aspects of his work?

▶ *LEARNING ACTIVITIES*

7. Interview a minority member or woman about his or her attitudes in relation to the work he or she is doing or planning to do. This activity should be done in collaboration with two or three other students. Develop one set of interview questions and then each of you interview one person. Once the interviews have been conducted, go back and compare notes with your group; do an interpretation of each subject.

8. Respond to one opinion in Bambara's essay, for example, her opinion on the role of women in today's society. Pick an opinion that Bambara treats persuasively, informatively, or entertainingly. Then write a one-paragraph response that either agrees or disagrees with Bambara but that matches her intention: if you have chosen a persuasive opinion, then be persuasive in response; if you have selected an informative opinion, be informative in response; if you have picked an entertaining opinion, be entertaining in response.

The Patented Gate and the Mean Hamburger

ROBERT PENN WARREN

Robert Penn Warren, for many years a teacher at Yale University, has combined the careers of scholar and writer. He has written novels, short fiction, poetry, plays, general interest essays, history, and criticism of other writers' work. He has also written a number of textbooks for college students. As a critic, he has been associated with the New Criticism, a critical movement that places emphasis on the critic's focus on relationships within a literary work itself, rather than on external historical, social, or philosophical influences. His literary work is strongly regional, often drawing its inspiration from the land, the people, and the history of the South. Penn Warren often bases his work on historical events (an example is his novel *All the King's Men,* which is based on the life of Huey Long, a Louisiana politician), which he reshapes into fiction or poetry whose significance is wider than its inspiration. Penn Warren has received Pulitzer Prizes for both fiction and poetry; he has won the National Book Award and is America's first poet laureate.

Penn Warren was born in 1905 in Guthrie, Kentucky, and spent his early life in Kentucky and Tennessee. During the 1920s, he was a member of two influential literary groups: the Fugitives (at Vanderbilt University, from which he graduated in 1925 with a degree in literature), and the Agrarians (former Fugitives who banded together again in the late 1920s). The Fugitives encouraged his interest in critical theory and influenced his later technical experiments in fiction and poetry. The Agrarians encouraged his lifelong literary interest in regional themes, rural life, and nature.

Several of Penn Warren's characteristic interests have influenced "The Patented Gate and the Mean Hamburger." The story is set in the rural South and reflects the author's preoccupation with the relationship between freedom and determinism. Think about these interests as you read the story:

1. Do you think Penn Warren wants his readers to feel that Jeff York and his wife were free to choose their fates? Or does he see them as being guided by forces outside themselves?
2. What is Penn Warren trying to tell his readers about life among people of Jeff York's and Slick Hardin's class in a small Southern town?

3. Is Jeff York happy in his farmwork? Is his wife unhappy as a farm wife? How can you tell? Why does change seem threatening to Jeff York but alluring to his wife?

▶ ————————————————————

    You have seen him a thousand times. You have seen him standing on the street corner on Saturday afternoon, in the little county-seat towns. He wears blue jean pants, or overalls washed to a pale pastel blue like the color of sky after a shower in spring, but because it is Saturday he has on a wool coat, an old one, perhaps the coat left from the suit he got married in a long time back. His long wrist bones hang out from the sleeves of the coat, the tendons showing along the bone like the dry twist of grapevine still corded on the stove-length of a hickory sapling you would find in his wood box beside his cookstove among the split chunks of gum and red oak. The big hands, with the knotted, cracked joints and the square, horn-thick nails, hang loose off the wrist bone like clumsy, home-made tools hung on the wall of a shed after work. If it is summer, he wears a straw hat with a wide brim, the straw fraying loose around the edge. If it is winter, he wears a felt hat, black once, but now weathered with streaks of dark gray and dull purple in the sunlight. His face is long and bony, the jawbone long under the drawn-in cheeks. The flesh along the jawbone is nicked in a couple of places where the unaccustomed razor has been drawn over the leather-coarse skin. A tiny bit of blood crusts brown where the nick is. The color of the face is red, a dull red like the red clay mud or clay dust which clings to the bottom of his pants and to the cast-iron-looking brogans on his feet, or a red like the color of a piece of hewed cedar which has been left in the weather. The face does not look alive. It seems to be molded from the clay or hewed from the cedar. When the jaw moves, once, with its deliberate, massive motion on the quid of tobacco, you are still not convinced. That motion is but the cunning triumph of a mechanism concealed within. 1

    But you see the eyes. You see that the eyes are alive. They are pale blue or gray, set back under the deep brows and thorny eyebrows. They are not wide, but are squinched up like eyes accustomed to wind or sun or to measuring the stroke of the ax or to fixing the object over the rifle sights. When you pass, you see that the eyes are alive and are warily and dispassionately estimating you from the ambush of the thorny brows. Then you pass on, and he stands there in that stillness which is his gift. 2

3   With him may be standing two or three others like himself, but they are still, too. They do not talk. The young men, who will be like these men when they get to be fifty or sixty, are down at the beer parlor, carousing and laughing with a high, whickering laugh. But the men on the corner are long past all that. They are past many things. They have endured and will endure in their silence and wisdom. They will stand on the street corner and reject the world which passes under their level gaze as a rabble passes under the guns of a rocky citadel around whose base a slatternly town has assembled.

4   I had seen Jeff York a thousand times, or near, standing like that on the street corner in town, while the people flowed past him, under the distant and wary and dispassionate eyes in ambush. He would be waiting for his wife and the three tow-headed children who were walking around the town looking into store windows and at the people. After a while they would come back to him, and then, wordlessly, he would lead them to the store where they always did their trading. He would go first, marching with a steady bent-kneed stride, setting the cast-iron brogans down deliberately on the cement; then his wife, a small woman with covert, sidewise, curious glances for the world, would follow, and behind her the towheads bunched together in a dazed, glory-struck way. In the store, when their turn came, Jeff York would move to the counter, accept the clerk's greeting, and then bend down from his height to catch the whispered directions of his wife. He would straighten up and say, ''Gimme a sack of flahr, if'n you please.'' Then when the sack of flour had been brought, he would lean again to his wife for the next item. When the stuff had all been bought and paid for with the grease-thick, wadded dollar bills which he took from an old leather coin purse with a metal catch to it, he would heave it all together into his arms and march out, his wife and towheads behind him and his eyes fixed level over the heads of the crowd. He would march down the street and around to the hitching lot where the wagons were, and put his stuff into his wagon and cover it with an old quilt to wait till he got ready to drive out to his place.

5   For Jeff York had a place. That was what made him different from the other men who looked like him and with whom he stood on the street corner on Saturday afternoon. They were croppers, but he, Jeff York, had a place. But he stood with them because his father had stood with their fathers and his grandfathers with their grandfathers, or with men like their fathers and grandfathers, in other towns, in settlements in the mountains, in towns beyond the mountains. They were the great-great-great-grandsons of men who, half woodsmen and half farmers, had been shoved into the sand hills, into the limestone hills, into the barrens, two hundred, two hundred and fifty years before and had learned there

the way to grabble a life out of the sand and the stone. And when the soil had leached away into the sand or burnt off the stone, they went on west, walking with the bent-kneed stride over the mountains, their eyes squinching warily in the gaunt faces, the rifle over the crooked arm, hunting a new place.

But there was a curse on them. They only knew the life they knew,   6
and that life did not belong to the fat bottom lands, where the cane was head-tall, and to the grassy meadows and the rich swale. So they passed those places by and hunted for the place which was like home and where they could pick up the old life, with the same feel in the bones and the squirrel's bark sounding the same after first light. They had walked a long way, to the sand hills of Alabama, to the red country of North Mississippi and Louisiana, to the Barrens of Tennessee, to the Knobs of Kentucky, and the scrub country of West Kentucky, to the Ozarks. Some of them had stopped in Cobb County, Tennessee, in the hilly eastern part of the country, and had built their cabins and dug up the ground for the corn patch. But the land had washed away there, too, and in the end they had come down out of the high land into the bottoms—for half of Cobb County is a rich, swelling country—where the corn was good and the tobacco unfurled a leaf like a yard of green velvet and the white houses stood among the cedars and tulip trees and maples. But they were not to live in the white houses with the limestone chimneys set strong at the end of each gable. No, they were to live in the shacks on the back of the farms, or in cabins not much different from the cabins they had once lived in two hundred years before over the mountains or, later, in the hills of Cobb County. But the shacks and the cabins now stood on somebody else's ground, and the curse which they had brought with them over the mountain trail, more precious than the bullet mold or grandma's quilt, the curse which was the very feeling in the bones and the habit in the hand, had come full circle.

Jeff York was one of those men, but he had broken the curse. It had   7
taken him more than thirty years to do it, from the time when he was nothing but a big boy until he was fifty. It had taken him from sun to sun, year in and year out, and all the sweat in his body, and all the power of rejection he could muster, until the very act of rejection had become a kind of pleasure, a dark, secret, savage dissipation, like an obsessing vice. But those years had given him his place, sixty acres with a house and barn.

When he bought the place, it was not very good. The land was run-   8
down from years of neglect and abuse. But Jeff York put brush in the gullies to stop the wash and planted clover on the run-down fields. He mended the fences, rod by rod. He patched the roof on the little house and propped up the porch, buying the lumber and shingles almost piece

by piece and one by one as he could spare the sweat-bright and grease-slick quarters and half-dollars out of his leather purse. Then he painted the house. He painted it white, for he knew that that was the color you painted a house sitting back from the road with its couple of maples, beyond the clover field.

9   Last, he put up the gate. It was a patented gate, the kind you can ride up to and open by pulling on a pull rope without getting off your horse or out of your buggy or wagon. It had a high pair of posts, well braced and with a high crossbar between, and the bars for the opening mechanism extending on each side. It was painted white, too. Jeff was even prouder of the gate than he was of the place. Lewis Simmons, who lived next to Jeff's place, swore he had seen Jeff come out after dark on a mule and ride in and out of that gate, back and forth, just for the pleasure of pulling on the rope and making the mechanism work. The gate was the seal Jeff York had put on all the years of sweat and rejection. He could sit on the porch on a Sunday afternoon in summer, before milking time, and look down the rise, down the winding dirt track, to the white gate beyond the clover, and know what he needed to know about all the years passed.

10   Meanwhile Jeff York had married and had had the three towheads. His wife was twenty years or so younger than he, a small, dark woman, who walked with her head bowed a little and from that humble and unprovoking posture stole sidewise, secret glances at the world from eyes which were brown or black—you never could tell which because you never remembered having looked her straight in the eye—and which were surprisingly bright in that sidewise, secret flicker, like the eyes of a small, cunning bird which surprise you from the brush. When they came down to town she moved along the street, with a child in her arms or later with the three trailing behind her, and stole her looks at the world. She wore a calico dress, dun-colored, which hung loose to conceal whatever shape her thin body had, and in winter over the dress a brown wool coat with a scrap of fur at the collar which looked like some tattered growth of fungus feeding on old wood. She wore black high-heeled shoes, slippers of some kind, which she kept polished and which surprised you under that dress and coat. In the slippers she moved with a slightly limping, stealthy gait, almost sliding them along the pavement, as though she had not fully mastered the complicated trick required to use them properly. You knew that she wore them only when she came to town, that she carried them wrapped up in a piece of newspaper until their wagon had reached the first house on the outskirts of town, and that, on the way back, at the same point, she would take them off and wrap them up again and hold the bundle in her lap

until she got home. If the weather happened to be bad, or if it was winter, she would have a pair of old brogans under the wagon seat.

It was not that Jeff York was a hard man and kept his wife in clothes   11
that were as bad as those worn by the poorest of the women of the croppers. In fact, some of the cropper women, poor or not, black or white, managed to buy dresses with some color in them and proper hats, and went to the moving picture show on Saturday afternoon. But Jeff still owed a little money on his place, less than two hundred dollars, which he had had to borrow to rebuild his barn after it was struck by lightning. He had, in fact, never been entirely out of debt. He had lost a mule which had got out on the highway and been hit by a truck. That had set him back. One of his towheads had been sickly for a couple of winters. He had not been in deep, but he was not a man, with all those years of rejection behind him, to forget the meaning of those years. He was good enough to his family. Nobody ever said the contrary. But he was good to them in terms of all the years he had lived through. He did what he could afford. He bought the towheads a ten-cent bag of colored candy every Saturday afternoon for them to suck on during the ride home in the wagon, and the last thing before they left town, he always took the lot of them over to the dogwagon to get hamburgers and orange pop.

The towheads were crazy about hamburgers. And so was his wife, for   12
that matter. You could tell it, even if she didn't say anything, for she would lift her bowed-forward head a little, and her face would brighten, and she would run her tongue out to wet her lips just as the plate with the hamburger would be set on the counter before her. But all those folks, like Jeff York and his family, like hamburgers, with pickle and onions and mustard and tomato catsup, the whole works. It is something different. They stay out in the country and eat hog-meat, when they can get it, and greens and corn bread and potatoes, and nothing but a pinch of salt to brighten it on the tongue, and when they get to town and get hold of beef and wheat bread and all the stuff to jack up the flavor, they have to swallow to keep the mouth from flooding before they even take the first bite.

So the last thing every Saturday, Jeff York would take his family over   13
to Slick Hardin's *Dew Drop Inn Diner* and give them the treat. The diner was built like a railway coach, but it was set on a concrete foundation on a lot just off the main street of town. At each end the concrete was painted to show wheels. Slick Hardin kept the grass just in front of the place pretty well mowed and one or two summers he even had a couple of flower beds in the middle of that shirttail-size lawn. Slick had a good business. For a few years he had been a prelim-fighter over in Nashville and had got his name in the papers a few times. So he was a

kind of hero, with the air of romance about him. He had been born, however, right in town and, as soon as he had found out he wasn't ever going to be good enough to be a real fighter, he had come back home and started the dogwagon, the first one ever in town. He was a slick-skinned fellow about thirty-five, prematurely bald, with his head slick all over. He had big eyes, pale blue and slick looking like agates. When he said something that he thought smart, he would roll his eyes around, slick in his head like marbles, to see who was laughing. Then he'd wink. He had done very well with his business, for despite the fact that he had picked up city ways and a lot of city talk, he still remembered enough to deal with the country people, and they were the ones who brought the dimes in. People who lived right there in town, except for school kids in the afternoon and the young toughs from the pool room or men on the night shift down at the railroad, didn't often get around to the dogwagon.

14   Slick Hardin was perhaps trying to be smart when he said what he did to Mrs. York. Perhaps he had forgotten, just for that moment, that people like Jeff York and his wife didn't like to be kidded, at least not in that way. He said what he did, and then grinned and rolled his eyes around to see if some of the other people present were thinking it was funny.

15   Mrs. York was sitting on a stool in front of the counter, flanked on one side by Jeff York and on the other by the three towheads. She had just sat down to wait for the hamburger—there were several orders in ahead of the York order—and had been watching in her sidewise fashion every move of Slick Hardin's hands as he patted the pink meat onto the hot slab and wiped the split buns over the greasy iron to make them ready to receive it. She always watched him like that, and when the hamburger was set before her she would wet her lips with her tongue.

16   That day Slick set the hamburger down in front of Mrs. York, and said, "Anybody likes hamburger much as you, Mrs. York, ought to git him a hamburger stand."

17   Mrs. York flushed up, and didn't say anything, staring at her plate. Slick rolled his eyes to see how it was going over, and somebody down the counter snickered. Slick looked back at the Yorks, and if he had not been so encouraged by the snicker he might, when he saw Jeff York's face, have hesitated before going on with his kidding. People like Jeff York are touchous, and they are especially touchous about the womenfolks, and you do not make jokes with or about their womenfolks unless it is perfectly plain that the joke is a very special kind of friendly joke. The snicker down the counter had defined the joke as not entirely friendly. Jeff was looking at Slick, and something was growing slowly in that hewed-cedar face, and back in the gray eyes in the ambush of thorny brows.

But Slick did not notice. The snicker had encouraged him, and so he said, "Yeah, if I liked them hamburgers much as you, I'd buy me a hamburger stand. Fact, I'm selling this one. You want to buy it?"   *18*

There was another snicker, louder, and Jeff York, whose hamburger had been about half way to his mouth for another bite, laid it down deliberately on his plate. But whatever might have happened at that moment did not happen. It did not happen because Mrs. York lifted her flushed face, looked straight at Slick Hardin, swallowed hard to get down a piece of the hamburger or to master her nerve, and said in a sharp, strained voice, "You sellen this place?"   *19*

There was complete silence. Nobody had expected her to say anything. The chances were she had never said a word in that diner in the couple of hundred times she had been in it. She had come in with Jeff York and, when a stool had come vacant, had sat down, and Jeff had said, "Gimme five hamburgers, if'n you please, and make 'em well done, and five bottles of orange pop." Then, after the eating was over, he had always laid down seventy-five cents on the counter—that is, after there were five hamburger-eaters in the family—and walked out, putting his brogans down slow, and his wife and kids following without a word. But now she spoke up and asked the question, in that strained, artificial voice, and everybody, including her husband, looked at her with surprise.   *20*

As soon as he could take it in, Slick Hardin replied, "Yeah, I'm selling it."   *21*

She swallowed hard again, but this time it could not have been hamburger, and demanded, "What you asken fer hit?"   *22*

Slick looked at her in the new silence, half shrugged, a little contemptuously, and said, "Fourteen hundred and fifty dollars."   *23*

She looked back at him, while the blood ebbed from her face. "Hit's a lot of money," she said in a flat tone, and returned her gaze to the hamburger on her plate.   *24*

"Lady," Slick said defensively, "I got that much money tied up here. Look at that there stove. It is a *Heat Master* and they cost. Them coffee urns, now. Money can't buy no better. And this here lot, lady, the diner sets on. Anybody knows I got that much money tied up here. I got more. This lot cost me more'n . . ." He suddenly realized that she was not listening to him. And he must have realized, too, that she didn't have a dime in the world and couldn't buy his diner, and that he was making a fool of himself, defending his price. He stopped abruptly, shrugged his shoulders, and then swung his wide gaze down the counter to pick out somebody to wink to.   *25*

But before he got the wink off, Jeff York had said, "Mr. Hardin."   *26*

Slick looked at him and asked, "Yeah?"   *27*

28   "She didn't mean no harm," Jeff York said. "She didn't mean to be messen in yore business."

29   Slick shrugged. "Ain't no skin off my nose," he said. "Ain't no secret I'm selling out. My price ain't no secret neither."

30   Mrs. York bowed her head over her plate. She was chewing a mouthful of her hamburger with a slow, abstracted motion of her jaw, and you knew that it was flavorless on her tongue.

31   That was, of course, on a Saturday. On Thursday afternoon of the next week Slick was in the diner alone. It was the slack time, right in the middle of the afternoon. Slick, as he told it later, was wiping off the stove and wasn't noticing. He was sort of whistling to himself, he said. He had a way of whistling soft through his teeth. But he wasn't whistling loud, he said, not so loud he wouldn't have heard the door open or the steps if she hadn't come gum-shoeing in on him to stand there waiting in the middle of the floor until he turned round and was so surprised he nearly had heart failure. He had thought he was there alone, and there she was, watching every move he was making, like a cat watching a goldfish swim in a bowl.

32   "Howdy-do," he said, when he got his breath back.

33   "This place still fer sale?" she asked him.

34   "Yeah, lady," he said.

35   "What you asken fer hit?"

36   "Lady, I done told you," Slick replied, "fourteen hundred and fifty dollars."

37   "Hit's a heap of money," she said.

38   Slick started to tell her how much money he had tied up there, but before he had got going, she had turned and slipped out of the door.

39   "Yeah," Slick said later to the men who came into the diner, "me like a fool starting to tell her how much money I got tied up here when I knowed she didn't have a dime. That woman's crazy. She must've walked that five or six miles in here just to ask me something she already knowed the answer to. And then turned right round and walked out. But I am selling me this place. I'm tired of slinging hash to them hicks. I got me some connections over in Nashville and I'm gonna open me a place over there. A cigar stand and about three pool tables and maybe some beer. I'll have me a sort of club in the back. You know, membership cards to git in, where the boys will play a little game. Just sociable. I got good connections over in Nashville. I'm selling this place. But that woman, she ain't got a dime. She ain't gonna buy it."

40   But she did.

41   On Saturday Jeff York led his family over to the diner. They ate hamburgers without a word and marched out. After they had gone, Slick

said, "Looks like she ain't going to make the invest-mint. Gonna buy a block of bank stock instead." Then he rolled his eyes, located a brother down the counter, and winked.

It was almost the end of the next week before it happened. What had been going on inside the white house out on Jeff York's place nobody knew or was to know. Perhaps she just starved him out, just not doing the cooking or burning everything. Perhaps she just quit attending to the children properly and he had to come back tired from work and take care of them. Perhaps she just lay in bed at night and talked and talked to him, asking him to buy it, nagging him all night long, while he would fall asleep and then wake up with a start to hear her voice still going on. Or perhaps she just turned her face away from him and wouldn't let him touch her. He was a lot older than she, and she was probably the only woman he had ever had. He had been too ridden by his dream and his passion for rejection during all the years before to lay even a finger on a woman. So she had him there. Because he was a lot older and because he had never had another woman. But perhaps she used none of these methods. She was a small, dark, cunning woman, with a sidewise look from her lowered face, and she could have thought up ways of her own, no doubt.

Whatever she thought up, it worked. On Friday morning Jeff York went to the bank. He wanted to mortgage his place, he told Todd Sullivan, the president. He wanted fourteen hundred and fifty dollars, he said. Todd Sullivan would not let him have it. He already owed the bank one hundred and sixty dollars and the best he could get on a mortgage was eleven hundred dollars. That was in 1935 and then farmland wasn't worth much and half the land in the country was mortgaged anyway. Jeff York sat in the chair by Todd Sullivan's desk and didn't say anything. Eleven hundred dollars would not do him any good. Take off the hundred and sixty he owed and it wouldn't be but a little over nine hundred dollars clear to him. He sat there quietly for a minute, apparently turning that fact over in his head. Then Todd Sullivan asked him, "How much you say you need?"

Jeff York told him.

"What you want it for?" Todd Sullivan asked.

He told him that.

"I tell you," Todd Sullivan said, "I don't want to stand in the way of a man bettering himself. Never did. That diner ought to be a good proposition, all right, and I don't want to stand in your way if you want to come to town and better yourself. It will be a step up from that farm for you, and I like a man has got ambition. The bank can't lend you the money, not on that piece of property. But I tell you what I'll do. I'll buy your place. I got me some walking horses I'm keeping out on my father's place. But I could use me a little place of my own. For my horses. I'll give you seventeen hundred for it. Cash.''

48   Jeff York did not say anything to that. He looked slow at Todd Sullivan as though he did not understand.

49   ''Seventeen hundred,'' the banker repeated. ''That's a good figure. For these times.''

50   Jeff was not looking at him now. He was looking out the window, across the alleyway—Todd Sullivan's office was in the back of the bank. The banker, telling about it later when the doings of Jeff York had become for a moment a matter of interest, said, ''I thought he hadn't even heard me. He looked like he was half asleep or something. I coughed to sort of wake him up. You know the way you do. I didn't want to rush him. You can't rush those people, you know. But I couldn't sit there all day. I had offered him a fair price.''

51   It was, as a matter of fact, a fair price for the times, when the bottom was out of everything in the section.

52   Jeff York took it. He took the seventeen hundred dollars and bought the dogwagon with it, and rented a little house on the edge of town and moved in with his wife and the towheads. The first day after they got settled, Jeff York and his wife went over to the diner to get instructions from Slick about running the place. He showed Mrs. York all about how to work the coffee machine and the stove, and how to make up the sandwiches, and how to clean the place up after herself. She fried up hamburgers for all of them, herself, her husband, and Slick Hardin, for practice, and they ate the hamburgers while a couple of hangers-on watched them. ''Lady,'' Slick said, for he had money in his pocket and was heading out for Nashville on the seven o'clock train that night, and was feeling expansive, ''Lady, you sure fling a mean hamburger.''

53   He wiped the last crumbs and mustard off his lips, got his valise from behind the door, and said, ''Lady, git in there and pitch. I hope you make a million hamburgers.'' Then he stepped out into the bright fall sunshine and walked away whistling up the street, whistling through his teeth and rolling his eyes as though there were somebody to wink to. That was the last anybody in town ever saw of Slick Hardin.

54   The next day, Jeff York worked all day down at the diner. He was scrubbing up the place inside and cleaning up the trash which had accumulated behind it. He burned all the trash. Then he gave the place a good coat of paint outside, white paint. That took him two days. Then he touched up the counter inside with varnish. He straightened up the sign out front, which had begun to sag a little. He had that place looking spic and span.

Then on the fifth day after they got settled—it was Sunday—he took   55
a walk in the country. It was along toward sun when he started out, not
late, as a matter of fact, for by October the days are shortening up. He
walked out the Curtisville pike and out the cut-off leading to his farm.
When he entered the cut-off, about a mile from his own place, it was
still light enough for the Bowdoins, who had a filling station at the corner, to see him plain when he passed.

The next time anybody saw him was on Monday morning about six   56
o'clock. A man taking milk into town saw him. He was hanging from
the main cross bar of the white patented gate. He had jumped off the
gate. But he had propped the thing open so there wouldn't be any
chance of clambering back up on it if his neck didn't break when he
jumped and he should happen to change his mind.

But that was an unnecessary precaution, as it developed. Dr. Stauffer   57
said that his neck was broken very clean. "A man who can break a neck
as clean as that could make a living at it," Dr. Stauffer said. And added,
"If he's damned sure it ain't ever his own neck."

Mrs. York was much cut up by her husband's death. People were   58
sympathetic and helpful, and out of a mixture of sympathy and curiosity she got a good starting trade at the diner. And the trade kept right on.
She got so she didn't hang her head and look sidewise at you and the
world. She would look straight at you. She got so she could walk in high
heels without giving the impression that it was a trick she was learning.
She wasn't a bad-looking woman, as a matter of fact, once she had
caught on how to fix herself up a little. The railroad men and the pool
hall gang liked to hang out there and kid with her. Also, they said, she
flung a mean hamburger.

Questions and Activities

▶ *COMPREHENSION QUESTIONS*

1. Why is Jeff York's patented gate so important to him? What does it
   represent? What does the "mean hamburger" represent to Mrs. York?
   Early in the story, why is her weekly hamburger so important to her?
2. What type of new life is foretold for Mrs. York in the conclusion of
   this story (paragraph 58)? In what ways is that new life a reaction
   against the life of "curse" and "rejection" that the Yorks led before

their move to town? Why did they consider that life, at least to some degree, one of curse and rejection?

3. What effects does Penn Warren's use of the second-person pronoun in the first three paragraphs of this story have on you as the reader? How does this more intimate form of address affect your attitude toward Jeff York? Do you feel superior to him? Do you see him as a social type, as the typical representative of a particular economic or social class, because of the story's point of view? (The *point of view* is the perspective a fiction writer gives the reader toward the experience contained in a story.) Some critics argue that the use of the second person can make readers feel uncomfortably button-holed. Is that the effect you feel here?

4. Write your impression of the character of the narrator (the person who is telling you this story). What kind of person is he? How do you know? Does he reveal himself in his description of Jeff York and his family? Do you think he is objective and neutral or biased in some way concerning the York family? Reread the story's first four paragraphs. Then, think about the narrator's function in these paragraphs. Finally, write without stopping for twenty minutes. Close your writing with an answer to the question of *why* the author used this kind of narrator.

5. Why does Penn Warren withhold the fact of Jeff York's suicide until the very end of the story? The story is narrated in the past tense; the author could have placed the suicide earlier in the story and still maintained a consistent point of view. Does the information, placed at the end, seem surprising to you? Why might the author have wanted you to feel surprised?

6. Why do you think Mrs. York finds working in the diner more to her liking than working on the farm? Does she show signs of discontent with her life before Slick Hardin mentions that he wants to sell his diner? What was missing in her work on the farm that is provided by her work in town?

7. Why do you think Jeff York killed himself after selling his farm and moving to town? Why was he unable to find satisfaction in buying the diner, repairing it, and working in it? Do you think York was trapped by his background? Was he negatively defined by his work? Is Mrs. York positively defined by her new work in the diner? Why?

8. Look through the employment opportunities section of a local news-paper. Find a job opportunity that interests you but is different from the kind of position you are qualified for by experience, general background, and education. Write a letter applying for this job; explain why you believe the job would be a good one for you, even though you do not have the specific training for it. You may have another member of your class play the role of the employer who would receive your letter. Both of you can discuss the kind of appeal that might work with this employer; then your classmate can write a response to your letter.

9. Reread the story through the end of paragraph 18. Then, spend twenty minutes free writing a description of how you think Mrs. York ought to have responded to Slick Hardin's question, given what you know of her through the first eighteen paragraphs. Finish by comparing your description of how Mrs. York should have responded to her actual response (paragraphs 19–22). Do you think the reader should be surprised by Mrs. York's actual response, or do you think her response is consistent with her character?

Writing Assignments

WORK AND SOCIETY

Respond to the following quotation (from Toni Cade Bambara's "What It Is I Think I'm Doing Anyhow") by writing an essay of three to four pages: "A writer, like any other cultural worker, like any other member of the community, ought to try to put her/his skills in the service of the community." Take Bambara's idea and relate it to similar or different ideas on the value and purpose of work from at least two other essays from this section.

VOCATION AND AVOCATION

This assignment is divided into three stages.

1. Read "Two Tramps in Mud Time" (pages 179–181) and respond to Frost's treatment of work and play. Write your response as a personal writing, aimed simply at helping you discover and clarify your thoughts about the theme of work and play in the poem. Provide an accurate summary of the speaker's attitude toward the relationship between work and play in his life. What parts of the poem contribute to your definition of the speaker's attitude?

2. Read your response to Frost's poem to another member of your class. Discuss it with him or her; listen to and make notes of his or her questions. Write an informal critique of your response to the poem based on your classmate's questions and your answers. Also, consider some of the ideas from the readings in this section as you write your critique. How can these ideas help you clarify, support, or expand the points in your response to Frost's poem? To help you plan the final writing that follows, you should make a list of these ideas from readings that you will use. Follow each idea on your list with at least one reason why you decided to use it in your essay.

3. As the final stage, write a formal personal essay. You are not expected to write as an expert in this essay. Assume the rest of your class is the essay's audience. They have read at least several of the readings in this section; they have done some careful thinking about the section's theme. But they are not sociologists or psychologists. Assume an appropriate style, use evidence from the readings and your own experiences to support your ideas, but write in a voice simi-

lar to your classroom voice. In your essay, respond to these questions:

a. Can an individual combine avocation and vocation in modern American life?

b. Can this combination, if it is possible, provide enough of the rewards that people normally expect from work in America? Does it provide advantages over work in which avocation and vocation are not combined?

Two Tramps in Mud Time
ROBERT FROST

Out of the mud two strangers came   *1*
And caught me splitting wood in the yard.
And one of them put me off my aim
By hailing cheerily 'Hit them hard!'
I knew pretty well why he dropped behind
And let the other go on a way.
I knew pretty well what he had in mind:
He wanted to take my job for pay.

Good blocks of oak it was I split,   *2*
As large around as the chopping block;
And every piece I squarely hit
Fell splinterless as a cloven rock.
The blows that a life of self-control
Spares to strike for the common good
That day, giving a loose to my soul,
I spent on the unimportant wood.

The sun was warm but the wind was chill.   *3*
You know how it is with an April day
When the sun is out and the wind is still,
You're one month on in the middle of May.
But if you so much as dare to speak,
A cloud comes over the sunlit arch,
A wind comes off a frozen peak,
And you're two months back in the middle of March.

A bluebird comes tenderly up to alight   *4*
And turns to the wind to unruffle a plume

His song so pitched as not to excite
A single flower as yet to bloom.
It is snowing a flake: and he half knew
Winter was only playing possum.
Except in color he isn't blue,
But he wouldn't advise a thing to blossom.

5   The water for which we may have to look
In summertime with a witching-wand,
In every wheelrut's now a brook,
In every print of a hoof a pond.
Be glad of water, but don't forget
The lurking frost in the earth beneath
That will steal forth after the sun is set
And show on the water its crystal teeth.

6   The time when most I loved my task
These two must make me love it more
By coming with what they came to ask.
You'd think I never had felt before
The weight of an ax-head poised aloft,
The grip on earth of outspread feet.
The life of muscles rocking soft
And smooth and moist in vernal heat.

7   Out of the woods two hulking tramps
(From sleeping God knows where last night,
But not long since in the lumber camps).
They thought all chopping was theirs of right.
Men of the woods and lumberjacks,
They judged me by their appropriate tool.
Except as a fellow handled an ax,
They had no way of knowing a fool.

8   Nothing on either side was said.
They knew they had but to stay their stay
And all their logic would fill my head:
As that I had no right to play
With what was another man's work for gain.
My right might be love but theirs was need.
And where the two exist in twain
Theirs was the better right—agreed.

9   But yield who will to their separation,
My object in living is to unite

My avocation and my vocation
As my two eyes make one in sight.
Only where love and need are one,
And the work is play for mortal stakes,
Is the deed ever really done
For Heaven and the future's sakes.

*I*n What Should
We Believe?

▶ ─────────────────────────────────

Introduction

▶ ─────────────────

The selections in this section explore the relationship between our private and public beliefs—our values and our morality. The readings fall into two general categories. The essays by Suzanne Gordon, Joan Didion, and David Abodaher describe the experiences and responses of individuals within particular social contexts. Gordon presents a case study of Jim Costello, a social activist and political radical of the 1960s whose change in consciousness and life style results in alienation from family and friends and in loneliness. Didion provides us with several portraits of California citizens who respond to their social situations with different degrees of superficiality and alienation. Abodaher tells how Lee Iacocca, a corporate executive and folk hero, directed the production of the Mustang, which captured the imagination of many American consumers.

The essays by Joseph Wood Krutch, Mark Twain, and Robert J. Lifton look at the larger social and moral situation within which we all as individuals live. Krutch, writing in the 1950s, argues that public morality has declined in the first half of this century, a decline reflected in the belief that individual actions have no effect on the social situations in which they find themselves. Twain, in a fictional letter from a recording angel in heaven to an American businessman, satirizes how individual greed disguises itself as public morality. Lifton provides a serious account of modern atrocities and their historical and psychological public effects.

These readings reveal a basic modern tension between self and society. How far can we push the desire to stand alone without creating loneliness and feelings of isolation? How far can we push the desire to belong to a group without threatening the individual's needs and beliefs? Can we believe in the same values when so many of us have such decidedly different experiences, listen to such different stories, grew up in such different kinds of families, or have experienced such different kinds of educations? The potential answers to the theme question of this section fall into three general areas: belief in the self, belief in a group, or belief in values formed by some combination of the two.

As you read, try to connect these writers' individual intentions with the overall theme of individual and public morality. In considering those writers who portray and analyze individuals, we must ask ourselves whether or not our society has a common set of beliefs and goals and, if so, how they affect our personal beliefs and actions.

1. Can individuals function effectively if their society has no commonly held beliefs?
2. Does a fate such as Jim Costello's await individuals who question society's moral and political customs?

In contrast, as we look at those writers who focus on society at large, we must ask ourselves whether or not the structure of social beliefs that organizes our everyday actions is in itself worth preserving.

1. Does Lifton's account of public immorality in the form of atrocities suggest that citizens must question society's values from the ground up?
2. Can individuals be skeptical of all public values and remain stable in their private lives?
3. Are there public values, such as the American dream of business success as described by David Abodaher, that cross economic and social lines to create a common mythology that people of all kinds can hold onto?

The New Immorality

JOSEPH WOOD KRUTCH

Joseph Wood Krutch (1893–1970) was born in Knoxville, Tennessee. As an undergraduate at the University of Tennessee, he concentrated on science and received a B.A. degree in 1915. Although he was never to lose his interest in science, his graduate work at Columbia University, where he got his M.A. in 1916 and his Ph.D. in 1924, concentrated on the humanities. In his career as a writer, Krutch was able to combine scientific and literary achievements to an extent that is rare among modern intellectuals.

Most of Krutch's nearly three dozen published books fall into two categories: literary criticism and nature and conservation from a scientific perspective. All of Krutch's works are characterized by his intensely moral concern with humanity's place in the world. Many of his books on literature argue that the technical specializations of science in the twentieth century have dehumanized us. *The Modern Temper* (1929), probably his most well-known and controversial book, argues that modern literature is characterized by the loss of that human sense of a noble purpose to life and that twentieth-century writers are not capable of producing tragic works because they have lost their awareness of an ordered world and the definite knowledge of right and wrong. Krutch believed that, like many scientists, the literary community had replaced emphasis on the human spirit with a tedious attention to physical detail and universal laws.

The essay included here is directed to a general reader. That reader is educated enough to know what Krutch means by the gentleman's way of "playing the game" (paragraph 9), to recognize Jonathan Swift's name and reputation, and to follow a closely reasoned argument. Yet Krutch demands no special moral credentials from his readers—those of the theologian, cleric, or moral historian, for example. He does assume his readers are interested enough in the moral state of the nation to weigh some evidence about conflicting interpretations of the national character in the 1950s. At the time this essay was written, in 1959 or 1960, serious people were concerned about apathy in American culture and about the social conformity apparent in the middle class. William Whyte's *The Organization Man* and David Riesman's *The Lonely Crowd* are examples of contemporary books that also raised these issues.

As you read, consider Krutch's purpose:

1. What does he want you, his reader, to do? Would he like you to change your opinion and believe what he says about Americans in

1960? Or would he like you simply to think more about the conditions that he describes?

2. Do you think his essay achieves its purpose?

▶ ─────────────

1   The provost of one of our largest and most honored institutions told me not long ago that a questionnaire was distributed to his undergraduates and that 40 percent refused to acknowledge that they believed cheating on examinations to be reprehensible.

2   Recently a reporter for a New York newspaper stopped six people on the street and asked them if they would consent to take part in a rigged television quiz for money. He reported that five of the six said yes. Yet most of these five, like most of the college cheaters, would probably profess a strong social consciousness. They may cheat, but they vote for foreign aid and for enlightened social measures.

3   These two examples exhibit a paradox of our age. It is often said, and my observation leads me to believe it true, that our seemingly great growth in social morality has oddly enough taken place in a world where private morality—a sense of the supreme importance of purely personal honor, honesty, and integrity—seems to be declining. Beneficent and benevolent social institutions are administered by men who all too frequently turn out to be accepting "gifts." The world of popular entertainment is rocked by scandals. College students put on their honor, cheat on examinations. Candidates for the Ph.D. hire ghost writers to prepare their theses.

4   But, one may object, haven't all these things always been true? Is there really any evidence that personal dishonesty is more prevalent than it always was?

5   I have no way of making a historical measurement. Perhaps these things are not actually more prevalent. What I do know is that there is an increasing tendency to accept and take for granted such personal dishonesty. The bureaucrat and disk jockey say, "Well, yes, I took presents, but I assure you that I made just decisions anyway." The college student caught cheating does not even blush. He shrugs his shoulders and comments: "Everybody does it, and besides, I can't see that it really hurts anybody."

6   Jonathan Swift once said: "I have never been surprised to find men wicked, but I have often been surprised to find them not ashamed." It is my conviction that though men may be no more wicked than they al-

ways have been, they seem less likely to be ashamed. If anybody does it, it must be right. Honest, moral, decent mean only what is usual. This is not really a wicked world, because morality means mores or manners and usual conduct is the only standard.

The second part of the defense, "it really doesn't hurt anybody," is equally revealing. "It doesn't hurt anybody" means it doesn't do that abstraction called society any harm. The harm it did the bribe-taker and the cheater isn't important; it is purely personal. And personal as opposed to social decency doesn't count for much. Sometimes I am inclined to blame sociology for part of this paradox. Sociology has tended to lay exclusive stress upon social morality, and tended too often to define good and evil as merely the "socially useful" or its reverse.   7

What social morality and social conscience leave out is the narrower but very significant concept of honor—as opposed to what is sometimes called merely "socially desirable conduct." The man of honor is not content to ask merely whether this or that will hurt society, or whether it is what most people would permit themselves to do. He asks, and he asks first of all, would it hurt him and his self-respect? Would it dishonor him personally?   8

It was a favorite and no doubt sound argument among early twentieth-century reformers that "playing the game" as the gentleman was supposed to play it was not enough to make a decent society. They were right: it is not enough. But the time has come to add that it is indeed inevitable that the so-called social conscience unsupported by the concept of personal honor will create a corrupt society. But suppose that it doesn't? Suppose that no one except the individual suffers from the fact that he sees nothing wrong in doing what everybody else does? Even so, I still insist that for the individual himself nothing is more important than this personal, interior sense of right and wrong and his determination to follow that rather than to be guided by what everybody does or merely the criterion of "social usefulness." It is impossible for me to imagine a good society composed of men without honor.   9

We hear it said frequently that what present-day men most desire is security. If that is so, then they have a wrong notion of what the real, the ultimate, security is. No one who is dependent on anything outside himself, upon money, power, fame, or whatnot, is or ever can be secure. Only he who possesses himself and is content with himself is actually secure. Too much is being said about the importance of adjustment and "participation in the group." Even cooperation, to give this thing its most favorable designation, is no more important than the ability to stand alone when the choice must be made between the sacrifice of one's own integrity and adjustment to or participation in group activity.   10

11   No matter how bad the world may become, no matter how much the mass man of the future may lose such of the virtues as he still has, one fact remains. If one person alone refuses to go along with him, if one person alone asserts his individual and inner right to believe in and be loyal to what his fellow men seem to have given up, then at least he will still retain what is perhaps the most important part of humanity.

Questions and Activities

▶ *COMPREHENSION QUESTIONS*

1. Do you think it is true that "no matter how much the mass man of the future may lose such of the virtues as he still has, one fact remains. If one person alone refuses to go along with him . . . then at least he will still retain what is perhaps the most important part of humanity" (paragraph 11)? What is, to Krutch, "the most important part of humanity"?

2. In popular magazines and newspapers of the times, find accounts of the specific types of personal immorality that Krutch mentions (paragraphs 1, 2, 3, and 5). Find a *New York Times* account of quiz show scandals, for example, or look at major newspapers for articles on what was then called "payola," the practice of disk jockeys' receiving kickbacks from record companies for promoting certain records and performers. Explain how knowing more about these events contributes to your understanding of Krutch's thesis.

▶ *QUESTIONS OF RHETORICAL PURPOSE AND STRATEGY*

3. As an informed reader of today, you know things about our culture that Krutch's original readers could not have known. In the late 1960s, the Vietnam War and the social problems at home combined to create a very different profile of the average American from Krutch's. This picture is one of participation in and intense reaction to public issues—anything but apathy. Now, in the 1980s, some social critics believe we are returning to the apathy and lack of personal conviction that Krutch observed in 1960. As you read, look for evidence of what Krutch calls a tendency toward unquestioning "cooperation" with the status quo. What support does Krutch provide for his opinion that the average American of the late 1950s put social above individual morality? Is his evidence convincing? Should he have presented more of it?

4. Describe the order in which Krutch presents his argument. Does he begin or end with examples? Where does he put his main idea? Are you influenced positively or negatively by the order of the ideas in this essay? Why might the order Krutch chose to use have a positive effect on his assumed reader? Does Krutch describe the possible opposition to his ideas? Where might he have treated these opposing ideas in this essay? What do you think of his conclusion?

5. Does Krutch seem to want to persuade his readers to change their attitude toward modern society? What attitude does Krutch expect his readers to hold toward modern culture? In what way does he want to change that attitude?

▶ *THEME QUESTIONS*

6. Can you explain the difference in what Krutch refers to as "social morality and social conscience" (paragraph 8) and "personal . . .decency" (paragraph 7) and "honor" (paragraph 8)? Describe to the class an incident in which you believe a person has used the argument "it really doesn't hurt anybody" as an excuse to do something dishonest or illegal. What about the example of cheating among college students that Krutch mentions—would today's students respond differently to such a questionnaire (paragraph 1)?

7. Can you think of current examples of personal and social immorality of the kind Krutch describes? Describe a few of these and tell why they are similar to Krutch's examples.

8. What would be Krutch's answer to this section's thematic question?

▶ *LEARNING ACTIVITIES*

9. Think back over your experiences as you began your first year in college. Select one incident that you believe characterizes how you felt during that period of time. Make some notes on that incident from memory. Then describe that incident as specifically as possible to another member of your class. Discuss with your classmate the incident as you have described it. Work together to define the emotion you both feel lies behind the incident.

   Finally, write a narrative that you believe combines the feeling behind the incident (perhaps loneliness, alienation, or exhilaration) and the description of the incident itself.

10. Explain why cheating on a test might be considered an immoral act. Is anyone besides the cheater hurt by the act of cheating? Who else is hurt? Do you think it's a crime to steal ideas? Why?

Jim Costello

Suzanne Gordon

Born in 1945, Suzanne Gordon graduated from Cornell University and earned her M.A. in French literature from Johns Hopkins. She has worked as a substitute school teacher and as an editor and translator for a French journalist. Gordon's book *Lonely in America* (1976), from which this essay is taken, is a sociological study of the phenomenon of loneliness in our modern culture. In the book, Gordon applies the case-study method, not as professional sociologists use it but as a basic tool to create the personal focus she wants on her subjects without sacrificing her objectivity. Gordon also employs this popular sociological method to a large degree in her articles, which have appeared in the *Washington Post, Newsweek, Ms.,* and the *Village Voice.* She is also the author of *Black Mesa: The Angel of Death* (1973).

Popular writers such as Gordon are often criticized by both general and professional readers. General readers sometimes find her objective methods tedious or annoyingly noncommittal. Professional sociologists sometimes criticize writers like Gordon for what they believe is superficial use of sociological methodology. As you read, you should decide where you stand on this issue, since many magazines you will read include articles that apply the methods of particular disciplines outside of their normal laboratory or technical contexts (*Psychology Today* and *Popular Science* are two examples of this type of magazine).

Answer these questions by locating textual excerpts and using them to support the generalities in your answers:

1. What do you think of Gordon's treatment of Jim Costello?
2. Is she precise enough in her recording of Costello's actions?
3. Are her implied conclusions drawn carefully enough? Are there times when you wish she had interpreted Costello's actions more openly? Are there times that you feel she has stacked the cards in favor of a particular interpretation?

But you need to take another line of inquiry as well. The following questions will lead you to an understanding of the kinds of generally educated audiences addressed by writers for serious journals and magazines.

1. What type of reader is interested in this type of writing? How much education does such a reader have? What degree of social awareness and social conscience does such a reader have?

2. In writing for this type of audience, to what shared qualities would you try to appeal?

Of course, there is also a general moral perspective at work in this essay, which can be appreciated by thinking about these questions:

1. Why does Jim Costello become a lonely and isolated man? Why does his search for a new set of values result in personal suffering rather than a new and better life?
2. How does Gordon's use of the narrative form affect you as the reader? Do you feel sympathy for Costello as a developed character in Gordon's story?
3. Was there a consistent and humane set of shared beliefs behind either Costello's old or his new way of life?

▶ ——————————————

They found him on a country road in Pennsylvania. The small car resting on its side in a ditch at the shoulder of the road looked like an insect desperately kicking its legs and trying to right itself. When the police came he was sitting about ten feet away from the wreck, rocking himself against the night. He took no notice of them or their questions, and they gentled their usual gruffness as they pulled him off the ground. It was a shock to see such a big man surrendering himself up to their care like a baby, repeating to himself over and over, ''My wife's going to leave me, she has a lover, right in our house.''

''Poor guy,'' one officer said, looking through the man's wallet for a license.

''Yeah—who do you think he is? Says here he comes from Cleveland. Sure is a weirdo.''

''We'd better take him in.''

They sat him down in a corner of the station house. No use locking him up. He was so quiet—docile almost. He noticed nothing—the officers walking by, the queer looks. After about fifteen minutes the phones began ringing more often, and the conversation, already dominated by the fact of a rare presence in the country precinct, grew more animated, more stares moving toward him.

''Say,'' one of the policemen shouted, putting down the phone, ''what do you know about this! They think he's the guy that broke those windows at the high school.''

''Hell—are you sure? He don't look like he could do nothing to no one.''

8   "Well," the other responded, "he fits the description of the guy seen near there, and his car was seen near the place. Better ask him some questions."

9   Do you know so and so, where were you at such and such a time, why did you come here. . . .?

10   He seemed to hear none of it. Finally they decided to put him in a cell, because he might, after all, be dangerous. They had telephoned his wife in Cleveland, who said she would leave for Pennsylvania immediately. And because of their description of his condition and the charges made against him, she said she would bring a friend with her, a psychiatrist. But it would take some time to get there.

11   It seemed for a moment, when she arrived, that he would recognize her. A tight-lipped, erect woman, whose carriage did not quite fit the loose, rather hippy-looking clothes she wore, she bent over him, repeating his name—"Jim, Jimmy, are you all right? Jimmy, what happened?" But his glance had closed in on itself. And so, after several hours and many consultations, it was decided that charges could be pressed later, after he had recovered from whatever it was that was troubling him. In the car, his wife, Meg, again tried to talk to him, to explain, and finally to apologize. But he remained silent and shut off—as he was when they took him into the hospital, as they left him when they locked the door to his room, to the ward, and to the world.

12   He had been a happy, boisterous man. The most outgoing in his whole group. At meetings of the antiwar group he and his friends had built into a large and influential force he outlined strategies with good-natured, almost naïve belief in whatever it was that was happening in the Movement around the country. There was always a cheerful assurance that things would work because he and his friends were behind them. He was a leader not because he had original ideas, or because he wanted any kind of power over others, but because he wanted to share his enthusiasms, be there at the front lines to cheer when change occurred. After the Revolution, they would proclaim to one another, all would be well. And since he knew that that revolution would not be long in coming, all would work out quite soon indeed. It was the pioneer's faith he had, the heritage of a large Italian family that laughed and fought with warmth and great self-confidence.

13   He brought that same enthusiasm to all his dealings; at parties he leaped into the center of the room and danced with the simplicity of a peasant dancing by the sea, moving round and round after the others had fallen from fatigue. He chided his wife for her waspish humors, for the stiffness that she could not, despite all her efforts, completely overcome. But he had great faith in her potential. They had been married al-

most ten years, and she had already come a long way. Politics and the sense of support he got from the community of people he worked and played with daily gave him an endless hope. He had only occasional bad moods—depressions. But, his friends assured him, if he had manic-depressive tendencies, they were mostly on the manic side. Nothing to worry about in that.

He had started out in politics as a liberal in the early sixties. An activist in the civil rights movement, he went on marches, read books on black/white problems. As a social worker he tried to bring his insights into the homes of the clients he could never help enough. Then came the Vietnam war, and he joined a small, peaceful protest group. As the war escalated, and teach-ins and marches began, he was stirred by the motion around him. He had been waiting only for a catalyst of the right proportions. *14*

Cleveland was a city that reminded one of the reality of racism and poverty. A city where integration was preached but prejudice was as pervasive as in any southern town. A city surrounded by black and blue-collar ghettos, there was something in the unremitting bleakness of Cleveland that made him recognize the maliciousness of American affluence, something that tied him to the city like a man trying to change the woman he has married. *15*

He soon saw that that change would not come if he remained a liberal. There was something too passive in that stance, something too cautious, that would not match the breadth of his hopes. He became a radical, expounding his new vision to his wife each night when he came home from work until she was pulled along by the buoyancy of his monologues. *16*

They set off in earnest—rallies, teach-ins, meetings. Political involvement had once taken up perhaps one evening a week. Now it took up almost every night and weekend. People were constantly at their house, some staying a couple of days, others a couple of months. These guests brought a flush of possibility to their marriage, which had, like most, settled into variations on a routine. Rarely having time for each other, they found themselves the center of a community they had never expected to find, where people began by sharing political ideas and ended sharing their entire lives. *17*

At first their social gatherings were enormous—large parties, with great platters of chili, and salads, and breads, contributed and consumed collectively. Beer and wine in great abundance. Soon, though, the parties grew so large that there was not a house big enough to accommodate all the people. And then grass made people less garrulous. Head trips were more comfortable with eight or ten than with a hundred. The large group broke into small ones, and Jim and Meg met con- *18* tinually with about four other couples, all with the same political penchant—for there were of course divisions within the Movement: those who favored Cuba or China, those who were too intellectual, too eagerly critical of every country whose socialism was not quite correct enough.

19   They came to be called a collective, formed opinions together, tried acid together, ate together at least two or three times a week. There were many hugs and great warmth and understanding. They of course recognized mutual attractions, such as jokes at which one cannot repress laughter. In different houses, on weekends, or on camping trips, they made of these attractions group games. Sitting on the floor, a man and woman, not mates, would face each other, legs crossed, eyes closed, hands running across each other's face, until laughter would break the stimulation, and then they would switch partners for two other people. They shared their excitement with the group. For it was the collective that was important. To move in new couples from the living room to the bedroom would bring more harm than the thrill of a new sexual experience was worth. Besides, they had a task to accomplish—to change the country—that was more important than any personal desires.

20   He was taken with the adventure of it all. No tactic seemed too outrageous, no attack on the enemy too ambitious. Neither he nor any of the other members of his group had ever engaged in violence, but they admired the courage of revolutionaries in other countries where change meant a rejection of every comfort he had ever known. He would have been pleased, almost, if he could have traded the paved streets of his city for the mountains of Cuba or Vietnam. Thus he believed there was a place for everything—teach-ins, terrorism, demonstrations, arrests, jail, even death. Some argued that America was not ready for too much revolutionary vigor, that it would require more time, more patience, more consistent and less dramatic effort. But he was an advocate of shock therapy for the country. Missing the connection, he did not understand that since he was against the use of such techniques on sick individuals he should be against its use on a sick society as well. But he was impatient with the vision of great possibilities—the potential of himself, his friends, and that buried in the land.

21   Others would have to accept that things would from now on be in constant flux. After all, he had accepted the turning around of his entire life. From liberal to radical, from working with blacks to working with whites, from working with students to working within a community that included white-, even blue-collar workers. Endless changes—in everything he had ever known. Now there was women's liberation, of which Meg had become a leader, meeting almost daily with the women

of their collective, who formed with her a consciousness-raising group. At night she and Jim talked about the reorganization of the society now that this dimension of women's rights had been added to the struggle. A reorganization that would have to begin right in their own marriage —with dishes and cleaning and sex roles. To all these innovations he brought unflagging approval, each new idea seeming a revolutionary advance on the past. They were exhausted, he and Meg. They had lost that exclusiveness and contact they had when they met and married. But they gained things they had never expected.

It was only after several years, near his thirtieth birthday, that depression set in. Not only his depression but Meg's and their friends' and that of the world around them. After all their work, day and night, little had changed. The troops were still in Vietnam, and President Nixon, despite protest after protest, had sent bombers into Cambodia, extending rather than ending the war. Things all over the world were moving to the right rather than to the left. Homosexuals arrested in Cuba; May, 1968, in France ended with Pompidou; there was subversion in Chile; dictatorships in Greece and Brazil. He did not want to stop fighting and was still as committed as ever. But he had grown tired—"burned out" was the expression. Both he and Meg wanted a rest. There were other people to carry on—younger people. It would not be an abandonment, just time to get back to themselves. The problem was, they discovered when the motors stopped, they no longer knew who they were. 22

The marriage had not been a particularly bad one. But what had brought them together had occurred so long ago, and times had changed so much since then. In their effort to keep track of all the external transformations, it seemed that they had lost whatever it was that had made them a unit when they were twenty. And then that unit had expanded so much over these past years, had included so many people moving into their lives, their home even, that its boundaries had cracked from the strain. The effort of learning to change the language of their relationship had been superseded by the need to relate honestly to their collective, their comrades and their friends. So many events had occupied their lives for so long that now they no longer knew how to occupy each other. 23

After things had slowed down in the Movement they decided that, to save themselves, they would move everyone from the house, withdraw from politics, and work on rebuilding their personal lives. No more discussions with their friends—they would talk only to each other. Sitting in the living room of the house that had served so long as a meeting place—a house they had never really spent time making their own, although it was theirs on all the proper papers—they dissected the problem. They had grown apart; he felt she was cold, and she that his 24 moods, rapid swings to high and low, prevented any serious discussions of things that troubled her. Were they incompatible, should they just split up? No, that would be too extreme, they still had too much feeling for each other. They would work it out if they just kept at it. But they always seemed to cover the same ground without finding a solution or a new problem on which to concentrate their energies and frustrations. The circle just seemed empty without others in it.

25   The group was still there when they came out again. They had begun a new adventure, a new revolution. Smashing monogamy, it was called. It had begun rather innocently, with one couple that had gone east for a year. He had slept with someone else, then she had slept with someone else. They were still together, they had talked it out, and since it had done little harm, it was something to share with the collective. Like all of them, this couple had married young; and after spending almost ten years exclusively with each other they felt liberated by their new experiment. An imported idea, it was worth testing among all of them. None of the couples involved wanted to separate. But to be making a revolution and to continue in bourgeois marital relations was not possible, was, in fact, hypocritical. They should be able to continue loving their mates and love others as well. Sex was not something that should split up a solid relationship. Their parents would perhaps divorce if one partner had an affair, but they—they were a new world.

26   Meg began. She found another man, Paul, whom she met at work. He was easy to get along with, not as political as she, but willing to change. And this new relationship was not complicated by years of problems. She had not slept with anyone but Jim in years, having been too young and moral to sleep around in college, and too old and attached for the sexual revolution. It was her turn now. She did not hide it from Jim. Being honest was what it was all about. You could not clandestinely smash monogamy. Jim appeared only a little jealous, a little more moody. And then he found someone else, a woman named Donna. The experience was new to him also, as he had had only one or two sexual encounters before marriage and certainly none after. It would be good for him, he tried to convince himself, good for both of them, all of them.

27   But he did not want to lose Meg, to simply find one day that in all the commotion they had ceased to mean anything to each other. He depended on her being there, cared about her, even though she was often too cold or preoccupied to return that feeling. He had hoped that with work they could move on. Maybe she needed the affair, and then, when she tired of it. . . . He had taken up with Donna mainly to keep up appearances, to make Meg think he was not against this temporary experiment. Now, however, he could see that it was not to be so temporary. Her friend, lover, Paul, grew more and more attached, as did Donna.

Each lover, or friend—there was no acceptable word in the vocabulary to describe those relationships—tried to edge out the husband or wife. He had not expected this, nor had Meg, but she was more willing to carry on and see where it took them. Their other friends also encouraged them to continue. They too were exchanging partners, trying out new forms.

Meg and Jim saw Donna and Paul more and more often. They laughed when they said "Good night, have a good time" as one or the other walked out the door, or as they called each other to the phone, or welcomed each other home in the morning or the next evening. Of course the situation was uncomfortable at times, but that was something that had to be dealt with and overcome. That would be the easiest thing to overcome. Less simple was Paul's desire to be with Meg more and more frequently, in fact, to live with her—a desire she reciprocated. It was just that she didn't want to leave Jim. There must be a way that she could be with them both—and they could find that way, the four of them, only together. They were all involved, after all.   28

The living room again became a meeting room, the four of them sitting together till late in the night, trying not to divide loyalties, to agree on all that would happen. So one night it was suggested, as if by all and yet by no one in particular, that they should live together, the four of them. The house was large enough. No one wanted to leave anyone, but all wanted to spend more time with their new friends. Meg wanted to be with Jim and Paul, and Jim wanted to be with Meg and Donna; Donna wanted to be with Jim and liked Paul, and Paul. . . . It seemed a valid idea, certainly one in keeping with their political beliefs. The decision was made. The foursome had absorbed their marriage.   29

They moved in together, cooked together, ate together. Said goodbye to one another as each new couple went out. Each person had his or her own room and was free to spend the night alone or with whomever he or she chose. It was always Meg who chose first—with Jim following, then Donna and Paul—Meg who directed those choices in subtle ways, like a player pushing a pin-ball machine ever so gently so as to get the best results. At night Jim could often hear Paul and Meg making love. He recognized her cries, and found it hard, when those cries were for him, to forget the times when he was only listening in. It grew harder and harder over those next two months to forget, harder and harder to be with her, to be with Donna, to be there in that house.   30

They all began to notice the change in him. He was more and more moody, laughed less. His best friend, a man uninvolved in this new sexual trend, tried to talk with him, bring him out. But the silence had moved from his eyes throughout his entire body. His walk was no longer an enthusiastic stride. Meg also tried to talk to him, as did   31

Donna and Paul. And then one day he took the car, and for hours, despite their phone calls to everyone they knew, they had no word. Until the police called from another state.

32   He got out of the mental hospital after eight months. They had given him shock, tranquilizers, groups, therapy. He knew more about himself. It was not all Meg's fault; there was his past—insecurities, his parents, sibling rivalry. He had thought a lot in the hospital, where he was alone not only because of his illness but because of political convictions no one shared. His politics made him almost laughable to the doctors and nurses, an example of where such things get you. He held to them, but less militantly. He no longer wanted to be that jubilant, rebelliously accepting person he had been. He would have to continue to see a doctor when he got home, as it was on that condition that charges were dropped regarding the high school windows he could not remember breaking.

33   Meg had asked Paul to go, and Donna had of course left after Jim entered the hospital. So Jim returned to their house. He tried to get back his old job, but his radical reputation and psychiatric history did not make him a favorable choice. Too unstable. He worked wherever he could and Meg contributed to their support. Since he had become ill she had gotten a good job that she liked. She had not returned to politics, and was a bit warmer, trying hard to be sympathetic to his needs. But the house was too small for the two of them and the memories of all that had happened. After several months they decided to split up. It was something, they agreed, they should have done long before. They had discovered very painfully that they couldn't be together and independent at the same time. And then, Jim's lingering depression was difficult for Meg to cope with. He understood.

34   He found a small place of his own where he could have quiet. He could not stand too much pressure. He had come out all right, but certain springs were weak and could not be replaced.

35   His friends had all expected that he would smile again. That his breakdown would be like that of a car, requiring extended repair time, of course, a large mechanics bill, continued care before those around could enjoy full use of the vehicle. The seventies had brought not peace and love but bad times for all of them. Broken marriages, broken friendships. They understood what he was going through. But after a while, even though they loved him, had such fond memories, it became too trying to be with him. They could no longer slough it off as recovery time or a bad mood. He had changed and would not change back. So finally he was left alone.

Questions and Activities

1. Aristotle maintained that a person's character is the sum of his or her choices. Apply this maxim to Jim Costello's story. Point to places where Costello had choices forced on him by social conditions or where he made choices without fully realizing their consequences. Do you think society was flexible enough in its response to Costello? At what points might the people around him have been more understanding and supportive?

2. Jim Costello is gregarious and outgoing at the beginning of his story. He has many acquaintances and friends; he has been married for quite a long time. Yet Gordon features him in a chapter in a book on loneliness. What definition of loneliness serves as a foundation for this analysis of Jim Costello? Why could Costello be lonely even while he was being outgoing and friendly? How is loneliness different from being alone? How might being alone be a positive experience whereas loneliness is always a negative one?

3. Why does Gordon begin her essay almost at the end of the story? Consider the effect of the first sentence: "They found him on a country road in Pennsylvania." Do you think this opening would appeal more to a professional audience of social scientists or to a general audience? Why?

4. This is an informative essay. Informative essays emphasize the new information on a subject that a writer can provide for a reader. This new information then becomes the basis for the reader's revised understanding of the essay's subject. Assuming that loneliness is the subject of this essay, what new information on that subject has Gordon provided? How has your understanding of loneliness been expanded or altered in reading the essay? What did you already know about loneliness that was simply confirmed by reading the essay?

5. The theme of this section focuses on moral beliefs. Is it true that Jim Costello's experimentation with moral values has to be seen as a cause of his loneliness at the end of his story? Why has Costello's moral experimentation had a negative effect on his life? Can you point to an occasion when Costello's lack of definiteness might

have caused his breakdown? Can you find places in the story where Costello's attempts to experiment met with selfish insensitivity from those around him?

6. In paragraph 19, Gordon describes the "collective" that Jim Costello, his wife, and their friends formed when they were in their twenties. What ideas and feelings served to organize this group of people? Why, in later paragraphs, did these ideas fail to hold this collective together in the face of larger social changes and pressures?

7. Why does Gordon seem to avoid calling the collective a community? What is missing in a collective that exists in a community?

8. Why is Costello's marriage threatened by the collective, even though both he and his wife were participating members in it? Does this question suggest an essential conflict between the modern family and more general social ties?

9. This essay raises various questions concerning the relation of the self to society. Consider Costello's marriage. Should he have been able to depend on his wife for support as he changed his beliefs? Or should he have expected her to become independent in ways that divided them further? Also consider Costello's relations with his social group. Should he have expected to receive ongoing support from others in his group as he changed his values? Or should he have expected others in the group to go their own ways as they became independent?

▶ *LEARNING ACTIVITIES*

10. Find at least two examples of newspaper, magazine, or television advertisements that exploit people's loneliness. Write a response in which you analyze the advertisement's appeal to a typical lonely person. Would strong moral beliefs make the lonely person less vulnerable to this appeal?

11. As you read this essay, did you see any similarity to an experience of yours of loneliness? Describe that experience in an informative narrative. Was your experience of loneliness very different from Jim Costello's? Refocus your narrative around an explanation of why your experience was different from or similar to Gordon's description of Costello's loneliness.

Good Citizens

JOAN DIDION

Born in 1934, Joan Didion is one of America's most well-known New Journalists. She was born in Sacramento, California, but as a child traveled from Army base to Army base with her father, who was in the military. She has always considered Sacramento her home, and she returned to California later in life. She graduated in 1956 from the University of California at Berkeley with a major in English literature. During her senior year at Berkeley, she won *Vogue* magazine's Prix de Paris contest for young writers, having submitted an essay on William Wurster, the father of the San Francisco style of architecture. A job with *Vogue* resulted from winning this prize; Didion began working for the magazine in New York City in the summer of 1956.

Didion has written several controversial books of essays on the moral impoverishment of the American middle class—of which she, her family, and her husband are very much a part. These books of essays include *Slouching Toward Bethlehem* (1969) and *The White Album* (1979). Her journalistic essays blend personal experience with a definite sense of place—often her native California or New York City, where she worked for many years as a journalist for *Vogue* and the *Saturday Evening Post*. Didion's novels—*Run River* (1978), *Play It as It Lays* (1978), and *A Book of Common Prayer* (1977)—also chronicle the moral degeneration apparent in different aspects of American culture, including California middle-class life and Hollywood.

To Didion, the effect of place on a modern individual's sense of reality, however, is seldom positive. New York City, for example, for all its allure and glamour, made Didion feel alienated and isolated from others during her stay there as a young journalist and publishing employee. California, the focus of attention in many of her books, for all its sunny pleasures, seems to cast people in busy but aimless lives. The American promised land, to Didion, seems not to have provided its inhabitants with the spiritual values that would make them able to withstand the temptations of physical pleasure and materialism.

As you read, consider Didion's concern with moral values, or the lack of them. If American life has become a dominantly materialistic dream of success, how can we know *what* to believe in, other than the objects we possess, the places in which we live, and the people we can control through wealth and power?

Didion's style has often been singled out for praise or criticism. She writes a fragmented, almost disconnected prose, which many critics believe is meant to reinforce her vision of the sterile inner lives of her subjects. Her prose is held together by often striking pairs of images within otherwise rather colorless or prosaic sentences. Take note of Didion's imagery as you read this essay:

1. How does Didion's imagery serve to reinforce what she is saying about the people she is describing?
2. Do her images seem drawn from a particular place? What are your personal associations with these images? Do those associations draw you into a specific pattern of response?
3. Do you consider the people and places that Didion describes in this essay far removed from your own experience? Are the people around you different from the people she describes? Does the place you live in affect you negatively or positively?

▶ ─────────────────────

1.

1   I was once invited to a civil rights meeting at Sammy Davis, Jr.'s house, in the hills above the Sunset Strip. "Let me tell you how to get to Sammy's," said the woman to whom I was talking. "You turn left at the old Mocambo." I liked the ring of this line, summing up as it did a couple of generations of that peculiar vacant fervor which is Hollywood political action, but acquaintances to whom I repeated it seemed uneasy. Politics are not widely considered a legitimate source of amusement in Hollywood, where the borrowed rhetoric by which political ideas are reduced to choices between the good (equality is good) and the bad (genocide is bad) tends to make even the most casual political small talk resemble a rally. "Those who cannot remember the past are condemned to repeat it," someone said to me at dinner not long ago, and before we had finished our *fraises des bois* he had advised me as well that "no man is an island." As a matter of fact I hear that no man is an island once or twice a week, quite often from people who think they are quoting Ernest Hemingway. "What a sacrifice on the altar of nationalism," I heard an actor say about the death in a plane crash of the president of the Philippines. It is a way of talking that tends to preclude further discussion, which may well be its intention: the public life of liberal Hollywood comprises a kind of dictatorship of good intentions, a social contract in which actual and irreconcilable disagreement is as

taboo as failure or bad teeth, a climate devoid of irony. "Those men are our unsung heroes," a quite charming and intelligent woman once said to me at a party in Beverly Hills. She was talking about the California State Legislature.

I remember spending an evening in 1968, a week or so before the   2
California primary and Robert Kennedy's death, at Eugene's in Beverly Hills, one of the "clubs" opened by supporters of Eugene McCarthy. The Beverly Hills Eugene's, not unlike Senator McCarthy's campaign itself, had a certain *déjà vu* aspect to it, a glow of 1952 humanism: there were Ben Shahn posters on the walls, and the gesture toward a strobe light was nothing that might interfere with "good talk," and the music was not 1968 rock but the kind of jazz people used to have on their record players when everyone who believed in the Family of Man bought Scandinavian stainless-steel flatware and voted for Adlai Stevenson. There at Eugene's I heard the name "Erich Fromm" for the first time in a long time, and many other names cast out for the sympathetic magic they might work ("I saw the Senator in San Francisco, where I was with Mrs. Leonard Bernstein. . ."), and then the evening's main event: a debate between William Styron and the actor Ossie Davis. It was Mr. Davis' contention that in writing *The Confessions of Nat Turner* Mr. Styron had encouraged racism ("Nat Turner's love for a white maiden, I feel my country can become psychotic about this"), and it was Mr. Styron's contention that he had not. (David Wolper, who had bought the motion picture rights to *Nat Turner*, had already made his position clear: "How can anyone protest a book," he had asked in the trade press," that has withstood the critical test of time since last October?") As the evening wore on, Mr. Styron said less and less, and Mr. Davis more and more ("So you might ask, why didn't *I* spend five years and write *Nat Turner*? I won't go into my reasons why, but. . ."), and James Baldwin sat between them, his eyes closed and his head thrown back in understandable but rather theatrical agony. Mr. Baldwin summed up: "If Bill's book does no more than what it's done tonight, it's a very important event." "Hear, hear," cried someone sitting on the floor, and there was general agreement that it had been a stimulating and significant evening.

Of course there was nothing crucial about that night at Eugene's in   3
1968, and of course you could tell me that there was certainly no harm and perhaps some good in it. But its curious vanity and irrelevance stay with me, if only because those qualities characterize so many of Hollywood's best intentions. Social problems present themselves to many of these people in terms of a scenario, in which, once certain key scenes are licked (the confrontation on the courthouse steps, the revelation that the opposition leader has an anti-Semitic past, the presentation of

the bill of particulars to the President, a Henry Fonda cameo), the plot will proceed inexorably to an upbeat fade. Marlon Brando does not, in a well-plotted motion picture, picket San Quentin in vain: what we are talking about here is faith in a dramatic convention. Things "happen" in motion pictures. There is always a resolution, always a strong cause-effect dramatic line, and to perceive the world in those terms is to assume an ending for every social scenario. If Budd Schulberg goes into Watts and forms a Writers' Workshop, then "Twenty Young Writers" must emerge from it, because the scenario in question is the familiar one about how the ghetto teems with raw talent and vitality. If the poor people march on Washington and camp out, there to receive bundles of clothes gathered on the Fox lot by Barbra Streisand, then some good must come of it (the script here has a great many dramatic staples, not the least of them a sentimental notion of Washington as an open forum, cf. *Mr. Deeds Goes to Washington*), and doubts have no place in the story.

4   There are no bit players in Hollywood politics: everyone makes things "happen." As it happens I live in a house in Hollywood in which, during the late thirties and early fifties, a screenwriters' cell of the Communist Party often met. Some of the things that are in the house now were in it then: a vast Stalinist couch, the largest rag rug I have ever seen, cartons of *New Masses*. Some of the people who came to meetings in the house were blacklisted, some of them never worked again and some of them are now getting several hundred thousand dollars a picture; some of them are dead and some of them are bitter and most of them lead very private lives. Things did change, but in the end it was not they who made things change, and their enthusiasms and debates sometimes seem very close to me in this house. In a way the house suggests the particular vanity of perceiving social life as a problem to be solved by the good will of individuals, but I do not mention that to many of the people who visit me here.

2.

5   Pretty Nancy Reagan, the wife then of the Governor of California, was standing in the dining room of her rented house on 45th Street in Sacramento, listening to a television newsman explain what he wanted to do. She was listening attentively. Nancy Reagan is a very attentive listener. The television crew wanted to watch her, the newsman said, while she was doing precisely what she would ordinarily be doing on a Tuesday morning at home. Since I was also there to watch her doing precisely what she would ordinarily be doing on a Tuesday morning at home, we seemed to be on the verge of exploring certain media frontiers: the television newsman and the two cameramen could

watch Nancy Reagan being watched by me, or I could watch Nancy Reagan being watched by the three of them, or one of the cameramen could step back and do a *cinéma vérité* study of the rest of us watching and being watched by one another. I had the distinct sense that we were on the track of something revelatory, the truth about Nancy Reagan at 24 frames a second, but the television newsman opted to overlook the moment's peculiar essence. He suggested that we watch Nancy Reagan pick flowers in the garden. "That's something you might ordinarily do, isn't it?" he asked. "Indeed it is," Nancy Reagan said with spirit. Nancy Reagan says almost everything with spirit, perhaps because she was once an actress and has the beginning actress's habit of investing even the most casual lines with a good deal more dramatic emphasis than is ordinarily called for on a Tuesday morning on 45th Street in Sacramento. "Actually," she added then, as if about to disclose a delightful surprise, "actually, I really *do* need flowers."

She smiled at each of us, and each of us smiled back. We had all been 6
smiling quite a bit that morning. "And then," the television newsman said thoughtfully, surveying the dining-room table, "even though you've got a beautiful arrangement right now, we could set up the pretense of your arranging, you know, the flowers."

We all smiled at one another again, and then Nancy Reagan walked 7
resolutely into the garden, equipped with a decorative straw basket about six inches in diameter. "Uh, Mrs. Reagan," the newsman called after her. "May I ask what you're going to select for flowers?"

"Why, I don't know," she said, pausing with her basket on a garden 8
step. The scene was evolving its own choreography.

"Do you think you could use rhododendrons?" 9

Nancy Reagan looked critically at a rhododendron bush. Then she 10
turned to the newsman and smiled. "Did you know there's a Nancy Reagan rose now?"

"Uh, no," he said. "I didn't." 11

"It's awfully pretty, it's a kind of, of, a kind of coral color." 12

"Would the. . .the Nancy Reagan rose be something you might be 13
likely to pick now?"

A silvery peal of laughter. "I could certainly *pick* it. But I won't be 14
using it." A pause. "I *can* use the rhododendron."

"Fine," the newsman said. "Just fine. Now I'll ask a question, and if 15
you could just be nipping a bud as you answer it. . ."

"Nipping a bud," Nancy Reagan repeated, taking her place in front of 16
the rhododendron bush.

"Let's have a dry run," the cameraman said. 17

The newsman looked at him. "In other words, by a dry run, you 18
mean you want her to fake nipping the bud."

"Fake the nip, yeah," the cameraman said. "Fake the nip." 19

3.

20   Outside the Miramar Hotel in Santa Monica a hard subtropical rain had been falling for days. It scaled still more paint from the faded hotels and rooming houses that front the Pacific along Ocean Avenue. It streamed down the blank windows of unleased offices, loosened the soft coastal cliffs and heightened the most characteristic Santa Monica effect, that air of dispirited abandon which suggests that the place survives only as illustration of a boom gone bankrupt, evidence of some irreversible flaw in the laissez-faire small-business ethic. In any imaginative sense Santa Monica seemed an eccentric place for the United States Junior Chamber of Commerce to be holding a national congress, but there they were, a thousand delegates and wives, gathered in the Miramar Hotel for a relentless succession of keynote banquets and award luncheons and prayer breakfasts and outstanding-young-men forums. Now it was the President's Luncheon and everyone was listening to an animated singing group called The New Generation and I was watching the pretty young wife of one delegate pick sullenly at her lunch. "Let someone else eat this slop," she said suddenly, her voice cutting through not only the high generalities of the occasion but The New Generation's George M. Cohan medley as well. Her husband looked away, and she repeated it. To my left another delegate was urging me to ask every man in the room how the Jaycees had changed his life. I watched the girl down the table and asked the delegate how the Jaycees had changed his life. "It saved my marriage and it built my business," he whispered. "You could find a thousand inspirational stories right here at this President's Luncheon." Down the table the young wife was sobbing into a pink napkin. The New Generation marched into "Supercalifragilisticexpialidocious." In many ways the Jaycees' 32nd Annual Congress of America's Ten Outstanding Young Men was a curious and troubling way to spend a few days in the opening weeks of 1970.

21   I suppose I went to Santa Monica in search of the abstraction lately called "Middle America," went to find out how the Jaycees, with their Couéistic emphasis on improving one's world and one's self simultaneously, had weathered these past several years of cultural shock. In a very real way the Jaycees have exemplified, usually so ingenuously that it was popular to deride them, certain ideas shared by almost all of the people in America's small cities and towns and by at least some of the people in America's large cities, ideas shared in an unexamined way even by those who laughed at the Jaycees' boosterism and pancake breakfasts and safe-driving Road-e-os. There was the belief in business success as a transcendent ideal. There was the faith that if one trans-

forms oneself from an "introvert" into an "extrovert," if one learns to "speak effectively" and "do a job," success and its concomitant, spiritual grace, follow naturally. There was the approach to international problems which construed the underdeveloped world as a temporarily depressed area in need mainly of People-to-People programs. ("Word of Operation Brotherhood swept through the teeming masses of Asia like a fresh wind from the sea," reads a Jaycee report on one such program in the late Fifties.) If only because these ideas, these last rattles of Social Darwinism, had in fact been held in common by a great many people who never bothered to articulate them, I wondered what the Jaycees were thinking now, wondered what their mood might be at a time when, as their national president put it one day at the Miramar, "so much of America seems to be looking at the negative."

At first I thought I had walked out of the rain into a time warp: the　*22* Sixties seemed not to have happened. All these Jaycees were, by definition, between 21 and 35 years old, but there was a disquieting tendency among them to have settled foursquare into middle age. There was the heavy jocularity, the baroque rhetoric of another generation entirely, a kind of poignant attempt to circumnavigate social conventions that had in fact broken down in the Twenties. Wives were lovely and forbearing. Getting together for drinks was having a cocktail reception. Rain was liquid sunshine and the choice of a table for dinner was making an executive decision. They knew that this was a brave new world and they said so. It was time to "put brotherhood into action," to "open our neighborhoods to those of all colors." It was time to "turn attention to the cities," to think about youth centers and clinics and the example set by a black policeman-preacher in Philadelphia who was organizing a decency rally patterned after Miami's. It was time to "decry apathy."

The word "apathy" cropped up again and again, an odd word to use　*23* in relation to the past few years, and it was a while before I realized what it meant. It was not simply a word remembered from the Fifties, when most of these men had frozen their vocabularies: it was a word meant to indicate that not enough of "our kind" were speaking out. It was a cry in the wilderness, and this resolute determination to meet 1950 head-on was a kind of refuge. Here were some people who had been led to believe that the future was always a rational extension of the past, that there would ever be world enough and time for "turning attention," for "problems" and "solutions." Of course they would not admit their inchoate fears that the world was not that way any more. Of course they would not join the "fashionable doubters." Of course they would ignore the "pessimistic pundits." Late one afternoon I sat in the Miramar lobby, watching the rain fall and the steam rise off the heated pool outside and listening to a couple of Jaycees discussing student unrest and whether the "solution" might not lie in on-campus Jaycee groups. I thought about this astonishing notion for a long time. It occurred to me finally that I was listening to a true underground, to the voice of all those who have felt themselves not merely shocked but personally betrayed by recent history. It was supposed to have been their time. It was not.

Questions and Activities

▶ *COMPREHENSION QUESTIONS*

1. What is the point of the report on the debate between William Styron and Ossie Davis (paragraph 2)? Is the debate itself important, or is Didion's point more directly related to the reactions it provokes from the Hollywood personalities?
2. Take one of the subjects of Didion's social analysis and reread the part of the essay that describes and analyzes that person. Then make a list of the characteristics of that person that seem to be important to Didion. What beliefs and values are found in or implied by your list?
3. Who is Eric Fromm (paragraph 2)? When was he popular? (You can find information about him in any biographical dictionary of contemporary authors in the reference section of a library.)
4. Identify the writers, musicians, artists, actors, and historical and political figures mentioned in this essay (Sammy Davis, Jr., Ernest Hemingway, Eugene McCarthy, Ben Shahn, Adlai Stevenson, William Styron, Ossie Davis, Nat Turner, etc.). Tell what each is best known for and why he or she fits in the context. Also, find out what you can about the California cities of Malibu and Sacramento. What kinds of people live there? What is the geography and climate? What industries or businesses, if any, are located there?

▶ *QUESTIONS OF RHETORICAL PURPOSE AND STRATEGY*

5. This essay has an expressive purpose. Expressive writers use writing as a means of discovering what they think about a subject. Most of the time expressive writing is intentionally incomplete and completely personal; it simply serves as a tool for writers as they discover their thoughts. Some talented writers polish their expressive writings and publish them as personal statements on general subjects.

Look back over Didion's essay and mark several places where you think she has made a personal discovery, as the climax to several pages of description and observation.

6. Expressive writing is often defined by the voice with which the writer decides to address his or her audience. Does Didion sound like someone who is arguing a point or more like someone who is thinking aloud about serious subjects? What in the language of the essay helps you answer this question?

▶ *THEME QUESTIONS*

7. What are the points of the reports on Nancy Reagan and the Jaycees convention? How do they relate to the point of the Hollywood vignette? Summarize this essay's overall view of contemporary society by combining the points Didion makes in each of its three parts.

8. What qualities do the people represented in this essay share? What, for example, does Nancy Reagan have in common with the Jaycees? Can you make a list of common characteristics shared by all three of the character types Didion describes? What do these common qualities reveal about how Didion sees the modern character?

▶ *LEARNING ACTIVITIES*

9. Think of a time when another person openly revealed his or her beliefs to you, much as the Jaycees do in this essay. Work that event into a story like the ones Didion uses in this essay. Imitate Didion's style as well as her method of organizing a story. To warm up for this activity, you might copy one of Didion's paragraphs word for word.

10. Look back over the story you wrote in Didion's style and mark those places where you feel you discovered a new perspective on or idea about your subject.

11. Didion's essay has no explicit thesis. Write a paragraph that might be used as an introduction to her essay if it were an academic assignment. The introduction should state the essay's thesis and orient the reader to Didion's subject. (You will be giving Didion's essay an informative rather than an expressive or personal purpose in doing this.) Discuss the effectiveness of your introduction with other members of your class.

Lee Iacocca and the Making of the Mustang

DAVID ABODAHER

David Abodaher has had a long and successful career as an advertising writer, a radio and television producer, and a writer of thirteen books for young adults. He began his career as program director and production manager for radio stations in Oklahoma City, Oklahoma, and Kalamazoo, Michigan. Next, he was radio director of several advertising firms in Detroit, Michigan. His work in Detroit soon brought him into contact with the automobile industry, first as an automobile account executive and writer for various advertising agencies and later as a freelance advertising writer and as the J. Walter Thompson agency's chief advertising writer for the Ford Motor Company account from 1964 to 1969, the years immediately following the Mustang's introduction. In the 1970s and 1980s, Abodaher has continued his career as an advertising writer in the Detroit area, serving as the Kenyon and Eckhardt agency's senior writer from 1977 to 1983.

Abodaher published his successful young-adult books about historical figures and automobiles during the time he was building his career in advertising. In 1982, he published his first book for an adult audience, a biography of automobile executive Lee Iacocca, from which the essay that follows was taken.

As you read this essay on how Lee Iacocca developed the Mustang, note Abodaher's facility with story telling. He is able, as a result of his years of experience in writing advertising copy, to describe a scene or event in a way that entertains while it clearly makes a point. In this essay, whenever Abodaher tells an anecdote or recreates a scene, he is careful to summarize in a way that makes a point about Lee Iacocca, his primary subject.

Lee Iacocca was born in Scranton, Pennsylvania, to Italian-American middle-class parents. He received engineering degrees from Lehigh University and Princeton, then went to work with the Ford Motor Company as a junior executive. His early success in the sales and promotion area brought him to the Ford central office in Dearborn, where he quickly rose to vice president and, later, president of the company. His most significant accomplishment as a Ford executive was his development and promotion of the highly successful Mustang. In 1978, however, because of a conflict with Henry Ford II, the chairman of the board, Iacocca was fired. Only three months later, he agreed to assume the presidency of the failing Chrysler Corporation. He was able in the following years to improve Chrysler's efficiency and sales sufficiently to acquire federal loans that enabled the corporation to survive and to regain most of its former stature in the automobile industry.

By introducing the Mustang and later saving Chrysler from bankruptcy, Iacocca became America's new model of the self-made man. As you read this description of Iacocca's work on the Mustang, notice how Abodaher emphasizes Iacocca's business virtues: his persistence in the face of denial, his self-assuredness, his ability to gauge the kind of automobile many Americans wanted, and his tough competitiveness in the face of opposition. Think about these questions as you read:

1. How does Abodaher accomplish his emphasis on Iacocca's particular virtues? How does he use combinations of anecdotes, direct quotations, narration, and specific description to create this emphasis?
2. How is Abodaher able to catalog the virtues of his subject without seeming preachy? Do you ever feel that Abodaher is manipulating facts to make Iacocca look better than he is? If so, what in Abodaher's writing causes that feeling?
3. Do you think Abodaher knows the automobile industry and its history well enough to be accepted as an expert on his subject? What in his writing makes you think that Abodaher is or is not an expert?

▶ ————————————————————

Unaware that he was creating a legend, Lee Iacocca initiated   1
plans for the first automobile he could call his own. His primary objective was to give American car buyers the kind of automobile they wanted. Iacocca was determined that his new car would be something special. It had to be, for he sensed that the American public had become more demanding and more quality conscious, that a change in public tastes was in the air.

A significant factor in Iacocca's thinking were the imports, which   2
were eating up an increasingly larger share of the American market. The import invasion had begun after World War II when England's manufacturers returned to car production before their counterparts in the United States were given the go-ahead by Washington.

The perky and sporty MG led the way, sending one-third of its 1946   3
production, 500 cars, across the Atlantic. Jaguar quickly followed. American GIs in Europe had been exposed to the sportier styling of British and European cars, many of which, like the MG, were smaller

than U.S. models, and they had learned to like them. Given a choice between a used American car and a new European model, many opted for the latter. In no time MG's most profitable market was the United States. Jaguar also found a bonanza on the western shores of the Atlantic. When its XK120, a stock car that sold for about $4,000, was delivered in the United States, it became an overnight sensation among fine-car buffs.

4   By 1948 the imports had achieved the modest American market penetration of 0.46 percent. It was so small, compared to GM's more than 40 percent, Chrysler's over 21 percent, and even Ford's near 19 percent, that American carmakers had not been concerned. Nor were they worried in 1956, when the import share climbed to 1.65 percent of American sales, even though it was more than double that of the previous year.

5   Volkswagen's Beetle and its smart Kharmann-Ghia coupe had hit American buyers in 1955, accounting for the sharp rise in import sales. Toyota and Datsun, from Japan, followed in 1957 and 1958, respectively. By the end of 1959 imports had achieved a startling 10.17 percent of American car sales, taking just over 4.25 percent from General Motors and over 2.5 percent from Chrysler. Thanks to Falcon, Ford earned a 1.68 percent increase.

6   A sharp diagnostician, Iacocca found further reinforcement for his concept of a new car in the sales figures for 1960, a year in which both GM and Chrysler introduced new compact cars to increase their shares of the American market at the expense of the imports and Ford.

7   Just a few months before Lee Iacocca's promotion to general manager of Ford Division—a pressure-laden responsibility since Ford Division produced 80 percent of the company's car—Chrysler had brought out its compact Plymouth Valiant, with a 101-horsepower, six-cylinder engine and a revolutionary electrical alternator. The new Valiant helped boost Plymouth sales by 55,486 in 1960.

8   At about the same time GM's Chevrolet Division offered its air-cooled, independently sprung, rear-engined Corvair. Corvair sold surprisingly well—it would be some time before Ralph Nader's book *Unsafe at Any Speed* would deal it a death blow—boosting Chevy's 1960 sales 277,794 over the previous year.

9   One factor in Corvair's sales charts particularly intrigued Iacocca. The highest number of Corvair sales went to its sporty version called Monza, a car that to a great degree reflected the styling of the European imports. But Lee was not totally convinced that the Corvair Monza provided a barometer for what Americans hungered for in an automobile. Certainly, Monza's success indicated that Ford Motor Company's lack of sportily styled automobiles had caused its decrease in 1960 of more

than 50,000 sales while Chevy registrations shot up over a quarter-million. Yet Iacocca felt that sportiness alone was not the complete answer.

A somewhat clearer picture emerged from a survey taken of the extra   10
equipment ordered for Ford Falcons. A great percentage of buyers had paid extra for more powerful engines, automatic transmissions, power features, and decorative items such as paint stripes and white sidewall tires. Americans, it seemed, did not want plain, unexciting cars.

Nonetheless, the picture of trends in American buyer wants in auto-   11
mobiles was still cloudy. Iacocca needed a sharper focus to avoid an Edsel fiasco. The Edsel's styling had not been thoroughly researched.

To get a handle on public preference Lee gathered a staff of twenty   12
young researchers and put them on a crash schedule. He told them to find out what kind of car Americans wanted. How big or small? How much power? What kind of styling? What special equipment?

His researchers polled students, young marrieds, the middle-aged,   13
Korean veterans, even Monza buyers. Surprisingly few interviewees cared for anything then on the market. Some pointed to the small, jazzy Europeans as ''maybe'' their kind of car. Most said only that they would like ''something different.''

Early on in his new position Lee Iacocca had put together a staff of ca-   14
pable aides, specialists in engineering, product planning, styling, and merchandising. Hal Sperlick was one. Gar Laux, Don Frey, and Joe Oros were others. Together with Lee they analyzed the research results in depth.

They soon noted that a new market segment, with its own buying   15
patterns, had been growing gradually among young buyers, the eighteen- and nineteen-year-olds ready for their first car, as well as the young marrieds who were then taking on family responsibilities at an earlier age. They wanted a car with flair in its styling.

As the Iacocca team dug further, it discovered that this same sporti-   16
ness was desired by a sizable percentage of the middle-aged and older, the ''young at heart'' who wanted to express their youthful spirit in a car with gusto. Television had proved to be the foundation of youth that washed away the stodgy and dull in their lives and instilled a passion for excitement and adventure.

The research revealed another important factor. A growing economy   17
was producing a more affluent middle class. The number of two-car families was growing, and they preferred a smaller, personalized automobile for their second car.

These multiple findings established a profile of the automobile Lee's   18
intuition told him would please American buyers. This would be his first contribution to the Ford product line. Plan a car that is easy to han-

dle, he ordered his team, a car styled with zip and class, lower and longer in front than other American makes, and shorter in the rear deck. Make it an automobile that performs with dash, that can go from zero to sixty in seven or eight seconds. And, very important, he emphasized, produce a car affordable for young America.

19   "Lee was very much personally involved in every phase of the car right from scratch," Hal Sperlick said. "He wanted to pave some fresh ground as the new vice-president of Ford Division. He wanted this car to hit a ready market and make the statement that Ford really was back in the mainstream of the automobile business."

20   Iacocca was not looking for a small car per se, Sperlick made clear. "There were some small cars out, like the Falcon and Monza," he said. "But Lee was looking for a distinctive kind of car. From cars already on the market you could buy only either a big car or a smaller, plain kind, and there wasn't a really nice smaller car available. If you wanted a nice car, you had to buy a Lincoln or Cadillac, but that was it."

21   In late October of 1961 Iacocca approved the specifications for the car as recommended by Sperlick and his product-planning team. It should weigh no more than 2,500 pounds and be no more than fifteen feet (180 inches) in overall length. And its retail price should be $2,500 or less.

22   The next step was to create a clay model based on the specifications. Lee discussed the matter with Eugene Bordinat, Ford Motor Company's chief designer. Bordinat arranged a competition between the company's three design studios, the Ford Division, Lincoln-Mercury, and Corporate studios. Each would take the specifications and come up with one or more clay models reflecting their individual conceptions of how the car should look.

23   Within two weeks the studios had seven clay models ready for inspection by Iacocca and his team. The one designed by Joe Oros, Ford Division's head stylist, had the lines and smart styling Lee wanted. It was a different, unique breed of automobile that measured less than twenty-nine inches from the ground to the top of the hood and only 154 inches in overall length, twenty-six inches shorter than the original specifications called for.

24   Lee was pleased with Oros's design at first sight. His initial plan had been a two-seater, much like the original Thunderbird, but he had changed his mind, asking that a small back seat be added. His gut reaction as he examined the clay model of a convertible was that they were on the right track.

25   But what about Henry Ford II? How would he look on this project, which had been put together secretly? It would take many millions of

dollars to tool up for and put into production such a car, and Henry's yes or no meant its life or death.

Protocol demanded that Iacocca approach Arjay Miller, the company   26
president, before going to Ford, the board chairman. But Lee, impatient at any small delay, went directly to Henry's suite in the Glass House. Henry all but literally threw him out of the office. He had absolutely no interest.

Lee returned to Ford Division undismayed. He knew he was right,   27
and however long it took, he would prove it. In a week he was back at the Glass House, trying to persuade Henry that the market was ready for this type of smaller car. An angry Henry again showed Lee the door, making it clear he was not interested in a small car.

A third and fourth trip found Henry gradually weakening, showing a   28
bit of interest, but still opposed. But Lee, realizing that he was developing a sort of inevitability for the success of his project, persisted. The fifth time at Henry's office he was able to outline details of the research he had conducted. Henry finally agreed to at least come and take a look.

At the Styling Center, surrounded by Iacocca, Sperlick, and other   29
Ford Division men, Henry still shook his head. Neither Lee Iacocca nor Hal Sperlick could convince Henry, however aggressively they sold the concept of the new automobile or the need for it in the marketplace. Henry was nervous over the failure of the Edsel and the resulting cash drain on the company, yet he finally agreed to think it over.

Iacocca already had set himself a timetable that would be shattered if   30
he had to wait for Henry's final decision. He took a chance and gave his team a go-ahead to proceed to the next phase, building an actual-size model from laminated hardwoods.

He had good reasons for his seeming impatience. As vital as secrecy is   31
in the highly competitive automobile business, where every security caution possible is taken, word of activity on anything new does leak out. Lee already knew that Chevrolet was considering a scaled-down version of the successful Corvette, and he was determined to beat them into the market.

Lee also realized that rumors were buzzing around Detroit about an   32
unusual new two-seater sports-type car on the Ford drawing boards. He hoped that these fast-spreading but unconfirmed reports would not send Chevrolet into a crash program that would upset his own schedule. He had to have a prototype ready the moment Henry approved funding for production—if, indeed, he gave the go-ahead.

Speculation about the new one from Ford escalated throughout the   33
industry, and Lee had a plan to feed those rumors. Dependent on Henry

II's decision, he intended to unveil a prototype of some kind during the annual running of the 1962 American Grand Prix at Watkins Glen, New York, on October 7.

34   Meanwhile Iacocca and his team busied themselves with deciding on a name for his creation. The name of a new car is vitally important to its marketability and sales success. In order to stir buyer enthusiasm it had to be catchy, memorable, and meaningful in terms of the car's image, a name that could be translated into advertising impact.

35   Merely for identification Iacocca's team referred to the new automobile as the Special Falcon. But nothing like the name Falcon was to be considered. Falcon was a Bob McNamara offering, and the all-new concept had to be perceived as an Iacocca production. Lee ordered the Ford Division advertising agency, J. Walter Thompson, to suggest names. The agency reported back with a list numbering more than 5,000. On the list were Colt, Bronco, Cheetah, Torino, Cougar, and Mustang.

36   Joe Oros had referred to his clay model as Cougar, and for a time that name was considered. Then a decision was made to call the car Torino, since it had a Ferrari flavor and Ferrari was built in Turin, a city the Italians call Torino. Torino was considered so seriously that J. Walter Thompson prepared potential advertisements using that name.

37   Despite all the pre-preparation the name Torino was suddenly dropped. One Ford executive said that the name had become an embarrassment since Henry Ford II was at the time pursuing Cristina all over Europe while his divorce was still pending. Iacocca, it was said, feared that the press would play the Italian connection to the hilt, making a mockery of the car's introduction.

38   Gar Laux, who was close to Lee throughout the car's development, is inclined to discount that story. "Look at the car," he said. "Look at the first prototype, then the second, and finally the car that was introduced. It looked, that first little one at Watkins Glen, like an Italian import. But when the car went on the market, it was all-American. Its looks had changed, so the name had to change. It became the Yankee-doodle car, and a name like Torino didn't fit. Mustang did. Made you think of wild charging horses and the wide-open west. The name and the car, they were both as American as all hell!"

39   Getting the approval of Henry Ford II to build Mustang took time and some doing on Lee Iacocca's part. As structured under Henry Ford II the Ford Motor Company was heavily financed-oriented, in sharp contrast to the fiscal looseness of the company under his grandfather. As a result every major investment was a difficult sell. Henry was not about to commit millions of dollars to produce anything but a sure hit. Undismayed, Iacocca collared Henry at every opportunity, either alone or

with Hal Sperlick's backing. Sperlick was as confident in, and as excited about, their planned car as was Lee. But Henry continued to hold out, demanding solid facts and figures to justify spending millions.

Yet, when Lee and Sperlick provided the facts and figures and peppered Henry with the results of their surveys, Henry remained opposed. Sure of his ground, Lee did not give up. 40

On September 10, 1962, Lee made another trip to the Glass House office of Henry Ford II. He again presented his case for a car that his gut feeling told him would bowl over the industry. 41

This time Henry, obviously weakening, agreed to take another look. He went with Lee to the Styling Center and examined the prototype from bumper to bumper. Finally he opened the passenger-side door and sat in the rear seat. 42

Henry, as the story goes, frowned for a moment. The back seat did not have enough room, he said. The car should provide an additional inch of space in the rear. 43

Iacocca, Sperlick, and the design team surrounding the car disagreed. Adding even that inch of space would destroy the styling, they all agreed. Henry would not listen. It had to be his way or there would be no new car. 44

Losing a small battle was better than total defeat. The designers and stylists added the extra space. Iacocca's persuasiveness had paid off at small cost. Henry approved an appropriation of $51 million for production of the new Mustang. 45

Iacocca and Sperlick were jubilant as they rushed back to Ford Division, but they had little time to savor their victory because a lot of work remained before the blue prototype could be shipped under wraps to Watkins Glen. After nearly a month's work around-the-clock, everything was ready. 46

The afternoon of October 7, 1962, 35,000 race buffs filled the Watkins Glen grandstand as a hard rain swept across the oval. They were there primarily to see some of the world's greatest race drivers compete in the American Grand Prix, but for hours curious eyes were focused on a platform in the infield where something was shrouded in canvas. 47

After Scotland's champion driver Jim Clark swept across the finish line as winner in his Lotus-Climax, the tarpaulin was removed. There it stood, now identified as Experimental Mustang I. In minutes thousands of spectators sloshed through mud and wet grass to get a close-up view of the little blue car with a Ferrari flair. 48

Standing no higher than a baby's crib, it had a long, sloping front end that ended hardly a foot from the platform floor. It had no headlights. It 49 was equipped with a V-4 engine installed, not under the hood like most American cars, not at the rear like a Volkswagen Beetle or Corvair, but in the middle like many classic European cars.

50   It had been planned as a smoke screen, a showcase car displayed to throw all competition off base, one with just enough of the future Mustang to whet the appetite—if indeed American car buyers reacted with pleasure. It was there to give Iacocca the assurance that he was on the right track.

51   At the unveiling Lee knew he was. The enthusiasm of the thousands crowding around the platform oblivious of the torrential rain gave him his answer. The hundreds in the crowd trying to place orders immediately buttressed his confidence.

52   Of course it was impossible to take orders, however loudly the crowd clamored. The real Mustang would not be ready for sale for almost two years.

53   After his return to Dearborn Iacocca realized that a way would have to be found to maintain and nourish the astounding interest generated at Watkins Glen in a car not yet ready for final production. A means had to be found for placating the media, which was bombarding him, Walter Murphy, and his Ford public relations staff with questions.

54   Iacocca could not afford to dampen this mounting Mustang momentum. Since he was not ready to release details about his final product, he decided on preparing another red herring to keep curiosity boiling. He ordered the building of a second Mustang prototype.

55   The front and back ends of Experimental Mustang I were chopped and pointed fenders added to give the new showpiece a different look. Since Mustang I, with its aerodynamic front end, had no headlights, recessed headlamps with glass covers were installed. Experimental Mustang II was also given an open-mouthed grille in which was centered the soon-to-become-ubiquitous galloping pony emblem.

56   Iacocca was playing a cloak-and-dagger game to give himself time to produce the real Mustang while throwing competition off. So he created Experimental Mustang II as another hybrid, part real Mustang and part fantasy, though less a phantom of the mind than the first.

57   No secret was made of the plan to reveal the new prototype. It was sent off with panoply and fanfare to the 1963 Watkins Glen American Grand Prix. Unlike 1962, this showing was not intended as a sneak preview. Newspapers, television, and radio reported the upcoming event. Journalists speculated as much about the car as about the race itself. Not surprisingly, attendance at Watkins Glen was far greater than in 1962.

58   Iacocca had hoped for a large crowd, for the reaction of the thousands at Watkins Glen would reassure him that his new car had what would

be needed to crowd Ford showrooms once the real Mustang was introduced.

Iacocca need not have worried. A hungry, eager crowd swarmed excitedly about the platform displaying his four-wheeled offspring. Not only young people, but men and women of middle age and older, shouted at anyone who appeared to be a Ford representative demanding, as hundreds had done the year before, to place orders.

The usually impassive Iacocca could not suppress a smile. If only Henry Ford II, who had fought production of Mustang for so long, were there to see.

Back at the Ford Division offices Iacocca, Sperlick, Laux, and others on his Mustang team sat around a conference table relishing their victory. They had many things to discuss, including the refinements that would transform Experimental Mustang II into the real thing. Just as important was the matter of Mustang's introduction.

New car models were at the time normally introduced in the fall, which would mean a year's wait. Iacocca was not about to have Mustang's debut diluted by other car intros. He put production on an all-out basis. "Make Mustang happen," he told his staff. "And make it quick."

Lee Iacocca had involved himself at all levels leading to the creation of the Mustang, a rarity in the industry. Now his primary efforts could be directed toward promotion and marketing, at which he was a master. The two exposures at Watkins Glen were just the forerunners of a promotion blitz unequaled in any area of the business world.

Lee did not permit any letdown after the smash success at Watkins Glen. Within weeks he had his staff invite fifty young, middle-income couples to the Ford Styling Center as a means of confirming consumer reactions to Mustang. They came in small groups, they looked and admired. Almost to a couple their only negative reaction was to what they believed such a fine car would cost. Their estimates ranged from $4,000–$7,000, hardly practical for middle-incomes of the time.

When they heard that the base price was somewhat under $2,500, they expressed amazement and disbelief. At such a price, all agreed, Mustang was a car that they would like to own. This simple master stroke sent 100 voices out of the Ford Styling Center to spread the word of Mustang through fifty American cities.

To further bridge the gap before Mustang's official introduction, Iacocca brought 200 of the nation's most listened-to radio disc jockeys to the Ford test track opposite Ford Division. Each test-drove a Mustang, and each was promised the use of a Mustang for a week after his return home. All any d.j. needed to do was contact the local Ford dealer and pick up the car.

67   At the turn of the year, Iacocca brought in Frank Zimmerman, who had joined Ford as a trainee just before Lee himself, to work with him as general marketing manager. As Mustang Day neared, promotions were stepped up. Mustangs were displayed at 200 Holiday Inns and in major airport terminals, shopping centers, and business lobbies.

68   On Monday April 13, 1964, Mustang Introduction Day, a press preview preceded the public showing in the Ford Pavilion at the New York World's Fair. Newspaper, radio, and television representatives from the United States and Canada heard briefings on Mustang and then participated in a road rally that took them from the pavilion to Ford headquarters in Dearborn, Michigan.

69   A reporter at the Ford Pavilion asked Lee Iacocca how many Mustangs he expected to sell in its first year.

70   "How many Falcons were sold?" Lee asked.

71   The automotive journalist rattled off the Falcon sales record, as yet unequaled in the industry. He told Lee, "417,174."

72   "Mustang will go 417,175." Lee said. (Actual sales figures for Mustang's first year were 417,800!)

73   Mustang mania took hold of America when the car was officially introduced to the public on April 17 at the New York World's Fair. Visitors packed into the Ford Pavilion in near hysteria. That same evening a Mustang served as pace car for a race in Huntsville, Alabama. More than 7,500 enthusiasts leaped over the retaining wall to form a phalanx around the Mustang, holding it in place and delaying the race for over an hour.

74   Car buffs swarmed into Ford dealerships from coast to coast in such numbers that business was halted. A Ford dealer in Pittsburgh was unable to get a Mustang off a wash rack because of people crowding around the car. In Chicago a dealer was forced to lock his doors, the crush of Mustang lookers was so great.

75   Henry Ford II was on hand at the Ford Pavilion, but Lee Iacocca was the man in demand. His picture made the cover of the April 17 issue of *Time*, and the cover feature of *Newsweek* was the Iacocca story. He had produced a spectacular car with a name that would soon be familiar in Rio, Rome, and Rangoon as well as Racine.

76   Mustang was quickly perceived as the all-American, all-purpose automobile. It could be seen at country clubs, outside famous restaurants and churches, as well as at drag strips and on boulevards. It was the right car at the right time, a sizzler with four-on-the-floor that appealed to a full spectrum of drivers from eighteen to eighty.

77   Such terms as "Mustang mystique," "Mustang mania," and "Mustang generation" became everyday expressions, the latter first used by a California real estate developer named Howard Ruby. In bro-

chures advertising apartments for young singles he offered "A country club atmosphere catering to the champagne tastes of the Mustang generation."

Mustanging became a way of life in America and throughout the world, and erased the dull and the humdrum replacing them with glamour and excitement. It was a Cinderella slipper on wheels, magically converting reserved Walter Mitty types into debonair men-about-town, as pictured in one of the early television commercials approved by Iacocca.   78

In the one-minute commercial Henry Foster, staid and prim in rimless pince-nez spectacles, derby hat, and dark suit, was seen leaving his shop. He was carrying something in a brown paper bag. He turned the sign that read "open" to "out to lunch" and securely locked the door. In the background was a wispy old lady who operated a nearby shop. "Have you heard about Henry Foster?" she asked.   79

Henry then walked stiffly until he turned the corner. There, in sight of his new red Mustang he became a different man. Off went his pince-nez glasses, his derby hat, his dark suitcoat. On went a bright plaid hat, red vest, and dark goggles, all taken from the brown paper bag. As he got behind the wheel of the Mustang, the old lady's voice was heard saying: "Something's happened to Henry."   80

The screen then showed Henry braking his Mustang in a park area as a soft, seductive voice said, "A Mustang's happened to Henry." On a grassy plot in the park a sexy young woman waited with a picnic basket and bottle of wine. Henry leaped from his Mustang to join the young lady, now totally uninhibited, happy and laughing.   81

"Mustang made it happen" became the battle cry of the "in" people of the mid-sixties, whatever their age. Lee Iacocca's desk at Ford Division was flooded with letters from young and old telling how much Mustang was loved. One forty-four-year-old bachelor from Texas wrote that he had a "pony V-8 in Rangoon Red with accent paint stripes, molding, and air conditioning, and man, this is the greatest. A widow with seven thousand acres came sixty miles so I could take her riding in it."   82

It was a Mustang world from its first day in the showroom, and Lee Iacocca took every advantage to keep the magic full force. The day Mustang was born he agreed to cooperate with the newly formed National Council of Mustang Clubs headquartered in the shadows of Ford Division. It was an extension of the firmly rooted car club traditions in Europe.   83

The National Council of Mustang Clubs brought the hundreds of such clubs throughout the United States under one umbrella, sponsoring activities that ran the gamut of motorsport action. Its big day   84

through the following years was April 17, a nationwide celebration of
Mustang's birthday.

85   On that day rallies were held by the hundreds of clubs associated
with the National Council. From the final results of each year's rallies a
national winner was determined and presented with a new Mustang.
All the proceeds generated by rallies supervised by the National Council
on that day were donated by the individual clubs to local charities.

86   Club activities took place year-round. On any weekend one might
find a beach gathering in Florida or California. There would be local sla-
loms, gymkhanas, and hill climbs almost anywhere. The National
Council even developed a "Braille rally" for youngsters at schools for
the blind. Club members would bring their Mustangs and each select a
blind boy or girl to serve as navigator using instructions prepared in
braille.

87   Iacocca also created the Society of Mustangers, a no-constitution and
no-by-laws group of Mustang owners brought together about the time
the millionth Mustang came off the assembly line. It was established
only after Mustang owners in Chicago, Philadelphia, and Los Angeles
were mailed a brochure explaining the plan and asking their reaction.

88   The only obligation, as stated in the brochure, was a two dollar annual fee, for which members would receive quarterly issues of *The
Mustanger*, a magazine that would serve as the official voice of the society, as well as a membership card and a decal for their car. Other incentives were discounted tour and travel rates; hotel, motel, restaurant,
and nightclub discounts; specially arranged Mustanger pleasure trips;
and quality merchandise items at about half the normal retail cost, all
explained and displayed in *The Mustanger*.

89   The recipients of the brochures were asked only to mail in a "no" or
"yes" indication of their interest in this type of organization. So strong
was the magnetism of Mustang that not only were "yes" votes unexpectedly large, 16 percent of those answering also included two dollars,
even though the society had not yet been established. One month later
an actual solicitation mailing was made, and over 35,000 Mustang owners became members of the Society of Mustangers.

90   One of the surprising facts discovered in the creation of the society
was that as many as 8 percent of members were between fifty-five and
sixty-five years of age, and 2 percent were over sixty-five. As was
expected, 67 percent were under forty-five. Not expected were such
revealing figures as those that showed 51 percent had annual incomes of
$10,000 or over, and 36 percent were professional or managerial types.
The college educated accounted for 58 percent.

91   Lee Iacocca had stunned the automobile industry with his Mustang,
the car that made its debut at a time when America was ready for an au-

tomobile with a change of pace in styling and performance. General Motors, Chrysler, and American Motors were not about to stand by stoically watching Mustang sales spiral steadily upward without doing something.

Chevrolet had a similar car on its drawing boards when Mustang exploded on the market, but it did not make its bow for two years. Mustang sales had soared past a half-million before Chevy brought out its Camaro, another jazzy, sleek machine that symbolized youthfulness.   92

To a degree the 1967 Camaro was a Mustang copy. It fit the long-hood, short-deck design and came on the scene gunning for Mustang's record. While 100,000 Camaros did hit the road within seven months, Chevy's entry was unable to outsell Mustang in any one sales period for almost three years.   93

General Motors tossed another competitor into the ring with its Pontiac Firebird. Chrysler entered the sports car field about the same time with refined versions of the Plymouth Barracuda and Dodge Charger, neither of which was a completely new car. A year after Camaro American Motors produced two "muscle" cars, as Mustang types were being called, the Javelin and the AMX. None came near matching Camaro, and Camaro was hard put to come close to Mustang in popularity.   94

The phenomenon that was Mustang, especially with spirited, powerful engines offered as options, could not be restricted to the street scene. Inevitably it progressed from street to drag strip and from drag strip to racing oval.   95

"Race 'em on Sunday, and sell 'em on Monday," was Lee Iacocca's philosophy. Mustangs raced and sold.   96

On drag strips, where it takes brute horsepower to eat up 1,320 feet of hot asphalt in the shortest time, Mustangs were fierce competitors, thanks to Iacocca's support and a supercharged 427-cubic-inch single overhead cam engine. Mustangs won class championships in the spring nationals of the National Hot Rod Association. In the American Hot Rod Association winter championship races a Mustang equipped with a 429-cubic-inch Cobra jet engine achieved an estimated 114 miles per hour, turning in an elapsed time of 12.5 seconds for the 1,320-foot dash.   97

From drag strip to road racing is a natural progression, and there, too, Mustang could not be denied. The Sports Car Club of America opened the door when it established the Trans-American sedan series. In a "24-hours at Daytona" race Mustang blew its Trans-Am competitors, including Camaro, figuratively into the Atlantic as it finished first in class, and fourth overall, behind three Porsche 907 coupes.   98

Ford Motor Company's reentry into the racing scene actually had taken place early in the summer of '64, two months after Mustang's in-   99 troduction. Henry Ford II, anxious to upstage Enzo Ferrari after the Italian carmaker's initial refusal to sell the Ferrari plant to Ford, had pressured Iacocca's Ford Division team to produce a car for the 1964 LeMans twenty-four hour race.

100   Iacocca's engineers produced three cars dubbed the Ford GT40 for the confrontation with Ferrari. The first Ford-built, Ford-sponsored cars ever to race on an international circuit, they were equipped with 4.2-liter (256-cubic-inch) V-8 engines. Their GT40 designation deceived few at the famous French race. Most saw them as experimental Mustangs with special bodies.

101   Also included among the fifty-five starters in the competition were two cars with 427-cubic-inch Ford Cobra Jet engines. Neither was an official Ford Motor Company entry. Enzo Ferrari's entries included two new V-12 Ferraris with 3.3- and 4-liter displacement. Triumphs, Porsches, Alfa Romeos, and Jaguars were among the other racers ready for the twenty-four-hour run.

102   As far as the press and the public were concerned, the focus of the race was on the Ferrari-Ford confrontation. Henry Ford II, in typical fashion, pulled no punches. He was out to humiliate Ferrari, and he was confident it could be done. In substance the race had developed into a struggle between American cars and the European.

103   For the first hour after the fall of the starter's flag—and despite two of the Ford GT40s being boxed in by other cars—the third GT40, driven by Richie Ginther and Gaston Gregory (both Americans), held the lead over a Ferrari 330P, handled by Lorenzo Bandini of Italy and England's John Surtees. Before it was over, however, all three GT40s had broken down, and Ferrari ran away with the honors.

104   It was a bitter defeat for Henry Ford II, tempered little by the fact that one of the unsponsored Cobra Jets had won first place in the GT category. Henry vowed to be back next year.

105   The defeat at LeMans in no way tarnished 1964 as Lee Iacocca's year of glory. Before year's end the Mustang was acclaimed an international success, visible almost everywhere in the free world. And everywhere the Ford Motor Company was perceived in connection with Lee Iacocca as much as Henry Ford. Iacocca was lauded as Mr. Mustang.

106   Everyone close to Lee Iacocca knows, however, that the birth of the Mustang was not his most treasured memory of 1964. On July 16 Mary Iacocca had presented him with his second daughter. She was named Lia, after her now famous father.

Questions and Activities

▶ *COMPREHENSION QUESTIONS*

1. Why did Ford executives finally decide to name the new car Mustang rather than Torino?
2. In paragraph 8, Abodaher mentions Ralph Nader's *Unsafe at Any Speed*. What can you find out about this book? How did it deal the Corvair "a death blow"?
3. In paragraph 11, Abodaher refers to the Edsel. When was the Edsel built? Why does Abodaher use the words "Edsel fiasco"? Why did Iacocca wish to avoid what happened with the Edsel as he developed the Mustang?
4. What influence did the "growing economy" and the "more affluent middle class" that Abodaher mentions in paragraph 17 have on the Mustang's success?
5. What type of automobiles are raced at Watkins Glen? To what international racing circuit does Watkins Glen belong? Why would a positive response to the Mustang from the crowd at Watkins Glen be an asset to Ford in promoting the car?

▶ *QUESTIONS OF RHETORICAL PURPOSE AND STRATEGY*

6. What is Abodaher's purpose in supplying the statistics given in paragraphs 4 through 8? How do these statistics help you understand Iacocca's ideas about developing the Mustang?
7. Many experts would describe Abodaher's writing as efficient, popular journalism. What do you think is meant by such a description? Are Abodaher's sentences easy or hard to read? Does their length and form have anything to do with their level of difficulty? Is Abodaher's vocabulary easy or difficult? Why?
8. What do you think is Abodaher's overall purpose in writing this piece? Is he trying to give a realistic portrait of Iacocca? Or is he more interested in praising Iacocca in an unqualified way? What evidence can you get from the text to support your answer?

▶ *THEME QUESTIONS*

9. From what you learn of Lee Iacocca's character in this piece, do you think he should be used as a role model by people in general, by businessmen and executives, or by young people who are considering business careers?
10. In paragraph 26, Abodaher tells us that Iacocca went over the head of the company president to present his plans for the Mustang to

Henry Ford II. Do you think an ambitious, hard-driving executive is justified in circumventing established lines of authority in order to communicate an important idea to someone higher up? Was Iacocca justified in doing this in this case? Can you imagine other situations in which such an action would or would not be justified?

▶ *LEARNING ACTIVITIES*

11. Compare Iacocca's acts during the development of the Mustang with the suggestions for how to achieve business success offered by Benjamin Franklin (pages 87–95). Does Iacocca seem to follow Franklin's suggestions? Does he ever act differently than Franklin might have acted in a similar situation? Interview a classmate using these questions.

12. Write a letter to an imaginary executive in which you describe, using Iacocca's success with the Mustang as a model, a plan you have for developing a new product. You might, for example, come up with a new line of jeans or a new type of exercise machine. What changes can you suggest making in the existing product? How are those changes geared to appeal to consumers? How can you make your letter appeal to an Iacocca type of executive?

Letter from the Recording Angel

MARK TWAIN

Popular lecturer, inventor, experienced traveler, newspaper reporter, riverboat pilot, novelist, and America's greatest humorist, Mark Twain (the pen name of Samuel Clemens) was born in Florida, Missouri, in 1835, and died in Redding, Connecticut, in 1910. His life and writings have fascinated both American and foreign readers since the late nineteenth century. His work includes some sixty-seven books, many published during his life, and others published posthumously and edited by scholars and critics.

Huckleberry Finn, thought by many to be *the* American literary classic, was published in 1884. It solidified Twain's fame and popularity with its original use of the common American vernacular, its creation in Huck Finn of the quintessential American character of innocence and practical ingenuity, its sensitive treatment of the moral problems of slavery, and its scathing satire of the gullibility, hypocrisy, and energy of the many mainstream American characters Huck and his friend Jim meet.

Twain perfected his satiric style by employing character stereotypes —the fancy-talking Eastern genteel dude and dialect-speaking Westerner predominated in his early works—enabling Americans to see their own weaknesses and superficialities without losing sight of their counterbalancing driving energy and will to live independently. The best of Twain's early journalistic satires of American frontier life and its observers from the more sophisticated East were *Roughing It* (1872) and *The Celebrated Jumping Frog of Calaveras County, and Other Sketches* (1867). Twain is also famous for *The Adventures of Tom Sawyer* (1876) and *The Prince and the Pauper* (1881). Works published later in his life include *The Man That Corrupted Hadleyburg and Other Stories and Essays* (1900) and the novels *Pudd'nhead Wilson* (1894) and *A Connecticut Yankee in King Arthur's Court* (1889).

In the following satiric piece, written in 1887 and published later in his career, Twain creates the persona of the "Recording Angel" who corresponds with a petitioning Christian. The Christian's prayers are the self-serving requests of an avaricious and hypocritical businessman; if granted, they would result in the suffering of many. Almost every one of the businessman's petitions also contradict his avowed Christian sentiments.

Underlying all of Twain's writing and perhaps explaining some of the major events in his life was what biographers have described as an extreme social conscience. This satiric piece raises questions of what we should believe and how we should act on our beliefs, as well as the question of whether or not orthodox religious beliefs are a cause rather than an alleviation of human suffering. Think about these questions as you read:

1. Do you find Twain's Christian, Andrew Langdon, too much of an exaggeration? Are his requests believable?
2. What are the motivating convictions behind Langdon's prayers? Why might Twain find such convictions dangerous?
3. What elements of American culture today are evocative of the behavior of Twain's Christian?

As you read, also think about Twain's use of language. In this piece, he is careful to write in a way that gives his Recording Angel the sound of a particular type of person.

1. How would you describe the character of the Recording Angel?
2. What is the angel's attitude toward human beings?

▶ ——————————————

Office of the Recording Angel,
Dept. of Petitions, Jan. 20.

Andrew Langdon,
    Coal Dealer, Buffalo, N.Y.

1   I have the honor, as per command, to inform you that your recent act of benevolence and self-sacrifice has been recorded upon a page by itself of the Book called Golden Deeds of Men; a distinction, I am permitted to remark, which is not merely extraordinary, it is unique.

2   As regards your prayers, for the week ending the 19th, I have the honor to report as follows:

3   1. For weather to advance hard coal 15 cents per ton. Granted.
4   2. For influx of laborers to reduce wages 10 percent. Granted.
5   3. For a break in rival soft-coal prices. Granted.
6   4. For a visitation upon the man, or upon the family of the man, who has set up a competing retail coal-yard in Rochester. Granted, as follows: diphtheria, 2, 1 fatal; scarlet fever, 1, to result in deafness and imbecility. NOTE: This prayer should have been directed against this subordinate's principals, the N.Y. Central RR Co.
7   5. For deportation to Sheol, of annoying swarms of persons who apply daily for work, or for favors of one sort or another. Taken under advisement for later decision and compromise, this petition appearing to conflict with another one of same date, which will be cited further along.
8   6. For application of some form of violent death to neighbor who threw brick at family cat, whilst the which was serenading. Re-

served for consideration and compromise, because of conflict with a prayer of even date to be cited further along.

7. To "damn the missionary cause." Reserved also—as above.   9

8. To increase December profits of $22,230 to $45,000 for January,   10 and perpetuate a proportionate monthly increase thereafter —"which will satisfy you." The prayer granted; the added remark accepted with reservations.

9. For cyclone, to destroy the works and fill up the mine of the North   11 Pennsylvania Co. NOTE: Cyclones are not kept in stock in the winter season. A reliable article of fire-damp can be furnished upon application.

Especial note is made of the above list, they being of particular moment. The 298 remaining supplications classifiable under the head of Special Providences, Schedule A, for week ending 19th, are granted in a body, except that 3 of the 32 cases requiring immediate death have been modified to incurable disease.   12

This completes the week's invoice of petitions known to this office under the technical designation of Secret Supplications of the Heart, and which for a reason which may suggest itself, always receive our first and especial attention.   13

The remainder of the week's invoice falls under the head of what we term Public Prayers, in which classification we place prayers uttered in Prayer Meeting, Sunday School, Class Meeting, Family Worship, etc. These kinds of prayers have value according to classification of Christian uttering them. By rule of this office, Christians are divided into two grand classes, to-wit: 1, Professing Christians; 2, Professional Christians. These, in turn, are minutely subdivided and classified by Size, Species, and Family; and finally, Standing is determined by carats, the minimum being 1, the maximum 1,000.   14

As per balance-sheet for quarter ending Dec. 31st, 1847, you stood classified as follows: 15

Grand Classification, Professing Christian.
Size, one-fourth of maximum.
Species, Human-Spiritual.
Family, A of the Elect, Division 16.
Standing, 322 carats fine.

As per balance-sheet for quarter just ended,—that is to say, forty years later,—you stand classified as follows: 16

Grand Classification, Professional Christian.
Size, six one-hundredths of maximum.
Species, Human-Animal.

Family, W of the Elect, Division 1547.
Standing, 3 carats fine.

17   I have the honor to call your attention to the fact that you seem to have deteriorated.

18   To resume report upon your Public Prayers—with the side remark that in order to encourage Christians of your grade and of approximate grades, it is the custom of this office to grant many things to them which would not be granted to Christians of a higher grade—partly because they would not be asked for:

19   Prayer for weather mercifully tempered to the needs of the poor and the naked. Denied. This was a Prayer-Meeting prayer. It conflicts with Item 1 of this Report, which was a Secret Supplication of the Heart. By a rigid rule of this office, certain sorts of Public Prayers of Professional Christians are forbidden to take precedence of Secret Supplications of the Heart.

20   Prayer for better times and plentier food "for the hard handed son of toil whose patient and exhausting labors make comfortable the homes, and pleasant the ways, of the more fortunate, and entitle him to our vigilant and effective protection from the wrongs and injustices which grasping avarice would do him, and to the tenderest offices of our grateful hearts." Prayer-Meeting Prayer. Refused. Conflicts with Secret Supplication of the Heart No. 2.

21   Prayer "that such as in any way obstruct our preferences may be generously blessed, both themselves and their families, we here calling our hearts to witness that in their worldly prosperity we are spiritually blessed, and our joys made perfect." Prayer-Meeting Prayer. Refused. Conflicts with Secret Supplications of the Heart Nos. 3 and 4.

22   "Oh, let none fall heir to the pains of perdition through words or acts of ours." Family Worship. Received fifteen minutes in advance of Secret Supplication of the Heart No. 5, with which it distinctly conflicts. It is suggested that one or the other of these prayers be withdrawn, or both of them modified.

23   "Be mercifully inclined toward all who would do us offence in our persons or our property." Includes man who threw brick at cat. Family Prayer. Received some minutes in advance of No. 6, Secret Supplications of the Heart. Modification suggested, to reconcile discrepancy.

24   "Grant that the noble missionary cause, the most precious labor entrusted to the hands of men, may spread and prosper without let or limit in all heathen lands that do as yet reproach us with their spiritual darkness." Uninvited prayer shoved in at meeting of American Board. Received nearly half a day in advance of No. 7, Secret Supplications of the Heart. This office takes no stock in missionaries, and is not connected in any way with the American Board. We should like to grant

one of these prayers, but cannot grant both. It is suggested that the American Board one be withdrawn.

This office desires for the twentieth time to call urgent attention to your remark appended to No. 8. It is a chestnut.

Of the 464 specifications contained in your Public Prayers for the week, and not previously noted in this report, we grant 2, and deny the rest. To-wit: Granted, (1), "that the clouds may continue to perform their office; (2), and the sun his." It was the divine purpose anyhow; it will gratify you to know that you have not disturbed it. Of the 462 details refused, 61 were uttered in Sunday School. In this connection I must once more remind you that we grant no Sunday School Prayers of Professional Christians of the classification technically known in this office as the John Wanamaker grade. We merely enter them as "words," and they count to his credit according to number uttered within certain limits of time, 3,000 per quarter-minute required, or no score; 4,200 in a possible 5,000 is a quite common Sunday School score, among experts, and counts the same as two hymns and a bouquet furnished by young ladies in the assassin's cell, execution-morning. Your remaining 401 details count for wind only. We bunch them and use them for head-winds in retarding the ships of improper people, but it takes so many of them to make an impression that we cannot allow anything for their use.

I desire to add a word of my own to this report. When certain sorts of people do a sizeable good deed, we credit them up a thousand-fold more for it than we would in the case of a better man—on account of the strain. You stand far away above your classification-record here, because of certain self-sacrifices of yours which greatly exceed what could have been expected of you. Years ago, when you were worth only $100,000, and sent $2 to your impoverished cousin the widow, when she appealed to you for help, there were many in heaven who were not able to believe it, and many more who believed that the money was counterfeit. Your character went up many degrees when it was shown that these suspicions were unfounded. A year or two later, when you sent the poor girl $4 in answer to another appeal, everybody believed it, and you were all the talk here for days together. Two years later you sent $6, upon supplication, when the widow's youngest child died, and that act made perfect your good fame. Everybody in heaven said, "Have you heard about Andrew?"—for you are now affectionately called Andrew here. Your increasing donation, every two or three years, has kept your name on all lips, and warm in all hearts. All heaven watches you Sundays, as you drive to church in your handsome carriage; and when your hand retires from the contribution plate, the glad shout is heard even to the ruddy walls of remote Sheol, "Another nickel from Andrew!" But the climax came a few days ago, when the widow wrote and said she could get a school in a far village to teach if she had $50 to get herself and her two surviving children over the long journey; and you counted up last month's clear profit from your three coal mines—$22,230—and added to it the certain profit for the current month—$45,000 and a possible fifty—and then got down your pen and your check-book and mailed her *fifteen whole dollars!* Ah, Heaven bless and keep you forever and ever, generous heart! There was not a dry eye in the realms of bliss; and amidst the hand-shakings, and embracings, and praisings, the decree was thundered forth from the shining mount, that this deed should out-honor all the historic self-sacrifices of men and angels, and be recorded by itself upon a page of its own, for that the strain of it upon you had been heavier and bitterer than the strain it costs ten thousand martyrs to yield up their lives at the fiery stake; and all said, "What is the giving up of life, to a noble soul, or to ten thousand noble souls, compared with the giving up of fifteen dollars out of the greedy grip of the meanest white man that ever lived on the face of the earth?"

28   And it was a true word. And Abraham, weeping, shook out the contents of his bosom and pasted the eloquent label there, "RESERVED;" and Peter, weeping, said, "He shall be received with a torchlight procession when he comes;" and then all heaven boomed, and was glad you were going there. And so was hell.

[Signed]
THE RECORDING ANGEL. [seal.]

By command.

Questions and Activities

▶ *COMPREHENSION QUESTIONS*

1. What do you think is Twain's attitude toward official language? Does he favor it, find it pretentious, or simply accept it as a necessity? What in this selection causes you to answer this question as you do?
2. What is the difference between "Professing Christians" and "Professional Christians" (paragraphs 14, 15, and 16)? Which type is good, and which bad? What has happened to a Professional Christian that has not happened to a Professing Christian?

3. This is a literary piece. Yet it is written in the form of an official letter from a governmental agency. Why does Twain use a form more often characteristic of informative prose for a religious and highly personal situation?

4. Suppose a serious Christian were to respond negatively to Twain's portrayal of Andrew Langdon as an example of Christianity. How would you convince this reader to be more open to Twain's point and purpose? What might this reader learn from this piece? Would that lesson necessarily make him or her less of a believing Christian? Is Twain saying that most Christians are like Andrew Langdon? Why might today's Christians be more materialistic than early ones?

5. What is the Recording Angel's real attitude toward Andrew Langdon and his prayers and requests? Provide evidence from the piece supporting your answer. Can you find examples of the use of sarcasm and irony in the Recording Angel's language?

6. Mark Twain deals with moral hypocrisy. What are the real motives for Andrew Langdon's actions? Do you find this satirical character representative of moral hypocrites you have known, read about, or seen on television?

7. Do you find elements of Andrew Langdon's character in people around you? Using professional or general categories such as businessman, clergyman, lawyer, student, housewife, or husband, describe the moral inconsistencies of at least two of the people you know. Are you ever inconsistent? Do you sometimes do things that contradict your principles? When are such inconsistent actions defensible, and when are they a sign of moral degeneracy?

8. Interview a practicing Christian on the subject of hypocrisy. Write up your interview as a pointed essay on "what it means to be morally hypocritical." Use the actual words of the person you interview, but be sure to interpret what he or she has to say in the context of this section's theme of moral beliefs.

9. Satirize a leading sports figure, religious leader, or politician who you believe speaks platitudes that he or she does not practice. Choose the voice you wish to create for your subject before you begin writing, and be sure to distinguish between your subject's voice and the interviewing narrator's voice.

Beyond Atrocity

ROBERT J. LIFTON

Born in 1926, Robert J. Lifton has taught at Yale since 1961. He has used concepts from the fields of psychiatry, behavioral psychology, and contemporary culture to form a new perspective on modern history that he and others have come to call "psychohistory." In psychohistory, current phenomena, such as nuclear bombings and what Lifton calls "atrocities," are interpreted using the methods of medicine, psychology, and history, and their effects on the psychologies of the people involved are analyzed. Sometimes in his studies Lifton focuses on the effects atrocities have on individuals, as in his study of the effects of the atomic bomb on the inhabitants of Hiroshima, *Death in Life: Survivors of Hiroshima* (1968). At other times his perspective is more general, as in his study of Vietnam veterans as a group, *Home from the War: Vietnam Veterans — Neither Victims nor Executioners* (1974). His seventeen published books include works on brainwashing in China, the Chinese cultural revolution, old age and dying, the effects of nuclear war, and women in America. He is considered an expert in the field of Asian studies.

All of Lifton's varied writings are structured by his central concern with developing our moral commitment to one another and to the maintenance of life on earth in as healthy a state as possible. "Beyond Atrocity," the essay that follows, focuses on the question of how people who have become accustomed to widespread suffering, inflicted by other human beings, can avoid becoming generally insensitive to the suffering of others. Lifton explains many events of recent history as the result of what he calls the feeling of "non-responsibility" among groups of people who feel they simply cannot do anything about the effects of technology, which has often been used to destroy rather than to help people.

This essay is addressed to a morally sensitive and serious reader, someone who is reasonably informed about recent political and social history and believes that people can do something to alter the way things are. Many observers argue that the college students of the 1980s find social involvement useless and frustrating and that they are more concerned with careers, money, and pleasure.

1. Think about the life styles of your friends and acquaintances. What are their worries? Are they going to school merely to get good jobs? Are they interested in how the government acts on issues such as

welfare, nuclear power, defense spending, and so on? Or do they seem cynical or apathetic about those issues?

2. What causes your friends' attitudes toward social involvement? Have they been affected by what Lifton calls the atrocities of modern life? Do they seem to feel cynical because of their inability to do something about universal dangers such as nuclear war, or the suffering of larger groups of people because of nuclear war? Or do they seem totally unaffected by Lifton's concerns?

▶ ————————————————

> *The landscape doesn't change much. For days and days you see just about nothing. It's unfamiliar—always unfamiliar. Even when you go back to the same place, it's unfamiliar. And it makes you feel as though, well, there's nothing left in the world but this. . . . You have the illusion of going great distances and traveling, like hundreds of miles . . . and you end up in the same place because you're only a couple of miles away. . . . But you feel like it's not all real. It couldn't possibly be. We couldn't still be in this country. We've been walking for days. You're in Vietnam and they're using real bullets. . . . Here in Vietnam they're actually shooting people for no reason. Any other time you think. It's such an extreme. Here you can go ahead and shoot them for nothing. As a matter of fact it's even . . . smiled upon, you know. Good for you. Everything is backwards. That's part of the kind of unreality of the thing. To the "grunt" [infantryman] this isn't backwards. He doesn't understand. . . . But something [at Mylai 4] was missing. Something you thought was real that would accompany this. It wasn't there. . . . There was something missing in the whole business that made it seem like it really wasn't happening. . . .*
> —American GI's recollections of Mylai.

When asked to speak on recent occasions, I have announced my title as "On Living in Atrocity." To be sure, neither I nor anyone else lives there all or even most of the time. But at this moment, in early 1971, an American investigator of atrocity finds himself dealing with something that has become, for his countrymen in general, a terrible subterranean image that can be neither fully faced nor wished away. There is virtue in bringing that image to the surface.   *1*

In one sense, no matter what happens in the external world, personal atrocity, for everyone, begins at birth. It can also be said that some of us have a special nose for atrocity. Yet I can remember very well, during the early stirrings of the academic peace movement taking place around   *2*

Harvard University during the mid- and late 1950s—about two hundred years ago, it now seems—how hard it was for us to *feel* what might happen at the other end of a nuclear weapon. Whatever one's nose for atrocities, there are difficulties surrounding the imaginative act of coming to grips with them.

3   After six months of living and working in Hiroshima, studying the human effects of the first atomic bomb, I found that these difficulties were partly overcome and partly exacerbated. On the one hand, I learned all too well to feel what happened at the other end of an atomic bomb. But on the other hand, I became impressed with the increasing gap we face between our technological capacity for perpetrating atrocities and our imaginative ability to confront their full actuality. Yet the attempt to narrow that gap can be enlightening, even liberating. For me, Hiroshima was a profoundly "radicalizing" experience—not in any strict ideological sense but in terms of fundamental issues of living and dying, of how one lives, of how one may die.

4   Whatever the contributing wartime pressures, Hiroshima looms as a paradigm of technological atrocity. Each of the major psychological themes discernible in Hiroshima survivors—death immersion, psychic numbing, residual guilt—has direct relationship to the atrocity's hideously cool and vast technological character. The specific technology of the bomb converted the brief moment of exposure into a lifelong encounter with death—through the sequence of the survivor's early immersion in massive and grotesque death and dying, his experiencing or witnessing bizarre and frequently fatal acute radiation effects during the following weeks and months, his knowledge of the increased incidence over the years of various forms (always fatal) of leukemia and cancer, and finally his acquisition of a death-tainted group identity, an "identity of the dead" or shared sense of feeling emotionally bound both to those killed by the bomb and to the continuing worldwide specter of nuclear genocide.

5   The experience of psychic numbing, or emotional desensitization—what some survivors called "paralysis of the mind"—was a necessary defense against feeling what they clearly knew to be happening. But when one looks further into the matter he discovers that those who made and planned the use of that first nuclear weapon—and those who today make its successors and plan their use—require their own form of psychic numbing. They too cannot afford to feel what they cognitively know would happen.

6   Victims and victimizers also shared a sense of guilt, expressed partly in a conspiracy of silence, a prolonged absence of any systematic attempt to learn about the combined physical and psychic assaults of the bomb on human beings. Survivors felt guilty about remaining alive

while others died, and also experienced an amorphous sense of having been part of, having imbibed, the overall evil of the atrocity. The perpetrators of Hiroshima (and those in various ways associated with them)—American scientists, military and political leaders, and ordinary people—felt their own forms of guilt, though, ironically, in less tangible ways than the victims. Yet one cannot but wonder to what extent Hiroshima produced in Americans (and others) a guilt-associated sense that if we could do this we could do anything, and that anyone could do anything to us—in other words, an anticipatory sense of unlimited atrocity.

If these are lessons of Hiroshima, one has to learn them personally. My own immersion in massive death during investigations in that city, though much more privileged and infinitely less brutal, will nonetheless be as permanent as that of Hiroshima survivors themselves. As in their case, it has profoundly changed my relationship to my own death as well as to all collective forms of death that stalk us. I had a similarly personal lesson regarding psychic numbing. During my first few interviews in Hiroshima I felt overwhelmed by the grotesque horrors described to me, but within the short space of a week or so this feeling gave way to a much more comfortable sense of myself as a psychological investigator, still deeply troubled by what he heard but undeterred from his investigative commitment. This kind of partial, task-oriented numbing now strikes me as inevitable and, in this situation, useful—yet at the same time potentially malignant in its implications.

By "becoming" a Hiroshima survivor (as anyone who opens himself to the experience must), while at the same time remaining an American, I shared something of both victims' and victimizers' sense of guilt. This kind of guilt by identification has its pitfalls, but I believe it to be one of the few genuine psychological avenues to confrontation of atrocity. For these three psychological themes are hardly confined to Hiroshima: Death immersion, psychic numbing, and guilt are a psychic trinity found in all atrocity.

Hiroshima also taught me the value and appropriateness of what I would call the apocalyptic imagination. The term offends our notions of steadiness and balance. But the technological dimensions of contemporary atrocity seem to me to require that we attune our imaginations to processes that are apocalyptic in the full dictionary meaning of the word—processes that are "wildly unrestrained" and "ultimately decisive," that involve "forecasting or predicting the ultimate destiny of the world in the shape of future events" and "foreboding imminent disaster or final doom."

In the past this kind of imagination has been viewed as no more than the "world-ending" delusion of the psychotic patient. But for the people of Hiroshima the "end of the world"—or something very close to it—became part of the actuality of their experience. Thus one survivor recalled: "My body seemed all black; everything seemed dark, dark all over...then I thought, 'The world is ending.'" And another: "The feeling I had was that everyone was dead....I thought this was the end of Hiroshima—of Japan—of humankind." Those witnessing Nazi mass murder—the greatest of all man's atrocities to date—called forth similar images, though they could usually perceive that the annihilating process was in some way selective (affecting mainly Jews or anti-Nazis or other specific groups). As Hiroshima took me to Auschwitz and Treblinka, however, I was struck mostly by the similarities and parallels in the overall psychology of atrocity.

11   Yet similar end-of-the-world impressions have been recorded in connection with "God-made" atrocities, as in the case of survivors' accounts of the plagues of the Middle Ages:

> How will posterity believe that there has been a time when without the lightings of heaven or the fires of earth, without wars or other visible slaughter, not this or that part of the earth, but well-nigh the whole globe, has remained without inhabitants....We should think we were dreaming if we did not with our eyes, when we walk abroad, see the city in mourning with funerals, and returning to our home, find it empty, and thus know that what we lament is real.

12   The plagues were God-made not only in the sense of being a mysterious and deadly form of illness outside of man's initiation or control but also because they could be comprehended as part of a God-centered cosmology. To be sure, scenes like the above strained people's belief in an ordered universe and a just God, but their cosmology contained enough devils, enough flexibility, and enough depth of imprint to provide, if not a full "explanation" of holocaust, at least a continued psychic framework within which to go on living. In contrast, Hiroshima and Auschwitz were carried out by men upon men, and at a time when old cosmologies had already lost much of their hold and could provide little explanatory power. Survivors were left with an overwhelming sense of dislocation and absurdity: Like the GI quoted earlier in relationship to Mylai, something for them was "missing"—namely, meaning, or a sense of reality. With Hiroshima and Auschwitz now part of man's historical experience, it is perilously naïve to insist that our imaginative relationship to world-destruction can remain unchanged—that we can continue to make a simple-minded distinction between psychotic proclivity for, and "normal" avoidance of, that image.

13   Yet, whatever the force of external events, there is a subjective, imaginative component to the perceived "end of the world." Hiroshi-

ma survivors had to call forth early inner images of separation and helplessness, of stasis and annihilation, images available from everyone's infancy and childhood, but with greater force to some than to others. There is, therefore, a danger, not just for Hiroshima survivors but for all of us, of being trapped in such images, bound by a psychic sense of doom to the point of being immobilized and totally unable or unwilling to participate in essential day-by-day struggles to counter atrocity and prevent the collective annihilation imagined.

Psychological wisdom, then, seems to lie in neither wallowing in, nor numbing ourselves to, our imaginings of apocalypse. A simple example of the constructive use of the apocalyptic imagination is recorded by Eugene Rabinowitch, from the beginning an articulate leader in scientists' anti-atomic bomb movements. Rabinowitch describes how, when walking down the streets of Chicago during the summer of 1945, he looked up at the city's great buildings and suddenly imagined a holocaust in which skyscrapers crumbled. He then vowed to redouble his efforts to prevent that kind of event from happening by means of the scientists' petition he and others were drawing up to head off the dropping of an atomic bomb, without warning, on a populated area. The effort, of course, failed, but this kind of apocalyptic imagination—on the part of Rabinowitch, Leo Szilard, and Bertrand Russell, among others—has made it possible for at least a small minority of men and women to name and face the true conditions of our existence. (Bertrand Russell had earlier exhibited the dangers of the apocalyptic imagination when he advocated that we threaten to drop atomic bombs on Russia in order to compel it to agree to a system of international control of nuclear weapons.) For we live in the shadow of the ultimate atrocity, of the potentially terminal revolution—and if that term is itself a contradiction, the same contradiction is the central fact of our relationship to death and life.

We perpetrate and experience the American atrocity at Mylai in the context of these apocalyptic absurdities and dislocations. The GI's quoted description suggests not only that atrocity can be a dreamlike affair (in this sense, resembling the quoted passage about the plague) but that it is committed by men living outside of ordinary human connection, outside of both society and history. Mylai was acted out by men who had lost their bearings, men wandering about in both a military and psychic no man's land. The atrocity itself can be seen as a grotesquely paradoxical effort to put straight this crooked landscape, to find order and significance in disorder and absurdity. There is at the same time an impulse to carry existing absurdity and disorder to their logical extremes as if both to transcend and demonstrate that aberrant existential state.

14

15

16   Atrocities are committed by desperate men—in the case of Mylai, men victimized by the absolute contradictions of the war they were asked to fight, by the murderous illusions of their country's policy. Atrocity, then, is a perverse quest for meaning, the end result of a spurious sense of mission, the product of false witness.

17   To say that American military involvement in Vietnam is itself a crime is also to say that it is an atrocity-producing situation. Or to put the matter another way, Mylai illuminates, as nothing else has, the essential nature of America's war in Vietnam. The elements of this atrocity-producing situation include an advanced industrial nation engaged in a counter-insurgency action, in an underdeveloped area, against guerrillas who merge with the people—precisely the elements that Jean-Paul Sartre has described as inevitably genocidal. In the starkness of its murders and the extreme dehumanization experienced by victimizers and imposed on victims, Mylai reveals to us how far America has gone along the path of deadly illusion.

18   Associated with this deadly illusion are three psychological patterns as painful to the sensitized American critic of the war as they are self-evident. The first is the principle of atrocity building upon atrocity, because of the need to deny the atrocity-producing situation. In this sense, Mylai itself was a product of earlier, smaller Mylais; and it was followed not by an ending of the war but by the American extension of the war into Laos and Cambodia.

19   The second principle involves the system of non-responsibility. One searches in vain for a man or group of men who will come forward to take the blame or even identify a human source or responsibility for what took place—from those who fired the bullets at Mylai (who must bear some responsibility, but were essentially pawns and victims of the atrocity-producing situation, and are now being made scapegoats as well); to the junior-grade officers who gave orders to do the firing and apparently did some of it themselves; to the senior-grade officers who seemed to have ordered the operation; to the highest military and civilian planners in Vietnam, the Pentagon, and the White House who created such things as a *"permanent free-fire zone"* (which, according to Richard Hammer, means "in essence. . . that any Americans operating within it had, basically, a license to kill and any Vietnamese living within it had a license to be killed"), planners who made even more basic decisions about continuing and even extending the war; to the amorphous conglomerate of the American people who, presumably, chose, or at least now tolerate, the aforementioned as their representatives. The atrocity-producing situation, at least in this case, depends upon what Masao Maruyama has called a "system of non-responsibility." Situation and system alike are characterized by a technology and a technicized bureaucracy not checked by sentient human minds.

The third and perhaps most terrible pattern is the psychology of   *20*
nothing happening. General Westmoreland gives way to General
Abrams, President Johnson to President Nixon, a visibly angry student
generation to one silent with rage—and the war, the atrocity-producing
situation, continues to grind out its thousands of recorded and
unrecorded atrocities. To be more accurate, something does happen:
The subliminal American perception of atrocity edges toward consciousness, making it more difficult but, unfortunately, not impossible
to defend and maintain the atrocity-producing situation. The widespread feeling of being stuck in atrocity contributes, in ways we can
now hardly grasp, to a national sense of degradation and a related attraction to violence, for nothing is more conducive to collective rage and
totalism than a sense of being bound to a situation perceived to be both
suffocating and evil.

Atrocity in general, and Mylai in particular, brings its perpetra-   *21*
tors—even a whole nation—into the realm of existential evil. That
state is exemplified by what another GI described to me as a working
definition of the enemy in Vietnam: "If it's dead, it's VC—because it's
dead. If it's dead, it *had* to be VC. And of course, a corpse couldn't defend itself anyhow." When at some future moment, ethically sensitive
historians get around to telling the story of the Vietnam War—
assuming that there will be ethically sensitive (or, for that matter, any)
historians around—I have no doubt that they will select the phenomenon of the "body count" as the perfect symbol of America's descent
into evil. What better represents the numbing, brutalizing illusion
(most of the bodies, after all, turn out to be those of civilians), grotesque
competition (companies and individuals vie for the highest body
counts), and equally grotesque technicizing (progress lies in the *count*)
characteristic of the overall American crime of the war in Vietnam.

Mylai is rather unusual in one respect. It combines two kinds of   *22*
atrocity: technological overkill (of unarmed peasants by Americans
using automatic weapons) and a more personal, face-to-face gunning-
down of victims at point-blank range. This combination lends the incident particular psychic force, however Americans may try to fend off
awareness of its implications. A participating GI could characterize
Mylai as "just like a Nazi-type thing" (as recorded in Seymour Hersh's
book *My Lai 4*), a characterization made by few if any pilots or crewmen
participating in the more technologically distanced killings of larger
numbers of Vietnamese civilians from the air.

The sense of being associated with existential evil is new to   *23*
Americans. This is so partly because such perceptions have been
suppressed in other atrocity-producing situations, but also because of
the humane elements of American tradition that contribute to a national self-image of opposing, through use of force if necessary, just this

kind of "Nazi-type thing." The full effects of the war in Vietnam upon this self-image are at this point unclear. The returns from Mylai are not yet in. Perhaps they never are for atrocity. But I for one worry about a society that seems to absorb, with some questioning but without fundamental self-examination, first Hiroshima and now Mylai.

24   For there is always a cost. Atrocities have a way of coming home. The killings by National Guardsmen of Kent State students protesting the extension of the war into Cambodia reflect the use of violence in defense of illusion and denial of evil—and the killings of blacks at Augusta, Georgia, and of black students at Jackson State in Mississippi reflect more indirectly that atmosphere. Indeed there is a real danger that the impulse to preserve illusion and deny evil could carry America beyond Vietnam and Cambodia into some form of world-destroying nuclear confrontation. In this sense, as well as in its relationship to existential evil, Mylai symbolized a shaking of the American foundations—a bitterly mocking perversion of what was left of the American dream. Like Hiroshima and Auschwitz, Mylai is a revolutionary event: Its total inversion of moral standards raises fundamental questions about the institutions and national practices of the nation responsible for it.

25   The problem facing Americans now is: What do we do with our atrocities? Do we simply try our best to absorb them by a kind of half-admission that denies their implications and prevents genuine confrontation? That is the classical method of governments for dealing with documented atrocities, and it is clearly the method now being used by the U.S. government and military in holding trials of individuals. Those who did the shooting and those who covered up the event are being labeled aberrant and negligent, so that the larger truth of the atrocity-producing situation can be avoided. The award of a Pulitzer Prize to Seymour Hersh for his journalistic feat in uncovering the story of Mylai and telling it in detail would seem to be a step in the direction of that larger truth. Yet one cannot but fear that such an award—as in the case of the National Book Award I received for my work on Hiroshima—can serve as a form of conscience-salving token recognition in place of confrontation. Surely more must be faced throughout American society, more must be articulated and given form by leaders and ordinary people, if this atrocity is to contribute to a national process of illumination instead of further degradation.

26   I am struck by how little my own profession has had to say about the matter—about the way in which aberrant *situations* can produce collective disturbance and mass murder. The psychiatry and psychohistory I would like to envisage for the future would put such matters at its center. It would also encourage combining ethical involvement with pro-

fessional skills in ways that could simultaneously shed light upon such crimes of war and contribute to the transformation our country so desperately requires. In dealing with our dislocations, we need to replace the false witness of atrocity with the genuine witness of new and liberating forms and directions. The task, then, is to confront atrocity in order to move beyond it.

Questions and Activities

▶ *COMPREHENSION QUESTIONS*

1. Define "technological atrocity" as Lifton uses the term in this essay (paragraph 4). What is the difference between a technological atrocity and a traditional atrocity, such as might have occurred during the Crusades, for example? How does the phenomenon of technological atrocity affect people today? According to Lifton, does it make them more or less sensitive to other people's suffering?

2. Paragraph 5 is critical to the point Lifton wants to make in this essay and also to the contribution this essay makes to our evolving sense of the moral situation in our society. Summarize what Lifton is saying about "psychic numbing" in this paragraph. Who else, besides the Hiroshima survivors, experiences this psychic numbing as this essay continues?

▶ *QUESTIONS OF RHETORICAL PURPOSE AND STRATEGY*

3. Lifton hopes to persuade his reader to change his or her attitude about the modern moral conscience. What new ideas and information does he provide to change that attitude? What overall form does his evidence take—reasons that support generalizations, facts, statistics, logic, or personal anecdote or experience?

4. Describe Lifton's voice in this essay. Does he sound like a psychologist writing as an expert, or does he sound like an educated citizen with information he thinks other educated citizens should have? Point to specific language devices that provide support for your characterization of Lifton's voice.

▶ *THEME QUESTIONS*

5. Explain the distinction Lifton makes in paragraph 12 between "God-made" and human-engendered atrocities. Why were medieval people, for example, better able to survive the plague with their sanity

intact than their modern counterparts are able to face the fact that "Hiroshima and Auschwitz [are] now part of man's historical experience"?

6. In paragraph 15, Lifton explains why otherwise normal men are capable of perpetrating an atrocity such as that at Mylai in Vietnam. What cause does he cite for the callousness of the American soldiers who followed orders and killed Vietnamese women and children? What does Lifton mean when he implies in paragraph 16 that Mylai was an example of a "perverse quest for meaning" in an otherwise chaotic situation?

7. Explain how a "system of non-responsibility" (paragraph 19) came into existence in Vietnam and America and speeded up American aggression during the war. Although it is treated rather humorously there, can you explain how this term applies to the television and movie versions of *M*A*S*H*? Does guilt cause us to deny responsibility for our actions?

▶ *LEARNING ACTIVITIES*

8. Do you agree with Lifton's conclusion in paragraph 6 that Americans felt about the bombing of Hiroshima that "if we could do this we could do anything"? Interview someone who was old enough in 1945 to remember reading or hearing the first reports of the dropping of the bomb. Find out how that person felt. Was he or she elated that a long war would soon be over, or horrified by the number of people killed, or both? Write a summary of your interview. Close it with a generalization explaining the effect of the bomb on the person you interviewed.

9. Study one or more newspaper, magazine, and book-length (for example, Seymour Hersh's *My Lai 4*) accounts of the Mylai massacre and its aftermath. Report to your class your opinion as to whether or not Lifton is right in his interpretation of that event.

10. Hold a debate in your class. One group should argue that those immediately involved in the massacre at Mylai were, as Lifton says, pawns in a bureaucratic-technological war and victims rather than criminals; the other group should argue that those who were involved were guilty, since if they had followed military discipline and law, the massacre would not have happened. This debate, of course, should occur after the class has heard and discussed several factual reports on Mylai.

11. Write down the propositions that you believe define the two opposing sides of the debate in the preceding activity. State the propositions as simple declarative sentences, either positive or negative.

Writing Assignments

MORALITY AND CHEATING

Respond to the following defense of several students who were caught cheating during a final examination: "Competition for jobs and places in professional schools is intense. Students have to get ahead any way they can. Cheating doesn't hurt others. If people are smart enough to get away with it, they are justified."

First, write a free response to this defense. Then, go back over your free writing and find a thesis that can be the focus for an essay in which you explore what at least three of the writers in this section would say about cheating in college exams. Write that essay, citing excerpts from those writers to support your thesis.

LOVE AND THE SINGLES GAME

This section has focused on the current moral context in America. Some writers—Suzanne Gordon, Joan Didion, and Joseph Wood Krutch —suggest that a kind of moral vacuum typifies modern life. People seem to be freer to act as their instincts and desires suggest, but they are unable to find direction or purpose within this relatively new freedom. Gordon's Jim Costello is a prime example of a person caught in a situation in which there are simply too many moral options. His ultimate response is a kind of catatonic paralysis, a total refusal to take hold of his life. Jim Costello is, of course, an extreme case. But many normal people reveal this moral unsureness in other ways.

One manifestation of the confusion and loneliness of modern American life is what many social scientists have come to call the "singles game." This game is played in many ways by various types of people—students, recently divorced people, urban professionals, and adolescents. However the game is played, the goal seems constant: to win the love of another person. In the singles game, sex is supposed to be a means to the end of total romantic and emotional involvement. But as the advertisement on pages 248–251 (which appeared in the magazine *Psychology Today*) implies, very few of the players of this game seem to have been able to achieve that goal. They fail and are left feeling stigmatized because they mistakenly believe themselves to be the only ones who have missed out on love.

Write an essay in which you explain why the need for love seems to have become *the* social concern of the late twentieth century. Follow a cause-and-effect pattern in writing this essay; explain the causes that drive people in search of love, as described in the readings in this section and in the advertisement reprinted here and others like it. Imagine yourself writing this essay for a college-age audience, perhaps for a magazine read by many young people, such as *Mademoiselle* or *Esquire*. You might wish to examine such a magazine before you write the final draft of your essay.

In planning this essay, you will need to do at least two things. First, you will need to read the advertisement and then reexamine the selections in this section to find the ones you believe will help you treat the topic of the search for love. As you reread, list the reasons why the individuals described in these essays seem to need love and companionship. What, for example, caused Jim Costello to need love? For the essays that are focused on society rather than on individuals, think about the social conditions that might cause people to place a very high value on having a lover. Do the causes that you find implied in these readings seem to be implied as well in the advertisement? Did the advertiser assume lost, lonely, and confused people were the audience for this advertisement?

Second, you will need to examine the causes and effects you discover in a classroom discussion, modifying your patterns in the light of others'. Do your own thinking on the topic first, and write up a first draft. Use that draft as the basis for your discussion with your classmates, revising it for your magazine audience after you have compared your observations with those of others. When you revise, consider how your style will need to be tailored to the magazine audience you have chosen to address.

How To Get The Love You Never Thought You Could.

1   Did you ever crawl into bed at night dreaming of a lover who was good-looking and sexy. Someone with great skin and beautiful eyes, thick lustrous hair and a trim well-formed body?

2   And did you ever walk into a discotheque or a restaurant and spot someone who was so incredibly attractive you actually hurt because you knew deep down inside you would never get to meet them?

3   The truth is, most of us are always falling madly in love with people we think are much too good for us, too attractive, too tall, too sexy, too glamorous. But instead of going after them with all our desire, energy

and creativity, we sit back and settle for a love that doesn't really turn us on, a love that may be ''okay'' but really isn't *great*. The kind of love, in short, that isn't really love at all.

Of course, not all people settle for the average. Oh, no, some people don't settle at all. Think about it. How many times have you seen a funny looking, knobby-kneed girl in glasses walk into a dance with a guy who looks like he could double for Robert Redford?   4

And how many times have you seen some short bald middle-aged man walking down the street with Sophia Loren's twin? The fact is, some people are always going beyond themselves in love. They know that it doesn't make any difference what you look like when it comes to attracting others. They know that the real key to finding a great lover is in the quality of love you show to the outside world. And that's why we think you ought to know about a brilliant new system from Symphony Press called *''CONNECTING'': How To Stop Losing and Start Winning At The Game Of Love.*   5

The Game Of Love

Love is a game. Some play it poorly. And some play it well. If you want to play it brilliantly—so brilliantly you win almost every time—then it's time you read the ''Connecting System.''   6

The ''Connecting System'' consists of two fabulous bestsellers, CONNECTING and GETTING TOGETHER. They'll show you exactly how to turn on and light up all the super sexy people you see almost everywhere you go. The ''Connecting System'' will teach you to open your eyes to the fact that people *want you to love them*, good-looking ones as well as not so good-looking ones. To show someone that you genuinely love them can be the biggest turn on in the world—for you *and* them.   7

Here are just a few of the scores of inventive and effective techniques you'll learn: 8

- How the raw *power* of your love can act like a magnet to attract the opposite sex.
- A fantastic way to turn a strictly sexual relationship into a deep, loving relationship *instantly*.
- A simple way to conquer your feelings of inadequacy so you project the personality of an exciting, passionate, irresistible lover.
- Why the flaws you feel so self-conscious about may very well be the most lovable things about you.
- An easy way to get out of a dead-end romance and move on to more exciting lovers.

- How to recognize "magic moments" in a relationship and how to use them to intensify feelings of love.
- How to "let yourself go" in love and why this can be a turn on to everyone you meet.
- A simple system that shows you how to pace yourself into a truly loving relationship and why "suffocating" your date with love too early can ruin a sure romance.
- Why the greatest lovers always learn the art of massage and the massage technique that will cause people to fall in love with you, often on the very first date (this technique has been called the "true" aphrodisiac touch by many experts).
- Why the "hate" vibrations you may think you feel from others might actually be their way of saying "I love you" . . . and how to know when this is happening.

9   And that's not all! The "Connecting System" is literally filled with over one hundred more fantastic techniques for finding, getting, and keeping love—not fleeting sexual encounters or one night stands, but true romantic, undying love.

10   If you want to fall in love, that's all you need—just a little bit of desire. The "Connecting System" will take care of the rest. You don't have to impress every girl or guy you meet with your accomplishments. You don't have to spend ridiculous amounts of money to win their love. You don't have to join an exercise class for a year so you look trim and sexy. You don't have to do any of these things. Our easy-to-read, enjoyable, inexpensive "Connecting System" will show you how to find love *the day you receive it*—not after you've lost 20 pounds, not after you've spent money on a new wardrobe, not after you've been rejected by fifty other people, but *the day you receive it!* Just the way you are. And the "Connecting System" doesn't promise you only one lover. It can show you how to have two, three, even four lovers at the same time—even if you've never had one before! And if you're presently involved in a sluggish, dull, unrewarding relationship that you don't know how to get out of, this revolutionary system will show you how to "unconnect" without anyone feeling bad or hurt. Or if you just want to energize your present, "unsatisfying" romance, you'll learn techniques that will turn your lover into the tempting, tantalizing, passionate, pulsating partner you always knew he or she could be.

One Year Guarantee

11   You're probably thinking "what if the 'Connecting System' doesn't work for me. I've never been able to find the love I want before, and I probably won't find it now, even if I do buy your system." Well,

we're so sure the "Connecting System" will work for you, that we guarantee it for one full year or your money back. That's right. Read it once, twice, five times...study it, memorize it, put the system to work for you...every day for 365 days. If after one full year you still don't think the "Connecting System" has helped, simply return the two volumes and we will send you a complete and immediate refund. No questions asked. Even if you secretly feel the system has helped you become more lovable.

Think about it. A system so good, so effective, so foolproof, that the　*12* publishers are willing to GUARANTEE that you will find love, even the love you never thought you could. That's an offer you simply can not afford to pass up.

Why spend another day of your life lonely and without love?　*13*

Holding hands in the moonlight with the most seductive woman in　*14* three states...strolling along the beach at sunset with a man that makes your heart pound with compassion...sitting in front of a glowing fire locked in an embrace of undying love...

Don't cheat yourself of the greatest emotion men and women experi-　*15* ence together. Fall in love with the "Connecting System".

*W*hat Do the Arts Tell Us About Ourselves?

▶ —————————————————————

Introduction

▶────────────────────

This section includes writings that explore the ways in which we are defined by the popular and fine arts. Many arts are represented. James Baldwin shows us the influence of music—jazz or blues—on the life of one man. Richard Rhodes focuses on greeting cards, a medium through which many of us express personal sentiments to friends, loved ones, relatives, and acquaintances. Robert Warshow looks at how the heroes of Western and gangster movies embody American values, our beliefs in good and bad, our particular ways of living together and apart. Both Jane Jacobs and Lewis H. Lapham analyze social arts that affect our everyday lives. Jacobs sees twentieth-century schools of public architecture as confused, too idealistic, or in outright conflict with people's needs. Lapham focuses on the political career and aspirations of Edward Kennedy as publicly produced theater in which major characters grow out of the psychological needs of the public psyche. Virginia Woolf brings us from a social context to a personal one, assuming an audience of readers of books. Rather than trying to tell us how books connect us with others, she emphasizes the creativity and control that reading books can give to the life of the individual. Honor Moore looks at the troubled life and painting career of her grandmother and explores the interrelationships among art, social position, and domestic ties in that one woman's life.

All of these writings assume a definition of art that may seem unconventional. Rather than as simple entertainment or pleasure, these writings see the arts as humanity's ways of organizing reality. These pictures of reality are our ways of knowing and understanding our world and, most importantly, ourselves. For James Baldwin's character Sonny, playing the blues expresses "all that hatred and misery and love" of his life growing up in Harlem. For Virginia Woolf, reading pulls together the otherwise disorganized perceptions of everyday life. Honor Moore makes sense of the relationship between creating art and being a woman by means of a perceptive analysis of her grandmother's life. Art represents the individual's struggle to express, in unique form, what living in his or her time and place is like.

The essays by Baldwin, Woolf, and Moore focus on individuals as they seek order through art. The rest of the essays in this section show us how people are often controlled by the popular arts. Richard Rhodes explains how greeting card verses shape our ways of expressing sentiment. Robert Warshow tells us how Western and gangster movie heroes both reflect and influence our personal values. Jane Jacobs argues that city planners shape our lives by creating the environments in which we live. Lewis H. Lapham suggests that the popular media shape our images of politicians and, ultimately, control our votes and our political views. Some of these forms of control are benign and useful; others are manipulative and harmful.

Three key ideas underlie the readings in this section: (1) that the arts often control the ways we perceive and think; (2) that popular arts reflect complex social problems and cannot be considered in isolation from society; (3) that people can exert some control over their lives and environments by seriously considering the implications of popular arts such as architecture, mass media, and politics.

Consider these questions as you read this section:

1. What might be the good and bad effects of particular popular arts on people? Can you think of arts that encourage negative tendencies in the people who consume them?
2. Should people simply take in the arts and their representations of life, or should they develop more selective and critical perspectives on them?
3. Do you think people's values and perspectives on others are influenced by the arts they are exposed to, or are most people simply entertained by the arts without being influenced by the values they express?
4. What popular arts are you most interested in? How might they be affecting your values?

Sonny's Blues

JAMES BALDWIN

James Baldwin (born 1924) is one of the most well-known, prolific, controversial, and socially active black writers in America. He has written seven novels, beginning with the largely autobiographical *Go Tell It on the Mountain* in 1953. Baldwin's first novel deals with its narrator's experiences with Christianity and the community in Harlem, the predominantly black section of New York City. At fourteen, Baldwin became a preacher at Harlem's Fireside Pentecostal Church. As an adolescent, he remained intensely involved in church affairs, following in his minister father's footsteps. By early adulthood, however, he had rejected the church because he felt it had limited and partially enslaved black people with its rigid codes and guilt-ridden morality. Nevertheless, the influence of Christianity never completely left Baldwin's work. In his latest novel, *Just Above My Head* (1979), the protagonist is a black gospel singer, and the subject is her experiences as a popular singing star. In the story "Sonny's Blues," the narrator spends a significant moment watching a sidewalk preacher and several women revivalists from an apartment window. This scene seems to help the narrator figure out his past experiences with religion.

Baldwin's talent as a writer, however, may be most apparent in the collections of his short stories — *Going To Meet the Man* (1965) and *This Morning, This Evening, So Soon* (1967) — and his personal essays — *Notes of a Native Son* (1955), *Nobody Knows My Name: More Notes of a Native Son* (1961), and *The Fire Next Time* (1963). In his stories and essays, Baldwin renders his experiences as a black American, intellectual, homosexual, and writer in arresting detail and in an impassioned yet reflective style. These works deal directly with racial and social issues, based on a careful rendering of personal experience, yet they never stray into ideological stereotyping.

In the 1960s and 1970s, Baldwin was intensely involved in the civil rights movement, the Black Power movement, and other human rights movements. Many critics believe his accomplishments as a writer would be far greater if his social activism had a somewhat smaller role in his life. But Baldwin has always strived to connect his literary accomplishments to the social context in which he writes.

As you read "Sonny's Blues," note the contrasting ways in which the story's narrator (Sonny's brother) and Sonny view their similar experiences. For most of the story, the narrator seems sure of his values

—seems to know that society approves of them. Sonny, on the other hand, seems sure that society will fail to appreciate his music and will find him worthless.

1. Why does Baldwin emphasize this contrast? What does Sonny's music express that the narrator's career as a mathematics teacher could not?
2. How might Sonny's jazz help other blacks just as much as his brother's teaching does?
3. Why do you think Baldwin chose to tell this story from Sonny's brother's viewpoint?

▶ ———————————————

1   I read about it in the paper, in the subway, on my way to work. I read it, and I couldn't believe it, and I read it again. Then perhaps I just stared at it, at the newsprint spelling out his name, spelling out the story. I stared at it in the swinging lights of the subway car, and in the faces and bodies of the people, and in my own face, trapped in the darkness which roared outside.

2   It was not to be believed and I kept telling myself that, as I walked from the subway station to the high school. And at the same time I couldn't doubt it. I was scared, scared for Sonny. He became real to me again. A great block of ice got settled in my belly and kept melting there slowly all day long, while I taught my classes algebra. It was a special kind of ice. It kept melting, sending trickles of ice water all up and down my veins, but it never got less. Sometimes it hardened and seemed to expand until I felt my guts were going to come spilling out or that I was going to choke or scream. This would always be at a moment when I was remembering some specific thing Sonny had once said or done.

3   When he was about as old as the boys in my classes his face had been bright and open, there was a lot of copper in it; and he'd had wonderfully direct brown eyes, and great gentleness and privacy. I wondered what he looked like now. He had been picked up, the evening before, in a raid on an apartment downtown, for peddling and using heroin.

4   I couldn't believe it: but what I mean by that is that I couldn't find any room for it anywhere inside me. I had kept it outside me for a long time. I hadn't wanted to know. I had had suspicions, but I didn't name them, I kept putting them away. I told myself that Sonny was wild, but he wasn't crazy. And he'd always been a good boy, he hadn't ever turned hard or evil or disrespectful, the way kids can, so quick, so quick, espe-

cially in Harlem. I didn't want to believe that I'd ever see my brother going down, coming to nothing, all that light in his face gone out, in the condition I'd already seen so many others. Yet it had happened and here I was, talking about algebra to a lot of boys who might, every one of them for all I knew, be popping off needles every time they went to the head. Maybe it did more for them than algebra could.

I was sure that the first time Sonny had ever had horse,* he couldn't   5
have been much older than these boys were now. These boys, now, were living as we'd been living then, they were growing up with a rush and their heads bumped abruptly against the low ceiling of their actual possibilities. They were filled with rage. All they really knew were two darknesses, the darkness of their lives, which was now closing in on them, and the darkness of the movies, which had blinded them to that other darkness, and in which they now, vindictively, dreamed, at once more together than they were at any other time, and more alone.

When the last bell rang, the last class ended, I let out my breath. It   6
seemed I'd been holding it for all that time. My clothes were wet—I may have looked as though I'd been sitting in a steam bath, all dressed up, all afternoon. I sat alone in the classroom a long time. I listened to the boys outside, downstairs, shouting and cursing and laughing. Their laughter struck me for perhaps the first time. It was not the joyous laughter which—God knows why—one associates with children. It was mocking and insular, its intent was to denigrate. It was disenchanted, and in this, also, lay the authority of their curses. Perhaps I was listening to them because I was thinking about my brother and in them I heard my brother. And myself.

One boy was whistling a tune, at once very complicated and very   7
simple, it seemed to be pouring out of him as though he were a bird, and it sounded very cool and moving through all that harsh, bright air, only just holding its own through all those other sounds.

I stood up and walked over to the window and looked down into the   8
courtyard. It was the beginning of the spring and the sap was rising in the boys. A teacher passed through them every now and again, quickly, as though he or she couldn't wait to get out of that courtyard, to get those boys out of their sight and off their minds. I started collecting my stuff. I thought I'd better get home and talk to Isabel.

The courtyard was almost deserted by the time I got downstairs. I   9
saw this boy standing in the shadow of a doorway, looking just like Sonny. I almost called his name. Then I saw that it wasn't Sonny, but somebody we used to know, a boy from around our block. He'd been

---

*"Horse" is a street name for heroin.

Sonny's friend. He'd never been mine, having been too young for me, and, anyway, I'd never liked him. And now, even though he was a grown-up man, he still hung around that block, still spent hours on the street corners, was always high and raggy. I used to run into him from time to time and he'd often work around to asking me for a quarter or fifty cents. He always had some real good excuse, too, and I always gave it to him, I don't know why.

10   But now, abruptly, I hated him. I couldn't stand the way he looked at me, partly like a dog, partly like a cunning child. I wanted to ask him what the hell he was doing in the school courtyard.

11   He sort of shuffled over to me, and he said, "I see you got the papers. So you already know about it."

12   "You mean about Sonny? Yes, I already know about it. How come they didn't get you?"

13   He grinned. It made him repulsive and it also brought to mind what he'd looked like as a kid. "I wasn't there. I stay away from them people."

14   "Good for you." I offered him a cigarette and I watched him through the smoke. "You come all the way down here just to tell me about Sonny?"

15   "That's right." He was sort of shaking his head and his eyes looked strange, as though they were about to cross. The bright sun deadened his damp dark brown skin and it made his eyes look yellow and showed up the dirt in his kinked hair. He smelled funky. I moved a little away from him and I said, "Well, thanks. But I already know about it and I got to get home."

16   "I'll walk you a little ways," he said. We started walking. There were a couple of kids still loitering in the courtyard and one of them said goodnight to me and looked strangely at the boy beside me.

17   "What're you going to do?" he asked me. "I mean, about Sonny?"

18   "Look. I haven't seen Sonny for over a year, I'm not sure I'm going to do anything. Anyway, what the hell *can* I do?"

19   "That's right," he said quickly, "ain't nothing you can do. Can't much help old Sonny no more, I guess."

20   It was what I was thinking and so it seemed to me he had no right to say it.

21   "I'm surprised at Sonny, though," he went on—he had a funny way of talking, he looked straight ahead as though he were talking to himself—"I thought Sonny was a smart boy, I thought he was too smart to get hung."

22   "I guess he thought so too," I said sharply, "and that's how he got hung. And how about you? You're pretty goddamn smart, I bet."

23   Then he looked directly at me, just for a minute. "I ain't smart," he said. "If I was smart, I'd have reached for a pistol a long time ago."

"Look. Don't tell *me* your sad story, if it was up to me, I'd give you one." Then I felt guilty—guilty, probably, for never having supposed that the poor bastard *had* a story of his own, much less a sad one, and I asked, quickly, "What's going to happen to him now?" 24

He didn't answer this. He was off by himself some place. 25

"Funny thing," he said, and from his tone we might have been discussing the quickest way to get to Brooklyn, "when I saw the papers this morning, the first thing I asked myself was if I had anything to do with it. I felt sort of responsible." 26

I began to listen more carefully. The subway station was on the corner, just before us, and I stopped. He stopped, too. We were in front of a bar and he ducked slightly, peering in, but whoever he was looking for didn't seem to be there. The juke box was blasting away with something black and bouncy and I half watched the barmaid as she danced her way from the juke box to her place behind the bar. And I watched her face as she laughingly responded to something someone said to her, still keeping time to the music. When she smiled one saw the little girl, one sensed the doomed, still-struggling woman beneath the battered face of the semi-whore. 27

"I never *give* Sonny nothing," the boy said finally, "but a long time ago I come to school high and Sonny asked me how it felt." He paused, I couldn't bear to watch him, I watched the barmaid, and I listened to the music which seemed to be causing the pavement to shake. "I told him it felt great." The music stopped, the barmaid paused and watched the juke box until the music began again. "It did." 28

All this was carrying me some place I didn't want to go. I certainly didn't want to know how it felt. It filled everything, the people, the houses, the music, the dark, quicksilver barmaid, with menace; and this menace was their reality. 29

"What's going to happen to him now?" I asked again. 30

"They'll send him away some place and they'll try to cure him." He shook his head. "Maybe he'll even think he's kicked the habit. Then they'll let him loose"—he gestured, throwing his cigarette into the gutter. "That's all." 31

"What do you mean, that's *all*?" 32

But I knew what he meant. 33

"I *mean*, that's *all*." He turned his head and looked at me, pulling down the corners of his mouth. "Don't you know what I mean?" he asked, softly. 34

"How the hell *would* I know what you mean?" I almost whispered it, I don't know why. 35

"That's right," he said to the air, "how would *he* know what I mean?" He turned toward me again, patient and calm, and yet I somehow felt him shaking, shaking as though he were going to fall apart. I 36 felt that ice in my guts again, the dread I'd felt all afternoon; and again I watched the barmaid, moving about the bar, washing glasses, and singing. "Listen. They'll let him out and then it'll just start all over again. That's what I mean."

37 "You mean—they'll let him out. And then he'll just start working his way back in again. You mean he'll never kick the habit. Is that what you mean?"

38 "That's right," he said, cheerfully. "*You* see what I mean."

39 "Tell me," I said at last, "why does he want to die? He must want to die, he's killing himself, why does he want to die?"

40 He looked at me in surprise. He licked his lips. "He don't want to die. He wants to live. Don't nobody want to die, ever."

41 Then I wanted to ask him—too many things. He could not have answered, or if he had, I could not have borne the answers. I started walking. "Well, I guess it's none of my business."

42 "It's going to be rough on old Sonny," he said. We reached the subway station. "This is your station?" he asked. I nodded. I took one step down. "Damn!" he said, suddenly. I looked up at him. He grinned again. "Damn it if I didn't leave all my money home. You ain't got a dollar on you, have you? Just for a couple of days, is all."

43 All at once something inside gave and threatened to come pouring out of me. I didn't hate him any more. I felt that in another moment I'd start crying like a child.

44 "Sure," I said. "Don't sweat." I looked in my wallet and didn't have a dollar, I only had a five. "Here," I said. "That hold you?"

45 He didn't look at it—he didn't want to look at it. A terrible, closed look came over his face, as though he were keeping the number on the bill a secret from him and me. "Thanks," he said, and now he was dying to see me go. "Don't worry about Sonny. Maybe I'll write him or something."

46 "Sure," I said. "You do that. So long."

47 "Be seeing you," he said. I went on down the steps.

48 And I didn't write Sonny or send him anything for a long time. When I finally did, it was just after my little girl died, he wrote me back a letter which made me feel like a bastard.

49 Here's what he said:

Dear brother,
    You don't know how much I needed to hear from you. I wanted to write you many a time but I dug how much I must have hurt you and so I didn't write. But now I feel like a man who's been trying to climb up out of some deep, real deep and funky hole and just saw the sun up there, outside. I got to get outside.
    I can't tell you much about how I got here. I mean I don't know how to tell you. I guess I was afraid of something or I was trying to escape from some-

thing and you know I have never been very strong in the head (smile). I'm glad Mama and Daddy are dead and can't see what's happened to their son and I swear if I'd known what I was doing I would never have hurt you so, you and a lot of other fine people who were nice to me and who believed in me.

I don't want you to think it had anything to do with me being a musician. It's more than that. Or maybe less than that. I can't get anything straight in my head down here and I try not to think about what's going to happen to me when I get outside again. Sometime I think I'm going to flip and *never* get outside and sometime I think I'll come straight back. I tell you one thing, though, I'd rather blow my brains out than go through this again. But that's what they all say, so they tell me. If I tell you when I'm coming to New York and if you could meet me, I sure would appreciate it. Give my love to Isabel and the kids and I was sure sorry to hear about Little Gracie. I wish I could be like Mama and say the Lord's will be done, but I don't know it seems to me that trouble is the one thing that never does get stopped and I don't know what good it does to blame it on the Lord. But maybe it does some good if you believe it.

Your brother,
Sonny

Then I kept in constant touch with him and I sent him whatever I   *50* could and I went to meet him when he came back to New York. When I saw him many things I thought I had forgotten came flooding back to me. This was because I had begun, finally, to wonder about Sonny, about the life that Sonny lived inside. This life, whatever it was, had made him older and thinner and it had deepened the distant stillness in which he had always moved. He looked very unlike my baby brother. Yet, when he smiled, when we shook hands, the baby brother I'd never known looked out from the depths of his private life, like an animal waiting to be coaxed into the light.

"How you been keeping?" he asked me.   *51*

"All right. And you?"   *52*

"Just fine." He was smiling all over his face. "It's good to see you   *53* again."

"It's good to see you."   *54*

The seven years' difference in our ages lay between us like a chasm: I   *55* wondered if these years would ever operate between us as a bridge. I was remembering, and it made it hard to catch my breath, that I had been there when he was born; and I had heard the first words he had ever spoken. When he started to walk, he walked from our mother straight to me. I caught him just before he fell when he took the first steps he ever took in this world.

"How's Isabel?"   *56*

"Just fine. She's dying to see you."   *57*

58   "And the boys?"

59   "They're fine, too. They're anxious to see their uncle."

60   "Oh, come on. You know they don't remember me."

61   "Are you kidding? Of course they remember you."

62   He grinned again. We got into a taxi. We had a lot to say to each other, far too much to know how to begin.

63   As the taxi began to move, I asked, "You still want to go to India?"

64   He laughed. "You still remember that. Hell, no. This place is Indian enough for me."

65   "It used to belong to them," I said.

66   And he laughed again. "They damn sure knew what they were doing when they got rid of it."

67   Years ago, when he was around fourteen, he'd been all hipped on the idea of going to India. He read books about people sitting on rocks, naked, in all kinds of weather, but mostly bad, naturally, and walking barefoot through hot coals and arriving at wisdom. I used to say that it sounded to me as though they were getting away from wisdom as fast as they could. I think he sort of looked down on me for that.

68   "Do you mind," he asked, "if we have the driver drive alongside the park? On the west side—I haven't seen the city in so long."

69   "Of course not," I said. I was afraid that I might sound as though I were humoring him, but I hoped he wouldn't take it that way.

70   So we drove along, between the green of the park and the stony, lifeless elegance of hotels and apartment buildings, toward the vivid, killing streets of our childhood. These streets hadn't changed, though housing projects jutted up out of them now like rocks in the middle of a boiling sea. Most of the houses in which we had grown up had vanished, as had the stores from which we had stolen, the basements in which we had first tried sex, the rooftops from which we had hurled tin cans and bricks. But houses exactly like the houses of our past yet dominated the landscape, boys exactly like the boys we once had been found themselves smothering in these houses, came down into the streets for light and air and found themselves encircled by disaster. Some escaped the trap, most didn't. Those who got out always left something of themselves behind, as some animals amputate a leg and leave it in the trap. It might be said, perhaps, that I had escaped, after all, I was a school teacher; or that Sonny had, he hadn't lived in Harlem for years. Yet, as the cab moved uptown through streets which seemed, with a rush, to darken with dark people, and as I covertly studied Sonny's face, it came to me that what we both were seeking through our separate cab windows was that part of ourselves which had been left behind. It's always at the hour of trouble and confrontation that the missing member aches.

71   We hit 110th Street and started rolling up Lenox Avenue. And I'd known this avenue all my life, but it seemed to me again, as it had

seemed on the day I'd first heard about Sonny's trouble, filled with a hidden menace which was its very breath of life.

"We almost there," said Sonny.   72

"Almost." We were both too nervous to say anything more.   73

We live in a housing project. It hasn't been up long. A few days after it   74
was up it seemed uninhabitably new, now, of course, it's already run-
down. It looks like a parody of the good, clean, faceless life—God
knows the people who live in it do their best to make it a parody. The
beat-looking grass lying around isn't enough to make their lives green,
the hedges will never hold out the streets, and they know it. The big
windows fool no one, they aren't big enough to make space out of no
space. They don't bother with the windows, they watch the TV screen
instead. The playground is most popular with the children who don't
play at jacks, or skip rope, or roller skate, or swing, and they can be
found in it after dark. We moved in partly because it's not too far from
where I teach, and partly for the kids; but it's really just like the houses
in which Sonny and I grew up. The same things happen, they'll have the
same things to remember. The moment Sonny and I started into the
house I had the feeling that I was simply bringing him back into the danger he had almost died trying to escape.

Sonny has never been talkative. So I don't why I was sure he'd be   75
dying to talk to me when supper was over the first night. Everything
went fine, the oldest boy remembered him, and the youngest boy liked
him, and Sonny had remembered to bring something for each of them;
and Isabel, who is really much nicer than I am, more open and giving,
had gone to a lot of trouble about dinner and was genuinely glad to see
him. And she's alway been able to tease Sonny in a way that I haven't. It
was nice to see her face so vivid again and to hear her laugh and watch
her make Sonny laugh. She wasn't, or, anyway, she didn't seem to be,
at all uneasy or embarrassed. She chatted as though there were no subject which had to be avoided and she got Sonny past his first, faint
stiffness. And thank God she was there, for I was filled with that icy
dread again. Everything I did seemed awkward to me, and everything I
said sounded freighted with hidden meaning. I was trying to remember
everything I'd heard about dope addiction and I couldn't help watching
Sonny for signs. I wasn't doing it out of malice. I was trying to find out
something about my brother. I was dying to hear him tell me he was
safe.

"Safe!" my father grunted, whenever Mama suggested trying to   76
move to a neighborhood which might be safer for children. "Safe, hell!
Ain't no place safe for kids, nor nobody."

He always went on like this, but he wasn't, ever, really as bad as he   77
sounded, not even on weekends, when he got drunk. As a matter of fact,

he was always on the lookout for "something a little better," but he died before he found it. He died suddenly, during a drunken weekend in the middle of the war, when Sonny was fifteen. He and Sonny hadn't ever got on too well. And this was partly because Sonny was the apple of his father's eye. It was because he loved Sonny so much and was frightened for him, that he was always fighting with him. It doesn't do any good to fight with Sonny. Sonny just moves back, inside himself, where he can't be reached. But the principal reason that they never hit it off is that they were so much alike. Daddy was big and rough and loud-talking, just the opposite of Sonny, but they both had—that same privacy.

78   Mama tried to tell me something about this, just after Daddy died. I was home on leave from the army.

79   This was the last time I ever saw my mother alive. Just the same, this picture gets all mixed up in my mind with pictures I had of her when she was younger. The way I always see her is the way she used to be on a Sunday afternoon, say, when the old folks were talking after the big Sunday dinner. I always see her wearing pale blue. She'd be sitting on the sofa. And my father would be sitting in the easy chair, not far from her. And the living room would be full of church folks and relatives. There they sit, in chairs all around the living room, and the night is creeping up outside, but nobody knows it yet. You can see the darkness growing against the windowpanes and you hear the street noises every now and again, or maybe the jangling beat of a tambourine from one of the churches close by, but it's real quiet in the room. For a moment nobody's talking, but every face looks darkening, like the sky outside. And my mother rocks a little from the waist, and my father's eyes are closed. Everyone is looking at something a child can't see. For a minute they've forgotten the children. Maybe a kid is lying on the the rug, half asleep. Maybe somebody's got a kid in his lap and is absent-mindedly stroking the kid's head. Maybe there's a kid, quiet and big-eyed, curled up in a big chair in the corner. The silence, the darkness coming, and the darkness in the faces frighten the child obscurely. He hopes that the hand which strokes his forehead will never stop—will never die. He hopes that there will never come a time when the old folks won't be sitting around the living room, talking about where they've come from, and what they've seen, and what's happened to them and their kinfolk.

80   But something deep and watchful in the child knows that this is bound to end, is already ending. In a moment someone will get up and turn on the light. Then the old folks will remember the children and they won't talk any more that day. And when light fills the room, the child is filled with darkness. He knows that every time this happens he's moved just a little closer to that darkness outside. The darkness outside is what the old folks have been talking about. It's what they've

come from. It's what they endure. The child knows that they won't talk any more because if he knows too much about what's happened to *them*, he'll know too much too soon, about what's going to happen to *him*.

The last time I talked to my mother, I remember I was restless. I wanted to get out and see Isabel. We weren't married then and we had a lot to straighten out between us.   81

There Mama sat, in black, by the window. She was humming an old church song, *Lord, you brought me from a long ways off*. Sonny was out somewhere. Mama kept watching the streets.   82

"I don't know," she said. "if I'll ever see you again, after you go off from here. But I hope you'll remember the things I tried to teach you."   83

"Don't talk like that," I said, and smiled. "You'll be here a long time yet."   84

She smiled, too, but she said nothing. She was quiet for a long time. And I said, "Mama, don't you worry about nothing. I'll be writing all the time, and you be getting the checks. . . ."   85

"I want to talk to you about your brother," she said, suddenly. "If anything happens to me he ain't going to have nobody to look out for him."   86

"Mama," I said, "ain't nothing going to happen to you *or* Sonny. Sonny's all right. He's a good boy and he's got good sense."   87

"It ain't a question of his being a good boy," Mama said, "nor of his having good sense. It ain't only the bad ones, nor yet the dumb ones that gets sucked under." She stopped, looking at me. "Your Daddy once had a brother," she said, and she smiled in a way that made me feel she was in pain. "You didn't never know that, did you?"   88

"No," I said, "I never knew that," and I watched her face.   89

"Oh, yes," she said, "your Daddy had a brother." She looked out of the window again. "I know you never saw your Daddy cry. But *I* did—many a time, through all these years."   90

I asked her, "What happened to his brother? How come nobody's ever talked about him?"   91

This was the first time I ever saw my mother look old.   92

"His brother got killed," she said, "when he was just a little younger than you are now. I knew him. He was a fine boy. He was maybe a little full of the devil, but he didn't mean nobody no harm."   93

Then she stopped and the room was silent, exactly as it had sometimes been on those Sunday afternoons. Mama kept looking out into the streets.   94

"He used to have a job in the mill," she said, "and, like all young folks, he just liked to perform on Saturday nights. Saturday nights, him and your father would drift around to different place, go to dances and things like that, or just sit around with people they knew, and your   95 father's brother would sing, he had a fine voice, and play along with himself on his guitar. Well, this particular Saturday night, him and your father was coming home from some place, and they were both a little drunk, and there was a moon that night, it was bright like day. Your father's brother was feeling kind of good, and he was whistling to himself, and he had his guitar slung over his shoulder. They was coming down a hill and beneath them was a road that turned off from the highway. Well, your father's brother, being always kind of frisky, decided to run down this hill, and he did, with that guitar banging and clanging behind him, and he ran across the road, and he was making water behind a tree. And your father was sort of amused at him and he was still coming down the hill, kind of slow. Then he heard a car motor and that same minute his brother stepped from behind the tree, into the road, in the moonlight. And he started to cross the road. And your father started to run down the hill, he says he don't know why. This car was full of white men. They was all drunk, and when they seen your father's brother they let out a great whoop and holler and they aimed the car straight at him. They was having fun, they just wanted to scare him, the way they do sometimes, you know. But they was drunk. And I guess the boy, being drunk, too, and scared, kind of lost his head. By the time he jumped it was too late. Your father says he heard his brother scream when the car rolled over him, and he heard the wood of that guitar when it give, and he heard them strings go flying, and he heard them white men shouting, and the car kept on a-going and it ain't stopped till this day. And, time your father got down the hill, his brother weren't nothing but blood and pulp."

96   Tears were gleaming on my mother's face. There wasn't anything I could say.

97   "He never mentioned it," she said, "because I never let him mention it before you children. Your Daddy was like a crazy man that night and for many a night thereafter. He says he never in his life seen anything as dark as that road after the lights of that car had gone away. Weren't nothing, weren't nobody on that road, just your Daddy and his brother and that busted guitar. Oh, yes. Your Daddy never did really get right again. Till the day he died he weren't sure but that every white man he saw was the man that killed his brother."

98   She stopped and took out her handkerchief and dried her eyes and looked at me.

99   "I ain't telling you all this," she said, "to make you scared or bitter or to make you hate nobody. I'm telling you this because you got a brother. And the world ain't changed."

100   I guess I didn't want to believe this. I guess she saw this in my face. She turned away from me, toward the window again, searching those streets.

"But I praise my Redeemer," she said at last, "that He called your   *101*
Daddy home before me. I ain't saying it to throw no flowers at myself,
but, I declare, it keeps me from feeling too cast down to know I helped
your father get safely through this world. Your father always acted like
he was the roughest, strongest man on earth. And everybody took him
to be like that. But if he hadn't had *me* there—to see his tears!"

She was crying again. Still, I couldn't move. I said, "Lord, Lord,   *102*
Mama, I didn't know it was like that."

"Oh, honey," she said, "there's a lot that you don't know. But you   *103*
are going to find out." She stood up from the window and came over to
me. "You got to hold on to your brother," she said, "and don't let him
fall, no matter what it looks like is happening to him and no matter how
evil you gets with him. You going to be evil with him many a time. But
don't you forget what I told you, you hear?"

"I won't forget," I said. "Don't you worry, I won't forget. I won't let   *104*
nothing happen to Sonny."

My mother smiled as though she were amused at something she saw   *105*
in my face. Then, "You may not be able to stop nothing from happening. But you got to let him know you's *there*."

Two days later I was married, and then I was gone. And I had a lot of   *106*
things on my mind and I pretty well forgot my promise to Mama until I
got shipped home on a special furlough for her funeral.

And, after the funeral, with just Sonny and me alone in the empty   *107*
kitchen, I tried to find out something about him.

"What do you want to do?" I asked him.   *108*

"I'm going to be a musician," he said.   *109*

For he had graduated, in the time I had been away, from dancing to   *110*
the juke box to finding out who was playing what, and what they were
doing with it, and he had bought himself a set of drums.

"You mean, you want to be a drummer?" I somehow had the feeling   *111*
that being a drummer might be all right for other people but not for my
brother Sonny.

"I don't think," he said, looking at me very gravely, "that I'll ever be   *112*
a good drummer. But I think I can play a piano."

I frowned. I'd never played the role of the older brother quite so   *113*
seriously before, had scarcely ever, in fact, *asked* Sonny a damn thing. I
sensed myself in the presence of something I didn't really know how to
handle, didn't understand. So I made my frown a little deeper as I asked:
"What kind of musician do you want to be?"

He grinned. "How many kinds do you think there are?"   *114*

"Be *serious*," I said.   *115*

He laughed, throwing his head back, and then looked at me. "I *am*   *116*
serious."

117   "Well, then, for Christ's sake, stop kidding around and answer a serious question. I mean, do you want to be a concert pianist, you want to play classical music and all that, or—or what?" Long before I finished he was laughing again. "For Christ's *sake*, Sonny!"

118   He sobered, but with difficulty. "I'm sorry. But you sound so— *scared!*" and he was off again.

119   "Well, you may think it's funny now, baby, but it's not going to be so funny when you have to make your living at it, let me tell you *that*." I was furious because I knew he was laughing at me and I didn't know why.

120   "No," he said, very sober now, and afraid, perhaps, that he'd hurt me, "I don't want to be a classical pianist. That isn't what interests me. I mean"—he paused, looking hard at me, as though his eyes would help me to understand, and then gestured helplessly, as though perhaps his hand would help—"I mean, I'll have a lot of studying to do, and I'll have to study *everything*, but, I mean, I want to play *with*—jazz musicians." He stopped. "I want to play jazz," he said.

121   Well, the word had never before sounded as heavy, as real, as it sounded that afternoon in Sonny's mouth. I just looked at him and I was probably frowning a real frown by this time. I simply couldn't see why on earth he'd want to spend his time hanging around nightclubs, clowning around on bandstands, while people pushed each other around a dance floor. It seemed—beneath him, somehow. I had never thought about it before, had never been forced to, but I suppose I had always put jazz musicians in a class with what Daddy called "good-time people."

122   "Are you *serious?*"

123   "Hell, *yes*, I'm serious."

124   He looked more helpless than ever, and annoyed, and deeply hurt.

125   I suggested, helpfully: "You mean—like Louis Armstrong?"

126   His face closed as though I'd struck him. "No. I'm not talking about none of that old-time, down home crap."

127   "Well, look, Sonny, I'm sorry, don't get mad. I just don't altogether get it, that's all. Name somebody—you know, a jazz musician you admire."

128   "Bird."*

129   "Who?"

*Charlie "Bird" Parker (1920–1955) was an almost legendary jazz saxophone player; Birdland, a famous jazz club in New York City, was named after him. Parker is often credited, along with Dizzy Gillespie, with having discovered the "New Jazz," or "bebop," in New York City. Parker was a narcotics addict, like Sonny in this story.

"Bird! Charlie Parker! Don't they teach you nothing in the goddamn   *130*
army?''

I lit a cigarette. I was surprised and then a little amused to discover   *131*
that I was trembling. "I've been out of touch," I said. "You'll have to be
patient with me. Now. Who's this Parker character?''

"He's just one of the greatest jazz musicians alive," said Sonny,   *132*
sullenly, his hands in his pockets, his back to me. "Maybe *the* greatest," he added, bitterly, "that's probably why *you* never heard of him.''

"All right," I said, "I'm ignorant. I'm sorry. I'll go out and buy all the   *133*
cat's records right away, all right?''

"It don't," said Sonny, with dignity, "make any difference to me. I   *134*
don't care what you listen to. Don't do me no favors.''

I was beginning to realize that I'd never seen him so upset before.   *135*
With another part of my mind I was thinking that this would probably
turn out to be one of those things kids go through and that I shouldn't
make it seem important by pushing it too hard. Still, I didn't think it
would do any harm to ask: "Doesn't all this take a lot of time? Can you
make a living at it?''

He turned back to me and half leaned, half sat, on the kitchen table.   *136*
"Everything takes time," he said, "and—well, yes, sure, I can make a
living at it. But what I don't seem to be able to make you understand is
that it's the only thing I want to do.''

"Well, Sonny," I said, gently, "you know people can't always do ex-   *137*
actly what they *want* to do—''

"*No*, I don't know that," said Sonny, surprising me. "I think people   *138*
ought to do what they want to do, what else are they alive for?''

"You getting to be a big boy," I said desperately, "it's time you   *139*
started thinking about your future.''

"I'm thinking about my future," said Sonny, grimly. "I think about   *140*
it all the time.''

I gave up. I decided, if he didn't change his mind, that we could al-   *141*
ways talk about it later. "In the meantime," I said, "you got to finish
school.'' We had already decided that he'd have to move in with Isabel
and her folks. I knew this wasn't the ideal arrangement because Isabel's
folks are inclined to be dicty* and they hadn't especially wanted Isabel
to marry me. But I didn't know what else to do. "And we have to get
you fixed up at Isabel's.''

There was a long silence. He moved from the kitchen table to the   *142*
window. "That's a terrible idea. You know it yourself.''

"Do you have a *better* idea?''   *143*

---

*"Dicty" is black slang describing a bossy or dictatorial person.

144   He just walked up and down the kitchen for a minute. He was as tall as I was. He had started to shave. I suddenly had the feeling that I didn't know him at all.

145   He stopped at the kitchen table and picked up my cigarettes. Looking at me with a kind of mocking, amused defiance, he put one between his lips. "You mind?"

146   "You smoking already?"

147   He lit the cigarette and nodded, watching me through the smoke. "I just wanted to see if I'd have the courage to smoke in front of you." He grinned and blew a great cloud of smoke to the ceiling. "It was easy." He looked at my face. "Come on, now. I bet you was smoking at my age, tell the truth."

148   I didn't say anything but the truth was on my face, and he laughed. But now there was something very strained in his laugh. "Sure. And I bet that ain't all you was doing."

149   He was frightening me a little. "Cut the crap," I said. "We already decided that you was going to go and live at Isabel's. Now what's got into you all of a sudden?"

150   "*You* decided it," he pointed out. "*I* didn't decide nothing." He stopped in front of me, leaning against the stove, arms loosely folded. "Look, brother. I don't want to stay in Harlem no more, I really don't." He was very earnest. He looked at me, then over toward the kitchen window. There was something in his eyes I'd never seen before, some thoughtfulness, some worry all his own. He rubbed the muscle of one arm. "It's time I was getting out of here."

151   "Where do you want to *go*, Sonny?"

152   "I want to join the army. Or the navy, I don't care. If I say I'm old enough, they'll believe me."

153   Then I got mad. It was because I was so scared. "You must be crazy. You goddamn fool, what the hell do you want to go and join the *army* for?"

154   "I just told you. To get out of Harlem."

155   "Sonny, you haven't even finished *school*. And if you really want to be a musician, how do you expect to study if you're in the *army?*"

156   He looked at me, trapped, and in anguish. "There's ways. I might be able to work out some kind of deal. Anyway, I'll have the G.I. Bill when I come out."

157   "*If* you come out." We stared at each other. "Sonny, please. Be reasonable. I know the setup is far from perfect. But we got to do the best we can."

158   "I ain't learning nothing in school," he said. "Even when I go." He turned away from me and opened the window and threw his cigarette out into the narrow alley. I watched his back. "At least, I ain't learning

nothing you'd want me to learn.'' He slammed the window so hard I thought the glass would fly out, and turned back to me. ''And I'm sick of the stink of these garbage cans!''

''Sonny,'' I said, ''I know how you feel. But if you don't finish school   *159* now, you're going to be sorry later that you didn't.'' I grabbed him by the shoulders. ''And you only got another year. It ain't so bad. And I'll come back and I swear I'll help you do *whatever* you want to do. Just try to put up with it till I come back. Will you please do that? For me?''

He didn't answer and he wouldn't look at me.   *160*

''Sonny. You hear me?''   *161*

He pulled away. ''I hear you. But you never hear anything *I* say.''   *162*

I didn't know what to say to that. He looked out of the window and   *163* then back at me. ''OK,'' he said, and sighed. ''I'll try.''

Then I said, trying to cheer him up a little, ''They got a piano at   *164* Isabel's. You can practice on it.''

And as a matter of fact, it did cheer him up for a minute. ''That's   *165* right,'' he said to himself. ''I forgot that.'' His face relaxed a little. But the worry, the thoughtfulness, played on it still, the way shadows play on a face which is staring into the fire.

But I thought I'd never hear the end of that piano. At first, Isabel   *166* would write me, saying how nice it was that Sonny was so serious about his music and how, as soon as he came in from school, or wherever he had been when he was supposed to be at school, he went straight to that piano and stayed there until suppertime. And, after supper, he went back to that piano and stayed there until everybody went to bed. He was at the piano all day Saturday and all day Sunday. Then he bought a record player and started playing records. He'd play one record over and over again, all day long sometimes, and he'd improvise along with it on the piano. Or he'd play one section of the record, one chord, one change, one progression, then he'd do it on the piano. Then back to the record. Then back to the piano.

Well, I really don't know how they stood it. Isabel finally confessed   *167* that it wasn't like living with a person at all, it was like living with sound. And the sound didn't make any sense to her, didn't make any sense to any of them—naturally. They began, in a way, to be afflicted by this presence that was living in their home. It was as though Sonny were some sort of god, or monster. He moved in an atmosphere which wasn't like theirs at all. They fed him and he ate, he washed himself, he walked in and out of their door; he certainly wasn't nasty or unpleasant or rude, Sonny isn't any of those things; but it was as though he were all wrapped up in some cloud, some fire, some vision all his own; and there wasn't any way to reach him.

168 　　At the same time, he wasn't really a man yet, he was still a child, and they had to watch out for him in all kinds of ways. They certainly couldn't throw him out. Neither did they dare to make a great scene about that piano because even they dimly sensed, as I sensed, from so many thousands of miles away, that Sonny was at that piano playing for his life.

169 　　But he hadn't been going to school. One day a letter came from the school board and Isabel's mother got it—there had, apparently, been other letters but Sonny had torn them up. This day, when Sonny came in, Isabel's mother showed him the letter and asked where he'd been spending his time. And she finally got it out of him that he'd been down in Greenwich Village, with musicians and other characters, in a white girl's apartment. And this scared her and she started to scream at him and what came up, once she began—though she denies it to this day —was what sacrifices they were making to give Sonny a decent home and how little he appreciated it.

170 　　Sonny didn't play the piano that day. By evening, Isabel's mother had calmed down but then there was the old man to deal with, and Isabel herself. Isabel says she did her best to be calm but she broke down and started crying. She says she just watched Sonny's face. She could tell, by watching him, what was happening with him. And what was happening was that they penetrated his cloud, they had reached him. Even if their fingers had been a thousand times more gentle than human fingers ever are, he could hardly help feeling that they had stripped him naked and were spitting on that nakedness. For he also had to see that his presence, that music, which was life or death to him, had been torture for them and that they had endured it, not at all for his sake, but only for mine. And Sonny couldn't take that. He can take it a little better today than he could then but he's still not very good at it and, frankly, I don't know anybody who is.

171 　　The silence of the next few days must have been louder than the sound of all the music ever played since time began. One morning, before she went to work, Isabel was in his room for something and she suddenly realized that all of his records were gone. And she knew for certain that he was gone. And he was. He went as far as the navy would carry him. He finally sent me a postcard from some place in Greece and that was the first I knew that Sonny was still alive. I didn't see him any more until we were both back in New York and the war had long been over.

172 　　He was a man by then, of course, but I wasn't willing to see it. He came by the house from time to time, but we fought almost every time we met. I didn't like the way he carried himself, loose and dreamlike all the time, and I didn't like his friends, and his music seemed to be merely an excuse for the life he led. It sounded just that weird and disordered.

Then we had a fight, a pretty awful fight, and I didn't see him for   *173*
months. By and by I looked him up, where he was living, in a furnished
room in the Village, and I tried to make it up. But there were lots of
other people in the room and Sonny just lay on his bed, and he wouldn't
come downstairs with me, and he treated these other people as though
they were his family and I weren't. So I got mad and then he got mad,
and then I told him that he might just as well be dead as live the way he
was living. Then he stood up and he told me not to worry about him any
more in life, that he *was* dead as far as I was concerned. Then he pushed
me to the door and the other people looked on as though nothing were
happening, and he slammed the door behind me. I stood in the hallway,
staring at the door. I heard somebody laugh in the room and then the
tears came to my eyes. I started down the steps, whistling to keep from
crying, I kept whistling to myself, *You going to need me, baby, one of
these cold, rainy days.*

I read about Sonny's trouble in the spring. Little Grace died in the   *174*
fall. She was a beautiful little girl. But she only lived a little over two
years. She died of polio and she suffered. She had a slight fever for a
couple of days, but it didn't seem like anything and we just kept her in
bed. And we would certainly have called the doctor, but the fever
dropped, she seemed to be all right. So we thought it had just been a
cold. Then, one day, she was up, playing, Isabel was in the kitchen
fixing lunch for the two boys when they'd come in from school, and she
heard Grace fall down in the living room. When you have a lot of children you don't always start running when one of them falls, unless they
start screaming or something. And, this time, Gracie was quiet. Yet,
Isabel says that when she heard that *thump* and then that silence, something happened in her to make her afraid. And she ran to the living room
and there was little Grace on the floor, all twisted up, and the reason she
hadn't screamed was that she couldn't get her breath. And when she did
scream, it was the worst sound, Isabel says, that she'd ever heard in all
her life, and she still hears it sometimes in her dreams. Isabel will sometimes wake me up with a low, moaning, strangled sound and I have to
be quick to awaken her and hold her to me and where Isabel is weeping
against me seems a mortal wound.

I think I may have written Sonny the very day that little Grace was   *175*
buried. I was sitting in the living room in the dark, by myself, and I
suddenly thought of Sonny. My trouble made his real.

One Saturday afternoon, when Sonny had been living with us, or   *176*
anyway, been in our house, for nearly two weeks, I found myself wandering aimlessly about the living room, drinking from a can of beer, and
trying to work up courage to search Sonny's room. He was out, he was
usually out whenever I was home, and Isabel had taken the children to
see their grandparents. Suddenly I was standing still in front of the

living room window, watching Seventh Avenue. The idea of searching Sonny's room made me still. I scarcely dared to admit to myself what I'd be searching for. I didn't know what I'd do if I found it. Or if I didn't.

177   On the sidewalk across from me, near the entrance to a barbecue joint, some people were holding an old-fashioned revival meeting. The barbecue cook, wearing a dirty white apron, his conked* hair reddish and metallic in the pale sun, and a cigarette between his lips, stood in the doorway, watching them. Kids and older people paused in their errands and stood there, along with some older men and a couple of very tough-looking women who watched everything that happened on the avenue, as though they owned it, or were maybe owned by it. Well, they were watching this, too. The revival was being carried on by three sisters in black, and a brother. All they had were their voices and their Bibles and a tambourine. The brother was testifying† and while he testified two of the sisters stood together, seeming to say, amen, and the third sister walked around with the tambourine outstretched and a couple of people dropped coins into it. Then the brother's testimony ended and the sister who had been taking up the collection dumped the coins into her palm and transferred them to the pocket of her long black robe. Then she raised both hands, striking the tambourine against the air, and then against one hand, and she started to sing. And the two other sisters and the brother joined in.

178   It was strange, suddenly, to watch, though I had been seeing these meetings all my life. So, of course, had everybody else down there. Yet, they paused and watched and listened and I stood still at the window. " 'Tis the old ship of Zion," they sang, and the sister with the tambourine kept a steady, jangling beat, *"it has rescued many a thousand!"* Not a soul under the sound of their voices was hearing this song for the first time, not one of them had been rescued. Nor had they seen much in the way of rescue work being done around them. Neither did they especially believe in the holiness of the three sisters and the brother, they knew too much about them, knew where they lived, and how. The woman with the tambourine, whose voice dominated the air, whose face was bright with joy, was divided by very little from the woman who stood watching her, a cigarette between her heavy, chapped lips, her hair a cuckoo's nest, her face scarred and swollen from many beatings, and her black eyes glittering like coal. Perhaps they both knew this, which was why, when, as rarely, they addressed each other, they addressed each other as Sister. As the singing filled the air the watching,

*Conked hair is heavily greased.
†Testifying is the act of publicly expressing religious belief.

listening faces underwent a change, the eyes focusing on something within; the music seemed to soothe a poison out of them; and time seemed, nearly, to fall away from the sullen, belligerent, battered faces, as though they were fleeing back to their first condition, while dreaming of their last. The barbecue cook half shook his head and smiled, and dropped his cigarette and disappeared into his joint. A man fumbled in his pockets for change and stood holding it in his hand impatiently, as though he had just remembered a pressing appointment further up the avenue. He looked furious. Then I saw Sonny, standing on the edge of the crowd. He was carrying a wide, flat notebook with a green cover, and it made him look, from where I was standing, almost like a schoolboy. The coppery sun brought out the copper in his skin, he was very faintly smiling, standing very still. Then the singing stopped, the tambourine turned into a collection plate again. The furious man dropped in his coins and vanished, so did a couple of the women, and Sonny dropped some change in the plate, looking directly at the woman with a little smile. He started across the avenue, toward the house. He has a slow, loping walk, something like the way Harlem hipsters walk, only he's imposed on this his own half-beat. I had never really noticed it before.

I stayed at the window, both relieved and apprehensive. As Sonny   179
disappeared from my sight, they began singing again. And they were still singing when his key turned in the lock.

"Hey," he said.   180

"Hey, yourself. You want some beer?"   181

"No. Well, maybe." But he came up to the window and stood beside   182
me, looking out. "What a warm voice," he said.

They were singing *If I could only hear my mother pray again!*   183

"Yes," I said, "and she can sure beat that tambourine."   184

"But what a terrible song," he said, and laughed. He dropped his   185
notebook on the sofa and disappeared into the kitchen. "Where's Isabel and the kids?"

"I think they went to see their grandparents. You hungry?"   186

"No." He came back into the living room with his can of beer. "You   187
want to come some place with me tonight?"

I sensed, I don't know how, that I couldn't possibly say no. "Sure.   188
Where?"

He sat down on the sofa and picked up his notebook and started   189
leafing through it. "I'm going to sit in with some fellows in a joint in the Village."

"You mean, you're going to play, tonight?"   190

"That's right." He took a swallow of his beer and moved back to the   191
window. He gave me a sidelong look. "If you can stand it."

192   "I'll try," I said.

193   He smiled to himself and we both watched as the meeting across the way broke up. The three sisters and the brother, heads bowed, were singing *God be with you till we meet again.* The faces around them were very quiet. Then the song ended. The small crowd dispersed. We watched the three women and the lone man walk slowly up the avenue.

194   "When she was singing before," said Sonny, abruptly, "her voice reminded me for a minute of what heroin feels like sometimes—when it's in your veins. It makes you feel sort of warm and cool at the same time. And distant. And—and sure." He sipped his beer, very deliberately not looking at me. I watched his face. "It makes you feel—in control. Sometimes you've got to have that feeling."

195   "Do you?" I sat down slowly in the easy chair.

196   "Sometimes." He went to the sofa and picked up his notebook again. "Some people do."

197   "In order," I asked, "to play?" And my voice was very ugly, full of contempt and anger.

198   "Well"—he looked at me with great, troubled eyes, as though, in fact, he hoped his eyes would tell me things he could never otherwise say—"they *think* so. And *if* they think so—!"

199   "And what do *you* think?" I asked.

200   He sat on the sofa and put his can of beer on the floor. "I don't know," he said, and I couldn't be sure if he were answering my question or pursuing his thoughts. His face didn't tell me. "It's not so much to *play.* It's to *stand* it, to be able to make it at all. On any level." He frowned and smiled: "In order to keep from shaking to pieces."

201   "But these friends of yours," I said, "they seem to shake themselves to pieces pretty goddamn fast."

202   "Maybe." He played with the notebook. And something told me that I should curb my tongue, that Sonny was doing his best to talk, that I should listen. "But of course you only know the ones that've gone to pieces. Some don't—or at least they haven't *yet* and that's just about all *any* of us can say." He paused. "And then there are some who just live, really, in hell, and they know it and they see what's happening and they go right on. I don't know." He sighed, dropped the notebook, folded his arms. "Some guys, you can tell from the way they play, they on something *all* the time. And you can see that, well, it makes something real for them. But of course," he picked up his beer from the floor and sipped it and put the can down again, "they *want* to, too, you've got to see that. Even some of them that say they don't—*some,* not all."

203   "And what about you?" I asked—I couldn't help it. "What about you? Do *you* want to?"

He stood up and walked to the window and I remained silent for a   *204*
long time. Then he sighed. "Me," he said. Then: "While I was downstairs before, on my way here, listening to that woman sing, it struck
me all of a sudden how much suffering she must have had to go
through—to sing like that. It's *repulsive* to think you have to suffer that
much."

I said: "But there's no way not to suffer—is there, Sonny?"   *205*

"I believe not," he said and smiled, "but that's never stopped any-   *206*
one from trying." He looked at me. "Has it?" I realized, with this
mocking look, that there stood between us, forever, beyond the power
of time or forgiveness, the fact that I had held silence—so long!—when
he had needed human speech to help him. He turned back to the window. "No, there's no way not to suffer. But you try all kinds of ways to
keep from drowning in it, to keep on top of it, and to make it seem
—well, like *you*. Like you did something, all right, and now you're suffering for it. You know?" I said nothing. "Well you know," he said,
impatiently, "why *do* people suffer? Maybe it's better to do something
to give it a reason, *any* reason."

"But we just agreed," I said, "that there's no way not to suffer. Isn't   *207*
it better, then, just to—take it?"

"But nobody just takes it," Sonny cried, "that's what I'm telling   *208*
you! *Everybody* tries not to. You're just hung up on the *way* some people try—it's not *your* way!"

The hair on my face began to itch, my face felt wet. "That's not   *209*
true," I said, "that's not true. I don't give a damn what other people do.
I don't even care how they suffer. I just care how *you* suffer." And he
looked at me. "Please believe me," I said, "I don't want to see you
—die—trying not to suffer."

"I won't," he said flatly, "die trying not to suffer. At least, not any   *210*
faster than anybody else."

"But there's no need," I said, trying to laugh, "is there? in killing   *211*
yourself."

I wanted to say more, but I couldn't. I wanted to talk about will   *212*
power and how life could be—well, beautiful. I wanted to say that it was
all within; but was it? or, rather, wasn't that exactly the trouble? And I
wanted to promise that I would never fail him again. But it would all
have sounded—empty words and lies.

So I made the promise to myself and prayed that I would keep it.   *213*

"It's terrible sometimes, inside," he said, "that's what's the trou-   *214*
ble. You walk these streets, black and funky and cold, and there's not
really a living ass to talk to, and there's nothing shaking, and there's no
way of getting it out—that storm inside. You can't talk it and you can't

make love with it, and when you finally try to get with it and play it, you realize *nobody's* listening. So *you've* got to listen. You got to find a way to listen.''

215   And then he walked away from the window and sat on the sofa again, as though all the wind had suddenly been knocked out of him. ''Sometimes you'll do *anything* to play, even cut your mother's throat.'' He laughed and looked at me. ''Or your brother's.'' Then he sobered. ''Or your own.'' Then: ''Don't worry. I'm all right now and I think I'll *be* all right. But I can't forget—where I've been. I don't mean just the physical place I've been, I mean where I've *been*. And *what* I've been.''

216   ''What have you been, Sonny?'' I asked.

217   He smiled—but sat sideways on the sofa, his elbow resting on the back, his fingers playing with his mouth and chin, not looking at me. ''I've been something I didn't recognize, didn't know I could be. Didn't know anybody could be.'' He stopped, looking inward, looking help-lessly young, looking old. ''I'm not talking about it now because I feel *guilty* or anything like that—maybe it would be better if I did, I don't know. Anyway, I can't really talk about it. Not to you, not to anybody,'' and now he turned and faced me. ''Sometimes, you know, and it was actually when I was most *out* of the world, I felt that I was in it, that I was *with* it, really, and I could play or I didn't really have to *play*, it just came out of me, it was there. And I don't know how I played, thinking about it now, but I know I did awful things, those times, sometimes, to people. Or it wasn't that I *did* anything to them—it was that they weren't real.'' He picked up the beer can; it was empty; he rolled it be-tween his palms: ''And other times—well, I needed a fix, I needed to find a place to lean, I needed to clear a space to *listen*—and I couldn't find it, and I—went crazy, I did terrible things to *me*, I was terrible *for* me.'' He began pressing the beer can between his hands, I watched the metal begin to give. It glittered, as he played with it like a knife, and I was afraid he would cut himself, but I said nothing. ''Oh well. I can never tell you. I was all by myself at the bottom of something, stinking and sweating and crying and shaking, and I smelled it, you know? *my* stink, and I thought I'd die if I couldn't get away from it and yet, all the same, I knew that everything I was doing was just locking me in with it. And I didn't know,'' he paused, still flattening the beer can, ''I didn't know, I still *don't* know, something kept telling me that maybe it was good to smell your own stink, but I didn't think that *that* was what I'd been trying to do—and—who can stand it?'' and he abruptly dropped the ruined beer can, looking at me with a small, still smile, and then rose, walking to the window as though it were the lodestone rock. I watched his face, he watched the avenue. ''I couldn't tell you when

Mama died—but the reason I wanted to leave Harlem so bad was to get away from drugs. And then, when I ran away, that's what I was running from—really. When I came back, nothing had changed, *I* hadn't changed, I was just—older." And he stopped, drumming with his fingers on the windowpane. The sun had vanished, soon darkness would fall. I watched his face. "It can come again," he said, almost as though speaking to himself. Then he turned to me. "It can come again," he repeated. "I just want you to know that."

"All right," I said, at last. "So it can come again. All right."   218

He smiled, but the smile was sorrowful. "I had to try to tell you," he   219
said.

"Yes," I said. "I understand that."   220

"You're my brother," he said, looking straight at me, and not smil-   221
ing at all.

"Yes," I repeated, "yes. I understand that."   222

He turned back to the window, looking out. "All that hatred down   223
there," he said, "all that hatred and misery and love. It's a wonder it doesn't blow the avenue apart."

We went to the only nightclub on a short, dark street, downtown. We   224
squeezed through the narrow, chattering, jampacked bar to the entrance of the big room, where the bandstand was. And we stood there for a moment, for the lights were very dim in this room and we couldn't see. Then, "Hello, boy," said a voice and an enormous black man, much older than Sonny or myself, erupted out of all that atmospheric lighting and put an arm around Sonny's shoulder. "I been sitting right here," he said, "waiting for you."

He had a big voice, too, and heads in the darkness turned toward us.   225

Sonny grinned and pulled a little away, and said, "Creole, this is my   226
brother. I told you about him."

Creole shook my hand. "I'm glad to meet you, son," he said, and it   227
was clear that he was glad to meet me *there*, for Sonny's sake. And he smiled, "You got a real musician in *your* family," and he took his arm from Sonny's shoulder and slapped him, lightly, affectionately, with the back of his hand.

"Well. Now I've heard it all," said a voice behind us. This was an-   228
other musician, and a friend of Sonny's, a coal-black, cheerful-looking man, built close to the ground. He immediately began confiding to me, at the top of his lungs, the most terrible things about Sonny, his teeth gleaming like a lighthouse and his laugh coming up out of him like the beginning of an earthquake. And it turned out that everyone at the bar knew Sonny, or almost everyone; some were musicians, working there, or nearby, or not working, some were simply hangers-on, and some

were there to hear Sonny play. I was introduced to all of them and they were all very polite to me. Yet, it was clear that, for them, I was only Sonny's brother. Here, I was in Sonny's world. Or, rather: his kingdom. Here, it was not even a question that his veins bore royal blood.

229   They were going to play soon and Creole installed me, by myself, at a table in a dark corner. Then I watched them, Creole, and the little black man, and Sonny, and the others, while they horsed around, standing just below the bandstand. The light from the bandstand spilled just a little short of them and, watching them laughing and gesturing and moving about, I had the feeling that they, nevertheless, were being most careful not to step into that circle of light too suddenly: that if they moved into the light too suddenly, without thinking, they would perish in flame. Then, while I watched, one of them, the small black man, moved into the light and crossed the bandstand and started fooling around with his drums. Then—being funny and being, also, extremely ceremonious—Creole took Sonny by the arm and led him to the piano. A woman's voice called Sonny's name and a few hands started clapping. And Sonny, also being funny and being ceremonious, and so touched, I think, that he could have cried, but neither hiding it nor showing it, riding it like a man, grinned, and put both hands to his heart and bowed from the waist.

230   Creole then went to the bass fiddle and a lean, very bright-skinned brown man jumped up on the bandstand and picked up his horn. So there they were, and the atmosphere on the bandstand and in the room began to change and tighten. Someone stepped up to the microphone and announced them. Then there were all kinds of murmurs. Some people at the bar shushed others. The waitress ran around, frantically getting in the last orders, guys and chicks got closer to each other, and the lights on the bandstand, on the quartet, turned to a kind of indigo. Then they all looked different there. Creole looked about him for the last time, as though he were making certain that all his chickens were in the coop, and then he—jumped and struck the fiddle. And there they were.

231   All I know about music is that not many people ever really hear it. And even then, on the rare occasions when something opens within, and the music enters, what we mainly hear, or hear corroborated, are personal, private, vanishing evocations. But the man who creates the music is hearing something else, is dealing with the roar rising from the void and imposing order on it as it hits the air. What is evoked in him, then, is of another order, more terrible because it has no words, and triumphant, too, for that same reason. And his triumph, when he triumphs, is ours. I just watched Sonny's face. His face was troubled, he was working hard, but he wasn't with it. And I had the feeling that, in a

way, everyone on the bandstand was waiting for him, both waiting for him and pushing him along. But as I began to watch Creole, I realized that it was Creole who held them all back. He had them on a short rein. Up there, keeping the beat with his whole body, wailing on the fiddle, with his eyes half closed, he was listening to everything, but he was listening to Sonny. He was having a dialogue with Sonny. He wanted Sonny to leave the shoreline and strike out for the deep water. He was Sonny's witness that deep water and drowning were not the same thing—he had been there, and he knew. And he wanted Sonny to know. He was waiting for Sonny to do the things on the keys which would let Creole know that Sonny was in the water.

And, while Creole listened, Sonny moved, deep within, exactly like   *232* someone in torment. I had never before thought of how awful the relationship must be between the musician and his instrument. He has to fill it, this instrument, with the breath of life, his own. He has to make it do what he wants it to do. And a piano is just a piano. It's made out of so much wood and wires and little hammers and big ones, and ivory. While there's only so much you can do with it, the only way to find this out is to try; to try and make it do everything.

And Sonny hadn't been near a piano for over a year. And he wasn't on   *233* much better terms with his life, not the life that stretched before him now. He and the piano stammered, started one way, got scared, stopped; started another way, panicked, marked time, started again; then seemed to have found a direction, panicked again, got stuck. And the face I saw on Sonny I'd never seen before. Everything had been burned out of it, and, at the same time, things usually hidden were being burned in, by the fire and fury of the battle which was occurring in him up there.

Yet, watching Creole's face as they neared the end of the first set, I   *234* had the feeling that something had happened, something I hadn't heard. Then they finished, there was scattered applause, and then, without an instant's warning, Creole started into something else, it was almost sardonic, it was *Am I Blue.** And, as though he commanded, Sonny began to play. Something began to happen. And Creole let out the reins. The dry, low, black man said something awful on the drums, Creole answered, and the drums talked back. Then the horn insisted, sweet and high, slightly detached perhaps, and Creole listened, commenting now and then, dry, and driving, beautiful and calm and old. Then they all came together again, and Sonny was part of the family again. I could tell this from his face. He seemed to have found, right there beneath his

---

*Am I Blue was sung by Ethel Waters in the 1929 film *On with the Show.* It was written by Grant Clark and Harry Akst and later recorded by Billie Holiday. It is a blues classic.

fingers, a damn brand-new piano. It seemed that he couldn't get over it. Then, for a while, just being happy with Sonny, they seemed to be agreeing with him that brand-new pianos certainly were a gas.

235   Then Creole stepped forward to remind them that what they were playing was the blues. He hit something in all of them, he hit something in me, myself, and the music tightened and deepened, apprehension began to beat the air. Creole began to tell us what the blues were all about. They were not about anything very new. He and his boys up there were keeping it new, at the risk of ruin, destruction, madness, and death, in order to find new ways to make us listen. For, while the tale of how we suffer, and how we are delighted, and how we may triumph is never new, it always must be heard. There isn't any other tale to tell, it's the only light we've got in all this darkness.

236   And this tale, according to that face, that body, those strong hands on those strings, has another aspect in every country, and a new depth in every generation. Listen, Creole seemed to be saying, listen. Now these are Sonny's blues. He made the little black man on the drums know it, and the bright, brown man on the horn. Creole wasn't trying any longer to get Sonny in the water. He was wishing him Godspeed. Then he stepped back, very slowly, filling the air with the immense suggestion that Sonny speak for himself.

237   Then they all gathered around Sonny and Sonny played. Every now and again one of them seemed to say, amen. Sonny's fingers filled the air with life, his life. But that life contained so many others. And Sonny went all the way back, he really began with the spare, flat statement of the opening phrase of the song. Then he began to make it his. It was very beautiful because it wasn't hurried and it was no longer a lament. I seemed to hear with what burning he had made it his, with what burning we had yet to make it ours, how we could cease lamenting. Freedom lurked around us and I understood, at last, that he could help us to be free if we would listen, that he would never be free until we did. Yet, there was no battle in his face now, I heard what he had gone through, and would continue to go through until he came to rest in earth. He had made it his: that long line, of which we knew only Mama and Daddy. And he was giving it back, as everything must be given back, so that, passing through death, it can live forever. I saw my mother's face again, and felt, for the first time, how the stones of the road she had walked on must have bruised her feet. I saw the moonlit road where my father's brother died. And it brought something else back to me, and carried me past it, I saw my little girl again and felt Isabel's tears again, and I felt my own tears begin to rise. And I was yet aware that this was only a moment, that the world waited outside, as hungry as a tiger, and that trouble stretched above us, longer than the sky.

Then it was over. Creole and Sonny let out their breath, both soaking 238
wet, and grinning. There was a lot of applause and some of it was real. In
the dark, the girl came by and I asked her to take drinks to the bandstand. There was a long pause, while they talked up there in the indigo
light and after awhile I saw the girl put a Scotch and milk on top of the
piano for Sonny. He didn't seem to notice it, but just before they started
playing again, he sipped from it and looked toward me, and nodded.
Then he put it back on top of the piano. For me, then, as they began to
play again, it glowed and shook above my brother's head like the very
cup of trembling.*

Questions and Activities

▶ *COMPREHENSION QUESTIONS*

1. Explain the significance of the story's title. In this story, blues is a
   type of black jazz. But it is also a name for Sonny's particular way of
   looking at his experience as a black man. Consider, for example,
   Sonny's and his brother's attention to the street revivalists who are
   described in paragraphs 177 and 178. Do these musicians seem to be
   expressing in their music sentiments similar to those Sonny strives to
   express through his more complex jazz? Why are both of these
   seemingly very different kinds of music evocative of the "blues"?
2. Why does Sonny feel it is so important to have his brother see him
   perform? What attitudes does Sonny wish to change? Paragraphs
   194 through 219 should help you understand what Sonny wishes to
   explain to his brother. But he cannot explain it in words; he must, instead, explain it through his music. Why?
3. What do you associate with the name Harlem? When did the name
   first come to your attention?
4. Why does Sonny join the Navy after his disagreement with the family with which he was living (see paragraphs 167–171)?

---

*The "cup of trembling" is a biblical phrase from *Isaiah* 51:17, 22–23: "Awake, awake,
stand up, O Jerusalem, which hast drunk at the hand of the Lord the cup of his fury; thou
hast drunken the dregs of the cup of trembling, and wrung them out. . . . Behold, I have
taken out of thine hand the cup of trembling, even the dregs of the cup of my fury; thou
shalt no more drink it again: But I will put it into the hand of them that afflict thee . . ."

5. Reread the story's first paragraph. Then compare the narrator's attitude and tone in the first paragraph to the same elements in the
final paragraph. *Attitude* is the opinion or feeling a person has toward a subject, in this case, the narrator's opinion about what has
happened to his brother. *Tone* is the way a charactor talks about
something, in this case, the narrator's experience with his brother; it
is created by the words the author puts into the narrator's mouth.
The way a person talks often tells what he or she thinks. Has the narrator changed his attitude toward Sonny? Has his tone changed as
he describes his responses to Sonny's performance? Has he become
more or less sympathetic to Sonny?

6. Baldwin's meaning in this story is expressed through a narrator who
has led a very different life from that of his brother. What advantages are there in Baldwin's choice of narrator? Why does seeing
Sonny through his older brother's eyes give us a more complex view
of him than we would get if Sonny had narrated his own story? What
limits are there to this narrator's viewpoint? How might he, because
of his own background and experience, not see Sonny accurately?
Can you give an example from the story where the narrator makes a
biased judgment of Sonny?

► *THEME QUESTIONS*

7. Several of the footnotes for this story provide facts about Charlie
Parker and other musicians and songs. Use these facts as a basis for
further research on blues music. What emotions and attitudes do
the blues convey? When and where did the blues originate? How
does this kind of music fit in with the theme of this section? What
does the blues tell us about the people who create and perform it?

8. Reread the footnote on page 285 that quotes the passage from the
Bible from which the phrase "cup of trembling" comes. How does
what is expressed in the biblical passage support the theme of
"Sonny's Blues"? Has the "cup of trembling" passed from Sonny at
the end of the story?

9. What parts of black life does Baldwin suggest are expressed in the
blues? Why is this expression important to the narrator of this story?
Why might this expression be important to blacks in general? What
kind of universal appeal is captured by the blues?

► *LEARNING ACTIVITIES*

10. Reread the first paragraph of the story. Then, build your response to
this first paragraph into a free writing in which you tell what it suggests about the character of the story's narrator, Sonny's older

brother. Write for only twenty minutes. Do not worry about spelling or punctuation—simply put down all your thoughts. How is the narrator responding to what he has read about his younger brother? What does this response tell you about the narrator? What does it tell you about the narrator's relationship with Sonny? Does the first paragraph suggest anything to you about the story that will follow? What kind of story do you expect—a mystery, a comedy, a serious story, or a light story? Is your expectation fulfilled by the story?

11. Read your free-written response to the first paragraph of this story to the rest of the class. Compare your response to some of your classmates'. Did you seem to respond to things in the text that others ignored? Did you expect a different kind of story than was expected by others in the class? Was your interpretation of the narrator's character different from some of your classmates' interpretations? What were the reasons behind these differences? Choose one of those differences and explain in a few paragraphs why your response was different from other responses.

12. Write a brief sketch about a past experience you shared with a sister or brother. Focus as specifically as you can on the details of this experience. Then, draw inferences of a general kind from the experience. What do these inferences suggest about your relationship with your sister or brother?

Packaged Sentiment

RICHARD RHODES

Richard Rhodes, the son of a laborer, was born in 1937 in Kansas City, Kansas, and graduated from Yale in 1957. He has had extensive experience in magazine journalism (with *Newsweek, Harper's,* and *Playboy*), broadcasting (with Radio Free Europe), and commercial publishing (with Hallmark, 1962–1970). His published writings include nonfiction books on the American Midwest, four novels, a Time-Life book on the Ozark mountain area, and an autobiographical sketch of his own life as a writer. His novel *The Last Safari* (1980) has been compared by one critic to the African writings of Ernest Hemingway. He has contributed more than fifty essays to popular magazines, including *Harper's, Redbook, Esquire, Playboy, Audience,* and *Reader's Digest.*

Rhodes has two purposes in this essay. He wishes to involve his reader in his descriptions of work at Hallmark in Kansas City. Rhodes captures the details and the established tradition of the company and briefly profiles the company's founder, who hoped to provide busy people with easy access to expressions of sentiment.

Rhodes's second purpose is more difficult to achieve. He wishes to use Hallmark as an example of American commercial and industrial ingenuity, as a company whose product, although easy to criticize for its seemingly stereotyped sentiments, meets a real need in contemporary life. Since average people seem not to have the time or inclination to write letters, Rhodes suggests, greeting cards are a convenient way to keep in touch with others. But to many educated readers, greeting cards are typical examples of stereotyped emotions, of a desire to have others think and speak for us—on television, in films, in books and magazines. These readers, Rhodes knows, are not going to be sympathetic to his position.

Rhodes never mentions this skeptical assumed reader directly. But many of his writing strategies are directed to changing this reader's mind. He begins his essay, for example, by describing the Christmas card deluge and other card-sending occasions in a way that seems to be critical of Americans' obsessive card buying. This opening allows him to create a sense of agreement with his assumed audience. And, of course, the negative connotations of the essay's title figure here, too. By the end of the opening few paragraphs, Rhodes has a trusting reader ready to hear a specific account of Hallmark cards. The way is open for the rest of the essay to present Rhodes's positive attitudes toward the greeting card business.

As you read this essay, you should consider your place among its assumed readership:

1. What do you think about greeting card sentiments? Are they sincere? By sending greeting cards, do you feel that you are letting someone else function for you in an area of your life that should reflect your most personal feelings? Would you communicate with others in more personal ways — through letters, for example — if greeting cards were not available?
2. Do you think greeting cards work the same way as television commercials, doing consumers' thinking for them, making them more passive, more reliant on the media?
3. Are you more positive about greeting cards? Do they allow you to keep in touch with people you care about, despite a busy schedule? Are they sincere expressions of sentiment? Do they express your thoughts better than you could yourself?

▶ ——————————————————

Christmas is come, the holiday season, and with it our annual   1
deluge of cards, whose successful dispersal across the land the Postal Service heralds to justify failing us for the rest of the year. "By God, we moved the Christmas cards!" Well, half of all the personal mail moved annually in the United States is greeting cards. Cards for Christmas but also cards for New Year's, Valentine's Day, Easter, Mother's Day, Father's Day, Independence Day and Thanksgiving and Halloween, the official holidays of the American year. And for the occasions greeting-card people call "Everyday," though they are not, births and birthdays, graduations, weddings, anniversaries, showers, vacations, friendship, promotion, hello, love, thanks, goodbye, illness and bereavement, and even to have Thought O' You and for a Secret Pal. We are a nation not of letter writers but of card signers. If the personal letter is long dead, maimed by the penny post and murdered by the telephone, the mass-produced card thrives, picturing what we haven't skill to picture, saying what we haven't words to say. Cards knot the ties that bind in a land where a fourth of us change residence with every change of calendar and where grown children no longer live at home. They show us at our best, if in borrowed finery. You may buy a card made of pansies and doggerel or you may buy a card made of da Vinci and the Sermon on the Mount. Whoever receives it will understand what you meant, and that you meant well.

2   The Christmas card was an English invention, but the greeting card
an American one. One hundred twenty-eight years ago this season, an
Englishman distracted by business matters failed to get his Christmas
cards written. Boldly he turned an embarrassment into an opportunity,
commissioned a paper tableau of Pickwickians, their glasses raised in
toast, and inside each engraved and colored folio he printed a verse. His
friends' reactions were not recorded. No doubt some found the idea
distastefully impersonal and lamented the decline of manners in a
declining age. Others, alert for new twists, thought it charming. The
sensible saw its efficiency. It met the first requirement of all mechanical inventions: it saved time.

3   We have taken the idea and made it ours. The English send few cards
today, and Europeans fewer still. We send cards for everything, mechanizing and standardizing the complex relationships we maintain with
one another, to give us time to breathe. We needn't be ashamed of our
custom. Elegant mechanizing is what we do best. It is the form our national character has taken. Look at our office buildings raised on narrow
pillars ten feet off the ground as if someone had dared us to float a fifty-
story building in the air. Compare our white and graceful moon rockets
to the Soviet Union's drab boiler plate. Look at our cards, little shuttles
of sentiment weaving across the land.

4   Some of the old cards, the nineteenth-century cards that borrowed
the Englishman's invention, were masterpieces of reproduction, printed in as many as twelve colors with verses selected in national contests
with cash prizes, verses no better than they should be for all the fanfare.
The Victorian Age produced German cards that opened up into three-
dimensional sleighing scenes of marvelous intricacy, cards with moving parts, cards fringed like a love-seat pillow with gaudy silks, cards as
ornate as any gingerbread house. Cards, one presumes, for the wealthy,
because the rest of us hadn't begun sending them in today's incredible
numbers, today's fifteen or twenty *billion* cards a year. Now that we do,
the special effects that delicate handwork once supplied have had to be
scaled down, though the cards we send today carry their weight of
handwork too, and with it their weight of amusing stories, cautionary
tales of American ingenuity gone berserk. I remember a humorous card
that required for its gag a small plastic sack of what it called "belly-
button fuzz" stapled below its punch line. No supplier could thumb out
enough of the authentic material to meet the demand, so the manufacturer turned to the clothes dryers of a nearby college town, bought
up the lint franchise, sterilized the lint to meet health regulations, and
bagged it and stapled it on, by hand, and got the effect it was seeking
and probably, college towns being college towns, got some belly-
button fuzz too. "Attachments," such devices are called—plastic

tears, toy scissors,, miniature boxes of crayons, feathers, spring-and-paper jumping jacks, pencils, beans, the detritus of industrial civilization shrunk to card size. An attachment will sell a humorous card all by itself if it isn't stolen first, a problem for greeting-card manufacturers as surely as it is a problem for the sellers of screws and beads and hair ribbons in dime stores. Like children we lust to get our hands on little things, finding magic in tiny representations of the lumbering world.

The business of greeting cards began in the ambitions of hungry men, and they improvised as they went. There are schools of nursing and schools of nuclear physics, but there are no schools for the makers of greeting cards, only apprenticeships. When Joyce Hall of country Nebraska began his enterprise in Kansas City, Missouri, more than sixty years ago, there weren't even many kinds of cards. Christmas, Easter, birthdays, and weddings were about the only occasions we announced. Hall, Fred Rust of Rust Craft, and a few people like them had to teach us to send cards by making cards we wanted to send. In that work, Hall's career strikingly parallels the career of another Midwesterner, Walt Disney, for both men learned to parse our emotions and recast them in visual and verbal form. Disney, for example, took some shadowy figures from a fairy tale, clothed them in universals, and gave us the Seven Dwarfs. Hall and his people took our need to signal our degrees of social familiarity and our various notions of good taste and gave us a choice among greeting cards.

For any given social occasion, depending on how well you know someone and what you want him to think of you, you may select a card for him that is Formal, Traditional, Humorous, Floral, Cute, Contemporary, or some other among Hallmark's many categories of mood. Two cards for a friend who is hospitalized give the flavor. One, an embossed vase of flowers, says, "Glad your Operation's Over," on the cover, and inside:

> *You're thought of so often*
> *As days come and go*
> *That this card comes to tell you,*
> *And then let you know*
> *How much you are wished*
> *A recovery that's quick—*
> *For someone like you*
> *Is too nice to be sick!*

The other card, a photograph of a cotton bunny in a flower-bedecked four-poster, opens with, "Hope you'll soon be out of that *blooming bed!*" and carries the flower pun through:

Sure like to see you back in the pink,
So just take it easy, 'cause then
You'll soon be in clover,
Feeling just rosy,
And fresh as a daisy *again!*

Moods and tones and levels, you see. You are not likely to send a Contemporary card to your maiden aunt nor a Formal card to your spouse. The greeting-card people give you a range of choices. It may be a narrower range than you would prefer, but if you are a sender of cards at all, the choices will not be so narrow that you turn away in disgust and write a letter. You may choose frank sentiment; humor ranging from the modestly ethnic (hillbillies, Indians, Dead End Kids—blacks, Italians, and Eastern Europeans are out today, though they used to be a staple) to the heavily punned to the backward compliment to the gentle slap; simple statement, favored for Christmas and sympathy cards, both occasions being to some people matters serious enough for prose; and a number of alternatives between. Visually, you may choose flowers, cartoons, arabesque gilding, photographs, even reproductions of fine art, though few enough of those because few people buy them. Or stylized little children with ink-drop eyes, or encrustations of plastic jewels, or velvet flocking, or metallic glitter. Variations in texture and surface are legion—and the pride of the older generation of greeting-card men, who believed in making a quality product, who learned what would sell by selling, and who relied for their judgment in such matters on what Joyce Hall once called "the vapors of past experience."

7   Even if you have never given thought to such matters as categories of emotion and levels of taste, greeting-card people know you operate by them, and know how many cards to make to meet your needs. Such is the variety, of cards and of needs, that the largest of the manufacturers, Hallmark Cards, would have collapsed a decade ago if the computer hadn't come along to speed their sorting. The company claims 12,000 products, counting each separate design a product, and the figure is certainly conservative. Twelve thousand different products in quantities of six to perhaps 20,000 different stores: you can do the multiplication yourself, but count in the envelopes; count in as many as ten or twenty different manufacturing operations on every card; count in all the designs being prepared for future publication, designs that pass through hundreds of hands at drawing boards and typewriters and approval committees and lithographic cameras and printing plants; count in all these different bits of information and many more besides, and you arrive at a total that demands the kind of machines that track astronauts to the moon.

And count in one thing more: every display in every store is a modest   8
computer of its own, each of its pockets filled with designs that favor
the social and cultural biases of the neighborhood around the store, and
among those favored designs the best sellers of the day. "Tailoring,"
Hallmark calls it—loading the display to favor the preferences of the
young or old or black or white or Catholic or Jewish or rich or poor who
regularly shop there. The salesman sets up the display with the help of
the owner; after that the computer in Kansas City keeps track. The
point, of course, is to give you a maximum range of choice among the
choices available. Tucked away in the stock drawer below the display,
quietly humming, an IBM card meters every design.

Despite appearances, then, greeting-card manufacture is no work of   9
hand coloring performed by elderly ladies in lace. The Hallmark plant
in Kansas City occupies two city blocks, and the company doesn't even
do its own printing. Times Square would fit nicely inside the new distribution center Hallmark is building on a railroad spur outside of town.
More than one printing firm in the United States owes its giant color
presses to Hallmark orders, which is why the company gets the kind of
quality it is known for—because it has the heft to stop the presses and
pull a proof. It claims 400 artists in residence, the largest art department
in the world, and if you include the girls who separate out the colors of a
design by hand, a procedure that still costs less for certain designs than
separating the colors by machine, the claim is fair.

So many different operations go into the production of greeting cards   10
that even a glimpse of them boggles the mind, serene and simple as the
cards look when they finally reach the store. Hallmark buys paper by
the boxcar, paper of every imaginable texture and weight, parchment,
deckle, bond, pebble-grained, leather-grained, cloth-grained, board,
brown wrapping, hard-finished, soft-finished, smooth. Special committees earnestly debate the future popularity of roses or ragamuffins. An
artist conceives a group of cards that feature cartoon mice, and the cards
sell and the artist is rewarded with a trip to San Francisco. Down in the
bowels of the building, behind a secret door, a master photographer labors as he has labored for most of a decade to perfect flat three-dimensional photography using a camera on which Hallmark owns the license, a camera that rolls around in a semicircle on model railroad
tracks, its prisms awhirr. In California a contract artist makes dolls of
old socks and ships them to Kansas City to be photographed for children's cards. Market-research girls carry cards mounted on black panels
to meetings of women's clubs, where the ladies, at a charitable fifty
cents a head, choose among different designs with the same verses, or
different verses with the same design, helping Hallmark determine

the very best that you might care to send. An engineer, a stack of hand-made designs before him on his desk, struggles to arrange them on a lithography sheet to get the maximum number of designs per sheet so that they can be printed all at once with minimum waste of paper—"nesting," the process is called. Artists roam the streets of major cities at Christmastime, studying shop windows and the offerings of art galleries to discover new trends in visual design. A deputation of sales managers retreats to an Ozark resort for a multimedia presentation of next year's line. A mechanical genius grown old in the service of the firm remembers the tricks he has taught mere paper cards to do: walking, talking, sticking out their tongues, growling, snoring, squeaking, issuing forth perfume at the scratch of a fingernail across microscopic beads. An engineer sits down at a hand-work table and conducts a motion study and designs a system and lines and lines of young girls in gray smocks follow the system to assemble a complicated card by hand, their hands making the memorized motions while they dream of boyfriends or listen to the rhythm of the gluing machines interweaving fugally along the line. A master engraver puts the finishing touches on a die that will punch a dotted line around a paper puppet on a get-well card. A committee of executives meets and decides that the pink of a card isn't cheerful enough and the cartoon figure on another card not sufficiently neuter to appeal both to men and to women. A shipment of paper for a line of children's books is frozen into a harbor in Finland when it should be steaming its way to a printing plant in Singapore. A baby leopard runs loose in the photography department while an editor upstairs sorts through another shipment of amateur verse mailed in by the card lovers of America. He has not found a writer worth encouraging in three years. Greeting cards aren't simply manufactured, like soap or breakfast cereal. They are rescued from the confusing crosscurrents of American life, every one of them a difficult recovery. John Donne found the King's likeness on a coin: greeting-card manufacturers must discover Everyman's likeness and somehow fix it on paper with all its idiosyncrasies smoothed away.

11   Hallmark employs far fewer writers than artists, about fifteen or twenty. Unlike designs, verses enjoy a long half-life if they are adjusted for minor changes in the language along the way. These days they are often selected—selected entire, not written—by computer from a stock of the most popular verses of the past. The writers try to think up new words, and from time to time they do. Greeting-card verse has come in for its share of ridicule, which perhaps it deserves, but before it is ridiculed its distinction ought to be explained. Most song lyrics look equally ridiculous when printed bald, because the rhetoric of a song lyric, the source of its emotional impact, is the music that accompanies

it. The rhetoric of greeting-card verse is the card, the physical and visual accompaniment to the verse. A few greeting-card makers have caught on to the similarity between song lyrics and greeting-card verse and have begun to borrow effects they can use, as in this verse from one of American Greetings' new "Soft Touch" cards, cards for young people that feature soft-focus photography:

> *untold the times i've kissed you*
> *in the moments i have missed you*
> *and our love goes on forever. . .*
> *with you softly on my mind*

If that doesn't quite make sense, well, neither do most lyrics away from their music, or greeting-card verses away from their cards. A poem, a real poem, the thing itself, works no better on a greeting card or in a song, because it contains its own orchestration and goes dissonant when larded with the scrapings of Mantovani strings.

Modern young people don't like eight-line rhymed verses, preferring   12
song words or evocative sentences. One card on my desk is captioned merely "Peace," which makes it appropriate to almost every occasion except Halloween. Finding the right words for a card is harder today than it used to be because a generation trained on the film expects the words and images to subtly interlock. Getting new words approved by management is harder still. Like most American corporations of healthy middle age, Hallmark has discovered the benefits of redundant personnel and of a certain resistance to fad. Good ideas don't come along every morning, and they must always be weighed against the success of the old; there are only so many pockets in a greeting-card display. Joyce Hall, a tall, spare man with a W. C. Fields nose and a lifetime of practical experience, used to approve every card Hallmark made, words, music, and all; and his son, Donald Hall, who is now president of the firm, still approves every Contemporary card that gets past his secretary, or did when I worked there. A friend of mine who freelanced for Hallmark once earned that secretary's enmity with a design she thought in questionable taste. "It's nice, Bill," she told him, "but it's not Hallmark." You cannot be too careful, and who is to say she wasn't right?

If the process of selection was once a matter of subjective judgment,   13
it is today at least outwardly scientific. For reasons that only statisticians understand, Kansas City is a superb test market. If products sell in Kansas City, they will sell to the nation, a fact that city sophisticates might soberly consider the next time they buy a card. The formula doesn't always work—the East Coast prefers the word "Pop" to the

word "Dad" on its Father cards, for example—but it works often enough to keep Hallmark researchers close to home. Yet market research is often discounted at Hallmark. The vapors of past experience still blow through the halls, and men whose only business experience has been with greeting cards still ignore the information of market tests if it conflicts with the information of the gut.

14   Daring subjectivity was Joyce Hall's genius, and remains a legacy of sorts in the hands of less remarkable men now that he has reluctantly relinquished command. Like every successful self-made man he has found retirement difficult. He is a man of quirks and crotchets and always was, but the enterprise he began out of a suitcase stashed under his bed at the Kansas City YMCA now ranks high on *Fortune* magazine's list of the 500 leading privately owned American corporations. The Hall family still owns the place lock, stock, and barrel. It is one of the few privately owned companies of any size left in Kansas City, where wealthy sons of fathers who sweated their way up from poverty tend to sell out to national conglomerations and pass their time at Martha's Vineyard or Harbor Point or Cannes. "You can teach your children everything but poverty," Hall once said, but he taught his son to care about the family firm; and today Hallmark thrives, branching out into gift books, stationery, party goods, calendars and albums, puzzles, candy, pens, urban redevelopment, retail stores on the Neiman-Marcus model, and whatever other enterprises it can find that fit its broad conception of its business, which it calls, modestly enough, "social expression."

15   I could complain against greeting cards. It isn't difficult to do in a world where more people feel pain than feel pleasure. There is even the risk that if I don't complain you will take me for a patsy. The greeting card's contribution to literacy will not be decisive, but I don't believe it does us that much harm. By definition, popular art can only be defended numerically, and to those who equate numbers with mediocrity, to the antipopulists, a numerical defense amounts to a certain conviction. Television is mediocre because it caters to popular taste, and greeting cards too. No. If either of them has a glaring weakness, it is that among their plethora of choices they do not give us all the choices we might want, or need. That is the effect of the marketplace, lopping off the ends of the bell curve, but the marketplace pays our bills. And if you would like to consider an opposing view, consider Joyce Hall's, who remembers this nation when it was largely rural and uneducated, and who believed that one of Hallmark's responsibilities was the elevation of American taste, a view that might seem didactic of him, but I was a

country boy too, and the first play I ever saw, chills running down my back, was *Macbeth,* on television's *Hallmark Hall of Fame.*

Hallmark established its considerable reputation with thought and care, spending far less on advertising than most companies that make consumer products do. It sponsors television specials and between the acts simply shows its cards. Can you remember a year when the *Hall of Fame* didn't come in for at least one Emmy? Do you know how many Americans traipsed through art galleries they had never visited before to see the collection of paintings by Winston Churchill that Hallmark shipped around the land? No breath of public scandal has ever blown through the organization. It does not make napalm and until very recently was old-fashioned enough to pay its bills in cash. One of its best men, now retired, a German Jew named Hans Archenhold whose printing plant was seized by the Nazis, came to Kansas City in its gangster years and found the printing industry there a sty of kickbacks and corruption. With the leverage of Hallmark printing orders he helped to clean it up. Hall himself switched his employees from coffee to milk breaks during the Depression, reasoning, in memory of his own hungry years, that they probably ate no breakfast and might not be sure of lunch, and I doubt that many complained of paternalism. By all means rail against the size and impersonality of American corporations—your arguments will be well taken—but remember also that most are little Swedens now, dispensing profits and medical care and life insurance and retirement funds with a cheerful hand.   16

Today Hallmark's brand identity, an elusive commodity in a competitive society, approaches 100 per cent. Schoolchildren, asked to make cards in class, often draw a crown on the back of their productions or attempt the famous slogan, "When you care enough to send the very best," in sturdy Big Chief print. There are other greeting-card companies, American, Buzza-Cardozo, Rust Craft, and Hallmark's own poor cousin, Ambassador Cards, to name only the biggest, but the one giant has come to stand for them all.   17

Strangely, 80 per cent of the buyers of greeting cards are women. That is why cards are tested at women's clubs. Even cards for men are designed with a woman buyer in mind, featuring scenes so romantically masculine that only the coldest feminine heart would not be touched: pipes and slippers, a red-capped hunter knocking down a brace of ducks, a fleet of galleons in harbor unaccountably full-sailed, knightly shields and lordly crests, racy automobiles, workshop tools, or smiling Dad (Pop) himself. Why do women buy most of the cards? The answer may be simpler than it seems. Men think themselves too busy running the nation to find time for the smaller amenities, but they rationalize. The   18 truth is that they are locked into an office or on a production line all day. Running an office, doing a job, no more takes all day than housework—few of us have brains that run so uniformly by the clock—but when the housework is done the woman who does it is free to go visiting or wander through the shops, while the man must shuffle papers and watch the clock. The woman may feel uncomfortable with her freedom, may feel she buys it at too high a price. It is hers nonetheless, and she uses it, among other good works, to buy cards. The new cards, by the way, the cards for young people, don't draw such sharp distinctions between masculine and feminine roles. They are androgynous. We all are, underneath: the kids have found us out.

19   I suspect we send each other cards partly from guilt, believing we haven't kept our friendships in good repair. If we are gregarious, we are also shy, uneasy as only a people raised in a society straining toward egalitarianism can be. Most of us were never rich and never desperately poor. We never learned our place: we started this country so we wouldn't have to, but our mobility leaves us unsure of where our elbows belong. We are known for our humor, but not for our wit; for our ability, but not for our style; for our strength, but not for our grace. We find ourselves harried and we fumble, or think we do.

20   Our guilt is misplaced. Thoreau's three chairs for company and two for friendship nicely defines our human limits. They are no longer limits to which we can comfortably adhere. We would hurt too many feelings if we did, the feelings of the people we work with, of our relatives and our neighbors and the neighbors we left behind. Anyone who has moved recently knows how much sheer matter we accumulate in our houses, but imagine also the long list of acquaintances we have accumulated, back to our earliest years. If we are fond of people at all, we have met thousands in our lives. Perhaps that is why so few of us read. Perhaps our culture is really oral, despite the science fiction of our media, satellites above and wires and presses below and the air itself in fervent vibration. One recalls the theory that ghetto children have difficulty in school not because of deprivation but because of excess, of overstimulation by the teeming world in which they live. It is true to some degree of us all. With China and the Soviet Union, and for much of the same reasons of origin and purpose, we are a national people far more than we are local. Our traditions and our associations extend from ocean to ocean, and our burden of communication too. The Communist nations, not having finished their first industrial revolution, turn to party meetings and rallies to stay in touch; with a more ritualized social structure, we send cards.

21   Making greeting cards to suit us isn't easy. Try to imagine a card that would please both your grandmother and your revolutionary son—and

yet your Christmas card probably did. For reasons no one knows, green cards don't sell. Writers of greeting cards must search their verses for unintentional double entendres, and because of that danger, the word "it" used as a direct object is taboo. "Today's your day to get *it!*" It won't do. St. Patrick's Day cards that kid Irish drinking habits elicit indignant letters from Hibernian Societies, a sign that the Irish are ready to melt the rest of the way into the pot. A card is two years in the making: what if hemlines change? Superman cards reached the stores the day the Superman fad collapsed. And what do you say, in a card, in mere words, to a widow whose world has emptied of the life she loved? (You say, in rhymed verse, that words can't express your sympathy.)

When I worked at Hallmark I sometimes thought of cards as pretty   22
packages with nothing inside, but I am a year older now and I wonder. Perhaps, ephemeral though they are, they carry a greater weight of emotion to a greater number of people than we can bear to carry ourselves. They are tactful, discreet; they strike the right tone. Their designers sweat blood, believe me, to make them so. Even when they fail we forgive the sender and blame the card, as we forgive a caller a bad connection on the phone. Greeting cards have inertia. Like Santa's bag they hang a little behind. They are innately conservative because the occasions of our lives are too important for fads, of style or of spirit. Hallmark has discovered that the young people who buy its breezily pessimistic Contemporary cards return to more traditional forms when they acquire families and careers. Pessimism becomes a luxury they can no longer afford.

We grow older; the cards for our stops along the way await us in the   23
store. They are not dangerous or subversive or mean; they espouse no causes except the old mute causes of life itself, birth and marriage and begetting and death, and these gently. I celebrate them as E. M. Forster celebrated democracy, with a hearty two cheers. Merry Christmas.

Questions and Activities

▶ COMPREHENSION QUESTIONS

1. Rhodes often makes his points with straightforward use of examples. Paragraph 10, in fact, is a long series of examples of what goes on in producing Hallmark cards. What general point is Rhodes making with this series?

2. Summarize the "belly-button fuzz" example in paragraph 4. What generalization about the greeting card industry does it support?

3. Which paragraph provides historical background on the greeting card industry? Why does Rhodes include historical background in this essay?

   ▶ *QUESTIONS OF RHETORICAL PURPOSE AND STRATEGY*

4. Do you think that the purpose of this essay is informative? Do you find any evidence that Rhodes is treating his subject ironically and trying to persuade his readers to curb their consumption of greeting cards because they are the product of an industry that exploits personal needs or because they are superficial expressions of sentiment? Or is Rhodes simply providing factual information on the greeting card industry?

5. Reread paragraph 3, which contains Rhodes's explanation of why Americans have developed greeting cards to an art form while Europeans have not. What type of reader does Rhodes have in mind here? Is that reader well-informed? Does that reader know immediately what Rhodes means when he says that Americans "send cards for everything, mechanizing and standardizing the complex relationships we maintain with one another"? Why does Rhodes, in the next sentence, say that we need not be ashamed of this tendency? Why *would* his assumed reader be ashamed of this tendency?

6. *Clichés* are familiar phrases that often cause readers to criticize a writer for lack of originality. With this definition in mind, analyze the first paragraph of Rhodes's essay. Point out the clichés in this paragraph, then tell whether or not you feel that they lower your estimation of Rhodes's writing ability.

   ▶ *THEME QUESTIONS*

7. Relate the first sentence of paragraph 7 to the theme question of this section. Do you think it good or bad that greeting card manufacturers exploit the subconscious emotions of consumers, that they even go further and package these emotions in marketable categories of sentiments? Why might this marketing be harmful? What aspects of human character might it diminish?

8. All the essays and stories in this section focus in one way or another on the question of whether or not we are defining ourselves or are defined by the arts. Can you think of another example in which a popular art form seems to be telling people how to think rather than engaging them in pursuing their own thought processes? Consider, for example, television soap operas. Do they define those who watch them, or are they simply used as entertainment? Do you know anyone who takes soap operas too seriously? Does this person seem to imitate or take on the values of soap opera characters?

▶ *LEARNING ACTIVITIES*

9. Reread this essay, stopping after paragraph 8. Free-write in response to this much of the essay for fifteen minutes. Put down anything that comes into your head, but do try to keep your thoughts in some way related to the essay. You might, for example, develop a personal experience that what you have read reminds you of. Or you might simply show how Rhodes, at this point in the essay, seems to be changing his purpose. Or you might explain why he has chosen to use a given example. Or you might simply describe a personal opinion or feeling that you have in reaction to what is said in one of the paragraphs that you read.

10. Write a description of an occasion on which you sent someone an inappropriate greeting card. Tell the occasion in story form. Include in it the reasons that led you to make the inappropriate choice. Do you think that you would have made the same type of mistake had you written a letter rather than sent a card?

11. Think of a situation in which a personal letter would be far more effective than a greeting card as an expression of feeling. Describe that occasion, and tell why the letter would be so much better than a card.

The Westerner

ROBERT WARSHOW

Robert Warshow was born in New York City in 1917 and graduated from the University of Michigan in 1938. From 1946 through 1955, he published a broad range of essays on popular American culture, particularly movies. Most of his articles appeared in *Commentary, Partisan Review,* and *American Mercury* and have been collected and published in *Immediate Experience* (1962). He worked from 1942 to 1946 with the Army Security Agency in Washington and then moved back to New York City to become an editor of *Commentary* magazine. He was working at *Commentary* when he died of a heart attack in 1955, at the age of thirty-seven.

Warshow's movie reviews and essays are distinguished by his total involvement with and love for the medium. They represent some of the best of this kind of writing, early criticism of film's potential to express the subconscious desires and social myths of the American character.

In this essay, Warshow compares two classic American movie heroes: the gangster and the Western hero. He examines their actions, gestures, and situations and analyzes the effects of these characteristics on movie-goers. Warshow finds common patterns in the plots of Westerns and gangster movies and reveals how these patterns portray the inner responses of Americans to the pressures of modern life. The gangster, he says, refuses to play by the rules because he shares the average person's knowledge of the futility of normal paths to happiness and success. The Westerner, Warshow says, is a loner and a man of leisure who recognizes the seriousness of life, its essential loneliness and isolation.

Toward the close of his essay, Warshow discusses the American preoccupation with violence, as exemplified in popular films. Yet he does not find the violence in Western movies threatening or psychologically damaging. Think about this issue of violence as you read this essay.

1. Why does Warshow have an accepting attitude concerning the violence in Western movies?
2. Do Warshow's concluding remarks on style help answer the preceding question?
3. Do you think the focus in today's films is on the style of rather than the consequences of violent acts? Can you think of popular film stars

who evince a great deal of style in their violent actions? Does a Clint Eastwood, a Burt Reynolds, or a Sylvester Stallone demonstrate a style that diminishes the potentially negative social effects of the violence these stars' movies present?

▶ _____

The two most successful creations of American movies are the gangster and the Westerner: men with guns. Guns as physical objects, and the postures associated with their use, form the visual and emotional center of both types of films. I suppose this reflects the importance of guns in the fantasy life of Americans; but that is a less illuminating point than it appears to be.   *1*

The gangster movie, which no longer exists in its "classical" form, is a story of enterprise and success ending in precipitate failure. Success is conceived as an increasing power to work injury, it belongs to the city, and it is of course a form of evil (though the gangster's death, presented usually as "punishment," is perceived simply as defeat). The peculiarity of the gangster is his unceasing, nervous activity. The exact nature of his enterprises may remain vague, but his commitment to enterprise is always clear, and all the more clear because he operates outside the field of utility. He is without culture, without manners, without leisure, or at any rate his leisure is likely to be spent in debauchery so compulsively aggressive as to seem only another aspect of his "work." But he is graceful, moving like a dancer among the crowded dangers of the city.   *2*

Like other tycoons, the gangster is crude in conceiving his ends but by no means inarticulate; on the contrary, he is usually expansive and noisy (the introspective gangster is a fairly recent development), and can state definitely what he wants: to take over the North Side, to own a hundred suits, to be Number One. But new "frontiers" will present themselves infinitely, and by a rigid convention it is understood that as soon as he wishes to rest on his gains, he is on the way to destruction.   *3*

The gangster is lonely and melancholy, and can give the impression of a profound worldly wisdom. He appeals most to adolescents with their impatience and their feeling of being outsiders, but more generally he appeals to that side of all of us which refuses to believe in the "normal" possibilities of happiness and achievement; the gangster is the "no" to that great American "yes" which is stamped so big over our official culture and yet has so little to do with the way we really feel about our lives. But the gangster's loneliness and melancholy are not   *4* "authentic"; like everything else that belongs to him, they are not honestly come by: he is lonely and melancholy not because life ultimately demands such feelings but because he has put himself in a position where everybody wants to kill him and eventually somebody will. He is wide open and defenseless, incomplete because unable to accept any limits or come to terms with his own nature, fearful, loveless. And the story of his career is a nightmare inversion of the values of ambition and opportunity. From the window of Scarface's bullet-proof apartment can be seen an electric sign proclaiming: "The World Is Yours," and, if I remember, this sign is the last thing we see after Scarface lies dead in the street. In the end it is the gangster's weakness as much as his power and freedom that appeals to us; the world is not ours, but it is not his either, and in his death he "pays" for our fantasies, releasing us momentarily both from the concept of success, which he denies by caricaturing it, and from the need to succeed, which he shows to be dangerous.

5   The Western hero, by contrast, is a figure of repose. He resembles the gangster in being lonely and to some degree melancholy. But his melancholy comes from the "simple" recognition that life is unavoidably serious, not from the disproportions of his own temperament. And his loneliness is organic, not imposed on him by his situation but belonging to him intimately and testifying to his completeness. The gangster must reject others violently or draw them violently to him. The Westerner is not thus compelled to seek love; he is prepared to accept it, perhaps, but he never asks of it more than it can give, and we see him constantly in situations where love is at best an irrelevance. If there is a woman he loves, she is usually unable to understand his motives; she is against killing and being killed, and he finds it impossible to explain to her that there is no point in being "against" these things: they belong to his world.

6   Very often this woman is from the East and her failure to understand represents a clash of cultures. In the American mind, refinement, virtue, civilization, Christianity itself, are seen as feminine, and therefore women are often portrayed as possessing some kind of deeper wisdom, while the men, for all their apparent self-assurance, are fundamentally childish. But the West, lacking the graces of civilization, is the place "where men are men"; in Western movies, men have the deeper wisdom and the women are children. Those women in the Western movies who share the hero's understanding of life are prostitutes (or, as they are usually presented, bar-room entertainers)—women, that is, who have come to understand in the most practical way how love can be an irrelevance, and therefore "fallen" women. The gangster, too, associates with prostitutes, but for him the important things about a prostitute are her passive availability and her costliness: she

is part of his winnings. In Western movies, the important thing about a prostitute is her quasi-masculine independence: nobody owns her, nothing has to be explained to her, and she is not, like a virtuous woman, a "value" that demands to be protected. When the Westerner leaves the prostitute for a virtuous woman—for love—he is in fact forsaking a way of life, though the point of the choice is often obscured by having the prostitute killed by getting into the line of fire.

The Westerner is *par excellence* a man of leisure. Even when he wears the badge of a marshal or, more rarely, owns a ranch, he appears to be unemployed. We see him standing at a bar, or playing poker—a game which expresses perfectly his talent for remaining relaxed in the midst of tension—or perhaps camping out on the plains on some extraordinary errand. If he does own a ranch, it is in the background; we are not actually aware that he owns anything except his horse, his guns, and the one worn suit of clothing which is likely to remain unchanged all through the movie. It comes as a surprise to see him take money from his pocket or an extra shirt from his saddlebags. As a rule we do not even know where he sleeps at night and don't think of asking. Yet it never occurs to us that he is a poor man; there is no poverty in Western movies, and really no wealth either: those great cattle domains and shipments of gold which figure so largely in the plots are moral and not material quantities, not the objects of contention but only its occasion. Possessions too are irrelevant.

Employment of some kind—usually unproductive—is always open to the Westerner, but when he accepts it, it is not because he needs to make a living, much less from any idea of "getting ahead." Where could he want to "get ahead" to? By the time we see him, he is already "there": he can ride a horse faultlessly, keep his countenance in the face of death, and draw his gun a little faster and shoot it a little straighter than anyone he is likely to meet. These are sharply defined acquirements, giving to the figure of the Westerner an apparent moral clarity which corresponds to the clarity of his physical image against his bare landscape; initially, at any rate, the Western movie presents itself as being without mystery, its whole universe comprehended in what we see on the screen.

Much of this apparent simplicity arises directly from those "cinematic" elements which have long been understood to give the Western theme its special appropriateness for the movies: the wide expanses of land, the free movement of men on horses. As guns constitute the visible moral center of the Western movie, suggesting continually the possibility of violence, so land and horses represent the movie's material basis, its sphere of action. But the land and the horses have also a moral significance: the physical freedom they represent belongs to the moral "openness" of the West—corresponding to the fact that guns are carried where they can be seen. (And, as we shall see, the character of land and horses changes as the Western film becomes more complex.)

10   The gangster's world is less open, and his arts not so easily identifiable as the Westerner's. Perhaps he too can keep his countenance, but the mask he wears is really no mask: its purpose is precisely to make evident the fact that he desperately wants to "get ahead" and will stop at nothing. Where the Westerner imposes himself by the appearance of unshakable control, the gangster's pre-eminence lies in the suggestion that he may at any moment lose control; his strength is not in being able to shoot faster or straighter than others, but in being more willing to shoot. "Do it first," says Scarface expounding his mode of operation, "and keep on doing it!" With the Westerner, it is a crucial point of honor *not* to "do it first"; his gun remains in its holster until the moment of combat.

11   There is no suggestion, however, that he draws the gun reluctantly. The Westerner could not fulfill himself if the moment did not finally come when he can shoot his enemy down. But because that moment is so thoroughly the expression of his being, it must be kept pure. He will not violate the accepted forms of combat though by doing so he could save a city. And he can wait. "When you call me that—smile!" the villain smiles weakly, soon he is laughing with horrible joviality, and the crisis is past. But it is allowed to pass because it must come again: sooner or later Trampas will "make his play," and the Virginian will be ready for him.

12   What does the Westerner fight for? We know he is on the side of justice and order, and of course it can be said he fights for these things. But such broad aims never correspond exactly to his real motives; they only offer him his opportunity. The Westerner himself, when an explanation is asked of him (usually by a woman), is likely to say that he does what he "has to do." If justice and order did not continually demand his protection, he would be without a calling. Indeed, we come upon him often in just that situation, as the reign of law settles over the West and he is forced to see that his day is over; those are the pictures which end with his death or with his departure for some more remote frontier. What he defends, at bottom, is the purity of his own image—in fact his honor. That is what makes him invulnerable. When the gangster is killed, his whole life is shown to have been a mistake, but the image the Westerner seeks to maintain can be presented as clearly in defeat as in victory: he fights not for advantage and not for the right, but to state what he is, and he must live in a world which permits that statement. The Westerner is the last gentleman, and the movies which over and

over again tell his story are probably the last art form in which the concept of honor retains its strength.

Of course I do not mean to say that ideas of virtue and justice and   *13*
courage have gone out of culture. Honor is more than these things: it is a style, concerned with harmonious appearances as much as with desirable consequences, and tending therefore toward the denial of life in favor of art. "Who hath it? he that died o' Wednesday." On the whole a world that leans to Falstaff's view is a more civilized and even, finally, a more graceful world. It is just the march of civilization that forces the Westerner to move on; and if we actually had to confront the question it might turn out that the woman who refuses to understand him is right as often as she is wrong. But we do not confront the question. Where the Westerner lives it is always about 1870—not the real 1870, either, or the real West—and he is killed or goes away when his position becomes problematical. The fact that he continues to hold our attention is evidence enough that, in his proper frame, he presents an image of personal nobility that is still real for us.

Clearly, this image easily becomes ridiculous: we need only look at   *14*
William S. Hart or Tom Mix, who in the wooden absoluteness of their virtue represented little that an adult could take seriously; and doubtless such figures as Gene Autry or Roy Rogers are no better, though I confess I have seen none of their movies. Some film enthusiasts claim to find in the early, unsophisticated Westerns a "cinematic purity" that has since been lost; this idea is as valid, and finally misleading, as T. S. Eliot's statement that *Everyman* is the only play in English that stays within the limitations of art. The truth is that the Westerner comes into the field of serious art only when his moral code, without ceasing to be compelling, is seen also to be imperfect. The Westerner at his best exhibits a moral ambiguity which darkens his image and saves him from absurdity; this ambiguity arises from the fact that, whatever his justifications, he is a killer of men.

In *The Virginian*, which is an archetypal Western movie as *Scarface*   *15*
or *Little Caesar* are archetypal gangster movies, there is a lynching in which the hero (Gary Cooper), as leader of a posse, must supervise the hanging of his best friend for stealing cattle. With the growth of American "social consciousness," it is no longer possible to present a lynching in the movies unless the point is the illegality and injustice of the lynching itself; *The Ox-Bow Incident*, made in 1943, explicitly puts forward the newer point of view and can be regarded as a kind of "anti-Western." But in 1929, when *The Virginian* was made, the present inhibition about lynching was not yet in force; the justice, and therefore the necessity, of the hanging is never questioned—except by the school-teacher from the East, whose refusal to understand serves as usual to set

forth more sharply the deeper seriousness of the West. The Virginian is thus in a tragic dilemma where one moral absolute conflicts with another and the choice of either must leave a moral stain. If he had chosen to save his friend, he would have violated the image of himself that he had made essential to his existence, and the movie would have had to end with his death, for only by his death could the image have been restored. Having chosen instead to sacrifice his friend to the higher demands of the "code"—the only choice worthy of him, as even the friend understands—he is none the less stained by the killing, but what is needed now to set accounts straight is not his death but the death of the villain Trampas, the leader of the cattle thieves, who had escaped the posse and abandoned the Virginian's friend to his fate. Again the woman intervenes: Why must there be *more* killing? If the hero really loved her, he would leave town, refusing Trampas's challenge. What good will it be if Trampas should kill him? But the Virginian does once more what he "has to do," and in avenging his friend's death wipes out the stain on his own honor. Yet his victory cannot be complete: no death can be paid for and no stain truly wiped out; the movie is still a tragedy, for though the hero escapes with his life, he has been forced to confront the ultimate limits of his moral ideas.

16   This mature sense of limitation and unavoidable guilt is what gives the Westerner a "right" to his melancholy. It is true that the gangster's story is also a tragedy—in certain formal ways more clearly a tragedy than the Westerner's—but it is a romantic tragedy, based on a hero whose defeat springs with almost mechanical inevitability from the outrageous presumption of his demands: the gangster is *bound* to go on until he is killed. The Westerner is a more classical figure, self-contained and limited to begin with, seeking not to extend his dominion but only to assert his personal value, and his tragedy lies in the fact that even this circumscribed demand cannot be fully realized. Since the Westerner is not a murderer but (most of the time) a man of virtue, and since he is always prepared for defeat, he retains his inner invulnerability and his story need not end with his death (and usually does not); but what we finally respond to is not his victory but his defeat.

17   Up to a point, it is plain that the deeper seriousness of the good Western films comes from the introduction of a realism, both physical and psychological, that was missing with Tom Mix and William S. Hart. As lines of age have come into Gary Cooper's face since *The Virginian*, so the outlines of the Western movie in general have become less smooth, its background more drab. The sun still beats upon the town, but the camera is likely now to take advantage of this illumination to seek out more closely the shabbiness of buildings and furniture, the loose, worn hang of clothing, the wrinkles and dirt of the faces.

Once it has been discovered that the true theme of the Western movie is not the freedom and expansiveness of frontier life, but its limitations, its material bareness, the pressures of obligation, then even the landscape itself ceases to be quite the arena of free movement it once was, but becomes instead a great empty waste, cutting down more often than it exaggerates the stature of the horseman who rides across it. We are more likely now to see the Westerner struggling against the obstacles of the physical world (as in the wonderful scenes on the desert and among the rocks in *The Last Posse*) than carelessly surmounting them. Even the horses, no longer the "friends" of man or the inspired chargers of knight-errantry, have lost much of the moral significance that once seemed to belong to them in their careering across the screen. It seems to me the horses grow tired and stumble more often than they did, and that we see them less frequently at the gallop.

In *The Gunfighter*, a remarkable film of a couple of years ago, the   *18* landscape has virtually disappeared. Most of the action takes place indoors, in a cheerless saloon where a tired "bad man" (Gregory Peck) contemplates the waste of his life, to be senselessly killed at the end by a vicious youngster setting off on the same futile path. The movie is done in cold, quiet tones of gray, and every object in it—faces, clothing, a table, the hero's heavy mustache—is given an air of uncompromising authenticity, suggesting those dim photographs of the nineteenth-century West in which Wyatt Earp, say, turns out to be a blank untidy figure posing awkwardly before some uninteresting building. This "authenticity," to be sure, is only aesthetic; the chief fact about nineteenth-century photographs, to my eyes at any rate, is how stonily they refuse to yield up the truth. But that limitation is just what is needed: by preserving some hint of the rigidity of archaic photography (only in tone and decor, never in composition), *The Gunfighter* can permit us to feel that we are looking at a more "real" West than the one the movies have accustomed us to—harder, duller, less "romantic"—and yet without forcing us outside the boundaries which give the Western movie its validity.

We come upon the hero of *The Gunfighter* at the end of a career in   *19* which he has never upheld justice and order, and has been at times, apparently, an actual criminal; in this case, it is clear that the hero has been wrong and the woman who has rejected his way of life has been right. He is thus without any of the larger justifications, and knows himself a ruined man. There can be no question of his "redeeming" himself in any socially constructive way. He is too much the victim of his own reputation to turn marshal as one of his old friends has done, and he is not offered the sentimental solution of a chance to give up his life for some good end; the whole point is that he exists outside the field of social value. Indeed, if we were once allowed to see him in the days of his "success," he might become a figure like the gangster, for his career has been aggressively "anti-social" and the practical problem he faces is the gangster's problem: there will always be somebody trying to kill him. Yet it is obviously absurd to speak of him as "anti-social," not only because we do not see him acting as a criminal, but more fundamentally because we do not see his milieu as a society. Of course it has its "social problems" and a kind of static history: civilization is always just at the point of driving out the old freedom; there are women and children to represent the possibility of a settled life; and there is the marshal, a bad man turned good, determined to keep at least his area of jurisdiction at peace. But these elements are not, in fact, a part of the film's "realism," even though they come out of the real history of the West; they belong to the conventions of the form, to that accepted framework which makes the film possible in the first place, and they exist not to provide a standard by which the gunfighter can be judged, but only to set him off. The true "civilization" of the Western movie is always embodied in an individual, good or bad is more a matter of personal bearing than of social consequences, and the conflict of good and bad is a duel between two men. Deeply troubled and obviously doomed, the gunfighter is the Western hero still, perhaps all the more because his value must express itself entirely in his own being—in his presence, the way he holds our eyes—and in contradiction to the facts. No matter what he has done, he *looks* right, and he remains invulnerable because, without acknowledging anyone else's right to judge him, he has judged his own failure and has already assimilated it, understanding—as no one else understands except the marshal and the bar-room girl—that he can do nothing but play out the drama of the gun fight again and again until the time comes when it will be he who gets killed. What "redeems" him is that he no longer believes in this drama and nevertheless will continue to play his role perfectly: the pattern is all.

20   The proper function of realism in the Western movie can only be to deepen the lines of that pattern. It is an art form for connoisseurs where the spectator derives his pleasure from the appreciation of minor variations within the working out of a pre-established order. One does not want too much novelty: it comes as a shock, for instance, when the hero is made to operate without a gun, as has been done in several pictures (e.g., *Destry Rides Again*), and our uneasiness is allayed only when he is finally compelled to put his "pacifism" aside. If the hero can be shown to be troubled, complex, fallible, even eccentric, or the villain given some psychological taint or, better, some evocative physical mannerism, to shade the colors of his villainy, that is all to the good. Indeed, that kind of variation is absolutely necessary to keep the type

from becoming sterile: we do not want to see the same movie over and over again, only the same form. But when the impulse toward realism is extended into a "reinterpretation" of the West as a developed society, drawing our eyes away from the hero if only to the extent of showing him as the one dominant figure in a complex social order, then the pattern is broken and the West itself begins to be uninteresting. If the "social problems" of the frontier are to be the movie's chief concern, there is no longer any point in re-examining these problems twenty times a year; they have been solved, and the people for whom they once were real are dead. Moreover, the hero himself, still the film's central figure, now tends to become its one unassimilable element, since he is the most "unreal."

The Ox-Bow Incident, by denying the convention of the lynching, presents us with a modern "social drama" and evokes a corresponding response, but in doing so it almost makes the Western setting irrelevant, a mere backdrop of beautiful scenery. (It is significant that *The Ox-Bow Incident* has no hero; a hero would have to stop the lynching or be killed in trying to stop it, and then the "problem" of lynching would no longer be central.) Even in *The Gunfighter* the women and children are a little too much in evidence, threatening constantly to become a real focus of concern instead of simply part of the given framework; and the young tough who kills the hero has too much the air of juvenile criminality: the hero himself could never have been like that, and the idea of a cycle being repeated therefore loses its sharpness. But the most striking example of the confusion created by a too conscientious "social" realism is in the celebrated *High Noon*. 21

In *High Noon* we find Gary Cooper still the upholder of order that he was in *The Virginian*, but twenty-four years older, stooped, slower moving, awkward, his face lined, the flesh sagging, a less beautiful and weaker figure, but with the suggestion of greater depth that belongs almost automatically to age. Like the hero of *The Gunfighter*, he no longer has to assert his character and is no longer interested in the drama of combat: it is hard to imagine that he might once have been so youthful as to say, "When you call me that—smile!" In fact, when we come upon him he is hanging up his guns and his marshal's badge in order to begin a new, peaceful life with his bride, who is a Quaker. But then the news comes that a man he had sent to prison has been pardoned and will get to town on the noon train; three friends of this man have come to wait for him at the station, and when the freed convict arrives the four of them will come to kill the marshal. He is thus trapped; the bride will object, the hero himself will waver much more than he would have done twenty-four years ago, but in the end he will play out the drama because it is what he "has to do." All this belongs to 22 the established form (there is even the "fallen woman" who understands the marshal's position as his wife does not). Leaving aside the crudity of building up suspense by means of the clock, the actual Western drama of *High Noon* is well handled and forms a good companion piece to *The Virginian*, showing in both conception and technique the ways in which the Western movie has naturally developed.

23   But there is a second drama along with the first. As the marshal sets out to find deputies to help him deal with the four gunmen, we are taken through the various social strata of the town, each group in turn refusing its assistance out of cowardice, malice, irresponsibility, or venality. With this we are in the field of "social drama"—of a very low order, incidentally, altogether unconvincing and displaying a vulgar anti-populism that has marred some other movies of Stanley Kramer's. But the falsity of the "social drama" is less important than the fact that it does not belong in the movie to begin with. The technical problem was to make it necessary for the marshal to face his enemies alone; to explain *why* the other townspeople are not at his side is to raise a question which does not exist in the proper frame of the Western movie, where the hero is "naturally" alone and it is only necessary to contrive the physical absence of those who might be his allies, if any contrivance is needed at all. In addition, though the hero of *High Noon* proves himself a better man than all around him the actual effect of this contrast is to lessen his stature: he becomes only a rejected man of virtue. In our final glimpse of him, as he rides away through the town where he has spent most of his life without really imposing himself on it, he is a pathetic rather than a tragic figure. And his departure has another meaning as well: the "social drama" has no place for him.

24   But there is also a different way of violating the Western form. This is to yield entirely to its static quality as legend and to the "cinematic" temptations of its landscape, the horses, the quiet men. John Ford's famous *Stagecoach* (1938) had much of this unhappy preoccupation with style, and the same director's *My Darling Clementine* (1946), a soft and beautiful movie about Wyatt Earp, goes further along the same path, offering indeed a superficial accuracy of historical reconstruction, but so loving in execution as to destroy the outlines of the Western legend, assimilating it to the more sentimental legend of rural America and making the hero a more dangerous Mr. Deeds. (*Powder River*, a recent "routine" Western shamelessly copied from *My Darling Clementine*, is in most ways a better film; lacking the benefit of a serious director, it is necessarily more concerned with drama than with style.)

25   The highest expression of this aestheticizing tendency is in George Stevens' *Shane*, where the legend of the West is virtually reduced to its essentials and then fixed in the dreamy clarity of a fairy tale. There never was so broad and bare and lovely a landscape as Stevens puts be-

fore us, or so unimaginably comfortless a "town" as the little group of buildings on the prairie to which the settlers must come for their supplies and to buy a drink. The mere physical progress of the film, following the style of *A Place in the Sun*, is so deliberately graceful that everything seems to be happening at the bottom of a clear lake. The hero (Alan Ladd) is hardly a man at all, but something like the Spirit of the West, beautiful in fringed buckskins. He emerges mysteriously from the plains, breathing sweetness and a melancholy which is no longer simply the Westerner's natural response to experience but has taken on spirituality; and when he has accomplished his mission, meeting and destroying in the black figure of Jack Palance a Spirit of Evil just as metaphysical as his own embodiment of virtue, he fades away again into the more distant West, a man whose "day is over," leaving behind the wondering little boy who might have imagined the whole story. The choice of Alan Ladd to play the leading role is alone an indication of this film's tendency. Actors like Gary Cooper or Gregory Peck are in themselves, as material objects, "realistic," seeming to bear in their bodies and their faces mortality, limitation, the knowledge of good and evil. Ladd is a more "aesthetic" object, with some of the "universality" of a piece of sculpture; his special quality is in his physical smoothness and serenity, unworldly and yet not innocent, but suggesting that no experience can really touch him. Stevens has tried to freeze the Western myth once and for all in the immobility of Alan Ladd's countenance. If *Shane* were "right," and fully successful, it might be possible to say there was no point in making any more Western movies: once the hero is apotheosized, variation and development are closed off.

Shane is not "right," but it is still true that the possibilities of fruitful variation in the Western movie are limited. The form can keep its freshness through endless repetitions only because of the special character of the film medium, where the physical difference between one object and another—above all, between one actor and another—is of such enormous importance, serving the function that is served by the variety of language in the perpetuation of literary types. In this sense, the "vocabulary" of films is much larger than that of literature and falls more readily into pleasing and significant arrangements. (That may explain why the middle levels of excellence are more easily reached in the movies than in literary forms, and perhaps also why the status of the movies as art is constantly being called into question.) But the advantage of this almost automatic particularity belongs to all films alike. Why does the Western movie especially have such a hold on our imagination? 26

Chiefly, I think, because it offers a serious orientation to the problem of violence such as can be found almost nowhere else in our culture. 27

One of the well-known peculiarities of modern civilized opinion is its refusal to acknowledge the value of violence. This refusal is a virtue, but like many virtues it involves a certain willful blindness and it encourages hypocrisy. We train ourselves to be shocked or bored by cultural images of violence, and our very concept of heroism tends to be a passive one: we are less drawn to the brave young men who kill large numbers of our enemies than to the heroic prisoners who endure torture without capitulating. In art, though we may still be able to understand and participate in the values of the *Iliad,* a modern writer like Ernest Hemingway we find somewhat embarrassing; there is no doubt that he stirs us, but we cannot help recognizing also that he is a little childish. And in the criticism of popular culture, where the educated observer is usually under the illusion that he has nothing at stake, the presence of images of violence is often assumed to be in itself a sufficient ground for condemnation.

28   These attitudes, however, have not reduced the element of violence in our culture but, if anything, have helped to free it from moral control by letting it take on the aura of "emancipation." The celebration of acts of violence is left more and more to the irresponsible: on the higher cultural levels to writers like Céline, and lower down to Mickey Spillane or Horace McCoy, or to the comic books, television, and the movies. The gangster movie, with its numerous variations, belongs to this cultural "underground" which sets forth the attractions of violence in the face of all our higher social attitudes. It is a more "modern" genre than the Western, perhaps even more profound, because it confronts industrial society on its own ground—the city—and because, like much of our advanced art, it gains its effects by a gross insistence on its own narrow logic. But it is anti-social, resting on fantasies of irresponsible freedom. If we are brought finally to acquiesce in the denial of the fantasies, it is only because they have been shown to be dangerous, not because they have given way to a better vision of behavior.[1]

29   In war movies, to be sure, it is possible to present the uses of violence within a framework of responsibility. But there is the disadvantage that modern war is a co-operative enterprise; its violence is largely impersonal, and heroism belongs to the group more than to the individual. The hero of a war movie is most often simply a leader, and his superiority is likely to be expressed in a denial of the heroic: you are not supposed

---

[1] I am not concerned here with the actual social consequences of gangster movies, though I suspect they could not have been so pernicious as they were thought to be. Some of the compromises introduced to avoid the supposed bad effects of the old gangster movies may be, if anything, more dangerous, for the sadistic violence that once belonged only to the gangster is now commonly enlisted on the side of the law and thus goes undefeated, allowing us (if we wish) to find in the movies a sort of "confirmation" of our fantasies.

to be brave, you are supposed to get the job done and stay alive (this too, of course, is a kind of heroic posture. But a new—and practical—one). At its best, the war movie may represent a more civilized point of view than the Western, and if it were not continually marred by ideological sentimentality we might hope to find it developing into a higher form of drama. But it cannot supply the values we seek in the Western.

Those values are in the image of a single man who wears a gun on his thigh. The gun tells us that he lives in a world of violence, and even that he "believes in violence." But the drama is one of self-restraint: the moment of violence must come in its own time and according to its special laws, or else it is valueless. There is little cruelty in Western movies, and little sentimentality; our eyes are not focused on the sufferings of the defeated but on the deportment of the hero. Really, it is not violence at all which is the "point" of the Western movie, but a certain image of man, a style, which expresses itself most clearly in violence. Watch a child with his toy guns and you will see: what most interests him is not (as we so much fear) the fantasy of hurting others, but to work out how a man might look when he shoots or is shot. A hero is one who looks like a hero.

Whatever the limitations of such an idea in experience, it has always been valid in art, and has a special validity in an art where appearances are everything. The Western hero is necessarily an archaic figure; we do not really believe in him and would not have him step out of his rigidly conventionalized background. But his archaicism does not take away from his power; on the contrary, it adds to it by keeping him just a little beyond the reach of common sense and of absolutized emotion, the two usual impulses of our art. And he has, after all, his own kind of relevance. He is there to remind us of the possibility of style in an age which has put on itself the burden of pretending that style has no meaning, and, in the midst of our anxieties over the problem of violence, to suggest that even in killing or being killed we are not freed from the necessity of establishing satisfactory modes of behavior. Above all, the movies in which the Westerner plays out his role preserve for us the pleasure of a complete and self-contained drama—and one which still effortlessly crosses the boundaries which divide our culture—in a time when other, more consciously serious art forms are increasingly complex, uncertain, and ill-defined.

Questions and Activities

▶ COMPREHENSION QUESTIONS

1. Look up in a film encyclopedia one of the Western movies that Warshow analyzes in detail. When was it made? Who starred in it? How did its original reviewers respond to it? Fit your information onto a five-by-eight card and use it as a basis for a report to your class.
2. Make lists of the contrasting characteristics of the Western and gangster movie heroes, as they are described in this essay. Compare your lists with those produced by your classmates.
3. Provide a paraphrase of Warshow's definition of "honor"in paragraphs 12 and 13. (A paraphrase is a rewrite of an existing passage that captures the sense of the original while altering its style.) How is his definition different from the popular definition of the word? How is that distinction important to his interpretation of the Western hero?

▶ QUESTIONS OF RHETORICAL PURPOSE AND STRATEGY

4. How much background knowledge does Warshow assume his readers have? Are his examples fully enough explained? Can you point to places where you require more information about the movie he is discussing? Would a movie-goer who had not seen most of the movies on which Warshow bases his discussion be able to follow his reasoning?
5. This essay's purpose is informative. Informative writing should always provide its readers with new information within the context of known facts. Taking yourself as an example, what did you already know about movies that you found simply reproduced and reorganized by Warshow? On the other hand, what new information did you get from Warshow? Did the new and old information fit together in a way that made your reading of the essay flow easily while allowing you to enjoy its originality? Select one paragraph and illustrate your answer by examining its mix of new and old information.
6. This essay makes extensive use of the comparative format. How does Warshow's opening description of the gangster (paragraphs 2, 3, and 4) function as a contrast to his longer discussion of the Western hero? What elements do these heroes have in common? How do they differ?

► *THEME QUESTIONS*

7. Describe one of the characteristics Warshow attributes to the pre-1955 Western hero. Then analyze that characteristic in a more recent Western character in a movie such as *The Wild Bunch, Butch Cassidy and the Sundance Kid, Blazing Saddles,* or a Clint Eastwood Western. Has the characteristic changed, disappeared, or remained the same? Why might it have done this?

8. Do the same analysis you did in response to the preceding question for a gangster movie character instead. A movie such as *Scarface, The Godfather I* or *II, Down These Mean Streets,* or *Raging Bull* could provide useful material for this analysis. Take Sylvester Stallone's Rocky and Rambo characters as examples. Is Rocky or Rambo ever the typical American "lonely" hero? How are Stallone's gestures, actions, and words either similar to or different from those of earlier American film heroes, as described by Warshow?

9. Do you believe that movie-goers might actually model their behavior after Western heroes? Certainly this modeling, if it does happen, would not be literal or direct. How might a businessman, truck driver, or teacher subconsciously adapt his or her behavior to the model of the Western hero? What would a person do that would indicate the influence of Westerns? Do you know anyone who seems to uphold frontier or Western values? What does this person do that suggests the influence of these values?

10. Can you use Westerns, gangster movies, or any other popular type of movie to answer this section's theme question? First, choose a type of movie and explain its general influence on the modern person's self-image. Then choose one example of this type of movie and tell how the behavior represented in that movie has been copied by movie-goers. A movie such as *Staying Alive,* any of the Clint Eastwood or Burt Reynolds films, any movie by or about a popular musician, or any of the four *Rocky* films would be good material for answering these questions.

► *LEARNING ACTIVITIES*

11. Make a list of characteristics that describe a new type of film hero or heroine. Then write a paragraph in which you develop a generalization that explains why this new type has caught the viewer's eye. Has a particular version, for example, of the character of the independent woman caught on in recent films? Is there a new stereotype of the sensitive and more dependent man? Or do contemporary

movie roles, despite recent attention to sexual roles, seem to reflect traditional male and female characteristics?

12. In his writing, Warshow moves from general definition of a type to illustrative example. Each paragraph of this essay moves gracefully from generality to particular example—a specific film, actor, or setting. Write a paragraph similar to one of Warshow's, but focused on a more contemporary type of movie character. What are the defining characteristics, for example, of space-age heroes and heroines portrayed in a movie such as *E.T., Star Wars, The Empire Strikes Back, Close Encounters of the Third Kind, Dune,* or *Space Camp?* What social values do current movie heroes and heroines have in common? How are they similar to and different from those of gangsters and Western heroes? Give particular examples, as Warshow does for Westerns, of the heroic actions and themes of the movies you mention.

Modern City Planning: The Victory over Vitality

JANE JACOBS

Born in 1916 in Syracuse, New York, Jane Jacobs is the daughter of a physician and married an architect in 1944. She never attended college. Immediately after high school, she spent a year as a reporter for the *Scranton Tribune*. She then went to work as a stenographer in New York and spent her free time writing free-lance articles about the city's working districts. Later, she took on a number of professional writing and editing jobs, which ranged in subject matter from metallurgy to the geography of the United States for foreign readers. She also served as associate and senior editor of *Architecture Forum* from 1952 to 1962. The year 1961 marked the publication of *The Death and Life of Great American Cities,* the book from which this essay was taken. In addition, Jacobs has written *The Exploding Metropolis* (1958) and *The Economy of Cities* (1969).

The fact that Jacobs is not a professional architect may account for her willingness to criticize conventional city planning. She has always refused to consider buildings and physical structures as separate from the people who use them. Her articles and books argue that people should be given more attention in the planning of urban architecture than most architects and city planners have in the past been willing to give them. She has combined her writing with social action: in the 1960s she opposed the construction of an expressway that would displace the families and businesses along the route from the Manhattan Tunnel to the Holland Tunnel.

The most effective way to begin reading this essay is to clarify Jacobs's purpose. She assumes her reader knows the problems of cities and knows that city environments often make these problems worse. First, she wishes to give these readers background information. Paragraphs 8 through 31 summarize the major influences on urban architecture and planning from the end of the nineteenth century to approximately 1960. Second, Jacobs wishes to persuade her readers that the assumptions behind these city-planning philosophies were wrong. They put environment before people, rather than seeing environment as an adjunct or complement to people's everyday activities. Jacobs, then, uses history and analysis to try to persuade her readers that people's activities should define their environment, not the reverse. She has in mind a reader who is concerned with life in cities and knows something about recent developments, but will accept change.

Here are some questions that you should keep in mind as you read Jacobs's essay:

1. What does our city architecture tell us about ourselves?
2. What do skyscrapers, enclosed gardens, mammoth but sometimes sterile civic centers and malls indicate about how we live or want to live? What do they indicate about the ideas and concerns of architects and city planners?
3. Jacobs's essay was published in 1961. Can you point to evidence that in recent years city governments have begun to take her arguments seriously as they plan rebuilding programs? Are neighborhood people given more say in decisions on how and where to rebuild? Do city planners seem to consider the life styles of the people who live in neighborhoods that are to be rehabilitated?

▶ _____

1   There is a wistful myth that if only we had enough money to spend—the figure is usually put at $100,000,000,000—America could wipe out all her slums in ten years, reverse decay in the great, dull Gray Belts that were yesterday's and day-before-yesterday's suburbs, anchor the wandering middle class and its wandering tax money, and perhaps even solve the traffic problem.

2   But look what we have built with the first several billions: Low-income housing projects that become worse centers of delinquency, vandalism and general social hopelessness than the slums they were supposed to replace. Middle-income housing projects which are perfect marvels of dullness and regimentation, sealed against any buoyancy or urban vitality. Luxury housing projects that mitigate their inanity, or try to, with a vapid vulgarity. "Cultural centers" that are unable to support a good book store. "Civic centers" that are avoided by everyone but the leisured indigent, who have fewer choices of loitering place than others. "Commercial centers" that are lackluster imitations of standardized suburban chain emporia. Promenades that go from no place to nowhere and have no promenaders. Expressways that eviscerate the metropolis.

3   This is not the rebuilding of cities. This is the sacking of cities.

4   These accomplishments are poorer than their poor pretentious surfaces. They seldom aid the city around them, as in theory they are supposed to do. The amputated neighborhoods around them typically develop galloping gangrene. To house people in this planned fashion, price tags are fastened to the population, and each sorted-out chunk comes to live in growing suspicion and tension against the surrounding

city. When two or more such hostile islands are juxtaposed, the result is called "a balanced neighborhood." Monopolistic shopping centers and monumental cultural centers cloak, under the public relations hoo-ha, the subtraction of commerce, and of culture too, from the intimate and casual life of cities.

To accomplish such wonders as these, it is necessary to push about the people marked with the planners' hex, to uproot them much as if they were the subjects of a conquering power. Thousands upon thousands of small businesses are destroyed, and their proprietors ruined, with hardly a gesture at compensation. Whole communities are ripped apart and sown to the winds, with a harvest of cynicism, resentment and despair that must be heard and seen to be believed. A group of clergymen in Chicago, appalled at the fruits of planned city-rebuilding there, asked, "Could Job have been thinking of Chicago when he wrote: 5

> Here are men that alter their neighbor's landmark...shoulder the poor aside, conspire to oppress the friendless.
> Reap they the field that is none of theirs, strip the vineyard wrongfully seized from its owner...
> A cry goes up from the city streets, where wounded men lie groaning..."

If so, he was also thinking of New York, Philadelphia, Boston, Washington, St. Louis, San Francisco, and a number of other places.

The economic rationale of current city rebuilding does not rest solely and soundly on reasoned investment of public tax subsidies, as the theory of "urban renewal" proclaims, but also on vast, involuntary subsidies wrung out of helpless site victims. And the increased tax returns from such sites, accruing to the cities as a result of this "investment," are a mirage, a pitiful gesture against the ever-increasing sums of public money needed to combat the disintegration and instability that flow from the cruelly shaken-up city. The means to planned city-rebuilding are as deplorable as the ends. 6

Meantime, all the art and science of city planning seem to be helpless to stem decay—and the spiritlessness that precedes decay—in ever more massive swathes. Nor can this decay be laid, reassuringly, to lack of opportunity for the arts of planning. It seems to matter little whether they are applied or not. The foregoing is what I believe they have achieved. And the history of the most influential ideas informing orthodox city planning—and urban architecture—seem by their very nature to predict this awful achievement. 7

The most important thread of influence may be said to begin with Ebenezer Howard, an English court reporter for whom planning was an avocation. Howard looked at the living conditions of the poor in late nineteenth-century London and understandably did not like what he 8 smelled, saw or heard. It was not simply that he hated the wrongs and mistakes of the city, he hated the city. He thought it an outright evil and an affront to nature that so many people should get themselves into an agglomeration. His prescription for saving the people was to do the city in.

9   The program he proposed, in 1898, was to halt the growth of London and also repopulate the declining country villages by building a new kind of town—the Garden City, where the city poor might again live close to nature. So they might earn their livings, industry was to be set up in the Garden City, for while Howard was not planning cities, he was not planning dormitory suburbs either. His aim was the creation of self-sufficient small towns—very nice towns if the citizen were docile, had no plans of his own and did not mind spending his life among others with no plans of their own. For, as in all Utopias, the right to have originality and force of any significance belonged only to the planners in charge. The Garden City was to be encircled with a belt of agriculture. Industry was to be in its planned preserves; schools, housing and greens in their planned preserves; and in the center were to be commercial, club and cultural places, held in common. The town and greenbelt, in their totality, were to be permanently controlled by the public authority under which the town was developed, to prevent speculation or supposedly irrational changes in land use, and also to do away with temptations to increase its density—in brief, to prevent it from ever becoming a city. The maximum population was to be held to thirty thousand.

10   Nathan Glazer has summed up the vision well in *Architectural Forum:* "The image was the English country town—with the manor house and its park replaced by a community center, and with some factories hidden behind a screen of trees, to supply work."

11   The closest American equivalent would probably be the model company town, but with profit-sharing, and the Parent-Teacher Associations in charge of the routine, custodial political life. For Ebenezer Howard was envisioning not simply a new physical environment and social life, but a paternalistic political and economic society.

12   Nevertheless, as Glazer has pointed out, the Garden City was essentially "conceived as an alternative to the city, and as a solution to city problems; this was, and is still, the foundation of its immense power as a planning idea." Howard managed to get two garden cities built, Letchworth and Welwyn, and of course England and Sweden have, since the War, built a number of satellite towns based on Garden City principles. In the United States, the suburb of Radburn, N. J., and the depression-built, Government-sponsored greenbelt towns (actually suburbs) were all modifications on the idea. But Howard's success in the literal, or reasonably literal, acceptance of his program was as noth-

ing compared to his success in influencing American city planning today. City planners and designers with no interest in the Garden City pure are thoroughly governed by its underlying principles.

Howard set spinning powerful and city-destroying ideas: He con-   13
ceived that the way to deal with the city's functions was to sort and sift out of the whole certain simple land-uses, and to arrange each of these in relative self-containment. He believed the provision of wholesome housing to be the central problem, to which everything else was subsidiary; further, he defined wholesome housing according to suburban physical qualities and small-town social qualities. He conceived of commerce as the routine, standardized supply of goods, and as serving a self-limited market. He conceived of good planning as a settling of things once for all; in each case, the plan must anticipate all that is needed and be protected, after it is executed, against any but the most minor subsequent changes. He conceived of planning also as essentially paternalistic, if not authoritarian. He was uninterested in those aspects of the city which could not be abstracted to serve his Utopia. In particular, he simply wrote off the intricate, many-faceted, cultural life of the metropolis. He was uninterested in such problems as the way great cities unofficially police themselves, or allow for the exchange of ideas, or operate politically, or invent new economic arrangements. In short, he was not designing for city life at all.

Howard's influence on American city planning converged on the city   14
from two directions: from town and regional planners on the one hand, and from architects on the other. Along the avenue of planning, Sir Patrick Geddes, a Scots biologist and philosopher, saw the Garden City idea not as a fortuitous way to absorb population growth otherwise destined for a great city, but as the starting point of a much grander and more encompassing pattern. He thought of the planning of cities as part of the planning of whole regions. Under regional planning, Garden Cities would be rationally distributed throughout large territories, dovetailing into natural resources, balanced against agriculture and woodland, forming one far-flung logical whole.

Howard's and Geddes' ideas were enthusiastically adopted in Ameri-   15
ca during the 1920's, and developed further by a group of extraordinarily effective and dedicated people—among them Lewis Mumford, Clarence Stein, the late Henry Wright, and Catherine Bauer. While they thought of themselves as regional planners, Catherine Bauer has more recently called this group the "Decentrists," and this name is more apt, for the primary result of regional planning, as they saw it, would be to decentralize great cities, thin them out, and disperse their enterprises and populations into smaller, separated cities, or, better yet, towns. At

the time, it appeared that the American population was both leveling off in numbers and increasing in median age, and the problem appeared to be not one of accommodating a rapidly growing population, but simply of redistributing a static one.

16   As with Howard, this group's effect was less in getting literal acceptance of its program—that got nowhere—than in influencing city planning, and legislation affecting housing and housing finance. Model housing schemes by Stein and Wright, built mainly in suburban settings or at the fringes of cities, together with the writings, diagrams, sketches and photographs presented by Mumford and Bauer, demonstrated and popularized ideas such as these, which are now taken for granted in orthodox planning:

1) The street is bad as an environment for humans; houses should be turned away from it and faced inward, toward sheltered greens.
2) Frequent streets are wasteful, of advantage only to real estate speculators who measure value by the front foot.
3) The basic unit of city design is not the street, but the block and more particularly the superblock.
4) Commerce should be segregated from residences and greens.
5) A neighborhood's demand for goods should be calculated "scientifically," and this much and no more commercial space allocated.
6) The presence of many other people is, at best, a necessary evil, and good city planning must aim for at least an illusion of isolation and quasi-suburban privacy. The Decentrists also hammered home, and with equal success, Howard's basic premises that the planned community must be islanded off as a self-contained unit, that it must resist future change, and that every significant detail must be controlled by the planners from the start and then stuck to. In short, good planning was project planning.

17   To reinforce and dramatize the necessity for the new order of things, the Decentrists incessantly cried down the bad old city.

18   They were incurious about its successes. They were interested only in failures, and all was failure. A book like Mumford's *The Culture of Cities* was largely a morbid and biased catalogue of ills. The great city was Megalopolis, Tyrannopolis, Necropolis, a monstrosity, a tyranny, a living death. New York's midtown was "solidified chaos" (Mumford). The shape and appearance of cities was nothing but "a chaotic accident...the summation of the haphazard, antagonistic whims of many self-centered, ill-advised individuals" (Stein). The centers of cities amounted to "a foreground of noise, dirt, beggars, souvenirs and shrill competitive advertising" (Bauer).

How could anything so bad be worth the attempt to understand it? And in the schools of planning and architecture, and in Congress, state legislatures and City Halls too, the Decentrists' ideas were gradually accepted as basic doctrine for working *constructively*.

The man with the most dramatic idea of how to get all this anti-city planning right into the cities themselves was the European architect Le Corbusier. He devised in the 1920's a dream city, which he called the Radiant City, composed not of the low buildings beloved of the Decentrists, but instead mainly of skyscrapers within a park. ''Suppose we are entering the city by way of the Great Park,'' Le Corbusier wrote. ''Our fast car takes the special elevated motor track between the majestic skyscrapers: as we approach nearer, there is seen the repetition against the sky of the twenty-four skyscrapers; to our left and right on the outskirts of each particular area are the municipal and administrative buildings; and enclosing the space are the museums and university buildings. The whole city is a Park.'' In Le Corbusier's vertical city, the common run of mankind was to be housed at 1,200 inhabitants to the acre, a fantastically high city density. But by building up so high, planners could leave 95 per cent of the ground open. The skyscrapers would occupy only 5 per cent of the ground. The high-income inhabitants would be in lower, luxury housing around courts, with 85 per cent of their ground left open. Here and there would be restaurants and theaters.

Le Corbusier was planning not only a physical environment, he was planning for a social Utopia as well. Le Corbusier's Utopia was a state of what he called maximum individual liberty, by which he seems to have meant not liberty to do anything much, but liberty from ordinary responsibility. In his Radiant City nobody, presumably, was going to have to be his brother's keeper anymore. Nobody was going to have to struggle with plans of his own. Nobody was going to be tied down.

The Decentrists and other loyal advocates of the Garden City were aghast at Le Corbusier's city of towers in a park, and still are. Their reaction to it was, and remains, much like that of progressive nursery school teachers confronting an utterly institutional orphanage. And yet, ironically, the Radiant City comes directly out of the Garden City. Le Corbusier accepted the Garden City's fundamental image, and worked to make it practical for high densities. He described his creation as the Garden City made attainable.

In another sense, too, in its relatively easy public reception, Le Corbusier's Radiant City depended upon the Garden City. The Garden City planners and their ever-increasing following among housing reformers, students and architects were tirelessly popularizing the idea of the superblock, the project neighborhood, the unchangeable plan, and grass, grass, grass. Le Corbusier really did not have to justify his vision in either humane or functional terms. The Decentrists' cries of institutionalization, mechanization, depersonalization seemed to others foolishly sectarian.

24   Le Corbusier's dream city has had an immense effect on our own cities. It was hailed deliriously by architects, and has gradually been embodied in scores of projects, ranging from low-income public housing to office building projects. Aside from making at least the superficial Garden City principle superficially practicable in dense cities, Le Corbusier attempted to make the automobile an integral part of his scheme, and this was, in the 1920's and early 1930's, a new and exciting idea. He included great arterial roads for express one-way traffic. He cut the number of streets because ''cross-roads are an enemy to traffic.'' He proposed underground streets for heavy vehicles and deliveries, and of course, like the Garden City planners, he kept the pedestrians off the streets and in the parks. It was like a wonderful mechanical toy. Furthermore, his conception, as an architectural work, had a dazzling clarity, simplicity and harmony. It was orderly, visible, easy to understand. It said everything in a flash, like a good advertisement. This vision and its bold symbolism have been all but irresistible to planners, housers, designers, and to developers, lenders and mayors too. It exerts a great pull on ''progressive'' zoners, who write rules calculated to encourage non-project builders to reflect, if only a little, the dream.

25   Although the Decentrists, with their devotion to the ideal of a cozy town life, have never made peace with the Le Corbusier vision, most of their disciples have. Virtually all sophisticated city designers today combine the two conceptions in various permutations. The rebuilding technique variously known as ''selective removal'' or ''spot removal'' or ''renewal planning'' or ''planned conservation''—meaning that total clearance of an area is avoided—is largely the trick of seeing how many old buildings can be left standing and the area still converted into a passable version of Radiant Garden City. Zoners, highway planners, legislators, land-use planners, and park and playground planners—none of whom live in an ideological vacuum—constantly use, as fixed points of reference, these two powerful visions and the more sophisticated merged vision. They may wander from the visions, they may compromise, they may vulgarize, but these are the points of departure.

26   Let us look briefly at one other, less important, line of ancestry in orthodox planning. This one begins, more or less, with the great Columbian Exposition in Chicago in 1893, just about the same time that Howard was formulating his Garden City ideas. The Chicago fair snubbed the exciting modern architecture which had begun to emerge

in Chicago and instead dramatized a retrogressive imitation-Renaissance style. One heavy, grandiose monument after another was arrayed in the exposition park, like frosted pastries on a tray, in a sort of squat, decorated forecast of Le Corbusier's later repetitive ranks of towers in a park. This ensemble of the rich and monumental captured the imagination of both planners and public. It gave impetus to a movement called the City Beautiful, and indeed the planning of the exposition was dominated by the man who became the leading City Beautiful planner, Daniel Burnham of Chicago.

The aim of the City Beautiful was the City Monumental. Great   27
schemes were drawn up for systems of baroque boulevards, which mainly came to nothing. What did come out of the movement was the Center Monumental, modeled on the fair. City after city built its Civic Center or its Cultural Center. These buildings were arranged along a boulevard (as at Benjamin Franklin Parkway in Philadelphia), or along a mall (as is the Government Center in Cleveland), or were bordered by park (as is the Civic Center at St. Louis), or were interspersed with park (as is the Civic Center at San Francisco). However they were arranged, the important point was that the monuments had been sorted out from the rest of the city, and assembled into the grandest effect thought possible, a complete unit, separate and well defined.

People were proud of them, but the Centers were not a success. In-   28
variably the ordinary city around them ran down instead of being uplifted, and they always acquired an incongruous rim of tattoo parlors and second-hand clothing stores, or else just nondescript, dispirited decay. The people stayed away from them remarkably. Somehow, when the fair became part of the city, it did not work like the fair.

The architecture of the City Beautiful centers went out of style. But   29
the idea behind the centers was not questioned, and it has never had more force than it does today. The idea of sorting out certain cultural or public functions and decontaminating their relationship with the workaday city dovetailed nicely with the Garden City teachings. The conceptions have harmoniously merged, much as the Garden City and the Radiant City merged, into a sort of Radiant Garden City Beautiful. Witness the immense Lincoln Square project for New York, in which a Monumental City Beautiful cultural center is one among a series of adjoining Radiant City and Radiant Garden City housing, shopping and campus centers.

And by analogy, the principles of sorting out—and of bringing order   30
by repression of all plans but the planners'—have been easily extended to all manner of city functions, until today a land-use master plan for a big city is largely a matter of the proposed placement of many series of decontaminated sortings.

31   From beginning to end, from Howard and Burnham to the latest amendment to Urban Renewal law, the entire concoction is, of course, quite irrelevant to the workings of genuine cities.

32   When we deal with cities we are dealing with life at a complex and intense level. Because this is so, there is a basic esthetic limitation on what can be done: *A city cannot be a work of art.*

33   Art has its own peculiar forms of order, and they are rigorous. Artists, whatever their medium, *make selections* from the abounding materials of life, and organize these selections into works that are under the control of the artist. The rather miraculous result of this work—if the selectivity, the organization and the control are consistent within themselves—can be art. But the essence of such work is disciplined, highly discriminatory selectivity *from* life. In relation to the inclusiveness and the literally endless intricacy of life, art is arbitrary, symbolic and abstracted. That is its value and the source of its own kind of order and coherence.

34   To approach a city, or even a city neighborhood, as if it were a larger architectural problem, capable of being given order by converting it into a disciplined work of art, is to make the mistake of attempting to substitute art for life. The results of such profound confusion between art and life are neither life nor art. They are taxidermy.

35   Nineteenth-century Utopians, with their revulsion at urbanized and industrialized society, and with their inheritance of eighteenth-century romanticist ideas about the nobility and simplicity of "natural" or primitive man, were much attracted to the idea of simple environments that were works of art by a harmonious consensus. To get back to this condition has been one of the hopes incorporated in our tradition of Utopian reform.

36   This futile (and deeply reactionary) hope tinctured the Utopianism of the Garden City planning movement too, and, at least ideologically, somewhat gentled its more dominant theme of harmony and order imposed and frozen by authoritarian planning.

37   The hope for an eventual, simple environment formed of art-by-consensus—or rather, a ghostly vestige of that hope—has continued to flit through Garden City planning theory when it has kept itself pure from Radiant City and City Beautiful planning. Thus, as late as the 1930's, Lewis Mumford in *The Culture of Cities* gave an importance (which would be puzzling indeed in the absence of this tradition) to pursuits like basket-weaving, pottery-making and blacksmithing in the planned communities he envisioned for us. As late as the 1950's, Clarence Stein, the leading American Garden City planner, on the occasion of receiving the American Institute of Architects' gold medal for

his contributions to architectural progress, was casting about for some object which might suitably be created by harmonious consensus in the ideal communities he envisioned. He suggested that citizens could be allowed to build a nursery school with their own hands. Aside from the conceded nursery school, the complete physical environment of a community and all the arrangements that compose it must be in the total, absolute and unchallenged control of the project's architects.

This is, of course, no different from the Radiant City and City Beautiful assumptions.   38

Like the housers who face a blank if they try to think what to build besides income-sorting projects, or the highwaymen who face a blank if they try to think what to do besides accommodate more cars, just so, architects who venture into city design often face a blank in trying to create order in cities except by substituting the order of art for the very different order of life.   39

We are constantly being told simple-minded lies about cities, being assured that duplication represents order. It is the easiest thing in the world to seize hold of a few forms, give them a regimented regularity, and try to palm them off in the name of order. Yet regimented regularity and significant systems of functional order are seldom coincident in this world.   40

To see complex systems of functional order as order, and not as chaos, takes understanding. The leaves dropping from the trees in the autumn, the interior of an airplane engine, the entrails of a dissected rabbit, all appear to be chaos if they are seen without comprehension. Once they are understood as systems of order, they actually *look* different.   41

When city designers and planners try to find a design device that will express, in a clear and easy way, the "skeleton" of city structure (expressways and promenades are current favorites), they are on the wrong track. A city is not put together like a mammal or a steel frame building, or even like a honeycomb or a coral. *A city's very structure consists of mixture of uses, and we get closest to its structural secrets when we deal with the conditions that generate diversity.*   42

If the slippery shorthand of analogy can help, perhaps the best analogy is this: imagine a large field in darkness. In the field, many fires are burning. They are of many sizes, some great, others small; some far apart, others dotted close together; some are brightening, some are slowly going out. Each fire, large or small, extends its radiance into the surrounding murk, and thereby carves out a space. But the space and the shape of that space exist only to the extent that the light from the fire creates it.   43

44   The murk has no shape or pattern except where it is carved into space by the light. Where the murk between the lights becomes deep and undefinable and shapeless, the only way to give it form or structure is to kindle new fires in the murk or sufficiently enlarge the nearest existing fires.

45   Only intricacy and use give to the parts of a city appropriate structure and shape. Wherever the fires of use and vitality fail to extend in a city is a place in the murk, a place essentially without city form and structure. Without that vital light, no seeking for "skeletons" or "frameworks" or "cells" can bring a city into form.

46   These metaphoric space-defining fires are formed—to get back to tangible realities—by areas where *diverse* city uses and users give each other close and lively support. This is the essential order which city design can assist. These areas of vitality need to have their remarkable functional order clarified. As cities have more such areas, and less gray area or murk, the need and the opportunities for clarification of this order will increase.

47   Whatever is done to clarify this order, this intricate life, has to be done mainly by tactics of emphasis and suggestion. Instead of attempting to substitute art for life, city designers should return to a strategy ennobling both to art and to life: a strategy of illuminating and clarifying life and helping to explain to us its meanings and order—in this case, helping to illuminate, clarify and explain the spontaneous order of cities.

48   All the various tactics for capturing city order are concerned with bits and pieces—bits and pieces which are, to be sure, knit into a city fabric of use that is as continuous and little cut apart as possible. Emphasis on bits and pieces is of the essence: this is what a city is, bits and pieces that supplement each other and support each other.

49   Perhaps this all seems very commonplace compared with the sweep and swoop of highways, or the eerily beautiful beehive huts of tribal kraals. But what we have to express in expressing our cities is not to be scorned. Their intricate order—a manifestation of the freedom of countless numbers of people to make and carry out countless plans—is in many ways a great wonder; we ought not to be reluctant to make this living collection of interdependent uses, this freedom, this life, more understandable for what it is, nor so unaware that we do not know what it is.

Questions and Activities

► *COMPREHENSION QUESTIONS*

1. Analyze the vocabulary of the first sentence of paragraph 5. How is Jacobs using the word "wonders"? What does she mean by the phrase "marked with the planners' hex"? Why does she choose the word "uproot" over a more objective one, such as "relocate"? How does her comparison "much as if they were the subjects of a conquering power" fit into this sentence and help develop her general intention?

2. Explain the essential differences between Le Corbusier's and Mumford's philosophies of city planning. Why were these theories particularly inappropriate ones to try to combine into one approach to city planning? What, according to Jacobs, were the results of this combination?

3. Define "Radiant City," "Garden City," "Decentrists," and "City Beautiful."

4. What does Jacobs mean by the phrase "the workings of genuine cities" in paragraph 31? How are these workings harmed by "the City Beautiful"?

5. Explain how the phrase "Radiant Garden City Beautiful" (paragraph 29) serves to summarize all the developments in city planning that have influenced modern cities. Who were the sources of each of the parts of this phrase? Why does Jacobs believe that the combined effect of all these developments was negative?

► *QUESTIONS OF RHETORICAL PURPOSE AND STRATEGY*

6. What do you think Jacobs wants her readers to do after reading this essay? Is she advocating a change in attitude or a change in behavior? What, for example, do you think the author wants her readers to think about skyscrapers, about large civic centers, or about carefully manicured but peopleless public gardens? Does she hope they will go to city-planning meetings to register their concerns? Do you think this essay is written for a specialized (architects, city planners) or a general audience?

7. This essay provides a great deal of new information for general readers. Yet the overall purpose of the essay is persuasive. Considering your answers to questions 1 and 4 above, what do you think makes this essay predominantly persuasive? Might the author's style, choice of words, sentence structure, and particular techniques such as use of metaphor have a good deal to do with the essay's persuasiveness?

8. What is the purpose underlying the first seven paragraphs of this essay? What type of perspective on the subject of modern city planning does it give the reader?

▶ *THEME QUESTIONS*

9. Does this essay suggest an answer to this section's theme question? If you feel it does, where in the essay do you find this answer suggested? Is urban architecture or city planning an art form in the same way that greeting cards or television soap operas are? How does the design of a building or a park express and shape the life styles and values of the people who live in it or use it?
10. In paragraph 6, Jacobs reminds us that urban planning does affect people, whether we want it to or not. She points out that urban renewal often abruptly uproots people who are living in the affected areas. Can you think of examples of people who have been directly affected by civic rehabilitation? How did these people feel about their situation? Did they think of themselves as victims?

▶ *LEARNING ACTIVITIES*

11. Write in your class notebook or journal (see the appendix "Keeping a Journal") a description of a building, small park, mall, or area in a nearby neighborhood. Can you find evidence of either the "City Beautiful" or the "Decentrist" school of planning? What effects do these elements have on the people's activities in the area that you are analyzing? Are the people there alienated from their environment? Are they isolated from each other by this environment? Do they seem to be conscious of their environment? Do they seem content with their environment? Keep your description as objective as you can. Imagine yourself contributing this description to an organization that is responding to citizens' concerns about the urban environment.
12. Look back over your objective description of a local building or place. Rewrite it with the aim of persuading someone that people are either happy or unhappy in that environment.
13. Describe, in your own words, Le Corbusier's "Radiant City." Then explain how a city you know well might be changed to fit the image of the "Radiant City."
14. Apply Jacobs's idea that cities are made up of "bits and pieces that supplement each other and support each other" (paragraph 48) to a city you know well. Describe some of the bits and pieces of the city you choose and show how they supplement and support each other.

Edward Kennedy and the Romance of Death

LEWIS H. LAPHAM

Born in 1935, Lewis H. Lapham graduated from Yale in 1956. He has spent his career in newspaper and magazine journalism. He was a reporter for the *San Francisco Examiner* and the *New York Herald Tribune;* he was a regular writer for the *Saturday Evening Post* and *Life* from 1963 to 1970. He has worked in the editorial offices of *Harper's* magazine since 1971, and has been the editor since 1975. Lapham often contributes timely essays to *Harper's* on social and political issues. The essay included here, published in 1979, is a good example of his freewheeling, imaginative social commentary.

This essay assumes an audience that possesses a great deal of background information. First, it assumes its reader takes for granted the image-consciousness of American politics. Edward Kennedy, from a family of politicians, is the product, Lapham argues, of a legendary kind of political image making. His brother, John, a popular and charismatic president—who became almost mythical after he was assassinated—casts a shadow of vulnerability over everything Senator Kennedy does. The long history of Boston and Massachusetts politics, which even people from other regions know something about, also colors Kennedy's public image. His identification with Democratic liberal issues, his support of labor unions, social welfare programs, and modified socialized medical care has made him a hero to some, a villain to others.

Edward Kennedy's personal life has gradually become more a part of his public legend than the private lives of either of his brothers were. The death of Mary Jo Kopechne at Chappaquiddick under extremely suspicious and unexplained circumstances and his domestic problems, such as his ex-wife Joan's alcoholism, have cast an aura of doubt over all that Kennedy does in private and public life. Is he the jet-setting, high liver who has little regard for the less powerful, or is he a sincere and serious man who occasionally lapses into careless good times?

Lapham assumes that his readers know the general Kennedy lore, although he does not necessarily assume a detailed knowledge of Edward Kennedy's political career. Readers of this essay must be ready to connect this Kennedy lore with contemporary political life in America. Television and magazines are probably as instrumental in creating our images of politicians as are their stands on issues or their voting records. We often assemble our image of a politician from bits and pieces of media-produced information. In this essay, Lapham argues that much of what we make of a politician derives from our need for heroes who might, at a stroke, solve problems that we subconsciously know cannot be solved that easily. It is this piecing together of fact into myth that Lapham finds so frightening. This essay, then, is not solely about Edward Kennedy; it is about our propensity to manufacture mythical figures who embody our fears and hopes rather than accepting realistic assessments of public figures.

Here, again, we have an example of a popular art—the making of a politician—in which we see ourselves reflected in the product of the art. We make ourselves over, we tell ourselves who we are by projecting our own needs into the political context. When we analyze political figures and myths, we learn—as Lapham shows us—more about ourselves than about politics.

1. Do you find yourself identifying with media-created myths about public figures?
2. Do you think it is morally right to vote for a political candidate on the basis of his or her popular myth?
3. Can you describe the mythical characteristics of some other famous politician?

▶ ————————————————

The Making of a Minotaur

Woe to thee, O land, when thy king is a child.
—Ecclesiastes 10:16

1   By choosing to campaign for the Presidency next year, Sen. Edward Kennedy permits his fellow citizens to enjoy the guilty pleasure of guessing at his chance of being murdered. Prolonged over a period of months, the intoxicating horror of this calculation will impart to the election the excitement of a gladiatorial show in the Roman arena. No matter what issues the candidates discuss, whether they choose to talk about arms-limitation agreements or the care of the nation's children, the public mind will remain fixed on the promise of blood-stained spectacle. Every airport, every shopping center and hotel lobby, every banquet hall through which Senator Kennedy passes on his perilous journey will be suffused in the flat and lurid light of a prospective killing ground.

2   As recently as twenty years ago the American electorate was content with balloons and platitudes and silly hats. But the times have gone

from bad to worse, and these innocent amusements no longer satisfy a people that feels itself baffled and betrayed. To the extent that the electorate deteriorates into a frightened mob, it grows restive and savage, demanding entertainments as deadly as its fears. The publishing and television syndicates distract the public mind with pornography and sadomasochistic violence, and the managers of the national political circus, distributing their handbills to coincide with the advent of the Christmas season, announce the entrance into the amphitheater of a man recognized by the crowd as both victim and devourer of victims. The desire that such a man should campaign for the Presidency bears witness to the debasement of the republican idea of government. Senator Kennedy so obviously stands within the penumbra of death, a smiling and Dionysian figure playing out the last act of a fearful tragedy, that it is fair to ask why anyone would follow him across a street, much less elect him to an office charged with the duty of protecting the life of a nation. Is it the man or the name, and, if a name, then a name for what?

In the iconography of his person, Senator Kennedy embodies the   3
whole of his family's history and character—its courage and licentiousness as well as the ruthlessness of its ambition, its corruption, laughter, greed, wealth, privilege, and cruelty. His place in the public imagination he owes to the death of three brothers, two of them assassinated. He can talk about the post office or the color of the rain, but even the whisper of his voice brings to mind not only the despairing alcoholism of his wife and the drowning of Mary Jo Kopechne, but also the suicide of Marilyn Monroe, the drug addiction of the nephew for whom he stands as surrogate father, his own father's thievery, and the rumors of sexual orgy that run like a soft counterpoint through the ballad of the Kennedys. The iconography has little or nothing to do with Senator Kennedy's own character or attainments. The armorers of the media force it over his head like a terrible helmet, both monstrous and beautiful. Senator Kennedy can do nothing to dislodge it. He inherits the reputation, the legend, and the iron mask of power.

Figures of Inferior Clay

Among the other candidates who so far have made themselves   4
available to next year's election, only President Carter and Gov. John Connally provide comparable opportunities for the dream of omnipotence. Mr. Carter presents himself as the agent of a spiritual supremacy. Having been elected on a promise to redeem the country rather than to govern it, and having so manifestly failed in this mission to the hea-

then, Mr. Carter now wanders through the countryside in search of a convenient Golgotha. He struggles up and down the hills of Maryland, wearing his jogger's sweatband as if it were a crown of thorns, perhaps thinking that by the sacrifice of his own sublime and twice-born self he yet might rescue the nation from all the evils that have befallen it. Unfortunately for Mr. Carter, this approach to the business of redemption inspires as little enthusiasm among the electorate as did Christ's disappointing news that he had come riding into Jerusalem on the foal of an ass not with an army but with a host of words. Governor Connally at least appreciates the uses of war and shows a proper regard for the money changers in the temple. His wealth and cynicism provide a scaffolding for a public fantasy almost as grotesque as the one that supports the effigy of Senator Kennedy.

5   To the citizen consumed by envy (that most democratic of emotions), Governor Connally offers the inspirational example of an adventurer grown rich in the service of the law. The envious citizen can say to himself that if only he possessed Governor Connally's contempt for scruple, then he, too, could enjoy the freedoms granted by the Constitution. Governor Connally inherits his place in the public imagination through the line of criminal descent that begins with the fur traders of the early nineteenth century and then, by degrees of subtlety and refinement, extends itself forward in time through the robber barons, the Harding Administration, the Teapot Dome scandal, Al Capone and the Chicago syndicate, Spiro Agnew, Richard Nixon, and George Steinbrenner. Although as equally uninterested as Senator Kennedy in the idea of republican government, Governor Connally cannot excite a crowd to the same fever of devotion. Perhaps this is because his crimes, whether real or imagined, tend toward a financial rather than a sexual expression. He lacks the Dionysian element, and this makes him less of a wanton child and more of an adult, ruthless enough and mean, but still too much associated with the tedious commercial realities of contracts, monetary rates, and bribes. Governor Connally has something about him of the romance of death, but for the most impersonal of reasons—because murder might be necessary to protect the money, not because of the pleasure of killing. By appealing to the basest motives of the American people, he grounds his campaign on the secure platform of fear and greed.

6   At this point in the campaign, none of the other candidates seems to be made of the kind of clay out of which it is possible to model figures hideous enough to divert the attention not only of the mob but also of the official and intellectual classes, who confuse the lost American Eden with the spaciousness of empire. The other candidates are too easily recognizable as mere men, and so they fail to satisfy the urgent de-

sire to establish gods and heroes in place of magistrates. In his essay on repentance, Montaigne remarks on the folly of assigning too much value to the illusions of omnipotence, and I think the passage worth quoting at some length:

> To storm a breach, conduct an embassy, govern a people, those are brilliant actions. To scold, laugh, sell, pay, love, hate, and deal gently and justly with one's family and oneself, not to relax or contradict oneself: that is something rarer, more difficult and less noticed by the world. . . . Private persons, says Aristotle, do virtue a higher and more difficult service than men in authority. We prepare to meet outstanding occasions rather for glory than for conscience' sake. The shortest way to gain a great name, however, would be to do for conscience' sake what we now do for glory. Alexander's virtue seems to me to show somewhat less strength on his great stage than that of Socrates in his humble and obscure activities. I can easily imagine Socrates in Alexander's place, but Alexander in that of Socrates, I cannot. If Alexander were asked what he could do, he would reply, "Conquer the world"; but if the same question were put to Socrates, his answer would be, "Lead a man's life according to its natural conditions," a much more general, more important, and more legitimate undertaking.
>
>   . . . As those who judge and test our inner being attach no great importance to the brilliance of our public acts, and see that these are no more than jets and beads of clear water spurting from an otherwise thick and muddy bottom; so, under similar circumstances, those who judge us by our brave outward show come to a like conclusion about our inner character. They cannot reconcile common faculties, just like their own, with these other faculties, which astound them and are so far beyond their vision.
>
>   Therefore we endow demons with monstrous shapes. And who does not picture Tamerlane with arched brows, open nostrils, a grim visage, and a prodigious stature, in accordance with the picture that the imagination has conceived of him from the report of his fame? . . . From such high thrones, it seems to us, men do not descend so low as to live.

A republican government assumes that it can get along without the   7
services of Alexander or Tamerlane. It assumes further that things change and men fail not because they are evil but because they are men. The attitude of mind requires the courage to admit that the future will not resemble the past and that the principle of uncertainty, as variously defined by Darwin, Freud, Jefferson, Einstein, and Heisenberg, is implicit in the nature of things. Under a republican form of government, men supposedly accept the responsibility of managing their own affairs, but over the past twenty years the heirs to the American fortune have lost interest in governing themselves. The country still flatters itself with the affectation that it enjoys the government of a sovereign people, but for at least a generation the conduct of its business has been left in the hands of the servants, both public and domestic.

The Servant Problem

8   In the private sectors of society, the well-to-do gentry rely upon a retinue of quack doctors, tennis professionals, hairdressers, astrologers, gossip mongers, and metaphysicians wearing the liveries of the American Enterprise Institute or the Ford Foundation. The American democracy as a whole maintains an equally lavish establishment in Washington, employing a staff of functionaries, orators, regulatory officials, aides-de-camp, and assistant chamberlains who perform the chores and ceremonies of government.

9   Rather than vote or read the Constitution (a document as tiresome as the trust agreements the family lawyers occasionally ask them to sign), the heirs prefer to go to Acapulco or Aspen to practice macrobiotic breathing and play sexual charades. They have better things to do with their lives than to bother with the details of preserving their freedom, and so they spend their time making themselves beautiful, holding themselves in perpetual readiness for the incarnations promised by the dealers in cosmetics and religion.

10   The servants meanwhile go about the increasingly expensive task of maintaining the illusions of grace and favor. The family lawyers sell off the assets of the estate (land, houses, corporations, jewelry, and technical information), and the resident intellectuals explain that among the best people the idea of scarcity has become fashionable, that it is a proof of good breeding and refined sensibility to own a windmill or a wood-burning stove. Politicians and Cabinet ministers appear in the role of the butler who finds phrases of art with which to conceal the embarrassments of the young master's profligacy and reduced circumstances. If the young master no longer belongs to the hunt club, that is not because the young master cannot pay his bills but because the hunt club has been admitting the wrong sorts of people; if the chauffeur has to be let go, that is not because the young master cannot afford to buy gas for his Duesenberg but because the chauffeur took to drink and Marxism.

11   By abdicating their authority and responsibility, the sovereign people also relinquish their courage. Like rich old women in Palm Beach, or a committee of dithering bankers, they become easily frightened by rumors of cancer in the rain or Russian ogres in the woods beyond the tennis courts. Their servants take advantage of the fear and trembling in the drawing room, and so they bring further proofs of all the dreadful things that can happen to a child who loses sight of his nurse. Pretty soon the heirs to fortune come to imagine themselves threatened by enemies of infinite number and variety; their fearfulness persuades them of the need for more regulation, more bureaucracy, more weapons, more places in the federal household for the cook's impoverished

cousins—anything and everything the butler wants if only he will consent not to abandon them. Every now and then the heirs make self-pitying remarks about their own weakness, but they have become too frightened, and, at the same time, too comfortable, to do anything to regain their independence of mind. In the library after dinner they might confide to one another their doubts about this fellow Kissinger or about David Rockefeller's manservant, Brzezinski, but then, as the family lawyer inevitably points out, who else does anybody know who can speak Russian or remember who was present at the Treaty of Versailles?

Given the disinclination of the sovereign people to think for themselves (thought, like celebrity, being the province of the servants), they seek to elect constitutional deities whom they can endow with godlike powers and dominions. Senator Kennedy seems to promise the restoration of an aristocratic Presidency, something along the lines of a freebooting monarchy in which the king's cousins and familiars can take part in the looting of the Spanish Coast. Governor Connally bears comparison to one of the magnificent condottieri of the Italian Renaissance, willing to save the sum of things for a percentage. The ruling prince pays him well enough to afford the luxury of despising him.

Within the political and intellectual classes the fear of death apparently has become very great. As the decade of the 1970s expires amidst a chorus of recrimination, the prolonged anxiety of the past ten years gives way to a feeling of pervasive dread. By now even the most well-informed sources understand that nobody knows how to figure all the factors into the equations of life and death. They console one another with exquisite discussions of their paralysis and failure to act, working the computations of despair through an infinite series. The American inflation rate of 14 percent possibly has something to do with the human flesh in Emperor Bokassa's icebox, but who can formulate the arithmetic or metaphysical principle of equivalence? What has disease in Ethiopia got to do with rebellion in Costa Rica, or Somoza's exiled parrots with Soviet naval vessels in the Indian Ocean?

The biologists say that one gram of bacteria judiciously placed within the ecosystem of the upper atmosphere could exterminate the human race; in New York City the water mains have been so corroded that only the rush of water through the pipes prevents them from falling apart. During the past eighteen months wars have been fought in Uganda, northwest Africa, Angola, Rhodesia, the Congo, Vietnam, Cambodia, Nicaragua, South Yemen, Iran, Libya, Ireland, China, and Iraq. Around the council tables at Geneva and the United Nations the ushers provide chairs for an increasingly sullen crowd of new and hostile states. Armed with nuclear weapons, the nations of the earth stalk one another across the Strait of Hormuz and through the maze of the London gold market. The workers on the currency exchanges begin to speculate whether the years between 1945 and 1980 might not come to be known as the Thirty-Five Years' Peace.

15   No wonder people cry out for gods to kill and die for them. If bestial apparitions slouch toward Jerusalem to be born, then men feel the need for monsters of their own. "Our old God," said William II on the eve of World War I, speaking affectionately of the deity as if it were a shambling dog.

16   If the history of the past twenty years has proved to the American Republic the inadequacies of its public servants, so also it has demonstrated the failures of its institutions. Even though the institutions have been made so huge and so complex as to seem the work of divinity, they cannot perform the tasks imposed on them. Consider the requests made of the American Presidency. If the office consisted of a board of directors, and if the board counted among its members Lincoln, Sophocles, and Newton, still it could not move the Persian Gulf to Florida or transform black people into white.

17   Although a boon to the writers of newspaper editorials, the recognition of inadequacy provides little in the way of comfort, at least as long as the recognition doesn't carry with it the acknowledgment of both the strength and the weakness of the merely human. For the time being, the American Republic appears unwilling to make such a concession, or in Montaigne's phrase to "descend so low as to live." Americans don't like to be reminded of the humanity they share with the less fortunate people of the world, particularly if their humiliation gains them nothing in the international currency markets and if it doesn't make less real the consequences of their mortality.

18   If a bureaucrat makes a mistake with his strategic doctrine, then it is conceivable that the population of Brentwood or Georgetown might burn to death. This state of affairs is intolerable and un-American. The denial of it results in the birth of an unnatural child, who, like the minotaur, represents the attempt to domesticate the destructive and antisocial instincts that make of every individual an enemy of civilization. Perhaps this explains why none of the candidates stands on the side of life, why nobody speaks for the love between men and women, for the republican virtues of modesty, optimism, patience, and self-restraint.

19   People who become too fearful of death seek to rid themselves of their fear by embracing death. Given the intensity of his family's will to death, Senator Kennedy cannot help drawing to himself those elements of rage and fear, in the collective mind as well as among individuals, that constitute the impulse toward self-annihilation. His birth as a can-

didate is as unnatural as that of the minotaur. He unites in his own person a number of opposed principles that, in conjunction, all but guarantee the destruction of a man or a republic. By seeming to represent the worst as well as the best that can be found in a man, the chronicle of his suffering somehow excusing his wealth and his sensuality, he allows people to hope, against all the laws of probability, for the best. If Senator Kennedy makes it plausible to believe that anything is possible, he gives the further impression that whatever is possible also can be done at once.

Behind the Mask

During presidential campaigns everybody makes a great show   20
of talking about the so-called issues; no matter how they get defined (usually by accident, in an offhand remark at an airport in Wichita or Duluth), these tortured questions of policy serve as the flickering lamps and fairy lights by which the country looks at itself in the mirror. Every four years the country stares into the depths of the glass, hoping to find a face that it can recognize as its own. The hideous beauty of the mask forced over Senator Kennedy's head makes him scarcely identifiable as human. The minotaur conjoins the monstrousness of the modern world with the loss of confidence in democracy.

I don't know how it is possible to make any judgment of the man, and   21
yet, if Senator Kennedy runs for the Presidency, the campaign will make of his character the only issue of substance. What else can anyone talk about? So much has been written and said of him, and so many of the reports so contradictory, that he remains invisible. The gossip about him varies according to the preoccupations of New York and Washington. The New York sources prefer to speak of Mr. Kennedy as a dull-witted rich kid, well-meaning and fond of women, forced against his will into the campaign by the Democratic political machine and by the ambition of political mercenaries, among them the worthy gentlemen who helped him frame the television statement excusing the incident at Chappaquiddick. The Washington sources portray Senator Kennedy as a man of keen intelligence, industrious and concerned, a paragon among Senators, who attends committee meetings, memorizes briefing papers, feels compassion for the constituency of the poor. I assume that all these reports contain elements of truth. Over the past twenty years I have seen Mr. Kennedy on no more than a score of occasions; sometimes he was drunk and sometimes sober, but he always gave the impression of a man who had lived his life for everybody except himself. I don't know how it is possible not to feel sympathy for the

man, and I'm sure that he possesses all the virtues that his admirers ascribe to him—courage, fortitude, sentimental good nature, and a bewildered decency of intent.

22   But I also don't know how it is possible to imagine a man more surely condemned to live within the isolation of the present. His past bears the marks of terrible suffering, and his future must be seen as demonic. If this is true, then Senator Kennedy deserves to be feared as well as pitied. The isolation of the present has a way of imparting to people an indifference to life that is as characteristic of victorious generals as it is of evangelists.

23   To the extent that Senator Kennedy remains invisible, he can be defined as a gravitational field, drawing to himself devotees who imagine that their own lives acquire meaning only insofar as they fall within the sphere of a magical object. The same kind of adulation attaches itself to rock stars and celebrated criminals. On the few occasions when I have come across Senator Kennedy in a private circumstance I have found him, as in his public persona, besieged by flatterers and hangers-on, by the Bacchantes who would devour him and yet, at the same time, who protect him as if he were the reflection of a god. In particular I remember a birthday party given for Senator Kennedy in the spring of 1963 by Stephen Smith, his brother-in-law and newly appointed campaign manager. Not knowing more than a few of the other guests in the room, most of them celebrities of large magnitude, I spent some time talking to a girl who had come to the party with the hope of making of herself a birthday present. As we watched Mr. Kennedy blunder back and forth across the dance floor in a game of bull-fighting (the band playing the *paso doble* and Mr. Smith holding the jacket of his tuxedo as if it were the *capa torera*), the girl fretted about her clothes and hair. She had dyed her hair blond for the occasion, but she had begun to think that this might have been a mistake. The Senator's wife was a blond, and maybe he was tired of blond; maybe he wanted something in a redhead or a brunette. No matter how often I reassured her, she refused to be consoled, worrying whether her dress was pretty enough, or the wrong color, or too obvious, or whether the Senator had any known preferences in fetishes. During the entire conversation she never took her eyes from Mr. Kennedy's person, and I remember thinking that the voracious emptiness in her face was as deadly and as terrifying a thing as I had ever seen. I understood what the Greeks had meant by the Gorgon turning people into stone.

24   This kind of adoration has an unhappy effect on the people subjected to it, and I can imagine that Senator Kennedy must be sick of being admired for reasons that have nothing to do with himself—because of his name, because people look to him for miracles, preferment, or relief

from boredom. Suetonius describes the Emperor Tiberius during the first years of his reign as a just and able administrator of the Roman state. But he soon became disgusted with the fawning of the court and with the business of governing a people who had so little respect for themselves that they could proclaim him a god. Corroded by self-loathing, he retired to Capri, where, during the last nine years of his life, he abandoned himself to the sexual atrocities for which he has been chiefly remembered.

But if the adulation of the mob has a dissolving effect on its victims, it has an equally dissolving effect on the people so eager to negate themselves in the fires of self-immolation. The expression on the face of the girl at Senator Kennedy's birthday party I have seen in the faces of the disciples of Hare Krishna as well as in the faces of the correspondents who followed the Kennedy campaigns of the 1960s and wrote the dispatches from Camelot. I noticed it most recently at the Council on Foreign Relations, among the leading citizens who had come to listen to Senator Kennedy's views on foreign policy. As is his custom, he said nothing of substance, choosing instead to propound a series of platitudes. But the distinguished ladies and gentlemen who composed the Senator's audience had come to be taken out of themselves, to be transformed in the presence of power, and so they listened to a banal speech as if it were a song sung by Mick Jagger.   25

The worship of man as god is the worship of god as beast. If the minotaur feeds within the labyrinth of the White House, then who but a fool or a moralist would think to argue with the beauty of death dancing? The pleasures of self-destruction are as dear to the American people as they have been to everybody else who ever had to relinquish his cherished bestiality to something so bloodless and abstract as an idea of civilization. Who else is the American hero if not the adventurer who proclaims himself the enemy of the society that reared him, shrugging off the restraints of law, art, science, and family as he wanders farther west into the wilderness of the Dakotas or the sea? His descendants crowd through the turnstiles of the nation's gambling casinos and orgiastic spas; resentful of the obligations necessary to the survival of a civilization, they constitute what Freud described as ''the hostile majority.'' Together with the Ayatollah Khomeini and the late Jim Jones of the Jonestown settlement, they prefer to believe that they command the world by magical wish, and they take as their motto Manes Sperber's summation of narcissism, ''Let them die who will not love me.'' Over against this majority the republican idea of government opposes the minority of citizens willing to defend the bridges between time past and time future. But what happens if the minority becomes   26

sick and dispirited, wondering if what little civilization it has acquired
is worth defending at all? As I watch Senator Kennedy's triumphal progress through the newspapers, I think of the mood of fatalism that over-
took the Wilhelmine Empire of Germany before the advent of World
War I. The other day I was reading John Rohl's introduction to the collected correspondence of two German diplomats of the period. Rohl observes that Bethmann Hollweg, the German chancellor, understood
that by encouraging Austria to go to war against Serbia he accepted the
condition that whatever the war's result, it would lead to the destruction of the existing order. Such a possibility did not appear to him to
have been entirely unwelcome, for he regarded the existing order as
lifeless and void of ideas. "Everything," he said to a friend, "has become so very old."

27   Over the past twenty years the mere willingness to campaign for the
office of the American Presidency has come to be understood as a self-
destructive act. John Kennedy was assassinated, Lyndon Johnson
villified and forced to retire from office, Richard Nixon disgraced,
Jimmy Carter reduced to an object of scorn and derision. The American
electorate apparently seeks to elect constitutional deities on whom it
confers absolute power for a brief period of time and then, discovering
itself betrayed, it tears the god to pieces. If the king must die, then only
a man as detached from life as Senator Kennedy, cast in the image of
every man but himself, could be persuaded to set forth on so perilous a
journey. Unfortunately Senator Kennedy does not go alone into the
arena. He takes with him as his hostages the idea of the republic as well
as the lives of his countrymen.

Questions and Activities

▶ COMPREHENSION QUESTIONS

1. Read the entire passage of Ecclesiastes 10:16, from which the opening quote is taken. Why does Lapham start his article with this
   quote? How does it tie in with his thesis on American politics and
   election campaigns?
2. What is a minotaur? Go to the reference desk of a library and look
   up this term in a reference book or dictionary of classical mythology. How does Lapham's mention of the minotaur help explain his
   thesis about contemporary American politicians?

3. Paragraph 3 is built around the word "iconography." What does this word mean? How might Senator Kennedy function as an icon? What does the Kennedy icon represent, according to Lapham?
4. Summarize Lapham's definition of republican government (paragraph 7). Why does Lapham believe that our current government is not republican?

▶ *QUESTIONS OF RHETORICAL PURPOSE AND STRATEGY*

5. What is the point behind Lapham's description of the female admirer of Senator Kennedy in paragraph 23? How does this description lead into the first sentence of paragraph 24?
6. Why does Lapham compare the members of the Council on Foreign Relations as they listen to Senator Kennedy to an audience of Mick Jagger's (paragraph 25)? How are these audiences similar to one another? What does Lapham achieve by focusing on this similarity?
7. Do you think the following sentence from paragraph 27 captures Lapham's thesis? "Over the past twenty years the mere willingness to campaign for the office of the American Presidency has come to be understood as a self-destructive act." Does this sentence leave one or more of Lapham's major points out? If yes, which ones?
8. Do you think that fifty or sixty years ago readers would have understood Lapham's point about the mythologizing of politicians? Remember that these readers would have been unfamiliar with the effects of television on people's images of politicians. Do you think these hypothetical readers would have constructed their images of politicians differently than we do today? Would they have spent more time reading rational analyses of character and objective positions on issues? Or would handshaking, campaigning from the platforms of railroad cars, and parades have filled the role of television in creating public images of politicians? Does Lapham assume more sophisticated readers than it would have been possible to assume fifty years ago? What factors might make today's educated readers more sophisticated than their predecessors about the influence of myth in politics?
9. What is the point of Lapham's allusions in paragraph 13 to current events, such as "Soviet naval vessels in the Indian Ocean"? Can you recall any of these events? Can you identify the point of the paragraph even without clear knowledge of the allusions?
10. This essay is more expressive and personal than it is persuasive or informative. It presents the complex thinking through of an issue by an experienced writer who has spent a good deal of time analyzing American politics. Its primary purpose is not the persuasion of

readers to a particular attitude or belief. Nor is its purpose simply to inform its readers of political facts or ideas. Rather, almost in the form of thinking aloud, Lapham expresses fears that many Americans have held at one time or another over the past twenty or thirty years, due to assassinations and attempted assassinations, an unpopular war, and Watergate. What benefit does a reader get from these very personal observations on American politics? Why did this essay appear in the editorial section of a magazine?

▶ *THEME QUESTIONS*

11. Before the past few decades, politics were not considered a popular art. Do you think this essay on politics belongs in this section of this book? What has happened over the past fifty or sixty years to make the development of a politician an art rather than a matter of traditional political strategy? Is it still possible to change the making of politicians from an image-conscious process to a more rational process?

12. Did the most recent election campaign between Ronald Reagan and Walter Mondale continue the pattern of the confusion of myth and fact that Lapham defines? What myths did Reagan and Mondale rely on in their campaigns? How were those myths used to win votes?

13. In retrospect, and in light of what Lapham says, do you think Edward Kennedy's decision not to run for the presidency in 1984 was a good one? How might the myths called up in a Kennedy campaign have been different from those called up by Reagan or Mondale?

14. If Lapham is right that political myth making is a popular art, what does this fact tell us about our values and beliefs?

▶ *LEARNING ACTIVITIES*

15. What you have read in this section asks you to consider the effects public arts have on your private beliefs and behavior. To further that consideration, write an essay on the popular mythology surrounding Ronald Reagan. Interview several people, asking them what they think of Reagan. How has his acting and movie background contributed to their image of his character? Has his private life on his California ranch influenced that image? Does his polished television and podium presence affect that image? Write up your interview as a rough draft in which you summarize and paraphrase the responses of the people you have interviewed.

16. Discuss the rough draft from the preceding activity with some other people in your class. After your discussions, develop a thesis that defines Reagan's image as it was defined by your interviewees. Then go back over your rough draft and underline the comments in the interviews that would help you write a paper in which you explain and support your thesis. Make notes explaining why you selected those comments.

How Should One Read a Book?

VIRGINIA WOOLF

Virginia Woolf (1882–1941) was a prolific and influential British writer and intellectual. She was born in London, the daughter of the Victorian critic and philosopher Leslie Stephen. Accustomed to learned discussion and serious intellectual endeavor from a very early age, Woolf educated herself primarily by reading from her father's extensive library. After her father's death, she lived with her sister and two brothers in Bloomsbury, a district of London that came to be identified with her, her family, and the group of writers and artists she entertained. She married journalist Leonard Woolf in 1912, and together they founded the Hogarth Press, which later published her novels and the works of other writers in the Bloomsbury Group.

Woolf's novels were experimental. She refined the narrative techniques of stream of consciousness and interior monologue and established them in modern fiction. She was interested in using fiction to capture the inner consciousness, the psychological reality of modern human life. Her novels include *Mrs. Dalloway* (1925), *To the Lighthouse* (1927), and *Orlando* (1928). Woolf's essays and reviews, which are collected in books such as *The Common Reader* (1925), also enjoy a wide audience. Another of her nonfiction books, *A Room of One's Own* (1929) has become very popular in recent years because it explores the subject of women and creativity.

The essay included here demonstrates Woolf's ongoing interest in how the individual experiences the world, as opposed to how society and the world shape the individual. She sees reading as a highly individualized process, with the reader's creative participation being a key element in any book's meaning. It is the reader, Woolf suggests, who constructs a personal meaning out of the facts and ideas on the page.

This essay has two general purposes. First (paragraphs 1–6), Woolf defines the reading process—how reading works, how it affects what we think and believe—and then she describes several different kinds of books. Woolf's second purpose (developed primarily in paragraphs 7–9) is to explain reading as it affects individual readers. The facts and details we find in biographies and histories can become the material from which we create our own ideas, values, and opinions. This emphasis on a second, creative aim of reading for information, Woolf goes on to explain, can lead us to the most difficult type of reading, poetry.

In paragraphs 10 through 13, Woolf gets to the real point of her essay, the point that is also most closely related to the theme of this section.

Here Woolf explains what our minds do with the material we read. Reading creates a reflective frame of mind. It helps people make sense of their experiences. It puts them in the habit, as Woolf suggests, of judging their experiences, of deciding what kinds of experience have most value, of constructing a set of values by which to judge the quality of life. Reading, then, becomes a way of taking in new experiences without sacrificing control or direction.

Think about these questions as you read the following essay:

1. How does Woolf's definition of reading as a creative process contribute to our understanding of the arts and their influences on us, individually or socially?

2. Other arts discussed in this section — movies, politics, urban architecture, and greeting cards — more actively and physically involve people in the artistic event itself. Their senses are engaged, but their minds may be disengaged. Consider the differences and similarities between how these arts explain and shape people and the detachment and judgment that Woolf suggests is formed by reading.

3. Are we a society of reflective and judgmental readers? Or are we a society of responsive but nonanalytical participants in the sensory aspects of the arts? Or is each of us a complex mixture of both the participatory and the judgmental?

4. How might reading books and articles analyzing a political figure's beliefs and actions become a means of offsetting the unreflective acceptance of mythical qualities that Lewis Lapham describes in his article in this section?

▶ ─────────────────────────────

In the first place, I want to emphasise the note of interrogation   *1*
at the end of my title. Even if I could answer the question for myself, the answer would apply only to me and not to you. The only advice, indeed, that one person can give another about reading is to take no advice, to follow your own instincts, to use your own reason, to come to your own conclusions. If this is agreed between us, then I feel at liberty to put forward a few ideas and suggestions because you will not allow them to fetter that independence which is the most important quality that a reader can possess. After all, what laws can be laid down about books? The battle of Waterloo was certainly fought on a certain day; but is *Hamlet* a better play than *Lear*? Nobody can say. Each must decide that question for himself. To admit authorities, however heavily furred and gowned, into our libraries and let them tell us how to read, what to read, what

value to place upon what we read, is to destroy the spirit of freedom which is the breath of those sanctuaries. Everywhere else we may be bound by laws and conventions—there we have none.

2   But to enjoy freedom, if the platitude is pardonable, we have of course to control ourselves. We must not squander our powers, helplessly and ignorantly, squirting half the house in order to water a single rose-bush; we must train them, exactly and powerfully, here on the very spot. This, it may be, is one of the first difficulties that faces us in a library. What is "the very spot"? There may well seem to be nothing but a conglomeration and huddle of confusion. Poems and novels, histories and memoirs, dictionaries and blue-books; books written in all languages by men and women of all tempers, races, and ages jostle each other on the shelf. And outside the donkey brays, the women gossip at the pump, the colts gallop across the fields. Where are we to begin? How are we to bring order into this multitudinous chaos and so get the deepest and widest pleasure from what we read?

3   It is simple enough to say that since books have classes—fiction, biography, poetry—we should separate them and take from each what it is right that each should give us. Yet few people ask from books what books can give us. Most commonly we come to books with blurred and divided minds, asking of fiction that it shall be true, of poetry that it shall be false, of biography that it shall be flattering, of history that it shall enforce our own prejudices. If we could banish all such preconceptions when we read, that would be an admirable beginning. Do not dictate to your author; try to become him. Be his fellow-worker and accomplice. If you hang back, and reserve and criticise at first, you are preventing yourself from getting the fullest possible value from what you read. But if you open your mind as widely as possible, then signs and hints of almost imperceptible fineness, from the twist and turn of the first sentences, will bring you into the presence of a human being unlike any other. Steep yourself in this, acquaint yourself with this, and soon you will find that your author is giving you, or attempting to give you, something far more definite. The thirty-two chapters of a novel—if we consider how to read a novel first—are an attempt to make something as formed and controlled as a building: but words are more impalpable than bricks; reading is a longer and more complicated process than seeing. Perhaps the quickest way to understand the elements of what a novelist is doing is not to read, but to write; to make your own experiment with the dangers and difficulties of words. Recall, then, some event that has left a distinct impression on you—how at the corner of the street, perhaps, you passed two people talking. A tree shook; an electric light danced; the tone of the talk was comic, but also tragic; a whole vision, an entire conception, seemed contained in that moment.

But when you attempt to reconstruct it in words, you will find that it   4
breaks into a thousand conflicting impressions. Some must be subdued;
others emphasised; in the process you will lose, probably, all grasp
upon the emotion itself. Then turn from your blurred and littered pages
to the opening pages of some great novelist—Defoe, Jane Austen,
Hardy. Now you will be better able to appreciate their mastery. It is not
merely that we are in the presence of a different person—Defoe, Jane
Austen, or Thomas Hardy—but that we are living in a different world.
Here, in *Robinson Crusoe*, we are trudging a plain high road; one thing
happens after another; the fact and the order of the fact is enough. But if
the open air and adventure mean everything to Defoe they mean nothing to Jane Austen. Hers is the drawing-room, and people talking, and
by the many mirrors of their talk revealing their characters. And if,
when we have accustomed ourselves to the drawing-room and its reflections, we turn to Hardy, we are once more spun round. The moors are
round us and the stars are above our heads. The other side of the mind is
now exposed—the dark side that comes uppermost in solitude, not the
light side that shows in company. Our relations are not towards people,
but towards Nature and destiny. Yet different as these worlds are, each
is consistent with itself. The maker of each is careful to observe the
laws of his own perspective, and however great a strain they may put
upon us they will never confuse us, as lesser writers so frequently do, by
introducing two different kinds of reality into the same book. Thus to
go from one great novelist to another—from Jane Austen to Hardy, from
Peacock to Trollope, from Scott to Meredith—is to be wrenched and
uprooted; to be thrown this way and then that. To read a novel is a difficult and complex art. You must be capable not only of great fineness of
perception, but of great boldness of imagination if you are going to
make use of all that the novelist—the great artist—gives you.

But a glance at the heterogeneous company on the shelf will show   5
you that writers are very seldom "great artists"; far more often a book
makes no claim to be a work of art at all. These biographies and
autobiographies, for example, lives of great men, of men long dead and
forgotten, that stand cheek by jowl with the novels and poems, are we
to refuse to read them because they are not "art"? Or shall we read
them, but read them in a different way, with a different aim? Shall we
read them in the first place to satisfy that curiosity which possesses us
sometimes when in the evening we linger in front of a house where the
lights are lit and the blinds not yet drawn, and each floor of the house
shows us a different section of human life in being? Then we are
consumed with curiosity about the lives of these people—the servants
gossiping, the gentlemen dining, the girl dressing for a party, the old
woman at the window with her knitting. Who are they, what are

they, what are their names, their occupations, their thoughts, and adventures?

6   Biographies and memoirs answer such questions, light up innumerable such houses; they show us people going about their daily affairs,
toiling, failing, succeeding, eating, hating, loving, until they die. And
sometimes as we watch, the house fades and the iron railings vanish
and we are out at sea; we are hunting, sailing, fighting; we are among
savages and soldiers; we are taking part in great campaigns. Or if we like
to stay here in England, in London, still the scene changes; the street
narrows; the house becomes small, cramped, diamond-paned, and
malodorous. We see a poet, Donne, driven from such a house because
the walls were so thin that when the children cried their voices cut
through them. We can follow him, through the paths that lie in the
pages of books, to Twickenham; to Lady Bedford's Park, a famous
meeting-ground for nobles and poets; and then turn our steps to Wilton,
the great house under the downs, and hear Sidney read the *Arcadia* to
his sister; and ramble among the very marshes and see the very herons
that figure in that famous romance; and then again travel north with
that other Lady Pembroke, Anne Clifford, to her wild moors, or plunge
into the city and control our merriment at the sight of Gabriel Harvey in
his black velvet suit arguing about poetry with Spenser. Nothing is
more fascinating than to grope and stumble in the alternate darkness
and splendour of Elizabethan London. But there is no staying there. The
Temples and the Swifts, the Harleys and the St. Johns beckon us on;
hour upon hour can be spent disentangling their quarrels and
deciphering their characters; and when we tire of them we can stroll on,
past a lady in black wearing diamonds, to Samuel Johnson and Gold-
smith and Garrick; or cross the channel, if we like, and meet Voltaire
and Diderot, Madame du Deffand; and so back to England and
Twickenham—how certain places repeat themselves and certain
names!—where Lady Bedford had her Park once and Pope lived later, to
Walpole's home at Strawberry Hill. But Walpole introduces us to such a
swarm of new acquaintances, there are so many houses to visit and
bells to ring that we may well hesitate for a moment, on the Miss
Berrys' doorstep, for example, when behold, up comes Thackeray; he is
the friend of the woman whom Walpole loved; so that merely by going
from friend to friend, from garden to garden, from house to house, we
have passed from one end of English literature to another and wake to
find ourselves here again in the present, if we can so differentiate this
moment from all that have gone before. This, then, is one of the ways in
which we can read these lives and letters; we can make them light up
the many windows of the past; we can watch the famous dead in their
familiar habits and fancy sometimes that we are very close and can sur-

prise their secrets, and sometimes we may pull out a play or a poem that they have written and see whether it reads differently in the presence of the author. But this again rouses other questions. How far, we must ask ourselves, is a book influenced by its writer's life—how far is it safe to let the man interpret the writer? How far shall we resist or give way to the sympathies and antipathies that the man himself rouses in us—so sensitive are words, so receptive of the character of the author? These are questions that press upon us when we read lives and letters, and we must answer them for ourselves, for nothing can be more fatal than to be guided by the preferences of others in a matter so personal.

But also we can read such books with another aim, not to throw light   7
on literature, not to become familiar with famous people, but to refresh and exercise our own creative powers. Is there not an open window on the right hand of the bookcase? How delightful to stop reading and look out! How stimulating the scene is, in its unconsciousness, its irrelevance, its perpetual movement—the colts galloping round the field, the woman filling her pail at the well, the donkey throwing back his head and emitting his long, acrid moan. The greater part of any library is nothing but the record of such fleeting moments in the lives of men, women, and donkeys. Every literature, as it grows old, has its rubbish-heap, its record of vanished moments and forgotten lives told in faltering and feeble accents that have perished. But if you give yourself up to the delight of rubbish-reading you will be surprised, indeed you will be overcome, by the relics of human life that have been cast out to moulder. It may be one letter—but what a vision it gives! It may be a few sentences—but what vistas they suggest! Sometimes a whole story will come together with such beautiful humour and pathos and completeness that it seems as if a great novelist had been at work, yet it is only an old actor, Tate Wilkinson, remembering the strange story of Captain Jones; it is only a young subaltern serving under Arthur Wellesley and falling in love with a pretty girl at Lisbon; it is only Maria Allen letting fall her sewing in the empty drawing-room and sighing how she wishes she had taken Dr. Burney's good advice and had never eloped with her Rishy. None of this has any value; it is negligible in the extreme; yet how absorbing it is now and again to go through the rubbish-heaps and find rings and scissors and broken noses buried in the huge past and try to piece them together while the colt gallops round the field, the woman fills her pail at the well, and the donkey brays.

But we tire of rubbish-reading in the long run. We tire of searching for   8
what is needed to complete the half-truth which is all that the Wilkinsons, the Bunburys, and the Maria Allens are able to offer us. They had not the artist's power of mastering and eliminating; they could not tell the whole truth even about their own lives; they have

disfigured the story that might have been so shapely. Facts are all that they can offer us, and facts are a very inferior form of fiction. Thus the desire grows upon us to have done with half-statements and approximations; to cease from searching out the minute shades of human character, to enjoy the greater abstractness, the purer truth of fiction. Thus we create the mood, intense and generalised, unaware of detail, but stressed by some regular, recurrent beat, whose natural expression is poetry; and that is the time to read poetry when we are almost able to write it.

> *Western wind, when wilt thou blow?*
> *The small rain down can rain.*
> *Christ, if my love were in my arms,*
> *And I in my bed again!*

9   The impact of poetry is so hard and direct that for the moment there is no other sensation except that of the poem itself. What profound depths we visit then—how sudden and complete is our immersion! There is nothing here to catch hold of; nothing to stay us in our flight. The illusion of fiction is gradual; its effects are prepared; but who when they read these four lines stops to ask who wrote them, or conjures up the thought of Donne's house or Sidney's secretary; or enmeshes them in the intricacy of the past and the succession of generations? The poet is always our contemporary. Our being for the moment is centred and constricted, as in any violent shock of personal emotion. Afterwards, it is true, the sensation begins to spread in wider rings through our minds; remoter senses are reached; these begin to sound and to comment and we are aware of echoes and reflections. The intensity of poetry covers an immense range of emotion. We have only to compare the force and directness of

> *I shall fall like a tree, and find my grave,*
>   *Only remembering that I grieve,*

with the wavering modulation of

> *Minutes are numbered by the fall of sands,*
> *As by an hour glass; the span of time*
> *Doth waste us to our graves, and we look on it;*
> *An age of pleasure, revelled out, comes home*
> *At last, and ends in sorrow; but the life,*
> *Weary of riot, numbers every sand,*
> *Wailing in sighs, until the last drop down,*
> *So to conclude calamity in rest,*

or place the meditative calm of

> *whether we be young or old,*
> *Our destiny, our being's heart and home,*
> *Is with infinitude, and only there;*
> *With hope it is, hope that can never die,*
> *Effort, and expectation, and desire,*
> *And something evermore about to be,*

beside the complete and inexhaustible loveliness of

> *The moving Moon went up the sky,*
> *And no where did abide:*
> *Softly she was going up,*
> *And a star or two beside—*

or the splendid fantasy of

> *And the woodland haunter*
> *Shall not cease to saunter*
> *When, far down some glade,*
> *Of the great world's burning,*
> *One soft flame upturning*
> *Seems, to his discerning,*
> *Crocus in the shade.*

to bethink us of the varied art of the poet; his power to make us at once actors and spectators; his power to run his hand into character as if it were a glove, and be Falstaff or Lear; his power to condense, to widen, to state, once and for ever.

"We have only to compare"—with those words the cat is out of the bag, and the true complexity of reading is admitted. The first process, to receive impressions with the utmost understanding, is only half the process of reading; it must be completed, if we are to get the whole pleasure from a book, by another. We must pass judgment upon these multitudinous impressions; we must make of these fleeting shapes one that is hard and lasting. But not directly. Wait for the dust of reading to settle; for the conflict and the questioning to die down; walk, talk, pull the dead petals from a rose, or fall asleep. Then suddenly without our willing it, for it is thus that Nature undertakes these transitions, the book will return, but differently. It will float to the top of the mind as a whole. And the book as a whole is different from the book received currently in separate phrases. Details now fit themselves into their places. We see the shape from start to finish; it is a barn, a pig-sty, or a cathedral. Now then we can compare book with book as we com-

10

pare building with building. But this act of comparison means that our attitude has changed; we are no longer the friends of the writer, but his judges; and just as we cannot be too sympathetic as friends, so as judges we cannot be too severe. Are they not criminals, books that have wasted our time and sympathy; are they not the most insidious enemies of society, corrupters, defilers, the writers of false books, faked books, books that fill the air with decay and disease? Let us then be severe in our judgments; let us compare each book with the greatest of its kind. There they hang in the mind the shapes of the books we have read solidified by the judgments we have passed on them—*Robinson Crusoe, Emma, The Return of the Native.* Compare the novels with these—even the latest and least of novels has a right to be judged with the best. And so with poetry—when the intoxication of rhythm has died down and the splendour of words has faded a visionary shape will return to us and this must be compared with *Lear,* with *Phèdre,* with *The Prelude;* or if not with these, with whatever is the best or seems to us to be the best in its own kind. And we may be sure that the newness of new poetry and fiction is its most superficial quality and that we have only to alter slightly, not to recast, the standards by which we have judged the old.

11   It would be foolish, then, to pretend that the second part of reading, to judge, to compare, is as simple as the first—to open the mind wide to the fast flocking of innumerable impressions. To continue reading without the book before you, to hold one shadow-shape against another, to have read widely enough and with enough understanding to make such comparisons alive and illuminating—that is difficult; it is still more difficult to press further and to say, "Not only is the book of this sort, but it is of this value; here it fails; here it succeeds; this is bad; that is good". To carry out this part of a reader's duty needs such imagination, insight, and learning that it is hard to conceive any one mind sufficiently endowed; impossible for the most self-confident to find more than the seeds of such powers in himself. Would it not be wiser, then, to remit this part of reading and to allow the critics, the gowned and furred authorities of the library, to decide the question of the book's absolute value for us? Yet how impossible! We may stress the value of sympathy; we may try to sink our own identity as we read. But we know that we cannot sympathise wholly or immerse ourselves wholly; there is always a demon in us who whispers, "I hate, I love", and we cannot silence him. Indeed, it is precisely because we hate and we love that our relation with the poets and novelists is so intimate that we find the presence of another person intolerable. And even if the results are abhorrent and our judgments are wrong, still our taste, the nerve of sensation that sends shocks through us, is our chief illuminant; we learn

through feeling; we cannot suppress our own idiosyncrasy without impoverishing it. But as time goes on perhaps we can train our taste; perhaps we can make it submit to some control. When it has fed greedily and lavishly upon books of all sorts—poetry, fiction, history, biography—and has stopped reading and looked for long spaces upon the variety, the incongruity of the living world, we shall find that it is changing a little; it is not so greedy, it is more reflective. It will begin to bring us not merely judgments on particular books, but it will tell us that there is a quality common to certain books. Listen, it will say, what shall we call *this*? And it will read us perhaps *Lear* and then perhaps the *Agamemnon* in order to bring out that common quality. Thus, with our taste to guide us, we shall venture beyond the particular book in search of qualities that group books together; we shall give them names and thus frame a rule that brings order into our perceptions. We shall gain a further and a rarer pleasure from that discrimination. But as a rule only lives when it is perpetually broken by contact with the books themselves—nothing is easier and more stultifying than to make rules which exist out of touch with facts, in a vacuum—now at last, in order to steady ourselves in this difficult attempt, it may be well to turn to the very rare writers who are able to enlighten us upon literature as an art. Coleridge and Dryden and Johnson, in their considered criticism, the poets and novelists themselves in their unconsidered sayings, are often surprisingly relevant; they light up and solidify the vague ideas that have been tumbling in the misty depths of our minds. But they are only able to help us if we come to them laden with questions and suggestions won honestly in the course of our own reading. They can do nothing for us if we herd ourselves under their authority and lie down like sheep in the shade of a hedge. We can only understand their ruling when it comes in conflict with our own and vanquishes it.

If this is so, if to read a book as it should be read calls for the rarest   *12* qualities of imagination, insight, and judgment, you may perhaps conclude that literature is a very complex art and that it is unlikely that we shall be able, even after a lifetime of reading, to make any valuable contribution to its criticism. We must remain readers; we shall not put on the further glory that belongs to those rare beings who are also critics. But still we have our responsibilities as readers and even our importance. The standards we raise and the judgments we pass steal into the air and become part of the atmosphere which writers breathe as they work. An influence is created which tells upon them even if it never finds its way into print. And that influence, if it were well instructed, vigorous and individual and sincere, might be of great value now when criticism is necessarily in abeyance; when books pass in review like the procession of animals in a shooting gallery, and the critic has only one second in which to load and aim and shoot and may well be pardoned if he mistakes rabbits for tigers, eagles for barndoor fowls, or misses altogether and wastes his shot upon some peaceful cow grazing in a further field. If behind the erratic gunfire of the press the author felt that there was another kind of criticism, the opinion of people reading for the love of reading, slowly and unprofessionally, and judging with great sympathy and yet with great severity, might this not improve the quality of his work? And if by our means books were to become stronger, richer, and more varied, that would be an end worth reaching.

13   Yet who reads to bring about an end however desirable? Are there not some pursuits that we practise because they are good in themselves, and some pleasures that are final? And is not this among them? I have sometimes dreamt, at least, that when the Day of Judgment dawns and the great conquerors and lawyers and statesmen come to receive their rewards—their crowns, their laurels, their names carved indelibly upon imperishable marble—the Almighty will turn to Peter and will say, not without a certain envy when He sees us coming with our books under our arms, ''Look, these need no reward. We have nothing to give them here. They have loved reading.''

Questions and Activities

▶ *COMPREHENSION QUESTIONS*

1. What habits of mind does this essay attribute to readers? Are readers generally more critical of what someone else says than nonreaders are? Are readers, to Woolf, more reflective and serious than nonreaders? Are readers more imaginative than nonreaders?

2. What does Woolf suggest happens to the category a library uses to classify a book once we actually start to read that book? Why is this point about the classifications into which we place books an important one later when Woolf begins to explain the fact-gathering and creative functions of reading?

3. Explain what Woolf means when she says that 'writers are very seldom "great artists"' (paragraph 5)? How does this statement fit in with Woolf's general explanation of why we read factual material such as biography, history, or newspapers?

▶ *QUESTIONS OF RHETORICAL PURPOSE AND STRATEGY*

4. This essay was originally delivered as a public lecture. What type of people do you think made up the audience for this lecture? What

does it seem to be trying to convince this audience to become? Look closely at the final paragraph. What does Woolf tell this audience is the most important result of a life of reading? Might someone who had read many books learn something from this lecture?

5. This essay blends two purposes: the informative and the persuasive. The first half or so of the essay explains the fact-gathering and creative functions of reading and the difficulty of classifying many books. But Woolf's writing becomes more persuasive in the essay's second half. How does Woolf want her audience to change their ideas and attitudes about reading? Does she believe that the ability to comprehend the facts of a book is sufficient to get the most from reading? Is the development of new perspectives and ideas in itself sufficient?

▶ *THEME QUESTIONS*

6. Can you explain the connection Woolf makes in paragraph 10 between simply comprehending what one reads and judging the value of one's reading? Why is it more difficult to judge the value of a book than it is to describe a book or put it into a category? Do you think that people should worry about judging the value of books? Or should they simply read, take in information, learn, and enjoy — no matter what the source? Might the value of a book vary depending on the reader? Why?

7. Are there any similarities in overall perspective between Jane Jacobs's argument that people should be more involved in planning city environments and Woolf's argument that reading is good because it gives people a way to be active, involved thinkers, rather than simple reflectors of the values they see around them? Do we really think about and judge our environments, or do we often simply passively accept them? Use your city or town as an example. Do the people there feel that they can become involved in the process of city planning — much as Woolf says a practiced reader might become involved in the ideas of an author? Or do they respond to public issues as if they were viewers of a television news program, in that all they can do is passively receive information? How do *you* respond to such public issues? What blend of critical and creative energies is appropriate when a person responds to a social problem?

8. Reading, like architecture, political campaigns, movies, greeting cards, and music, shapes the thinking of those who are exposed to it. Do you think Woolf believes that reading is a less dangerous influence on readers than other arts and media? What might make reading dangerous? When might reading be susceptible to the misuses that affect other arts? What protections do readers have against fakery, propaganda, sensationalism, distortion, or inaccuracy?

▶ *LEARNING ACTIVITIES*

9. Think back over your reading experiences. Do you usually read simply to get information, or do you ever read critically, disagreeing
with or elaborating on the information the writer gives you? If you
do recall reading critically at one time or another, what were you
reading? Were you reading a textbook in preparation for an examination in school? Were you reading a magazine to get more information about a personal hobby? Were you reading a self-help book
in order to improve your credentials for a job? Why did the particular situation surrounding your critical reading encourage you to ask
questions of the author, to compare his or her ideas with your own,
or to criticize the logic of what you were reading?

10. Write a narrative in the first person describing your responses to a
particular story, essay, letter, or newspaper article. Then go back
over your narrative and analyze it, using Woolf's fact-gathering and
creative functions as checkpoints. How many facts find their way
into your narrative? Does your narrative seem to produce new ideas
out of ones contained in the piece you read?

My Grandmother Who Painted

HONOR MOORE

Honor Moore was born in 1945 to wealthy parents. Her father was an Episcopal bishop; her mother, Jenny, was a writer. In this essay, she traces the life of her maternal grandmother, Margarett Sargent McKean, whose family had a long and illustrious New England ancestry. Moore is an established poet with one book — *Leaving and Coming Back* (1979) — and many magazine publications, an award-winning dramatist, an editor of an anthology of women's plays, and a winner of several fellowships and awards. She graduated from Radcliffe College in 1967 and attended Yale University for two years. She has been intensely involved in the women's movement since 1968, and has said that "writers, especially writers working with risky and controversial subject matter, need community and context. I wrote out of the women's movement."*

The essay that follows demonstrates Moore's concern with the issue of women's independence. In this essay, she uses her grandmother's struggles to pursue her artistic endeavors *and* fulfill her domestic responsibilities to develop in her readers an understanding of what it is like for a woman to give up a career because of societal and familial pressures. Her grandmother's drinking and excessive behavior, Moore suggests, were her means of coping with her frustrated desire to express herself through her art. As you read, note how Moore's telling of her grandmother's story is carefully combined with her evolving sense of her own career as a writer. What do you think she has done differently from her grandmother? How is her situation, from the start, different from her grandmother's in her younger days?

This essay touches on another issue related to this section's theme. Both Moore and her grandmother were able to pursue their careers without financial worry. Yet Moore is careful to point out that, although money does create the opportunity for independence, it does not ensure the accomplishment of independent expression. Think about this issue as you read about Moore and her grandmother:

1. How might someone unfamiliar with a wealthy person's inner struggles oversimplify that person's life?
2. Why did access to governesses, travel, and private schooling not guarantee a successful career for Moore's grandmother?

*Contemporary Authors, Vol. 85–88, p. 413.

3. Do the popular arts—particularly television soap operas and romance novels such as the Harlequin books—make us feel that wealth and family status guarantee success?
4. What satisfactions do Honor Moore and her grandmother find in their art that cannot be supplied by wealth or status?

▶ ─────────────────────────

1   I can see from where I write, on the back porch of an old house, the dark form of a Japanese beetle burrowing, devouring to the heart of a pink-edged white rose. The urge to rescue the bloom taunts my concentration like radio static. Get up, pursue him with digging fingers to the center where the sweet is, pull him from the flower, plunge him into fatal kerosene. The garden is just two feet outside the porch. The rose is the largest this summer, "Garden Party," a cream-colored mauve-edged dress billowing against green. The beetle will eat all the petals, turn the rose to skeletal lace. If I get up, I will putter in the garden all afternoon, and I must work, burrow toward this piece of writing still to move my hand.

2   I work sitting on the large, wood-framed loggia couch which belonged to Margarett, my mother's mother, a woman who stopped painting and sculpting after thirty years because, as she put it, "It got too intense." She said it that way at eighty-two, having survived five strokes, manic-depression, divorce, years in and out of sanitariums. "It got too intense," she answers, gravelly rasp rendered nearly incomprehensible by partial paralysis. "I turned to horticulture."

3   I am thirty-three. I have been a poet ten years. At twenty-two, I turned to psychoanalysis because, as I wrote in a journal: "I'm always afraid I'll turn into a manic-depressive like my grandmother." Winters I live and write in New York, summers in an eccentric white clapboard house in Connecticut, site of my nine rosebushes and small salad garden. My grandmother Margarett was born in 1892 in Boston. Her father was a Sargent, her mother a Hunnewell, daughter of Hollis Horatio Hunnewell, who made a fortune in railroads and copper. Margarett always had gardeners to keep Japanese beetles from eating her pink-edged roses, to keep the lavender and white blossoms of her tree wisteria elegantly weeping, to plant and tend the copper beeches which still stand on the grounds of what was her estate in Prides Crossing, Massachusetts. The resources that supported her gardeners, maids, cook, and chauffeur have thinned in the intervening generation: I can

afford the young man who charges six dollars an hour to mow my small lawn, but I do the gardening. Last winter, after losing all but four of thirty lilies because I didn't take time to mulch them against the heaves of winter frost, I decided to limit my flowers to roses, for which I have a passion, and wild daylilies, which require no maintenance. I would not call myself a horticulturalist.

"It got too intense." This is the first and only time in my relationship with Margarett, a friendship that begins and grows in the last seven years of her life, long after she has become bedridden, that we speak of her art. "Too intense." The closest we come to speaking of her manic-depression, the madness I interpret as the inevitable result of conflict between art and female obligation in upper-class, "old-family" Boston. Margarett had no role models. John Singer Sargent, the painter, was a fourth cousin, but from a part of the family from which she was separated by the previous generation's feud over abolition. Her parents were not artists, her father perhaps in rebellion against his father Henry Jackson Sargent, who is mythologized as a husband and father negligent because he wrote poetry, its only issue *Feathers from a Moulting Muse*, published in 1854. Serious art goes against the grain of this milieu; horticulture does not. Knowledge of plants, especially trees, runs strong in Margarett's blood on both sides. Charles Sprague Sargent, the painter's cousin and friend, made the Arnold Arboretum a force in American horticulture, inspiring Hollis Hunnewell to plant his "pinetum" whose ancient evergreens still tower, with careful Latin labels, near Lake Waban in Wellesley. When his coveted stand of India hardy azaleas bloomed each spring, Hunnewell put up a huge tent to enclose the bushes, so the assembled, sipping tea and eating cakes, could better drink in the glory of the hot pink blooms.

"I turned to horticulture." Turned. And returned, to childhood, to Grandfather Hunnewell's Wellesley estate, the white pillared mansion, his children and grandchildren in their own houses nearby—an enclave, self-sufficient. Margarett and two Hunnewell girl cousins grow up there together, are tutored by a succession of governesses until each Thanksgiving when all move to Boston townhouses, the children to Boston private schools. The house in Wellesley, where Margarett and four brothers and sisters spent springs and falls, still stands, inhabited by Hunnewells, painted the same soft gray it was eighty years ago, peak-roofed icehouse no longer used but still in good repair. And, down a lane, Hollis Hunnewell's white mansion, inhabited by a cousin in her nineties, still reigns in early Victorian splendor over acres of lawn, rivaled in impressiveness only by a front-yard stand of weeping copper beeches that forms a giant, voluptuous, dark red leafy tent, under which five generations have played hide-and-seek.

6   But Margarett leaves, leaves in 1910 for Florence, again in 1914 for New York. "She went to Florence an ugly duckling," her lifelong friend declaims seventy-seven years later, passionate octogenarian insistence fleshing out the cliché, "and returned a lovely swan." Not ugly, but certainly plain: posing grinning with the handlebar-moustached captain of the ocean liner, "Sept.–1910–Oct." scribbled below the photo; and with two big-hatted chums on deck chairs, she wears a sailor blouse, hand over giggling mouth—"all busy being silly." Margarett got accepted to the Florentine School by telegraphing, "Please reconsider our marvellous daughter" and signing her parents' names, which surprised no one who knew the girl who at seven threw a ruler at the governess with the harelip and, when asked if she regretted it, replied, "Only that I missed." Two years abroad: photographs of Margarett, awkward, and her schoolmates: Fiesole, Capri, Côte d'Azur, and "London 1911 Coronation Day." And then come the 1914 pictures: a chic young woman, silk draped from handsome delicate shoulders, feathered hat, fur stole. The finishing school has done its work. There is a coming-out party at the Somerset Hotel in Boston, and Margarett is crowded with aspiring partners. A beauty, "lovely swan." And what doesn't show, the young woman artist soon to leave home to study painting, soon to pursue her talent in New York. When manic-depression and drinking become evident in the early 1930s, Margarett's mother cries, "If only we hadn't sent her to Europe!" Repeats this to many people. In her agony.

7   I can uncover no evidence of overt resistance to Margarett's journey to Florence or her move to New York, but she is the only girl in her family and group of Boston friends to show such independence. One Farmington schoolmate told me that Margarett came to the finishing school in Connecticut pompadoured as conservatively as any Boston girl, and that a roommate's thirty pairs of slippers opened her fourteen-year-old eyes. Margarett does learn about the Florentine School at Farmington, and a Boston friend's mother introduces her to Gutzon Borglum, the sculptor, in whose studio she works her first years in New York. But there is no particular encouragement from her family or sanction from her milieu to become a serious artist. "I don't understand my daughter at all," her mother exclaims to a friend of Margarett's when Margarett returns from Florence, paints her bedroom walls black, and hangs theater posters.

8   Margarett was unusual for her time. I am not for mine. I have become a writer in an era of advantage for women and am supported in my vocation by lovers, family, friends, colleagues. A community.

> *. . .I am not alone as my grandmother*
> *was who painted, was free and talented and*
> *who for some M-A-D reason married, had kids, went mad and*
> *stopped finishing her paintings at thirty-five. . . .*

Forty-five actually, but ten years don't matter; what matters is she stopped. No one says I must stop writing to pluck a Japanese beetle from a rose or wash the breakfast dishes, and yet there is a force in me that resists my work, and I connect that force to Margarett. I wrote that poem, "Polemic #1," in 1972, groping to name that resistance:

> *This male-approval-desire filter and its*
> *attached hook, abbreviated M-A-D filter and hook,*
> *have driven many women mad. . . .*

exhorting women artists, my new community

> *M-A-D is the filter through which we're pressed to see our-*
> *   selves—*
> *if we don't, we won't get published, sold or exhibited—*
> *I blame none of us for not challenging it*
> *except not challenging it may drive us mad. . . .*

exhorting them and myself to risk expression, responding with expression to my grandmother's life: What made her stop? There is not a day I do not think of Margarett when I sit down to write, her half-finished canvases as viscerally present as if they are my wound, vibrating like the ghost of an amputated limb a heat-sensitive microscope picks up months after its removal.

When Margarett was nine years old, she wrote on the back page of a   *9* half-finished journal:

When thirty am going to have a house & millions of animals. Am going to be a nice cantankerous old maid. . . .

When she was twenty, she broke a year-long engagement and began to study art in earnest. But in 1920, when she was twenty-eight, her father died and her favorite older brother rode his horse into the woods and slit his throat. Shortly after she returned to Boston from New York, she sent a telegram to Shaw McKean, her beau of nine years, which comes down in family lore as "I guess I will marry you."

They stayed married twenty-seven years. "Perhaps the first five,"   *10* my aunt says in answer to my question, "Were they ever happy?" This aunt is the oldest of Margarett and Shaw's children, born in 1921, her mother's namesake, followed in 1923 by my mother, Jenny, named for Margarett's mother. In 1925, Margarett had twin boys.

11   "Margarett and Shaw were an incredibly beautiful couple. People would gasp when they walked into a party. Papa played polo. Once in Europe he played polo with the King of Spain!" Every fall they went to Europe, leaving the children with Senny, the governess. There is a 1928 photograph of Margarett, chin resting on her hand, elbow on knee, staring at us, directly but not comfortably. The blue stamp on the back of the photograph reads "Berenice Abbott, Paris, 1928."* In Europe, they bought paintings which they hung in the Prides Crossing house. Shaw imported the first Afghan hounds to this country, bred and raised them—they named the estate Prides Hill Kennels. There are scores of photographs, house in the background, Margarett and Shaw, four children at various ages, anywhere from three to a dozen elegantly clipped blond dogs.

12   "She was not a very cozy mother," my aunt tells me. "We'd visit her at her studio. We wouldn't stay long. She'd be intent on her work." Margarett showed paintings and sculpture in New York every year from 1926 through 1931. It was not just marriage and children that made her stop. There was always the governess, and Shaw was supportive of her art, even began himself to paint. But in the 1930s the balance in her life between marriage, motherhood, career, was thrown. Her mental illness—periods of depression when she drank heavily, followed by manic periods when she did not drink at all—intensified. The marriage grew increasingly unhappy. George Luks, the painter, her mentor and friend, died.

13   At a conference of women artists and writers late in 1978, fifty years after the Paris photograph, I meet Berenice Abbott, the photographer. I bring a small print, Margarett's staring face. "Do you remember her?" Immediate recognition. "Of course I do! How is she?" "She died last January. Did you know her well?" "I knew her in Paris. Then I lost her. Where did I lose her? Something about a play. She sent me to a play in New York and I didn't like it. I lost her in New York." She asks me what happened to her. "Well," I say, "she stopped painting. She was a manic-depressive. I don't know whether she stopped because she got sick or got sick because she stopped." Immediate response. "She got sick because she stopped. They all did and they didn't know it."

14   I write about Margarett to find out, concretely, for myself. That silence, that unused canvas, thwarted passion and talent passed down a matrilineage to me. My mother has nine children, survives a near-fatal

*Berenice Abbott (born 1898), a famous American woman photographer, is best known for her realistic sequence of photographs of New York City, done in 1935–1939 and published as *Changing New York* in 1939.

automobile accident, a nervous breakdown to put herself first, to commit herself to writing. She publishes one book, but in two more years, at fifty, she dies of cancer. Talent. And failure. Failure to hold, failure to focus, failure to hold the focus to the hot place so the transformation can occur, carry you out of self, so what you create may support, steady, nurture, and protect you.

I write to understand this moment: my relief when sitting in my   15
aunt's living room after Margarett has left her eightieth birthday party, my relief that when I defend her evening-long silence—there were toasts to her wit, the beauty of her house, the dynamism of her personality, none to her art, and she did not speak all evening: ''She is not selfish, she was driven crazy,...'' I hesitate, ''...by the conflict between being an artist and being a wife and mother''—my relief that when I in my late twenties say this, my mother, newly committed to her autonomy, her writing, sitting under one of Margarett's paintings, everyone silent waiting for her to speak, my relief that with fear in her voice, a tremor, she agrees with me, and I see, for the first time, love of her mother in her eyes.

Margarett's art begins eight years before her marriage. Soon after she   16
returns to Boston from Florence in 1910, she starts to study with a Mr. Bird, St. Botolph Street. Summers until the war she goes up to Ogunquit, Maine, to study painting with Charles Woodbury, later meets Gutzon Borglum who would become famous for his presidential faces on Mount Rushmore. She moves first to Stamford, Connecticut, then to New York to work with Borglum. Her early work is sculpture. In New York she lives and works in a studio on Fifth Avenue across from the Plaza Hotel. Fanny Brice* lives downstairs. She and Margarett are friends, and Fanny spends one night, having argued with Nicky Arnstein, sleeping on the floor of Margarett's apartment. Once Arnstein gives Margarett a shirt, silk with his initials on the pocket, because he feels it's an improvement over her smock. I know more about this shirt (and the day Margarett at Fanny's request spends a morning in Central Park returning to find Nicky gone, arrested—they had not wanted her implicated) than I do about her growth as an artist, or her first one-woman show in New York six years after her marriage.

*Fanny Brice (1891–1951) was the most famous female star of the American stage from 1915 until her death. From 1910 to 1936, she starred in the ''Ziegfeld Follies.'' She made five feature films between 1928 and 1946 and was featured as ''Baby Snooks'' on national radio broadcasts from 1937 to 1951. She was best known for her sentimental ethnic songs and humor. Brice was married and divorced three times. She was with her second husband, Nick Arnstein, from 1918 to 1927 and had two children with him.

17   The first show got very good reviews. "Sculpture and water colors by Margarett Sargent are on view at the Kraushaar Galleries. It is refreshing to find work that is so personal in its expression as this is" (*New York Evening Post*, March 6, 1926). "Margarett Sargent is that rare apparition in the local art world, a stranger coming here wholly unheralded and yet with an astonishing number of things to say for herself in her watercolors and sculptures. Her pictures have the delicacy of Marie Laurencin in color, yet in the case of this Boston artist, it is used for exquisite and unconventional expression. . . . Her head of George Luks is a veritable tour de force in its effect" (*New York City American*, March 14, 1926). George Luks's "open enthusiasm for the work of the gifted Bostonian Margarett Sargent—now known to New Yorkers—is quite disinterested because she is not a follower in any sense . . ." (*New York Telegram*).

18   Reviews of the Kraushaar shows build in enthusiasm each year until 1931, and late that year the headline of a Boston paper proclaims, "Margarett Sargent Exhibition Popular: Pictures Attract Hundreds at Gloucester." I find no reviews after 1932. I remember her drawing, and my aunt tells me she does not stop until her first stroke in 1965, but she stops exhibiting, and her painting tapers off during the late thirties and early forties. "I think she hated herself for not continuing."

19   And here the stories of the madness begin. Shaw's brother and his wife arrive for Christmas Eve with their children. Margarett is drunk. "We all went home." This at five in the afternoon. Margarett driving down to Wareham with her brother Harry. At first she is her bright, charming, intelligent self, and then, in a flashing moment, she seems drunk. They arrive at their mother's seashore house. Margarett rushes to the long wood pier, Harry follows. The tide is out. She walks to the end of the pier. "All I want to do is dive in," she says to Harry, who is horrified. Dive in. The tide is out. The rocks glisten, wet. But there is no water. Harry takes her into the house. The rest of the family hears of it from their mother. "If only we hadn't sent her to Europe."

20   After the five strokes she has in the last thirteen years of her life, Margarett is moved to a high-rise apartment in Boston so she'll be closer to doctors and twenty-four-hour nurses. The apartment has a view of the whole Boston Common, but the curtains are always kept pulled. I arrive one evening for a visit. Wearing a fuchsia satin jacket and makeup as porcelain as I imagine Empress Josephine's to have been, Margarett is sitting up in bed, scrapbooks crammed with yellowed reviews overflowing onto sheets the color of daffodils, a salmon satin blanket cover. She looks up. "Why I'd forgotten these!" she exclaims, shocked, genuine. I stand there mute in the face of a degree of pain no one, much less a healthy granddaughter fifty-three years younger, can

console. I am afraid of physical incapacity and I know it. Since she can hardly make her speech comprehensible, would she understand the questions I might ask? Grandma, why did you stop? When she answers, "It got too intense," why don't I say, "But why else? Was it because of the children? Was it because your marriage was unhappy? Something in your childhood? Grandma, what did it feel like when you began to go crazy? Did you go crazy? Was it craziness or just something in you that needed to be understood and wasn't?"

Margarett's sister-in-law sits, eighty-eight years old, on the window   21
seat overlooking the ocean in the house built by her grandfather, her return to this family place an affirmation of her ease in the life to which she was born, an ease Margarett never had. "She was so clever, one of the funniest people alive! Once at Christmas Eve dinner at my house—I knew but no one else did—Margarett, dressed as a maid, wore a red wig, blacked out three of her teeth, put the most hideous slippers on her feet." She spoke "with a ghastly Irish accent" and kept passing hors d'oeuvres "within an inch of my mother's nose." Mrs. Lee was polite for a while, but Margarett the maid kept jeering, "Have ye had too much to drink, m'um?" Finally Mrs. Lee's indignation overcame her. "If you don't behave, I'm going to tell Mrs. McKean to throw you out!"

And the other outrageous stories.   22

Once at a party she hired wrestlers for after-dinner entertainment.   23

Once she greeted two gentlemen guests in the bathroom. She was in   24
the tub, nude, bath water thick with floating gardenias. Someone passed champagne.

For another party she hired special waiters. Someone would ask,   25
"May I have a bit of ice for my drink, please?" and the waiter would go off to return from the pantry struggling with a chunk of uncut ice "practically the size of a boulder!" His companion, an acrobat disguised as a waiter, did pratfalls while passing champagne, not spilling a drop.

Once Margarett ran off to Europe with another man. No one knew of   26
her departure until the children appeared at breakfast. Pinned to each pair of pajamas was a luggage tag scrawled with the name of the person to whom each child should be sent in her absence.

In answer to my question, "Were you and Margarett close?" her   27
sister-in-law shakes her head. "Margarett was too bright for me, just too bright. A terrible waste. She could have been an actor. A writer! A painter!"

An eight-by-ten photograph mounted on an eleven-by-fourteen   28
board. Margarett stands painting. 1931. Large wooden easel. Intent on the canvas. Face blurred, for her whole body moves as she paints, and

the photographer from Bachrach has asked her actually to paint. Brush in right hand, palette nearly hidden in the left. Hair pulled back at her neck, sleeves of the knee-length, high-necked smock rolled to the elbow.

29   A November morning forty-seven years later. I am back at work after weeks of interruption: *Mourning Pictures*, my play about my mother's death, performed in Minneapolis. I am called overprotective because I am offended at the addition of someone else's lyrics, the cutting of the play without my permission. Two days ago there was a reading of my new play: two women in their twenties, their friendship, their search, each for her creative impulse, how that search is deflected again and again before a commitment is made. Forty-seven years later, to keep Margarett at her easel, I write about the woman at her art.

30   This photograph of Margarett is one of a series of her by Bachrach. The newspaper article that accompanies it: "Society woman turned artist." Headline: "Applies her artistic skill to make her home beautiful. Mrs. McKean's hobbies, modern paintings and old doors." She painted as Margarett Sargent. "Mrs. McKean in private life. . . ." How is the family more private than the woman intent on her canvas? "Mrs. McKean herself—black-haired, blue-eyed, lovely, gentle and questioning—but forceful and courageous on the subject of her work." The woman artist whom no interruption deflects. "Despite her big family and her large household, Mrs. McKean is always worrying about her work. She is unaggressive and gentle in her worry, but she is always thinking about her next painting, about the next thing to be done. And about her house, nothing escapes her notice, so sensitive is she to the beautiful that a drooping flower registers immediately."

31   In these past months I've moved after separation from a long relationship. Half my belongings are in packing boxes. I learn to let things escape my notice, but it is not easy. If it were not for two deadlines, I would not work. "The urge to rescue the bloom taunts. . . . The garden is just two feet outside. . . ."

32   In another photo in the Bachrach series, the finished painting sits on the easel. A self-portrait. Yearning, not eagerness in the wide-open, light-blue eyes. And sadness. Nothing gentle unless you can call pain gentle. Margarett's face in the photograph not girl-beautiful as in this self-portrait. Thickening neck. Thickening cheeks. A puffiness, probably from drinking. "As children we didn't really know about the sickness," my aunt tells me. "All we knew was that some mornings we were told we could tiptoe in and kiss our mother, but that she was sleeping late because she was tired. And we would go in, and the shades would be drawn."

33   I imagine two women in 1931, who, reading the morning *Globe*, might have seen Margarett's photograph and read the article. One has

children and no one to care for them, should she want or need just to go to bed and draw the shades. This is a woman whose dreams—to be a painter, a writer, an actress—were put aside when she married at sixteen, had her first baby at seventeen. In the photograph, Margarett stands, uninterrupted, brush raised. A quilt slung over a screen encloses the space where she works in her studio. The other woman I imagine is an artist Margarett's age, single, who works unphotographed, without money, no high-necked smock, no studio. When these women read the article, do they become angry with this woman who is an artist with children, with the money to work as she pleases? Would they realize that Margarett Sargent resents this description of her house at the expense of her work, that this "socialite" is also a serious artist? Would they have sympathy with the difficulty I share with Margarett, learning to work if you don't have to work to earn a living? There is no way either of my imagined women will learn that Margarett Sargent stops painting. But she does stop. Would either of these women, each in her own difficult circumstance, have imagined that something in Margarett's situation would stop her art?

"We would go up and visit her in her studio. She would say hello, but *34* she would be intent on her work." "It got too intense." Too intense. That feeling in me. At the moment of perfection in the work, life is balanced. Then some event, some moment, throws the balance, and I do not work for days, feel what Margarett felt standing at the end of the pier. "She got sick because she stopped. They all did, and they didn't know it." The urge to stop: to call someone, or to eat, or to weep. These interruptions are more staunchly supported inside me than perseverance. The battle is to hold to the vision I know I must express, but the confidence to do it, where does that come from?

"You will have a bosom like your grandmother's," my mother says. *35* I am eleven, standing with her near the brass-fixtured highboy on the second-floor landing of our house in Indianapolis. My mother, black-haired, olive-skinned. My brother teases me for being too pale, too round—"white and gooshy, white and gooshy"—and I reassure myself: I am like my grandmother. She had black hair and very white skin. Like mine. She is not called pale. She is called wonderfully fair.

"I was flat-chested until I had children," my mother says, pulling *36* my first bra from the underwear drawer. "I envy you your bosom." Thirteen. Ever since the blue-plaid straight skirt would not pass my hips that day we shopped in Indianapolis, I call myself fat. Alone in the mirrored dressing room I share with two sisters, I cup new breasts with small, wide hands. Bosom like my grandmother's. The bosom grows. And the buttocks. "What's that behind you?" my mother jokes as we walk together down a midwestern street. Fat. Fat as Margarett's face in the picture she sent from Brittany in 1952. The only picture of her in our house. Framed. A fat face. Too fat for the Breton headdress. Too sad to look at for long. I finger the red felt jacket she sent from Saint-Malo. It lasts. Grandma sent it from France! The fat face. Whimsy of the red jacket. She taught me to draw. To want to write letters in strange colored inks on unusual paper.

37   It could have been any day in the years before the truce my mother and I reached when I left home. It happened a lot in the years my bosom was becoming like my grandmother's. Standing in the twenties vintage maroon bathroom so the other children wouldn't hear, my mother and I scream at each other for "reasons" having to do with hair—"Sweetie, keep it away from your face!" And she pushes it from my face. And I yank her hand away. And there is silence, then, "There, that's lovely," the side of my face revealed when the hair goes behind the ear. Bitch. Under my breath. Messy room. A slap. My face. Not often. Punctuation to the fights with my mother. Not fights. One long fight. She is cool. I am not. Margarett's fat face. Too sad to look at for long. My mother dead now. I am left with reports of witnesses, war correspondents. "All the time," my brother says. "Screaming at you. Screaming." And my sister. "Once I asked Mom, why are you so mean to Honor?" "What did she say?" "Nothing." And my father. "My psychiatrist told me to stay out of it: mothers and daughters. . . ." My brother twenty years later: "She was fighting something back in you. Definitely. Tamping it down. It was her mother in you. She saw Margarett growing in you."

38   "Grandma was selfish," my mother says. "She and Papa fought. Terrible being at home. Away as much as I could be." And my aunt: "Jenny and I tried to talk Papa into leaving her sooner, getting a divorce. But he said he couldn't leave us with her. Nearly impossible in those days for fathers to get custody." So he waited to divorce her until the children grew up, we grandchildren were told. As if it was a civilized agreement. "Your grandparents don't get along, so . . ." Nothing about pain, her shock at his announcement. "I don't think she ever thought he would leave her," his brother's wife tells me. There are those who say she didn't love him. There are those who say she never loved anyone else.

39   My mother on the telephone when telephones were black. She hangs up: "Grandma's in the hospital again." "What's wrong with her?" "Mentally ill." My mother standing there touching her head. "It means her mind is sick." Her brain? The feeling inside my own head. Nothing in my mother's voice telling me her fear. Fifteen years later. A white telephone. My mother telling me she herself is going into a sanitarium, "depressed," Margarett's sad face. Oh, yes, her brain. Fat. Her

mind. Oh, yes, kernel of pain in my own head. Yes, I understand. That feeling starting to hurt. No words for it.

My mother is giving a dinner party. I help. From the high cupboard   40
we bring down white china cupids holding luscious fake grapes, gift from Margarett, to decorate the long dining room table, Margarett's wedding present. "You know the story of this," my mother says as we place the silver and the red goblets. "She promised it as a wedding present, then she had more shock treatments, and when we went to claim it, she wouldn't give it to us! Shock treatments made her forget even our wedding!" My mother talks in a perfectly normal voice. "Finally we got it, but the whole thing was *just* awful."

My mother wants to keep me from going to Radcliffe. "I don't want   41
you to have to cope with Mama." Cambridge is just an hour from Prides Crossing. Of course I want to go nowhere but Radcliffe. The time comes, Margarett is in a sanitarium, I go there. Brick Cambridge. Old trees. At Radcliffe I am a midwestern immigrant even though all the men in my mother's family have gone to Harvard for generations, even though Radcliffe was founded in 1879 by my mother's great-grandmother. I cry from fear the night before my first exam. *King Lear* seems written in an alien language. I am too ashamed ever to speak the wish: I want to write. My cover is the theater. I audition, voice failing when I must speak. Work backstage. Skate a surface, the dark water of possible creativity well below, frozen from me. Unspoken, even unthought is the fear: If I thaw, plunge, will I go mad? You look just like Margarett! Crazy like my grandmother?

Crazy is not romantic for me in spite of the romance of tortured fe-   42
male madness as creativity, Sylvia Plath et al. Crazy fighting with my mother. Crazy after crying—the feeling no one can comfort. Crazy Margarett, the woman always described as startlingly beautiful, bestially fat, stuffed into high heels, still attempting chic. Crazy. Scent of her perfume cut with heavy, nausea smell. Image of my mother on the phone, the news again and again of Margarett drunk, manic, sent, for a few weeks, to this or that sanitarium. I see her once with my parents in the room she has taken at the Gladstone Hotel during a New York visit. She doesn't talk much, look at us much, fiddles with gladioli in a vase, and afterward, my mother on the phone, "Mama was in terrible shape—" something about drinking, but I don't remember Margarett's drinking, just her very long, very dark red, very shiny fingernails.

At seventeen I do not want to be fat, but I want to love to drink the   43
way she does, to laugh the way she does. I do not want to be crazy, and yet I love this grandmother. Everything she does, she does with taste so original its sensuality is palpable: letters written in brown ink on

butcher's paper; a green satin purse with cream satin lining, a Christmas present for the granddaughter she barely knows; the feathery sketches she does of children; the extravagant love she expresses in the arched, rising vowels of a North Shore accent—"Dahling, I *adore* you."

44   "That week at Grandma's wrecked my life," I say. My father laughs. "We were all so worried, but you had a great time." Wrecked my life. What mystery, what example, what illusion, what ultimate would have formed the yearning of my imagination had I not, at the age of four, visited that grandmother in that house?

45   That house. A dark saltbox bought by my grandfather while he was still at Harvard. Built in 1630. Lived in first by the king's tax collector for the Massachusetts Bay Colony, then during the Revolution by General Burgoyne. Added onto by Margarett and Shaw after their marriage. Old part left intact, restored, then whole wings built so that it becomes, to a small girl's eye, a castle. Entrance hall first Margarett's studio, then, with later additions, a mammoth living room. Tower room off one corner, octagonal, walled with mirrors Margarett left outdoors for a winter to weather their silver to an appropriate cloudiness. Furniture that looks exotic, extreme versions of many styles. Spanish. Louis XIV. Arcane Americana. Copies so skillfully made it doesn't matter that they're copies. Dark clapboard. Pool surrounded by trimmed boxtree. Entrance hidden so the hedge seems a maze. Apple trees like candelabra, espaliered against the house. Windows crisscross leaded, tiny handblown panes.

46   I remember the dress with the lace collar. The photographs are black and white, but my dress was purple, the collar wide like a clown's. I am small, my hair pulled back from my face with barrettes. I sit below George Luks's portrait of my mother at four dressed as a Spanish infanta. My grandmother directs as the photographer, a small, wiry man who says little, positions me. I stand below the portrait. My child face. My child mother's painted grin. Flash. The photographer changes the plate in the old-fashioned camera. I turn and look up at my mother. In the photograph my small body twisting, the back of my head. My mother, tiny in a brocade gown, mischievous. Not the serious mother I know who always carried a baby—my brother, my sister—on her hip.

47   We move down the long tile corridor to Grandma's Spanish bedroom. I sit pasting paper, intent. Grandma looks on. Flash. I ride a tiny antique rocking horse. On the wall above the mantle behind me, the di Chirico, two stallions rampant, creamy manes lifted by desert wind, creamy tails streaming to the ground. Nearby sits Grandma, pen in hand, sketchpad on knee. Flash. Outdoors, arm around the neck of one of the Labradors she sculpted early at Stamford with Borglum. My little

gray hat makes my head round as the stone dog's. I become part of the landscape of that house.

That house. I remember running down the long hall. Pink. Windows onto the garden, the pool. I remember sleeping in a pink room. I remember hurrying down narrow, winding back stairs to a kitchen. I remember a kind cook with a long gray braid. I remember a man, plaster on his trousers, stumbling through a door onto the loggia from I didn't know where and I knew not to ask. ''There was always some parasite artist or other staying with Margarett after the divorce. Some were nice. Some were simply *awful*.'' Grandma sitting near my bed. Navy blue suit. Tight black pumps. Sketching me as I fall asleep. When I wake from the nap, she is gone. I remember Jack, the green macaw, screaming ''Margarett!!!'' over and over. ''Maaaggrrett. Marrggrrett!'' And the darkened bedroom. ''Shhhh. Quiet,'' the cook says. ''Your grandmother up late, sleeping.'' I remember shafts of sun coming through skylights breaking the gloom of the living room. The quiet. But I don't remember my grandmother's voice. Or what she sketched. I don't think I ever saw the drawing.

To write Margarett ''I want one you painted'' takes until I have my first apartment. My letter to her says something about lots of blank white walls. Tentative because I have seen only one drawing of hers, never a painting. Tentative because I know she stopped and don't know how many paintings there are, if any. *The Blue Girl*, its arrival announced weeks before by a note scrawled in pink on hot turquoise stationery, comes crated. I unwind thirty gleaming screws. ''It has a wonderful Spanish frame,'' she writes. Unwind, place the screws, one by one, in an ashtray, lift the lid, whiff of wood, fresh, peel back the cardboard: yes, the old frame and dazed black eyes staring as if interrupted. A stranger, huge black hat's shadows smudge the white forehead, lips set, red, disturbed. Color. Color. Light blue collars a pale neck, behind writhe thick green vines, exploding ultramarine blooms. Brown hair to the shoulder she sits, volcanic, holds the graceful white arm of an orange chair with both hands, as if to hold her to the canvas. I am twenty-one. This is my first adult intimacy with a woman who has given up.

''Who is she?'' I ask Margarett later. Her voice is already muffled by the first paralytic stroke. ''A model.'' Of despair. Hands badly articulated. After the stroke, Margarett's hands shake too much to draw, *The Blue Girl*'s hands, painted in 1929, splay like fans, prophetic.

Intense color. By ''too intense,'' Margarett, what do you mean? Too hot? The hot color blooming, blooming across canvas after canvas, gets hotter, hotter, then too hot for any brush and explodes, burns out, leaving just a tiny pile of ash? ''Who did that frightening painting?'' A visitor asks. I am twenty-one. ''My crazy grandmother,'' I laugh, knowing that at night when I sit down at my blue typewriter I won't be able to dismiss her piercing disturbance as I type, fingers splaying across the keyboard, drumming, drumming to tame, to come to know that countenance, the steady acidic gaze that follows me everywhere in the room watching, communicating some warning I cannot yet hear.

52   But those drummings begin my writing. First inchoate raging and need, then, finally, poems, prose. The earliest readable piece begins: ''In the pouring rain one day I drive my friend Jonathan out to see Grandma at her house. She has not lived there for years, but she has recovered enough from three strokes to go 'out to the country' several mornings a week. We drive through torrents to the house. Grandma has not yet arrived. I push open the huge door. The long entrance hall, living room bereft of paintings and furniture except for a few huge hard-to-move pieces. A rose brocade, outsized altar piece which Grandma bought once at an auction in Spain, still hangs at the end of the room, maintaining its handsome shape but well past beginning to crumble. Jack, her green macaw, is long dead, but because of the storm, I think I hear him screaming ''MMmmaaaaaggrrett'' from somewhere up-stairs.''

53   That visit to her house is my first since childhood. Margarett comes, escorted by her lawyer. By this time this lawyer and my aunt are her legal guardians. The windows of the long black limousine are fogged. ''Hello, dahling, you've arrived,'' she says, ignoring her weight, crippled body, the grossness of her face. She is dressed in hot pink jersey, perfectly made up. Lawyer and chauffeur begin to lift her into the wheelchair, she grasps for her cane, diamonds glinting in the car's overhead light, perfume wafting the air. ''Be careful!'' she yelps, snaps, continuing to smile at Jonathan and me. ''Your aunt called and begged me not to go out in the storm, but I told her you were coming and that I wouldn't miss it for the world.'' We wheel her into the house, and when we are settled in the cold, dark living room, Jonathan says, ''This house is beautiful. It's the most beautiful house I've ever seen.'' And she answers, ''This house is me. I devoted my life to it, and now I come out here and keep up the work on the grounds, the planting, the trees.'' The copper beech, gigantic, swaying in the storm. The wisteria unrecognizable without blooms.

54   It is on this visit that I see the paintings, by some fluke brought in from the studio on the hill before the fire. The paintings saved, and all her sculpture burned. The pile of ash. In the dark room the paintings. I have seen only *The Blue Girl*, don't know how many she did before she stopped, have no conception. Paintings in a room off the living room.

Canvas after canvas after canvas stacked against the walls. Too many to look at. Eyes. Wide open eyes. Color. Two little girls in red woolen caps. Margie. Jenny. One of her twins, my Uncle Harry, a little boy, recognizable around the eyes. A child on her side stretched out on a pink chaise longue, green plain dress, reading. Still life with cyclamen and clock. A cloche-hatted woman winking, the word "whoopee" dashed across the canvas. Women with tortured eyes, half-finished hands. Women with finished hands. Three children on a green ground, backs to us, wandering in some dream game of hide-and-seek. A man in a tux. The intense dark boy in the golden chair. Too many to see. Hundreds. Stacked in layers against the wall. A body of work. And for the first time Margarett is more than an inspiration. For the first time she is an example. "Why did I ever stop?" The asking voice. "For years I worked. Hard. And then it got too intense. I turned to horticulture."

"Still a worthy cage, ladies and gentlemen. Let's start this fine antique cage at twenty-five, ladies and gentlemen." The bullet rhythm of the auctioneer's voice. Festive green and white tent set up on the lawn near where the stone Labradors, long gone to my aunt's house, once stood. The box hedge overgrown, the pool drained. Tent crowded with people on folding chairs, standing, craning, peering at each piece that comes up. "Refreshments for sale, ladies and gentlemen. Luncheon." A table near the wisteria. Cars surround the copper beech. "And who will start this important, no this magnificent Shaker table at $800, ladies and gentlemen?" And Margarett no longer visits. She has been in a nursing home twenty miles from here for six months. "I hope she doesn't know about this. It's tragic," a woman in a flowered dress says to her companion. And she doesn't know that the house has been sold to a developer who has promised to preserve at least the original saltbox, or that the furniture, dishes, rugs, mirrored fixtures from the art deco bathroom, and everything her children didn't take, that didn't rot, is being auctioned off this sunny summer day, two weeks before her eighty-fifth birthday. I see Margarett's sister-in-law across the crowd, and one of Shaw's sons from his second marriage buys a silver tray. A small Queen Anne wing chair is hoisted to the front and quickly sold. "Aren't they divine!" the lady in the flowered dress says about the Spanish beds from the di Chirico bedroom. "Everything she had was good! Margarett had a great eye."

Her blue eyes, still like lakes. Skinny, shriveled back to her bones, hair no longer dyed, no makeup. Vulnerable as a child, she lies on her side on a hospital bed. "Hello, Grandma," I say, hating that I speak as if to a child to this woman who has lived eighty-five years. "Oh, hello, dahling,'' her voice is very low. ''Hello. Hello.'' She's been repeating things since she came here. A new drug? Oakwood, mansion turned nursing home, on a bluff overlooking the ocean. ''How are you?'' ''Not very well. Not very well.'' It is August. There are five photographs of my mother in the bare but spacious room, one of me. Beside her bed is a copy of the anthology I've edited, my first book, new plays by women. I'd sent a first copy to her four months ago. A week later had come her call: ''I read your book, read your book, read your book. I've read it twice. Twice. Wonderful. Wonderful.'' The nurse, worrying I haven't understood, says before hanging up, ''When she finishes reading it, she begins all over again.'' The book of plays about women, each play about a woman struggling to be autonomous. Margarett's greatest compliment to me is the book lying there, the only book beside her in this barren room with a view of the ocean, blue on this sparkling day. ''I love you,'' I say, ''love you, love you, love you,'' repeating like her, biting my tongue not to thank her for the things of hers I've bought at the auction. I am not speaking the truth and it is the last time I see her. New Year's Day I telephone. ''I love you so much. So much. So much,'' she repeats, voice barely audible. ''How are you?'' I ask. ''The same. The same. The same. The same,'' voice fading with each repetition. She dies three weeks later. Months afterward I ask for her copy of my book, and it arrives, dog-eared, tattered, fattened by repeated readings, in a legal envelope. My inscription reads, ''For Grandma, with intense love and great thanks for her example.''

Questions and Activities

▶ *COMPREHENSION QUESTIONS*

1. Why does Moore begin this essay with a paragraph describing how her urge to garden threatens to disturb her concentration as a writer? How does this paragraph tie in with Moore's description of her grandmother?

2. What is ''manic-depression'' (paragraph 2)? How did Moore's grandmother show symptoms of manic-depression? How is this illness related to her struggles to reconcile her life and her art, according to Moore?

3. Paragraphs 4 through 12 of this essay contain an account of some facts about Margarett McKean's life. Do these facts allow you to place her in a particular social class? Do you feel that her class

background was a hindrance or a help to Margarett McKean? How did it hinder or help her?

4. In paragraphs 17 and 18, Moore cites reviews of her grandmother's shows. Do these reviews suggest that Margarett had talent? What qualities do the reviews emphasize?

5. Do you think Moore would have persisted in her artistic career if she had not had the example of her grandmother behind her? Do all people need role models as they pursue careers? Why would women who pursue careers that have previously not had many women in them especially need female role models?

▶ *QUESTIONS OF RHETORICAL PURPOSE AND STRATEGY*

6. Why did Moore choose to write this essay in the first person? Might we have gotten a more objective view of Margarett McKean if the essay had been written in the third person?

7. How would you describe the assumed audience of this essay? Are the intended readers male or female or both? Is Moore assuming that her readers share her interests — in art, in artists, in women and their roles? Does Moore assume her readers are from a particular age group? Where in the essay do you find evidence of these assumptions?

8. Can you point out a place where you feel Moore provides an objective perspective on her grandmother? In what ways is the language Moore uses in presenting this perspective different from the language she uses in her more subjective descriptions?

▶ *THEME QUESTIONS*

9. Why is the fact that her grandmother found her art "too intense" important to Moore? Do you think that Moore believes her grandmother made the right choice in giving up her artistic career? Does Moore seem to suggest that her grandmother's eccentricities of dress and unconventional decor were in some way related to her forsaken career?

10. Both the fine arts and the popular arts help shape how people perceive the world. Do you think that Margarett McKean missed a real chance to influence how others see the world when she gave up her painting and sculpturing? What parts of the essay seem to support your answer to this question?

▶ *LEARNING ACTIVITIES*

11. Describe an eccentric or unconventional relative or friend. Do your subject's eccentricities seem to evolve from a past experience or decision, or are they simply a natural part of his or her personality?

12. Interview a housewife or househusband. Does your subject find the role somewhat creative? Or is it strictly a routine one?
13. Condense paragraph 55 into a factual two-or-three-sentence newspaper report describing the auction of Margarett McKean's possessions. What is lost in this translation?

Writing Assignments

ART AND MONEY

Using at least three of the readings in this section, argue for or against the following assertion: "The arts have a negative effect on our lives. They make us wish for pleasures and material things that only a few well-established people can have."

Be sure to provide specific examples to support your argument, to organize those examples and the generalities that develop from them into a form that readers who disagree with you could easily follow, to consider opposing arguments, and to write in a style that will not offend or patronize your readers.

IMAGE MAKING

Analyze a character or personality from a television drama, commercial, news program, or talk show. Write a first draft in which you record your detailed observations of this character or personality from at least three or four appearances (in other words, you will need to choose a subject who appears on a weekly or syndicated show, a popular commercial, or some kind of repeated program). Organize your observations around what you believe to be the image this person is trying to convey to the audience. Discuss your draft with others who have written the same type of paper. Do they remember the same types of details, gestures, or aspects of physical appearance or clothing? After your discussions with other students, go back over your draft to fill in revealing details.

As a second stage of this assignment, write a two-or-three-page analysis of the audience that you think your subject assumes. Base this analysis on the details you recorded in the first stage. What in your subject's physical appearance suggests that he or she is trying to appeal to particular age groups, values, or income brackets? Do the actions of your subject suggest a certain character type or personality? Do these actions seem to appeal to particular types or groups of people? On a more general level, why do you think the image your subject is projecting is one that the producers of this show or commercial believe will appeal successfully to its assumed audience?

Your final draft of this assignment should answer this last question, and it should relate that answer to the theme question of this section. In other words, reconsider your detailed observations of a television character or personality and your description of an assumed audience; then develop a statement that explains how popular arts such as television often appeal to and shape the attitudes of their audiences. Use your character analysis to illustrate this thesis. Imagine yourself writing this article for a serious media magazine, one read by people who want to understand how the popular arts and the public interact.

Essays that illustrate a point using an extended example should possess several qualities. First, the point should be clearly stated and the illustration should be closely related to it. Second, the illustration should be described in detail, and each part of the description should clearly develop part of the point. Third, the writer should order the parts of the essay so that the reader can easily follow the connection between general point and specific example. Sometimes, for example, sentences or phrases that make a point or an example should be alternated so that the reader never loses sight of one or the other. At other times, the point can be developed in an opening paragraph, the example in several following paragraphs, and the point reemphasized in the closing. The ordering strategy that is used should suit the purpose and the audience.

How Does Language Define Our Identities?

▶ ———————————————————————

Introduction

▶ ——————————————————

The essays in this section explore the relationship between the language we hear, speak, read, and write and our social and personal identities. Some of the writers look directly at how the public sphere of our lives manipulates and distorts language to make us see ourselves and our world in certain ways. Arthur Schlesinger, Jr., writing in 1974, analyzes how the corruption of language, and therefore of ideas and people, during Vietnam and Watergate created a "linguistic as well as political crisis." Stuart Berg Flexner looks at how advertising uses a language of "scare tactics" to sell products. Tom Wolfe tells how a new, sensational "pornography of violence" pervades journalistic reporting. The other writers explore cultural and personal dimensions of the role of language in our lives. Alleen Pace Nilsen surveys the entries in a standard dictionary and finds a fundamental sexism embodied in our language and culture. In her diary, Susan Griffin chronicles her struggle, through writing, to find a woman's language, one with a world view of joy and faith. Geneva Smitherman argues that the lack of public acceptance of black English is another form of racism and classism, a denial of black cultural and personal identity; however, Richard Rodriguez recalls his experiences growing up in a Spanish-speaking family and argues against bilingual education, against denying minorities a mainstream, English-speaking life. In Dorothy Parker's short story, "Arrangement in Black and White," the main character's speech reveals her racism and class-consciousness.

We may assume that language is merely a tool of communication, which we can readily control. But, like all the writers in this section, Arthur Schlesinger, Jr., acknowledges how fundamental language is to our perception of ourselves as individuals and as members of society and to our understanding of the world: "Language colors and penetrates the depths of our consciousness. It is the medium that dominates perceptions, organizes categories of thought, shapes the development of ideas, and incorporates a philosophy of existence." Each of the writers explores an important way in which language penetrates and shapes our lives. Alleen Pace Nilsen begins her essay "Sexism in English: A Feminist View" with the questions "Does culture shape language? Or does language shape culture?" Pace Nilsen sees language and culture as inseparable. Her survey of words in a standard American desk dictionary categorizes instances of sexism in a language and culture that value a woman's body but a man's mind or activities, that expect women to be passive but men to be active, that connect positive qualities with the concept of masculine but negative or trivial ones with the concept of feminine. Pace Nilsen recognizes the accepted principle "that as culture changes so will the language," but she notes that the "reverse of this—as a language changes so will the culture—is not so readily accepted." Susan Griffin, a contemporary feminist writer, believes that language creates change. Her diary, much of which is about writing her long prose poem *Woman in Nature: The Roaring Inside Her,* records her struggle to find a personal, female language that readily expresses faith in nature and the universe, apart from the language of patriarchy with its despair concerning the universe. She relates how this new language changes how she organizes her book and how she perceives her world.

Just as language shapes our perceptions and values, it can also reveal them, as it does for the woman in Dorothy Parker's short story. At a party in honor of a noted black singer, this "woman with the pink velvet poppies wreathed round the assisted gold of her hair" proclaims the difference between her own and her husband's feelings toward "colored people," but as she nervously chatters, she exposes her true feelings. In their essays, both Geneva Smitherman and Richard Rodriguez are directly concerned with the issue of how language shapes how members of a social minority can think about themselves and be thought of. In his autobiographical excerpt, Rodriguez remembers his experiences as a child of Mexican immigrants. He recreates scenes, sounds, and feelings associated with his giving up Spanish, the private language of his family, for English, the public language of school and culture. Rodriguez sees this change from private to public language, from family to school, as the necessary experience of all children. As a minority, as a "socially disadvantaged" child, Rodriguez particularly felt how the private "ghetto language" of his family's Spanish "deepened and strengthened my feeling of public separateness." He had to speak English to have a public identity. Rodriguez argues for linguistic assimilation, but Geneva Smitherman argues for the recognition of black English and black cultural identity and heritage. Smitherman uses historical and linguistic evidence to show how black English is labeled inferior in order to maintain white supremacy. Our society preaches equal opportunity and class mobility, but Smitherman exposes how a notion of "standard," "correct" English acts as a means of oppression. Smitherman's own writing—moving between standard academic writing and expressive black English—promotes a different standard of "dynamic," "contextually appropriate," and "truthful" language.

The inseparable relationship between language and culture seems to leave no area of our lives unaffected by our language. Americans are concerned, even obsessed, by common physical conditions like bad breath and perspiration. Stuart Berg Flexner looks at how advertising has coined and popularized a pseudoscientific language of ailments, such as halitosis and B.O., that buying certain products will, of course, cure. Tom Wolfe, a journalist and social critic, looks at how a new pornography of violence has come to pervade most forms of journalism. Once the exclusive style of tabloids with headlines like "Teenager Twists Off Corpse's Head," a language of sensational action, "gory details," and violence as "status competition" is seen even in accounts of the assassination of a president. Does such writing shape, or is it shaped by, the views of the reading public? While Wolfe raises such questions through his exposé of a brand of journalism, the historian Arthur Schlesinger, Jr., bitterly reflects on the relationship between language and politics. Schlesinger analyzes, historically and politically, "the spreading dissociation of words from meaning, of language from reality," so that words become "instruments less of communication than of deception." Schlesinger calls on writers and teachers to "expose the attack on meaning and discrimination in language" and contribute to the ongoing struggle for "the redemption of politics."

These essays offer multiple perspectives on the relationship of our language and our culture to our identities. As you read these essays, consider how language penetrates and shapes your life and thinking:

1. Have you ever been in a situation in which you felt you were being judged by the way you talked? Do you ever judge others by the way they talk?
2. Do you think there is a single right way to use language?
3. Do you feel that public institutions such as schools and government agencies should require their employees to use a standard language?
4. Do you ever discount the importance of a public figure's ideas because of the way he or she uses language? Have you ever changed your opinion on an issue because of language that you heard or read in talking or reading about the issue?
5. Do you ever feel insulted by the language in an advertisement? Do you ever allow an advertisement's language to persuade you to buy a product that you really do not need?
6. Are you ever offended by the language that is used in a newspaper or magazine sold at a grocery store check-out counter?

Where It's At

GENEVA SMITHERMAN

Geneva Smitherman is a professor in the communications department of Wayne State University in Detroit. She was born in Brownsville, Tennessee, in 1940 and has been an educator, scholar, and writer. She taught English and Latin in the Detroit public schools from 1960 to 1965 and has taught English and speech at Eastern Michigan University and at Wayne State University from 1966 to the present. From 1971 to 1973, she was a visiting lecturer in Afro-American studies at Harvard University; from 1973 to 1977, she directed the Center for Black Studies at Wayne State University. She earned her B.A. and M.A. degrees from Wayne State and her Ph.D. from the University of Michigan. In 1975, she received the Richard Wright–Woodie King Award for drama criticism from *Black World Magazine;* in the same year, she was honored by the Education Press Association for excellence in educational journalism. She has written and edited six books, including *Talkin & Testifyin: The Language of Black America* (1977), many articles on education and language theory, and a regular column called "Soul n' Style" for the *English Journal* from 1974 to 1976.

Smitherman combines scholarly precision with colorful, everyday language in her essays and books. She has consistently written for audiences of teachers at all levels in an accessible and entertaining style without sacrificing the conventions of her profession as linguistic scholar and university researcher. Her work emphasizes the necessity of analyzing and teaching language as it is used by people, not as an objective, self-contained system of rules.

The key to understanding the essay included here lies in being open to new attitudes about language. First, Smitherman believes that most people simply do not think very much about language. They assume that it works by simple rules and that educated people and people who hold important jobs know those rules and use "correct" language. People often assume as well that language is simply a transparent cover on thought, a relatively unimportant medium through which we exchange ideas. Finally, and most important to this essay, most people judge others at least partially by the way they speak and write. If someone sounds right, in other words, he or she must be smart and knowledgeable. If a person sounds odd, he or she must be dumb and ignorant. Of course, if we stop and think about how language works, these common opinions may seem too simplistic.

These general truths about how language influences people should be, in your reading of this essay, related to the history of oppression and poverty that black people have experienced in America. Having experienced slavery and segregation, blacks are subject to having their language maligned and ridiculed. Whereas white dialects often go unnoticed or are accepted as regional variations of standard English, black dialects often stigmatize their speakers as uneducated and unintelligent. Smitherman attempts in this essay a historical and cultural analysis of language use and its connections with political power and social hierarchy. Smitherman hopes that this analysis will cause readers like yourself — educated and willing to consider historical information about language and dialects — to revise long-held attitudes toward the dialects that are spoken by blacks and to see dialects as highly structured and complex languages in themselves.

The point of Smitherman's essay is to get you to think about the nature of language and how people use it. First, she shows by example how people are often stereotyped by their language. Then, she argues that all English-speakers speak dialects, that some dialects have more social prestige than others but all work by sophisticated linguistic rules. Finally, she goes over the recent history of prestige dialects, pointing out that the social status of the speakers often determined the esteem in which a particular English or American dialect was held. Among these consecutive treatments of language function and history, Smitherman intersperses information on current black writers and their desire to uphold the spoken dialects of their people, because they believe this to be the only natural route to the appreciation of black culture in general.

As you read, keep in mind the fact that Smitherman is able to read and write both standard English and dialect, and consider these questions:

1. How do you think she was able to develop fluency in both areas?
2. What advantages does she have over those people who feel they must reject their own language backgrounds in order to be successful? What advantages might she have over a speaker or writer who is unable to switch from a minority dialect to the standard one?
3. Do you ever find yourself in situations in which you are self-conscious about your language? What does Smitherman seem to suggest you should do in these situations?

▶ ————————————————

SIMPLE: What're you doing with all those timetables and travel books, baby? [1]

JOYCE: Just in case we ever should get married, maybe I'm picking out a place to spend our honeymoon — Niagara Falls, the Grand Canyon, Plymouth Rock...

SIMPLE: I don't want to spend no honeymoon on no rock. These books is pretty, but, baby, we ain't ready to travel yet.

JOYCE: We can dream, can't we?

SIMPLE: Niagara Falls makes a mighty lot of noise falling down. I likes to sleep on holidays.

JOYCE: Oh, Jess! Then how about the far West? Were you ever at the Grand Canyon?

SIMPLE: I were. Fact is, I was also at Niagara Falls, after I were at Grand Canyon.

JOYCE: I do not wish to criticize your grammar, Mr. Simple, but as long as you have been around New York, I wonder why you continue to say, I were, and at other times, I was?

SIMPLE: Because sometimes I were, and sometimes I was, baby. I was at Niagara Falls and I were at the Grand Canyon—since that were in the far distant past when I were a coachboy on the Santa Fe. I was more recently at Niagara Falls.

JOYCE: I see. But you never were "I were"! There is no "were." In the past tense, there is only "I was." The verb *to be* is declined, "I am, I was, I have been."

SIMPLE: Joyce, baby, don't be so touchous about it. Do you want me to talk like Edward R. Murrow?

JOYCE: No! But when we go to formals I hate to hear you saying, for example, "I taken" instead of "I took." Why do colored people say, "I taken," so much?

SIMPLE: Because we are taken—taken until we are undertaken, and, Joyce, baby, funerals is high!

JOYCE: Funerals *are* high.

SIMPLE: Joyce, what difference do it make?

JOYCE: Jess! What difference *does* it make? Does is correct English.

SIMPLE: And do ain't?

JOYCE: Isn't—not ain't.

SIMPLE: Woman, don't tell me ain't ain't in the dictionary.

JOYCE: But it ain't—I mean—it isn't correct.

SIMPLE: Joyce, I gives less than a small damn! What if it aren't?

JOYCE: You say what if things aren't. You give less than a damn. Well, I'm tired of a man who gives less than a damn about "What if things aren't." I'm tired! Tired! You hear me? Tired! I have never known any one man so long without having some kind of action out of him. You have not even formally proposed to me; let alone writing my father for my hand.

SIMPLE: I did not know I had to write your old man for your hand.

JOYCE: My father, Jess, not my old man. And don't let it be too long. After all, I might meet some other man.

SIMPLE: You better not meet no other man. You better not! Do and I will marry you right now this June in spite of my first wife, bigamy, your old man—I mean your father. Joyce, don't you know I am not to be trifled with? I'm Jesse B. Simple.

JOYCE: I know who you are. Now, just sit down and let's spend a nice Sunday evening conversing, heh?...Oh, Sweety! Let me make you a nice cool drink. Lemonade?

SIMPLE: Yes, Joyce, lemonade. Lemonade! Baby, you ain't mad with me, is you? (*Joyce smiles and shakes her head, no*) Because I know you know what I mean when I say, "I is"—or "I are" or "was" or whatever it be. Listen, Joyce, honey please. (*He sings.*)

> *When I say "I were" believe me.*
> *When I say "I was" believe me, too—*
> *Because I were, and was, and I am*
> *Deep in love with you.*
>
> *If I say "You took" or "taken,"*
> *Just believe I have been taken, too,*
> *Because I were, and am, and I is*
> *Taken by you.*
>
> *If it is or it ain't well stated,*
> *And it ain't or it aren't said right,*
> *My love still must be rated*
> *A love that don't fade over night.*
>
> *When I say "I am" believe me.*
> *When I say "I is" believe me, too—*
> *Because I were, and was, and I is*
> *Deep in love with you.*
>
> *Damn if I ain't!*

JOYCE: A small damn?

Once again, Langston Hughes's folk hero, Jesse B. Simple, uses his rappin ability and verbal quickness to win an argument (and his woman as well). But life, unlike literature, rarely provides us with such happy endings. The conflict between the two characteristic language attitudes Simple and Joyce represent continues unresolved in Black American life.

On the one hand, you have those blacks who feel that black speech is just as functional as white speech in communicating meanings.

"Ain't" or "isn't"—as Simple says, "what difference do it make?" Within this group you have many blacks who argue that our Africanized English should be retained because it's part of the black cultural heritage. Besides, Black English expressions are often superior to those of Americanized English because black talk captures certain subtleties and expressive nuances more effectively. This is the point Simple attempts to make by distinguishing the pastness of "were" from that of "was." While his particular example should not be taken seriously, there is, of course, a kernel of truth in what Simple is saying. That is, some Africanized English verb patterns do convey nuances and subtle meanings that Americanized English verbs do not—the difference in meaning between *be* and *non-be*, for instance.

4   The other characteristic language attitude you find in the black community is represented by Simple's girlfriend Joyce. This is the notion that "colored people" should use "correct English," meaning, of course, "correct" by White English standards. Furthermore, so holders of this view argue, black speech is associated with being "country," down-Southish. This is the underlying point Joyce is hitting on when she wonders why, as long as Simple has been around New York, he continues to use bad grammar. ("You can take the nigguh out of the country, but you cain't take the country out of the nigguh," as the black saying goes.) Note too that Joyce not only objects to Simple's Black English syntax, but his vocabulary as well. For instance, she checks him for referring to her father as her "old man." Thus Joyce reflects the typical black attitude that rejects the totality of black speech, whether linguistic or stylistic. (There is a message in the fact that many whites reading the Joyce-Simple dialogue assume that Joyce is white.)

5   Joyce and Simple's two distinctly different language attitudes reflect continuance of the "push-pull" dynamic in Black American history. The ambivalence they symbolize not only exists in the black group at large, it can be found in any *one* black individual. As DuBois said in *Souls of Black Folk:**

> After the Egyptian and Indian, the Greek and Roman, the Teuton and Mongolian, the Negro is a sort of seventh son, born with a veil, and gifted with second-sight in this American world—a world which yields him no true self-consciousness, but only lets him see himself through the revelation of the other world. It is a peculiar sensation, this double-consciousness, this sense of always looking at one's self through the eyes of others, of measuring one's soul by the tape of a world that looks on in amused contempt and pity.

*W. E. B. DuBois (1868–1963) was a black educator and sociologist who founded the National Association for the Advancement of Colored People (NAACP) in 1910. *Souls of Black Folk* was his most influential and well-known book.

One ever feels his two-ness—an American, a Negro; two souls, two thoughts, two unreconciled strivings; two warring ideals in one dark body, whose dogged strength alone keeps it from being torn asunder.

[Understanding the living] conditions in the slave community [is one] way of understanding this "double-consciousness" in black language attitudes. Further insight can be provided by locating these ambivalent linguistic attitudes in the psychology of the colonized personality.   6

An individual's language is intricately bound up with his or her sense of identity and group consciousness. In the history of man's inhumanity to man, it is clearly understandable why the conqueror forces his victim to learn his language, for as black psychiatrist Frantz Fanon said, "every dialect is a way of thinking." Certainly this principle has been operative in the history of colonized people, where the colonizer's language and culture occupy a position superior to that of the colonized, even among the oppressed persons themselves. (The fact that America was once a colony of England goes a long way toward explaining why British English still commands such great prestige in this country—despite the real communication barrier it poses for most Americans. Fanon would label this the "colonized mentality" of White America.)   7

In analyzing the colonized African mind, Fanon points to the denigration of the African's native language (and subsequent Creole versions) as a basic manifestation of the cultural rejection of Africa by both Europeans and Africans. Speaking of the "Negro and language" in the French West Indies, Fanon characterized the situation thus: 8

To speak means. . .to assume a culture. . .The Negro of the Antilles will be proportionately whiter. . .in direct ratio to his mastery of the French language. . .Every colonized people—in other words, every people in whose soul an inferiority complex has been created by the death and burial of its local cultural originality—finds itself face to face with the language of the civilizing nation. . .The middle class in the Antilles never speak Creole except to their servants. In school the children. . .are taught to scorn the dialect. . .Some families completely forbid the use of Creole. . .The educated Negro adopts such a position with respect to European languages. . .because he wants to emphasize the rupture that has now occurred. He is incarnating a new type of man that he imposes on his associates and his family.

In the American context, the negative attitude toward black speech is but a variation on this same theme. Historically, Black English has been the usage pattern associated with plantation figures like Uncle Remus and Uncle Tom. Contemporaneously, it is the dialect associated with black urban "ghetto" types. Consistently, it has been labeled "poor English." While blacks have demonstrated ambivalence about it,   9 whites have characteristically rejected it out of hand. In a 1973 article on the subject, a white professor denounced Black English as the "shuffling speech of slavery." In earlier times, whites believed that Black English was the result of lazy lips and tongues, or at best the result of a kind of baby talk. For instance, toward the end of the nineteenth century, writer Ambrose Gonzales collected black stories from the Georgia-Carolina area and later published them in *Black Border*. In the preface to that work he stated:

> The [Gullah] words are, of course, not African, for the African brought over or retained only a few words of his jungle-tongue, and even these few are by no means authenticated as part of the original scant baggage of the negro slaves...Slovenly and careless of speech, these Gullahs seized upon the peasant English used by some of the early settlers and by the white servants of the wealthier Colonists, wrapped their clumsy tongues about it as well as they could, and, enriched with certain expressive African words, it issued through their flat noses and thick lips as so workable a form of speech that it was gradually adopted by the other slaves and became in time the accepted Negro speech of the lower districts of South Carolina and Georgia. With characteristic laziness, these Gullah Negroes took short cuts to the ears of their auditors, using as few words as possible, sometimes making one gender serve for three, one tense for several, and totally disregarding singular and plural numbers.

10   In a 1924 article, "The English of the Negro," and later in his 1925 *English Language in America*, linguist George Philip Krapp attributed the origin of Black English to "archaic" Old English forms and to "baby-talk" between master and slave.

> ...from the very beginning the white overlords addressed themselves in English to their black vassals. It is not difficult to imagine the kind of English this would be. It would be a very much simplified English—the kind of English some people employ when they talk to babies. It would probably have no tenses of the verb, no distinctions of case in nouns or pronouns, no marks of singular or plural. Difficult sounds would be eliminated, as they are in baby-talk. Its vocabulary would be reduced to the lowest possible elements...As the Negroes imported into America came from many unrelated tribes, speaking languages so different that one tribe could not understand the language of another, they themselves were driven to the use of this infantile English in speaking to one another...it is reasonably safe to say that not a single detail of Negro pronunciation or Negro syntax can be proved to have any other than an English origin.

11   Since the Civil War, and in the twentieth century especially, upward mobility for Black Americans has come to mean the eradication of black language (and black culture) and the adoption of the linguistic norms of the white middle class. (In point of fact, other minority groups

and lower-class whites as well have had to assimilate the language patterns of the dominant white middle class. . . . As one black writer put it in 1963, "Negro dialect" was the "last barrier to integration." Even the young are not exempt from these negative attitudes toward black speech. A 1968 study of the speech of inner-city black junior high students asked the students what they thought about their language. Most felt that the way they spoke was "wrong," and that black people "broke verbs," and "didn't talk right." (Yet when asked if they would change their patterns of speech, all said, in effect, "ain no way.")

The recent push for bi-dialectalism (fluency in both Black and White   *12* English) aims at being a mitigating force against the rejection of black language. This view would have blacks using Black English with black people and White English with whites. Yet that does not really solve the linguistic dilemma. In fact, bi-dialectalism has been termed the "linguistics of white supremacy" (by a white linguist, no less) who argues that whites don't have to learn to talk like blacks to gain upward mobility in America. Moreover, some blacks contend that being bi-dialectal not only causes a schism in the black personality, but it is also like saying black talk is "good enough" for blacks but not for whites. A striking example is provided by black writer Claude Brown. He comments positively about the "language of soul" both in his autobiography *Manchild in the Promised Land* and in an article on the subject:

> The language of soul—or, as it might also be called, "Spoken Soul" or "Colored English"—is simply an honest vocal portrayal of Black America. . . "Spoken Soul" is more a sound than a language. It generally possesses a pronounced lyrical quality which is frequently incompatible to any music other than that ceaseless and relentlessly driving rhythm that flows from poignantly spent lives. Spoken soul has a way of coming out metered without the intention of the speaker to invoke it. There are specific phonetic traits. To the soulless ear the vast majority of these sounds are dismissed as incorrect usage of the English language and, not infrequently, as speech impediments. To those so blessed as to have had bestowed upon them at birth the lifetime gift of soul, these are the most communicative and meaningful sounds ever to fall upon human ears: the familiar "mah" instead of "my," "gonna" for "going to," "yo" for "your." "Ain't" is pronounced "ain"; "bread" and "bed," "bray-ud" and "bay-ud"; "baby" is never "bay-bee" but "bay-buh"; Sammy Davis, Jr., is not "Sammee" but a kind of "Sammeh"; the same goes for "Eddeh" Jefferson. No matter how many "man's" you put into your talk, it isn't soulful unless the word has the proper plaintive, nasal "maee-yun."

Yet in virtually the same breath, Brown tells us how he was ashamed of his parents when they went to juvenile court, before a white judge, using the pronunciation and other dialect features of Black English.

13   Some blacks try to solve the linguistic ambivalence dilemma by accepting certain features or types of black speech and rejecting others. This amounts to the exclusion of those black subgroups using the nonacceptable features of Africanized English. You know, a lil bit of blackness is cool, but not too much. Obviously, this does not solve the problem, for it leads to even greater disunity in what the Reverend Jesse Jackson has called the "great divide" in the community—middle class blacks, for example, accepting the black semantics of musicians and hipsters but rejecting the black syntax of working class blacks—despite the fact that all are, as the Rev would say, "still in slavery."

14   It continues to be the painful and trying task of the black consciousness movement to destroy the ambivalence about black language and culture and replace the old pejorative associations with new positive ones. Throughout the 1960s and on into the seventies, the clarion call of black politicians, artists, leaders, and intellectuals has been ethnic, their style revolutionary, their language black. Undoubtedly this has been in recognition of the fact that language is interwoven with culture and psychic being. Thus to deny the legitimacy of Africanized English is to deny the legitimacy of black culture and the black experience. The father of the black arts literary movement and leader-spokesman for the National Black Political Assembly, Imamu Baraka, speaks to the unity of black language with black identity:

> I heard an old Negro street singer last week, Reverend Pearly Brown, singing, "God don't never change!" This is a precise thing he is singing. He does not mean "God does not ever change!" He means "God don't never change!" The difference is in the final human reference . . . the form of passage through the world. A man who is rich and famous who sings, "God don't never change," is confirming his hegemony and good fortune . . . or merely calling the bank. A blind hopeless black American is saying something very different. Being told to "speak proper," meaning that you become fluent with the jargon of power, is also a part of not "speaking proper." That is, the culture which desperately understands that it does not "speak proper," or is not fluent with the terms of social strength, also understands somewhere that its desire to gain such fluency is done at a terrifying risk. The bourgeois Negro accepts such risk as profit. But does *close-ter* (in the context of "jes a close-ter, walk wi-thee") mean the same thing as *closer? Close-ter*, in the term of its user is, believe me, exact. It means a quality of existence, of actual physical disposition perhaps . . . in its manifestation as a *tone* and *rhythm* by which people live, most often in response to common modes of thought best enforced by some factor of environmental emotion that is exact and specific. Even the picture it summons is different, and certainly the 'Thee' that is used to connect the implied 'Me' with, is different. The God of the damned cannot know the God of the damner, that is, cannot know he is God. As no Blues person can really believe emotionally in Pascal's God, or

Wittgenstein's question, "Can the concept of God exist in a perfectly logical language?" Answer: "God don't never change."

Fanon spoke in a similar vein in describing the situation of the   *15*
Creole-speaking Antilles Negro educated in France:

> In every country of the world there are climbers, "the ones who forget who they are," and, in contrast to them, "the ones who remember where they came from." The Antilles Negro who goes home from France expresses himself in the dialect if he wants to make it plain that nothing has changed.

In coming home to the community that gave them birth and nour-   *16*
ished them till they got ovuh, E. Franklin Frazier's "black bourgeoisie" and W. E. B. DuBois's "talented tenth" bees makin it plain that nothin done change by using a mode of speech that reflects not only those who have not yet got ovuh but themselves as well. Some examples have been noted earlier in discussing the Black English speaking style of spokesmen like Rap Brown, Malcolm X, Martin Luther King, Jr., and Jesse Jackson. Some blacks have gone even further to incorporate the style and flavor of black speech into their writings (as much as this bees possible at least!). For instance, in a piece of literary criticism by Carolyn Rodgers, one finds the following:

> . . .all black poems ain't the same kind. . .certain poets hip you to something, pull the covers off of something or run it down to you, or ask you to just dig it—your coat is being pulled. . .every poet has written a bein poem. In fact, most poets start off writing them. Just writing about the way they be, they friends be, they lovers be, the world be. . .We do not want subhumans defining what we be doing. . .black poetry is becoming what it has always been but has not quite beed.

And in a sociological essay on the need for an "ideology of black social science," Gerald McWorter, holder of a doctorate from the University of Chicago, says:

> Robert Park was just another cat walkin' and workin'. . .now this was a white dude trying to trick us into diggin' what some slave owners developed about us (remember that they counted us as three-fifths of a man). . .Park was the man most responsible in the social sciences for developing a liberal white game to run on Black people. . .in other words, we need to get this shit on, and for that we need a revolutionary script for the terrible black drama of cosmic forces that we're about to rain down on these pitiful ofays.

It is perhaps the new black poets who have not only made most ex-   *17*
tensive use of Black English in written form, but have also had the greatest impact on black readers. To give them they propers in this respect, we should say a word about their contributions to the eradication of negative black attitudes toward Black English.

18   The Black Arts Movement emerged during the past decade as the appropriate artistic counterpart to the politics of black power. The black arts writer redefined the role of the artist and presented a new perspective on what constitutes art. The creator of black arts literature envisions himself or herself as a necromancer, a skillful manipulator of the art of shonuff black magic whose job it is to "heal" black folks through the evocative power of art, and transform their suffering into constructive political action. According to black fiction writer Ishmael Reed, in his introduction to *19 Necromancers from Now,*

> the condition of the Afro-American writer in this country is so strange that one has to go to the supernatural for an analogy. Manipulation of the word has always been related in the mind to manipulation of nature. One utters a few words and stones roll aside, the dead are raised and the river beds emptied of their content...The Afro-American artist is similar to the Necromancer...He is a conjuror who works JuJu upon his oppressors; a witch doctor who frees his fellow victims from the psychic attack launched by demons of the outer and inner worlds.

19   There is a striking difference between this contemporary black arts revival and an earlier literary trend, the Harlem Renaissance movement of the 1920s. This movement brought to the fore what Alain Locke termed a "new Negro," and established Harlem as a literary mecca for such black writers as Countee Cullen, Claude McKay, and Langston Hughes.* The Harlem Renaissance was a period when, according to Locke, the "Negro was in vogue." It was a time when whites flocked to Harlem clubs and cabarets to soak up the sensual energy and live-for-today vitality of black life, and to hear the creative expressions of the new black artists—artists who, having thrown off the shackles of black self-rejection, were loudly proclaiming their African ancestry and heaping curses and threats of vengeance upon whites. "If we must die, let it not be like hogs / Hunted and penned in an inglorious spot / While round us bark the mad and hungry dogs / Making their mock at our accursed lot." And so on, like that, said Claude McKay, in his famous "If We Must Die" poem of 1919, a sort of landmark protest poem, undoubtedly motivated by all the black blood that flowed in the race riots of what W. E. B. DuBois termed the "Red Summer" of 1919. (Ironically, the late Sir Winston Churchill used this poem in his public appeals for Allied support during World War II, and further, a white American soldier, who had died on the Russian front, purportedly had this poem among his possessions.)

---

*Countee Cullen, Claude McKay, and Langston Hughes are black lyrical poets who had wide readerships during the Harlem Renaissance of the 1920s. They helped black dialects gain acceptance among educated people.

Both the Harlem Renaissance and the Black Arts Movement are sim-   20
ilar in that each involved a rediscovery and legitimizing of the black
cultural heritage and a more vigorous political protest stance on the
part of black writers. However, the movements differ in two major respects.

First, the Harlem writers conceived of themselves as writers first,   21
last, and only. They were a rather cliquish group, sharing their works
mainly with other black writers and their white patrons. They made no
attempts to align themselves with the black community and would
never have thought of taking their works there. Today's black artists,
by contrast, are not content to be simply writers, sounding their protests only through their art. They see themselves as black first, and thus
as active participants in the struggle for black liberation (which explains why an artist like Baraka became involved in local and national
black politics).

In the second place, the Renaissance artists, for all they bad-mouthin   22
of America and white folks, apparently "loved this cultured hell that
tested [they] youth," for the literature they created is very much in the
Euro-American tradition. During a period when the Lost Generation
crowd of the White American literati-intelligentsia was experimenting
with new verse forms, Claude McKay, for instance, consistently cast
his protest in the conventional sonnet form. And so it was with most of
his black contemporaries: their versification styles were very Western,
and in their art they quite consciously neglected the rich reservoir of
Afro-American folk forms and the black cultural tradition. (Of all the
Renaissance "niggerati," Langston Hughes and poet-teacher Sterling
Brown stand out as important exceptions who opted for poems about
common black folk expressed in the "forms of things unknown.")

Today's black writers are making Herculean efforts to create a   23
literature that will reach and reflect common black folks. They are
going into the community—on the street, in the churches, in the recreation centers, and wherever black folk be. The art they are taking with
them, they have decided, must be functional and relevant to the lives
and daily struggles of black people. This art, which is to be born out of
the agony and sweat of the black spirit, must manifest a cultural reality
that is uniquely Afro-American. The objective is to prevent today's
black consciousness movement from becoming like that of the Harlem
Renaissance, which, according to Langston Hughes, ordinary Harlem-
ites had not even heard of, and if they had, "it hadn't raised their wages
any."

The new black poetry is the dominant creative expression of this   24
present-day literary renaissance. While the black theater movement,
with Ed Bullins at its head, and excellent works of fiction by Ishmael

Reed and John Oliver Killens are clearly in the mainstream of the Black Arts Movement, it is the poetic genre which has seen the most prolific outpouring of the new art. To examine why this is so, recall the highly oral nature of black culture. To get the written word to the black nonreading, still essentially preliterate community, the new black writer must, as Haki Madhubuti says,

> move into the small volume direction. . . small black works that can be put into back pockets and purses, volumes that can be conveniently read during the 15 minute coffee break or during the lunch hour. . . we as black poets and writers are aware of the fact that the masses (and I do not use the word lightly for I am part of the masses) of black people *do not read books.*

25   Then there is the importance of music as a cultural dynamic in Black America. Black writer-critic Larry Neal put it this way:

> . . . the key to where the black people have to go is in the music. Our music has always been the most dominant manifestation of what we are and feel, literature was just an afterthought, the step taken by the Negro bourgeoisie who desired acceptance on the white man's terms. And that is precisely why the literature has failed. It was the case of one elite addressing another elite.
>
> But our music is something else. The best of it has always operated at the core of our lives, forcing itself upon us as in a ritual. It has always, somehow, represented the collective psyche. Black Literature must attempt to achieve that same sense of the collective ritual. . .

As a literary genre, poetry, both traditionally and now, is written to be recited, even in a sense "sung," in such a way that its creator becomes a kind of performing bard before the group. Thus poetry is the form that can most effectively go where black people are at, for it combines orality, music, verbal performance, and brevity—and when performed before a black audience it evokes the "collective ritual."

26   In taking their poetry to the people, the new black poets recognize that the grass roots, since they lack the black bourgeoisie's white middle-class aspirations, have been the bearers and sustainers of black culture through the centuries. In representing the masses, this new art is expressive of the uniqueness of Afro-American culture. It has a style rooted in the artistic trappings of the Afro-American cultural sensibili-ty—a style that has emerged as an identifiable black aesthetic. On no level is this aesthetic more strikingly revealed than in the *language* of the new black poetry: the poets bees not only tappin the reservoir of the black cultural universe but doing so in the Black Idiom. Within the limitations of written form, today's poets are attempting to capture the flavor of Black American speech—its rhythms and sounds, its dialect and style. They use Black English not only to project the voice of a black character in a poem, but even when they are speaking in their own poet-

ic voices in a given poem. Through their artistic efforts, the poets seem
to be saying: if the message is new, the medium must be new also. As
Haki put it, "blackpoets [will] deal in...black language or Afro-
American language in contrast to standard english...will talk of king-
doms of Africa, will speak in Zulu and Swahili, will talk in muthafuck-
as and 'can you dig it.' "

[Elsewhere I have] cited some poetry written in the black, and poetry   *27*
performances utilizing the dynamics of black communication (such as
call-response). Here we might note additional examples. In her collection *We a BaddDDD People*, Sonia Sanchez uses Black English language
features extensively in her "chant for young brothas & sistuhs" in
which she warns them of the destructiveness of dope in the black community:

> *yall*
> > > *out there.*   *looooken so cooool*
> *in yo / highs.*
> > > > > *yeah yall*
> > > > > > *rat there*
> > > > *listen to me*
> *screeaamen this song.*
> > > > > > > > > *did u know i've*
> > *seen yo / high*
> > > > > *on every blk / st in*
> *wite / amurica...*
> > > > > *listen to this drummen.*
> *this sad / chant.*
> > > > > > *listen to the tears*
> *flowen down my blk / face*
> > > > > > > > > *listen to a*
> *death/song being sung on thick/lips*
> *by a blk/woman...*
> *yall*
> > > *out there*   *looooken so cooool*
> *in yo / highs.*
> > > > *yeah.*   *yall*
> > > > > > *rat there*
> *c'mon down from yo / wite / highs*
> > > > *and live.*

In a poetic tribute to Malcolm X, Haki Madhubuti uses Black Seman-   *28*
tics throughout, but especially when he describes Malcolm as being
"from a long line of super-cools, doo-rag lovers and revolutionary
pimps." Super-cools and pimps, living outside the bounds of the white

man's laws and customs, are often viewed as culture heroes, and in the old pre-naturals days they were distinguished by their meticulously coiffured "do's." What Haki is alluding to, of course, is Malcolm X's early life as a criminal, dope pusher, and pimp. However, the fact that Haki calls him a "revolutionary" pimp suggests that the leadership and black political consciousness Malcolm later exhibited lay within him all the time. By extension, the poet is also implying that the same revolutionary potential lies in other black pimps.

29   In her collection *Just Give Me a Cool Drink of Water 'fore I Diiie,* Maya Angelou plays not the Dozens, but the Thirteens, with separate but stylistically parallel versions denouncing the untogetha actions of both blacks and whites.

THE THIRTEENS (BLACK)

Your Momma took to shouting
Your Poppa's gone to war,
Your sister's in the streets
Your brother's in the bar,
The thirteens. Right On.

Your cousin's taking smack
Your Uncle's in the joint,
Your buddy's in the gutter
Shooting for his point
The thirteens. Right On.

And you, you make me sorry
You out here by yourself,
I'd call you something dirty,
But there just ain't nothing left,
cept
The thirteens. Right On.

THE THIRTEENS (WHITE)

Your Momma kissed the chauffeur,
Your Poppa balled the cook,
Your sister did the dirty,
in the middle of the book,
The thirteens. Right On.

Your daughter wears a jock strap,
Your son he wears a bra
Your brother jonesed your cousin
in the back seat of the car.
The thirteens. Right On.

Your money thinks you're something
But if I'd learned to curse,
I'd tell you what your name is
But there just ain't nothing worse
than
The thirteens. Right On.

In *Poems From Prison*, poet Etheridge Knight has two outstanding   *30*
Toast poems, one of which, mentioned earlier, is a poetic version of
"Shine and the Sinking of the Titanic." The other is a Toast to black
prisoner Hard Rock, who was "known not to take no shit / From
nobody . . . and he had the scars to prove it." I mean Hard Rock was so
bad that "he had once bit / A screw on the thumb and poisoned him
with syphilitic spit." But bad as this black hero had done been, the
"WORD was that Hard Rock wasn't a mean nigger / Anymore, that the
doctors had bored a hole in his head / Cut out part of his brain, and shot
electricity / Through the rest." With a sensitive stroke of poetic under-
statement, Knight portrays the effect of the dethroning of this new-
style black hero, the black prisoner:

The testing came to see if Hard Rock was really tame.
A hillbilly called him a black son of a bitch
And didn't lose his teeth, a screw who knew Hard Rock
From before shook him down and barked in his face.
And Hard Rock did nothing. Just grinned and looked silly.
His eyes empty like knot holes in a fence.

And even after we discovered that it took Hard Rock
Exactly 3 minutes to tell you his first name,
We told ourselves that he had just wised up,
Was being cool; but we could not fool ourselves for long,
And we turned away, our eyes on the ground. Crushed.
He had been our Destroyer, the doer of things
We dreamed of doing but could not bring ourselves to do.
The fears of years, like a biting whip,
Had cut grooves too deeply across our backs.

31   As a final, really outstanding poetic example, I cite Haki's "But he was cool: or he even stopped for green lights," a signifyin poem, showing all the features of heavy signification and rich in Black Semantics, sound, and syntax.

> *super-cool*
> *ultrablack*
> *a tan/purple*
> *had a beautiful shade.*
>
> *he had a double-natural*
> *that wd put the sisters to shame.*
> *his dashikis were tailor made*
> *his beads were imported sea shells*
>   *(from some blk/country i never heard of)*
> *he was triple-hip*
>
> *his tikis were hand carved*
> *out of ivory*
> *& came express from the motherland.*
> *he would greet u in swahili*
> *& say good-by in yoruba.*
> *wooooooooooooo-jim he bes so cool & ill tel li gent*
>   *cool-cool is so cool he was un-cooled by*
>   *other niggers' cool*
>   *cool-cool ultracool was bop-cool/ice box*
>   *cool so cool cold cool*
>   *his wine didn't have to be cooled, him was*
>   *air conditioned cool*
>   *cool-cool/real cool made me cool—now*
>   *ain't that cool*
>   *cool-cool so cool him nick-named refriger-*
>   *ator.*
> *cool-cool so cool*
> *he didn't know,*
> *after detroit, newark, chicago &c.,*
> *we had to hip*
>   *cool-cool/ super-cool/ real cool*
>   *that*
> *to be black*
> *is*
> *to be*
> *very-hot.*

32   What the new black poets have done, then, is to take for their conceptual and expressive tools a language firmly rooted in the black experience. Such terms and expressions enable the poets to use cultural im-

ages and messages familiar to their black audiences, and with great strokes of brevity, Black English lines and phrases reveal a complete story. (Such, of course, is the way any good poet operates; what is unique here is the effective execution of the operation in a black way.)

I alluded earlier to the linguistic assimilation forced upon other "outsiders" in American life. While much of the contemporary sound and fury on "nonstandard" speech focuses on the linguistic behavior of the largest minority group (blacks), traditionally there has always been a significant social dimension undergirding the racial component which throws the whole question of standard-nonstandard English into a wider realm ultimately affecting whites as well. Although our focus here has been on racial and oppressive attitudes toward *black* language behavior, language has been a tool of oppression wielded against other social and ethnic groups. Anyone familiar with Mark Twain's masterpiece *Huckleberry Finn* can recall that Huck's rebellion against the slavocracy is foreshadowed early in the novel by Huck's resistance to corrections of his Pike County Missouri dialect. What linguist Donald Lloyd has labeled the "national mania for correctness" stems from a long-standing tradition of elitism in American life and language matters. Let us take a brief look at this tradition in hopes of clarifying some popular misconceptions about American English, Black English, and language in general.   33

Though Americans preach individualism and class mobility, they practice conformity and class stasis. The individual pioneer spirit is held in check by the need to keep up with the Joneses. Any number of American social critics—among them Norman Mailer, James Baldwin, Vance Packard—have dealt extensively with the rather schizophrenic nature of the American social sensibility. Paralleling this social class consciousness is the class anxiety that is reflected in the area of language, as is evident by surveying the American schoolroom grammar tradition which had its beginnings in England.   34

Language conventions and the English grammar handbooks—which anyone who passes through the American educational system is exposed to—are based on a preoccupation with the all-engrossing question "What is correct English?" Not: What is dynamic and vivid language? Not: What is contextually appropriate language? Not even: What is truthful language? But simply: What is "correct" language? Such uptight language attitudes, which are fostered in the schools, are grounded in the "doctrine of correctness" that emerged during the eighteenth century. The correctness obsession was a logical consequence of the coming to power of the "primitive" middle classes and the decline of the "refined" aristocracy in post-Middle Ages Europe. Whereas Latin had enjoyed centuries of prestigious use and admiration, the Roman   35

Empire had, after all, declined, and practical considerations dictated the necessity for British children to be instructed in their own vernacular, the Anglo-Saxon tongue. Richard Mulcaster, in his educational writings of the sixteenth century, had decided to write in English because "though I appeal to the learned who understand Latin, I wish to reach also the unlearned, who understand only English, and whose interests are to be the more considered that they have fewer chances of information." The problem with the vernacular of the "unlearned," however, was that it was not in accord with Latin grammatical rules and considered quite disorderly. As Mulcaster himself had said, "our Sparta must be spunged, [there is a need to bring] our tung to Art and form of disapline."

36   Pushed into prominence by the Industrial Revolution and expanding technology, the newly risen middle class posed a potentially powerful threat to the declining aristocracy. The fears, though, were unfounded because the new group wanted only to ape and be accepted by their "betters," and they wanted neither themselves nor their children to reflect any kinship with those they had left behind. Instead, they wanted rules of conduct, linguistic and social, so as not to belie their rural or lower-class origins. (The eighteenth century also saw the rise of Emily Post–type social etiquette books.) From our contemporary vantage point in history, the imitational behavior of these fresh-from-the-bottom speakers of the "barbaric" tongue is especially ironic. After all, it had been the aristocracy, the feudal lords, that had oppressed their forefathers, and it had been the immoral greed of this power elite that had led to wars over land and property (as well as initiated the slave trade). Nonetheless, England was becoming an important world power, London the center of commercial life, and the middle-class rush was on. Certainly it was to the advantage of the elite to have their manners and speech adopted by these new social hordes. It would help to civilize them into the established values of the fallen monarchs and secure for that aristocratic set a permanent place in the upper ranks of the social order. Imitation is not only the highest form of flattery but a well-traveled road to sociopolitical co-optation.

37   The early grammarians who envisioned their task as one of "regularizing" and "purifying" common speech unwittingly became part of the grand design to perpetuate the centuries-old class system. One popular text, the Port Royal grammarians' *The Art of Speaking* translated from French into English in 1668, railed against the "depraved language of common people" and contended that

> the best Expressions grow low and degenerate, when profan'd by the populace, and applied to mean things. The use they make of them, infecting them with a mean and abject Idea, causes that we cannot use them without

sullying and defiling those things, which are signified by them. But it is no hard matter to discern between the depraved Language of common People, and the noble refin'd expressions of the Gentry, whose condition and merits have advanced them above the other.

Bishop Robert Lowth's *Short Introduction to English Grammar* (1763) denigrated the "unruly, barbarous tongue of the Anglo-Saxons" and sought to give it "order and permanence" by superimposing upon it his own Latin-based standards. Even though in theory Lowth rejected the Latinate model, in actual practice, his *ipse dixit* rules and pronouncements for correct English usage came straight out of the Latin-Classical tradition. Not only did these self-appointed preservers and polishers of the national tongue find the language of everyday people at variance with Latinate and elitist norms, but even, according again to Lowth, the lingo of "the politest part of the nation. . .[and] writings of our most approved authors often offends against every part of Grammar." The English "doctrine of correctness" tradition was clearly undergirded by the belief that matters of English usage, like the divine right to rule, were decreed from on high.

Although Americans supposedly severed their colonial ties with the Mother Country in 1776, and although this country was founded in repudiation of the European class system, still the class-biased attitudes toward grammatical amenities came right on with the Mayflower. The American counterparts of British grammarians are strikingly exemplified in Gold Brown, in his *Grammar of English Grammars* (1851), and Lindley Murray in his *English Grammar* (1795). Murray, who even railed against contractions, wrote his grammar not simply to introduce the "proper" method of English usage among the young, but to inculcate in them all the morals and virtues commensurate with "proper" English. Dig Murray:

38

> The author of the following work wishes to promote the cause of virtue as well as of learning: and with this view, he has been studious, through the whole of the work, not only to avoid every example and illustration, which might have an improper effect on the minds of youth, but also to introduce on many occasions such as have a moral and religious tendency.

Thus Lindley Murray reiterated the English (and French) notion that there was something intrinsically virtuous and personally superior in those who used "correct" language forms. (Of course, on the face of it, there is nothing wrong with teaching moral and religious precepts. But what code of ethics could have any validity which excludes "correct" English examples about the evils of the slavocracy that was running rampant in a country which had just fought a war for liberty and justice? Like, everybody talkin bout Heaven ain goin there!)

39   Subsequent American English grammars tended merely to mirror these early elitist ones and to perpetuate the myth that language, like the Trinity, should never change. But it is not only that Latinate-prescriptive grammars helped to perpetuate a way of life built upon class discrimination and bias. This approach to the structure of English is linguistically invalid. Whereas the Latin-Classical model fits an inflected language, it cannot explain an uninflected language whose structure and meaning is dependent, in large part, on word position. For example, in English, *The boy loves the girl* is differentiated from *The girl loves the boy* by moving the elements of the sentence around, since certainly a different meaning is possible in the two sentences—after all, just cause he love her don't mean she love him! However, in Latin, *Puer puellam amat* is the same as *Puellam puer amat*. Despite reversed word order, the two mean the same, since in Latin, inflectional endings, not position, are keys to word meanings.

40   Or consider the rule that prepositions are not to be used to end sentences with. In Latin, this isn't possible, since Latin prepositions are not separable from the verb. For instance, Latin *voro*, "swallow," but *devoro* for "swallow down," in the sense of "put up with." (Sir Winston Churchill must be credited with the last word on this rule. When told not to end sentences with prepositions, he quipped: "This is the kind of nonsense up with which I will not put.")

41   The Latinate-prescriptive tradition enjoyed unchallenged longevity until the early years of the twentieth century and the rise of structural grammarians. Influenced by scientific-empirical thought, structuralists approached the study of English on the premise that language was in people, not in grammar handbooks. Emphasizing the primacy of spoken language, they argued that the linguist's task is to survey the social scene, collect representative samples of language in action, and *describe*, rather than *prescribe*. A grammar should be a description of the structure and operation of a language, not a list of social etiquette do's and don'ts. By codifying observable, empirical data, the structuralists insured that their descriptions were valid. Their analyses revealed numerous disparities between grammar-book dictates and the actual language practices of Americans. Departures from Latinate rules included such "errors" as ending sentences with prepositions and using objective case after copula (*It is me* for *It is I*). In their approach to the structure of English, the structuralists contributed a grammar describing the language in terms of its *own* signals and structural cues—use of word order, determiners, intonation patterns, and so on, to signal meaning. They demonstrated incontrovertibly that the Latinate model was inapplicable to an understanding of the structure of English.

In their attempt to free speakers from outmoded strictures and   42
eighteenth-century norms, the structuralist-descriptivists induced the
new "standard English" norms from the linguistic data of actual speakers. But the twentieth-century language pacesetters were invariably
persons in upper- and middle-class positions. For example, in Charles
C. Fries's *American English Grammar* (1940), he surveyed some 3,000
letters of veterans of varying class status and arrived at his Class I standard speakers on the basis of socioeconomic indices. Thus "standard
English" became, as Fries defined it, the class dialect of the "socially
acceptable . . . those who carry on the affairs of the country." The new
standard thus didn't make thangs no better for common (and minority
culture) folk. Instead of freeing speakers and writers from petty linguistic amenities, the immediate educational application of structuralist
research was towards sociolinguistic conformity for the children whose
parents had immigrated to this country in massive numbers around the
turn of the century. (No broken English in this class, Antonio, and so
on, like that.) The melting pot has never been a reality, not even for
whites. Black poet Haki Madhubuti has said it melted and we blacks
burned. But so did a lot of other "divergent" languages and cultures, for
the immigrants' kids became ashamed of they mommas and daddies
who had sweated and toiled to bring they families to this country and
then turned round and sweated some more to send they kids to school
only to find them kids embarrassed bout them and they speech! Thus
the descriptivist standard merely involved the substitution of one elitist norm for another—the white Anglo-Saxon Protestant group standard
of America for the individualist "divinely inspired" Latinate standard
of England. The contemporary emphasis on linguistic conformity to the
dominant ethic of this new twentieth-century American aristocracy
has the same objective as the old: to make the rising plebeian outsiders
talk and thereby think and act like the ruling-class insiders.

Despite the American ideal of equal opportunity for all, the oppres-   43
sive "doctrine of correctness" still abounds. It is kept alive not only by
popular misconceptions about "standard" English and "correct"
speech, but also by persistent myths about languages in general. Perhaps one of the most prevalent myths is the notion that there are "primitive," "underdeveloped," or "inferior" languages. Another myth has
to do with the belief that in any given country, some people are speaking "*the* language" while others are merely speaking "dialect" versions of "*the* language." Still another persistent myth is that the speech
of certain persons in society is sloppy and unsystematic, while that of
others is governed by rules and regulations. Through their study and
knowledge of the various languages and cultures of the world,

linguists have put the lie to all such myths, and have arrived at a number of "linguistic universals" underlying all languages. Unfortunately much of this important work by linguists is framed in the jargon and concepts of modern linguistic science, with terminology that is confusing, technical, and often unintelligible to those outside the field of linguistics. Thus, despite linguistic truths now well over a century old, this vitally needed scientific information has not filtered down to precisely the place where it could have the greatest impact—the public school. For, as stated earlier, the public school is the main institution that continues to perpetuate myths and inaccuracies about language. In an effort to redress this situation, the following discussion of linguistic universals is offered in what I hope is clear, nontechnical language.

44   First, we should note that all languages have variations which are properly called "dialects." Now in a popular sense, the term "dialect" suggests some form of speech that is substandard or inferior, but in a scientific, linguistic sense, a dialect is simply a variation of a language. Since everybody speaks a variation of "*the* language," everybody can be said to be speaking a dialect. The only way we can apprehend "*the* language" is through listening to, recording, or reading its many variations among the people who speak it. What is popularly termed the "real" language, then, exists only in the abstract. All we can point to or observe are the specific manifestations of the "real" English language in its multiplicity of speakers, all of whom represent varying and legitimate dialects of English.

45   This linguistic principle applied to English might be represented graphically as follows:

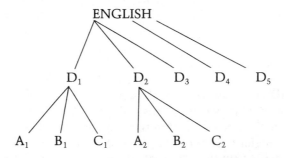

The D's in the diagram suggest the dialect groups comprising English throughout the English-speaking world—for example, Canadian English, American English, British English, and Australian English. Each of these different kinds of English has some forms of pronunciation, vocabulary, and idioms unique to the speakers in those countries. For example, in Canadian English, the *sch* of the word *schedule* is pronounced like the *sh* of *shoe*. In British English, a T.V. is a "telly." A speaker of Australian English refers to himself as an Austr*EYE*lian.

The ABC's in the diagram are used to suggest the various subgroups   *46* of a given dialect group of English. The number of dialects and subdialects varies, of course, depending on the language and the method of classification. For example, the American English dialect group might be broken down into geographical groupings representing the different regions of the United States, such as Southern American English dialect, Midwestern American English dialect, New England American English dialect, and so on. Or we might categorize American English dialects by social or ethnic groupings, such as Black English, white working-class English, upper-class Black and White English, and so forth. As with the larger groups of English speakers, each of these subgroups of American English speakers has some forms of pronunciation and idiomatic usage unique to its speakers. But I repeat: all these English dialect groups and subgroups represent varying and legitimate dialects of the English language; all the speakers can be said to be speaking the "real" English language. (As a matter of fact, one well-known linguist sigged: "Who's speaking '*the*' language and who's speaking only a dialect of '*the*' language depends on who has the army.")

The question arises: how do these different English dialect groups   *47* communicate with and understand one another? Here the modern linguistic concepts of "deep" and "surface" structure can help us.

All languages may be said to consist of deep and surface structures.   *48* The notion of deep structure is an abstract, intuitive concept that may be said to be like your gut-level understanding of what somebody says, and it is based on your understanding and knowledge of your native language. Though abstract, deep structure is where the true meaning of a given language resides. Through ordered linguistic rules, deep structures of a language are transformed into surface structures. These are the concrete manifestations of the deep structure, that is, what *actually* gets expressed in speech or writing. Although each speaker of a language has his or her unique way of talking, the speakers all share common deep structures; otherwise, they could not understand one another, and there would be no communication. For example, one American English speaker might say, *John hit the ball*. Another might say, *The ball was hit by John*. In the deep structure of English, these two sentences are really the same; thus despite being expressed in different ways, their meaning is clear to speakers of English. Similarly, one speaker might say, *He do know it*. And another might say, *He does know it.* Again, both statements are the same in the deep structure, and the two different versions are simply two ways of saying the same thing.

49   Shared deep structure is what helps us to understand one another even when surface structure doesn't indicate precisely what people mean. For instance, check out the following sentence, which was spoken by a highly educated American English speaker:

> He told her he was going to Greece—which he went.

Or consider the following sentence, written by another highly educated American English speaker:

> Dr. John Jones has been selected by President Smith to serve on the Advisory Committee to recommend a Dean for the College of Liberal Arts as a replacement for Clarence Johnson.

In both examples, despite the fact that the surface structure is confusingly worded, the statements are linguistically intelligible and we can understand the meaning because we share the deep structure of the speaker and writer.

50   Shared deep structures help in still other instances in communication. One example is the notion of "understood" meanings, as in the sentence: *Look out!* The listener is supposed to understand that the speaker means *You look out!* Such sentences are possible in American English because of shared deep structure. Another example concerns differences in vocabulary and pronunciation. For instance, in Boston's prestigious Beacon Hill area, one hears *pahk the cah.* In Grosse Pointe, home-of-Henry-Ford, Michigan, it's *park the car.* Depending on the region of the country, carbonated beverages are *soda, tonic, soda pop,* or *pop.* In southern Indiana and Ohio you say *he took sick.* In California and the Midwest you say *he got sick.* Despite such differences in surface structures, all the speakers of these different states can understand one another, all are speaking the English language, and they can all communicate because the various dialects have the same source of meaning: English deep structure.

51   Since all languages consist of dialect variations, and since the "real" language is an abstraction, one may well ask: where does the notion of a national standard language come from? Although many people speak of the standard dialect in hallowed tones, there are *no* national standard languages which are decreed from on high. Rather, one particular dialect of a language may get to be elevated over other variations due to an arbitrary decision by the speakers of that language. Well, not truly "arbitrary," since the dialect that becomes the standard is generally the

same dialect spoken by those with political and economic power. This, for instance, was the case with the many British dialects of Old and Middle English. In the years between 1150 and 1500 A.D., at least five different English dialects were spoken in the British Isles: Northern, West Midland, East Midland, Southern and Kentish. As mentioned earlier, by the eighteenth century, London had emerged as the commercial center of Britain, and thus, the dialect spoken there—a citified version of East Midland—evolved as the British national standard. It is that dialect which is the basis of present-day Received Standard British, that is, the British English speech of the universities of the Crown and Parliament, of the BBC radio and television commentators, and of the "refined gentry" of England. In similar fashion, what has evolved as today's national standard American English dialect is the dialect of those Americans of economic and political power, namely the white, Anglo-Saxon, Protestant middle and upper classes.

Another important linguistic universal is the principle that every language is systematic and represents rule-governed behavior on the part of its speakers. Since dialects are the real, concrete reflection of the abstract language, it obviously follows that all dialect variations represent rules and patterned regularities of speakers. Related to this principle is the fact that all speakers, barring those with physiological defects, will acquire their native language and intuitive competence in its underlying principles without any formal, programmatic kind of instruction. Thus in America, small children quickly learn to go from "sentences" like "up" to "Pick me up." They learn principles of English word order like *The book is here*, not *Is here book the*. In Black America, speakers learn how to manipulate the rules for *be/non-be* without anybody telling them that "*be* is to express habitual conditions." (Because of these universal language behavior patterns, one school of modern linguists contends that language is a biological, creative human act, universally separating man from other animals.) 52

All native speakers of a language have an underlying competence in the forms of their language and thus can produce sentences they've never said before as well as understand those they've never heard before. Of course, we don't always perform at our maximum competence—not in any phase of life really, whether speech-making, music-making, or, for that matter, love-making. Still the potential ability is there, though oftentimes the linguistic computer of the mind is working faster than that of the mouth, as demonstrated in the sentences quoted earlier by those very highly educated and fluent speakers of American English. This principle is true for all speakers, regardless of how "quaint," "sloppy," "unpleasant"—or even "colored"—their speech sounds to someone else's ear. 53

54   Finally, a language reflects a people's culture and their world view, and thus each group's language is suited to the needs and habits of its users. The Eskimos have several words for and make verbal distinctions about various kinds of snow, whereas for English-speaking Americans, snow is snow. Obviously this does not make American English a "primitive" language—rather it's one in which the experience of snow is not an important reality. The Hopi Indians in the southwestern part of the United States are said to have a "timeless" language because Hopi verbs are not concerned with the time of any action (the tense), only with its truth or validity. And in some cultures, talking is not even valued at all: the Paliyans of South India communicate very little at all times and become almost silent by the age of forty—in their world, people who are verbal and communicative are regarded as abnormal and often as offensive. By the same token, despite the linguistic chauvinism of the literate West, oral and written language are of similar value and function to a culture, neither taking precedence over the other. Since all languages change, all are modified and modifiable according to the dictates, customs, and habits of their users; American English, for example, has added a multiplicity of words germane to the space age, such as "A-O.K."

55   Despite these important linguistic universals, studies of language attitudes show that people continue to make judgments—usually erroneous—about others, purely on the basis of their speech. As an example, Canadian researchers Lambert and Tucker compared personality ratings of various American speakers. Black and white college students were asked to listen to voices on tape and to rank the speakers on the basis of intelligence, friendliness, faith in God, honesty, determination, and a whole host of other terms that Lambert and Tucker found people using to stereotype and categorize others. The speech of network newscasters was ranked higher than that of college-educated blacks or whites. That is, despite the fact that there is no correlation between one's style of speech and their intelligence or honesty, these newscasters were considered to be more friendly, intelligent, and honest simply because of the way they spoke! As to the speakers ranked the lowest, the black students judged the educated white Southern speakers least favorably, and the white students ranked the Southern black college student speakers the lowest. (In an earlier study, Lambert and Tucker found that speakers of Canadian English were ranked higher than the SAME voices speaking Canadian French, by both French and English Canadians—a striking demonstration of the correlation between language and politics.)

56   What is so deep about this matter of language attitudes is the unspoken rule especially pronounced among the power-holders, that

those folks "over there" must do as I *say*, not necessarily as I *do*. Labov asked middle-class New Yorkers to rank the employability of other New Yorkers on the basis of speech samples. For any speaker they rejected, they were asked to indicate the feature of that person's speech that would cause him or her to get rejected. Yeah, y'all way ahead of me...Cause what Labov found was that they rejected the speaker for using forms of speech that they themselves used!

In a similar study, Robert Pooley surveyed the language of public   57
school English teachers and college English professors speaking in quasi-formal situations, that is, during class sessions and in faculty meetings conducted by parliamentary procedure. Pooley found the English teachers and profs using many of the same forms of speech that they were attempting to drill their students out of in classroom composition and grammar assignments! Yeah, dig that.

An experience of mine brought out this attitude in stark clarity. I had   58
approached the head of research at a large urban university where I was on the faculty. I was trying to solicit support for a study of attitudes of potential employers toward black speech. This white research man, in a salary range well above $30,000, contended that such a study would only prove the obvious since everybody knew that you had to speak the King's English to get ahead in America. With my research proposal thus dismissed, I started to leave. As I did so, the research division head turned to his assistant and said, "Listen, can you stay a few minutes? You and me have some work to do." Now, me bein me, I *had* to correct my man's "bad grammar." I said, "Hey, watch yo dialect—it's you and *I* have some some work to do." He turned fifty shades o' red, and I split. Naturally, that siggin of mine had shonuff blowed the possibility of me gittin any grant money!

As America completes the Bicentennial and looks forward to moving   59
toward the tricentennial, we find contemporary linguistic realities not much different from those of old. The "national mania for correctness" is, after all, a useful tool. The speech of blacks, the poor, and other powerless groups is used as a weapon to deny them access to full participation in the society. Teachers harp on the "bad" English of their students; potential employees are denied jobs because they don't talk "right"; future college graduates become force-outs because they write in "nonstandard" English. Yet what is "nonstandard" English is simply the language of "nonstandard" people. Their linguistic usage deviates from the collective dialect of the dominant culture—nothing more, as simple and yet as complex as that. For your language and the dialect in which it is actualized was acquired at around age two, pretty firmly fixed by about age five or six, and by adolescence your basic speech patterns have become a well-ingrained habit. Nearly impossible to change

(except maybe over inordinately long periods of time—and then you have to be willing to surrender whole chunks of your identity to do so). What better weapon, then, with which to keep the outsiders out than the obstacle of speech?

60   From the viewpoint of Black Americans, it seems that White America's use of black speech as an economic impediment is, on the one hand, a new form of racism, a way to hinder blacks from gittin it on in America, even if they acquire the education and skills; and on the other, a manifestation of White America's class bias. As James Baldwin has said, America is a country where everybody has status, and in a place where everybody has status, it is possible that *nobody* has status. Thus Americans in general, lacking a fixed place in the society, don't know where they be in terms of social class and personal identity. But, as Baldwin concludes, with nigguhs round, at least they always knows where the bottom bees.

Questions and Activities

▶ *COMPREHENSION QUESTIONS*

1. Who is Langston Hughes (paragraph 2)? Go to the reference section of a library and look up the basic facts about his life, what he accomplished, and a general description of the period in which he lived. Does this information help to explain why Smitherman chose Hughes's dialogue to open her essay?
2. Explain, in your own language, 'the "push-pull" dynamic in Black American history' (paragraph 5). How do the Joyce and Simple characters of the opening dialogue represent that general dynamic?
3. Why was Claude Brown "ashamed of his parents when they went to juvenile court" (paragraph 12)? What social conditions might have led to Brown's feelings about his parents? Also, what do Brown's feelings about his parents in that situation tell you about his own sense of identity? Do you think he had a positive self-image?
4. Why does Smitherman feel that the new black poetry will help blacks solve the problem of finding cultural identity through their language?
5. Why do all native speakers of a language have an "underlying competence in the forms of their language" (paragraph 53)? How should this competence affect our attitudes toward speakers of other dialects?

6. Why does Smitherman use black dialect in some places in her essay? What effect does that dialect have on you as you read? Does its use confuse or clarify her points? Why do you respond as you do to her use of dialect?

7. Describe, as specifically as you can, Smitherman's purpose in writing this essay. In what ways does she hope her readers will change their attitudes toward language? Define one of those hoped-for changes, and explain whether or not she has succeeded in her purpose in your case. How does the organization of this essay help Smitherman develop her purpose?

8. Analyze the function of one of the quotations in this essay. Is Smitherman using it as a negative or positive example concerning attitudes toward language?

▶ *THEME QUESTIONS*

9. Is Smitherman arguing that the way people speak should or should not play a major role in how others define them? Point out examples in the essay that support your answer. Is Smitherman suggesting that blacks should use dialect at all times and refuse to use standard written English? Or is she suggesting that blacks (or any other group of people) should respect their dialects *and* be able to use standard written English?

10. What happens, according to Smitherman, when someone looks down on his or her own dialect and speech patterns? What happens to such a person's self-image, or identity as an individual and social being? What happens to a person's attitude toward the culture from which he or she came if he or she rejects that culture's way of speaking? Why might a negative attitude toward the language of one's social group affect an individual's identity?

▶ *LEARNING ACTIVITIES*

11. Tape-record the conversation of a friend, relative, or acquaintance. Keep your tape recorder hidden as you record, although your subject should know he or she is being recorded. Listen to the tape carefully, making notes of what you think are good examples of your subject's personal manner of speaking. Wait until your subject has become immersed in the conversation before you begin to take note of specific speech patterns. Organize your examples under categories, such as words, sayings, grammar usages, slang, personal idioms, and dialect usages; then use your categories to write a

sketch about your subject's speaking habits. Present your sketch to your subject and discuss it with him or her.

12. Listen carefully to the speech during discussion sessions in one of your classes. Take notes, recording exact phrases and bits of dialogue. Then pick one person in this class as your subject and write a short paper characterizing that person's speech—his or her dialect, uses of slang or formal diction, physical gestures and action while speaking. Close your essay by making a generalization about the effect the person's speech has on other people in the class.

13. Listen closely to the language of a newscaster on network television. Does it seem that this newscaster is studiously avoiding any usages of dialect? What signs of dialect are most obviously missing?

14. Write down what someone says who is actively engaged in an interesting conversation. Use a tape recorder if you have access to one. Compare the transcription you create with a piece of published or polished writing—a newspaper article, an essay from this book, a final draft of another student's paper. What differences do you observe? Is the sample of speech less correct and more repetitious than the edited piece of writing? Is the piece of writing lacking some of the color and spontaneity of the transcribed speech?

A Consumer's Guide to Social Offenses

STUART BERG FLEXNER

Stuart Berg Flexner has worked as an editor, bookseller, and publisher. Since 1949, he has made his living by studying everyday uses of the American language. His most well-known and famous book, the *Dictionary of American Slang* (1960), is a scholarly yet humorous study of the origins of American slang. Flexner's accounts of word derivations often simultaneously provide fascinating social history. His other books are also very entertaining. *I Hear America Talking: An Illustrated History of American Words and Phrases* (1977) and *Listening to America: An Illustrated History of Words and Phrases from Our Lively and Splendid Past* (1982) provide a fascinating record of the voices of American people from all occupations, social levels, and periods of history. Flexner has also worked on the editing of the authoritative *Random House Dictionary of the English Language.*

In the following excerpt from *Listening to America,* Flexner traces the commercial origins of many of the technical-sounding words advertisers use to talk about personal hygiene, common ailments, or "a merely socially embarrassing condition." As you read, note Flexner's careful combination of historical facts about word origins with interpretation of the social significance of those facts. These historical and etymological accounts should convince you that much of the "science" that is heard and seen on television and in magazines is not science at all. What it is is pseudoscience—technical-sounding language used to describe simple bodily functions. The deodorant ad that uses pseudoscientific language to support the claim that the product produces drier underarms is actually using language to shape—in this case, *distort*—reality.

Ask yourself, as you read, what point underlies Flexner's description and analysis of technical language in advertising:

1. Can you think of more recent examples where pseudoscientific words appear in advertising for personal hygiene products? Do you think Flexner believes that such products should be used by most people, or does he believe that the advertisers are simply trying to make consumers feel they need these products to achieve social acceptance?

2. Do you use any personal hygiene products whose advertisements employ technical-sounding language? Do you think men or women use such products more?
3. What do you think is Flexner's purpose in writing this essay? Does he hope to persuade, inform, or explain? Does his style of writing suggest his intention?

▶ ─────────────────────

1   B.O., athlete's foot, and halitosis are unknown to most of the world outside the United States—not because other people don't suffer from them but because the terms have been coined or popularized here by advertising men. Since our 1840s patent medicine men, American advertisers have used scare tactics to sell their wares. When there hasn't been a well-known disease their products could cure they have often invented one or made a merely socially embarrassing condition sound like a dread disease by giving it a name.

2   In 1895, C. W. Post introduced his all-grain brew Postum, claiming not only that it made "red blood" but that it cured *coffee nerves*, a malady then unknown both to doctors and to the general public, but which we have been aware of ever since. Thus the advertisement for the cure gave birth to the term, if not the ailment.

3   *Dandruff* (1545 in English, akin to Old Norse *hurf*, scab, scurf) and *psoriasis* (1684 in English from the Greek *psōriasis*, to have the itch) are old words and ailments that have been made part of the popular vocabulary by the advertising of preparations to cure them. *Ringworm* (an English word of about 1425) of the foot is also a real ailment though it was seldom mentioned until it was widely called *athlete's foot* (1928) when Absorbine Jr. first advertised itself as a remedy for it. More recently, a manufacturer of a preparation to relieve itching in the groin area has popularized the term *jock strap itch* (mid 1970s, soon shortened by the public to *jock itch*) for this ailment which, now that it has a pithy, masculine name, is also talked about more than before.

4   *Halitosis* (an 1874 English word, from Latin *helitus*, breath, plus *-osis*, condition, especially a pathological condition) was a little-known medical word referring to specific breath odors that doctors could use to diagnose patients' diseases until Listerine mouthwash ads claimed it fought "insidious *halitosis*" and defined it as bad breath in general, beginning in 1921 (for the first ten years Listerine ads followed the word *halitosis* with the explanation "bad breath" or "unpleasant breath" in parentheses, knowing full well that most people had never heard of the word before).

The worst social offense, however, was not scratching one's head, el- 5
bows, feet, or groin, or even having bad breath, but underarm odor,
caused by underarm perspiration—and this was indeed offensive and
widespread before the routine daily shower and home washing machine. By clogging the pores, masking the odor, or combining with the
perspiration, various preparations could eliminate this offense. Such
preparations became available and were widely advertised in the 1920s,
the advertisements then mainly being aimed at women, both because
sleeveless dresses were the style, making the odor more obvious, and
because many men thought their own odor was somehow manly. Thus
as early as 1924 liquid Odorono was advertised as a "perspiration
corrective"—for both the underarms and the feet—whose protection
could last for days. Its ads popularized a blunt new term, saying that
when Odorono was used under the arms it would prevent *underarm
odor*. Similar liquids and creams joined the war against underarm odor
and underarm perspiration stains on clothing so that during the 1930s
both women and men were removing the underarm *shields* they had
added to their dresses and suits to absorb perspiration and using an *underarm deodorant*, often a cream such as Mum, whose early advertising
slogan was the punning *Mum's the word*. Not until the 1960s did
manufacturers call the all-too-vivid yet somewhat passive sounding *underarm deodorant* by the more active, scientific sounding name *anti-
perspirant*, and now that almost everyone took daily showers, deemphasized underarm odor in favor of emphasizing that the product
stopped *wetness*, a new euphemism for underarm clothing stains.

The hallmark of scare ads against underarm and other body perspira- 6
tion odors, however, was Lifebuoy Health Soap's campaign. In 1933,
millions of Americans began to laugh at and use the abbreviation *B.O.*
to mean *body odor*, as popularized by the advertising of this orange-
colored, peculiar-smelling (the ads said it had a "crisp odor"), oddly
shaped bathsoap. Soon the two-note foghorn warning B_O was known to
everyone through radio ads—and Lifebuoy was the best-selling soap in
America. By 1935, *body odor* was such an accepted term that Lux laundry soap was advertising that women should "Lux underthings after
each wearing to wash away stale body odors."

With the success of *halitosis* and *body odor*, modern advertising 7
continued to coin and popularize terms for both real and imaginary ailments and embarrassing conditions. In the 1930s and 40s there were ads
for products which would help prevent everything from *irregularity* (a
euphemism for constipation) to *pink toothbrush* (caused by bleeding
gums), followed by ads for products that could prevent that horror of
horrors *tattletale gray* (left on laundry from using too mild a laundry
soap), *dishpan hands* (in general use by 1944, red hands from using too

strong a dishwashing soap), *tired blood* (from not having enough iron in one's diet), and, echoing the earlier "tattletale gray," *ring around the collar* (mid 1970s, from not using a liquid detergent that removed collar grime from shirts in a home washing machine).

8   If there was any doubt after the 1920s, 30s, and 40s that advertising could popularize a term, the history of *chlorophyll* set it to rest. Only scientists had heard of *chlorophyll* (from the Greek *chlor/chloro*, light green, greenish yellow, plus *-phyll/phyllo*, leaf), the green coloring matter in plants essential for photosynthesis, until the late 1940s, when the substance was first claimed to be able to "fight unwanted odors." Soon there were Nullo pills, advertised as a product that "kills body odors and bad breath...Safe as a lettuce leaf...contains nature's chlorophyll." Next came the 1951 ads for the lozengelike Clorets "makes breath kissing sweet...contains chlorophyll," and by 1952 a torrent of products advertising chlorophyll as their special ingredient, including at least 30 tablets and lozenges sold as breath sweeteners, 11 toothpastes and tooth powders, 9 chewing gums, 8 brands of dogfood, 4 mouthwashes (for humans), and one brand of cigarette. The chlorophyll fad began to fade the following year, though some of the products are still with us and the word has become a part of the general vocabulary, now found in all desk dictionaries and known to almost every school child from basic science classes.

Questions and Activities

▶ COMPREHENSION QUESTIONS

1. What is meant in paragraph 2 by "coffee nerves," a phrase from an advertisement written in 1895? In what ways have we become more aware of coffee nerves since 1895? Was our increased awareness of this "ailment" the result of the advertiser's coinage of the new term, or was it caused by an increased consumption of coffee, creating nervous reactions?

2. Look up the word "chlorophyll" in a scientific dictionary. How is the scientific definition different from the meaning attached to this word in advertisements? Does this difference support Flexner's idea about media manipulation through the use of pseudoscientific language? How might the use of pseudoscientific language lead to consumers developing obsessions with disease and body malfunctions? How might these obsessions be exploited by advertisers to sell products?

► *QUESTIONS OF RHETORICAL PURPOSE AND STRATEGY*

3. What is Flexner's purpose in writing this piece? Is he trying to persuade readers not to use the products he describes? Or is his purpose to show his readers how language can shape their sense of their physical and social needs?
4. Describe Flexner's voice. Does he sound like a language scientist, a friendly expert, or an irate consumer? Refer to specific examples of his vocabulary and sentence structure to support your answer.

► *THEME QUESTIONS*

5. Explain the moral implications of Flexner's assertion about advertisers: "When there hasn't been a well-known disease their products could cure they have often invented one or made a merely socially embarrassing condition sound like a dread disease by giving it a name" (paragraph 1). How far should advertisers be allowed to go in making consumers feel a need for their products? Would better education for consumers alleviate the problem of media manipulation?
6. Consider the consumers toward whom the advertisements that Flexner describes in this piece are directed. How might their identities have been affected by these advertisements? Do you think that advertisements such as these might make people overly concerned with how others perceive their bodies? What might be the good and bad effects of such self-consciousness?
7. How have women been stereotyped in some advertisements for personal hygiene products? What bodily obsessions have women been encouraged by these advertisements to develop? Do you think that women's images are permanently affected by these advertisements?

► *LEARNING ACTIVITIES*

8. Look through some copies of magazines and newspapers from the 1920s or 1930s. Can you find other examples of the types of advertisements that Flexner describes in this piece? Bring one such advertisement to class and explain how it is similar to and/or different from one of Flexner's examples.
9. Find a contemporary advertisement that does the same thing Flexner's examples do. Write a brief explanation of how your current example fits into one of Flexner's categories, how it corresponds to one of Flexner's examples, and how it might affect consumers in a similar way. Be sure to comment on both the text and pictures used in the advertisement.

Politics and the American Language

ARTHUR SCHLESINGER, JR.

Arthur Schlesinger, Jr. has had a distinguished career as historian, teacher, political advisor, scholarly writer, and political and social analyst. He has written speeches for five presidents or presidential candidates. He was President John F. Kennedy's special assistant from 1960 to 1963 and served as Democratic presidential nominee Adlai Stevenson's advisor in the elections of 1952 and 1956. He has always supported liberal politics: he had a major influence on the "New Frontier" programs of John F. Kennedy and the "Great Society" programs of Lyndon Johnson in the 1960s. Through this influence Schlesinger was able to make a significant contribution to the Peace Corps, Medicare and Medicaid, and the Civil Rights Act.

Many experts have praised his three-volume study *The Age of Roosevelt* (1957–1960) as the best and most complete treatment of New Deal politics. Schlesinger won both a National Book Award and a Pulitzer Prize for the biography *A Thousand Days* (1966), his personal account of decision making during John F. Kennedy's administration. He also won a Pulitzer Prize in history for *The Age of Jackson* (1946) and a National Book Award for *Robert Kennedy and His Times* (1979). He has published more than thirty nonfiction books and numerous magazine and journal articles on history and politics.

All of Schlesinger's writing combines his eye for pointed, accurate detail with his driving sense of social and political purpose. "Politics and the American Language," first published in the *American Scholar,* addresses its audience forthrightly about what Schlesinger sees as the deterioration of American language. When language deteriorates, Schlesinger argues, social and political life deteriorates along with it because citizens can no longer distinguish truth from falsehood or honest promise from corrupt slogan. Schlesinger is careful to back his moral criticism with historical fact, referring to *The Federalist Papers* (1785–1790), written shortly after the Revolution, as the standard against which American political writing should be judged.

Above all other virtues, Schlesinger values a writer's ability to say what he or she means in plain language that does not oversimplify reality. He admires the elegance of directness and abhors the tendency to dress up ideas in overly technical or formal language. His exemplars for this kind of clear, direct prose are writers such as Ralph Waldo Emerson in the nineteenth century and George Orwell in the twentieth. Both of these writers, Schlesinger thinks, knew how to make complex ideas understandable in simple language, and both often criticized writers who lacked these virtues. Thus, they helped to clean up the language pollution around them.

Think about Schlesinger's position on the need for a policing of our language as you read:

1. Do you find Schlesinger's voice persuasive? Is he sufficiently clear to be convincing? Does his desire to persuade ever get in the way of his handling of facts or his objectivity?
2. Does his established position as a spokesperson for liberal causes ever seem to bias his discussion of the deterioration of the American language?
3. Can you think of current examples when politicians intentionally confused citizens by the use of vague or overcomplicated language? What were these politicians hiding when they used this language, or were they simply confused?

▶ ——————————————————

> *In our time, political speech and writing are largely the defense of the indefensible.*
>
> —George Orwell

It takes a certain fortitude to pretend to amend Orwell on this   *1*
subject. But "Politics and the English Language"—which I herewith incorporate by reference—was written more than a generation ago. In the years since, the process of semantic collapse has gathered speed, verified all of Orwell's expectations, and added new apprehensions for a new age. Americans in particular have found this a painful period of self-recognition. In 1946 we comfortably supposed that Orwell was talking about other people—Nazis and Stalinists, bureaucrats and sociologists, Professor Lancelot Hogben and Professor Harold Laski.* Now recent history has obliged us to extend his dispiriting analysis to ourselves.

Vietnam and Watergate: these horrors will trouble the rest of our   *2*
lives. But they are not, I suppose, unmitigated horrors. "Every act rewards itself," said Emerson. As Vietnam instructed us, at terrible cost,

*Lancelot Hogben and Harold Laski were writers whose writing was criticized by George Orwell in a famous essay, "Politics and the English Language," published in 1946.

in the limit of our wisdom and power in foreign affairs, so Watergate instructed us, at considerably less cost, in the limits of wisdom and power in the presidency. It reminded us of the urgent need to restore the original balance of the Constitution—the balance between presidential power and presidential accountability. In doing this, it has, among other things, brought back into public consciousness the great documents under which the American government was organized.

3   The Constitution, the debates of the Constitutional Convention, *The Federalist Papers*—how many of us read them with sustained attention in earlier years? A few eccentrics like Justice Black and Senator Ervin pored over them with devotion. The rest of us regarded them, beyond an occasional invocation of the Bill of Rights or the Fourteenth Amendment, as documents of essentially historical interest and left them undisturbed on the shelf. Then, under the goad first of Vietnam and then of Watergate, legislators, editors, columnists, even political scientists and historians—everyone, it would seem, except for presidential lawyers—began turning the dusty pages in order to find out what Madison said in the convention about the war-making power or how Hamilton defined the grounds for impeachment in the sixty-fifth *Federalist*. Vietnam and Watergate are hardly to be compared. One is high tragedy, the other low, if black, comedy. But between them they have given the American people a spectacular reeducation in the fundamentals of our constitutional order.

4   One cannot doubt that this experience will have abiding political significance. The effect of Vietnam in exorcising our illusions and chastening our ambitions in foreign affairs has long been manifest. Now we begin to see the effect of Watergate in raising the standards of our politics. But I am less concerned initially with the political than with the literary consequences of this return to our constitutional womb. For, in addition to their exceptional qualities of insight and judgment, the historic documents must impress us by the extraordinary distinction of their language.

5   This was the age of the Enlightenment in America. The cooling breeze of reason tempered the hot work of composition and argument. The result was the language of the Founding Fathers—lucid, measured, and felicitous prose, marked by Augustan virtues of harmony, balance, and elegance. People not only wrote this noble language. They also read it. The essays in defense of the Constitution signed Publius appeared week after week in the New York press during the winter of 1787–88; and the demand was so great that the first thirty-six Federalist papers were published in book form while the rest were still coming out in the papers. One can only marvel at the sophistication of an audience that consumed and relished pieces so closely reasoned, so thoughtful and an-

alytical. To compare *The Federalist Papers* with their equivalents in the press of our own day—say, with the contributions to the Op Ed page of the *New York Times*—is to annotate the decay of political discourse in America.

No doubt the birth of a nation is a stimulus to lofty utterance. The Founding Fathers had a profound conviction of historical responsibility. "The people of this country, by their conduct and example," Madison wrote in *The Federalist*, "will decide the important question, whether societies of men are really capable or not of establishing good government from reflection and choice, or whether they are forever destined to depend for their political constitutions on accident and force." The substitution of reflection and choice for accident and force proposed a revolution in the history of government; and the authors of *The Federalist* were passionate exemplars of the politics of reason.

The Founding Fathers lived, moreover, in an age when politicians could say in public more or less what they believed in private. If their view of human nature was realistic rather than sentimental, they were not obliged to pretend otherwise. *The Federalist*, for example, is a work notably free of false notes. It must not be supposed, however, that even this great generation was immune to temptation. When the Founding Fathers turned to speak of and to the largest interest in a primarily agricultural nation, they changed their tone and relaxed their standards. Those who lived on the soil, Jefferson could inanely write, were "the chosen people of God... whose breasts He has made His peculiar deposit for substantial and genuine virtue." Such lapses from realism defined one of the problems of American political discourse. For, as society grew more diversified, new interests claimed their place in the sun; and each in time had to be courted and flattered as the Jeffersonians had courted and flattered the agriculturists. The desire for success at the polls thus sentimentalized and cheapened the language of politics.

And politics was only an aspect of a deeper problem. Society as a whole was taking forms that warred against clarity of thought and integrity of language. "A man's power to connect his thought with its proper symbol, and so to utter it," said Emerson, "depends on the simplicity of his character, that is, upon his love of truth, and his desire to communicate it without loss. The corruption of man is followed by the corruption of language. When simplicity of character and the sovereignty of ideas is broken up by the prevalence of secondary desires, the desire of riches, of pleasure, of power, and of praise... words are perverted to stand for things which are not."

"The prevalence of secondary desires," the desire of riches, pleasure, power, and praise—this growing social complexity began to divert the function of words from expression to gratification. No one observed the impact of a mobile and egalitarian society on language more acutely than Tocqueville.* Democracy, he argued, inculcated a positive preference for ambiguity and a dangerous addiction to the inflated style. "An abstract term," Tocqueville wrote, "is like a box with a false bottom; you may put in what you please, and take them out again without being observed." So words, divorced from objects, became instruments less of communication than of deception. Unscrupulous orators stood abstractions on their head and transmuted them into their opposites, aiming to please one faction by the sound and the contending faction by the meaning. They did not always succeed. "The word *liberty* in the mouth of Webster," Emerson wrote with contempt after the Compromise of 1850, "sounds like the word *love* in the mouth of a courtezan." Watching Henry Kissinger babbling about his honor at his famous Salzburg press conference, one was irresistibly reminded of another of Emerson's nonchalant observations: "The louder he talked of his honor, the faster we counted our spoons."

10   Other developments hastened the spreading dissociation of words from meaning, of language from reality. The rise of mass communications, the growth of large organizations and novel technologies, the invention of advertising and public relations, the professionalization of education—all contributed to linguistic pollution, upsetting the ecological balance between words and their environment. In our own time the purity of language is under unrelenting attack from every side—from professors as well as from politicians, from newspapermen as well as from advertising men, from men of the cloth as well as from men of the sword, and not least from those indulgent compilers of modern dictionaries who propound the suicidal thesis that all usages are equal and all correct.

11   A living language can never be stabilized, but a serious language can never cut words altogether adrift from meanings. The alchemy that changes words into their opposites has never had more adept practitioners than it has today. We used to object when the Communists described dictatorships as "people's democracies" or North Korean aggression as the act of a "peace-loving" nation. But we are no slouches ourselves in the art of verbal metamorphosis. There was often not much that was "free" about many of the states that made up what we used to call, sometimes with capital letters, the Free World; as there is, alas, very often little that is gay about many of those who seek these days to kidnap that sparkling word for specialized use. Social fluidity,

*Alexis de Tocqueville (1805–1859) was a French politician, traveler, and historian whose writings on American life greatly influenced later interpretations of the culture. His two-volume study, *Democracy in America* (1835), remains a classic.

moral pretension, political and literary demagoguery, corporate and academic bureaucratization, and a false conception of democracy are leading us into semantic chaos. We owe to Vietnam and Watergate a belated recognition of the fact that we are in linguistic as well as political crisis and that the two may be organically connected. As Emerson said, "We infer the spirit of the nation in great measure from the language."

For words are not neutral instruments, pulled indifferently out of a   *12* jumbled tool kit. "Language," wrote Coleridge, "is the armoury of the human mind; and at once contains the trophies of its past, and the weapons of its future conquests."* Language colors and penetrates the depths of our consciousness. It is the medium that dominates perceptions, organizes categories of thought, shapes the development of ideas, and incorporates a philosophy of existence. Every political movement generates its own language-field; every language-field legitimizes one set of motives, values, and ideals and banishes the rest. The language-field of the Founding Fathers directed the American consciousness toward one constellation of standards and purposes. The language-field of Vietnam and Watergate has tried to direct the national consciousness toward very different goals. Politics in basic aspects is a symbolic and therefore a linguistic phenomenon.

We began to realize this in the days of the Indochina War. In the mid-   *13* dle 1960s Americans found themselves systematically staving off reality by allowing a horrid military-bureaucratic patois to protect our sensibilities from the ghastly things we were doing in Indochina. The official patter about "attrition," "pacification," "defoliation," "body counts," "progressive squeeze-and-talk," sterilized the frightful reality of napalm and My Lai. This was the period when television began to provide a sharper access to reality, and Marshall McLuhan had his day in court.

But the military-bureaucratic jargon could be blamed on generals,   *14* who, as General Eisenhower reminded us at every press conference, habitually speak in a dialect of their own. What we had not perhaps fully realized before Watergate was the utter debasement of language in the mouths of our recent civilian leaders. How our leaders really talk is not, of course, easy to discover, since their public appearances are often veiled behind speeches written by others. I know that President Kennedy spoke lucidly, wittily and economically in private. President Johnson spoke with force and often in pungent and inventive frontier idiom. President Nixon's fascinating contribution to oral history suggests, however, a recent and marked decline in the quality of presiden-

---

*Samuel Taylor Coleridge (1772–1834) was one of the most influential and widely read thinkers and writers of the British Romantic period (1790–1830).

tial table talk. "A man cannot speak," said Emerson, "but he judges himself."

15   Groping to describe that degenerate mélange of military, public relations and locker-room jargon spoken in the Nixon White House, Richard N. Goodwin aptly wrote of "the bureaucratization of the criminal class." It was as if the Godfather spoke in the phrases of the secretary of health, education and welfare. When one read of "stroking sessions," of "running out of the bottom line," of "toughing it out," of going down "the hang-out road," or "how do you handle that PR-wise," one felt that there should be one more impeachable offense; and that is verbicide. But what was worse than the massacre of language, which after all displayed a certain low ingenuity, was the manipulation of meaning. The presidential speech preceding the release of the expurgated transcripts was syntactically correct enough. But it proclaimed in tones of ringing sincerity that the transcripts showed exactly the opposite of what in fact the transcripts did show. "He unveils a swamp," as the *New Yorker* well put it, "and instructs us to see a garden of flowers." In the Nixon White House, language not only fled the reality principle but became the servant of nightmare.

16   "The use of words," wrote Madison in the thirty-seventh *Federalist*, "is to express ideas. Perspicuity, therefore, requires not only that the ideas should be distinctly formed, but that they should be expressed by words distinctly and exclusively appropriate to them." Madison was under no illusion that this condition of semantic beatitude was easy to attain. "No language is so copious," he continued, "as to supply words and phrases for every complex idea, or so correct as not to include many equivocally denoting different ideas. . . . When the Almighty himself condescends to address mankind in their own language, his meaning, luminous as it must be, is rendered dim and doubtful by the cloudy medium through which it is communicated." Nevertheless, Madison and his generation thought the quest for precision worth the effort. It is an entertaining but morbid speculation to wonder what the Founding Fathers, returning to inspect the Republic on the eve of the two-hundredth anniversary of the independence they fought so hard to achieve, would make of the White House tapes.

17   The degradation of political discourse in America is bound to raise a disturbing question. May it be, as Tocqueville seemed to think, that such deterioration is inherent in democracy? Does the compulsion to win riches, pleasure, power, and praise in a fluid and competitive society make the perversion of meaning and the debasement of language inevitable? One can certainly see specific American and democratic traits that have promoted linguistic decay. But a moment's reflection suggests that the process is by no means confined to the United States nor

to democracies. Language degenerates a good deal more rapidly and thoroughly in communist and fascist states. For the control of language is a necessary step toward the control of minds, as Orwell made so brilliantly clear in *1984*. Nowhere is meaning more ruthlessly manipulated, nowhere is language more stereotyped, mechanical, implacably banal, and systematically false, nowhere is it more purged of personal nuance and human inflection, than in Russia and China. In democracies the assault on language is piecemeal, sporadic, and unorganized. And democracy has above all the decisive advantage that the preservation of intellectual freedom creates the opportunity for counterattack. Democracy always has the chance to redeem its language. This may be an essential step toward the redemption of its politics.

One must add that it is idle to expect perfection in political discourse. The problem of politics in a democracy is to win broad consent for measures of national policy. The winning of consent often requires the bringing together of disparate groups with diverging interests. This inescapably involves a certain oracularity of expression. One remembers de Gaulle before the crowd in Algeria, when the *pieds-noirs** chanted that Algeria belonged to France, replying solemnly, "Je vous comprends, mes camarades"†—hardly a forthright expression of his determination to set Algeria free. Besides, oracularity may often be justified since no one can be all that sure about the future. The Founding Fathers understood this, which is why the Constitution is in many respects a document of calculated omission and masterful ambiguity whose "real" meaning—that is, what it would mean in practice—only practice could disclose. Moreover, as Lord Keynes,‡ who wrote even economics in English, once put it, "Words ought to be a little wild, for they are an assault of thought upon the unthinking."

Keynes immediately added, however: "But when the seats of power and authority have been attained, there should be no more poetic license." Madison described the American experiment as the replacement of accident and force by reflection and choice in the processes of government. The responsibility of presidents is to define real choices and explain soberly why one course is to be preferred to another—and, in doing so, to make language a means not of deception but of communication, not an enemy but a friend of the reality principle.

---

*The *pieds-noirs*, or "blackfeet," were a group of Algerian nationalists and their French supporters who opposed French President Charles de Gaulle's policies in French-run Algeria in the 1950s.
†"I understand you, my friends."
‡John Maynard Keynes (1883–1946) was a British economist who developed a new theory about the capitalist economic system, often referred to as "Keynesian economics."

20   Yet presidents cannot easily rise above the society they serve and lead. If we are to restore the relationship between words and meaning, we must begin to clean up the whole linguistic environment. This does not mean a crusade for standard English or a campaign to resurrect the stately rhythms of *The Federalist Papers*. Little could be more quixotic than an attempt to hold a rich and flexible language like American English to the forms and definitions of a specific time, class, or race. But some neologisms are better than others, and here one can demand, particularly in influential places, a modicum of discrimination. More important is that words, whether new or old, regain a relationship to reality. Vietnam and Watergate have given a good many Americans, I believe, a real hatred of double-talk and a hunger for bluntness and candor. Why else the success of the posthumous publication of President Truman's gaudy exercise in plain speaking?

21   The time is ripe to sweep the language-field of American politics. In this season of semantic malnutrition, who is not grateful for a public voice that appears to blurt out what the speaker honestly believes? A George Wallace begins to win support even among blacks (though ambition is already making Wallace bland, and blandness will do him in too). Here those who live by the word—I mean by the true word, like writers and teachers; not by the phony word, like public relations men, writers, and teachers—have their peculiar obligation. Every citizen is free under the First Amendment to use and abuse the words that bob around in the swamp of his mind. But writers and teachers have, if anyone has, the custodianship of the language. Their charge is to protect the words by which they live. Their duty is to expel the cant of the age.

22   At the same time, they must not forget that in the recent past they have been among the worst offenders. They must take scrupulous care that indignation does not lead them to the same falsity and hyperbole they righteously condemn in others. A compilation of political pronouncements by eminent writers and learned savants over the last generation would make a dismal volume. One has only to recall the renowned, if addled, scholars who signed the full page advertisement in the *New York Times* of October 15, 1972, which read, as the *New Yorker* would say, in its entirety: "Of the two major candidates for the Presidency of the United States, we believe that Richard Nixon has demonstrated the superior capacity for prudent and responsible leadership. Consequently, we intend to vote for President Nixon on November 7th and we urge our fellow citizens to do the same."

23   The time has come for writers and teachers to meet the standards they would enforce on others and rally to the defense of the word. They must expose the attack on meaning and discrimination in language as an attack on reason in discourse. It is this rejection of reason itself that

underlies the indulgence of imprecision, the apotheosis of usage, and the infatuation with rhetoric. For once words lose a stable connection with things, we can no longer know what we think or communicate what we believe.

One does not suggest that the restoration of language is all that easy   24
in an age when new issues, complexities, and ambiguities stretch old forms to the breaking point.

> . . . *Words strain*
> *Crack and sometimes break, under the burden,*
> *Under the tension, slip, slide, perish,*
> *Decay with imprecision, will not stay in place,*
> *Will not stay still.* *

Each venture is therefore the new beginning, the raid on the inarticulate with shabby equipment always deteriorating in the general mess of imprecision of feeling. Yet, as Eliot went on to say, "For us, there is only the trying. The rest is not our business." As we struggle to recover what has been lost ("and found and lost again and again"), as we try our own sense of words against the decay of language, writers and teachers make the best contribution they can to the redemption of politics. Let intellectuals never forget that all they that take the word shall perish with the word. "Wise men pierce this rotten diction," said Emerson, "and fasten words again to visible things; so that picturesque language is at once a commanding certificate that he who employs it, is a man in alliance with truth and God."

Questions and Activities

▶ *COMPREHENSION QUESTIONS*

1. Why does Schlesinger argue for renewed attention to *The Federalist Papers?* Do you know who authored *The Federalist Papers?* Where were they originally published, and what type of people read them? You can find this kind of information in the introduction to any standard edition of *The Federalist Papers.*

2. Why does Schlesinger believe that the authors of *The Federalist Papers* were "passionate exemplars of the politics of reason" (paragraph 6)?

---

*From "Burnt Norton," section V of *Four Quartets*, by T. S. Eliot. T. S. Eliot (1888–1965) was one of the most accomplished and recognized of modern English poets and playwrights.

3. What is Schlesinger saying about Henry Kissinger in paragraph 9? How does the quotation "The louder he talked of his honor, the faster we counted our spoons" apply to Kissinger as Schlesinger describes him?

▶ *QUESTIONS OF RHETORICAL PURPOSE AND STRATEGY*

4. What elements of Schlesinger's style make this a persuasive essay? What is Schlesinger trying to persuade his readers to do?
5. To whom is this essay directed? What evidence is there in the essay that your definition of its audience is correct?
6. Look closely at the way paragraph 17 is written. What convinces you that Schlesinger is taking on a particular voice for this occasion? What kind of image do Schlesinger's sentences create? Note the repetition of parallel phrases, the series of descriptive adjectives, the use of rhetorical questions, and the abstract vocabulary. What do these devices contribute to your knowledge of Schlesinger's character?

▶ *THEME QUESTIONS*

7. Why is it teachers and writers who must "expel the cant of the age" (paragraph 21)? Why does Schlesinger suggest that in recent years these professionals have not been living up to their responsibility?
8. Assuming language does contribute a great deal to people's sense of personal and social identity, what is Schlesinger implying has happened to our national identity because of Watergate and Vietnam? What has happened at the same time to our understanding and use of language, and how has that change influenced our national self-image?
9. Do you feel that Schlesinger gives too much or too little attention to how political ideas are expressed? Does he seem to ignore content, or "what" questions? Do we need to attend as carefully as Schlesinger says we should to the word usage of our political representatives? Consider these questions in the light of what Coleridge says about the power of words in paragraph 12. How might political language be a "medium that dominates perceptions"? How might the way a politician talks about an issue be as important as what he or she says about the issue?
10. Why does Schlesinger believe that a democracy has more hope of cleaning up its language than does a country with a totalitarian government?

▶ *LEARNING ACTIVITIES*

11. Focus on a catchword or slogan used recently by the current administration. Does that catchword or slogan distort reality? Is it

simply a neutral term, not calling for in-depth analysis? Is it an accurate representation of the political reality behind it?

12. Write a personal response to a speech by a major political figure. Organize this response into the following four sections, which can be rearranged in a way that seems logical to you:
    a. Summarize the purpose of the speech.
    b. Describe your personal reaction to the speech.
    c. Relate your personal reaction to the speech's purpose.
    d. Tell what part the language used in the speech played in producing your reaction.

Porno-Violence

TOM WOLFE

Tom Wolfe (Thomas Kennerly Wolfe, Jr.) is one of the most colorful and innovative of contemporary journalists. He was born in Richmond, Virginia in 1931; he graduated from Washington and Lee University in 1951 and received his Ph.D. from Yale in 1957. He spent several years as a newspaper and magazine reporter before he began free-lancing as a journalist in the early 1960s for magazines such as *New York Magazine* and *Esquire.*

Wolfe popularized the New Journalism in the 1960s and 1970s in several best-selling books: *The Kandy-Kolored Tangerine-Flake Streamline Baby* (1965), *The Pump House Gang* (1968), *The Electric Kool-Aid Acid Test* (1968), *Radical Chic and Mau-Mauing the Flak Catchers* (1970), and *The Painted Word* (1975). In these books, Wolfe presented essays and longer studies of contemporary social movements and patterns; all these works were based on careful investigative reporting and firsthand experience. He has often spent a great deal of time living with, observing, and interviewing his subjects, as he did in the late sixties with Ken Kesey and the Merry Pranksters—the hippies and intellectuals who were the subjects of *The Electric Kool-Aid Acid Test.*

Wolfe expanded the reporter's role to incorporate that of social critic. His comments on contemporary social phenomena, such as custom car clubs, motorcycle clubs, surfers, and the liberal in-group of New York City society, became synonymous with fashionable criticism of modern society in general. His style—often called a "tabloid" style—uses large bold type and free-form punctuation much like that in weekly tabloids such as *The National Enquirer.* He frequently parodies the language and actions of his subjects. His book *The Right Stuff* (1979) tells the story of the first American astronauts, combining factual material and social commentary and presenting the astronauts as the new American heroes.

In the essay included here, Wolfe presents *his perception* of a modern trend in print journalism—the pornography of violence. He does not emphasize factual information. Rather, Wolfe organizes his observations to serve his purpose: to convince his readers that even relatively sophisticated people are increasingly attracted by a new combination of pornography and violence. In other words, Wolfe writes *persuasively* here, rather than informatively. He wants his readers to agree with him by the time they have finished reading the piece.

A persuasive essay, of course, demands certain reading strategies. You will need to question Wolfe's opinions and logical conclusions critically. Wolfe begins his essay by establishing factual credibility (in the first ten paragraphs). He describes a journalistic convention of *Enquirer* stringers in Manhattan realistically, despite the fact that he wasn't there. He includes made-up dialogue, snippets of *Enquirer* headlines, and a good deal of specialized journalistic language. All these elements help you accept Wolfe's authority concerning his subject; however, his imaginative rather than logical approach should lead you to expect his persuasive goal from the beginning. By paragraph 11, then, where Wolfe introduces his opinion, the critical reader ought to be prepared for the hard sell. Even though Wolfe does not emphasize the logic of his position, logical analysis is necessary to evaluate his argument. In order, however, to apply logic, the reader has to know where Wolfe is going: a fast reading of the entire essay can establish Wolfe's thesis; a rereading of those parts of the essay where Wolfe provides the logical support for that thesis provides the basis for judging his reasoning.

As you read, think about the following aspects of Wolfe's use of language:

1. Do you think Wolfe's unconventional journalistic style weakens the logic of his argument? Does his careful attention to detail and fact seem to offset the sensational quality of his writing and create a balance between emotional and logical appeals?
2. Is it right for a journalist to dress up his subject, as Wolfe does?
3. What part of a newspaper is best suited to Wolfe's type of journalism? In what types of magazines would you expect to find Wolfe's journalism? Is Wolfe's writing suitable for a news magazine such as *Time* or *Newsweek*? Is it objective enough for most daily newspapers?

Also consider how this essay relates to this section's theme:

1. Do newspapers that publish tabloid journalism permanently change their readers' perceptions of reality? How might a reader's perception of reality be changed by reading such journalism?
2. What kinds of identity definitions are encouraged by tabloid journalism? Might tabloid journalism cause the average reader to strive for self-definition of a sensational kind?
3. What would be the differences between sensational and objective news reports of a president's assassination? Would the reports look

different? Would their vocabularies differ? Would different information be included in the two articles?

▶ ─────────────────────────────────

1   *"Keeps His Mom-in-law in Chains,* meet *Kills Son and Feeds
Corpse to Pigs.* Pleased to meet you. *Teenager Twists Off Corpse's
Head... To Get Gold Teeth,* meet *Strangles Girl Friend, then Chops
Her to Pieces.* Likewise, I'm sure. *Nurse's Aide Sees Fingers Chopped
Off in Meat Grinder,* meet...."

2   In ten years of journalism I have covered more conventions than I
care to remember. Podiatrists, theosophists, Professional Budget Finance dentists, oyster farmers, mathematicians, truckers, dry cleaners,
stamp collectors, Esperantists, nudists and newspaper editors—I have
seen them all, together, in vast assemblies, sloughing through the wall-
to-wall of a thousand hotel lobbies (the nudists excepted) in their
shimmering grey-metal suits and Nicey Short Collar white shirts with
white Plasti-Coat name cards on their chests, and I have sat through
their speeches and seminars (the nudists included) and attentively
endured ear baths such as you wouldn't believe. And yet some of the
truly instructive conventions of our times I seem to have missed altogether. One, for example, I only heard about from one of the many
anonymous men who have labored in... a curious field. This was a convention of the stringers for *The National Enquirer.*

3   *The Enquirer* is a weekly newspaper that is probably known by sight
to millions more than know it by name. In fact, no one who ever came
face-to-face with *The Enquirer* on a newsstand in its wildest days is
likely to have forgotten the sight: a tabloid with great inky shocks of
type all over the front page saying something on the order of *Gouges
Out Wife's Eyes to Make Her Ugly, Dad Hurls Hot Grease in
Daughter's Face, Wife Commits Suicide After 2 Years of Poisoning Fails
to Kill Husband....*

4   The stories themselves were supplied largely by stringers, i.e., correspondents, from all over the country, the world, for that matter, mostly
copy editors and reporters on local newspapers. Every so often they
would come upon a story, usually via the police beat, that was so grotesque the local sheet would discard it or run it in a highly glossed form
rather than offend or perplex its readers. The stringers would preserve
them for *The Enquirer,* which always rewarded them well and respectfully.

In fact, one year *The Enquirer* convened and feted them at a hotel in   5
Manhattan. It was a success in every way. The only awkward moment
was at the outset when the stringers all pulled in. None of them knew
each other. Their hosts got around the problem by introducing them by
the stories they had supplied. The introductions, I am told, went like
this:

"Harry, I want you to meet Frank here. Frank did that story, you re-   6
member that story, *Midget Murderer Throws Girl Off Cliff After She
Refuses To Dance With Him.*"

"Pleased to meet you. That was some story."   7

"And Harry did the one about *I Spent Three Days Trapped at Bottom*   8
of Forty-foot-deep Mine Shaft and Was Saved by a Swarm of Flies."

"Likewise, I'm sure."   9

And *Midget Murderer Throws Girl Off Cliff* shakes hands with *I*   10
Spent Three Days Trapped at Bottom of Forty-foot-deep Mine Shaft,
and *Buries Her Baby Alive* shakes hands with *Boy, Twelve, Strangles
Two-year-old Girl*, and *Kills Son and Feeds Corpse to Pigs* shakes hands
with *He Strangles Old Woman and Smears Corpse with Syrup, Ketch-
up, and Oatmeal*...and....

...There was a great deal of esprit about the whole thing. These men   11
were, in fact, the avant-garde of a new genre that since then has become
institutionalized throughout the nation without anyone knowing its
proper name. I speak of the new pornography, the pornography of
violence.

Pornography comes from the Greek word *porne*, meaning harlot, and   12
pornography is literally the depiction of the acts of harlots. In the new
pornography, the theme is not sex. The new pornography depicts practitioners acting out another, murkier drive: people staving teeth in, ripping guts open, blowing brains out and getting even with all those bastards....

The success of *The Enquirer* prompted many imitators to enter the   13
field, *Midnight, The Star Chronicle, The National Insider, Inside
News, The National Close-up, The National Tattler, The National Ex-
aminer*. A truly competitive free press evolved, and soon a reader could
go to the newspaper of his choice for *Kill the Retarded! (Won't You Join
My Movement!)* and *Unfaithful Wife! Burn Her Bed!, Harem Master's
Mistress Chops Him with Machete, Babe Bites Off Boy's Tongue*, and
Cuts Buddy's Face to Pieces for Stealing His Business and Fiancée.

And yet the last time I surveyed the Violence press, I noticed a curi-   14
ous thing. These pioneering journals seem to have pulled back. They
seem to be regressing to what is by now the Redi-Mix staple of literate
Americans, plain old lust-o-lech sex. *Ecstasy and Me (By Hedy Lamarr)*,

says *The National Enquirer. I Run A Sex Art Gallery*, says *The National Insider.* What has happened, I think, is something that has happened to avant-gardes in many fields, from William Morris and the Craftsmen to the Bauhaus group.* Namely, their discoveries have been preempted by the Establishment and so thoroughly dissolved into the mainstream they no longer look original.

15   Robert Harrison, the former publisher of *Confidential*, and later publisher of the aforementioned *Inside News*, was perhaps the first person to see it coming. I was interviewing Harrison early in January of 1964 for a story in *Esquire* about six weeks after the assassination of President Kennedy, and we were in a cab in the West Fifties in Manhattan, at a stoplight, by a newsstand, and Harrison suddenly pointed at the newsstand and said, "Look at that. They're doing the same thing *The Enquirer* does."

16   There on the stand was a row of slick-paper, magazine-size publications, known in the trade as one-shots, with titles like *Four Days That Shook the World, Death of a President, An American Tragedy* or just *John Fitzgerald Kennedy (1921–1963)*. "You want to know why people buy those things?" said Harrison. "People buy those things to see a man get his head blown off."

17   And, of course, he was right. Only now the publishers were in many cases the pillars of the American press. Invariably, these "special coverages" of the assassination bore introductions piously commemorating the fallen President, exhorting the American people to strength and unity in a time of crisis, urging greater vigilance and safeguards for the new President, and even raising the nice metaphysical question of collective guilt in "an age of violence."

18   In the three and a half years since then, of course, there has been an incessant replay, with every recoverable clinical detail, of those less than five seconds in which a man got his head blown off. And throughout this deluge of words, pictures and film frames, I have been intrigued with one thing. The point of view, the vantage point, is almost never that of the victim, riding in the Presidential Lincoln Continental. What you get is . . . the view from Oswald's rifle. You can step right up here and look point-blank right through the very hairline cross in Lee Harvey Oswald's Optics Ordinance four-power Japanese

---

*William Morris (1834–1896) was a Victorian intellectual, artist, craftsman, social commentator, and writer who was best known for his descriptions and advocacy of utopian societies. The Bauhaus was German institute established in Weimar in 1919 for the study of functional design and architecture. Many intellectuals of the 1920s and 1930s saw this style as a prototype for utopian architecture.

telescopic sight and watch, frame by frame by frame by frame by frame, as that man there's head comes apart. Just a little History there before your very eyes.

The television networks have schooled us in the view from Oswald's rifle and made it seem a normal pastime. The TV viewpoint is nearly always that of the man who is going to strike. The last time I watched *Gunsmoke*, which was not known as a very violent Western in TV terms, the action went like this: The Wellington agents and the stagecoach driver pull guns on the badlands gang leader's daughter and Kitty, the heart-of-gold saloonkeeper, and kidnap them. Then the badlands gang shoots two Wellington agents. Then they tie up five more and talk about shooting them. Then they desist because they might not be able to get a hotel room in the next town if the word got around. Then one badlands gang gunslinger attempts to rape Kitty while the gang leader's younger daughter looks on. Then Kitty resists, so he slugs her one in the jaw. Then the gang leader slugs him. Then the gang leader slugs Kitty. Then Kitty throws hot stew in a gang member's face and hits him over the back of the head with a revolver. Then he knocks her down with a rock. Then the gang sticks up a bank. Here comes the sheriff, Matt Dillon. He shoots a gang member and breaks it up. Then the gang leader shoots the guy who was guarding his daughter and the woman. Then the sheriff shoots the gang leader. The final exploding bullets signal The End.

It is not the accumulated slayings and bone-crushings that make this porno-violence, however. What makes it porno-violence is that in almost every case the camera angle, therefore the viewer, is with the gun, the fist, the rock. The pornography of violence has no point of view in the old sense that novels do. You do not live the action through the hero's eyes. You live with the aggressor, whoever he may be. One moment you are the hero. The next, you are the villain. No matter whose side you may be on consciously, you are in fact with the muscle, and it is you who disintegrate all comers, villains, lawmen, women, anybody. On the rare occasions in which the gun is emptied into the camera—i.e., into your face—the effect is so startling that the pornography of violence all but loses its fantasy charm. There are not nearly so many masochists as sadists among those little devils whispering into your ears.

In fact, sex—"sadomasochism"—is only a part of the pornography of violence. Violence is much more wrapped up, simply, with status. Violence is the simple, ultimate solution for problems of status competition, just as gambling is the simple, ultimate solution for economic competition. The old pornography was the fantasy of easy sexual delights in a world where sex was kept unavailable. The new pornography is the fantasy of easy triumph in a world where status competition has become so complicated and frustrating.

22   Already the old pornography is losing its kick because of overexposure. In the late Thirties, Nathaniel West published his last and best-regarded novel, *The Day of the Locust,* and it was a terrible flop commercially, and his publisher said if he ever published another book about Hollywood it would "have to be *My Thirty-nine Ways of Making Love by Hedy Lamarr."* *Ecstasy and Me* is not quite that . . . but maybe it is. I stopped counting. I know her account begins: "The men in my life have ranged from a classic case history of impotence, to a whip-brandishing sadist who enjoyed sex only after he tied my arms behind me with the sash of his robe. There was another man who took his pleasure with a girl in my own bed, while he thought I was asleep in it."

23   Yawns all around. The sin itself is wearing out. Pornography cannot exist without certified taboo to violate. And today Lust, like the rest of the Seven Deadly Sins—Pride, Sloth, Envy, Greed, Anger, and Glutony—is becoming a rather minor vice. The Seven Deadly Sins, after all, are only sins against the self. Theologically, the idea of Lust—well, the idea is that if you seduce some poor girl from Akron, it is not a sin because you are ruining her, but because you are wasting your time and your energies and damaging your own spirit. This goes back to the old work ethic, when the idea was to keep every able-bodied man's shoulder to the wheel. In an age of riches for all, the ethic becomes more nearly: Let him do anything he pleases, as long as he doesn't get in my way. And if he does get in my way, or even if he doesn't . . . well . . . we have *new* fantasies for that. *Put hair on the walls.*

24   *Hair on the Walls* is the invisible subtitle of Truman Capote's book, *In Cold Blood.* The book is neither a who-done-it nor a will-they-be-caught, since the answers to both questions are known from the outset. It does ask why-did-they-do-it, but the answer is soon as clear as it is going to be. Instead, the book's suspense is based largely on a totally new idea in detective stories: the promise of gory details, and the with-holding of them until the end. Early in the game one of the two murderers, Dick, starts promising to put "plenty of hair on them-those walls" with a shotgun. So read on, gentle readers, and on and on; you are led up to the moment before the crime on page 60—yet the specifics, what happened, the gory details, are kept out of sight, in grisly dangle, until page 244.

25   But Dick and Perry, Capote's killers, are only a couple of lower-class bums. With James Bond the new pornography has already reached dead center, the bureaucratic middle class. The appeal of Bond has been explained as the appeal of the lone man who can solve enormously com-

plicated, even world problems through his own bravery and initiative. But Bond is not a lone man at all, of course. He is not the Lone Ranger. He is much easier to identify than that. He is a salaried functionary in a bureaucracy. He is a sport, but a believable one; not a millionaire, but a bureaucrat on expense account. He is not even a high-level bureaucrat. He is an operative. This point is carefully and repeatedly made by having his superiors dress him down for violations of standard operating procedure. Bond, like the Lone Ranger, solves problems with guns and fists. When it is over, however, the Lone Ranger leaves a silver bullet. Bond, like the rest of us, fills out a report in triplicate.

Marshall McLuhan says we are in a period in which it will become   26
harder and harder to stimulate lust through words and pictures—i.e., the old pornography. In an age of electronic circuitry, he says, people crave tactile, all-involving experiences. The same thing may very well happen to the new pornography of violence. Even such able craftsmen as Truman Capote, Ian Fleming, NBC and CBS may not suffice. Fortunately, there are historical models to rescue us from this frustration. In the latter days of the Roman Empire, the Emperor Commodus became jealous of the celebrity of the great gladiators. He took to the arena himself, with his sword, and began dispatching suitably screened cripples and hobbled fighters. Audience participation became so popular that soon various *illuminati* of the Commodus set, various boys and girls of the year, were out there, suited up, gaily cutting a sequence of dwarves and feebles down to short ribs. Ah, swinging generations, what new delights await?

Questions and Activities

▶ *COMPREHENSION QUESTIONS*

1. Why does Wolfe feel that tabloid newspapers such as *The National Enquirer* have toned down their treatment of sensational violence in recent years?
2. Look at the *New York Times* issue reporting on John F. Kennedy's assassination. Does Wolfe's description of the coverage of the assassination seem accurate?
3. What does Wolfe mean by the phrase "the new pornography, the pornography of violence"? How does this new pornography differ from the "old" pornography? How does this new pornography engage its readers—their perspectives, desires, and feelings?

▶ *QUESTIONS OF RHETORICAL PURPOSE AND STRATEGY*

4. Consider the purpose of the second paragraph of this essay. How does the information in this paragraph function in relation to the rest of the essay? How is the background Wolfe provides in this paragraph important to his later analysis of *The National Enquirer* and other tabloids? Does this paragraph also help to establish Wolfe's credentials for writing this essay?

5. Describe Wolfe's voice in this essay (his personality as it is embodied in the words). What kind of person does he sound like — sophisticated, wise, intelligent, flashy? Choose an adjective for Wolfe and defend your choice by referring to the words and structure of this essay. Does his voice make Wolfe's essay more or less convincing?

6. Point out the places in this essay where Wolfe's purpose seems to be primarily informative. Are these informative passages clearly connected to Wolfe's persuasive thesis? Are the connections primarily logical or emotional? What new information is given in these passages? (An informative essay aims to provide new information on a defined subject; a persuasive essay informs in a way that also attempts to change the attitudes or behavior of readers.)

7. What does Wolfe want his readers to do after they have read his essay? Does he hope they will avoid magazines and newspapers such as *The National Enquirer*? Does he simply wish to alert his readers to the perverse appeal of these publications? Does he see a need for censorship? Is he simply trying to show how our identities are reflected in what we like to read?

▶ *THEME QUESTIONS*

8. Wolfe appeals to his readers' emotions, to their respect for his record as a journalist, and to their reasoning abilities. The logical appeal is summarized in paragraph 21, where Wolfe states his thesis. Put his thesis into your own words, then go back over the first twenty paragraphs and indicate those that seem to appeal to readers' emotions, those that are built on the readers' acceptance of the author's credentials, and those that rest on logic.

9. What is the logic behind Wolfe's criticism of the mass media and its treatment of John F. Kennedy's assassination? Did the media, according to Wolfe, help shape the average person's response to President Kennedy's assassination? How, according to Wolfe, did the media accomplish this? Or did the media simply cater to Americans' already established appetite for violence?

10. Does this essay suggest an answer to this section's theme question?

11. Make a list of at least five ways in which reading persuasive essays differs from reading informative essays. Your list should be written from the reader's perspective, as a group of dos and don'ts to follow in a recipe for critical reading. What should a reader watch out for in a persuasive essay? What should a reader be wary of in reading an informative (primarily factual) essay? How do the writer's tone and voice affect the reader's response to an essay's content? How do choice of words and sentence structure affect a reader's attitude toward a writer's subject?

12. Write a brief letter to a friend in which you explain how publications such as *The National Enquirer* should be read. What should a reader look for; what should he or she be ready to question?

13. Compare a recent issue of *The National Enquirer* to Wolfe's description of the newspaper. Has the newspaper changed? Has it changed in a way that makes it more palatable to supermarket consumers? Does this change suggest that alterations are necessary for Wolfe's thesis?

14. Go over a recent issue of a local newspaper. Put an X next to the headline or title of any article, column, or feature story that deals with violence in any way. When you have finished marking the paper, count the total number of pieces in the issue and the total number that deal with violence. Is the percentage of articles on violence high? Does that percentage reflect a high degree of violence in our society or an exaggerated concern with the subject in the media?

Sexism in English: A Feminist View

ALLEEN PACE NILSEN

Born in 1936, Alleen Pace Nilsen is a linguist and a professor of education at Arizona State University, Tempe. Throughout her career she has focused on language as it affects and is affected by the sex roles of individuals in English-speaking societies, especially American society. She has analyzed sexist language in children's schoolbooks, in professions and workplaces, and in classrooms. Her books include *Sexism in English: A Feminist View* (1971), the co-authored *Sexism and Language* (1977), and several books on language for young adults. She is a specialist in the linguistic field of semantic theory and co-authored the book *Semantic Theory: A Linguistic Perspective* (1975). Pace Nilsen also taught at Northern Iowa University and Eastern Michigan University and spent two years (1967–1969) teaching in Afghanistan.

In this essay, Pace Nilsen raises the question of whether language shapes us or we shape language. Then she narrows this question to how American language influences a woman's image of herself and her intended role in life. Culture, who we are and the way we think, certainly exerts some influence on language. Consider, for example, the changes in words already caused by recent attention to sexism by educated users of the English language, such as to have the affix -*man* replaced by -*person* in public contexts, resulting in chair*person* rather than chair*man*. Also, endings of words indicating the female version of a name have been dropped: both males and females are *poets,* not *poets* and *poetesses;* or *actors,* not *actors* and *actresses.* Many people must now think twice before they verbally represent an activity done by both men and women.

We may feel that what we think controls our use of language. Pace Nilsen argues the reverse of this idea. Her categories and analyses of a dictionary's entries illustrate how our language subtly suggests that women and men play very different cultural roles. Because we seldom are aware, on a conscious level, of this subtle influence of language, we are generally powerless to change or control it.

As you read this essay, think about your own language experience:

1. Do you think the language you hear and use at home, in school, or in your community has influenced your choice of college or career or your general self-image?

2. Have you ever felt that the language someone else used in describing you was stereotyped or superficial? Do you belong to a group of people who have been verbally stereotyped by others?
3. Do you feel that people can become too sensitive to how others respond to them through language?

▶ ————————————————————

Does culture shape language? Or does language shape culture? This is as difficult a question as the old puzzler of which came first, the chicken or the egg, because there's no clear separation between language and culture.

A well-accepted linguistic principle is that as culture changes so will the language. The reverse of this—as a language changes so will the culture—is not so readily accepted. This is why some linguists smile (or even scoff) at feminist attempts to replace *Mrs.* and *Miss* with *Ms.* and to find replacements for those all-inclusive words which specify masculinity, e.g., *chairman, mankind, brotherhood, freshman,* etc.

Perhaps they are amused for the same reason that it is the doctor at a cocktail party who laughs the loudest at the joke about the man who couldn't afford an operation so he offered the doctor a little something to touch up the X-ray. A person working constantly with language is likely to be more aware of how really deep-seated sexism is in our communication system.

Last winter I took a standard desk dictionary and gave it a place of honor on my night table. Every night that I didn't have anything more interesting to do, I read myself to sleep making a card for each entry that seemed to tell something about male and female. By spring I had a rather dog-eared dictionary, but I also had a collection of note cards filling two shoe boxes. The cards tell some rather interesting things about American English.

First, in our culture it is a woman's body which is considered important while it is a man's mind or his activities which are valued. A woman is sexy. A man is successful.

I made a card for all the words which came into modern English from somebody's name. I have a two-and-one-half inch stack of cards which are men's names now used as everyday words. The women's stack is less than a half inch high and most of them came from Greek mythology. Words coming from the names of famous American men include *lynch, sousaphone, sideburns, Pullman, rickettsia, Schick test, Winchester rifle, Franklin stove, Bartlett pear, teddy bear,* and *boysen-*

berry. The only really common words coming from the names of American women are *bloomers* (after Amelia Jenks Bloomer) and *Mae West jacket*. Both of these words are related in some way to a woman's physical anatomy, while the male words (except for *sideburns* after General Burnside) have nothing to do with the namesake's body.

7   This reminded me of an earlier observation that my husband and I made about geographical names. A few years ago we became interested in what we called "Topless Topography" when we learned that the Grand Tetons used to be simply called *The Tetons* by French explorers and *The Teats* by American frontiersmen. We wrote letters to several map makers and found the following listings: *Nippletop* and *Little Nipple Top* near Mt. Marcy in the Adirondacks, *Nipple Mountain* in Archuleta County, Colorado, *Nipple Peak* in Coke County, Texas, *Nipple Butte* in Pennington, South Dakota, *Squaw Peak* in Placer County, California (and many other places), *Maiden's Peak* and *Squaw Tit* (they're the same mountain) in the Cascade Range in Oregon, *Jane Russell Peaks* near Stark, New Hampshire, and *Mary's Nipple* near Salt Lake City, Utah.

8   We might compare these names to Jackson Hole, Wyoming, or Pikes Peak, Colorado. I'm sure we would get all kinds of protests from the Jackson and Pike descendants if we tried to say that these topographical features were named because they in some way resembled the bodies of Jackson and Pike, respectively.

9   This preoccupation with women's breasts is neither new nor strictly American. I was amused to read the derivation of the word *Amazon*. According to Greek folk etymology, the *a* means "without" as in *atypical* or *amoral* while *mazon* comes from *mazōs* meaning "breast." According to the legend, these women cut off one breast so that they could better shoot their bows. Perhaps the feeling was that the women had to trade in part of their femininity in exchange for their active or masculine role.

10   There are certain pairs of words which illustrate the way in which sexual connotations are given to feminine words while the masculine words retain a serious, businesslike aura. For example, being a *callboy* is perfectly respectable. It simply refers to a person who calls actors when it is time for them to go on stage, but being a *call girl* is being a prostitute.

11   Also we might compare *sir* and *madam*. *Sir* is a term of respect while *madam* has acquired the meaning of a brothel manager. The same thing has happened to the formerly cognate terms, *master* and *mistress*. Because of its acquired sexual connotations, *mistress* is now carefully avoided in certain contexts. For example, the Boy Scouts have *scoutmasters* but certainly not *scoutmistresses*. And in a dog show the fe-

male owner of a dog is never referred to as the *dog's mistress*, but rather as the *dog's master*.

Master appears in such terms as *master plan, concert master, schoolmaster, mixmaster, master charge, master craftsman*, etc. But *mistress* appears in very few compounds. This is the way it is with dozens of words which have male and female counterparts. I found two hundred such terms, e.g., *usher-usherette, heir-heiress, hero-heroine*, etc. In nearly all cases it is the masculine word which is the base with a feminine suffix being added for the alternate version. The masculine word also travels into compounds while the feminine word is a dead end; e.g., from *king-queen* comes *kingdom* but not *queendom*, from *sportsman-sportslady* comes *sportsmanship* but not *sportsladyship*, etc. There is one—and only one—semantic area in which the masculine word is not the base or more powerful word. This is in the area dealing with sex and marriage. Here it is the feminine word which is dominant. *Prostitute* is the base word with *male prostitute* being the derived term. *Bride* appears in *bridal shower, bridal gown, bridal attendant, bridesmaid*, and even in *bridegroom*, while *groom* in the sense of *bridegroom* does not appear in any compounds, not even to name the groom's attendants or his prenuptial party.

At the end of a marriage, this same emphasis is on the female. If it ends in divorce, the woman gets the title of *divorcée* while the man is usually described with a statement, such as, "He's divorced." When the marriage ends in death, the woman is a *widow* and the *-er* suffix which seems to connote masculine (probably because it is an agentive or actor type suffix) is added to make *widower*. *Widower* doesn't appear in any compounds (except for *grass widower*, which is another companion term), but *widow* appears in several compounds and in addition has some acquired meanings, such as the extra hand dealt to the table in certain card games and an undesirable leftover line of type in printing.

If I were an anthropological linguist making observations about a strange and primitive tribe, I would duly note on my tape recorder that I had found linguistic evidence to show that in the area of sex and marriage the female appears to be more important than the male, but in all other areas of the culture, it seems that the reverse is true.

But since I am not an anthropological linguist, I will simply go on to my second observation, which is that women are expected to play a passive role while men play an active one.

One indication of women's passive role is the fact that they are often identified as something to eat. What's more passive than a plate of food? Last spring I saw an announcement advertising the Indiana University English Department picnic. It read "Good Food! Delicious Women!" The publicity committee was probably jumped on by local feminists, but it's nothing new to look on women as "delectable morsels." Even women compliment each other with "You look good enough to eat," or "You have a peaches and cream complexion." Modern slang constantly comes up with new terms, but some of the old standbys for women are: *cute tomato, dish, peach, sharp cookie, cheese cake, honey, sugar,* and *sweetie-pie.* A man may occasionally be addressed as *honey* or described as a *hunk of meat,* but certainly men are not laid out on a buffet and labeled as women are.

17   Women's passivity is also shown in the comparisons made to plants. For example, to *deflower* a woman is to take away her virginity. A girl can be described as a *clinging vine, a shrinking violet,* or a *wall-flower.* On the other hand, men are too active to be thought of as plants. The only time we make the comparison is when insulting a man we say he is like a woman by calling him a *pansy.*

18   We also see the active-passive contrast in the animal terms used with males and females. Men are referred to as *studs, bucks,* and *wolves,* and they go *tomcatting around.* These are all aggressive roles, but women have such pet names as *kitten, bunny, beaver, bird, chick, lamb,* and *fox.* The idea of being a pet seems much more closely related to females than to males. For instance, little girls grow up wearing *pigtails* and *ponytails* and they dress in *halters* and *dog collars.*

19   The active-passive contrast is also seen in the proper names given to boy babies and girl babies. Girls are much more likely to be given names like *Ivy, Rose, Ruby, Jewel, Pearl, Flora, Joy,* etc., while boys are given names describing active roles such as *Martin* (warlike), *Leo* (lion), *William* (protector), *Ernest* (resolute fighter), and so on.

20   Another way that women play a passive role is that they are defined in relationship to someone else. This is what feminists are protesting when they ask to be identified as *Ms.* rather than as *Mrs.* or *Miss.* It is a constant source of irritation to women's organizations that when they turn in items to newspapers under their own names, that is, Susan Glascoe, Jeanette Jones, and so forth, the editors consistently rewrite the item so that the names read Mrs. John Glascoe, Mrs. Robert E. Jones.

21   In the dictionary I found what appears to be an attitude on the part of editors that it is almost indecent to let a respectable woman's name march unaccompanied across the pages of a dictionary. A woman's name must somehow be escorted by a male's name regardless of whether or not the male contributed to the woman's reason for being in the dictionary, or in his own right, was as famous as the woman. For example, Charlotte Brontë is identified as Mrs. Arthur B. Nicholls, Amelia Earhart is identified as Mrs. George Palmer Putnam, Helen Hayes is identified as Mrs. Charles MacArthur, Zona Gale is identified

as Mrs. William Llwelyn Breese, and Jenny Lind is identified as Mme. Otto Goldschmidt.

Although most of the women are identified as Mrs. _____ or as the wife of _____ , other women are listed with brothers, fathers, or lovers. Cornelia Otis Skinner is identified as the daughter of Otis, Harriet Beecher Stowe is identified as the sister of Henry Ward Beecher, Edith Sitwell is identified as the sister of Osbert and Sacheverell, Nell Gwyn is identified as the mistress of Charles II, and Madame Pompadour is identified as the mistress of Louis XV.   *22*

The women who did get into the dictionary without the benefit of a masculine escort are a group sort of on the fringes of respectability. They are the rebels and the crusaders: temperance leaders Frances Elizabeth Caroline Willard and Carry Nation, women's rights leaders Carrie Chapman Catt and Elizabeth Cady Stanton, birth control educator Margaret Sanger, religious leader Mary Baker Eddy, and slaves Harriet Tubman and Phillis Wheatley.   *23*

I would estimate that far more than fifty percent of the women listed in the dictionary were identified as someone's wife. But of all the men—and there are probably ten times as many men as women—only one was identified as "the husband of..." This was the unusual case of Frederic Joliot who took the last name of Joliot-Curie and was identified as "husband of Irene." Apparently Irene, the daughter of Pierre and Marie Curie, did not want to give up her maiden name when she married and so the couple took the hyphenated last name.   *24*

There are several pairs of words which also illustrate the more powerful role of the male and the relational role of the female. For example a *count* is a high political officer with a *countess* being simply the wife of a count. The same is true for a *duke* and a *duchess* and a *king* and a *queen*. The fact that a king is usually more powerful than a queen might be the reason that Queen Elizabeth's husband is given the title of *prince* rather than *king*. Since *king* is a stronger word than *queen*, it is reserved for a true heir to the throne because if it were given to someone coming into the royal family by marriage, then the subjects might forget where the true power lies. With the weaker word of *queen*, this would not be a problem; so a woman marrying a ruling monarch is given the title without question.   *25*

My third observation is that there are many positive connotations connected with the concept of masculine, while there are either trivial or negative connotations connected with the corresponding feminine concept.   *26*

Conditioning toward the superiority of the masculine role starts very early in life. Child psychologists point out that the only area in which a girl has more freedom than a boy is in experimenting with an appropri-   *27* ate sex role. She is much freer to be a *tomboy* than is her brother to be a *sissy*. The proper names given to children reflect this same attitude. It's perfectly all right for a girl to have a boy's name, but not the other way around. As girls are given more and more of the boys' names parents shy away from using boy names that might be mistaken for girl names, so the number of available masculine names is constantly shrinking. Fifty years ago *Hazel, Beverly, Marion, Francis*, and *Shirley* were all perfectly acceptable boys' names. Today few parents give these names to baby boys and adult men who are stuck with them self-consciously go by their initial or by abbreviated forms such as *Haze* or *Shirl*. But parents of little girls keep crowding the masculine set and currently popular girls' names include *Jo, Kelly, Teri, Cris, Pat, Shawn, Toni*, and *Sam*.

28   When the mother of one of these girls tells her to *be a lady*, she means for her to sit with her knees together. But when the father of a little boy tells him to *be a man*, he means for him to be noble, strong, and virtuous. The whole concept of manliness has such positive connotations that it is a compliment to call a male a *he-man*, a *manly man*, or a *virile man* (*virile* comes from the Indo-European *vir*, meaning "man"). In each of these three terms, we are implying that someone is doubly good because he is doubly a man.

29   Compare *chef* with *cook, tailor* and *seamstress*, and *poet* with *poetess*. In each case, the masculine form carries with it an added degree of excellence. In comparing the masculine *governor* with the feminine *governess* and the masculine *major* with the feminine *majorette*, the added feature is power.

30   The difference between positive male and negative female connotations can be seen in several pairs of words which differ denotatively only in the matter of sex. For instance compare *bachelor* with the terms *spinster* and *old maid*. *Bachelor* has such positive connotations that modern girls have tried to borrow the feeling in the term *bachelor-girl*. *Bachelor* appears in glamorous terms such as *bachelor pad, bachelor party*, and *bachelor button*. But *old maid* has such strong negative feelings that it has been adopted into other areas, taking with it the feeling of undesirability. It has the metaphorical meaning of shriveled and unwanted kernels of popcorn, and it's the name of the last unwanted card in a popular game for children.

31   *Patron* and *matron* (Middle English for *father* and *mother*) are another set where women have tried to borrow the positive masculine connotations, this time through the word *patroness*, which literally means "female father." Such a peculiar term came about because of the high prestige attached to the word *patron* in such phrases as "*a patron of the arts*" or "*a patron saint*." *Matron* is more apt to be used in talking about a woman who is in charge of a jail or a public restroom.

Even *lord* and *lady* have different levels of connotation. *Our Lord* is 32
used as a title for deity, while the corresponding *Our Lady* is a relational
title for Mary, the mortal mother of Jesus. *Landlord* has more dignity
than *landlady* probably because the landlord is more likely to be
thought of as the owner while the landlady is the person who collects
the rent and enforces the rules. *Lady* is used in many insignificant
places where the corresponding *lord* would never be used, for example,
ladies room, ladies sizes, ladies aid society, ladybug, etc.

This overuse of *lady* might be compared to the overuse of *queen* 33
which is rapidly losing its prestige as compared to *king*. Hundreds of
beauty queens are crowned each year and nearly every community in
the United States has its *Dairy Queen* or its *Freezer Queen*, etc. Male
homosexuals have adopted the term to identify the "feminine" partner. And advertisers who are constantly on the lookout for euphemisms
to make unpleasant sounding products salable have recently dealt what
might be a death blow to the prestige of the word *queen*. They have
begun to use it as an indication of size. For example, *queen-size* panty
hose are panty hose for fat women. The meaning comes through a comparison with *king-size*, meaning big. However, there's a subtle difference in that our culture considers it desirable for males to be big because
size is an indication of power, but we prefer that females be small and
petite. So using *king-size* as a term to indicate bigness partially enhances the prestige of *king*, but using *queen-size* to indicate bigness
brings unpleasant associations to the word *queen*.

Another set that might be compared are *brave* and *squaw*. The word 34
brave carries with it the connotations of youth, vigor, and courage,
while *squaw* implies almost opposite characteristics. With the set *wizard* and *witch*, the main difference is that *wizard* implies skill and wisdom combined with magic, while *witch* implies evil intentions combined with magic. Part of the unattractiveness of both *squaw* and *witch*
is that they suggest old age, which in women is particularly undesirable. When I lived in Afghanistan (1967–1969), I was horrified to hear a
proverb stating that when you see an old man you should sit down and
take a lesson, but when you see an old woman you should throw a
stone. I was equally startled when I went to compare the connotations
of our two phrases *grandfatherly advice* and *old wives' tales*. Certainly
it isn't expressed with the same force as in the Afghan proverb, but the
implication is similar.

In some of the animal terms used for women the extreme undesira- 35
bility of female old age is also seen. For instance consider the unattractiveness of *old nag* as compared to *filly*, of *old crow* or *old bat* as
compared to *bird*, and of being *catty* as compared to being *kittenish*.
The chicken metaphor tells the whole story of a girl's life. In her youth

she is a *chick*, then she marries and begins feeling *cooped up*, so she goes to *hen parties* where she *cackles* with her friends. Then she has her *brood* and begins to *henpeck* her husband. Finally she turns into *an old biddy*.

Questions and Activities

▶ *COMPREHENSION QUESTIONS*

1. What is the general point behind the examples of geographical names given in paragraph 7?
2. Why does the doctor laugh the loudest in response to the joke in paragraph 3? Explain the relevance of this analogy to Pace Nilsen's main point about sexism, language, and culture.

▶ *QUESTIONS OF RHETORICAL PURPOSE AND STRATEGY*

3. Why does Pace Nilsen fail to give support for her generalizations in paragraph 5? Does she think these generalizations are self-evident? Can you think of exceptions to these generalizations? Do you agree that they are self-evident? Does she deal with these generalizations later in this essay?
4. Do you think this essay has been written for an audience of men, women, or both? What elements of Nilsen's style (word choice, sentence structure, uses of metaphor and image, etc.) cause you to choose the answer you do?
5. What do you think of Pace Nilsen's method of analysis as represented in this essay? Do you think her use of a dictionary is scientific and precise enough to support her conclusions concerning sexism? What are the flaws in her method? Is a dictionary the best source to use in judging how language is used in a culture? What other sources might have been used, and would they have provided better or more complete data for Pace Nilsen's study? On the other hand, what are the strengths of Nilsen's method of analysis? What sources of data might have been a worse choice than a dictionary? Is her choice of data and method of analysis persuasive to a professional or scientific reader? Why or why not?
6. Has Pace Nilsen written a persuasive or an informative essay? Would you say that her purpose is to make readers agree that language shapes culture or simply to show how our language is sexist?

7. Are Pace Nilsen's examples convincing? Does she spend sufficient time examining them? Does she clarify the logical connections between the various examples and her generalizations on sexism? Will her examples of *how* language is sexist convince her readers that language shapes culture?

▶ *THEME QUESTIONS*

8. Do you agree that the way we use language can shape our attitudes and values, or do you think thought always controls our use of words? Would young girls raised in a culture in which women's breasts are a fixation necessarily grow up thinking that breasts are the most important part of the female body? Might it be true that our language is sexist because our thought patterns are inherently sexist?

9. Can you think of other specific ways that the American language embodies social stereotypes and prejudices? Do these examples support Pace Nilsen's idea that our language often shapes our attitudes?

▶ *LEARNING ACTIVITIES*

10. Make a list summarizing the ways in which the first five essays of this section portray language's influence on the thinking of individuals and on culture in general. Be as precise as you can in wording the items in your list. Compare your list with those of your classmates. Once you are satisfied with your list, write a paragraph that briefly explains why you are or are not convinced that language does influence thinking and culture.

11. Choose an occupation, such as waitress or nurse, that has traditionally been filled by women. Interview a person who has begun to train for or is already working in that occupation. Find out how sensitive your subject is to the potential for sexual stereotyping of his or her occupation. Rework the results of your interview as a short informative essay.

Aria: A Memoir of a Bilingual Childhood

RICHARD RODRIGUEZ

Born in San Francisco in 1944, son of Leopoldo Rodriguez (a dental technician) and Victoria Rodriguez (a clerk-typist), Richard Rodriguez graduated from Stanford University in 1969. He has been awarded several prestigious fellowships, including Fulbright and National Endowment for the Humanities fellowships. Rodriguez was studying for his Ph.D. in England in 1977, when he decided to leave academic life in order to re-establish his ties with Spanish-American culture. He held various jobs, including a janitorial one, and supported himself on freelance writing from 1977 to 1981. Since 1981, he has been a full-time writer. His book *Hunger of Memory: The Education of Richard Rodriguez* (1982) is an autobiographical account of his experience as a Spanish-speaking citizen in American schools. It won several awards, including the 1982 Christopher Award.

In this memoir, Rodriguez looks at how he was encouraged to replace Spanish, which he spoke and heard at home, with English, the language of school and public social-political life. Even though he felt that this pressure to speak English somewhat harmed his relations with his family and Spanish friends, he has come to steadfastly oppose bilingual education. He feels that these policies do not help the poor and uneducated who are trapped by their subculture's language and kept from gaining status in American society. Rodriguez believes that Americans whose first language is not English can learn English without necessarily diminishing the value of their native language, and he believes that the process of adapting to an English-speaking culture provides the bilingual speaker with valuable social and cultural strengths.

This memoir presents a private voice speaking on a public issue. The writer reviews his childhood experience to find and make accessible to others a truth he has perceived about language. Rodriguez takes us on a private journey to a public discovery. As readers, we must first become part of his experience, remembering the sounds he remembers, recalling the conversations he recalls, but, like him, reseeing childhood from an adult's point of view. We must also appreciate how the points he makes build up to discoveries; in paragraph 29, for example, he sees that the insistence that he speak English led to his finally becoming, at eight years old, a part of public life in America. The rest of the essay works in the same way, with personal experience punctuated by sudden but calculated narrative discoveries.

We may see Rodriguez's experience with English and Spanish as an intense version of what many Americans go through as they learn to become part of the larger, public culture. The language of our homes, private and intimately affectionate, dominates our lives from birth until the age of five or six. But gradually, from this age, or often earlier in children whose parents work, this intimate language of home comes in conflict with or is expanded or replaced by the socialized language of school and public life.

As you read Rodriguez's memoir, think about the private-public language dichotomy:

1. Do you feel that the move from home to school and its effects on the language one speaks have to be traumatic? How was your experience different from Rodriguez's?
2. Do you think that people who are pressured to make their language conform to some public standard are less willing to assert themselves in all areas of life?
3. What would Geneva Smitherman say about Rodriguez's childhood experiences with language? Would she agree with his perspective on and conclusions about bilingual education?

▶ ───────────────────────

I remember, to start with, that day in Sacramento, in a California now nearly thirty years past, when I first entered a classroom—able to understand about fifty stray English words. The third of four children, I had been preceded by my older brother and sister to a neighborhood Roman Catholic school. But neither of them had revealed very much about their classroom experiences. They left each morning and returned each afternoon, always together, speaking Spanish as they climbed the five steps to the porch. And their mysterious books, wrapped in brown shopping-bag paper, remained on the table next to the door, closed firmly behind them.

An accident of geography sent me to a school where all my classmates were white and many were the children of doctors and lawyers and business executives. On that first day of school, my classmates must certainly have been uneasy to find themselves apart from their families, in the first institution of their lives. But I was astonished. I was fated to be the "problem student" in class.

3   The nun said, in a friendly but oddly impersonal voice: "Boys and girls, this is Richard Rodriguez." (I heard her sound it out: *Rich-heard Road-ree-guess.*) It was the first time I had heard anyone say my name in English. "Richard," the nun repeated more slowly, writing my name down in her book. Quickly I turned to see my mother's face dissolve in a watery blur behind the pebbled-glass door.

4   Now, many years later, I hear of something called "bilingual education"—a scheme proposed in the late 1960s by Hispanic-American social activists, later endorsed by a congressional vote. It is a program that seeks to permit non-English-speaking children (many from lower class homes) to use their "family language" as the language of school. Such, at least, is the aim its supporters announce. I hear them, and am forced to say no: It is not possible for a child, any child, ever to use his family's language in school. Not to understand this is to misunderstand the public uses of schooling and to trivialize the nature of intimate life.

5   Memory teaches me what I know of these matters. The boy reminds the adult. I was a bilingual child, but of a certain kind: "socially disadvantaged," the son of working-class parents, both Mexican immigrants.

6   In the early years of my boyhood, my parents coped very well in America. My father had steady work. My mother managed at home. They were nobody's victims. When we moved to a house many blocks from the Mexican-American section of town, they were not intimidated by those two or three neighbors who initially tried to make us unwelcome. ("Keep your brats away from my sidewalk!") But despite all they achieved, or perhaps because they had so much to achieve, they lacked any deep feeling of ease, of belonging in public. They regarded the people at work or in crowds as being very distant from us. Those were the others, *los gringos*. That term was interchangeable in their speech with another, even more telling: *los americanos*.

7   I grew up in a house where the only regular guests were my relations. On a certain day, enormous families of relatives would visit us, and there would be so many people that the noise and the bodies would spill out to the backyard and onto the front porch. Then for weeks no one would come. (If the doorbell rang, it was usually a salesman.) Our house stood apart—gaudy yellow in a row of white bungalows. We were the people with the noisy dog, the people who raised chickens. We were the foreigners on the block. A few neighbors would smile and wave at us. We waved back. But until I was seven years old, I did not know the name of the old couple living next door or the names of the kids living across the street.

In public, my father and mother spoke a hesitant, accented, and not   8
always grammatical English. And then they would have to strain, their
bodies tense, to catch the sense of what was rapidly said by *los gringos*.
At home, they returned to Spanish. The language of their Mexican past
sounded in counterpoint to the English spoken in public. The words
would come quickly, with ease. Conveyed through those sounds was
the pleasing, soothing, consoling reminder that one was at home.

During those years when I was first learning to speak, my mother and   9
father addressed me only in Spanish; in Spanish I learned to reply. By
contrast, English (*inglés*) was the language I came to associate with
gringos, rarely heard in the house. I learned my first words of English
overhearing my parents speaking to strangers. At six years of age, I
knew just enough words for my mother to trust me on errands to stores
one block away—but no more.

I was then a listening child, careful to hear the very different sounds   10
of Spanish and English. Wide-eyed with hearing, I'd listen to sounds
more than to words. First, there were English (gringo) sounds. So many
words still were unknown to me that when the butcher or the lady at
the drugstore said something, exotic polysyllabic sounds would bloom
in the midst of their sentences. Often the speech of people in public
seemed to me very loud, booming with confidence. The man behind the
counter would literally ask, "What can I do for you?" But by being so
firm and clear, the sound of his voice said that he was a gringo; he
belonged in public society. There were also the high, nasal notes of
middle-class American speech—which I rarely am conscious of hearing
today because I hear them so often, but could not stop hearing when I
was a boy. Crowds at Safeway or at bus stops were noisy with the
birdlike sounds of *los gringos*. I'd move away from them all—all the
chirping chatter above me.

My own sounds I was unable to hear, but I knew that I spoke English   11
poorly. My words could not extend to form complete thoughts. And the
words I did speak I didn't know well enough to make distinct sounds.
(Listeners would usually lower their heads to hear better what I was trying to say.) But it was one thing for *me* to speak English with difficulty; it
was more troubling to hear my parents speaking in public: their high-
whining vowels and guttural consonants; their sentences that got stuck
with "eh" and "ah" sounds; the confused syntax; the hesitant rhythm
of sounds so different from the way gringos spoke. I'd notice, moreover,
that my parents' voices were softer than those of gringos we would meet.

I am tempted to say now that none of this mattered. (In adulthood I   12
am embarrassed by childhood fears.) And, in a way, it didn't matter
very much that my parents could not speak English with ease. Their
linguistic difficulties had no serious consequences. My mother and fa-

ther made themselves understood at the county hospital clinic and at government offices. And yet, in another way, it mattered very much. It was unsettling to hear my parents struggle with English. Hearing them, I'd grow nervous, and my clutching trust in their protection and power would be weakened.

13   There were many times like the night at a brightly lit gasoline station (a blaring white memory) when I stood uneasily hearing my father talk to a teenage attendant. I do not recall what they were saying, but I cannot forget the sounds my father made as he spoke. At one point his words slid together to form one long word—sounds as confused as the threads of blue and green oil in the puddle next to my shoes. His voice rushed through what he had left to say. Toward the end, he reached falsetto notes, appealing to his listener's understanding. I looked away at the lights of passing automobiles. I tried not to hear any more. But I heard only too well the attendant's reply, his calm, easy tones. Shortly afterward, headed for home, I shivered when my father put his hand on my shoulder. The very first chance that I got, I evaded his grasp and ran on ahead into the dark, skipping with feigned boyish exuberance.

14   But then there was Spanish: *español*, the language rarely heard away from the house; *español*, the language which seemed to me therefore a private language, my family's language. To hear its sounds was to feel myself specially recognized as one of the family, apart from *los otros*. A simple remark, an inconsequential comment could convey that assurance. My parents would say something to me and I would feel embraced by the sounds of their words. Those sounds said: *I am speaking with ease in Spanish. I am addressing you in words I never use with los gringos. I recognize you as someone special, close, like no one outside. You belong with us. In the family. Ricardo.*

15   At the age of six, well past the time when most middle-class children no longer notice the difference between sounds uttered at home and words spoken in public, I had a different experience. I lived in a world compounded of sounds. I was a child longer than most. I lived in a magical world, surrounded by sounds both pleasing and fearful. I shared with my family a language enchantingly private—different from that used in the city around us.

16   Just opening or closing the screen door behind me was an important experience. I'd rarely leave home all alone or without feeling reluctance. Walking down the sidewalk, under the canopy of tall trees, I'd warily notice the (suddenly) silent neighborhood kids who stood warily watching me. Nervously, I'd arrive at the grocery store to hear there the sounds of the gringo, reminding me that in this so-big world I was a foreigner. But if leaving home was never routine, neither was coming

back. Walking toward our house, climbing the steps from the sidewalk, in summer when the front door was open, I'd hear voices beyond the screen door talking in Spanish. For a second or two I'd stay, linger there listening. Smiling, I'd hear my mother call out, saying in Spanish, "Is that you, Richard?" Those were her words, but all the while her sounds would assure me: *You are home now. Come closer inside. With us.* "*Sí*," I'd reply.

Once more inside the house, I would resume my place in the family.   *17*
The sounds would grow harder to hear. Once more at home, I would grow less conscious of them. It required, however, no more than the blurt of the doorbell to alert me all over again to listen to sounds. The house would turn instantly quiet while my mother went to the door. I'd hear her hard English sounds. I'd wait to hear her voice turn to soft-sounding Spanish, which assured me, as surely as did the clicking tongue of the lock on the door, that the stranger was gone.

Plainly it is not healthy to hear such sounds so often. It is not healthy   *18*
to distinguish public from private sounds so easily. I remained cloistered by sounds, timid and shy in public, too dependent on the voices at home. And yet I was a very happy child when I was at home. I remember many nights when my father would come back from work, and I'd hear him call out to my mother in Spanish, sounding relieved. In Spanish, his voice would sound the light and free notes that he never could manage in English. Some nights I'd jump up just hearing his voice. My brother and I would come running into the room where he was with our mother. Our laughing (so deep was the pleasure!) became screaming. Like others who feel the pain of public alienation, we transformed the knowledge of our public separateness into a consoling reminder of our intimacy. Excited, our voices joined in a celebration of sounds. *We are speaking now the way we never speak out in public—we are together*, the sounds told me. Some nights no one seemed willing to loosen the hold that sounds had on us. At dinner we invented new words that sounded Spanish, but made sense only to us. We pieced together new words by taking, say, an English verb and giving it Spanish endings. My mother's instructions at bedtime would be lacquered with mock-urgent tones. Or a word like *sí*, sounded in several notes, would convey added measures of feeling. Tongues lingered around the edges of words, especially fat vowels: And we happily sounded that military drum roll, the twirling roar of the Spanish *r*. Family language, my family's sounds: the voices of my parents and sisters and brother. Their voices insisting: *You belong here. We are family members. Related. Special to one another. Listen!* Voices singing and sighing, rising and straining, then surging, teeming with pleasure which burst syllables

into fragments of laughter. At times it seemed there was steady quiet only when, from another room, the rustling whispers of my parents faded and I edged closer to sleep.

19   Supporters of bilingual education imply today that students like me miss a great deal by not being taught in their family's language. What they seem not to recognize is that, as a socially disadvantaged child, I regarded Spanish as a private language. It was a ghetto language that deepened and strengthened my feeling of public separateness. What I needed to learn in school was that I had the right, and the obligation, to speak the public language. The odd truth is that my first-grade classmates could have become bilingual, in the conventional sense of the word, more easily than I. Had they been taught early (as upper middle-class children often are taught) a "second language" like Spanish or French, they could have regarded it simply as another public language. In my case, such bilingualism could not have been so quickly achieved. What I did not believe was that I could speak a single public language.

20   Without question, it would have pleased me to have heard my teachers address me in Spanish when I entered the classroom. I would have felt much less afraid. I would have imagined that my instructors were somehow "related" to me; I would indeed have heard their Spanish as my family's language. I would have trusted them and responded with ease. But I would have delayed—postponed for how long?—having to learn the language of public society. I would have evaded—and for how long?—learning the great lesson of school: that I had a public identity.

21   Fortunately, my teachers were unsentimental about their responsibility. What they understood was that I needed to speak public English. So their voices would search me out, asking me questions. Each time I heard them I'd look up in surprise to see a nun's face frowning at me. I'd mumble, not really meaning to answer. The nun would persist. "Richard, stand up. Don't look at the floor. Speak up. Speak to the entire class, not just to me!" But I couldn't believe English could be my language to use. (In part, I did not want to believe it.) I continued to mumble. I resisted the teacher's demands. (Did I somehow suspect that once I learned this public language my family life would be changed?) Silent, waiting for the bell to sound, I remained dazed, diffident, afraid.

22   Because I wrongly imagined that English was intrinsically a public language and Spanish was intrinsically private, I easily noted the difference between classroom language and the language at home. At school, words were directed to a general audience of listeners. ("Boys and girls . . .") Words were meaningfully ordered. And the point was not self-expression alone, but to make oneself understood by many others. The teacher quizzed: "Boys and girls, why do we use that word in this

sentence? Could we think of a better word to use there? Would the sentence change its meaning if the words were differently arranged? Isn't there a better way of saying much the same thing?" (I couldn't say. I wouldn't try to say.)

Three months passed. Five. A half year. Unsmiling, ever watchful, my teachers noted my silence. They began to connect my behavior with the slow progress my brother and sisters were making. Until, one Saturday morning, three nuns arrived at the house to talk to our parents. Stiffly they sat on the blue living-room sofa. From the doorway of another room, spying on the visitors, I noted the incongruity, the clash of two worlds, the faces and voices of school intruding upon the familiar setting of home. I overheard one voice gently wondering, "Do your children speak only Spanish at home, Mrs. Rodriguez?" While another voice added, "That Richard especially seems so timid and shy."   23

That Rich-heard!   24

With great tact, the visitors continued, "Is it possible for you and your husband to encourage your children to practice their English when they are home?" Of course my parents complied. What would they not do for their children's well-being? And how could they question the Church's authority which those women represented? In an instant they agreed to give up the language (the sounds) which had revealed and accentuated our family's closeness. The moment after the visitors left, the change was observed. "*Ahora*, speak to us only *en inglés*," my father and mother told us.   25

At first, it seemed a kind of game. After dinner each night, the family gathered together to practice "our" English. It was still then *inglés*, a language foreign to us, so we felt drawn to it as strangers. Laughing, we would try to define words we could not pronounce. We played with strange English sounds, often overanglicizing our pronunciations. And we filled the smiling gaps of our sentences with familiar Spanish sounds. But that was cheating, somebody shouted, and everyone laughed.   26

In school, meanwhile, like my brother and sisters, I was required to attend a daily tutoring session. I needed a full year of this special work. I also needed my teachers to keep my attention from straying in class by calling out, "*Rich-heard*"—their English voices slowly loosening the ties to my other name, with its three notes, *Ri-car-do*. Most of all, I needed to hear my mother and father speak to me in a moment of seriousness in "broken"—suddenly heartbreaking—English. This scene was inevitable. One Saturday morning I entered the kitchen where my parents were talking, but I did not realize that they were talking in Spanish until, the moment they saw me, their voices changed and they began speaking English. The gringo sounds they uttered   27 startled me. Pushed me away. In that moment of trivial misunderstanding and profound insight, I felt my throat twisted by unsounded grief. I simply turned and left the room. But I had no place to escape to where I could grieve in Spanish. My brother and sisters were speaking English in another part of the house.

28   Again and again in the days following, as I grew increasingly angry, I was obliged to hear my mother and father encouraging me: "Speak to us *en inglés.*" Only then did I determine to learn classroom English. Thus, sometime afterward it happened: one day in school, I raised my hand to volunteer an answer to a question. I spoke out in a loud voice and I did not think it remarkable when the entire class understood. That day I moved very far from being the disadvantaged child I had been only days earlier. Taken hold at last was the belief, the calming assurance, that I *belonged* in public.

29   Shortly after, I stopped hearing the high, troubling sounds of *los gringos*. A more and more confident speaker of English, I didn't listen to how strangers sounded when they talked to me. With so many English-speaking people around me, I no longer heard American accents. Conversations quickened. Listening to persons whose voices sounded eccentrically pitched, I might note their sounds for a few seconds, but then I'd concentrate on what they were saying. Now when I heard someone's tone of voice—angry or questioning or sarcastic or happy or sad—I didn't distinguish it from the words it expressed. Sound and word were thus tightly wedded. At the end of each day I was often bemused, and always relieved, to realize how "soundless," though crowded with words, my day in public had been. An eight-year-old boy, I finally came to accept what had been technically true since my birth: I was an American citizen.

30   But diminished by then was the special feeling of closeness at home. Gone was the desperate, urgent, intense feeling of being at home among those with whom I felt intimate. Our family remained a loving family, but one greatly changed. We were no longer so close, no longer bound tightly together by the knowledge of our separateness from *los gringos*. Neither my older brother nor my sisters rushed home after school any more. Nor did I. When I arrived home, often there would be neighborhood kids in the house. Or the house would be empty of sounds.

31   Following the dramatic Americanization of their children, even my parents grew more publicly confident—especially my mother. First she learned the names of all the people on the block. Then she decided we needed to have a telephone in our house. My father, for his part, continued to use the word gringo, but it was no longer charged with bitterness or distrust. Stripped of any emotional content, the word simply became a name for those Americans not of Hispanic descent. Hearing

him, sometimes, I wasn't sure if he was pronouncing the Spanish word *gringo*, or saying gringo in English.

There was a new silence at home. As we children learned more and more English, we shared fewer and fewer words with our parents. Sentences needed to be spoken slowly when one of us addressed our mother or father. Often the parent wouldn't understand. The child would need to repeat himself. Still the parent misunderstood. The young voice, frustrated, would end up saying, "Never mind"—the subject was closed. Dinners would be noisy with the clinking of knives and forks against dishes. My mother would smile softly between her remarks; my father, at the other end of the table, would chew and chew his food while he stared over the heads of his children.

My mother! My father! After English became my primary language, I no longer knew what words to use in addressing my parents. The old Spanish words (those tender accents of sound) I had earlier used—*mamá* and *papá*—I couldn't use any more. They would have been all-too-painful reminders of how much had changed in my life. On the other hand, the words I heard neighborhood kids call their parents seemed equally unsatisfactory. "Mother" and "father," "ma," "papa," "pa," "dad," "pop" (how I hated the all-American sound of that last word)—all these I felt were unsuitable terms of address for *my* parents. As a result, I never used them at home. Whenever I'd speak to my parents, I would try to get their attention by looking at them. In public conversations, I'd refer to them as my "parents" or my "mother" and "father."

My mother and father, for their part, responded differently, as their children spoke to them less. My mother grew restless, seemed troubled and anxious at the scarceness of words exchanged in the house. She would question me about my day when I came home from school. She smiled at my small talk. She pried at the edges of my sentences to get me to say something more. ("What . . .?") She'd join conversations she overheard, but her intrusions often stopped her children's talking. By contrast, my father seemed to grow reconciled to the new quiet. Though his English somewhat improved, he tended more and more to retire into silence. At dinner he spoke very little. One night his children and even his wife helplessly giggled at his garbled English pronunciation of the Catholic "Grace Before Meals." Thereafter he made his wife recite the prayer at the start of each meal, even on formal occasions when there were guests in the house.

Hers became the public voice of the family. On official business it was she, not my father, who would usually talk to strangers on the phone or in stores. We children grew so accustomed to his silence that years later we would routinely refer to his "shyness." (My mother often tried to explain: both of his parents died when he was eight. He was raised by an uncle who treated him as little more than a menial servant. He was never encouraged to speak. He grew up alone—a man of few words.) But I realized my father was not shy whenever I'd watch him speaking Spanish with relatives. Using Spanish, he was quickly effusive. Especially when talking with other men, his voice would spark, flicker, flare alive with varied sounds. In Spanish he expressed ideas and feelings he rarely revealed when speaking English. With firm Spanish sounds he conveyed a confidence and authority that English would never allow him.

36   The silence at home, however, was not simply the result of fewer words passing between parents and children. More profound for me was the silence created by my inattention to sounds. At about the time I no longer bothered to listen with care to the sounds of English in public, I grew careless about listening to the sounds made by the family when they spoke. Most of the time I would hear someone speaking at home and didn't distinguish his sounds from the words people uttered in public. I didn't even pay much attention to my parents' accented and ungrammatical speech—at least not at home. Only when I was with them in public would I become alert to their accents. But even then their sounds caused me less and less concern. For I was growing increasingly confident of my own public identity.

37   I would have been happier about my public success had I not recalled, sometimes, what it had been like earlier, when my family conveyed its intimacy through a set of conveniently private sounds. Sometimes in public, hearing a stranger, I'd hark back to my lost past. A Mexican farm worker approached me one day downtown. He wanted directions to some place. *"Hijito, . . ."* he said. And his voice stirred old longings. Another time I was standing beside my mother in the visiting room of a Carmelite convent, before the dense screen which rendered the nuns shadowy figures. I heard several of them speaking Spanish in their busy, singsong, overlapping voices, assuring my mother that, yes, yes, we were remembered, all our family was remembered, in their prayers. Those voices echoed faraway family sounds. Another day a dark-faced old woman touched my shoulder lightly to steady herself as she boarded a bus. She murmured something to me I couldn't quite comprehend. Her Spanish voice came near, like the face of a never-before-seen relative in the instant before I was kissed. That voice, like so many of the Spanish voices I'd hear in public, recalled the golden age of my childhood.

38   Bilingual educators say today that children lose a degree of "individuality" by becoming assimilated into public society. (Bilingual schooling is a program popularized in the seventies, that decade when mid-

dle-class "ethnics" began to resist the process of assimilation—the "American melting pot.") But the bilingualists oversimplify when they scorn the value and necessity of assimilation. They do not seem to realize that a person is individualized in two ways. So they do not realize that, while one suffers a diminished sense of *private* individuality by being assimilated into public society, such assimilation makes possible the achievement of *public* individuality.

Simplistically again, the bilingualists insist that a student should be reminded of his difference from others in mass society, of his "heritage." But they equate mere separateness with individuality. The fact is that only in private—with intimates—is separateness from the crowd a prerequisite for individuality; an intimate "tells" me that I am unique, unlike all others, apart from the crowd. In public, by contrast, full individuality is achieved, paradoxically, by those who are able to consider themselves members of the crowd. Thus it happened for me. Only when I was able to think of myself as an American, no longer an alien in gringo society, could I seek the rights and opportunities necessary for full public individuality. The social and political advantages I enjoy as a man began on the day I came to believe that my name is indeed *Rich-heard Road-ree-guess*. It is true that my public society today is often impersonal; in fact, my public society is usually mass society. But despite the anonymity of the crowd, and despite the fact that the individuality I achieve in public is often tenuous—because it depends on my being one in a crowd—I celebrate the day I acquired my new name. Those middle-class ethnics who scorn assimilation seem to me filled with decadent self-pity, obsessed by the burden of public life. Dangerously, they romanticize public separateness and trivialize the dilemma of those who are truly socially disadvantaged.

39

If I rehearse here the changes in my private life after my Americanization, it is finally to emphasize a public gain. The loss implies the gain. The house I returned to each afternoon was quiet. Intimate sounds no longer greeted me at the door. Inside there were other noises. The telephone rang. Neighborhood kids ran past the door of the bedroom where I was reading my schoolbooks—covered with brown shopping-bag paper. Once I learned the public language, it would never again be easy for me to hear intimate family voices. More and more of my day was spent hearing words, not sounds. But that may only be a way of saying that on the day I raised my hand in class and spoke loudly to an entire roomful of faces, my childhood started to end.

40

I grew up the victim of a disconcerting confusion. As I became fluent in English, I could no longer speak Spanish with confidence. I continued to understand spoken Spanish, and in high school I learned how to read and write Spanish. But for many years I could not pro-

41

nounce it. A powerful guilt blocked my spoken words; an essential glue was missing whenever I would try to connect words to form sentences. I would be unable to break a barrier of sound, to speak freely. I would speak, or try to speak, Spanish, and I would manage to utter halting, hiccupping sounds which betrayed my unease. (Even today I speak Spanish very slowly, at best.)

42   When relatives and Spanish-speaking friends of my parents came to the house, my brother and sisters would usually manage to say a few words before being excused. I never managed so gracefully. Each time I'd hear myself addressed in Spanish, I couldn't respond with any success. I'd know the words I wanted to say, but I couldn't say them. I would try to speak, but everything I said seemed to me horribly anglicized. My mouth wouldn't form the sounds right. My jaw would tremble. After a phrase or two, I'd stutter, cough up a warm, silvery sound, and stop.

43   My listeners were surprised to hear me. They'd lower their heads to grasp better what I was trying to say. They would repeat their questions in gentle, affectionate voices. But then I would answer in English. No, no, they would say, we want you to speak to us in Spanish ("*en español*"). But I couldn't do it. Then they would call me *Pocho*. Sometimes playfully, teasing, using the tender diminutive—*mi pochito*. Sometimes not so playfully but mockingly, *pocho*. (A Spanish dictionary defines that word as an adjective meaning "colorless" or "bland." But I heard it as a noun, naming the Mexican-American who, in becoming an American, forgets his native society.) "*¡Pocho!*" my mother's best friend muttered, shaking her head. And my mother laughed, somewhere behind me. She said that her children didn't want to practice "our Spanish" after they started going to school. My mother's smiling voice made me suspect that the lady who faced me was not really angry at me. But searching her face, I couldn't find the hint of a smile.

44   Embarrassed, my parents would often need to explain their children's inability to speak fluent Spanish during those years. My mother encountered the wrath of her brother, her only brother, when he came up from Mexico one summer with his family and saw his nieces and nephews for the very first time. After listening to me, he looked away and said what a disgrace it was that my siblings and I couldn't speak Spanish, "*su propria idioma.*" He made that remark to my mother, but I noticed that he stared at my father.

45   One other visitor from those years I clearly remember: a long-time friend of my father from San Francisco who came to stay with us for several days in late August. He took great interest in me after he realized that I couldn't answer his questions in Spanish. He would grab me, as I started to leave the kitchen. He would ask me something. Usually he wouldn't bother to wait for my mumbled response. Knowingly, he'd

murmur, "*¿Ay pocho, pocho, donde vas?*" And he would press his thumbs into the upper part of my arms, making me squirm with pain. Dumbly I'd stand there, waiting for his wife to notice us and call him off with a benign smile. I'd giggle, hoping to deflate the tension between us, pretending that I hadn't seen the glittering scorn in his glance.

I recount such incidents only because they suggest the fierce power 46
that Spanish had over many people I met at home, how strongly Spanish was associated with closeness. Most of those people who called me a *pocho* could have spoken English to me, but many wouldn't. They seemed to think that Spanish was the only language we could use among ourselves, that Spanish alone permitted our association. (Such persons are always vulnerable to the ghetto merchant and the politician who have learned the value of speaking their clients' "family language" so as to gain immediate trust.) For my part, I felt that by learning English I had somehow committed a sin of betrayal. But betrayal against whom? Not exactly against the visitors to the house. Rather, I felt I had betrayed my immediate family. I knew that my parents had encouraged me to learn English. I knew that I had turned to English with angry reluctance. But once I spoke English with ease, I came to feel guilty. I sensed that I had broken the spell of intimacy which had once held the family so close together. It was this original sin against my family that I recalled whenever anyone addressed me in Spanish and I responded, confounded.

Yet even during those years of guilt, I was coming to grasp certain 47
consoling truths about language and intimacy—truths that I learned gradually. Once, I remember playing with a friend in the backyard when my grandmother appeared at the window. Her face was stern with suspicion when she saw the boy (the *gringo* boy) I was with. She called out to me in Spanish, sounding the whistle of her ancient breath. My companion looked up and watched her intently as she lowered the window and moved (still visible) behind the light curtain, watching us both. He wanted to know what she had said. I started to tell him, to translate her Spanish words into English. The problem was, however, that though I knew how to translate exactly what she had told me, I realized that any translation would distort the deepest meaning of her message: it had been directed only to me. This message of intimacy could never be translated because it did not lie in the actual words she had used but passed through them. So any translation would have seemed wrong; the words would have been stripped of an essential meaning. Finally I decided not to tell my friend anything—just that I didn't hear all she had said.

This insight was unfolded in time. As I made more and more friends 48
outside my house, I began to recognize intimate messages spoken in English in a close friend's confidential tone or secretive whisper. Even

more remarkable were those instances when, apparently for no special reason, I'd become conscious of the fact that my companion was speaking *only to me*. I'd marvel then, just hearing his voice. It was a stunning event to be able to break through the barrier of public silence, to be able to hear the voice of the other, to realize that it was directed just to me. After such moments of intimacy outside the house, I began to trust what I heard intimately conveyed through my family's English. Voices at home at last punctured sad confusion. I'd hear myself addressed as an intimate—in English. Such moments were never as raucous with sound as in past times, when we had used our "private" Spanish. (Our English-sounding house was never to be as noisy as our Spanish-sounding house had been.) Intimate moments were usually moments of soft sound. My mother would be ironing in the dining room while I did my homework nearby. She would look over at me, smile, and her voice sounded to tell me that I was her son, *Richard*.

49   Intimacy thus continued at home; intimacy was not stilled by English. Though there were fewer occasions for it—a change in my life that I would never forget—there were also times when I sensed the deep truth about language and intimacy: *Intimacy is not created by a particular language; it is created by intimates*. Thus the great change in my life was not linguistic but social. If, after becoming a successful student, I no longer heard intimate voices as often as I had earlier, it was not because I spoke English instead of Spanish. It was because I spoke public language for most of my day. I moved easily at last, a citizen in a crowded city of words.

50   As a man I spend most of my day in public, in a world largely devoid of speech sounds. So I am quickly attracted by the glamorous quality of certain alien voices. I still am gripped with excitement when someone passes me on the street, speaking in Spanish. I have not moved beyond the range of the nostalgic pull of those sounds. And there is something very compelling about the sounds of lower-class blacks. Of all the accented versions of English that I hear in public, I hear theirs most intently. The Japanese tourist stops me downtown to ask me a question and I inch my way past his accent to concentrate on what he is saying. The eastern European immigrant in the neighborhood delicatessen speaks to me and, again, I do not pay much attention to his sounds, nor to the Texas accent of one of my neighbors or the Chicago accent of the woman who lives in the apartment below me. But when the ghetto black teenagers get on the city bus, I hear them. Their sounds in my society are the sounds of the outsider. Their voices annoy me for being so loud—so self-sufficient and unconcerned by my presence, but for the same reason they are glamorous: a romantic gesture against public

acceptance. And as I listen to their shouted laughter, I realize my own quietness. I feel envious of them—envious of their brazen intimacy.

I warn myself away from such envy, however. Overhearing those 51 teenagers, I think of the black political activists who lately have argued in favor of using black English in public schools—an argument that varies only slightly from that of foreign-language bilingualists. I have heard ''radical'' linguists make the point that black English is a complex and intricate version of English. And I do not doubt it. But neither do I think that black English should be a language of public instruction. What makes it inappropriate in classrooms is not something in the language itself but, rather, what lower-class speakers make of it. Just as Spanish would have been a dangerous language for me to have used at the start of my education, so black English would be a dangerous language to use in the schooling of teenagers for whom it reinforces feelings of public separateness.

This seems to me an obvious point to make, and yet it must be said. 52 In recent years there have been many attempts to make the language of the alien a public language. ''Bilingual education, two ways to understand...'' television and radio commercials glibly announce. Proponents of bilingual education are careful to say that above all they want every student to acquire a good education. Their argument goes something like this: Children permitted to use their family language will not be so alienated and will be better able to match the progress of English-speaking students in the crucial first months of schooling. Increasingly confident of their ability, such children will be more inclined to apply themselves to their studies in the future. But then the bilingualists also claim another very different goal. They say that children who use their family language in school will retain a sense of their ethnic heritage and their family ties. Thus the supporters of bilingual education want it both ways. They propose bilingual schooling as a way of helping students acquire the classroom skills crucial for public success. But they likewise insist that bilingual instruction will give students a sense of their identity apart from the English-speaking public.

Behind this scheme gleams a bright promise for the alien child: one 53 can become a public person while still remaining a private person. Who would not want to believe such an appealing idea? Who can be surprised that the scheme has the support of so many middle-class ethnic Americans? If the barrio or ghetto child can retain his separateness even while being publicly educated, then it is almost possible to believe that no private cost need be paid for public success. This is the consolation offered by any of the number of current bilingual programs. Consider, for example, the bilingual voter's ballot. In some American cities one can cast a ballot printed in several languages. Such a document implies that it is possible for one to exercise that most public of rights—the right to vote—while still keeping oneself apart, unassimilated in public life.

54   It is not enough to say that such schemes are foolish and certainly doomed. Middle-class supporters of public bilingualism toy with the confusion of those Americans who cannot speak standard English as well as they do. Moreover, bilingual enthusiasts sin against intimacy. A Hispanic-American tells me, "I will never give up my family language," and he clutches a group of words as though they were the source of his family ties. He credits to language what he should credit to family members. This is a convenient mistake, for as long as he holds on to certain familiar words, he can ignore how much else has actually changed in his life.

55   It has happened before. In earlier decades, persons ambitious for social mobility, and newly successful, similarly seized upon certain "family words." Workingmen attempting to gain political power, for example, took to calling one another "brother." The word as they used it, however, could never resemble the word (the sound) "brother" exchanged by two people in intimate greeting. The context of its public delivery made it at best a metaphor; with repetition it was only a vague echo of the intimate sound. Context forced the change. Context could not be overruled. Context will always protect the realm of the intimate from public misuse. Today middle-class white Americans continue to prove the importance of context as they try to ignore it. They seize upon idioms of the black ghetto, but their attempt to appropriate such expressions invariably changes the meaning. As it becomes a public expression, the ghetto idiom loses its sound, its message of public separateness and strident intimacy. With public repetition it becomes a series of words, increasingly lifeless.

56   The mystery of intimate utterance remains. The communication of intimacy passes through the word and enlivens its sound, but it cannot be held by the word. It cannot be retained or ever quoted because it is too fluid. It depends not on words but on persons.

57   My grandmother! She stood among my other relations mocking me when I no longer spoke Spanish. *Pocho*, she said, but then it made no difference. She'd laugh, and our relationship continued because language was never its source. She was a woman in her eighties during the first decade of my life—a mysterious woman to me, my only living grandparent, a woman of Mexico in a long black dress that reached down to her shoes. She was the one relative of mine who spoke no word of English. She had no interest in gringo society and remained completely aloof from the public. She was protected by her daughters, protected even by me when we went to Safeway together and I needed to act as her translator. An eccentric woman. Hard. Soft.

When my family visited my aunt's house in San Francisco, my grand-   58
mother would search for me among my many cousins. When she found
me, she'd chase them away. Pinching her granddaughters, she would
warn them away from me. Then she'd take me to her room, where she
had prepared for my coming. There would be a chair next to the bed, a
dusty-jellied candy nearby, and a copy of *Life en Español* for me to examine. "There," she'd say. And I'd sit content, a boy of eight. *Pocho*,
her favorite. I'd sift through the pictures of earthquake-destroyed Latin-
American cities and blonde-wigged Mexican movie stars. And all the
while I'd listen to the sound of my grandmother's voice. She'd pace
around the room, telling me stories of her life. Her past. They were stories so familiar that I couldn't remember when I'd heard them for the
first time. I'd look up sometimes to listen. Other times she'd look over
at me, but she never expected a response. Sometimes I'd smile or nod. (I
understood exactly what she was saying.) But it never seemed to matter
to her one way or the other. It was enough that I was there. The words
she spoke were almost irrelevant to that fact. We were content. And the
great mystery remained: intimate utterance.

I learn nothing about language and intimacy listening to those social   59
activists who propose using one's family language in public life. I learn
much more simply by listening to songs on a radio, or hearing a great
voice at the opera, or overhearing the woman downstairs at an open
window singing to herself. Singers celebrate the human voice. Their
lyrics are words, but, animated by voice, those words are subsumed
into sounds. (This suggests a central truth about language: all words are
capable of becoming sounds as we fill them with the "music" of our
life.) With excitement I hear the words yielding their enormous power
to sound, even though their meaning is never totally obliterated. In
most songs, the drama or tension results from the way that the singer
moves between words (sense) and notes (song). At one moment the
song simply "says" something; at another moment the voice stretches
out the words and moves to the realm of pure sound. Most songs are
about love: lost love, celebrations of loving, pleas. By simply being occasions when sounds soar through words, however, songs put me in
mind of the most intimate moments of life.

Finally, among all types of music, I find songs created by lyric poets   60
most compelling. On no other public occasion is sound so important for
me. Written poems on a page seem at first glance a mere collection of
words. And yet, without musical accompaniment, the poet leads me to
hear the sounds of the words that I read. As song, a poem moves between the levels of sound and sense, never limited to one realm or the
other. As a public artifact, the poem can never offer truly intimate
sound, but it helps me to recall the intimate times of my life. As I read
in my room, I grow deeply conscious of being alone, sounding my voice

in search of another. The poem serves, then, as a memory device; it forces remembrance. And it refreshes; it reminds me of the possibility of escaping public words, the possibility that awaits me in intimate meetings.

61   The child reminds the adult: to seek intimate sounds is to seek the company of intimates. I do not expect to hear those sounds in public. I would dishonor those I have loved, and those I love now, to claim anything else. I would dishonor our intimacy by holding on to a particular language and calling it my family language. Intimacy cannot be trapped within words; it passes through words. It passes. Intimates leave the room. Doors close. Faces move away from the window. Time passes, and voices recede into the dark. Death finally quiets the voice. There is no way to deny it, no way to stand in the crowd claiming to utter one's family language.

62   The last time I saw my grandmother I was nine years old. I can tell you some of the things she said to me as I stood by her bed, but I cannot quote the message of intimacy she conveyed with her voice. She laughed, holding my hand. Her voice illumined disjointed memories as it passed them again. She remembered her husband—his green eyes, his magic name of Narcissio, his early death. She remembered the farm in Mexico, the eucalyptus trees nearby (their scent, she remembered, like incense). She remembered the family cow, the bell around its neck heard miles away. A dog. She remembered working as a seamstress, how she'd leave her daughters and son for long hours to go into Guadalajara to work. And how my mother would come running toward her in the sun—in her bright yellow dress—on her return. "MMMMAAAAMMMMÁÁÁÁ," the old lady mimicked her daughter (my mother) to her daughter's son. She laughed. There was the snap of a cough. An aunt came into the room and told me it was time I should leave. "You can see her tomorrow," she promised. So I kissed my grandmother's cracked face. And the last thing I saw was her thin, oddly youthful thigh, as my aunt rearranged the sheet on the bed.

63   At the funeral parlor a few days after, I remember kneeling with my relatives during the rosary. Among their voices I traced, then lost, the sounds of individual aunts in the surge of the common prayer. And I heard at that moment what since I have heard very often—the sound the women in my family make when they are praying in sadness. When I went up to look at my grandmother, I saw her through the haze of a veil draped over the open lid of the casket. Her face looked calm—but distant and unyielding to love. It was not the face I remembered seeing most often. It was the face she made in public when the clerk at Safeway asked her some question and I would need to respond. It was her public face that the mortician had designed with his dubious art.

Questions and Activities

▶ *COMPREHENSION QUESTIONS*

1. Define "bilingual education." Why is Rodriguez opposed to it?
2. What is an aria? How does the meaning of the word help define the kind of writing Rodriguez is doing in this essay? Does the word "aria" also help define Rodriguez's attitude toward his childhood conflict between Spanish and English? What is that attitude?
3. Why does Rodriguez feel that music comes closer than any verbal language to expressing intimacy?

▶ *QUESTIONS OF RHETORICAL PURPOSE AND STRATEGY*

4. Why does Rodriguez devote so much of this piece to simply describing his childhood experience with language? Might this emphasis on unadorned description give readers more of an interest and involvement in the subject than a straightforward exposition of the subject would? Does making the descriptive purpose dominant seem to enhance or weaken the writing's persuasiveness?
5. To whom do you think this essay is addressed—Spanish-Americans, educators, all Americans, or linguists? Support your choice with references to the essay.
6. Why does Rodriguez put his linguistic arguments in paragraphs that are separate from his descriptions of his past experience? Compare, for example, paragraph 19 with the paragraphs that precede it. Are there differences in the style and voice? How does the voice in paragraph 19 differ from the voice in the earlier paragraphs?

▶ *THEME QUESTIONS*

7. Why is the incident in which Rodriguez's grandmother appears at the window while he is playing with a gringo boy (paragraph 47) significant to the author? Explain how he uses this example to show that his ongoing intimacy with his Spanish-speaking grandmother and his growing confidence in his ability to communicate with his friends in English were equally important?
8. What do you believe would be Rodriguez's answer to the theme question of this section? Has his identity been shaped by his languages? Or has he shaped his identity through his language experiences?
9. Geneva Smitherman, in the essay that starts off this section (pages 389–416), argues that we should accept and appreciate dialects. She also suggests that the friction between home and outside language is usually a negative influence on a child because it creates a sense of inferiority. Would Rodriguez disagree with Smitherman on this

point? Does his attitude toward Spanish suggest a rejection of it? Does he believe the friction between one's home language and one's school or work language is, generally, a good or a bad thing? Why was it necessary for Rodriguez to speak English at home as well as at school during the early part of his schooling?

► *LEARNING ACTIVITIES*

10. Recall a childhood incident when the language you were used to at home seemed to conflict with the language of school or public life. Write a sketch about that incident, using concrete details and some dialogue to bring the scene alive. Use the first person.
11. Rodriguez uses the first person in this essay. Compare your use of the first person in the sketch you wrote for the preceding activity with Rodriguez's. Does he seem more distant from and objective about his childhood self than you do? Did you organize your experience chronologically, as he did? (However, note that in certain key paragraphs, paragraph 5, for example, Rodriguez uses the present tense: "Memory teaches me what I know of these matters.")
12. Write an introduction and a conclusion for the sketch about a childhood incident of language conflict. These added elements should provide a more objective analysis of what happened in the incident. Imitate Rodriguez's shifts in style in your transitions from objective analysis to more personal description.
13. Work with another student to review your work on your sketch up to this point. Make a list combining the arguments for and against bilingual education that are implied or directly stated in your sketch and in Rodriguez's memoir. You might also wish to reconsider Geneva Smitherman's argument against bilingual education (pages 389–416). As a final step, write a generalization defining your position on this issue.

Thoughts on Writing: A Diary

SUSAN GRIFFIN

Susan Griffin is one of the most cited and productive of contemporary feminist poets. She has degrees from San Francisco State University, has taught drama and English at several universities, colleges, and community agencies, and has worked as a waitress, switchboard operator, and housepainter to support herself while writing. Griffin has also been an editor for *Ramparts* magazine. Most of her poetry — *Dear Sky* (1971) and *Let Them Be Said* (1973) — was published by small presses. Her later works, published by Harper and Row, have received a much wider reading: *Like the Iris of an Eye* (1976), *Rape: The Power of Consciousness* (1979), and *Woman and Nature: The Roaring inside Her* (1981). The latter is a work in poetic prose in which feminist philosophy is explained in terms of woman's relationship with nature and man. A great deal of Griffin's poetry has been reprinted in anthologies, and many of her essays have appeared in magazines such as *Ramparts, Sundance,* and *Aphra.*

The piece that follows is an excerpt from Griffin's diary. This writing is thus more personal and self-involved than Richard Rodriguez's more formal autobiographical essay (pages 457–474). Griffin here describes her anxiety as she wrote her long prose poem about women and creativity. She felt this tension because her creative role as a woman writer exploring her inner consciousness came into perpetual conflict with societal roles of male authority. In this diary excerpt, she describes how she tried to resolve this problem by projecting two contending voices into her poem: the voice of female openness and creativity versus the voice of patriarchal rationality and science. The open feminine voice wins out. Griffin, in subduing male rationality, gives herself over entirely to the process of discovery through language. She delays final interpretations until she has gone through a full range of experience. And even then her conclusions are always subject to revision, and for the most part purposely ambiguous.

How does this exploration of conflicting voices tie in with the question of whether language is defined by or defines reality? Griffin's view of the role writing plays in her life provides the link. Writing is a way of controlling and developing thoughts, a way for the introspective person to become more conscious of inner sensations. By following her feelings and thoughts in her writing, Griffin gradually discovers that they are different from those of men; she learns as well that reality is *not* always what others tell us it is. It is a creation of our own and others' language. The experience of writing "renders a precise meaning" out of what otherwise would be either suppressed by other realities or lost in vagueness and generality.

Through writing and reading, Griffin learns to transform her internal dialogue into an expression of life as she sees it. Unlike many of the other writers represented in this section, she does not despair because of the degeneration of language. In contrast, she celebrates language's ability to capture personal visions and make them public.

As you read, consider how Griffin uses style to create a personal voice:

1. What is her point of view as she writes?
2. Does Griffin want to share her ideas with her readers or persuade them to change their way of thinking about writing?
3. For whom was Griffin writing this piece?

▶ ————————————————

August 7, 1979

1   Last night I dreamed that I wrote the beginning of this diary in Sanskrit. The night before in a lecture (not in a dream) Sanskrit was explained to me as "the mother of all language." And perhaps poetry is also the mother of language. And thought. And once again, I have solved a problem in writing by falling asleep and dreaming. So here I pose another principle which after all is not irrelevant. Above all the act of writing calls on faith.

2   Here, a voice in my head, with whom I am always having a dialogue, asks, "Faith in what?"

3   But I tell the voice, "Wait, that will come. Stay with the experience because this experience renders a precise meaning."

4   For instance, when I was writing *Woman and Nature: The Roaring inside Her*, which is a kind of extended, long prose poem, after several months of writing little paragraphs and doing research and making plans I came across what I thought was a terrible problem. There were sides to reality that this voice could not utter. Now the idea of creating another voice, of an entirely different tone, seems obvious. But it was not then, although even then there were two other voices in me. One was the voice of despair, which said, "This will not work." And another, that calm writer of poetry, said simply, "Wait."

A few nights later I dreamt the solution: I woke with a clear idea that   5
I needed two voices posing conflicted visions of reality.

Now in fact (and this, in retrospect, is what I find most interesting   6
about writing that book, which took me five years), the voice of despair
and the calm voice of poetry correspond exactly to those two different
world views which, roughly speaking, in my book I designated as the
voice of patriarchy and the voice of woman and nature, and which came
to me first in a dream.

Woman and Nature: In the chapter called "Terror" a man tells a   7
woman of the meaninglessness of the heavens. He speaks of the void.
He quantifies the vastness and the void. He tells her the human body
would perish in that space, and that, in that magnitude, all human
meaning becomes insignificant. "He tells her how perishable she is and
how little there is to perish." The voice of woman and nature answers
in that chapter that the stars "are unmerciful witnesses" to his delusions, and later sings, "...we know these meanings reach you...the
stars and their light we hold in our hands...." Because this voice does
not despair. And does not despair because it sees the physical universe
as embodying meaning.

When I wrote this chapter I had in mind a poem whose first lines   8
("You if you were sensible/When I tell you the stars flash signals, each
one dreadful,") have admonished me for years. The poem is "Under
the Oak" by D. H. Lawrence. In the poem, a man speaks in an intense
and anguished voice to a woman whose silliness is implied when the
speaker must ask her to refrain from turning and saying to him, "The
night is wonderful," after he has described his terror of the stars to her.

In the last verse of this poem Lawrence creates out of this same   9
woman an inhuman being ("What thing better are you, what worse?"),
and, linking her to the dreadful signals of the stars, he asks what she has
to do with "the mysteries" of this earth, or with his "ancient curse."
Finally, in words that reverberate to woman, the stars, and what we
know as chance, Lawrence asks, "What place have you in my
histories?"

Lawrence's words are much more complex than my voice of the pa-   10
triarch in *Woman and Nature*. Still, what the stars give him is dread,
and as a being in the universe he feels cursed. The woman with whom
he speaks is variously insensitive and foolish ("twittering to and
fro/Beneath the oak...") or part of the mystery that has cursed him.
As all these, she is either better than him or worse, but not kindred.

This emotional tone, a kind of ambivalent bitterness toward the uni-   11
verse and woman, informs much of modern poetry, such that there is a
range from the anguished and ambivalent despair of Lawrence to the al-

most scientific usage of words, as sound units without sense, that is called concrete poetry. It is more or less the official artistic dogma of our age against which feminism, as an influence on poetry, is in rebellion.

12   But this split view of the universe and of woman is not new. Someone/thing better or worse than myself. Nature as divine or devilish. The muse, who is feminine, as cruel or benevolent.

13   And now the words "mother tongue," language, widen out for me, as I see that our relationship to the one who has given us birth, and to that universe which engendered our being, might be the same as our relationship to language: we must trust words and the coming of words.

14   And how the conflict between these two attitudes (or voices)—that of despair toward language, the muse and the universe; and that of love of language, of faith in the universe to render meaning—how this has raged in myself. And how it is played out daily in my work.

15   The voice of despair arrives as a kind of terror (just as I called it in *Woman and Nature*). I am certain before I begin writing a piece that I will not be able to put sentences together, or worse, that all I have to say has been said before, that there is no purpose, that there is no intrinsic authority to my own words. And that is where the struggle begins. Because I must then find the place in myself where my words have authority, some true and untouched place that does not mutter what has been said before, that speaks feelingly, enough to electrify the rhythms of speech, and make in the very telling a proof of authenticity.

16   This process can take days, and during those days one looks as though one is doing nothing. Here is where despair enters.

17   I, for instance, clean off my desk. I make telephone calls. I know I am avoiding the typewriter. I know that in my mind, where there might be words, there is simply a blankness. I may try to write and then my words bore me. At such times the whole world of words seems to be irrelevant, as if my faith in language itself had gone. And my faith cannot be restored by any sort of reasoning or logic. Now, I am in another world and I am deaf to singing.

August 9, 1979

18   I come back to this problem of despair in writing, myself caught up in it today, feeling a dullness about all language. In the morning I am irritable. I feel as if my sleep had been disturbed, as if a dream were intruded upon, and I am not quite certain how to proceed. This is a profound disorientation. When I am not giving forth words, I am not cer-

tain any longer who I am. But it is not like the adolescent searching for an identity; no, this state of mind has an entirely different quality, because in it there is a feeling of loss, as if my old identity, which had worked so well, which seemed to be the whole structure of the universe, were now slipping away, and all my attempts to retrieve it seem graceless, or angry, or blaming. And the old voice of protection and order in me whispers like an Iago that I betray myself.

And now I remember the substance of a revelation about faith I had a   19
few months ago. I was walking in the woods and became aware suddenly of a knowledge that enters me in that kind of silence, especially in the presence of an organic life that is not controlled by man. This is a knowledge of a deeply peaceful kinship with all that is alive, a state of mind that language struggles to render, and yet that, paradoxically, makes me want to sing. And at the same time I became aware that the whole impulse to science in western civilization must have been born of doubt. Indeed, all the great questions of science (what is the nature of matter, what is the origin of life, what is the cause of all motion in the universe, what is light) all these began as religious questions, and remained essentially religious until the nineteenth century. So one doubts the feeling of presence, the feeling of unity with all beings, in oneself; one seeks instead a proof, "scientific," quantifiable. Sense data. So perhaps this accounts for the poetic quality of many scientific truths, and yet, also, the fact that the scientific method abolishes intuition (although indeed intuition has solved many "scientific" problems).

In *Woman and Nature* I made the voice of science, hostile to intu-   20
ition, the voice of patriarchy, and all the time I wrote that book, the patriarchal voice was in me, whispering to me (the way the voice of order whispers to me now), that I had no proof for any of my writing, that I was wildly in error, that the vision I had of the whole work was absurd.

And what is this state of mind that the voice of order brings about in   21
myself, and that is akin to scientific doubt, and to patriarchal disapproval? I want to draw a portrait of this creature of despair who inhabits me, capture her, name her. Write a phenomenology of her.

She is, for one thing, concerned with the question of efficiency. She   22
would not have me "waste" any time. And so, to that end, she would have me know what I am going to write during any day's work before I write it.

And now seeing these words here, I see again how similar this crea-   23
ture is in every way to the patriarchal voice of science, which defends its very existence with arguments of efficiency, saving labor, use, production. But underneath this rationale is fear of the loss of control, and fear of death.

24   Because each time I write, each time the authentic words break through, I am changed. The older order that I was collapses and dies. I lose control. I do not know exactly what words will appear on the page. I follow language. I follow the sound of the words, and I am surprised and transformed by what I record.

25   And so perhaps despair hides a refusal and perhaps in this refusal is that terror born of faithlessness, which keeps a guard over my thoughts, will not let dreams reach the surface of my mind.

26   When I had written the first draft of *Woman and Nature* the book had a disorganized quality. I had several small chapters, some a paragraph, some a few pages, and no final sequence for them. And so I put the little pieces all in a logical order, by topic, or chronology or whatever seemed most reasonable. But this order did not "work." It was like a well-built bench that had no grace, and so one did not want to sit on it.

27   So I began again putting the pieces together, but this time I simply followed the words intuitively, putting pieces next to one another where the transition seemed wonderful, and that was when the shape of the book began to seem beautiful to me.

28   I read this in a book on Jewish mysticism: "Language in its purest form, Hebrew, according to the Kabbalists, reflects the fundamental spiritual nature of the world."

29   Before I wrote *Woman and Nature* I knew I wanted a kind of symmetry and a kind of repetition built into the structure. At first I began to create these purposefully. But very soon they began to occur in the work quite unbidden. So, as more and more in the work I began to oppose science with a mystical view of the universe, my work took on a life of its own, and began to resemble the patterns of the universe that it envisioned.

30   There is a meditation that is also an old Shamanistic practice in which one concentrates on the body of an animal, or a shell, or a tree, or a mountain, until one becomes that mountain. (This going into and becoming the other is the way of knowledge directly opposite to scientific objectification.) And when one writes *about* a phenomenon, one's words begin to mimic that phenomenon, to become that which they describe.

31   I remember here the Buddhist formulation: you are what you see.

32   *The phenomenology of despair.* She tells me words cannot change the world. She says there is not enough time. She wants to know a pur-

pose for every act. She is impressed only by the quantifiable material phenomenon. She is like a scale. Or a weighing machine. How many pages have been written? She is a judge without vision. She cannot play. She above all cannot *be*. She shares with the voice of patriarchy in *Woman and Nature* this idea that forests ought to grow near sawmills, that trees are good for lumber. As I write about her, large spaces of white ought to appear on the page indicating silence.

So much is sacrificed, in this civilization in which I write, to the en-   *33*
gine God of despair. But still, the other voice, the intuitive, returns, like grass forcing its way through concrete.

> *So much gladness, mother*
> *I am afraid I will break, oh,*
> *why was it*
> *You never spoke to me of this?*

This poem that entered my mind a few nights ago and until now I   *34*
have not written down and suddenly, for no reason I can see, wants to be written on this page here.

Too much an imitation of Sappho, the voice of despair says. Because   *35*
she is also wholly absorbed with ideas of authorship, and who said what, and one's reputation, and respectability. She is prideful and out of her mouth speaks a whole chorus of social disapproval which ranges all the way from professors, and male doctors of law, and male authorities with awards on their breasts, such as those Virginia Woolf envisioned, to feminists, different factions of the movement, to a friend I know who disapproves of a word I find I want to use.

Too much an imitation of Sappho, she says, and no one, she says,   *36*
will understand what you are saying. And this, she says, has been said over and over again. What you wanted to say is inexpressible.

That moment (last week), watching the film, when I knew the   *37*
filmmaker had captured a certain shape to life, which I had seen too, felt, and then tears in my eyes, crying both for the heroine in the film and that my soul was touched this way, by this film, and that also, this feeling, which perhaps has become too rare, is, nevertheless, not unique, but old, very, very old. And no, there is no logical train of words, no scientific proof, formulating what this film is saying. No, instead, the faltering words of a young boy, which on repetition seem almost sentimental—"We cannot live without love"—these evoke in us this deep, old, old knowledge which we know, suddenly, must belong to every creature.

August 11, 1979

38   Now I begin the day wondering if the voice of the "other" in society (the lesbian, the Black, the Jew) takes on, both in herself and as a
characteristic projected by the dominant ones, the meaning of the voice
of poetry (or woman, or nature, or wildness, or darkness). Thus it is we
in the class of the rejected who, it is argued, must be controlled. We *are*
the problem, the scapegoat for all impulses that might change the
accepted order.

39   The voice of despair, similarly, sees the voice of poetry (joy, playful-
ness, rebellious vision) as the problem. I encounter this particular kind
of drama almost every day I write. I may hour after hour put off going
into my study, or perhaps only for a few minutes, but the dialogue is the
same. The voice of protection and order shouts at me "necessity," as if I
must go to my desk and record reason's preordained words. But if I can
listen past this voice, inside is another voice—accused of laziness and
childishness and too many emotions—who wants to speak, who is
overflowing with language, and whose words, in some unpredictable
ways, always afterward, *after* they have been spoken, seem necessary to
reason.

40   (Similarly, if women, blacks, lesbians, Jews were given "what they
want," enormous social problems might be solved.)

41   This correlation might explain why the most interesting creative
work is being done at the moment by those who are excluded and have
departed from the dominant culture—women, people of color, homosexuals. And this work, unlike the decadent, and abstract, and dadaist,
and concrete, and mechanist work of the dominant culture, is not despairing. This work is radiant with will, with the desire to speak; it
sings with the clear tones of long-suppressed utterance, is brilliant with
light, with powerful and graceful forms, with forms that embody feeling and enlarge the capacity of the beholder, of the listener, to feel.

42   I find myself staying away, on the whole, unless they have been
recommended to me as an exception, from work by white men, because
this work seems to need to blunt or even bludgeon the sensibilities of its
audience. This is also true of work by women or blacks who imitate
that white male contemporary tradition. And there are of course
abundant examples of art by white men that depart from this tradition.

43   This voice of departure from protection and order is what I value
most in myself. She is the one who loves, and loves fiercely (and perhaps that is why so much of poetry is love poetry). She has a sense of the
largest meanings of life and can find these in the smallest actualities. If

there is a tragedy, a weeping in her, this is always a grief for the loss of herself, her burial, her muteness.

Silences. Not the silences between notes of music, or the silences of a   44
sleeping animal, or the calm of a glassy surfaced river witnessing the outstretched wings of a heron. Not the silence of an emptied mind. But this other silence. That silence which can feel like a scream, in which there is no peace. The grim silence between two lovers who are quarreling. The painful silence of the one with tears in her eyes who will not cry. The silence of the child who knows she will not be heard. The silence of a whole people who have been massacred. Of a whole sex made mute, or not educated to speech. The silence of a mind afraid to admit truth to itself. This is the silence the poet dreads.

And now I think of the wonderful laughter of a room full of women,   45
the excited talking. The joy. Or the almost blistering crackle of energy in a room full of women when one is singing or reading her work to the others. Every word counts.

Think of the difference between these two phrases, that "things   46
count" or to "count things."

And what of rigor, or discipline, or training? Do these belong to the   47
voice of protection or to the voice of departure? To both now, I think, sitting here, having forced myself to come to my study before going out on errands. Because I know I will have more energy now. But perhaps the key to the difference here is intent. I speak now of the kind of joyful rigor—and now perhaps is the time to make a distinction between pleasure and joy. When one is working very hard, it may at any moment be more pleasurable to go from the work and sleep, or eat or lie in the sun. But joy, which is a different, deeper, more thrilling kind of pleasure, joy which is an experience of embodied meaning, joy may be had from working on. Even when the body complains, or the mind aches and claims it cannot go on. To find joy, even in the erotic, one must push past resistances, both in the psyche and the physical, and above all this is significant to the process of writing. But one does not intend to push past a resistance to punish oneself. Rather, one has a hunger for this joy, for this meaning that will pierce experience, and make one suddenly close to all being.

So in writing *Woman and Nature* I moved toward joy but often with   48
great weariness and full of fear and even sometimes anguish. Because indeed the voice of protection and order *is* a resistance, and it takes

great strength (courage, rigor, discipline, decisiveness) to struggle with this voice. But finally the joy was in the writing itself, to witness and be part of this process whereby the words and shape of the book began to embody its meaning, so that the very process of writing seemed a proof and to illuminate existence.

49   And finally I was changed by the writing of the book.

50   Synchronicities, the voices of trees, rivers, the wind, coincidental openings of books, a larger knowledge that seemed available to me only through ''intuition'' (a mode of listening to the universe) all these in my writing of the book changed me so that in my acts, in my daily acts, I was no longer a child of the age of science and rational thought. Now, writing this diary even, I still live in a profound state of disorientation. I know I find my power only when I trust language and follow words, moving with them musically, but I cannot always do this. I find myself stopping. Looking about to see where I am. Who I am. And what I am doing.

51   Faith in what? Only in what I know most certainly and in what can never be proved except through joy. But in this sense a diary about writing is not about writing at all. Or at least, not uniquely about writing. And if this were not so, poets would have no readers.

52   So all that I ask of my writing I ask of the rest of my life too. *Here (I say) the words are too thin. I have heard this before, I say, and there is more to this than is being revealed. I have said the obvious and expected. But beyond this must be something shocking, something satisfying.* And so I mark out these old words and write again. I cross out all the words except those that affect me deeply, those for which I have some ''irrational'' love. I keep those and build again. And again. All the while knowing that deeper meaning will rise to the surface like the form in a piece of stone, or the grain of a polished wood, if I have faith in this knowledge inside me. If I keep working. And over and over the words do not fail me. Over and over I come to a clarifying end. A circle is made. A pattern of sense is given to those words I loved for no apparent reason. I trust my own heart again. *This experience renders a precise meaning.*

Questions and Activities

► *COMPREHENSION QUESTIONS*

1. Why does Griffin begin her piece with a reference to Sanskrit as "the mother of all language"? How does the idea of motherhood tie in with what Griffin has to say about women and their writing? How does the idea of language tie in with what Griffin goes on to say about writing?

2. What place does dreaming have in Griffin's writing process? Find a place in this selection where Griffin tells how a dream became a part of her writing.

3. Who are the Kabbalists, mentioned in paragraph 28? Why are they an appropriate group for Griffin to mention at this point in her explanation of what writing means to her?

4. In paragraph 32, Griffin discusses the "phenomenology of despair." Restate this phrase in your own words. Why does Griffin put this phrase in these precise terms at this point in her diary? (You may need to reread the preceding and following paragraphs for Griffin's discussion of the despairing voice in Shamanistic practices and the God of despair of Western civilization.)

► *QUESTIONS OF RHETORICAL PURPOSE AND STRATEGY*

5. What in the physical layout of this selection tells you that it is from a diary? Who is writing to whom in a diary? What is usually the purpose of a diary?

6. Two writing voices are used in this selection. Define them; then point to specific places where one voice or the other is speaking. How would you describe the differences in style (word choice, sentence structure, etc.) of these two voices? How are the two voices set off against one another?

7. How does Griffin organize this writing? Are there groups of paragraphs that develop one significant point? Does the repetition of "precise meaning" in paragraphs 3 and 52 (the final paragraph) help pull the main ideas together?

8. Why, in paragraph 52, are certain words italicized? Who is speaking these italicized words?

► *THEME QUESTIONS*

9. Many of the other selections in this section argue that people are shaped by their own and others' language. Does Griffin seem to believe that a writer can use language to shape her identity, to fight against others who would shape it for her? Who does Griffin feel

would shape her identity if she did not strive to do it herself? How would these others shape her identity, perhaps without even trying to do so?

10. Why is the personal form of a diary better suited to what Griffin has to say about writing than a more objective form might be?

11. Describe the "voice of patriarchy" as Griffin uses the term (paragraph 6). How is that voice different from Griffin's voice in this diary? Does this difference between Griffin's voice and the dominant voice of the patriarchal culture help define her point about writing and its true purpose?

► *LEARNING ACTIVITIES*

12. Write your own diary entry in response to your reading of Griffin's. Do this by stopping yourself at certain points as you reread the selection. At each stopping point create a paragraph that explains or describes a question, feeling, or idea that Griffin's writing has created in you.

13. Discuss your written diary entry with others in your class. What points in the selection caused others to stop and make a diary entry? Are other students' diary entries more or less personal than yours? What do all the entries taken together tell you about Griffin's piece? What do they tell you and your classmates about yourselves as readers?

Arrangement in Black and White

DOROTHY PARKER

Dorothy Parker died in 1967 at the age of seventy-four. Her career was a fascinating and prolific one. She worked as an editor for *Vogue* and *Vanity Fair* from 1916 to 1920; she was fired as the drama critic of *Vanity Fair* in 1920 for writing three unfavorable reviews of current plays. She was a book reviewer and columnist for *The New Yorker* from 1925 to 1957; she then reviewed books for *Esquire* from 1958 to 1965. She married, divorced, and remarried screenwriter Alan Campbell, with whom she co-authored twenty-one screenplays for full-length films between 1934 and 1949 (including *A Star Is Born* in 1937). She produced several volumes of witty and satiric poetry and many widely read and sophisticated short stories, and adapted three of the latter for television. Her writings are collected in *The Portable Dorothy Parker* (1973), *Collected Poetry* (1944), *Constant Reader* (1970), and *A Month of Saturdays* (1971). Parker won the O. Henry Award for short fiction in 1929 for her short story "Big Blond."

Parker was most popular in the 1930s and 1940s. She seemed to personify a popular need to display wit, cynicism, and sophistication in the face of the hardship and tragedy of those decades. She often treated tragedy and suffering with a satiric sense of humor and a stiff-upper-lip attitude. All of these characteristics are apparent in the story that follows.

In "Arrangement in Black and White," Parker offers readers the opportunity to observe a woman who must respond to a new social situation. Nothing much happens in the story; the setting is a party in New York, and the main character, a woman with "pink velvet poppies" in her dyed blond hair, chatters away about her husband and her excitement about meeting the guest of honor, a famous black singer. Neither her host nor the singer have much chance or inclination to respond to her. The readers are expected to analyze the woman's character almost entirely from her language:

1. How does the main character's manner of speaking reveal her inner feelings and mental state? Is the woman trying to seem more confident than she really is?
2. What does the woman really think about black people? Does her language suggest feelings and attitudes that she is unaware of?
3. What is the significance of the title of this story?

▶ ─────────────────────────

1   The woman with the pink velvet poppies wreathed round the assisted gold of her hair traversed the crowded room at an interesting gait combining a skip with a sidle, and clutched the lean arm of her host.

2   "Now I got you!" she said. "Now you can't get away!"

3   "Why, hello," said her host. "Well. How are you?"

4   "Oh, I'm finely," she said. "Just simply finely. Listen. I want you to do me the most terrible favor. Will you? Will you please? Pretty please?"

5   "What is it?" said her host.

6   "Listen," she said. "I want to meet Walter Williams. Honestly, I'm just simply crazy about that man. Oh, when he sings! When he sings those spirituals! Well, I said to Burton, 'It's a good thing for you Walter Williams is colored,' I said, 'or you'd have lots of reason to be jealous.' I'd really love to meet him. I'd like to tell him I've heard him sing. Will you be an angel and introduce me to him?"

7   "Why, certainly," said her host. "I thought you'd met him. The party's for him. Where is he, anyway?"

8   "He's over there by the bookcase," she said. "Let's wait till those people get through talking to him. Well, I think you're simply marvelous, giving this perfectly marvelous party for him, and having him meet all these white people, and all. Isn't he terribly grateful?"

9   "I hope not," said her host.

10   "I think it's really terribly nice," she said. "I do. I don't see why on earth it isn't perfectly all right to meet colored people. I haven't any feeling at all about it—not one single bit. Burton—oh, he's just the other way. Well, you know, he comes from Virginia, and you know how they are."

11   "Did he come tonight?" said her host.

12   "No, he couldn't," she said. "I'm a regular grass widow tonight. I told him when I left, 'There's no telling what I'll do,' I said. He was just so tired out, he couldn't move. Isn't it a shame?"

13   "Ah," said her host.

14   "Wait till I tell him I met Walter Williams!" she said. "He'll just about die. Oh, we have more arguments about colored people. I talk to him like I don't know what, I get so excited. 'Oh, don't be so silly,' I say. But I must say for Burton, he's heaps broader-minded than lots of these Southerners. He's really awfully fond of colored people. Well, he says himself, he wouldn't have white servants. And you know, he had this old colored nurse, this regular old nigger mammy, and he just simply loves her. Why, every time he goes home, he goes out in the kitchen to see her. He does, really, to this day. All he says is, he says he hasn't

got a word to say against colored people as long as they keep their place. He's always doing things for them—giving them clothes and I don't know what all. The only thing he says, he says he wouldn't sit down at the table with one for a million dollars. 'Oh,' I say to him, 'you make me sick, talking like that.' I'm just terrible to him. Aren't I terrible?''

''Oh, no, no, no,'' said her host. ''No, no.''   15

''I am,'' she said. ''I know I am. Poor Burton! Now, me, I don't feel   16
that way at all. I haven't the slightest feeling about colored people. Why, I'm just crazy about some of them. They're just like children —just as easy-going, and always singing and laughing and everything. Aren't they the happiest things you ever saw in your life? Honestly, it makes me laugh just to hear them. Oh, I like them. I really do. Well, now, listen, I have this colored laundress, I've had her for years, and I'm devoted to her. She's a real character. And I want to tell you, I think of her as my friend. That's the way I think of her. As I say to Burton, 'Well, for Heaven's sakes, we're all human beings!' Aren't we?''

''Yes,'' said her host. ''Yes, indeed.''   17

''Now this Walter Williams,'' she said. ''I think a man like that's a   18
real artist. I do. I think he deserves an awful lot of credit. Goodness, I'm so crazy about music or anything, I don't care what color he is. I honestly think if a person's an artist, nobody ought to have any feeling at all about meeting them. That's absolutely what I say to Burton. Don't you think I'm right?''

''Yes,'' said her host. ''Oh, yes.''   19

''That's the way I feel,'' she said. ''I just can't understand people   20
being narrow-minded. Why, I absolutely think it's a privilege to meet a man like Walter Williams. Now, I do. I haven't any feeling at all. Well, my goodness, the good Lord made him, just the same as He did any of us. Didn't He?''

''Surely,'' said her host. ''Yes, indeed.''   21

''That's what I say,'' she said. ''Oh, I get so furious when people are   22
narrow-minded about colored people. It's just all I can do not to say something. Of course, I do admit when you get a bad colored man, they're simply terrible. But as I say to Burton, there are some bad white people, too, in this world. Aren't there?''

''I guess there are,'' said her host.   23

''Why, I'd really be glad to have a man like Walter Williams come to   24
my house and sing for us, some time,'' she said. ''Of course, I couldn't ask him on account of Burton, but I wouldn't have any feeling about it at all. Oh, can't he sing! Isn't it marvelous, the way they all have music in them? It just seems to be right *in* them. Come on, let's go on over and talk to him. Listen, what shall I do when I'm introduced? Ought I to shake hands? Or what?''

25   "Why, do whatever you want," said her host.

26   "I guess maybe I'd better," she said. "I wouldn't for the world have him think I had any feeling. I think I'd better shake hands, just the way I would with anybody else. That's just exactly what I'll do."

27   They reached the tall young Negro, standing by the bookcase. The host performed introductions; the Negro bowed.

28   "How do you do?" he said.

29   The woman with the pink velvet poppies extended her hand at the length of her arm and held it so for all the world to see, until the Negro took it, shook it, and gave it back to her.

30   "Oh, how do you do, Mr. Williams," she said. "Well, how do you do. I've just been saying, I've enjoyed your singing so awfully much. I've been to your concerts, and we have you on the phonograph and everything. Oh, I just enjoy it!"

31   She spoke with great distinctness, moving her lips meticulously, as if in parlance with the deaf.

32   "I'm so glad," he said.

33   "I'm just simply crazy about that 'Water Boy' thing you sing," she said. "Honestly, I can't get it out of my head. I have my husband nearly crazy, the way I go around humming it all the time. Oh, he looks just as black as the ace of—Er. Well, tell me, where on earth do you ever get all those songs of yours? How do you ever get hold of them?"

34   "Why," he said, "there are so many different ——"

35   "I should think you'd love singing them," she said. "It must be more fun. All those darling old spirituals—oh, I just love them! Well, what are you doing, now? Are you still keeping up your singing? Why don't you have another concert, some time?"

36   "I'm having one the sixteenth of this month," he said.

37   "Well, I'll be there," she said. "I'll be there, if I possibly can. You can count on me. Goodness, here comes a whole raft of people to talk to you. You're just a regular guest of honor! Oh, who's that girl in white? I've seen her some place."

38   "That's Katherine Burke," said her host.

39   "Good Heavens," she said, "is that Katherine Burke? Why, she looks entirely different off the stage. I thought she was much better-looking. I had no idea she was so terribly dark. Why, she looks almost like—Oh, I think she's a wonderful actress! Don't you think she's a wonderful actress, Mr. Williams? Oh, I think she's marvelous. Don't you?"

40   "Yes, I do," he said.

41   "Oh, I do, too," she said. "Just wonderful. Well, goodness, we must give someone else a chance to talk to the guest of honor. Now, don't forget, Mr. Williams, I'm going to be at that concert if I possibly can. I'll be

there applauding like everything. And if I can't come, I'm going to tell everybody I know to go, anyway. Don't you forget!"

"I won't," he said. "Thank you so much."   42

The host took her arm and piloted her into the next room.   43

"Oh, my dear," she said. "I nearly died! Honestly, I give you my   44
word, I nearly passed away. Did you hear that terrible break I made? I
was just going to say Katherine Burke looked almost like a nigger. I just
caught myself in time. Oh, do you think he noticed?"

"I don't believe so," said her host.   45

"Well, thank goodness," she said, "because I wouldn't have embar-   46
rassed him for anything. Why, he's awfully nice. Just as nice as he can
be. Nice manners, and everything. You know, so many colored people,
you give them an inch, and they walk all over you. But he doesn't try
any of that. Well, he's got more sense, I suppose. He's really nice. Don't
you think so?"

"Yes," said her host.   47

"I liked him," she said. "I haven't any feeling at all because he's a   48
colored man. I felt just as natural as I would with anybody. Talked to
him just as naturally, and everything. But honestly, I could hardly keep
a straight face. I kept thinking of Burton. Oh, wait till I tell Burton I
called him 'Mister'!"

Questions and Activities

▶ *COMPREHENSION QUESTIONS*

1. Reread the first paragraph of this story. How does the description in this paragraph help to set up your response to the main character? What do you expect of this woman after reading this paragraph?

2. Reread the woman's speech in paragraph 4. What do the phrases "just simply finely" and "the most terrible favor" tell you about the character who speaks them?

3. What does the speaker's description of her husband in paragraph 14 tell you about his character? Is he broad-minded?

4. Is the speaker as different from her husband as she tells us she is? Does what the speaker reveals about herself through her language make her seem more bigoted than her husband?

▶ *QUESTIONS OF RHETORICAL PURPOSE AND STRATEGY*

5. Why did Parker choose to tell this story from the third-person point of view? What do you think the host is thinking as he listens to the

"woman with the pink velvet poppies"? Do his brief responses to her suggest his feelings about what she says? How should the host's brief responses be interpreted? Is he passing judgment on the woman? Does Parker want her readers to share his judgment?

6. Why is this story titled "Arrangement in Black and White"? What is the meaning of the word "arrangement" in this title? Does the word bring up connotations of flower arrangements or still-life paintings?

► THEME QUESTIONS

7. Does the woman reveal herself through the way she talks? Does Walter Williams reveal himself through the way he talks?
8. What general social criticism underlies Parker's treatment of blacks and whites in this story?
9. How do you think the woman would have responded if Walter Williams had spoken to her in black dialect?

► LEARNING ACTIVITIES

10. Think of someone you have known who has a memorable and unique way of talking. Spend a half-hour writing down that person's speech as you remember it; your memory will be clearer if you recall this person's speech as it occurred in some specific situation. Do not concentrate on form or correctness during this transcription stage. Follow the transcription stage by writing a page in which you show how this person's speech defined his or her identity for those who heard it.
11. Write a dialogue in which the person you observed and analyzed in the previous activity is having a conversation with a different kind of speaker. Follow the forms of punctuation that Parker uses in dialogue.
12. Have someone in your class edit the dialogue from the preceding activity so it follows Parker's forms in this story.
13. Trade written and edited dialogues with another student. Each of you should produce a list of traits describing the main speaker's character.

Writing Assignments

PRIVATE AND PUBLIC LANGUAGE

Using several of the readings in this section, argue for or against the following proposition: "The language that children use in school should be different from the language they use at home."

Begin the writing process by creating a sketch describing a situation in which a child's use of the language in the home might lessen that child's chances of becoming a successful member of society. Refer to readings from this section as you do this sketch, but use your own past experience as the primary basis for your writing.

Rewrite your sketch as an argument for or against the above proposition. Use the descriptions in your sketch along with references to specific readings to support your reaction to the proposition.

THE LANGUAGE OF ADVERTISING

Choose a series of three or four advertisements for similar products (for example, automobiles, cigarettes, or deodorants) that represent a stereotyped image of men or women. In a first draft for a paper, explain the stereotype and why you think the advertisers feel the stereotype will appeal to their consumers. Turn your first draft into an informative essay in which you show your readers how the language and pictures in the advertisements appeal to this stereotyped image held by men and/or women.

When writing your first draft, imagine yourself addressing an audience of your peers. Before you begin writing, discuss with other students their responses to a few common stereotypes in advertisements. What stereotypes most offend them, and why? What stereotypes seem to them harmless, and why? Use your discussions as a base for defining the audience to whom you will address your first draft.

When writing your final draft, imagine yourself addressing a larger more public audience. You might, for example, wish to address women concerning the negative female stereotypes that appear in certain advertisements. Or you might wish to address men or women of a particular socioeconomic class concerning the methods certain advertisers use to appeal to them via a stereotyped image. You should use the same material that you used in your first draft, but it should be couched in more general and analytical terms appropriate to the final draft's more public audience.

Before you write your final draft, you may wish to write an informal sketch of your intended audience, describing their likes and dislikes (and the causes for them) and analyzing their sensitivity and sophistication concerning the appeals and language of advertising. (This audience profile might also be discussed with other students in your class.)

What Does It Mean To Be a Woman?

▶ ———————————————————————

Introduction

▶ ─────────────────────

This section of this book focuses on questions of identity for women in our society. A woman's identity is the product of many influences and personality traits, and it is also subject to a continuous process of development. The influence of family and school on the child, the pressures exerted by peers of a certain class and neighborhood, the examples set and the ideas promoted by the media all have important effects on individual identity. Every woman inherits particular psychological and physical qualities that contribute to the formation of her identity. These external and internal, or social and individual, influences on a woman's developing identity have been compounded in our culture by the historical changes women as a group have lived through in recent years. The result is what psychologist Erik Erikson has called an identity crisis for many modern women. Most women, to a greater or lesser degree, are having a difficult time arriving at a stable sense of identity amidst this process of social and individual change.

How do the essays and story in this section treat the question of women's identity crises? Bruno Bettelheim's essay on growing up female provides this section's central perspective. Bettelheim describes in detail the variety of pressures that are exerted on women by family, friends, and institutions such as schools and churches. He also describes the individual woman's need to reconcile these outside influences with a growing awareness of inner needs. Bettelheim provides, in nontechnical terms, a psychological and sociological perspective on the theme of woman's identity. He also introduces the concept of the past influencing the present, a theme that winds its way through every selection in this section. For Bettelheim, all women are, at least partially, products of their social pasts.

Maya Angelou and Patricia Hampl provide different individual perspectives on growing up female and on Bettelheim's theme of the past's influence on the present. Angelou, a black actress and writer, describes

499

a group of confidence men with whom she grew up in and around her mother's boarding house in San Francisco. The Angelou who narrates this piece has drawn her image of men partly from her experiences as a child, and we can infer that many of her attitudes as an adult toward the roles of men and women in our society have been shaped by her experiences as a girl with Mr. Red Leg and his fellow confidence men. If we take a more general view of Angelou's autobiographical sketch, we can see it as a portrait of a black woman's education through personal experience, one showing us how a woman's past can influence her present. As a child, a woman learns to understand the people around her in ways that influence her attitudes and behavior toward others as an adult.

Patricia Hampl, a white middle-class woman from St. Paul, Minnesota, describes the last years of her Czech grandmother's life and some changes that affect her own sense of her grandmother's value as a person. We can see how Hampl's adult identity has been influenced in an important way by her grandmother's life and death. Her respect for her grandmother, intensified after her death, influences Hampl's attitude toward women's particular toughness and interpersonal qualities and toward her own nature as a woman.

Nora Ephron also works from personal experience. But in her discussion of her hang-up about breasts, she generalizes from her experience far more than Angelou and Hampl do in their memoirs. She ranges over her childhood and young adulthood to give us a specific impression of the history of her hang-up, and in the process gives us some understanding of why many women, to one degree or another, seem to share it. Ephron, through humorous and specific references to past personal experiences, shows us how a woman can feel oppressed by society's attitudes concerning what constitute ideal female physical characteristics.

Jan Brunvand shifts us from the personal perspective of Angelou, Hampl, and Ephron back to the sociological perspective of Bettelheim. But unlike Bettelheim, who applied clinical experience in developing his ideas about women, Brunvand presents a view of woman as she appears in popular culture. He describes and analyzes the story of "The Boyfriend's Death," a tale told orally by teenagers across the country. This story treats its female character in a way that Brunvand believes represents many of our culture's stereotyped attitudes toward women. He shows us how traditional social values concerning women are propagated by popular legends, and he suggests that these seemingly innocuous legends might have lasting effects on our attitudes toward women.

Finally, Eudora Welty's story, "A Worn Path," is a revelation of the character of an atypical woman. Phoenix Jackson is a representative of an earlier and decidedly unique type of Southern black woman. We see her juxtaposed with a modern, urban setting, providing us with a basis for some interesting considerations of woman's individual and social identity. Welty, like Hampl, gives us a portrait of a traditional grandmother, but instead of a Czech immigrant, this time she is a rural black. It is interesting to relate these two traditional portraits to the images this section gives us of modern women—in the selections by Hampl, Ephron, and Bettelheim, in particular.

What types of questions should you ask as you read the selections in this section? If you are female, ask yourself whether or not there are similar pressures and experiences in your life. If you are male, ask yourself whether or not you know any women who are like those represented in these works. On a more general and sociological level, consider the influence of media images of women on both women's attitudes toward themselves and society's attitudes toward women. As you read, also keep in mind the concept of identity. Remember that identity is both an individual and social phenomenon, that a stable identity reflects a balancing of external and internal influences, and that a person with a stable identity is usually able to respond more flexibly to a given situation than is a person whose identity is unstable—perhaps controlled to too great an extent by external or internal influences. The following questions should help focus your thinking about identity:

1. Can you recall situations in which you were torn between social pressures and personal needs or desires?
2. In what ways might the women represented in this section be caught between social conventions and individual needs?
3. Do men's and women's ideas about the struggle to express personal identity in social situations differ?

You should also consider the influence of past experience on present behavior and attitudes:

1. How does a woman's past experience shape her current values, identity, and behavior?
2. How has your past shaped your self-image?
3. Do you know any men or women who seem excessively controlled by their pasts?
4. What are the good and bad effects of Madison Avenue stereotypes on the individual woman?

Growing Up Female

Bruno Bettelheim

Bruno Bettelheim is one of the most fascinating and popular of twentieth-century writers on psychology. He was born in Austria in 1903. In his thirties, Bettelheim was arrested by the Nazis and sent to concentration camps at Dachau and Buchenwald. While in these camps, he carefully observed other prisoners; after being freed and moving to the United States, he wrote a now-famous article, "Individual and Mass Behavior in Extreme Situations," which became required reading for all U.S. military officers and government officials serving in Europe. Later, he wrote a highly acclaimed book, *The Informed Heart: Autonomy in a Mass Age* (1960), in which he argues that modern societies must strive to maintain individual freedom in the face of depersonalization. In this book, Bettelheim first displayed a quality that was to become central to all his later psychological writings: his ability to describe his experiments and state his analyses in rigorous language that never sacrifices human appeal or emotional involvement. Bettelheim's writing is always based on careful observation and reasoning, yet it consistently underlines the need to improve the conditions under which men and women live.

Bettelheim has spent most of his career studying and writing about children. His writing evolves from his work with emotionally disturbed children at the Sonia Shankman Orthogenic School at the University of Chicago. He has developed an influential theory of autism: that autism occurs when a child develops the belief that none of his or her acts has any effect on the outside world. Four well-known books report on Bettelheim's work with disturbed children: *Love Is Not Enough* (1950), *Truants from Life* (1955), *The Empty Fortress* (1967), and *A Home for the Heart* (1974). In 1976, he published *The Uses of Enchantment: The Meaning and Importance of Fairy Tales,* a book in which he argues that children living in a technological society such as ours need the fantasy experience of fairy tales to sustain their imaginations and to help them develop independent personalities. In another book, *The Children of the Dream* (1969), Bettelheim used his observations of children living in a kibbutz (a collective farm owned and managed by the workers) in Israel to outline the positive and negative effects of communal child-rearing.

The essay that follows typifies Bettelheim's use of scientific research in developing humane and compassionate approaches to basic social problems. In the nine introductory paragraphs of this essay, Bettelheim explains how society's attitudes toward women changed between 1962, when the original essay was published in *Harper's* magazine, and 1978, when the essay, with introduction added, was republished in an anthology.

As you read, ask yourself whether you agree with Bettelheim when he asserts that the problem of finding a personal identity continues to be a woman's central problem in adjusting to modern life. Also consider these questions:

1. Have the facts that women more often pursue careers, raise children by themselves, and have freedom to express themselves sexually made finding one's personal identity less or more of a problem in the 1980s than it was in the 1960s?
2. Are our personal identities created by external social conditions or by internal drives and feelings or by both?
3. Do you feel that Bettelheim provides sufficient facts to support his argument that women, despite their new freedoms, are still having a difficult time achieving stable identities? Do you feel that his argument depends too heavily on an emotional appeal? Do you trust his voice? Do you feel that a scientist should be more objective than Bettelheim is in this piece of writing?

▶ ——————————————————————

In the sixteen years since this essay was first published—it was   1
written a few years earlier—the problems it deals with have become, if anything, more acute. Greater numbers of women are now working. They have made significant strides toward achieving social, economic, and occupational equality with males, and women now more frequently hold positions of considerable importance and prestige. With all this, women have gained much more independence—but they have had to pay a price for it.

An increasing number of marriages now end in divorce, and many   2
more women are having to raise their children without the help of a husband—in general, the number of single parents has jumped significantly in the last decade or so. While women have made great progress towards sexual equality and have achieved considerably greater sexual freedom, this has not necessarily made for greater enjoyment of sex; sexual freedom does not seem to offer deeper and more lasting emotional satisfactions than a good marriage.

The achievements of the women's movement have led to severe   3
identity confusion among many women. The change in social roles women fulfill in society and the home, and changes in their views of themselves and of their relations to males, have led to parallel and

equally widespread identity confusion among males regarding their relations to females and their sexual role. All this has made social and sexual relations more problematic for both females and males.

4   *While a traditionally ordered society tightly shackled both females and males to narrowly defined social and sexual roles, society thus provided people with certainty regarding their identities. A few always revolted against being forced to live a life contrary to their desires and suffered, or were made to suffer, for it. But the vast majority had neither the strength nor the opportunity to revolt, and so they more or less accepted and settled into the roles which society decreed. Where there is no doubt, there is also little insecurity. While such tightly regulated social and sexual roles did not permit much freedom or individuality, there was also little need for developing a strong personal identity; identity was settled at the moment of birth.*

5   *The historical role for each sex allowed only restricted satisfactions. But as long as nothing better was thought possible, and religion sanctioned these roles, it was easier to make one's peace with the considerable deprivations they imposed, even when there was little satisfaction in sex or the relations to one's partner.*

6   *With the breaking down of ancient customs and traditional sex-related traits, and the new freedom to be oneself in whatever way one wishes, comes the difficult task of achieving personal identity, and the related task of gaining autonomy. This is what a technologically advanced society requires of one, if we are not to risk eventually being forced back into rigid patterns of living by a totalitarian system.*

7   *The externals of women's lives have changed since this article was written, and so have the externals of male attitudes towards females. Therefore some of what is said here about external arrangements in women's lives no longer applies to the same degree. But the internal difficulties of achieving a secure personal and sexual identity have, if anything, become even more of a problem. Persons who have not achieved a secure identity for themselves cannot provide each other with those complementary experiences that make for a happy marital relationship. Although in many more cases both partners in a marriage now have an independent life in society, this has not necessarily made it easier for them to be happier with each other.*

8   *The greatest happiness in marriage can come about only when true independence as socially equal human beings is enriched and made continually fascinating and satisfying for both partners by their being sexually completely secure with each other. This security is based on a complementary attraction, enriched by the specific differences in personality and sexual experiences that come from one partner being female, and the other male.*

In the last analysis, it is very difficult to attain one's full identity as a person all by oneself, as in a vacuum—one must relate to others. I believe that the essence of a healthy heterosexual identity requires that it be proven again and again by the depth of satisfaction that a relation which is close emotionally and completely gratifying sexually provides when the particular female qualities bring out the best in the male; and simultaneously the particular male qualities bring out the best in the female.

By what models is a modern girl to measure herself in her growth? Many a psychologist or educator today will find few questions more recurrent or troubling than this one. On every side one encounters growing girls and educated women who seem to have followed out the respected modern formulas: they have "done well" at school, at finding jobs, at finding husbands, at running homes, at planning activities of all sorts. And yet they remain, as Veblen put it, "touched with a sense of grievance too vivid to put them at rest."* They are frequently baffled by this and so, unhappily, are some of the psychologists they consult. In trying to help women—to "accept the womanly role," for example —counselors often seem to aggravate the grievance, rather than cure it.

What I shall try to show in this article is that the grievance is very real and justified, although it is barely understood. The ways in which we bring up girls in America, and the goals we set for them, are so strangely—and often painfully—contradictory that it is only too predictable that their expectations of love and work and marriage should frequently be confused, and that deep satisfactions should elude them. Very few human problems have been so transformed by the convulsive growth and evolution of modern society as those of women; but the parents and psychologists and educators who guide young women today have scarcely begun to inquire into what a modern and satisfying female life might really be.

Many of women's special difficulties spring from the distorted images of females that preoccupy so many men. Freud was probably right in thinking that the male infant's overattachment to his mother projects him into a continuing emotional predicament that is peculiarly difficult for most men to solve, and often warps the demands they make on women. Bound emotionally to the infantile image of his mother as unassailably pure, a man may seek out a superior woman he can worship. Or, trying to break the infantile bond, he may choose a woman who ap-

*Thorstein Bunde Veblen (1857–1929) was an American sociologist and economist who wrote *The Theory of the Leisure Class* (1899). Veblen attacked the new industrial, leisure classes in all his writing.

pears inferior to himself. The different kinds of emotional balm men seek from women are as various as their frustrations when they do not find it. But the female who needs and wants a man—and all normal women do—is often placed in a sadly absurd position: she must shape herself to please a complex male image of what she should be like—but alas, it is often an image having little to do with her own real desires or potentialities; these may well be increasingly stunted or concealed as she grows into womanhood.

13   Such irrational demands on women are nothing new, as we can learn from the Bible. In the purely psychological sphere, relations between the sexes have always been difficult. But we often forget that until the modern industrial era, the great majority of people had little time or energy to devote to purely emotional "satisfactions" and "relationships." Life was still taken up with the basic necessities of food, clothing, and shelter. To secure them, most men and women and their children worked extremely hard—and often worked together—in their homes and shops and fields. If the family was to survive and prosper, the women and girls simply had to do their heavy share, and this earned them a certain respect. It would seem from the available evidence that enough good feeling existed between the sexes to make their emotional difficulties manageable—especially if sex as such was satisfying. What we call "psychological satisfactions" today was frosting on the cake—the cake of economic survival and simple sex.

14   Now the technological revolution has brought us to precisely the opposite situation. Many women no longer need be bound to men by economic necessity; they rarely share any work with their husbands, and their time is often their own. Women are at last reaching that stage where they can shape their personal relations the way they choose. What choices are they making, and how successful are they?

15   Most women claim to base their personal relations on what they conceive to be "love"—on "emotional satisfaction." In this, they are clearly the children of modern technology and the easy life it brings. So too is psychoanalysis itself, which aims to make emotional satisfaction more possible. But now a savage paradox is slowly—all too slowly —dawning on the psychoanalysts and many of their female patients: it appears that relations entered into chiefly to gain psychological satisfaction more often than not end in psychological despair. "Love," as Saint-Exupéry put it, "does not consist in gazing at each other, but in looking outward in the same direction." For what kind of love, and what kind of life, are we preparing our girls today?

16   Paul Goodman has suggested that boys today are growing up in ways that he calls "absurd." But how much more absurd are the ways in which we raise our daughters! We tell them early that they are very dif-

ferent from little boys and give them dolls to play with rather than base-balls. But we also provide them, from kindergarten on through college, with exactly the same education given to boys—an education clearly designed to prepare boys for a life of competition and independent responsibility.

Consider the contradictions that are thrust upon the growing girl.   *17*
For fifteen years or more she is officially encouraged to compete with boys in the schoolroom, to develop her mind and her initiative, to be second to none. She may study the same physics and history as her boy-friends, work part-time at jobs not too different from theirs, share many of the same political and social interests. And then our curious system insists she "fall in love" with a potential husband: she is, in fact, expected to enjoy giving up what she may have loved until then, and suddenly find deep fulfillment in taking care of a child, a home, a mate. Her life is to be filled with what are, to her husband, after-hours occupations, and the training of her youth is seemingly intended to fall away like an afterbirth. After years of apparent equality, it is made clear that males are more equal, and most females resent this, as they should. Our educational system has ostensibly prepared them for a kind of liberated marital and occupational life that in fact rarely exists in our society; at the same time it celebrates the values of an antiquated form of marriage inherited from a time when women were prepared for little else.

If many girls seem to accept these hypocrisies calmly, perhaps it is   *18*
because they have been made aware, quite early in the game, that their role in society will in fact be very different from that of the boys sitting next to them in the classroom. The boys have no doubt that their schooling is intended to help them succeed in their mature life, to enable them to accomplish something in the outside world. But the girl is made to feel that she must undergo precisely the same training only because she may need it if she is a failure—an unfortunate who somehow cannot gain admission to the haven of marriage and motherhood where she properly belongs.

Actually, the gravest damage is done long before this. The little girl's   *19*
first storybooks and primers, for example, hardly ever show a woman as working or active outside the home. It makes no difference that many millions of American children under twelve have full-time working mothers. A little girl is expected to shape herself in the image of the maternal housekeeper of these ridiculous primer stories, and never mind what certain unfortunate mothers may be obliged to do. As if to emphasize society's ambivalence, this image of the stay-at-home is usually presented by a female teacher, who may well be a working mother, a contradiction that is not lost on the little girl and tends to teach her that she will have to live a life of contradictions. In these early

years, it is rare indeed for girls to hear the slightest suggestion that they might one day do the interesting work of this world quite as well as many men, or even better.

20   It is little wonder then that as adolescence approaches, many girls are already convinced that what really counts is not any commitment to their studies—although they may be conscientious about them—but their ability to carry on social, emotional, and sexual relations that will make them popular and ultimately attract the right boys. Here matters are made more difficult by the fact that young girls tend to mature faster physically and emotionally than boys, although the boys may do better academically.

21   The girls soon perceive that they are ahead of the boys in the maturity and sophistication of their desires. The boys seem more childish, less grown up, less certain about their ability to cope with the other sex. What is more, the boys often come from homes where Mother knows best, and they find themselves ruled by female teachers who day after day impress upon them their authority and competence. In this situation it is not easy for a boy to gain confidence in his maleness, to say the least. (Later on, of course, both sexes are exposed to male teachers in high school and college, but by then it is often too late to undo the damage.)[1]

22   The high school and college girl must face a frequently awful predicament. She—and usually her mother also—feels she must be popular with boys. To get the dates she wants, the girl must try to reassure the boys that they are really superior to her; but deep down she cannot believe in this pretense, and she may well resent the necessity for it. Once she has gained the ultimate objective and is safely married, she will, as likely as not, drop the mask and begin to assert in her home what she is convinced is a superior maturity. By then, however, it may no longer exist, for boys typically catch up with girls in this respect during their mid-twenties. And in the meantime the boys are generally given a good deal more freedom to experiment—to "sow their wild oats."

23   A good many young men, for example, may skirt marriage until they are into their thirties; they are allowed to go their own way, suffering no more than a mild nagging and some teasing from their friends. It is tacitly acknowledged that they need more time to find themselves in

---

[1]Many boys drop out of school before they meet with many male teachers; in order to protect their own male image, they reject this continuing domination by females. Similarly, the aggressive delinquency which gets boys into trouble is often no more than a desperate attempt to assert their maleness. Since the girls in school are often more mature socially and sexually, the boys find that they can clearly assert male superiority in school only through aggressive and competitive sports. Having learned this, they choose aggressive ways to prove themselves male when outside the school.

their work before they settle down, and they remain popular in both married and unmarried circles. Such men are considered failures only when they cannot support themselves, or make headway in their careers. By contrast, the situation of an unmarried young woman is altogether different, often cruelly so. No matter how gifted she may be in her work—or how brilliantly she has put her education to use—a woman bears a suspicion of failure if she does not marry young.

Indeed, the pressures upon the young girl to marry safely and quickly   24
may seem inexorable just when she is trying to embark on her own path; and these pressures are exerted in ways unfamiliar to boys. During his first years at college, for example, a boy is likely to undergo a "crisis of identity," exposed as he is to conflicting new ideas and ways of acting, and given chances to experiment. As a junior or senior, however, he may start to find himself through serious academic work. A girl may undergo a parallel experience, only to discover that her new dedication to scholarship may rule her out of the marriage market. Fearing that her single-minded absorption will allow her chances to slip by, she stops dead in her tracks; or worse, she cannot make up her mind about what she wants, and she may suffer a college-girl "breakdown."

Nor does this happen only in college. Many a girl emerges from high   25
school with a vague feeling that she can, she should make something of herself. But everyone around her insists that she will find fulfillment through marriage—and her friends are getting married. So she buckles down to a brief course in beauty culture or secretarial work. Later, as the wife of a clerk or skilled worker, she is as restless and bewildered as the college girl who gave up an interest that was becoming "too absorbing," so that she could marry off into the suburbs. Neither girl can quite understand what has gone wrong—she is, after all, an undoubted success in the eyes of others.

And what in fact has gone wrong? What happens when the young   26
bride at last enters the home she has been taught to think of as her true domain? In truth, she may find that the much-touted labors and pleasures of the hearth are among the sad delusions of our times. For if it is hard for male youth nowadays to find meaningful work, as Paul Goodman has argued, the fate of the homebound wife is surely harder.

Of course, modern labor-saving devices have abolished most of the   27
backbreaking housework of the past—and good riddance; but at the same time they are doing away with the real satisfactions this work once yielded. Using her husband's money to buy machine-made clothes for her family involves no unique or essential labors on a woman's part. Much the same can be said about cooking with prepackaged ingredients. What remain, apart from child-rearing, are the most stultifying mechanical tasks—dusting, making beds, washing, and picking up.

And beyond these lie chiefly the petty refinements of "homemaking"
—what Veblen described as the occupation of ceremonial futility.

28   The very people who sell women products for the home are shrewdly
aware of this futility. A study by the sociologist Florence Kluckhohn
has shown that advertising aimed at the housewife often subtly describes the home as a kind of penal colony from which she should escape as quickly and for as long as possible. Typically, an ad for an automatic stove shows a woman putting on her hat, leaving, and coming
back hours later to find the dinner all cooked. The advertiser, as Mrs.
Kluckhohn points out, does not say where the woman has been; just to
get away, it is implied, is a blessing.

29   Since work around the house is often less than interesting, children
are the natural target for the young wife's energies. Here, at least, she
feels considerably more sophisticated than her mother. After all, she
has had extensive schooling, and has perhaps worked briefly at a
demanding job, and motherhood has been depicted to her as another tre-
mendous and enlarging experience—the climax, somehow, to all that
has gone before. Yet, in fact, the care of an infant forces a woman to give
up most of her old interests, and unless she is fascinated by the minute
developments of the baby, she seldom finds that any new and different
enrichment has entered her life to replace her relinquished satisfactions.

30   This impoverishment is particularly acute when a woman has her
first child. Later on, the concerns of her older children may enliven her
days while she cares for a newcomer. Then, as the time for nurturing
babies and taking care of small children passes, many middle-class
mothers come to find existence empty without small children to care
for. Reluctant to return to the outer world—or lacking confidence in her
ability to do so—the housewife must find something to occupy her
which seems vital and demanding of her concentration, so she continues to devote herself to her children.

31   Things change when children become of school age—and change
once again when they are in their teens. Schoolchildren certainly need a
mother, but they actually need far less of her than she may devote to
them. Chauffeuring children around the suburbs, for example, takes
time and requires someone who drives a car, but this person need not be
a mother. The children themselves would prefer to be free of arranged
rides and the tight scheduling this imposes. The same goes for arranging
children's social life, which again they would much prefer to do themselves.

32   Of course the professed concern of many mothers is to watch over
their children's educational life, and help them with their problems in
growing up. But in these things, too, the children would often rather be

on their own, except for those occasional crises when the parents are needed for support. And sadly enough, the modern mother is often in a poor position to give support when her child is doing badly in school or is not very popular or feels defeated. Having invested so much emotionally in her child's achievement, a mother's pride suffers at his failure and as likely as not, she administers a bawling-out when understanding and compassion are needed. Thus she may fail as a mother because her inner needs make her work at it too hard. The children of women who do interesting work of their own during the day often find more sensible and sympathetic mothers to help them with their studies and problems in the evening. On the other hand, the mother who urges her girl on toward intellectual achievement while staying at home herself poses a contradiction that is probably not lost on the girl.

When motherhood does not bring satisfaction, the woman turns to her husband with the demand, spoken or unspoken, that he somehow make up to her for what she is missing in life. She waits for him to come home with word of the outside world and its events. At the same time, she may work hard at being a wife, trying to advance her husband's career, plotting to get him ahead socially. But even if this sort of thing works, he may resent it—it will not be his success, but hers.   33

Sometimes a wife will spend her husband's money heedlessly and push him to achieve higher earnings and status, blindly demanding things to make up for her empty feelings about her life. Other wives simply nag, or they repress their resentment altogether and accept the prospect of a stultifying life. The husband begins in turn to resent his nagging wife and even his family life; or he may resent his wife for her passive dreariness. In either case both suffer, often without in the least knowing why. Living with such parents, a growing girl may well absorb and keep for life a distorted view of what a man is for, and how he can be used.   34

No doubt it will be argued that there is more to a modern woman's life than this—that labor-saving devices have so freed housewives from their chores that they can undertake useful and interesting activities of all sorts without actually taking jobs. Such claims seem questionable. Undeniably, a good many housewives do find time for activities outside the home, but all too often the activities themselves are really frivolous or makework, creating futile and unrewarding experiences. Such activities often include gardening—which has replaced the conspicuous embroidery of an earlier age—or the ubiquitous bridge circle and country-club life. There are also activities like the PTA, the League of Women Voters, and charity work which pass as "constructive" and "valuable." Close examination, however, reveals that these pursuits are often used to cover up a lack of really serious and interesting   35 involvement. And according to a recent study, "Volunteer workers are increasingly being assigned to fund-raising or low level routine, from which little achievement satisfaction is possible."

36   To quote Veblen again, "Woman is endowed with her share—which there is reason to believe is more than an even share—of the instinct of workmanship, to which futility of life or of expenditure is obnoxious." When this impulse is denied expression, a woman feels that sense of grievance which runs like a vivid current through the lives of so many women today.

37   If the instincts for workmanship are widely frustrated in many modern women, this is even more true in regard to their sexual instincts. Of course, sexual difficulties are neither a recent curse of the young, nor limited to girls. But the way we prepare our children for sexual life has burdened girls far more than boys.

38   In Latin countries, as in many other lands, girls are prepared from early childhood to accept a yielding and passive role, not only in sexual relations, but in the life of the family, where the man traditionally dominates. But the American girl is raised in contradiction. On the one hand, she is told that to be feminine means to be yielding and courted, and that she must respect this norm. She certainly cannot, for example, ask a boy she likes for a date, nor can she pay the expenses when she goes out with him (although she may sometimes "go dutch"). She may feel most reluctant simply to call up a boy to talk with him, or to ask him to take a walk with her.

39   Yet at the same time today's young girl has been taught from childhood to think and act for herself; to strive for success, and compete equally with boys at school. What she has *not* been taught is that men and women are neither wholly similar, nor wholly opposite, but complementary. She has never been encouraged to quietly consider the ways in which she and the boys she knows are alike—the talents and aspirations they could build up together and the emotional needs they share—and the ways in which they are not alike, as in their sexual functions. As a result, the girl does not know where and when to be "feminine" and where and when to be "equal."

40   The adult world has led her to think that the "active woman" is somehow an unfeminine and sexually inadequate woman—something patently untrue. Women who strive to "wear the pants" do so for defensive and neurotic reasons, just as the very need to be dominant, whether in man or woman, is due to feelings of inferiority or to thwarted desires. But it is quite a different thing for a girl to do purposeful work, not because of some twisted drive, but because she wants to realize her own potentials. Unless we distinguish clearly between the two kinds of striving we stifle the healthy growth of girls by labeling natural ambition as unfeminine.

At the same time, girls are led into an equally dangerous misunderstanding about the sexual act itself. While men and women need not be so different in their personal aspirations as our society now pretends, they are different in the way they experience sex. Here much confusion was created by Wilhelm Reich* and his rather too facile following among the intelligentsia; he led both partners to expect that they could and should have a parallel orgastic experience. Too often, a parallel experience is mistakenly thought to mean a similar if not identical experience; the emphasis upon the desirability of orgasm may lead to frustration in both man and woman.   41

This problem is very different in some societies, where modern technology has not affected the lives of women and their expectations. There it is still sufficient for a woman if her lover or husband enjoys sex with her. Since his enjoyment proves her a good woman, she too can enjoy herself; she does not worry whether she is frigid or torrid, and as likely as not she achieves total release. Since her lover is not obliged by any conscious code to provide her with an orgasm, he can enjoy himself, experience orgasm, and thus help her to feel fully satisfied herself.   42

In our own society, boys need as much as ever to have their virility attested to by their sexual partners; and girls have a parallel need. But today the boy wants his girl to prove him a man by her so-called orgastic experience, and the girl is even worse off. She not only has to prove him a man by making him experience orgasm; she must also prove her femininity by orgastic release or else fear she is frigid.   43

She is quite used to performing with males on equal grounds, but she has too little sense of how to complement them. She cannot suddenly learn this in bed. Trying to make sure that the man has an orgastic experience, and also wondering if they can have one themselves, many women become so worried that they truly experience little satisfaction, and end up pretending. Sexual intercourse cannot often bear the burden of *proving* so many things in addition to being enjoyable. It becomes another competition between man and woman: who can make whom have an orgastic experience. And the lovers cannot even enjoy their mutual desire or the forgetting of self in the act.   44

With both sex and household work often less than satisfying, it is not surprising that so many modern marriages turn sour, and that the phenomenon of homosexuality looms as importantly as it does today.   45

Many young wives soon realize that their husbands are neither willing nor able to complement them in their motherly tasks in any sat-   46

---

*Wilhelm Reich (1897–1957) was an Austrian psychologist and psychoanalyst. He believed that free expression of sexual instincts would lead to a more healthy individual and that men and women should gain equal pleasure from sexual encounters.

isfying way. Resentful, in many cases, of her husband's fuller life, a young wife may nevertheless try to force him to share motherhood with her. But irrespective of whether or not he attempts to do so, and however hard she may try, a woman cannot find compensation in marriage itself for her own thwarted aspirations.

47   The results are often men who want women, but don't know what to do with them when they get them; and women who get men, but who are disappointed in them and in themselves when they live together. Mutually disappointed, it is natural that each sex should seek out its own as company; for only then can they really be themselves on a truly equal basis, freed of anxiety, disappointment, or inferiority-feeling. Who has not observed the tendency of the sexes to segregate themselves in certain married circles? However, when relations between the sexes are so plagued, then a kind of homosexuality may also become rampant. And indeed, psychiatrists have recently been noticing an alarming rise in both female and male homosexuality.

48   Higher statistics concerning "female homosexuality" may reflect an increasing number of women who are unwilling to pretend they enjoy having a role forced on them that frustrates their aspirations; and so they seek the company of a partner who can share them. Sometimes two such women find it convenient to live together, whether sex is involved or not, and slowly, as in a good marriage, the partners blend their lives.

49   In some cases—but much less often than is sometimes assumed—this leads to a desire for sexual relations. But unlike most male homosexuals, such women can often switch their sexual attention to the other sex if they can find a male who really wants and needs to "look outward with them" (and I would add inward) in the same direction. (This, of course, does not hold true for a hard core of female homosexuals.)

50   The upbringing of most girls today also fosters something resembling female homosexuality. This is because the old intimacy between mothers and daughters who actually worked together for the survival of the family has now practically vanished. As discussed, many women now feel compelled to prove themselves good mothers by making sure their daughters are "successes" in life, and so it is difficult for warm confidence to grow between them. The daughter of such a woman naturally longs for real affection, for the sharing closeness to another woman, for the tender loving care that she wanted from her mother, and never got. When they meet with a rewarding response to this need on the part of a mature woman—which need not, and preferably should not, be of a gross sexual nature—some young women are enriched by it, and are then better able to move on to a successful heterosexual relation.

51   At this point the prospects for the young female hoping for a satisfying marriage may seem fairly bleak. Whether marriage as we know it

is obsolete, I do not know, but frankly I doubt it. Despite its shortcomings, marriage is still the best institution we have developed to combat loneliness and to provide a structure within which two adults can find intimate satisfaction and continue to grow; not to mention the child's need for two parents.

But no institution can provide intimacy or anything else; it can at   52
best provide a framework. This framework itself cannot ensure that youthful love will be transmitted into two fulfilled lives, since our children need to be prepared for marriage by a kind of upbringing very different from the ones they are getting. People must learn to expect far less of the institution itself and much more of themselves in the way of hard work to help each other live interesting and satisfying lives. They must not marry so early that they peg each other to permanent immaturity, out of anxiety, emptiness, or because they feel unable to make a go of life all by themselves. And they must recognize that a woman's place cannot automatically be confined to the home.

Fortunately, there are more than a few mature marriages to be found.   53
In these, the partners have come to see that the feelings of love—and the affection for idiosyncracies of personality—which lie between them can count for very little by themselves in making their relations work. In the long run, the crucial questions for a married couple concern the kinds of worlds in which they can actively interest themselves as man and woman, and as parents—very much including their connections to their work as well as to each other. If these connections act to bring the members of the family together, then the marriage has a strong chance of survival.

But, of course, this is not so easy. Often the husband's work may   54
split him off from his wife instead of bringing them together. A rather extreme form of this dilemma was presented in a novel called *Command the Morning* by Pearl Buck. She wrote about the wives of scientists working on the secret atomic project at Los Alamos during the war, all of whom were tiresomely caught up in the usual antiquated variety of American marriage. These women had to live lonely lives with secretive husbands who could not share with them the excitement of their work. The only other alternative was to look for some secret excitement of their own, in promiscuous adventure. Only the heroine, a female physicist, is shown to have a complete life, for she shares the creative suspense of the scientists. As she and one of the scientists become involved in work together, they inevitably fall in love. Unfortunately Miss Buck was unable to conceive of any outcome for this affair except a conventional homebound marriage, or no marriage at all. It was apparently beyond her to imagine a marriage where both partners could still love each other and remain part of the same working world. And so, of course, she had the female physicist reject her lover and the prospect

of imprisonment in domesticity, so that she didn't have to give up her science.

55   Obviously I do not think these are the only choices to be made. But I have no doubt that Miss Buck speaks for a great many people who do think so. When such choices do arise, how do we advise young girls to deal with them?

56   Recently I discussed this problem with some psychoanalytic friends. The majority of these analysts still embraced a nineteenth-century solution to the problem similar to Miss Buck's: a woman belongs in the home, at least for the sake of her children while she is raising them. Her life can be made more bearable if she is helped to gain some meaning from her after-hours community activities, from aesthetic pursuits, and from her sexual life with her husband—or, if need be, from some extramarital sexual adventures.

57   Such analysts advise a woman to seek meaningful work until the time she gets married or pregnant. Then, she should make an about-face in her way of life, if not also in her emotions. She should then accept the so-called womanly role, stay at home, and raise her children for a decade or longer, during the very years when she is in the prime of life. During this period she must be helped to be not too frustrated a wife, so that when the children are at last in grade or high school, she can make another about-face, recognize the limitations of the PTA life, and return to the more satisfying occupation she pursued before her marriage and children.

58   What such advice disregards is that having a mother at home who is dissatisfied with her life is no help to the child, even if she does not take it out on the child that his presence prevents her from having a more interesting life. A mother unhappy about the limitations imposed on her life will not be able to make her child happy in his.

59   Nevertheless the route of working before childbirth, and again after the children have become adolescents, is actually the one that many mothers—voluntarily or involuntarily—have chosen to follow. But one result of such switching back and forth in their major commitments is that many women resentfully feel that they lived a meaningful life only before they got married—a feeling that can have disastrous effects on them, their marriages, and their children. This "switching" solution, in short, leaves the conflict between self-realization and child care unexamined.

60   I am convinced that modern women will have to confront this conflict, and solve it. It might mean adopting the system found in some other societies where women work—i.e., entrusting part of the infant care to the older children, or sharing it with relatives. It might well mean more arrangements whereby young children are entrusted to the care of well-qualified professional people, at least for part of the time.

Some kind of change along these lines is badly needed, but it will not 61 be an easy reform to make, given the resistance which may be expected. In trying to bring such a change about, women unfortunately will not be able to count on much support from their therapists. For, as we have seen, the preconceptions of many a psychologist about the proper feminine role prevent him from really helping a girl to grow up successfully female—that is, generically female in her sexual and emotional relations and in child-rearing, and yet able to develop as fully as a male can in all other respects.

Psychoanalysts' inability to do full justice to this female situation 62 stems from the very nature of psychoanalysis as a method essentially concerned with the exploration of the unconscious recesses of the mind and of infantile fixations. Psychoanalytic therapy is little concerned with how society ought to be organized or even how the patient ought to organize his life in society—its proper task is to help the individual solve some problem which prevents him from being what he wants to be. How the patient arranges his life after this has been achieved is entirely up to him, for enabling the patient to live an independent life is the goal of therapy.

This is why psychoanalysis may help a girl greatly in dealing with 63 problems of sexual repression or preoedipal and oedipal fixations, just as it may help a young student overcome his inability to study—these are problems of personal self-realization. But it cannot help a girl decide what kind of woman she wants to be or what role she wants to play in the community, any more than it can help a student decide what subject to study or what career to choose. These are problems of social self-realization, and to deal with them as personal psychoanalytic problems may muddle and aggravate them.

Since each different female must find her unique solution to the 64 problem of whether or not to combine marriage and motherhood with work, we cannot look to psychoanalysis as such for leadership in solving this issue. But paradoxically enough, hope for a more rational approach to the problems of women can be found in the discoveries of Freud himself.

Freud felt rather uneasy in discussing the psychology of women. Ba- 65 sically he remained caught up in his own nineteenth-century middle-class background, with his typical overesteem for his mother and his compensatory feeling that he should dominate his wife. He accepted this view as part of the "natural order of things," and, as we have seen, its shadow still hovers over today's psychoanalysts, and our society generally.

But it is worth noting that Freud himself, while always the courteous 66 gentleman when with his wife, often turned for companionship to intellectually active women who, according to his own view, had chosen the unfeminine role in life. He lived domestically as superior male, but in his work sought the company of women he treated as equals.

67   Freud thus stood at the threshold of a new era in the relations of man and woman, and was not able to cross it. But he did forge the tools that now might enable us to take the steps impossible for him. He was able to demonstrate that the repressive sex taboos of his time were in fact a counterpart of the Victorian overvaluation of the forbidden woman. By showing us how to uncover these repressions, he opened a way for healthier and more satisfying sexual relations to develop between men and women in the years that followed.

68   Like most great reforms in man's thinking, this one grew from the most honest and most searching examination possible of the contradictions between what people glibly profess, anxiously evade, and blindly do. We should by now be capable of extending a similar self-examination to the contradictions in our attitudes toward women.

69   If we do this, I suggest we shall find that although women have been accorded votes and education and jobs over the years, our view of them and their potentials is still far from psychologically mature. Indeed, it is in many ways still biased in the unhappy limitations it imposes on the possibilities for women to make the most of their capacities. A rational and psychologically balanced view would appreciate and enjoy the ways that women are truly different from men, but it would recognize that in most respects women have far more in common with men than our society is now willing to grant.

70   Above all, such a reform in attitudes must take place among those who have anything whatever to do with bringing up the young. For until parents, teachers, and psychologists honestly perceive the prejudice in their assumptions about the proper roles for women, equal education of the sexes will continue to be a mockery, and we must expect the continuing disintegration of young marriages as emotional distance grows between immature couples. Only a thorough effort by their elders to grow up in their thinking will enable our boys to become adults so secure in their masculinity that they can be truly male in their relations to their female partners, very much including in the sexual relation; and this without any need to assert what used to be viewed as the traditional male role in home or society—because maleness and femaleness reside in how one feels about oneself and the partner, in short in who one is, and not in what one happens to do in the home or society. Only efforts to raise boys and girls to this realization will enable our girls to accept marriage and motherhood as an important part of their future, but a part that will not waste—in desperation, resignation, or boredom—the best of their lives and possibilities.

Questions and Activities

▶ *COMPREHENSION QUESTIONS*

1. The word "identity" plays a large role in this essay. What does it mean? Does Bettelheim use the word in any special way? What does it mean to say that someone has a clear sense of his or her identity?
2. The word "role" also has an important function in this essay. How does the idea of one's role in life relate to one's behavior? What is the difference between identity and role?
3. What are some of the "distorted images of females that preoccupy so many men" (paragraph 12)?
4. What, to Bettelheim, is "absurd" about the way Americans raise their daughters (see paragraphs 16 and 17)?

▶ *QUESTIONS OF RHETORICAL PURPOSE AND STRATEGY*

5. How does Bettelheim organize the support for his contention that growing up female in our culture is an absurd experience? Explain how Bettelheim's organizational strategy controls the structure of large sections of this essay as well as particular paragraphs.
6. Does Bettelheim state any idea as a fact that is actually an opinion? Consider his assertion that "all normal women" need and want a man (paragraph 12). Might some psychologists take issue with this assertion? What are the results of Bettelheim's treating this assertion as a fact rather than an opinion?

▶ *THEME QUESTIONS*

7. What does Bettelheim suggest is the overall effect on men of the feminine control over children and the home in our society? Is that effect positive or negative?
8. Once people begin to free themselves of some of the constraints associated with traditional male and female roles, what potentially negative element begins to enter their lives? What does such freedom threaten? Consider Bettelheim's discussion of the effects of labor-saving technology on the housewife (paragraphs 26–28) as an example of the potentially negative effect of freedom from traditional sex roles.
9. What response does Bettelheim offer to the argument that a woman can find meaningful and satisfying work without having a career (paragraph 35)?
10. What is Bettelheim's attitude toward homosexuality (paragraphs 45–50)? Does he believe that it is a threat to social and psychologi-

cal stability? Or is homosexuality, to Bettelheim, simply an alternative means of sexual expression?

11. What is Bettelheim's attitude toward marriage? Does he feel that it has become a threatened institution? Does he feel that the institution is salvageable? Does Bettelheim believe that partners pursuing separate careers can make a marriage work?

12. Why does Bettelheim argue that psychotherapy cannot help an individual woman gain "social self-realization" (paragraph 63)? What is Bettelheim's alternative to individual psychoanalysis as a remedy for women's problems of self-realization and identity?

▶ *LEARNING ACTIVITIES*

13. Interview one of your female classmates to discover her response to the question of choosing a career and the effects of that choice on her decision as to whether or not to marry. Write up a set of questions before you do the interview. Be sure that the questions you develop are clearly related to Bettelheim's essay and are logically ordered with respect to one another.

14. Tape-record or transcribe the responses of your interview subject. Then write a brief interpretation of these responses, using Bettelheim's essay as a frame of reference. Has your subject evolved a solution to the problem of choosing a career? Does that solution include plans for marriage? Is there any reason to believe that some unanticipated problem will force a change in plans or goals later in your subject's life?

Mr. Red Leg

MAYA ANGELOU

Maya Angelou has had a distinguished career in the performing arts and as a writer. She acted and sang in *Porgy and Bess* during a twenty-two nation tour sponsored by the U.S. Department of State. She has co-authored, authored, or acted in three successful off-Broadway plays. She has done extensive work in Africa at the University of Ghana, where she appeared in the play *Mother Courage* by Bertoldt Brecht, worked with the Institute of African Studies, and served as assistant administrator of the School of Music and Drama. She has also been a free-lance correspondent for the *Ghanaian Times* and the Ghanaian Broadcasting Company. Angelou has taught writing as a visiting professor or writer-in-residence at Wake Forest University, Wichita State University, California State University at Sacramento, and the University of Kansas. She has received honorary degrees from Mills College, Lawrence University, and Smith College. She was a member of President Gerald Ford's American Bicentennial Council from 1975 to 1976.

Angelou's most well-known work is her autobiography, *I Know Why the Caged Bird Sings,* which was nominated for the National Book Award in 1970. Her book of poems, *Just Give Me a Cool Drink of Water 'Fore I Die,* was nominated for a Pulitzer Prize in 1972. She has also published articles and stories in *Redbook, Mademoiselle, Black Scholar, Harper's,* and *Ebony.*

The following excerpt from *I Know Why the Caged Bird Sings* demonstrates Angelou's unique blend of story-telling ability with astute social commentary. Angelou employs a realistic story to make a central point: her past experiences as a black woman have influenced her present identity. What she has become also helps her give shape and form to what she was in the past. Her career in the performing arts prepares her to understand and value the confidence games of Just Black and Mr. Red Leg; her writing abilities enable her to describe these confidence men and their endeavors in entertaining detail; her ability to analyze the stories that she tells enables her to communicate their meaning to people who are unfamiliar with the values of black Americans who have grown up in ghettoes.

To connect this selection to the theme question for this section, you will need to consider the effect this experience with Mr. Red Leg and the other black confidence men had on the woman who narrates this piece:

1. Is she entertained by the story of Mr. Red Leg's and Just Black's con game?
2. Does she feel that the confidence game is justified, even though it results in the theft of forty thousand dollars? If so, why?
3. Consider the values of the essay's narrator as you read. Why, for example, does she say that the combination of necessity and intelligence is unbeatable "when unblunted by formal education" (paragraph 2)? How might formal education blunt someone's intelligence? Is Mr. Red Leg's intelligence blunted by formal education?

▶ ───────────────────────

1   Our house was a fourteen-room typical San Franciscan post-Earthquake affair. We had a succession of roomers, bringing and taking their different accents, and personalities and foods. Shipyard workers clanked up the stairs (we all slept on the second floor except Mother and Daddy Clidell) in their steel-tipped boots and metal hats, and gave way to much-powdered prostitutes, who giggled through their make-up and hung their wigs on the door-knobs. One couple (they were college graduates) held long adult conversations with me in the big kitchen downstairs, until the husband went off to war. Then the wife who had been so charming and ready to smile changed into a silent shadow that played infrequently along the walls. An older couple lived with us for a year or so. They owned a restaurant and had no personality to enchant or interest a teenager, except that the husband was called Uncle Jim, and the wife Aunt Boy. I never figured that out.

2   The quality of strength lined with tenderness is an unbeatable combination, as are intelligence and necessity when unblunted by formal education. I was prepared to accept Daddy Clidell as one more faceless name added to Mother's roster of conquests. I had trained myself so successfully through the years to display interest, or at least attention, while my mind skipped free on other subjects that I could have lived in his house without ever seeing him and without his becoming the wiser. But his character beckoned and elicited admiration. He was a simple man who had no inferiority complex about his lack of education and, even more amazing, no superiority complex because he had succeeded despite that lack. He would say often, "I been to school three years in my life. In Slaten, Texas, times was hard, and I had to help my daddy on the farm."

3   No recriminations lay hidden under the plain statement, nor was there boasting when he said, "If I'm living a little better now, it's because I treats everybody right."

He owned apartment buildings and, later, pool halls, and was famous *4*
for being that rarity "a man of honor." He didn't suffer, as many "honest men" do, from the detestable righteousness that diminishes their virtue. He knew cards and men's hearts. So during the age when Mother was exposing us to certain facts of life, like personal hygiene, proper posture, table manners, good restaurants and tipping practices, Daddy Clidell taught me to play poker, blackjack, tonk and high, low, Jick, Jack and the Game. He wore expensively tailored suits and a large yellow diamond stickpin. Except for the jewelry, he was a conservative dresser and carried himself with the unconscious pomp of a man of secure means. Unexpectedly, I resembled him, and when he, Mother and I walked down the street his friends often said, "Clidell, that's sure your daughter. Ain't no way you can deny her."

Proud laughter followed those declarations, for he had never had *5*
children. Because of his late-arriving but intense paternal sense, I was introduced to the most colorful characters in the Black underground. One afternoon, I was invited into our smoke-filled dining room to make the acquaintance of Stonewall Jimmy, Just Black, Cool Clyde, Tight Coat and Red Leg. Daddy Clidell explained to me that they were the most successful con men in the world, and they were going to tell me about some games so that I would never be "anybody's mark."

To begin, one man warned me, "There ain't never been a mark yet *6*
that didn't want something for nothing." Then they took turns showing me their tricks, how they chose their victims (marks) from the wealthy bigoted whites and in every case how they used the victims' prejudice against them.

Some of the tales were funny, a few were pathetic, but all were *7*
amusing or gratifying to me, for the Black man, the con man who could act the most stupid, won out every time over the powerful, arrogant white.

I remember Mr. Red Leg's story like a favorite melody. *8*

"Anything that works against you can also work for you once you understand the Principle of Reverse. *9*

"There was a cracker in Tulsa who bilked so many Negroes he could *10*
set up a Negro Bilking Company. Naturally he got to thinking, Black Skin means Damn Fool. Just Black and I went to Tulsa to check him out. Come to find out, he's a perfect mark. His momma must have been scared in an Indian massacre in Africa. He hated Negroes only a little more than he despised Indians. And he was greedy.

"Black and I studied him and decided he was worth setting up against *11*
the store. That means we were ready to put out a few thousand dollars in preparation. We pulled in a white boy from New York, a good con artist, and had him open an office in Tulsa. He was supposed to be a

Northern real estate agent trying to buy up valuable land in Oklahoma. We investigated a piece of land near Tulsa that had a toll bridge crossing it. It used to be part of an Indian reservation but had been taken over by the state.

12   "Just Black was laid out as the decoy, and I was going to be the fool. After our friend from New York hired a secretary and had his cards printed, Black approached the mark with a proposition. He told him that he had heard that our mark was the only white man colored people could trust. He named some of the poor fools that had been taken by that crook. It just goes to show you how white folks can be deceived by their own deception. The mark believed Black.

13   "Black told him about his friend who was half Indian and half colored and how some Northern white estate agent had found out that he was the sole owner of a piece of valuable land and the Northerner wanted to buy it. At first the man acted like he smelled a rat, but from the way he gobbled up the proposition, turns out what he thought he smelled was some nigger money on his top lip.

14   "He asked the whereabouts of the land but Black put him off. He told his cracker that he just wanted to make sure that he would be interested. The mark allowed how he was being interested, so Black said he would tell his friend and they'd get in touch with him. Black met the mark for about three weeks in cars and in alleys and kept putting him off until the white man was almost crazy with anxiety and greed and then accidentally it seemed Black let drop the name of the Northern real estate agent who wanted the property. From that moment on we knew we had the big fish on the line and all we had to do was to pull him in.

15   "We expected him to try to contact our store, which he did. That cracker went to our setup and counted on his whiteness to ally him with Spots, our white boy, but Spots refused to talk about the deal except to say the land had been thoroughly investigated by the biggest real estate concern in the South and that if our mark did not go around raising dust he would make sure that there would be a nice piece of money in it for him. Any obvious inquiries as to the rightful ownership of the land could alert the state and they would surely push through a law prohibiting the sale. Spots told the mark he would keep in touch with him. The mark went back to the store three or four times but to no avail, then just before we knew he would crack, Black brought me to see him. That fool was as happy as a sissy in a C.C.C. camp. You would have thought my neck was in a noose and he was about to light the fire under my feet. I never enjoyed taking anybody so much.

16   "Anyhow, I played scary at first but Just Black told me that this was one white man that our people could trust. I said I did not trust no white man because all they wanted was to get a chance to kill a Black man le-

gally and get his wife in the bed. (I'm sorry, Clidell.) The mark assured me that he was the only white man who did not feel like that. Some of his best friends were colored people. In fact, if I didn't know it, the woman who raised him was a colored woman and he still sees her to this day. I let myself be convinced and then the mark began to drag the Northern whites. He told me that they made Negroes sleep in the street in the North and that they had to clean out toilets with their hands in the North and even things worse than that. I was shocked and said, 'Then I don't want to sell my land to that white man who offered seventy-five thousand dollars for it.' Just Black said, 'I wouldn't know what to do with that kind of money,' and I said that all I wanted was to have enough money to buy a home for my old mom, to buy a business and to make one trip to Harlem. The mark asked how much would that cost and I said I reckoned I could do it on fifty thousand dollars.

"The mark told me no Negro was safe with that kind of money. That white folks would take it from him. I said I knew it but I had to have at least forty thousand dollars. He agreed. We shook hands. I said it would do my heart good to see the mean Yankee go down on some of 'our land.' We met the next morning and I signed the deed in his car and he gave me the cash. 17

"Black and I had kept most of our things in a hotel over in Hot Springs, Arkansas. When the deal was closed we walked to our car, drove across the state line and on to Hot Springs. 18

"That's all there was to it." 19

When he finished, more triumphant stories rainbowed around the room riding the shoulders of laughter. By all accounts those storytellers, born Black and male before the turn of the twentieth century, should have been ground into useless dust. Instead they used their intelligence to pry open the door of rejection and not only became wealthy but got some revenge in the bargain. 20

It wasn't possible for me to regard them as criminals or be anything but proud of their achievements. 21

The needs of a society determine its ethics, and in the Black American ghettos the hero is that man who is offered only the crumbs from his country's table but by ingenuity and courage is able to take for himself a Lucullan feast.* Hence the janitor who lives in one room but sports a robin's-egg-blue Cadillac is not laughed at but admired, and the domestic who buys forty-dollar shoes is not criticized but is appreciated. We know that they have put to use their full mental and physical powers. Each single gain feeds into the gains of the body collective. 22

---

*The adjective "Lucullan" means lavish or luxurious. The word derives from Lucullus (110–57 B.C.), a Roman general who was famous for his extravagant feasts.

23   Stories of law violations are weighed on a different set of scales in the Black mind than in the white. Petty crimes embarrass the community and many people wistfully wonder why Negroes don't rob more banks, embezzle more funds and employ graft in the unions. ''We are the victims of the world's most comprehensive robbery. Life demands a balance. It's all right if we do a little robbing now.'' This belief appeals particularly to one who is unable to compete legally with his fellow citizens.

24   My education and that of my Black associates were quite different from the education of our white schoolmates. In the classroom we all learned past participles, but in the streets and in our homes the Blacks learned to drop s's from plurals and suffixes from past-tense verbs. We were alert to the gap separating the written word from the colloquial. We learned to slide out of one language and into another without being conscious of the effort. At school, in a given situation, we might respond with ''That's not unusual.'' But in the street, meeting the same situation, we easily said, ''It be's like that sometimes.''

Questions and Activities

▶ *COMPREHENSION QUESTIONS*

1. What does the word "cracker" mean as it is used in paragraph 15? Does the use of this word seem fitting to the character of the person telling the story? How?
2. What is the significance behind the names Stonewall Jimmy, Just Black, Cool Clyde, Tight Coat, and Red Leg? Are these names meant to tell something about the characters of these men? How do their life styles as con men fit in with their names? What does the "I" of this narrative, the young Angelou, think about these names?
3. Mr. Red Leg is an expert con man. How is his experience representative of a skill Angelou feels blacks must develop if they are to survive in American culture?

▶ *QUESTIONS OF RHETORICAL PURPOSE AND STRATEGY*

4. Describe the teller of this story. How old is she when she is telling the story? How old was she when the events in it happened? What does she think of the confidence men she describes? How did she feel about them when she first heard Mr. Red Leg's story? Have her feelings about these characters changed over the years?

5. Why do you think the narrator tells Mr. Red Leg's story in his own words? What might have been lost if she had summarized his story rather than quoted him directly?

6. Do you think you would feel differently about the confidence game if it had been reported by its victim rather than by someone sympathetic to Mr. Red Leg and Just Black?

▶ *THEME QUESTIONS*

7. Explain how the following sentence from paragraph 2 is supported by the story that is told by Mr. Red Leg: "The quality of strength lined with tenderness is an unbeatable combination, as are intelligence and necessity when unblunted by formal education." What is Angelou trying to get across to her readers concerning human nature and the relationship between blacks and whites by retelling Mr. Red Leg's story?

8. What does Angelou say about men in general in this piece? When are they at their best and their worst?

9. Does Angelou suggest any ideal female qualities in this piece? Can you infer ideal female qualities from her portrayal of what she believes are ideal male qualities?

▶ *LEARNING ACTIVITIES*

10. Write a one-page monologue in which someone you know well tells a story. Be sure to make your story-teller speak in his or her own voice. Punctuate your monologue in the same way that Angelou punctuates Mr. Red Leg's (paragraphs 9 through 19).

11. Practice reading your monologue aloud until you feel confident that you are capturing the speech patterns of your story-teller. Then read it aloud to the class.

Teresa

PATRICIA HAMPL

Patricia Hampl has lived all her life in St. Paul, Minnesota. She has been a visiting assistant professor of English at the University of Minnesota in Minneapolis. She also has earned an advanced creative writing degree from the University of Iowa and has won a creative writing grant from the National Endowment of the Arts, a grant from the Bush Foundation, and a Houghton Mifflin literary fellowship. The fellowship supported her while she was writing her memoirs, *A Romantic Education,* from which the following selection is taken. Her book of poems, *Woman Before an Aquarium,* was published in 1978.

Hampl has always been interested in expressing personal discoveries in her writings. Her memoirs are filled with well-constructed descriptions of significant events in her life, to which she is able to give wider social significance. In the selection that follows, note how Hampl recounts her grandmother's aging and death in a way that connects this particular experience with the theme of aging and death as it applies to all people. What particular aspects of Teresa's death is Hampl suggesting are experienced by all those who reach old age and must deal with the imminence of death for an extended period of time?

To relate this selection to the theme of this section, you will need to consider its perspective on women. Note that all the principal figures in this memoir are women, and, of course, the narrator is Teresa's granddaughter. Keep these questions in mind as you read:

1. How does the younger woman come to learn from the older one? Is she ever told anything directly by her grandmother?
2. What does the narrator's delayed grief for her grandmother's death come to mean to her? Why does she feel, later, that she should have gone to her grandmother's funeral?
3. Has the narrator learned to value a part of her past that seemed unimportant to her before her grandmother's death?

▶ ────────────────

1   And my grandmother, the elderly art nouveau* figure, finally disappeared. She ended up in a nursing home, in the modern way. We all hated it. My father cried and made a fist in his pocket. My mother,

---

*"Art nouveau" is a French term meaning "new art." It is applied to an elaborate style of decorative art that became popular in the 1890s.

who got her household back after years of the ignorant lowness ruining her roses, ruining her role as chatelaine, was not happy and wanted her back, and did not root up the chive plant in the back yard but allowed it to take over so that even today there are chives everywhere, even in the chinks of the sidewalk. My aunts said, "What else can we do?" And what else could we.

I wasn't living at home anymore, but I got letters from my mother. 2 The card parties and Czech lodge meetings with other old ladies who spoke some nineteenth-century version of Czech known only to themselves had come to an end. There weren't even any wakes or funerals for my grandmother to go to anymore; apparently everyone was dead, except for her. She had kept up her relentless cooking and the deep concern for her looks, a discipline held so long it had become a kind of honor. But slowly, steadily, as if they followed a plot, my mother's letters led to the nursing home: Grandma had burned herself one day when she didn't notice she'd left the gas flame on the stove. Her housedresses, cotton flower-print dresses with rickrack trim (her uniform at home), were often not clean: unbelievable.

Then an account of how Grandma had gotten into the bathtub and 3 couldn't hoist herself out; she had sat there, her skin puckering in the water for three hours until my mother heard strange heave-ho noises in the apartment and came in to pull her out. Later, another report that Aunt Sylvia had decided to come every week to clean the apartment ("the kitchen is filthy"). Then Aunt Sylvia suggested that my grandmother should take a bath only when someone was with her. There was a follow-up report that Aunt Sylvia, cleaning the apartment, had been unable to pull Grandma out of the tub and had started to cry. My grandmother began to laugh. It was a stand-off, one of them too weak from crying, the other from laughing. Finally, my aunt called in my mother from next door, and the hoist was accomplished, their big elderly baby laughing because there was nothing else to do.

Then a letter came saying Grandma had fallen down the basement 4 stairs. It might be a stroke. She would have to go to a nursing home: for a while, maybe for longer. She couldn't take care of herself. My mother and father both worked; no one was at home during the day.

A few days later I got a brief note from my mother saying my grand- 5 mother was in the nursing home (address included, suggestion that I send a card) and was confined to a wheelchair. She of the endless avidity and the boundless faith that work was life. My grandmother *sitting*—it was a contradiction in terms. Maybe it was an effect of the stroke, no one seemed sure. But she said she couldn't walk and sank into the wheelchair with no apparent intention of walking again.

For several months she was taken to physical therapy, but finally the 6 head nurse told my father he might as well buy a wheelchair; the rented one was not economical for long-term cases. Then the therapy ended and she had a catheter as a permanent appendage, and showed it to her visitors, unasked, with a kind of wonder at its obvious functionalism. There was no more talk of her walking.

7   I think she went through some kind of nervous breakdown. It's strange to think of a dark night of the soul coming to someone eighty-seven or eighty-eight. By then it would seem that the husk of the personality has rigidified so that if it splits apart at all, it is only into the splinters of senility. I would not have thought of a very old person cracking the personality open and hurling out its pain and experience in sorrow and then, as if there were a future, turning upward in a huge cleansing wave, leaving the soul spent but free and wise at the last shore of its life. But something like that happened to my grandmother.

8   It took about two years. There are several indications that she went through the spiritual cleansing that saints and mystics describe. I was most struck when my father told me that she had said, apropos of nothing (not even of pain: there wasn't a lot of pain at the end), "Well, I think it's time to die tonight." And she did. Her body and soul were that finely meshed by the end. As my aunt said, she knew *what she was*. She knew she was about to be dead.

9   At first, in the nursing home, she fought like a tiger. She did not fight the good fight the physical therapy people wanted her to fight. She must have sensed that there was no future in being a goody-goody. She was out to break the joint. She fought her roommates who, each in turn, asked to be moved out. She fought the medication. She fought being put in bed and then snarled when she was taken out again and put in her wheelchair. She hated the food, but complained that she didn't get enough. She cried and demanded to go home; she sulked and then said casually that when she got home she intended to buy herself a new bed like the one she had in the nursing home—the best bed of her life, she said. She spoke authoritatively, as if acquisition implied mobility. And when no one, out of kindness, reminded her that she wouldn't be going back to her apartment, she reported to her next visitor that she was soon going home.

10   Her children or grandchildren and their children came every day to visit. Everyone talked to her, to each other, about what a nice place the nursing home was, how friendly the staff was, how clean the rooms were, how there were lots of people around to play cards with, and that the best part was that they could take her home anytime for dinners, picnics, holidays. And then they left, and hardly got out the front door before they burst into tears and cried aloud: why did their mother have to be there, in that nice, clean, friendly place?

11   This was not one of the miserable holes for the aged, gigantic and crowded, with loudspeakers blatting endless messages, not one of the

sleazy places that is marginally in the news because of some legislative inquiry about mishandling of public funds. It was what we told her, told each other: a nice, clean, friendly place, modern and light with lots of windows, a yard too small and too near busy traffic perhaps, but the staff was competent, not cruelly overworked, often affectionate. The rooms were not large but were bigger than hospital rooms, and there were only two beds in each one, with a certain commitment to privacy. Large windows, a bath for each room, bright and tiled. I never saw or tasted the food, but my aunts said it was all right. My grandmother was diagnosed as a diabetic soon after arriving so her diet was restricted, probably bland. My family, always clannish, liked to visit her, liked to be with her, and it was generally agreed that even though the place was *very nice*, it didn't do any harm to make it clear that Mrs. Hampl in 106 had four children, innumerable other relatives, and that they came, one or another of them, every day to visit her. *If* the staff merely put on an act for visitors, our endless parade would keep them busily at it. This was the watchful thought.

In an effort to get her interested in the world around her, away from the apartment she kept refurnishing in her mind and conversation, her children and the staff tried to introduce her to other people. They got her to play cards, always her favorite pastime. But years of playing five hundred with indulgent children who let her cheat without much comment had blunted her technique, of playing and of cheating. She was hurt and angry, as chronic cheaters always are, when her new companions bluntly told her to cut it out. Besides, she said, some of them didn't talk right. This was the beginning of her acquaintance with those who, as she put it, were touched. Eventually, if she saw one of her visitors foolishly attempting conversation with someone woefully touched, she discreetly tapped her finger on her own forehead and shook her head, more savvy than her children about the signs around her.

Her wild-tiger time, when she fought the place, lasted less than a year, but it continued in occasional energetic jags for two years. It was a denial of the place and its purpose. She never talked about death or dying. Nor about illness or infirmity. She wanted to go home.

One of the last times I visited her, while I was home for a vacation, I noticed a change. It frightened me; I thought she was going to become one of the touched. She was sitting in her wheelchair moaning when I came in. This was something I hadn't seen her do before. She didn't stop or try to cover her tears. I thought she might be in physical pain, might need a nurse. But that wasn't it. She kept moaning and crying, rocking herself back and forth, not oblivious to my presence, but somewhere out of reach of the conventions of etiquette, the charm that had been one of her enduring principles, deep in her own anguish, not about to abandon her intimacy with it. She took my hand (any hand), stroked her own cheek with it, cried that she was lonely, lonely, looonely, hanging on to the *o* sound. She wanted to die. She made me promise I would come to her funeral. But mostly she did not talk. She moaned and rocked back and forth, like one of the anonymous touched. She wouldn't talk and acknowledged my inept affection (I held her hand, stroked her hair) only from a great distance. That is when she said, more greenhorn than grandmother, "You're good, you're kind."

15   When I left she didn't have me wheel her down to the big lounge picture window, as she had every other time, so that she could wave to me as I drove off—a procedure that always made me feel like a culprit and, really a culprit, made me glad to get away fast. This time she stayed where she was and continued to moan. I felt guilty, I still feel wrong, but I left her moaning there. Anything to get away from that mantra* of sorrow, that awful moaning, toneless, impersonal, not *her*. It—if not she—seemed prepared to go on moaning endlessly. That was the worst part: the eternity in that moan.

16   When I got home one of my aunts was visiting my mother; everybody was glad to see me: coffee, Christmas cookies, kisses around. I didn't want to tell them about the moaning. In some odd, callous way, I was already seeing it as less important than it had seemed at the time. And then my aunt said—mostly to my mother, for my mother—how good I was to take time during my vacation to visit my grandmother, and I began to focus, by degrees, on that aspect of the visit: my kindness. It had been my grandmother's comment too.

17   I thought this was the beginning of her descent into senility and mindlessness. And that the next time I went to visit her she would be babbling and incoherent, her mind woolly with bent memories. I thought her sadness had no bottom, or that there was no trap door to that moan, no escape but death. It occurred to me that she might arrive, in senility, back in Bohemia, the life and country she had had so little memory of, and that she would live there alone in her antiquated, mashed form of the language, mumbling, back in the embrace of the peasantry, lumpen. I didn't want to visit her again. I only saw her once or twice more.

18   But she wasn't senile and she didn't, ever again, moan that way. The curtain in her heart that split in half from top to bottom that day had mended—or hadn't been rent? I almost wondered if I had imagined it. She had become calm and humorous, patient, not the same as be-

---

*"Mantra" is a Hindu term that refers to a sacred formula that is used in prayers. A mantra type of prayer is believed by Hindus to embody the divinity being invoked through breath rhythms and incantations. Hampl is using the term loosely here to describe her grandmother's complaining.

fore—she had always been feisty—but not senile. After her death, my father wrote me about the end. There was a tone of wonder in his letter. The last six months of her life, he wrote, something strange had happened. He didn't know what to call it, he wrote. She just became, after her tiger period, very *kind*. It was she who talked sensibly and naturally to those who were touched in the worst, most unreachable ways; she who held a hand, wheeled herself over to someone sitting vacant and weird in a corner. She cheered the nurses (the nurses said; it was beyond a polite remark, my father wrote). She seemed to understand everybody's troubles, asked for nothing, gave amazing light. Everyone wanted to be around her. Teresa, they called her: her name, of course, but unusual to be called by one's most personal, authentic name in these end-of-the-line places where false affection makes everyone Grandma or, more courteously, more coolly, Mrs. this or that. She died Teresa, a person.

I didn't see any of this. I wasn't around during those last months. I know it from my father who was amazed, bemused by this turn of events. She had gone down and down, and, then, when everyone had every reason to expect her to go even more desperately down—into senility, into woeful bitterness—she made that strange, luminous turn. She glittered at the end not with charm, but with pure spirit, more than a brave salute. Our immigrant became a noble.   *19*

I did not go home for her funeral. I was living in a tiny river town in Illinois, right on the river in fact, so close to the bank that in spring the channel flooded the narrow frontage road and almost reached the strand of houses facing the water. There was no getting away from St. Paul; we were still connected, in a direct line, by the river. In St. Paul the Mississippi is not the Father of Waters; it is narrow and threads its unromantic way past industrial plants. But in Illinois where it begins to become the river of Mark Twain and billows out in a wider, plainlike channel, it becomes aloof and serious.   *20*

After my mother called with the news of my grandmother's death—it hadn't been expected—I went outside by the river. I felt a satisfying finality, what I took to be acceptance. The river glided by, still, grand, metaphoric. I didn't go home for the funeral because a friend of mine had just had twin babies and I felt, solemnly and sincerely, that I was choosing life over death, staying near my friend who wanted me there. My grandmother, who had had twins herself, would have approved, I thought.   *21*

She would not have approved. But I was impervious to the last to her personality. I considered, philosophically, the misty middle ground between life and death that old people inhabit at the end. It was almost   *22* pleasant, this idea of fading. I thought I had probably already said my good-bye to her years before when she first began to get really old, or when she went to the nursing home. Or maybe the day in her room when she had moaned and moaned, as if she were no one in particular, just that grievous sound. She died a long time ago, I thought, as I stood by the wide river, and this recent death is just the expression of it. She had just made it into her tenth decade: she had been ninety on Columbus Day and she died in November. A long life, such a long life as hers, cannot end all of a sudden, I felt. She is at peace, I thought. And so am I.

23   Several weeks later I woke, jolted out of deep sleep in the middle of the night by nothing at all. I was drenched in sweat. I hadn't been dreaming, or hadn't remembered that I was. I was sobbing—I had no idea why at first. Then I focused: I had made a *terrible mistake* and should have gone to her funeral. This was the knowledge—not a dream—that had awakened me. And not having gone, there was no way to undo it.

24   I cried at sudden, unpredictable moments for two weeks after that, sobbing as I drove home, hunched over the steering wheel, unable to see through the tears, as if I were beating my way through a Minnesota blizzard. I moaned aloud in the public library stacks one day, again to my utter surprise. There was an elderly man on the other side of the stacks who peered through a chink in the wall of books to see what the matter was. He was wearing rimless glasses. Those are the cleanest glasses I've ever seen, I thought, and stared at them, fascinated, as if he were the apparition and not I.

25   I must have looked more astonished than miserable; my attacks (as I thought of them) were the advance guard of my emotions. I sobbed, I moaned stupidly, and only after the sound did I think, "Oh, it's Grandma. Because she's dead." The sobbing and moaning were acts dissociated from feeling. It was a weird sensation: to moan aloud in a supermarket check-out line, and then to look sheepishly at the bemused, unsobbing people around me. Yet I didn't miss her. And after a while the sobbing and my sudden public moans diminished and finally, left me entirely.

26   The picture of the luscious art nouveau girl with her lute* went to my Aunt Therese. There was no will, nothing that self-conscious. Things just went, of their own accord, to the family members who wanted or needed them. My cousin ended up with the purple satin eiderdown, perhaps the most Bohemian of my grandmother's posses-

---

*Hampl is referring here to a painting that had hung above her grandmother's sofa for years. To Hampl, the painting represented the ideal of feminine beauty of her grandmother's generation.

sions: the great goose-down quilt of middle Europe. My father wrote in his letter that it seemed as if Grandma had everything beautifully timed: her savings left exactly enough for her burial and for checks of $500 to each of her four children and to Frank's daughter: she had left heirs. If she had lived a few more months, her money would have run out. Nothing would have changed, but welfare—or some version of it—would have paid her way. Ever the housekeeper, she had arranged to the end, tidily. She stopped on a dime.

I asked for the album of Prague views. My aunt wrote back that no-   27
body could find it; somehow or other it was lost. She sent me instead my grandmother's ring, a Bohemian garnet set in white gold with an art nouveau design. I felt someone else should have had it, Frank's daughter perhaps, but this was the object that came to me, apparently it was what I was meant to have. I put it on my finger, the one on which the other women in the family wear their wedding rings; I was the only unmarried one among them.

Then, our personal Europe dead and buried, I decided I must go there.   28

Questions and Activities

▶ *COMPREHENSION QUESTIONS*

1. What does the phrase "elderly art nouveau figure" (paragraph 1) mean? Does this phrase suggest anything about the grandmother's physical appearance, dress, speech, or behavior?

2. What does Hampl mean by "a dark night of the soul" (paragraph 7)? How did Hampl know that her grandmother was going through such a trial? Is "a dark night of the soul" the same as "the spiritual cleansing" that Hampl mentions in paragraph 8, or did the one experience grow out of the other?

3. Does Hampl suggest that the nursing home in which her grandmother was placed was a nice place? How does your answer to this question influence your evaluation of the Hampl family's treatment of Teresa?

4. Did Teresa serve as a link with the past for her family? What about the past might she have represented to her family?

▶ *QUESTIONS OF RHETORICAL PURPOSE AND STRATEGY*

5. Why does Hampl divide her memories of her grandmother's later years into phases such as "a dark night of the soul," "the spiritual cleansing," "wild-tiger time" (paragraph 13), and periods of moaning and kindness? Do you think these divisions are used because

they help Hampl's readers follow along as Hampl describes her experience of her grandmother's later years? Do they have other rhetorical purposes as well?

6. Why does Hampl describe how she is treated back at home after one of her visits to her grandmother in the nursing home (paragraph 16)? Does this description make you feel that Hampl is more or less in tune with her grandmother's feelings?

7. What effect does Hampl's description of her thoughts when she heard of her grandmother's death (paragraphs 21 and 22) have on you? What is the function of the river in this description? What feelings are emphasized in this description? How does Hampl rationalize not going to her grandmother's funeral?

▶ *THEME QUESTIONS*

8. Consider the information that this selection contains concerning Hampl's grandmother. What role did Teresa play within the family? What evidence is there that the family missed the grandmother's daily presence when she was moved to the nursing home? Compare the grandmother's role in the family with the narrator's. How is the narrator, as a young, unmarried female, treated specially or differently by her family?

9. What is the significance of the fact that people at the nursing home began to call the grandmother "Teresa" toward the very end of her life? Does her being thought of and known as Teresa have anything to do with her female qualities?

10. Why does Hampl react to her grandmother's death as she does? There is no "sobbing and moaning" until several months after Teresa's death. How does this fact tie in with Hampl's role as the young, single woman in the family? Does the fact that Hampl's grief is personal and private explain its difference from other modes of grieving for loved ones?

▶ *LEARNING ACTIVITIES*

11. Look up St. Theresa. [Most reference sections in large libraries have Alban Butler's *Lives of the Saints* (four volumes, 1956), which gives brief descriptions of all canonized saints.] For what virtues was she elevated to sainthood? What were the facts of her life? Are any of these facts relevant to what happens to the grandmother in this selection?

12. Have you had any experience to which you wish you had paid more attention or participated in more fully than you did? Why do you feel this way now? Write an informal sketch describing the experience and explaining its significance for you.

New Legends for Old

JAN BRUNVAND

Jan Brunvand is a professor of folklore at the University of Utah who earned his Ph.D. from Indiana University in 1961. His most well-known and widely read book is *The Vanishing Hitchhiker* (1981), which recounts and interprets examples of the phenomenon Brunvand calls the "urban legend." Urban legends are brief stories told over and over again in various regions of the United States. Although these stories are believed by those who tell and hear them, they usually have little or no authenticity. In this selection, in prose that is informative, easy-to-read, and sensible, Brunvand first explains what an urban legend is, describes and interprets "The Boyfriend's Death" (an exemplary urban legend), and finishes by telling how urban legends can be interpreted. Brunvand believes that urban legends contain indirect statements concerning the typical hopes, fears, and values of modern individuals and that interpretations of these legends can tell us a great deal about ourselves and our culture.

Brunvand has published more than a hundred articles in professional folklore journals, a basic folklore textbook, and a second book of urban legends, *The Choking Doberman* (1984).

The urban legend "The Boyfriend's Death" reflects many of society's values concerning the behavior of men and women. Note, for example, that it is the boy who ventures out of the car for help, that it is the girl who is the most frightened by the situation, that the girl is saved by male authority figures, and that the whole story seems to suggest that young people, particularly girls, should not venture away from home, school, or community into isolated places. All these "facts" can be looked at as representative of very definite societal attitudes about the roles of women.

Brunvand also suggests a way for you to gather your own data on male and female roles in our society. You can be attentive to the way women's roles are described in the stories and jokes that your friends and family share. Keep these questions in mind as you read this essay:

1. What do the stories that you hear and tell reveal about the roles of women?
2. Do these roles indicate any changes occurring in traditional values?
3. Do the roles women play in oral stories and jokes seem potentially restricting?

▶ ────────────────────────

1   We are not aware of our own folklore any more than we are of the grammatical rules of our language. When we follow the ancient practice of informally transmitting "lore"—wisdom, knowledge, or accepted modes of behavior—by word of mouth and customary example from person to person, we do not concentrate on the form or content of our folklore; instead, we simply listen to information that others tell us and then pass it on—more or less accurately—to other listeners. In this stream of unselfconscious oral tradition the information that acquires a clear story line is called *narrative folklore,* and those stories alleged to be true are *legends.* This, in broad summary, is the typical process of legend formation and transmission as it has existed from time immemorial and continues to operate today. It works about the same way whether the legendary plot concerns a dragon in a cave or a mouse in a Coke bottle.

2   It might seem unlikely that legends—*urban* legends at that—would continue to be created in an age of widespread literacy, rapid mass communications, and restless travel. While our pioneer ancestors may have had to rely heavily on oral traditions to pass the news along about changing events and frontier dangers, surely we no longer need mere "folk" reports of what's happening, with all their tendencies to distort the facts. A moment's reflection, however, reminds us of the many weird, fascinating, but unverified rumors and tales that so frequently come to our ears—killers and madmen on the loose, shocking or funny personal experiences, unsafe manufactured products, and many other unexplained mysteries of daily life. Sometimes we encounter different oral versions of such stories, and on occasion we may read about similar events in newspapers or magazines; but seldom do we find, or even seek after, reliable documentation. The lack of verification in no way diminishes the appeal urban legends have for us. We enjoy them merely as stories, and we tend at least to half-believe them as possibly accurate reports. And the legends we tell, as with any folklore, reflect many of the hopes, fears, and anxieties of our time. In short, legends are definitely part of our modern folklore—legends which are as traditional, variable, and functional as those of the past.

3   Folklore study consists of collecting, classifying, and interpreting in their full cultural context the many products of everyday human interaction that have acquired a somewhat stable underlying form and that are passed traditionally from person to person, group to group, and generation to generation. Legend study is a most revealing area of such research because the stories that people believe to be true hold an important place in their worldview. "If it's true, it's important" is an axiom

to be trusted, whether or not the lore really *is* true or not. Simply becoming aware of this modern folklore which we all possess to some degree is a revelation in itself, but going beyond this to compare the tales, isolate their consistent themes, and relate them to the rest of the culture can yield rich insights into the state of our current civilization. Such is the premise of this book, and from it derives the method which it follows.*

Urban Legends as Folklore

Folklore subsists on oral tradition, but not all oral communication is folklore. The vast amounts of human interchange, from casual daily conversations to formal discussions in business or industry, law, or teaching, rarely constitute straight oral folklore. However, all such "communicative events" (as scholars dub them) are punctuated routinely by various units of traditional material that are memorable, repeatable, and that fit recurring social situations well enough to serve in place of original remarks. "Tradition" is the key idea that links together such utterances as nicknames, proverbs, greeting and leave-taking formulas, wisecracks, anecdotes, and jokes as "folklore"; indeed, these are a few of the best known "conversational genres" of American folklore. Longer and more complex folk forms—fairy tales, epics, myths, legends, or ballads, for example—may thrive only in certain special situations of oral transmission. All true folklore ultimately depends upon continued oral dissemination, usually within fairly homogeneous "folk groups," and upon the retention through time of internal patterns and motifs that become traditional in the oral exchanges. The corollary of this rule of stability in oral tradition is that all items of folklore, while retaining a fixed central core, are constantly changing as they are transmitted, so as to create countless "variants" differing in length, detail, style, and performance technique. Folklore, in short, consists of oral tradition in variants.

Urban legends belong to the subclass of folk narratives, legends, that—unlike fairy tales—are believed, or at least believable, and that—unlike myths—are set in the recent past and involve normal human beings rather than ancient gods or demigods. Legends are folk history, or rather quasi-history. As with any folk legends, urban legends gain credibility from specific details of time and place or from references to source authorities. For instance, a popular western pioneer leg-

*The book referred to here is *The Vanishing Hitchhiker* (see headnote).

end often begins something like, "My great-grandmother had this strange experience when she was a young girl on a wagon train going through Wyoming when an Indian chief wanted to adopt her . . ." Even though hundreds of different great-grandmothers are supposed to have had the same doubtful experience (being desired by the chief because of her beautiful long blond hair), the fact seldom reaches legend-tellers; if it does, they assume that the family lore has indeed spread far and wide. This particular popular tradition, known as "Goldilocks on the Oregon Trail," interests folklorists because of the racist implications of a dark Indian savage coveting a fair young civilized woman—this legend is familiar in the *white* folklore only—and it is of little concern that the story seems to be entirely apocryphal.*

6   In the world of modern urban legends there is usually no geographical or generational gap between teller and event. The story is *true*; it really occurred, and recently, and always to someone else who is quite close to the narrator, or at least "a friend of a friend." Urban legends are told both in the course of casual conversations and in such special situations as campfires, slumber parties, and college dormitory bull sessions. The legends' physical settings are often close by, real, and sometimes even locally renowned for other such happenings. Though the characters in the stories are usually nameless, they are true-to-life examples of the kind of people the narrators and their audience know firsthand.

7   One of the great mysteries of folklore research is where oral traditions originate and who invents them. One might expect that at least in modern folklore we could come up with answers to such questions, but this is seldom, if ever, the case. . . . most leads pointing to possible authors or original events lying behind urban legends have simply evaporated.

The Performance of Legends

8   Whatever the origins of urban legends, their dissemination is no mystery. The tales have traveled far and wide, and have been told and retold from person to person in the same manner that myths, fairy tales, or ballads spread in earlier cultures, with the important difference that today's legends are also disseminated by the mass media. Groups of age-mates, especially adolescents, are one important American

---

*"Apocryphal" means of questionable authorship or authenticity. The Apocrypha were fourteen books of the Septuagint that appeared in the Latin Vulgate versions of the Bible but were considered inauthentic by later Protestant interpreters because they were not part of the Hebrew scripture. Brunvand uses the word here to mean "unfounded."

legend channel, but other paths of transmission are among office work-ers and club members, as well as among religious, recreational, and re-gional groups. Some individuals make a point of learning every recent rumor or tale, and they can enliven any coffee break, party, or trip with the latest supposed "news." The telling of one story inspires other peo-ple to share what they have read or heard, and in a short time a lively ex-change of details occurs and perhaps new variants are created.

Tellers of these legends, of course, are seldom aware of their roles as   9
"performers of folklore." The conscious purpose of this kind of storytelling is to convey a true event, and only incidentally to entertain an audience. Nevertheless, the speaker's demeanor is carefully orches-trated, and his or her delivery is low-key and soft-sell. With subtle ges-tures, eye movements, and vocal inflections the stories are made dra-matic, pointed, and suspenseful. But, just as with jokes, some can tell them and some can't. Passive tellers of urban legends may just report them as odd rumors, but the more active legend tellers re-create them as dramatic stories of suspense and, perhaps, humor.

"The Boyfriend's Death"

With all these points in mind about folklore's subject-matter,   10
style, and oral performance, consider this typical version of a well-known urban legend that folklorists have named "The Boyfriend's Death," collected in 1964 (the earliest documented instance of the story) by folklorist Daniel R. Barnes from an eighteen-year-old fresh-man at the University of Kansas. The usual tellers of the story are adolescents, and the normal setting for the narration is a college dormi-tory room with fellow students sprawled on the furniture and floors.

> This happened just a few years ago out on the road that turns off 59 highway by the Holiday Inn. This couple were parked under a tree out on this road. Well, it got to be time for the girl to be back at the dorm, so she told her boyfriend that they should start back. But the car wouldn't start, so he told her to lock herself in the car and he would go down to the Holiday Inn and call for help. Well, he didn't come back and he didn't come back, and pretty soon she started hearing a scratching noise on the roof of the car. "Scratch, scratch...scratch, scratch." She got scareder and scareder, but he didn't come back. Finally, when it was almost daylight, some people came along and stopped and helped her out of the car, and she looked up and there was her boyfriend hanging from the tree, and his feet were scraping against the roof of the car. This is why the road is called "Hangman's Road."

Here is a story that has traveled rapidly to reach nationwide oral cir-   11
culation, in the process becoming structured in the typical manner of

folk narratives. The traditional and fairly stable elements are the parked couple, the abandoned girl, the mysterious scratching (sometimes joined by a dripping sound and ghostly shadows on the windshield), the daybreak rescue, and the horrible climax. Variable traits are the precise location, the reason for her abandonment, the nature of the rescuers, murder details, and the concluding placename explanation. While "The Boyfriend's Death" seems to have captured teenagers' imaginations as a separate legend only since the early 1960s, it is clearly related to at least two older yarns, "The Hook" and "The Roommate's Death." All three legends have been widely collected by American folklorists, although only scattered examples have been published, mostly in professional journals. Examination of some of these variations helps to make clear the status of the story as folklore and its possible meanings.

12   At Indiana University, a leading American center of folklore research, folk-narrative specialist Linda Dégh and her students have gathered voluminous data on urban legends, especially those popular with adolescents. Dégh's preliminary published report on "The Boyfriend's Death" concerned nineteen texts collected from IU students from 1964 to 1968. Several storytellers had heard it in high school, often at parties; others had picked it up in college dormitories or elsewhere on campus. Several students expressed some belief in the legend, supposing either that it had happened in their own hometowns, or possibly in other states, once as far distant as "a remote part of Alabama." One informant reported that "she had been sworn to that the incident actually happened," but another, who had heard some variations of the tale, felt that "it seemed too horrible to be true." Some versions had incorporated motifs from other popular teenage horror legends or local ghost stories; one text evidently drew some influence from the urban legend "The Runaway Grandmother," since the characters are "a lady and her husband. . .driving in the desert of New Mexico."

13   One of the Indiana texts, told in the state of Washington, localizes the story there near Moses Lake, "in the country on a road that leads to a dead-end right under a big weeping willow tree. . .about four or five miles from town." As in most American versions of the story, these specific local touches make believable what is essentially a traveling legend. In a detail familiar from other variants of "The Boyfriend's Death," the body—now decapitated—is left hanging upside down from a branch of the willow tree with the fingernails scraping the top of the car. Another version studied by the Indiana researcher is somewhat aberrant, perhaps because the student was told the story by a friend's parents who claimed that "it happened a long time ago, probably thirty or forty years." Here a murderer is introduced, a "crazy old lady" on

whose property the couple has parked. The victim this time is skinned rather than decapitated, and his head scrapes the car as the corpse swings to and fro in the breezy night.

A developing motif in "The Boyfriend's Death" is the character and role of the rescuers, who in the 1964 Kansas version are merely "some people." The standard identification later becomes "the police," authority figures whose presence lends further credence to the story. They are either called by the missing teenagers' parents, or simply appear on the scene in the morning to check the car. In a 1969 variant from Leonardtown, Maryland, the police give a warning, "Miss, please get out of the car and walk to the police car with us, but don't look back." (Concerning the murderer, this storyteller added, "Everyone supposed it was the Hook Man who had done this"...) In a version from Texas collected in 1971, set "at this lake somewhere way out in nowhere," a policeman gets an even longer line: "Young lady, we want you to get out of the car and come with us. Whatever you do, don't turn, don't turn around, just keep walking, just keep going straight and don't look back at the car." The more detailed the police instructions are, the more plausible the tale seems to become. Of course the standard rule of folk-narrative plot development now applies: the taboo must be broken (or the "interdiction violated," as some scholars put it). The girl always *does* look back, like Orpheus in the underworld,* and in a number of versions her hair turns white from the shock of what she sees, as in a dozen other American legends.

14

In a Canadian version of "The Boyfriend's Death," told by a four-teen-year-old boy from Willowdale, Ontario, in 1973, the words of the policemen are merely summarized, but the opening scene of the legend is developed more fully, with several special details, including one usually found in the legend "The Hook"—a warning heard on the car radio. The girl's behavior when left behind is also described in more detail.

15

> A guy and his girlfriend are on the way to a party when their car starts to give them some trouble. At that same time they catch a news flash on the radio warning all people in the area that a lunatic killer has escaped from a local criminal asylum. The girl becomes very upset and at that point the car stalls completely on the highway. The boyfriend gets out and tinkers around with the engine but can't get the car to start again. He decides that he is going to have to walk on up the road to a gas station and get a tow truck but wants his girlfriend to stay behind in the car. She is frightened and pleads with him to

---

*Orpheus, a character in Greek mythology, went to Hades to bring back his dead wife. She was allowed to follow him out of the underworld on the condition that he not look back at her. He was unable to fulfill the condition and lost her forever.

take her, but he says that she'll be safe on the floor of the car covered with a blanket so that anyone passing will think it is an abandoned car and not bother her. Besides he can sprint along the road and get back more quickly than if she comes with him in her high-heeled shoes and evening dress. She finally agrees and he tells her not to come out unless she hears his signal of three knocks on the window . . .

She does hear knocks on the car, but they continue eerily beyond three; the sound is later explained as the shoes of the boyfriend's corpse bumping the car as the body swings from a limb above the car.

16   The style in which oral narratives are told deserves attention, for the live telling that is dramatic, fluid, and often quite gripping in actual folk performance before a sympathetic audience may seem stiff, repetitious, and awkward on the printed page. Lacking in all our examples of "The Boyfriend's Death" is the essential ingredient of immediate context—the setting of the legend-telling, the storyteller's vocal and facial expression and gestures, the audience's reaction, and the texts of other similar tales narrated at the same session. Several of the informants explained that the story was told to them in spooky situations, late at night, near a cemetery, out camping, or even "while on a hayride or out parked," occasionally near the site of the supposed murder. Some students refer to such macabre legends, therefore, as "scary stories," "screamers," or "horrors."

17   A widely-distributed folk legend of this kind as it travels in oral tradition acquires a good deal of its credibility and effect from the localized details inserted by individual tellers. The highway and motel identifications in the Kansas text are good examples of this, and in a New Orleans version, "The Boyfriend's Death" is absorbed into a local teenage tradition about "The Grunch"—a half-sheep, half-human monster that haunts specific local sites. One teenager there reported, "A man and lady went out by the lake and in the morning they found 'em hanging upside down on a tree and they said grunches did it." Finally, rumors or news stories about missing persons or violent crimes (as mentioned in the Canadian version) can merge with urban legends, helping to support their air of truth, or giving them renewed circulation after a period of less frequent occurrence.

18   Even the bare printed texts retain some earmarks of effective oral tradition. Witness in the Kansas text the artful use of repetition (typical of folk narrative style): "Well, he didn't come back and he didn't come back. . . . but he didn't come back." The repeated use of "well" and the building of lengthy sentences with "and" are other hallmarks of oral style which give the narrator complete control over his performance, tending to squeeze out interruptions or prevent lapses in attention among the listeners. The scene that is set for the incident—lonely road, night, a tree looming over the car, out of gas—and the sound effects

—scratches or bumps on the car—contribute to the style, as does the dramatic part played by the policeman and the abrupt ending line: "She looked back, and she saw. . . .!" Since the typical narrators and auditors of "The Boyfriend's Death" themselves like to "park" and may have been alarmed by rumors, strange sights and noises, or automobile emergencies (all intensified in their effects by the audience's knowing other parking legends), the abrupt, unresolved ending leaves open the possibilities of what "really happened."

Urban Legends as Cultural Symbols

Legends can survive in our culture as living narrative folklore if   *19* they contain three essential elements: a strong basic story-appeal, a foundation in actual belief, and a meaningful message or "moral." That is, popular stories like "The Boyfriend's Death" are not only engrossing tales, but also "true," or at least so people think, and they teach valuable lessons. Jokes are a living part of oral tradition, despite being fictional and often silly, because of their humor, brevity, and snappy punch lines, but legends are by nature longer, slower, and more serious. Since more effort is needed to tell and appreciate a legend than a joke, it needs more than just verbal art to carry it along. Jokes have significant "messages" too, but these tend to be disguised or implied. People tell jokes primarily for amusement, and they seldom sense their underlying themes. In legends the primary messages are quite clear and straightforward; often they take the form of explicit warnings or good examples of "poetic justice." Secondary messages in urban legends tend to be suggested metaphorically or symbolically; these may provide deeper criticisms of human behavior or social conditions.

People still tell legends, therefore, and other folk take time to listen   *20* to them, not only because of their inherent plot interest but because they seem to convey true, worthwhile, and relevant information, albeit partly in a subconscious mode. In other words, such stories are "news" presented to us in an attractive way, with hints of larger meanings. Without this multiple appeal few legends would get a hearing in the modern world, so filled with other distractions. Legends survive by being as lively and "factual" as the television evening news, and, like the daily news broadcasts, they tend to concern deaths, injuries, kidnappings, tragedies, and scandals. Apparently the basic human need for meaningful personal contact cannot be entirely replaced by the mass media and popular culture. A portion of our interest in what is occurring in the world must be filled by some face-to-face reports from other human beings.

21   On a literal level a story like "The Boyfriend's Death" simply warns young people to avoid situations in which they may be endangered, but at a more symbolic level the story reveals society's broader fears of people, especially women and the young, being alone and among strangers in the darkened world outside the security of their own home or car. Note that the young woman in the story (characterized by "her high-heeled shoes and evening dress") is shown as especially helpless and passive, cowering under the blanket in the car until she is rescued by men. Such themes recur in various forms in many other popular urban legends. . . .

22   In order to be retained in a culture, any form of folklore must fill some genuine need, whether this be the need for an entertaining escape from reality, or a desire to validate by anecdotal examples some of the culture's ideals and institutions. For legends in general, a major function has always been the attempt to explain unusual and supernatural happenings in the natural world. To some degree this remains a purpose for urban legends, but their more common role nowadays seems to be to show that the prosaic contemporary scene is capable of producing shocking or amazing occurrences which may actually have happened to friends or to near-acquaintances but which are nevertheless explainable in some reasonably logical terms. On the one hand we want our factual lore to inspire awe, and at the same time we wish to have the most fantastic tales include at least the hint of a rational explanation and perhaps even a conclusion. Thus an escaped lunatic, a possibly *real* character, not a fantastic invader from outer space or Frankenstein's monster, is said to be responsible for the atrocities committed in the gruesome tales that teenagers tell. As sometimes happens in real life, the car radio gives warning, and the police get the situation back under control. (The policemen's role, in fact, becomes larger and more commanding as the story grows in oral tradition.) Only when the young lovers are still alone and scared are they vulnerable, but society's adults and guardians come to their rescue presently.

23   In common with brief unverified reports ("rumors"), to which they are often closely related, urban legends gratify our desire to know about and to try to understand bizarre, frightening, and potentially dangerous or embarrassing events that *may* have happened. (In rumors and legends there is always some element of doubt concerning where and when these things *did* occur.) These floating stories appeal to our morbid curiosity and satisfy our sensation-seeking minds that demand gratification through frequent infusions of new information, "sanitized" somewhat by the positive messages. Informal rumors and stories fill in the gaps left by professional news reporting, and these marvelous, though generally false, "true" tales may be said to be carrying the folk-news—along

with some editorial matter—from person to person even in today's highly technological world.

Interpreting Urban Legends

Collections of verbatim oral texts from their natural contexts, along with background information about storytellers and their listeners, are the basis for reliable interpretations of folk stories' meanings and functions in the societies in which they are found. Texts from the mass media need to be identified by date and place of publication as well as to their likely audiences. Insofar as possible, the history and distribution of any given tale should be made clear from the collected examples of it. Unfortunately, these ideals were not always met in past folk-narrative studies, but it should be the goal of all present and future collectors to secure the fullest possible data on stories and their human sources. For urban legends this ought to become standard procedure, since they belong to an ongoing tradition that is easily observed. 24

Even with incomplete data, some worthwhile conclusions about the meanings of urban legend are possible when the existing information is evaluated and compared. Folklorists assume that no cultural data is devoid of meaning, and that any data from a culture may cast some light on the meaning of other data from the same culture. A few observations about the folkloristic methods of analysis applicable to urban legend research are in order.... 25

As already noted, in any living oral tradition, such as storytelling, certain stable elements persist at the same time that other elements are in constant variation. By the process sometimes referred to as "communal re-creation," people in a folk community absorb new material into their oral culture, then remake it through repetition and creative retelling. The resulting oral narratives are somewhat stereotyped and formalized in broad terms, but also they are always fluid and changing in details. The first step in identifying and classifying an oral-narrative tradition such as that of an urban legend is to distinguish the stable elements from the variable units. 26

For the purpose of study, the stable parts of urban legends are usually stated as generalized descriptions of basic stages in the plot, such as the couple parking, the threat from outside, the rescue, and the final revelation of the crime in "The Boyfriend's Death." These abstracted actions are then compared to the story units of other traditional legends . . . and their underlying structural patterns described. Often, for example, sets of opposites dominate urban legend plots; these may be expressed in 27 such paired terms as old/young, life/death, home/away, good/bad, reality/fantasy, and the like. Another typical pattern, common in many kinds of folk narratives, is threefold repetition, with the climax at the third stage. In these repeated standardized patterns of oral tradition we find solid clues as to the meanings stories convey, whether explicitly as straightforward warnings, or less directly in symbolic form.

28   Like other narrative folklore, urban legends develop two kinds of variations. Many changes are predictable adaptations to make the stories fit local conditions. Especially in an oral tradition that is considered true (like legends), circumstantial details of name, place, time, and situation often enter into narrators' performances. More significant variations, however, go beyond local color to introduce new characters, objects, or plot elements, and especially attempts on the part of storytellers to explain the story (sometimes called "oral-literary criticism"). When other narrators repeat and expand upon these variable elements, they become accepted into a wider tradition and further shape legends as cultural symbols. In "The Boyfriend's Death," for example, we saw how the details of the girl's reaction to stress and the enlargement of the policemen's part in the story both reflect how American society expects young women and authority figures to behave in times of crisis. Comparative folklore research has also shown us how such older traditional "motifs"—individual plot elements—as violation of a taboo ("Don't look back!") and hair turning white from fear became attached to this newer legend. . . .

29   Along with material from the urban legend tradition itself, other social and cultural aspects of modern life related to the subject matter of legends are considered in an interpretation. Folklorists ask what else the culture says about the same subjects in expressive forms other than folklore. Evidence may be sought in popular culture, institutions (such as school and church), patterns of family life, social interaction, and the like. What are the standards of behavior that the characters in legends either conform to or disregard? Do the messages of legends support or attack society's expectations?

30   Perhaps the most telling aspect of legend interpretation—but often the most lacking in past collections—is solid information about the narration of legends in their natural contexts. What little we know about *who* tells the stories, *when, to whom,* and *why* invariably contributes towards understanding how legends function and what they mean. Too frequently, however, our contextual and background information is limited to the name, age, sex, and address of informants; seldom do we find scholarly studies that give close descriptions of actual storytelling events. As a result, we must make the best of what we

have . . . and we must encourage the further study of urban legends in much more depth and with better social, cultural, and performance data. . . .

Questions and Activities

► *COMPREHENSION QUESTIONS*

1. What does Brunvand mean when he says that urban legends have a "stable underlying form" (paragraph 3)? What is the stable underlying form of "The Boyfriend's Death"?
2. How are urban legends disseminated?
3. Do folklorists know anything about how urban legends originate? What makes discovering the source of an urban legend difficult?
4. What does Brunvand mean when he talks about how urban legends are "localized" (paragraph 17)? Use "The Boyfriend's Death" to explain your answer.
5. What are the three essential elements that a legend must possess if it is to become a part of living narrative folklore?

► *QUESTIONS OF RHETORICAL PURPOSE AND STRATEGY*

6. Why does Brunvand put his discussion of "The Boyfriend's Death" between a general introduction explaining urban legends in technical terms and a general conclusion explaining how folklorists interpret legends? Does this structure suggest a particular audience and purpose for this essay?
7. Reread the subheadings that appear throughout this essay. Do they seem more appropriate to a textbook or a newspaper? Why?
8. Consider Brunvand's voice. Is it adapted to informative or persuasive writing? What qualities make it either informative or persuasive?

► *THEME QUESTIONS*

9. Brunvand offers a few tentative interpretations of "The Boyfriend's Death." What implications about male and female roles in our culture are contained in those interpretations? Are the young women who hear this legend being told, for example, to avoid lonely and isolated locations? Are they being told not to stray from male protection? If a young woman heard many legends of this type as she grew up, might she end up limiting herself to the behavior that was advocated by the social conventions implied in these legends?

10. Consider the function of oral folklore in developing the beliefs and values of your friends and family. Does your family ever engage in story-telling as a way of proving the truth of a particular value? Do your friends ever tell stories that seem to reinforce specific social values? Do these groups' stories have implications for the roles played by men and women? What are those implications?

   ▶ *LEARNING ACTIVITIES*

11. Be an amateur folklorist. Work together with a small group of your classmates to find, transcribe, and interpret an urban legend that you believe says something about the roles of men and women in our society. Each group should report its findings to the whole class.

12. Discuss the following proposition with a small group of your classmates: "Our folk culture stereotypes men and women." Then write an essay in which you argue either for or against the proposition.

A Few Words about Breasts: Shaping Up Absurd

NORA EPHRON

Nora Ephron grew up in Beverly Hills, California. The child of two Hollywood screenwriters, she wanted to be a writer from an early age. At Wellesley College, where she received her bachelor's degree, her letters home were turned by her parents into a successful play, *Take Her, She's Mine*. From that point in the early 1960s up to the present, Ephron's private life and writing career have never been separate. She has become a very well-known journalist, and most of her writing focuses on characters and experiences drawn from her own life. She has written columns on the experience of being a woman and on the influence and inner workings of the media for *Esquire* and *New York Magazine,* and she worked for five years as a reporter for the *New York Post*. Many of her columns and personal essays have been published in the best-selling books *Wall-Flower at the Orgy* (1970), *Crazy Salad* (1975), and *Scribble, Scribble* (1979). Ephron employs a witty, humorous voice and keen observations of character to create interesting commentaries on modern life. In 1983, Ephron co-authored the screenplay for the film *Silkwood,* which adapted the true story of Karen Silkwood, who was exposed to radiation while working in an Oklahoma nuclear power plant. (Many people believe that Silkwood was murdered while en route to a secret meeting with a newspaper reporter about conditions in that plant.)

Ephron's most controversial book is *Heartburn* (1983), a novel that deals with the break-up of her marriage to Carl Bernstein, the co-author of *All the President's Men* and one of the *Washington Post* reporters who first investigated the Watergate incident. This novel, like her columns, combines extremely detailed accounts of the author's personal life with indirect commentary on contemporary relations between men and women.

The following essay on what it's like growing up as a flat-chested female comes from *Crazy Salad*. It serves as an excellent example of Ephron's ability to make personal experience publicly relevant. As you read the essay, note how Ephron's voice creates a definite attitude toward her subject:

1. How does her language communicate Ephron's perception of the absurdity of putting so much emphasis on a single physical characteristic?

2. Why does she continue to feel self-conscious about the size of her breasts even though she obviously considers it absurd to give breasts so much significance?
3. Do you feel that the tendency to value a woman according to the size of her breasts has increased or diminished since 1975? What evidence do you have for your answer to this question?

▶ ——————————————————

1   I have to begin with a few words about androgyny. In grammar school, in the fifth and sixth grades, we were all tyrannized by a rigid set of rules that supposedly determined whether we were boys or girls. The episode in *Huckleberry Finn* where Huck is disguised as a girl and gives himself away by the way he threads a needle and catches a ball—that kind of thing. We learned that the way you sat, crossed your legs, held a cigarette and looked at your nails, your wristwatch, the way you did these things instinctively was absolute proof of your sex. Now obviously most children did not take this literally, but I did. I thought that just one slip, just one incorrect cross of my legs or flick of an imaginary cigarette ash would turn me from whatever I was into the other thing; that would be all it took, really. Even though I was outwardly a girl and had many of the trappings generally associated with the field of girldom—a girl's name, for example, and dresses, my own telephone, an autograph book—I spent the early years of my adolescence absolutely certain that I might at any point gum it up. I did not feel at all like a girl. I was boyish. I was athletic, ambitious, outspoken, competitive, noisy, rambunctious. I had scabs on my knees and my socks slid into my loafers and I could throw a football. I wanted desperately not to be that way, not to be a mixture of both things but instead just one, a girl, a definite indisputable girl. As soft and as pink as a nursery. And nothing would do that for me, I felt, but breasts.

2   I was about six months younger than everyone in my class, and so for about six months after it began, for six months after my friends had begun to develop—that was the word we used, develop—I was not particularly worried. I would sit in the bathtub and look down at my breasts and know that any day now, any second now, they would start growing like everyone else's. They didn't. "I want to buy a bra," I said to my mother one night. "What for?" she said. My mother was really hateful about bras, and by the time my third sister had gotten to that point where she was ready to want one, my mother had worked the whole business into a comedy routine. "Why not use a Band-Aid in-

stead?'' she would say. It was a source of great pride to my mother that she had never even had to wear a brassiere until she had her fourth child, and then only because her gynecologist made her. It was incomprehensible to me that anyone would ever be proud of something like that. It was the 1950s, for God's sake. Jane Russell. Cashmere sweaters. Couldn't my mother see that? *"I am too old to wear an undershirt."* Screaming. Weeping. Shouting. "Then don't wear an undershirt," said my mother. "But I want to buy a bra." "What for?"

I suppose that for most girls, breasts, brassieres, that entire thing, has   3
more trauma, more to do with the coming of adolescence, of becoming a woman, than anything else. Certainly more than getting your period, although that too was traumatic, symbolic. But you could *see* breasts; they were there; they were visible. Whereas a girl could claim to have her period for months before she actually got it and nobody would ever know the difference. Which is exactly what I did. All you had to do was make a great fuss over having enough nickels for the Kotex machine and walk around clutching your stomach and moaning for three to five days a month about The Curse and you could convince anybody. There is a school of thought somewhere in the women's lib/women's mag/ gynecology establishment that claims that menstrual cramps are purely psychological, and I lean toward it. Not that I didn't have them finally. Agonizing cramps, heating-pad cramps, go-down-to-the-school-nurse-and-lie-on-the-cot cramps. But unlike any pain I had ever suffered, I adored the pain of cramps, welcomed it, wallowed in it, bragged about it. "I can't go. I have cramps." "I can't do that. I have cramps." And most of all, gigglingly, blushingly: "I can't swim. I have cramps." Nobody ever used the hard-core word. Menstruation. God, what an awful word. Never that. "I have cramps."

The morning I first got my period, I went into my mother's bedroom   4
to tell her. And my mother, my utterly-hateful-about-bras mother, burst into tears. It was really a lovely moment, and I remember it so clearly not just because it was one of the two times I ever saw my mother cry on my account (the other was when I was caught being a six-year-old kleptomaniac), but also because the incident did not mean to me what it meant to her. Her little girl, her firstborn, had finally become a woman. That was what she was crying about. My reaction to the event, however, was that I might well be a woman in some scientific, textbook sense (and could at least stop faking every month and stop wasting all those nickels). But in another sense—in a visible sense—I was as androgynous and as liable to tip over into boyhood as ever.

I started with a 28AA bra. I don't think they made them any smaller   5
in those days, although I gather that now you can buy bras for five year

olds that don't have any cups whatsoever in them; trainer bras they are called. My first brassiere came from Robinson's Department Store in Beverly Hills. I went there alone, shaking, positive they would look me over and smile and tell me to come back next year. An actual fitter took me into the dressing room and stood over me while I took off my blouse and tried the first one on. The little puffs stood out on my chest. "Lean over," said the fitter (to this day I am not sure what fitters in bra departments do except to tell you to lean over). I leaned over, with the fleeting hope that my breasts would miraculously fall out of my body and into the puffs. Nothing.

6   "Don't worry about it," said my friend Libby some months later, when things had not improved. "You'll get them after you're married."

7   "What are you talking about?" I said.

8   "When you get married," Libby explained, "your husband will touch your breasts and rub them and kiss them and they'll grow."

9   That was the killer. Necking I could deal with. Intercourse I could deal with. But it had never crossed my mind that a man was going to touch my breasts, that breasts had something to do with all that, petting, my God they never mentioned petting in my little sex manual about the fertilization of the ovum. I became dizzy. For I knew instantly—as naïve as I had been only a moment before—that only part of what she was saying was true: the touching, rubbing, kissing part, not the growing part. And I knew that no one would ever want to marry me. I had no breasts. I would never have breasts.

10   My best friend in school was Diana Raskob. She lived a block from me in a house full of wonders. English muffins, for instance. The Raskobs were the first people in Beverly Hills to have English muffins for breakfast. They also had an apricot tree in the back, and a badminton court, and a subscription to *Seventeen* magazine, and hundreds of games like Sorry and Parcheesi and Treasure Hunt and Anagrams. Diana and I spent three or four afternoons a week in their den reading and playing and eating. Diana's mother's kitchen was full of the most colossal assortment of junk food I have ever been exposed to. My house was full of apples and peaches and milk and homemade chocolate-chip cookies—which were nice, and good for you, but-not-right-before-dinner-or-you'll-spoil-your-appetite. Diana's house had nothing in it that was good for you, and what's more, you could stuff it in right up until dinner and nobody cared. Bar-B-Q potato chips (they were the first in them, too), giant bottles of ginger ale, fresh popcorn with melted butter, hot fudge sauce on Baskin-Robbins jamoca ice cream, powdered-sugar doughnuts from Van de Kamps. Diana and I had been best friends since we were seven; we were about equally popular in school (which is

to say, not particularly), we had about the same success with boys (extremely intermittent) and we looked much the same. Dark. Tall. Gangly.

It is September, just before school begins. I am eleven years old, about to enter the seventh grade, and Diana and I have not seen each other all summer. I have been to camp and she has been somewhere like Banff with her parents. We are meeting, as we often do, on the street midway between our two houses and we will walk back to Diana's and eat junk and talk about was has happened to each of us that summer. I am walking down Walden Drive in my jeans and my father's shirt hanging out and my old red loafers with the socks falling into them and coming toward me is . . . I take a deep breath . . . a young woman. Diana. Her hair is curled and she has a waist and hips and a bust and she is wearing a straight skirt, an article of clothing I have been repeatedly told I will be unable to wear until I have the hips to hold it up. My jaw drops, and suddenly I am crying, crying hysterically, can't catch my breath sobbing. My best friend has betrayed me. She has gone ahead without me and done it. She has shaped up.   *11*

Here are some things I did to help: *12*
Bought a Mark Eden Bust Developer.   *13*
Slept on my back for four years.   *14*
Splashed cold water on them every night because some French actress said in *Life* magazine that that was what *she* did for her perfect bustline.   *15*

Ultimately, I resigned myself to a bad toss and began to wear padded bras. I think about them now, think about all those years in high school I went around in them, my three padded bras, every single one of them with different sized breasts. Each time I changed bras I changed sizes: one week nice perky but not too obtrusive breasts, the next medium-sized slightly pointed ones, the next week knockers, true knockers; all the time, whatever size I was, carrying around this rubberized appendage on my chest that occasionally crashed into a wall and was poked inward and had to be poked outward—I think about all that and wonder how anyone kept a straight face through it. My parents, who normally had no restraints about needling me—why did they say nothing as they watched my chest go up and down? My friends, who would periodically inspect my breasts for signs of growth and reassure me—why didn't they at least counsel consistency?   *16*

And the bathing suits. I die when I think about the bathing suits. That was the era when you could lay an uninhabited bathing suit on the beach and someone would make a pass at it. I would put one on, an absurd swimsuit with its enormous bust built into it, the bones from   *17* the suit stabbing me in the rib cage and leaving little red welts on my body, and there I would be, my chest plunging straight downward absolutely vertically from my collarbone to the top of my suit and then suddenly, wham, out came all that padding and material and wiring absolutely horizontally.

18   Buster Klepper was the first boy who ever touched them. He was my boyfriend my senior year of high school. There is a picture of him in my high-school yearbook that makes him look quite attractive in a Jewish, horn-rimmed glasses sort of way, but the picture does not show the pimples, which were air-brushed out, or the dumbness. Well, that isn't really fair. He wasn't dumb. He just wasn't terribly bright. His mother refused to accept it, refused to accept the relentlessly average report cards, refused to deal with her son's inevitable destiny in some junior college or other. "He was tested," she would say to me, apropos of nothing, "and it came out 145. That's near-genius." Had the word underachiever been coined, she probably would have lobbed that one at me, too. Anyway, Buster was really very sweet—which is, I know, damning with faint praise, but there it is. I was the editor of the front page of the high-school newspaper and he was editor of the back page; we had to work together, side by side, in the print shop, and that was how it started. On our first date, we went to see *April Love* starring Pat Boone. Then we started going together. Buster had a green coupe, a 1950 Ford with an engine he had handchromed until it shone, dazzled, reflected the image of anyone who looked into it, anyone usually being Buster polishing it or the gas-station attendants he constantly asked to check the oil in order for them to be overwhelmed by the sparkle on the valves. The car also had a boot stretched over the back seat for reasons I never understood; hanging from the rearview mirror, as was the custom, was a pair of angora dice. A previous girl friend named Solange who was famous throughout Beverly Hills High School for having no pigment in her right eyebrow had knitted them for him. Buster and I would ride around town, the two of us seated to the left of the steering wheel. I would shift gears. It was nice.

19   There was necking. Terrific necking. First in the car, overlooking Los Angeles from what is now the Trousdale Estates. Then on the bed of his parents' cabana at Ocean House. Incredibly wonderful, frustrating necking, I loved it, really, but no further than necking, please don't, please, because there I was absolutely terrified of the general implications of going-a-step-further with a near-dummy and also terrified of his finding out there was next to nothing there (which he knew, of course; he wasn't that dumb).

20   I broke up with him at one point. I think we were apart for about two weeks. At the end of that time I drove down to see a friend at a boarding

school in Palos Verdes Estates and a disc jockey played *April Love* on the radio four times during the trip. I took it as a sign. I drove straight back to Griffith Park to a golf tournament Buster was playing in (he was the sixth-seeded teen-age golf player in Southern California) and presented myself back to him on the green of the 18th hole. It was all very dramatic. That night we went to a drive-in and I let him get his hand under my protuberances and onto my breasts. He really didn't seem to mind at all.

> *"Do you want to marry my son?" the woman asked me.*   21
> *"Yes," I said.*   22
> *I was nineteen years old, a virgin, going with this woman's son, this*   23
> *big strange woman who was married to a Lutheran minister in New Hampshire and pretended she was Gentile and had this son, by her first husband, this total fool of a son who ran the hero-sandwich concession at Harvard Business School and whom for one moment one December in New Hampshire I said—as much out of politeness as anything else—that I wanted to marry.*
> *"Fine," she said. "Now, here's what you do. Always make sure*   24
> *you're on top of him so you won't seem so small. My bust is very large, you see, so I always lie on my back to make it look smaller, but you'll have to be on top most of the time."*
> *I nodded. "Thank you," I said.*   25
> *"I have a book for you to read," she went on, "Take it with you when*   26
> *you leave. Keep it." She went to the bookshelf, found it, and gave it to me. It was a book on frigidity.*
> *"Thank you," I said.*   27

That is a true story. Everything in this article is a true story, but I feel   28
I have to point out that that story in particular is true. It happened on December 30, 1960. I think about it often. When it first happened, I naturally assumed that the woman's son, my boyfriend, was responsible. I invented a scenario where he had had a little heart-to-heart with his mother and had confessed that his only objection to me was that my breasts were small; his mother then took it upon herself to help out. Now I think I was wrong about the incident. The mother was acting on her own, I think: that was her way of being cruel and competitive under the guise of being helpful and maternal. You have small breasts, she was saying; therefore you will never make him as happy as I have. Or you have small breasts; therefore you will doubtless have sexual problems. Or you have small breasts; therefore you are less woman than I am. She was, as it happens, only the first of what seems to me to be a never-ending string of women who have made competitive remarks to me about breast size. "I would love to wear a dress like that," my friend Emily says to me, "but my bust is too big." Like that. Why do women

say these things to me? Do I attract these remarks the way other women attract married men or alcoholics or homosexuals? This summer, for example. I am at a party in East Hampton and I am introduced to a woman from Washington. She is a minor celebrity, very pretty and Southern and blonde and outspoken and I am flattered because she has read something I have written. We are talking animatedly, we have been talking no more than five minutes, when a man comes up to join us. "Look at the two of us," the woman says to the man, indicating me and her. "The two of us together couldn't fill an A cup." Why does she say that? It isn't even true, dammit, so why? Is she even more addled than I am on this subject? Does she honestly believe there is something wrong with her size breasts, which, it seems to me, now that I look hard at them, are just right. Do I unconsciously bring out competitiveness in women? In that form? What did I do to deserve it?

29   As for men.

30   There were men who minded and let me know they minded. There were men who did not mind. In any case, I always minded.

31   And even now, now that I have been countlessly reassured that my figure is a good one, now that I am grown up enough to understand that most of my feelings have very little to do with the reality of my shape, I am nonetheless obsessed by breasts. I cannot help it. I grew up in the terrible Fifties—with rigid stereotypical sex roles, the insistence that men be men and dress like men and women be women and dress like women, the intolerance of androgyny—and I cannot shake it, cannot shake my feelings of inadequacy. Well, that time is gone, right? All those exaggerated examples of breast worship are gone, right? Those women were freaks, right? I know all that. And yet, here I am, stuck with the psychological remains of it all, stuck with my own peculiar version of breast worship. You probably think I am crazy to go on like this: here I have set out to write a confession that is meant to hit you with the shock of recognition and instead you are sitting there thinking I am thoroughly warped. Well, what can I tell you? If I had had them, I would have been a completely different person. I honestly believe that.

32   After I went into therapy, a process that made it possible for me to tell total strangers at cocktail parties that breasts were the hang-up of my life, I was often told that I was insane to have been bothered by my condition. I was also frequently told, by close friends, that I was extremely boring on the subject. And my girl friends, the ones with nice big breasts, would go on endlessly about how their lives had been far more miserable than mine. Their bra straps were snapped in class. They couldn't sleep on their stomachs. They were stared at whenever the word "mountain" cropped up in geography. And *Evangeline*, good God what they went through every time someone had to stand up and recite the Prologue to Longfellow's *Evangeline:* "*. . . stand like druids of*

eld . . . / With beards that rest on their bosoms." It was much worse for them, they tell me. They had a terrible time of it, they assure me. I don't know how lucky I was, they say.

I have thought about their remarks, tried to put myself in their place,   33
considered their point of view. I think they are full of shit.

Questions and Activities

▶ *COMPREHENSION QUESTIONS*

1. Look up "androgyny" in a dictionary. Then explain how the definition of this term applies to Ephron's discussion of female anatomy.
2. What was Ephron's mother's response to the news that her daughter had gotten her period? How did this response contrast with her usual attitude about physical changes in her daughter? Why does Ephron think her mother responded differently to this change?
3. What is "a Mark Eden Bust Developer" (paragraph 13)? Where are they usually advertised? How does someone get one?
4. Why does Ephron remember the remark made to her by the pretty Southern woman at a party in East Hampton (paragraph 28)? What does this remark signify to Ephron about women, and about herself?

▶ *QUESTIONS OF RHETORICAL PURPOSE AND STRATEGY*

5. Describe Ephron's voice. Point to phrases and words that create this voice. What effect does her voice have on your attitude toward her subject?
6. What is Ephron's primary means for supporting her ideas in this essay? Does she use statistics, facts, examples, or particular devices of style? Does she cite any authorities to support her claims?
7. What is Ephron's primary purpose in this essay? Does she want to change her readers' minds, simply entertain them, or give a scientific explanation for her hang-up concerning breasts?
8. For whom did Ephron write this essay? Was it written primarily for women? Do you think it first appeared in a popular or a serious magazine? Was it written for younger or older women, or both?

▶ *THEME QUESTIONS*

9. Do you feel that men are affected as much as women by a need to project certain physical qualities? Are men, for example, expected to have large muscles or a particular sort of smell? Are men as bothered by these expectations as Ephron is, as most women are?

10. Do you agree with Ephron that it is absurd for women to worry about physical characteristics such as breast size? Why might such a worry be an understandable one in our culture?
11. Does a woman's worrying about developing certain female physical characteristics necessarily mean that she would have to deemphasize her intellectual, athletic, or artistic endeavors?

   ▶ *LEARNING ACTIVITIES*

12. Free-write an essay in which you describe some aspect of your physical appearance that you worried over a great deal earlier in your life. Were you, for example, very worried at one time about being overweight or underweight, about the size of your nose, or feet, or breasts? Were you ever concerned about being too short or too tall? After you have described this worry, tell what you think about it now.
13. Make a list of physical characteristics that the media present as ideals for men and women in our culture. Compare your list with those of other students. Are these characteristics touted in advertisements for particular products? Are they reinforced by being apparent in popular film and television personalities? Do you think Ephron was influenced by similar kinds of media images as she grew up?

A Worn Path

EUDORA WELTY

Eudora Welty, born in 1909, is widely recognized as one of the South's most talented writers of fiction. Her stories and novels usually deal with Southern life and the relationship of family to society and include characterizations that are both realistic and original. She is a master at capturing the sound of the speech of all social classes, and she is able to portray the friction between social values and individual needs and desires without devaluing either her individual characters or the society in which they live.

Welty herself has said that she writes two kinds of stories. Her "inside" stories convey directly the thoughts and emotions of her characters. Their purpose is to provide readers with clear portraits of characters whose contradictions, deep feelings, and voices represent the wide range of individuals who populate the South. Her characters are never all good or all bad, but are realistic combinations of a variety of motives, values, and qualities. The novels *Delta Wedding* (1946) and *The Optimist's Daughter* (1972) and many of the stories included in *The Wide Net* (1943) and *The Bride of Innisfallen* (1955) are "inside" stories.

Welty's "outside" stories, in contrast, emphasize action, plot, and description of setting rather than the inner thoughts of characters. Dialogue, story-telling, and events reveal character indirectly in these stories. *A Robber Bridegroom* (1942), *Ponder Heart* (1954), *Losing Battles* (1970), and *A Curtain of Green and Other Stories* (1941) represent Welty's "outside" stories. (This inside/outside distinction in Eudora Welty's fiction comes from *Contemporary Literary Criticism,* Vol. 33, p. 413.)

In 1984, Welty published *One Writer's Beginnings,* an autobiography in which she tells of how her early propensity for listening closely to the talk of her parents, family, and friends and her voracious reading formed the basis for the different forms of story-telling and character-creating in her fiction. Her fascination with the locales of her Mississippi childhood and the people she knew and loved and her memories of family journeys back to Ohio and West Virginia created the foundation for the settings and characters of her fiction.

"A Worn Path," the story that follows, is an "inside" story. In it, Welty focuses on the character of Phoenix Jackson, a very old black woman living outside of Natchez, Mississippi. We learn about Phoenix's character through her actions and what she says when she talks to herself. Also, as she completes her trip into town, she meets and talks with four white people (the hunter, the lady in the street, the attendant, and the nurse). Actions, thoughts, and dialogue combine to give us a striking portrait of a woman who is of an earlier time.

What does Phoenix's character suggest to us about the meaning of being a woman? Perhaps the best answer would be to point out how Phoenix is different from the middle-class white characters that she meets on her journey. Phoenix, despite her poverty and age, is totally independent, living by her own sense of time and place. Those she meets seem driven by exterior values, always judging Phoenix by society's standards. Phoenix's love of her grandson, for whom she has made her journey, and her own stubborn will to survive seem to place her in an earlier, simpler social structure in which both women and men had to struggle similarly to survive. Phoenix provides us with the opportunity to reconsider the identities of modern women.

Consider the modern versus traditional status of women as you read:

1. Does this story suggest that technological societies have developed restricted ideas of a woman's physical, emotional, and intellectual capacities?
2. Does Phoenix demonstrate a variety of qualities that many modern women would never be asked to demonstrate?
3. Are we all constrained in our social roles by "civilized" expectations?

▶ ────────────────

1   It was December—a bright frozen day in the early morning. Far out in the country there was an old Negro woman with her head tied in a red rag, coming along a path through the pinewoods. Her name was Phoenix Jackson. She was very old and small and she walked slowly in the dark pine shadows, moving a little from side to side in her steps, with the balanced heaviness and lightness of a pendulum in a grandfather clock. She carried a thin, small cane made from an umbrella, and with this she kept tapping the frozen earth in front of her. This made a grave and persistent noise in the still air, that seemed meditative, like the chirping of a solitary little bird.

2   She wore a dark striped dress reaching down to her shoetops, and an equally long apron of bleached sugar sacks, with a full pocket; all neat and tidy, but every time she took a step she might have fallen over her shoelaces, which dragged from her unlaced shoes. She looked straight ahead. Her eyes were blue with age. Her skin had a pattern all its own of

numberless branching wrinkles and as though a whole little tree stood in the middle of her forehead, but a golden color ran underneath, and the two knobs of her cheeks were illuminated by a yellow burning under the dark. Under the red rag her hair came down on her neck in the frailest of ringlets, still black, and with an odor like copper.

Now and then there was a quivering in the thicket. Old Phoenix said, "Out of my way, all you foxes, owls, beetles, jack rabbits, coons, and wild animals!...Keep out from under these feet, little bob-whites....Keep the big wild hogs out of my path. Don't let none of those come running my direction. I got a long way." Under her small black-freckled hand her cane, limber as a buggy whip, would switch at the brush as if to rouse up any hiding things. 3

On she went. The woods were deep and still. The sun made the pine needles almost too bright to look at, up where the wind rocked. The cones dropped as light as feathers. Down in the hollow was the mourning dove—it was not too late for him. 4

The path ran up a hill. "Seem like there is chains about my feet, time I get this far," she said, in the voice of argument old people keep to use with themselves. "Something always take a hold on this hill—pleads I should stay." 5

After she got to the top she turned and gave a full, severe look behind her where she had come. "Up through pines," she said at length. "Now down through oaks." 6

Her eyes opened their widest and she started down gently. But before she got to the bottom of the hill a bush caught her dress. 7

Her fingers were busy and intent, but her skirts were full and long, so that before she could pull them free in one place they were caught in another. It was not possible to allow the dress to tear. "I in the thorny bush," she said. "Thorns, you doing your appointed work. Never want to let folks past—no sir. Old eyes thought you was a pretty little *green* bush." 8

Finally, trembling all over, she stood free, and after a moment dared to stoop for her cane. 9

"Sun so high!" she cried, leaning back and looking, while the thick tears went over her eyes. "The time getting all gone here." 10

At the foot of this hill was a place where a log was laid across the creek. 11

"Now comes the trial," said Phoenix. 12

Putting her right foot out, she mounted the log and shut her eyes. Lifting her skirt, leveling her cane fiercely before her, like a festival figure in some parade, she began to march across. Then she opened her eyes and she was safe on the other side. 13

"I wasn't as old as I thought," she said. 14

15   But she sat down to rest. She spread her skirts on the bank around her and folded her hands over her knees. Up above her was a tree in a pearly cloud of mistletoe. She did not dare to close her eyes, and when a little boy brought her a little plate with a slice of marble-cake on it she spoke to him. "That would be acceptable," she said. But when she went to take it there was just her own hand in the air.

16   So she left that tree, and had to go through a barbed-wire fence. There she had to creep and crawl, spreading her knees and stretching her fingers like a baby trying to climb the steps. But she talked loudly to herself: she could not let her dress be torn now, so late in the day, and she could not pay for having her arm or her leg sawed off if she got caught fast where she was.

17   At last she was safe through the fence and risen up out in the clearing. Big dead trees, like black men with one arm, were standing in the purple stalks of the withered cotton field. There sat a buzzard.

18   "Who you watching?"

19   In the furrow she made her way along.

20   "Glad this not the season for bulls," she said, looking sideways, "and the good Lord made his snakes to curl up and sleep in the winter. A pleasure I don't see no two-headed snake coming around that tree, where it come once. It took a while to get by him, back in the summer."

21   She passed through the old cotton and went into a field of dead corn. It whispered and shook, and was taller than her head. "Through the maze now," she said, for there was no path.

22   Then there was something tall, black, and skinny there, moving before her.

23   At first she took it for a man. It could have been a man dancing in the field. But she stood still and listened, and it did not make a sound. It was as silent as a ghost.

24   "Ghost," she said sharply, "who be you the ghost of? For I have heard of nary death close by."

25   But there was no answer, only the ragged dancing in the wind.

26   She shut her eyes, reached out her hand, and touched a sleeve. She found a coat and inside that an emptiness, cold as ice.

27   "You scarecrow," she said. Her face lighted. "I ought to be shut up for good," she said with laughter. "My senses is gone. I too old. I the oldest people I ever know. Dance, old scarecrow," she said, "while I dancing with you."

28   She kicked her foot over the furrow, and with mouth drawn down shook her head once or twice in a little strutting way. Some husks blew down and whirled in streamers about her skirts.

29   Then she went on, parting her way from side to side with the cane, through the whispering field. At last she came to the end, to a wagon

track, where the silver grass blew between the red ruts. The quail were walking around like pullets, seeming all dainty and unseen.

"Walk pretty," she said. "This the easy place. This the easy going." 30

She followed the track, swaying through the quiet bare fields, 31 through the little strings of trees silver in their dead leaves, past cabins silver from weather, with the doors and windows boarded shut, all like old women under a spell sitting there. "I walking in their sleep," she said, nodding her head vigorously.

In a ravine she went where a spring was silently flowing through a 32 hollow log. Old Phoenix bent and drank. "Sweetgum makes the water sweet," she said, and drank more. "Nobody knows who made this well, for it was here when I was born."

The track crossed a swampy part where the moss hung as white as 33 lace from every limb. "Sleep on, alligators, and blow your bubbles." Then the track went into the road.

Deep, deep the road went down between the high green-colored 34 banks. Overhead the live-oaks met, and it was as dark as a cave.

A black dog with a lolling tongue came up out of the weeds by the 35 ditch. She was meditating, and not ready, and when he came at her she only hit him a little with her cane. Over she went in the ditch, like a little puff of milk-weed.

Down there, her senses drifted away. A dream visited her, and she 36 reached her hand up, but nothing reached down and gave her a pull. So she lay there and presently went to talking. "Old woman," she said to herself, "that black dog come up out of the weeds to stall you off, and now there he sitting on his fine tail, smiling at you."

A white man finally came along and found her—a hunter, a young 37 man, with his dog on a chain.

"Well, Granny!" he laughed. "What are you doing there?" 38

"Lying on my back like a June-bug waiting to be turned over, mis- 39 ter," she said, reaching up her hand.

He lifted her up, gave her a swing in the air, and set her down, 40 "Anything broken, Granny?"

"No sir, them old dead weeds is springy enough," said Phoenix, 41 when she had got her breath. "I thank you for your trouble."

"Where do you live, Granny?" he asked, while the two dogs were 42 growling at each other.

"Away back yonder, sir, behind the ridge. You can't even see it from 43 here."

"On your way home?" 44

"No, sir, I going to town." 45

"Why that's too far! That's as far as I walk when I come out myself, 46 and I get something for my trouble." He patted the stuffed bag he carried, and there hung down a little closed claw. It was one of the bob-whites, with its beak hooked bitterly to show it was dead. "Now you go on home, Granny!"

47   "I bound to go to town, mister," said Phoenix. "The time come around."

48   He gave another laugh, filling the whole landscape. "I know you colored people! Wouldn't miss going to town to see Santa Claus!"

49   But something held Old Phoenix very still. The deep lines in her face went into a fierce and different radiation. Without warning she had seen with her own eyes a flashing nickel fall out of the man's pocket on to the ground.

50   "How old are you, Granny?" he was saying.

51   "There is no telling, mister," she said, "no telling."

52   Then she gave a little cry and clapped her hands, and said, "Git on away from here, dog! Look! Look at that dog!" She laughed as if in admiration. "He ain't scared of nobody. He a big black dog." She whispered, "Sick him!"

53   "Watch me get rid of that cur," said the man. "Sick him, Pete! Sick him!"

54   Phoenix heard the dogs fighting and heard the man running and throwing sticks. She even heard a gunshot. But she was slowly bending forward by that time, further and further forward, the lids stretched down over her eyes, as if she were doing this in her sleep. Her chin was lowered almost to her knees. The yellow palm of her hand came out from the fold of her apron. Her fingers slid down and along the ground under the piece of money with the grace and care they would have in lifting an egg from under a sitting hen. Then she slowly straightened up, she stood erect, and the nickel was in her apron pocket. A bird flew by. Her lips moved. "God watching me the whole time. I come to stealing."

55   The man came back, and his own dog panted about them. "Well, I scared him off that time," he said, and then he laughed and lifted his gun and pointed it at Phoenix.

56   She stood straight and faced him.

57   "Doesn't the gun scare you?" he said, still pointing it.

58   "No, sir, I seen plenty go off closer by, in my day, and for less what I done," she said, holding utterly still.

59   He smiled, and shouldered the gun. "Well, Granny," he said, "you must be a hundred years old, and scared of nothing. I'd give you a dime if I had any money with me. But you take my advice and stay home, and nothing will happen to you."

60   "I bound to go on my way, mister," said Phoenix. She inclined her head in the red rag. Then they went in different directions, but she could hear the gun shooting again and again over the hill.

She walked on. The shadows hung from the oak trees to the road like   61
curtains. Then she smelled wood-smoke, and smelled the river, and she
saw a steeple and the cabins on their steep steps. Dozens of little black
children whirled around her. There ahead was Natchez shining. Bells
were ringing. She walked on.

In the paved city it was Christmas time. There were red and green   62
electric lights strung and crisscrossed everywhere, and all turned on in
the daytime. Old Phoenix would have been lost if she had not distrusted
her eyesight and depended on her feet to know where to take her.

She paused quietly on the sidewalk, where people were passing by. A   63
lady came along in the crowd, carrying an armful of red-, green-, and
silver-wrapped presents; she gave off perfume like the red roses in hot
summer, and Phoenix stopped her.

"Please, missy, will you lace up my shoe?" She held up her foot.   64

"What do you want, Grandma?"   65

"See my shoe," said Phoenix. "Do all right for out in the country,   66
but wouldn't look right to go in a big building."

"Stand still then, Grandma," said the lady. She put her packages   67
down carefully on the sidewalk beside her and laced and tied both shoes
tightly.

"Can't lace 'em with a cane," said Phoenix. "Thank you, missy. I   68
doesn't mind asking a nice lady to tie up my shoe when I gets out on the
street."

Moving slowly and from side to side, she went into the stone build-   69
ing and into a tower of steps, where she walked up and around and
around until her feet knew to stop.

She entered a door, and there she saw nailed up on the wall the docu-   70
ment that had been stamped with the gold seal and framed in the gold
frame which matched the dream that was hung up in her head.

"Here I be," she said. There was a fixed and ceremonial stiffness over   71
her body.

"A charity case, I suppose," said an attendant who sat at the desk be-   72
fore her.

But Phoenix only looked above her head. There was sweat on her   73
face; the wrinkles shone like a bright net.

"Speak up, Grandma," the woman said. "What's your name? We   74
must have your history, you know. Have you been here before? What
seems to be the trouble with you?"

Old Phoenix only gave a twitch to her face as if a fly were bothering   75
her.

"Are you deaf?" cried the attendant.   76

But then the nurse came in.   77

"Oh, that's just old Aunt Phoenix," she said. "She doesn't come for   78
herself—she has a little grandson. She makes these trips just as regular

as clockwork. She lives away back off the Old Natchez Trace.'' She bent down. ''Well, Aunt Phoenix, why don't you just take a seat? We won't keep you standing after your long trip.'' She pointed.

79   The old woman sat down, bolt upright in the chair.

80   ''Now, how is the boy?'' asked the nurse.

81   Old Phoenix did not speak.

82   ''I said, how is the boy?''

83   But Phoenix only waited and stared straight ahead, her face very solemn and withdrawn into rigidity.

84   ''Is his throat any better?'' asked the nurse. ''Aunt Phoenix, don't you hear me? Is your grandson's throat any better since the last time you came for the medicine?''

85   With her hand on her knees, the old woman waited, silent, erect and motionless, just as if she were in armor.

86   ''You mustn't take up our time this way, Aunt Phoenix,'' the nurse said. ''Tell us quickly about your grandson, and get it over. He isn't dead, is he?''

87   At last there came a flicker and then a flame of comprehension across her face, and she spoke.

88   ''My grandson. It was my memory had left me. There I sat and forgot why I made my long trip.''

89   ''Forgot?'' The nurse frowned. ''After you came so far?''

90   Then Phoenix was like an old woman begging a dignified forgiveness for waking up frightened in the night. ''I never did go to school—I was too old at the Surrender,'' she said in a soft voice. ''I'm an old woman without an education. It was my memory fail me. My little grandson, he is just the same, and I forgot it in the coming.''

91   ''Throat never heals, does it?'' said the nurse, speaking in a loud, sure voice to Old Phoenix. By now she had a card with something written on it, a little list. ''Yes. Swallowed lye. When was it—January—two—three years ago—''

92   Phoenix spoke unasked now. ''No, missy, he not dead, he just the same. Every little while his throat begin to close up again, and he not able to swallow. He not get his breath. He not able to help himself. So the time come around, and I go on another trip for soothing medicine.''

93   ''All right. The doctor said as long as you came to get it you could have it,'' said the nurse. ''But it's an obstinate case.''

94   ''My little grandson, he sit up there in the house all wrapped up, waiting by himself,'' Phoenix went on. ''We is the only two left in the world. He suffer and it don't seem to put him back at all. He got a sweet look. He going to last. He wear a little patch quilt and peep out, holding his mouth open like a little bird. I remembers so plain now. I not going to forget him again, no, the whole enduring time. I could tell him from all the others in creation.''

"All right." The nurse was trying to hush her now. She brought her a 95 bottle of medicine. "Charity," she said, making a check mark in a book.

Old Phoenix held the bottle close to her eyes and then carefully put it 96 into her pocket.

"I thank you," she said. 97

"It's Christmas time, Grandma," said the attendant. "Could I give 98 you a few pennies out of my purse?"

"Five pennies is a nickel," said Phoenix stiffly. 99

"Here's a nickel," said the attendant. 100

Phoenix rose carefully and held out her hand. She received the nickel 101 and then fished the other nickel out of her pocket and laid it beside the new one. She stared at her palm closely, with her head on one side.

Then she gave a tap with her cane on the floor. 102

"This is what come to me to do," she said. "I going to the store and 103 buy my child a little windmill they sells, made out of paper. He going to find it hard to believe there such a thing in the world. I'll march myself back where he waiting, holding it straight up in this hand."

She lifted her free hand, gave a little nod, turned round, and walked 104 out of the doctor's office. Then her slow step began on the stairs, going down.

Questions and Activities

▶ *COMPREHENSION QUESTIONS*

1. Does the time of year tie in with Phoenix's age in this story? Explain the connection between the season and Phoenix's age.
2. Does Phoenix's dress help you define her character?
3. Do you think it odd that Phoenix talks to herself on her journey? What might make this behavior ordinary in Phoenix's situation, when it would be considered odd in other situations?
4. Why does Phoenix ask the woman in the street to tie her shoe before she enters the doctor's building (paragraph 64)? Does this request, although it seems simple on the surface, indicate a real social sophistication on Phoenix's part?

▶ *QUESTIONS OF RHETORICAL PURPOSE AND STRATEGY*

5. This story is told entirely from Phoenix's viewpoint. Yet it is not told in the first person. What does the narrator of this story think of Phoenix? Is the narrator sympathetic, neutral, or unsympathetic?

Point to places in the story where the narrator reveals an attitude toward Phoenix.

6. Throughout this story, you overhear Phoenix as she talks to herself and to others. What impression does Phoenix's way of talking leave on you? How is that impression similar to or different from the impressions that the hunter, the woman in the street, and the receptionist and nurse have of Phoenix?
7. What is Welty's overall purpose in telling this story? What or who does she hope to give her readers a better understanding of? Is the story meant simply to entertain?

▶ *THEME QUESTIONS*

8. Phoenix is not a typical woman. Does Welty's portrayal of her character suggest female qualities that mainstream American society has chosen to deemphasize? What are those qualities? Why have they been deemphasized?
9. What strengths do you think Phoenix demonstrates? Are they general human strengths, or are they the kinds of strengths that are found only in men or only in women?
10. Contrast Phoenix with a typical modern woman. What characteristics do these two types share, if any? Is there a pattern to the differences between the two? You might want to draw your example of the modern woman directly from an advertisement, film, or television show.

▶ *LEARNING ACTIVITIES*

11. Describe to the rest of your class an example of a woman who seems to you different from the typical modern woman. What qualities make this woman different? Are all the differences good? Do they make your subject's life easier or more difficult? Is your subject aware of these differences and of their effects on others?
12. As an experiment, write a page or two of dialogue in which a typical modern woman and Phoenix discuss a specific issue. Try to capture Phoenix's voice as it is portrayed in this story, and put her voice in conflict with the modern woman's. Read your dialogue to a couple of your classmates.

Writing Assignments

HAPPINESS IN MARRIAGE

Write a three-stage response to the following quotation from Bruno Bettelheim's "Growing Up Female" (page 504):

> The greatest happiness in marriage can come about only when true independence as socially equal human beings is enriched and made continually fascinating and satisfying for both partners by their being sexually completely secure with each other. This security is based on a complementary attraction, enriched by the specific differences in personality and sexual experiences that come from one partner being female, and the other male.

Your first writing should be a straightforwardly personal response. Simply write down how you feel and what you think about Bettelheim's assertion. Does any part of it make you angry, frustrated, or irritated? What aspects of the quotation evoke positive responses in you?

After rereading and thinking over your personal response, write a more objective interpretation of Bettelheim's assertion. Use ideas from at least three of the selections in this section as counterpoints to Bettelheim's.

Finally, combine your personal and objective responses into a final essay in which you develop a balanced (both personal and objective) interpretation of Bettelheim's assertion.

GOALS FOR WOMEN

Imagine yourself explaining the meaning of Marge Piercy's "Barbie Doll" (page 572) to a group of female high school students. You have been asked to talk to this group because they have been considering, in a social studies class, the need to make decisions concerning their personal and career goals.

You must first discuss the poem line by line, to show your audience how it works. You can prepare for this part of your talk by outlining your reactions to each stanza of the poem, and by noting which specific parts of the poem support or explain your reactions. You will also need to consider how this poem might affect your audience. Will they be likely to respond as you did? How and why are their responses apt to be different from yours? What do you know about your audience's background (you can make this up, of course) that might help you imagine their responses? In what ways are high school and college students different?

After you have done a line-by-line analysis of the poem with your audience in mind, you should conclude your talk by explaining the social significance of the poem. Prepare this part of your speech by imagining how your audience would evaluate the poem's significance and by considering how your interpretation differs. What advice would you give your audience, based on your interpretation of the poem? Would you, for example, suggest that women should not develop goals based only on what society suggests they should do? How does the poem support that suggestion? How receptive do you think your audience would be to your advice, considering their age level, their gender, and the situation in which you would be speaking to them?

Barbie Doll
MARGE PIERCY

1 This girlchild was born as usual
and presented dolls that did pee-pee
and miniature GE stoves and irons
and wee lipsticks the color of cherry candy.
Then in the magic of puberty, a classmate said:
You have a great big nose and fat legs.

2 She was healthy, tested intelligent,
possessed strong arms and back,
abundant sexual drive and manual dexterity.
She went to and fro apologizing.
Everyone saw a fat nose on thick legs.

3 She was advised to play coy,
exhorted to come on hearty,
exercise, diet, smile and wheedle.
Her good nature wore out
like a fan belt.
So she cut off her nose and her legs
and offered them up.

4 In the casket displayed on satin she lay
with the undertaker's cosmetics painted on,
a turned-up putty nose,
dressed in a pink and white nightie.
Doesn't she look pretty? everyone said.
Consummation at last.
To every woman a happy ending.

*In What Ways
Must We Change?*

▶ ────────────────────────────

Introduction

▶ ─────────────────────

The selections in this section offer different perspectives on change. In the essay by Wendell Berry that begins the section, personal experience is used to persuade readers to believe that a simpler, rural life is preferable to an urban one. Berry uses the occasion of a walk in the country to offer his insights into why human beings need to consider, privately, their changing relationships with their environment and one another. Carol Bly's essay is another personal response to the question of change, but her essay is based on her reading of Bruno Bettelheim's analysis of modern culture and on her application of that analysis to the social conditions under which she lives in a small Midwestern town. For Bly, people need to be jarred out of complacency by ideas that are drawn from a larger context; for Berry, the problem is maintaining one's sense of individuality in a society in which one is bombarded by too many conflicting outside influences. Berry suggests a change from the outside in; Bly, a change from the inside out.

"Outside in" changes are those that are primarily caused by external forces in a person's environment: the pressures exerted by other people and their values, changes in the natural environment, or altered social, economic, and political conditions. "Inside out" changes are those caused by a person's inner reactions to his or her social or natural environment, gradual or sudden alterations in perception or changed states of mind and values. For most people, change is a matter of interaction of outside in and inside out influences.

Gail Sheehy and Daniel Boorstin shift the focus from personal to social perspectives on the process of change, drawing from sociology and history as they do so. Sheehy, using the work of psychologists and sociologists, theorizes that adults go through stages of development that are similar to those for children. These stages often produce unexpected, and therefore traumatic, changes in people's goals and values; Sheehy suggests that treating such changes as normal will help people learn how to adapt to them and to develop new goals and values, without trauma.

Daniel Boorstin, in contrast to Sheehy, seems to distrust what sociologists and psychologists have to say about change and development. He argues that human beings can learn how to adapt to change by learning how to appreciate the past. Boorstin says that our present culture is imprisoned in the here and now; as a result, we often feel that our problems are more traumatic than they really are simply because we lack a sense of what previous generations have experienced.

Arthur Koestler provides a far broader perspective on twentieth-century culture than does any other writer represented in this section. He tells us that modern societies are living by a new calendar that began with the dropping of the atomic bomb on Hiroshima in 1945. This new sense of time has brought changes in values that influence, to some degree, every individual's and every culture's experience. Koestler suggests how internationally significant events can have a measurable effect on our responses to more immediate aspects of our social and personal lives. The changes we experience, Koestler suggests, are usually the result of both public and individual contexts.

Richard Wright brings us back to a personal situation. "The Library Card" is an excerpt from his autobiography. As autobiography, it can be read as simply an honest rendition of events from his past. But his personal experience becomes socially significant when we consider it in relation to the general question of human identity. Wright lives through a series of incidents that brings him to the point of making a major change in his life. Growing up as a Southern black, Wright would like to use the local library to find information on social-racial relations in America; he wants to formulate his own ideas on these relations. But his desire to learn is thwarted until he persuades a white co-worker to secretly help him get library books. Wright learns from the experience of getting the books as much as he learns from reading them. By analyzing Wright's experiences, we begin to understand how identity changes occur in all people and how day-to-day experiences combine to bring about major turning points.

Everyone changes. This section's readings provide a range of personal and social, regional and international, historical and sociological perspectives on change. As you sift through these readings, you must bring your own experience to bear on them and use them to form your own perspective on change. Consider these questions as you read the selections in this section:

1. Is change primarily motivated by psychological, social, or physical needs and processes?
2. Can the ideas on change from two or three of the selections in this section be integrated into a more general attitude on change? How

do your own experiences support or modify the attitudes expressed in these essays?
3. Can you think of attitudes toward change that are wrong or harmful? Do you know of people who exemplify these wrong or harmful attitudes? Does your explanation as to why these attitudes are wrong or harmful have any bearing on the ideas expressed in these essays?
4. Can people avoid change? What are some specific changes that are avoidable or unavoidable?

A Native Hill

WENDELL BERRY

Wendell Berry was born in 1933 and is now a writer and farmer in Port Royal, Kentucky, a small river town in an agricultural district. He has written several novels, several books of poems, and several collections of personal essays. He has been a professor at the University of Kentucky. Berry won the Bess Hokin Prize for "Six Poems" in 1967 and a Guggenheim fellowship and a Rockefeller grant earlier in his career. Of his writings, his essays have received the greatest critical praise; they have been published in *Recollected Essays, 1965–1980* (1982), which many critics have called Berry's best book of prose. The essay that follows was first published in *The Long-Legged House* (1969).

Berry is unabashedly opinionated and straightforwardly moralistic in all his writings. He believes that a return to simpler agricultural and rural values could remedy many of the ills of our modern, technological civilization. In a time when the scientific approach to solving social problems is dominant, Berry advocates an independence of thought and action that would result in a society of landed laborers who were bound together in a network of separate but interdependent farms. Berry has directly attacked what he calls "agribusiness" and has argued for a return to small, predominantly self-sufficient farms. Men and women, Berry asserts, can learn to live cooperatively only after they have learned to find their own individual places in nature's cycle.

In this essay, Berry takes his readers on a walk on a path near the town he lives in. He has traveled the path many times, using the journey to figure out his relationships with nature and other human beings. In one sense, the path Berry travels and the observations that he makes while walking are a means for him to get from one mental place to another; in a second sense, his physical journey is symbolic of all attempts to connect human life and nature, to find meaning in the ongoing process of living. Berry believes that industrial and commercial ways of life give human beings the idea that they can change natural processes to fit their own ends. What Berry wants is a more unaffected and innocent acceptance of those natural processes, with less imposition of human goals on the natural world.

As you read "A Native Hill," note Berry's ability to connect concrete observations of his local surroundings to moral arguments that he wishes his readers to accept. This essay shows Berry at his best, attempting to persuade modern readers to accept a new morality based on traditional values. These values, however, are never simply pushed at readers, rather they are expressed through the narrator's experiences with the natural environment.

As you read this selection, think about these questions:

1. Do you find Berry's style preachy?
2. Do you think that Berry spends sufficient time developing his examples?
3. Do you feel that Berry's life is too far removed from the average American life style to serve as a meaningful example for his readers?
4. Do you think Berry chooses an appropriate point of view from which to accomplish his intentions in this piece? Would, for example, the choice of a more formal, perhaps third-person, point of view have been more effective?

▶ ─────────────────────

I start down from one of the heights of the upland, the town of Port Royal at my back. It is a winter day, overcast and still, and the town is closed in itself, humming and muttering a little, like a winter beehive.

The dog runs ahead, prancing and looking back, knowing the way we are about to go. This is a walk well established with us—a route in our minds as well as on the ground. There is a sort of mystery in the establishment of these ways. Any time one crosses a given stretch of country with some frequency, no matter how wanderingly one begins, the tendency is always toward habit. By the third or fourth trip, without realizing it, one is following a fixed path, going the way one went before. After that, one may still wander, but only by deliberation, and when there is reason to hurry, or when the mind wanders rather than the feet, one returns to the old route. Familiarity has begun. One has made a relationship with the landscape, and the form and the symbol and the enactment of the relationship is the path. These paths of mine are seldom worn on the ground. They are habits of mind, directions and turns. They are as personal as old shoes. My feet are comfortable in them.

From the height I can see far out over the country, the long open ridges of the farmland, the wooded notches of the streams, the valley of the river opening beyond, and then more ridges and hollows of the same kind.

Underlying this country, nine hundred feet below the highest ridgetops, more than four hundred feet below the surface of the river, is sea level. We seldom think of it here; we are a long way from the coast, and the sea is alien to us. And yet the attraction of sea level dwells in this country as an ideal dwells in a man's mind. All our rains go in search of it and, departing, they have carved the land in a shape that is fluent and falling. The streams branch like vines, and between the branches the land rises steeply and then rounds and gentles into the long narrowing fingers of ridgeland. Near the heads of the streams even the steepest land was not too long ago farmed and kept cleared. But now it has been given up and the woods is returning. The wild is flowing back like a tide. The arable ridgetops reach out above the gathered trees like headlands into the sea, bearing their human burdens of fences and houses and barns, crops and roads.

5   Looking out over the country, one gets a sense of the whole of it: the ridges and hollows, the clustered buildings of the farms, the open fields, the woods, the stock ponds set like coins into the slopes. But this is a surface sense, an exterior sense, such as you get from looking down on the roof of a house. The height is a threshold from which to step down into the wooded folds of the land, the interior, under the trees and along the branching streams.

6   I pass through a pasture gate on a deep-worn path that grows shallow a little way beyond, and then disappears altogether into the grass. The gate has gathered thousands of passings to and fro that have divided like the slats of a fan on either side of it. It is like a fist holding together the strands of a net.

7   Beyond the gate the land leans always more steeply toward the branch. I follow it down, and then bear left along the crease at the bottom of the slope. I have entered the downflow of the land. The way I am going is the way the water goes. There is something comfortable and fit-feeling in this, something free in this yielding to gravity and taking the shortest way down. The mind moves through the watershed as the water moves.

8   As the hollow deepens into the hill, before it has yet entered the woods, the grassy crease becomes a raw gully, and along the steepening slopes on either side I can see the old scars of erosion, places where the earth is gone clear to the rock. My people's errors have become the features of my country.

9   It occurs to me that it is no longer possible to imagine how this country looked in the beginning, before the white people drove their plows into it. It is not possible to know what was the shape of the land here in this hollow when it was first cleared. Too much of it is gone, loosened by the plows and washed away by the rain. I am walking the route of the departure of the virgin soil of the hill. I am not looking at the same land the firstcomers saw. The original surface of the hill is as extinct as the

passenger pigeon. The pristine America that the first white man saw is a lost continent, sunk like Atlantis in the sea. The thought of what was here once and is gone forever will not leave me as long as I live. It is as though I walk knee-deep in its absence.

The slopes along the hollow steepen still more, and I go in under the trees. I pass beneath the surface. I am enclosed, and my sense, my interior sense, of the country becomes intricate. There is no longer the possibility of seeing very far. The distances are closed off by the trees and the steepening walls of the hollow. One cannot grow familiar here by sitting and looking as one can up in the open on the ridge. Here the eyes become dependent on the feet. To see the woods from the inside one must look and move and look again. It is inexhaustible in its standpoints. A lifetime will not be enough to experience it all. Not far from the beginning of the woods, and set deep in the earth in the bottom of the hollow, is a rock-walled pool not a lot bigger than a bathtub. The wall is still nearly as straight and tight as when it was built. It makes a neatly turned narrow horseshoe, the open end downstream. This is a historical ruin, dug here either to catch and hold the water of the little branch, or to collect the water of a spring whose vein broke to the surface here—it is probably no longer possible to know which. The pool is filled with earth now, and grass grows in it. And the branch bends around it, cut down to the bare rock, a torrent after heavy rain, other times bone dry. All that is certain is that when the pool was dug and walled there was deep topsoil on the hill to gather and hold the water. And this high up, at least, the bottom of the hollow, instead of the present raw notch of the stream bed, wore the same mantle of soil as the slopes, and the stream was a steady seep or trickle, running most or all of the year. This tiny pool no doubt once furnished water for a considerable number of stock through the hot summers. And now it is only a lost souvenir, archaic and useless, except for the bitter intelligence there is in it. It is one of the monuments to what is lost.

Wherever one goes along the streams of this part of the country, one is apt to come upon this old stonework. There are walled springs and pools. There are the walls built in the steeper hollows where the fences cross or used to cross; the streams have drifted dirt in behind them, so that now where they are still intact they make waterfalls that have scooped out small pools at their feet. And there used to be miles of stone fences, now mostly scattered and sifted back into the ground.

Considering these, one senses a historical patience, now also extinct in the country. These walls were built by men working long days for little wages, or by slaves. It was work that could not be hurried at, a meticulous finding and fitting together, as though reconstructing a previous wall that had been broken up and scattered like puzzle pieces along

10

11

12

the stream beds. The wall would advance only a few yards a day. The pace of it could not be borne by most modern men, even if the wages could be afforded. Those men had to move in closer accord with their own rhythms, and nature's, than we do. They had no machines. Their capacities were only those of flesh and blood. They talked as they worked. They joked and laughed. They sang. The work was exacting and heavy and hard and slow. No opportunity for pleasure was missed or slighted. The days and the years were long. The work was long. At the end of this job the next would begin. Therefore, be patient. Such pleasure as there is, is here, now. Take pleasure as it comes. Take work as it comes. The end may never come, or when it does it may be the wrong end.

13   Now the men who built the walls and the men who had them built have long gone underground to be, along with the buried ledges and the roots and the burrowing animals, a part of the nature of the place in the minds of the ones who come after them. I think of them lying still in their graves, as level as the sills and thresholds of their lives, as though resisting to the last the slant of the ground. And their old walls, too, re-enter nature, collecting lichens and mosses with a patience their builders never conceived of.

14   Like the pasture gates, the streams are great collectors of comings and goings. The streams go down, and paths always go down beside the streams. For a while I walk along an old wagon road that is buried in leaves—a fragment, beginningless and endless as the middle of a sentence on some scrap of papyrus. There is a cedar whose branches reach over this road, and under the branches I find the leavings of two kills of some bird of prey. The most recent is a pile of blue jay feathers. The other has been rained on and is not identifiable. How little we know. How little of this was intended or expected by any man. The road that has become the grave of men's passages has led to the life of the woods.

> *And I say to myself: Here is your road*
> *without beginning or end, appearing*
> *out of the earth and ending in it, bearing*
> *no load but the hawk's kill, and the leaves*
> *building earth on it, something more*
> *to be borne. Tracks fill with earth*
> *and return to absence. The road was worn*
> *by men bearing earth along it. They have come*
> *to endlessness. In their passing*
> *they could not stay in, trees have risen*
> *and stand still. It is leading to the dark,*
> *to mornings where you are not. Here*
> *is your road, beginningless and endless as God.*

Now I have come down within the sound of the water. The winter   *15*
has been rainy, and the hill is full of dark seeps and trickles, gathering finally, along these creases, into flowing streams. The sound of them is
one of the elements, and defines a zone. When their voices return to the
hill after their absence during summer and autumn, it is a better place
to be. A thirst in the mind is quenched.

I have already passed the place where water began to flow in the little   *16*
stream bed I am following. It broke into the light from beneath a rock
ledge, a thin glittering stream. It lies beside me as I walk, overtaking me
and going by, yet not moving, a thread of light and sound. And now from
below comes the steady tumble and rush of the water of Camp
Branch—whose nameless camp was it named for?—and gradually as I
descend the sound of the smaller stream is lost in the sound of the
larger.

The two hollows join, the line of the meeting of the two spaces   *17*
obscured even in winter by the trees. But the two streams meet precisely as two roads. That is, the stream *beds* do; the one ends in the other.
As for the meeting of the waters, there is no looking at that. The one
flow does not end in the other, but continues in it, one with it, two
clarities merged without a shadow.

All waters are one. This is a reach of the sea, flung like a net over the   *18*
hill, and now drawn back to the sea. And as the sea is never raised in the
earthly nets of fishermen, so the hill is never caught and pulled down by
the watery net of the sea. But always a little of it is. Each of the
gathering strands of the net carries back some of the hill melted in it.
Sometimes, as now, it carries so little that the water seems to flow
clear; sometimes it carries a lot and is brown and heavy with it.
Whenever greedy or thoughtless men have lived on it, the hill has
literally flowed out of their tracks into the bottom of the sea.

There appears to be a law that when creatures have reached the level   *19*
of consciousness, as men have, they must become conscious of the creation; they must learn how they fit into it and what its needs are and
what it requires of them, or else pay a terrible penalty: the spirit of the
creation will go out of them, and they will become destructive; the very
earth will depart from them and go where they cannot follow.

My mind is never empty or idle at the joinings of streams. Here is the   *20*
work of the world going on. The creation is felt, alive and intent on its
materials, in such places. In the angle of the meeting of the two streams
stands the steep wooded point of the ridge, like the prow of an upturned
boat—finished, as it was a thousand years ago, as it will be in a thousand
years. Its becoming is only incidental to its being. It will be because it
is. It has no aim or end except to be. By being, it is growing and wearing
into what it will be. The fork of the stream lies at the foot of the slope
like hammer and chisel laid down at the foot of a finished sculpture. But

the stream is no dead tool; it is alive, it is still at its work. Put your hand to it to learn the health of this part of the world. It is the wrist of the hill.

21   Perhaps it is to prepare to hear some day the music of the spheres that I am always turning my ears to the music of streams. There is indeed a music in streams, but it is not for the hurried. It has to be loitered by and imagined. Or imagined *toward*, for it is hardly for men at all. Nature has a patient ear. To her the slowest funeral march sounds like a jig. She is satisfied to have the notes drawn out to the lengths of days or weeks or months. Small variations are acceptable to her, modulations as leisurely as the opening of a flower.

22   The stream is full of stops and gates. Here it has piled up rocks in its path, and pours over them into a tiny pool it has scooped at the foot of its fall. Here it has been dammed by a mat of leaves caught behind a fallen limb. Here it must force a narrow passage, here a wider one. Tomorrow the flow may increase or slacken, and the tone will shift. In an hour or a week that rock may give way, and the composition will advance by another note. Some idea of it may be got by walking slowly along and noting the changes as one passes from one little fall or rapid to another. But this is a highly simplified and diluted version of the real thing, which is too complex and widespread ever to be actually heard by us. The ear must imagine an impossible patience in order to grasp even the unimaginableness of such music.

23   But the creation is musical, and this is a part of its music, as bird song is, or the words of poets. The music of the streams is the music of the shaping of the earth, by which the rocks are pushed and shifted downward toward the level of the sea.

24   And now I find lying in the path an empty beer can. This is the track of the ubiquitous man Friday of all our woods. In my walks I never fail to discover some sign that he has preceded me. I find his empty shotgun shells, his empty cans and bottles, his sandwich wrappings. In wooded places along roadsides one is apt to find, as well, his overtraveled bedsprings, his outcast refrigerator, and heaps of the imperishable refuse of his modern kitchen. A year ago, almost in this same place where I have found his beer can, I found a possum that he had shot dead and left lying, in celebration of his manhood. He is the true American pioneer, perfectly at rest in his assumption that he is the first and the last whose inheritance and fate this place will ever be. Going forth, as he may think, to sow, he only broadcasts his effects.

25   As I go on down the path alongside Camp Branch, I walk by the edge of croplands abandoned only within my own lifetime. On my left are the south slopes where the woods is old, long undisturbed. On my right, the more fertile north slopes are covered with patches of briars and sumacs and a lot of young walnut trees. Tobacco of an extraordinary quali-

ty was once grown here, and then the soil wore thin, and these places were given up for the more accessible ridges that were not so steep, where row cropping made better sense anyway. But now, under the thicket growth, a mat of bluegrass has grown to testify to the good nature of this ground. It was fine dirt that lay here once, and I am far from being able to say that I could have resisted the temptation to plow it. My understanding of what is best for it is the tragic understanding of hindsight, the awareness that I have been taught what was here to be lost by the loss of it.

We have lived by the assumption that what was good for us would be good for the world. And this has been based on the even flimsier assumption that we could know with any certainty what was good even for us. We have fulfilled the danger of this by making our personal pride and greed the standard of our behavior toward the world—to the incalculable disadvantage of the world and every living thing in it. And now, perhaps very close to too late, our great error has become clear. It is not only our own creativity—our own capacity for life—that is stifled by our arrogant assumption; the creation itself is stifled. 26

We have been wrong. We must change our lives, so that it will be possible to live by the contrary assumption that what is good for the world will be good for us. And that requires that we make the effort to *know* the world and to learn what is good for it. We must learn to co-operate in its processes, and to yield to its limits. But even more important, we must learn to acknowledge that the creation is full of mystery; we will never entirely understand it. We must abandon arrogance and stand in awe. We must recover the sense of the majesty of creation, and the ability to be worshipful in its presence. For I do not doubt that it is only on the condition of humility and reverence before the world that our species will be able to remain in it. 27

Standing in the presence of these worn and abandoned fields, where the creation has begun its healing without the hindrance or the help of man, with the voice of the stream in the air and the woods standing in silence on all the slopes around me, I am deep in the interior not only of my place in the world, but of my own life, its sources and searches and concerns. I first came into these places following the men to work when I was a child. I knew the men who took their lives from such fields as these, and their lives to a considerable extent made my life what it is. In what came to me from them there was both wealth and poverty, and I have been a long time discovering which was which. 28

It was in the woods here along Camp Branch that Bill White, my grandfather's Negro hired hand, taught me to hunt squirrels. Bill lived in a little tin-roofed house on up nearer the head of the hollow. And this was, I suppose more than any other place, his hunting ground. It was 29 the place of his freedom, where he could move without subservience, without considering who he was or who anybody else was. On late summer mornings, when it was too wet to work, I would follow him into the woods. As soon as we stepped in under the trees he would become silent and absolutely attentive to the life of the place. He was a good teacher and an exacting one. The rule seemed to be that if I wanted to stay with him, I had to make it possible for him to forget I was there. I was to make no noise. If I did he would look back and make a downward emphatic gesture with his hand, as explicit as writing: Be quiet, or go home. He would see a squirrel crouched in a fork or lying along the top of a branch, and indicate with a grin and a small jerk of his head where I should look; and then wait, while I, conscious of being watched and demanded upon, searched it out for myself. He taught me to look and to listen and to be quiet. I wonder if he knew the value of such teaching or the rarity of such a teacher.

30   In the years that followed I hunted often here alone. And later in these same woods I experienced my first obscure dissatisfactions with hunting. Though I could not have put it into words then, the sense had come to me that hunting as I knew it—the eagerness to kill something I did not need to eat—was an artificial relation to the place, when what I was beginning to need, just as inarticulately then, was a relation that would be deeply natural and meaningful. That was a time of great uneasiness and restlessness for me. It would be the fall of the year, the leaves would be turning, and ahead of me would be another year of school. There would be confusions about girls and ambitions, the wordless hurried feeling that time and events and my own nature were pushing me toward what I was going to be—and I had no notion what it was, or how to prepare.

31   And then there were years when I did not come here at all—when these places and their history were in my mind, and part of me, in places thousands of miles away. And now I am here again, changed from what I was, and still changing. The future is no more certain to me now than it ever was, though its risks are clearer, and so are my own desires: I am the father of two young children whose lives are hostages given to the future. Because of them and because of events in the world, life seems more fearful and difficult to me now than ever before. But it is also more inviting, and I am constantly aware of its nearness to joy. Much of the interest and excitement that I have in my life now has come from the deepening, in the years since my return here, of my relation to this countryside that is my native place. For in spite of all that has happened to me in other places, the great change and the great possibility of change in my life has been in my sense of this place. The major difference is perhaps only that I have grown able to be wholeheartedly pres-

ent here. I am able to sit and be quiet at the foot of some tree here in this woods along Camp Branch, and feel a deep peace, both in the place and in my awareness of it, that not too long ago I was not conscious of the possibility of. This peace is partly in being free of the suspicion that pursued me for most of my life, no matter where I was, that there was perhaps another place I *should* be, or would be happier or better in; it is partly in the increasingly articulate consciousness of being here, and of the significance and importance of being here.

After more than thirty years I have at last arrived at the candor neces-   32
sary to stand on this part of the earth that is so full of my own history and so much damaged by it, and ask: What *is* this place? What is in it? What is its nature? How should men live in it? What must I do?

I have not found the answers, though I believe that in partial and frag-   33
mentary ways they have begun to come to me. But the questions are more important than their answers. In the final sense they *have* no answers. They are like the questions—they are perhaps the same questions—that were the discipline of Job.* They are a part of the necessary enactment of humility, teaching a man what his importance is, what his responsibility is, and what his place is, both on the earth and in the order of things. And though the answers must always come obscurely and in fragments, the questions must be persistently asked. They are fertile questions. In their implications and effects, they are moral and aesthetic and, in the best and fullest sense, practical. They promise a relationship to the world that is decent and preserving.

They are also, both in origin and effect, religious. I am uneasy with   34
the term, for such religion as has been openly practiced in this part of the world has promoted and fed upon a destructive schism between body and soul, heaven and earth. It has encouraged people to believe that the world is of no importance, and that their only obligation in it is to submit to certain churchly formulas in order to get to heaven. And so the people who might have been expected to care most selflessly for the world have had their minds turned elsewhere—to a pursuit of ''salvation'' that was really only another form of gluttony and self-love, the desire to perpetuate their own small lives beyond the life of the world. The heaven-bent have abused the earth thoughtlessly, by inattention, and their negligence has permitted and encouraged others to abuse it deliberately. Once the creator was removed from the creation, divinity became only a remote abstraction, a social weapon in the hands of the religious institutions. This split in public values produced or was accompanied by, as it was bound to be, an equally artificial and ugly

---

*Job, an Old Testament figure, questioned God concerning his suffering here on earth. He had to learn the discipline necessary to submit to God's will concerning his fate.

division in people's lives, so that a man, while pursuing heaven with the sublime appetite he thought of as his soul, could turn his heart against his neighbors and his hands against the world. For these reasons, though I know that my questions *are* religious, I dislike having to *say* that they are.

35   But when I ask them my aim is not primarily to get to heaven. Though heaven is certainly more important than the earth if all they say about it is true, it is still morally incidental to it and dependent on it, and I can only imagine it and desire it in terms of what I know of the earth. And so my questions do not aspire beyond the earth. They aspire *toward* it and *into* it. Perhaps they aspire *through* it. They are religious because they are asked at the limit of what I know; they acknowledge mystery and honor its presence in the creation; they are spoken in reverence for the order and grace that I see, and that I trust beyond my power to see.

36   The stream has led me down to an old barn built deep in the hollow to house the tobacco once grown on those abandoned fields. Now it is surrounded by the trees that have come back on every side—a relic, a fragment of another time, strayed out of its meaning. This is the last of my historical landmarks. To here, my walk has had insistent overtones of memory and history. It has been a movement of consciousness through knowledge, eroding and shaping, adding and wearing away. I have descended like the water of the stream through what I know of myself, and now that I have there is a little more to know. But here at the barn, the old roads and the cow paths—the formal connections with civilization—come to an end.

37   I stoop between the strands of a barbed-wire fence, and in that movement I go out of time into timelessness. I come into a wild place. I walk along the foot of a slope that was once cut bare of trees, like all the slopes of this part of the country—but long ago; and now the woods is established again, the ground healed, the trees grown big, their trunks rising clean, free of undergrowth. The place has a serenity and dignity that one feels immediately; the creation is whole in it and unobstructed. It is free of the strivings and dissatisfactions, the partialities and imperfections of places under the mechanical dominance of men. Here, what to a housekeeper's eye might seem disorderly is nonetheless orderly and within order; what might seem arbitrary or accidental is included in the design of the whole as if by intention; what might seem evil or violent is a comfortable member of the household. Where the creation is whole nothing is extraneous. The presence of the creation here makes this a holy place, and it is as a pilgrim that I have come—to give the homage of awe and love, to submit to mystification. It is the creation that has attracted me, its perfect interfusion of life and design. I have made myself its follower and its apprentice.

One early morning last spring, I came and found the woods floor   *38*
strewn with bluebells. In the cool sunlight and the lacy shadows of the
spring woods the blueness of those flowers, their elegant shape, their
delicate fresh scent kept me standing and looking. I found a rich delight
in them that I cannot describe and that I will never forget. Though I had
been familiar for years with most of the spring woods flowers, I had
never seen these and had not known they grew here. Looking at them, I
felt a strange feeling of loss and sorrow that I had never seen them before. But I was also exultant that I saw them now—that they were here.

For me, in the thought of them will always be the sense of the joyful   *39*
surprise with which I found them—the sense that came suddenly to me
then that the world is blessed beyond my understanding, more abun-
dantly than I will ever know. What lives are still ahead of me here to be
discovered and exulted in, tomorrow, or in twenty years? What wonder
will be found here on the morning after my death? Though as a man I inherit great evils and the possibility of great loss and suffering, I know
that my life is blessed and graced by the yearly flowering of the bluebells. How perfect they are! In their presence I am humble and joyful. If I
were given all the learning and all the methods of my race I could not
make one of them, or even imagine one. Solomon in all his glory was
not arrayed like one of these.* It is the privilege and the labor of the apprentice of creation to come with his imagination into the unimaginable, and with his speech into the unspeakable.

Questions and Activities

▶ *COMPREHENSION QUESTIONS*

1. Describe the narrator's physical relationship with what he observes
   in this essay. Is he usually observing from a short distance? Does he
   direct his journey so that he must notice details of his environment?
   What tense does he use to describe his journey?
2. Describe Bill White and his relationship to the narrator of this essay
   (paragraph 29). Why was White significant in Berry's life? How does
   his significance tie in with Berry's point in telling of this journey?
3. Explain Berry's use of the word "religious" in paragraph 34. How is
   Berry's use of this word different from the way many others use it?

*Solomon, the son of King David, was king of Israel in the tenth century B.C. He was
noted for his wisdom and magnificence. Berry is here paraphrasing an Old Testament
metaphor comparing a flower's beauty to Solomon's.

4. Have you ever seen bluebells? If you have, describe them and the occasion when you saw them to your class. If you have not, look them up in a horticultural encyclopedia and report to the class on their appearance and habitat.

▶ *QUESTIONS OF RHETORICAL PURPOSE AND STRATEGY*

5. Why does Berry place his finding of the bluebells at the end of this essay? Does his experiencing of the bluebells have a more general significance concerning his perceptions of humanity's relations with nature?
6. Berry intermittently narrates an experience and explains the significance of that experience. Find a paragraph in which he both describes something in an objective way and tells the general significance of what he describes. Does his interpretation of his experience seem convincing? Can you think of other interpretations of the experience?
7. Berry's style has often been called "simple" and "biblical." Does this essay seem to justify those labels? Is his vocabulary always common and conversational? Are his sentences fairly short? Is normal word order usually used, rather than extraordinary patterns of words? Does Berry's style fit his message about people and nature?
8. Is Berry trying to persuade or explain? Do you feel that he wants his readers to change their way of life to more closely resemble his?

▶ *THEME QUESTIONS*

9. What is Berry's attitude toward change? What kinds of change would he be against? Does he think some change is natural and should be accepted?
10. What types of change does Berry observe as he completes his walk? How would someone who lived in a city respond to these changes? Would such a person, a visitor to the area, even notice them?
11. How was the work of wall building that Berry describes in paragraph 12 different from the work done today in factories and on mechanized farms?

▶ *LEARNING ACTIVITIES*

12. Many of Berry's sentences read as though they were proverbs or maxims. (A proverb is a short, well-known saying that expresses a common truth or accepted fact. A maxim is a more formal and concise formulation of a basic principle or rule of conduct, often passed from teacher to student or from master to apprentice.) Take one of the sentences from this essay that you think could serve

as a proverb or maxim and use it as the first sentence of a two-or-three-page essay. You might follow the quoted sentence with a related anecdote, an analysis of something you have recently read, or a general discussion of its point.

13. Choose a walk or ride that you often take. Try to be more observant than you normally are the next time you take it. Then report any new observations to a workshop group of your classmates. Are you able to attach any general significance to your observations?

Bruno Bettelheim: Three Ideas To Try in Madison, Minnesota

CAROL BLY

Carol Bly has lived in rural Minnesota most of her life. She graduated from Wellesley College and has done graduate work at the University of Minnesota at Minneapolis. She has done a great deal of editorial work for literary magazines, has served as a humanities consultant and theme developer for the American Farm Project, has developed a humanities program for rural high school students, and has taught at the University of Wisconsin, the University of Minnesota (at Duluth, Minneapolis, and Morris), Carleton College, and Mankato State University. She has won grants and awards from the Minnesota Arts Board and the Bush Foundation for her writing and her work in the humanities. Bly has published short stories and essays in magazines such as *The New Yorker, American Review, Ploughshares,* and *Twin Cities.* Her poems have been published in *Poetry Northwest* and *Coastlines.*

Bly's writing has always been closely tied to public service and community involvement. In 1981, she published *Letters from the Country,* a widely praised collection of essays about her life in rural Minnesota. This book describes both the positive and the negative aspects of small-town life, treating rural people's love of family and community with a good deal of sympathy, while asserting at the same time the inhibiting effect small-town life often has on the individual's critical judgment and independence of mind.

As the essay included here illustrates, Bly wants the people around her to become more involved in national intellectual and political life. She suggests that people's secure small-town lives can make them complacent and closed to the potential for change. She wants the people with whom she associates to develop more active and critical thought processes. To do this, she suggests, these people will need to fight the tendency to squelch all dissenting opinion and ignore depressing news. Reading, thinking, and writing, she argues, will keep one alive and open to change, even in the midst of the securities of family, job, and community.

As you read, consider Bly's voice:

1. Bly has lived in small Minnesota towns for about twenty-five years. Do you think her voice has a tone that her neighbors would find sufficiently pleasant to be persuasive?

2. Is the discussion of Bruno Bettelheim's work clear enough to educate even as it entertains?
3. Does Bly actually hope that some of the neighbors she describes in this essay will change their ways?
4. How is the sense of community expressed in this essay related to the need for isolation that Bly feels is necessary for the full development of any human being?

▶ ─────────────────────────────

It is exhilarating to spend a few days thinking about the ideas of   *1*
Bruno Bettelheim,[1] not just because he has such energy and moral genius, but because he is so out of style at the moment. The attention, and certainly the affections, of the liberal intelligentsia are somewhere else, and I feel private and quiet among Bettelheim's findings, instead of feeling like one of a cheering crowd at the arena. There is no distraction.

I expect Bettelheim owes his unpopularity to the fact that he is such   *2*
a mixed bag: he gets off some of the coarsest censures of young people, leftists, and women that you can come across. He is good and out of fashion. What I like and honor in him is his constant work on *decency*. In a decade given to opening up the unconscious almost as an end in itself, Bettelheim still goes on working on decency between people, decency based squarely on the moral well-being within each person. He calls this moral well-being "individual autonomy." Roughly, it means that no matter how sensibly some insane or cruel proposition is presented to you, you make up your own mind that it is not acceptable, and you do not do the insane or cruel thing.

Applying Bruno Bettelheim's perspective to life in rural Minnesota   *3*
means taking ideas learned *in great straits* (in the concentration camp at Dachau and later, in the Orthogenic School of the University of Chicago, where he treated autistic children) and deliberately using them *in little straits*. I commend this idea because the countryside, despite its apparent culture lag, is doomed to be wrecked in the mass culture just as surely as the cities are being wrecked. We need major thinking, but our habit is to listen only to the local prophets—mild-mannered provincial professionals living among us, regional poets with their evident faith in nature, local administrators of community educa-

[1]Dr. Bettelheim has written many books. I've taken some of his ideas here from *The Informed Heart*, *The Empty Fortress*, and some recent newspaper interviews [author's note].

tion projects. Our habit is to listen to those nearby who are affable and low-key. They can't save our personalities, though, any better than fervent quilt making can save our artistic nature or Solarcaine can set a broken leg.

4   Certainly life in western Minnesota must be about as untroublesome as life anywhere in the twentieth century. It is only luck; we haven't ourselves done anything, psychically or morally, to protect us from the coarsening of life that comes with more population. We are all set to become "mass men"—or at least we have no proofs that we won't give way to impersonal relations, increasing rudeness, increasing distrust, ill-temper while queuing up for everything from tennis courts to funeral reservations. Bettelheim's ideas—and I've chosen three of them to think about—have to do with how to keep the self from succumbing to the mass state. The three ideas are (1) replacing the feeling of "business as usual" with crisis thinking, (2) forcing ourselves to have a sense of time in our lives, and (3) understanding the power of negative thinking.

5   Even when the Germans began arresting Jews in the 1930s, many of the Jews refused to leave Germany because the aura of their possessions—the rooms, the rugs, the paintings—gave them a sense of normalcy in things: they'd projected some of themselves into these objects around them, so if the objects were still there, surely everything was usual? What they needed to do was to switch to *crisis thinking:* they needed to say to themselves, "This is *not* business as usual. We must run away at night, or join the Underground, or separate and plan to meet in Switzerland."

6   Bettelheim says we must speak or fight, whichever is called for, at the *first moment of our anxiety.* National Socialism looked like "business as usual" in 1932 and 1933; by 1934 it was too late. The Gestapo's intention to terrify eighty million Germans through the constant threat of the camps was published long before they actually did it, but few paid attention. *Mein Kampf*[2] should have been lots of warning: very few people took it seriously. So Bettelheim suggests we must ask ourselves at every other moment, Is this business as usual? Is this a crisis? Is it O.K. to go on just maintaining my life today, or must I act in a political way? So here are some questions we can ask in rural Minnesota:

1. Should the President[3] be impeached? Now in the moment of our anxiety over his crookedness: should we impeach? If not, is there something else we should be doing? Is it really O.K. just to be sitting here?
2. Is TV watching turning our children into mass men or is it not? Many parents in Madison have said explicitly they think TV watching is

---

[2]Adolf Hitler's statement of his theories and program, published 1925–27.
[3]Richard M. Nixon, who resigned the presidency in 1974.

bad for their children, but only two families I know of have got rid of the set. Somehow, the course of each day's activity disperses the parents' anxiety. Since they do not act in the moment of anxiety, then the children go on dully taking in the commercials and the vulgarity of feeling and another week goes by, a year goes by, and the day after tomorrow, or perhaps it was yesterday, the children are eighteen and they have been watching television for seventeen years. They saw eighteen thousand murders by the time they were fourteen (according to *TV Generation*, by Gerald Loomey), and all the while the parents sincerely felt that TV watching was bad for them.

3. Is the American diet really "well balanced" as the Department of Agriculture would have us believe, or have the grain-milling companies (who systematically began degerminating all wheat flour on the market in the second decade of the century) caused a deficiency of Vitamin E (and other vitamins as well) which is responsible for the multiplying incidence of certain diseases and a sharp rise in fatalities from them? Does it mean anything that in the pamphlets given 4-H children, telling them how to make bread, the picture credits are nearly all to those very grain-milling companies?

A sense of time warns that now is the time; it is not business as usual. Thinking of time leads to the second idea of Bettelheim's I'd like to bring in: a sense of *time left*. The Gestapo cleverly realized that if you never know *when* something will happen, such as the release of a prisoner from camp or the end of a slave-work detail, you can't organize your own thoughts. A crude example that comes to my mind is the dilemma of a runner; if he doesn't know how many laps remain, how shall he husband his diminishing strength? When shall he make his final spurt? Christianity feels the sense of *time left* so strongly that the Church teaches that you must regard every moment as your last, so that you will make the final, mortal spurt always. But mass society, which tends to make people relaxed and low-key and unambitious, encourages a slack time sense. Here's an example from my town.

As soon as a Madison girl marries she will be asked to join most if not all of the following groups:

1. A circle of church women
2. The large Ladies' Aid, which meets monthly
3. A homemakers' group
4. An auxiliary of the American Legion or the VFW
5. Mrs. Jaycees
6. A study club (Federated Women's Clubs of America)
7. Women's—or couples'—bridge club

I have omitted community groups that do useful work, such as teaching released-time school, or shampooing at the Home, filling hospital bird-feeding stations, or working in the hospital auxiliary. These projects are self-justifying.

9   If the young woman doesn't say to herself: I am twenty-five and in seventy years I will probably be dead, she is likely to join the organizations listed. If she has a sense of *time left*, however, she may ask the right questions: How much of my life do I want to spend in solitude? Most women in town also drink coffee with two or more other women at 10 A.M. and at 3 P.M. every day. This means another three hours a day of time spent in idle social intercourse. Yet, whenever we ask these young women if they think they might on their deathbeds regret this casual frittering away of time, they grin and say, "Oh, let's not be morbid now!"

10   Still, forty-five-year-old women do start dropping out of the artificially structured social life in Madison: people who have dazedly accepted belonging to clubs for twenty years now choose to topple into their own inner lives instead. They simply have finally learned a sense of *time left*—and the tragedy of it is that a spiritually dormant society ever allowed them to waste twenty years.

11   A few years ago we had a constantly cheerful minister in town; no one was less apprehensive than he. He wasn't nervous about the hydrogen bomb and he wasn't nervous about our participation in the Vietnam War. Then he became critically ill, and upon recovery he preached for an entire winter the first serious, thoughtful sermons of his life, or at least of his life here. Any number of people complained that the sermons had gone morbid and "negative." They hadn't. He simply had learned a sense of *time left*.

12   Complaints about "negative" sermons bring me to the third of Bettelheim's ideas: the usefulness of negative or critical thinking. Bettelheim objects to everyone's seizing on Anne Frank's "All men are basically good."* He argues that they wish to derive comfort from their admiration of her positive attitude under such awful circumstances, instead of feeling uncomfortable with the truth—which is that men are basically good and they are basically bad. They can be ghastly. Stanley Milgram's *Obedience to Authority* describes an experiment in which subjects were directed to "administer pain" to people strapped in chairs in the next room who were visible through the window. The subjects believed that the dials they operated gave pain whenever the people

---

*Anne Frank (1929–1945?) has become famous for her diary, published in 1952 as *Anne Frank: The Diary of a Young Girl*. It records her thoughts and experiences while hiding from the Nazis in an Amsterdam warehouse. Anne and her family were captured by the Nazis in 1944; she was sent to the concentration camp at Belsen, where she died just before World War II ended.

strapped to the chair failed to learn a given piece of information. Some of the subjects repeatedly turned the dial to the "danger" markings on the machine. They were sadistic without even noticing. If we keep in mind such left-handed inhumanity—Americans just obeying orders—and then repeat to ourselves Anne Frank's remark about men being basically good, we are irritated: naïveté, which ever wants to preserve its artless high, is ignoring rank cruelty. Positive thinking is that kind of naïveté. People who practice or commend it are interested in feeling no pain and in preserving a high. Sometimes a whole culture wishes to preserve this high: then its art and doctrines turn not into positive thinking but into positive pretending.

We haven't got a Germany here, but we do have a TV space-selling   13
society. Hence a generation has grown up on mostly happy, bland, evasive propaganda. No wonder this beastly positive thinking, which means positive *pretending*, has become the crutch of church and club. The other day a clergyman told me he "preferred to think of the Ten Commandments as positive, not negative." Marvelous! What is the *positive* way not to commit adultery? How do you *positively* not covet your neighbor's husband? How do you *positively* not steal from the Klein National Bank?

Bettelheim noted that, when he first wrote his interpretations of the   14
concentration camps, his readers told him they felt "a strange relief," gruesome as the subject was. No matter how oppressive the facts, facing them, calling evil evil, safeguards our personalities.

Why read a set of ideas based on imprisonment in Dachau in 1938?   15
When I first began reading Bettelheim years ago I had the uncanny sensation he was handing me a beautifully thought-out set of bright tools, to keep me (or anyone) in one piece. He showed a way not to sit around absent-mindedly while a gross society raveled away decency like a yarn ball. As much as anyone I've read, Bettelheim helps us not to be wrecked. It takes affection to keep preventing wrecks, and saving people already wrecked. You feel this tough affection in his ideas.

Questions and Activities

▶ COMPREHENSION QUESTIONS

1. Why does Bly say that Bruno Bettelheim is "out of style" (paragraph 1) at the time she is writing (the early 1970s)?
2. What effects do the social organizations that Bly lists in paragraph 8 have on young women in the town of Madison, Minnesota? Are these effects positive, according to Bly?

3. Why does Bly say that life in western Minnesota is "about as untroublesome as life anywhere in the twentieth century" (paragraph 4)? Might her evaluation of western Minnesota apply equally to many American towns and suburbs? To whom might Minnesota small-town life be troublesome?

4. Why do Bly's neighbors call the minister's sermons after his illness "negative" (paragraph 12)? Do they mean this as serious criticism?

▶ *QUESTIONS OF RHETORICAL PURPOSE AND STRATEGY*

5. What ideas of Bruno Bettelheim does Bly use? Why does she use these ideas as the basis for her essay? How do these ideas help Bly structure and organize this piece? How do they help her fulfill her purpose?

6. To whom is this essay addressed? Do you think the style of the essay suggests it is meant for an audience of experts or one of educated general readers? Would this essay be most appropriate for readers who live in small towns, in cities, or in rural areas? Is it geared more toward male or female readers?

7. What type of person would find this essay enjoyable and informative? What type of person would like Bly's writing style? Give a specific description of this imagined reader.

▶ *THEME QUESTIONS*

8. What attitudes toward change are held by Bly's neighbors in Minnesota? Do they seem to welcome some types of change, but not others? Does Bly seem to agree or disagree with their attitudes toward change?

9. What might be the relationship between what Bly calls "the usefulness of negative or critical thinking" (paragraph 13) and society's general response to change? Might those practiced in negative thinking be more apt to question the value of change? Might those practiced in negative thinking be more apt to support a change actively if they were convinced of its value?

10. In paragraph 6, Bly suggests that her Minnesota neighbors should take more seriously than they have several current social or political issues: the effects of television watching on children, President Nixon's possible impeachment, and the American diet. Can you list several current issues to which you believe people should be paying greater attention? Why are people not giving these issues enough attention? Are there psychological and social reasons for this avoidance, just as Bly claims psychological and social reasons for her neighbors' complacency?

▶ *LEARNING ACTIVITIES*

11. Record some of the reactions of classmates, friends, or relatives to questions that you ask them about current events. Once you have written the reactions down, compare them to the responses Bly found in her community. Do your questions seem to elicit some of the same responses that Bly reports? Did some of your respondents seem to be indulging in negative thinking, for example? Did some want to put off thinking about these issues because of an exaggerated sense of what Bly calls "time left" (paragraph 7)?

12. Use your transcription of friends', relatives', or classmates' responses to questions on current events to write a personal essay in which you explain what you believe to be some of the reasons for those responses. Some of these reasons may be personal and others social. For example, might our culture's emphasis on positive thinking and progress cause some people to avoid questioning what goes on around them or what they see in the news?

Predictable Crises of Adulthood

GAIL SHEEHY

Gail Sheehy has written a novel about the break-up of her marriage (*Lovesounds,* 1970), a nonfiction book on race relations (*Panthermania,* 1971), and several nonfiction books on subjects such as prostitution (*Hustling,* 1973). She has also contributed feature essays to *Cosmopolitan, McCall's, Good Housekeeping, The London Sunday Telegraph, Paris Match,* and the *New York Times Magazine.* She has concentrated on a career in journalism since her graduation from the University of Vermont in 1958, having served as contributing and fashion editor for some major magazines early in her career.

By far her best-known and most controversial book is *Passages* (1976), from which the essay presented here was taken. The controversy arose when several of the experts from whom she derived information for the book, including Roger Gould, a psychologist from the University of California at Los Angeles, complained that Sheehy relied too heavily on their unpublished research and interpretations. Gould later sued and won rights to ten percent of the book's royalties. Most critics agree, however, that Sheehy did an outstanding job of organizing the experts' information into a highly readable and clearly presented argument.

In *Passages,* Sheehy explains how many of the domestic and career difficulties experienced by men and women today are the manifestations of predictable and natural periods of transition in adult life. It is the exception, not the rule, she argues, when a person decides on a career and a partner early in life and then feels content and fulfilled ever after. More expected, Sheehy says, is a life marked by several common and predictable stages. The well-adjusted adult recognizes his or her natural need for change and treats life as a series of passages from one emotional-physical condition to another.

Sheehy's best talent is her ability to translate the jargon and technicalities of the social sciences into clear, readable, and interesting prose. As you read, note how she puts complex ideas into accessible words. Think about these questions in particular:

1. How does her point of view (first-person plural) contribute to readability?
2. Does her sentence structure seem uncomplicated?
3. Can you find any examples of specialized vocabulary? How are those specialized words used?

4. Have you ever found it possible to predict changes in your own life? Would it be advantageous to be able to predict how you will feel at a future age? Is it beneficial to know that change is inevitable in everyone's life?

▶ ————————————————————

We are not unlike a particularly hardy crustacean. The lobster   *1*
grows by developing and shedding a series of hard, protective shells. Each time it expands from within, the confining shell must be sloughed off. It is left exposed and vulnerable until, in time, a new covering grows to replace the old.

With each passage from one stage of human growth to the next we,   *2*
too, must shed a protective structure. We are left exposed and vulnerable—but also yeasty and embryonic again, capable of stretching in ways we hadn't known before. These sheddings may take several years or more. Coming out of each passage, though, we enter a longer and more stable period in which we can expect relative tranquility and a sense of equilibrium regained. . . .

As we shall see, each person engages the steps of development in his   *3*
or her own characteristic *step-style.* Some people never complete the whole sequence. And none of us "solves" with one step—by jumping out of the parental home into a job or marriage, for example—the problems in separating from the caregivers of childhood. Nor do we "achieve" autonomy once and for all by converting our dreams into concrete goals, even when we attain those goals. The central issues or tasks of one period are never fully completed, tied up, and cast aside. But when they lose their primacy and the current life structure has served its purpose, we are ready to move on to the next period.

Can one catch up? What might look to others like listlessness, con-   *4*
trariness, a maddening refusal to face up to an obvious task may be a person's own unique detour that will bring him out later on the other side. Developmental gains won can later be lost—and rewon. It's plausible, though it can't be proven, that the mastery of one set of tasks fortifies us for the next period and the next set of challenges. But it's important not to think too mechanistically. Machines work by units. The bureaucracy (supposedly) works step by step. Human beings, thank God, have an individual inner dynamic that can never be precisely coded.

Although I have indicated the ages when Americans are likely to go   *5*
through each stage, and the differences between men and women where

they are striking, do not take the ages too seriously. The stages are the thing, and most particularly the sequence.

6   Here is the briefest outline of the developmental ladder.

Pulling Up Roots

7   Before 18, the motto is loud and clear: "I have to get away from my parents." But the words are seldom connected to action. Generally still safely part of our families, even if away at school, we feel our autonomy to be subject to erosion from moment to moment.

8   After 18, we begin Pulling Up Roots in earnest. College, military service, and short-term travels are all customary vehicles our society provides for the first round trips between family and a base of one's own. In the attempt to separate our view of the world from our family's view, despite vigorous protestations to the contrary—"I know exactly what I want!"—we cast about for any beliefs we can call our own. And in the process of testing those beliefs we are often drawn to fads, preferably those most mysterious and inaccessible to our parents.

9   Whatever tentative memberships we try out in the world, the fear haunts us that we are really kids who cannot take care of ourselves. We cover that fear with acts of defiance and mimicked confidence. For allies to replace our parents, we turn to our contemporaries. They become conspirators. So long as their perspective meshes with our own, they are able to substitute for the sanctuary of the family. But that doesn't last very long. And the instant they diverge from the shaky ideals of "our group," they are seen as betrayers. Rebounds to the family are common between the ages of 18 and 22.

10   The tasks of this passage are to locate ourselves in a peer group role, a sex role, an anticipated occupation, an ideology or world view. As a result, we gather the impetus to leave home physically and the identity to *begin* leaving home emotionally.

11   Even as one part of us seeks to be an individual, another part longs to restore the safety and comfort of merging with another. Thus one of the most popular myths of this passage is: We can piggyback our development by attaching to a Stronger One. But people who marry during this time often prolong financial and emotional ties to the family and relatives that impede them from becoming self-sufficient.

12   A stormy passage through the Pulling Up Roots years will probably facilitate the normal progression of the adult life cycle. If one doesn't have an identity crisis at this point, it will erupt during a later transition, when the penalties may be harder to bear.

The Trying Twenties

The Trying Twenties confront us with the question of how to take hold in the adult world. Our focus shifts from the interior turmoils of late adolescence—"Who am I?" "What is truth?"—and we become almost totally preoccupied with working out the externals. "How do I put my aspirations into effect?" "What is the best way to start?" "Where do I go?" "Who can help me?" "How did *you* do it?" | 13

In this period, which is longer and more stable compared with the passage that leads to it, the tasks are as enormous as they are exhilarating: To shape a Dream, that vision of ourselves which will generate energy, aliveness, and hope. To prepare for a lifework. To find a mentor if possible. And to form the capacity for intimacy, without losing in the process whatever consistency of self we have thus far mustered. The first test structure must be erected around the life we choose to try. | 14

Doing what we "should" is the most pervasive theme of the twenties. The "shoulds" are largely defined by family models, the press of the culture, or the prejudices of our peers. If the prevailing cultural instructions are that one should get married and settle down behind one's own door, a nuclear family is born. If instead the peers insist that one should do one's own thing, the 25-year-old is likely to harness himself onto a Harley-Davidson and burn up Route 66 in the commitment to have no commitments. | 15

One of the terrifying aspects of the twenties is the inner conviction that the choices we make are irrevocable. It is largely a false fear. Change is quite possible, and some alteration of our original choices is probably inevitable. | 16

Two impulses, as always, are at work. One is to build a firm, safe structure for the future by making strong commitments, to "be set." Yet people who slip into a ready-made form without much self-examination are likely to find themselves *locked in.* | 17

The other urge is to explore and experiment, keeping any structure tentative and therefore easily reversible. Taken to the extreme, these are people who skip from one trial job and one limited personal encounter to another, spending their twenties in the *transient* state. | 18

Although the choices of our twenties are not irrevocable, they do set in motion a Life Pattern. Some of us follow the lock-in pattern, others the transient pattern, the wunderkind pattern, the caregiver pattern, and there are a number of others. Such patterns strongly influence the particular questions raised for each person during each passage.... | 19

Buoyed by powerful illusions and belief in the power of the will, we commonly insist in our twenties that what we have chosen to do is the | 20 one true course in life. Our backs go up at the merest hint that we are like our parents, that two decades of parental training might be reflected in our current actions and attitudes.

21   "Not me," is the motto, "I'm different."

Catch-30

22   Impatient with devoting ourselves to the "shoulds," a new vitality springs from within as we approach 30. Men and women alike speak of feeling too narrow and restricted. They blame all sorts of things, but what the restrictions boil down to are the outgrowth of career and personal choices of the twenties. They may have been choices perfectly suited to that stage. But now the fit feels different. Some inner aspect that was left out is striving to be taken into account. Important new choices must be made, and commitments altered or deepened. The work involves great change, turmoil, and often crisis—a simultaneous feeling of rock bottom and the urge to bust out.

23   One common response is the tearing up of the life we spent most of our twenties putting together. It may mean striking out on a secondary road toward a new vision or converting a dream of "running for president" into a more realistic goal. The single person feels a push to find a partner. The woman who was previously content at home with children chafes to venture into the world. The childless couple reconsiders children. And almost everyone who is married, especially those married for seven years, feels a discontent.

24   If the discontent doesn't lead to a divorce, it will, or should, call for a serious review of the marriage and of each partner's aspirations in their Catch-30 condition. The gist of that condition was expressed by a 29-year-old associate with a Wall Street law firm:

25   "I'm considering leaving the firm. I've been there four years now; I'm getting good feedback, but I have no clients of my own. I feel weak. If I wait much longer, it will be too late, too close to that fateful time of decision on whether or not to become a partner. I'm success-oriented. But the concept of being 55 years old and stuck in a monotonous job drives me wild. It drives me crazy now, just a little bit. I'd say that 85 percent of the time I thoroughly enjoy my work. But when I get a screwball case, I come away from court saying, 'What am I doing here?' It's a *visceral* reaction that I'm wasting my time. I'm trying to find some way to make a social contribution or a slot in city government. I keep saying, 'There's something more.' "

26   Besides the push to broaden himself professionally, there is a wish to expand his personal life. He wants two or three more children. "The concept of a home has become very meaningful to me, a place to get

away from troubles and relax. I love my son in a way I could not have anticipated. I never could live alone.''

Consumed with the work of making his own critical life-steering decisions, he demonstrates the essential shift at this age: an absolute requirement to be more self-concerned. The self has new value now that his competency has been proved.   27

His wife is struggling with her own age-30 priorities. She wants to go to law school, but he wants more children. If she is going to stay home, she wants him to make more time for the family instead of taking on even wider professional commitments. His view of the bind, of what he would most like from his wife, is this: 28

''I'd like not to be bothered. It sounds cruel, but I'd like not to have to worry about what she's going to do next week. Which is why I've told her several times that I think she should do something. Go back to school and get a degree in social work or geography or whatever. Hopefully that would fulfill her, and then I wouldn't have to worry about her line of problems. I want her to be decisive about herself.''   29

The trouble with his advice to his wife is that it comes out of concern with *his* convenience, rather than with *her* development. She quickly picks up on this lack of goodwill: He is trying to dispose of her. At the same time, he refuses her the same latitude to be ''selfish'' in making an independent decision to broaden her own horizons. Both perceive a lack of mutuality. And that is what Catch-30 is all about for the couple.   30

Rooting and Extending

Life becomes less provisional, more rational and orderly in the early thirties. We begin to settle down in the full sense. Most of us begin putting down roots and sending out new shoots. People buy houses and become very earnest about climbing career ladders. Men in particular concern themselves with ''making it.'' Satisfaction with marriage generally goes downhill in the thirties (for those who have remained together) compared with the highly valued, vision-supporting marriage of the twenties. This coincides with the couple's reduced social life outside the family and the in-turned focus on raising their children.   31

The Deadline Decade

In the middle of the thirties we come upon a crossroads. We have reached the halfway mark. Yet even as we are reaching our prime, we begin to see there is a place where it finishes. Time starts to squeeze.   32

The loss of youth, the faltering of physical powers we have always taken for granted, the fading purpose of stereotyped roles by which we   33 have thus far identified ourselves, the spiritual dilemma of having no absolute answers—any or all of these shocks can give this passage the character of crisis. Such thoughts usher in a decade between 35 and 45 that can be called the Deadline Decade. It is a time of both danger and opportunity. All of us have the chance to rework the narrow identity by which we defined ourselves in the first half of life. And those of us who make the most of the opportunity will have a full-out authenticity crisis.

34   To come through this authenticity crisis, we must reexamine our purposes and reevaluate how to spend our resources from now on. "Why am I doing all this? What do I really believe in?" No matter what we have been doing, there will be parts of ourselves that have been suppressed and now need to find expression. "Bad" feelings will demand acknowledgment along with the good.

35   It is frightening to step off onto the treacherous footbridge leading to the second half of life. We can't take everything with us on this journey through uncertainty. Along the way, we discover that we are alone. We no longer have to ask permission because we are the providers of our own safety. We must learn to give ourselves permission. We stumble upon feminine or masculine aspects of our natures that up to this time have usually been masked. There is grieving to be done because an old self is dying. By taking in our suppressed and even our unwanted parts, we prepare at the gut level for the reintegration of an identity that is ours and ours alone—not some artificial form put together to please the culture or our mates. It is a dark passage at the beginning. But by disassembling ourselves, we can glimpse the light and gather our parts into a renewal.

36   Women sense this inner crossroads earlier than men do. The time pinch often prompts a woman to stop and take an all-points survey at age 35. Whatever options she has already played out, she feels a "my last chance" urgency to review those options she has set aside and those that aging and biology will close off in the *now foreseeable* future. For all her qualms and confusion about where to start looking for a new future, she usually enjoys an exhilaration of release. Assertiveness begins rising. There are so many firsts ahead.

37   Men, too, feel the time push in the mid-thirties. Most men respond by pressing down harder on the career accelerator. It's "my last chance" to pull away from the pack. It is no longer enough to be the loyal junior executive, the promising young novelist, the lawyer who does a little *pro bono* work on the side. He wants now to become part of top management, to be recognized as an established writer, or an active politician with his own legislative program. With some chagrin, he discovers that he has been too anxious to please and too vulnerable to criticism. He wants to put together his own ship.

During this period of intense concentration on external advancement, it is common for men to be unaware of the more difficult, gut issues that are propelling them forward. The survey that was neglected at 35 becomes a crucible at 40. Whatever rung of achievement he has reached, the man of 40 usually feels stale, restless, burdened, and unappreciated. He worries about his health. He wonders, "Is this all there is?" He may make a series of departures from well-established lifelong base lines, including marriage. More and more men are seeking second careers in midlife. Some become self-destructive. And many men in their forties experience a major shift of emphasis away from pouring all their energies into their own advancement. A more tender, feeling side comes into play. They become interested in developing an ethical self.

Renewal or Resignation

Somewhere in the mid-forties, equilibrium is regained. A new stability is achieved, which may be more or less satisfying.

If one has refused to budge through the midlife transition, the sense of staleness will calcify into resignation. One by one, the safety and supports will be withdrawn from the person who is standing still. Parents will become children; children will become strangers; a mate will grow away or go away; the career will become just a job—and each of these events will be felt as an abandonment. The crisis will probably emerge again around 50. And although its wallop will be greater, the jolt may be just what is needed to prod the resigned middle-ager toward seeking revitalization.

On the other hand...

If we have confronted ourselves in the middle passage and found a renewal of purpose around which we are eager to build a more authentic life structure, these may well be the best years. Personal happiness takes a sharp turn upward for partners who can now accept the fact: "I cannot expect *anyone* to fully understand me." Parents can be forgiven for the burdens of our childhood. Children can be let go without leaving us in collapsed silence. At 50, there is a new warmth and mellowing. Friends become more important than ever, but so does privacy. Since it is so often proclaimed by people past midlife, the motto of this stage might be "No more bullshit."

Questions and Activities

▶ *COMPREHENSION QUESTIONS*

1. Explain how the metaphor in the first two paragraphs works to set up Sheehy's point in this essay. How are human beings, to Sheehy, like crustaceans?
2. Why are the traumas that many adults experience predictable, according to Sheehy? Are the reasons for this predictability psychological or social or both?
3. Paraphrase the six headings that appear throughout this selection. What does each one say about a particular age group of adults?

▶ *QUESTIONS OF RHETORICAL PURPOSE AND STRATEGY*

4. Explain why Sheehy's style has often been called "journalistic."
5. Is Sheehy's voice that of an expert in the field of psychology or sociology or that of an educated interpreter of the work of such experts?
6. Does Sheehy make references to the sources of her information? Do you think that formal documentation is necessary in this type of writing? What might be the dangers of not including sources in a piece such as this? What might the addition of sources do to Sheehy's voice and style?
7. Explain the organizational strategy underlying this essay. How does Sheehy set up her categories? Is the essay easy to follow? Does its organization do justice to the complexity of the topic?
8. Do you think Sheehy's purpose was to convince her readers that their problems are shared by other adults? What reasons would there be to justify such a purpose?
9. Would it be accurate to say that Sheehy's essay is meant to serve as a psychological primer on how to deal with change in the various stages of adult life? Considered as such a primer, do you think Sheehy's essay includes a sufficient number of examples and a sufficient amount of analysis of those examples to be useful to its readers?

▶ *THEME QUESTIONS*

10. What do you think Wendell Berry would say about Sheehy's essay? Would individuals in his rural, agricultural world also go through the kinds of passages described by Sheehy? Is Sheehy's essay, in other words, relevant only to a certain type of American?
11. Does Sheehy feel that change is inevitable? Could a person, according to Sheehy, avoid change and remain well-adjusted and healthy? What types of change are inevitable, and what types are avoidable?

► *LEARNING ACTIVITIES*

12. Interview an adult you know about the idea of passages. You might ask your subject to describe a recent stage, or passage, in his or her life. Base your questions for the interview on what Sheehy has to say about typical adult passages.

13. In a workshop group with some of your classmates, analyze the results of your interview and compare those results to Sheehy's descriptions of adult passages. Does your subject's response match one of Sheehy's typical passages? If not, how is it different? Does your subject's response raise questions about Sheehy's entire approach? Do you feel that this type of popular psychology is useful or useless when applied to particular individuals?

Reflections on the Year 15 p.H.

ARTHUR KOESTLER

Arthur Koestler died of a drug overdose in 1983, the victim of an apparent suicide pact with his third wife. He was seventy-eight years old and a firm believer in euthanasia when he died. He suffered from Parkinson's disease and leukemia.

His most famous book, *Darkness at Noon* (1940), was an indictment of Soviet Communism. Koestler had been a member of the Communist Party from 1931 to 1938 but had been disillusioned by what he felt was its extreme internal strife, competition, and social hypocrisy. *Darkness at Noon* was transformed into a successful Broadway play in 1951, and it has been translated into thirty languages.

Koestler's work as a journalist took him on an arctic expedition in 1931, on a journey through central Asia in the 1930s, to Russia for a year of political activity and correspondence, and to Spain as a news correspondent in 1936 during the Spanish Civil War. He was tried, convicted, and sentenced to death by the Franco government in 1937 and released through British intervention in 1938. In 1939, he was imprisoned in France after war was declared; he was released in 1940 and escaped to England. He later served in the French Foreign Legion and the British Pioneer Corps. He lived most of the later part of his life in Britain, where he continued his writing career.

In the 1940s, his books focused on the effects of international politics on the individual. These books used Koestler's own experience with different parties and movements to develop general commentary on modern political life. His writing during this period included two autobiographical works that were best-sellers: *Scum of the Earth* (1941) and *Dialogue with Death* (1942).

Later Koestler broadened his interests to produce books on human creativity (*The Act of Creation,* 1964) and psychology (*Studies in Psychology,* 1965), on capital punishment (*Hanged by the Neck,* 1961), on British culture (*Suicide of a Nation,* 1963), on the idea of coincidence (*The Roots of Coincidence,* 1972), on the possibility of an after-life (*Life after Death,* 1976), and on mental telepathy (*The Challenge of Chance,* 1973). In these later works, Koestler was able to translate his extensive reading background and personal experience into arguments on a wide range of subjects. Through all this later writing, he continued to focus on the theme of individual independence and identity in an age of mass political movements and increased dependence on technology.

In the essay here, Koestler asks readers to consider the effects the coming of the nuclear age has had on our sense of history. Once the modern world experienced nuclear holocaust, Koestler suggests, internationalism became a recurrent theme. A new sense of imminent destruction both drew nations together and instilled a terrible mutual fear. Individuals living in this era of a new social consciousness are inextricably bound up with their societies. As you read, ask yourself what social, personal, and political events have marked off periods of change in your life:

1. Were the changes that you recall in relation to social events traumatic? What actually changed?
2. Is there any pattern to the events that have motivated changes in your life? Did these events affect your daily life? Did they change the way you thought of your future, of your role in the future?
3. Do any relatively recent events, for example, concerning the space program or nuclear power, seem to follow the pattern Koestler says was begun with the bombing of Hiroshima?

In this essay, Koestler marks off what he believes is a new era for human society. Here, as in all his writing, Koestler analyzes the effects of an international event—the dropping of the first atomic bomb at Hiroshima—on the development of the individual human psyche. This analysis also represents an attitude toward individual and social change. As you read, ask yourself whether or not Koestler might be offering an overview on human cultural development that is similar to the overview Gail Sheehy takes of individual development (pages 600–609):

1. How is what Koestler says about modern society similar to what Sheehy says is true of the individual's development?
2. How are Sheehy's and Koestler's views of individual and social development different? Does Sheehy seem to suggest a final stage of stability for the individual that is the opposite of what Koestler indicates will characterize society's final stage?

In light of the information provided about Koestler's writing in this headnote, consider his style in this essay:

1. Are there places in the essay where Koestler's broad range of background experience is apparent?
2. Does Koestler demonstrate knowledge far beyond what would be required to write an essay on the effects of dropping a bomb on Hiroshima? Where specifically does Koestler demonstrate his knowledge of history, of science, and of technology?

▶ ────────────────

1   Nineteen sixty means to me anno 15 p.H., where "p" stands for post—after—and "H" stands for Hiroshima. I say that not because I like to remember that episode, nor as an act of penance—for after all we were not consulted—but for a factual and unsentimental reason. Calendars imply convictions about the importance of certain events—the first Olympiad for the Greeks, the foundation of the city of Rome, the birth of a child in Nazareth, the flight of Mohammed from Mecca. The positing of a year Zero provides a time-scale, the measure of the age, of the distance covered, from the real or assumed starting point of a given civilization.

2   There is, I believe, a strong case to be made for keeping a kind of second calendar in our minds which indicates the distance traveled from that decisive moment when a man-made flash of light outshone the sun. Fifteen years are but a few seconds on the dials of history and it is not surprising that this new-born civilization of ours is as yet unaware of its own separate existence.

3   More precisely, its awareness is still of that inchoate, shapeless, nebulous kind which precedes the conscious discovery of one's identity. On the surface we find no sharp, decisive break between life before and after *anno* Zero. There have been some social, political, cultural changes, but if these were all, there would be no justification for suggesting this kind of new calendar.

4   My feeling that all that happened before 1945 belongs to a quasi-prehistorical epoch is based on a rather simple consideration which, however, is not quite simple to explain. Let me proceed by steps. The fact that mankind has acquired the power to destroy itself does enter into it, but merely as a preliminary step.

5   The next question is what this fact does to the human psyche. I think that so far it has affected it but very little, at least on the conscious level. The simple proof is that everybody went on manufacturing the thing. There were protests and involved controversies, but no global outcry powerful enough to stop it.

6   The somewhat clownish character of some of the protest demonstrations was particularly revealing. The voluble phrases about the possibility of blowing the whole planet to glory sounded at first both frightening and subtly flattering to our vanity; but soon they became clichés divorced from emotional meaning. Then everybody got bored with this insoluble problem until the sputniks* brought a new thrill

───────────────

*The sputniks were the first Russian satellites to be put into orbit. Sputnik I was launched in 1957, and it inspired a worldwide emphasis on space exploration and science.

and the pleasant hope that these things might develop a tendency to keep going upward and not coming down.

And thus, *anno* 15 p.H., we have apparently settled down to business as usual. But, I believe, only apparently. There are periods of incubation. The Copernican theory of the earth's motion* took eighty years before it sank in. The unconscious has its own clock, and its own ways of digesting what the conscious mind has rejected as indigestible. There are signs that, on a limited scale and in an oblique way, this process of assimilation has already begun, a process which, I believe, is bound to transform completely the mental make-up of our race.

The essence of this transformation could be defined as follows: hitherto man had to live with the idea of his death as an individual; from now onward mankind will have to live with the idea of its death as a species.

This is an entirely novel prospect, but not necessarily a gloomy one. To realize its implications one must try to bear in mind that we are not dealing in abstractions but with hard, obstinate facts; in other words, we must try to achieve a psychological break-through across the multiple smoke-screens of our own mental defenses against reality. If we succeed in achieving that, we may discover a rather breathtaking vision beyond the screen, which will make human destiny appear in a new light.

We, who have been brought up in the Western way of thinking, have always been taught to accept the transitoriness of existence as individuals, while taking the survival of our species axiomatically for granted. And this was a perfectly reasonable belief, barring some unlikely cosmic catastrophe. But it has ceased to be a reasonable belief since the day, fifteen years ago, when the feasibility of just such a cosmic catastrophe was tested and proved. It pulverized the assumptions on which all philosophy, from Socrates onward, was based, that is to say, the potential immortality of our species.

Let us consider the implications of this turn of events from a completely detached, that is, inhuman, point of view. Let us imagine that among the hidden works of the Lord Almighty there functions a kind of intergalactic insurance company which periodically surveys the insurance risks the various intelligent species on the various inhabited planets represent.

The company knows no more about the intellectual progress and psychological kinks of its individual clients—which number perhaps half a million in our galaxy alone—than a terrestrial insurance company does. It simply watches them from a distance. Before its observers

7

8

9

10

11

12

---

*The Copernican theory of the earth's motion around the sun, now accepted as astronomical fact, was first promulgated by the Polish astronomer Nicholas Copernicus in 1543.

noted that certain flash fifteen years ago, they would probably have given the inhabitants of this planet quite a reasonable life span.

13   This planet has, by cosmic standards, just the right size of a middle-aged sun, in a stable, middle-aged galaxy, safe by all probability standards from any local or intergalactic collision. Its dominant race, which emerged relatively late after the beginning of organic life on the planet, seemed to be intellectually too precocious compared to its emotional retardation, and accordingly maladjusted.

14   But, against this, it enjoyed the considerable advantage of having no serious biological competitors for the mastery of the planet. So far, so good. Then came the familiar flash which the company's watchman had so frequently observed in other parts of the sky, and the computers were set to work.

15   The computers worked on the principle, based on past experience, that the gadgets which cause the flash will undergo the process known as progressive miniaturization: They will become ever smaller and more elegant, as suitcases and transistor radios and satellite equipment did. The computers took it for granted that an effective global control of the gadgets was in the long run impracticable on these grounds alone, and that in the foreseeable future they will be produced and stored in large quantities, from windswept Alaska to sunny Cairo and Tel Aviv.

16   The computers were then fed relevant samples of the past behavior of the race, and a long tape showing the location and intensity and frequency of the various potential and open conflicts on various parts of the planet. Finally, they were fed the old but useful analogy about the problem child left with a matchbox in a room filled with inflammable material, and were then asked to compute from these data: firstly, the chances of indefinite survival for *Homo sapiens;* and secondly, its probable remaining life-span.

17   I think that all of us imagine from time to time that we hear the computers clicking—not in outer space, but in the equally puzzling inner spaces of the human mind, with its private clocks, and private calendars. For that, of course, is the space—call it the collective psyche, if you like—where our collective destiny is being computed. However, let me revert for another moment to my allegory, for at this point it takes an unexpected turn.

18   The computers had finished their work; the attendant extracted the tape, looked at the figures and took it in to the boss; "pretty grim," he said, shaking his head in sympathy. The boss did not look at the tape; instead he dictated the following message to the planet:

19   "Congratulations. The results look pretty grim, but the company can only compute statistical probabilities, and the final outcome still depends on the individual client. We congratulate you, as usual on

these occasions, on the mere fact that you have reached the age of majority. Before that turning point you were assured of your survival, regardless of the nasty things you did. You were potentially immortal as a race, and in this secure knowledge you could indulge in all kinds of irresponsible behavior.

"This is now changed, though you do not realize it yet. Your survival [20] now depends on you and you alone. The company can do nothing for you. Nature can do nothing for you. Nature nursed and protected you before you reached majority, even to the extent of producing a surplus of male births to replenish your stock depleted by wars. Now you are stronger than Nature and entirely on your own.

"The way you celebrated your reaching maturity was not pretty. But [21] let it pass; there have been worse scandals in the galaxy. The company does not judge and does not punish because once you are past the turn-ing point you are your own judge and your own executioner. At this stage, justice works by automatic back-feed.

"Your race will never again feel quite safe, just as its individual [22] members never have felt safe since the first of them ate the forbidden fruit of knowledge. But you need not be frightened about that; there are compensations. By learning to live with the sober awareness of its possible extinction, your race may derive the same spiritual benefits which the individual derived from coming to terms with his own mortality.

"These benefits were of course considerable. You no doubt remem- [23] ber your old sage who said that philosophy is the history of man's endeavors to come to terms with death. And since philosophy is a Good Thing, death must be a Good Thing—or at least awareness thereof. Take the word 'death' out of your vocabulary and your great works of literature become meaningless; take that awareness away and your cathedrals collapse, the pyramids vanish into the sand and the great organs become silent.

"You know all this, but since you live in an age of anxiety and transi- [24] tion, you condemn all concern with death as morbid in the indignant tones of your Victorian prudes. You deny Thanatos as the Victorians denied Eros;* you shrink from the facts of death as they shrank from the facts of life. And yet the philosophy of man, the art of man, the dignity of man is derived from his brave endeavors to reconcile Eros and Thanatos.

---

*"Eros" and "Thanatos" were the terms first used by Sigmund Freud to describe the human being's constructive and destructive impulses. Freud believed that these contrary instincts were in constant battle within the human psyche. They are often called the life and death wishes.

25   "You are entering as an adult the large family of our clients—around half a million in your galaxy alone; I always forget their exact figure because they come and vanish so fast, much quicker than a single galactic rotation. Nobody interferes with them; those who vanish are their own executioners because they prove in the long run unfit for existence. Those who survive flourish because they have discovered their cosmic *raison d'être*. The rest is up to you. All the company can do is to wish you good luck as we always do on these occasions."

26   To come back to earth—though I do not think we have really left it for a moment—let me conclude by a brief comparison between our present outlook and that of roughly 500 years before Hiroshima.

27   The medieval universe was like a walled-in city with firm boundaries in space and time, a few million miles in diameter and a few thousand years in duration. In this closed universe a well-ordered drama was taking its course which began with the Creation and would end when the trumpet sounded and the four horsemen appeared in the sky.

28   In one sense we have reverted to that vision: we are no longer sure that *Homo sapiens* will go on forever and we again feel that the Last Judgment may take place in the foreseeable future. But in another sense we have moved away from that vision: for we know that the end of *Homo sapiens* would not be the end of the world, merely the end of an episode in a drama on an incomparably larger scale than the medieval shape allowed for. In other words, the necessity of getting reconciled with the idea of his possible extinction may breed a new humility and may rid man of that biological jingoism which made him regard himself as the crown of creation.

29   The idea that the world will go on, even if mankind does not, may prove an antidote to that cosmic anxiety which has held us in its grip since the burning star fell on Hiroshima, distorted our sense of values, exposed us to various forms of blackmail, undermined our dignity and our power of decision.

30   Schopenhauer,* wrongly described as a pessimist, regarded himself as a mortal leaf on an immortal tree, a leaf to be replaced next year by another, nourished by the same sap. Gradually we shall perhaps learn that the leaves which bud into life and sail away in the autumn symbolize not only individuals but other great civilizations dotted along the vaporous branches of the expanding universe. We shall be more peaceful then. But it will take some time. After all, we have only just entered the fifteenth year of the new era.

---

*Arthur Schopenhauer (1788–1860) was a German philosopher whose world view was one in which the conflict of individual wills and desires produced pain and frustration.

Questions and Activities

1. What is the antecedent, or referent, for the pronoun "its" in the first sentence of paragraph 3? What do the words "inchoate, shapeless, and nebulous" mean as they are used in this sentence? *What* is still inchoate, shapeless, and nebulous?
2. What is "a quasi-prehistorical epoch" (paragraph 4)? How was life before 1945 such a quasi-prehistorical epoch?
3. What kind of language is Koestler using in paragraph 13? Is it the language of science or poetry, of a particular field of study?
4. What do Eros and Thanatos mean in paragraph 24? Why are these words capitalized? How are the ideas of Eros and Thanatos connected to our living in "an age of anxiety and transition" (paragraph 24)?

▶ *QUESTIONS OF RHETORICAL PURPOSE AND STRATEGY*

5. Koestler builds this entire essay around an extended analogy. He asks readers to imagine a cosmic insurance company doing a statistical analysis of the human race's chances for survival. Why do you think Koestler builds on this analogy rather than on logical or factual appeals? What type of reader is apt to be most persuaded by this type of argument?
6. What does the sentence "So far, so good" (paragraph 14) suggest about Koestler's writing style? Does this sentence make his style more personal? Why?
7. Why do you think Koestler wrote this essay? Did he want to jar people into a new frame of mind concerning the future of the human race? Did he want them to recognize the enormous significance of the dropping of the atomic bomb on Hiroshima?

▶ *THEME QUESTIONS*

8. Exactly how did Hiroshima change the future of the human race, according to Koestler? Was the change primarily an individual or a social one?
9. Explain the meaning of the leaf-and-tree metaphor in paragraph 30, the essay's final paragraph. Why might some people find this a pessimistic image? Are readers to imagine that civilizations, like individuals, are "mortal" and therefore transient, whereas the tree is immortal and permanent? What does the tree stand for?

10. This essay was published in 1960. We are now in what Koestler would call the year 42 p.H. Working with some of your classmates in a group, list at least ten major world events from 1960 to the present. Date the items on the list according to Koestler's new calendar.

    Review your group's list of events and pick those that are most closely related to the dropping of the atomic bomb on Hiroshima. Discuss these selected events in relation to Koestler's argument that from 1945 on human destiny is in the hands of human beings, not in the hands of a higher being or under the control of some natural force. Do these events suggest that humanity can be its own worst enemy, as Koestler says that Hiroshima proves?

11. Consider Koestler's main point in relation to some current event. Does this event seem created by human, natural, or supernatural forces? Write a brief analysis of a news article describing the event. Use Koestler's thesis as the perspective underlying your analysis.

The Prison of the Present

Daniel J. Boorstin

Daniel J. Boorstin has been Librarian of Congress since 1975. A *summa cum laude* graduate of Harvard University, Boorstin was a Rhodes scholar at Balliol College, Oxford University, where he earned a law degree in 1936. He continued his study of law at Yale and was admitted to the Massachusetts bar in 1942. From 1942 to 1969, he was a professor of history, mostly at the University of Chicago. Boorstin has published more than thirty books, has edited many volumes of history, and has published in many scholarly journals and popular magazines.

Boorstin has always been an outspoken student of American history. He has been able to combine thorough research with an elegant writing style to construct persuasive interpretations of whole periods of American history. His most ambitious and well-known project was his three-part cultural history of the United States: *The Colonial Experience* (1958), *The National Experience* (1965), and *The Democratic Experience* (1973). Whereas many contemporary scholars have been critical of American materialism and commercialism, Boorstin consistently finds positive value in American practicality and inventiveness. Boorstin's supporters feel that he is able to see beyond the crass surface of much of American culture to the essential pragmatism that has helped to establish the United States as a world power in a relatively short time. This positive response, unlike many historians' criticisms of almost every traditional American institution, is developed most forcefully in *The Decline of Radicalism: Reflections of America Today* (1969) and in the book from which the essay that follows was taken, *Democracy and Its Discontents: Reflections on Everyday America* (1974).

As you read this essay, note how Boorstin's sharp, critical intelligence first establishes a thesis on current American culture, "our imprisonment in the present." Then he shows how that thesis explains Americans' current preoccupation with social problems such as poverty and corruption. If people do not have a sense of the past, Boorstin suggests, they too quickly develop the idea that their problems are unsolvable. Because they are unaware that their problems have existed before, they become bogged down in negativism when they might be constructing solutions.

Boorstin seems to opt for gradual social and political change controlled by a strong sense of history. As you read, compare his position with those of Arthur Koestler and Gail Sheehy:

1. What are the similarities or differences between Koestler's sense that our culture was irrevocably and traumatically altered by the dropping of the first atomic bomb and Boorstin's implicit faith in American institutions?
2. How might Sheehy's concept of adult passages be regarded by Boorstin, who feels that the contemporary individual is dominated by the present and unaware of the past?
3. Might someone fascinated by Sheehy's ideas be apt to miss what Boorstin has to say about the relationship between past and present? As one moves from one developmental stage to another, is one ever truly free of previous stages?

▶ ————————————————

1   Our inventive, up-to-the-minute, wealthy democracy makes new tests of the human spirit. Our very instruments of education, of information and of "progress" make it harder every day for us to keep our bearings in the larger universe, in the stream of history and in the whole world of peoples who feel strong ties to their past. A new price of our American standard of living is our imprisonment in the present.

2   That imprisonment tempts us to a morbid preoccupation with ourselves, and so induces hypochondria. That, the dictionary tells us, is "an abnormal condition characterized by a depressed emotional state and imaginary ill health; excessive worry or talk about one's health." We think we are the beginning and the end of the world. And as a result we get our nation and our lives, our strengths and our ailments, quite out of focus.

3   We will not be on the way to curing our national hypochondria unless we first see ourselves in history. This requires us to accept the unfashionable possibility that many of our national ills are imaginary and that others may not be as serious as we imagine. Unless we begin to believe that we won't be dead before morning, we may not be up to the daily tasks of a healthy life. By recalling some of the premature obituaries pronounced on other nations, we may listen more skeptically to the moralists and smart alecks who pretend to have in their pocket a life-expectancy chart for nations.

4   Overwhelmed by the instant moment—headlined in this morning's newspaper and flashed on this hour's newscast—we don't see the whole real world around us. We don't see the actual condition of our long-lived body national.

In a word, we have lost our sense of history. In our schools the story   5
of our nation has been displaced by "social studies"—which is often
the story only of what ails us. In our churches the effort to see man *sub
specie aeternitatis** has been displaced by a "social gospel"—which is a
polemic against the supposed special evils of our time. Our book publishers and literary reviewers no longer seek the timeless and the dura-
ble, but spend much of their efforts in fruitless search for à la mode
"social commentary"—which they pray won't be out of date when the
issue goes to press in two weeks or when the manuscript becomes a
book in six months. Our merchandisers frantically devise their semi-
annual models which will cease to be voguish when their sequels appear a few months hence. Neither our classroom lessons nor our sermons nor our books nor the things we live with nor the houses we live
in are any longer strong ties to our past. We have become a nation of
short-term doomsayers.

Without the materials of historical comparison, having lost our tra-   6
ditional respect for the wisdom of ancestors and the culture of kindred
nations, we are left with little but abstractions, baseless utopias, to
compare ourselves with. No wonder, then, that some of our distraught
citizens libel us as the worst nation in the world, or the bane of human
history. For we have wandered out of history.

We have nearly lost interest in those real examples from the human   7
past which alone can help us shape standards of the humanly possible.
So we compare ours with a mythical Trouble-Free World, where all
mankind was at peace. We talk about the war in Vietnam as if it were
the first war in American history to which many Americans were
opposed. We condemn our nation for not yet having attained perfect
justice, and we forget that ours is the most motley and miscellaneous
great nation in history—the first to use the full force of law and constitutions and to enlist the vast majority of its citizens in a strenuous
quest for justice for all races and ages and religions.

We flagellate ourselves as "poverty-ridden"—by comparison with   8
some mythical time when there was no bottom 20 percent in the economic scale. We sputter against the Polluted Environment—as if it had
come with the age of the automobile. We compare our smoggy air not
with the odor of horse dung and the plague of flies and the smells of garbage and human excrement which filled cities in the past, but with the
honeysuckle perfumes of some nonexistent City Beautiful. We forget
that even if the water in many cities today is not as spring-pure nor as

*This Latin phrase means "under the aspect of eternity."

palatable as we would like, still for most of history the water of the cities (and of the countryside) was undrinkable. We reproach ourselves for the ills of disease and malnourishment, and forget that until recently, enteritis and measles and whooping cough, diphtheria and typhoid, were killing diseases of childhood, puerperal fever plagued mothers in childbirth, polio was a summer monster.

9   Flooded by screaming headlines and televised "news" melodramas of dissent, of shrill cries for "liberation," we haunt ourselves with the illusory ideal of some "whole nation" which had a deep and outspoken "faith" in its "values."

10   We become so obsessed by where we are that we forget where we came from and how we got here. No wonder that we begin to lack the courage to confront the normal ills of modern history's most diverse, growing, burbling Nation of Nations.

11   Our national hypochondria is compounded by distinctively American characteristics. The American belief in speed, which led us to build railroads farther and faster than any other nation, to invent "quick-lunch" and self-service to save that intolerable ten-minute wait, to build automobiles and highways so we can commute at 70 miles an hour, and which made us a nation of instant cities, instant coffee, and TV dinners, has bred in us a colossal impatience. Any social problem that can't be solved instantly by money and legislation seems fatal. Our appliances and our buildings—and our very lives—seem out of date even before we know it. What can't be done right now seems hardly worth doing at all.

12   Some of these current attitudes are themselves the late-twentieth-century perversions of the old American Booster Spirit, which has had no precise parallel anywhere else. Totalitarian nations have been marked by their obsession with "planning"—with five-year plans and ten-year plans. But planning expresses willingness to accept a sharp distinction between present and future, between the way things are and the way they might be. And that distinction has never been too popular in the U.S.A. The nineteenth-century Boosters of Western cities defended their extravagant boasts by saying there was no reason to wait, if you were actually bragging only about things that were certain to happen. To them the beauties of Oleopolis or Gopher City were not less real just because they had "not yet gone through the formality of taking place."

13   This Booster-Vagueness has always made Americans wonderfully unpedantic about the distinction between the present and the future. The amiable vagueness, which once gave an optimistic nineteenth-century America the energy and the hope to go on, still survives. But in a hypochondriac twentieth-century America its effects can be disastrous.

Now that very same extravagant vagueness leads some Americans to believe that every battle is Armageddon* and that the nation is not less dead just because the national demise also has "not yet gone through the formality of taking place."

An immigrant nation, without an established religion and without   *14* political dogma, has had to depend heavily on its sense of a shared past (and a shared future). American history itself was an antidote to dogmatism and utopianism. It proved that a nation did not need to be altogether one thing or another. Federalism was a way of combining local control with national government. Ethnic pluralism was a way of allowing people to keep as much as they wanted of their Old World language, religion, and cuisine—to live among themselves as much as they wished. The immigrant was not compelled either to keep or to abandon his Old World identity. Despite flagrant exceptions expressing prejudices of race, religion, and sex, nevertheless, in the nation as a whole free public schools, and the American innovations of the free high school and the public college, have tried to have standards and yet give everybody the same commodity. The nation aimed to preserve "free private enterprise" (freer and on a larger scale than anywhere else) and yet to provide social security, farm price supports, and other insurance against the free market. On a priori grounds, each and all of these would have seemed impossible, and they were all messy, philosophically speaking.

The best antidote, then, against ruthless absolutes and simple-   *15* minded utopias has been American history itself. But that history becomes more and more inaccessible when the technology and institutions of our time imprison us in the present. How can we escape the prison?

First, we must awaken our desire to escape. To do this we must   *16* abandon the prevalent belief in the superior wisdom of the ignorant. Unless we give up the voguish reverence for youth and for the "culturally deprived," unless we cease to look to the vulgar community as arbiters of our schools, of our art and literature, and of all our culture, we will never have the will to de-provincialize our minds. We must make every effort to reverse the trend in our schools and colleges—to move away from the "relevant" and toward the cosmopolitanizing, the humanizing, and the unfamiliar. Education is learning what you didn't even know you didn't know. The vogue for "Black Studies" itself grew out of the ghetto, and ironically enough, unwittingly became an

---

*Armageddon was a plain where the Israelites in the Old Testament experienced many military victories and disasters. The word has since come to refer to any scene of a momentous test, and especially to the scene of the great battle between good and evil at the end of the world.

effort to idealize the ways of the ghetto. The last thing the able young Negro needs is "Black Studies"—which simply reinforces the unfortunate narrowness of his experience and confines him in *his* provincial present. He does need a better, more cosmopolitan educational system, from kindergarten on up, and a freer opportunity to grasp the opportunities in the whole nation. While he has suffered more than most other Americans from imprisonment in his provincial present, ultimately we all have the same need. We need liberation, too, from the White Ghetto. We all need more ancient history, more medieval history, more of the history and culture of Asia and Africa.

17   Then, we must enlarge and widen and deepen what we mean by our history. The preoccupation with politics, which has been the bane of the history classroom, fosters unreasonable notions that today governments are the root of all good and evil. The self-righteous effort by self-styled prophets of self-vaunted new "schools" of history would make history a mere tool of contemporary polemics, and so destroy the reason for exploring our past. They would make men of all other ages into the slaves of our conceit—to be used only for our purposes. We must make our history more total by incorporating the past that people lived but that historians have not talked much about. In the United States this means an effort to make more of the history of immigrants, of the history of technology, of the history of everyday life, of business and advertising and housing and eating and drinking and clothing. Democratizing our history does not mean perverting it to the current needs of demagogic or "revolutionary" politics. It does mean enlarging its once-pedantic scope to include the whole spectrum of the ways of life of all men and women and children.

18   When we allow ourselves to be imprisoned in the present, to be obsessed by the "relevant," we show too little respect for ourselves and our possibilities. We assume that we can properly judge our capacities by the peculiar tests of our own day. But we must look into the whole Historical Catalogue of man's possiblities. To be really persuaded that things can be otherwise, we must see how and when and why they actually have been otherwise.

19   To revive our sense of history is no panacea for current ills. But it surely is a palliative. It may help us discover what is now curable, may help us define the timetable of the possible, and so help us become something that we are not. If history cannot give us panaceas, it is the best possible cure of the yen for panaceas. And the only proven antidote for utopianism.

20   "The voice of the intellect," observed Sigmund Freud (who did not underestimate the role of the irrational) in 1928, "is a soft one, but it does not rest until it has gained a hearing. Ultimately, after endlessly

repeated rebuffs, it succeeds. This is one of the few points in which one may be optimistic about the future of mankind." Beneath the strident voice of the present we must try to hear the insistent whisper of reason. It does not sound "with it." It speaks only to the attentive listener. It speaks a language always unfamiliar and often archaic. It speaks the language of all past times and places, which is the language of history.

Questions and Activities

▶ *COMPREHENSION QUESTIONS*

1. In paragraph 5, Boorstin argues that a "social gospel" has replaced the religious gospel in contemporary American churches. What do you think Boorstin means by "social gospel"? How does the fact that social studies is more often taught than American history in American schools fit into this pattern?

2. What is Boorstin saying about what he believes is our national preoccupation with poverty in paragraph 8? What is he implying when he says that we 'flagellate ourselves as "poverty-ridden" '?

3. Why has the United States, according to Boorstin, had to rely more than most countries on a shared sense of the past? Why does this fact make our current fascination with the present seem even more threatening to Boorstin?

▶ *QUESTIONS OF RHETORICAL PURPOSE AND STRATEGY*

4. Is this primarily a persuasive or an informative essay? Does the fact that the final five paragraphs of the essay make recommendations for solving the problem defined in the first fifteen paragraphs suggest a persuasive purpose?

5. Most of this essay is written in the first-person plural point of view. Why do you think Boorstin chooses this point of view rather than, specifically, the conventional third person of formal essays on history? Does Boorstin's use of the first person suggest that this essay appeared in a book that was not intended solely for historians?

▶ *THEME QUESTIONS*

6. In paragraph 14, Boorstin describes social conditions that he says are unique to the United States. How do the facts that it is an immigrant nation, has free high schools and public colleges, and has fostered free enterprise while trying to assure basic social security

contribute to its uniqueness? Does Boorstin see these conditions positively or negatively? Why would these social conditions cause Americans to rely more heavily than do many traditional societies on a sense of a shared past?

7. Does Boorstin's analysis of American culture make you feel that any society that radically changes the conditions under which people live will also need to soften the effects of those changes? Does Boorstin feel that using the past as a means of developing a sense of tradition is one effective way of softening the trauma of social changes; that people, in other words, must have some sense of security, even when they live in a progressive culture?

8. Is it possible that contemporary American culture's fascination with the present is a stage, or phase, of development? If you believe it is, give what might be some causes for this phase. If you believe it is a more permanent characteristic, tell why you think Americans have always been present-oriented. Might a present-orientation be common to technological societies, which are always attempting to achieve better products and processes?

   ▶ *LEARNING ACTIVITIES*

9. Find an advertisement that represents our culture's fascination with the here and now. Show the advertisement to your classmates and explain to them how the ad writers have appealed to Americans' preoccupation with the here and now.

10. Find advertisements — for life insurance or investments, for example — that have a future-orientation, rather than a past or present one. Do even these advertisements have some reference as well to the here and now? Or do these advertisements constitute real exceptions to or contradictions of Boorstin's thesis?

11. Write a free response to an advertisement or commercial that you believe demonstrates our society's youth orientation. You can criticize, praise, or simply describe the advertisement or commercial.

The Library Card

RICHARD WRIGHT

Few American writers of this century have had a more interesting career than Richard Wright, who is recognized as one of our most influential black writers. Born in Natchez, Mississippi, in 1908 and sporadically educated in Southern schools, Wright established his reputation by writing both autobiography and fiction about the frustrations he felt as a young Southern black man. His autobiography, *Black Boy* (1945), which includes the piece reprinted here, received generally favorable reviews for its realistic and moving accounts of the effects of racism on Wright as a child and young man. Wright's most well-known book, the novel *Native Son* (1940), is a fictional treatment of the effects of racism on black consciousness. Similar themes are dealt with in his short fiction, most notably in the widely praised collection *Uncle Tom's Children* (1938).

Wright was involved in political and social movements throughout his adult life. He moved from Memphis to Chicago when he was a young man, joining the American Communist Party in 1932 and resigning from it in disappointment in 1944. In his young adulthood, Wright seemed caught between his own vigorous individuality and a desire to subjugate his personality to some kind of socialist cause. Invited to Paris by the French government in 1946, Wright lived there from 1947 until his death in 1960. His life in Paris brought him into close association with French existentialist philosophers and sociologists; existentialism, with its emphasis on individual consciousness in an otherwise meaningless world, came to dominate Wright's later fiction, particularly his novels *The Outsider* (1953) and *The Long Dream* (1958). Wright devoted much of his later writing career to producing nonfictional accounts of national independence movements in Africa. His book on Ghana, *Black Power* (1954), won praise for its accurate and moving reporting, although his political interpretations were controversial.

Wright's writing is characterized by descriptive and narrative power. He is able to render his experience dramatically, and he is able to use that experience to support his interpretations of the modern individual's problems in dealing with impersonal, amoral, and evil social systems. These descriptive and narrative skills are apparent in the autobiographical piece that follows. As you read this memoir, think about Wright's use of his experience:

1. Does Wright present himself as a victim of a racist society? Is there anything he could do to change the system under which he lives?

2. Do you think Wright is justified in feeling that the whites in his environment are unable, even if they would like to, to change the racist system under which they live?
3. Wright's story suggests a question that has been central in much modern literature: Is it possible to develop social systems that will assure stability and security and at the same time encourage individual growth and change?

▶ ─────────────────────────

1   One morning I arrived early at work and went into the bank lobby where the Negro porter was mopping. I stood at a counter and picked up the Memphis *Commercial Appeal* and began my free reading of the press. I came finally to the editorial page and saw an article dealing with one H. L. Mencken. I knew by hearsay that he was the editor of the *American Mercury*, but aside from that I knew nothing about him. The article was a furious denunciation of Mencken, concluding with one, hot, short sentence: Mencken is a fool.

2   I wondered what on earth this Mencken had done to call down upon him the scorn of the South. The only people I had ever heard denounced in the South were Negroes, and this man was not a Negro. Then what ideas did Mencken hold that made a newspaper like the *Commercial Appeal* castigate him publicly? Undoubtedly he must be advocating ideas that the South did not like. Were there, then, people other than Negroes who criticized the South? I knew that during the Civil War the South had hated northern whites, but I had not encountered such hate during my life. Knowing no more of Mencken than I did at that moment, I felt a vague sympathy for him. Had not the South, which had assigned me the role of a non-man, cast at him its hardest words?

3   Now, how could I find out about this Mencken? There was a huge library near the riverfront, but I knew that Negroes were not allowed to patronize its shelves any more than they were the parks and playgrounds of the city. I had gone into the library several times to get books for the white men on the job. Which of them would now help me to get books? And how could I read them without causing concern to the white men with whom I worked? I had so far been successful in hiding my thoughts and feelings from them, but I knew that I would create hostility if I went about this business of reading in a clumsy way.

4   I weighed the personalities of the men on the job. There was Don, a Jew; but I distrusted him. His position was not much better than mine and I knew that he was uneasy and insecure; he had always treated me

in an offhand, bantering way that barely concealed his contempt. I was afraid to ask him to help me to get books; his frantic desire to demonstrate a racial solidarity with the whites against Negroes might make him betray me.

Then how about the boss? No, he was a Baptist and I had the suspicion that he would not be quite able to comprehend why a black boy would want to read Mencken. There were other white men on the job whose attitudes showed clearly that they were Kluxers or sympathizers, and they were out of the question.

There remained only one man whose attitude did not fit into an anti-Negro category, for I had heard the white men refer to him as a "Pope lover." He was an Irish Catholic and was hated by the white Southerners. I knew that he read books, because I had got him volumes from the library several times. Since he, too, was an object of hatred, I felt that he might refuse me but would hardly betray me. I hesitated, weighing and balancing the imponderable realities.

One morning I paused before the Catholic fellow's desk.

"I want to ask you a favor," I whispered to him.

"What is it?"

"I want to read. I can't get books from the library. I wonder if you'd let me use your card?"

He looked at me suspiciously.

"My card is full most of the time," he said.

"I see," I said and waited, posing my question silently.

"You're not trying to get me into trouble, are you, boy?" he asked, staring at me.

"Oh, no, sir."

"What book do you want?"

"A book by H. L. Mencken."

"Which one?"

"I don't know. Has he written more than one?"

"He has written several."

"I didn't know that."

"What makes you want to read Mencken?"

"Oh, I just saw his name in the newspaper," I said.

"It's good of you to want to read," he said. "But you ought to read the right things."

I said nothing. Would he want to supervise my reading?

"Let me think," he said. "I'll figure out something."

I turned from him and he called me back. He stared at me quizzically.

"Richard, don't mention this to the other white men," he said.

"I understand," I said. "I won't say a word."

A few days later he called me to him.

5

6

7

8

9

10

11

12

13

14

15

16

17

18

19

20

21

22

23

24

25

26

27

28

29

30

31   "I've got a card in my wife's name," he said. "Here's mine."

32   "Thank you, sir."

33   "Do you think you can manage it?"

34   "I'll manage fine," I said.

35   "If they suspect you, you'll get in trouble," he said.

36   "I'll write the same kind of notes to the library that you wrote when you sent me for books," I told him. "I'll sign your name."

37   He laughed.

38   "Go ahead. Let me see what you get," he said.

39   That afternoon I addressed myself to forging a note. Now, what were the names of books written by H. L. Mencken? I did not know any of them. I finally wrote what I thought would be a foolproof note: *Dear Madam: Will you please let this nigger boy*—I used the word "nigger" to make the librarian feel that I could not possibly be the author of the note—*have some books by H. L. Mencken?* I forged the white man's name.

40   I entered the library as I had always done when on errands for whites, but I felt that I would somehow slip up and betray myself. I doffed my hat, stood a respectful distance from the desk, looked as unbookish as possible, and waited for the white patrons to be taken care of. When the desk was clear of people, I still waited. The white librarian looked at me.

41   "What do you want, boy?"

42   As though I did not possess the power of speech, I stepped forward and simply handed her the forged note, not parting my lips.

43   "What books by Mencken does he want?" she asked.

44   "I don't know, ma'am," I said, avoiding her eyes.

45   "Who gave you this card?"

46   "Mr. Falk," I said.

47   "Where is he?"

48   "He's at work, at the M———Optical Company," I said. "I've been in here for him before."

49   "I remember," the woman said. "But he never wrote notes like this."

50   Oh, God, she's suspicious. Perhaps she would not let me have the books? If she had turned her back at that moment, I would have ducked out the door and never gone back. Then I thought of a bold idea.

51   "You can call him up, ma'am," I said, my heart pounding.

52   "You're not using these books, are you?" she asked pointedly.

53   "Oh, no, ma'am. I can't read."

54   "I don't know what he wants by Mencken," she said under her breath.

55   I knew now that I had won; she was thinking of other things and the race question had gone out of her mind. She went to the shelves. Once

or twice she looked over her shoulder at me, as though she was still doubtful. Finally she came forward with two books in her hand.

"I'm sending him two books," she said. "But tell Mr. Falk to come   *56* in next time, or send me the names of the books he wants. I don't know what he wants to read."

I said nothing. She stamped the card and handed me the books. Not   *57* daring to glance at them, I went out of the library, fearing that the woman would call me back for further questioning. A block away from the library I opened one of the books and read a title: *A Book of Prefaces.* I was nearing my nineteenth birthday and I did not know how to pronounce the word "preface." I thumbed the pages and saw strange words and strange names. I shook my head, disappointed. I looked at the other book; it was called *Prejudices.* I knew what that word meant; I had heard it all my life. And right off I was on guard against Mencken's books. Why would a man want to call a book *Prejudices?* The word was so stained with all my memories of racial hate that I could not conceive of anybody using it for a title. Perhaps I had made a mistake about Mencken? A man who had prejudices must be wrong.

When I showed the books to Mr. Falk, he looked at me and frowned.   *58*

"That librarian might telephone you," I warned him.   *59*

"That's all right," he said. "But when you're through reading those   *60* books, I want you to tell me what you get out of them."

That night in my rented room, while letting the hot water run over   *61* my can of pork and beans in the sink, I opened *A Book of Prefaces* and began to read. I was jarred and shocked by the style, the clear, clean, sweeping sentences. Why did he write like that? And how did one write like that? I pictured the man as a raging demon, slashing with his pen, consumed with hate, denouncing everything American, extolling everything European or German, laughing at the weaknesses of people, mocking God, authority. What was this? I stood up, trying to realize what reality lay behind the meaning of the words . . . Yes, this man was fighting, fighting with words. He was using words as a weapon, using them as one would use a club. Could words be weapons? Well, yes, for here they were. Then, maybe, perhaps, I could use them as a weapon? No. It frightened me. I read on and what amazed me was not what he said, but how on earth anybody had the courage to say it.

Occasionally I glanced up to reassure myself that I was alone in the   *62* room. Who were these men about whom Mencken was talking so passionately? Who was Anatole France? Joseph Conrad? Sinclair Lewis, Sherwood Anderson, Dostoevski, George Moore, Gustave Flaubert, Maupassant, Tolstoy, Frank Harris, Mark Twain, Thomas Hardy, Arnold Bennett, Stephen Crane, Zola, Norris, Gorky, Bergson, Ibsen, Balzac, Bernard Shaw, Dumas, Poe, Thomas Mann, O. Henry, Dreiser, H. G. Wells, Gogol, T. S. Eliot, Gide, Baudelaire, Edgar Lee Masters,

Stendhal, Turgenev, Huneker, Nietzsche, and scores of others? Were these men real? Did they exist or had they existed? And how did one pronounce their names?

63   I ran across many words whose meanings I did not know, and I either looked them up in a dictionary or, before I had a chance to do that, encountered the word in a context that made its meaning clear. But what strange world was this? I concluded the book with the conviction that I had somehow overlooked something terribly important in life. I had once tried to write, had once reveled in feeling, had let my crude imagination roam, but the impulse to dream had been slowly beaten out of me by experience. Now it surged up again and I hungered for books, new ways of looking and seeing. It was not a matter of believing or disbelieving what I read, but of feeling something new, of being affected by something that made the look of the world different.

64   As dawn broke I ate my pork and beans, feeling dopey, sleepy. I went to work, but the mood of the book would not die; it lingered, coloring everything I saw, heard, did. I now felt that I knew what the white men were feeling. Merely because I had read a book that had spoken of how they lived and thought, I identified myself with that book. I felt vaguely guilty. Would I, filled with bookish notions, act in a manner that would make the whites dislike me?

65   I forged more notes and my trips to the library became frequent. Reading grew into a passion. My first serious novel was Sinclair Lewis's *Main Street.** It made me see my boss, Mr. Gerald, and identify him as an American type. I would smile when I saw him lugging his golf bags into the office. I had always felt a vast distance separating me from the boss, and now I felt closer to him, though still distant. I felt now that I knew him, that I could feel the very limits of his narrow life. And this had happened because I had read a novel about a mythical man called George F. Babbitt.

66   The plots and stories in the novels did not interest me so much as the point of view revealed. I gave myself over to each novel without reserve, without trying to criticize it; it was enough for me to see and feel something different. And for me, everything was something different. Reading was like a drug, a dope. The novels created moods in which I lived for days. But I could not conquer my sense of guilt, my feeling that the white men around me knew that I was changing, that I had begun to regard them differently.

*Sinclair Lewis (1885–1951) was a famous American writer of realistic fiction. *Babbitt* (1922) satirized the business values of its main character, George F. Babbitt. *Main Street* (1920) satirized small-town midwestern life. Lewis won the Nobel Prize for literature in 1930, the first American novelist so honored.

Whenever I brought a book to the job, I wrapped it in newspaper—a 67
habit that was to persist for years in other cities and under other circumstances. But some of the white men pried into my package when I was
absent and they questioned me.

"Boy, what are you reading those books for?" 68

"Oh, I don't know, sir." 69

"That's deep stuff you're reading, boy." 70

"I'm just killing time, sir." 71

"You'll addle your brains if you don't watch out." 72

I read Dreiser's *Jennie Gerhardt* and *Sister Carrie** and they revived 73
in me a vivid sense of my mother's suffering; I was overwhelmed. I grew
silent, wondering about the life around me. It would have been impossible for me to have told anyone what I derived from these novels, for it
was nothing less than a sense of life itself. All my life had shaped me for
the realism, the naturalism of the modern novel, and I could not read
enough of them.

Steeped in new moods and ideas, I bought a ream of paper and tried to 74
write; but nothing would come, or what did come was flat beyond telling. I discovered that more than desire and feeling were necessary to
write and I dropped the idea. Yet I still wondered how it was possible to
know people sufficiently to write about them? Could I ever learn about
life and people? To me, with my vast ignorance, my Jim Crow station in
life, it seemed a task impossible of achievement. I now knew what
being a Negro meant. I could endure the hunger. I had learned to live
with hate. But to feel that there were feelings denied me, that the very
breath of life itself was beyond my reach, that more than anything else
hurt, wounded me. I had a new hunger.

In buoying me up, reading also cast me down, made me see what was 75
possible, what I had missed. My tension returned, new, terrible, bitter,
surging, almost too great to be contained. I no longer *felt* that the world
about me was hostile, killing; I *knew* it. A million times I asked myself
what I could do to save myself, and there were no answers. I seemed forever condemned, ringed by walls.

I did not discuss my reading with Mr. Falk, who had lent me his li- 76
brary card; it would have meant talking about myself and that would
have been too painful. I smiled each day, fighting desperately to maintain my old behavior, to keep my disposition seemingly sunny. But
some of the white men discerned that I had begun to brood.

---

*Theodore Dreiser (1871–1945) was an important and popular realistic American
novelist. *Jennie Gerhardt* (1911) was his first successful novel. *Sister Carrie* (1900), his
first novel, was suppressed because of its controversial portrayal of its heroine. Dreiser's
classic was *An American Tragedy* (1925).

77   "Wake up there, boy!" Mr. Olin said one day.

78   "Sir!" I answered for the lack of a better word.

79   "You act like you've stolen something," he said.

80   I laughed in the way I knew he expected me to laugh, but I resolved to be more conscious of myself, to watch my every act, to guard and hide the new knowledge that was dawning within me.

81   If I went north, would it be possible for me to build a new life then? But how could a man build a life upon vague, unformed yearnings? I wanted to write and I did not even know the English language. I bought English grammars and found them dull. I felt that I was getting a better sense of the language from novels than from grammars. I read hard, discarding a writer as soon as I felt that I had grasped his point of view. At night the printed page stood before my eyes in sleep.

82   Mrs. Moss, my landlady, asked me one Sunday morning:

83   "Son, what is this you keep on reading?"

84   "Oh, nothing. Just novels."

85   "What you get out of 'em?"

86   "I'm just killing time," I said.

87   "I hope you know your own mind," she said in a tone which implied that she doubted if I had a mind.

88   I knew of no Negroes who read the books I liked and I wondered if any Negroes ever thought of them. I knew that there were Negro doctors, lawyers, newspapermen, but I never saw any of them. When I read a Negro newspaper I never caught the faintest echo of my preoccupation in its pages. I felt trapped and occasionally, for a few days, I would stop reading. But a vague hunger would come over me for books, books that opened up new avenues of feeling and seeing, and again I would forge another note to the white librarian. Again I would read and wonder as only the naïve and unlettered can read and wonder, feeling that I carried a secret, criminal burden about with me each day.

89   That winter my mother and brother came and we set up housekeeping, buying furniture on the installment plan, being cheated and yet knowing no way to avoid it. I began to eat warm food and to my surprise found that regular meals enabled me to read faster. I may have lived through many illnesses and survived them, never suspecting that I was ill. My brother obtained a job and we began to save toward the trip north, plotting our time, setting tentative dates for departure. I told none of the white men on the job that I was planning to go north; I knew that the moment they felt I was thinking of the North they would change toward me. It would have made them feel that I did not like the life I was living, and because my life was completely conditioned by what they said or did, it would have been tantamount to challenging them.

I could calculate my chances for life in the South as a Negro fairly   *90*
clearly now.

I could fight the southern whites by organizing with other Negroes,   *91*
as my grandfather had done. But I knew that I could never win that way;
there were many whites and there were but few blacks. They were
strong and we were weak. Outright black rebellion could never win. If I
fought openly I would die and I did not want to die. News of lynchings
were frequent.

I could submit and live the life of a genial slave, but that was impossi-   *92*
ble. All of my life had shaped me to live by my own feelings, and
thoughts. I could make up to Bess* and marry her and inherit the house.
But that, too, would be the life of a slave; if I did that, I would crush to
death something within me, and I would hate myself as much as I knew
the whites already hated those who had submitted. Neither could I ever
willingly present myself to be kicked, as Shorty had done. I would rather have died than do that.

I could drain off my restlessness by fighting with Shorty and   *93*
Harrison. I had seen many Negroes solve the problem of being black by
transferring their hatred of themselves to others with a black skin and
fighting them. I would have to be cold to do that, and I was not cold and I
could never be.

I could, of course, forget what I had read, thrust the whites out of my   *94*
mind, forget them; and find release from anxiety and longing in sex and
alcohol. But the memory of how my father had conducted himself made
that course repugnant. If I did not want others to violate my life, how
could I voluntarily violate it myself?

I had no hope whatever of being a professional man. Not only had I   *95*
been so conditioned that I did not desire it, but the fulfillment of such
an ambition was beyond my capabilities. Well-to-do Negroes lived in a
world that was almost as alien to me as the world inhabited by whites.

What, then, was there? I held my life in my mind, in my conscious-   *96*
ness each day, feeling at times that I would stumble and drop it, spill it
forever. My reading had created a vast sense of distance between me and
the world in which I lived and tried to make a living, and that sense of
distance was increasing each day. My days and nights were one long,
quiet, continuously contained dream of terror, tension, and anxiety. I
wondered how long I could bear it.

---

*The names Bess, Shorty, and Harrison mentioned in this selection refer to important
figures in Wright's life. Bess was the girlfriend he rejected for a life as a writer. Shorty and
Harrison were childhood friends from Wright's old neighborhood.

Questions and Activities

▶ *COMPREHENSION QUESTIONS*

1. What was H. L. Mencken's general reputation as a journalist? Why did many Americans have highly emotional reactions to his articles? (You can find information on Mencken in the biographical and reference sections of any library.)
2. Why was Wright so surprised to find out that white Southerners harbored such hatred for H. L. Mencken? What had he previously assumed about whites' relations with other whites that his new knowledge of Southerners' responses to Mencken forced him to question?
3. What does reading books do for Wright's understanding of the world around him? How does it, for example, help him to understand better the white people with whom he must work and live?
4. Why does Wright try to keep secret his new experience with books? Why would this experience be threatening to many of the white people around him?

▶ *QUESTIONS OF RHETORICAL PURPOSE AND STRATEGY*

5. Why do you think Wright includes in his story the fact that he cooked his pork and beans by running hot water over the can (paragraph 61)? How does this autobiographical fact help shape your response to his character?
6. Consider the overall organization of this story. How does Wright order the actions so that they lead up to his main point? Where does he insert commentary? What effects does his commentary have on your reactions to the action and other characters?
7. Do you like the person who tells this story? How would you describe the personality of this narrator? What language devices does Wright use to create his narrative personality?

▶ *THEME QUESTIONS*

8. Do you think that books changed Wright's life? If so, do you think that this change was for the better or the worse? Does the final paragraph of this piece suggest a different type of life style for Wright from the one he had in Memphis?
9. What does Wright mean when he says in paragraph 95 that he does not want to be a professional man? What professions do you think he has in mind when he says this? Why, when Wright considers a new life, does he avoid considering professions that might bring him substantial material gain?

10. Write a personal response to one of Wright's descriptive passages. Close your free response by defining the emotion you experienced in reaction to the passage: anger, frustration, satisfaction, etc.

    Reread the entire story and reconsider your personal response to one passage in light of your reaction to the whole piece. Do you think that the response you had to a single passage is compatible with the response Wright intended you to have to the whole piece?

11. Reread the headnote that precedes Wright's story. Select one of the facts of Wright's career and consider the relevance of the experience related in this story to that fact. In other words, did Wright's experience in the library in Memphis seem to influence his career, or did his reading of Mencken set him off in a particular direction as a writer, or did his relations with whites on his job in Memphis affect his treatment of whites in his writing? Report the results of this activity to the rest of the class.

Writing Assignments

THE SELF VERSUS THE MASS

Write an essay in which you apply to yourself one of the three ideas Carol Bly chose for keeping "the self from succumbing to the mass state" (page 594, paragraph 4). How would the idea affect your everyday behavior, your relations with others, your daily schedule? Would the application of this idea cause you to be more responsive than usual to political and social concerns?

THE CHANGE TO COLLEGE

Write an essay addressed to college students in which you define several important ways in which individuals change when they go from high school or job to college. Your essay should reflect the influence of at least three of the selections from this section. Your purpose in this writing is to explain important patterns of change that are commonly experienced by new college students, so that your readers will better understand the changes going on in their lives.

You should do this assignment in three stages. First, write a brief sketch of a personal experience that demonstrates one or more of the types of change that are commonly experienced by first-year college students. This draft should be a narrative, with careful attention given to concrete detail and well-developed action. In this narrative draft, let the story itself make your point.

In a second draft, use your first draft as the basis for an informative essay. To accomplish this transition from a descriptive and narrative sketch to a more formal informative essay, you will need to summarize your personal experience and relate it more directly to the central point. You will need to keep in mind the following question: "Why have I described this experience for this audience?"

Your third draft should be an expanded version of the second in which you make the connections between your narrative material and your central point about the changes of the first year of college pointedly clear to your audience. As you write this third and final draft, you'll need to consider questions such as the following:

1. Am I providing sufficient context for my readers to understand why I am writing this essay in the first place? (Context is any background information that a reader might require to interpret what he or she is reading.)

2. Do I begin the essay in a way that will be interesting to my audience?
3. Will my readers understand the significance of each part of my experience?
4. Will my readers follow my transitions from specific descriptions to general points about change in the first year of college?
5. Are my ideas on change in the first year of college organized into patterns that my readers will understand?
6. Do I close my essay in a way that makes my central point perfectly clear?

How Should We Use Power?

▶ ——————————————————————————————

Introduction

▶ ────────────────────────

The essays in this section revolve around two axes: the personal and the public. One group of essays looks at the personal effects of power. Barbara Grizutti Harrison describes the effects of a particular consciousness-raising movement, est, on the individuals who enroll in its courses. In the process, she argues against the misuse of power that can take place when a well-organized group takes in vulnerable individuals. Margaret Walker describes how being born black and female has led her as a writer to look at the world, how that world treats her as a black woman and a writer, and the results produced by this tension between social context and individual condition. N. Scott Momaday gives a complex portrait of two American Indians separated from their tribe and land and unsuccessfully struggling in an alien society with mixed rules and often hidden values. Momaday suggests that this problem is more acute than in the past due to the existence of large, impersonal cities that often threaten to swallow individuals who come there seeking work.

The essays by George Orwell, Jan Morris, John Jay and Alexander Hamilton, and Gerard Piel provide analyses and commentary on the public use and function of power. Orwell and Morris look closely at the experiences of individuals confronted by political power. Orwell recounts his experience as a representative of the British government in Burma; ironically, he finds that, as a member of the ruling class, he is forced into public displays of power by those he supposedly rules. Reading Orwell's essay helps us understand that those who set themselves up to rule over people of a different culture have to rule, to some degree, by overt physical force rather than by the power of commonly held values and traditions. Jan Morris surveys official Washington with wit and understanding from her perspective as a British visitor and journalist. She focuses on the scenes and customs of explicit political situations, where, in one sense, everyone is trying to find the most effective ways to gain access to power. Washington, Morris suggests, is controlled by this overt sense of a political power struggle. Morris herself seems half dazzled and half alienated by what she sees and hears in Washington.

The essays by John Jay and Alexander Hamilton as well as that by Gerard Piel offer more abstract and systematic accounts of how power is part of our political and economic institutions. They locate the causes and effects of power in abstract documents such as the United States Constitution, and in machines such as the computer, rather than in people. In 1787, when the United States was still a loose confederation, the air was filled with arguments for and against strong federal government. Both Jay and Hamilton believed in the necessity for a strong federal government to offset the threat of foreign invasion or interference, to build up a national treasury, and to settle territorial disputes between states. Hamilton goes further than Jay in describing the means such a federal government might use to ensure the public's trust in its elected officials. Piel's essay is an objective, scientific analysis of the effects twentieth-century technology has had on economic power structures, particularly in labor and business. Piel is far more interested in how economic and technological systems function than in the immediate effects of those systems on individuals. He does close his essay, however, with a moral evaluation of the general economic conditions that have been created by the computer and its related technology.

As you read these essays, you will want to explore how these varying perspectives on the uses and effects of power can be integrated with your own ideas and experiences. Consider this sequence of questions as you develop your response to the question of how we should use power:

1. What types of social conditions encourage individuals to feel they have some form of personal power in their everyday lives?
2. When do individuals have too much power?
3. What happens when a social system makes it difficult for a large number of people to have or use power?
4. What types of power does a strong central government hold? How are those types of power different from the types of power held by individuals?
5. Who in a society should determine the existence and limits of the power of nonhuman agents such as computers and other technical tools? Should individuals adapt themselves to these tools, or should the tools be adapted to them?
6. Must power corrupt?
7. How is power used well? What concerns does the leader who uses power well have?

8. How can a society balance an individual's sense of civil or political power with his or her sense of personal power, as derived from religion or literature? When does personal power interfere unjustly with political processes or civil rights?
9. Is separation of individual and social contexts always a good thing?
10. Should a person's productive potential define the power he or she has in a social context?

Shooting an Elephant

George Orwell

George Orwell, whose real name was Eric Arthur Blair, was born in Bengal, India, in 1903 and died in London in 1950. After being educated in England, Orwell went to Burma to work as a British official in the imperial police. He was never able to adapt successfully to his role as an enforcer of British rule in a foreign land, in which he was called upon to regulate the lives of people whose culture he didn't completely understand. After five difficult years, he returned to England, where for several years he lived in poverty. He began at this point in his life to publish both personal and journalistic accounts of his responses to social institutions and political organizations and their effects on the people they controlled.

All of Orwell's major writings had social purposes. In his earlier works, including *The Road to Wigan Pier* (1937), he recorded his observations of the working classes and of the subjects of imperial governments, such as that in India. Orwell consistently espoused a socialistic middle ground between the extremes of pure democracy, which he thought encouraged too much individualism and insufficient social consciousness, and pure totalitarianism, including Russian communism, which he thought repressive and materialistic. Orwell is now best known for his two political novels, *Animal Farm* (1945) and *Nineteen Eighty-Four* (1949), in which he bitterly criticized the insensitivity and authoritarianism of rigid totalitarian governments.

In the essay included here, Orwell uses an experience with the Burmese to explain his negative response to British imperialism. Orwell, as narrator, looks back at a particular past experience, retelling it from a later vantage point, and turns it into a message opposing all forms of rule in which a more powerful group of people governs a larger group who are less powerful. Orwell skillfully mixes personal narrative and social commentary; note how his generalizations about the meaning of his experience grow naturally out of his narration of the events.

Orwell directs his attention to the possibilities for abusing power that are inherent in certain authoritarian forms of government. As you read, you will be able to get more out of Orwell's interpretation if you consider these questions:

1. What type of language does the narrator use in describing the Burmese? Is he condescending, patronizing, or sympathetic?
2. What type of reader did Orwell assume for this essay? How much does that reader know about Burma, about British rule in the empire,

about social conditions in the world in general? What in the language of the essay influences your answers to these questions?

3. When you finish reading paragraph 1, characterize the narrator. What type of person do you think he is? Is he different from the person who wrote the essay? How is he different?

▶ ───────────────────

In Moulmein, in lower Burma, I was hated by large numbers of people—the only time in my life that I have been important enough for this to happen to me. I was sub-divisional police officer of the town, and in an aimless, petty kind of way anti-European feeling was very bitter. No one had the guts to raise a riot, but if a European woman went through the bazaars alone somebody would probably spit betel juice over her dress. As a police officer I was an obvious target and was baited whenever it seemed safe to do so. When a nimble Burman tripped me up on the football field and the referee (another Burman) looked the other way, the crowd yelled with hideous laughter. This happened more than once. In the end the sneering yellow faces of young men that met me everywhere, the insults hooted after me when I was at a safe distance, got badly on my nerves. The young Buddhist priests were the worst of all. There were several thousands of them in the town and none of them seemed to have anything to do except stand on street corners and jeer at Europeans. 1

All this was perplexing and upsetting. For at that time I had already made up my mind that imperialism was an evil thing and the sooner I chucked up my job and got out of it the better. Theoretically—and secretly, of course—I was all for the Burmese and all against their oppressors, the British. As for the job I was doing, I hated it more bitterly than I can perhaps make clear. In a job like that you see the dirty work of Empire at close quarters. The wretched prisoners huddling in the stinking cages of the lock-ups, the grey, cowed faces of the long-term convicts, the scarred buttocks of the men who had been flogged with bamboos—all these oppressed me with an intolerable sense of guilt. But I could get nothing into perspective. I was young and ill-educated and I had had to think out my problems in the utter silence that is imposed on every Englishman in the East. I did not even know that the British Empire is dying, still less did I know that it is a great deal better than the younger empires that are going to supplant it. All I knew was that I was stuck between my hatred of the empire I served and my rage against the evil-spirited little beasts who tried to make my job impossible. With one part of my mind I thought of the British Raj as an unbreakable 2

tyranny, as something clamped down, in *saecula saeculorum,** upon
the will of prostrate peoples; with another part I thought that the
greatest joy in the world would be to drive a bayonet into a Buddhist
priest's guts. Feelings like these are the normal by-products of imperialism; ask any Anglo-Indian official, if you can catch him off duty.

3   One day something happened which in a roundabout way was enlightening. It was a tiny incident in itself, but it gave me a better
glimpse than I had had before of the real nature of imperialism—the real
motives for which despotic governments act. Early one morning the
sub-inspector at a police station the other end of the town rang me up on
the 'phone and said that an elephant was ravaging the bazaar. Would I
please come and do something about it? I did not know what I could do,
but I wanted to see what was happening and I got on to a pony and
started out. I took my rifle, an old .44 Winchester and much too small to
kill an elephant, but I thought the noise might be useful *in terrorem.*†
Various Burmans stopped me on the way and told me about the
elephant's doings. It was not, of course, a wild elephant, but a tame one
which had gone "must."‡ It had been chained up, as tame elephants always are when their attack of "must" is due, but on the previous night
it had broken its chain and escaped. Its mahout, the only person who
could manage it when it was in that state, had set out in pursuit, but
had taken the wrong direction and was now twelve hours' journey
away, and in the morning the elephant had suddenly reappeared in the
town. The Burmese population had no weapons and were quite helpless
against it. It had already destroyed somebody's bamboo hut, killed a
cow and raided some fruit-stalls and devoured the stock; also it had met
the municipal rubbish van and, when the driver jumped out and took to
his heels, had turned the van over and inflicted violences upon it.

4   The Burmese sub-inspector and some Indian constables were waiting
for me in the quarter where the elephant had been seen. It was a very
poor quarter, a labyrinth of squalid bamboo huts, thatched with palm-
leaf, winding all over a steep hillside. I remember that it was a cloudy,
stuffy morning at the beginning of the rains. We began questioning the
people as to where the elephant had gone and, as usual, failed to get any
definite information. That is invariably the case in the East; a story always sounds clear enough at a distance, but the nearer you get to the
scene of events the vaguer it becomes. Some of the people said that the
elephant had gone in one direction, some said that he had gone in another, some professed not even to have heard of any elephant. I had almost

---

*Loosely translated from Latin, this phrase means "in the spirit of the times."
†This phrase is Latin for "during a time of terror."
‡"Must" is an Indian term for a periodic frenzy of bull elephants during the mating
season.

made up my mind that the whole story was a pack of lies, when we heard yells a little distance away. There was a loud, scandalized cry of "Go away, child! Go away this instant!" and an old woman with a switch in her hand came round the corner of a hut, violently shooing away a crowd of naked children. Some more women followed, clicking their tongues and exclaiming; evidently there was something that the children ought not to have seen. I rounded the hut and saw a man's dead body sprawling in the mud. He was an Indian, a black Dravidian coolie, almost naked, and he could not have been dead many minutes. The people said that the elephant had come suddenly upon him round the corner of the hut, caught him with its trunk, put its foot on his back and ground him into the earth. This was the rainy season and the ground was soft, and his face had scored a trench a foot deep and a couple of yards long. He was lying on his belly with arms crucified and head sharply twisted to one side. His face was coated with mud, the eyes wide open, the teeth bared and grinning with an expression of unendurable agony. (Never tell me, by the way, that the dead look peaceful. Most of the corpses I have seen looked devilish.) The friction of the great beast's foot had stripped the skin from his back as neatly as one skins a rabbit. As soon as I saw the dead man I sent an orderly to a friend's house nearby to borrow an elephant rifle. I had already sent back the pony, not wanting it to go mad with fright and throw me if it smelt the elephant.

The orderly came back in a few minutes with a rifle and five cartridges, and meanwhile some Burmans had arrived and told us that the elephant was in the paddy fields below, only a few hundred yards away. As I started forward practically the whole population of the quarter flocked out of the houses and followed me. They had seen the rifle and were all shouting excitedly that I was going to shoot the elephant. They had not shown much interest in the elephant when he was merely ravaging their homes, but it was different now that he was going to be shot. It was a bit of fun to them, as it would be to an English crowd; besides they wanted the meat. It made me vaguely uneasy. I had no intention of shooting the elephant—I had merely sent for the rifle to defend myself if necessary—and it is always unnerving to have a crowd following you. I marched down the hill, looking and feeling a fool, with the rifle over my shoulder and an ever-growing army of people jostling at my heels. At the bottom, when you got away from the huts, there was a metalled road and beyond that a miry waste of paddy fields a thousand yards across, not yet ploughed but soggy from the first rains and dotted with coarse grass. The elephant was standing eight yards from the road, his left side towards us. He took not the slightest notice of the crowd's approach. He was tearing up bunches of grass, beating them against his knees to clean them and stuffing them into his mouth.

6   I had halted on the road. As soon as I saw the elephant I knew with perfect certainty that I ought not to shoot him. It is a serious matter to shoot a working elephant—it is comparable to destroying a huge and costly piece of machinery—and obviously one ought not to do it if it can possibly be avoided. And at that distance, peacefully eating, the elephant looked no more dangerous than a cow. I thought then and I think now that his attack of "must" was already passing off; in which case he would merely wander harmlessly about until the mahout came back and caught him. Moreover, I did not in the least want to shoot him. I decided that I would watch him for a little while to make sure that he did not turn savage again, and then go home.

7   But at that moment I glanced round at the crowd that had followed me. It was an immense crowd, two thousand at the least and growing every minute. It blocked the road for a long distance on either side. I looked at the sea of yellow faces above the garish clothes—faces all happy and excited over this bit of fun, all certain that the elephant was going to be shot. They were watching me as they would watch a conjurer about to perform a trick. They did not like me, but with the magical rifle in my hands I was momentarily worth watching. And suddenly I realized that I should have to shoot the elephant after all. The people expected it of me and I had got to do it; I could feel their two thousand wills pressing me forward, irresistibly. And it was at this moment, as I stood there with the rifle in my hands, that I first grasped the hollowness, the futility of the white man's dominion in the East. Here was I, the white man with his gun, standing in front of the unarmed native crowd—seemingly the leading actor of the piece; but in reality I was only an absurd puppet pushed to and fro by the will of those yellow faces behind. I perceived in this moment that when the white man turns tyrant it is his own freedom that he destroys. He becomes a sort of hollow, posing dummy, the conventionalized figure of a sahib. For it is the condition of his rule that he shall spend his life in trying to impress the "natives," and so in every crisis he has got to do what the "natives" expect of him. He wears a mask, and his face grows to fit it. I had got to shoot the elephant. I had committed myself to doing it when I sent for the rifle. A sahib has got to act like a sahib; he has got to appear resolute, to know his own mind and do definite things. To come all that way, rifle in hand, with two thousand people marching at my heels, and then to trail feebly away, having done nothing—no, that was impossible. The crowd would laugh at me. And my whole life, every white man's life in the East, was one long struggle not to be laughed at.

8   But I did not want to shoot the elephant. I watched him beating his bunch of grass against his knees, with that preoccupied grandmotherly air that elephants have. It seemed to me that it would be murder to

shoot him. At that age I was not squeamish about killing animals, but I had never shot an elephant and never wanted to. (Somehow it always seems worse to kill a *large* animal.) Besides, there was the beast's owner to be considered. Alive, the elephant was worth at least a hundred pounds; dead, he would only be worth the value of his tusks, five pounds, possibly. But I had got to ack quickly. I turned to some experienced-looking Burmans who had been there when we arrived, and asked them how the elephant had been behaving. They all said the same thing: he took no notice of you if you left him alone, but he might charge if you went too close to him.

It was perfectly clear to me what I ought to do. I ought to walk up to   9
within, say, twenty-five yards of the elephant and test his behavior. If he charged, I could shoot; if he took no notice of me, it would be safe to leave him until the mahout came back. But also I knew that I was going to do no such thing. I was a poor shot with a rifle and the ground was soft mud into which one would sink at every step. If the elephant charged and I missed him, I should have about as much chance as a toad under a steam-roller. But even then I was not thinking particularly of my own skin, only of the watchful yellow faces behind. For at that moment, with the crowd watching me, I was not afraid in the ordinary sense, as I would have been if I had been alone. A white man mustn't be frightened in front of "natives"; and so, in general, he isn't frightened. The sole thought in my mind was that if anything went wrong those two thousand Burmans would see me pursued, caught, trampled on and reduced to a grinning corpse like that Indian up the hill. And if that happened it was quite probable that some of them would laugh. That would never do. There was only one alternative. I shoved the cartridges into the magazine and lay down on the road to get a better aim.

The crowd grew very still, and a deep, low, happy sigh, as of people   10
who see the theatre curtain go up at last, breathed from innumerable throats. They were going to have their bit of fun after all. The rifle was a beautiful German thing with cross-hair sights. I did not then know that in shooting an elephant one would shoot to cut an imaginary bar running from ear-hole to ear-hole. I ought, therefore, as the elephant was sideways on, to have aimed straight at his ear-hole; actually I aimed several inches in front of this, thinking the brain would be further forward.

When I pulled the trigger I did not hear the bang or feel the kick—one   11
never does when a shot goes home—but I heard the devilish roar of glee that went up from the crowd. In that instant, in too short a time, one would have thought, even for the bullet to get there, a mysterious, terrible change had come over the elephant. He neither stirred nor fell, but every line of his body had altered. He looked suddenly stricken, shrunk-

en, immensely old, as though the frightful impact of the bullet had paralysed him without knocking him down. At last, after what seemed a long time—it might have been five seconds, I dare say—he sagged flabbily to his knees. His mouth slobbered. An enormous senility seemed to have settled upon him. One could have imagined him thousands of years old. I fired again into the same spot. At the second shot he did not collapse but climbed with desperate slowness to his feet and stood weakly upright, with legs sagging and head drooping. I fired a third time. That was the shot that did for him. You could see the agony of it jolt his whole body and knock the last remnant of strength from his legs. But in falling he seemed for a moment to rise, for as his hind legs collapsed beneath him he seemed to tower upward like a huge rock toppling, his trunk reaching skywards like a tree. He trumpeted, for the first and only time. And then down he came, his belly towards me, with a crash that seemed to shake the ground even where I lay.

12   I got up. The Burmans were already racing past me across the mud. It was obvious that the elephant would never rise again, but he was not dead. He was breathing very rhythmically with long rattling gasps, his great mound of a side painfully rising and falling. His mouth was wide open—I could see far down into caverns of pale pink throat. I waited a long time for him to die, but his breathing did not weaken. Finally I fired my two remaining shots into the spot where I thought his heart must be. The thick blood welled out of him like red velvet, but still he did not die. His body did not even jerk when the shots hit him, the tortured breathing continued without a pause. He was dying, very slowly and in great agony, but in some world remote from me where not even a bullet could damage him further. I felt that I had got to put an end to that dreadful noise. It seemed dreadful to see the great beast lying there, powerless to move and yet powerless to die, and not even to be able to finish him. I sent back for my small rifle and poured shot after shot into his heart and down his throat. They seemed to make no impression. The tortured gasps continued as steadily as the ticking of a clock.

13   In the end I could not stand it any longer and went away. I heard later that it took him half an hour to die. Burmans were bringing dahs and baskets even before I left, and I was told they had stripped his body almost to the bones by the afternoon.

14   Afterwards, of course, there were endless discussions about the shooting of the elephant. The owner was furious, but he was only an Indian and could do nothing. Besides, legally I had done the right thing, for a mad elephant has to be killed, like a mad dog, if its owner fails to control it. Among the Europeans opinion was divided. The older men

said I was right, the younger men said it was a damn shame to shoot an elephant for killing a coolie, because an elephant was worth more than any damn Coringhee coolie. And afterwards I was very glad that the coolie had been killed; it put me legally in the right and it gave me a sufficient pretext for shooting the elephant. I often wondered whether any of the others grasped that I had done it solely to avoid looking a fool.

Questions and Activities

▶ *COMPREHENSION QUESTIONS*

1. In what way might Orwell have been a fool in acting as he did in this incident? To whom might he have looked foolish if he had not shot the elephant?
2. Why was Orwell hated by "large numbers of people" (paragraph 1) in Burma? Did he do anything himself to warrant this hatred? What did his role as a British official have to do with this hatred? What particular groups hated him?
3. Why did Orwell have such a difficult time getting the facts of the elephant's rampage straight (paragraph 4)? How was this difficulty symptomatic of the relations between the Burmese and British?

▶ *QUESTIONS OF RHETORICAL PURPOSE AND STRATEGY*

4. Why does Orwell use the word "grandmotherly" to describe the elephant in paragraph 8? Does this make the subsequent event more ironic than it might otherwise be?
5. Describe the way in which this story is told. How is the narrator of the story different from the person who wrote it down? What are the physical and intellectual differences between the narrator and the author? Look at the first paragraph. What tense does the narrator use? Does it suggest an older narrator who is looking back at a past experience? How does this narrator's language reveal his attitude toward the story he is telling?
6. What is the effect of Orwell's use of the past tense on your reaction to this essay? What might have been gained or lost by use of the present tense?
7. Why do you think that this piece is generally classified as an essay rather than as fiction? What particular rhetorical qualities make this an essay and not a short story?

► *THEME QUESTIONS*

8. What point does Orwell wish to make about imperialistic governments? Why does he think they are doomed to fail even if the people who govern are well intentioned and basically decent?
9. Who really held the power in the situation described in this piece,
   the ruler or the ruled? Why do you feel that power was situated
   there? What do your answers to these questions suggest about the
   conditions under which governments use power?
10. Do you think it is true that Orwell's lack of knowledge of the cul-
    ture—the customs and values—of the Burmese eroded his power in
    this situation? Why might that be the case?

► *LEARNING ACTIVITIES*

11. Choose an example of a system of human relationships that is
    obviously based on power. (You might consider your church,
    school, job, or family.) Think about how power is distributed and
    justified in this system. Then write a narrative in which you describe
    a single interaction between two individuals within this power struc-
    ture.
12. Discuss your narrative describing a power-related interaction with
    others in your class. Take notes on your classmates' analyses. Then
    write an analysis of the power structure represented in your narra-
    tive. Who holds the power and why? What is the source of that
    power? Do you think the rules constraining the participants in the
    situation that you describe are fairly and consistently applied?

The Computer as Sorcerer's Apprentice

GERARD PIEL

Gerard Piel is best known as the founder (in 1948) and publisher of *Scientific American*. After working in the editorial offices of *Life* and *Time* magazines, and as an assistant to the president at Henry J. Kaiser Company, he started *Scientific American* as a periodical for the reader who was capable of entering into an educated but nonspecialized dialogue about recent scientific advancements. Over the years, Piel has developed the magazine into a highly respected forum for essays on the social significance of current scientific research and for lucid explanations of complex scientific theories. For his work in forwarding the public's understanding of science through *Scientific American,* Piel has received many honors, including twelve honorary doctorates from universities and colleges, the Rosenberger Medal from the University of Chicago, and the George K. Polk Award for excellence in journalism. Piel has also written two books, *Science in the Cause of Man* (1962) and *The Acceleration of History* (1972).

In "The Computer as Sorcerer's Apprentice," first published in 1966, Piel judges the future using an analysis of the past and present. Piel focuses on the computer's effect of accelerating the transformation of the United States from a labor to a management society. The computer, Piel argues, integrates the gains in production of different parts of the economy and provides the means to consolidate these gains more rapidly. Through the use of the computer, more goods are made available to more people in less time. The result is a decrease in blue-collar employment and a corresponding expansion of the service and white-collar areas of the economy. The United States is becoming less a working and more a managing, serving, and distributing society.

Piel's essay makes a pointed contrast with George Orwell's (pages 646–654). Orwell sees power in human terms; Piel, in theoretical and technical terms. For Piel, human beings are snared in a network of impersonal scientific and economic forces that must be seen, at least partially, as inevitable and separate from human interaction. Only after these processes have been analyzed and understood can human beings adapt their actions to them. Like most scientists, Piel assumes an impersonal world, run by principles that have little to do with human causation or motivation. Power, for the objective social scientist, lies in understanding how technology shapes social conditions. Only with that understanding can human action be directed toward changing existing conditions.

Consider Piel's overall perspective. He writes in the voice of a scientific analyzer of economic and social patterns. As you read, think about these questions:

1. What gives Piel's essay its emphasis on objective analysis? (Note his uses of statistics and logic.)
2. At what points does this essay move into moral considerations? What relationship do these concerns with values have to Piel's more objective discussion of economic theory?
3. At the close of this essay, Piel argues that social, technological, and economic forces are "manmade" and can be changed by the force of "human will." Does this position conflict with his earlier description of how economic and technical systems control our lives? Or is that control the result of our ignorance of how these systems work? Could a more educated and motivated populace alter these systems and their effects?

▶ ─────────────────────────

1   The computer is the engine of this latest phase in the acceleration of the industrial revolution. The role of the computer cannot be measured in the simple terms of the number of computers at work in the American economy or even in the extraordinary variety of functions in which the computer has found work to do—from accounting routines to industrial process control to creative enterprise in mathematics itself. More significantly, computer technology gathers in and brings to intense focus the most diverse discoveries on the frontiers of knowledge—from investigation into the nature of matter to speculations at the foundation of knowledge. It is the agency through which the advance of human understanding now finds its way to the control of natural forces in time intervals that grow shorter year by year and month by month.

2   Because the time lag between invention and application now diminishes so swiftly, it becomes possible—and necessary—to forecast the ethical, social and economic implications of this development. Today in our country and in certain other industrial nations, men are compelled to recognize and give assent to a profound transformation in human values. Technological change has already largely eliminated people from production; it has sundered the hitherto socially essential connection of work to consumption. The citizens and the institutions

of these nations must accommodate themselves to the law of material abundance: each individual can secure increase in his own well-being only through action that secures increase in the well-being of others.

This novel dispensation stands in contrast to the law of scarcity   3
which, in the words of Alexander Herzen (1812–1870), declares: "Slavery is the first step toward civilization. In order to develop, it is necessary that things should be much better for some and much worse for others; then those who are better off can develop at the expense of the others."

The iron law of scarcity underlies the ethical dilemma of political   4
economy which has sought for nearly three centuries to discover or to rationalize equity in social institutions long ago designed to secure the inequitable distribution of goods in scarce supply. Adam Smith, the first great systematizer of economic theory, was foremost a moral philosopher. In his *Theory of Moral Sentiments*, published in 1759 and the work which brought him his principal contemporary fame, he traced the roots of moral action to the "passion of sympathy"—"which leads us into the situations of other men and to partake with them in the passions which those situations have a tendency to excite." It was later, in the *Wealth of Nations* published in 1776, that he undertook to explore "those political regulations which are founded, not upon the principles of justice, but that of expediency, and which are calculated to increase the riches, the power and the property of the state." Against the princely mercantilism of the autocratic continental powers, Smith asserted the labor theory of value: "Labour is the real measure of the exchangeable value of all commodities . . . Equal quantities of labour at all times and places are of equal value to the labourer . . . Labour alone, therefore, never varying in its own value, is alone the ultimate and real standard by which the value of all commodities can at all times and places be estimated and compared." In the free play of supply and demand in the open market, the products of human labor found the just and equitable price at which they were to be exchanged. In the market labor, itself a commodity in consequence of the division of labor, also found its fair price. Under the sure guidance of the "invisible hand" each man could seek his private interest, confident in the knowledge that he thereby secured the public weal.

For the generations that launched the industrial revolution in 18th   5
century England, Adam Smith and his successors in political economy furnished not only the guidelines to practical action but the moral assurance necessary to the taking of action. Before the middle of the 19th century, however, it had become impossible to conceal—in the blight laid upon green England by the carboniferous phase of industrialization—the failure of their enterprise. Benjamin Jowett, Master of Balliol

and translator of Plato, spoke for the alienation of the humanities from the sciences when he said: "I have always felt a certain horror of political economists since I heard one of them say that the famine in Ireland would not kill more than a million people, and that would scarcely be enough to do much good."

6   Even as Jowett wrote, the first phase of the industrial revolution had made such computations obsolete as well as patently immoral. In 1864, the year of the Emancipation Proclamation, mechanical horsepower generated by steam engines in the U.S. economy exceeded for the first time the output of biological horsepower by horses and men. As early as 1900, only 75 per cent of the U.S. labor force was employed as "producers of goods"; more than half of these producers were engaged in farming and the next largest percentage in unskilled labor functions. By 1960, human muscle had been all but eliminated from the production process. The census for that year shows that less than half (46 per cent) of the labor force was now employed as producers of goods; farmers (7 per cent) and unskilled laborers (5 per cent) were approaching statistically negligible percentages of the labor force. More than half of the producers were classified as "operatives," that is human nervous systems still interposed in process control feedback loops not yet completely closed by electronics.

7   In the present phase of acceleration, as is well known, the industrial revolution is eliminating nervous systems from the production process. Robots—artificial sensory organs and mechanical controllers linked by feedback circuits—have been taking over from human workers in all of the fluid process industries. In at least 85 plants in the U.S., computers at the center of control networks have transformed the process streams into truly self-regulating systems. The computer and the feedback control loops have now begun a corresponding transformation of the discontinuous processes of the metalworking industry. The same revolution in technology—for example, transcontinental pipeline transportation of fluid commodities under computer and feedback-loop controls—is under way or impends in all of the production sectors of the economy.

8   During the past decade, blue-collar employment in American manufacturing has actually declined, while the output of these industries has nearly doubled. The rate of increase in productivity in the production sectors of the economy, which has averaged 5.6 per cent over the decade and has been accelerating, is grossly understated by productivity figures applied to the entire labor force. These, the figures given widest circulation, have shown an annual improvement of only about 2.5 to 3 per cent.

9   Until recently increase in employment in trade and distribution and in the services has compensated for disemployment from production.

The computer, however, finds application even more readily in the functions that employ human beings in these sectors. The "white collar" computer, equipped with a typewriter on its input and output side, is conceptually a much simpler organism than the computer equipped with sensory organs and muscles that displaces the blue collar worker. A conservatively estimated million-fold increase in the data-processing capacity of organizations equipped with computers as compared to organizations manned by human beings and assigned to comparable tasks has already been demonstrated in military command and control systems. Although computer technology has just begun to find its way into trade and distribution and the services, increase in employment in these sectors has already begun to slacken. In the private sector of the economy it now barely offsets disemployment from the production industries. During the five-year period from 1957 through 1962, the private enterprise economy generated less than 300,000 additional new jobs.

The creation of new jobs in the economy as a whole has now lagged   10
the growth of the labor force for more than a decade. This is a polite way of saying that the economy is afflicted with a constant and insidious increase in unemployment. Ever since 1952, the rate of unemployment has been larger at the peak of each ripple or boomlet in the economic cycle, and each recession has left a larger percentage of the labor force high on the beach.

Debate continues as to whether the country's rising unemployment   11
is "cyclical" or "structural". Classical economists—and nowadays Keynesian economists are "classical"—assure us that the unemployment is cyclical. They point to the history of the past 60 years in stubborn support of the thesis that the labor-saving effect of technological progress merely frees labor from one task for employment in another. It is conceded that frictions make for unemployment in this turnover of the labor force, especially when progress goes forward rapidly. But sooner or later new jobs, generated by ever greater economic activity and an ever expanding Gross National Product, soak up the unemployed. By tried and tested and now generally sanctioned counter-cyclical measures—for example, by the recent Federal tax cut—the fluctuations of the system can be damped and the peaks and valleys of unemployment smoothed out. When the Kennedy Administration took office, its official economists were arguing that unemployment at the rate of 4 per cent could be regarded as normal. Despite the tax cut and the prolongation of the present boom, unemployment now ranges above 5 per cent.

Increase in unemployment accompanying expansion of economic   12
activity would seem to indicate that a rising percentage of the unemployment is indeed structural—that people, in other words, are being

displaced from the economic system in ever larger numbers by mechanization, more specifically by the computer and its accessory and allied
technologies. Consider, for example, the computer industry itself, thus
broadly defined. If employment were to expand in any industry during
this period of intensive mechanization, one would think first of the
payroll of the industry that is doing the mechanizing. What is more, the
technology of electronics that furnishes your hardware has been notably, if paradoxically, highly labor-intensive. Until a few years ago, labor
would represent up to 60 per cent of the production cost of a piece of
electronic hardware. Engineering would constitute the major investment; materials would be a minor cost and capital equipment a negligible item on the balance sheet. In these respects electronics was like the
garment industry: a business anybody could get into, providing he had a
bright idea and could finance his payroll long enough to get his product
on the market. Within the last 10 years, as I need not tell you, electronics has gone solid state. The transistor and the micromodule are even
now yielding to the integrated circuit. With this development, acre
after acre of work benches at which housewives and high school girls
wield pliers and soldering irons have been disappearing. Labor cost is
vanishing in the economics of electronics. Material costs have now become significant; engineering and plant costs, transcendent.

13   In other words, the prevailing relationships among the factors of production in electronics are being turned 180 degrees around. With people
being exiled from the computer industry as rapidly as the computer itself is promoting the disengagement of people from jobs in other sectors
of the economy, the expansion of this industry will not generate anything approaching a corresponding buildup of its payroll.

14   It cannot be said, any longer, that the industrial revolution is the
same old story. The acceleration of technological change, driven by the
accelerating advance of human understanding, reaches to the very heart
of the institutions of our society; that is, to the value system upon
which those institutions rest.

15   The unemployment figures present a profoundly misleading measure of the degree to which our capacity to produce material abundance
has outrun the capacity of our institutions to secure the distribution of
that abundance. It must be reckoned, in the first place, that some 8 million persons are employed in the war economy and contribute nothing
whatever to the flow of material abundance from the cornucopia of our
non-military productive system. If the production workers in the war
economy are subtracted from the productive work force, then the percentage employed as producers of goods falls below 40 per cent. But this
figure still overstates the truth because most of the goods circulating in
commerce and consumed by American citizens are produced by the

very much smaller percentage of the labor force that is employed by our most efficient production organizations.

Consider, for example, our farms. Some 85 per cent of the food that moves from the farms to the markets comes from less than one million farms. And the same is true of industry. The few large and efficient corporations in each industry, with their relatively smaller payrolls, produce the overwhelming percentage of our industrial output. If a small minority of our working force is today doing most of the production then, in the future, we can expect to see an even smaller minority of our working force account for all of the production of goods in our economy. The sorcerer's apprentice has thrown the switch.* The great test of our democracy is to find ways to distribute the mounting flood of abundance.   16

Actually, by the kind of improvisations that are so characteristic of democracy, we have had some success in coping with this task starting from the turn of the century. In 1900, 40 per cent of the adults of our country were not employed; that is to say, they were either unemployed or they were not in the labor force. In those good old days, 57 per cent of the adults of the country were employed in the private sector of the economy. Our country still approximated the description it gave of itself in the Declaration of Independence, as a people engaged in the pursuit of happiness—in the pursuit of private interest, either their own or that of their employers. Only 3 per cent of the American people were on the public payroll. In 1960, the same 40 per cent of our population was not employed, either unemployed or not in the labor force. But only 40 per cent of the population was now employed in the private sector of our economy. A full 20 per cent of the American people found their employment either directly on the public payroll or indirectly through the increasingly huge expenditures of governmental agencies for the product and services of private corporations—not only in the war economy but in the construction of highways and other major public works ventures. In other words, one-third of the working force now owes its employment to public expenditure.   17

Direct employment in the public sector has been increasing at five times the rate of increase in the private sector. During the past five years the public sector generated more than a million of the less than 1.5 million new jobs in the economy. Since the Federal payroll   18

---

*"The Sorcerer's Apprentice" was originally the title of a ballad by the German poet Johann Goethe. It was set to music by Paul Dukas; Michael Fokine used Dukas's music in his ballet *The Sorcerer's Apprentice* (1959). Walt Disney Studios produced the feature film *Fantasia*, which contained an animated version of the story using Dukas's music and based on Fokine's ballet. The story is as follows: a sorcerer's apprentice, left on his own, remembers the magic words that will get objects to work for him to do his chores; however, he fails to remember the words that will stop the objects and havoc results.

remained constant during this period, this gain must be credited to state and local governments. It can be declared with pride, furthermore, that the biggest part of the gain was in the payroll of our public education system. This, in turn, may be taken as an indication of the responsiveness of our value system to the evolutionary pressure of abundance.

19   The national accounts also indicate, however, that the evolution of our social institutions is falling further and further behind the accelerating pace of technological change. It turns out that the magnificent industrial apparatus of America has been producing as much poverty as wealth. Poverty is now officially acknowledged to be the lot of at least 25 per cent of our population. Contemporary American poverty is selective, as Michael Harrington has pointed out. It tends to settle in places where it disappears from sight—hidden away geographically, for example, in Appalachia and in the central cities from which more fortunate members of our society have fled to set up their new settlements in the suburbs. In New York and Chicago, the third generation of families on relief has already begun its blighted existence.

20   Poverty is selective also with respect to age. Unemployment rates, which for the labor force as a whole are officially acknowledged to exceed 5 per cent, exceed that rate among the youth by at least twice, and among Negro youths it exceeds the rate among white youths by more than twice again. In fact, the prevailing rate of unemployment among Negro youths in the ghettoes of our central cities runs from 40 to 50 per cent. The high-school drop-out may spend five years or more in empty limbo between school and his first job. Out of such alienation of so many of our young people has come the rise in juvenile delinquency, and out of the rejection of our Negro youth came the riots in the streets of the north during the past summer. Poverty is equally selective with respect to age at the other end of life. The 40 per cent of our adult population not counted in the labor force now includes several million men and women retired to live on the pittance of monthly social security checks under contract not to seek gainful employment.

21   Such are the shameful facts that confront us in the midst of the most prolonged boom since the crash of 1929. Forecasters predict the boom will hold up well into the first quarter of the new year. Against the expectations of myself as well as a few other pessimists, the tax cut has had a strongly stimulating effect on the economic system. It has encouraged a remarkably high rate of investment by industry in new capital equipment—one-third of the investment going to modernization thereby also accelerating the rate of mechanization. Through the action of the familiar Keynesian multiplier, these expenditures on the capital investment side have helped to sustain consumer expenditures

at new highs. The argument that fiscal measures may help to reduce unemployment, therefore, finds support in the current movement of the economy. Although these measures and the prolongation of the boom have not actually reduced unemployment below the 5 per cent line, a catastrophic increase in unemployment has been forestalled.

The financial pages all agree, however, that this boom has a terminal date; most set it around the end of the first half of 1965. As the boom runs out, the application of mere counter-cyclical measures—a further cut in Federal taxes, for example—will be of no avail. At the same time, responsible citizens and public officials must face up to the question of the armaments budget. Even in advance of that distant date when we may see some substantial measure of disarmament, the military budget has got to be cut back. Our country long since acquired the capability of overkill, counting all the targets in China as well as in the U.S.S.R. Yet, with the business cycle turning downward, it will take brave men to cope with the fact that eight million jobs hang directly upon the size of the military budget. 22

Plainly, the termination of the present boom will require not a tax cut but, on the contrary, a considerable expansion in public expenditure. That expansion has got to come, moreover, in the Federal budget. It is perfectly plain that the payrolls of local governments are not equal to short run challenges; they cannot respond as flexibly and with the same massive effect as Federal expenditures can. The next Administration will be compelled to seek, therefore, a vigorous expansion in Federal expenditures on public works and public welfare. 23

I don't think I betray the security of the present Administration at this point in the national election campaign by telling you that task forces in every department in Washington are at work on the question of how to spend increased sums on non-military undertakings of the Federal Government. The house economists of the Kennedy Administration observed some time ago that the nation had accumulated a backlog of demand for public works and welfare equal in magnitude to the backlog of demand for consumer goods and capital goods at the end of World War II. According to the National Planning Association, such neglected tasks as urban redevelopment, mass transportation, control of environmental pollution and restoration of natural resources could absorb additional public investment at the rate of $60 billion per year. The Arms Control and Disarmament Agency, which is principally responsible for analyzing the prospective impact of disarmament on the economy, predicts an easy transition from huge outlays for warfare to huge outlays for welfare—it points to this backlog of unmet public needs. Soviet economists join their American colleagues in forecasting an easy transition; they assure us that capitalism is equal to the task. 24

25   All of this is cheering to hear. And it is especially considerate of the Soviet economists to give us their encouragement. But, against a value system that stoutly resists every increase in Federal expenditure except those that carry the absolute sanction of the national defense, any effort to increase public expenditures for public welfare will encounter heavy political opposition.

26   The backward state of our value system is suggested by the following figures describing the condition of our society: America has, in fact, the highest rate of unemployment among all the industrial nations of the world. If the maintenance of adequate nutrition is taken to establish the poverty line, then Department of Agriculture studies show that not one-quarter but one-third of our fellow citizens remain not only ill-fed but ill-clothed and ill-housed as well. Our country has the lowest ratio of public to private expenditures, even with our gigantic war budget. In the public sector—in Federal, state and local budgets—our economy turns over 25 per cent of its Gross National Product. The lowest figure you find in any other industrial society is 30 per cent. America has the lowest rate of public expenditure on public welfare and public works; it comes to something less than 10 per cent for the country as a whole. The lowest figure in any other industrial nation is nearly three times this percentage.

27   Last spring, the Johnson Administration took its first tentative steps to meet the impending short-run economic crisis. It assembled from already on-going and funded activities of the Federal Government an anti-poverty program. Meanwhile private institutions and individuals were attempting to draw the lines of long-run perspective. One group of concerned citizens—the self-styled Ad Hoc Committee on the Triple Revolution, which included political economists, historians, former public officials, labor leaders, civil rights workers and at least two men who have met payrolls—looked rather more deeply into the widening gap between the productive capacity of our industrial system and the effective demand of our consumer economy. In one conclusion to their analysis, they envisioned a day when: "Society, through its appropriate legal and governmental institutions, must undertake an unqualified commitment to provide every individual and every family with an adequate income as a matter of right."

28   The idea of paying people incomes whether they work or not captured attention in newspaper city rooms all across the country. It seems scarcely necessary to add that the idea also won a great deal of unfavorable comment. Setting aside the ephemeral essays of the commentators and pundits who explain the news to the rest of us, the comments of two distinguished public figures are illuminating. The Secretary of Labor, Willard Wirtz, declared: "I think the analysis is right but the

prognosis and the prescription is wrong." He added: "I don't believe the world owes me a living and I don't believe it owes anyone else a living."

The other comment comes from a man who was at the time candidate for the Republican Presidential nomination. You may recognize his voice. He said, "Our job as Republicans is to get rid of people who will even listen to people who say we should pay people whether they work or not!"

These two statements, taken together, speak faithfully for the austere premises of classical political economy and the tenacity of their grip upon the conscience of many members of our society. Yet the preposterous notion of a guaranteed annual income (or G.A.I., as it has come to be called) has found its way onto the agenda of public issues. Upon deeper reflection over the summer, *Life* magazine returned to the subject for the second time on its editorial page. This time, *Life* conceded that there is technological disemployment: " . . . experts can't agree whether technological unemployment is growing by 4,000 or 40,000 jobs a week. But it is growing fast enough to see that the seeming logic of the . . . plan for free incomes, or instant socialism, may grow too."

Having frightened itself with this prospect *Life* goes on to say that there can be "more than one radical alternative" and puts forward one of its own: "It is private capitalism, after all, that has brought us to the brink of this daunting affluence, and there is an obvious capitalist solution to the problem that the success of capitalism is creating. It lies in the ownership of the machines and the processes that are destroying the old jobs and creating the new wealth." *Life's* proposal is that the ownership be spread—to everybody! Endorsing the analysis set forth in *"The New Capitalists"* by Mortimer Adler and Louis Kelso, *Life* would " . . . guarantee bank loans for new stock acquisitions through a Capital Diffusion Insurance Corporation modeled on FHA."

Let us tarry a moment, here, to contemplate the prospects of instant capitalism. The figures indicate that it would be much more difficult to achieve *Life's* worthy purpose by instant capitalism than by what it calls instant socialism. Consider these disparities in the wealth of our citizenry: As is well known, the bottom 20 per cent of our population gets only 5 per cent of the national income—at the summit of society these percentages are precisely reversed. The bottom 20 per cent thus does poorly enough as income earners. But they show up even worse as capitalists: they hold no liquid assets whatever, except the cash they may happen to have in their jeans. The next 30 per cent of the population above holds liquid assets not exceeding $500 per family. So the bottom 50 per cent of our society holds less than 3 per cent of our liquid assets. It scarcely need be added that these people have no equity or debt interest in the productive system of our land; for 87 per cent of the people have no such stake in the system. As for real property, 50 per cent of our population has an equity of less than $1,000 in the homes in which they live. You have to go to the top 10 per cent of income earners before you find people whose assets begin to equal their annual income; you have to go to the top 1 per cent before you find people whose equity and property holdings keep them in the style to which they are accustomed. Plainly the proposal that we seek a more equitable distribution of affluence through the redistribution of ownership presents a more radical alternative than the achievement of that end by the redistribution of incomes.

33   *Life* is not alone in its concern with the question of how American society might now go about the equitable distribution of the abundance that overburdens institutions framed for the opposite purpose. That soft-spoken quarterly *The American Scholar*, the journal of Phi Beta Kappa, devotes most of this quarter's pages to a symposium on "the problems that unite us." Out of six articles in this symposium, four plainly reflect thoughtful consideration of the possibility of guaranteeing incomes to people. I will quote from one author, August Heckscher, a perceptive and sensitive student of American life who served the Kennedy Administration as the President's special assistant in cultural affairs. He begins by saying: "The objections to this approach [guaranteed annual income] are obvious," and declares: "The very idea of large populations doing nothing but pleasing themselves goes against the American grain." Nonetheless he comes forward with a radical alternative of his own: "Suppose the monetary rewards of society went, as now, to those who work—and also to those who study. Would this not be a means of assuring their being saved from a bored and barren existence?"

34   This author then goes on to suggest other ways in which the surplus of human capacity might be soaked up: "At the simplest level one can readily conceive efforts to organize personal or household services more imaginatively so that the work can be done more efficiently. Hours can be made regular and wages can be more nearly commensurate with those earned in other fields." A little later in his analysis, touching on the question of how these increased wages to domestics are to be financed, he comes up with a truly radical alternative: "The salaries . . . could be supplemented so as to keep the supply adequate and yet not put the wage out of reach of those who require such services. To supplement in a similar way the rate which people are ready to pay handymen or gardeners could substantially cut relief rolls."

35   This surely goes beyond either instant socialism or instant capitalism; you might call it instant feudalism. In fact, the vision of instant

feudalism comes clearer in this author's next still "more far-reaching" suggestion: "It assumes retirement from the industrial work force at a considerably earlier age than now, together with pensions and social security which would be clearly conceived as 'deferred wages' . . . From such a pool we could draw a host of talents and services which would make our common life more various, colorful and pleasant. . . We can indeed conceive a whole second economy—the economy of craftsmanship and service—growing up alongside the economy of the machine."

Probably, this vision could be more swiftly and effectively realized in certain of the underdeveloped countries where the economy of craftsmanship still exists and where it is threatened by destruction through the infectious spread of the industrial revolution. In America we would have to reconstruct the economy of craftsmanship from the ground up.   *36*

Before we start designing Utopias or building the Great Society, it seems to me, we ought to turn to a more searching and possibly painful re-examination of our inexplicit premises—our values. A good way to begin is to ask what we mean by work and what we mean by leisure. With these two words we precipitate the crisis. The proposal of a guaranteed annual income presses the underlying issue in its sharpest and most uncomfortable form.   *37*

The objection to the Heckscher vision of the dual craftsmanship-machine society rests upon its hierarchical character, implicit in the compulsion that relates the services of the handyman and the gardener to "us." This defect could, in fact, be cured by the guarantee of an annual income, paid as a matter of right and not in compensation for services rendered. There would then be no reason why the cultures of craftsmanship and machines could not flourish side by side in moral parity. And there could even be a third culture—of leisure, which would include, I hope, dry-fly fishing.   *38*

On the other hand, criticism of the G.A.I. notion from the left expresses the dark suspicion that this is a middle class stratagem to tranquilize the proletariat by putting the poor on the dole. Apparently, most people are troubled by the question of what *other* people are likely to do with their leisure time!   *39*

Except for the attention the guaranteed annual income has so recently won in public discussion there is nothing very novel or profound about the idea. Nor is it so novel in practice. A substantial portion of our society is already living not on a guaranteed and not on a securely annual income, but living on an income from the public treasury. These people get these incomes on the most humiliating and degrading terms. They get their dole because they present themselves for certification by the appropriate authorities as indigents or paupers. Or they get their monthly checks from Uncle Sam because they take an oath not   *40* to go back to work and earn more than a stated percentage of their Social Security income. In other words, the American society today offers an income without work to a large number of its members but makes the offer on terms that shame us all. The ugly transactions involved derive their ethical justification from the deep unconscious of society—from the institutional memory of the days when the lash drove 80 per cent of the population to work in the fields and mines in order that the few might get on with the high occupations of making history and civilization. The cruelty and inhumanity that persists in our system from those days must be extirpated if we are to resolve successfully the issues that confront us in the tide of abundance set running in America by the present culmination of the industrial revolution.

41   In my opinion, the issues must be met under two major headings. First, we must recognize that economic and social institutions are man-made and so subject to human will. We cannot see the invisible hand because, in truth, it is not there! The enormous power conferred upon modern societies by industrial technology must be brought under the witting* and rational control of democratic institutions still to be perfected.

42   Second, we must recognize that abundance sets the foundations of an entirely new ethical and moral order. The cultural deprivation that blights the life of a single child in the racial ghettoes of our central cities ultimately exacts its cost in the lives of every other citizen. The prolongation of the agony of economic development threatens to destroy the frail parliamentary institutions of India and bring that poverty-stricken nation into the nuclear club under military dictatorship. At this turn in human affairs it is plain that each man's well being can increase only to the degree that the well being of all other men is increased. The work of the world still remains in large part to be done. But the instruments to accomplish it are now in our hands. The work that needs most to be done, especially here in America, is in tasks that enrich society as generously as the individuals who undertake them.

---

*"Witting" means "intentional," or "performed deliberately or knowingly."

Questions and Activities

1. Explain in your own words what Piel means in paragraph 1: "The computer is the engine of this latest phase in the acceleration of the industrial revolution."
2. What is the "law of scarcity," as Piel uses the term (paragraph 3)? How has the computer helped to change our society from one governed by scarcity to one governed by "the law of material abundance" (paragraph 2)?
3. Define the difference between "cyclical" and "structural" unemployment (paragraph 11). How might a reader of this essay see the computer as a cause of structural rather than cyclical unemployment? Why would this be a negative interpretation of the effects of the computer on the economy?
4. In your own words, tell exactly what Piel is suggesting in paragraph 23. Why does Piel believe that increased federal spending is necessary to offset local unemployment? Why is Piel sympathetic to unemployed people in the first place? Has computer technology created their unemployment?

▶ *QUESTIONS OF RHETORICAL PURPOSE AND STRATEGY*

5. Note Piel's use of statistics in paragraph 32. What general idea do the statistics in this paragraph support? How does that general idea fit into Piel's overall argument concerning the effects of the computer on the economy?
6. How is the support that Piel provides for his general idea in paragraph 33 different from the statistics he uses in paragraph 32?
7. What are Piel's grounds for dismissing what he calls "designing Utopias or building the Great Society" (paragraph 37) as solutions for economic problems?
8. What type of voice does Piel establish in this essay? Does he project a serious and scholarly voice, a voice of moral outrage or concern, or the objective voice of science? How does Piel's use of factual evidence in support of his ideas contribute to the quality of his voice?

▶ *THEME QUESTIONS*

9. Far more than George Orwell, Piel considers power as being controlled by social systems. Explain, in your own words, why Piel emphasizes the economic system's influence over the distribution of power rather than the individual's efforts to influence his or her social conditions.

10. How does the computer contribute to the economic system's control over individuals in our society? Do you think the influence that Piel says the computer has had on labor economics is unavoidable?
11. At the close of this essay, Piel argues for a moral interpretation of the dilemmas created by the law of material abundance. Restate this moral argument in your own words. What are its two central points?

▶ *LEARNING ACTIVITIES*

12. Interview a classmate concerning the effects of the computer on his or her life. Fashion your questions carefully, dividing them in the process into two groups: ones on how computers have affected your subject's everyday life (for example, does he or she own, or operate on a daily basis, a personal computer), and ones on how computers have affected more general aspects of life, such as career planning or the financing of major purchases (for example, most department stores now use computerized billing, and most universities employ computerized recordkeeping).
13. As a member of a collaborative writing team, analyze the results of the interviews that were conducted for the preceding activity. Your team will need to first divide the responses of the interview subjects into useful categories, and then use the categorized responses as the basis for a team-written report on the effects of computers on college students.

est: The Invasion of the Mind-Stealers

BARBARA GRIZZUTI HARRISON

Barbara Grizzuti Harrison was born in Brooklyn, New York, in 1934, a member of an Italian-American family. When she was nine years old, she and her mother became Jehovah's Witnesses. Her commitment to this fundamentalist and apocalyptical religion lasted until she was twenty-two years old, and it was the subject of her second and best-known book, *A History and a Memory of Jehovah's Witnesses* (1978). This book set the pattern for which her writing subsequently became known. Harrison's work consistently combines personal expression with objective analysis of fact into readable, opinionated, and well-informed books and articles on current trends and social issues.

Harrison's first book, *Unlearning the Lie: Sexism in School* (1969), describes and analyzes an experiment in which the school Harrison's child attended attempted to alter the sexist upbringing of its students. Harrison has also published a novel, *Foreign Bodies* (1984), and has contributed many essays to magazines such as *Harper's, The Nation, The New York Times Book Review, Ms.,* and *The New Republic.* A collection of her journalistic essays, *Off-Center* (1980), received critical acclaim and has helped to establish her as one of the most talented and controversial of contemporary journalists.

Traditionally, journalists have tried to use a style that was thought to be appropriate for the objective observer of human actions and social events. Personal feeling, opinion, and argument were subordinated to the stories that were being reported. Even on the editorial pages, many traditional journalists tried to weigh alternatives, to balance others' opinions rather than feature their own. However, many of today's journalists, Harrison included, do not believe that totally objective reporting is either possible or accessible to readers. These "New Journalists" incorporate their own feelings and ideas in the articles they write.

This essay on est illustrates Harrison's desire to provide carefully researched and personally experienced responses to contemporary issues. This essay leaves readers in no doubt about Harrison's opinions on her subject. Yet she is careful to provide concrete facts about her subject and descriptions of her experiences to make readers understand why and how she came to hold those opinions. The result is lively, entertaining, and informative prose.

As you read, consider Harrison's treatment of the theme of power. The leaders and "trainers" of the est program seem, as Harrison describes them, to enjoy their control over their students. And they seem to feel that this control is justified by the fact that they are helping their students achieve a sense of control and personal responsibility. Think about this exercise of power as you read:

1. Why do you think that Harrison feels justified in criticizing the actions and goals of the est program?
2. Do you think the est leaders use power in responsible ways?
3. Do you feel that Harrison sufficiently explains the theory behind est? Do you think, for example, that she should have included some objective analysis of the movement's reading material and a few carefully conducted interviews with est leaders?

▶ ————————————————

1   It's both silly and sinister. It's as if the Wizard of Oz had set up business in Dachau and invited victims to pay $250 a marked head for the privilege of being stripped naked and dynamited. Or, it's like being on a tour of a minefield with an insane guide who, speaking in tongues, leads his passive charges unerringly to exactly those mines that will explode in their beseeching faces. It is like being born again at the hands of a witch doctor who, during the bloodied Hallelujah-birthing, wears leering masks: in his several manifestations, he appears to be a small-town Booster, Houdini, Billy Graham, the Marquis de Sade; finally, to his grateful creatures, he appears in the likeness of God. It's like having the top of your head blown off and being rewarded with a prescription for aspirin.

2   (The metaphors shift and change, because the experience, like one's worst nightmare, is both muddy and electrifying; it is like being imprisoned in sticky black cotton candy and being obliged to draw sustenance from that appalling shroud.)

3   Over seventy-five thousand people—most of whom are seemingly no more cranky or crazy than you or I—have in fact shelled out $250 for the Erhard Seminars Training. Est, which has been touted by its graduates as the sixty-hour intensive training that will change your life (or, in est-eze, "transform your ability to experience living"), was founded, as everybody now knows, by Werner Erhard, a forty-one-year-old Gucci-Pucci-Bally California-style guru who "got it" while driving along the California freeway, and promptly packaged "it," and is, as a consequence, awfully rich.

What is "it"? You may well ask. "It," so far as one can figure out, is a   4
synonym for enlightenment—or, as one est graduate put it, "the ability
to experience the world without the benefit of human understanding."
(And I used to think "it" was something Clara Bow had.) Werner, as his
devotees familiarly and reverentially call him, speaks in riddles. (Perhaps that's one reason he changed his name from the decidedly prosaic
and unsphinxlike Jack Rosenberg. The other reason is that he was running away from his first wife and kids.) Anyway, it's no good asking
Werner what "it" is: you have to take the training to find out.

The wonder is that so many people should want to. Why should   5
thousands—among whom are Cloris Leachman, Joanne Woodward,
Valerie Harper, and John Denver—pay to enter what is essentially a
larger version of Patty Hearst's closet? I took the est training to find out.

Most of what I knew about the est technique I'd gleaned from *Mary*   6
Hartman, Mary Hartman,* which had satirized this Big Daddy of the
"consciousness movement." Then I ran into my old friend Nancy, who
had, since I'd seen her last, taken the training and avowedly gotten
"it." Like many of the Human Potential Movement camp-followers est
attracts, Nancy is a kind of barometer for what's happening on the
psychic-panacea market. The last time we'd met, she was muttering
om on her way to a Rolf massage after a lunch of soybeans and curds that
she'd shared with her astrologer who'd confirmed her feeling that she'd
been a Mongolian horseman in a previous incarnation. Now she was on
her way to an est graduate seminar. She greeted me with this remarkable sentence: "I haven't been able to find the energy to clean my cellar,
and at the sharing at the seminar I'll be assisted into my space to look at
the barrier that stands between me and my spring cleaning and I'll disappear the barrier." I had no idea what she was talking about. Was
Nancy satirizing Mary Hartman? "You've probably never experienced
your experience," Nancy said. "I have no idea what you're talking
about," I said. "You feel empty," she said, "right? Your life doesn't
work. You don't like yourself." "Nonsense," I said. "*Good,*" Nancy
said. "You're anxious and tense for sure. You probably have a dark-
brown headache the size of a walnut between your eyes." "Well," I
said, "I'm certainly anxious and tense. My father is very ill." "*Fab-*
ulous," Nancy said. "What is, is. Come to the seminar. It'll blow your
mind."

I did; and it didn't. I ought to say right now that I was expelled from   7
est—after twenty-four hours that didn't change my life. More about
that later. For now, suffice it to say that whatever "it" is, it isn't worth

---

**Mary Hartman, Mary Hartman* was a weekly television situation comedy, the first of
what have come to be called late-night soap operas. It often satirized fads such as est.

what one has to go through to get it. I'm convinced that no good end can possibly result from est's scary (*evil*, is what I really want to say) means.

8   *Monday, April 12, 9:30 A.M., the ballroom of a hotel on Central Park West.* Est graduates convene to hear a lecture called *Be Here Now.* Everyone is issued a first-name tag, yellow for graduates, white for guests.

9   After being received with applause and grins by est graduates in a reception so warm it suggests we've all done something terribly clever, eight guests (all women) are quickly shunted off to a small room where we meet Jonathan, an est staffer who will answer our questions and encourage us to plunk down a $30 deposit against the training fee. Jonathan looks hand-pressed, deodorized, and sexless—not, as a matter of fact, unlike John Denver.

10   Guest: "I'm unemployed, and what I want to know is, why does est cost so much?"

11   Jonathan: "Because it does. . . .I had no money and no job when I signed up for the training—and a week after I registered, I had a job. Est makes it possible for you to know that you have control over your life. *You cause your own experience.*"

12   Is Jonathan talking about control? or about magic? The minute one commits oneself to est, he implies, terrific things happen. He tells us about a fat man who began to lose weight as soon as he'd signed the est registration form. . ."without trying to."

13   "After my training," Jonathan says, "I took responsibility for my life. I cleared up the most rotten thing I'd ever done: when I was in prep school, I lost a manuscript for the senior yearbook. After my training, I wrote a letter of apology to my headmaster." Jonathan beams.

14   That's his nasty secret? The world is blowing up and he's worried about a prep-school essay? As if reading my thoughts, the preppie says, "You can't change the world. The way things are is the way things are. Life is what it is. There is no now and no then. There is no Marxism and no capitalism. Mass protests don't *work*—shouting and sulking don't work. Your life doesn't *work*. Werner's life works. Werner is the Source, the Synthesizer; it's Werner's intention to transform the world. By signing up for the training, *you* are transforming the world—without trying."

15   Guest: "But what will I learn if I take the training?"

16   Jonathan: "You will know what you already know."

17   Guest: "I'm really angry because you just don't seem to be answering the question."

18   Jonathan: "Good. It's not bad to be angry. It's just being angry. You're making moral judgments out of your belief system. Belief sys-

tems are what you get stuck in to prove you're right. And that's not bad either.''

Guest: ''Is *anything* bad?''   19

Jonathan: ''No. And nothing's not bad, either.''   20

Guest: ''But what will I get from the est training?''   21

Jonathan: ''You'll get what you get.''   22

Jonathan explains that the training consists of *data* from the trainer,   23
processes, and *sharing* the experience of the processes. He takes us
through a sample process:

''Uncross your arms and legs, take everything off your lap, relax, and   24
close your eyes. Thank you. . . . Recall a time when you were really
happy with someone and notice what that experience was like for you.
Great. . . . Now recall a time when someone was really happy with you.
Notice how your body felt. Fabulous. . . . Now bring a stranger into the
picture and notice what happens to the experience. How do you feel
now? Good. . . . Now notice if there is any tension in your body. See if
you have tension in the area of your forehead between your eyes. Is it
the size of a pea? Is it the size of a walnut? Good. . . . Look at the tension
and see if it's okay with you to release it. Great. . . . Now get a sense of
the space you would like to be in with yourself. When you feel good
about that space, smile and open your eyes into that space. Great.''

''What I experienced,'' a woman said, ''is that I have no friends. I   25
have never been happy.'' ''Thank you for sharing,'' Jonathan said.

''You will experience in the est training that you are powerful, and   26
that people are really loving. Do you know that nobody has ever been
mugged after leaving an est session, even at two in the morning?''

''Did somebody alert the muggers?'' I asked.   27

''You might want to look at whether, if you're mugged, you want to   28
be mugged,'' the preppie said.

''That sounds to me like, 'If she was raped, she was asking for it,' '' I   29
said. ''Thank you for sharing,'' Jonathan said.

Jonathan attempts to shame his audience into paying $250, to ma-   30
nipulate vacillating (and unemployed) guests.

''Barbara signed up for the training. Isn't anyone else as brave and   31
courageous as she is?''

''I'm not brave. I'm apprehensive. I think you ought to tell people   32
that I'm here because I'm writing an article.''

''*Good.* Fear is good. When you get on an airplane, you're frightened,   33
but you know you're going to get there.''

''No, I don't. That's why I'm frightened.''   34

''What you don't get,'' Jonathan said, ''is that people who go through   35
their barriers die with smiles on their faces. Even if you crashed and
splattered on a rock in the Grand Canyon, you'd have gotten there.''

36   In the taxi coming home, I say to Nancy, "Doesn't it strike you that all this self-absorption is dangerous? Shouldn't you think about the social implications of all of this? Does a napalmed baby 'cause his own experience'? If, as Jonathan suggests, there is no evil, then we're not obliged to resist evil. Think of Hitler, for goodness' sake."

37   "Good," Nancy said. "You're resisting. What you resist, you 'get.'"

38   What I was getting was a headache the size of a watermelon.

39   *Friday, April 16, 2 P.M., est Manhattan office.* Everyone to whom I speak is brusque, purposeful, heads turn with bright, birdlike motions, revealing clear, determined eyes. Est staffers, when they speak to each other, pitch their voices just above conversational level, so that people sitting in the lobby can hear their conversations, which are, as we used to say in Sunday school, "edifying and uplifting." Everything is done for effect; the proselytizing has begun.

40   The young woman who greets me ("Hi! I'm Diane. How may I assist you?") refers me to an office worker who will process my application form ("Hi! I'm Suzie. How may I assist you?"). I am alarmed by a clause in the form that reads: "I understand that the material of the training, including, but not limited to, the names of the participants and their remarks, is private and confidential, and I agree to keep all such material private and confidential." I tell Suzie that I want to call my agent and my editor before I sign what looks to be a very dicey—and possibly illegal—disclaimer. Unfortunately, it is lunchtime, and Good Friday to boot, so neither person is likely to be in.

41   "If you call them with the intention of finding them in," Suzie says, a Delphic smile lighting her face, "you will find that they will be in." Can she be suggesting that I can *cause* them to be in? That my thoughts are a magic carpet that will transport them from East Hampton to midtown Manhattan? I would find that kind of power abhorrent.

42   "What if I woke up tomorrow morning with the intention of making the sun stand still?"

43   "It is Werner's destiny," Suzie replies cryptically, "to make the physical universe work."

44   When I return from a fruitless visit to a phone booth, Suzie says, "You didn't call with the intention of finding them in, did you? And they were out." It is impossible to assail her est-enlightened smile with logic.

45   During the week before I was scheduled to take the est training, I talked to a lot of my friends about the cloud-cuckoo-land encounters I'd had with est staffers. Many were loath to believe that anybody in real

life talked and behaved as I said est-ers had; they implied I must be exaggerating. In the next breath, however, they expressed the fear that est would somehow "get" to me. (The media-hype—193 articles were written about est in 1975—had, I'm afraid, gotten to *them*. I felt as if I were being viewed as a candidate for the Mind-Stealers.) I knew that, on one level, est could and would get to me: the rules of the training were that no one could leave the room (even to go to the bathroom) for four-hour stretches; I considered that senseless deprivation an invitation to cystitis and claustrophobia. I figured that keeping my eyes closed for a sixty-minute process might very well precipitate a massive anxiety attack. (Who isn't afraid of the unfriendly dark?) I was afraid, most of all, that I would be bored into somnolence by mystical clichés and dreary encounter-group platitudes.

My friends said, "Look at all the skeptics who go into est and come out claiming that it's worked for them. Why should you be any different?" Why, indeed? Intelligence, I admit, is no safeguard if one is determined to leap into belief. My armor against est, I thought to myself (and it's hard, even with one's friends, to say things like this aloud—it's often perceived as a lack of humility), is that, while my life is far from perfect, I like myself. I can't in honesty say, as I heard people say in the pretraining, "I have never loved anybody, touched anybody, been loved; I am nothing; I am empty." The fact that est "works" (supposing it does have benevolent long-range effects) doesn't make it, as a social philosophy, good or true. Behavior modification worked for Hitler Youth, too—it gave their lives purpose, and they smiled a lot; that didn't make the behavior modifiers any less reprehensible. I was fully prepared to have a couple of insights during the training. So what? I've had insights on Amtrak parlor cars. If you sit long enough in one place, you have an insight. And what was all this relentless railing against belief systems I'd heard from est-ers? Why bother to empty people of their concepts, beliefs, judgments, and evaluations unless you planned to replace one system of beliefs with another? If I wanted a new belief system, I'd choose to believe in God—He's been in business longer than Werner, and He has better music. To say nothing of the fact that I'm a snob—and est, with its gobbledygook, supersalesmanship, and peach-faced gurus in bodysuits, struck me as ineffably tacky.

Monday, April 26, 7 P.M., the ballroom of a midtown hotel. The training begins. We are calculatedly divided into Us (250 of us) and Them. We exhibit various signs of nervous anticipation; they greet us with stern, unsmiling visages, impervious to pleasantries or chagrin. We are ordered, in loud, declamatory tones, to leave all watches and timepieces in an anteroom. (Phooey. I slip my watch into my bra.) We

46

47

are then ordered to sit on hard-backed, dainty chairs, arranged so that flesh—there is no more than a quarter of an inch between me and the people on either side of me—touches unfamiliar flesh. Est staffers are posted at the sealed doors. It is uncomfortably hot.

48   Marvin, an unprepossessing young man who has total control of his facial muscles, which never once arrange themselves into a semblance of a smile, takes his place on the podium and drones out a series of rules that he calls agreements: no alcohol and no medication other than that specifically prescribed by doctors is to be taken by trainees for two weeks ("Is that clear?"); no snacking during the training sessions; no milk is to be drunk during the breaks ("Is that clear?"); nobody may leave the room to go to the bathroom; no notes may be taken; est staffers may tape-record the proceedings, trainees may not ("Is that clear?"). The hour-long recitation is so boring, so repetitive, so infantilizing—"When you can't hear, raise your hand and say, 'I can't hear.' Is that clear?"—it amounts to an assault.

49   Trainee: "I'm going to the dentist on Wednesday to have a tooth pulled. Can I take Novocain?"

50   Marvin: "The trainer will explain body pain on Tuesday. In the meantime, be where you are."

51   Trainee: "Is it all right for me to relate to my husband during the training?"

52   Marvin (after a long pause in which irony has no part): "Yes."

53   Up through the center aisle bounds a pretty, athletic man, something disturbingly concave about his mouth, sexless: "I'm Landon, and you're all assholes."

54   Landon is our trainer. His voice alternately oily and icy, he bludgeons, anticipating our objections: "You think Marvin is a Nazi, don't you, assholes? You think we're the antichrist. You're being *reasonable*. Where has reason gotten you? It's gotten you nowhere, and you're nothing. If you weren't nothing, why would you be here? Spending good money to be called assholes. If you assholes keep your agreements with me, your life will work. If you don't, it won't. A lot of what's wrong in this country is that people don't follow rules. The rules do not have to be explained. They're just rules. Is that clear? They are not reasonable. The training is not reasonable. Is that clear?"

55   Landon literally unsettles us: he shifts us around so that nobody winds up in the chair he or she had chosen. People look as if the chairs had been pulled out from under them, as indeed they have.

56   Trainee: "Why are no blacks taking the training?"

57   Landon: "*You* hate *niggers*, you asshole!"

58   (This technique, that of putting the questioner on the defensive and placing everything in the trainer's frame of reference, is consistently

and brilliantly used by Landon to blunt all adversary questions . . . and to make the questioner feel like an ass.)

For hours, stopping only to answer questions with riddles or with contempt, Landon, with gathering momentum, sneers at and assaults logic, intellectual curiosity, reason, independence, belief systems, and "concepts"—all of which, according to him, keep our lives from "working." He draws complicated charts to illustrate his theses: none of us has "experienced our experience," and we are therefore doomed to repeat our experience forever and ever, like rats going through the same moldy tunnels for the same piece of stale cheese; catatonics are smarter than we are—at least they don't pretend to know anything; in order to be "truly knowing," we have first to be empty, to *accept*—to accept Landon, and est; if we're not here to accept, why are we here at all? Landon, a steamroller, knocks down everybody's props—including belief in God: "God is a *concept*. God is bullshit." [59]

Trainee: "How can you say I haven't experienced my experience? My mother just died. . . ." She is racked with bitter sobs. [60]

Landon: "Your *mother* didn't die, you asshole. *You* died . . . it's killing *you*." [61]

Trainee (currying favor): "My son died two years ago, and I felt fine." [62]

Landon: "Very good. Did you feel a sense of completion? What is, is. You experienced that experience, so you're not stuck with it anymore." [63]

This denial of grief is obscene, the ultimate in nihilism. Est refuses to confront the fact of mortality by denying that death exists (death is a "concept"). Landon says, "People choose their deaths. *You cause your own experience.*" Again, he is talking about control, but he really means magic: if people can be sold on the idea that they cause their own deaths, they can go through life armored with the invincible belief that no accident can ever befall them, that they need never fear the terrible black horseman who can ride through our lives, taking us surprised and unaware. I am reminded of what Nancy said when a friend died grotesquely: a flower pot (I wish this didn't sound funny—but life, contrary to est, is full of funny-terrible accidents) fell on her head as she was strolling down Fifth Avenue. Nancy said, "She must really have wanted to die." [64]

Trainee: "What do you mean, we cause our own experience? If a drunk comes up and punches me in the nose, am I responsible? If a bus runs me over, am I responsible?" [65]

Landon: "Yes. . . . *You* think of life as a punch in the nose, you asshole, you *look* as if you've been run over by a bus." Landon creates a world in which there are victims, but no victimizers. [66]

The corollary to one's causing one's own experience is that one may never *help* anyone else. *Help* is a dirty word. "Why do you think Latin [67]

Americans hate us?'' Landon asks triumphantly. "Because,'' he says, dangerously simplifying complex political and economic issues, "we *help* them! Nobody can help anybody. We can *assist* people to find their own space.'' (Werner has been quoted as saying, "There are only two things in this world, semantics and nothing.'' Language is being restructured in this room. People are being given a new vocabulary, and a new belief system—Werner's.)

68   A trainee shouts: "Stop, you're killing me! I've studied philosophy for twenty years, and you're stripping it all away! You're leaving me with nothing!''

69   How to explain the hysteria of her response? It can't be attributed to Landon's "philosophy,'' which is an unimpressive mishmash of psychiatric truisms and Eastern conundrums. (Landon even manages to confuse *mysticism* with *superstition*, which ought to tell serious scholars of Eastern philosophy something.) It is his technique, derived, in part, from Gestalt,* Mind Dynamics, Scientology† (and from Fuller Brush Company sales techniques), that is dazzlingly effective, combined, as it is, with a high degree of physical discomfort, approaching exhaustion—it is now 12 A.M.—and the terrible neediness that brought people here in the first place, looking for instant salvation.

70   Landon: "*Good.* This lady is far ahead of the rest of you assholes. She knows she's dying in this room. What she doesn't know is that she'll be born again.''

71   Shortly after midnight, we are given a twenty-five-minute bathroom break . . . but since nobody is wearing a watch, and since everybody has trouble following complicated verbal directions to crowded bathrooms, the exodus has all the earmarks of panic. What should have been a release is another degradation.

72   When we return, the feeling in the room has palpably changed. People are tired of resisting, there is a sense of capitulation, of will-less surrender. People have understood that their comfort—perhaps their survival—depends on their giving Landon what he demands. This is what boot camp must be like. It's almost restful to do what the man says. Landon said he would dynamite our souls and suck us out like oranges. . . . There is a kind of sublimated sexuality in this submission to a dominant force.

*"Gestalt'' describes a unified configuration that has properties that cannot be derived from its parts. It is used in psychology to refer to a whole personality or entity that cannot be explained by its constituent parts.
†Scientology is a religious philosophy combining scientific principles and mysticism. It has developed a relatively large following in the past two decades.

Trainee: "I have an ulcer, and..."   73

Landon: "Asshole, an ulcer is just a concept, can you *see* your ulcer,   74
can you *feel* it?"

Trainee: "...and when you said I couldn't have milk during the   75
break, I tried to understand why not. But I should have just accepted it.
So I decided to believe what you said because you told me to, is that
right? I accept."

Like born-again Christians at a revival meeting, the trainees offer the   76
sorry evidence of their lives to Landon. It is selected evidence, because
Landon is an unwholesome saint: his followers' suppurating sores are
his imprimatur. Everybody wants to bell the leper, everybody wants to
be the leper; they want Landon to lick their wounds with his sandpaper
tongue.

"My baby died a crib death, and I didn't feel anything. Do I have a   77
problem with feeling, or did I experience my experience?"

"All my life I thought I was happy, now I realize I was just a rat going   78
down tunnels for rotten cheese. I'm empty. I'm nothing."

Landon is as emotionless as if his charges were reciting the multipli-   79
cation tables; he makes no compassionate connection.

I feel desolate, as if I'm in a sci-fi movie—the kind where seedpods   80
from Mars take over minds and bodies, and one turns to familiar faces
and sees only alien vacuous stares. I feel nausea rising in me. An image
flashes through my mind—my grandmother's room, dark poverty-
brown and airless, the sick-sweet smell of incense contending with the
smell of death, and around my grandmother's bed churchy crones in
black, wailing, while my grandfather's vivid curses echo from another
room...that smell is in this room now; it stinks, in here, of defeat.

A voice saying real words breaks the spell. A young woman has risen   81
to her feet. "How can you be so arrogant?" she demands of Landon.
"Was *Mozart* an asshole? There must be people in this room who are
kind and courageous. Is *everybody* a shit?"

Landon, who has set up a situation in which only weakness is   82
rewarded, says, "Thank you for sharing.... Mozart was an asshole. Everybody in this room is an asshole, and you're the biggest asshole because you're a *right*-machine—you have to believe you're right."

A small, insignificant-looking man says, slowly and carefully, "I'm a   83
compulsive gambler, and I need every bit of ego I have to fight my
addiction. I have a delicate balance of mental health, and you're destroying my ego. I'm leaving."

As he walks out, head bowed, Landon—without deigning to address   84
him directly—says, "Mental health? What does he know about mental
health? *I'll* tell you how the mind works on Sunday. He's just putting up
defenses and justifying himself—the way you are, you assholes."

85   Ten minutes later, the gambler reenters. He stands at attention while an est woman runs down the aisle to bring him a mike. (The est running-crouch is a cross between Namath's quarterback sprint and the White Rock nymph in bionic motion.) "I want to say that Marvin assisted me to come back, and I'm glad I'm here." The sustained applause that greets the prodigal's return is proof—if more were needed —that the group has solidified behind Landon. Anyone who challenges Landon now will have the group to contend with. It is a peculiarly dispiriting realization. If there are any protestors left here, they have been quarantined, isolated by the group's disapproval.

86   It is now 3 A.M. The temperature has dropped dramatically. It is uncomfortably cold. Landon takes us through a process. (The timing is exquisite—all mental and physical resources have been eroded, everyone is totally suggestible.) We close our eyes. From hidden loudspeakers comes the sound of surf. Landon's disembodied voice suggests that we are not tired, our aches and pains are disappearing, we are *relaaaaxed*, we will sleep well and wake refreshed, we are *relaaaaaxed*. Est people soundlessly prowl the aisles. . . I know they do, I peep. At Landon's cue, everyone surfaces from a hypnotic trance, as if from a communal wet dream.

87   *Tuesday, April 27.* I have asked Suzanne, the young woman who endeared herself to me by asking the Mozart question, to have dinner with me at the Oyster Bar. (I have oysters, white wine—thus breaking an est rule—and strawberries. Being good to oneself is the best revenge.) Suzanne, a network TV producer, is, on the face of it, an unlikely candidate for coercive persuasion. Her lover, an est convert, has paid her $250 tuition, and she is hanging in, she says, because she is fascinated by group dynamics. Well read in Eastern philosophy, she is appalled that Landon should "vulgarize mystical concepts—and charge all those poor people so much to be punished." She giggles: "I feel like a kid playing Simon Says, don't you? . . . You won't let them get to you, will you? They won't be able to get to you? I don't think they can get to me. . . . I'm so tired. I had two hours' sleep last night, I'm really flakey, I'm frightened."

88   *April 27, 7 P.M., the ballroom of a midtown hotel.* My body aches. I feel as if I'd been beaten with a rubber hose. All around me people are standing up to testify that they have slept well, they are refreshed, they have never had so little sleep and so much energy. . . . Well, of course! Their nerve ends are exposed, they're experiencing the illusory clarity and high that comes with total physical exhaustion, and, I suspect, they

are acting out of posthypnotic suggestion. . . . The woman sitting next to me is rocking herself back and forth, crying. A man behind me says he has never felt better in his life, he doesn't know what's happening to him, he's gay and a jealous lover, and could he please have a bag to vomit in.

Landon says, "Everybody is perfect *and* has barriers to perfection [there are no *buts* in est-land, no on-the-other-hands, no complexities or shades of gray]; what you try to change persists; if you just *observe* a problem, you 'disappear' it; if you try to *understand* a problem, you get the booby prize." The killings at Kent State and at Attica, he says, and revolutions everywhere, are a result of assholes trying to change things, examples of the futility of struggle; *he* never gets upset when he reads the news—what is, is.   89

(Is Rockefeller financing est? Is the CIA financing est? Hardly likely, but: if you can get a well-drilled army of good soldiers to believe that all struggles to bring about change are puerile and counterproductive, what a wonderful way to maintain the status quo, to prepare people for withdrawal, to encourage narcissism in the midst of social unrest. Werner demands that all est staffers give up their "own intentions, purposes, desires, and objectives in life" in order to serve him. Will est be used to create a Werner-world where each man is an island, where intellectual vitality and political action are perceived as moral defects? Is Werner creating a whole school of social dropouts who will obey his will? Werner, his disciples rumor, may some day wish to be President.)   90

Panacea time. Landon takes us through a process to teach us how to "disappear" physical pain: "Close your eyes and go into your space. Good. Locate a space in your right ankle. Good. Locate a space in your left ankle. Good. Locate your pain. Is it the size of an orange? Is it round? Is it square? Is it triangular? Good. What color is it? Good. Now look at the pain. Observe it. Experience it. Re-create it. Good. The pain you have re-created will enter the space of the pain you are observing and will disappear it. Good. Relax. Open your eyes."   91

(Nancy says that since she's taken the training she no longer has migraines. Actually, what she says is, "I go *through* my migraines and *experience* them, so I don't experience them as pain." . . . It sounds to me as if she still has migraines.)   92

All over the room people are testifying that their aches and pains have been "disappeared." Without even the laying on of hands. . . . Well, why not? As long as they don't claim to cure cancer. . . .   93

The Cancer Lady Speaks: "I have cancer. And a heart condition. And my family and friends live in Philadelphia, but my husband made me   94 move to New York, and I'm terrified of New York, all the buildings close around me, I'm all alone here, and my doctors said my husband was killing me. . . . Why is he killing me?"

95   "Your husband isn't killing *you*, you're killing *him*. *You* caused your experience—you caused pieces of yourself to be cut out—so you could kill him, so you could prove you were right and he was wrong. Cancer," Landon says, "is a concept." A concept for which she is responsible. A concept that can be "disappeared."

96   We are to go through a "truth process." Everyone is to get in touch with an unwanted "item" in his or her experience, in order to "disappear" it.

97   "What is your item?"

98   "Guilt?"

99   "Guilt is a concept. Pick an item, any item."

100   "Sadness? I'm sad because my mother. . . ."

101   "Your item is sadness. Don't assign a cause to that item. Your life is like a vegetable stew . . . reach in and grab one item . . . and remember, peas don't cause *carrots*."

102   Item: Sadness.

103   Item: Fear.

104   Item: Despair.

105   We close our eyes. The recorded surf pounds again. "You are on a beach. . . . Experience what it was like to be on that beach. Good. Experience what comes up for you. Is it a person? Good. Experience that person. Now look at how you are feeling. . . ."

106   During the process, I play these (unauthorized) games: I imagine a passage of Job written in est-eze (item: despair); and I understand that the reduction of all human emotions to single-word "items" makes art—and emotion itself—impossible. . . . I think of people I would like to have sitting around me: novelist Muriel Spark, for her iconoclastic intelligence, her irony, her absolute faith in an absolute God; Ralph Nader and a whole bunch of his Raiders; my Marxist friend Sol Yurick (part of what is going on in this room is a denial of cause and effect, which is a denial of history); a Jesuit; Woody Allen; and anybody at all who will make a convincing case for human reciprocity—who will convince people that people do hurt one another, help one another, drive one another crazy, and make one another happy. . . . I try to imagine what would happen if anyone introduced the following things into this room: somebody with a gun. A Beethoven quartet. Somebody having a heart attack. A crying baby. . . . I cast my eyes down, but do not close them, anxiety nibbling at my nerves. . . . Landon, his voice now soothing and syrupy (creepy, is what it is), chants: "You are powerful. And

you have the power to project your consciousness anywhere in the universe, and into the space [the mind?] of any other person. Relaaax. Open your eyes and come out of your space." The process has lasted one hour. It is now 3 A.M.

Wednesday, April 28, 7 P.M., the ballroom of the midtown hotel.   107
Landon has drawn complicated charts on two blackboards—circles, squares, and arrows that purport to illustrate how est can "transform your ability to experience living so that the situations you have been trying to change, or have been putting up with, clear up just in the process of life itself."

Before the formal session begins, I copy the charts and the struggle-   108
free recipe for Happy Living. Marvin appears at my shoulder: "Is there anything in your space that prevents you from keeping your agreement not to take notes?"

"Are you telling me you don't want me to take notes? I won't take   109
notes."

"I'll take the book you're writing in."   110

"No, you can't have the book."   111

Marvin orders me to the back of the room, where he hands me a pen-   112
cil. "Erase the notes," he says.

"You do it. You're the one who wants the notes erased."   113

Grim, Marvin hands my book and the eraser to an est woman, whose   114
ability to erase for the cause is second only to that of Rose Mary Woods's.

"Now take that book and put it over there in the cloak room."   115

"Do you want my fillings, too?"   116

"No, just your book. . . . Now I want to know what there is in your   117
space that is a barrier keeping you from obeying the agreements. Is it your intention to keep the agreements?"

"I've said I wouldn't take notes, and I've said I would put my book   118
away."

Marvin has to be satisfied with my oblique answers. It's clear, how-   119
ever, that what he expected was for me to dither about "spaces" and "agreements" and "barriers," for me to question, not him, but myself. He's counted on my being on the defensive. A look of pure fury contorts his face and is just as quickly erased as he orders me roughly back to my seat.

Tonight people are "sharing" what they "got" in the "truth pro-   120
cess." These are some of the words one doesn't hear in their mouths: courage, loyalty, goodness, economics, hope, joy. When love is mentioned, it is only in a negative context: "*I got that I had never loved*

anybody"; "I got that I am afraid to love men"; "I got that what I thought was love was bullshit." Landon is well pleased.

121   *Thursday, April 29, back at the ballroom.* The Gambler/Prodigal speaks again: "I can't go through another process. It's too painful. Too much terrible stuff comes up. I've had two heart attacks, and my doctor says that it's bad for my heart for me to go through this."

122   Landon: "Your *heart?* You don't even know where your heart *is,* asshole. Can you *feel* it? The only way to know something is experientially. Are you experiencing a heart attack right now? You're walking out of this room because of a bullshit concept. You're leaving because of your bullshit doctor. You don't know your heart from your asshole."

123   The Gambler stays.

124   Suzanne, my dinner partner, is in a rage: "How dare you!" she shouts. "How can you manipulate vulnerable people like this?"

125   A woman turns to shush her: "We're here because we want to be here. We're not vulnerable, we're assholes."

126   Landon says, "Suzanne, you might want to look at your arrogance. You just have to be right, don't you? You have to win. You don't care about these people, you just care about winning. Arrogant. Asshole. Suzanne is an arrogant asshole."

127   Everybody applauds.

128   Suzanne, teary and trembling, pleads with me to say something in her support. I don't want to blow my journalistic cool, but Suzanne's stricken face is hard to deny.

129   "Did the people in Hiroshima cause their own experience?" I ask. "If they had 'observed' the bomb, would they have 'disappeared' it?"

130   Landon says, "Let Werner and me worry about the world. I'll tell you what caused Hiroshima on Sunday. And you know what? You're not really concerned with Hiroshima at all, you're angry. You're so angry you can't see . . . anger is your item, asshole."

131   He's right, of course, to this extent: wild horses wouldn't have dragged anything personal out of me at that moment; I had an almost fetishistic horror of revealing anything of my personal life to Landon. I find that I am shaking with anger, I can barely stand, hardly contain it. I think of what Simone Weil said about the Warsaw uprising—"indignation is the fiercest form of love"*—and I try to tell Landon that, in this

---

*Simone Weil (1909–1943) was a French religious and political philosopher, teacher, and writer. Not a Communist, she consistently supported working class causes; her sixteen books and many articles are all dedicated to improving the lot of the working classes in an industrial society. She has recently become a favorite of feminist and liberal intellectuals in the United States. The Warsaw uprising involved the Jewish occupants of that Polish city, who tried unsuccessfully to oust Nazi troops in 1943.

situation, anger is entirely appropriate. "But your anger is hurting you, asshole, it's not hurting me. Your anger is killing *you*." I do in fact feel murderous.

During the break, the Cancer Lady says, "Don't worry about Hiroshima, honey, he'll explain it to you on Sunday."   132

And if, on Sunday, he told them that the niggers and the kikes caused Hiroshima? He won't, of course; but if he did, what are they not prepared to accept?   133

After the break, we go into a process designed to take us into our sadness, fear, and pain and, by "looking at it," to exorcise it. It is 2 A.M., and uncomfortably cold. We are instructed to lie prone on the floor. Landon preps us for hypnosis: people will shout, vomit, and scream during this process, he says, and under no circumstances may anyone come to the aid of another—everyone's alone on this roller-coaster ride. This is payoff time. (And everyone who's paid $250 is eager to be complicit in his own victimization.)   134

The surf again. The beach again. Landon's voice: "Remember a time when you were sad. Good. Remember a time when you were terrified."   135

I hear the most awful wails I have ever heard in my life. Like a hundred Arab women keening. Over and over and over again. People pound the carpet with their fists, drum the floor with their heels, writhe. Voices scream, *no! no! no!* People are infatuated with their own suffering, their faces closed to what is going on around them, absorbed in the violent satisfactions of their fantasies.   136

I can't keep my eyes closed. There's no way I'm going to put my sanity to this test, no way I'm going to put my welfare in Landon's fleshy white manicured hands. Too much violence is being done in this room. How can anyone learn anything good from the brutal indifference that is being inculcated here? Demons could appear to drink the blood of virgins—Werner could appear to drink the blood of virgins—and this crowd would still be on their beaches, experiencing their experience.   137

A woman lying near me stiffens; her arms, then her legs, shoot up in the air, her head twists uncontrollably. Est staffers gather round, nod and smile at one another, make cabalistic signs over her body—apparently she is not dying. Landon sees that I see. He comes over to me: "*Shut your eyes.*" "I can't." "You're not going to shut your eyes?" "I can't." "Get out."   138

Navigating over people's heads, stepping over people's bodies, I make my way through this writhing obstacle course, to the door, and the safety of the world.   139

It is 3 A.M. Acting on an impulse I don't understand, I telephone my children from a phone booth in the lobby. An extravagant call to match   140 an extravagant mood: it is noon in Bombay, where they are visiting their father. *"Mommy?"* As soon as their voices leap over the transatlantic cable I know why I've called them. Their safe, sane voices, happy and alive with warm curiosity and affection, call me back beautifully to the world.

141   The streets are deserted, the air is rain-fresh; I've never been so happy to be going home.

142   Suzanne called me after she finished her training to tell me what I'd missed. Landon had taken the group through a "fear process"—he'd sent them into their space to "experience" being mugged, raped, strangled, knifed. They were choking on their fears, Suzanne said, and then, when it seemed that they would die of it, Landon said, "Assholes, don't you know that the person next to you is afraid of *you?* Doctors are afraid of you—that's why they write in Latin; cops are afraid of you—that's why they have guns. *You are powerful.* Now *you* go out and give someone *else* an ulcer. There is nobody in the universe more powerful than you."

143   Wonderful. Nothing like mystifying the sources of temporal power.

144   Next, the group got the est word about love: "Love is bullshit. When you're hot, you're hot; when you're not, you're not." That's a slogan to *live* by? "Well," Suzanne said, "it's certainly a slogan to fuck by."

145   On the final Sunday, the group had learned what "it" was: "What is, is. What ain't, ain't." Talk of a dying fall. It all seemed sadly anticlimactic.

146   I told Suzanne that I'd been pretty scared. "Oh, no," she said, "I can't bear that they got to you. It's so *silly.*" I took that to mean that they hadn't gotten to her. Then she said, "I did get that I was arrogant...that I always wanted to win, that I had to be right...."

147   "The impression I got was that you wanted to be good," I said.

148   "...and I got that Landon loved me," she said.

149   So I thought Suzanne was lost to the est world of endless graduate-seminar fixes, garbage-language, beach-spaces, disappearing fruit-shaped headaches, and Werner-love. Then she called me again: She felt "spacey," she said. She hadn't been able to sleep. "Nothing matters. I feel like a machine, I feel hollow. I feel like what Landon said I was—a mechanical asshole. I try to remember what I was like before the training, but I feel like a collection of empty spaces. In my head, I'm always back on that beach."

150   It's not the River Jordan, it isn't even Malibu. That beach is a cold and lonely place. I wonder how many est graduates have been stranded there, and who will help them back to the real world of struggle and pain and love.

Questions and Activities

▶ *COMPREHENSION QUESTIONS*

1. What is meant by the phrase "consciousness movement" (paragraph 6)? What is supposed to happen to a person who joins a consciousness movement?

2. What does Landon mean when he says that the woman who asks him about Mozart is "a *right*-machine" (paragraph 82)? Why does Landon continually use slogans and catch-phrases? What do these ways of addressing the seminar students tell you about the est program's attitudes toward them?

3. Why does Harrison mention the River Jordan and Malibu in the same sentence in her last paragraph? What do these two very different places have in common? How does this commonality tie in with earlier parts of the essay?

▶ *QUESTIONS OF RHETORICAL PURPOSE AND STRATEGY*

4. Harrison makes her attitude toward est apparent from the start of this essay. Do you enjoy this straightforward approach, or would you have preferred a more subtle one? Do you think that Harrison's approach allows you to consider the value of the est movement objectively?

5. Why does Harrison arrange her material in the way she does? Why, for example, does she use subheadings that give the time of day, date, and place? Why does she choose to present her material in a combined expository and narrative form, mixing the presentation of ideas with stories of her est experience?

▶ *THEME QUESTIONS*

6. Describe in your own words the kind of power that est trainers have over their students. How is this power different from the kind of power teachers have in traditional classrooms? Do you agree with Harrison that there is something immoral about est's use of power? Is this exercise of power justified by the fact that the students of est voluntarily join the seminar?

7. Do you think that the experience and study Harrison went through to produce her book on the Jehovah's Witnesses was good preparation for writing her essay on the est movement? Why?

8. Is there any relationship between Gerard Piel's idea that the computer industry has caused people to feel alienated from the work they do (because they are not directly involved in production, but are more often using computers to manage someone else's work)

and the kind of people who sign up for est? Reread the profiles of est students that Harrison gives. Do these profiles have any connection with the socioeconomic conditions presented by Piel?

▶ *LEARNING ACTIVITIES*

9. Brainstorm with a group of your classmates to locate and analyze other places in our society where "the mind-stealers" may be functioning. With your group, define the social context in which mind-stealing seems to be occurring and explain how it is carried out. Report back to the whole class on your findings.

10. Do some independent research on est. Does what you find in other journals and magazines seem to contradict or confirm Harrison's point of view? Can you find *facts* that seem to contradict those offered by Harrison?

11. Find some biographical information about Werner Erhard, the founder of the est movement. Give a brief report to the class on what you find.

The Federalist No. 3 and The Federalist No. 65

JOHN JAY AND ALEXANDER HAMILTON

In order to understand the two essays that follow, you will need to know something about the context within which they were written. The *Federalist Papers* were written by John Jay, Alexander Hamilton, and James Madison. Many Americans had responded negatively to the Constitution that was written by the politicians who attended the Philadelphia Convention of 1787. Hamilton, a framer and supporter of the Constitution, proposed to Madison and Jay that the three of them write a series of open letters defending the Constitution. The three began working together several months after the Constitution had been drafted at the Philadelphia Convention, and their essays were subsequently published as the *Federalist Papers* in a variety of New York City newspapers from the fall of 1787 through August of 1788. Two books that included all eighty-five of the essays were published during the spring of 1789.

On what authority did Hamilton, Jay, and Madison address the issues involved in gaining the public's acceptance of the Constitution? All three had helped write the Constitution. All three had spent at least part of their lives in public life. Jay was the chief justice of the New York Supreme Court, a diplomatic ambassador to Spain and France, and a representative to the first two Continental Congresses. Hamilton was an assistant to George Washington during the War for Independence, the secretary and treasurer of the first revolutionary government, and a representative to the Continental Congress. Madison (later America's fourth president) also served in the Continental Congress, was active in politics and territorial affairs in Virginia, and was involved in American relations with Britain, Spain, and France after the War for Independence.

What common concern motivated Hamilton, Jay, and Madison? All three hoped the new Constitution would unify the loose confederacy of states into an organized federation. Hamilton saw in the Constitution a way to establish financial support through taxation and licensing fees; Jay was especially interested in developing a strong national defense against the encroachments of Spain, France, and Britain; Madison, who later switched his support to the principles of Jeffersonian democracy and increased state sovereignty, supported federalist causes in the late 1780s as a way to stop the fighting among states over territories, boundaries, and rights to seaports and rivers.

The papers were first published anonymously under pseudonyms such as "Publius," but many of New York's "informed" readers recognized the ideas of Hamilton and his co-authors. Discussion of the Constitution was common. Some citizens were afraid that their independence would be threatened by federalism; others feared chaos and weakness would result if separatism were carried too far. Over the years the *Federalist Papers* have come to be known as the single most informed and cogent defense of the United States Constitution. Consider these questions as you read:

1. Are possible abuses of power implied in any of Jay's arguments for a strong, federal government?
2. At the time these essays were written, what types of communities might have been threatened by a strong, central government?
3. Can you think of present-day politicians who are opposed to the kind of federalism proposed here? What might be the grounds for their opposition?
4. What arguments might there be for placing the responsibility for conducting impeachment proceedings in the citizens themselves, rather than in their elected representatives, as Hamilton proposes?

▶ ─────────────────────

The Federalist No. 3
JOHN JAY

November 3, 1787

To the People of the State of New York.

1   It is not a new observation that the people of any country (if like the Americans intelligent and well informed) seldom adopt, and steadily persevere for many years in, an erroneous opinion respecting their interests. That consideration naturally tends to create great respect for the high opinion which the people of America have so long and uniformly entertained of the importance of their continuing firmly united under one Fœderal Government, vested with sufficient powers for all general and national purposes.

2   The more attentively I consider and investigate the reasons which appear to have given birth to this opinion, the more I become convinced that they are cogent and conclusive.

Among the many objects to which a wise and free people find it nec-   3
essary to direct their attention, that of providing for their *safety* seems
to be the first. The *safety* of the people doubtless has relation to a great
variety of circumstances and considerations, and consequently affords
great latitude to those who wish to define it precisely and comprehen-
sively.

At present I mean only to consider it as it respects security for the   4
preservation of peace and tranquility, as well against dangers from *foreign arms and influence,* as from dangers of the *like kind* arising from
domestic causes. As the former of these comes first in order, it is proper
it should be the first discussed. Let us therefore proceed to examine
whether the people are not right in their opinion, that a cordial Union
under an efficient national Government, affords them the best security
that can be devised against *hostilities* from abroad.

The number of wars which have happened or will happen in the   5
world, will always be found to be in proportion to the number and
weight of the causes, whether *real* or *pretended,* which *provoke* or *invite* them. If this remark be just, it becomes useful to inquire, whether
so many *just* causes of war are likely to be given by *United America,* as
by *disunited* America; for if it should turn out that United America will
probably give the fewest, then it will follow that, in this respect, the
Union tends most to preserve the people in a state of peace with other
nations.

The *just* causes of war for the most part arise either from violations of   6
treaties, or from direct violence. America has already formed treaties
with no less than six foreign nations, and all of them, except Prussia,
are maritime, and therefore able to annoy and injure us: She has also extensive commerce with Portugal, Spain, and Britain, and with respect
to the two latter, has in addition the circumstance of neighbourhood to
attend to.

It is of high importance to the peace of America, that she observe the   7
laws of nations towards all these Powers, and to me it appears evident
that this will be more perfectly and punctually done by one national
Government, than it could be either by thirteen separate States, or by
three or four distinct confederacies.

Because when once an efficient national government is established,   8
the best men in the country will not only consent to serve, but also will
generally be appointed to manage it; for altho' town or country, or other
contracted influence may place men in state assemblies, or senates, or
courts of justice, or executive departments; yet more general and extensive reputation for talents and other qualifications, will be necessary to
recommend men to offices under the national government—especially
as it will have the widest field for choice, and never experience that
want of proper persons, which is not uncommon in some of the States.

Hence it will result, that the administration, the political counsels, and the judicial decisions of the national Government will be more wise, systematical and judicious, than those of individual States, and consequently more satisfactory with respect to other nations, as well as more *safe* with respect to us.

9   Because under the national Government, treaties and articles of treaties, as well as the laws of nations, will always be expounded in one sense, and executed in the same manner—whereas adjudications on the same points and questions, in thirteen States, or in three or four confederacies, will not always accord or be consistent; and that as well from the variety of independent courts and judges appointed by different and independent Governments, as from the different local laws and interests which may affect and influence them. The wisdom of the Convention in committing such questions to the jurisdiction and judgment of courts appointed by, and responsible only to one national Government, cannot be too much commended.

10   Because the prospect of present loss or advantage, may often tempt the governing party in one or two States to swerve from good faith and justice; but those temptations not reaching the other States, and consequently having little or no influence on the national government, the temptation will be fruitless, and good faith and justice be preserved. The case of the treaty of peace with Britain, adds great weight to this reasoning.*

11   Because even if the governing party in a State should be disposed to resist such temptations, yet as such temptations may, and commonly do result from circumstances peculiar to the State, and may affect a great number of the inhabitants, the governing party may not always be able if willing to prevent the injustice meditated, or to punish the aggressors. But the national Government, not being affected by those local circumstances, will neither be induced to commit the wrong themselves, nor want power or inclination to prevent, or punish its commission by others.

12   So far therefore as either designed or accidental violation of treaties and of the laws of nations afford *just* causes of war, they are less to be apprehended under one general government, than under several lesser ones, and in that respect, the former most favors the *safety* of the people.

13   As to those just causes of war which proceed from direct and unlawful violence, it appears equally clear to me, that one good national gov-

*The United States and Great Britain signed a treaty of peace in 1783. Some of the states had already violated the terms of the treaty by 1787, when this essay was written. These states allowed their citizens to ignore their debts to British creditors, who had been assured in the treaty that they would receive the money owed to them.

ernment affords vastly more security against dangers of that sort, than can be derived from any other quarter.

Because such violences are more frequently caused by the passions   *14* and interests of a part than of the whole, of one or two States than of the Union. Not a single Indian war has yet been occasioned by aggressions of the present Fœderal Government, feeble as it is, but there are several instances of Indian hostilities having been provoked by the improper conduct of individual States, who either unable or unwilling to restrain or punish offences, have given occasion to the slaughter of many innocent inhabitants.

The neighbourhood of Spanish and British territories, bordering on   *15* some States, and not on others, naturally confines the causes of quarrel more immediately to the borderers. The bordering States if any, will be those who, under the impulse of sudden irritation, and a quick sense of apparent interest or injury, will be most likely by direct violence, to excite war with those nations; and nothing can so effectually obviate that danger, as a national Government, whose wisdom and prudence will not be diminished by the passions which actuate the parties immediately interested.

But not only fewer just causes of war will be given by the national   *16* Government, but it will also be more in their power to accommodate and settle them amicably. They will be more temperate and cool, and in that respect, as well as in others, will be more in capacity to act advisedly than the offending State. The pride of States as well as of men, naturally disposes them to justify all their actions, and opposes their acknowledging, correcting or repairing their errors and offences. The national Government in such cases will not be affected by this pride, but will proceed with moderation and candour to consider and decide on the means most proper to extricate them from the difficulties which threaten them.

Besides it is well known that acknowledgments, explanations and   *17* compensations are often accepted as satisfactory from a strong united nation, which would be rejected as unsatisfactory if offered by a State or Confederacy of little consideration or power.

In the year 1685 the State of Genoa having offended Louis the XIVth   *18* endeavoured to appease him. He demanded that they should send their *Doge* or chief magistrate, accompanied by four of their Senators to *France* to ask his pardon and receive his terms. They were obliged to submit to it for the sake of peace. Would he on any occasion either have demanded, or have received the like humiliation from Spain, or Britain, or any other *powerful* nation?

Publius.

The Federalist No. 65
ALEXANDER HAMILTON

March 7, 1788

To the People of the State of New York.

1   The remaining powers, which the plan of the Convention allots to the Senate, in a distinct capacity, are comprised in their participation with the Executive in the appointment to offices, and in their judicial character as a court for the trial of impeachments. As in the business of appointments the Executive will be the principal agent, the provisions relating to it will most properly be discussed in the examination of that department. We will therefore conclude this head with a view of the judicial character of the Senate.

2   A well constituted court for the trial of impeachments, is an object not more to be desired than difficult to be obtained in a government wholly elective. The subjects of its jurisdiction are those offenses which proceed from the misconduct of public men, or in other words from the abuse or violation of some public trust. They are of a nature which may with peculiar propriety be denominated POLITICAL, as they relate chiefly to injuries done immediately to the society itself. The prosecution of them, for this reason, will seldom fail to agitate the passions of the whole community, and to divide it into parties, more or less friendly or inimical, to the accused. In many cases, it will connect itself with the pre-existing factions, and will inlist all their animosities, partialities, influence and interest on one side, or on the other; and in such cases there will always be the greatest danger, that the decision will be regulated more by the comparative strength of parties than by the real demonstrations of innocence or guilt.

3   The delicacy and magnitude of a trust, which so deeply concerns the political reputation and existence of every man engaged in the administration of public affairs, speak for themselves. The difficulty of placing it rightly in a government resting entirely on the basis of periodical elections will as readily be perceived, when it is considered that the most conspicuous characters in it will, from that circumstance, be too often the leaders, or the tools of the most cunning or the most numerous faction; and on this account can hardly be expected to possess the requisite neutrality towards those, whose conduct may be the subject of scrutiny.

4   The Convention, it appears, thought the Senate the most fit depositary of this important trust. Those who can best discern the intrinsic

difficulty of the thing will be least hasty in condemning that opinion; and will be most inclined to allow due weight to the arguments which may be supposed to have produced it.

What it may be asked is the true spirit of the institution itself? Is it not designed as a method of NATIONAL INQUEST into the conduct of public men? If this be the design of it, who can so properly be the inquisitors for the nation, as the representatives of the nation themselves? It is not disputed that the power of originating the inquiry, or in other words of preferring the impeachment ought to be lodged in the hands of one branch of the legislative body; will not the reasons which indicate the propriety of this arrangement, strongly plead for an admission of the other branch of that body to a share in the inquiry? The model, from which the idea of this institution has been borrowed, pointed out that course to the Convention: In Great Britain, it is the province of the house of commons to prefer the impeachment; and of the house of lords to decide upon it. Several of the State constitutions have followed the example. As well the latter as the former seem to have regarded the practice of impeachments, as a bridle in the hands of the legislative body upon the executive servants of the government. Is not this the true light in which it ought to be regarded?

Where else, than in the Senate could have been found a tribunal sufficiently dignified, or sufficiently independent? What other body would be likely to feel *confidence enough in its own situation*, to preserve unawed and uninfluenced the necessary impartiality between an *individual* accused, and the *representatives of the people, his accusers?*

Could the Supreme Court have been relied upon as answering this description? It is much to be doubted whether the members of that tribunal would, at all times, be endowed with so eminent a portion of fortitude, as would be called for in the execution of so difficult a task; & it is still more to be doubted, whether they would possess the degree of credit and authority, which might, on certain occasions, be indispensable, towards reconciling the people to a decision, that should happen to clash with an accusation brought by their immediate representatives. A deficiency in the first would be fatal to the accused; in the last, dangerous to the public tranquillity. The hazard in both these respects could only be avoided, if at all, by rendering that tribunal more numerous than would consist with a reasonable attention to œconomy. The necessity of a numerous court for the trial of impeachments is equally dictated by the nature of the proceeding. This can never be tied down by such strict rules, either in the delineation of the offence by the prosecutors, or in the construction of it by the Judges, as in common cases serve to limit the discretion of courts in favor of personal security. There will be no jury to stand between the Judges, who are to pronounce the sentence of the law and the party who is to receive or suffer it. The awful discretion, which a court of impeachments must necessarily have, to doom to honor or to infamy the most confidential and the most distinguished characters of the community, forbids the commitment of the trust to a small number of persons.

8   These considerations seem alone sufficient to authorise a conclusion, that the Supreme Court would have been an improper substitute for the Senate, as a court of impeachments. There remains a further consideration which will not a little strengthen this conclusion. It is this. The punishment, which may be the consequence of conviction upon impeachment, is not to terminate the chastisement of the offender. After having been sentenced to a perpetual ostracism from the esteem and confidence, and honors and emoluments of his country; he will still be liable to prosecution and punishment in the ordinary course of law. Would it be proper that the persons, who had disposed of his fame and his most valuable rights as a citizen in one trial, should in another trial, for the same offence, be also the disposers of his life and his fortune? Would there not be the greatest reason to apprehend, that error in the first sentence would be the parent of error in the second sentence? That the strong bias of one decision would be apt to overrule the influence of any new lights, which might be brought to vary the complexion of another decision? Those, who know any thing of human nature, will not hesitate to answer these questions in the affirmative; and will be at no loss to perceive, that by making the same persons Judges in both cases, those who might happen to be the objects of prosecution would in a great measure be deprived of the double security, intended them by a double trial. The loss of life and estate would often be virtually included in a sentence, which, in its terms, imported nothing more than dismission from a present, and disqualification for a future office. It may be said, that the intervention of a jury, in the second instance, would obviate the danger. But juries are frequently influenced by the opinions of Judges. They are sometimes induced to find special verdicts which refer the main question to the decision of the court. Who would be willing to stake his life and his estate upon the verdict of a jury, acting under the auspices of Judges, who had predetermined his guilt?

9   Would it have been an improvement of the plan, to have united the Supreme Court with the Senate, in the formation of the court of impeachments? This Union would certainly have been attended with several advantages; but would they not have been overballanced by the signal disadvantage, already stated, arising from the agency of the same Judges in the double prosecution to which the offender would be liable? To a certain extent, the benefits of that Union will be obtained from making the Chief Justice of the Supreme Court the President of the court of impeachments, as is proposed to be done in the plan of the Con-

vention; while the inconveniences of an intire incorporation of the former into the latter will be substantially avoided. This was perhaps the prudent mean. I forbear to remark upon the additional pretext for clamour, against the Judiciary, which so considerable an augmentation of its authority would have afforded.

Would it have been desirable to have composed the court for the trial   10
of impeachments of persons wholly distinct from the other departments of the government? There are weighty arguments, as well against, as in favor of such a plan. To some minds, it will not appear a trivial objection, that it would tend to increase the complexity of the political machine; and to add a new spring to the government, the utility of which would at best be questionable. But an objection, which will not be thought by any unworthy of attention, is this—A court formed upon such a plan would either be attended with heavy expence, or might in practice be subject to a variety of casualties and inconveniencies. It must either consist of permanent officers stationary at the seat of government, and of course entitled to fixed and regular stipends, or of certain officers of the State governments, to be called upon whenever an impeachment was actually depending. It will not be easy to imagine any third mode materially different, which could rationally be proposed. As the court, for reasons already given, ought to be numerous; the first scheme will be reprobated by every man, who can compare the extent of the public wants, with the means of supplying them; the second will be espoused with caution by those, who will seriously consider the difficulty of collecting men dispersed over the whole union; the injury to the innocent, from the procrastinated determination of the charges which might be brought against them; the advantage to the guilty, from the opportunities which delay would afford to intrigue and corruption; and in some cases the detriment to the State; from the prolonged inaction of men, whose firm and faithful execution of their duty might have exposed them to the persecution of an intemperate or designing majority in the House of Representatives. Though this latter supposition may seem harsh, and might not be likely often to be verified; yet it ought not to be forgotten, that the demon of faction will at certain seasons extend his sceptre over all numerous bodies of men.

But though one or the other of the substitutes which have been   11
examined, or some other that might be devised, should be thought preferable to the plan, in this respect, reported by the Convention, it will not follow, that the Constitution ought for this reason to be rejected. If mankind were to resolve to agree in no institution of government, until every part of it had been adjusted to the most exact standard of perfection, society would soon become a general scene of anarchy, and the world a desert. Where is the standard of perfection to be found? Who

will undertake to unite the discordant opinions of a whole community, in the same judgment of it; and to prevail upon one conceited projector to renounce his *infallible* criterion, for the *fallible* criterion of his more *conceited neighbor?* To answer the purpose of the adversaries of the Constitution, they ought to prove, not merely, that particular provisions in it are not the best, which might have been imagined; but that the plan upon the whole is bad and pernicious.

Publius.

Questions and Activities

▶ *COMPREHENSION QUESTIONS*

1. Jay argues for a strong central government. In order to understand his argument, however, you need to be aware that there are other possible ways to distribute power in a democratic government. In 1787, for example, many citizens were suspicious of a strong federal government because they wished to keep power situated in the states. Can you think of some arguments against concentrating power in a centralized government?

2. What does Jay mean when he uses the word "just" to qualify "causes of war" (paragraphs 5 and 6)? Does he mean morally fair, legally warrantable, or politically allowable?

3. Explain Hamilton's use and emphasis of the word "political" in paragraph 2 of No. 65. How does his definition of political parallel his general position as to how impeachment should be handled in a democracy?

4. What kind of trust does Hamilton argue is placed in public officials in a democracy? Who places that trust? Why is the Senate, according to Hamilton, the most appropriate body to handle misuses or abuses of that public trust?

▶ *QUESTIONS OF RHETORICAL PURPOSE AND STRATEGY*

5. Describe the voices of Jay and Hamilton. How are their voices at least partially made necessary by the context in which the pieces appeared? Remember that these essays were first published in New York City newspapers in 1787 and 1788, shortly after the Constitution had been drafted and passed in convention. Remember, also, that the United States was a much smaller country then, with a

larger percentage of its citizens directly involved in government. How might these considerations have affected Jay's and Hamilton's choice of language?

6. Compare Jay's and Hamilton's styles to the speaking or writing style of a current politician. Use as a basis such characteristics as elegance, formality, clarity, accessibility, etc.

▶ *THEME QUESTIONS*

7. Evaluate the validity of Hamilton's argument in paragraph 11 of No. 65: "If mankind were to resolve to agree in no institution of government, until every part of it had been adjusted to the most exact standards of perfection, society would soon become a general scene of anarchy, and the world a desert." What are the implications of this statement for the interpretation of a document like a constitution? Where does it place power—in the words of a constitution or in those who interpret it?

8. Contrast these two essays on power in government with George Orwell's more personal account of the effects of political power structures on individuals (pages 647–653). What are the main differences between imperialistic power in Burma in the 1920s and centralized power in the United States in 1787? Why, according to Orwell, would a more natural relationship between those who ruled and those who were ruled be possible in the United States? Why would that more natural relationship betwen leaders and citizens make the likelihood of centralized government stronger in the United States than in Burma?

▶ *LEARNING ACTIVITIES*

9. Work together with others from your class to devise a list of counterarguments to those of Jay and Hamilton on the necessity of centralized government. Spend some time discussing how the items on the list can be connected into a strong general argument against a too powerful federal government.

10. Working alone, combine your group's list of counterarguments and your interpretation of Jay's and Hamilton's arguments in favor of strong central government into a plan for a balanced essay on the problems of centralizing power in a democracy. Even if you do not write the essay, keep your plan as a record of your response to the *Federalist Papers*.

Washington, D.C.:
The Morning After

JAN MORRIS

Formerly James Morris, Jan Morris has written more than twenty-four history and travel books. Born in Britain in 1926 and graduated from Oxford University, James Morris began taking hormone pills in 1964 to bring about a sex change that was completed by surgery in 1972. Having changed her name to Jan Morris, she published *Conundrum* (1974), an autobiographical account of the feelings and experiences that led to and resulted from her sexual transformation.

Morris's most famous early book was an account of a 1953 expedition to an altitude of twenty-two thousand feet on Mount Everest in the Himalayas. Four years later, when Morris was twenty-seven and working as a *London Times* reporter, *Coronation Everest* (1958) was published. Several of Morris's books—*Cities* (1963), *Travels* (1976), and *Destinations* (1980), from which the essay reprinted here is taken—draw from earlier travels to make observations on the character of particular places in the contemporary world. *Pax Britannica* (1968) and *The Outsiders* (1963), two of Morris's books on England, provide fresh and informative perspectives on that country in the twentieth century.

Morris brings together in her writings a rare blend of an eye for detail and a sense of social significance. Her keen observations help her to create for her readers a strong sense of having been to the places that she describes. At the same time, Morris's quick and penetrating intelligence enables her to capture the significance of the things she observes and to convey it in a convincing and often controversial way.

Washington, to Morris, is a fascinating paradox: a place possessed by monuments, official forms and ceremonies, and famous names and places, and yet also the real center of political power in the twentieth century. By the close of this essay, Morris has come to understand and accept this paradox. Power, she argues, produces a conventional language and a degree of artificial posturing in public dialogue, but it bears close analysis, for its complexity lies beneath the official and public surface of a city such as Washington.

You need to remember, as you read this essay, that Jan Morris shares in the cultural traditions of Great Britain, a country that was once the foremost imperialist power in the world. Recall George Orwell's essay on this theme (pages 647–653). Orwell felt uncomfortable with British imperialism in Burma in the 1920s. Morris, some fifty years later, represents the British perspective in a world no longer subject to British international presence, a world in which power is concentrated in Washington. All of Morris's observations are influenced to one degree or another by her British sense of the past. Her feeling, for example, that people's obsession with power in Washington seems uncontrolled and highly individualistic might derive from her sense that, in the past, British governing bureaucracies were more efficient but less apparent in their day-to-day operations.

Morris's essay adds another dimension to the theme of this section. As a careful observer and systematic interpreter of culture, Morris provides us with a first-hand but dispassionate analysis of how place and power combine in the contemporary world. She makes us raise such questions as the following:

1. How are people's attitudes toward power influenced by the context in which they live?
2. Might a person living in Washington be more apt than other Americans to take political history seriously?
3. Are important political or historical figures usually less impressive in person, as Morris suggests?
4. How might knowing public figures such as Henry Kissinger on a first-name basis affect one's attitudes toward the wielding of power in our society?

▶ ───────────────────

There was an unmistakable feeling of hangover to Washington,   1
D.C., in the fall of 1974. The long revelation of Watergate, partly so horrible, partly so beguiling, had left the capital shaken but oddly nostalgic for its months of disclosure. President Ford, having pardoned Richard Nixon for his goings-on, was trying to restore to the political scene some of its supposed wholesomeness, not to say alleged sanity. Washington society was still obsessed with the minutiae of the great scandal. By the time I got there the macabre party was over: this is a portrait of the morning after.

Failing to solve any of the problems in the airline magazine's   2
puzzle page, and soon exhausting all the faces upon which I could superimpose buckteeth or sideburns, as we approached Washington, D.C., I

turned to that beloved standby of the experienced traveler, the application for Diners Club credit cards. With a practiced hand I registered my name as Ethelreda B. Goering, my Amount and Source of Other Income as $8 million, Gold Mine, Transvaal, and as we landed I was delightfully debating whether to use as my personal reference His Holiness the Pope, Windsor Castle, Lhasa, or J. P. Morgan at the University of Lapland.

3   Imagine then my pleasure when, arriving at my hotel that evening and opening the Washington Directory, I discovered the mayor of Washington to be Mayor Washington, the treasurer of the White House Correspondents Association Mr. Edgar A. Poe, and the doorkeeper of the House of Representatives Mr. William (Fish Bait) Miller. A concomitant of power is the privilege of eccentricity, and though in recent years Americans may have pined for rulers of more orthodox method, still to visitors from smaller and less potent states an early intimation of quirk is more a comfort than a threat—the gods make their victims mad, but their favorites unconventional.

4   Besides, it has a healthily deflationary effect on the stranger. The great Moslem travelers of the Middle Ages, when they approached the capital of some unimaginable Caliph or omniscient Sultan, fell as a matter of form or policy into a ceremonial prose, matching their cadences to the Master of the World, or adjusting their punctuation to the Commander of the Faithful. I had wondered myself, as I set off for Washington this time, what avedictory style might be best suited for the present Sublimity of the White House. When I first came to the city, President Eisenhower sat in the Hall of a Thousand Ears, and his style was easily, as you might say, approximated to. President Kennedy no less obviously demanded a mixed pastiche of Hemingway, Tolkien and Zane Grey, while President Nixon, of course, could only in courtesy be addressed in his own meaningful communicational media.

5   But President Ford offered the wanderer no text. Something faintly sanctimonious, perhaps? Something brisk and sporting? Something bland, something soothing, some literary equivalent of orange juice or rubdown, to honor his role as the Great Jogger? I could not make up my mind: and so, abandoning the precedents of ibn-Khaldun and ibn-Batuta, and encouraged by the evidence of the Washington Directory, I decided to skip the honorifics altogether, and simply say hi to Fish Bait—who turned out to be, by the way, an inescapable figure of Washington life, and who earned his nickname, so his office told me, during a shrimp- or worm-sized boyhood on the Mississippi shore.

6   Unreality, of course, whether comic, paranoiac or simply bizarre, is an attribute of capital cities, because power itself is so illusory. We look

on the face of Nixon as of Ozymandias, and even Haroun-al-Raschid survives only in the fancy of his storytellers.* At least, though, the Caliph could disguise himself when he wished, and walk anonymously through the marketplace of Baghdad, where the poets declaimed, the merchants haggled and all the jostle of the real world was available outside his palace gates. When President Nixon wished to do the same, he could only go to the Lincoln Memorial, slightly drugged it seems, and talk to the students in its sepulchral glow.

The idea of an artificial capital is, I believe, specifically American, though the nature of Washington is of course another legacy of those damned French. It was a rotten idea, disastrously copied in such dumps as Canberra, Brasilia and Islamabad, and inevitably creating in the nation's capital just the same blinkered introspection as one finds in new universities started from scratch on virgin rural sites. But though everyone claims to miss the stimulus of variety in Washington, like academics, politicians are terrified of outside competition, so that in practice all conspire to maintain the shrinelike posture of the place. It is a posture, altogether spurious, of dedicated zeal and memorial—a necromantic attitude, in fact, sustained by the commanding presence of the Arlington National Cemetery, Fame's Camping Ground as it says on its triumphal arch, and suggesting to me sometimes, not least when the carillon of the Central Union Mission rings out its hymns twice daily across the Mall, a premature hush of general elegy (though I was sorry to discover, when I inquired at the Mission door, that there was in fact no glazed lady carillonneur playing "Abide with Me" on the roof, only a man with a tape recorder at the reception desk).

From the center of that allegoric cemetery one may look out across the Potomac to the grand sweep of the capital beyond. Nothing could appear much less American, for while America is above all a country of verticals, artistic, economic, symbolic, phallic, imposed splendidly upon the passive landscape, Washington, D.C., is all horizontal. Nowhere is much flatter than Washington. The ground is flat. The style is flat. The architecture is deliberately flat. From up there in the Arlington cemetery the whole city seems to lie in a single plane, without depth or perspective, its layered strips of blue, green and white broken only by the obelisk of the Washington Monument and the Capitol dome, as the

7

8

---

*Ozymandias was the name given to Egyptian Pharoah Rameses II by the Greek historian Didorus Siculus; in the nineteenth century, English Romantic poet Percy Bysshe Shelley wrote a poem about the transiency of power and called it "Ozymandias." Haroun-al-Raschid was the hero of *The Arabian Nights*; this character was based on the life of Harun the Just, who was the caliph, or ruler, of the Saracens from 765 to 809. Morris uses these references to set up her theme of the illusory nature of power.

massed ranks of Arlington are interrupted only by the graves of specially important corpses. It looks like a city of slabs, reverently disposed,
and only the jets from the National Airport, straining themselves with
difficulty out of the ambiance, throw a bold diagonal across the scene.

9   "Are all these," said a child to me outside Arlington House, surveying Fame's Camping Ground around us, "are all these *dead* guys?"
"Dead," said I, "as mutton"—but at that moment her grandmother
arrived, direct I would guess from Kalamazoo, and throwing me a
distinctly accusatory look, as though I were undermining the loyalty of
the young, she gave the child's nose a necessary wipe and hurried her
down the hill to catch the Tour-Mobile.

10   The sentries at the Tomb of the Unknown Soldier are mounted by an
infantry regiment known as the Old Guard, and I found them more
haunting than the shades. I suppose new arrivals at Arlington are, so to
speak, cosmeticized before burial, but however assiduously they are
touched up for their last roll call, they could hardly be more theatrical
than those soldiers still alive. Apparently shaven headed beneath their
peaked caps, ominously sunglassed when the day is bright, expression-
less, ritually stooped, they move with an extraordinary gliding motion
that seems to require no muscular activity at all, but is controlled electronically perhaps from some distant command post—a slow, lunar
motion, to and fro before the gaping crowds—a halt, a click of the boots,
a stylized shift of the rifle from one shoulder to the other, a long pause
as though the electrodes are warming up, and then, with an almost per-
ceptible hiss, that slow spectral lope back to the other side of the memorial, while the tourists suppress a shudder.

11   Behind their dark glasses, I suppose, the soldiers know nothing of the
sinister chill that surrounds them, and indeed when I later came across
some of the Old Guard off duty at their barracks, they seemed nice,
cheerful fellows. In the same way the obsessive nature of Washington is
not always apparent to those who form part of it. "When I was just a
little kid," a friend of mine told me at lunch one day, "I guess I wasn't
more than ten or eleven years old, I used to dream to myself I could see
my name there on the bedroom door—Senator W—!" I could hardly
conceive such a fancy in a child's mind, but she saw nothing remarkable about it, and it is probably commonplace in Washington. Politicians are politicians everywhere, but only here is the political addiction
so ingrained and so frank. Here one can observe its pursuit in every fanatic detail, from the gleam in the collective eye of the visiting debating
society to the attendant stiffening when the great man speaks, from the
swiveling heads over the cocktail canapés to the sweep of the big black
cars at the Senate side.

To avoid getting hooked myself, for it is catching as well as habit-   *12*
forming, sometimes I took the day off from politics, and did the tourist
rounds: but for all the grandeur and meaning of the city, for all the
endearing pride of my fellow visitors, still these experiences only
heightened my sense of intrusion upon some immense private performance. Inorganic by origin, Washington is unnatural in behavior; but
far from heightening everything as New York does, it spreads everything out, memorializes it, puts it in a park and reflects it in an orna-
mental pool. In New York I feel more myself than usual, in Washington
much less, for when I look for my own reflection in this city, statues
and symbols look back at me.

It is an alienating city. It lacks the corporate gift of hospitality. It is   *13*
like one vast smokeless zone. Was ever genius less at home than in the
National Gallery of Art, where the enigmatic Giorgione, the mad Van
Gogh, the lusty Picasso hang forever antiseptically among the Garden
Courts? Did ever Marlow or Molière find a less likely stage than the
Center for the Performing Arts, which suggests to me a cross between a
Nazi exhibition and a more than usually ambitious hairdresser? I
thanked my good fortune that this time I had arrived in September; at
least those interminable cherries weren't out.

Nowhere in the world is so inexorably *improving.* Elevating texts   *14*
and aphorisms, quotations from statesmen and philosophers,
Thoughts for All Eternity nag one from every other downtown wall,
and make one feel, especially perhaps if one has come in a high-school
excursion bus, awfully insignificant. What giants there were in those
days! How grandly they expressed themselves! How thickly they stand
about! Innocent III, Napoleon, Moses and St. Louis supervise the Senate subway; clumps of heroes wrestle with their standards, horseback
generals plan their strategies again on plinth and plaza across the capital. "Where Law Ends," booms the Department of Justice, "Tyranny
Begins." "Taxes Are What We Pay for a Civilized Society," retorts the
Department of Internal Revenue. "Here Are the Ties That Bind the
Life of Our People," the National Archives cry, and across the avenue
the Mission responds, with an unctuous chime of the carillon: "Come
to Me!"

When we came down from the top of the Washington Monument,   *15*
even the elevator operator dismissed us with an injunction. "Let's all
work," he said, "to clean up our country for the 200th anniversary just
coming up." "Yes sir," we dutifully replied, "you're darned right—you
hear that, kids?" He had not, however, finished yet. "And I'm talking,"
he darkly added, "about the mental aspects as well as the physical."

We had no answer to that.   *16*

17   Let me insert, if you will forgive me, two anecdotes of Westminster Abbey.* One I report firsthand. I was standing once in a cluttered alcove of the fane, romantically topsy-turvy with statues of forgotten admirals, judges and miscellaneous rulers of the world, when I heard behind me the comment of an American visitor. "All it needs," she observed *sotto voce* but decisively, "is a good museum curator from the Middle West." A second quotation was given me by one of the Abbey's guides. "Sir," another American remarked politely to him one morning, "it occurs to me that this building looks remarkably like a church."

18   I throw them in because I am aware of a prejudice in my reaction to the Washington aesthetic. I stand with Chesterton for the rolling road, and prefer even the symmetry of the Greeks or the Georgians to have its nooks and serendipities. This is, I know, a taste common in my own particular culture, but rarer elsewhere, and I must bear in mind that the singular beauties of Washington, more than the beauties of less significant cities, lie in the eyes of their beholders. I can see that, for example, the motto inscribed on the Seabees memorial—*Can Do*—which seems slick or cheap to me, translates with perfect dignity as *On Peut*, and to a visitor from Rome, Vienna or Castile the Beaux Arts monumentality of Washington is no doubt only to be expected. We all see ourselves in America, and we see our own countries, our own civilizations, confirmed, denied or parodied in Washington, D.C.

19   The fantasy of the place is nourished, indeed, by the foreigners who frequent it. The presidents and prime ministers succeeding each other day by day at Blair House are like pilgrims come to consult the great oracle across the way. The embassies strung out among their flags and gardens on Massachusetts Avenue are pavilions of make-believe. It is all a parade! The Shah is indistinguishable from the Chairman to the maid who makes their beds. The embassies are built on air, with their agency-supplied manservants or K.G.B.† chauffeurs, their government-issue carpets or regulation icons, their signed portraits of king or dictator among the dahlias on the grand piano, their ineffable hostesses, their suitable oil paintings, their envoys brought to this heady eminence by a lifetime of slog or a magazine of bullets, and the universal

---

*Westminster Abbey, originally a Benedictine monastery, was built by William the Conqueror in 1065 and added to by famous British and French architects throughout subsequent centuries. From the time of William the Conqueror until 1760, every British monarch but two was buried there. The Abbey is crowded with the tombs of famous British subjects.
†The K.G.B. is the secret police organization of Soviet Russia, members of which are here serving as chauffeurs for Soviet diplomats and their visitors.

convention, sacrosanct in Washington, that their inhabitants are in some measure recipients of a divine or at least presidential grace.

I gave myself a walking tour of the Washington embassies, and highly diverting it was, being less an architectural exhibition than a display of national images. The most endearing building, I thought, was the Icelandic, which looks like a very comfortable boardinghouse in the outskirts of Reykjavik. The most alluring seemed to me the Turkish, which was designed in fact by the American, George Totten, but speaks deliciously of hookah and seraglio, and ought to be overlooking the Golden Horn instead of the Rock Creek Parkway. The most anthropomorphic is the Yugoslav, which bears a distinct physical resemblance to Marshal Tito, the most geographic is the Canadian, which bears a distinct physical resemblance to Canada.   20

Old-school loyalist that I am, of course I like the British embassy best, and am not in the least resentful, though perhaps a *little* surprised, to hear that in these difficult times they have installed in the ambassador's house that enervating contemporary device, air conditioning. No wonder a Washington posting no longer qualifies for hazard pay! Still, up there in Lutyens's country house, red Sussex brick in Washington NW, the diplomatic masque is unashamed, and English gentlemen still stand fastidious and self-amused beneath their chandeliers. When I first came to Washington, twenty years ago, that easy Oxford manner was a local cynosure. Ambitious Americans affected it, American aristocrats wore it like a uniform, Washington hostesses talked incessantly about dukely cousins or ancestral homes in Wiltshire.*   21

Fashion is doubly fickle, though, when it partners power, and today most of the local Wasps, if they have not buzzed away altogether, have discreetly folded their wings. I met a few. I had coffee with A—, more indelibly English of accent, more unswervingly patrician of style, than any Englishman I have met for years. I renewed my acquaintance with B—, who spoke kindly of Harold Macmillan and asked what Lord Caccia was doing these days. I ran into the chairman of the Episcopalian Cathedral Garden Committee, who complained about the *dreadful* mess people made with Coca-Cola cans, adjured her dog Flicker to obey the garden regulations, and begged me not to notice the weeds. I met a retired colonel who told me to look out for an interesting essay he had contributed to the journal of the D.A.R.† But gone, or at least adeptly modified, are the Anglophile enthusiasms which, only a generation   22

---

*Wiltshire is a county in southern England famous for its prehistoric monuments, Stonehenge in particular.
†D.A.R. stands for Daughters of the American Revolution.

ago, so largely set the social tone of the city. For better or worse, America has found itself since then, and the pretensions are home-grown now.

23   An ambassador nevertheless, as Sir Henry Wotton wrote, is a man sent abroad to lie for his country, and in every one of those plushy embassies, turreted or curtain-walled, rich in monarchic symbols or austere with socialist dogma, the envoys are doing their best to sustain their own deceptions. I went to the British embassy one evening to see the pianist Vladimir Horowitz presented with the Gold Medal of the Royal Philharmonic Society, brought to him on a cushion by a marvel-ously suave young secretary, and handed over with a graceful ambassa-dorial speech about violent times and the meaning of art. Mr. Horowitz seemed pleased, but instead of replying in kind sat down at the piano and played in a highly vibrant and indeed imperial manner *God Save the Queen*, making full use of the sustaining pedal.

24   There was a pause at the end of it, and instantly, as the last notes faded, I clicked the scene in my memory: and so I have held it there like a flash from a dream, the ambassador benignly at attention, the young diplomats rigid all about, the American guests clutching their cham-pagne glasses, the great room aglow with carpets and portraits, the pianist's hand raised in a last grandiloquence—an ornate little vignette of Washington, where life so often shimmers through a gauze curtain, insubstantially.

25   Often time itself seems suspended in Washington. Superficially the current mutations show, from floppy moustaches in the National Press Building to mock folk art on the Georgetown sidewalks. Physically few cities have changed more radically in a lifetime: there are cabdrivers still on the road who remember the building of the Lincoln Memorial, and a city which fifty years ago was no more than an appendage to the Capitol is now a metropolis in its own right. Yet in the political heart of it, though the Presidents come and go, though the administrative style allegedly changes and the stance of government shifts, still the essence seems to stay the same. I was taken to lunch one day to a restaurant po-litical people favor, and looking around at the other tables, seemed to see there precisely the same sober-tied lobbyists, identically the same boyish congressmen, with just the same haircuts and almost the same suits, as I had seen there eating unquestionably the same rockfish twen-ty years before.

26   They were *not* the same men. If I could see them side by side with their predecessors of 1954, I would doubtless notice differences of manner, dress, even bone structure. But set against the monumental presence of government, like mutes in a mausoleum they assumed a common identity. Even Nelson Rockefeller, one of the richest men in

the world from one of history's most debatable dynasties, assumed it as to the manner born when he appeared before the committee inquiring into his suitability for the vice-presidency. So absolutely was he disguised in the capital's livery that seeing him sitting there among the humdrum rest of us, the world-weary reporters, the sycophantic senators, the policemen and the ushers, really I could hardly differentiate the Rockefeller person from all the others. More disturbing still, when I went to the theater that night, and saw Robert Preston belting out the opening song of the musical *Mack and Mabel* against a frenetic back-projection of the Keystone Kops,* falling through manholes, sliding off roofs, driving cars into rivers and leaping from burning hospitals, at first it seemed to me that it was not Preston at all singing away amidst the chaos, but Rockefeller yet again.

In Georgetown especially, which is I suppose the most obsessively   27
political residential enclave in the world, an extraordinary sense of sameness sometimes overcomes me. Georgetown is an innocent exterior disguising an immensely worldly, not to say tigerish community. Most of its houses are poky, inconvenient and unbeautiful, but a sort of rich inner glue of common interest and influence has permeated them, sticking them together through cracks in the brickwork, and making many of them feel less like individual houses than wings of some awkwardly dismembered mansion. Outside, too, their often undistinguished fronts have been successfully disguised with foliage, shutters and colonial lamps, giving the whole district so powerful a sense of unity that its streets have become more or less interchangeable, and I came to feel that if I got the address confused, and went to the wrong house for dinner, nobody would notice anyway.

There are spontaneous parts of Georgetown, modest parts too, but   28
the dominant characteristic of the quarter is a rich premeditation. Good taste is everywhere: original style, not often. Georgetown's culture is the culture of politics. It is all in the game. It flows watchfully with the tide, abstract to pop, kinetic to representational, *Time* one year to *Rolling Stone* the next. I doubt if there are, for instance, just at the moment anyway, many Victorian narrative pictures in the Georgetown drawing rooms; I wonder how often Mendelssohn, for example, is played on the Georgetown hi-fis; I doubt if, let us say, Somerset Maugham is prominently displayed in many Georgetown bookcases. Washington taste is much like Washington ambition: calculated.

Within the cramped opulence of the Georgetown setting, which is a   29
kind of lush mirror image of the Capitol scene, the faces of the

---

*The Keystone Kops were zany policemen who participated in wild chases in many silent movie comedies of the 1920s.

Washington activists are shaded still further into anonymity, lost among their peers and followers, so that even the affection of marriage, parenthood or friendship seems to lose its truth. It is like a shadow world. At one Georgetown dinner I was introduced to a man I seemed to think I knew. Had I met him in Europe somewhere? Was he a colleague from the distant past? Or was he, as so often happens these days, not a personal acquaintance at all, but an actor from some television serial whose face is familiar to us all? He seemed a nice man and I did not like to hurt his feelings, but I did venture to ask what was the name again. ''George McGovern,'' I was told.* Ah yes.

30   The ultimate self-deception is the deception of permanence, and Heaven knows this is not unique to Washington. Every empire has assumed its own eternity: within a decade of each other both Churchill and Hitler spoke of their respective empires lasting a thousand years apiece. I am sure there are many people in Washington who have envisaged their capital destroyed by a nuclear missile, a fate for which it seems almost expressly designed, but I suspect there are a few politicians who see their ambitions, their successes and their professional sorrows merely as transient contributions to decay. It seems so important, no doubt, when your name goes on that door at last; it seems so desperate, when you lose that election; it seems so magic a moment, when the House Majority Leader recognizes you in the elevator, or the *Washington Post* profiles you, or you get that job on the senatorial staff or the committee payroll. It is all a parade! Nowhere in the world, I think, do people take themselves more seriously than they do in Washington, or seem so indifferent to other perceptions than their own. Whether they are granite reactionaries or raging revolutionaries, they find it hard to see beyond.

31   As a corrective to this most fundamental error, I used sometimes to go and sit on the grass beside the Mall, where the tourist coaches stop beside the great round pool below Grant's statue, and the white mass of the Capitol looms portentously above it all. I am a cultist of the *genii loci*, those misty and marvelous spirits which are, I believe, literally conjured into being by the force of human experience: and though the Capitol is not very old by mystic standards, still there can be few buildings on earth more compelling to such sprites, so that on the right day I could almost see their vaporous trails circling the great dome, or intercepting each other with comic gestures above the crowning figure

---

*George McGovern, a senator from South Dakota known for his liberal views, was the unsuccessful Democratic candidate for the presidency in 1972. He was defeated by Richard Nixon.

of freedom (for they know better than any of us how little liberty has to do with politics). I was awed by the thought of them there, and the high intentions which had for nearly two centuries attended that site, and when I found the ground a little dusty, and cast around for something to sit on, for a moment I really wondered if it would be improper to place my bottom on a map of The Nation's Capital.

The point about the *genii loci*, though, is that they outlive their creators. I could not easily imagine Washington actually deserted, but as I sat there in the hot sun I did not find it hard to imagine the city past its heyday. There is an Indian feeling to Washington on a hot fall day, when the grass is browned by the long summer, the trees have lost their flowers, and the taxis are bouncing desolately through the dust of the new subway excavations—a slight sense of Calcutta, say, where the monuments of another greatness look out forlornly across the parched Maidan. Then I saw Washington too frayed in decline: the gleaming white of the Capitol gray and fretted, the pool blotched with scum, the cherry trees dead in their twos and threes, litter blowing across the grass and slogans scrawled on the statues' plinths. Then I saw the remaining spaces of the Washington plan filled in not with ostentatious halls and galleries, but with the jerry-buildings of an impoverished bureaucracy, and I saw potholes in those ceremonial boulevards, and beggars sleeping disregarded in the shade of the Washington Monument, and two or three mangy dogs nosing about the rubbish outside the Federal Court House.

But as I sat engrossed in this melancholy fancy, I heard a camera click. "Thanks, ma'am," said the cheerful young man with his girl, and instantly I remembered that illusion is a prism: for to them, who was I but your perennial Washington tourist, from Iowa or Arkansas, sitting on her map to keep her skirt clean, a history teacher perhaps, or a realtor's wife of artistic yearnings, sketching the Capitol in her notebook, recording patriotic emotions, or resolving once more to keep America beautiful in a mental as well as physical sense?

The Elder Statesman, being rather deaf, had to lean over the sofa to conduct the conversation, but was not deterred.* "Who's that? What? Sure, I remember when Jack cut off aid there. Sam didn't agree. Ted did. De Gaulle didn't want it. I thought we should. What? Who's that? Sure. I remember that very well—the Bay of Pigs—the U-2—Eisenhower

32

33

34

---

*In the simulated monologue here, Morris inserts the names of various political leaders from a number of countries. She is making the point that, in everyday talk, Washingtonians drop names of world leaders, even using first names whether they know the figures personally or not.

didn't have any idea—Khrushchev didn't know—Sam said yes—Dulles said no—I told the committee it couldn't be done. When? Who d'you say? Sure, some people say it was the Truman Doctrine, but it wasn't, only Jack/Sam/Lyndon/Harry said look, if we don't get there as sure as hell there'll be trouble with Nasser/Chiang/Nehru/Thieu. Which? When d'you say? Sure, I met him that evening. Macmillan was there, Gromyko was there, Winston was there, Stalin was there, Napoleon said look, Gladstone said wait a minute, Robert E. Lee was there, Lincoln said to me, I said to the Kaiser, Metternich said not on your sweet life, Bismarck walked out—he was a very difficult guy to deal with. ...What's that? Which? Sure, yes, I'd love some, no sugar thanks. ...''

35   For of course there is to the gigantic fantasy of Washington a hardly less enormous element of truth. If I have romanticized that monologue toward the end, I have not distorted its message—which is that like it or not, Washington is the summit of the Western world. The great seldom seem so great when one meets them face to face, and in Washington especially they seem to shrink in the flesh—the only man I saw in the city who struck me at once with the magic aura of leadership was the cantor or precentor of a group of Hare Krishna devotees. Nevertheless the names that Washington so loves to drop really are the names that will survive in the history books, and that statesman across the sofa was truly reminiscing about the stuff of legend. His wife was there too, and her conversation was hardly less Pepysian or Nicolsonian.* ''I do think,'' she said ''—and I've just this minute run into him at the Italian Embassy reception—I really do think Henry's getting a *little* too fat.''†

36   My own sense of hierarchy is skeptical, even condescending, so that this kind of small talk raises in me more a giggle than a gasp: but I pulled myself together whenever I could and reminded myself that in Washington more than anywhere, perhaps, the great game of politics is played for human lives and happiness. So infectious is the rhythm of the capital, so compelling, I can well see, is the fascination of its charades, that it takes a conscious effort of the will to translate its illusions into reality (not least, as I later discovered, in the presence of Henry, who is not too fat at all, I don't think, and who is so genuinely entertaining a man, with so smoky a wit, that one can hardly grasp the titanesque na-

*Samuel Pepys (1633–1703) was a famous British diarist who provided personal descriptions of court life in England from 1660 to 1669. Sir Harold Nicolson was most famous for his three-volume *Diaries and Letters* (1966–1968), which provide a valuable record of British social and political life from 1930–1964. Both men were famous, then, for their social ''conversation.''
†The Henry referred to is Henry Kissinger, former President Nixon's Secretary of State.

ture of his employment). There is a car that drives around the town towing a coffin inscribed with the text "The Death of Philippine Democracy." In a city accustomed to the comings and goings of Immortals, such a little cortège goes unremarked. I obliged myself, though, when it passed me one day, to wonder just what it meant, and what tenuous chain of appeal it represented. At one end of the demonstration stood the White House, the fount of all mercy, whose incumbent was commonly supposed to have achieved office by a deal with his predecessor, a common crook, but who would one day be honored in this city, no doubt, whatever his shortcomings, with a Memorial Grove, Archive or Sculpture Garden. At the other end of the message lay—what? Men in prison? Wives distraught? The knock at the midnight door? I did not, to be honest, know much about the state of Philippine democracy, but just to speculate about the connection between the state of human happiness in the Manila backstreets and the condition of human power in the Oval Office was a useful exercise in perspectives.

Here is another. I shared a taxi into town one day with a lady in a blue   *37*
silk turban who was visiting Washington and was about to meet her daughter for lunch at a Hot Shoppe. Down the great thoroughfares we drove, and all the memorials of the American splendor passed us one by one, granite and concrete, obelisk and colonnade. My companion drew my attention now and then to a White House or a Treasury, but it was as we approached the Capitol itself, and were deploring the state of things in general, that she spoke the words I best remember: "I sometimes wonder, oh, what kind of a world are we bringing our children into, when you have to pay 20¢ for a donut?"

Twenty cents for a donut! Even Americans bleed. . . .   *38*

Questions and Activities

▶ COMPREHENSION QUESTIONS

1. Why does Morris say, in her introductory paragraph to this essay, that there was a feeling of hangover to Washington, D.C., in the fall of 1974? How does this comment flavor everything that is said about Washington in the essay that follows?
2. What type of "prejudice" does Morris admit to having about Washington in paragraph 18? How is that prejudice explained by the Westminster Abbey anecdotes in paragraph 17? What does Morris do to assure her readers that this prejudice does not disqualify her as a commentator on the city of Washington?

3. Define what Morris means by the phrase *genii loci* in paragraph 31. (A loose translation of the Latin phrase is "local spirits.") How is the phrase used to describe Morris's response to Washington? Why do these local spirits outlive the real people who try to shape political destiny in Washington?

▶ *QUESTIONS OF RHETORICAL PURPOSE AND STRATEGY*

4. Why does Morris begin this essay with a description of her arrival in Washington? Why, instead, did she not begin with some factual information on the population and geography of Washington? How does her more personal opening establish the essay's overall purpose?
5. Can you discern the purpose behind Morris's inclusion of so many names of politicians and statesmen in this essay? Is Morris using these individuals to represent what she thinks are typical Washington types? If so, what general impression is she creating by emphasizing these types?
6. Most readers would agree that this is not primarily a persuasive essay. Why do you think this is true? What elements of Morris's style seem to indicate her purpose is a personal and expressive interpretation of Washington rather than persuading her readers to change their attitudes toward the city?
7. Consider Morris's use of references to famous people and places in this essay. What do they add to the essay's overall effect on you as reader? Are they often sarcastically used? In what ways do the references to places and people suggest Morris's attitude toward official Washington?

▶ *THEME QUESTIONS*

8. Washington, as Morris describes it, seems most interested in what might be called official, or formal, power. Morris also seems to suggest that there is a kind of personal and spiritual power that Washington seems to ignore or deemphasize. Can you point to a place in this essay where personal and official power seem to be contrasted?
9. What, in the atmosphere of the city of Washington, encourages public figures to leave their personal lives behind when they come to the city? How might this atmosphere have contributed to a scandal such as Watergate?

▶ *LEARNING ACTIVITIES*

10. Contrast the kind of power Morris finds in Washington to the kind of power described in another selection in this section. Create an out-

line for an essay, organizing your ideas around three categories: the sources of power, the people who share power, and the results of power.

11. If you have previously experienced an exposure to power, describe that experience to the rest of this class. (Your experience could involve local as well as regional or national power groups, school government, city or town politics, neighborhood groups, etc.) What were the sources, who were the people involved, and what were the results of the power you experienced?

12. Report to the class on a book you have recently read that dealt in one way or another with the theme of using power. A political biography or a nonfictional account or novel about high finance or science would qualify. Organize your report around the categories of sources, people, and results used in the previous two activities.

On Being Female, Black, and Free

MARGARET WALKER

Margaret Walker has had a productive career as a college teacher and writer. She has also remained consistently involved in black political and social movements and, more recently, has been active in supporting women writers. She was educated at Northwestern University and the University of Iowa and taught at Jackson State College, Mississippi, from 1949 until her retirement in 1982.

Her novel, *Jubilee* (1972), won her critical acclaim for its sensitive portrayal of the effects of social conditions on its black characters. She won the Yale Series of Younger Poets Award for her first book of poems, *For My People* (1942), and has published three other books of poems. She has received a Fulbright fellowship and honorary doctorates from Rush College, Northwestern University, Dennison University, and Morgan State University.

In the essay included here, Walker describes her career as one divided among allegiances to family and church on a personal level, to colleges and students on a professional level, and to her writing and general human causes on a national and international level. These different levels of allegiance have made her life interesting and worthwhile, but anxiety-ridden and painful at the same time. It is from this context of conflict, triumph, and suffering that Walker draws the energy for her writing, and it is from the expressive power of her writing that she seems to draw the energy for her involvement in social and political movements.

In contrast to the rest of the essays in this section, Walker's piece focuses on the power of individual expression in the midst of social, political, and economic forces. Writing, teaching, and social action are Walker's means of stabilizing and redirecting the forces that might otherwise direct her life. As you read, consider these questions:

1. Jan Morris emphasized a power that is connected with place, with a physical location in space and time. What is the center of power for Walker?
2. What might Walker think of John Jay's and Alexander Hamilton's arguments for a more centralized form of governmental power?
3. What might Walker think of Barbara Grizzuti Harrison's description of the est program and its treatment of individuals (pages 672–688)?

4. How might Walker feel about the narrator's situation in George Orwell's "Shooting an Elephant" (pages 647–653)? Would she describe Orwell's narrator as a victim of political circumstances, a simple fool, or an insensitive British official in a colonial country?
5. How do you think Walker would respond to Gerard Piel's analysis of the effects of the computer on economic realities? Do you think Walker would warn against overreliance on the computer? Or would she consider the computer a positive extension of individual effort and talent?

▶ ————————————

My birth certificate reads female, Negro, date of birth and place. Call it fate or circumstance, this is my human condition. I have no wish to change it from being female, black, and free. I like being a woman. I have a proud black heritage, and I have learned from the difficult exigencies of life that freedom is a philosophical state of mind and existence. The mind is the only place where I can exist and feel free. In my mind I am absolutely free.

My entire career of writing, teaching, lecturing, yes, and raising a family is determined by these immutable facts of my human condition. As a daughter, a sister, a sweetheart, a wife, a mother, and now a grandmother, my sex or gender is preeminent, important, and almost entirely deterministic. Maybe my glands have something to do with my occupation as a creative person. About this, I am none too sure, but I think the cycle of life has much to do with the creative impulse and the biorhythms of life must certainly affect everything we do.

Creativity cannot exist without the feminine principle, and I am sure God is not merely male or female but He-She—our Father-Mother God. All nature reflects this rhythmic and creative principle of feminism and femininity: the sea, the earth, the air, fire, and all life whether plant or animal. Even as they die, are born, grow, reproduce, and grow old in their cyclic time, so do we in lunar, solar, planetary cycles of meaning and change.

Ever since I was a little girl I have wanted to write and I have been writing. My father told my mother it was only a puberty urge and would not last, but he encouraged my early attempts at rhyming verses just the same, and he gave me the notebook or daybook in which to keep my poems together. When I was eighteen and had ended my junior year in college, my father laughingly agreed it was probably more than a puberty urge. I had filled the 365 pages with poems.

5   Writing has always been a means of expression for me and for other black Americans who are just like me, who feel, too, the need for freedom in this "home of the brave, and land of the free." From the first, writing meant learning the craft and developing the art. Going to school had one major goal, to learn to be a writer. As early as my eighth year I had the desire, at ten I was trying, at eleven and twelve I was learning, and at fourteen and fifteen I was seeing my first things printed in local school and community papers. I have a copy of a poem published in 1930 and an article with the caption, "What Is to Become of Us?" which appeared in 1931 or 1932. All of this happened before I went to Northwestern.

6   I spent fifteen years becoming a poet before my first book appeared in 1942. I was learning my craft, finding my voice, seeking discipline as life imposes and superimposes that discipline upon the artist. Perhaps my home environment was most important in the early stages—hearing my mother's music, my sister and brother playing the piano, reading my father's books, hearing his sermons, and trying every day to write a poem. Meanwhile, I found I would have to start all over again and learn how to write prose fiction in order to write the novel I was determined to create to the best of my ability and thus fulfill my promise to my grandmother. A novel is not written exactly the same way as a poem, especially a long novel and a short poem. The creative process may be basically the same—that is, the thinking or conceptualization—but the techniques, elements, and form or craft are decidedly and distinctively different.

7   It has always been my feeling that writing must come out of living, and the writer is no more than his personality endures in the crucible of his times. As a woman, I have come through the fires of hell because I am a black woman, because I am poor, because I live in America, and because I am determined to be both a creative artist and maintain my inner integrity and my instinctive need to be free.

8   I don't think I noticed the extreme discrimination against women while I was growing up in the South. The economic struggle to exist and the racial dilemma occupied all my thinking until I was more than an adult woman. My mother had undergone all kinds of discrimination in academia because of her sex; so have my sisters. Only after I went back to school and earned a doctorate did I begin to notice discrimination against me as a woman. It seems the higher you try to climb, the more rarefied the air, the more obstacles appear. I realize I had been naïve, that the issues had not been obvious and that as early as my first employment I felt the sting of discrimination because I am female.

9   I think it took the women's movement to call my attention to cases of overt discrimination that hark back to my WPA days on the Writers'

Project.* It did not occur to me that Richard Wright as a supervisor on the project made $125 per month and that he claimed no formal education, but that I had just graduated from Northwestern University and I was a junior writer making $85 per month. I had no ambitions to be an administrator; I was too glad to have a job; I did not think about it. Now I remember the intense antagonism on the project toward the hiring of a black woman as a supervisor, none other than the famous Katherine Dunham, the dancer, but it never occurred to me then that she was undergoing double discrimination.

When I first went to Iowa and received my master's degree that year   10 there were at least five or six women teaching English in the university. When I returned to study for the doctorate, not a single woman was in the department. At Northwestern my only woman teacher had taught personal hygiene. I did not expect to find women at Yale, but it slowly dawned on me that black women in black colleges were more numerous than white women in coed white universities.

And then I began looking through the pages of books of American and   11 English literature that I was teaching, trying in vain to find the works of many women writers. I have read so many of those great women writers of the world—poets, novelists, and playwrights: Sigrid Undset and Selma Lagerlof, Jane Austen, George Sand, George Eliot, and Colette. All through the ages women have been writing and publishing, black and white women in America and all over the world. A few women stand out as geniuses of their times, but those are all too few. Even the women who survive and are printed, published, taught and studied in the classroom fall victim to negative male literary criticism. Black women suffer damages at the hands of every male literary critic, whether he is black or white. Occasionally a man grudgingly admits that some woman writes well, but only rarely.

Despite severe illness and painful poverty, and despite jobs that al-   12 ways discriminated against me as a woman—never paying me equal money for equal work, always threatening or replacing me with a man, or men who were neither as well educated nor experienced but just men—despite all these examples of discrimination I have managed to work toward being a self-fulfilling, re-creating, reproducing woman, raising a family, writing poetry, cooking food, doing all the creative things I know how to do and enjoy. But my problems have not been simple; they have been manifold. Being female, black, and poor in America

*WPA is an abbreviation for the Work Projects Administration, the public works program of Franklin Roosevelt's administration in the 1930s, used to curb unemployment after the Great Depression of 1929–1933. The WPA included a Writers' Project along with several manual labor programs.

means I was born with three strikes against me. I am considered at the bottom of the social class-caste system in these United States, born low on the totem pole. If "a black man has no rights that a white man is bound to respect," what about a black woman?

13   Racism is so extreme and so pervasive in our American society that no black individual lives in an atmosphere of freedom. The world of physical phenomena is dominated by fear and greed. It consists of pitting the vicious and the avaricious against the naïve, the hunted, the innocent, and the victimized. Power belongs to the strong, and the strong are BIG in more ways than one. No one is more victimized in this white male American society than the black female.

14   There are additional barriers for the black woman in publishing, in literary criticism, and in promotion of her literary wares. It is an insidious fact of racism that the most highly intellectualized, sensitized white person is not always perceptive about the average black mind and feeling, much less the creativity of any black genius. Racism forces white humanity to underestimate the intelligence, emotion, and creativity of black humanity. Very few white Americans are conscious of the myth about race that includes the racial stigmas of inferiority and superiority. They do not understand its true economic and political meaning and therefore fail to understand its social purpose. A black, female person's life as a writer is fraught with conflict, competitive drives, professional rivalries, even danger, and deep frustrations. Only when she escapes to a spiritual world can she find peace, quiet, and hope of freedom. To choose the life of a writer, a black female must arm herself with a fool's courage, foolhardiness, and serious purpose and dedication to the art of writing, strength of will and integrity, because the odds are always against her. The cards are stacked. Once the die is cast, however, there is no turning back.

15   In the first place, the world of imagination in which the writer must live is constantly being invaded by the enemy, the mundane world. Even as the worker in the fires of imagination finds that the world around her is inimical to intellectual activity, to the creative impulse, and to the kind of world in which she must daily exist and also thrive and produce, so, too, she discovers that she must meet that mundane world head-on every day on its own terms. She must either conquer or be conquered.

16   A writer needs certain conditions in which to work and create art. She needs a piece of time; a peace of mind; a quiet place; and a private life.

17   Early in my life I discovered I had to earn my living and I would not be able to eke out the barest existence as a writer. Nobody writes while hungry, sick, tired, and worried. Maybe you can manage with one of

these but not all four at one time. Keeping the wolf from the door has been my full-time job for more than forty years. Thirty-six of those years I have spent in the college classroom, and nobody writes to full capacity on a full-time teaching job. My life has been public, active, and busy to the point of constant turmoil, tumult, and trauma. Sometimes the only quiet and private place where I could write a sonnet was in the bathroom, because that was the only room where the door could be locked and no one would intrude. I have written mostly at night in my adult life and especially since I have been married, because I was determined not to neglect any members of my family; so I cooked every meal daily, washed dishes and dirty clothes, and nursed sick babies.

I have struggled against dirt and disease as much as I have against sin,   18
which, with my Protestant and Calvinistic background, was always to be abhorred. Every day I have lived, however, I have discovered that the value system with which I was raised is of no value in the society in which I must live. This clash of my ideal with the real, of my dream world with the practical, and the mystical inner life with the sordid and ugly world outside—this clash keeps me on a battlefield, at war, and struggling, even tilting windmills. Always I am determined to overcome adversity, determined to win, determined to be me, myself at my best, always female, always black, and everlastingly free. I think this is always what the woman writer wants to be, herself, inviolate, and whole. Shirley Chisholm,* who is also black and female, says she is unbossed and unbought. So am I, and I intend to remain that way. Nobody can tell me what to write because nobody owns me and nobody pulls my strings. I have not been writing to make money or earn my living. I have taught school as my vocation. Writing is my life, but it is an avocation nobody can buy. In this respect I believe I am a free agent, stupid perhaps, but *me* and still free.

When I was younger I considered myself an emancipated woman,   19
freed from the shackles of mind and body that typified the Victorian woman, but never would I call myself the liberated woman in today's vernacular; never the bohemian; never the completely free spirit living in free love; never the lesbian sister; always believing in moderation and nothing to excess; never defying convention, never radical enough to defy tradition; not wanting to be called conservative but never moving beyond the bounds of what I consider the greatest liberty within law, the greatest means of freedom within control. I have lived out my female destiny within the bonds of married love. For me, it could not have been otherwise. In the same way I refuse to judge others, for if tol-

*Shirley Chisholm is a black politician and leader of women's causes from New York City. She has been very involved in national Democratic politics.

erance is worth anything, love is worth everything. Everyone should dare to love.

20   I am therefore fundamentally and contradictorily three things. I am religious almost to the point of orthodoxy—I go to church, I pray, I believe in the stern dogma and duty of Protestant Christianity; I am radical but I wish to see neither the extreme radical left nor the radical right in control. And I am like the astrological description of a crab, a cancer—quick to retreat into my shell when hurt or attacked. I will wobble around circuitously to find another way out when the way I have chosen has been closed to me. I believe absolutely in the power of my black mind to create, to write, to speak, to witness truth, and to be heard.

21   Enough for a time about being female and black. What about freedom? The question of freedom is an essential subject for any writer. Without freedom, personal and social, to write as one pleases and to express the will of the people, the writer is in bondage. This bondage may seem to be to others outside oneself but closely related by blood or kinship in some human fashion; or this bondage may appear to be to the inimical forces of the society that so impress or repress that individual.

22   For the past twenty years or longer I have constantly come into contact with women writers of many different races, classes, nationalities, and degrees. I look back on more than forty years of such associations. Whether at a cocktail party for Muriel Rukeyser at *Poetry* magazine or at Yaddo where Carson MacCullers, Jean Stafford, Karen Blixen, Caroline Slade, and Katherine Anne Porter were guests; or meeting Adrienne Rich and Erica Jong in Massachusetts at Amherst, or having some twenty-five of my black sister-poets at a Phillis Wheatley poetry festival here in Mississippi, including many of the young and brilliant geniuses of this generation; or here in Mississippi where I have come to know Eudora Welty and Ellen Douglas, or having women from foreign countries journey to Jackson to see me, women like Rosey Pool from Amsterdam and a young woman writer a few weeks ago from Turkey or Bessie Head from South Africa—all these experiences have made me know and understand the problems of women writers and our search for freedom.

23   For the nonwhite woman writer, whether in Africa, Asia, Latin America, the islands of the Caribbean, or the United States, her destiny as a writer has always seemed bleak. Women in Africa and Asia speak of hunger and famine and lack of clean water at the same time that their countries are riddled with warfare. Arab women and Jewish women think of their children in a world that has no hope of peace. Irish women, Protestant and Catholic, speak of the constant threat of bombs and being blown to bits. The women of southern Africa talk of their lives apart from their husbands and their lives in exile from their home-

lands because of the racial strife in their countries. A Turkish woman speaks of the daily terrorism in her country, of combing the news each evening to see if there are names known on the list of the murdered.

I have read the works of scores of these women. I saw Zora Neale Hurston when I was a child and I know what a hard life she had. I read the works of a dozen black women in the Harlem Renaissance, who despite their genius received only a small success. Langston Hughes translated Gabriela Mistral, and I read her before she won the Nobel Prize for Literature. Hualing Nieh Engle tells of her native China, and my friends in Mexico speak of the unbelievable poverty of their people. Each of these internationally known women writers is my sister in search of an island of freedom. Each is part of me and I am part of her.

Writing is a singularly individual matter. At least it has historically been so. Only the creative, original individual working alone has been considered the artist working with the fire of imagination. Today, this appears no longer to be the case. In America, our affluent, electronic, and materialistic society does not respect the imaginative writer regardless of sex, race, color, or creed. It never thought highly of the female worker, whether an Emily Dickinson or Amy Lowell, Phillis Wheatley, or Ellen Glasgow. Our American society has no respect for the literary values of intellectual honesty nor for originality and creativity in the sensitive individual. Books today are managed, being written by a committee and promoted by the conglomerate, corporate structures. Best sellers are designed as commodities to sell in the marketplace before a single word is written. Plastic people who are phony writers pretending to take us into a more humanistic century are quickly designated the paper heroes who are promoted with super-HYPE. Do I sound bitter? A Black Woman Writer who is free? Free to do what? To publish? To be promoted? Of what value is freedom in a money-mad society? What does freedom mean to the racially biased and those bigots who have deep religious prejudices? What is my hope as a woman writer?

I am a black woman living in a male-oriented and male-dominated white world. Moreover, I live in an American Empire where the financial tentacles of the American Octopus in the business-banking world extend around the globe, with the multinationals and international conglomerates encircling everybody and impinging on the lives of every single soul. What then are my problems? They are the pressures of a sexist, racist, violent, and most materialistic society. In such a society life is cheap and expendable; honor is a rag to be scorned; and justice is violated. Vice and money control business, the judicial system, government, sports, entertainment, publishing, education, and the church. Every other arm of this hydra-headed monster must render lip service and yeoman support to extend, uphold, and perpetuate the syndicated world-system. The entire world of the press, whether broadcast or print journalism, must acquiesce and render service or be eliminated. And what have I to do with this? How do I operate? How long can I live under fear before I too am blown to bits and must crumble into anonymous dust and nonentity?

27   Now I am sixty-three. I wish I could live the years all over. I am sure I would make the same mistakes and do all the things again exactly the same way. But perhaps I might succeed a little more; and wistfully I hope, too, I might have written more books.

28   What are the critical decisions I must make as a woman, as a writer? They are questions of compromise, and of guilt. They are the answers to the meaning and purpose of all life; questions of the value of life lived half in fear and half in faith, cringing under the whip of tyranny or dying, too, for what one dares to believe and dying with dignity and without fear. I must believe there is more wisdom in a righteous path that leads to death than an ignominious path of living shame; that the writer is still in the avant-garde for Truth and Justice, for Freedom, Peace, and Human Dignity. I must believe that women are still in that humanistic tradition and I must cast my lot with them.

29   Across the world humanity seems in ferment, in war, fighting over land and the control of people's lives; people who are hungry, sick, and suffering, most of all fearful. The traditional and historic role of womankind is ever the role of the healing and annealing hand, whether the outworn modes of nurse, and mother, cook, and sweetheart. As a writer these are still her concerns. These are still the stuff about which she writes, the human condition, the human potential, the human destiny. Her place, let us be reminded, is anywhere she chooses to be, doing what she has to do, creating, healing, and always being herself. Female, Black, and Free, this is what I always want to be.

Questions and Activities

▶ *COMPREHENSION QUESTIONS*

1. Walker links writing with power. Define the kind of power that Walker associates with writing in paragraph 4 as well as the kind of power she identifies with writing in paragraph 11.
2. Look up Sigrid Undset and Selma Lagerlof (paragraph 11) in biographical dictionaries in the reference section of the library. What nationalities are they? What have they written? What is Walker's point in listing their names with those of the four better-known women writers?

3. What is Walker's point when she compares her salary with Richard Wright's in paragraph 9? Reread the headnote on Wright (pages 627–628) before you answer this question.

▶ *QUESTIONS OF RHETORICAL PURPOSE AND STRATEGY*

4. How would you describe Walker's first sentence? What type of relationship does it establish between Walker and her readers? Is that relationship maintained throughout the essay?
5. Why does Walker choose to write this essay in the first person? How might the use of the third person (either "she" or the more formal "one") have changed Walker's relationship with her readers?
6. Walker arranges her material in this essay so that it flows from more personal experiences in the earlier parts to more public issues in its later parts. What was Walker's purpose in choosing such an arrangement?

▶ *THEME QUESTIONS*

7. Many of the selections included in this section deal with the relationship between personal and public uses of power. What do you think is Walker's general position concerning this relationship?
8. Do you think Walker would agree with someone who argued that writers do not need to concern themselves with political or social issues or with the situations of other writers in their communities?
9. Why does Walker say that "the world of imagination in which the writer must live is constantly being invaded by the enemy, the mundane world" (paragraph 15)? What is "the mundane world"? How has it interfered in Walker's life as a writer? Do all writers (and people) share this problem of interference from the mundane world?

▶ *LEARNING ACTIVITIES*

10. Record the ways in which the mundane world interferes in your life. Share your list with some of your classmates. Do their lists have any items in common with yours?
11. Write a brief sketch in which you describe how mundane affairs interfere with some important goal or activity. Read your sketch to the class. Listen and respond to others as they read their sketches.
12. Make a list of arguments against Walker's contention that writers should have a strong sense of social purpose. Might, for example, someone argue that writers should function in ivory towers, as isolated from social conditions as possible? Or might someone argue that a writer should specialize in a particular field in order to become an expert and that political and social concerns would impede the development of that special expertise?

The Night Chanter
N. SCOTT MOMADAY

N. Scott Momaday, a member of the Kiowa tribe, was born in Oklahoma in 1934. One of the foremost native American writers, he currently teaches English at the University of Arizona, has previously taught at the University of California at Berkeley and Santa Barbara, and received degrees from Stanford University and the University of New Mexico. He has won a Guggenheim Fellowship and the Academy of American Poets Prize.

Momaday's poetry, fiction, and essays are all devoted to portraying the effects of the American Indian heritage on the Indian world view in this century. In *The Way to Rainy Mountain* (1969), Momaday combines myth, history, and personal recollection in a story about the Kiowa tribe. In *House Made of Dawn* (1968), which won a Pulitzer Prize for fiction, Momaday tells the story of a displaced Kiowa Indian, who experiences military service, prison, rehabilitation, and a final return to his tribal homeland, where he reunites with his grandfather and nature in a climactic Indian ritual. These books, as well as Momaday's poetry and essays, strive to explain Kiowa culture and sensibility and to contrast that sensibility to what Momaday feels is the alienation of most Americans from nature and from one another. The Kiowa, Momaday suggests, for all their displacement and suffering in modern cities, have managed to hold onto tribal myths and beliefs that enable them to connect with each other and with the world around them.

Momaday's messages are always conveyed in writing that is innovative and powerful. *House Made of Dawn,* for example, is narrated by several different voices, and the chronology of events is distorted and reshaped to fit the thematic intention of the novel. The result is both a dramatic rendering of the main character's experiences and a more universal view of the Indian experience in modern America.

The following piece is taken from *House Made of Dawn.* It is narrated by a citified Indian, who befriends another Indian in Los Angeles, shortly after the latter's release from prison. As the piece begins, the narrator is describing his friend's departure from Los Angeles, and he proceeds to combine a specific account of his own actions during the rest of the day with his recollections of his friend's experiences during his stay in the city. The result is a curious mixture of the narrator's loneliness and his friend's struggles with himself and the authorities. The modern Indian and the tribal Indian are contrasted, and both are unhappy and out of place in Los Angeles.

Momaday's story gives us a picture of the dispossessed in a large city. The Indians have no power to alter their situation, at least as Momaday presents it, because they have no real sense of connection to the society within which they live and work. Both men are driven, during their free time, back to Indian religious rituals. But these rituals, experienced among small groups of displaced fellow Indians during times after work, serve to emphasize their alienation from the culture of Los Angeles.

Some general questions should be kept in mind in order to connect the view on power offered in Momaday's story to the other perspectives in the rest of this section:

1. Must individual power be dependent on the role that is assigned to a person by the larger society?
2. How can people maintain a connection with their past when they live in environments that seem to have no relationship with that past?
3. Do feelings of personal power evolve from participation in group rituals and myths, or do they evolve primarily from individual imagination, knowledge, or strength?

▶ ——————————————————

Los Angeles, February 20, 1952

He left today. It was raining, and I gave him my coat. You know, I hated to give it up; it was the only one I had. We stood outside on the platform. He was looking down, and I was trying to think of something to say. The tracks were all wet—you know how the rails shine in the rain—and there were people all around, saying goodbye to each other. He had a sack and a suitcase—you know, one of those little tin boxes with three stripes painted on it. We had walked all the way in the rain, and the shoulders of that coat—his coat—were all wet and stained. He tried to keep the sack inside of his coat, but part of it got wet. He took it out and tried to dry it when we got to the station, but it was already getting soft. I guess it fell apart afterward. He looked pretty bad. His hands were still bandaged, and he couldn't use them very well. It took us a long time to get there. He couldn't walk very fast. It was a good coat, gray gabardine, but it was old and it hadn't been cleaned in a long time. I don't remember where I got it. I got it secondhand, and there was a big hole in the right pocket. You don't really need a coat like that around here, except when it rains.

1

2   It was getting dark when I came back, and it stopped raining for a while. I got downtown and the streets were wet and all the lights were going on. You know, it's dark down there all the time, even at noon, and the lights are always on. But at night when it rains the lights are everywhere. They shine on the pavement and the cars. They are all different colors; they go on and off and move all around. The stores are all lighted up inside, and the windows are full of shiny things. Everything is clean and bright and new-looking.

3   You have to watch where you're going. There's always a big crowd of people down there, especially after it rains, and a lot of noise. You hear the cars on the wet streets, starting and stopping. You hear a lot of whistles and horns, and there's a lot of loud music all around. Those old men who stand around on the corners and sell papers, they're always yelling at you, but you can't understand them. I can't, anyway.

4   I walked right along because it was going to rain again, and I was getting cold. I didn't want to be down there anyway. I kept thinking about him being sick like that on the train. He looked pretty bad, like he might need some help. There was still a lot of blue and swelling around his eyes, and you could see that his nose was broken. His hands were all bandaged up. Now you know you're not going to help a man who's all beat up like that, not if you don't know him. You're going to be afraid of him. I kept thinking about that, how nobody was going to help him, and I got to feeling bad; I got lonesome, too, I guess. It started to rain again, and it was kind of lonesome down there in the streets, everybody going someplace, going home.

5   I came out of the tunnel on 3rd Street and turned around toward Bunker Hill Avenue. It was raining pretty hard again, and my shirt was all wet and sticky—you know how wool smells when it gets all wet—and I went into The Silver Dollar, Henry's place. It was warm in there. It's a pretty good place; there's a juke box, and there's always some Indians, drinking and fooling around. You can get drunk in there, and as long as you don't get sick or start a fight or something, nobody says anything. Martinez comes in there sometimes, and then everybody gets real quiet. You know, they call him *culebra*.* He's a cop, and a bad one. He's always looking for trouble, and if he's got it in for you—if you make him mad—you better look out. But Henry always gives him a bottle—and money, too, I guess. He's good to him, you know? And if you behave yourself in there, he lets you alone.

6   It was pretty crowded on account of the rain. I wanted a drink, but I didn't have any money, so I asked Manygoats if he could pay me back.

---

*"Culebra" is the Spanish word for "snake."

He was with some girl I didn't know—she's new around here, from Oklahoma, I think—and he's owed me some money for a long time. He gets paid by the week, and he gets some lease money from home, too. He was acting pretty big, because of that girl, I guess, and he gave me three dollars. She was good-looking, that girl—you know, great big breasts—and I kind of wanted to meet her. I could have talked to her, I guess; she seemed real nice and friendly, but I could tell that Manygoats wanted me to leave. He was making out all right; he had some plans, I guess. So I told him I had to meet somebody outside, and he sure was glad. If he hadn't paid me back, I could have had some fun with him. Right away I was sorry I said that—about meeting somebody, I mean —because then I had to leave. There were some other guys I knew, Howard and Tosamah and Cruz and those guys, but they were all having a big time together. They had some plans, I guess. I guess I didn't care much, either. I didn't feel like going anyplace, so I bought a bottle of wine and came on home.

You could see the rain around the streetlights. They made funny yellow circles against the clouds and the buildings, and the rain was steady and fine. It was dark out there, except for the streetlights, and there was nobody around, just a car now and then. And it would go along pretty slow and sound like it does in the rain, and when it passed you could see the taillights, how they make those wavy red lines in the street. 7

There's no light downstairs; it blew out a long time ago. There was nobody around. I couldn't hear anybody, and the stairs were dark. I forgot to get some matches at Henry's place, and I had to feel my way up the stairs. When I came in here, the window was open. That's the first thing I saw, that the window was open and the rain was coming in and the sill was dripping inside. I felt bad about that, forgetting to close the window, because the floor leaks and that old woman Carlozini downstairs, she gets pretty mad. It leaks on her bed, I guess, and one time she told the landlord about it. I turned on the light and, sure enough, there was a big wet spot on the floor. I tried to wipe it up, but it was pretty well soaked in. She's out someplace again, and I hope she really ties one on. She's going to tell the landlord as sure as anything. Well, it's the only window in here, you know, and it gets pretty stale if you don't keep it open. You have to open the door, too, so there's a draft. I remember how I was sitting there this afternoon with my feet up on the sill. It was just beginning to sprinkle a little, and he had that little suitcase out on the bed, and I could hear him moving around behind me. There was a big pigeon flying around out there in the street, and I was trying to get it to come up on the sill. You know, you can do that sometimes if you put some crumbs around. But that one—it was a great big one, with a lot of 8 blue and purple on its neck—it couldn't seem to make up its mind. It just sailed around for a while, and finally it flew up on the roof across the street. There were some others over there, a lot of them. We just forgot about that window, that's all.

9   It was pretty cold in here when I came in, and I took off that wet shirt and turned the radiator on. I was afraid the furnace wasn't on, but pretty soon the pipes began knocking and there was a little heat coming out. I put my shirt over the radiator, and pretty soon you could really smell the wool. It got almost dry, and I was afraid it was going to get burned, so I put it on again. It was all warm, and it really felt good. I thought about eating something. Milly brought some groceries up here yesterday; she's always doing that, and it comes out of her own pocket, too. We put some cheese and crackers and a couple of candy bars in that sack he had. There's quite a bit left, I guess, some bread and some cans of chili and stuff. But I wasn't very hungry, and I had that bottle of wine. Now that he's gone, I don't know if Milly's going to come around anymore. I guess she will. It got pretty hot in here after a while, and I had to turn the heat off. It's funny how those pipes make all that noise. You can hear them all over the building, especially when there's nobody around.

10   I kept thinking about him. I wish Milly was here. She liked him a whole lot, and she's always talking to me about him. She thought he was going to be O.K. around here, I guess. She wouldn't get drunk with us or anything like that, but she would always come around with some groceries and we would eat together, the three of us. She was always asking him about the reservation and the army and prison and all at first, but he didn't like to talk about it much, and she caught on after a while. And then she talked about other things. We kidded her a lot, and she liked it, and pretty soon she didn't bring all those papers around anymore. She was new on the job, and at first she used to bring a lot of questionnaires and read them to us, a lot of silly questions about education and health and the kind of work we were doing and all, and she would write down a lot of that stuff. I didn't care, but he got mad about it and said it wasn't any of her business. She took it all right, and that's when she stopped bringing all those forms and things around. He started to like her after that, and I was glad. We got along pretty well together. She was sorry to see him go. She wouldn't let on, but I could tell that she felt pretty bad. She had to work today, or I guess she would have gone down to the station with us. Maybe she'll come around tomorrow. Maybe not.

11   I kept thinking about last night, too. We went up there on the hill, him and me, with Tosamah and Cruz. There were a lot of Indians up there, and we really got going after a while. We were all pretty drunk by that time, and there were a couple of drums, and some guy had a flute.

There was a lot of liquor up there, and everybody was feeling pretty good. We started singing some of those real old-time songs, and it was still and cool up there. Somebody built a fire, and we heated the drums until they were good and tight and you could really hear them. And pretty soon they started to dance. Mercedes Tenorio had some turtle shells and she started a stomp dance. You know, she was going all around with those shells in the firelight and calling out just like an old-timer, "Ee he! Oh ho! Ah ha!" And everybody started to answer in the same way, and they all got behind her and she was leading them all around. I kind of wanted to get in there, too, but he didn't care much about it, and he couldn't dance anyway on account of being all banged up like that, so we just stood back and watched.

You can forget about everything up there. We could see all the lights   12
down below, a million lights, I guess, and all the cars moving around, so small and slow and far away. We could see one whole side of the city, all the way to the water, but we couldn't hear anything down there. All we could hear was the drums and the singing. There were some stars, and it was like we were way out in the desert someplace and there was a squaw dance or a sing going on, and everybody was getting good and drunk and happy.

He wanted to tell me something, and we went off a little way by our-   13
selves. We were both pretty drunk, and we just stood around out there in the dark, listening. I guess we were thinking the same thing. I don't know what he wanted to say. I guess he wanted me to say something first, so I started to talk about the way it was going to be. We had some plans about that. We were going to meet someplace, maybe in a year or two, maybe more. He was going home, and he was going to be all right again. And someday I was going home, too, and we were going to meet someplace out there on the reservation and get drunk together. It was going to be the last time, and it was something we had to do. We were going out into the hills on horses and alone. It was going to be early in the morning, and we were going to see the sun coming up. It was going to be good again, you know? We were going to get drunk for the last time, and we were going to sing the old songs. We were going to sing about the way it used to be, how there was nothing all around but the hills and the sunrise and the clouds. We were going to be drunk and, you know, peaceful—beautiful. We had to do it a certain way, just right, because it was going to be the last time.

I told him about that. It was a plan we had. You know, I made all of   14
that up when he was in the hospital, and it was just talk at first. But he believed in it, I guess, and the next day he asked me about it. I had to remember what it was, and then I guess I started to believe in it, too. It was a plan we had, just the two of us, and we weren't ever going to tell anybody about it.

15   "House made of dawn." I used to tell him about those old ways, the stories and the sings, Beautyway and Night Chant. I sang some of those things, and I told him what they meant, what I thought they were about. We would get drunk, both of us, and then he would want me to sing like that. Well, we were up there on the hill last night, and we could hear the drums and the flute away off, and it was dark and cool and peaceful. I told him about the plan we had, and we were getting pretty drunk, and I started to sing all by myself. The others were singing, too, but it was the wrong kind of thing, and I wanted to pray. I didn't want them to hear me, because they were having a good time, and I was ashamed, I guess. I kept it down because I didn't want anybody but him to hear.

> Tségihi.
> *House made of dawn,*
> *House made of evening light,*
> *House made of dark cloud,*
> *House made of male rain,*
> *House made of dark mist,*
> *House made of female rain,*
> *House made of pollen,*
> *House made of grasshoppers,*
> *Dark cloud is at the door.*
> *The trail out of it is dark cloud.*
> *The zigzag lightning stands high upon it.*
> *Male deity!*
> *Your offering I make.*
> *I have prepared a smoke for you.*
> *Restore my feet for me,*
> *Restore my legs for me,*
> *Restore my body for me,*
> *Restore my mind for me,*
> *Restore my voice for me.*
> *This very day take out your spell for me.*
> *Your spell remove for me.*
> *You have taken it away for me;*
> *Far off it has gone.*
> *Happily I recover.*
> *Happily my interior becomes cool.*
> *Happily I go forth.*
> *My interior feeling cool, may I walk.*
> *No longer sore, may I walk.*
> *Impervious to pain, may I walk.*

With lively feelings, may I walk.
As it used to be long ago, may I walk.
Happily may I walk.
Happily, with abundant dark clouds, may I walk.
Happily, with abundant showers, may I walk.
Happily, with abundant plants, may I walk.
Happily, on a trail of pollen, may I walk.
Happily may I walk.
Being as it used to be long ago, may I walk.
May it be beautiful before me,
May it be beautiful behind me,
May it be beautiful below me,
May it be beautiful above me,
May it be beautiful all around me.
In beauty it is finished.

He was unlucky. You could see that right away. You could see that   16
he wasn't going to get along around here. Milly thought he was going to
be all right, I guess, but she didn't understand how it was with him. He
was a longhair, like Tosamah said. You know, you have to change.
That's the only way you can live in a place like this. You have to forget
about the way it was, how you grew up and all. Sometimes it's hard, but
you have to do it. Well, he didn't want to change, I guess, or he didn't
know how. He came here from prison, too, and that was bad. He was on
parole, and he had to do everything right the first time. That made it a
lot harder for him; he wasn't as lucky as the rest of us. He was going to
get us all in trouble, Tosamah said. Tosamah sized him up right away,
and he warned me about him. But, you know, Tosamah doesn't understand either. He talks pretty big all the time, and he's educated, but he
doesn't understand.

One night I was up here by myself—he was out someplace—and   17
Tosamah came in. I didn't much want to talk to him, you know, because he's always showing off and making fun of things. He was feeling
pretty good, I guess, and he started right in the way he does. "You take
that poor cat," he said. "They gave him every advantage. They gave
him a pair of shoes and told him to go to school. They deloused him and
gave him a lot of free haircuts and let him fight on their side. But was he
grateful? Hell, no, man. He was too damn dumb to be civilized. So what
happened? They let him alone at last. They thought he was harmless.
They thought he was going to plant some beans, man, and live off the
fat of the land. Oh, he was going to make his way, all right. He would
get some fat little squaw all knocked up, and they would lie around all
day and get drunk and raise a lot of little government wards. They

would make some pottery, man, and boost the economy. But it didn't turn out that way. He turned out to be a real primitive sonuvabitch, and the first time he got hold of a knife he killed a man. That must have embarrassed the hell out of them.

18   "And do you know what he said? I mean, do you have any *idea* what that cat said? A *snake*, he said. He killed a goddam *snake! The corpus delicti,* * see, he threatened to turn himself into a snake, for crissake, and rattle around a little bit. Now ain't that something, though? Can you *imagine* what went on at that trial? There was this longhair, see, cold sober, of sound mind, and the goddam judge looking on, and the prosecutor trying to talk sense to that poor degenerate Indian: 'Tell us about it, man. Give it to us straight.' 'Well, you honors, it was this way, see? I cut me up a little snake meat out there in the sand.' Christ, man, that must have been our finest hour, better than Little Bighorn. That little no-count cat must have had the whole Jesus scheme right in the palm of his hand. Think of it! *What's-His-Name v. United States.* I mean, where's the legal precedent, man? When you stop to think about it, due process is a hell of a remedy for snakebite.

19   "They put that cat away, man. They *had* to. It's part of the Jesus scheme. *They,* man. They put all of us renegades, us diehards, away sooner or later. They've got the right idea. They put us away before we're born. They're an almighty wise and cautious bunch, those cats, full of discretion. You've got to admire them, man; they know the score. I mean they see through us. They know what we're waiting for. We don't fool them for a minute. Listen here, Benally, one of these nights there's going to be a full red moon, a hunter's moon, and we're going to find us a wagon train full of women and children. Now you won't believe this, but I drink to that now and then."

20   He's always going on like that, Tosamah, talking crazy and showing off, but he doesn't understand. I got to thinking about it, though, anyway. About *him*; about him being afraid of that man out there, so afraid he didn't know what to do. That, you know, being so scared of something like that—that's what Tosamah doesn't understand. He's educated, and he doesn't believe in being scared like that. But he doesn't come from the reservation. He doesn't know how it is when you grow up out there someplace. You grow up out there, you know, someplace like Kayenta or Lukachukai. You grow up in the night, and there are a lot of funny things going on, things you don't know how to talk about. A baby dies, or a good horse. You get sick, or the corn dries up for no good reason. Then you remember something that happened the week before,

---

*"Corpus delicti" is Latin for "the whole body or nature of the case." In this context, the phrase means "to sum it up."

something that wasn't right. You heard an owl, maybe, or you saw a funny kind of whirlwind; somebody looked at you sideways and a moment too long. And then you *know*. You just know. Maybe your aunt or your grandmother was a witch. Maybe you knew she was, because she was always going around at night, around the corrals; maybe you saw her sometimes, like she was talking to the dogs or the sheep, and when you looked again she wasn't there. You just know, and you can't help being scared. It was like that with him, I guess. It might have been like that.

We got along all right; we had some pretty good times. I remember the first time he came around. It was pretty early. I had been there about an hour, I guess, and the foreman called me. I thought he was going to bawl me out because I had punched in late, but I guess he didn't know about that. I went into the office, and there *he* was, with the foreman and some other guy, a Relocation officer. We shook hands and the foreman said he was going to start him out on my line, and would I show him around? I was glad, because DeBenedictus had been laid off the week before, and there was nobody across from me on the line and I didn't have anybody to talk to. I needed a stapler pretty bad, too, because I was having to do two jobs and a lot of orders were piling up. Well, I showed him how to punch in and took him around to meet some of the guys. I could tell he was kind of shy and scared—you know how it is when you start to work in a new place—and then I took him over to my line and showed him how to staple. He was good with his hands, and he caught on all right. He was just learning, you know, and it was kind of slow at first. He made some mistakes, too, but I played like I didn't notice, and after a while we were turning those things out pretty good.

He was looking right down at his work all the time, like I wasn't even there. I knew how he felt, so I didn't try to talk to him, and every time it slowed up we just stood there looking up the line for the next piece, like we were really busy thinking about it, you know, and it was part of the job. It was getting on toward noon, and I noticed that he hadn't brought a lunch bag. I was trying to think what I ought to do about that. I didn't know if he had any money. It's funny, but I hadn't thought about that before, and I got to worrying about it. I didn't want to embarrass him or anything, and I guess he was thinking about it, too, because when the whistle blew he acted like he didn't know what it was and went right on working. Anyway, it turned out all right. We punched out, and I took him over to the Coke machine. He had some Relocation money, I guess. He had some change, anyway, and I was glad. We got a couple of Cokes and went on out into the yard. Everybody was sitting around out there eating lunch. They were being pretty friendly, too, but I didn't want to get in with them because I knew he would have been embarrassed. They kid around a lot down there, those guys. They're always calling you chief and talking about firewater and everything. I don't mind, but I didn't know how he would take it. I was afraid it might hurt his feelings or something. He was used to it, though, because he had been in the army, and in prison, too, but I didn't know that then. Right away we went off by ourselves. I had a sandwich, and I asked him if he wanted to split it with me, but he said he wasn't hungry. I ate about half of it and acted like I didn't want any more. I put the rest of it down on the plank between us and kept hoping he would change his mind and take it, but he didn't. Finally, I had to throw it away.

23   He didn't have anyplace to stay. The Relocation people were looking around, I guess, but they hadn't found a place, and he was going to spend the night at the Indian Center. There's a storeroom down there in the alley, where they keep the food and clothing that people have donated, you know. You can stay there sometimes if you don't have anyplace else to go. It's just an old frame building, and you can see through the cracks in the walls, but you can make a pretty good bed out of those old coats and things, and you can keep warm. But there's no toilet and no lights, and somebody's always bringing a girl in there to fool around. A lot of guys get sick in there, too, and it always smells kind of sour and bad. I told him about that and said he could move in with me if he wanted to. He didn't say anything, but after work he went down and talked to the Relocation people, and that night he came with that little suitcase up to my room. . . .

Questions and Activities

▶ *COMPREHENSION QUESTIONS*

1. What is the frame of mind of the narrator of this story during its opening paragraphs? What physical elements (light and dark colors, cold or heat) help to create the sense of the narrator's frame of mind?
2. What type of basic human need are the Indians filling when they join each other in the middle of the night on a hillside overlooking Los Angeles? Why is that need not filled in the city, at the bar, for example?
3. What is a "longhair," which is how the narrator describes his now-departed friend (paragraph 16)?
4. Why does the narrator's friend refuse the narrator's offer of part of a sandwich in paragraph 22 even though he has no lunch?

5. Why do you think Momaday chooses to tell this story through the eyes of a close friend of the main character? What might have been gained or lost by using either a more distant, less involved, narrator or the more involved first person?

6. Why did Momaday choose to work backward in time in telling this story? Why did Momaday place the most recent events first (the friend's departure and the narrator's actions after his departure), the flashback to the Indian evening gathering in the middle, and the narrator's recollection of his friend's first day at work last? Does this arrangement arouse your sympathy for the narrator's friend by placing you more directly in his place in the story?

7. What is Tosamah's function in this story? How is he different from either the narrator or his friend?

8. Why do most of the Indians in this story seem powerless? Do you think Momaday is suggesting that there are socioeconomic or cultural reasons for the alienation of the narrator and his friend? Would, for example, better jobs and more schooling solve their problems? Or does their problem lie in their separation from their tribal customs and their disconnection from nature?

9. In this section, only George Orwell's "Shooting an Elephant" emphasizes the individual's reaction to power as much as Momaday does in this story. Compare and contrast Orwell's situation with that of the narrator of "The Night Chanter." How are their situations similar or different? To what degrees do they have or lack power? Why does Orwell, who ostensibly holds a great deal of power, seem to be, in the end, even more powerless than Momaday's narrator? Why does Momaday's narrator, who on the surface seems powerless, sometimes possess a kind of power that Orwell never feels?

10. Rewrite one of Momaday's paragraphs in a more formal and distant voice. Read your rewritten passage aloud to the rest of the class. Discuss with them whether or not your rewrite gives them a different feel for the narrator's character than the original language did.

11. Working with a partner, write a description of how the song transcribed in paragraph 15 would be performed in an authentic Indian religious context. You may look up information on Kiowa culture if you wish, but most of your description can be based on information found in paragraph 15 and nearby paragraphs.

Writing Assignments

EXPERIENCES WITH THE ABUSE OF POWER

Write an essay in which you describe and explain a specific abuse of power that you know of or have experienced. Your essay should contain the following parts, arranged in the order you believe will be most effective for your audience of people like your classmates who have shared the readings in this section:

> a description of the situation in which power was abused
> a definition of the way in which power should have been used in this situation
> a recommendation for a plan of action that would discourage similar abuses of power in the future

POWER RELATIONSHIPS IN ORGANIZATIONS

Imagine yourself addressing a group of new professionals about the importance of power relationships to the organizations within which they are working. You must explain how individuals in an organization influence and are influenced by power and show how organizations can develop responsible ways of influencing the power relationships of people who work in them. To ensure that your essay includes sufficient and well-rounded support, use at least one example of each of the following kinds of evidence:

> a personal experience in which you had either a good or a bad reaction to someone else's use or abuse of power
> an extended reference to a piece from this section by which you show how a particular kind of power affected an individual or how a particular social structure encouraged or discouraged responsible uses of power
> a reference to an article on power relationships that appeared in a professional journal for the field within which your audience works
> a quote from an interview with someone who is now working in the field in which your audience works

You will need to combine this material into an essay that provides its readers with a well-informed assessment of how power relationships should work in an organization. Remember that your readers will be relatively inexperienced members of their profession, they will possess some first-hand experience of organizational relationships, they will have read some of the selections included in this section, and they will be motivated to read your piece because they will want to improve their chances of career success. To strike the right tone with them, you should avoid the extremes of condescension and flattery.

What Does It Mean To Be Independent?

▶ ────────────────────────

Introduction

▶ ————————————————————

Some people would argue that independence is a state of mind. Others would argue that independence is defined by social conditions. Still others would argue that independence is not really achievable because we are always controlled by the laws and customs of the context in which we live.

The essays in this section focus on the meaning of independence, as defined by the friction between individuals and their social situations. Two of the essays represent the extremes of individual versus social views of independence. Henry David Thoreau, in his famous essay on civil disobedience, places the source of independence squarely in the individual. For Thoreau, a person's moral conscience must dictate his or her social actions, and the individual must hold out in matters of conscience against the conforming pressures of convention and peer pressure. In contrast to Thoreau, Lewis Thomas views human beings as social animals; he takes the biologist's perspective on animal behavior and applies it to human beings in their social contexts. For Thomas, no individual action seems ever to be completely free of social constraints.

The other selections in this section fall between these extremes. Noel Perrin explains three country codes that underlie the independence of rural New Englanders. For Perrin, independence depends on social customs that assure individuals some degree of freedom and autonomy. Often these customs, his essay asserts, are partially hidden in ways that keep outsiders from understanding how a group's codes work to assure individual independence.

Walter White and Hunter S. Thompson provide first-person narratives describing individual and group efforts to achieve a sense of independence. White tells of his experience as a thirteen-year-old boy in Atlanta during the race riots of 1906. This experience leads him to commit his life to working for racial equality and human rights. White, who became a well-known civil rights leader and black activist, decided at a young age to assert his independence through a commitment to a community and its social welfare. Thompson relates a story about the Hell's Angels, a motorcycle gang that received a great deal of attention from the media in the 1960s and early 1970s. His observations of the gang demonstrate the idea that even the most radical assertions of independence have their own conventionality. The Angels, a group bent on radical independence, are in fact rather strictly bound by the rules and assumptions of their outlaw code.

Russell Baker and Erica Jong provide another set of views on independence. Baker satirizes the useless work of corporate executives and managers who are tied together in a meaningless chain of paper exchanges. Because their work offers little opportunity for defining individuality, office workers may have problems seeing its worth. Jong, in contrast, sees modern women as having gained the opportunity to assert and explore their individuality as writers. The women's movement of the late 1960s and early 1970s provided many women with the courage to vent their rage at a patriarchal society that entrapped and degraded them. But Jong argues that women writers cannot be limited by political dogma and anger, that they must now enter a new period of exploration fueled by "emotional and intellectual curiosity."

As you read these essays, think about these questions concerning social and individual perspectives on independence:

1. When do the customs and laws of a society become negative influences on individual independence?
2. Can individuals be independent only when they live in societies that restrain individual freedom?
3. Can you recall situations in which you felt that your independence was threatened by others? Can you recall situations in which you felt that your independence was preserved or protected by the customs of the group to which you belonged?
4. How highly do you value independence? How much do the people who belong to the same social groups you do value independence?
5. Does independence necessarily imply some sacrifice of group feeling? Does an individual have to become or feel less a part of a group to achieve independence?
6. What are the differences in dependence, independence, and interdependence? When is one person dependent on another? When are two people independent of one another? When do two people have an interdependent relationship?

Country Codes

NOEL PERRIN

Noel Perrin teaches English at Dartmouth College in Hanover, New Hampshire, and writes about life in rural New England and the ways of its farmers and townspeople. Perrin has lived in New England for more than twenty-five years, yet, as he says in one of his essays, he is still learning the ways of the natives. Originally a city boy (New York City), the son of an advertising executive, Perrin has learned in his writing to keep a low profile, to report objectively on his subjects, and to allow his readers to construct their own interpretations of the society he describes. His essays have been published in *Country Journal* and *The New Yorker;* the one reprinted here comes from one of his most popular books, *Second Person Rural* (1980).

In this essay, Perrin explains three country codes. These codes, as Perrin understands them, are rural New Englanders' means of creating a social foundation for individualism and self-reliance. A central irony of Perrin's descriptions of New England characters is the fact that each one's independence is the result of social agreements, customs, or conventions — never the result of simple rebellion or romantic introspection. Perrin exhibits the same kind of socially defined independence in his writing. His simple voice belies an ironic but sympathetic perspective on the ways of both city and country people. As you read, note how Perrin creates a sense of familiarity and trust in his readers. Note, also, how this familiarity enables Perrin to tell his stories and to develop his interpretations without argument or contention.

Thematically, this essay introduces the idea that an individual's sense of independence is often established by the codes and customs of the social group to which he or she belongs. Also, it establishes the idea that outsiders can come into conflict with the codes of independence that exist within groups. As you read, keep the following general questions in mind:

1. Do you belong to social groups that encourage a particular form of independence? What are the groups' codes for fostering that sense of independence?
2. What is the difference between freedom and independence? Are the New England characters in Perrin's essay free or independent?
3. How do outsiders learn the codes of a social group to which they wish to belong? How much of himself or herself does a person have to give up in order to accept new codes?

▶ _____

1   Robert Frost once wrote a poem about a 'townbred' farmer who was getting his hay in with the help of two hired men, both locals. As they're working, the sky clouds over, and it begins to look like rain. The farmer instructs the two hired men to start making the haycocks especially carefully, so that they'll shed water. About half an hour later (it still isn't raining), one of them abruptly shoves his pitchfork in the ground and walks off. He has quit.

2   The farmer is utterly baffled. The hired man who stays explains to him that what he said was a major insult.

> *'He thought you meant to find fault with his work.*
> *That's what the average farmer would have meant.'*

This hired man goes on to say that he would have quit, too—if the order had been issued by a regular farmer. But seeing as it was a city fellow, he made allowances.

> *'I know you don't understand our ways.*
> *You were just talking what was in your mind,*
> *What was in all our minds, and you weren't hinting.'*

Frost called that poem 'The Code.' He published it in 1914.

3   Sixty-four years later, the country code is still going strong, and it is still making trouble for town-bred people who live in rural areas. Only I think the code is even more complicated than Frost had room to describe in his poem. In fact, there isn't just one country code, there are at least three. What they all have in common is that instead of saying things out plainly, the way you do in the city, you approach them indirectly. You hint.

4   I am going to call these three the Power Code, the Non-Reciprocity Code, and the Stoic's Code. These are not their recognized names; they don't *have* recognized names. Part of the code is that you never speak of the code, and I am showing my own town-bredness in writing this exposition. (As Frost showed his in writing the poem. He was a city kid in San Francisco before he was a farmer in New Hampshire.)

5   In Frost's poem, it was the Power Code that the townie violated. Under the rules of the Power Code, you *never* give peremptory orders, and you ordinarily don't even make demands. You make requests. What the code says is that everybody is to be treated as an equal, even when financially or educationally, or whatever, they're not. Treat them as either inferiors or superiors, and you can expect trouble.

Just recently, for example, a young city doctor moved to our town, and began violating the Power Code right and left. Take the way he treated the boss of the town road crew. The house the doctor was renting has a gravel driveway that tends to wash out after storms. It washed out maybe a month after he had moved in. He is said to have called the road commissioner and given him a brisk order. 'I want a culvert installed, and I want it done by this weekend.'

Now in the city that would be a quite sensible approach. You're calling some faceless bureaucrat, and you use standard negotiating technique. You make an outrageous demand; you throw your weight around, if you have any; and you figure on getting part of what you ask for. You're not surprised when the bureaucrat screams, *'This week!* Listen, we got a hunnert and sixty-two jobs aheada you right now. If you're lucky, we'll get to you in October.' You scream back and threaten to call the mayor's office. Then you finally compromise on August.

But it doesn't work that way in the country. The code doesn't encourage throwing your weight around. Our road commissioner had been given an order, and he instantly rejected it. ' 'Tain't the town's job to look after folks' driveways. If you want a culvert, you can buy one down to White River Junction.'

I happened to hear what the road commissioner told some friends later. The doctor had actually called at a good time. The town had several used culverts lying around—road culverts they had replaced, which were still good enough to go at the end of a driveway. 'If he'd asked decent, we'd have been glad to put one in for him, some day when work was slack.' If he'd used the code, that is.

That's nothing, though, compared with the way the young doctor handled one of our retired farmers. When the doctor decided to live in our town—it meant a fifteen-mile drive to the hospital where he worked—it was because he had gotten interested in country things. He wanted to have a garden, burn wood, learn how to scythe a patch of grass, all those things. During his first spring and summer in town, he probably asked the old farmer a hundred questions. He got free lessons in scything. He consulted on fencing problems. Learned how thick to plant peas.

Then one day the farmer asked *him* a question: 'I understand you know suthin' about arthritis,' the farmer said. 'Well, my wife's is actin' up.' And he went on to ask a question about medication.

The young doctor's answer was quick and smooth. 'I'll be glad to see her in office hours,' he said.

Again, normal city practice. You've got to protect yourself against all the people at cocktail parties who want free medical advice. Furthermore, you probably really should examine a patient before you do any prescribing. All the same, what he was saying loud and clear in the country code was, 'My time is worth more than yours; I am more important than you are. So I can ask you free questions, but you must pay for any you ask me.' Not very polite. What he should have done was put down the scythe and say, 'Let's go have a look at her.'

14   Actually, if he had done that, he probably would have muffed it anyway. Because then he would have come up against the Non-Reciprocity Code, and he didn't understand that, either. The Non-Reciprocity Code says that you never take any favors for granted (or call in your debts, as city politicians say). Instead, you always pretend that each favor done you is a brand-new one. In the case of the young doctor, suppose he *had* stopped his free scythe lesson and gone to examine the farmer's wife. When he was ready to leave, the farmer would have said to him, 'What do I owe you?' And then one of two things would have happened. Old habits would have asserted themselves, and he would have said smoothly, 'That will be twenty-five dollars, please.' Or else, a little cross with the farmer for not recognizing his generous motive (does the old fool think I make *house calls?*), he would have said that it was free, in a sort of huffy, look-what-a-favor-I'm-doing-you voice.

15   Both answers would have been wrong. The correct response would be to act as if the farmer was doing *you* a favor in letting you not charge. Something like, 'Come on, if you can teach me to scythe, and how to plant peas, I guess there's no harm in my taking a look at your wife.'

16   One of the funniest instances in which you see the Non-Reciprocity Code operating is after people get their trucks stuck, which during mud season in Vermont is constantly. You're driving along in your pickup, and there's your neighbor with two wheels in the ditch, unable to budge. You stop, get out your logging chain, hook on, and pull him out. 'How much will that be?' he asks, as if his cousin Donald hadn't just pulled you out the week before. In a way it's a ritual question. He would be surprised out of his mind if you thought a minute and said, 'Oh, I guess five dollars would be about right.'

17   But it's not entirely ritual. He would be surprised. But he would hand over the five dollars. The point of the question is to establish that you don't *have* to pull him out just because he's a friend and will someday pull you out. It's treated as an act of free will, a part of New England independence.

18   The third code, the Stoic's Code, is sometimes confused with machismo, but really has no connection with it. Country people of both sexes practice it with equal fervency. Basically, it consists of seeing who can go without complaining longest.

I first became aware of the Stoic's Code when I was helping two people put hay bales into a barn loft about fifteen years ago. It was a hot day in late June, with the humidity running at least ninety percent. I function badly in hot weather. Within ten minutes I was pouring sweat—as were my coworkers. The difference was that I kept bitching about it. Finally, after three-quarters of an hour, I flopped down and announced I'd have to cool off before I touched another bale.   19

To me this just seemed common sense. We had no special deadline to meet in loading that hay. What I really thought was that all three of us should go take a dip in the river.   20

But the Stoic's Code doesn't stress common sense. It stresses endurance. Maybe that's because to survive at all as a farmer in New England you need endurance. In any case, the other two flicked me one quick scornful look and kept on working. One of them has never really respected me again to this day. The other, like the second hired man in Frost's poem, made allowances for my background and forgave me. We have since become fast friends. I have never dared to ask, but I think he thinks I have made real progress in learning to shut my mouth and keep working.   21

I could never be a stoic on the true native level, though. Consider the story of Hayden Clark and Rodney Palmer, as Rodney tells it. A good many years ago, before there were any paved roads in town, Hayden ran a garage. (Rodney runs it now.) He also sold cordwood.   22

One day when there wasn't much doing at the garage, Hayden was sawing cordwood just across the road, where he could keep an eye on the gas pumps. If you saw with a circular saw, and do it right, it takes three men. One person lifts up the logs, one does the actual cutting, and one throws the cut pieces into a pile. The three jobs are called putting on, sawing, and taking off. In all three you are doing dangerous work at very high speed.   23

On this day a man named Charlie Raynes was putting on, Hayden was sawing, and young Rodney was taking off. Hayden kept the wood coming so fast that Rodney was always a beat behind. He never paused a second to let Rodney catch up, and this torture went on for nearly an hour. No one spoke. (Not that you could hear over a buzz saw, anyway.)   24

Then finally a customer pulled in for gas. Hayden left the other two sawing, and went over to pump it. Charlie continued to put on, and Rodney sawed in Hayden's place.   25

Rather than interrupt their rhythm when he came back, Hayden began to take off. Rodney and Charlie exchanged a quick glance, and began putting the wood to Hayden so fast that *he* was off balance the whole time, and not infrequently in some danger of getting an arm cut   26 off. At this speed and in this way they finished the entire pile. It was Rodney's revenge, and as he told me about it, his eyes gleamed.

27   It was only a year or two ago that Rodney told me the story. In the very act of telling it, he included me as one who knew the code. But I instantly betrayed it. My city background is too strong. I'm too verbal, too used to crowing over triumphs.

28   'After you were done sawing, Hayden never said anything about it?' I asked.

29   'Oh, *no*,' Rodney answered, looking really shocked. 'Any more than I'd have said anything to him.'

30   So, next time you're in a country store and you get a sense that the locals are avoiding you as if you had the worst case of B.O. in the county, you can be pretty sure of the reason. You've probably just said some dreadful thing in code.

Questions and Activities

▶ *COMPREHENSION QUESTIONS*

1. What is Perrin's point, in paragraphs 6 through 9, when he describes how the new doctor, who was used to living in a city, violated the "Power Code"? Was it the doctor's or the townspeople's insensitivity, or both, that caused the problems?

2. Explain what Perrin calls the "Non-Reciprocity Code" in your words. Why do the people of the town always offer to pay for favors that they know were done as acts of good will?

▶ *QUESTIONS OF RHETORICAL PURPOSE AND STRATEGY*

3. Describe Perrin's voice in this essay. Does he sound like a town-bred person? What particular word choices help to establish his voice? Do you think his voice is directed at urban or rural readers?

4. Describe the overall strategy used for developing ideas in this essay. What kinds of evidence does Perrin offer in support of his ideas? How is this evidence arranged? How is the evidence related to his generalizations?

5. Why does Perrin close his essay with the anecdote about Rodney and Hayden? What does it tell you about country codes and about Noel Perrin?

6. Why does Perrin begin with a description of and quotations from Robert Frost's poem "The Code"? How does the situation that is described in the poem fit in with Perrin's ideas about country living?

▶ *THEME QUESTIONS*

7. Are the natives of Perrin's New England town truly independent, or are they more bound by social conventions than they realize? In what ways are the natives Perrin describes more independent than individuals who work in corporations or factories, for example? In what ways are they less independent?
8. Perrin emphasizes the unspoken, read-between-the-lines nature of country codes. Do you think this hidden aspect encourages more or less independence? Is, for example, the new doctor more or less independent because of the unspokenness of the code? Are the townfolk, because they are more aware than the newcomers, better able to use the code to express their own individual goals? If the code were more openly expressed and acknowledged, would people be freer to express themselves?

▶ *LEARNING ACTIVITIES*

9. Think about a social group to which you have belonged. Did that group have its codes? How were those codes expressed? Did the codes enable members of the group to exclude some and include others? Did it take newcomers some time to learn the codes? Why? Report to the rest of the class on your answers to these questions.
10. Write a brief dialogue between two of the people that Perrin describes in this essay. In the dialogue, you should try to suggest the operation of one of the three codes.
11. Listen to a conversation between two or three people in one of the social groups to which you belong. Is there any evidence that an explicit or implicit code is operating to control the conversation?

On Societies as Organisms

LEWIS THOMAS

Lewis Thomas, born in 1913, is perhaps the best-known example of a new breed of science writer. His accomplishments as a biological and medical researcher and physician are numerous: a B.S. from Princeton; an M.D. from Harvard; research fellowships from Johns Hopkins, Yale, and the Rockefeller Institute for Medical Research; faculty and administrative positions at the medical schools of New York University, Tulane, the University of Minnesota, and Yale; and, most recently, president and chief executive officer of the prestigious Sloan-Kettering Cancer Center in New York City.

During all of his medical career, Thomas has published numerous professional articles in prestigious medical and science journals. In 1971, however, he began doing what was for him a new kind of writing, a popular column for the *New England Journal of Medicine* called "Notes of a Biology Watcher." In these columns, Thomas turned his scientifically specialized observations of natural phenomena into essays about the notions of interdependency and symbiosis. These columns suggest that both humanity and the natural world follow laws of connection and interlinkage that only modern science, with its refined methods of observation and analysis, could have made known to us. There are, Thomas says, complex social purposes behind even seemingly independent human actions and behaviors. Thomas collected some of these columns and published them as *Lives of a Cell* in 1974; this book received a National Book Award. Thomas has followed *Lives of a Cell* with two more books of essays that combine literary style with scientific observation and knowledge: *The Medusa and the Snail* (1979) and *Late Night Thoughts on Listening to Mahler's Ninth Symphony* (1983).

In the essay here, Thomas argues that scientific observations of ant, bee, and wasp societies reveal an astonishing degree of social purposefulness, and he suggests that this group orientation in lower organisms might tell us a great deal about human societies and their underlying processes and purposes. Throughout this essay, Thomas demonstrates what has become the central quality of his style: the voice of a learned and careful scientist who, nonetheless, is willing to take on a poet's visionary perspective.

Like Noel Perrin in "Country Codes" (pages 748–752), Thomas looks at how individuality is dependent on partially hidden social agreements. Independence, to Perrin and Thomas, must be traced back to the social and biological conditions that both support and constrain it.

These general questions should guide your thinking as you read this piece:

1. Why do ants or wasps seem to exhibit random behavior when they are viewed in isolation but purposeful behavior when in groups? Is the difference in the ants or wasps, or in the scientist who is observing them?
2. Should scientists make analogies, as Thomas does, between aspects of the natural world and the human condition? If so, when should they make these analogies?
3. Why might it be dangerous to confuse the roles of scientist and poet?

▶ ──────────────────

Viewed from a suitable height, the aggregating clusters of medi-   1
cal scientists in the bright sunlight of the boardwalk at Atlantic City, swarmed there from everywhere for the annual meetings, have the look of assemblages of social insects. There is the same vibrating, ionic movement, interrupted by the darting back and forth of jerky individuals to touch antennae and exchange small bits of information; periodically, the mass casts out, like a trout-line, a long single file unerringly toward Childs's. If the boards were not fastened down, it would not be a surprise to see them put together a nest of sorts.

It is permissible to say this sort of thing about humans. They do re-   2
semble, in their most compulsively social behavior, ants at a distance. It is, however, quite bad form in biological circles to put it the other way round, to imply that the operation of insect societies has any relation at all to human affairs. The writers of books on insect behavior generally take pains, in their prefaces, to caution that insects are like creatures from another planet, that their behavior is absolutely foreign, totally unhuman, unearthly, almost unbiological. They are more like perfectly tooled but crazy little machines, and we violate science when we try to read human meanings in their arrangements.

It is hard for a bystander not to do so. Ants are so much like human   3
beings as to be an embarrassment. They farm fungi, raise aphids as livestock, launch armies into wars, use chemical sprays to alarm and confuse enemies, capture slaves. The families of weaver ants engage in child labor, holding their larvae like shuttles to spin out the thread that

sews the leaves together for their fungus gardens. They exchange information ceaselessly. They do everything but watch television.

4   What makes us most uncomfortable is that they, and the bees and termites and social wasps, seem to live two kinds of lives: they are individuals, going about the day's business without much evidence of thought for tomorrow, and they are at the same time component parts, cellular elements, in the huge, writhing, ruminating organism of the Hill, the nest, the hive. It is because of this aspect, I think, that we most wish for them to be something foreign. We do not like the notion that there can be collective societies with the capacity to behave like organisms. If such things exist, they can have nothing to do with us.

5   Still, there it is. A solitary ant, afield, cannot be considered to have much of anything on his mind; indeed, with only a few neurons strung together by fibers, he can't be imagined to have a mind at all, much less a thought. He is more like a ganglion on legs. Four ants together, or ten, encircling a dead moth on a path, begin to look more like an idea. They fumble and shove, gradually moving the food toward the Hill, but as though by blind chance. It is only when you watch the dense mass of thousands of ants, crowded together around the Hill, blackening the ground, that you begin to see the whole beast, and now you observe it thinking, planning, calculating. It is an intelligence, a kind of live computer, with crawling bits for its wits.

6   At a stage in the construction, twigs of a certain size are needed, and all the members forage obsessively for twigs of just this size. Later, when outer walls are to be finished, thatched, the size must change, and as though given new orders by telephone, all the workers shift the search to the new twigs. If you disturb the arrangement of a part of the Hill, hundreds of ants will set it vibrating, shifting, until it is put right again. Distant sources of food are somehow sensed, and long lines, like tentacles, reach out over the ground, up over walls, behind boulders, to fetch it in.

7   Termites are even more extraordinary in the way they seem to accumulate intelligence as they gather together. Two or three termites in a chamber will begin to pick up pellets and move them from place to place, but nothing comes of it; nothing is built. As more join in, they seem to reach a critical mass, a quorum, and the thinking begins. They place pellets atop pellets, then throw up columns and beautiful, curving, symmetrical arches, and the crystalline architecture of vaulted chambers is created. It is not known how they communicate with each other, how the chains of termites building one column know when to turn toward the crew on the adjacent column, or how, when the time comes, they manage the flawless joining of the arches. The stimuli that set them off at the outset, building collectively instead of shifting

things about, may be pheromones* released when they reach commit-tee size. They react as if alarmed. They become agitated, excited, and then they begin working, like artists.

Bees live lives of organisms, tissues, cells, organelles, all at the same time. The single bee, out of the hive retrieving sugar (instructed by the dancer: "south-southeast for seven hundred meters, clover—mind you make corrections for the sundrift") is still as much a part of the hive as if attached by a filament. Building the hive, the workers have the look of embryonic cells organizing a developing tissue; from a distance they are like the viruses inside a cell, running off row after row of symmetri-cal polygons as though laying down crystals. When the time for swarm-ing comes, and the old queen prepares to leave with her part of the popu-lation, it is as though the hive were involved in mitosis.† There is an agitated moving of bees back and forth, like granules in cell sap. They distribute themselves in almost precisely equal parts, half to the departing queen, half to the new one. Thus, like an egg, the great, hairy, black and golden creature splits in two, each with an equal share of the family genome.‡

The phenomenon of separate animals joining up to form an organism is not unique in insects. Slime-mold cells do it all the time, of course, in each life cycle. At first they are single amebocytes swimming around, eating bacteria, aloof from each other, untouching, voting straight Re-publican. Then, a bell sounds, and acrasin§ is released by special cells toward which the others converge in stellate ranks, touch, fuse togeth-er, and construct the slug, solid as a trout. A splendid stalk is raised, with a fruiting body on top, and out of this comes the next generation of amebocytes, ready to swim across the same moist ground, solitary and ambitious.

Herring and other fish in schools are at times so closely integrated, their actions so coordinated, that they seem to be functionally a great multi-fish organism. Flocking birds, especially the seabirds nesting on the slopes of offshore islands in Newfoundland, are similarly attached, connected, synchronized.

8

9

10

---

*Pheromones are chemical substances that are given off by members of the same species and that affect their behavior. Examples of pheromones are sex attractants that encourage mating, alarm substances that warn of danger, and territorial markers that alert one mem-ber of a species of the territorial prerogative of another.

†Mitosis is the division of one cell into two during genetic reformation.

‡A genome is a single set of chromosomes. Each chromosome contains a set number of genes. Genomes reform and change their basic structure. When they are divided and then united with other genomic structures, they create new forms of cellular life.

§Acrasin is a biochemical that is emitted by independent amebocytes and that attracts other amebocytes, producing formations known as slugs. Slugs are shell-less snails, found in fairly wet climates, that are pests to cultivated plants.

11   Although we are by all odds the most social of all social animals —more interdependent, more attached to each other, more inseparable in our behavior than bees—we do not often feel our conjoined intelligence. Perhaps, however, we are linked in circuits for the storage, processing, and retrieval of information, since this appears to be the most basic and universal of all human enterprises. It may be our biological function to build a certain kind of Hill. We have access to all the information of the biosphere, arriving as elementary units in the stream of solar photons. When we have learned how these are rearranged against randomness, to make, say, springtails, quantum mechanics, and the late quartets, we may have a clearer notion how to proceed. The circuitry seems to be there, even if the current is not always on.

12   The system of communications used in science should provide a neat, workable model for studying mechanisms of information-building in human society. Ziman, in a recent *Nature* essay, points out, "the invention of a mechanism for the systematic publication of *fragments* of scientific work may well have been the key event in the history of modern science." He continues:

> A regular journal carries from one research worker to another the various . . . observations which are of common interest. . . . A typical scientific paper has never pretended to be more than another little piece in a larger jigsaw—not significant in itself but as an element in a grander scheme. *This technique, of soliciting many modest contributions to the store of human knowledge, has been the secret of Western science since the seventeenth century, for it achieves a corporate, collective power that is far greater than any one individual can exert* [italics mine].

13   With some alternation of terms, some toning down, the passage could describe the building of a termite nest.

14   It is fascinating that the word "explore" does not apply to the searching aspect of the activity, but has its origins in the sounds we make while engaged in it. We like to think of exploring in science as a lonely, meditative business, and so it is in the first stages, but always, sooner or later, before the enterprise reaches completion, as we explore, we call to each other, communicate, publish, send letters to the editor, present papers, cry out on finding.

Questions and Activities

▶ *COMPREHENSION QUESTIONS*

1. What is the point of Thomas's comparison of an aerial view of medi-cal scientists attending a convention in Atlantic City and the behav-ior of "social insects" (paragraph 1)?
2. Why does Thomas believe that certain insects "accumulate intelli-gence as they gather together" (paragraph 7)? On what types of evi-dence does he base this generalization? Could this evidence be called scientific?
3. What is the point of the material quoted in paragraph 12? How are the actions of scientists and the functions of their professional jour-nals as described in this quotation similar to the behavior of the ants, termites, and bees that Thomas describes earlier in this essay?

▶ *QUESTIONS OF RHETORICAL PURPOSE AND STRATEGY*

4. What is the overall purpose behind Thomas's comparisons of human, insect, and animal impulses toward social integration? What is Thomas saying about human beings via this comparison?
5. Ethical appeal occurs when writers manage to convince their readers that they are honest, sincere, and well-informed commenta-tors on a subject. How does Thomas try to set up an ethical appeal in this essay? Do his observations of insects and animals seem care-ful and intelligent? Does what he says about human beings seem the result of careful comparison and analysis? Does the language he uses indicate that he is a thinker you can trust? Why?
6. Would a natural scientist call the kind of metaphorical reasoning that Thomas uses in his essay scientific reasoning? Why or why not?

▶ *THEME QUESTIONS*

7. If human beings, like many insects or animals, seem to have a swarming or herding instinct, what does that fact suggest about tra-ditional attitudes concerning individualism and independence? Should those traditional attitudes be revised? Is individualism an overrated quality? Are we far more dependent on others than we re-alize?
8. Would the assemblage of medical scientists in Atlantic City be seen by social scientists as individuals? In what ways might the individual actions in such a "swarm" be seen as being motivated by social situ-ation?
9. Do you think Thomas believes that we can actually separate indi-viduals from the societies within which they live? Why or why not?

▶ *LEARNING ACTIVITIES*

10. Try Thomas's perspective yourself. Find a vantage point from which you can observe individuals who are engaged in pursuing one general activity and who belong to an identifiable social group. Find, for example, a balcony or upper-story window from which you can look down on a group of students as they register for classes, attend a lecture or seminar, or work in a laboratory situation. Or go to a local exposition grounds or arena during a new car or recreation vehicle show or a business convention. Find a place from which you can look down from above on the show's or convention's proceedings. Write an essay in which you compare your response to this event with Thomas's view of the convention of medical scientists in Atlantic City.

11. Observe and record the behavior of an insect. Does that behavior seem to have a social purpose (food gathering, nest building, or the like)? Or does the insect seem nondeterministic? Report your observations to the class.

Hoodlum Circus, Statutory Rape of Bass Lake

HUNTER S. THOMPSON

Hunter S. Thompson, the son of an insurance agent, was born in Louisville, Kentucky, in 1939. He never attended college, and he describes his politics as "anarchist" and his religion as "none." Thompson has become famous for what he has called "gonzo journalism." While writing *Hell's Angels: A Strange and Terrible Saga* (1966), he virtually lived with the Hell's Angels motorcycle gang for a year. Shortly before Thompson's stay with the Angels, they had been featured in a *Life* magazine cover story; during that year, the Angels had confrontations with communities in the entire country. The middle class developed almost an obsession with the Angels, whose wild and violent behavior seemed to both terrify and fascinate ordinary citizens.

Like certain other journalists of the 1960s, such as Tom Wolfe and Gay Talese, Thompson wrote news reports in which he was emotionally involved in what he described. He purposely included his opinions and feelings in his reports on the Angels and also in his two most famous later books: *Fear and Loathing on the Campaign Trail '72* (1973) (written while following the Nixon and McGovern presidential campaigns in 1972) and *Fear and Loathing in Las Vegas* (1972) (written while living in Las Vegas and in response to the city's life styles).

Thompson's presence is obvious in all his reporting. He is not the objective reporter and commentator on social events that the traditional newswriter tried to be; he takes on the feeling, responding, and editorializing voice of the concerned individual who is at the center of a social drama. All these characteristics of Thompson's style of journalism are apparent in the selection included here, which was originally published as a chapter of *Hell's Angels*. Thompson places himself somewhere in the middle, between the Angels and the townspeople of Bass Lake. He does not stand back to observe; instead, he writes out of the center of the action, and he projects his opinions and interpretations into his descriptions of what he experiences.

Thompson's Hell's Angels are literally hell-bent on establishing their independence from middle-class values, from established religions, governments, and institutions. In this, the Angels are typically American, since this country was founded on revolutionary and frontier values — values firmly based on concepts of individualism. The Angels are different only in the ways in which they express their independence.

Furthermore, the Angels are not the only people who receive Thompson's attention in this piece. The police who protect the town during the invasion of the Angels, the vigilantes who are hired by one of the town's businessmen, and the tourists who travel from place to place to observe the Angels are all part of Thompson's drama. He is just as interested in reporting their reactions to the phenomenon of the Hell's Angels as he is in the Angels themselves.

As you read, consider these questions:

1. Why are the tourists so fascinated with the Angels? What do the Angels have that might be missing in the tourists' lives? Does society's obsession with the Angels suggest that most people are unable to attain independence in their lives?
2. Why do the vigilantes exhibit such an intense desire to fight the Angels? What need would be filled by a confrontation with the Angels?
3. How does Tiny Baxter, the local sheriff, benefit from the situation that is created by the Angels?

▶ ─────────────────────

1   Bass Lake is not really a town, but a resort area—a string of small settlements around a narrow, picture-postcard lake that is seven miles long and less than a mile wide at any point. The post office is on the north side of the lake in a cluster of stores and buildings all owned by a man named Williams. This was the Angels' rendezvous point . . . but the local sheriff, a giant of a man named Tiny Baxter, had decided to keep them out of this area by means of a second roadblock about a half mile from the center of downtown. It was Baxter's decision and he backed it with his three-man force and a half dozen local forest rangers.

2   By the time I got there the outlaws were stopped along both sides of the highway, and Barger was striding forth to meet Baxter. The sheriff explained to the Angel chieftain and his Praetorian Guard* that a spacious campsite had been carefully reserved for them up on the mountain above town, where they wouldn't "be bothered." Baxter is six-foot-six and built like a defensive end for the Baltimore Colts. Barger is barely six feet, but not one of his followers had the slightest doubt that he would swing on the sheriff if things suddenly came down to the hard

─────────────────────

*The Praetorian Guard was an elite group of bodyguards for the Roman emperors; they often determined the imperial succession.

nub. I don't think the sheriff doubted it either, and certainly I.didn't. There is a steely, thoughtful quality about Barger, an instinctive restraint that leads outsiders to feel they can reason with him. But there is also a quiet menace, an egocentric fanaticism tempered by eight years at the helm of a legion of outcasts who, on that sweaty afternoon, were measuring the sheriff purely by his size, his weapon and the handful of young rangers who backed him up. There was no question about who would win the initial encounter, but it was up to Barger to decide just what that victory would be worth.

He decided to go up the mountain, and his legion followed without question or bitterness. The ranger who pointed out the route made it sound like a ten-minute drive up a nearby dirt road. I watched the outlaw horde boom off in that direction, then talked for a while with two of the rangers who stayed to man the roadblock. They seemed a little tense but smiled when I asked if they were afraid the Hell's Angels might take over the town. They had shotguns in the cab of their truck, but during the confrontation the guns had remained out of sight. Both were in their early twenties, and they seemed very cool, considering the much-publicized threat they had just met and sidetracked. I chalked it up later to the influence of Tiny Baxter, the only cop I've ever seen put Sonny Barger on the defensive.

It was about 3:30 P.M. when I started up the dirt road to the designated Angel campground. Thirty minutes later I was still following motorcycle tracks up a fresh bulldozer cut that looked like something hacked out of a Philippine jungle. The angle was low gear all the way, it zigzagged like a deer trail and the campsite itself was so high that when I finally arrived it seemed that only a heavy ground fog lay between us and a clear view of Manhattan Island, at the other end of the continent. There was no trace of water, and by this time the Angels had worked up a serious thirst. They had been shunted off to a parched meadow nine or ten thousand feet up in the Sierras and it was obviously a bum trip. They hadn't minded the climb, but now they felt deceived and they wanted to retaliate. The prevailing ugly mood was shared by Barger, who felt the sheriff had duped him. The campsite was fit only for camels and mountain goats. The view was excellent, but a camp without water on a California Fourth of July is as useless as an empty beer can.

I listened to the war talk and shouting for a while, then hustled down the mountain to call a Washington newspaper I was writing for at the time, to say I was ready to send one of the great riot stories of the decade. On the way down the road I passed outlaw bikes coming the other way. They'd been stopped at the Bass Lake roadblock and pointed up to the campsite. The Frisco swastika truck came by in first gear, with two bikes in the back and a third trailing twenty feet behind at the end of a long rope in a cloud of dust. Its rider was hanging on grimly behind green goggles and a handkerchief tied over his nose and mouth. Following the truck was a red Plymouth that erupted with shouts and horn blasts as I passed. I stopped, not recognizing the car, and backed up. It was Larry, Pete and Puff, the new president of the Frisco chapter. I hadn't seen them since the night of the meeting at the DePau. Pete, the drag racer, was working as a messenger in the city, and Larry was carving totem poles out of tree stumps in other Angels' front yards. They had broken down on the freeway near Modesto and been picked up by three pretty young girls who stopped to offer help. This was the Plymouth, and now the girls were part of the act. One was sitting on Pete's lap in the back seat, half undressed and smiling distractedly, while I explained the problem of the campsite. They decided to push on, and I said I'd see them later in town . . . or somewhere, and at that point I thought it would probably be in jail. A very bad scene was building up. Soon the Angels would be coming down the mountain en masse, and in no mood for reasonable talk.

6   In the Carolinas they say "hill people" are different from "flatlands people," and as a native Kentuckian with more mountain than flatlands blood, I'm inclined to agree. This was one of the theories I'd been nursing all the way from San Francisco. Unlike Porterville or Hollister, Bass Lake was a mountain community . . . and if the old Appalachian pattern held, the people would be much slower to anger or panic, but absolutely without reason or mercy once the fat was in the fire. Like the Angels, they would tend to fall back in an emergency on their own native sense of justice—which bears only a primitive resemblance to anything written in law books. I thought the mountain types would be far more tolerant of the Angels' noisy showboating, but—compared to their flatlands cousins—much quicker to retaliate in kind at the first evidence of physical insult or abuse.

7   On the way down the mountain I heard another Monitor newscast, saying the Hell's Angels were heading for Bass Lake and big trouble. There was also mention of a Los Angeles detective who had shot one of the suspects rounded up for questioning about the rape of his daughter the day before. The sight of the suspect being led through the hall of the police station was too much for the detective, who suddenly lost control and began firing point blank. The victim was said to be a Hell's Angel, and newspapers on sale in Bass Lake that afternoon were headlined: HELL'S ANGEL SHOT IN RAPE CASE. (The suspect, who survived, was a twenty-one-year-old drifter. He was later absolved of any connection with either the Angels or the rape of the detective's daughter . . . who had been selling cookbooks, door to door, when she was lured into a house known to be frequented by dragsters and hot-rod

types. The detective admitted losing his head and shooting the wrong man; he later pleaded temporary insanity and was acquitted of all charges by a Los Angeles grand jury.) It took several days, however, for the press to separate the rape-shooting from the Hell's Angels, and in the meantime the headlines added fuel to the fire. On top of the Laconia stories, including the one in *Life*, the radio bulletins and all the frightening predictions in the daily press—now this, a Hell's Angels rape in Los Angeles, and just in time for the July 3 papers.

Given all these fiery ingredients, I didn't feel a trace of alarmist guilt   8
when I finally got a Bass Lake–Washington connection and began outlining what was about to happen. I was standing in a glass phone booth in downtown Bass Lake—which consists of a small post office, a big grocery, a bar and cocktail lounge, and several other picturesque redwood establishments that look very combustible. While I was talking, Don Mohr pulled up on his bike—having breached the roadblock with his press credentials—and indicated that he was in a hurry to call the *Tribune*. My editor in Washington was telling me how and when to file, but I was not to do so until the riot was running under its own power, with significant hurt to both flesh and property . . . and then I was to send no more than an arty variation of the standard wire-service news blurb: Who, What, When, Where and Why.

I was still on the phone when I saw a big burr-haired lad with a pistol   9
on his belt walk over to Mohr and tell him to get out of town. I couldn't hear much of what was going on, but I saw Mohr produce a packet of credentials, stringing them out like a card shark with a funny deck. I could see that he needed the phone, so I agreed with my man in Washington that first things would always come first, and hung up. Mohr immediately occupied the booth, leaving me to deal with the crowd that had gathered.

Luckily, my garb was too bastard for definition. I was wearing Levis,   10
Wellington boots from L. L. Bean in Maine, and a Montana sheepherder's jacket over a white tennis shirt. The burr-haired honcho asked me who I was. I gave him my card and asked why he had that big pistol on his belt. "You know why," he said. "The first one of these sons-of-bitches that gives me any lip I'm gonna shoot right in the belly. That's the only language they understand." He nodded toward Mohr in the phone booth, and there was nothing in his tone to make me think I was exempted. I could see that his pistol was a short-barreled Smith & Wesson .357 Magnum—powerful enough to blow holes in Mohr's BSA cylinder head, if necessary—but at arm's length it hardly mattered. The gun was a killer at any range up to a hundred yards, and far beyond that in the hands of a man who worked at it. He was wearing it in a police-type holster on the belt that held up his khaki pants, high on his right

hip and in an awkward position for getting at it quickly. But he was very conscious of having the gun and I knew he was capable of raising bloody hell if he started waving it around.

11   I asked him if he was a deputy sheriff.

12   "No I'm workin for Mr. Williams," he said, still studying my card. Then he looked up. "What are you doin with this motorcycle crowd?"

13   I explained that I was only a journalist trying to do an honest day's work. He nodded, still fondling my card. I said he could keep it, which seemed to please him. He dropped it in the pocket of his khaki shirt, then tucked his thumbs in his belt and asked me what I wanted to know. The tone of the question implied that I had about sixty seconds to get the story.

14   I shrugged. "Oh, I don't know. I just thought I'd look around a bit, maybe write a few things."

15   He chuckled knowingly. "Yeah? Well, you can write that we're ready for em. We'll give em all they want."

16   The dusty street was so crowded with tourists that I hadn't noticed the singular nature of the group that surrounded us. They weren't tourists at all; I was standing in the midst of about a hundred vigilantes. There were five or six others wearing khaki shirts and pistols. At a glance they looked like any bunch of country boys at any rustic hamlet in the Sierras. But as I looked around I saw that many carried wooden clubs and others had hunting knives on their belts. They didn't seem mean, but they were obviously keyed up and ready to bust some heads.

17   The merchant Williams had hired a few private gunmen to protect his lakefront investment; the rest were volunteer toughs who'd been waiting all day for a fight with a bunch of hairy city boys who wore chains for belts and stank of human grease. I remembered the mood of the Angels up on the mountain and I expected at any moment to hear the first of the bikes coming down the hill into town. The scene had all the makings of a king-hell brawl, and except for the pistols it looked pretty even.

18   Just then the door of the phone booth opened behind me, and Mohr stepped out. He looked curiously at the mob, then raised his camera and took a picture of them. He did it as casually as any press photographer covering an American Legion picnic. Then he straddled his bike, kicked it to life and roared up the hill toward the roadblock.

19   Burr-head seemed confused and I took the opportunity to stroll off toward my car. Nobody said anything and I didn't look back, but at any instant I expected to be whacked on the kidneys with a big stick. Despite the press credentials, both Mohr and I had been firmly identified with the outlaws. We were city boys, intruders, and under these circumstances the only neutrals were the tourists, who were easily identifi-

able. On my way out of town I wondered if anybody in Bass Lake might take one of my aspen-leaf checks for a fluorescent Hawaiian beach suit and some stylish sandals.

The scene at the roadblock was surprisingly peaceful. The bikes were again parked along both sides of the highway, and Barger was talking to the sheriff. With them was the chief forest ranger for the area, who was explaining cheerfully that another campsite had been set aside for the Angels... Willow Cove, about two miles down the main road and right on the edge of the lake. It sounded too good to be true, but Barger signaled his people to follow the rangers' jeep and check it out. The strange procession moved slowly down the highway, then veered into the pines on a narrow jeep trail that led to the campsite.   *20*

There were no complaints this time. Willow Cove lacked only a free-beer machine to make it perfect. A dozen of the Angels leaped off their bikes and rushed into the lake fully clothed. I parked under a tree and got out to look around. We were on a small peninsula jutting into Bass Lake and cut off from the highway by a half mile of pine forest. It was an idyllic kind of setting and a very unlikely place to be put aside for an orgy. But it was, and the outlaws set about occupying it like a victorious army. Sheriff Baxter and the head ranger explained to Barger that there were only two conditions on their use of the site: (1) that they would leave it as clean and unlittered as they found it and (2) that they would keep to themselves and not menace the campgrounds on the other side of the lake, which were full of tourists. Sonny agreed, and the weekend's first crisis was over. The outlaw clan, which now numbered about two hundred, was agreeably settled in a private kingdom, with nothing of substance to bitch about. Beyond that, the Maximum Angel was committed to the task of keeping his people under control. It was an unnatural situation for Barger to find himself in. Instead of spending the weekend rallying his boozy legion from one piece of unfriendly turf to another, beset at all times by a cruel authority wearing guns and badges, he now found his people in a pleasant cul-de-sac... a state of rare equality with the rest of humanity, which they could only disturb by committing some deliberate outrage—by violating an agreement that the Prez had honored with his word.   *21*

The transaction had been carried out in Hollywood Indian style. There was a childlike simplicity in the dialogue between Barger and the lawmen: *22*

> "If you play straight with us, Sonny, we'll play straight with you. We don't want any trouble and we know you guys have as much right to camp on this lake as anybody else. But the minute you cause trouble for us or anyone else, we're gonna come down on you hard, it's gonna be powder valley for your whole gang."

Barger nods, seeming to understand. "We didn't come here for trouble, Sheriff. The way we heard it, you had trouble waitin for us."

"Well, what did you expect? We heard you were coming in for a rumble, to tear things up." Baxter forces a smile. "But there's no reason why you can't enjoy yourselves here like everybody else. You guys know what you're doing. There's nothing wrong with you. We know that."

Then Barger smiles, very faintly, but he smiles so seldom that even a grimace means he thinks something is very funny. "Come off it, Sheriff. You know we're all fuck-ups or we wouldn't be here."

23   The sheriff shrugged and walked back to his car, but one of the deputies picked up the conversation and soon found himself telling five or six grinning Angels what basically decent fellows they were. Barger went off to get a beer kitty going. He stood in the middle of the big clearing and called for donations. We had been there about half an hour and by this time I'd suffered a fatal run on my own stock. Puff had spotted the cooler in my car. I hadn't planned to roll into camp and instantly dispose of my beer supply for the weekend, but under the circumstances I had little choice. There was no hint of intimidation, but neither was there any question in anyone's mind that I'd brought the beer for any other purpose than to share it at this crucial, bone-dry time. As it happened, I had barely enough money for gas back to San Francisco. Once my two cases were gone I couldn't buy a single can all weekend without cashing a check, and that was out of the question. Beyond that, I was—and might still be—the only journalist the Angels had ever seen who didn't have an expense account, so I was a little worried at their reaction when I'd be forced to plead poverty and start drinking out of the kitty. My own taste for the hops is very powerful, and I had no intention of spending a beerless weekend in the withering sun.

24   In retrospect this seems like a small point, but it didn't at the time. It was an ill-chosen moment to cast my bread on the waters . . . the sucktide was running. Somewhere in the cacophony of foaming and hissing that followed the discovery of my cache, I recall saying, to nobody in particular: "All right, goddamnit, this thing had better work both ways." But there was no reason to believe it would. At that stage of their infamy the Angels equated all reporters with *Time* and *Newsweek*. Only a few of them knew me, and the others were not going to be happy when I began lurking around the beer supply, draining one can after another in a feverish effort to even the score.

25   Many hours later, after the beer crisis had passed, I felt a little foolish for having worried. The outlaws gave it no thought. To them it was just as natural for me to have their beer as for them to have mine. By the end of the weekend I'd consumed three or four times as much as I'd brought with me . . . and even now, looking back on nearly a year of drinking with the Angels, I think I came out ahead. But that isn't the way they

balance the books. Despite their swastika fetish, the fiscal relationship between Angels is close to pure communism: "from each according to his abilities and to each according to his needs." The timing and the spirit of the exchange are just as important as the volume. Much as they claim to admire the free enterprise system, they can't afford it among themselves. Their working ethic is more on the order of "He who has, shares." There is nothing verbal or dogmatic about it; they just couldn't make it any other way.

But none of this was apparent that afternoon in Bass Lake as I watched my stock disappear while Barger called for funds. Although Sheriff Baxter had left, six deputies had attached themselves to the camp on what appeared to be a permanent basis. I was talking to one of them when Barger joined us with a handful of money. "The sheriff said that place by the post office will sell us all the beer we want," he said. "How about using your car? There's likely to be trouble if we take one of the trucks." *26*

I didn't mind and the deputy said it was a socko idea, so we counted out the money on the hood of the car. It came to $120 in bills and roughly $15 in change. Then, to my astonishment, Sonny handed me the whole bundle and wished me well. "Try to hustle," he said. "Everybody's pretty thirsty." *27*

I insisted that somebody come with me to help load the beer in the car . . . but my real reason for not wanting to go alone had nothing to do with loading problems. I knew all the outlaws lived in cities, where the price of a six-pack ranges from $.79 to $1.25. But we were nowhere near a city, and I also knew, from long experience, that small stores in remote areas sometimes get their pricing policy from *The Gouger's Handbook*. *28*

Once, near the Utah-Nevada border, I had to pay $3.00 for a six-pack, and if that was going to be the case at Bass Lake, I wanted a reliable witness—like Barger himself. At normal city prices, $135 would fetch about thirty cases of beer, but up in the Sierras it would only cover twenty, or maybe fifteen if the merchants were putting up a solid front. The Angels were in no position to do any comparison shopping, and if they were about to be taught a harsh lesson in socioeconomics, I figured they'd be more receptive to the bad news if it came from one of their own people. There was also the fact that sending a penniless writer to get $135 worth of beer was—as Khrushchev* said of Nixon—"like sending a goat to tend the cabbage." *29*

---

*Nikita S. Khrushchev (1894–1964) was First Secretary of the Communist Party and Premier of the Soviet Union from 1953 to 1964. While Vice-President of the United States, Richard M. Nixon had a series of meetings with Khrushchev.

30   I mentioned this on the way to town, after Sonny and Pete had agreed to come with me. "You'd of come back with it," Sonny said. "A person would have to be awful stupid to run off with our beer money." Pete laughed. "Hell, we even know where you live. And Frenchy says you got a boss-lookin old lady, too." He said it jokingly, but I noted that raping my wife was the first form of retaliation that came to his mind.

31   Barger, like the politician he is, hastened to change the subject. "I read that article you wrote about us," he said. "It was okay."

32   The article had appeared a month or so earlier, and I remembered a night in my apartment when one of the Frisco Angels had said, with a beery smile, that if they didn't like what I wrote they'd come over some night to kick down my door, throw gasoline into the hall and then put a match to it. We were all in good spirits at the time, and I recall pointing to the loaded double-barreled shotgun on my wall and replying, with a smile, that I would croak at least two of them before they got away. But none of this violence had come to pass, so I assumed they either hadn't read the article or had managed to live with what it said. Nonetheless, I was leery of having it mentioned, and especially by Barger, whose opinions automatically become the Hell's Angels' official line. I had written the piece with the idea that I would never again have any contact with motorcycle outlaws, whom I'd referred to as "losers," "ignorant thugs" and "mean hoodlums." None of these were terms I looked forward to explaining while surrounded at a remote Sierra campsite by two hundred boozing outlaws.

33   "What are you doin now?" Barger asked. "Are you writin somethin else?"

34   "Yeah," I said. "A book."

35   He shrugged. "Well, we don't ask for nothin but the truth.[1] Like I say, there's not much good you can write about us, but I don't see where that gives people the right to just make up stuff. . . all this bullshit, hell, ain't the truth bad enough for em?"

36   We were almost to Williams' store, and I suddenly remembered my burr-haired inquisitor with his high-powered language barrier. We made the turn at the bottom of the hill and I parked the car as inconspicuously as possible about thirty yards from the store. According to the deputy at the campsite, the sale was already arranged. All we had to do was pay, load the beer and leave. Sonny had the cash, and as far as I was concerned, I was just the chauffeur.

37   It took about fifteen seconds to understand that something had boggled the plan. As we stepped out of the car the vigilantes began mov-

[1]Several months later they decided that truth was not enough. There would have to be money too. This created tension, which blossomed into resentment and finally violence.

ing toward us. It was very hot and quiet, and I could taste the dust that hung over the parking area. A Madera County paddy wagon was parked at the other end of the shopping center, with two cops in the front seat. The mob stopped short of the car and formed a bristling human wall on the boardwalk outside the store. Apparently they hadn't been informed of the pending transaction. I opened the trunk of my car, thinking that Sonny and Pete would go in for the beer. If things got serious I could jump into the trunk and lock it behind me, then kick out the back seat and drive away when it was all over.

Neither Angel made a move toward the store. Traffic had stopped and the tourists were standing off at a safe distance, watching. The scene reeked of Hollywood: the showdown, *High Noon, Rio Bravo.* But without cameras or background music it didn't seem quite the same. After a long moment of silence the burr-haired fellow took a few steps forward and shouted, "You better get your asses out of here. You don't have a chance." 38

I walked over to talk with him, thinking to explain the beer agreement. I wasn't particularly opposed to the idea of a riot, but I didn't want it to happen right then, with my car in the middle and me a participant. It would have been ugly: two Hell's Angels and a writer against a hundred country toughs on a dusty street in the Sierras. Burr-head listened to my reasoning, then shook his head. "Mr. Williams changed his mind," he said. And then I heard Sonny's voice right behind me: "Well, fuck that! We can change our minds too." He and Pete had walked out to join the argument, and now the vigilantes moved forward to support Burr-head, who didn't look at all worried. 39

Well, I thought, here we go. The two cops in the paddy wagon hadn't moved; they were in no hurry to break the thing up. Getting beaten by a mob is a very frightening experience. . .like being caught in a bad surf: there is not much you can do except try to survive. It has happened to me twice, in New York and San Juan, and it came within seconds of happening again at Bass Lake. All that prevented it was the suspiciously timely arrival of Tiny Baxter. The crowd parted to make room for his big car with the flashing red light on top. "I thought I told you to stay out of town," he snapped. 40

"We came for the beer," Sonny replied. 41

Baxter shook his head. "No, Williams says he's running low. You gotta go over to the market on the other side of the lake. They have plenty." 42

We left instantly. Like the first campsite, the first beer contact had all the signs of a calculated botch. Baxter may or may not have known what he was doing, but if he did he deserves credit for coming up with a subtle and ingenious strategy. He made a limited number of appear- 43 ances during that weekend, but each one came at a critical moment and he always arrived with a solution. After the fixing of the beer crisis the Angels began to view him as a secret sympathizer, and by midnight of the first day Barger had been made to feel almost personally responsible for the welfare of everybody in Bass Lake. Each time Baxter fixed something he put the Angels more in his debt. The strange burden eventually ruined Barger's holiday. The vagaries of the restraining order and the numerous agreements he'd made with the sheriff caused him to worry constantly. One of his few pleasures was the knowledge that Baxter wasn't getting any sleep either.

44   On the way around the lake we speculated about what sort of mob might be waiting at the next store. "Those bastards were gonna stomp us," said Pete.

45   "Yeah, and that would have been it," Sonny muttered. "That sheriff don't know how close he was to havin a war on his hands."

46   I didn't take his remark very seriously, but by the time the weekend was over I knew he hadn't been kidding. If Barger had been stomped by a mob of locals, nothing short of a company of armed militia could have kept the main body of outlaws from swarming into town for vengeance. An attack on the Prez would have been bad enough, but under those circumstances—a police-planned beer run—it would have been evidence of the foulest treachery, a double cross, and the Angels would have done exactly what they all came to Bass Lake expecting to do. Most would have finished the weekend in jail or the hospital, but they were expecting that too. It would have been a good riot, but looking back, I no longer think the initial clash would have been evenly matched. Many of the vigilantes would have lost their taste for the fight the moment they realized that their opponents meant to inflict serious injury on anybody they could reach. Big Frank from Frisco,[2] for instance, is a black belt in karate who goes into any fight with the idea of jerking people's eyeballs out of their sockets. It is a traditional karate move and not difficult for anyone who knows what he's doing...although it is not taught in "self-defense" classes for housewives, businessmen and hot-tempered clerks who can't tolerate bullies kicking sand in their faces. The intent is to demoralize your opponent, not blind him. "You don't really jerk out the eyeball," Big Frank explained. "You just sorta *spring* it, so it pops outta the socket. It hurts so much that most guys just faint."

47   Red-blooded American boys don't normally fight this way. Nor do they swing heavy chains on people whose backs are turned...and when they find themselves in a brawl where things like this are happening,

[2]Or Frank Number Two—not legendary Frank, ex-outlaw and -president.

they have good reason to feel at a disadvantage. It is one thing to get punched in the nose, and quite another to have your eyeball sprung or your teeth shattered with a wrench.

So if there had been a full-strength fight that afternoon, the locals would probably have been routed after the first clash. But it would have taken a while for the police to muster enough strength to prevail, and in the meantime the outlaws would have wreaked all manner of destruction on the merchant Williams' property—breaking windows, looting beer coolers and probably rifling some cash registers. A few would have been shot by Burr-head and his crew, but most would have tried to flee at the first sign of serious police action. This would have led to wild chases and skirmishing, but Bass Lake is a long way from Angel turf and not many of them could have made it all the way home without being captured at roadblocks.

Barger knew this and he didn't want it to happen. But he also knew that it was not a sense of hospitality or concern for social justice that had got them a campsite. Tiny Baxter had a bomb on his hands, and he had to tread carefully to keep it from going off. This was Barger's leverage—the certainty that his people would behave like wild beasts if they were pushed too far. But it would last only as long as things stayed quiet. John Foster Dulles* might have called it a "balance of terror," a volatile stand-off which neither side wanted to upset. Whether this was a just or desirable situation for a woodsy American community to find itself in is, again, pretty much beside the point. As weird and unreal as the Bass Lake confrontation might have sounded to radio listeners in New York or Chicago, nobody on the scene had any doubt about what they were seeing. Right or wrong, it was happening, and by the time the Angels were settled at Willow Cove, even the locally made restraining order was irrelevant. The outlaws simply had to be dealt with in terms of moment-to-moment reality.

I hadn't planned to get physically involved, but after the narrow escape at Williams' store I was so firmly identified with the Angels that I saw no point in trying to edge back to neutrality. Barger and Pete seemed to take me for granted. As we drove around the lake they tried earnestly to explain the importance of the colors. Pete seemed puzzled that the question had ever come up. "Hell," he said, "that's what it's all about."

The other market was in the center of the main tourist area, and when we got there the crowd was so dense that the only place to park was between the gas pump and the side door. If trouble broke out we'd

*John Foster Dulles (1888–1959) was an American lawyer and diplomat who was Secretary of State from 1953 to 1959.

be hopelessly penned in. At a glance the scene looked even worse than the one we'd just been rescued from.

52   But this was a different crowd. They'd apparently been waiting for hours to see the Angels in action, and now, as the two stepped out of the car, a murmur of gratification went up. These were not locals, but tourists—city people, from the valley and the coast. The store was full of newspapers featuring the Hell's Angels rape in Los Angeles, but nobody looked frightened. A curious crowd gathered as the outlaws bargained with the owner, a short moon-faced man who kept saying, "Sure thing, boys—I'll take care of you." He was aggressively friendly, even to the point of putting his arm around Pete's grimy shoulders as they made their way to the beer vault.

53   I bought a paper and went to the bar and lunch counter at the far end of the store. While I was reading the rape story I heard a little girl behind me ask, "Where are they, Mommy? You said we were going to see them." I turned to look at the child, a bandy-legged pixie just getting her permanent teeth, and felt thankful once again that my only issue is male. I glanced at the mother and wondered what strange grooves her mind had been fitted to in these wonderfully prosperous times. She was a downbeat thirty-five, with short blond hair and a sleeveless blouse only half tucked into her tight bermuda shorts. It was a vivid Pepsi Generation tableau...on a hot California afternoon a sag-bellied woman wearing St. Tropez sunglasses is hanging around a resort-area market, trailing her grade-school daughter and waiting in the midst of an eager crowd for the arrival of The Hoodlum Circus, as advertised in *Life*.

54   I remembered the previous spring, when I was driving one night from San Francisco to Big Sur and heard a radio bulletin about a tidal wave due to strike the California coast around midnight. Shortly before eleven I got to Hot Springs Lodge—which sits on a cliff just above the ocean—and rushed inside to sound the alarm. It was a slow night, and the only people still awake were a half dozen locals sitting around a redwood table with some bottles of wine. They had already heard the warnings and were waiting for the thing to hit. A tidal wave was a sight worth waiting up for. That same night, according to anguished police reports, more than ten thousand people flocked to Ocean Beach in San Francisco, creating a night-long traffic jam on the Coast Highway. They too were curious, and if the wave had come up on schedule most of them would have been killed. Luckily it petered out somewhere between Honolulu and the West Coast...

55   A crowd of about fifty people gathered to watch us load the beer. Several teen-agers got up the nerve to help. A man wearing madras shorts and black business socks kept asking Pete and Sonny to pose while he backed off for panoramic sequences with his home-movie camera. An-

other man, also wearing bermudas, sidled up to me and asked quietly, "Say, are you guys really Nazis?"

"Not me," I said. "I'm Kiwanis."   56

He nodded wisely, as if he had known all along. "Then what's all this   57
stuff you read?" he asked. "You know, this stuff about swastikas."

I called to Sonny, who was showing our helpers how to stack the   58
cases in the back seat. "Hey, this man wants to know if you're a Nazi."
I expected him to laugh, but he didn't. He made the usual disclaimers
regarding the swastikas and Iron Crosses ("That don't mean nothin, we
buy that stuff in dime stores"), but just about the time the man seemed
satisfied that it was all a rude put-on, Barger unloaded one of those jar-
ring ad libs that have made him a favorite among Bay area newsmen.
"But there's a lot about that country we admire," he said, referring to
pre-war Germany. "They had discipline. There was nothing chicken-
shit about em. They might not of had all the right ideas, but at least
they respected their leaders and they could depend on each other."

The audience seemed to want to mull this over, and in the meantime   59
I suggested we get back to Willow Cove. At any moment I expected
somebody to start yelling about Dachau and then to see some furious
Jew lay Barger out with a campstool. But there was no sign of anything
like that. The atmosphere was so congenial that we soon found ourselves back inside the store, eating hamburgers and sipping draft beer. I
was beginning to feel almost relaxed when we heard motorcycles outside and saw the crowd surge toward the door. Seconds later, Skip from
Richmond appeared, saying he'd waited as long as he could for the beer
and had finally decided to seek it on his own. Several more Angels
arrived, for the same reason, and the owner scurried around behind the
bar, serving up the mugs with a nice enthusiasm: "Drink up, boys, and
take it easy—I bet you're thirsty as hell after that long ride, eh?"

The man's attitude was very odd. As we left he stood by the car and   60
told us to come back real soon, "with the other fellas." Considering the
circumstances, I listened closely for a telltale lilt of craziness in his
voice. Maybe he's not even the owner, I thought...Maybe the owner
had fled with his family to Nevada, leaving the village loony to mind
the store and deal with the savages in his own way. Whoever he was, the
eager little person had just sold eighty-eight six-packs of beer at $1.50
each and guaranteed himself a booming trade for the rest of the weekend...Without spending a penny, he'd landed the West Coast's top animal act, a sure-fire crowd-pleaser that would put the traditional
lakeside fireworks display in deep shade. All he had to worry about was
the good possibility that the act might go haywire at any moment,
destroying both the profits and the customers in a brutal eruption
which the next day's newspapers would describe as:

THE RAPE OF BASS LAKE: FIRE AND PANIC IN MOUNTAIN RESORT;
COPS BATTLE HELL'S ANGELS AS RESIDENTS FLEE

61   The locals seemed resigned to it, and it was no surprise to find them armed and surly. Nor was it strange to find the police unusually tense. This was the first major rally since Monterey, and the vast publicity surrounding it was a factor that neither the outlaws nor the police had ever had to contend with. Things like roadblocks and restraining orders were new problems for both sides. The idea of a carefully reserved campsite had been tried before, but it had never been effective except late at night, when the outlaws were not likely to move around anyway. The real shocker, however, was the beer situation. The Angels have always prided themselves on the one contribution they inevitably make to any community they visit. In spite of the terror they inspire, they leave many dollars in local taverns. Because of this, they found it unthinkable that anyone would refuse to sell them beer—and especially without fair warning, which would have caused them to bring a whole truck load from the city.

62   But Bass Lake was a different scene. The locals had had nearly a week to work themselves into a swivet, and by Saturday morning they were braced for the worst. Among the safety measures they were counting on was the knowledge that the hoodlums would be much less dangerous if denied large quantities of drink. This was evident to everyone concerned—even the beer-sellers—and besides, it was going to be a bad money weekend anyway, since the rotten publicity would cause large numbers of vacationers to go elsewhere. What manner of man would bring his family to camp on a battleground, a place almost certain to be invaded by an army of vicious rabble?

63   The question still pertains, but it doesn't alter the fact that people came from all over California that weekend to enjoy the rustic pleasures of Bass Lake. When they were turned away from motels or regular campsites they slept in roadside turn-outs and dirty ravines. By Monday morning the lakefront looked like the White House lawn after Andrew Jackson's inaugural ball.* The crowd was abnormal even for a big summer holiday.

64   Californians are known to be enthusiastic outdoorsmen; in 1964, near Los Angeles, thousands of weekend campers had to be restrained by barriers from moving into an area that had just been gutted by a forest fire. When it was under control and the barriers were opened, the blackened campsite quickly filled to capacity. A reporter on the scene

---

*Andrew Jackson (1767–1845) was the seventh president of the United States and was known as "Old Hickory." He invited many of his old cronies and friends from his home state to his inauguration ball in 1829, and they camped on the White House lawn.

said the campers were "pitching their tents among smoking stumps." One man who had brought his family explained that there was "no place else to go, and we only have two days."

As a pathetic comment, it made a pathetic kind of sense. But nothing that simple and tangible could explain the capacity crowd at Bass Lake. Anybody who really wanted no part of the outlaws had plenty of time to find a safer vacation spot. Police reports of possible "Hell's Angels strikes" had Bass Lake near the top of every list.   65

So it must have been a giddy revelation for the Bass Lake Chamber of Commerce to discover that the Hell's Angels' presence—far from being a plague—was in fact a great boon to the tourist trade. It is eerie to consider the meaning of it. If the Hell's Angels draw standing room only, any half-hip chamber-of-commerce entertainment chairman should see the logical follow-up; next year, bring in two fighting gangs from Watts and pit them against each other on one of the main beaches . . . with fireworks overhead while the local high school band plays *Bolero* and "They Call the Wind Maria."   66

Questions and Activities

▶ *COMPREHENSION QUESTIONS*

1. Are there similarities between Bass Lake and the New England town represented in Noel Perrin's "Country Codes" (pages 748–752)? How are these two towns similar and different? How much are the differences between the two towns due to the different intentions of the two authors?

2. What is the difference between "hill people" and "flatlands people" as Thompson describes them in paragraph 6? How does Thompson explain that difference? How does that difference apply to the contending parties in this piece?

3. What is the difference between the crowd that is waiting for the Angels in paragraph 51 and the groups the Angels encountered at earlier points in this narrative? Where was most of this crowd from? What were their motives in coming to observe the Angels?

▶ *QUESTIONS OF RHETORICAL PURPOSE AND STRATEGY*

4. Why does Thompson focus so much of his attention on the relationship between Sheriff Tiny Baxter ("a giant of a man," paragraph 1) and Sonny Barger, the leader of the Hell's Angels? What basic American legends are brought to mind by this confrontation? Does

this focusing create a sense of theater that readers might otherwise not feel when they read about the events at Bass Lake?

5. Why does Thompson give himself an active role in the events he describes? A more traditional reporter might have maintained a more distant or objective stance by writing a third-person account of these events. What does Thompson gain by this strategy? What does he lose? What are the effects of this strategy on the reader?

6. What writing devices does Thompson use to establish the characters of Sonny Barger and Tiny Baxter in this essay? For example, what descriptions help to bring their characters alive? What parts do their dialogues with each other and with the townspeople play in shaping your impressions of their characters? How does the background information that Thompson provides help develop their characters?

7. What is Thompson's purpose in explaining the behavior of the tourists who came to Bass Lake to see the Angels (paragraphs 63–66)? What danger is implied, to Thompson, in the tourists' curious lack of emotional involvement in what they are observing? Do they seem to be looking for an entertaining spectacle, something like an interesting television show or a movie to spice up their vacations? Why might Thompson find such an attitude worrisome or dangerous?

▶ *THEME QUESTIONS*

8. Are the Hell's Angels totally free, or are they constrained more than they might admit by the actions and values of those around them? Give examples that support both positive and negative answers to this question.

9. Lewis Thomas (pages 755–758) suggests that human beings, like many insects and animals, have strong social instincts. In what ways do the Angels demonstrate the swarming or herding instincts of insects or animals? In what ways do they demonstrate a drive toward independence from others of their species?

10. When does the Angels' avowed intention to be free of society's "hang-ups" become unethical or immoral? Give specific examples from the essay to support your answer.

▶ *LEARNING ACTIVITIES*

11. Bring to class a current news article concerning what might be considered an antisocial or radical group. Discuss your article with some of your classmates. How does the article differ in form and style from Thompson's essay? Is it more or less objective? Does it give as dramatic an account of events as Thompson's essay does?

12. Tell the rest of the class a story about a past experience with an anti-social group, either as a member yourself or as an observant outsider. Why were you attracted to and/or repulsed by the group? Did the group seem to have clear reasons for its behavior? Were the members of the group from a definable social or economic class, or were they bonded by their reaction against some particular social conventions?

The Atlanta Riot

WALTER WHITE

Walter White (1893–1955) spent his life working for human rights for blacks. His father, a letter carrier, and his mother, a teacher before her marriage, were both light-skinned. White was light enough to pass for a Caucasian; yet at thirteen years old, during the Atlanta riots of 1906 described in the autobiographical sketch reprinted here, he resolved to live as a black man and to dedicate himself to furthering human rights. He spent the early part of his career as a reporter for several black newspapers and as an organizer of protests against racial discrimination in American schools. He often posed as a white reporter from an Eastern newspaper in order to gain access to news that white communities would otherwise have kept hidden. In 1918, White began working for the NAACP, and he soon became famous for his investigative reporting and writings on lynchings in the South. This work resulted in the book *Rope and Faggot: A Biography of Judge Lynch* (1929), a study of the complex causes of lynching, and eventually led to the passage of federal antilynching legislation.

White also wrote the book *A Rising Wind* (1945) about his experiences with international human rights movements, particularly in the U.S. armed forces. In the 1920s he wrote two novels, *The Fire in the Flint* (1924) and *Flight* (1926), which described his experiences with lynchings and with passing for white. But by far his most well-known book is his autobiography, *A Man Called White* (1948), in which he gives a sensitive and compelling first-hand account of the violence that was done to blacks in many situations. White won many awards, including the Springarn Medal in 1938 for his work on human rights and a Guggenheim Fellowship in 1927 for his writing. Perhaps his greatest social accomplishment was the influence he had on American politicians in the 1940s, particularly President Roosevelt and President Truman. This political influence resulted in antidiscrimination laws concerning defense industries during World War II and in the establishing of the Fair Employment Practices Commission during the late 1940s.

The selection featured here comes from *A Man Called White* and relates the author's memories of the Atlanta riots of 1906. During these riots, rampaging gangs of whites attacked black pedestrians and threatened to burn White's family's house. Perhaps the most significant quality of this autobiographical essay is White's ability to create a controlled, almost serene voice with which to narrate an intensely violent series of events; the reader shares in both an appreciation of the riot's barbarism and the emotional response that the thirteen-year-old White had to the event.

As you read and think about this essay, you might focus on the young narrator's decision, described in paragraph 19, to dedicate his life to fostering human rights, particularly racial equality:

1. What causes White to make this decision?
2. Do you think he became more independent because of his decision? In what particular ways might White have become more independent because of his dedication to establishing human rights?
3. Did this dedication take away some of his freedom? Did his community have more control over him than it would have, for example, if he had decided to write about subjects other than race?

▶ ─────────────────

There were nine light-skinned Negroes in my family: mother, father, five sisters, an older brother, George, and myself. The house in which I discovered what it meant to be a Negro was located on Houston Street, three blocks from the Candler Building, Atlanta's first skyscraper, which bore the name of the ex-drug clerk who had become a millionaire from the sale of Coca-Cola. Below us lived none but Negroes; toward town all but a very few were white. Ours was an eight-room, two-story frame house which stood out in its surroundings not because of its opulence but by contrast with the drabness and unpaintedness of the other dwellings in a deteriorating neighborhood.

Only Father kept his house painted, the picket fence repaired, the board fence separating our place from those on either side whitewashed, the grass neatly trimmed, and flower beds abloom. Mother's passion for neatness was even more pronounced and it seemed to me that I was always the victim of her determination to see no single blade of grass longer than the others or any one of the pickets in the front fence less shiny with paint than its mates. This spic-and-spanness became increasingly apparent as the rest of the neighborhood became more down-at-heel, and resulted, as we were to learn, in sullen envy among some of our white neighbors. It was the violent expression of that resentment against a Negro family neater than themselves which set the pattern of our lives.

On a day in September 1906, when I was thirteen, we were taught that there is no isolation from life. The unseasonably oppressive heat of an Indian summer day hung like a steaming blanket over Atlanta. My sisters and I had casually commented upon the unusual quietness. It seemed to stay Mother's volubility and reduced Father, who was more taciturn, to monosyllables. But, as I remember it, no other sense of impending trouble impinged upon our consciousness.

4   I had read the inflammatory headlines in the *Atlanta News* and the more restrained ones in the *Atlanta Constitution* which reported alleged rapes and other crimes committed by Negroes. But these were so standard and familiar that they made—as I look back on it now—little impression. The stories were more frequent, however, and consisted of eight-column streamers instead of the usual two- or four-column ones.

5   Father was a mail collector. His tour of duty was from three to eleven P.M. He made his rounds in a little cart into which one climbed from a step in the rear. I used to drive the cart for him from two until seven, leaving him at the point nearest our home on Houston street, to return home either for study or sleep. That day Father decided that I should not go with him. I appealed to Mother, who thought it might be all right, provided Father sent me home before dark because, she said, "I don't think they would dare start anything before nightfall." Father told me as we made the rounds that ominous rumors of a race riot that night were sweeping the town. . . .

6   During the afternoon preceding the riot little bands of sullen evil-looking men talked excitedly on street corners all over downtown Atlanta. Around seven o'clock my father and I were driving toward a mail box at the corner of Peachtree and Houston Streets when there came from near-by Pryor Street a roar the like of which I had never heard before, but which sent a sensation of mingled fear and excitement coursing through my body. I asked permission of Father to go and see what the trouble was. He bluntly ordered me to stay in the cart. A little later we drove down Atlanta's main business thoroughfare, Peachtree Street. Again we heard the terrifying cries, this time near at hand and coming toward us. We saw a lame Negro bootblack from Herndon's barber shop pathetically trying to outrun a mob of whites. Less than a hundred yards from us the chase ended. We saw clubs and fists descending to the accompaniment of savage shouting and cursing. Suddenly a voice cried, "There goes another nigger!" Its work done, the mob went after new prey. The body with the withered foot lay dead in a pool of blood on the street.

7   Father's apprehension and mine steadily increased during the evening, although the fact that our skins were white kept us from attack. Another circumstance favored us—the mob had not yet grown violent enough to attack United States government property. But I could see Father's relief when he punched the time clock at eleven P.M. and got

into the cart to go home. He wanted to go the back way down Forsyth Street, but I begged him, in my childish excitement and ignorance, to drive down Marietta to Five Points, the heart of Atlanta's business district, where the crowds were densest and the yells loudest. No sooner had we turned into Marietta Street, however, than we saw careening toward us an undertaker's barouche. Crouched in the rear of the vehicle were three Negroes clinging to the sides of the carriage as it lunged and swerved. On the driver's seat crouched a white man, the reins held taut in his left hand. A huge whip was gripped in his right. Alternately he lashed the horses and, without looking backward, swung the whip in savage swoops in the faces of members of the mob as they lunged at the carriage determined to seize the three Negroes.

There was no time for us to get out of its path, so sudden and swift   8
was the appearance of the vehicle. The hub cap of the right rear wheel of the barouche hit the right side of our much lighter wagon. Father and I instinctively threw our weight and kept the cart from turning completely over. Our mare was a Texas mustang which, frightened by the sudden blow, lunged in the air as Father clung to the reins. Good fortune was with us. The cart settled back on its four wheels as Father said in a voice which brooked no dissent, "We are going home the back way and not down Marietta."

But again on Pryor Street we heard the cry of the mob. Close to us and   9
in our direction ran a stout and elderly woman who cooked at a downtown white hotel. Fifty yards behind, a mob which filled the street from curb to curb was closing in. Father handed the reins to me and, though he was of slight stature, reached down and lifted the woman into the cart. I did not need to be told to lash the mare to the fastest speed she could muster.

The church bells tolled the next morning for Sunday service. But no   10
one in Atlanta believed for a moment that the hatred and lust for blood had been appeased. Like skulls on a cannibal's hut the hats and caps of victims of the mob the night before had been hung on the iron hooks of telegraph poles. None could tell whether each hat represented a dead Negro. But we knew that some of those who had worn hats would never again wear any.

Later in the afternoon friends of my father's came to warn of more   11
trouble that night. They told us that plans had been perfected for a mob to form on Peachtree Street just after nightfall to march down Houston Street to what the white people called "Darktown," three blocks or so below our house, to "clean out the niggers." There had never been a firearm in our house before that day. Father was reluctant even in those circumstances to violate the law, but he at last gave in at Mother's insistence.

12   We turned out the lights, as did all our neighbors. No one removed his clothes or thought of sleep. Apprehension was tangible. We could almost touch its cold and clammy surface. Toward midnight the unnatural quiet was broken by a roar that grew steadily in volume. Even today I grow tense in remembering it.

13   Father told Mother to take my sisters, the youngest of them only six, to the rear of the house, which offered more protection from stones and bullets. My brother George was away, so Father and I, the only males in the house, took our places at the front windows. The windows opened on a porch along the front side of the house, which in turn gave onto a narrow lawn that sloped down to the street and a picket fence. There was a crash as Negroes smashed the street lamp at the corner of Houston and Piedmont Avenue down the street. In a very few minutes the vanguard of the mob, some of them bearing torches, appeared. A voice which we recognized as that of the son of the grocer with whom we had traded for many years yelled, ''That's where the nigger mail carrier lives! Let's burn it down! It's too nice for a nigger to live in!'' In the eerie light Father turned his drawn face toward me. In a voice as quiet as though he were asking me to pass him the sugar at the breakfast table, he said, ''Son, don't shoot until the first man puts his foot on the lawn and then—don't you miss!''

14   In the flickering light the mob swayed, paused, and began to flow toward us. In that instant there opened within me a great awareness; I knew then who I was. I was a Negro, a human being with an invisible pigmentation which marked me a person to be hunted, hanged, abused, discriminated against, kept in poverty and ignorance, in order that those whose skin was white would have readily at hand a proof of their superiority, a proof patent and inclusive, accessible to the moron and the idiot as well as to the wise man and the genius. No matter how low a white man fell, he could always hold fast to the smug conviction that he was superior to two-thirds of the world's population, for those two-thirds were not white.

15   It made no difference how intelligent or talented my millions of brothers and I were, or how virtuously we lived. A curse like that of Judas was upon us, a mark of degradation fashioned with heavenly authority. There were white men who said Negroes had no souls, and who proved it by the Bible. Some of these now were approaching us, intent upon burning our house.

16   Theirs was a world of contrasts in values: superior and inferior, profit and loss, cooperative and noncooperative, civilized and aboriginal, white and black. If you were on the wrong end of the comparison, if you were inferior, if you were noncooperative, if you were aboriginal, if you were black, then you were marked for excision, expulsion, or extinction. I was a Negro; I was therefore that part of history which opposed

the good, the just, and the enlightened. I was a Persian, falling before the hordes of Alexander, I was a Carthaginian, extinguished by the Legions of Rome. I was a Frenchman at Waterloo, an Anglo-Saxon at Hastings, a Confederate at Vicksburg. I was defeated, wherever and whenever there was a defeat.

Yet as a boy there in the darkness amid the tightening fright, I knew   17
the inexplicable thing—that my skin was as white as the skin of those who were coming at me.

The mob moved toward the lawn. I tried to aim my gun, wondering   18
what it would feel like to kill a man. Suddenly there was a volley of shots. The mob hesitated, stopped. Some friends of my father's had barricaded themselves in a two-story brick building just below our house. It was they who had fired. Some of the mobsmen, still blood-thirsty, shouted, "Let's go get the nigger." Others, afraid now for their safety, held back. Our friends, noting the hesitation, fired another volley. The mob broke and retreated up Houston Street.

In the quiet that followed I put my gun aside and tried to relax. But a   19
tension different from anything I had ever known possessed me. I was gripped by the knowledge of my identity, and in the depths of my soul I was vaguely aware that I was glad of it. I was sick with loathing for the hatred which had flared before me that night and come so close to making me a killer; but I was glad I was not one of those who hated; I was glad I was not one of those made sick and murderous by pride. I was glad I was not one of those whose story is in the history of the world, a record of bloodshed, rapine, and pillage. I was glad my mind and spirit were part of the races that had not fully awakened, and who therefore still had before them the opportunity to write a record of virtue as a memorandum to Armageddon.

It was all just a feeling then, inarticulate and melancholy, yet reas-   20
suring in the way that death and sleep are reassuring, and I have clung to it now for nearly half a century.

Questions and Activities

▶ *COMPREHENSION QUESTIONS*

1. Describe the conditions under which White and his family lived while he was growing up in Atlanta at the turn of the century. Were they living in poverty? Did they live solely among people of their own race? What were White's biggest problems as he grew up, and who created those problems?

2. How did the color of White's skin seem to affect white people and other black people? Give examples to support your answer.

▶ *QUESTIONS OF RHETORICAL PURPOSE AND STRATEGY*

3. How old is White when this story occurs? Is the narrator speaking in the voice of an adult looking back at a past experience? Does the narrator seem to have the advantages of hindsight? Does the narrator seem to have full awareness of the significance of the events that he describes? What does the older narrator understand that the boy may not have understood at the time?
4. Describe the tone the narrator uses to tell this story. Does the narrator seem angry, sad, resigned, or indignant as he relates his brief accounts of white cruelty and violence? What language devices are employed to create the narrator's tone?
5. The first sentence of paragraph 3 states the main point of this piece. Why does the main point first appear in paragraph 3 rather than at the very beginning?

▶ *THEME QUESTIONS*

6. Consider the situation of White's family in this story. Are they fighting for independence or simply for survival? Why does the young White realize that he will spend his entire life dedicated to fighting for human rights during his family's struggle for survival in a race riot? Do the violence and sense of threat cause White to see racism in a way that might not have been possible otherwise?
7. White dedicated his life to improving individual rights and working for human equality. Does this self-dedication suggest that White continued to be trapped to some extent by his background? Would White have been truly independent of racism only if he no longer needed to fight for equality?

▶ *LEARNING ACTIVITIES*

8. In a workshop group, discuss your reactions to this narrative. When do you feel the most empathy for White and his family? At what points in the narrative do you first note the narrator's more mature voice, and in what ways do you respond to this voice?
9. Go back and reread the first eight paragraphs of this selection. Write about the event described in paragraph 8 from the point of view of White's father. Describe the thoughts that might lie behind the father's statement: "We are going home the back way and not down Marietta." What do you think White's father was thinking when he said this? Do you think he also felt humiliated at being forced to alter his normal route home, especially in front of his son?

Work in Corporate America
RUSSELL BAKER

Born in 1925 in Virginia, Russell Baker is a very popular political satirist and humorist. He has won two Pulitzer Prizes, one in 1979 for social commentary for a series of newspaper columns and the other in 1982 for his autobiography. He has worked for the *Baltimore Sun* and the *New York Times,* where he wrote columns covering White House and State Department politics from 1954 to 1962. He grew tired of political reporting in 1962 and began to write his "Observer" columns for the *Times,* which made him one of the most widely read political columnists in the country by 1974. From that point on, his columns' subject matter was expanded to include general social as well as political issues.

Baker's writing combines an astute critical sense, an analytical intelligence, and an entertaining and sensitive perspective on human behavior. His autobiography conveys deep feeling without sentimentality, and his columns, even when satiric, are never cruel or insensitive. Critics often praise Baker's writing because it criticizes American life without being cynical or one-sided. His columns have been collected in several best-selling books, including *Baker's Dozen* (1964), *Poor Russell's Almanac* (1972), and *The Rescue of Miss Yaskell and Other Pipe Dreams* (1983). His prize-winning autobiography, *Growing Up,* was published in 1982.

In the article reprinted here, Baker, half seriously and half satirically, tells why corporate workers have such a difficult time describing their work to their children. Work, for today's manager or executive, produces no tangible results; its goal is usually the production of paper reports or ledger accounts. The result, Baker suggests, is very little positive identification with one's work and a lost opportunity for personal expression and independence.

Like other selections in this section, this article raises questions about the social basis for individual independence. Workers, Baker suggests, must be valued by the society for which they work; without that social esteem, they may feel unimportant and useless. Each of us depends, in other words, on others to some degree for our sense of worth.

As you read, ask yourself these questions:

1. Would the corporate workers Baker describes agree with him about their work? Do you think they would agree that the goal of their work was to push paper? Or would they see other values in their jobs?

2. Why might a worker who produces tangible products feel a greater sense of independence than a paper-pusher?
3. In what ways has your work—as a student or at a job—made you feel, or not feel, independent?

▶ ————————————————

1   It is not surprising that modern children tend to look blank and dispirited when informed that they will someday have to "go to work and make a living." The problem is that they cannot visualize what work is in corporate America.

2   Not so long ago, when a parent said he was off to work, the child knew very well what was about to happen. His parent was going to make something or fix something. The parent could take his offspring to his place of business and let him watch while he repaired a buggy or built a table.

3   When a child asked, "What kind of work do you do, Daddy?" his father could answer in terms that a child could come to grips with. "I fix steam engines." "I make horse collars."

4   Well, a few fathers still fix steam engines and build tables, but most do not. Nowadays, most fathers sit in glass buildings doing things that are absolutely incomprehensible to children. The answers they give when asked, "What kind of work do you do, Daddy?" are likely to be utterly mystifying to a child.

5   "I sell space." "I do market research." "I am a data processor." "I am in public relations." "I am a systems analyst." Such explanations must seem nonsense to a child. How can he possibly envision anyone analyzing a system or researching a market?

6   Even grown men who do market research have trouble visualizing what a public relations man does with his day, and it is a safe bet that the average systems analyst is as baffled about what a space salesman does at the shop as the average space salesman is about the tools needed to analyze a system.

7   In the common everyday job, nothing is made any more. Things are now made by machines. Very little is repaired. The machines that make things make them in such a fashion that they will quickly fall apart in such a way that repairs will be prohibitively expensive. Thus the buyer is encouraged to throw the thing away and buy a new one. In effect, the machines are making junk.

8   The handful of people remotely associated with these machines can, of course, tell their inquisitive children "Daddy makes junk." Most of

the work force, however, is too remote from junk production to sense any contribution to the industry. What do these people do?

Consider the typical twelve-story glass building in the typical   9
American city. Nothing is being made in this building and nothing is being repaired, including the building itself. Constructed as a piece of junk, the building will be discarded when it wears out, and another piece of junk will be set in its place.

Still, the building is filled with people who think of themselves as   10
working. At any given moment during the day perhaps one-third of them will be talking into telephones. Most of these conversations will be about paper, for paper is what occupies nearly everyone in this building.

Some jobs in the building require men to fill paper with words. There   11
are persons who type neatly on paper and persons who read paper and jot notes in the margins. Some persons make copies of paper and other persons deliver paper. There are persons who file paper and persons who unfile paper.

Some persons mail paper. Some persons telephone other persons and   12
ask that paper be sent to them. Others telephone to ascertain the whereabouts of paper. Some persons confer about paper. In the grandest offices, men approve of some paper and disapprove of other paper.

The elevators are filled throughout the day with young men carrying   13
paper from floor to floor and with vital men carrying paper to be discussed with other vital men.

What is a child to make of all this? His father may be so eminent that   14
he lunches with other men about paper. Suppose he brings his son to work to give the boy some idea of what work is all about. What does the boy see happening?

His father calls for paper. He reads paper. Perhaps he scowls at paper.   15
Perhaps he makes an angry red mark on paper. He telephones another man and says they had better lunch over paper.

At lunch they talk about paper. Back at the office, the father orders   16
the paper retyped and reproduced in quintuplicate, and then sent to another man for comparison with paper that was reproduced in triplicate last year.

Imagine his poor son afterwards mulling over the mysteries of work   17
with a friend, who asks him, "What's your father do?" What can the boy reply? "It beats me," perhaps, if he is not very observant. Or if he is, "Something that has to do with making junk, I think. Same as everybody else."

Questions and Activities

► *COMPREHENSION QUESTIONS*

1. What would it mean to call this piece tongue-in-cheek? Find a sentence to which this adjective applies. Explain to someone else why this sentence is tongue-in-cheek.
2. Can you give informal definitions of the jobs that Baker mentions in paragraph 5? Can you give an example of a specific activity a person holding one of these jobs would do?
3. In what sense does Baker use the word "vital" in paragraph 13 to describe the men that carry paper? Is he being satirical when he uses this word? Are these men, to Baker, really vital?
4. Why, according to Baker, do children find it difficult to understand what their parents do?

► *QUESTIONS OF RHETORICAL PURPOSE AND STRATEGY*

5. Many people agree that Baker writes effective political and social satire. How would a first-time reader of Baker's work know that he is treating his subject satirically in this article? What clues are there that Baker means something other than what his words literally say?
6. Why does Baker use the word "junk" in paragraph 8 to describe what the workers and machines in factories produce? Why didn't he use "products," "commodities," or "consumer goods" instead?
7. Does Baker's established reputation as a social commentator, humorist, and political satirist help readers to understand his intentions in this essay? How might that reputation help them?
8. Do you think Baker exaggerates the negative qualities of corporate work? Is his exaggeration too extreme to be believable, or is it just enough to make his point?

► *THEME QUESTIONS*

9. White-collar or office workers, as Baker describes them, do not produce tangible products. Outline a defense of the work that is done by office workers and managers. What important services and functions do they provide or carry out? Be as specific as you can in justifying the usefulness of this kind of work.
10. Office workers are extremely dependent on one another in their jobs. Do you think that this fact makes them less independent in other ways—less creative or assertive, for example?
11. Lewis Thomas uses a biological perspective from which to describe the social dependency of all individuals on others in their species or social group (pages 755–758). Could such a biological perspective

be applied to office workers? How are office workers like the convention-attending medical scientists that Thomas describes in the opening of his essay? Would a biological perspective, in contrast to Baker's satirical view, make office workers seem just as independent as any other workers?

▶ *LEARNING ACTIVITIES*

12. Organize a debate around the following proposition: "Office workers do indispensable and useful work." Three people should defend the proposition, and three should oppose it. Each team of three can divide themselves into three roles: one person presents the team's argument for or against the proposition; the second counters the opposing team's position on the proposition; and the third student sums up the pro and con arguments that have been presented by previous speakers from both teams. The rest of the class should be divided into supporting research groups. Supporting groups will provide arguments and outside information that can be used by members of either team to shore up their positions. The teacher can choose two or three students to judge the debate and decide on the winning team.

    In the process of preparing for this debate, write a short paper that develops criteria for judging the debate. Each criterion should be accompanied by a supporting paragraph that explains why it should be applied. The judges can then use these criteria to reach a decision as to which team wins the debate.

13. List the reasons behind Baker's criticism of modern office work. Discuss your list with others in your class, and combine items to produce a list as complete as it can be. Compare this list with opposing arguments used in the debate of the preceding activity.

On the Duty of Civil Disobedience

HENRY DAVID THOREAU

Henry David Thoreau lived in and around Concord, Massachusetts, in the middle of the nineteenth century. He spent two years in 1845 and 1846 living in a sturdy but simple one-room cabin next to Walden Pond, a small lake about two miles south of Concord village. He first described his experiences at Walden Pond in a series of public lectures in Concord in 1846. These lectures were so well received that he turned them into a book by 1849, revising them extensively into *Walden,* which was finally published in 1854. It sold only moderately well at the time, around 2,000 copies in its first five years in print.

A century later, immediately after World War II, *Walden* gained Thoreau an international reputation for independent, principled thinking and for social and political individualism that was essentially spiritual in its origins. *Walden* is valued for its quotable style, its advocacy of a combination of oriental spiritualism and Yankee materialism, and its essentially moral perspective on natural and social life. In the late 1960s, *Walden* and the essay reprinted here, "On the Duty of Civil Disobedience," became popular documents among Americans who protested the Vietnam War. "On the Duty of Civil Disobedience" was also used in this century by Dr. Martin Luther King, Jr., and Mahatma Gandhi as support for their advocacy of nonviolent civil disobedience in the cause of human rights and racial equality.

In "On the Duty of Civil Disobedience," Thoreau argues that it is the individual's moral duty to oppose the laws and actions of government when those laws and actions break higher laws. In 1849, the year this essay was first published, the United States was involved in two activities—slavery and a war with Mexico—that Thoreau felt were not justified by higher natural and moral laws. This piece of writing is his justification of his refusal to pay poll taxes, which he sees as a means of protesting these governmental actions. At the same time as it makes this specific political argument, the essay also makes the larger argument that only individuals who have the discipline to live simple, uncluttered, and relatively unmaterialistic lives will be able to use civil disobedience effectively against a government. Only such individuals will have little to lose in opposing government.

Thoreau also wrote books on natural science, journals describing his expeditions into nature, for example, the Maine woods, and some poetry. He is now accepted as a classic American nature writer and literary philosopher. He died of tuberculosis in 1862, at forty-five years of age, without experiencing any of the widespread fame that his books were to bring him in this century.

In treating the theme of independence, Thoreau emphasizes the need for the individual to stand up against the prevailing social context. Unlike most of the other writers represented in this section, Thoreau argues that an ideal social system depends on the individual's refusal to cooperate with customs or laws, rather than passively supporting or quietly opposing them. As you read, consider these larger questions:

1. What might be the source of the individual's sense of higher moral laws?
2. Did Thoreau believe that human beings are essentially good?
3. Many traditional religions assume the innate evil of human beings (for example, the Christian concept of original sin). What do you think believers in such religions would say in reaction to Thoreau's statement, "That government is best which governs least"?
4. Do you find it to be true that the more eventful and successful your life becomes the less you are able to oppose the institutions around you?

▶ ────────────────────

I heartily accept the motto—"That government is best which   1
governs least"; and I should like to see it acted up to more rapidly and systematically. Carried out, it finally amounts to this, which also I believe,—"That government is best which governs not at all"; and when men are prepared for it, that will be the kind of government which they will have. Government is at best but an expedient; but most governments are usually, and all governments are sometimes, inexpedient. The objections which have been brought against a standing army, and they are many and weighty, and deserve to prevail, may also at last be brought against a standing government. The standing army is only an arm of the standing government. The government itself, which is only the mode which the people have chosen to execute their will, is equally liable to be abused and perverted before the people can act through it. Witness the present Mexican war, the work of comparatively a few individuals using the standing government as their tool; for, in the outset, the people would not have consented to this measure.

This American government—what is it but a tradition, though a re-   2
cent one, endeavoring to transmit itself unimpaired to posterity, but

each instant losing some of its integrity? It has not the vitality and force of a single living man; for a single man can bend it to his will. It is a sort of wooden gun to the people themselves. But it is not the less necessary for this; for the people must have some complicated machinery or other, and hear its din, to satisfy that idea of government which they have. Governments show us how successfully men can be imposed on, even impose on themselves, for their own advantage. It is excellent, we must all allow. Yet this government never of itself furthered any enterprise, but by the alacrity with which it got out of its way. *It* does not keep the country free. *It* does not settle the West. *It* does not educate. The character inherent in the American people has done all that has been accomplished; and it would have done somewhat more, if the government had not sometimes got in its way. For government is an expedient by which men would fain succeed in letting one another alone; and, as has been said, when it is most expedient, the governed are most let alone by it. Trade and commerce, if they were not made of India-rubber, would never manage to bounce over the obstacles which legislators are continually putting in their way; and, if one were to judge these men wholly by the effects of their actions and not partly by their intentions, they would deserve to be classed and punished with those mischievous persons who put obstructions on the railroads.

3   But, to speak practically and as a citizen, unlike those who call themselves no-government men, I ask for, not at once no government, but *at once* a better government. Let every man make known what kind of government would command his respect, and that will be one step toward obtaining it.

4   After all, the practical reason why, when the power is once in the hands of the people, a majority are permitted, and for a long period continue, to rule is not because they are most likely to be in the right, nor because this seems fairest to the minority, but because they are physically the strongest. But a government in which the majority rule in all cases cannot be based on justice, even as far as men understand it. Can there not be a government in which majorities do not virtually decide right and wrong, but conscience—in which majorities decide only those questions to which the rule of expediency is applicable? Must the citizen ever for a moment, or in the least degree, resign his conscience to the legislator? Why has every man a conscience, then? I think that we should be men first, and subjects afterward. It is not desirable to cultivate a respect for the law, so much as for the right. The only obligation which I have a right to assume is to do at any time what I think right. It is truly enough said, that a corporation has no conscience; but a corporation of conscientious men is a corporation *with* a conscience. Law never made men a whit more just; and, by means of their respect for it, even the well-disposed are daily made the agents of injustice. A com-

mon and natural result of an undue respect for law is, that you may see a file of soldiers, colonel, captain, corporal, privates, powder-monkeys, and all, marching in admirable order over hill and dale to the wars, against their wills, ay, against their common sense and consciences, which makes it very steep marching indeed, and produces a palpitation of the heart. They have no doubt that it is a damnable business in which they are concerned; they are all peaceably inclined. Now, what are they? Men at all? or small movable forts and magazines, at the service of some unscrupulous man in power? Visit the Navy-Yard, and behold a marine, such a man as an American government can make, or such as it can make a man with its black arts—a mere shadow and reminiscence of humanity, a man laid out alive and standing, and already, as one may say, buried under arms with funeral accompaniments, though it may be,—

> *Not a drum was heard, not a funeral note,*
> *As his corpse to the rampart we hurried;*
> *Not a soldier discharged his farewell shot*
> *O'er the grave where our hero we buried.*

The mass of men serve the state thus, not as men mainly, but as machines, with their bodies. They are the standing army, and the militia, jailors, constables, posse comitatus, etc. In most cases there is no free exercise whatever of the judgment or of the moral sense; but they put themselves on a level with wood and earth and stones; and wooden men can perhaps be manufactured that will serve the purpose as well. Such command no more respect than men of straw or a lump of dirt. They have the same sort of worth only as horses and dogs. Yet such as these even are commonly esteemed good citizens. Others—as most legislators, politicians, lawyers, ministers, and office-holders—serve the state chiefly with their heads: and, as they rarely make any moral distinctions, they are as likely to serve the Devil, without *intending* it, as God. A very few, as heroes, patriots, martyrs, reformers in the great sense, and *men*, serve the state with their consciences also, and so necessarily resist it for the most part; and they are commonly treated as enemies by it. A wise man will only be useful as a man, and will not submit to be "clay," and "stop a hole to keep the wind away," but leave that office to his dust at least:—

> *I am too high-born to be propertied,*
> *To be a secondary at control,*
> *Or useful serving-man and instrument*
> *To any sovereign state throughout the world.*

6   He who gives himself entirely to his fellow-men appears to them use-less and selfish; but he who gives himself partially to them is pronounced a benefactor and philanthropist.

7   How does it become a man to behave toward this American government to-day? I answer, that he cannot without disgrace be associated with it. I cannot for an instant recognize that political organization as *my* government which is the *slave's* government also.

8   All men recognize the right of revolution; that is, the right to refuse allegiance to, and to resist, the government, when its tyranny or its inefficiency are great and unendurable. But almost all say that such is not the case now. But such was the case, they think, in the Revolution of '75. If one were to tell me that this was a bad government because it taxed certain foreign commodities brought to its ports, it is most probable that I should not make an ado about it, for I can do without them. All machines have their friction; and possibly this does enough good to counterbalance the evil. At any rate, it is a great evil to make a stir about it. But when the friction comes to have its machine, and oppression and robbery are organized, I say, let us not have such a machine any longer. In other words, when a sixth of the population of a nation which has undertaken to be the refuge of liberty are slaves, and a whole country is unjustly overrun and conquered by a foreign army, and subjected to military law, I think that it is not too soon for honest men to rebel and revolutionize. What makes this duty the more urgent is the fact that the country so overrun is not our own, but ours is the invading army. . . .

> A drab of state, a cloth-o'-silver slut,
>   To have her train borne up, and her soul trail in the dirt

Practically speaking, the opponents to a reform in Massachusetts are not a hundred thousand politicians at the South, but a hundred thousand merchants and farmers here, who are more interested in commerce and agriculture than they are in humanity, and are not prepared to do justice to the slave and to Mexico, *cost what it may*. I quarrel not with far-off foes, but with those who, near at home, coöperate with, and do the bidding of, those far away, and without whom the latter would be harmless. We are accustomed to say, that the mass of men are unprepared; but improvement is slow, because the few are not materially wiser or better than the many. It is not so important that many should be as good as you, as that there be some absolute goodness somewhere; for that will leaven the whole lump. There are thousands who are *in opinion* opposed to slavery and to the war, who yet in effect do nothing to put an end to them; who, esteeming themselves children of Washington and Franklin, sit down with their hands in their pockets, and say that they know not what to do, and do nothing; who even postpone the question of freedom to the question of free-trade, and quietly read the prices-current along with the latest advices from Mexico, after dinner, and, it may be, fall asleep over them both. What is the price-current of an honest man and patriot to-day? They hesitate, and they regret, and sometimes they petition; but they do nothing in earnest and with effect. They will wait, well disposed, for others to remedy the evil, that they may no longer have it to regret. At most, they give only a cheap vote, and a feeble countenance and God-speed, to the right, as it goes by them. There are nine hundred and ninety-nine patrons of virtue to one virtuous man. But it is easier to deal with the real possessor of a thing than with the temporary guardian of it.

All voting is a sort of gaming, like checkers or backgammon, with a   9
slight moral tinge to it, a playing with right and wrong, with moral questions; and betting naturally accompanies it. The character of the voters is not staked. I cast my vote, perchance, as I think right; but I am not vitally concerned that that right should prevail. I am willing to leave it to the majority. Its obligation, therefore, never exceeds that of expediency. Even voting *for the right* is *doing* nothing for it. It is only expressing to men feebly your desire that it should prevail. A wise man will not leave the right to the mercy of chance, nor wish it to prevail through the power of the majority. There is but little virtue in the action of masses of men. When the majority shall at length vote for the abolition of slavery, it will be because they are indifferent to slavery, or because there is but little slavery left to be abolished by their vote. *They* will then be the only slaves. Only *his* vote can hasten the abolition of slavery who asserts his own freedom by his vote.

I hear of a convention to be held at Baltimore, or elsewhere, for the   10
selection of a candidate for the Presidency, made up chiefly of editors, and men who are politicians by profession; but I think, what is it to any independent, intelligent, and respectable man what decision they may come to? Shall we not have the advantage of his wisdom and honesty, nevertheless? Can we not count upon some independent votes? Are there not many individuals in the country who do not attend conventions? But no: I find that the respectable man, so called, has immediately drifted from his position, and despairs of his country, when his country has more reason to despair of him. He forthwith adopts one of the candidates thus selected as the only *available* one, thus proving that he is himself *available* for any purposes of the demagogue. His vote is of no more worth than that of any unprincipled foreigner or hireling native, who may have been bought. O for a man who is a *man*, and, as my neighbor says, has a bone in his back which you cannot pass your hand

through! Our statistics are at fault: the population has been returned too large. How many *men* are there to a square thousand miles in this country? Hardly one. Does not America offer any inducement for men to settle here? The American has dwindled into an Odd Fellow,—one who may be known by the development of his organ of gregariousness, and a manifest lack of intellect and cheerful self-reliance; whose first and chief concern, on coming into the world, is to see that the Alms-houses are in good repair; and, before yet he has lawfully donned the virile garb, to collect a fund for the support of the widows and orphans that may be; who, in short, ventures to live only by the aid of the Mutu-al Insurance company, which has promised to bury him decently.

11   It is not a man's duty, as a matter of course, to devote himself to the eradication of any, even the most enormous wrong; he may still proper-ly have other concerns to engage him; but it is his duty, at least, to wash his hands of it, and, if he gives it no thought longer, not to give it practi-cally his support. If I devote myself to other pursuits and contempla-tions, I must first see, at least, that I do not pursue them sitting upon another man's shoulders. I must get off him first, that he may pursue his contemplations too. See what gross inconsistency is tolerated. I have heard some of my townsmen say, "I should like to have them order me out to help put down an insurrection of the slaves, or to march to Mexico;—see if I would go"; and yet these very men have each, di-rectly by their allegiance, and so indirectly, at least, by their money, furnished a substitute. The soldier is applauded who refuses to serve in an unjust war by those who do not refuse to sustain the unjust govern-ment which makes the war; is applauded by those whose own act and authority he disregards and sets at naught; as if the state were penitent to that degree that it hired one to scourge it while it sinned, but not to that degree that it left off sinning for a moment. Thus, under the name of Order and Civil Government, we are all made at last to pay homage to and support our own meanness. After the first blush of sin comes its in-difference; and from immoral it becomes, as it were, *unmoral*, and not quite unnecessary to that life which we have made.

12   The broadest and most prevalent error requires the most disinterest-ed virtue to sustain it. The slight reproach to which the virtue of patrio-tism is commonly liable, the noble are most likely to incur. Those who, while they disapprove of the character and measures of a government, yield to it their allegiance and support are undoubtedly its most consci-entious supporters, and so frequently the most serious obstacles to re-form. Some are petitioning the state to dissolve the Union, to disregard the requisitions of the President. Why do they not dissolve it them-selves—the union between themselves and the state,—and refuse to

pay their quota into its treasury? Do not they stand in the same relation to the state that the state does to the Union? And have not the same reasons prevented the state from resisting the Union which have prevented them from resisting the state?

How can a man be satisfied to entertain an opinion merely, and enjoy   13
it? Is there any enjoyment in it, if his opinion is that he is aggrieved? If you are cheated out of a single dollar by your neighbor, you do not rest satisfied with knowing that you are cheated, or with saying that you are cheated, or even with petitioning him to pay you your due; but you take effectual steps at once to obtain the full amount, and see that you are never cheated again. Action from principle, the perception and the performance of right, changes things and relations; it is essentially revolutionary, and does not consist wholly with anything which was. It not only divides states and churches, it divides families; ay, it divides the *individual*, separating the diabolical in him from the divine.

Unjust laws exist: shall we be content to obey them, or shall we en-   14
deavor to amend them, and obey them until we have succeeded, or shall we transgress them at once? Men generally, under such a government as this, think that they ought to wait until they have persuaded the majority to alter them. They think that, if they should resist, the remedy would be worse than the evil. But it is the fault of the government itself that the remedy *is* worse than the evil. *It* makes it worse. Why is it not more apt to anticipate and provide for reform? Why does it not cherish its wise minority? Why does it cry and resist before it is hurt? Why does it not encourage its citizens to be on the alert to point out its faults, and *do* better than it would have them? Why does it always crucify Christ, and excommunicate Copernicus and Luther, and pronounce Washington and Franklin rebels?

One would think, that a deliberate and practical denial of its authori-   15
ty was the only offense never contemplated by government; else, why has it not assigned its definite, its suitable and proportionate penalty? If a man who has no property refuses but once to earn nine shillings for the state, he is put in prison for a period unlimited by any law that I know, and determined only by the discretion of those who placed him there; but if he should steal ninety times nine shillings from the state, he is soon permitted to go at large again.

If the injustice is part of the necessary friction of the machine of gov-   16
ernment, let it go, let it go: perchance it will wear smooth,—certainly the machine will wear out. If the injustice has a spring, or a pulley, or a rope, or a crank, exclusively for itself, then perhaps you may consider whether the remedy will not be worse than the evil; but if it is of such a nature that it requires you to be the agent of injustice to another, then, I

say, break the law. Let your life be a counter friction to stop the machine. What I have to do is to see, at any rate, that I do not lend myself to the wrong which I condemn.

17   As for adopting the ways which the state has provided for remedying the evil, I know not of such ways. They take too much time, and a man's life will be gone. I have other affairs to attend to. I came into this world, not chiefly to make this a good place to live in, but to live in it, be it good or bad. A man has not everything to do, but something; and because he cannot do *everything*, it is not necessary that he should do *something* wrong. It is not my business to be petitioning the Governor or the Legislature any more than it is theirs to petition me; and if they should not hear my petition, what should I do then? But in this case the state has provided no way: its very Constitution is the evil. This may seem to be harsh and stubborn and unconciliatory; but it is to treat with the utmost kindness and consideration the only spirit that can appreciate or deserves it. So is all change for the better, like birth and death, which convulse the body.

18   I do not hesitate to say, that those who call themselves Abolitionists should at once effectually withdraw their support, both in person and property, from the government of Massachusetts and not wait till they constitute a majority of one, before they suffer the right to prevail through them. I think that it is enough if they have God on their side, without waiting for that other one. Moreover, any man more right than his neighbors constitutes a majority of one already.

19   I meet this American government, or its representative, the state government, directly, and face to face, once a year—no more—in the person of its tax-gatherer; this is the only mode in which a man situated as I am necessarily meets it; and it then says distinctly, Recognize me; and the simplest, most effectual, and, in the present posture of affairs, the indispensablest mode of treating with it on this head, of expressing your little satisfaction with and love for it, is to deny it then. My civil neighbor, the tax-gatherer, is the very man I have to deal with,—for it is, after all, with men and not with parchment that I quarrel,—and he has voluntarily chosen to be an agent of the government. How shall he ever know well what he is and does as an officer of the government, or as a man, until he is obliged to consider whether he shall treat me, his neighbor, for whom he has respect, as a neighbor and well-disposed man, or as a maniac and disturber of the peace, and see if he can get over this obstruction to his neighborliness without a ruder and more impetuous thought or speech corresponding with his action. I know this well, that if one thousand, if one hundred, if ten men whom I could name,—if ten *honest* men only,—ay, if *one* HONEST man, in this State of Massa-

chusetts, *ceasing to hold slaves,* were actually to withdraw from this copartnership, and be locked up in the county jail therefor, it would be the abolition of slavery in America. For it matters not how small the beginning may seem to be: what is once well done is done forever. But we love better to talk about it: that we say is our mission. Reform keeps many scores of newspapers in its service, but not one man. If my esteemed neighbor, the State's ambassador, who will devote his days to the settlement of the question of human rights in the Council Chamber, instead of being threatened with the prisons of Carolina, were to sit down the prisoner of Massachusetts, that State which is so anxious to foist the sin of slavery upon her sister,—though at present she can discover only an act of inhospitality to be the ground of a quarrel with her,—the Legislature would not wholly waive the subject the following winter.

Under a government which imprisons any unjustly, the true place for a just man is also a prison. The proper place to-day, the only place which Massachusetts has provided for her freer and less desponding spirits, is in her prisons, to be put out and locked out of the State by her own act, as they have already put themselves out by their principles. It is there that the fugitive slave, and the Mexican prisoner on parole, and the Indian come to plead the wrongs of his race should find them; on that separate, but more free and honorable ground, where the State places those who are not *with* her, but *against* her,—the only house in a slave State in which a free man can abide with honor. If any think that their influence would be lost there, and their voices no longer afflict the ear of the State, that they would not be as an enemy within its walls, they do not know by how much truth is stronger than error, nor how much more eloquently and effectively he can combat injustice who has experienced a little in his own person. Cast your whole vote, not a strip of paper merely, but your whole influence. A minority is powerless while it conforms to the majority; it is not even a minority then; but it is irresistible when it clogs by its whole weight. If the alternative is to keep all just men in prison, or give up war and slavery, the State will not hesitate which to choose. If a thousand men were not to pay their tax-bills this year, that would not be a violent and bloody measure, as it would be to pay them, and enable the State to commit violence and shed innocent blood. This is, in fact, the definition of a peaceable revolution, if any such is possible. If the tax-gatherer, or any other public officer, asks me, as one has done, "But what shall I do?" my answer is, "If you really wish to do anything, resign your office." When the subject has refused allegiance, and the officer has resigned his office, then the revolution is accomplished. But even suppose blood should flow. Is there not a sort of

20

blood shed when the conscience is wounded? Through this wound a man's real manhood and immortality flow out, and he bleeds to an ever-lasting death. I see this blood flowing now.

21

I have contemplated the imprisonment of the offender, rather than the seizure of his goods,—though both will serve the same purpose, —because they who assert the purest right, and consequently are most dangerous to a corrupt State, commonly have not spent much time in accumulating property. To such the State renders comparatively small service, and a slight tax is wont to appear exorbitant, particularly if they are obliged to earn it by special labor with their hands. If there were one who lived wholly without the use of money, the State itself would hesitate to demand it of him. But the rich man—not to make any invidious comparison—is always sold to the institution which makes him rich. Absolutely speaking, the more money, the less virtue; for money comes between a man and his objects, and obtains them for him; and it was certainly no great virtue to obtain it. It puts to rest many questions which he would otherwise be taxed to answer; while the only new question which it puts is the hard but superfluous one, how to spend it. Thus his moral ground is taken from under his feet. The opportunities of living are diminished in proportion as what are called the ''means'' are increased. The best thing a man can do for his culture when he is rich is to endeavor to carry out those schemes which he entertained when he was poor. Christ answered the Herodians according to their condition. ''Show me the tribute-money,'' said he;—and one took a penny out of his pocket;—if you use money which has the image of Caesar on it and which he has made current and valuable, that is, *if you are men of the State*, and gladly enjoy the advantages of Caesar's government, then pay him back some of his own when he demands it. ''Render therefore to Caesar that which is Caesar's, and to God those things which are God's,''—leaving them no wiser than before as to which; for they did

22

not wish to know. . . .

I have paid no poll-tax for six years. I was put into a jail once on this account, for one night; and, as I stood considering the walls of solid stone, two or three feet thick, the door of wood and iron, a foot thick, and the iron grating which strained the light, I could not help being struck with the foolishness of that institution which treated me as if I were mere flesh and blood and bones, to be locked up. I wondered that it should have concluded at length that this was the best use it could put me to, and had never thought to avail itself of my services in some way. I saw that, if there was a wall of stone between me and my townsmen, there was a still more difficult one to climb or break through before they could get to be as free as I was. I did not for a moment feel confined, and the walls seemed a great waste of stone and mortar. I felt as if I alone of all my townsmen had paid my tax. They plainly did not know how to treat me, but behaved like persons who are underbred. In every threat and in every compliment there was a blunder; for they thought that my chief desire was to stand the other side of that stone wall. I could not but smile to see how industriously they locked the door on my meditations, which followed them out again without let or hindrance, and *they* were really all that was dangerous. As they could not reach me, they had resolved to punish my body; just as boys, if they cannot come at some person against whom they have a spite, will abuse his dog. I saw that the State was half-witted, that it was timid as a lone woman with her silver spoons, and that it did not know its friends from its foes, and I lost all my remaining respect for it, and pitied it.

23

Thus the State never intentionally confronts a man's sense, intellectual or moral, but only his body, his senses. It is not armed with superior wit or honesty, but with superior physical strength. I was not born to be forced. I will breathe after my own fashion. Let us see who is the strongest. What force has a multitude? They only can force me who obey a higher law than I. They force me to become like themselves. I do not hear of *men* being *forced* to live this way or that by masses of men. What sort of life were that to live? When I meet a government which says to me, "Your money or your life," why should I be in haste to give it my money? It may be in a great strait, and not know what to do: I cannot help that. It must help itself; do as I do. It is not worth the while to snivel about it. I am not responsible for the successful working of the machinery of society. I am not the son of the engineer. I perceive that, when an acorn and a chestnut fall side by side, the one does not remain inert to make way for the other, but both obey their own laws, and spring and grow and flourish as best they can, till one, perchance, overshadows and destroys the other. If a plant cannot live according to its nature, it dies; and so a man. . . .

24

When I came out of prison,—for some one interfered, and paid that tax,—I did not perceive that great changes had taken place on the common, such as he observed who went in a youth and emerged a tottering and gray-headed man; and yet a change had to my eyes come over the scene,—the town, and State, and country,—greater than any that mere time could effect. I saw yet more distinctly the State in which I lived. I saw to what extent the people among whom I lived could be trusted as good neighbors and friends; that their friendship was for summer weather only; that they did not greatly propose to do right; that they were a distinct race from me by their prejudices and superstitions, as the Chinamen and Malays are; that in their sacrifices to humanity they ran no risks, not even to their property; that after all they were not so noble but they treated the thief as he had treated them, and hoped, by a

certain outward observance and a few prayers, and by walking in a particular straight though useless path from time to time, to save their souls. This may be to judge my neighbors harshly; for I believe that many of them are not aware that they have such an institution as the
25   jail in their village.

It was formerly the custom in our village, when a poor debtor came out of jail, for his acquaintances to salute him, looking through their fingers, which were crossed to represent the grating of a jail window. ''How do ye do?'' My neighbors did not thus salute me, but first looked at me, and then at one another, as if I had returned from a long journey. I was put into jail as I was going to the shoemaker's to get a shoe which was mended. When I was let out the next morning, I proceeded to finish my errand, and, having put on my mended shoe, joined a huckleberry party, who were impatient to put themselves under my conduct; and in half an hour,—for the horse was soon tackled,—was in the midst of a huckleberry field, on one of our highest hills, two miles off, and then
26   the State was nowhere to be seen. . . .

I have never declined paying the highway tax, because I am as desirous of being a good neighbor as I am of being a bad subject; and as for supporting schools, I am doing my part to educate my fellow-countrymen now. It is for no particular item in the tax-bill that I refuse to pay it. I simply wish to refuse allegiance to the State, to withdraw and stand aloof from it effectually. I do not care to trace the course of my dollar, if I could, till it buys a man or a musket to shoot with,—the dollar is innocent,—but I am concerned to trace the effects of my allegiance. In fact, I quietly declare war with the State, after my fashion, though I will still make what use and get what advantage of her I can, as is usual in such
27   cases.

If others pay the tax which is demanded of me, from a sympathy with the State, they do but what they have already done in their own case, or rather they abet injustice to a greater extent than the State requires. If they pay the tax from a mistaken interest in the individual taxed, to save his property, or prevent his going to jail, it is because they have not considered wisely how far they let their private feelings interfere with
28   the public good.

This, then, is my position at present. But one cannot be too much on his guard in such a case, lest his action be biased by obstinacy or an undue regard for the opinions of men. Let him see that he does only
29   what belongs to himself and to the hour.

I think sometimes, Why, this people mean well, they are only ignorant; they would do better if they knew how: why give your neighbors this pain to treat you as they are not inclined to? But I think again, This is no reason why I should do as they do, or permit others to suffer much greater pain of a different kind. Again, I sometimes say to myself, When many millions of men, without heat, without ill will, without personal feeling of any kind, demand of you a few shillings only, without the possibility, such is their constitution, of retracting or altering their present demand, and without the possibility, on your side, of appeal to any other millions, why expose yourself to this overwhelming brute force? You do not resist cold and hunger, the winds and the waves, thus obstinately; you quietly submit to a thousand similar necessities. You do not put your head into the fire. But just in proportion as I regard this as not wholly a brute force, but partly a human force, and consider that I have relations to those millions as to many millions of men, and not of mere brute or inanimate things, I see that appeal is possible, first and instantaneously, from them to the Maker of them and, secondly, from them to themselves. But if I put my head deliberately into the fire, there is no appeal to fire or to the Maker of fire, and I have only myself to blame. If I could convince myself that I have any right to be satisfied with men as they are, and to treat them accordingly, and not according, in some respects, to my requisitions and expectations of what they and I ought to be, then, like a good Mussulman* and fatalist, I should endeavor to be satisfied with things as they are, and say it is the will of God. And, above all, there is this difference between resisting this and a purely brute or natural force, that I can resist this with some effect; but I cannot expect, like Orpheus,† to change the nature of the rocks and trees and beasts.

30

I do not wish to quarrel with any man or nation. I do not wish to split hairs, to make fine distinctions, or set myself up as better than my neighbors. I seek rather, I may say, even an excuse for conforming to the laws of the land. I am but too ready to conform to them. Indeed, I have reason to suspect myself on this head; and each year, as the tax-gatherer comes round, I find myself disposed to review the acts and position of the general and State governments, and the spirit of the people, to discover a pretext for conformity.

> *We must affect our country as our parents,*
> *And if at any time we alienate*
> *Our love or industry from doing it honor,*
> *We must respect effects and teach the soul*
> *Matter of conscience and religion,*
> *And not desire of rule or benefit.*

*A Mussulman is a Moslem; the name is derived from Turkish. Moslems put a great deal of emphasis on fate rather than free will as the directing force over life.
†Orpheus was a mythical Greek musician who played music so beautiful that it charmed animals, trees, and rivers.

I believe that the State will soon be able to take all my work of this sort out of my hands, and then I shall be no better a patriot than my fellow-countrymen. Seen from a lower point of view, the Constitution, with all its faults, is very good; the law and the courts are very respectable; even this State and this American government are, in many respects, very admirable, and rare things, to be thankful for, such as a great many have described them; but seen from a point of view a little higher, they are what I have described them; seen from a higher still, and the highest, who shall say what they are, or that they are worth looking at or thinking of at all?

31   However, the government does not concern me much, and I shall bestow the fewest possible thoughts on it. It is not many moments that I live under a government, even in this world. If a man is thought-free, fancy-free, imagination-free, that which *is not* never for a long time appearing *to be* to him, unwise rulers or reformers cannot fatally interrupt him.

32   I know that most men think differently from myself; but those whose lives are by profession devoted to the study of these or kindred subjects content me as little as any. Statesmen and legislators, standing so completely within the institution, never distinctly and nakedly behold it. They speak of moving society, but have no resting-place without it. They may be men of a certain experience and discrimination, and have no doubt invented ingenious and even useful systems, for which we sincerely thank them; but all their wit and usefulness lie within certain not very wide limits. They are wont to forget that the world is not governed by policy and expediency. Webster* never goes behind government, and so cannot speak with authority about it. His words are wisdom to those legislators who contemplate no essential reform in the existing government; but for thinkers, and those who legislate for all time, he never once glances at the subject. I know of those whose serene and wise speculations on this theme would soon reveal the limits of his mind's range and hospitality. Yet, compared with the cheap professions of most reformers, and the still cheaper wisdom and eloquence of politicians in general, his are almost the only sensible and valuable words, and we thank Heaven for him. Comparatively, he is always strong, original, and, above all, practical. Still, his quality is not wisdom, but prudence. The lawyer's truth is not Truth, but consistency or a consistent expediency. Truth is always in harmony with herself, and is not concerned chiefly to reveal the justice that may consist with wrong-doing. He well deserves to be called, as he has been called, the Defender of the

*Daniel Webster (1782–1852) was an American political leader and diplomat who was involved in the issues of slavery and states' rights.

Constitution. There are really no blows to be given by him but defensive ones. He is not a leader, but a follower. His leaders are the men of '87. "I have never made an effort," he says, "and never propose to make an effort; I have never countenanced an effort, and never mean to countenance an effort, to disturb the arrangement as originally made, by which the various States came into the Union." Still thinking of the sanction which the Constitution gives to slavery, he says, "Because it was a part of the original compact,—let it stand." Notwithstanding his special acuteness and ability, he is unable to take a fact out of its merely political relations, and behold it as it lies absolutely to be disposed of by the intellect,—what, for instance, it behooves a man to do here in America to-day with regard to slavery,—but ventures, or is driven, to make some such desperate answer as the following while professing to speak absolutely, and as a private man,—from which what new and singular code of social duties might be inferred? "The manner," says he, "in which the governments of those States where slavery exists are to regulate it is for their own consideration, under their responsibility to their constituents, to the general laws of propriety, humanity, and justice, and to God. Associations formed elsewhere, springing from a feeling of humanity, or other cause, have nothing whatever to do with it. They have never received any encouragement from me, and they never will."

They who know of no purer sources of truth, who have traced up its stream no higher, stand, and wisely stand, by the Bible and the Constitution, and drink at it there with reverence and humility; but they who behold where it comes trickling into this lake or that pool, gird up their loins once more, and continue their pilgrimage toward its fountainhead. 33

No man with a genius for legislation has appeared in America. They are rare in the history of the world. There are orators, politicians, and eloquent men, by the thousand; but the speaker has not yet opened his mouth to speak who is capable of settling the much-vexed questions of the day. We love eloquence for its own sake, and not for any truth which it may utter, or any heroism it may inspire. Our legislators have not yet learned the comparative value of free-trade and of freedom, of union, and of rectitude, to a nation. They have no genius or talent for comparatively humble questions of taxation and finance, commerce and manufactures and agriculture. If we were left solely to the wordy wit of legislators in Congress for our guidance, uncorrected by the seasonable experience and the effectual complaints of the people, America would not long retain her rank among the nations. For eighteen hundred years, though perchance I have no right to say it, the New Testament has been written; yet where is the legislator who has wisdom and prac- 34

35   tical talent enough to avail himself of the light which it sheds on the science of legislation?

The authority of government, even such as I am willing to submit to,—for I will cheerfully obey those who know and can do better than I, and in many things even those who neither know nor can do so well,—is still an impure one: to be strictly just, it must have the sanction and consent of the governed. It can have no pure right over my person and property but what I concede to it. The progress from an absolute to a limited monarchy, from a limited monarchy to a democracy, is a progress toward a true respect for the individual. Even the Chinese philosopher was wise enough to regard the individual as the basis of the empire. Is a democracy, such as we know it, the last improvement possible in government? Is it not possible to take a step further towards recognizing and organizing the rights of man? There will never be a really free and enlightened State until the State comes to recognize the individual as a higher and independent power, from which all its own power and authority are derived, and treats him accordingly. I please myself with imagining a State at last which can afford to be just to all men, and to treat the individual with respect as a neighbor; which even would not think it inconsistent with its own repose if a few were to live aloof from it, not meddling with it, nor embraced by it, who fulfilled all the duties of neighbors and fellow-men. A State which bore this kind of fruit, and suffered it to drop off as fast as it ripened, would prepare the way for a still more perfect and glorious State, which also I have imagined, but not yet anywhere seen.

Questions and Activities

▶ COMPREHENSION QUESTIONS

1. What two specific issues prompted Thoreau to refuse to pay his poll tax and to write this essay? Do you think those issues were important enough to warrant his civil disobedience?

2. Thoreau was opposed to violence of any kind. What type of opposition to unjust laws might he advocate, other than nonpayment of taxes?

3. Does Thoreau display much faith in majority rule? When does he think an individual is justified in opposing the majority? The majority often enforces its power by force. How would an individual opposed in conscience to the majority express his or her power?

4. Why was Thoreau released after being imprisoned for nonpayment of taxes? Considering his principles, do you think he should have refused to be released?

▶ *QUESTIONS OF RHETORICAL PURPOSE AND STRATEGY*

5. Examine Thoreau's persuasive strategies in this essay. Does he seem to try to convince his readers to agree with his position primarily through logical, emotional, or moral-ethical arguments? Find one specific example of each of these argumentative appeals in the essay.
6. Give one or two examples of Thoreau's occasional use of unsupported personal opinion. Why does he choose to leave some opinions unsupported? Are these unsupported opinions founded on assumptions that are established elsewhere in the essay? What are those assumptions?
7. Describe Thoreau's voice. Does he sound like an independent thinker from a small town? What in his language creates his voice? Are there some types of readers who would be put off by Thoreau's voice? Who would those readers be?

▶ *THEME QUESTIONS*

8. Examine the logic that takes Thoreau from the assertion "That government is best which governs least" to "That government is best which governs not at all." Might someone opposed to these assertions argue that some government is necessary to ensure that individuals can act freely without being restrained by others' actions? How much government would be too little or too much?
9. Thoreau is an enthusiastic and idealistic supporter of individual independence. Explain why Thoreau believes that the individual can act according to his or her own sense of right and wrong without threatening the social order. (Other thinkers might argue that to encourage people to act on their consciences might result in anarchy and chaos.)
10. Compared to Lewis Thomas's biological perspective on human behavior (pages 755–758), Thoreau's focus on individual behavior might seem to be overly simple and unscientific. How would you defend Thoreau against the charge that he has a simplistic view of social interaction? Does Thoreau's argument for civil disobedience seemed to ignore the ways in which all human action is socially conditioned? Or is his position basically in line with Thomas's?
11. Thoreau organizes this essay around his own thinking processes rather than in a way that is oriented to the reader's need to categorize and structure his ideas. There are no headings; most of the para-

graphs do not have explicit connections with those surrounding them; there are not very many summarizing generalizations. Connections, headings, and generalizations would make it easier for readers to connect the parts of the essay, to remember its main outline, and to retain its details. Why, given his general argument, do you think Thoreau chose to organize his essay in a more personal and unconventional way? What are some of his less explicit organizing strategies?

▶ *LEARNING ACTIVITIES*

12. Discuss with your classmates the question of whether or not your university or college has the right to require you to do things that may go against your conscience. If a university, for example, has made investments in foreign governments or corporations that support social, religious, or political positions to which a student is morally opposed, has that student the right to withhold payment of fees or to protest in ways that adversely affect others' education?

13. Free-write a response to Thoreau's contention: "All voting is a sort of gaming, like checkers or backgammon, with a slight moral tinge to it, a playing with right and wrong, with moral questions; and betting naturally accompanies it" (paragraph 9). (Free-writing is an open form of writing, unrestrained by conscious use of formal rules of grammar or logic.) Compare your response with those of two or three of your classmates.

Blood and Guts: The Tricky Problem of Being a Woman Writer in the Late Twentieth Century

ERICA JONG

Erica Jong, born in New York City in 1942 and educated at Barnard College and Columbia University, became a best-selling author with the publication of *Fear of Flying* (1973), a novel that caused her to be called the pioneer of woman's pornography by some critics. Some reviewers celebrated *Fear of Flying* as a true sign of women's liberation; others condemned it as a lowering of the ideals of the women's movement. Both before and after the publication of *Fear of Flying*, however, Jong wrote and has continued to publish critically praised poetry: *Fruits and Vegetables* (1971), *Loveroot* (1975), and *The Poetry of Erica Jong* (1976). Her later works of fiction have continued to pursue themes of erotic love, sexuality, and the individual's need for freer forms of emotional expression. *How To Save Your Own Life* (1977) was a personal account of Jong's struggles with her own identity after she had gained fame and fortune from *Fear of Flying*. *Fanny* (1980) is a fictionalized account of the life of an eighteenth-century female alter-ego of Tom Jones, the famous hero of Henry Fielding's novel of that century.

Jong's writing career has consistently focused on questions of the relationship of female identity, sexual expression, and personal freedom. In the essay that follows, Jong expresses her views on the problems faced by women writers of this generation. Women writers, Jong feels, have gone through periods of meekness and rage and must now enter a "phase of empathy." Jong sees women writers courageously exploring all dimensions of their "emotional and intellectual curiosity," creating unique and collectively female visions of experience.

Here, again, the tension between community and individuality is touched on. Jong, as a writer, has needed the encouragement and sense of shared experience that she found in the women's movement. Without that sharing, she says, she would have grown discouraged and possibly given up. But she has also needed to have a strong sense of her own worth and individuality, for without those qualities her writing would have been dominated by what others felt and thought and not by her own sense of the significance of her experience. Somewhere between the extremes of total community domination and total individuality lies the right blend of dependence and independence.

As you read, consider these questions:

1. Can a woman go too far in the direction of excluding men from her life and work?
2. At what point might Jong say that a career woman had allowed men to influence her to too great a degree?
3. Do you feel committed to a community of people? How far are you willing to go in allowing that community to define your plans? Do you feel any need to lessen a particular community's influence on your thoughts? Why?
4. What might it mean to enter a "phase of empathy" in your development of relations with others? How might empathy make you behave differently than anger or introspection would? How might empathy help you become more independent?

▶ ─────────────────────

1   The question of whether or not writers are affected by the politics of the times in which they live has always been a tricky one. Some part of them assuredly is—but whether it is the part that tunes into the communal unconscious and makes poems and novels is doubtful. Yet a writer is a person of his or her age and must live in it. For women writers the systematic discouragement even to *attempt* to become writers has been so constant and pervasive a force that we cannot consider their literary productions without somehow assessing the effects of that barrage of discouragement. Often discouraged in the home, often at school, often by families and spouses, the rare woman writer who does not lose her determination along the way is already a survivor. That one should next have to face the systematic discouragement of a male-oriented literary establishment is absurd and sad but nonetheless a real fact of life for many women writers.[1] The truth is that many of us are doomed to do our best work in an atmosphere of condescension and loneliness. Yet perhaps there is some sense in which that lack of establishment approval is a blessing, for an artist must learn (the sooner the better) that he or she works for the work itself, not for approval, and it is easier to establish that sense of creative independence when approval is lacking

[1]No one has chronicled this repression better than Tillie Olsen in her splendid book *Silences* (1978).

than when one is seduced by it. Prizes, awards, rave reviews are, after all, snares, and perhaps they are more destructive to one's sense of creative independence than the systematic discouragement the perpetual outsider receives. Still, we cannot truly understand the situation of the woman writer unless we are honest about this systematic discouragement, and unless we try to see clearly the form it takes, and the strategies of survival it imposes upon the individual artist. School is as good a place to start as any, for school is a microcosm of our society's values.

One of the most notable (and faintly horrifying) memories from my college years is the time a Distinguished Critic came to my creative writing class and delivered himself of the following thundering judgment: "Women can't be writers. They don't know blood and guts, and puking in the streets, and fucking whores, and swaggering through Pigalle at 5 A.M...." But the most amazing thing was the *response*—or lack of it. It was 1961 or '62, and we all sat there—aspiring women writers that we were—and listened to this Maileresque* claptrap without a word of protest. Our hands folded on our laps, our eyes modestly downcast, our hearts cast even lower than our eyes, we listened meekly—while the male voice of authority told us what women could or couldn't write.

Things have changed since then. When I went to college (from 1959 to 1963), there were no women's studies courses, no anthologies that stressed a female heritage, no public women's movement. Poetry meant Yeats, Lowell, James Dickey. Without even realizing it, I assumed that the voice of the poet had to be male. Not that I didn't get a good literary education. I did. Barnard was a miraculous place where they actually gave you a degree for losing yourself in a library with volumes of Byron and Keats, Shakespeare and Chaucer, but the whole female side of the library heritage was something I would have to discover for myself years later, propelled by the steam generated by the women's movement.

No Distinguished Critic would dare say such things to a college class today (however much he might think them). Sexism is somewhat better hidden now—though it is far from eradicated. And no college class would sit meekly listening to such rubbish. That is one of the things that has happened in the years since I graduated from college, and I am proud to have been part of the process. Now, when I go to read my work at colleges, I find the students reading and discussing contemporary writing by women as if there never had been a time when a Distin-

2

3

4

---

*Norman Mailer, born in 1923, is a well-known American novelist who is famous for his male-oriented perspective and macho attitude.

guished Critic could say "Women can't be writers"—even in jest. I am grateful and glad for that change, but it has not been won without pain. Nor is it necessarily a lasting change. Like the feminists of the twenties, we could easily see the interest in female accomplishments once again eclipsed by reactionary sexism, only to have to be passionately rediscovered yet again, several decades later.

5   It's ironic that Mr. Distinguished Critic should have identified Blood and Guts as the thing that women writers supposedly lacked,[2] because in the first years of the women's movement, there was so *much* Blood and Guts in women's writing that one wondered if women writers ever did anything but menstruate and rage. Released from the prison of propriety, blessedly released from having to pretend meekness, gratefully in touch with our own cleansing anger, we raged and mocked and menstruated through whole volumes of prose and poetry. This was fine for writers who had a saving sense of irony, but in many cases the rage tended to eclipse the writing. Also, as years went by, literary feminism tended to ossify into convention. Rage became almost as compulsory to the generation of writers who came of age in the late sixties and early seventies as niceness and meekness had been to an earlier generation. Feminists proved that they could be as rigidly dogmatic as any other group. They did not hesitate to criticize works of art on political grounds and to reject poems and novels for dealing with supposedly counterrevolutionary subjects.

6   This was unfortunate. It was also, I suppose inevitable. Anger against patriarchal stifling of talent had been so proscribed for so many centuries that in letting it loose, many women completely lost their sense of humor. Nor could anyone maintain that getting in touch with anger was unimportant. It was, in fact, a vitally important phase for women's writing to go through. Nothing is more destructive of the spirit and ultimately of creativity than false meekness, anger that does not know its own name. And nothing is more freeing for a woman (or for a woman writer) than giving up the pleasures of masochism and beginning to fight. But we must always remember that fighting is only a first

---

[2]This is indeed a curious metaphor for what women writers supposedly lack, since of course it is obvious that women are the sex most in tune with the entrails of life, as it were. But we can understand the great critic's condemnation better if we remember that in the nineteenth century women writers were denigrated for their delicacy, their excessive propriety (which supposedly precluded greatness), while in the past decade or so they have been condemned by male critics for their *im*propriety—which also supposedly precludes greatness. The whole issue is a red herring. Whatever women writers do or do not do precludes greatness (in the mind of the chauvinist) simply because they are women. We must see this sort of reasoning for what it is: namely, misogyny. See Mary Ellmann's wonderful book, *Thinking about Women* (1968) on the subjects of sexual stereotypes and phallic criticism. She exposes the hypocrisies of phallic criticism with great wit.

step. As Virginia Woolf points out in *A Room of One's Own*, many women's books have been destroyed by the rage and bitterness at their own centers. Rage opens the doors into the spirit, but then the spirit must be nurtured. This is hardly easy because women writers (like women) tend to be damned no matter what they do. If we are sweet and tender, we are damned for not being "powerful" enough (not having "blood and guts"), and if we rage, we are said to be "castrating," Amazonian, lacking in tenderness. It is a real dilemma. What is the authentic voice of the woman writer? Does anyone *know?* Does anyone know what the authentic voice of woman is? Is it sweet and low like the voice of Shakespeare's Cordelia, or is it raging and powerful like the voice of Lady Macbeth? Is it an alternation of the two?

The problem is, I suppose, that women have never been left alone to   7
be themselves and to find out for themselves. Men need them so badly and are so terrified of losing them that they have used their power to imprison them. To imprison them in castles of stone as long as that was possible, and to imprison them in castles of myth thereafter. The myths were mostly ways of keeping us out of touch with our own strength, and this confused many generations of women. We were told we were weak, yet as we grew older, we increasingly sensed we were strong. We were told that men loved us for our dependency, yet as we grew older, we observed that, despite themselves, they loved us for our independence, and if they didn't—we didn't always care! We found that we could grow only by loving ourselves a little, and loving our strengths, and so, paradoxically, we found we could only grow up by doing the opposite of all the things our culture told us to do. We were told our charm lay in weakness; yet in order to survive, we had to be strong. We were told we were by nature indecisive; and yet, having been told that, our very existence often seemed to depend on our decisiveness. We were told that certain mythic definitions of women were immutable natural laws, biological "facts"; yet so often our very endurance depended upon changing those supposedly unchangeable things, and upon embracing a life credo of change.

In fact, when I look back on the years since I left college, and I try to   8
sum up what I have learned, it is precisely that: not to fear change, not to expect my life to be immutable. All the good things that have happened to me in the last several years have come, without exception, from a willingness to change, to risk the unknown, to do the very things I feared the most. Every poem, every page of fiction I have written, has been written with anxiety, occasionally panic, always uncertainty about its reception. Every life decision I have made—from changing jobs, to changing partners, to changing homes—has been taken with trepidation. I have not ceased being fearful, but I have ceased to let fear

control me. I have accepted fear as a part of life, specifically the fear of change, the fear of the unknown, and I have gone ahead despite the pounding in the heart that says: turn back, turn back, you'll die if you venture too far.

9   I regard myself as a fairly typical member of the female sex, and as a fairly typical member of the class of '63. I may have a greater talent for self-expression, but in my fears and feelings, I am the same. My talent to write may propel me into places and situations I wouldn't otherwise find myself in, but in the dark of night, having insomnia, I think the same thoughts as you or you. I get impatient with successful women who feel that their success has lifted them out of the ordinary stream of women's lives and who say to their fearful, unfledged sisters: I did it against the odds; you can, too. As a writer, I feel that the very source of my inspiration lies in my never forgetting how much I have in common with other women, how many ways in which we are all—successful or not—similarly shackled. I do not write about superwomen who have transcended all conflict; I write about women who are torn, as most of us are torn, between the past and the future, between our mothers' frustrations and the extravagant hopes we have for our daughters. I do not know what a writer would write about if all her characters were superwomen, cleansed of conflict. Conflict is the soul of literature.

10   I know I would not mind envisioning a world in which my daughter were free *not* to be a feminist,[3] were free (if she chose to be a writer) not to write about women's conflicts, not to assume that the accident of her gender compelled her work to have a specific creative bias. But I would also like to see a world in which male writers wrote without masculinist bias, in which for example Hemingway's masculinist mythology (and that of many other contemporary American male writers) was perceived as quite as bizarre and hysterical as the most absurd excesses of militant feminist fiction, and in which consciousness had become so truly androgynous that the adjective itself would be puzzlingly obsolete. Alas, I do not think our culture is heading in this direction. I think, rather, that after a brief flirtation with sensitivity to patriarchal attitudes (brought about by what has been termed the "second wave" of the women's movement—roughly that fleeting half-decade from 1969 to 1974) the culture is sliding back into its habitual sexism (with perhaps a few new wrinkles of equality, created more by the birth-control revolution and the ravages of inflation upon the average family income than by feminist theory). Radical feminists have, in a sense, abetted

[3]I assume here that feminism is necessitated by our patriarchal culture. In a truly egalitarian culture, feminism would be obsolete. Let us all pray for such obsolescence.

this process of backsliding by becoming quite as simple-mindedly dogmatic as the most dogmatic male chauvinists, by disassociating themselves from the realities of most women's lives: i.e., a desire for children and warm affective relationships with men. It is unrealistic to assume that after living in families and tribes for millions of years of human evolution, women will suddenly cease to need affective relationships with men and children and become either solitaries or feminist communards. The human need for companionship and sexuality is far stronger than any intellectual theory, and the point is not to keep women from establishing families (a desire that may even be instinctual) but rather to make their *position* in families less that of semislaves and more that of autonomous individuals within the protection of the group.

Where does all this leave the woman writer of our age? Usually in a quandary. As a sharp observer of her society she cannot fail to see that it discriminates against women (often in emotionally crippling and physically murderous ways), but as an artist she cannot allow her vision to be polluted by the ephemeral dogmas of political movements. It is simply not possible to write a good book that "proves" the essential righteousness of either lesbianism or heterosexuality, childbearing or its avoidance, man-loving or man-hating. Righteousness has, in fact, no place in literature. Of course the keen observer of her culture will feel deeply about the oppression she sees around her, the inhumanity of man to man, of man to woman, but her vision of it must be essentially personal, not abstractly political. Books are not written by committees—at least not good books. And the woman writer has as much right as any other artist to an essentially individual and idiosyncratic vision. If we judge her books according to their political "correctness," we are doing her as great a disservice as if we judged them according to her looks or her behavior in the voting booth. Certainly human history is full of such judgmentalism—most of it not coming from women—but always it is antithetical to the creation of works of art.

After saying all of this, I must also gratefully acknowledge that the second wave of the feminist movement liberated my writing and was a liberating influence upon my whole life. How? Not by supplying me with dogma, but by making it easier for me to look into myself and assume that what I felt as a woman was also shared by other women (and men). For one of the most positive by-products of the so-called second wave of the feminist movement was its discovery of a new audience of readers—readers both female and male—who came to realize that literary history as we previously knew it was the history of the literature of the white, the affluent, the male, and that the female side of experience had been almost completely omitted (except as seen through the eyes of the traditional victors in the war between the sexes[4]—men). And this audience was suddenly passionately interested in dispatches from the center of the female heart which represented a sort of dark continent, a *terra incognita*, the exploration of which was necessary to a full understanding of human consciousness in all its permutations.

13   From the courage the women's movement gave and from the reinforcement I received from grateful and passionate readers, I learned the daring to assume that my thoughts, nightmares, and daydreams were the same as my readers'. I discovered that whenever I wrote about a fantasy I thought was wholly private, bizarre, kinky—(the fantasy of the Zipless Fuck in *Fear of Flying* is perhaps the best example of this)—I invariably discovered that thousands of other people had experienced the same private, bizarre, and kinky fantasy.

14   In the past several years, I have learned, in short, to trust myself. Not to eradicate fear but to go on in spite of fear. Not to become insensitive to distinguished critics but to follow my own writer's instinct despite what they say women should or should not write. My job is not to paralyze myself by anticipating judgment but to do the best I can and let the judgment fall where it may. The difference between the woman who is writing this essay and the girl sitting in that creative writing class in 1961 is mostly a matter of nerve and daring—the nerve to trust my own instincts and the daring to be a fool. No one ever found wisdom without also being a fool. Writers, alas, have to be fools in public, while the rest of the human race can cover its tracks. But it is also painfully true that no one avoids being a fool without also avoiding growth, and growth does not, alas, stop with the current feminist vision of reality. It goes on far beyond it.

15   It seems to me that having now created an entire literature of female rage, an entire literature of female introspection, women writers are ready to enter the next phase—the phase of empathy. Without forgetting how hard-won our rage was, without forgetting how many puritanical voices would still like to censor our sexuality, I think we must consider ourselves free to explore the whole world of feeling in our writings—and not to be trapped forever in the phase of discovering buried anger. The anger has been discovered, unearthed, anatomized, and catalogued. It may be a strong propellant to the creation of literature,

---

[4]The question of whether or not men are really victors in the war between the sexes is older than Aristophanes' *Lysistrata*. In terms of the distribution of society's material goodies and power, they are clearly victors, but there is much reason to believe that their very status as victors has robbed them emotionally—and robbed them of the sort of flexibility and emotional openness women more usually possess. Still, this is the price they pay for their own dominance, and the fact that the underdog has certain emotional advantages should never obscure the fact that she *is* the underdog.

but it is hardly the only propellant. Stronger even than anger is curiosity—emotional and intellectual curiosity—the vehicles through which we enter into other states of being, other lives, other historical periods, other galaxies. Patriarchy will have truly crippled women if it prevents us from experiencing our native human curiosity (because that curiosity has been so overlaid with rage at our position in society). The time has come to let go of that rage; the time has come to realize that curiosity is braver than rage, that exploration is a nobler calling than war. As artists, the unknown beckons to us, singing its siren song* and making our hearts pound with fear and desire. Let us not tie ourselves to the mast of anger but sail into the unknown, fearful of the future, yet not paralyzed into immobility by fear; *feeling* the fear, yet not letting the fear control us. This is the ultimate test of our blood and guts. Those who pass it will discover new worlds and create a new literature by women truly worthy of our courage, our imagination, and our craft.

Questions and Activities

▶ *COMPREHENSION QUESTIONS*

1. What does Jong think is the most difficult aspect of being a woman with a career? How does Jong's experience as a woman writer support your answer?
2. Why did the women in the creative writing class sit quietly while they were told by a visiting "Distinguished Critic" that they could never be professional writers (paragraph 2)?
3. Does Jong support or oppose the idea, which is held by some feminists, that writing done by women must support particular feminist values and philosophies? Or does she believe that women writers should support their own personal beliefs and values and refuse to be systematized by anyone, male or female?
4. How are all women "similarly shackled" (paragraph 9)? What in our social system keeps women from fulfilling their intellectual, emotional, and physical potential? Why are men not subject to some or most of these shackles?

*The sirens were mythical nymphs who tried to lure men to shipwreck on their rocky island by singing enchanting songs. In Homer's *Odyssey*, Odysseus and his ship got by because he ordered his crew to stop up their ears and tie him to the mast.

5. In paragraph 10, Jong tries to develop a balanced perspective on contemporary feminism and the conditions of women in the larger society. Do you think that she manages to create a voice of sufficient openness and conviction to make her argument persuasive?
6. Jong's essay is focused on defining and clarifying a problem. What is the "tricky" problem that woman writers face today? How does this essay define and explain this problem? Explain how this essay can be divided into two parts: a first half that defines the problem of women today and a second half that offers a solution to that problem, at least for some women. Can you point to other possible ways of describing the organization of this essay?

7. Jong argues that women must refuse to be controlled by their anger and frustration as they fight for greater independence in our society. Why do you think Jong feels that a woman's anger might cut into her independence and put her more rather than less under the control of forces outside herself? Can you think of any situation in which someone who was angry was manipulated by others using that anger?
8. When and how might anger be a necessary step toward independence? Why might a woman need to feel anger before she could pass beyond it to more constructive social action?
9. Are men also stereotyped and restrained by the social situation? Are male stereotypes less constraining than female ones? Are men's social stereotypes less apt than women's to keep them from achieving personal and professional goals?

10. Interview a woman and a man concerning their future aspirations. When you have finished the interviews, note those places where you were surprised by the responses of your subjects. Do these points suggest attitudes on your part that you were previously unaware of? Discuss these attitudes with others in your class.
11. Write a brief character sketch of some truly independent person you have known. Be sure that you know or remember the character well enough to describe him or her in detail. After you have finished, compare your sketch with those of several of your classmates, and work together to extract a general definition of an independent person.

Writing Assignments

PORTRAIT OF AN INDEPENDENT PERSON

Write a five-to-seven-page essay in which you define and then describe an independent person. Use at least three of the essays in this section as support for your definition. Be sure to consider both social and individual perspectives on independence as you plan and write your essay.

THE INTERDEPENDENCY OF MEN AND WOMEN

Read Kate Chopin's "The Story of an Hour" (pages 822–824). Discuss the story with several classmates, using the following list of questions to direct the discussion:

1. What kind of life has Mrs. Mallard had before this story begins?
2. On what and whom had Mrs. Mallard depended for security before the story opens?
3. Would Mrs. Mallard's real response to the news of her husband's death have seemed odd to her sister or her husband's friend Richards? What is odd about it to readers, who know her inner thoughts? What does the narrator of this story do to ensure that readers will understand the oddness of Mrs. Mallard's response to the news of her husband's death?
4. Why does Brently Mallard's appearance in paragraph 21 shock Mrs. Mallard? How would a reader's answer to this question differ from that of the observers in the story?
5. Did Mrs. Mallard really die of "joy that kills" (paragraph 23)?

Pull together your discussion group's answers to these questions into an interpretation of the meaning of the story. What significance does the story have for readers who are interested in the possibilities for independence in the relationships between men and women?

Working on your own, write an essay addressed to a group of college students in which you explain why men and women should be interdependent rather than either dependent or independent. Utilize at least two essays from this section and "The Story of an Hour" for source material for your essay. You can assume that your audience has done some thinking about sexual identity, marriage, and questions of dependence and independence, but you cannot assume that they have read your sources.

As you write your essay, remember to address your audience with a voice and tone appropriate to their age, status, and experience. These students are interested in sexual identity and independence. They have not read the pieces you have read in this section, however. You will need to refer specifically and accurately to your sources, and you must be sure to define clearly the context in which those sources are being discussed. Also, you will be writing to equals who will respond negatively to condescension on your part. Finally, your readers will resent their time being wasted; make your point and support it, but do not pad.

The Story of an Hour
KATE CHOPIN

1   Knowing that Mrs. Mallard was afflicted with a heart trouble, great care was taken to break to her as gently as possible the news of her husband's death.

2   It was her sister Josephine who told her, in broken sentences; veiled hints that revealed in half concealing. Her husband's friend Richards was there, too, near her. It was he who had been in the newspaper office when intelligence of the railroad disaster was received, with Brently Mallard's name leading the list of "killed." He had only taken the time to assure himself of its truth by a second telegram, and had hastened to forestall any less careful, less tender friend in bearing the sad message.

3   She did not hear the story as many women have heard the same, with a paralyzed inability to accept its significance. She wept at once, with sudden, wild abandonment, in her sister's arms. When the storm of grief had spent itself she went away to her room alone. She would have no one follow her.

4   There stood, facing the open window, a comfortable, roomy armchair. Into this she sank, pressed down by a physical exhaustion that haunted her body and seemed to reach into her soul.

5   She could see in the open square before her house the tops of trees that were all aquiver with the new spring life. The delicious breath of rain was in the air. In the street below a peddler was crying his wares. The notes of a distant song which some one was singing reached her faintly, and countless sparrows were twittering in the eaves.

6   There were patches of blue sky showing here and there through the clouds that had met and piled one above the other in the west facing her window.

7   She sat with her head thrown back upon the cushion of the chair, quite motionless, except when a sob came up into her throat and shook

her, as a child who has cried itself to sleep continues to sob in its dreams.

She was young, with a fair, calm face, whose lines bespoke repression and even a certain strength. But now there was a dull stare in her eyes, whose gaze was fixed away off yonder on one of those patches of blue sky. It was not a glance of reflection, but rather indicated a suspension of intelligent thought.   8

There was something coming to her and she was waiting for it, fearfully. What was it? She did not know; it was too subtle and elusive to name. But she felt it, creeping out of the sky, reaching toward her through the sounds, the scents, the color that filled the air.   9

Now her bosom rose and fell tumultuously. She was beginning to recognize this thing that was approaching to possess her, and she was striving to beat it back with her will—as powerless as her two white slender hands would have been.   10

When she abandoned herself a little whispered word escaped her slightly parted lips. She said it over and over under her breath: "free, free, free!" The vacant stare and the look of terror that had followed it went from her eyes. They stayed keen and bright. Her pulses beat fast, and the coursing blood warmed and relaxed every inch of her body.   11

She did not stop to ask if it were or were not a monstrous joy that held her. A clear and exalted perception enabled her to dismiss the suggestion as trivial.   12

She knew that she would weep again when she saw the kind, tender hands folded in death; the face that had never looked save with love upon her, fixed and gray and dead. But she saw beyond that bitter moment a long procession of years to come that would belong to her absolutely. And she opened and spread her arms out to them in welcome.   13

There would be no one to live for her during those coming years; she would live for herself. There would be no powerful will bending hers in that blind persistence with which men and women believe they have a right to impose a private will upon a fellow-creature. A kind intention or a cruel intention made the act seem no less a crime as she looked upon it in that brief moment of illumination.   14

And yet she had loved him—sometimes. Often she had not. What did it matter! What could love, the unsolved mystery, count for in face of this possession of self-assertion which she suddenly recognized as the strongest impulse of her being!   15

"Free! Body and soul free!" she kept whispering.   16

Josephine was kneeling before the closed door with her lips to the keyhole, imploring for admission. "Louise, open the door! I beg; open   17 the door—you will make yourself ill. What are you doing, Louise? For heaven's sake open the door."

18   "Go away. I am not making myself ill." No; she was drinking in a very elixir of life through that open window.

19   Her fancy was running riot along those days ahead of her. Spring days, and summer days, and all sorts of days that would be her own. She breathed a quick prayer that life might be long. It was only yesterday she had thought with a shudder that life might be long.

20   She rose at length and opened the door to her sister's importunities. There was a feverish triumph in her eyes, and she carried herself unwittingly like a goddess of Victory. She clasped her sister's waist, and together they descended the stairs. Richards stood waiting for them at the bottom.

21   Some one was opening the front door with a latchkey. It was Brently Mallard who entered, a little travel-stained, composedly carrying his grip-sack and umbrella. He had been far from the scene of the accident, and did not even know there had been one. He stood amazed at Josephine's piercing cry; at Richards' quick motion to screen him from the view of his wife.

22   But Richards was too late.

23   When the doctors came they said she had died of heart disease—of joy that kills.

*I*s Education
What It Should Be?

▶ ──────────────────

Introduction

▶ ────────────────

The essays in this section focus on formal, public education. Every essay, in one way or another, raises the question of whether the goal of public education in America has been to shape individuals to fit into the roles their culture has prepared for them or to help individuals reach their potential independently, to help them shape the culture in which they live.

The first selection in the section is Alfred Kazin's detailed description of the effects his schooling in the Brownsville section of Brooklyn had on him as a child and adult. A Jewish son of recent immigrants, Kazin was subjected, along with Italian, German, Irish, and Polish children, to drudgery, hard work, and the authoritarian rule of teachers and administrators whose main aim was to fit their students for a productive life within the American system. There was, in Kazin's school, no talk of having students discover their inner potential or their ethnic heritage. School was a place where immigrant children learned to survive and achieve in the competitive American economic and social environment.

Jonathan Kozol describes an urban Boston school some thirty years after Kazin was an elementary school student. Kozol is a teacher, and his pupils are black children who are treated by other teachers and administrators as the second-class citizens of the Boston public school system. He befriends his students, gains their trust and respect, and has some small success in helping them learn. But all his personal rapport with his students is nullified when he is fired because he had his students read a Langston Hughes poem about the suffering of blacks in America. This experience was to bring Kozol to argue for alternative, community-controlled public schools, where parents, teachers, and students might share control of the learning process.

Jules Henry, a cultural anthropologist writing on the purposes of public schools, provides a more general picture of how these institutions strive to introduce students to their cultural roles. Providing detailed portraits of both traditional and progressive classrooms, Henry convincingly argues that public schools, whatever their educational philosophies, exist to subvert the individual impulses of students and to condition students to take their places in the technologically oriented, free-enterprise society. Henry goes so far as to suggest that teachers who emphasize affectionate and open relationships with children may actually be hurting the children's chances of competing successfully in the larger, more competitive society.

John Dewey, a famous American philosopher and progressive educator, raises another general educational issue. A believer in the benefits of science and technology, Dewey argues that modern educational systems have failed to curtail war and human suffering primarily because they have failed to apply the rigorous methods of scientific analysis to the important moral and social questions of the twentieth century. Dewey suggests that the arguments between those who would foster the development of the individual and those who would objectively impart knowledge are pointless ones. What is more important is the question of how students can be taught to apply the disciplined and rigorous forms of thought characteristic of modern science to every aspect of their lives. For Dewey, the methods of science can help us solve moral and social problems, but only if we close the gap that presently exists between the sciences and humanities.

Caroline Bird and James Thurber criticize one of America's most respected institutions — its universities and colleges. In their very different essays, one serious and the other satirical, Bird and Thurber raise the question of why students should attend college in the first place. Bird argues that too many students go to college simply in order to get a good job, or a meaningful one. Because only a relatively small number of these types of jobs exist, however, many college students are destined for disappointment and frustration. Thurber, in describing his own college days at Ohio State University during World War I, captures the absurdity of going through seemingly meaningless rituals to earn a degree. Both Bird and Thurber suggest that people should attend college only when they have a personal thirst for knowledge and a desire to study for its own sake. Otherwise, academic life can be senseless.

This section, then, poses two central questions: Should formal education promote individual creativity or cultural indoctrination? Is it possible to combine these two general aims of education? The authors represented in this section offer three perspectives on these questions.

Kazin and Kozol emphasize a personal perspective, writing from their own experiences as student and teacher in large, public, urban school systems. Their essays are convincing because of the deeply felt, honestly expressed, and dramatically detailed qualities of their writing. Henry and Dewey take a broad, intellectual approach to the subject of education. They develop theories that explain why education has sometimes failed to address particular social problems, and they explain how more accurate ideas about what education is all about might lead to more successful approaches to solving problems through education. Bird and Thurber adopt critical perspectives on a particular aspect of formal education. Bird, in a straightforwardly critical analysis, attacks the assertion that college should be for everyone. Thurber, in a humorous satire, tells us why college often seemed absurd to him. Their writing is effective because of the clarity with which they analyze facts and relate personal experiences.

As you read the selections in this section, the following questions will prepare you to respond actively to the issues that are raised:

1. Can you imagine an educational system that effectively combines individualism and cultural orientation? What would students do in such a combined system?
2. Should formal schooling leave individual development to other social contexts and emphasize the teaching of skills and knowledge? Is it possible to learn when personal involvement has been left out of the learning environment?
3. Can skills such as writing and mathematical reasoning be learned in the abstract, without students actually doing them? Should teachers provide all the answers to student questions?
4. Who should control the school curriculum—professional educators, parents, students, communities, government leaders? How should students participate in their educations?
5. Has your own education ever seemed absurd? Have you ever felt you had a purpose in going to school, beyond the fact that you were required to go?

Brownsville Schooldays

ALFRED KAZIN

Alfred Kazin (born in 1915) throughout his career has written mixed journalism, literary criticism, autobiography, and biographical criticism. In some cases, he has mixed these genres in one book; he has never been a writer that reviewers could easily pigeon-hole. A lifelong native of New York City, where he graduated from City College and Columbia University, Kazin has written a sensitive and humane study of his own experiences growing up in New York (*A Walker in the City,* 1951); a major interpretation of the effects of American culture on American literature (*On Native Grounds,* 1942); perceptive and balanced accounts of other literary personalities and the effects of American culture on them (*Contemporaries,* 1962); and a book on the sociocultural and literary environment of the 1930s in New York City (*Starting Out in the Thirties,* 1965). In 1978, his Jewish heritage and New York background came together to create a fascinating cultural and literary autobiography (*New York Jew*). Kazin has also published many essays on current events, literary and otherwise, in the politically liberal *New Republic* magazine, in the more literary *Atlantic Monthly,* and in many other periodicals.

Kazin is another writer who uses personal experience heavily in his writings. In "Brownsville Schooldays," which is taken from *A Walker in the City,* Kazin builds up a detailed narrative about his schooldays. He attempts to make his readers understand his school experience from his personal perspective, but he also works hard to convey the general educational significance of that experience. Kazin, an ethnic boy growing up in a public school in Brooklyn, becomes a symbol of children of American immigrants who worked their way through schools like Kazin's Brownsville school. The authority figures, hard work, fear, and social climbing found in Kazin's school can all be seen as elements of the American dream of social opportunity, by which individuals might achieve untold success or fall to depths of failure.

Kazin provides a detailed, personal portrait of the traditional city school in America, where the emphasis is on conforming to established codes of behavior and where individuals of radically different backgrounds learn to adapt to the American way. Kazin also gives an analysis of the effects on one individual of that pressure to conform, compete, and win at an intense educational game. Think about these effects of education as you read this selection:

1. Is Kazin's school experience from the 1920s similar in any way to school experiences today?
2. Although the scene may have changed, do American cities continue to produce highly competitive school environments in which learning is something of a contest? Do other kinds of schools—private, rural, suburban—also emphasize these competitive and conforming traits, perhaps in different ways?
3. Must education be competitive?
4. Must personal fulfillment always be at odds with public measures of success?

▶ ─────────────────────

All my early life lies open to my eye within five city blocks. When I passed the school, I went sick with all my old fear of it. With its standard New York public-school brown brick courtyard shut in on three sides of the square and the pretentious battlements overlooking that cockpit in which I can still smell the fiery sheen of the rubber ball, it looks like a factory over which has been imposed the façade of a castle. It gave me the shivers to stand up in that courtyard again; I felt as if I had been mustered back into the service of those Friday morning "tests" that were the terror of my childhood.

It was never learning I associated with that school: only the necessity to succeed, to get ahead of the others in the daily struggle to "make a good impression" on our teachers, who grimly, wearily, and often with ill-concealed distaste watched against our relapsing into the natural savagery they expected of Brownsville boys. The white, cool, thinly ruled record book sat over us from their desks all day long, and had remorselessly entered into it each day—in blue ink if we had passed, in red ink if we had not—our attendance, our conduct, our "effort," our merits and demerits; and to the last possible decimal point in calculation, our standing in an unending series of "tests"—surprise tests, daily tests, weekly tests, formal midterm tests, final tests. They never stopped trying to dig out of us whatever small morsel of fact we had managed to get down the night before. We had to prove that we were really alert, ready for anything, always in the race. That white thinly ruled record book figured in my mind as the judgment seat; the very thinness and remote blue lightness of its lines instantly showed its cold authority over me; so much space had been left on each page, columns and columns in which to note down everything about us, implacably and forever. As it lay there on a teacher's desk, I stared at it all day long with such fear and anxious propriety that I had no trouble believing that God, too, did nothing but keep such record books, and that on the final day He would face me with an account in Hebrew letters whose phonetic dots and dashes looked strangely like decimal points counting up my every sinful thought on earth.

3   All teachers were to be respected like gods, and God Himself was the greatest of all school superintendents. Long after I had ceased to believe that our teachers could see with the back of their heads, it was still understood, by me, that they knew everything. They were the delegates of all visible and invisible power on earth—of the mothers who waited on the stoops every day after three for us to bring home tales of our daily triumphs; of the glacially remote Anglo-Saxon principal, whose very name was King; of the incalculably important Superintendent of Schools who would someday rubberstamp his name to the bottom of our diplomas in grim acknowledgment that we had, at last, given satisfaction to him, to the Board of Superintendents, and to our benefactor the City of New York—and so up and up, to the government of the United States and to the great Lord Jehovah Himself. My belief in teachers' unlimited wisdom and power rested not so much on what I saw in them—how impatient most of them looked, how wary—but on our abysmal humility, at least in those of us who were "good" boys, who proved by our ready compliance and "manners" that we wanted to get on. The road to a professional future would be shown us only as we pleased *them. Make a good impression the first day of the term, and they'll help you out. Make a bad impression, and you might as well cut your throat.* This was the first article of school folklore, whispered around the classroom the opening day of each term. You made the "good impression" by sitting firmly at your wooden desk, hands clasped; by silence for the greatest part of the live-long day; by standing up obsequiously when it was so expected of you; by sitting down noiselessly when you had answered a question; by "speaking nicely," which meant reproducing their painfully exact enunciation; by "showing manners," or an ecstatic submissiveness in all things; by outrageous flattery; by bringing little gifts at Christmas, on their birthdays, and at the end of the term—the well-known significance of these gifts being that they came not from us, but from our parents, whose eagerness in this matter showed a high level of social consideration, and thus raised our standing in turn.

4   It was not just our quickness and memory that were always being tested. Above all, in that word I could never hear without automatically seeing it raised before me in gold-plated letters, it was our *character.* I always felt anxious when I heard the word pronounced. Satisfactory as

my "character" was, on the whole, except when I stayed too long in the playground reading; outrageously satisfactory, as I can see now, the very sound of the word as our teachers coldly gave it out from the end of their teeth, with a solemn weight on each dark syllable, immediately struck my heart cold with fear—they could not believe I really had it. Character was never something you had; it had to be trained in you, like a technique. I was never very clear about it. On our side *character* meant demonstrative obedience; but teachers already had it—how else could they have become teachers? They had it; the aloof Anglo-Saxon principal whom we remotely saw only on ceremonial occasions in the assembly was positively encased in it; it glittered off his bald head in spokes of triumphant light; the President of the United States had the greatest conceivable amount of it. Character belonged to great adults. Yet we were constantly being driven onto it; it was the great threshold we had to cross. *Alfred Kazin, having shown proficiency in his course of studies and having displayed satisfactory marks of character.*. . . Thus someday the hallowed diploma, passport to my further advancement in high school. But there—I could already feel it in my bones—they would put me through even more doubting tests of character; and after that, if I should be good enough and bright enough, there would be still more. *Character* was a bitter thing, racked with my endless striving to please. The school—from every last stone in the courtyard to the battlements frowning down at me from the walls—was only the stage for a trial. I felt that the very atmosphere of learning that surrounded us was fake—that every lesson, every book, every approving smile was only a pretext for the constant probing and watching of me, that there was not a secret in me that would not be decimally measured into that white record book. All week long I lived for the blessed sound of the dismissal gong at three o'clock on Friday afternoon.

I was awed by this system, I believed in it, I respected its force. The   5 alternative was "going bad." The school was notoriously the toughest in our tough neighborhood, and the dangers of "going bad" were constantly impressed upon me at home and in school in dark whispers of the "reform school" and in examples of boys who had been picked up for petty thievery, rape, or flinging a heavy inkwell straight into a teacher's face. Behind any failure in school yawned the great abyss of a criminal career. Every refractory attitude doomed you with the sound "Sing Sing."* Anything less than absolute perfection in school always

---

*Sing Sing was a federal prison in Ossining, New York. At the time Kazin was growing up, it had been made famous through references to it in gangster movies of the 1930s. It is now closed.

suggested to my mind that I might fall out of the daily race, be kept back in the working class forever, or—dared I think of it?—fall into the criminal class itself.

6   I worked on a hairline between triumph and catastrophe. Why the odds should always have felt so narrow I understood only when I realized how little my parents thought of their own lives. It was not for myself alone that I was expected to shine, but for them—to redeem the constant anxiety of their existence. I was the first American child, their offering to the strange new God; I was to be the monument of their liberation from the shame of being—what they were. And that there was shame in this was a fact that everyone seemed to believe as a matter of course. It was in the gleeful discounting of themselves—what do we know?—with which our parents greeted every fresh victory in our savage competition for "high averages," for prizes, for a few condescending words of official praise from the principal at assembly. It was in the sickening invocation of "Americanism"—the word itself accusing us of everything we apparently were not. Our families and teachers seemed tacitly agreed that we were somehow to be a little ashamed of what we were. Yet it was always hard to say why this should be so. It was certainly not—in Brownsville!—because we were Jews, or simply because we spoke another language at home, or were absent on our holy days. It was rather that a "refined," "correct," "nice" English was required of us at school that we did not naturally speak, and that our teachers could never be quite sure we would keep. This English was peculiarly the ladder of advancement. Every future young lawyer was known by it. Even the Communists and Socialists on Pitkin Avenue spoke it. It was bright and clean and polished. We were expected to show it off like a new pair of shoes. When the teacher sharply called a question out, then your name, you were expected to leap up, face the class, and eject those new words fluently off the tongue.

7   There was my secret ordeal: I could never say anything except in the most roundabout way; I was a stammerer. Although I knew all those new words from my private reading—I read walking in the street, to and from the Children's Library on Stone Avenue; on the fire escape and the roof; at every meal when they would let me; read even when I dressed in the morning, propping my book up against the drawers of the bureau as I pulled on my long black stockings—I could never seem to get the easiest words out with the right dispatch, and would often miserably signal from my desk that I did not know the answer rather than get up to stumble and fall and crash on every word. If, angry at always being put down as lazy or stupid, I did get up to speak, the black wooden floor would roll away under my feet, the teacher would frown at me in amazement, and in unbearable loneliness I would hear behind me the groans and laughter: *tuh-tuh-tuh-tuh.*

The word was my agony. The word that for others was so effortless   8
and so neutral, so unburdened, so simple, so exact, I had first to medi-
tate in advance, to see if I could make it, like a plumber fitting together
odd lengths and shapes of pipe. I was always preparing words I could
speak, storing them away, choosing between them. And often, when
the word did come from my mouth in its great and terrible birth,
quailing and bleeding as if forced through a thornbush, I would not be
able to look the others in the face, and would walk out in the silence,
the infinitely echoing silence behind my back, to say it all cleanly back
to myself as I walked in the streets. Only when I was alone in the open
air, pacing the roof with pebbles in my mouth, as I had read
Demosthenes* had done to cure himself of stammering; or in the street,
where all words seemed to flow from the length of my stride and the
color of the houses as I remembered the perfect tranquillity of a phrase
in Beethoven's *Romance In F* I could sing back to myself as I
walked—only then was it possible for me to speak without the infinite
premeditations and strangled silences I toiled through whenever I got
up at school to respond with the expected, the exact answer.

It troubled me that I could speak in the fullness of my own voice only   9
when I was alone on the streets, walking about. There was something
unnatural about it; unbearably isolated. I was not like the others! I was
not like the others! At midday, every freshly shocking Monday noon,
they sent me away to a speech clinic in a school in East New York,
where I sat in a circle of lispers and cleft palates and foreign accents
holding a mirror before my lips and rolling difficult sounds over and
over. To be sent there in the full light of the opening week, when everyone else was at school or going about his business, made me feel as if I
had been expelled from the great normal body of humanity. I would gob-
ble down my lunch on my way to the speech clinic and rush back to the
school in time to make up for the classes I had lost. One day, one unfor-
gettable dread day, I stopped to catch my breath on a corner of Sutter Avenue, near the wholesale fruit markets, where an old drugstore rose up
over a great flight of steps. In the window were dusty urns of colored
water floating off iron chains; cardboard placards advertising hairnets,
Ex-Lax; a great illustrated medical chart headed THE HUMAN FACTORY,
which showed the exact course a mouthful of food follows as it falls
from chamber to chamber of the body. I hadn't meant to stop there at
all, only to catch my breath; but I so hated the speech clinic that I
thought I would delay my arrival for a few minutes by eating my lunch
on the steps. When I took the sandwich out of my bag, two bitterly hard
pieces of hard salami slipped out of my hand and fell through a grate

---

*Demosthenes (384–322 B.C.) was a famous Greek orator and politician whose speeches
were known for their powerful delivery, emotional appeal, and patriotism.

onto a hill of dust below the steps. I remember how sickeningly vivid an odd thread of hair looked on the salami, as if my lunch were turning stiff with death. The factory whistles called their short, sharp blasts stark through the middle of noon, beating at me where I sat outside the city's magnetic circle. I had never known, I knew instantly I would never in my heart again submit to, such wild passive despair as I felt at that moment, sitting on the steps before THE HUMAN FACTORY, where little robots gathered and shoveled the food from chamber to chamber of the body. They had put me out into the streets, I thought to myself; with their mirrors and their everlasting pulling at me to imitate their effortless bright speech and their stupefaction that a boy could stammer and stumble on every other English word he carried in his head, they had put me out into the streets, had left me high and dry on the steps of that drugstore staring at the remains of my lunch turning black and grimy in the dust.

10   In the great cool assembly hall, dominated by the gold sign above the stage, KNOWLEDGE IS POWER, the windowsills were lined with Dutch bulbs, each wedged into a mound of pebbles massed in a stone dish. Above them hung a giant photograph of Theodore Roosevelt. Whenever I walked in to see the empty assembly hall for myself, the shiny waxed floor of the stage dangled in the middle of the air like a crescent. On one side was a great silk American flag, the staff crowned by a gilt eagle. Across the dry rattling of varnish-smelling empty seats bowing to the American flag, I saw in the play of the sun on those pebbles wildly sudden images of peace. *There* was the other land, crowned by the severe and questioning face of Theodore Roosevelt, his eyes above the curiously endearing straw-dry mustache, behind the pince-nez glittering with light, staring and staring me through as if he were uncertain whether he fully approved of me.

11   The light pouring through window after window in that great empty varnished assembly hall seemed to me the most wonderful thing I had ever seen. It was that thorough varnished cleanness that was of the new land, that light dancing off the glasses of Theodore Roosevelt, those green and white roots of the still raw onion-brown bulbs delicately flaring up from the hill of pebbles into which they were wedged. The pebbles moved me in themselves, there were so many of them. They rose up around the bulbs in delicately strong masses of colored stone, and as the sun fell between them, each pebble shone in its own light. Looking across the great rows of empty seats to those pebbles lining the windowsills, I could still smell summer from some long veranda surrounded by trees. On that veranda sat the family and friends of Theodore Roosevelt. I knew the name: Oyster Bay. Because of that picture, I had read *The*

Boy's Life of Theodore Roosevelt; knew he had walked New York streets night after night as Police Commissioner, unafraid of the Tenderloin gangsters; had looked into *Theodore Roosevelt's Letters to His Children*, pretending that those hilarious drawings on almost every page were for me. *There* was America, I thought, the real America, *his* America, where from behind the glass on the wall of our assembly hall he watched over us to make sure we did right, thought right, lived right.

"Up, boys! Up San Juan Hill!" I still hear our roguish old civics teacher, a little white-haired Irishman who was supposed to have been with Teddy in Cuba, driving us through our Friday morning tests with these shouts and cries. He called them "Army Navy" tests, to make us feel big, and dividing the class between Army and Navy, got us to compete with each other for a coveted blue star. Civics was city government, state government, federal government; each government had functions; you had to get them out fast in order to win for the Army or the Navy. Sometimes this required filling in three or four words, line by line, down one side of the grimly official yellow foolscap that was brought out for tests. (In the tense silence just before the test began, he looked at us sharply, the watch in his hand ticking as violently as the sound of my heart, and on command, fifty boys simultaneously folded their yellow test paper and evened the fold with their thumbnails in a single dry sigh down the middle of the paper.) At other times it meant true-or-false tests; then he stood behind us to make sure we did not signal the right answers to each other in the usual way—for true, nodding your head; for false, holding your nose. You could hear his voice barking from the rear. *"Come on now, you Army boys! On your toes like West Point cadets! All ready now? Get set! Go! Three powers of the legislative branch? The judiciary? The executive? The subject of the fifteenth amendment? The capital of Wyoming? Come on, Navy! Shoot those landlubbers down! Give 'em a blast from your big guns right through the middle! The third article of the Bill of Rights? The thirteenth amendment? The sixteenth? True or false, Philadelphia is the capital of Pennsylvania. Up and at 'em, Navy! Mow them down! COME ON!!!"* Our "average" was calculated each week, and the boys who scored 90 per cent or over were rewarded by seeing *their own names* lettered on the great blue chart over the blackboard. Each time I entered that room for a test, I looked for my name on the blue chart as if the sight of it would decide my happiness for all time.

Down we go, down the school corridors of the past smelling of chalk, lysol out of the open toilets, and girl sweat. The staircases were a gray stone I saw nowhere else in the school, and they were shut in on both sides by some thick unreflecting glass on which were pasted travel post-

ers inviting us to spend the summer in the Black Forest. Those staircases created a spell in me that I had found my way to some distant,
cool, neutral passageway deep in the body of the school. There, enclosed within the thick, green boughs of a classic summer in Germany,
I could still smell the tense probing chalk smells from every classroom,
the tickling high surgical odor of lysol from the open toilets, could still
hear that continuous babble, babble of water dripping into the bowls.
Sex was instantly connected in my mind with the cruel openness of
those toilets, and in the never-ending sound of the bowls being flushed I
could detect, as I did in the maddeningly elusive fragrance of cologne
brought into the classroom by Mrs. B., the imminence of something severe, frightening, obscene. Sex, as they said in the "Coney Island"
dives outside the school, was like going to the toilet; there was a great
contempt in this that made me think of the wet rings left by our sneak-
ers as we ran down the gray stone steps after school.

14   Outside the women teachers' washroom on the third floor, the tough
guys would wait for the possible appearance of Mrs. B., whose large
goiterous eyes seemed to bulge wearily with mischief, who always
looked tired and cynical, and who wore thin chiffon dresses that
affected us much more than she seemed to realize. Mrs. B. often went
about the corridors in the company of a trim little teacher of mathematics who was a head shorter than she and had a mustache. Her chiffon dresses billowed around him like a sail; she seemed to have him in
tow. It was understood by us as a matter of course that she wore those
dresses to inflame us; that she *was* tired and cynical, from much practice in obscene lovemaking; that she was a "bad one" like the young
Polish blondes from East New York I occasionally saw in the "Coney
Island" dives sitting on someone's lap and smoking a cigarette. How
wonderful and unbelievable it was to find this in a teacher; to realize
that the two of them, after we had left the school, probably met to rub
up against each other in the faculty toilet. Sex was a grim test where
sooner or later you would have to prove yourself doing things to
women. In the smell of chalk and sweat and the unending smirky babble of the water as it came to me on the staircase through my summer's
dream of old Germany, I could feel myself being called to still another
duty—to conquer Mrs. B., to rise to the challenge she had whispered to
us in her slyness. I had seen pictures of it on the block—they were always passing them around between handball games—the man's face furious, ecstatic with lewdness as he proudly looked down at himself; the
woman sniggering as she teased him with droplets from the contracep-
tive someone had just shown me in the gutter—its crushed, filmy
slyness the very sign of the forbidden.

They had never said anything about this at home, and I thought I   *15*
knew why. Sex was the opposite of books, of pictures, of music, of the
open air, even of kindness. They would not let you have both. Something always lingered to the sound of those toilets to test you. In and out
of the classroom they were always testing you. *Come on, Army! Come
on, Navy!* As I stood up in that school courtyard and smelled again the
familiar sweat, heard again the unending babble from the open toilets, I
suddenly remembered how sure I had always been that even my failures
in there would be entered in a white, thinly ruled, official record book.

Questions and Activities

▶ *COMPREHENSION QUESTIONS*

1. Describe the attitude toward students that Kazin attributes to his
   teachers. How did this attitude affect Kazin as a child? How does it
   affect him later, as the narrator of this piece?
2. Define "character," as Kazin uses the word in paragraph 4. Did
   Kazin believe as a child that people were born with character or
   that one had to be trained to have character?
3. What did the phrase "going bad" mean to Kazin as a child
   (paragraph 5)? What happened to children who went bad?
4. Why was the young Kazin so obsessed with words? What fears and
   anxieties caused him to stammer?
5. Why does Kazin say that, as an adolescent, sex was a "grim test"
   (paragraph 14)? What was being tested by sex?

▶ *QUESTIONS OF RHETORICAL PURPOSE AND STRATEGY*

6. Kazin focuses on particular events, people, and images from his
   past to bring alive his ideas about the effects his schooling had on
   him. Choose one of the following events, people, or images and explain how it helps you understand the Brownsville school's effects
   on the young Kazin: "The Human Factory" chart, the dropping of
   his salami through a sidewalk grate, his trips to the speech clinic, the
   slogan "Knowledge is Power," the Irish civics teacher, the portrait
   of Theodore Roosevelt, or Mrs. B. and the "trim little teacher of
   mathematics."
7. Why does Kazin use the past tense in this essay? Why might he wish
   to emphasize the fact that these experiences happened a long time
   ago?

8. Single out a particular paragraph in this essay. Underline the words in it that you believe reveal Kazin's attitude toward school. Explain to others in your class how these words communicate Kazin's attitude toward school.

▶ *THEME QUESTIONS*

9. Kazin had what some contemporary educators might call a repressive or stifling school experience. Yet he went on to become a successful teacher and writer. Thinking back over Kazin's experiences, explain what his schooling might have taught him, despite its coldness and authoritarianism.

10. Was Kazin valued as an individual by teachers and school administrators? Why did he unquestioningly accept the treatment he received from his teachers?

11. Kazin, a Jewish immigrant, was taught by Americans who often had negative attitudes about ethnic groups. Do you think those negative attitudes had an effect on Kazin and his fellow students in their later lives?

12. Should schools attempt to accommodate the cultural backgrounds of students, or should they ignore individual background as they strive to educate students for roles in the dominant culture?

▶ *LEARNING ACTIVITIES*

13. Work in a group with other students to develop answers to the following set of questions. Report as a group to the rest of the class.
    a. Does your school or college recognize different cultural or social backgrounds?
    b. What types of minority, ethnic, and socioeconomic groups are represented in your school's student population?
    c. Do individual members of minority, ethnic, and socioeconomic groups feel equitably treated in your school environment? How can you find out?

14. Write a brief sketch describing a school experience in which you were treated insensitively by teachers or administrators. Or describe a situation in which teachers and administrators treated you with sensitivity and understanding. Use some of Kazin's methods in your writing—his point of view, his detailed narration of events, his focus on important images.

Teaching in an Inner-City School

JONATHAN KOZOL

Jonathan Kozol, born in 1936 in Boston, Massachusetts, graduated from Harvard in 1958. He was a Rhodes scholar studying at Oxford University, England, in 1958 and 1959 and published a novel, *The Fume of Poppies,* in 1958. But from that time on Kozol has focused his writing career on the American public school system, particularly those schools set in city environments.

Kozol became famous with the publication of *Death at an Early Age* (1967), a personal account of his experiences in the mid-1960s as a teacher in the Boston public schools, from which the selection included here is taken. This book is a compelling account of the situation leading up to and following Kozol's firing because he used a poem by a Negro writer, Langston Hughes, that the school administrators said was neither written in standard English nor optimistic enough in its content and tone. Kozol's personal account includes condemnatory descriptions of the physical and psychological abuse of black children by white teachers and administrators. Kozol argues that this mistreatment was widespread and also that it was the result of the public school system's being constructed to keep the poor poor and the rich rich.

In his later writings, Kozol broadened his scope to include impassioned and factually supported accounts of the problem of illiteracy in America. In *Free Schools* (1972), which was revised as *Alternative Schools* (1982), Kozol describes the process he went through in establishing a community alternative school in Roxbury, a black Boston neighborhood, and suggests a program that others interested in alternative schools might follow in building such a school. In *Illiterate America* (1985), Kozol assembles staggering statistics on American illiteracy — over a third of Americans are partially or fully illiterate — and then argues for a community-by-community approach to solving the problem. In this and other books on literacy, Kozol also argues that literacy must be understood as being far more than having the basic, or functional, reading and writing skills. Literacy is, rather, a change of consciousness, the development in a person of new and more productive ways of organizing and acting on experiences. It includes the ability to set one's own goals in life, to define one's own values, and to criticize the thinking of others, including powerful institutions such as schools or corporations.

Obviously, Kozol does not believe that education in America is what
it should be. His writings advocate a radical change from the conformity and authority that Alfred Kazin described (pages 831–839). For Kozol,
parents, who were so silent during Kazin's generation in Brooklyn, must
learn to take more control over the schools to which they send their
children. Think about the issue of control of learning as you read this selection:

1. What might more conservative educators or parents say in response
   to Kozol? Would they point to a need for stronger senses of authority
   and responsibility in the graduates of public schools than Kozol's
   more open system would encourage?
2. Is it necessary that correct forms of language and thought be learned
   before intellectual experimentation can occur?
3. Must the schools always teach people to adapt to the social system
   to which they will later belong?

▶ ─────────────────

1   One morning in the spring, as I was putting work up on the
blackboard, the Reading Teacher came into my room to chat with me.
There still were a few minutes before the children would come in. It
was a bright, cheerful morning and she was in a bright and cheerful
mood. Before her, on the table beside my desk, were several piles of new
books from the library and piles of mimeographed poetry, including the
poems by Frost and Langston Hughes. On the back of the door that led
into the room was the chart that gave my class's math and spelling
scores. The math grades stopped suddenly at the score of 36, then there
was a week's jump to 60, and the grade after that was 79.

2   Deleted from those averages, however, were the scores of five or six
pupils who were so hopelessly behind that it seemed no longer meaningful even to include their average in a final grade since they actually
could score no grade at all. Among those children, thus excluded from
our final reckonings, was the boy I have called Edward. Edward, that
week, was still learning to add nine and three and to subtract six from
eight. I also was trying hard to teach him to tell time. Some of the children who were doing well in math would take turns working with him.
At moments when some kind of small victory was made, his helper
would bring him back up to my desk to show me what he had learned.
When I saw how much could be done even in such a short time and in
such grimy circumstances, I used to wonder about the judgment of
those who said that a boy like Edward could not be taught within a nor-

mal room. He was having a hard time still and his day was a steady stream of disappointments. But he was learning something. He was learning to tell time.

While she still stood there, chatting, beside the doorway, and while I was hurrying to get all the morning's work up on the board, the Reading Teacher looked out at the sunshine and she said to me happily: "Spring is a wonderful season for a teacher, Johnny." She looked at me, and she added: "It's a time when all of the hard gains of the year's work come to view."

I knew what she meant by this and I knew that it was partly out of habit that she said it. But partly, once again, I was bothered by the tone of what she said. It suggested to me that she was unaware of too much of the pain and too much of the waste around us in this school and it was clear from the sound of her voice that she allowed herself no sense at all of the extent of the tragedy which this year had been for many children. A few days before, I had taken my children to the zoo and Edward, gazing in wonderment and envy at the monkey in the cage, had said to me unhesitantly: "I wish I could be him." The same day a toy snake I had given him broke in two somehow and he instantly collapsed on the ground and began squirming on his belly and writhing in pain. He wept and screamed. At length I bought him another toy snake and he picked it up in his hand and stopped crying. An occurrence of that sort seemed characteristic of his school career. Yet he, like Stephen, like Frederick, had been receiving regular rattannings* down in the cellar all year long. I wondered if the Reading Teacher was thinking of him, too, when she told me that spring was a wonderful season for a teacher.

On a day a week later, about fifteen minutes before lunchtime, I was standing in front of the class and they were listening to a record I had brought in. The record was a collection of French children's songs. We had been spending the month reading and talking about Paris and about France. As lunchtime drew near I decided to let the children listen to the music while they were having their meal. While the record was playing, a little signal on the wall began to buzz. I left the room and hurried to the Principal's office. A white man whom I had never seen before was sitting by the Principal's desk. This man, bristling and clearly hostile to me, as was the Principal, instantly attacked me for having read to my class and distributed at their wish the poem . . . that was entitled "Ballad of the Landlord." It turned out that he was the father of one of the white boys in the class. He was also a police officer. The mimeograph of the poem, in my handwriting, was waved before my eyes. The

---

*"Rattanning" is taken from the Malaysian rattan palm tree, whose stems are remarkable for their strength. "To rattan" means to punish by whipping with a rattan switch.

Principal demanded to know what right I had to allow such a poem—not in the official Course of Study—to be read and memorized by the children in my class. I said I had not asked anyone to memorize it but that I would defend the poem and its use against her or anyone on the basis that it was a good poem. The Principal became incensed with my answer and blurted out that she did not consider it a work of art. I remember that I knew right away I was not going to give in to her. I replied, in my own anger, that I had spent a good many years studying poetry and that I was not going to accept her judgment about a poem that meant that much to me and to my pupils. Although I did not say it in these words, it was really a way of telling her that I thought myself a better judge of poetry than she. I hope that I am.

6   The parent attacked me, as well, for having forced his son to read a book about the United Nations. I had brought a book to class, one out of sixty or more volumes, that told about the U.N. and its Human Rights Commission. The man, I believe, had mistaken "human rights" for "civil rights" and he was consequently in a patriotic rage. The Principal, in fairness, made the point that she did not think there was anything really wrong with the United Nations, although in the report that she later filed on the matter, she denied this for some reason and said, instead, "I then spoke and said that I felt there was no need for this material in the classroom." The Principal's report goes on to say that, after she dismissed me to my own room, she assured the parent that "there was not another teacher in the district who would have used this poem or any material like it. I assured him that his children would be very safe from such incidents."

7   As the Principal had instructed, I returned to my class, where the children had remained quiet and had not even opened up their lunch because I had not told them to and they were patiently waiting for me to come back. We had our lunch and listened to more music and did the rest of our lessons and at quarter to two, just before school ended, the Principal called me back again. She told me I was fired. This was about eight days before the end of school. I asked her whether this was due to the talk we had had earlier but she said it was not. I asked her if it was due to an evaluation, a written report, which I had sent in on the compensatory program about a week before. This was a report that I had written, as all teachers had, in answer to a request from the School Department and in which I had said that the program seemed to me to be very poor. I was told, at the time I passed it in, that the Principal had been quite angry. But again she said it was not that. I asked her finally if my dismissal was at her request and she said, No, it came from higher up and she didn't know anything about it except that I should close up my records and leave school and not come back. She said that I should

not say good-bye to the children in my class. I asked her if she really meant this and she repeated it to me as an order.

I returned to my class, taught for ten more minutes, then gave assignments for the following morning as if I would be there and saw the children file off. After all but one were gone, that one, a little girl, helped me to pile up the books and posters and pictures with which I had tried to fill the room. It took an hour to get everything out and when it was all in my car it filled up the back seat and the space behind it and the floor, as well as the floor and half the seat in front. Outside my car, on the sidewalk, I said good-bye to this one child and told her that I would not be back again. I told her I had had a disagreement with the Principal and I asked her to say good-bye to the other children. I regretted very much now that I had not disobeyed the Principal's last order and I wished that I could have had one final chance to speak to all my pupils. The little girl, in any case, took what I had said with great solemnity and promised that she would relay my message to the other children. Then I left the school.

The next morning, an official who had charge of my case at the School Department contradicted the Principal by telling me that I was being fired at her wish. The woman to whom I spoke said the reason was the use of the poem by Langston Hughes, which was punishable because it was not in the Course of Study. She also said something to me at the time that had never been said to me before, and something that represented a much harder line on curriculum innovation than I had ever seen in print. No literature, she said, which is not in the Course of Study can *ever* be read by a Boston teacher without permission from someone higher up. When I asked her about this in more detail, she said further that no poem anyway by any Negro author can be considered permissible if it involves suffering. I thought this a very strong statement and I asked her several times again if that was really what she meant. She insisted that it was.

I asked if there would be many good poems left to read by such a standard. Wouldn't it rule out almost all great Negro literature? Her answer evaded the issue. No poetry that described suffering was felt to be suitable. The only Negro poetry that could be read in the Boston schools, she indicated, must fit a certain kind of standard or canon. The kind of poem she meant, she said by example, might be a poem that "accentuates the positive" or "describes nature" or "tells of something hopeful." Nothing was wanted of suffering, nothing that could be painful, nothing that might involve its reader in a moment of self-questioning or worry. If this is an extremely conservative or eccentric viewpoint, I think that it is nonetheless something which has to be taken seriously. For an opinion put forward in the privacy of her office by a School

Department official who has the kind of authority that that woman had must be taken to represent a certain segment of educational opinion within the Boston school system and in some ways it seems more representative even than the carefully written and carefully prepared essays of such a lady as the Deputy Superintendent. For in those various writings Miss Sullivan unquestionably has had one ear tuned to the way they were going to come across in print and sound in public whereas, in the office of a central bureaucratic person such as the lady with whom I now was talking, you receive an absolutely innocent and unedited experience in what a school system really feels and believes.

11   The same official went on a few minutes later to tell me that, in addition to having made the mistake of reading the wrong poem, I also had made an error by bringing in books to school from the Cambridge Public Library. When I told her that there were no books for reading in our classroom, except for the sets of antiquated readers, and that the need of the children was for individual reading which they would be able to begin without delay, she told me that that was all very well but still this was the Boston school system and that meant that you must not use a book that the Cambridge Library supplied. She also advised me, in answer to my question, that any complaint from a parent means automatic dismissal of a teacher anyway and that this, in itself, was therefore sufficient grounds for my release. When I repeated this later to some Negro parents they were embittered and startled. For they told me of many instances in which they had complained that a teacher whipped their child black and blue or called him a nigger openly and yet the teacher had not been released. It seemed obvious to them, as it seems to me, and would to anyone, that a complaint from a white police officer carries more weight in the Boston school system than the complaint of the mother of a Negro child.

12   I asked this official finally whether I had been considered a good teacher and what rating I had been given. She answered that she was not allowed to tell me. An instant later, whimsically reversing herself, she opened her files and told me that my rating was good. The last thing she said was that deviation from a prescribed curriculum was a serious offense and that I would never be permitted to teach in Boston again. The words she used were these: "You're out. You cannot teach in the Boston schools again. If you want to teach why don't you try a private school someday." I left her office but, before I left the building, I stopped at a table and I took out a pad of paper and wrote down what she had said.

13   The firing of a "provisional teacher" from a large public school system is not generally much of an event. As Mr. Ohrenberger was to say later, it happens commonly. When the firing is attributed to something

as socially relevant and dramatically specific as a single poem by a well-known Negro poet, however, it is not apt to go unnoticed; and, in this case, I was not ready to let it go unnoticed. I telephoned one of the civil rights leaders of Roxbury and told him what had happened. He urged me to call Phyllis Ryan, press spokesman for the Boston chapter of CORE.* Mrs. Ryan decided to set up a press conference for the same day. That afternoon, sitting at the side of the Negro minister who had begun and carried on a lonely vigil for so many days outside the Boston School Committee, I described what had just happened.

The reaction of the reporters seemed, for the most part, as astonished   14
as my own, and the direct consequence of this was that Miss Sullivan and Mr. Ohrenberger were obliged in a hurry, and without checking carefully, to back up the assertions of their own subordinates. The consequence of this, in turn, was that both of them allowed themselves to repeat and to magnify misstatements. Mr. Ohrenberger came out with a statement that I had been "repeatedly warned" about deviation from the Course of Study. Miss Sullivan's statement on my dismissal was much the same as Mr. Ohrenberger's, adding, however, a general admonition about the dangers of reading to Negro children poems written in bad grammar. Although Langston Hughes "has written much beautiful poetry," she said, "we cannot give directives to the teachers to use literature written in native dialects." It was at this time that she also made the statement to which I have alluded earlier: "We are trying to break the speech patterns of these children, trying to get them to speak properly. This poem does not present correct grammatical expression and would just entrench the speech patterns we want to break." I felt it was a grim statement.

The reactions of a large number of private individuals were re-   15
counted in the press during the following weeks, and some of them gave me a better feeling about the city in which I grew up than I had ever had before. One school employee who asked, for his safety, to remain anonymous, gave a statement to the press in which he reported that the atmosphere at school on the civil rights subject was like the atmosphere of a Gestapo. I believe that the person in question was a teacher in my school, but the fact that he had felt it necessary to keep his name anonymous, and his position unspecified, made his statement even more revelatory than if his name and position had appeared.

Another thing that reassured me was the reaction of the parents of   16
the children in my class and in the school. I did not have any means of contacting them directly, but dozens of CORE members went out into

---

*CORE stands for Congress Of Racial Equality.

the neighborhood, knocked at doors, and told parents very simply that a teacher had been fired for reading their children a good poem written by a Negro. A meeting was called by the chairman of the parent group, a woman of great poise and courage, and the parents asked me if I would come to that meeting and describe for them what had gone on. I arrived at it late and I was reluctant to go inside but, when I did go in, I found one of the most impressive parent groups that I had ever seen gathered in one hall. Instead of ten or eleven or twelve or fifteen or even twenty or thirty, which was the number of parents that usually could be rallied for a meeting on any ordinary occasion during the year, there were in the church building close to two hundred people and I discovered that several of my pupils were in the audience as well as over half the parents of the children in my class.

17   I do not want to describe all the things that were said that night, what statements of strong loyalty came forward from those mothers and fathers, or how they developed, step by step, the plan of protest which they would put into effect on the following morning and which was to be the subject of intensive press attention for a good many days to come. Looking back on it, I am sure that it was one of the most important and most valuable and most straightforward moments in my life. A white woman who was present, and who has observed race relations in Roxbury for a long while, said to me after the meeting: "I hope that you understand what happened tonight between you and those parents. Very few white people in all of their lives are ever going to be given that kind of tribute. You can do anything in your life—and I don't know what plans you have. But you will never have a better reason to feel proud."

18   I believed that what she said was true. It is hard to imagine that any other event in my life can matter more.

19   In the days after that meeting, there were a number of demonstrations at the school which had a disruptive effect on certain classes. Whether this is a good thing or a bad thing, many people may not be sure. The question is whether it is a real loss to miss one or two or even three or four days of school when none of the days that you are spending in school is worth much anyway. The Art and Reading Teachers, as well as many of the other older teachers, I was told, went on teaching and talking and grading as if in total oblivion of the turmoil breaking all around them and as if they had no idea that anything out of the ordinary might be going on. On the Monday after my firing, the parents of many students in my class kept their children home from school and went up to sit all day at their children's desks themselves. This action brought the Deputy Superintendent to the school building, and she cajoled and pleaded with the parents to give up their protest but, for once perhaps in her career, diplomacy of that type just did not work. Although the par-

ents consented at last to leave the building at her request, they did not give up the demonstration and they returned to the school two days later to carry out a longer and larger protest. At length, it took a member of the School Committee, Mr. Eisenstadt, to persuade the parents to give up their sit-in at the school. He achieved this purpose by promising them a thorough investigation into the entire matter. Before he began the investigation, however, he told me on the telephone and he told the press as well that he felt the firing was completely justified. His announcement of such a pre-judgment, along with his expressed intention to investigate anyway, seemed to me to place him in an ambiguous position and I did not therefore expect a great deal from the investigation he now was about to undertake.

Questions and Activities

▶ *COMPREHENSION QUESTIONS*

1. Considering the rest of this essay, why do you think Kozol ends the first paragraph with an account of his class's rising math scores?
2. Considering Kozol's firing, do you find his inclusion of the reading teacher's remark about spring ironic? Explain why it is ironic.
3. What seemed to be the reasons behind the white parent's attack on Kozol's teaching of a poem by Langston Hughes (paragraph 5)? The man may also have confused "human rights" with "civil rights" (paragraph 6). Why would he have become enraged about civil rights? What recent events might have contributed to his rage?
4. What reasons did the Boston public school officials give for firing Kozol? Did their reasons contradict one another?
5. Why did Kozol end this essay by saying that he had little faith in the objectivity of the school committee member's investigation? What remark by the school committee member caused Kozol's skepticism?

▶ *QUESTIONS OF RHETORICAL PURPOSE AND STRATEGY*

6. Why does Kozol spend time describing Edward and his reactions to Edward? Do you think Kozol wants you to think about whether the school system's treatment of him will harm Edward?
7. Why does Kozol use a conversational writing style? What reaction is his style intended to provoke in his readers? Why might a more technical or formal style not have achieved this effect on Kozol's readers?
8. Is Kozol's voice honest and sincere? Why?

▶ *THEME QUESTIONS*

9. Kozol describes an inner-city school system in which very traditional methods seem to have repressed or stifled the children. Why was Alfred Kazin (pages 831–839) able to survive in a similar school, but students such as Edward in Kozol's class are not? What differences mark the two types of students and the two situations? Why did Kazin's parents accept teachers' and administrators' attitudes, while the parents of Kozol's children did not?

10. Do you think a good poem can be written in a spoken dialect? What was the school administrator's argument as to why a poem written in dialect should not be used in school (paragraph 14)? Why does Kozol make a point of describing this incident in detail? Do you think he is suggesting that racial prejudice rather than an advocacy of correct language usage lies behind the administrator's reasoning? Should a child's early education emphasize skills such as correct grammar, or should it expose the child to good literature?

11. What were the official grounds for Kozol's firing? Should a school system require a teacher to follow a standard curriculum?

12. To what degree does a school "belong" to the people who live in the community and send their children to it? To what degree does a school "belong" to its professional educators or the elected school board officials?

▶ *LEARNING ACTIVITIES*

13. Select one of the dialogues described by Kozol (see paragraphs 5 and 6, 7, 8, 9–12, or 19). Working with a classmate, write a more specific script for the dialogue than appears in Kozol's essay.

    Role play the speakers in the dialogue before the rest of the class. Have the class respond to your role playing by defining the educational issue behind the dialogue. What point, in other words, was Kozol trying to make by including the dialogue?

14. Write a free response to one paragraph in Kozol's essay, describing your emotional reaction to the paragraph. Then go on to define the reasons for your response.

Golden Rule Days: American Schoolrooms

JULES HENRY

Jules Henry was an anthropologist and educational theorist who taught at Washington University in St. Louis, Missouri, from 1947 until his death in 1969 at the age of sixty-five. He had a lasting interest in the question of how particular cultures educate their young to fit into the dominant cultural patterns. Henry researched such subjects as the American family and the customs of native tribes of Mexico, Brazil, and Argentina. His anthropological books include *Jungle People* (1969), *Pathways to Madness* (1972), and the highly praised *Culture Against Man* (1963), a book on American society's tendency to impose cultural patterns of competition and success over the inclinations of the individual for affection, personal expression, and the release of emotional impulses. Henry also wrote many essays for professional and popular journals.

The essay reprinted here is taken from *Culture Against Man*. In it, Henry provides many examples of classroom activity drawn from middle- and upper-class suburban classrooms in the late 1950s and early 1960s. These examples fall into two patterns. Early in the essay, Henry's examples describe teachers and students engaged in learning games that are used by teachers to instill competitive values in children. Skills such as spelling, arithmetic, and grammar are learned through games like "baseball spelling," in which those who master the skills win the game and those who do not lose. Later in the essay, Henry includes examples from progressive classrooms in which the teachers act as friends to the students, encouraging cooperation through affection, flexibility, and openness. Competition, in these classrooms, is replaced by friendly support and peer influence on student behavior.

Henry, as the objective anthropologist, does not favor one or the other of the classroom approaches. He argues that, whatever classroom methods are used, teachers must keep in mind the overall cultural contexts within which their students live. He brings up the question of whether it is good for individuals who are preparing to enter a competitive society to be placed in classrooms where they receive only positive responses and reinforcement from teachers.

Consider Henry's essay in the context of those by Alfred Kazin (pages 831–839) and Jonathan Kozol (pages 842–849). Kazin describes the negative aspects of his Brownsville schooling, yet he obviously came out of this repressive and authoritarian system with many important skills and with a burning desire to create his own expressions of significance and value. Could the skills he learned in school, along with this desire, have accounted for his later success as a writer and teacher? Kozol's highly critical account of a traditional, authoritarian system in which blacks are mistreated because of their color and socioeconomic background suggests the need for communities to control their own schools, in which children will be thought of as equals by teachers and administrators. You might ask yourself, considering Kazin's and Kozol's essays together, whether traditional authoritative approaches to teaching have to result in repressive classroom environments. Henry provides some pertinent material for developing your opinion on this issue of the balancing of freedom and discipline in education:

1. What are the benefits of a totally open classroom, one in which each student is encouraged to follow her or his own direction? On the other hand, are there any benefits to a repressive classroom, in which students speak only when called on and never move about on their own initiative?
2. What might be an ideal blend of the two? Can you imagine, in other words, a classroom where learning was carefully controlled but flexible enough to encourage creativity?

▶ ────────────────

Introduction

1   School is an institution for drilling children in cultural orientations. Educationists have attempted to free the school from drill, but have failed because they have gotten lost among a multitude of phantasms—always choosing the most obvious ''enemy'' to attack. Furthermore, with every enemy destroyed, new ones are installed among the old fortifications—the enduring contradictory maze of the culture. Educators think that when they have made arithmetic or spelling into a game; made it unnecessary for children to ''sit up straight''; defined the relation between teacher and children as democratic; and introduced plants, fish, and hamsters into schoolrooms, they have settled the problem of drill. They are mistaken.

Education and the Human Condition

Learning to Learn. The paradox of the human condition is ex-   2
pressed more in education than elsewhere in human culture, because
learning to learn has been and continues to be *Homo sapiens'* most for-
midable evolutionary task. Although it is true that mammals, as compared to birds and fishes, have to learn so much that it is difficult to say
by the time we get to chimpanzees what behavior is inborn and what is
learned, the learning task has become so enormous for man that today
learning—education—along with survival, constitutes a major preoccupation. In all the fighting over education we are simply saying that
we are not yet satisfied—after about a million years of struggling to become human—that we have mastered the fundamental human task,   ①
learning. It must also be clear that we will never quite learn how to
learn, for since *Homo sapiens* is self-changing, and since the *more* culture changes the *faster* it changes, man's methods and rate of learning
will never quite keep pace with his need to learn. This is the heart of the
problem of "cultural lag," for each fundamental scientific discovery
presents man with an incalculable number of problems which he cannot foresee. Who, for example, would have anticipated that the discoveries of Einstein would have presented us with the social problems of
the nuclear age, or that information theory would have produced unemployment and displacement in world markets?

Fettering and Freeing. Another learning problem inherent in the   3
human condition is the fact that we must conserve culture while
changing it; that we must always be *more* sure of surviving than of   ②
adapting—*as we see it.* Whenever a new idea appears our first concern
as *animals* must be that it does not kill us; then, and only then, can we
look at it from other points of view. While it is true that we are often
mistaken, either because we become enchanted with certain modes of
thought or because we cannot anticipate their consequences, this tendency to look first at survival has resulted in fettering the capacity to
learn new things. In general, primitive people solved this problem simply by walling their children off from new possibilities by educational
methods that, largely through fear (including ridicule, beating, and
mutilation) so narrowed the perceptual sphere that other than traditional ways of viewing the world became unthinkable. Thus throughout history the cultural pattern has been a device for binding the intellect. Today, when we think we wish to free the mind so it will soar, we
are still, nevertheless, bound by the ancient paradox, for we must hold
our culture together through clinging to old ideas lest, in adopting new
ones, we literally cease to exist.

4   In searching the literature on the educational practices of other civilizations I have found nothing that better expresses the need to teach and to fetter than the following, from an account by a traveler along the Niger River in Africa in the fourteenth century:

> . . . their zeal for learning the Koran by heart [is so great that] they put their children in chains if they show any backwardness in memorizing it, and they are not set free until they have it by heart. I visited the *qadi* in his house on the day of the festival. His children were chained up, so I said to him, "Will you not let them loose?" He replied, "I shall not do so until they learn the Koran by heart."[1]

Perhaps the closest material parallel we have to this from our own cultural tradition is the stocks in which ordinary English upper-class children were forced to stand in the eighteenth century while they pored over their lessons at home. The fettering of the mind while we "set the spirit free" or the fettering of the spirit as we free the mind is an abiding paradox of "civilization" in its more refined dimensions. It is obvious that chimpanzees are incapable of this paradox. It is this capacity to pass from the jungles of the animal world into the jungle of paradox of the human condition that, more than anything else, marks off human from animal learning. It is this jungle that confronts the child in his early days at school, and that seals his destiny—if it has not previously been determined by poverty—as an eager mind or as a faceless learner.

5   Since education is always against some things and for others, it bears the burden of the cultural obsessions. While the Old Testament extols without cease the glory of the One God, it speaks with equal emphasis against the gods of the Philistines; while the children of the Dakota Indians learned loyalty to their own tribe, they learned to hate the Crow; and while our children are taught to love our American democracy, they are taught contempt for totalitarian regimes. It thus comes about that most educational systems are imbued with anxiety and hostility, that they are against as many things as they are for. Because, therefore, so much anxiety inheres in any human educational system—anxiety that it may free when it should fetter; anxiety that it may fetter when it should free; anxiety that it may teach sympathy when it should teach anger; anxiety that it may disarm where it should arm—our contemporary education system is constantly under attack. When, in anxiety about the present state of our world, we turn upon the schools with even more venom than we turn on our government, we are "right" in the sense that it is in the schools that the basic binding and

---

[1]Ibn Battuta, *Travels in Asia and Africa*, London: Broadway House, Carter Lane, 1957, p. 330. (Translated and selected by H. A. R. Gibb, from the original written in 1325–54.)

freeing processes that will "save" us will be established. But being "right" derives not so much from the faults of our schools but from the fact that the schools are the central conserving force of the culture. The Great Fear thus turns our hostility unerringly in the direction of the focus of survival and change, in the direction of education.

Creativity and Absurdity. The function of education has never been to free the mind and the spirit of man, but to bind them; and to the end that the mind and spirit of his children should never escape *Homo sapiens* has employed praise, ridicule, admonition, accusation, mutilation, and even torture to chain them to the culture pattern. Throughout most of his historic course *Homo sapiens* has wanted from his children acquiescence, not originality. It is natural that this should be so, for where every man is unique there is no society, and where there is no society there can be no man. Contemporary American educators think they want creative children, yet it is an open question as to what they expect these children to create. And certainly the classrooms—from kindergarten to graduate school—in which they expect it to happen are not crucibles of creative activity and thought. It stands to reason that were young people truly creative the culture would fall apart, for originality, by definition, is different from what is given, and what is given is the culture itself. From the endless, pathetic, "creative hours" of kindergarten to the most abstruse problems in sociology and anthropology, the function of education is to prevent the truly creative intellect from getting out of hand. Only in the exact and the biological sciences do we permit unlimited freedom, for we have (but only since the Renaissance, since Galileo and Bruno underwent the Inquisition) found a way—or *thought* we had found a way—to bind the explosive powers of science in the containing vessel of the social system.

- American classrooms, like educational institutions anywhere, express the values, preoccupations, and fears found in the culture as a whole. School has no choice; it must train the children to fit the culture as it is. School can give training in skills; it cannot teach creativity. All the American school can conceivably do is nurture creativity when it appears. And who has the eyes to see it? Since the creativity that is conserved and encouraged will always be that which seems to do the most for the culture, which seems at the moment to do the most for the obsessions and the brutal preoccupations and anxieties from which we all suffer, schools nowadays encourage the child with gifts in mathematics and the exact sciences. But the child who has the intellectual strength to see through social shams is of no consequence to the educational system.

7

8   • Creative intellect is mysterious, devious, and irritating. An intellectually creative child may fail, for example, in social studies, simply because he cannot understand the stupidities he is taught to believe as "fact." He may even end up agreeing with his teachers that he is "stupid" in social studies. Learning social studies is, to no small extent, whether in elementary school or the university, learning to be stupid. Most of us accomplish this task before we enter high school. But the child with a socially creative imagination will not be encouraged to play among new social systems, values, and relationships; nor is there much likelihood of it, if for no other reason than that the social studies teachers will perceive such a child as a poor student. Furthermore, such a child will simply be unable to fathom the absurdities that seem transparent *truth* to the teacher. What idiot believes in the "law of supply and demand," for example? But the children who do tend to *become* idiots, and learning to be an idiot is part of growing up! Or, as Camus put it, learning to be *absurd*.* Thus the child who finds it impossible to learn to think the absurd the truth, who finds it difficult to accept absurdity as a way of life, the intellectually creative child whose mind makes him flounder like a poor fish in the net of absurdities flung around him in school, usually comes to think himself stupid.

9   • The schools have therefore never been places for the stimulation of young minds. If all through school the young were provoked to question the Ten Commandments, the sanctity of revealed religion, the foundations of patriotism, the profit motive, the two-party system, monogamy, the laws of incest, and so on, we would have more creativity than we could handle. In teaching our children to accept fundamentals of social relationships and religious beliefs without question we follow the ancient highways of the human race, which extend backward into the dawn of the species, and indefinitely into the future. There must therefore be more of the caveman than of the spaceman about our teachers.

10   Up to this point I have argued that learning to learn is man's foremost
Sum   evolutionary task, that the primary aim of education has been to fetter the mind and the spirit of man rather than to free them, and that nowadays we confront this problem in our effort to stimulate thought

---

*Albert Camus (1913–1960) was a French writer whose works established existential philosophy's emphasis on the idea that human life is essentially absurd.

while preventing the mind of the child from going too far. I have also urged that since education, as the central institution for the training of the young in the ways of the culture, is thus burdened with its obsessive fears and hates, contemporary attacks upon our schools are the reflection of a nervousness inherent in the school as a part of the central obsession. Finally, I argued that creativity is the last thing wanted in any culture because of its potentialities for disruptive thinking; that the primordial dilemma of all education derives from the necessity of training the mighty brain of *Homo sapiens* to be stupid; and that creativity, when it is encouraged (as in science in our culture), occurs only after the creative thrust of an idea has been tamed and directed toward socially approved ends. In this sense, then, creativity can become the most obvious conformity. In this sense we can expect scientists—our cultural maximizers—to be socially no *more* creative than the most humble elementary school teacher, and probably less creative socially than a bright second-grader.

Communication

Much of what I have to say in the following pages pivots on the inordinate capacity of a human being to learn more than one thing at a time. Although it is true that all the higher orders of animals can learn several things at a time, this capacity for polyphasic learning reaches unparalleled development in man. A child writing the word "August" on the board, for example, is not only learning to word "August" but also how to hold the chalk without making it squeak, how to write clearly, how to keep going even though the class is tittering at his slowness, how to appraise the glances of the children in order to know whether he is doing it right or wrong, et cetera. If the spelling, arithmetic, or music lesson were only what it appeared to be, the education of the American child would be much simpler; but it is all the things the child learns *along with* his subject matter that really constitute the drag on the educational process as it applies to the curriculum.

A classroom can be compared to a communications system, for certainly there is a flow of messages between teacher (transmitter) and pupils (receivers) and among the pupils; contacts are made and broken, messages can be sent at a certain rate of speed only, and so on. But there is also another interesting characteristic of communications systems that is applicable to classrooms, and that is their inherent tendency to generate *noise. Noise*, in communications theory, applies to all those random fluctuations of the system that cannot be controlled. They are the sounds that are not part of the message: the peculiar quality communicated to the voice by the composition of the telephone circuit, the static on the radio, and so forth. In a classroom lesson on arithmetic, for example, such *noise* would range all the way from the competitiveness of the students, the quality of the teacher's voice ("I remember exactly how she sounded when she told me to sit down"), to the shuffling of the children's feet. The striking thing about the child is that along with his arithmetic—his "messages about arithmetic"—he learns all the noise in the system also. It is this inability to avoid *learning the noise with the subject matter* that constitutes one of the greatest hazards for an organism so prone to polyphasic learning as man. It is this that brings it about that an objective observer cannot tell which is being learned in any lesson, the *noise* or the formal subject matter. But—and mark this well—it is *not* primarily the message (let us say, the arithmetic or the spelling) that constitutes the most important subject matter to be learned, but the noise! The most significant cultural learnings—primarily the cultural drives—are communicated as *noise.*

13   Let us take up these points by studying selected incidents in some of the suburban classrooms my students and I studied over a period of six years.

The Realm of Song

14   It is March 17 and the children are singing songs from Ireland and her neighbors. The teacher plays on the piano, while the children sing. While some children sing, a number of them hunt in the index, find a song belonging to one of Ireland's neighbors, and raise their hands in order that they may be called on to name the next song. The singing is of that pitchless quality always heard in elementary school classrooms. The teacher sometimes sings through a song first, in her off-key, weakishly husky voice.

The usual reason for having this kind of a song period is that the children are broadened, while they learn something about music and singing.

15   It is true that the children learn something about singing, but what they learn is to sing like everybody else, in the standard, elementary school pitchlessness of the English-speaking world—a phenomenon impressive enough for D. H. Lawrence to have mentioned it in *Lady Chatterly's Lover*. The difficulty in achieving true pitch is so pervasive among us that missionaries carry it with them to distant jungles, teaching the natives to sing hymns off key. Hence on Sundays we would hear

our Pilagá Indian friends, all of them excellent musicians in the Pilagá scale, carefully copy the missionaries by singing Anglican hymns, translated into Pilagá, off key exactly as sharp or as flat as the missionaries sang. Thus one of the first things a child with a good ear learns in elementary school is to be musically stupid; he learns to doubt or to scorn his innate musical capacities.

But possibly more important than this is the use to which teacher   16
and pupils put the lesson in ways not related at all to singing or to Ireland and her neighbors. To the teacher this was an opportunity to let the children somehow share the social aspects of the lesson with her, to democratically participate in the selection of the songs. The consequence was distraction from singing as the children hunted in the index and raised their hands to have their song chosen. The net result was to activate the competitive, achievement, and dominance drives of the children, as they strove with one another for the teacher's attention, and through her, to get the class to do what they wanted it to do. In this way the song period on Ireland and her neighbors was scarcely a lesson in singing but rather one in extorting the maximal benefit for the Self from *any* situation. The first lesson a child has to learn when he comes to school is that lessons are not what they seem. He must then forget this and act as if they were. This is the first step toward "school mental health"; it is also the first step in becoming absurd. In the first and second grades teachers constantly scold children because they do not raise their hands enough—the prime symbol of having learned what school is all about. After that, it is no longer necessary; the kids have "tumbled" to the idea.

The second lesson is to put the teachers' and students' criteria in   17
place of his own. He must learn that the proper way to sing is tunelessly and not the way *he* hears the music; that the proper way to paint is the way the teacher says, not the way he sees it; that the proper attitude is not pleasure but competitive horror at the success of his classmates, and so on. And these lessons must be so internalized that he will fight his parents if they object. The early schooling process is not sucessful unless it has accomplished in the child an acquiescence in its criteria, unless the child *wants* to think the way school has taught him to think. He must have accepted alienation as a rule of life. What we see in the kindergarten and the early years of school is the pathetic surrender of babies. How could it be otherwise?

Now, if children are taught to adopt alienation as a way of life, it fol-   18
lows that they must have feelings of inadequacy, for nothing so saps self-confidence as alienation from the Self. It would follow that school, the chief agent in the process, must try to provide the children with "ego support," for culture tries to remedy the ills it creates.

19   Hence the effort to give recognition; and hence the conversion of the songfest into an exercise in Self-realization. That anything essential was nurtured in this way is an open question, for the kind of individuality that was recognized as the children picked titles out of the index was mechanical, without a creative dimension, and under the strict control of the teacher. Let us conclude this discussion by saying that *school metamorphoses the child, giving it the kind of Self the school can manage, and then proceeds to minister to the Self it has made.*

20   Perhaps I have put the matter grossly, appearing to credit the school with too much formative power. So let us say this: let us grant that American children, being American, come to school on the first day with certain potentialities for experiencing success and failure, for enjoying the success of their mates or taking pleasure in their failure, for competitiveness, for cooperation, for driving to achieve or for coasting along, et cetera. But school cannot handle variety, for as an institution dealing with masses of children it can manage only on the assumption of a homogeneous mass. Homogeneity is therefore accomplished by defining the children in a certain way and by handling all situations uniformly. In this way no child is directly coerced. It is simply that the child must react in terms of the institutional definitions or he fails. The first two years of school are spent not so much in learning the rudiments of the three Rs, as in learning definitions.

21   It would be foolish to imagine that school, as a chief molder of character, could do much more than homogenize the children, but it does do more—it sharpens to a cutting edge the drives the culture needs.

22   If you bind or prune an organism so it can move only in limited ways, it will move rather excessively in that way. If you lace a man into a strait jacket so he can only wiggle his toes, he will wiggle them *hard.* Since in school children are necessarily constrained to limited human expression, under the direction of the teacher, they will have a natural tendency to do with exaggerated enthusiasm what they are permitted to do. They are like the man in the strait jacket. In class children are usually not permitted to talk much, to walk around much, to put their arms around each other during lessons, to whistle or sing. But they are permitted to raise their hands and go to the pencil sharpener almost at will. Thus hand-raising, going to the pencil sharpener, or hunting in the back of a song book for a song for the class to sing are not so much activities stemming from the requirements of an immediate situation as expressions of the intensified need of the organism for relief from the five-hour-a-day pruning and confining process. This goes under the pedagogical title of "release of tension"; but in our view the issue is that what the children are at length permitted—and invited—to do, and what they therefore often throw themselves into with the enthusiasm of multiple

pent-up feelings, are cultural drive-activities narrowly construed by the school. In that context the next example is not only an expression by the children of a wish to be polite, but an inflated outpouring of contained human capacities, released enthusiastically into an available—because approved—cultural channel.

On Hanging Up a Coat

The observer is just entering her fifth-grade classroom for the observation period. The teacher says, "Which one of you nice, polite boys would like to take [the observer's] coat and hang it up?" From the waving hands, it would seem that all would like to claim the title. The teacher chooses one child, who takes the observer's coat. The teacher says, "Now, children, who will tell [the observer] what we have been doing?"   *23*

The usual forest of hands appears, and a girl is chosen to tell. ... The teacher conducted the arithmetic lessons mostly by asking, "Who would like to tell the answer to the next problem?" This question was usually followed by the appearance of a large and agitated forest of hands, with apparently much competition to answer.   *24*

What strikes us here are the precision with which the teacher was able to mobilize the potentialities in the boys for proper social behavior, and the speed with which they responded. One is impressed also with the fact that although the teacher could have said, "Johnny, will you please hang up [the observer's] coat?" she chose rather to activate all the boys, and thus give *them* an opportunity to activate their Selves, in accordance with the alienated Selfhood objectives of the culture. The children were thus given an opportunity to exhibit a frantic willingness to perform an act of uninvolved solicitude for the visitor; in this way each was given also a chance to communicate to the teacher his eagerness to please her "in front of company."   *25*

The mere appearance of the observer in the doorway sets afoot a kind of classroom destiny of self-validation and actualization of pupil-teacher communion, and of activation of the cultural drives. In the observer's simple act of entrance the teacher perceives instantly the possibility of exhibiting her children and herself, and of proving to the visitor, and once again to herself, that the pupils are docile creatures, eager to hurl their "company" Selves into this suburban American tragi-comedy of welcome. From behind this scenery of mechanical values, meanwhile, the most self-centered boy might emerge a *papier*   *26* *maché* Galahad,* for what he does is not for the benefit of the visitor but for the gratification of the teacher and of his own culturally molded Self. The large number of waving hands proves that most of the boys have already become absurd; but they have no choice. Suppose they sat there frozen?

27   From this question we move to the inference that the skilled teacher sets up many situations in such a way that *a negative attitude can be construed only as treason.* The function of questions like, "Which one of you nice polite boys would like to take [the observer's] coat and hang it up?" is to bind the children into absurdity—to compel them to acknowledge that absurdity is existence, to acknowlege that it is better to exist absurd than not to exist at all.

28   It is only natural, then, that when the teacher next asks, "Now who will tell what we have been doing?" and "Who would like to tell the answer to the next problem?" there should appear "a large and agitated forest of hands," for failure to raise the hand could be interpreted only as an act of aggression. The "arithmetic" lesson, transformed by the teacher, had become an affirmation of her matriarchal charisma as symbol of the system.

29   The reader will have observed that the question is not put, "Who *has* the answer to the next problem?" but "Who *would like to tell*" it? Thus, what at one time in our culture was phrased as a challenge to skill in arithmetic, becomes here an invitation to group participation. What is sought is a sense of "groupiness" rather than a distinguishing of individuals. Thus, as in the singing lesson an attempt was made to deny that it was a group activity, in the arithmetic lesson the teacher attempts to deny that it is an individual one. The essential issue is that *nothing is but what it is made to be by the alchemy of the system.*

30   In a society where competition for the basic cultural goods is a pivot of action, people cannot be taught to love one another, for those who do cannot compete with one another, except in play. It thus becomes necessary for the school, without appearing to do so, to teach children how to hate, without appearing to do so, for our culture cannot tolerate the idea that babes should hate each other. How does the school accomplish this ambiguity? Obviously through competition itself, for what has greater potential for creating hostility than competition? One might say that this is one of the most "creative" features of school. Let us consider an incident from a fifth-grade arithmetic lesson.

---

*Galahad was one of the knights of King Arthur's Round Table. He succeeded in the quest for the Holy Grail and was known for his innocence and chastity. Henry is suggesting here that modern students are not true Galahads because their quests are not inspired by higher goals.

At the Blackboard

Boris had trouble reducing "12/16" to the lowest terms, and   *31*
could only get as far as "6/8". The teacher asked him quietly if
that was as far as he could reduce it. She suggested he "think."
Much heaving up and down and waving of hands by the other
children, all frantic to correct him. Boris pretty unhappy, probably mentally paralyzed. The teacher, quiet, patient, ignores
the others and concentrates with look and voice on Boris. She
says, "Is there a bigger number than two you can divide into the
two parts of the fraction?" After a minute or two, she becomes
more urgent, but there is no response from Boris. She then turns
to the class and says, "Well, who can tell Boris what the number is?" A forest of hands appears, and the teacher calls Peggy.
Peggy says that four may be divided into the numerator and the
denominator.

Thus Boris' failure has made it possible for Peggy to succeed; his depres-   *32*
sion is the price of her exhilaration; his misery the occasion for her
rejoicing. This is the standard condition of the American elementary
school, and is why so many of us feel a contraction of the heart even if
someone we never knew succeeds merely at garnering plankton in the
Thames: because so often somebody's success has been bought at the
cost of our failure. To a Zuñi, Hopi, or Dakota Indian, Peggy's performance would seem cruel beyond belief, for competition, the wringing
of success from somebody's failure, is a form of torture foreign to those
noncompetitive redskins. Yet Peggy's action seems natural to us; and
so it is. How else would you run our world? And since all but the
brightest children have the constant experience that others succeed at
their expense they cannot but develop an inherent tendency to hate—to
hate the success of others, to hate others who are successful, and to be
determined to prevent it. Along with this, naturally, goes the hope that
others will fail. This hatred masquerades under the euphemistic name
of "envy."

Looked at from Boris' point of view, the nightmare at the blackboard   *33*
was, perhaps, a lesson in controlling himself so that he would not fly
shrieking from the room under the enormous public pressure. Such experiences imprint on the mind of every man in our culture the *Dream of
Failure*, so that over and over again, night in, night out, even at the pin-
nacle of success, a man will dream not of success, but of failure. *The external nightmare is internalized for life*. It is this dream that, above all
other things, provides the fierce human energy required by technological drivenness. It was not so much that Boris was learning arithmetic,

but that he was learning the *essential nightmare. To be successful in our culture one must learn to dream of failure.*

34   From the point of view of the other children, of course, they were learning to yap at the heels of a failure. And why not? Have they not dreamed the dream of flight themselves? If the culture does not teach us to fly from failure or to rush in, hungry for success where others have failed, who will try again where others have gone broke? Nowadays, as misguided teachers try to soften the blow of classroom failure, they inadvertently sap the energies of success. The result will be a nation of chickens unwilling to take a chance.

35   When we say that "culture teaches drives and values" we do not state the case quite precisely. One should say, rather, that culture (and especially the school) provides the occasions in which drives and values are *experienced in events* that strike us with *overwhelming and constant force.* To say that culture "teaches" puts the matter too mildly. Actually culture invades and infests the mind as an obsession. If it does not, culture will not "work," for only an obsession has the power to withstand the impact of critical differences; to fly in the face of contradiction; to engulf the mind so that it will see the world only as the culture decrees that it shall be seen; to compel a person to be absurd. The central emotion in obsession is fear, and the central obsession in education is fear of failure. In order not to fail most students are willing to believe anything and to care not whether what they are told is true or false. Thus one becomes absurd through being afraid; but paradoxically, *only by remaining absurd can one feel free from fear.* Hence the immovableness of the absurd.

36   In examining education as a process of teaching the culture pattern, I have discussed a singing lesson, an arithmetic lesson, and the hanging up of a coat. Now let us consider a spelling lesson in a fourth-grade class.

"Spelling Baseball"

37   The children form a line along the back of the room. They are to play "spelling baseball," and they have lined up to be chosen for the two teams. There is much noise, but the teacher quiets it. She has selected a boy and a girl and sent them to the front of the room as team captains to choose their teams. As the boy and girl pick the children to form their teams, each child chosen takes a seat in orderly succession around the room. Apparently they know the game well. Now Tom, who has not yet been chosen, tries to call attention to himself in order to be chosen. Dick shifts his position to be more in the direct line of vision of the

choosers, so that he may not be overlooked. He seems quite
anxious. Jane, Tom, Dick, and one girl whose name the observer does not know, are the last to be chosen. The teacher even
has to remind the choosers that Dick and Jane have not been
chosen. . . .

The teacher now gives out words for the children to spell, and   38
they write them on the board. Each word is a pitched ball, and
each correctly spelled word is a base hit. The children move
around the room from base to base as their teammates spell the
words correctly. With some of the words the teacher gives a
little phrase: "Tongue, watch your tongue, don't let it say
things that aren't kind; butcher, the butcher is a good friend to
have; dozen, twelve of many things; knee, get down on your
knee; pocket, keep your hand out of your pocket, and anybody
else's. No talking! Three out!" The children say, "Oh, oh!"

The outs seem to increase in frequency as each side gets near   39
the children chosen last. The children have great difficulty
spelling "August." As they make mistakes, those in the seats
say, "No!" The teacher says, "Man on third." As a child at the
board stops and thinks, the teacher says, "There's a time limit;
you can't take too long, honey." At last, after many children
fail on "August" one child gets it right and returns, grinning
with pleasure, to her seat. . . . The motivation level in this
game seems terrific. All the children seem to watch the board,
to know what's right and wrong, and seem quite keyed up.
There is no lagging in moving from base to base. The child who
is now writing "Thursday" stops to think after the first letter,
and the children snicker. He stops after another letter. More
snickers. He gets the word wrong. There are frequent signs of
joy from the children when their side is right.

Since English is not pronounced as it is spelled, "language skills" are   40
a disaster for educators as well as for students. We start the problem of
"spelling baseball" with the fact that the spelling of English is so mixed
up and contradictory and makes such enormous demands on the capacity for being absurd that nowadays most people cannot spell. "Spelling
baseball" is an effort to take the "weariness, the fever, and the fret" out
of spelling by absurdly transforming it into a competitive game. Over
and over again it has seemed to our psychologist designers of curriculum scenery that the best way to relieve boredom is to transmute it into
competition. Since children are usually good competitors, though they
may never become good spellers, and although they may never learn to
spell "success" (which really should be written *sukses*), they know

what it *is*, how to go after it, and how it feels not to have it. A competitive game is indicated when children are failing, because the drive to succeed in the *game* may carry them to victory over the *subject matter*. At any rate it makes spelling less boring for the teacher and the students, for it provides the former with a drama of excited children, and the latter with a motivation that transports them out of the secular dreariness of classroom routine. ''Spelling baseball'' is thus a major effort in the direction of making things seem not as they are. But once a spelling lesson is cast in the form of a game of baseball a great variety of *noise* enters the system, because the sounds of *baseball* (the baseball ''messages'') cannot but be *noise* in a system intended to communicate *spelling*. Let us therefore analyze some of the baseball noise that has entered this spelling system from the sandlots and the bleachers.

41   We see first that a teacher has set up a choosing-rejecting system directly adopted from kid baseball. I played ball just that way in New York. The two best players took turns picking out teammates from the bunch, coldly selecting the best hitters and fielders first; as we went down the line it didn't make much difference who got the chronic muffers (the kids who couldn't catch a ball) and fanners (the kids who couldn't hit a ball). I recall that the kids who were not good players danced around and called out to the captains, ''How about me, Slim? How about me?'' Or they called attention to themselves with gestures and intense grimaces, as they pointed to their chests. It was pretty noisy. Of course, it didn't make any difference because the captains knew whom they were going to try to get, and there was not much of an issue after the best players had been sorted out to one or the other team. It was an honest jungle and there was nothing in it that didn't belong to the high tension of kid baseball. But nobody was ever left out; and even the worst were never permitted to sit on the sidelines.

42   ''Spelling baseball'' is thus sandlot baseball dragged into the schoolroom and bent to the uses of spelling. If we reflect that one could not settle a baseball game by converting it into a spelling lesson, we see that baseball is bizarrely *irrelevant* to spelling. If we reflect further that a kid who is a poor speller might yet be a magnificent ballplayer, we are even further impressed that learning spelling through baseball is learning by absurd association. In ''spelling baseball'' words become detached from their real significance and become assimilated to baseballs. Thus a spelling game that promotes absurd associations provides an indispensable bridge between the larger culture, where doubletalk is supreme, and the primordial meaningfulness of language. It provides also an introduction to those associations of mutually irrelevant ideas so well known to us from advertising—girls and vodka gimlets, people and billiard balls, lipstick and tree-houses, et cetera.

In making spelling into a baseball game one drags into the classroom   43
whatever associations a child may have to the impersonal sorting process of kid baseball, and in this way some of the *noise* from the baseball
system enters spelling. But there are differences between the baseball
world and the "spelling baseball" world also. Having participated in
competitive athletics all through my youth, I seem to remember that
we sorted ourselves by skills, and we recognized that some of us were
worse than others. In baseball I also seem to remember that if we struck
out or muffed a ball we hated ourselves and turned flips of rage, while
our teammates sympathized with our suffering. In "spelling baseball"
one experiences the sickening sensation of being left out as others are
picked—to such a degree that the teachers even have to remind team
captains that some are unchosen. One's failure is paraded before the
class minute upon minute, until, when the worst spellers are the only
ones left, the conspicuousness of the failures has been enormously
increased. Thus the *noise* from baseball is amplified by a *noise* factor
specific to the classroom.

It should not be imagined that I "object" to all of this, for in the first   44
place I am aware of the indispensable social functions of the spelling
game, and in the second place, I can see that the rendering of failure conspicuous, the forcing of it on the mind of the unchosen child by a process of creeping extrusion from the group, cannot but intensify the
quality of the essential nightmare, and thus render an important service
to the culture. Without nightmares human culture has never been possible. Without hatred competition cannot take place.

One can see from the description of the game that drive is heightened   45
in a complex competitive interlock: each child competes with every
other to get the words right; each child competes with all for status and
approval among his peers; each child competes with the other children
for the approval of the teacher; and, finally, each competes as a member
of a team. Here failure will be felt doubly because although in an ordinary spelling lesson one fails alone, in "spelling baseball" one lets
down the children on one's team. Thus though in the game the motivation toward spelling is heightened so that success becomes triumph, so
does failure become disaster. The greater the excitement the more intense the feeling of success and failure, and the importance of spelling
or failing to spell "August" becomes exaggerated. But it is in the nature
of an obsession to exaggerate the significance of events.

We come now to the *noise* introduced by the teacher. In order to   46
make the words clear she puts each one in a sentence: "Tongue: watch
your tongue; don't let it say things that aren't kind." "Butcher: the
butcher is a good friend to have." "Dozen: twelve of many things."
"Knee: get down on your knee." "Pocket: keep your hand out of your

pocket, and anybody else's.'' More relevant associations to the words would be, ''The leg bends at the knee.'' ''A butcher cuts up meat.'' ''I carry something in my pocket,'' etc. What the teacher's sentences do is introduce a number of her idiosyncratic cultural preoccupations, without clarifying anything; for there is no *necessary* relation between butcher and friend, between floor and knee, between pocket and improperly intrusive hands, and so on. In her way, therefore, the teacher establishes the same irrelevance between words and associations as the game does between spelling and baseball. She amplifies the *noise* by introducing ruminations from her own inner communication system.

Carping Criticism

47   The unremitting effort by the system to bring the cultural drives to a fierce pitch must ultimately turn the children against one another; and though they cannot punch one another in the nose or pull each other's hair in class, they can vent some of their hostility in carping criticism of one another's work. Carping criticism is so destructive of the early tillerings of those creative impulses we cherish, that it will be good to give the matter further review.

48   Few teachers are like Miss Smith in this sixth-grade class:

> The Parent-Teachers Association is sponsoring a school frolic, and the children have been asked to write jingles for publicity. For many of the children, the writing of a jingle seems painful. They are restless, bite their pencils, squirm in their seats, speak to their neighbors, and from time to time pop up with questions like, ''Does it have to rhyme, Miss Smith?'' At last she says, ''Alright, let's read some of the jingles now.'' Child after child says he ''couldn't get one,'' but some have succeeded. One girl has written a very long jingle, obviously the best in the class. However, instead of using ''Friday'' as the frolic day, she used ''Tuesday,'' and several protests were heard from the children. Miss Smith defended her, saying ''Well, she made a mistake. But you are too prone to criticize. If *you* could only do so well!''

49   In our six years of work, in hundreds of hours of observation in elementary and high schools, Miss Smith is unique in that she scolded the children for tearing down the work of a classmate. Other teachers support such attacks, sometimes even somewhat against their will.

50   ''For many of the children, the writing of a jingle seems painful'' says the record. ''They are restless, bite their pencils, squirm in their seats....'' What are they afraid of but failure? This is made clear by Miss Smith's angry defense of the outstanding child as she says to her

critics, "If only *you* could do so well!"

In a cooperative society carping is less likely to occur. Spiro says of   *51*
the *kibbutz:*

> ... The emphasis on group criticism can potentially engender competitive,
> if not hostile feelings among the children. Frequently, for example, the chil-
> dren read their essays aloud, and the others are then asked to comment. Only
> infrequently could we detect any hostility in the criticisms of the students,
> and often the evaluations were filled with praise.[2]

But in Miss Smith's class, because the children have failed while one of
their number has succeeded, they carp. And why not? However we may
admire Miss Smith's defense of the successful child, we must not let
our own "inner Borises" befog our thinking. A competitive culture endures by tearing people down. Why blame the children for doing it?

Let us now consider two examples of carping criticism from a fifth-   *52*
grade class as the children report on their projects and read original stories.

> Bill has given a report on tarantulas. As usual the teacher waits   *53*
> for volunteers to comment on the child's report.
>
> MIKE: The talk was well illustrated and well prepared.
> BOB: Bill had a *piece of paper* [for his notes] and teacher said he
>   should have them on *cards.* . . .
>
> Bill says he could not get any cards, and the teacher says he
> should tear the paper the next time he has no cards.
>
> BOB: He held the paper behind him. If he had had to look at it, it
>   wouldn't have been very nice.
>
> The children are taking turns reading to the class stories they   *54*
> have made up. Charlie's is called *The Unknown Guest.*
>
> "One dark, dreary night, on a hill a house stood. This house
> was forbidden territory for Bill and Joe, but they were going in
> anyway. The door creaked, squealed, slammed. A voice warned
> them to go home. They went upstairs. A stair cracked. They
> entered a room. A voice said they might as well stay and find
> out now; and their father came out. He laughed and they
> laughed, but they never forgot their adventure together."
>
> TEACHER: Are there any words that give you the mood of the
>   story?
> LUCY: He could have made the sentences a little better. . . .

[2]Melford Spiro, *Children of the Kibbutz.* Harvard University Press, 1958, p. 261.

TEACHER: Let's come back to Lucy's comment. What about his sentences?

GERT: They were too short.

55   Charlie and Jeanne have a discussion about the position of the word "stood" in the first sentence.

TEACHER: Wait a minute; some people are forgetting their manners....

JEFF: About the room: the boys went up the stairs and one "cracked," then they were in the room. Did they fall through the stairs, or what?

56   The teacher suggests Charlie make that a little clearer....

TEACHER: We still haven't decided about the short sentences. Perhaps they make the story more spooky and mysterious.

GWYNNE: I wish he had read with more expression instead of all at one time.

RACHEL: Not enough expression.

TEACHER: Charlie, they want a little more expression from you. I guess we've given you enough suggestions for one time. [Charlie does not raise his head, which is bent over his desk as if studying a paper.] Charlie! I guess we've given you enough suggestions for one time, Charlie, haven't we? [Charlie half raises his head, seems to assent grudgingly.]

57   It stands to reason that a competitive system must do this; and adults, since they are always tearing each other to pieces, should understand that children will be no different. School is indeed a training for later life not because it teaches the 3 Rs (more or less), but because it instills the essential cultural nightmare fear of failure, envy of success, and absurdity.

58   We pass now from these horrors to gentler aspects of school: impulse release and affection.

Impulse Release and Affection

59   The root of life is impulse, and its release in the right amount, at the proper time and place, and in approved ways, is a primary concern of culture. Nowadays, however, in the era of impulse release and fun, the problem of impulse release takes on a special character because of the epoch's commitment to it. This being the case, teachers have a task unique in the history of education: the fostering of impulse release rather than, as in past ages, the installation of controls. Everywhere controls are breaking down, and firmness with impulse is no part of contemporary pedagogy of "the normal child." Rather impulse release,

phrased as "spontaneity," "life adjustment," "democracy," "permissiveness," and "mothering," has become a central doctrine of education. It persists, despite protests from tough-minded critics from the Eastern Seaboard. In this sense education, often attacked for being "soft," is, as so often the case, far ahead of its detractors. Hardboiled critics of the educational system concentrate on curriculum. The teachers know better; the *real*, the persisting subject matter is noise.

How can a teacher face the whelming impulse life of children and yet discharge the task this period of history has assigned her? How can she release children's emotions without unchaining chaos? How can she permit the discharge of impulse and yet teach subject matter? How can she permit so much *noise* and not lose the message? Were they alive, the teachers I had in P.S. 10 and P.S. 186 in New York City, where we had to sit rigid and absolutely silent with our hands behind our backs or clasped before us on the desk, would say that chaos does prevail in many modern classrooms and that the message *is* lost. But then, each age has its own criteria of order, and what seems reasonable order to us nowadays might look and sound like chaos to them.

[margin: 60 Paradox]

In our research on this problem in suburban classrooms it became necessary to develop a rating for noisiness (not noise).[3] It is a problem whether at certain times classrooms committed to impulse release can be said to have *any* social structure. Indeed, the pivot of order can scarcely be, as under more traditional discipline, the teacher but must become the pupil. As a matter of fact the extent to which order in any logical sense can be present in the midst of impulse release is problematic. As one reads the observations that follow, one should bear in mind that these are not delinquents or disturbed children tearing the social structure from its hinges, but nice suburban boys and girls who are merely being given their heads. We are concerned, meanwhile, not so much with what the children do, but rather with the absurdity inherent in the situation; with how the teacher manages to prevent chaos while, in a sense, encouraging it; with how she controls impulse while indulging its release. The first example is from a second-grade classroom with 37 children. Rather full excerpts are taken from one typical day, and very brief materials from a day a month later.

[margin: 61]

> The observer[4] arrives in the classroom at 12:45 and remarks, "As has been the case in past observations, the *noise rating was 2*." The record continues: There are about seven children walking around, apparently doing nothing. There are about

---

[3]Very noisy, "mild uproar," 3; somewhat noisy, 2; a little noise, 1. Quiet, 0. Tending toward bedlam was rated 4. These ratings were established by creating the conditions experimentally in my own classroom and accustoming my students to use of the rating scale.
[4]Unless otherwise stated, observers are always students trained by me.

nine children sitting on the floor on the left side of the teacher's desk. Teacher is passing back some papers the children worked on yesterday. She says, "If you missed more than one of the questions on the board, it means that you either aren't reading carefully or that you aren't thinking enough. Betty, will you sit over here, please. Thank you."

This teacher, like most of the teachers in the area, uses "honey" and "dear" a great deal. Some examples recorded on this day are:

(1) Could you talk a little louder, Johnny dear?
(2) I'll have to ask you to go to your seat, honey.
(3) Honey, where were you supposed to go if you didn't have your paper?
(4) Bill, I think George can do that by himself, honey.
(5) Susie, honey, what's the name of it?
(6) It's up here, dear.

The record continues:

> 1:10. The reading period is over. Children return to their seats. Teacher begins to write four words on the board. As she does this the talking and moving around the room increase to a mild uproar. *Noise rating 3.* Teacher says, "May I have your eyes this way please? Bill, will you and Tommy please watch?"
> 1:20. "May I suggest that the people in John Burns' group, instead of doing this work with the vowels, read in *The Friendly Village?*"
> 1:40. Teacher is sitting at desk. Children seem to be busy at work. Everyone seems to be doing something different. *Noise rating has dropped to 2.* Fifteen out of 34 of the children present are not doing the assigned work. Most of the children in this group are doing absolutely nothing in the line of school work. Some are merely staring into space; some are playing with rubber bands, hankies, etc.
> 1:56. Presently there are 10 children out of their regular seats and seated in the rockers at the bookcase, at the library table, or just aimlessly walking around the room. Two girls in the back of the room are showing each other their scarves. There is a great deal of foot shuffling; everyone looks as if he is preparing to go home. Teacher comments, "Boys and girls, we do not go home at 2 o'clock, so please continue with your work. Doug, may I talk to you a minute?" Doug goes up to teacher, who says, "We're going to let you stay 5 minutes after school because of this talking."

A month later the record reads:

> 12:40. When the teacher reprimands the children, her voice in all instances is soft, almost hesitant. She informed me [the observer] that when she scolds she wants the children to feel she is disappointed in them. I can see how the sad tone of her voice would convey this message.
>
> 12:50. Teacher says, "May I have you in your seats, please?" During the collection of papers the *noise rate had increased to 2,* and 12 people were out of their seats.
>
> 1:04. Teacher returns and says, "Annie, would you sit down honey, and get busy. Whose feet are making so much noise?" One child says, "Pam's!" and teacher says, "Pam, that's very annoying, please don't." Observer remarks, "It's odd that this small noise should bother Mrs. Olan. I didn't even hear it." Teacher says, "Doug, will you turn around, please? Billy, do you understand the process—how to do it? I thought maybe Jimmy was helping you. Stephen, are you finished? Murray and Mickey! Boys and girls, let's tend to our own work, please." [At this point the observer remarks, "Watch it, Mrs. Olan, just a little bit of authority is creeping into your voice!"]
>
> 1:55. Five minutes before recess. Teacher says "Put your work away quietly." She sits back and with a completely expressionless face waits for the five minutes to pass. The number of children out of their seats increased to 17. Three boys were bouncing balls on the floor; one was throwing his against the wall of the cloakroom; three children were killing each other with imaginary guns.

The absence of nightmarish qualities is what repels us most in these observations. The children seem to be so at ease. Competitiveness and fear of failure seem minimal, and the only thing left seems to be absurdity—the absurdity of trying to teach subject matter, or, perhaps, of being in school at all. Everything seems to be subordinated to impulse release and fun. I have said that fun is a clowning saboteur; here we have it. In her own sweet, human way Mrs. Olan is chopping at the roots of the old system, but the children hold the hatchets. Of course, it is exhausting; in any one and a half-hour observation period Mrs. Olan was frequently in and out of the room, sometimes for as long as ten minutes. Who wouldn't be? Her withdrawal naturally resulted in increased noisiness, and she had to work at getting the sound level down when she came back. The social structure does not quite break down, because Mrs. Olan creates an affectionate atmosphere; because, by expressing disappointment rather than anger she makes the children feel evanescently guilty and afraid of losing love, and because the children's egos are remarkably firm. They seem to have an inner strength that does not permit the social structure to fall apart; and Mrs. Olan manipulates this strength with a kind, maternal skill. Lest old-fashioned readers argue that the social structure *has* fallen apart, I will point out what does *not* happen: the children do not fight or wrestle, run around the room, throw things, sing loudly, or whistle. The boys did not attack the girls or vice versa; and the children did not run in and out of the room. They did not make the teacher's life miserable. All this happens when the social structure *is* torn down. What this does to the subject matter, of course, is evident.

64   Let us now look at some parts of an interview with Mrs. Olan.

> In this day and age, she says, the children have more tensions and problems than when I first taught. In the one-room school-house in which I first taught the children came from calm homes. There was no worry about war, and there was no TV or radio. They led a calm and serene life. They came to school with their syrup pails for lunch buckets. Children of today know more about what is going on; they are better informed. So you can't hold a strict rein on them. It is bad for children to come in and sit down with their feet under the seat: you have to have freedom to get up and move around. When they do this they are more rested and have a greater attention span....
>
> Children need to enjoy school and like it. They also need their work to be done; it's not all play. You must get them to accept responsibility and doing work on their own.

Technological drivenness creates the problems and the needs that Mrs. Olan feels she has to meet in the children. To the question, "What would you say is your own particular way of keeping order in the classroom?" she says:

> Well, I would say I try to get that at the beginning of the year by getting this bond of affection and a relationship between the children and me. And we do that with stories; and I play games *with* them—don't just teach them how to play. It's what you get from living together comfortably. We have share times—that's the time a child can share with the teacher; and he gives whatever he wants to share: a bird's nest he has found; a tadpole that he and his dad got. Sometimes he may simply tell about something in his life—that his grandmother fell down and broke a leg and is not at home.... These are the things that contribute toward this discipline. Another thing in discipline: it took me a long time to learn it, too—I thought I was the boss, but I learned that even with a child, if you speak to him as you

would to a neighbor or a friend you would get a better response than if you say, "Johnny, do this or that." If you say "Mary, will you please cooperate, you are disturbing us; we want to finish our reading," rather than just giving a command, they feel they are working with you and not just taking orders.

Mrs. Olan has a philosophy: love is the path to discipline through permissiveness; and school is a continuation of family life, in which the values of sharing and democracy lead to comfortable living and ultimately to discipline. If you produce a comfortable atmosphere through affectionate sharing, she says the children will "cooperate." And her children do cooperate in producing that *quality* of order obtained by *that kind* of classroom management. But it is not the order educators of an earlier generation had in mind. It is the order of the imp—the order of impulse release and fun—with just enough old-fashioned order so the class does not completely disintegrate and achievement scores are somehow maintained. Sometimes they are not.

65

A motto for this kind of school would be "Discipline and knowledge through love." One for an earlier generation of public schools would be, "Discipline and knowledge through disciplined competition."

66

Love is very, very important to Mrs. Olan. She continues:

67

> With primary children the teacher is a mother during the day; they have to be able to bring their problems to you. They get love and affection at home, and I see no reason not to give it in school.
>
> If you have the right relationship between teacher and child or between parent and child he can take harsh words and the things you say in the right spirit; and if you don't have that bond of affection he just doesn't take it.

To Mrs. Olan, mother of a twenty-one-year-old son, second-grade children are pussy-cats, and you quiet them as you do kittens. For example, in answer to the question, "Do you think the children tend to be quieter if the teacher is affectionate?" she says:

> If a teacher has a well-modulated voice and a pleasing disposition her children are more relaxed and quiet. Children are like kittens: if kittens have a full stomach and lie in the sun they purr. If the atmosphere is such that the children are more comfortable, they are quiet. It is comfortable living that makes the quiet child. When you are shouting at them and they're shouting back at you it isn't comfortable living.

Observation has made clear that Mrs. Olan is no "boss," but lodges responsibility in the children. She clarifies the matter further:

It means a great deal to them to give them their own direction. When problems do come up in the room we talk them over and discuss what is the right thing to do when this or that happens. Usually you get pretty good answers. They are a lot harder on themselves than I would be; so if any punishment comes along like not going to an assembly you have group pressure.

68   As the interviewer was leaving Mrs. Olan remarked, "My children don't rate as high [on achievement tests] as other children. I don't push, and that's because I believe in comfortable living." *Noise* has indeed become subject matter.

69   As a result of the idea that elementary school teachers should be affectionate parents, tenderness has become a defense against the children's impulses; the teacher awakens affection and makes her children fear the loss of it if they behave badly. In this way one array of feelings—affection, fear of losing it, and guilt—becomes a containing wall against another.

70   From where comes the belief that teachers should be parents? The answer is from the circumstance that our children *do not have enough parents*, because parents are unable to do all that has to be done *by* parents nowadays. Two technologically driven parents are not enough for technologically driven children, and technological drivenness has made the two-parent family obsolete. The school teacher who acts like a parent is society's answer to the obsolescence of the two-parent family. It is the unheralded socialization of parenthood; it is the culture's feeble remedy for the anguish of being a parent.

71   While woman teachers seem repeatedly to control children's impulses through affection and fear of loss of it (like almost any middle-class mother) an interesting question is, "What does a male teacher do in this kind of school?"

72   In the classroom Mr. Jeffries, now principal of his school, takes the role of one type of contemporary middle-class American father: a puckish imp-of-fun, buddy of the boys and sweetheart of the girls, he addresses the latter with endearments and uses nicknames and diminutives for the former, as he pats them on the head or puts an arm around their shoulders. His room is a rough-and-tumble, happy-go-lucky, brink-of-chaos sort of place. Mr. Jeffries calls it a "rat-race" and says, "We get tired and ready to drop by the time it is over." Let us have a look at Mr. Jeffries' classroom:

> 11:05. The class is having a reading lesson. Teacher says, "Galapagos means tortoise. Where are 300-pound turtles found?" A boy says, "In the zoo," and Teacher says, "Where are they native in this country?" A girl says, with a grimace of disgust, "We saw them in Marine Land in Florida. They were

slaughtered and used for meat. Ugh!'' John has raised his hand and Teacher calls on him. ''We saw one in Wisconsin about the size of Bob's head.'' Teacher says, ''That's pretty big!'' and the class laughs.

Teacher asks, ''What was Douglas [a boy in the story] doing on the island? Have you ever been scared, John?'' ''Yes,'' replies John. ''So have I,'' says the teacher, and the class laughs. Teacher says, *''That's what I like about buddies.''*

11:25. Teacher says, ''Let's read the story silently.'' He says to a girl, ''Do you mind putting your beads away for the rest of the morning instead of tearing them apart?''

The room is now very quiet. He walks around the aisles as the children read.

Mr. Jeffries obviously runs a democratic classroom, and his pupils are spontaneous and effervescent. He tells them he is a buddy; he is no aloof figure, pretending to invulnerability, but like the children, he is capable of fear; he is ''scared'' *with* them. He is right down there on the floor with the kids, so to speak; like a contemporary American daddy, he has levelled the distance between himself and his children. Yet by command he can suddenly get quiet when he wants it, though rarely for long.   *73*

A week later we are at a grammar lesson: *74*

10:15. The class is discussing types of nouns. Teacher says, ''If I had lots of Ritas, she'd be a type. Maybe we're lucky we have only one.'' Class laughs. A girl raises her hand and Teacher says, ''What is it, honey?''

10:25. The room has grown noisy during the lesson and Teacher says, ''Can't hear you, Shirley. You're not going to find out a thing by looking in that direction.'' His voice has risen, getting louder in order to be heard above the classroom noise.

10:40. Clatter is increasing. Eight or nine pupils are walking around the room. One boy throws a paper wad at another. Four pupils are at the pencil sharpener. Noise grows louder but teacher ignores it.

10:45. Teacher says, ''It would seem to me that in the past five minutes you haven't accomplished a thing; you've been so busy wandering around.'' This creates complete silence. Then two boys stand to look at neighbor's work. Another goes to Teacher's desk to get help. Teacher and he confer. Noise is louder now.

10:55. Two boys raise hands. Two others stand next to teacher. One girl pats his back as he bends over. She giggles.

11:00. Teacher, ''O.K., put language books away, please!'' He giggles as a girl asks him a question. Pupils put books in desks. Teacher: "Take a couple of minutes here. Girl with the blue hair, get up. Stretch a bit." Loud laughter from the class. Teacher: "Get up and stretch." Most of the class stands. Two boys continue writing at their desks. A boy and girl push each other. The smallest boy in the class stands alone and looks on as two girls wrestle.

75   At the end of this observation period the observer wrote, "I feel that the pupils are truly fond of Mr. Jeffries. They enjoy laughing together; not *at* somebody, but *with* each other." Though we might question the last in view of the joshing, buddy-buddy jokes at the expense of Rita and Bob, there seems no doubt that Mr. Jeffries is a love object and that everybody has a wonderful time. Frequently the noise gets so loud that Mr. Jeffries has to shout and the students cannot hear. When children are pushing and wrestling, Mr. Jeffries ignores it. Suddenly, absurdly, even though he has permitted disorder and noise he may scold the children for not accomplishing anything. The following week, during a hilarious and noisy arithmetic lesson, when the children can barely hear what is going on, a girl takes a boy's paper, tears it up and throws it into the waste basket; but the teacher laughs, the class pays no attention, the paper is fished out and taped together, and the lesson continues.

76   One day five weeks later, Mr. Jeffries was sick and a substitute was on duty. The room was in its usual noisy state when the principal walked in and stood in the back of the room for a few minutes. No change took place in the class. The principal bent over one of the little girls, embraced her, whispered something to her, then turned to the observer and said, "Fine bunch of gals here," and left. Thus, in his own behavior the principal expresses the emphasis on impulse release. Teacher, principal, children, and community are one continuous cultural system.

77   As the school year entered the last month, evidence began to appear that impulse release and noisiness had reached a point beyond the endurance of the children, for the children, particularly the girls, began to *shush* the class.

> 10:40. The children have just finished singing. Teacher says, "Get paper, eraser, pencil." There is a loud buzz at this command, and a girl says, "What's the paper for?" Teacher says, "Now don't go wild just because you sang. Your pencils don't have to be so sharp." Observer notes that a bunch of kids is storming the pencil sharpener as Teacher says this. Someone *shushes* the class. Teacher says, "Fill this out the same as yes-

terday." He passes the sheets out very carefully, dropping the correct number on the first desk of each row. "Today's date is the eighth of May," says Teacher. "Sorry you're so noisy. Don't open your books till I tell you. Just fill out the first page. This is a reading test." The class reads in silent concentration. 11:01. The test is over. Teacher starts to issue instructions for the next activity and a girl says to the class, "*Shush!*"
11:06. A girl goes to the Teacher's desk for help in spelling. He spells a word aloud as she writes, leaning on his desk for support. A girl walks by John and smacks him playfully. He gets up, walks by her, smacks her on the back soundly and sprints away. Teacher says, "I notice that most of you have finished your papers promptly. I'm very pleased. Now devote your time, the next 15 minutes, to your spelling." A girl says, "*Shush!*" There is a loud buzz. Observer notes that this *shush*ing has occurred several times today, only from the girls.

These observations underscore a point made earlier, that in this kind 78 of class responsibility for maintenance of order has shifted, the children determining the controls. In the last observation, their efforts to hold the social structure together become audible; but throughout the term, the teacher's interest in order is so slight, he so often ignores the racket in his room that order would have disappeared entirely had not the children tacitly set their own limits.

It wasn't until two years later that we talked to Mr. Jeffries, now 79 principal of this school, about his theories of classroom management. His passionate involvement in teaching and in children easily won the interviewer.

At the very beginning of the year, says Mr. Jeffries, he expands the 80 boundaries of his own family to bring his sixth-graders close:

> The very first day, I introduce myself to the children and tell them about myself. I use my family a great deal. I talk about my boy and about my daughter. I tell them about certain of my experiences, just to give them an understanding that "here is an individual."

In this way he begins to draw closer to the children. He becomes almost one with them. Speaking of himself, he says,

> They know the teacher's a friend with whom they can exchange jokes and banter. But if the teacher says, "Come on, we must get to this or that," they say to themselves, "We must do it." Maybe they say, "He's a good Joe, he's a guy, so let's get the job done."

Mr. Jeffries is like Mrs. Olan in that he sees himself as working out the criteria for classroom management and discipline with the children in a democratic way, and he lets the children set their own punishments when they get into serious trouble, like fighting in the school yard. Mr. Jeffries' long explanation of how he goes about letting children set their own rules cannot be reproduced here, but what it amounts to is that he guides the children in the course of discussion to acceptance of his ideas.

81   We have seen that Mr. Jeffries' room is a buoyant, noisy, brink-of-chaos sort of milieu. "You can't hold children in a tight rein," he says, "no more than you can hold a racehorse in a tight rein. A racehorse needs freedom and so does a child." If you hold in a child in class he'll somehow break loose and "stomp" on somebody, just like a racehorse that breaks out into the spectators. Children are "God-given individuals" and have a right to get up and walk around whenever they please. As a matter of fact, he says, since in this way they may find their way to an encyclopedia or a map, mobility is closely related to creativity. To Mr. Jeffries "a quiet classroom is a dead classroom" where "the children are not thinking or are afraid to think." A stranger, he says, walking into his room might think it a "riot" or that "Mayhem was being committed," but he simply would not understand the basic thinking behind Mr. Jeffries' management. Furthermore

> A classroom with affection can be an awfully happy and joyous one. A quiet classroom may be an awfully fearful situation for someone.

Love, demonstrativeness, freedom, mobility, creativity, noisiness, and thoughtfulness all go together as Mr. Jeffries sees it. As a matter of fact, he is afraid of quietness and restraint.

82   In such classrooms the contemporary training for impulse release and fun is clear. There the children are not in uniform but in the jerkins and gossamer of *A Midsummer Night's Dream**; it is a sweet drilling without pain. Since impulse and release and fun are the requirements of the classroom, and since they must be contained within the four walls, the instrument of containment can only be affection. The teacher must therefore become a parent, for it is a parent above all who deals with the impulses of the child. In these circumstances male and female teachers adopt roles natural to the contemporary American parent. The classroom atmosphere becomes erotized as the children receive their first

---

*"Jerkins" were jackets or short coats worn by gentlemen in the early 1600s; "gossamer" refers both to the season of midsummer and to light or flimsy substances; *A Midsummer Night's Dream* is a Shakespearean comedy filled with fantasy and make-believe.

lessons in how to live in the "friendly," "relaxed" climates of the contemporary bureaucracies of business and government.

In these classrooms subject matter has a difficult time, for the noisiness and the low level of order make concentration problematic. Always *noise* is more important than subject matter; but in the era of impulse release and fun subject matter has trouble in surviving at all. Meanwhile, in these middle-class schools, the children's egos display remarkable firmness: they do not admit true chaos in spite of provocations to it. It is obvious that the classroom of fun and impulse release must remain a middle- and upper-class phenomenon, for the children's underlying controls are still strong enough there.

Today our emphasis on impulse release, spontaneity, and creativity goes hand in hand with culture-weariness, a certain tiredness and disillusionment with impulse restraint, and a feeling that the Self has been sold down the river. In these circumstances permissiveness has invaded many phases of work with children, so that in some schools there is a great relaxation of controls, the essential nightmare is impaired, and the teacher most highly regarded is the one who lets children be free. Of course, it is the *adult* Self that is really straining to be free, and when Mr. Jeffries says that a child held in tight rein may break loose and "stomp" on somebody, the racehorse tearing at the halter is his own inner Self.

It is hard for us to see, since we consider most people inherently replaceable, that there is anything remarkable in a parent-figure like a teacher showering the symbols of affection on a child for a year and then letting him walk out of her life, to be replaced next year and the next and the next by different children. However, this is almost unheard of outside the stream of Western civilization; and even in the West it is not common. As a matter of fact, the existence of *children* willing to accept such demonstrations is in itself an interesting phenomenon, based probably on the obsolescence of the two-parent family. The fact that a teacher can be thus demonstrative without inflicting deep wounds on *herself* implies a character structure having strong brakes on involvement. Otherwise how could the teacher not go to pieces? If she became deeply involved in the children in her classes she would have to give up teaching, for the hurt inflicted on her as she lost her beloved children each year would be too severe. It must be, then, that the expressions of tenderness imply also, "So far and no farther"; over the years, children must come to recognize this. It is a kind of mutual conspiracy of affectivity in which children and teacher hold themselves aloof, neither giving nor demanding more than the tacit rules permit. If this were not so children would have to be dragged shrieking from grade to grade, for they would become too deeply attached to teachers. This is

83

84

85

one of the first lessons a child has to learn in kindergarten or the first grade. From this regular replacement-in-affection they learn that the affection-giving figure, the teacher, is replaceable also. In this way children are drilled in uninvolvement: they are affectively weaned from the social system. Meanwhile they learn the symbols of affectivity; that they can be used ambiguously, and that they are not binding—that they can be scattered upon the world without commitment. Classroom demonstrativeness is a phantom commitment on which no one can collect.

86   The reader should not imagine I am "against" affectionate classrooms. They are a necessary adjunct to contemporary childhood and to the socialization of parenthood at this stage of our culture. They are also an indispensable training ground for the release of impulse and for the buddy-buddy relations of contemporary business, government, and university.

A Final Note on Learning and Creativity

87   In some areas of modern education theory (especially inside the heads of my education majors) democracy, permissiveness, originality, spontaneity, impulse release, learning, thinking, and adjustment to life are all mixed up together, so that, without any historic perspective at all, students come to me with the conviction that criticism of permissiveness is an attack on democracy itself. They have not been taught that the schoolrooms in which the originators of our American democracy received instruction were places of strict discipline. During the eighteenth and nineteenth centuries, when England was creating the industrial revolution and adding to her great literature, schools were anything but models of permissiveness. Although German schools have been among the most "authoritarian" in Europe, Germany was one of the most creative nations in the West—and also, before Hitler, a great political democracy. China is unparalleled in the tyranny with which schoolmasters ruled, yet China has given the world great poetry, drama, painting, and sculpture. France is one of the most turbulent and creative democracies of modern times, yet her classrooms are strict—much stricter, for example, than those of Czechoslovakia.[5]

88   What, then, is the central issue? The central issue is love of knowledge for its own sake, not as the creature of drive, exploited largely for survival and for prestige. When knowledge is loved for itself, *noise* is at a minimum and never endangers the subject matter. Creative cultures

---

[5]For these remarks on contemporary European classrooms I am deeply indebted to Professor David Rodnick's observations on the spot.

have loved the "beautiful person"—meditative, intellectual, and exalted. As for the creative individual, the history of the great civilizations seems to reveal little about creativity except that it has had an obstinate way of emerging only in gifted individuals, and that it has never appeared in the mass of the people. Loving the beautiful person more we might alter this.

Summary

The twentieth century is the period in history when man has at last set himself to thoroughly investigate the process of learning; his study has produced an enormous mass of literature. *Homo sapiens* has finally come consciously to grips with his most essential evolutionary task; for as his culture swept him on he discovered that he was moving rapidly in the current of new knowledge but yet had no efficient way of understanding its full implications or communicating its enormous mass to his children.   89

As he acquires new knowledge, modern man becomes perplexed by the fact that old ideas and preoccupations bind; that in the process of teaching his children he acts in ancient ways, fettering mind and spirit. But while acknowledging that this hampers the capacity to move, man is yet afraid that unchaining the young intellect will cause overthrow and chaos. Meanwhile culture, which must be impressed upon the young mind so that traditional ways will not be thrust aside by youthful rebellion or new ideas, has to have obsessive power, and convey its antagonisms and sympathies during learning. Thus education is burdened with the weight of cultural anxieties and hatreds to the degree, indeed, that what it *loves* is often obscured, and originality is thrust aside.   90

Children everywhere have been trained to fit culture as it exists; and to the end that they should not fail to fit, man has used the great ingenuity of which he is capable. As a device for teaching what was necessary and preventing deviation, education became an instrument for narrowing the perceptual sphere, thus defining the human condition of being absurd; of learning to be stupid; of learning to alienate one's Self from inner promptings.   91

Turning to the contemporary school we see it as a place where children are drilled in cultural orientations, and where subject matter becomes to a very considerable extent the instrument for instilling them. This comes about, however, not only because school, as the heartbeat of the culture, naturally embodies and expresses the central preoccupations, but also because schools deal with masses of children, and can manage therefore only by reducing them all to a common definition. Since it is in the nature of things that the definition should be deter-   92 mined by the cultural preoccupations, school creates what I have called the *essential nightmare.* The nightmare must be dreamed in order to provide the fears necessary to drive people away from something (in our case, failure) and toward something (success). In this way children, instead of loving knowledge become embroiled in the nightmare.

93   In this situation a modern trend to make school the habitat of impulse release and fun is an expected development. It is a therapy for the cultural obsession—educators' expression of their own disenchantment with the cultural nightmares—and they have made the trend synonymous with democracy itself. That a vital democracy can be the product of a disciplined and intelligent population only; that disorder and laxity are poison to democracy, they naturally cannot see because they are just as obsessed with destroying the nightmare as an older generation was with creating it.

Questions and Activities

► COMPREHENSION QUESTIONS

1. Most people believe schools are intended to teach children skills that they can use to develop their individual talents. Schools are, these people might say, intended to free people from the bonds of ignorance. What, according to Henry, is the purpose of formal education?

2. Explain why Henry believes that most education is "absurd" (paragraph 8)? What is absurd about what we learn in school? In what sense is a questioning student more rational than a quietly cooperative student who learns to accept absurdity?

3. According to Henry, what is "noise" in a classroom (paragraph 12)? If, for example, children were learning mathematics, would a classroom baseball game in which math questions were "pitched," contain what Henry would call "noise"?

4. What is the point of Henry's description in paragraph 31 of Boris at the blackboard doing math problems? How does Boris's experience reinforce the idea that what is primarily learned in the classroom is self-alienation and cultural orientation?

5. Why, according to Henry, does the teacher bring the rules and conventions of sandlot baseball into a spelling lesson? What is that teacher really teaching the children during that lesson?

6. When and how does a teacher encourage "impulse release" (paragraph 59)? Give an example of this phenomenon outside of this essay.

7. Why does Henry devote so much of this essay to describing and analyzing the teaching methods of Mrs. Olan and Mr. Jeffries? Is he using them to exemplify progressive methods of teaching, in contrast to his earlier examples from more explicitly competitive schoolrooms? What does Henry himself think of these teachers' classrooms?

8. Why does Henry organize his essay around direct observations of teachers in their classrooms? Does this approach seem more convincing to you than more formal methods of analysis—statistics or graphs, for example?

9. What is the function of the headings and the italicized phrases that mark the beginning of several paragraphs (see paragraph 2, for example)? If you look back over this essay, reading only these headings and phrases, what indication do you get of the author's intention?

10. Analyze Henry's word choices. He claims to be objective, but can you find words that suggest a positive or negative attitude toward the educational methods he describes?

11. How does Henry's analysis of the progressive classroom fit into his overall thesis of cultural orientation through education? Are Mrs. Olan and Mr. Jeffries orienting their students to the American culture just as much as more traditional teachers do? In what ways is their teaching orienting students to our culture?

12. Do you think any teacher can avoid the influence of our culture in his or her teaching? If your answer is negative, explain why cultural influences are impossible to avoid. If your answer is positive, explain what methods and approaches a teacher would use to avoid cultural influences. Would a teacher who simply posed questions and encouraged students to develop their own answers be avoiding cultural influence as much as possible?

13. What do you think is the main purpose of public education—the development of each individual's potential or the propagation of cultural and social values? Can the two be effectively integrated?

14. Conduct interviews with two or three first-year students at your college or university. Ask them the following questions, then summarize their answers in a report to the rest of the class.
    a. Do you expect to get a better job as a result of going to college?
    b. Do you expect to get a good job immediately after graduating?

    c. Do your parents' ideas about the value of a college education differ from yours? Explain how your ideas are similar to or different from your parents'.

    d. Do you believe college will enable you to discover and develop talents that you did not know you had before you came to college? What ideas or experiences cause you to answer this question as you did?

    e. Describe how one of your classmates, whose perspective is not the same as yours, thinks about the value of college. Explain how and why your perspectives are different.

15. After participating in a class discussion on the purpose of education, free-write two paragraphs, one describing what you believe are society's reasons for supporting colleges and universities and the second describing what you believe are the most common individual reasons for going to college. Are these views on the purpose of education similar or different? Are individuals unaware of the general social function of colleges and universities? Do colleges and universities often ignore the individual goals of students?

The Democratic Faith and Education

JOHN DEWEY

John Dewey (1859–1952) was an enormously influential philosopher of American education. He became famous in the latter part of the nineteenth century for a theory known as "instrumentalism." This theory assumed that human beings could manage their lives by developing goals in ways consistent with the scientific method. Rather than simply accepting traditional ways of seeing the world, Dewey felt that people should be more actively involved in constructing their perceptions of the world by examining, as a scientist might, the details of experience, by developing hypothetical goals based on those observations, and by working toward those goals in all everyday decisions. To Dewey, reality was in a constant state of change. The individual's only hope for organizing that reality was to develop methods of inquiry that were also open to change. Dewey made these ideas an accepted part of American educational theory through his many books, including *Reconstruction in Philosophy* (1920), *Experience and Nature* (1929), *Art as Experience* (1931), and *Logic: The Theory of Inquiry* (1938).

Dewey's emphasis on active, creative learning contrasts with traditional educational practice, as reported, for example, by Alfred Kazin (pages 831–839) and Jonathan Kozol (pages 842–849). Dewey advocated classrooms in which students learn to ask and answer their own questions, rather than memorizing facts or the theories of others. From 1894 to 1904, Dewey tried out his ideas at the University of Chicago, where his work was criticized by traditionalists. He found a more congenial environment for his ideas at Columbia University, where from 1904 until his death in 1952 he produced most of his major works.

In the piece that follows, originally an article published in the *Antioch Review* in 1941, Dewey argues that many modern educators have developed an oversimplified and negative attitude toward science and technology. Modern catastrophes have occurred, Dewey suggests, not because of the growth of science but because of its misuse, particularly where science has been unthinkingly applied to moral and social experience. Dewey's commitment to democracy never wavered but he believed that evil occurred when human beings responded passively to their environments.

Consider these questions as you read:

1. Does Dewey seem to you to offer a balanced alternative between the extremes of traditional and progressive classrooms? Would his students, using the scientific method, have a balance between discipline and freedom in their learning?
2. Can you think of ways in which science and technology, in themselves neutral, have been misapplied by human beings, leading to wars, ecological catastrophes, or repressive government?
3. How might people be taught to use the best aspects of the scientific method and technological tools without producing negative social, moral, or political consequences?

▶ ─────────────────────

1   Not even the most far-seeing of men could have predicted, no longer ago than fifty years, the course events have taken. The expectations that were entertained by men of generous outlook are in fact chiefly notable in that the actual course of events has moved, and with violence, in the opposite direction. The ardent and hopeful social idealist of the last century or so has been proved so wrong that a reaction to the opposite extreme has taken place. A recent writer has even proposed a confraternity of pessimists who should live together in some sort of social oasis. It is a fairly easy matter to list the articles of that old faith which, from the standpoint of today, have been tragically frustrated.

2   The first article on the list had to do with the prospects of the abolition of war. It was held that the revolution which was taking place in commerce and communication would break down the barriers which had kept the peoples of the earth alien and hostile and would create a state of interdependence which in time would insure lasting peace. Only an extreme pessimist ventured to suggest that interdependence might multiply points of friction and conflict.

3   Another item of that creed was the belief that a general development of enlightenment and rationality was bound to follow the increase in knowledge and the diffusion which would result from the revolution in science that was taking place. Since it had long been held that rationality and freedom were intimately allied, it was held that the movement toward democratic institutions and popular government which had produced in succession the British, American, and French Revolutions was bound to spread until freedom and equality were the foundations of political government in every country of the globe.

A time of general ignorance and popular unenlightenment and a time 4
of despotic and oppressive governmental rule were taken to be practically synonymous. Hence the third article of faith. There was a general belief among social philosophers that governmental activities were necessarily more or less oppressive; that governmental action tended to be an artificial interference with the operation of natural laws. Consequently the spread of enlightenment and democratic institutions would produce a gradual but assured withering away of the powers of the political state. Freedom was supposed to be so deeply rooted in the very nature of men that given the spread of rational enlightenment it would take care of itself with only a minimum of political action confined to insuring external police order.

The other article of faith to be mentioned was the general belief that 5
the vast, the almost incalculable, increase in productivity resulting from the industrial revolution was bound to raise the general standard of living to a point where extreme poverty would be practically eliminated. It was believed that the opportunity to lead a decent, self-respecting, because self-sufficient, economic life would be assured to everyone who was physically and morally normal.

The course of events culminating in the present situation suffice to 6
show without any elaborate argument how grievously these generous expectations have been disappointed. Instead of universal peace, there are two wars worldwide in extent and destructive beyond anything known in all history. Instead of uniform and steady growth of democratic freedom and equality, we have the rise of powerful totalitarian states with thoroughgoing suppression of liberty of belief and expression, outdoing the most despotic states of previous history. We have an actual growth in importance and range of governmental action in legislation and administration as necessary means of rendering freedom on the part of the many an assured actual fact. Instead of promotion of economic security and movement toward the elimination of poverty, we have had a great increase in the extent and the intensity of industrial crises with great increase of inability of workers to find employment. Social instability has reached a point that may portend revolution if it goes on unchecked.

Externally it looks as if the pessimists had the best of the case. But 7
before we reach a conclusion on that point, we have to inquire concerning the solidity of the premise upon which the idealistic optimists rested their case. This principle was that the desirable goals held in view were to be accomplished by a complex of forces to which in their entirety the name ''Nature'' was given. In practical effect, acceptance of this principle was equivalent to adoption of a policy of drift as far as human intelligence and effort were concerned. No conclusion is

warranted until we have inquired how far failure and frustration are consequences of putting our trust in a policy of drift; a policy of letting "George" in the shape of Nature and Natural Law do the work which only human intelligence and effort could possibly accomplish. No conclusion can be reached until we have considered an alternative: What is likely to happen if we recognize that the responsibility for creating a state of peace internationally, and of freedom and economic security internally, has to be carried by deliberate cooperative human effort? Technically speaking the policy known as *Laissez-faire** is one of limited application. But its limited and technical significance is one instance of a manifestation of widespread trust in the ability of impersonal forces, popularly called Nature, to do a work that has in fact to be done by human insight, foresight, and purposeful planning.

8   Not all the men of the earlier period were of the idealistic type. The idealistic philosophy was a positive factor in permitting those who prided themselves upon being realistic to turn events so as to produce consequences dictated by their own private and class advantage. The failure of cooperative and collective intelligence and effort to intervene was an invitation to immediate short-term intervention by those who had an eye to their own profit. The consequences were wholesale destruction and waste of natural resources, increase of social instability, and mortgaging of the future to a transitory and brief present of so-called prosperity. If "idealists" were misguided in what they failed to do, "realists" were wrong in what they did. If the former erred in supposing that the drift (called by them progress or evolution) was inevitably toward the better, the latter were more actively harmful because their insistence upon trusting to natural laws was definitely in the interest of personal and class profit.

9   The omitted premise in the case of both groups is the fact that neither science nor technology is an impersonal cosmic force. They operate only in the medium of human desire, foresight, aim, and effort. Science and technology are transactions in which man and nature work together and in which the human factor is that directly open to modification and direction. That man takes part along with physical conditions in invention and use of the devices, implements, and machinery of industry and commerce no one would think of denying.

10   But in practice, if not in so many words, it has been denied that man has any responsibility for the consequences that result from what he invents and employs. This denial is implicit in our widespread refusal to

---

*Laissez-faire is a French phrase meaning "let people do what they choose." Economists and politicians use it to refer to policies of noninterference or an avoidance of government regulations and rules.

engage in large-scale collective planning. Not a day passes, even in the present crisis, when the whole idea of such planning is not ridiculed as an emanation from the brain of starry-eyed professors or of others equally inept in practical affairs. And all of this in the face of the fact that there is not a successful industrial organization that does not owe its success to persistent planning within a limited field—with an eye to profit—to say nothing of the terribly high price we have paid in the way of insecurity and war for putting our trust in drift.

Refusal to accept responsibility for looking ahead and for planning in   *11* matters national and international is based upon refusal to employ in social affairs, in the field of human relations, the methods of observation, interpretation, and test that are matters of course in dealing with physical things, and to which we owe the conquest of physical nature. The net result is a state of imbalance, of profoundly disturbed equilibrium between our physical knowledge and our social-moral knowledge. This lack of harmony is a powerful factor in producing the present crisis with all its tragic features. For physical knowledge and physical technology have far outstripped social or humane knowledge and human engineering. Our failure to use in matters of direct human concern the scientific methods which have revolutionized physical knowledge has permitted the latter to dominate the social scene.

The change in the physical aspect of the world has gone on so rapidly   *12* that there is probably no ground for surprise in the fact that our psychological and moral knowledge has not kept pace. But there is cause for astonishment in the fact that after the catastrophe of war, insecurity, and the threat to democratic institutions have shown the need for new moral and intellectual attitudes and habits that will correspond with the changed state of the world, there should be a definite campaign to make the scientific attitude the scapegoat for present evils, while a return to the beliefs and practices of a prescientific and pretechnological age is urged as the road to our salvation.

II

The organized attack now being made against science and   *13* against technology as inherently materialistic and as usurping the place properly held by abstract moral precepts—abstract because divorcing ends from the means by which they must be realized—defines the issue we now have to face. Shall we go backwards or shall we go ahead to discover and put into practice the means by which science and technology shall be made fundamental in the promotion of human welfare? The failure to use scientific methods in creating understanding of human relationships and interests and in planning measures and policies that correspond in human affairs to the technologies in physical use is easily explained in historical terms. The new science began with things at the furthest remove from human affairs, namely with the stars of the heavens. From astronomy the new methods went on to win their victories in physics and chemistry. Still later science was applied in physiological and biological subject-matter. At every stage, the advance met determined resistance from the representatives of established institutions who felt their prestige was bound up with maintenance of old beliefs and found their class-control of others being threatened. In consequence, many workers in science found that the easiest way in which to procure an opportunity to carry on their inquiries was to adopt an attitude of extreme specialization. The effect was equivalent to the position that their methods and conclusions were not and could not be "dangerous," since they had no point of contact with man's serious moral concerns. This position in turn served to perpetuate and confirm the older separation of man as man from the rest of nature and to intensify the split between the "material" and the moral and "ideal."

14   Thus it has come about that when scientific inquiry began to move from its virtually complete victories in astronomy and physics and its partial victory in the field of living things over into the field of human affairs and concerns, the interests and institutions that offered resistance to its earlier advance are gathering themselves together for a final attack upon that aspect of science which in truth constitutes its supreme and culminating significance. On the principle that offense is the best defense, respect for science and loyalty to its outlook are attacked as the chief source of all our present social ills. One may read, for example, in current literature such a condescending concession as marks the following passage: "Of course, the scientific attitude, though often leading to such a catastrophe, is not to be condemned," the immediate context showing that the particular "catastrophe" in mind consists of "errors leading to war...derived from an incorrect theory of truth." Since these errors are produced by belief in the applicability of scientific method to human as well as physical facts, the remedy, according to this writer is to abandon "the erroneous application of the methods and results of natural science to the problems of human life."

15   In three respects the passage is typical of the organized campaign now in active operation. There is first the assertion that such catastrophes as that of the present war are the result of devotion to scientific method and conclusions. The denunciation of "natural" science as applied to human affairs carries, in the second place, the implication that man is outside of and above nature, and the consequent necessity of returning to the medieval prescientific doctrine of a supernatural foundation and outlook in all social and moral subjects. Then thirdly there

is the assumption, directly contrary to fact, that the scientific method has at the present time been seriously and systematically applied to the problems of human life.

I dignify the passage quoted by this reference to it because it serves   16
quite as well as a multitude of other passages from reactionaries would to convey a sense of the present issue. It is true that the *results* of natural science have had a large share, for evil as well as for good, in bringing the world to its present pass. But it is equally true that "natural" science has been identified with *physical* science in a sense in which the physical is set over against the human. It is true that the interests and institutions which are now attacking science are just the forces which in behalf of a supernatural center of gravity are those that strive to maintain this tragic split in human affairs. Now the issue, as is becoming clearer every day, is whether we shall go backward or whether we shall go forward toward recognition in theory and practice of the indissoluble unity of the humanistic and the naturalistic.

III

What has all this to do with education? The answer to this question   17
tion may be gathered from the fact that those who are engaged in assault upon science center their attacks upon the increased attention given by our schools to science and to its application in vocational training. In a world which is largely what it is today because of science and technology they propose that education should turn its back upon even the degree of recognition science and technology have received. They propose we turn our face to the medievalism in which so-called "liberal" arts were identified with literary arts: a course natural to adopt in an age innocent of knowledge of nature, an age in which the literary arts were the readiest means of rising above barbarism through acquaintance with the achievements of Greek-Roman culture. Their proposal is so remote from the facts of the present world, it involves such a bland ignoring of actualities, that there is a temptation to dismiss it as idle vaporing. But it would be a tragic mistake to take the reactionary assaults so lightly. For they are an expression of just the forces that keep science penned up in a compartment labelled "materialistic and antihuman." They strengthen all the habits and institutions which render that which is morally "ideal" impotent in action and which leave the "material" to operate without humane direction.

Let me return for the moment to my initial statement that the basic   18
error of social idealists was the assumption that something called "natural law" could be trusted, with only incidental cooperation by

human beings, to bring about the desired ends. The lesson to be learned is that human attitudes and efforts are the strategic center for promotion of the generous aims of peace among nations; promotion of economic security; the use of political means in order to advance freedom and equality; and the worldwide cause of democratic institutions. Anyone who starts from this premise is bound to see that it carries with it the basic importance of education in creating the habits and the outlook that are able and eager to secure the ends of peace, democracy, and economic stability.

19   When this is seen, it will also be seen how little has actually been done in our schools to render science and technology active agencies in creating the attitudes and dispositions and in securing the kinds of knowledge that are capable of coping with the problems of men and women today. Externally a great modification has taken place in subjects taught and in methods of teaching them. But when the changes are critically examined it is found that they consist largely in emergency concessions and accommodation to the urgent conditions and issues of the contemporary world. The standards and the controlling methods in education are still mainly those of a prescientific and pretechnological age. This statement will seem to many persons to be exaggerated. But consider the purposes which as a rule still govern instruction in just those subjects that are taken to be decisively "modern," namely science and vocational preparation. Science is taught upon the whole as a body of readymade information and technical skills. It is not taught as furnishing in its method the pattern for all effective intelligent conduct. It is taught upon the whole not with respect to the way in which it actually enters into human life, and hence as a supremely humanistic subject, but as if it had to do with a world which is "external" to human concerns. It is not presented in connection with the ways in which it actually enters into every aspect and phase of present human life. And it is hardly necessary to add that still less is it taught in connection with what scientific knowledge of human affairs might do in overcoming sheer drift. Scientific method and conclusions will not have gained a fundamentally important place in education until they are seen and treated as supreme agencies in giving direction to collective and cooperative human behavior.

20   The same sort of thing is to be said about the kind of use now made in education of practical and vocational subjects, so called. The reactionary critics are busy urging that the latter subjects be taught to the masses—who are said to be incapable of rising to the plane of the "intellectual" but who do the useful work which somebody has to do, and who may be taught by vocational education to do it more effective-

ly. This view is of course an open and avowed attempt to return to that dualistic separation of ideas and action, of the "intellectual" and the "practical," of the liberal and servile arts, that marked the feudal age. And this reactionary move in perpetuation of the split from which the world is suffering is offered as a cure, a panacea, not as the social and moral quackery it actually is. As is the case with science, the thing supremely needful is to go forward. And the forward movement in the case of technology as in the case of science is to do away with the chasm which ancient and medieval educational practice and theory set up between the liberal and the vocational, not to treat the void, the hole, constituted by this chasm, as if it were a foundation for the creation of free society.

There is nothing whatever inherent in the occupations that are so-   21
cially necessary and useful to divide them into those which are "learned" professions and those which are menial, servile, and illiberal. As far as such a separation exists in fact it is an inheritance from the earlier class structure of human relations. It is a denial of democracy. At the very time when an important, perhaps *the* important, problem in education is to fill education having an occupational direction with a genuinely liberal content, we have, believe it or not, a movement...to cut vocational training off from any contact with what is liberating by relegating it to special schools devoted to inculcation of technical skills. Inspiring vocational education with a liberal spirit and filling it with a liberal content is not a utopian dream. It is a demonstrated possibility in schools here and there in which subjects usually labelled "practically useful" are taught charged with scientific understanding and with a sense of the social-moral applications they potentially possess.

IV

If little is said in the foregoing remarks specifically upon the   22
topic of democratic faith, it is because their bearing upon a democratic outlook largely appears upon their very face. Conditions in this country when the democratic philosophy of life and democratic institutions were taking shape were such as to encourage a belief that the latter were so natural to man, so appropriate to his very being, that if they were once established they would tend to maintain themselves. I cannot rehearse here the list of events that have given this naive faith a shock. They are contained in every deliberate attack upon democracy and in every expression of cynicism about its past failures and pessimism about its future—attacks and expressions which have to be taken

seriously if they are looked at as signs of trying to establish democracy as an end in separation from the concrete means upon which the end depends.

23   Democracy is not an easy road to take and follow. On the contrary, it is as far as its realization is concerned in the complex conditions of the contemporary world a supremely difficult one. Upon the whole we are entitled to take courage from the fact that it has worked as well as it has done. But to this courage we must add, if our courage is to be intelligent rather than blind, the fact that successful maintenance of democracy demands the utmost in use of the best available methods to procure a social knowledge that is reasonably commensurate with our physical knowledge, and the invention and use of forms of social engineering reasonably commensurate with our technological abilities in physical affairs.

24   This then is the task indicated. It is, if we employ large terms, to humanize science. This task in the concrete cannot be accomplished save as the fruit of science, which is named technology, is also humanized. And the task can be executed in the concrete only as it is broken up into vital applications of intelligence in a multitude of fields to a vast diversity of problems so that science and technology may be rendered servants of the democratic hope and faith. The cause is capable of inspiring loyalty in thought and deed. But there has to be joined to aspiration and effort the formation of free, wide-ranging, trained attitudes of observation and understanding such as incorporate within themselves, as a matter so habitual as to be unconscious, the vital principles of scientific method. In this achievement science, education, and the democratic cause meet as one. May we be equal to the occasion. For it is our human problem and if a solution is found it will be through the medium of human desire, human understanding, and human endeavor.

Questions and Activities

▶ COMPREHENSION QUESTIONS

1. Summarize Dewey's reasons for the twentieth-century disillusionment with science and technology.
2. According to Dewey, what premise has been forgotten by both the defenders and critics of science and technology? How has this forgotten premise caused people to misuse what should be the beneficial aspects of science and technology?

3. What does Dewey think is the most important educational goal of the twentieth century? How does he suggest that this goal should be accomplished?

▶ *QUESTIONS OF RHETORICAL PURPOSE AND STRATEGY*

4. Why does Dewey begin his essay with a listing of some reasons behind the disillusionment with science and technology? How does this beginning fit in with the points he makes later about education?
5. Why does Dewey close his essay with a consideration of the implications of his thesis on education and science and technology for democracy? What effect was this closing intended to have on his readers?
6. What elements of language and style combine to make this the most formal of the essays in this section? Does Dewey's subject justify this more formal treatment? Why?

▶ *THEME QUESTIONS*

7. Was there any evidence of Dewey's scientific model of education in your background? Have you been asked to separate social and moral values from scientific and technical learning? Can you give specific classroom examples of this separation?
8. Both Alfred Kazin's and Jonathan Kozol's essays describe schools where skills were supposed to be learned, with no regard for moral or social considerations. Do you think Dewey would have been critical of such schools? Why?
9. Dewey suggests that the precision of thought that the modern world seems to reserve only for scientific inquiry must be applied to moral and social inquiry as well. Why are people prone to dismiss scientific methods when they deal with moral and social issues? How might schools work against this tendency?
10. What would Dewey say in response to the question of whether education can be both creative and practical? Do you think Dewey could supply concrete, practical examples of learning that was both theoretically valid and useful? Can you supply such an example?

▶ *LEARNING ACTIVITIES*

11. Discuss with a small group of your classmates the possibility of applying scientific reasoning to a moral or social issue such as capital punishment, abortion, or the taxation of churches. First, state the issue precisely. Then, work with your classmates to develop a set of questions and hypotheses you might use to study the issue.

12. Using the set of questions and hypotheses from the preceding activity, produce a report and deliver it as a group to the whole class. Consider the following questions in your report: What are the potential values of applying the more rigorous methods of science to social and moral issues? What might be the limitations of such an approach to social and moral inquiry?

Where College Fails Us

CAROLINE BIRD

Born in New York City in 1915, Caroline Bird spent many years as a journalistic researcher, newswriter, editor, and public relations writer. She worked for *Newsweek, Fortune,* and other publications. In 1966, she published *The Invisible Scar,* a book describing the effects of the Great Depression on American life. Since then, she has written *Born Female: The High Cost of Keeping Women Down* (1970), *Everything a Woman Needs to Know to Get Paid What She's Worth* (1972), and *The Case Against College* (1975). Since 1975, Bird has published several popular books on women in contemporary America, most recently, *The Good Years: Your Life in the Twenty-First Century* (1983), a book about the future of the women's movement and the lives of individual women in the next century.

Like other writers represented in this section, Bird selects problems in American life, writes books that describe those problems in detail, and then offers programs that she believes will help victims of those problems achieve solutions or outlets. Most of Bird's efforts have been directed toward women's issues. In the broadest sense of the term, Bird's writing attempts to educate women, to help them discover who they are, why they feel trapped or constrained, and how they can develop strategies for breaking out of traditional bonds. Bird's writing has been successful because she does solid research, assembles her facts into convincing support for her arguments, and offers functional and sensible solutions to problems. For example, in one of her latest books, *The Two-Paycheck Marriage: How Women at Work Are Changing Life in America* (1979), Bird painstakingly proves, with statistics and footnotes, that a broad spectrum of working couples are making major contributions to economic and social life in urban America. She then goes on to offer help with the problems of two-paycheck families: child care, domestic pressures, and changing sex and power roles.

In the essay included here, Bird argues that college is not the answer for everyone. She feels that too many young people go to college without having good reasons for doing so. And she argues that only people who have a thirst for knowledge for its own sake can justify spending four years away from productive work as they continue their schooling. College, in other words, is not vocational training.

Consider these questions as you read Bird's essay:

1. Why did you go to college? Were your reasons vocational (to get a good job) or educational (to learn and to improve yourself)? Why did most of the students you know go to college?
2. Does the college you attend seem to put a great deal of effort into vocational training? Should it?
3. Is it possible to make college education practical and at the same time personally enriching? Do you know any college programs that seem to do that?
4. Are Bird's arguments oversimplified? Does she leave out any important qualifications?

▶ ─────────────────

1   The case *for* college has been accepted without question for more than a generation. All high school graduates ought to go, says Conventional Wisdom and statistical evidence, because college will help them earn more money, become "better" people, and learn to be more responsible citizens than those who don't go.

2   But college has never been able to work its magic for everyone. And now that close to half our high school graduates are attending, those who don't fit the pattern are becoming more numerous, and more obvious. College graduates are selling shoes and driving taxis; college students sabotage each other's experiments and forge letters of recommendation in the intense competition for admission to graduate school. Others find no stimulation in their studies, and drop out—often encouraged by college administrators.

3   Some observers say the fault is with the young people themselves —they are spoiled, stoned, overindulged, and expecting too much. But that's mass character assassination, and doesn't explain all campus unhappiness. Others blame the state of the world, and they are partly right. We've been told that young people have to go to college because our economy can't absorb an army of untrained eighteen-year-olds. But disillusioned graduates are learning that it can no longer absorb an army of trained twenty-two-year-olds, either.

4   Some adventuresome educators and campus watchers have openly begun to suggest that college may not be the best, the proper, the only place for every young person after the completion of high school. We may have been looking at all those surveys and statistics upside down, it seems, and through the rosy glow of our own remembered college experiences. Perhaps college doesn't make people intelligent, ambitious, happy, liberal, or quick to learn new things—maybe it's just the other

way around, and intelligent, ambitious, happy, liberal, and quick-learning people are merely the ones who have been attracted to college in the first place. And perhaps all those successful college graduates would have been successful whether they had gone to college or not. This is heresy to those of us who have been brought up to believe that if a little schooling is good, more has to be much better. But contrary evidence is beginning to mount up.

The unhappiness and discontent of young people is nothing new, and   5 problems of adolescence are always painfully intense. But while traveling around the country, speaking at colleges, and interviewing students at all kinds of schools—large and small, public and private—I was overwhelmed by the prevailing sadness. It was as visible on campuses in California as in Nebraska and Massachusetts. Too many young people are in college reluctantly, because everyone told them they ought to go, and there didn't seem to be anything better to do. Their elders sell them college because it's good for them. Some never learn to like it, and talk about their time in school as if it were a sentence to be served.

Students tell us the same thing college counselors tell us—they go   6 because of pressure from parents and teachers, and stay because it seems to be an alternative to a far worse fate. It's "better" than the Army or a dead-end job, and it has to be pretty bad before it's any worse than staying at home.

College graduates say that they don't want to work "just" for the   7 money: They want work that matters. They want to help people and save the world. But the numbers are stacked against them. Not only are there not enough jobs in world-saving fields, but in the current slow-down it has become evident that there never were, and probably never will be, enough jobs requiring higher education to go around.

Students who tell their advisers they want to help people, for exam-   8 ple, are often directed to psychology. This year the Department of Labor estimates that there will be 4,300 new jobs for psychologists, while colleges will award 58,430 bachelor's degrees in psychology.

Sociology has become a favorite major on socially conscious cam-   9 puses, but graduates find that social reform is hardly a paying occupation. Male sociologists from the University of Wisconsin reported as gainfully employed a year after graduation included a legal assistant, sports editor, truck unloader, Peace Corps worker, publications director, and a stockboy—but no sociologist per se. The highest paid worked for the post office.

Publishing, writing, and journalism are presumably the vocational   10 goal of a large proportion of the 104,000 majors in Communications and Letters expected to graduate in 1975. The outlook for them is grim. All of the daily newspapers in the country combined are expected to hire a total of 2,600 reporters this year. Radio and television stations may hire a total of 500 announcers, most of them in local radio stations. Nonpublishing organizations will need 1,100 technical writers, and public-relations activities another 4,400. Even if new graduates could get all these jobs (they can't, of course), over 90,000 of them will have to find something less glamorous to do.

11   Other fields most popular with college graduates are also pathetically small. Only 1,900 foresters a year will be needed during this decade, although schools of forestry are expected to continue graduating twice that many. Some will get sub-professional jobs as forestry aides. Schools of architecture are expected to turn out twice as many as will be needed, and while all sorts of people want to design things, the Department of Labor forecasts that there will be jobs for only 400 new industrial designers a year. As for anthropologists, only 400 will be needed every year in the 1970s to take care of all the college courses, public-health research, community surveys, museums, and all the archaeological digs on every continent. (For these jobs graduate work in anthropology is required.)

12   Many popular occupations may seem to be growing fast without necessarily offering employment to very many. "Recreation work" is always cited as an expanding field, but it will need relatively few workers who require more special training than life guards. "Urban planning" has exploded in the media, so the U.S. Department of Labor doubled its estimate of the number of jobs to be filled every year in the 1970s—to a big, fat 800. A mere 200 oceanographers a year will be able to do all the exploring of "inner space"—and all that exciting underwater diving you see demonstrated on television—for the entire decade of the 1970s.

13   Whatever college graduates *want* to do, most of them are going to wind up doing what *there is* to do. During the next few years, according to the Labor Department, the biggest demand will be for stenographers and secretaries, followed by retail-trade salesworkers, hospital attendants, bookkeepers, building custodians, registered nurses, foremen, kindergarten and elementary-school teachers, receptionists, cooks, cosmetologists, private-household workers, manufacturing inspectors, and industrial machinery repairmen. These are the jobs which will eventually absorb the surplus archaeologists, urban planners, oceanographers, sociologists, editors, and college professors.

14   Vocationalism is the new look on campus because of the discouraging job market faced by the generalists. Students have been opting for medicine and law in droves. If all those who check "doctor" as their career goal succeed in getting their MDs, we'll immediately have ten times the target ratio of doctors for the population of the United States. Law schools are already graduating twice as many new lawyers every

year as the Department of Labor thinks we will need, and the oversupply grows annually.

Specialists often find themselves at the mercy of shifts in demand, and the narrower the vocational training, the more risky the long-term prospects. Engineers are the classic example of the "Yo-Yo" effect in supply and demand. Today's shortage is apt to produce a big crop of engineering graduates after the need has crested, and teachers face the same squeeze.

Worse than that, when the specialists turn up for work, they often find that they have learned a lot of things in classrooms that they will never use, that they will have to learn a lot of things on the job that they were never taught, and that most of what they have learned is less likely to "come in handy later" than to fade from memory. One disillusioned architecture student, who had already designed and built houses, said, "It's the degree you need, not everything you learn getting it."

A diploma saves the employer the cost of screening candidates and gives him a predictable product: He can assume that those who have survived the four-year ordeal have learned how to manage themselves. They have learned how to budget their time, meet deadlines, set priorities, cope with impersonal authority, follow instructions, and stick with a task that may be tiresome without direct supervision.

The employer is also betting that it will be cheaper and easier to train the college graduate because he has demonstrated his ability to learn. But if the diploma serves only to identify those who are talented in the art of schoolwork, it becomes, in the words of Harvard's Christopher Jencks, "a hell of an expensive aptitude test." It is unfair to the candidates because they themselves must bear the cost of the screening—the cost of college. Candidates without the funds, the academic temperament, or the patience for the four-year obstacle race are ruled out, no matter how well they may perform on the job. But if "everyone" has a diploma, employers will have to find another way to choose employees, and it will become an empty credential.

(Screening by diploma may in fact already be illegal. The 1971 ruling of the Supreme Court in *Griggs* v. *Duke Power Co.* contended that an employer cannot demand a qualification which systemically excludes an entire class of applicants, unless that qualification reliably predicts success on the job. The requiring of a high school diploma was outlawed in the *Griggs* case, and this could extend to a college diploma.)

The bill for four years at an Ivy League college is currently climbing toward $25,000; at a state university, a degree will cost the student and his family about $10,000 (with taxpayers making up the difference).*

*All monetary figures quoted in this article are much higher currently.

21   Not many families can afford these sums, and when they look for financial aid, they discover that someone else will decide how much they will actually have to pay. The College Scholarship Service, which establishes a family's degree of need for most colleges, is guided by noble principles: uniformity of sacrifice, need rather than merit. But families vary in their willingness to "sacrifice" as much as the bureaucracy of the CSS thinks they ought to. This is particularly true of middle-income parents, whose children account for the bulk of the country's college students. Some have begun to rebel against this attempt to enforce the same values and priorities on all. "In some families, a college education competes with a second car, a color television, or a trip to Europe—and it's possible that college may lose," one financial-aid officer recently told me.

22   Quite so. College is worth more to some middle-income families than to others. It is chilling to consider the undercurrent of resentment that families who "give up everything" must feel toward their college-age children, or the burden of guilt children must bear every time they goof off or receive less than top grades in their courses.

23   The decline in return for a college degree within the last generation has been substantial. In the 1950s, a Princeton student could pay his expenses for the school year—eating club and all—on less than $3,000. When he graduated, he entered a job market which provided a comfortable margin over the earnings of his agemates who had not been to college. To be precise, a freshman entering Princeton in 1956, the earliest year for which the Census has attempted to project lifetime earnings, could expect to realize a 12.5 percent return on his investment. A freshman entering in 1972, with the cost nearing $6,000 annually, could expect to realize only 9.3 percent, less than might be available in the money market. This calculation was made with the help of a banker and his computer, comparing college as an investment in future earnings with other investments available in the booming money market of 1974, and concluded that in strictly financial terms, college is not always the best investment a young person can make.

24   I postulated a young man (the figures are different with a young woman, but the principle is the same) whose rich uncle would give him, in cash, the total cost of four years at Princeton—$34,181. (The total includes what the young man would earn if he went to work instead of to college right after high school.) If he did not spend the money on Princeton, but put it in the savings bank at 7.5 percent interest compounded daily, he would have, at retirement age sixty-four, more than five times as much as the $199,000 extra he could expect to earn between twenty-two and sixty as a college man rather than a mere high school graduate. And with all that money accumulating in the bank, he

could invest in something with a higher return than a diploma. At age twenty-eight, when his nest egg had reached $73,113, he could buy a liquor store, which would return him well over 20 percent on his investment, as long as he was willing to mind the store. He might get a bit fidgety sitting there, but he'd have to be dim-witted to lose money on a liquor store, and right now we're talking only about dollars.

If the young man went to a public college rather than Princeton, the investment would be lower, and the payoff higher, of course, because other people—the taxpayers—put up part of the capital for him. But the difference in return between an investment in public and private colleges is minimized because the biggest part of the investment in either case is the money a student might earn if he went to work, not to college—in economic terms, his "foregone income." That he bears himself.

Rates of return and dollar signs on education are a fascinating brain teaser, and, obviously, there is a certain unreality to the game. But the same unreality extends to the traditional calculations that have always been used to convince taxpayers that college is a worthwhile investment.

The ultimate defense of college has always been that while it may not teach you anything vocationally useful, it will somehow make you a better person, able to do anything better, and those who make it through the process are initiated into the "fellowship of educated men and women." In a study intended to probe what graduates seven years out of college thought their colleges should have done for them, the Carnegie Commission found that most alumni expected the "development of my abilities to think and express myself." But if such respected educational psychologists as Bruner and Piaget are right, specific learning skills have to be acquired very early in life, perhaps even before formal schooling begins.

So, when pressed, liberal-arts defenders speak instead about something more encompassing, and more elusive. "College changed me inside," one graduate told us fervently. The authors of a Carnegie Commission report, who obviously struggled for a definition, concluded that one of the common threads in the perceptions of a liberal education is that it provides "an integrated view of the world which can serve as an inner guide." More simply, alumni say that college should have "helped me to formulate the values and goals of my life."

In theory, a student is taught to develop these values and goals himself, but in practice, it doesn't work quite that way. All but the wayward and the saintly take their sense of the good, the true, and the beautiful from the people around them. When we speak of students acquiring "values" in college, we often mean that they will acquire the values—and sometimes that means only the tastes—of their professors. The values of professors may be "higher" than many students will encounter elsewhere, but they may not be relevant to situations in which students find themselves in college and later.

30   Of all the forms in which ideas are disseminated, the college professor lecturing a class is the slowest and most expensive. You don't have to go to college to read the great books or learn about the great ideas of Western Man. Today you can find them everywhere—in paperbacks, in the public libraries, in museums, in public lectures, in adult-education courses, in abridged, summarized, or adapted form in magazines, films, and television. The problem is no longer one of access to broadening ideas; the problem is the other way around: how to choose among the many courses of action proposed to us, how to edit the stimulations that pour into our eyes and ears every waking hour. A college experience that piles option on option and stimulation on stimulation merely adds to the contemporary nightmare.

31   What students and graduates say that they did learn on campus comes under the heading of personal, rather than intellectual, development. Again and again I was told that the real value of college is learning to get along with others, to practice social skills, to "sort out my head," and these have nothing to do with curriculum.

32   For whatever impact the academic experience used to have on college students, the sheer size of many undergraduate classes in the 1970s dilutes faculty-student dialogue, and, more often than not, they are taught by teachers who were hired when colleges were faced with a shortage of qualified instructors, during their years of expansion and when the big rise in academic pay attracted the mediocre and the less than dedicated.

33   On the social side, colleges are withdrawing from responsibility for feeding, housing, policing, and protecting students at a time when the environment of college may be the most important service it could render. College officials are reluctant to "intervene" in the personal lives of the students. They no longer expect to take over from parents, but often insist that students—who have, most often, never lived away from home before—take full adult responsibility for their plans, achievements, and behavior.

34   Most college students do not live in the plush, comfortable country-clublike surroundings their parents envisage, or, in some cases, remember. Open dorms, particularly when they are coeducational, are noisy, usually overcrowded, and often messy. Some students desert the institutional "zoos" (their own word for dorms) and move into run-down, overpriced apartments. Bulletin boards in student centers are littered

with notices of apartments to share and the drift of conversation suggests that a lot of money is dissipated in scrounging for food and shelter.

Taxpayers now provide more than half of the astronomical sums that   35
are spent on higher education. But less than half of today's high school
graduates go on, raising a new question of equity: Is it fair to make all
the taxpayers pay for the minority who actually go to college? We decided long ago that it is fair for childless adults to pay school taxes because
everyone, parents and nonparents alike, profits by a literate population.
Does the same reasoning hold true for state-supported higher education? There is no conclusive evidence on either side.

Young people cannot be expected to go to college for the general good   36
of mankind. They may be more altruistic than their elders, but no great
numbers are going to spend four years at hard intellectual labor, let
alone tens of thousands of family dollars, for "the advancement of
human capability in society at large," one of the many purposes invoked by the Carnegie Commission report. Nor do any considerable
number of them want to go to college to beat the Russians to Jupiter,
improve the national defense, increase the Gross National Product,
lower the crime rate, improve automobile safety, or create a market for
the arts—all of which have been suggested at one time or other as benefits taxpayers get for supporting higher education.

One sociologist said that you don't have to have a reason for going to   37
college because it's an institution. His definition of an institution is
something everyone subscribed to without question. The burden of
proof is not on why you should go to college, but why anyone thinks
there might be a reason for not going. The implication—and some educators express it quite frankly—is that an eighteen-year-old high school
graduate is still too young and confused to know what he wants to do,
let alone what is good for him.

Mother knows best, in other words.   38

It had always been comfortable for students to believe that authori-   39
ties, like Mother, or outside specialists, like educators, could determine what was best for them. However, specialists and authorities no
longer enjoy the credibility former generations accorded them. Patients
talk back to doctors and are not struck suddenly dead. Clients question
the lawyer's bills and sometimes get them reduced. It is no longer self-
evident that all adolescents must study a fixed curriculum that was
constructed at a time when all educated men could agree on precisely
what it was that made them educated.

The same with college. If high school graduates don't want to contin-   40
ue their education, or don't want to continue it right away, they may
perceive more clearly than their elders that college is not for them.

41   College is an ideal place for those young adults who love learning for its own sake, who would rather read than eat, and who like nothing better than writing research papers. But they are a minority, even at the prestigious colleges, which recruit and attract the intellectually oriented.

42   The rest of our high school graduates need to look at college more closely and critically, to examine it as a consumer product, and decide if the cost in dollars, in time, in continued dependency, and in future returns, is worth the very large investment each student—and his family—must make.

Questions and Activities

► *COMPREHENSION QUESTIONS*

1. What do the job statistics Bird summarizes in paragraphs 8 through 12 suggest about the importance of college in ensuring its graduates good jobs? How do these statistics support Bird's overall argument?
2. According to Bird, do those who specialize in job-oriented areas in college necessarily do better in the long run than those who are generally educated? Give what you think are Bird's reasons for this.
3. What function does a college degree have for potential employers? Do you think Bird is limited in her thinking on this point? Are there other, broader benefits for employers in hiring college-educated applicants? What are they?

► *QUESTIONS OF RHETORICAL PURPOSE AND STRATEGY*

4. Bird attempts to persuade us that we place too much emphasis on college, and she provides statistics to back up her argument. Do you think her statistics tell the whole story? What arguments can you think of to offset them? What kinds of evidence would best support your arguments? Could you find statistics that would offset Bird's? Would you place greater emphasis on ethical or moral appeals than Bird does?
5. Bird uses the third-person point of view. Why does this point of view better support her form of argument than would the less formal and more personal first person or second person?
6. Choose two of Bird's paragraphs and use them to demonstrate how she organizes her material. How are general ideas and specific evidence related to one another in these paragraphs? How does she

establish a general line of reasoning as she moves from one set of statistics to another? Do you think her strategies of paragraphing are suitable for a persuasive essay? Why?

▶ *THEME QUESTIONS*

7. Bird suggests that most college students attend college for the wrong reasons. According to this essay and other selections in this section, what *are* good reasons for going to college?
8. Given Bird's arguments, what do you think she believes formal education should do for people? Should it ensure good jobs, open up new horizons, encourage creativity, or teach specific skills?
9. What about the general social and cultural aspects of education? Does Bird miss their importance? Perhaps, for example, college serves as an introduction to social groups that will benefit students later in professional or business life.
10. Should the job market control the college and university curriculum? Why, or why not?

▶ *LEARNING ACTIVITIES*

11. Review the selections you have read so far in this section. Then make a list of the pros and cons of today's formal education. In what ways is formal education good for the individual? In what ways does it serve a necessary social function?
12. Work two of the contrasting items on your list of pros and cons into a thesis statement on the value of formal education in our culture. Once you have developed your statement, explain the assumptions behind it (the values you are assuming your reader will share) and the kind of evidence you would use to support it (facts, statistics, examples, logic, or emotional or ethical appeals).

University Days

JAMES THURBER

James Thurber (1894–1961) was America's premier twentieth-century humorist. A native of Columbus, Ohio, Thurber attended Ohio State University, was a code clerk in Paris for the U.S. Department of State during World War I, and then held various journalistic jobs until 1927, when he began working for *The New Yorker*. He began as a managing editor, but quickly found a niche as a staff writer. His column "Talk of the Town" became famous for its wit, and from 1927 until his death in 1961 he published short stories, humorous fables, satires, essays, and cartoons in the magazine. He, Dorothy Parker, E. B. White, and John Updike, among others, were writers whose names were associated with *The New Yorker's* reputation for sophisticated and polished writing style.

Thurber gradually went blind, yet he was able to maintain a prolific writing and drawing career. His work is represented in twenty-eight adult books, six children's books, and numerous essays and short stories. His play, *The Male Animal,* was a success on Broadway. He did cartoon illustrations for three books written by others and wrote a widely read biography of Harold Ross, the founder and owner of *The New Yorker,* entitled *The Years with Ross* (1959).

Many critics argue that calling Thurber a humorist is an oversimplification. All his humor is based on a deeper pessimism concerning human nature, on a tragic sense of human possibilities curtailed by circumstance and vice. Much of his satire is directed against marriage and its effects on individual men and women or against the inventions of modern civilization that suppress human creativity and inspiration. One of his most famous stories, "The Secret Life of Walter Mitty" (published in 1942 in the collection *My World—and Welcome to It*), tells of a man who daydreams heroic adventures to escape from a bossy wife and a dull job. Still another famous story, "The Catbird Seat," tells of a nondescript bureaucrat who devises a plan to destroy a woman whose belligerent verbosity has threatened his secure routine. His fables, such as "The Unicorn in the Garden" and "The Seal in the Bedroom," deal with the effects of domestic life on the imagination of those who share that life.

In the brief piece that follows, Thurber uses his characteristically conversational, simple, and understated style to satirize his experiences at Ohio State University. He develops his satire by picturing himself as an inept victim of a university that seemingly requires him to do things just for the sake of doing them, whether he is actually learning anything or not.

Thurber's treatment of his college years raises questions that have been noted throughout this section:

1. Is formal education really just an indoctrination of individuals into the customs and values of society? Is it possible for formal education to encourage creativity as it indoctrinates?
2. Are college students often asked to maintain traditional forms at the expense of individual initiative and talent?
3. Should universities favor cultural indoctrination or individual freedom?

▶ ——————————————————

I passed all the other courses that I took at my university, but I could never pass botany. This was because all botany students had to spend several hours a week in a laboratory looking through a microscope at plant cells, and I could never see through a microscope. I never once saw a cell through a microscope. This used to enrage my instructor. He would wander around the laboratory pleased with the progress all the students were making in drawing the involved and, so I am told, interesting structure of flower cells, until he came to me. I would just be standing there. "I can't see anything," I would say. He would begin patiently enough, explaining how anybody can see through a microscope, but he would always end up in a fury, claiming that I could *too* see through a microscope but just pretended that I couldn't. "It takes away from the beauty of flowers anyway," I used to tell him. "We are not concerned with beauty in this course," he would say. "We are concerned solely with what I may call the *mechanics* of flars." "Well," I'd say, "I can't see anything." "Try it just once again," he'd say, and I would put my eye to the microscope and see nothing at all, except now and again a nebulous milky substance—a phenomenon of maladjustment. You were supposed to see a vivid, restless clockwork of sharply defined plant cells. "I see what looks like a lot of milk," I would tell him. This, he claimed, was the result of my not having adjusted the microscope properly, so he would readjust it for me, or rather, for himself. And I would look again and see milk.

I finally took a deferred pass, as they called it, and waited a year and tried again. (You had to pass one of the biological sciences or you

1

2

couldn't graduate.) The professor had come back from vacation brown as a berry, bright-eyed, and eager to explain cell-structure again to his classes. "Well," he said to me, cheerily, when we met in the first laboratory hour of the semester, "we're going to see cells this time, aren't we?" "Yes, sir," I said. Students to right of me and to left of me and in front of me were seeing cells; what's more, they were quietly drawing pictures of them in their notebooks. Of course, I didn't see anything.

3   "We'll try it," the professor said to me, grimly, "with every adjustment of the microscope known to man. As God is my witness, I'll arrange this glass so that you see cells through it or I'll give up teaching. In twenty-two years of botany, I—" He cut off abruptly for he was beginning to quiver all over, like Lionel Barrymore,* and he genuinely wished to hold onto his temper; his scenes with me had taken a great deal out of him.

4   So we tried it with every adjustment of the microscope known to man. With only one of them did I see anything but blackness or the familiar lacteal opacity, and that time I saw, to my pleasure and amazement, a variegated constellation of flecks, specks, and dots. These I hastily drew. The instructor, noting my activity, came back from an adjoining desk, a smile on his lips and his eyebrows high in hope. He looked at my cell drawing. "What's that?" he demanded, with a hint of a squeal in his voice. "That's what I saw," I said. "You didn't, you didn't, you *didn't!*" he screamed, losing control of his temper instantly, and he bent over and squinted into the microscope. His head snapped up. "That's your eye!" he shouted. "You've fixed the lens so that it reflects! You've drawn your eye!"

5   Another course that I didn't like, but somehow managed to pass, was economics. I went to that class straight from the botany class, which didn't help me any in understanding either subject. I used to get them mixed up. But not as mixed up as another student in my economics class who came there direct from a physics laboratory. He was a tackle on the football team, named Bolenciecwcz. At that time Ohio State University had one of the best football teams in the country, and Bolenciecwcz was one of its outstanding stars. In order to be eligible to play it was necessary for him to keep up in his studies, a very difficult matter, for while he was not dumber than an ox he was not any smarter. Most of his professors were lenient and helped him along. None gave him more hints in answering questions or asked him simpler ones than the economics professor, a thin, timid man named Bassum. One day

*Lionel Barrymore (1878–1954) was a noted stage, radio, and film actor, also well-known for his exaggerated physical actions on stage.

when we were on the subject of transportation and distribution, it came
Bolenciecwcz's turn to answer a question. "Name one means of transportation," the professor said to him. No light came into the big tackle's eyes. "Just any means of transportation," said the professor.
Bolenciecwcz sat staring at him. "That is," pursued the professor,
"any medium, agency, or method of going from one place to another."
Bolenciecwcz had the look of a man who is being led into a trap. "You
may choose among steam, horse-drawn, or electrically propelled vehicles," said the instructor. "I might suggest the one which we commonly take in making long journeys across land." There was a profound silence in which everybody stirred uneasily, including Bolenciecwcz and
Mr. Bassum. Mr Bassum abruptly broke this silence in an amazing
manner. "Choo-choo-choo," he said, in a low voice, and turned instantly scarlet. He glanced appealingly around the room. All of us, of
course, shared Mr. Bassum's desire that Bolenciecwcz should stay
abreast of the class in economics, for the Illinois game, one of the
hardest and most important of the season, was only a week off. "Toot,
toot, too-tooooooot!" some student with a deep voice moaned, and we
all looked encouragingly at Bolenciecwcz. Somebody else gave a fine
imitation of a locomotive letting off steam. Mr. Bassum himself rounded off the little show. "Ding, dong, ding, dong," he said, hopefully.
Bolenciecwcz was staring at the floor now, trying to think, his great
brow furrowed, his huge hands rubbing together, his face red.

"How did you come to college this year, Mr. Bolenciecwcz?" asked 　6
the professor. "*Chuffa* chuffa, *chuffa* chuffa."

"M' father sent me," said the football player. 　7

"What on?" asked Bassum. 　8

"I git an 'lowance," said the tackle, in a low, husky voice, obviously 　9
embarrassed.

"No, no," said Bassum. "Name a means of transportation. What did 　10
you *ride* here on?"

"Train," said Bolenciecwcz. 　11

"Quite right," said the professor. "Now, Mr. Nugent, will you tell 　12
us—"

If I went through anguish in botany and economics—for different rea- 　13
sons—gymnasium work was even worse. I don't even like to think
about it. They wouldn't let you play games or join in the exercises with
your glasses on and I couldn't see with mine off. I bumped into professors, horizontal bars, agricultural students, and swinging iron rings.
Not being able to see, I could take it but I couldn't dish it out. Also, in
order to pass gymnasium (and you had to pass it to graduate) you had to
learn to swim if you didn't know how. I didn't like the swimming pool,
I didn't like swimming, and I didn't like the swimming instructor, and

after all these years I still don't. I never swam but I passed my gym work anyway, by having another student give my gymnasium number (978) and swim across the pool in my place. He was a quiet, amiable blonde youth, number 473, and he would have seen through a microscope for me if we could have got away with it, but we couldn't get away with it. Another thing I didn't like about gymnasium work was that they made you strip the day you registered. It is impossible for me to be happy when I am stripped and being asked a lot of questions. Still, I did better than a lanky agricultural student who was cross-examined just before I was. They asked each student what college he was in—that is, whether Arts, Engineering, Commerce, or Agriculture. "What college are you in?" the instructor snapped at the youth in front of me. "Ohio State University," he said promptly.

14   It wasn't that agricultural student but it was another a whole lot like him who decided to take up journalism, possibly on the ground that when farming went to hell he could fall back on newspaper work. He didn't realize, of course, that that would be very much like falling back full-length on a kit of carpenter's tools. Haskins didn't seem cut out for journalism, being too embarrassed to talk to anybody and unable to use a typewriter, but the editor of the college paper assigned him to the cow barns, the sheep house, the horse pavilion, and the animal husbandry department generally. This was a genuinely big "beat," for it took up five times as much ground and got ten times as great a legislative appropriation as the College of Liberal Arts. The agricultural student knew animals, but nevertheless his stories were dull and colorlessly written. He took all afternoon on each of them, on account of having to hunt for each letter on the typewriter. Once in a while he had to ask somebody to help him hunt. "C" and "L," in particular, were hard letters for him to find. His editor finally got pretty much annoyed at the farmer-journalist because his pieces were so uninteresting. "See here, Haskins," he snapped at him one day, "why is it we never have anything hot from you on the horse pavilion? Here we have two hundred head of horses on this campus—more than any other university in the Western Conference except Purdue—and yet you never get any real low-down on them. Now shoot over to the horse barns and dig up something lively." Haskins shambled out and came back in about an hour; he said he had something. "Well, start it off snappily," said the editor. "Something people will read." Haskins set to work and in a couple of hours brought a sheet of typewritten paper to the desk; it was a two-hundred-word story about some disease that had broken out among the horses. Its opening sentence was simple but arresting. It read: "Who has noticed the sores on the tops of the horses in the animal husbandry building?"

Ohio State was a land grant university and therefore two years of mil-   15
itary drill was compulsory. We drilled with old Springfield rifles and
studied the tactics of the Civil War even though the World War was
going on at the time. At 11 o'clock each morning thousands of freshmen
and sophomores used to deploy over the campus, moodily creeping up
on the old chemistry building. It was good training for the kind of
warfare that was waged at Shiloh but it had no connection with what
was going on in Europe. Some people used to think there was German
money behind it, but they didn't dare say so or they would have been
thrown in jail as German spies. It was a period of muddy thought and
marked, I believe, the decline of higher education in the Middle West.

As a soldier I was never any good at all. Most of the cadets were   16
glumly indifferent soldiers, but I was no good at all. Once General
Littlefield, who was commandant of the cadet corps, popped up in front
of me during regimental drill and snapped, "You are the main trouble
with this university!" I think he meant that my type was the main trouble with the university but he may have meant me individually. I was
mediocre at drill, certainly—that is, until my senior year. By that time I
had drilled longer than anybody else in the Western Conference, having
failed at military at the end of each preceding year so that I had to do it
all over again. I was the only senior still in uniform. The uniform
which, when new, had made me look like an interurban railway con-
ductor, now that it had become faded and too tight made me look like
Bert Williams in his bellboy act.* This had a definitely bad effect on my
morale. Even so, I had become by sheer practice little short of wonderful at squad maneuvers.

One day General Littlefield picked our company out of the whole reg-   17
iment and tried to get it mixed up by putting it through one movement
after another as fast as we could execute them: squads right, squads left,
squads on right into line, squads right about, squads left front into line,
etc. In about three minutes one hundred and nine men were marching
in one direction and I was marching away from them at an angle of forty
degrees, all alone. "Company, halt!" shouted General Littlefield.
"That man is the only man who has it right!" I was made a corporal for
my achievement.

The next day General Littlefield summoned me to his office. He was   18
swatting flies when I went in. I was silent and he was silent too, for a
long time, I don't think he remembered me or why he had sent for me,

*Bert Williams was a popular vaudeville and silent movie star. He was known for a comic
routine in which he played a hotel porter in a shrunken suit.

but he didn't want to admit it. He swatted some more flies, keeping his eyes on them narrowly before he let go with the swatter. "Button up your coat!" he snapped. Looking back on it now I can see that he meant me although he was looking at a fly, but I just stood there. Another fly came to rest on a paper in front of the general and began rubbing its hind legs together. The general lifted the swatter cautiously. I moved restlessly and the fly flew away. "You startled him!" barked General Littlefield, looking at me severely. I said I was sorry. "That won't help the situation!" snapped the General, with cold military logic. I didn't see what I could do except offer to chase some more flies toward his desk, but I didn't say anything. He stared out the window at the faraway figures of co-eds crossing the campus toward the library. Finally, he told me I could go. So I went. He either didn't know which cadet I was or else he forgot what he wanted to see me about. It may have been that he wished to apologize for having called me the main trouble with the university; or maybe he had decided to compliment me on my brilliant drilling of the day before and then at the last minute decided not to. I don't know. I don't think about it much any more.

Questions and Activities

▶ *COMPREHENSION QUESTIONS*

1. What is the point behind Thurber's description of his experiences in botany class? Is Thurber making a similar point when he tells the story about Bolenciecwcz, the tackle on the football team? What do these two stories suggest is the point of Thurber's description of his university education?
2. What is the significance of the last sentence of this essay? Why does Thurber use "it" rather than a definite noun? Could "it" refer to university education in general, as well as to the story he tells in the last paragraph?

▶ *QUESTIONS OF RHETORICAL PURPOSE AND STRATEGY*

3. Why does Thurber repeat himself in several places, the opening sentences of paragraphs 3 and 4, for example? Do these repetitions emphasize the absurdity of Thurber's education?
4. Describe Thurber's style. Is it easy to read? Why? Why do you think Thurber chose to write in this style?

5. What kind of person does the writer of this essay seem to be? Is he a simpleton? How can you tell? Perhaps more important is whether you think Thurber is as simple as he makes himself *seem* in this essay.

▶ *THEME QUESTIONS*

6. Jules Henry argues that formal education teaches students to accept absurd ways of understanding and organizing experience in order to propagate culture (pages 852–884). Is there evidence of that type of educational-cultural orientation in Thurber's report of his experiences at Ohio State? Were behaviors that seemed absurd to Thurber part of the university scene simply because they bolstered cultural traditions?

7. Thurber never graduated from Ohio State, yet he became a successful writer. Do you think this fact justifies his feelings about the general absurdity of formal education? Or was college absurd only for him?

8. In what ways do you think Thurber had hoped college would make sense? Had he expected it to develop talents that he already possessed instead of attempting to develop skills for which he had no talent? Had he hoped to develop useful skills rather than abstract or obscure ways of analyzing the world?

▶ *LEARNING ACTIVITIES*

9. Write a two- or three-page satirical description of an activity you participated in in college or high school. Using Thurber's description of his botany class as a model, imitate his use of dialogue, his style, and his conversational tone.

10. Discuss your satire with other members of the class. Use the following set of questions as general guidelines for this discussion.
    a. What is the point of your satire?
    b. What does your satire suggest about higher education in general?
    c. What does your satire tell your readers about you?
    d. What does your satire tell your readers about the activity you describe?

Writing Assignments

EDUCATION: INDIVIDUALISM VERSUS SOCIETY

The essays in this section fall into three categories. Alfred Kazin and
Jonathan Kozol describe negative educational situations in concrete
detail. They attempt to show how schools can reduce learning by
placing children in contexts in which their natural inclinations to learn
new things are repressed by authoritarian systems. Jules Henry and
John Dewey write from more general perspectives than either Kazin or
Kozol does. Henry provides evidence for the assertion that schools
must be in the business of exposing children to the customs and rules of
the larger society and of subduing their creativity at the same time.
Dewey proposes the idea that the problem-solving methods of science
should be carefully applied to the social and moral dilemmas of life as
well. Both Henry and Dewey assume the cultural function of public education, and they claim to accept rather than to fight the limitations
such acculturation places on individuals. Caroline Bird and James
Thurber criticize the general belief that college is for everyone. Perhaps, Bird and Thurber suggest in their different ways, college is really
only meant for the relatively small number of people who want to pursue knowledge for its own sake.

   With these three categories in mind, write a three-to-five-page essay
in which you use at least two of the essays in this section to argue for or
against one of the following propositions:

> Schools are by definition repressive and in opposition to indi-
>   vidual expression and creativity.
> Schools could develop individual creativity if this became their
>   primary educational goal.
> Schools must foster social growth and maturity and downplay
>   individualism.
> Schools must combine techniques that foster individual cre-
>   ativity with those that foster cultural productivity.
> The growth of the individual is at the center of the American
>   school system.
> The propagation of the American way is at the center of the
>   American school system.

   Your argument should consist of four elements: a clear thesis, reasons for or against that thesis, evidence to support the reasons, and
some emotional support for the thesis.

In the school described in the following story by Donald Barthelme, everything seems to go wrong. But in the story's final line the children are cheering wildly because of the arrival of the new gerbil. Write an essay in which you explain to a group of would-be teachers the meaning of the last line of this story.

As you write, you should follow through on two lines of reasoning. First, consider the possibility that the last line of the story functions as a response to the long series of deaths that occur earlier. Second, consider as well the idea that this school, or all schools for that matter, must kill before they can educate. What must they kill, and are these killings literal or figurative? How can schools educate students by working from these killings?

Remember that your task is to convince your audience of future teachers that out of failure comes success, out of death comes life, out of suffering comes joy. Schooling can never be all joy and pleasure, nor should it be all suffering and pain. Assume that your audience has read essays like the ones in this section. They are not convinced that either progressive or traditional education is the answer to the need for effective schooling. You will, in other words, use Barthelme's story to explain the good and bad, the risks and pleasures, and the boredom and excitement of formal education to some potential teachers.

The School

DONALD BARTHELME

Well, we had all these children out planting trees, see, because we figured that...that was part of their education, to see how, you know, the root systems...and also the sense of responsibility, taking care of things, being individually responsible. You know what I mean. And the trees all died. They were orange trees. I don't know why they died, they just died. Something wrong with the soil possibly or maybe the stuff we got from the nursery wasn't the best. We complained about it. So we've got thirty kids there, each kid had his or her own little tree to plant, and we've got these thirty dead trees. All these kids looking at these little brown sticks, it was depressing.   1

It wouldn't have been so bad except that just a couple of weeks before the thing with the trees, the snakes all died. But I think that the   2

snakes—well, the reason that the snakes kicked off was that . . . you remember, the boiler was shut off for four days because of the strike, and
that was explicable. It was something you could explain to the kids because of the strike. I mean, none of their parents would let them cross
the picket line and they knew there was a strike going on and what it
meant. So when things got started up again and we found the snakes
they weren't too disturbed.

3   With the herb gardens it was probably a case of overwatering, and at
least now they know not to overwater. The children were very conscientious with the herb gardens and some of them probably . . . you know,
slipped them a little extra water when we weren't looking. Or maybe
. . . well, I don't like to think about sabotage, although it did occur to
us. I mean, it was something that crossed our minds. We were thinking
that way probably because before that the gerbils had died, and the
white mice had died, and the salamander . . . well, now they know not
to carry them around in plastic bags.

4   Of course we *expected* the tropical fish to die, that was no surprise.
Those numbers, you look at them crooked and they're belly-up on the
surface. But the lesson plan called for a tropical-fish input at that point,
there was nothing we could do, it happens every year, you just have to
hurry past it.

5   We weren't even supposed to have a puppy.

6   We weren't even supposed to have one, it was just a puppy the
Murdoch girl found under a Gristede's truck one day and she was afraid
the truck would run over it when the driver had finished making his delivery, so she stuck it in her knapsack and brought it to school with her.
So we had this puppy. As soon as I saw the puppy I thought, Oh Christ, I
bet it will live for about two weeks and then . . . And that's what it did. It
wasn't supposed to be in the classroom at all, there's some kind of regulation about it, but you can't tell them they can't have a puppy when
the puppy is already there, right in front of them, running around on the
floor and yap yap yapping. They named it Edgar—that is, they named it
after me. They had a lot of fun running after it and yelling, "Here,
Edgar! Nice Edgar!" Then they'd laugh like hell. They enjoyed the ambiguity. I enjoyed it myself. I don't mind being kidded. They made a
little house for it in the supply closet and all that. I don't know what it
died of. Distemper, I guess. It probably hadn't had any shots. I got it out
of there before the kids got to school. I checked the supply closet each
morning, routinely, because I knew what was going to happen. I gave it
to the custodian.

7   And then there was this Korean orphan that the class adopted
through the Help the Children program, all the kids brought in a quarter
a month, that was the idea. It was an unfortunate thing, the kid's name

was Kim and maybe we adopted him too late or something. The cause of death was not stated in the letter we got, they suggested we adopt another child instead and sent us some interesting case histories, but we didn't have the heart. The class took it pretty hard, they began (I think; nobody ever said anything to me directly) to feel that maybe there was something wrong with the school. But I don't think there's anything wrong with the school, particularly, I've seen better and I've seen worse. It was just a run of bad luck. We had an extraordinary number of parents passing away, for instance. There were I think two heart attacks and two suicides, one drowning, and four killed together in a car accident. One stroke. And we had the usual heavy mortality rate among the grandparents, or maybe it was heavier this year, it seemed so. And finally the tragedy.

The tragedy occurred when Matthew Wein and Tony Mavrogordo were playing over where they're excavating for the new federal office building. There were all these big wooden beams stacked, you know, at the edge of the excavation. There's a court case coming out of that, the parents are claiming that the beams were poorly stacked. I don't know what's true and what's not. It's been a strange year. 8

I forgot to mention Billy Brandt's father, who was knifed fatally when he grappled with a masked intruder in his home. 9

One day, we had a discussion in class. They asked me, where did they go? The trees, the salamander, the tropical fish, Edgar, the poppas and mommas, Matthew and Tony, where did they go? And I said, I don't know, I don't know. And they said, who knows? and I said, nobody knows. And they said, is death that which gives meaning to life? and I said, no, life is that which gives meaning to life. Then they said, but isn't death, considered as a fundamental datum, the means by which the taken-for-granted mundanity of the everyday may be transcended in the direction of— 10

I said, yes, maybe. 11

They said, we don't like it. 12

I said, that's sound. 13

They said, it's a bloody shame! 14

I said, it is. 15

They said, will you make love now with Helen (our teaching assistant) so that we can see how it is done? We know you like Helen. 16

I do like Helen but I said that I would not. 17

We've heard so much about it, they said, but we've never seen it. 18

I said I would be fired and that it was never, or almost never, done as a demonstration. Helen looked out of the window. 19

They said, please, please make love with Helen, we require an assertion of value, we are frightened. 20

21   I said that they shouldn't be frightened (although I am often frightened) and that there was value everywhere. Helen came and embraced me. I kissed her a few times on the brow. We held each other. The children were excited. Then there was a knock on the door, I opened the door, and the new gerbil walked in. The children cheered wildly.

Glossary of Rhetorical Terms

▶ ──────────────────

All the terms in this glossary appear in one form or another in this book. The definitions provided are functional, rather than technical. These terms should be sufficiently clear in the context of a reading question, activity, or writing assignment. However, you may find this glossary a handy reference for clarifying and conceptualizing the meaning of a term.

Aim. The effect that writing is intended to have on the reader. Typical aims are to *express* a feeling or opinion, to *persuade* to a point of view or attitude, to *inform* someone of a process, body of knowledge, or point of view, and to *entertain* or *instruct* through literature. Aims are usually attributed by readers to authors of written texts.

Appeal. The writer's attempt to engage the reader's emotional, intellectual, and critical faculties. Traditionally, writers have developed appeals to reason, emotion, and character. The appeal to reason encourages the reader's rational and logical response to a text; the appeal to emotion encourages some kind of felt response from the reader; the appeal to character encourages the reader's belief in the good intentions, intelligence, and honesty of the writer.

Argument. The kind of writing that attempts to persuade an audience or to prove or refute a point of view on an issue. An argument can be inserted into other types of writing, or it can control an entire piece of writing. Argument is one of the traditional *modes* of discourse.

Arrangement. The writer's strategy for ordering the parts of a piece of writing. Arrangement was the second of the five classical parts of rhetoric: invention, arrangement, style, delivery, and memory. See *form*.

Attitude.   The term used to describe the writer's emotional and intellectual perspective on a subject. Attitudes can be neutral, positive, negative, or mixed.

Audience.   The particular readers for whom the writer intended to write a particular piece. Classical rhetoric originally was meant to help orators deliver speeches, and the traditional term for a live group of listeners (*audience*) has now been applied by writing teachers to the readers of written works.

Body.   The term used to describe the middle of an academic essay. The body of an academic essay comes between the introduction and conclusion and usually contains the specific support for the main idea of the essay. See *introduction* and *conclusion.*

Brainstorming.   An invention device through which writers list and associate ideas on a subject as they come to mind. These lists are then organized into plans for writing. This activity can be done alone or in groups. See *invention.*

Classification.   A common pattern of thought in informative, persuasive, and argumentative writing; includes identifying a subject as part of a larger group with shared features. See *contrast, comparison,* and *definition.*

Coherence.   Describes an essay or other piece of writing in which all the parts are clearly related to the whole.

Collaboration.   The process that writers go through as they work together to produce final products. Collaboration usually includes responding to, critiquing, and evaluating another writer's efforts from the perspective of that writer's intended audience. (Collaboration does not mean the writing of parts of another student's essay unless the teacher has explicitly encouraged such a practice. When that practice has been encouraged by a teacher, collaboration can refer to the co-authoring of an essay.)

Comparison.   A common pattern of thought in informative, persuasive, and argumentative writing; includes pointing out ways in which a subject is similar to something else. The two subjects can be compared separately with their similarities noted after each has been discussed, or they can be compared point by point. Comparisons usually include considerations of degrees of similarity and difference. See *contrast, definition,* and *classification.*

Conclusion.   Describes the final section of an academic essay, following the introduction and body. The conclusion usually summarizes the essay's main point and primary evidence and closes with some general statement about the significance of the main point and subject. Conclusions of short essays do not simply repeat what has been said in the essay.

Context.   The general environment in which a piece of writing is produced and presented. The context can include a piece's audience, purpose, function, author, and the occasion for which it was composed.

Contrast.   A common pattern of thought in informative, persuasive, and argumentative writing; based on the assumption that a subject may be more clearly illustrated by pointing out ways in which the subject is unlike another subject. Like comparison, contrast can be carried out by separate discussions of each subject followed by a discussion of how the subjects are different or by point-by-point analysis of contrasting elements. Contrasts, also like comparisons, usually include considerations of degrees of similarity and difference. See *comparison, classification,* and *definition.*

Conversational style.   A style of writing that sounds much like everyday conversation. This style is usually reserved for personal and exploratory essays. It is characterized by the use of the first person (I), by concrete vocabulary and sentences that follow normal word order, by punctuation with dashes and commas, by the use of contractions, and by direct and familiar ways of addressing readers.

Critiquing.   The process of assessing the effective and ineffective qualities of another writer's efforts. Critiquing is more objective and analytical than simple *responding,* which usually includes only the gut reactions of the reader. Critiquing is less complete and formal than *evaluating,* which includes all the reasoning behind a reader's criticisms of a writer's draft.

Definition.   A common pattern of thought in informative, persuasive, and argumentative writing; includes placing a subject into an appropriate class and then differentiating it from other members of that class. Definition helps writers and readers distinguish one subject from all others. In prose, definitions are often extended by illustrations and examples. See *comparison, contrast,* and *classification.*

Description.   A kind of writing that pictures images verbally and arranges them according to spatial, temporal, or associational forms of organization. Traditionally, description is the second of the four modes of discourse: narration, description, argumentation, and exposition. Writers can organize a whole piece as description, or they can use description to develop only one part of a larger essay. See *modes.*

Dialoguing.   An invention device in which two or more writers talk freely about a subject in order to get ideas for a piece of writing. See *invention.*

Diction.   A formal term often used by writing teachers to refer to the word choices of a writer. Diction should be appropriate to meaning and intention. Diction is often contrasted with *vocabulary*, which refers to all the words that are used by a writer, regardless of purpose or appropriateness.

Drafting.   Refers to early, tentative efforts by writers to produce a complete essay. Drafts are written for the writer, fellow writers, and editors. They are expected to elicit responses, critiques, and evaluations that will help the writer achieve his or her intentions. Drafts should also be distinguished from notes, outlines, or responses, which are not first attempts at completed essays.

Editing.   Describes the final stage in the process of producing a piece of writing. Editing usually includes attention to word choice, correct usage, grammatical rules, punctuation, spelling, and mechanics. Editing is carried out after a rough draft has been revised for organization and content.

Evaluating.   One of the three ways that peers in a writing class can react to another student's writing. Evaluating is the judging of the quality of another's writing using standards that are prescribed by the class, defined by the writer, or both. See *responding* and *critiquing*.

Evidence.   The support a writer provides for a thesis in argumentative writing. Evidence for an argumentative thesis must be logically related to the premises of the argument, and it must be objective and factual. See *argument*.

Example.   One of the ways to support the thesis of an essay. An example is one instance of a general pattern or group of ideas or experiences. Examples are not as useful in argumentative academic essays as facts, statistics, or logical reasons are, but they are very useful in personal or informal academic essays.

Exposition.   A kind of writing that aims to inform readers by providing knowledge, by explaining, and by offering examples and illustrations. One of the four traditional modes of discourse: narration, description, exposition, and argument.

Form.   The intended structure of a complete piece of writing or of one of its parts. This structure is composed of an internal set of consistent relationships that guides the reader's response to the writer's text.

Formal style.   A style of writing characterized by technical or appropriately professional diction, by an avoidance of conversational markers (dashes, exclamation points, familiar diction, slang, contractions, and the like), and by periodic and balanced sentences.

Formal style is usually intended for presentation in some formal situation. See *informal style.*

Free-writing.   An invention device by which a writer writes without constraints of any kind for a prescribed amount of time. See *invention.*

Function.   What a piece of writing is intended to do once it is finished. Writings can function as legal documents, directions, personal statements, formal analyses, contracts, etc.

Illustration.   One of the ways to support the thesis of an essay. Illustrations are usually step-by-step descriptions of the processes by which ideas, experiences, projects, or analyses have been carried out.

Informal style.   A writing style characterized by a mixture of conversational and formal elements and by moderation in the choice of diction, sentence structure, and formal and conversational punctuation. This style is usually most appropriate for academic essays. See *conversational style* and *formal style.*

Introduction.   Describes the opening paragraphs of an academic essay. Academic introductions usually state the writer's thesis, suggest the form of the essay that will follow, and give some indication of the significance of the writer's topic and thesis. Occasionally, introductions include devices, such as anecdotes or rhetorical questions, for gaining the reader's attention. Introductions serve the function of orienting readers to the writer's subject and purpose in as pleasant and efficient a way as possible. See *body* and *conclusion.*

Invention.   The process of discovering ideas and methods for developing a piece of writing. Some processes of invention are open and flexible: free-writing, brainstorming, and dialoguing, for example. Other processes of invention are more systematic and mechanical: outlining, logical planning, and using authorities, for example. See *arrangement* and *style.*

Literary discourse.   One of the four major types of discourse: expressive, informative, persuasive, and literary. Literary discourse involves readers in an aesthetically pleasing verbal event in order to provide pleasure and instruction. It is often narrated in language that calls attention to itself. See *aim.*

Logic.   The use of rational demonstration to persuade an audience of the truth of a thesis; usually applied in informative and argumentative writing. See *argument.*

Modes of discourse.   Traditionally, divided into four general categories: *narration, description, exposition,* and *argument.* The modes are kinds of writing used to accomplish the different aims of discourse. See *aim, argument, description, exposition,* and *narration.*

Narration.   A kind of writing that tells a story or relates an event. Usually organized by spatial or temporal forms, or by the mental associations of a narrator or story-teller. Narration generally tells what happened, when it happened, and how it happened. Traditionally, narration is the first of the four modes of discourse: narration, description, exposition, and argument. See *argument, description,* and *exposition.*

Outlining.   A formal method of planning an essay in which main points and subpoints are numbered and indented. Outlines work best when they are constructed after the writer has had responses to a rough draft and before a final draft is written.

Paragraph.   An academic unit of prose including a central idea, either implied or explicit, with several supporting sentences. In an academic essay, paragraphs are set off from one another by spacing and indention. Academic paragraphs are often organized through the use of patterns of discourse (classification, comparison, contrast, and definition), which help readers connect main ideas and supporting sentences. Paragraphs in other media, particularly in newspapers, novels, or technical prose, for example, are often different from those in academic essays. See *classification, comparison, contrast, definition, supporting sentences,* and *topic sentence.*

Patterns of exposition.   Patterns of thought that are often used to organize paragraphs and whole essays, particularly in academic prose. The most common patterns are *classification, comparison, contrast,* and *definition.*

Persuasive discourse.   One of the four major kinds of discourse: expressive, informative, persuasive, and literary. Persuasive discourse focuses on the receiver of the message, or audience. Usually, it attempts to elicit a specific action or change of attitude in the reader. Persuasive style often emphasizes emotional, logical, and ethical appeals through connotative word and sentence choices. See *attitude.*

Point of view.   The stance or perspective that a writer takes on a subject. Also used technically to designate whether a writer uses the first person (I, we), second person (you), or third person (he, she, it, they) to write an essay. Points of view can be primarily subjective and personal or objective and impersonal, or a combination of the two.

Prewriting.   The activity of a writer's mind before writing, as he or she develops ideas, experiences, and plans for writing a specific piece.

Prewriting is that state of producing writing in which the writer defines himself or herself and his or her subject. Some prewriting strategies are open and flexible, and others are set and mechanical. See *invention*.

Process.   Current writing theory argues that writing is a process that includes a set of complex conventions and is characterized by stages that occur in nonlinear sequence: prewriting, writing, revising, and editing.

Purpose.   Describes the writer's ability to direct his or her writing to a clear set of goals; answers the question "Why was this writing done?" Usually, the answer comes from a variety of contextual considerations: For whom was this piece written? Why was it written for such an audience? What context motivated its writing? What does the piece hope to accomplish?

Responding.   One of the three ways that peers in a writing class can react to a student's writing. Responding includes the reader's initial reaction to another's writing, without the intervention of analysis or objective evaluation. Responses are usually influenced more than critiquing or evaluation is by personal background and emotions. See *critiquing* and *evaluating*.

Revising.   The act of reshaping structure and changing language to adapt to changes of intention during the process of producing a piece of writing. Revising is usually carried out after a rough draft has been written. Experienced writers often revise as they write, as well. Revising occurs in response to the reactions of readers or editors or because of rereading by the writer.

Rhetoric.   Traditionally, rhetoric means the art of discovering the available means of persuasion in a given situation. Rhetoric has been broadened to include the discovery and use of language forms that will create desired effects on audiences, in all types of writing. In popular culture, rhetoric is often a negative term, signifying the manipulative and deceptive language of advertisers, popular orators, politicians, and salesmen.

Rhetorical questions.   Questions asked by writers in order to get their readers to consider the implications of a subject, issue, or claim. Sometimes rhetorical questions are not explicitly answered by the writing itself, but are left for readers to answer on their own. Rhetorical questions are also used to emphasize a key issue, argument, or implication.

Statistics.   A form of evidence in which numerical data are used to establish the degree of truth of a proposition. This form is particularly appropriate for informative and argumentative writing on social issues. Statistics usually organize and interpret the meaning of the results from a population sample.

Style.   Traditionally, the third of the major divisions of rhetoric: invention, arrangement, and style. Style can mean (1) the ornaments that can be added to language to gain a particular response from readers, or (2) a writer's particular way of putting words together on paper. The key to the concept of style is the idea that a writer can create an effective style by choosing those words and sentence structures that are appropriate to intention, subject, audience, and purpose.

Support.   The means a writer uses to develop ideas: reasons, examples, illustrations, evidence, logic, demonstrations, statistics, facts, personal experiences, and the like.

Supporting sentences.   Those sentences that provide support for the topic sentence or main idea of a paragraph in an academic essay. See *paragraph* and *topic sentence.*

Theme.   A value or idea that runs through many works or a single work, by one or more writers.

Thesis.   The main or controlling idea of an argumentative or informative piece of writing. A thesis is an idea or proposition that a writer indicates his or her writing will attempt to prove, explain, illustrate, or demonstrate.

Tone.   Reflects the relationship assumed between the writer and his or her audience in any piece of writing. Tones are best described by analogy to degrees of acquaintance: a *familiar* tone is friendly, casual, and intimate, as if intended for a close friend; a *formal* tone is precise, objective, and distant, as if intended for a stranger; a *moderate* tone is concrete, simple, unadorned, but precise and objective, as if intended for an interested acquaintance.

Topic sentence.   The sentence in a paragraph that includes its controlling idea. Some paragraphs do not contain topic sentences; the controlling idea is implied rather than explicitly stated. Topic sentences can appear in any position within a paragraph, but are most often at the beginning of paragraphs in academic essays. See also *supporting sentences* and *paragraph.*

Voice.   Used to describe the impression a particular writer's style makes on readers. Writers may sound tough, or sweet, or stuffy, for example (see Walker Gibson's *Tough, Sweet, and Stuffy*, Bloomington, Indiana: Indiana University Press, 1966), because of the particular language choices that they make. Some writers argue that voices are developed from within rather than learned by imitation. This book assumes that readers can describe and analyze a writer's voice by identifying the language choices he or she has made.

Keeping a Journal

▶ ────────────────

A journal serves two purposes in a writing course. It provides a place where you can respond in a personal way to your surroundings, to course readings and discussions, and to themes and ideas important to you as an individual. It also provides a place where you can respond to the study questions and activities that appear at the end of each reading selection, either personally or analytically, and where you can write down your own reading queries and comments as you read. In general, keeping a journal will help you write by serving the following specific functions:

1. It provides a forum for repeated, informal writing that will not have to undergo outside evaluation.
2. It helps overcome writer's block by establishing the habit of writing.
3. It provides useful material for more formal writing.
4. It creates the opportunity to learn from experimentation.
5. It provides the occasion for opinionated and unanalytical responses to themes and issues that are brought up in reading and discussion.
6. It allows for practicing those writing skills that need refining or improving.
7. It acts as a specific record of personal responses that can be built into supportable interpretations.

Many of the learning activities that appear after each reading selection in this book provide good material for journals. These activities encourage students to respond to readings in creative ways, keeping the theme of the section in mind. Journals can also help students develop their own responses to a section's theme as they respond to readings, with one question or comment leading to another, resulting in a coherent, overall response. When students keep journals, they take advantage of writing as a means of directing personal inquiry. This advantage then ties in later with the students' use of writing to communicate the results of their personal inquiries. Personal response grows gradually into public communication.

Journal Keeping as Personal Expression

The following ideas for journal entries will help students develop writing as a medium of personal expression. They are adapted from my earlier text, *From Experience to Expression* (1981). These suggestions are meant to supplement the ones in the learning activities following the reading selections.

1. Put your responses to course readings in your journal. Begin by recording your immediate reactions. Once in a while go back and write a few paragraphs that pull together those reactions and form more unified impressions.

2. Be sure to try at least a few observation exercises. Imagine that you are a professional writer looking for material. Take notes on what you see; include concrete details and observe from several different perspectives.

3. Note details that you might ordinarily ignore. Go into a crowded department store and listen as well as look. Do you hear any peculiar or repetitive sounds that you hadn't noticed before? If you live in an apartment, a house, or a dormitory that overlooks a fairly busy street, look out the window for ten minutes. What do you see now for the first time? Go into a supermarket or corner store and record the smells.

4. As you go through daily experiences, keep your senses moving from the general to the specific. If you see a large tree, go on to look closely at its leaves, to smell its fragrance, to touch its bark. If you drive by a large billboard every day, read what is on it. If you ride a bicycle or a motorcycle, consciously evaluate what you feel as you ride—the bumps, the wind, the road beneath you.

5. Include some personal-feeling entries. Find words that you think accurately convey your feelings. Don't just say that something made you feel gloomy; instead, show how it feels inside to be gloomy.

6. To test whether your reactions to certain objects or people are caused by some prejudice in you or by the object or person, write an objective description of something or someone you dislike—that annoying person who sits next to you in history class, for example. Have another student read your description and tell you whether it is accurate.

7. Occasionally change your perspective on a common experience. If you're close enough, try walking to class instead of driving or riding. If you usually walk up a particular hill, try walking down it. Look up at your bedroom or dormitory window rather than down

from it. Record any significant discoveries produced by these changes in perspective.

8. Write a long journal entry in the style of your favorite political, society, or sports columnist. Or write a series of fictional "Dear Abby" columns, letters and all.

9. Record your observations of current events—elections, local issues, public meetings. Include entries written from different perspectives, in varying styles.

10. Make notes of language tidbits that you find interesting or instructive: a particularly apt advertising slogan, a clever piece of sarcasm you overheard at a party, a short descriptive phrase, an excerpt from a popular song. Occasionally you might explain why you like the selection.

11. Write some letters that you'll never send: a note introducing yourself to a person you saw only briefly, an ironic note to a store clerk or college official who treated you rudely, a letter of complaint to a public official about some bothersome rule or policy.

12. You may discover after a while that a theme keeps recurring in your journal. Maybe you constantly refer to particular kinds of people. Perhaps you enjoy describing busy department stores more than anything else. Or maybe you have come to feel that you are treated as a second-class citizen because you are a student. Make at least one entry, no matter how small, on that special subject every day. Later boil all these entries down into a short essay.

13. Every six or seven days, go back over what you have written and write approximately one page that pulls together those journal entries. These long entries should help you unify your experience as well as give you some idea of what to look for and what to emphasize as you continue to write in your journal.

Journal Keeping as Response to Reading

The following ideas for journal entries will help students develop writing as a means of turning responses to readings into materials and ideas for essays. These entries are also meant to supplement the ones suggested in the learning activities following the reading selections.

1. Write specific accounts of emotions you felt were called up by particular sections of a reading. Close your entry by telling why you experienced each emotion.

2. Write a series of brief, negative comments in response to parts of readings that you find particularly offensive. Shoot from the hip. Close by telling some of the objective reasons behind each of your negative responses.

3. Describe a past experience you've had that you feel is similar to one used in a reading. Close by telling how that experience affected you later in life and comparing your later response to your experience to the professional writer's response to his or her experience.

4. Write an entry in which you explain to a classmate why he or she is wrong about a particular part of a particular reading. Do not worry about polish or correctness, simply tell honestly how you feel. Then exchange your entry with one written by that classmate. This sequence could go back and forth for as long as you and your partner think it's worth it.

5. Take a comment by another student in a class discussion and use it as the basis of a personal response in your journal. Be sure to cite the comment as exactly as you can, give your response to it in as much detail as possible, and close your entry by saying something about what would be the commenter's response to your entry.

6. Mark off a particularly interesting part of a reading and rewrite it in your own words. Be sure that you think about the passage's meaning *before* you rewrite it. Compare the two versions when you are finished, or read both your rewrite and the original aloud to the rest of the class.

7. Write a series of questions that you think captures the line of reasoning in a particular reading. Show your list to another student, get his or her reaction to it, then explain how your list of questions follows the reasoning in the reading.

8. Write a hypothetical conversation between the author of one of the readings and yourself. Define the role each of you will play before you begin. Will you be opposed, sarcastic, and satirical or agreeable, supportive, and straightforward? What kind of role will the author of the reading play? What will be the point of your conversation?

9. Find a reading that makes its central point in its final paragraph. Write a paragraph to replace the original last paragraph. How does your paragraph change the meaning of the original essay? Or does your version of the last paragraph simply change the wording, but not the meaning?

10. Describe the character of an author of a reading. Close by telling why you have that impression of the author.

11. Review the personal responses to a particular reading you included in your journal; write a formal paper using these entries for support and evidence.

12. Outline a reading after you have finished reading and discussing it.
13. Write a deliberate misinterpretation of a particular reading. Close by explaining why this response is a misinterpretation.
14. Free-write a reaction to the theme question of one of the sections. Then pick out a reading that you think is relevant to your reaction. Summarize that reading, and tell how it either reinforces or undermines your initial reaction to the theme question.
15. Write a letter to a friend explaining how a particular reading in this book has changed your way of thinking on a theme. Before you begin, jot down some information about the person to whom you will be writing. Consider this information as you write the letter.

*A*cknowledgments

▶ ——————————————

937

of Writings'' by Susan Griffin. Copyright © 1982 by Susan Griffin. Reprinted by permission of Harper & Row, Publishers, Inc., and the Women's Press, Ltd.

HALLMARK CARDS Lines © Hallmark Cards, Inc. Reprinted by permission.

PATRICIA HAMPL ''Teresa'' from *A Romantic Education* reprinted by permission of Rhoda Weyr Agency.

BARBARA GRIZUTTI HARRISON ''est: The Invasion of the Mind-Stealers.'' Excerpts from *Off Center* by Barbara Grizutti Harrison. Copyright © 1980 by Barbara Grizutti Harrison. Reprinted by permission of Doubleday & Company, Inc.

JULES HENRY ''Golden Rule Days: American Schoolrooms'' from *Culture Against Man*, by Jules Henry. Copyright © 1963 by Random House, Inc. Reprinted by permission of the publisher.

LANGSTON HUGHES Selection from ''Simply Heavenly'' reprinted by permission of Indiana University Press.

JANE JACOBS ''Modern City Planning: The Victory over Vitality'' from *The Death and Life of Great American Cities*, by Jane Jacobs. Copyright © 1961 by Jane Jacobs. Reprinted by permission of Random House, Inc.

ERICA JONG Reprinted by permission of The Sterling Lord Agency, Inc. Copyright © 1980 Erica Jong.

PAULINE KAEL Reprinted by permission. © 1985 by Pauline Kael. Originally in *The New Yorker.*

ROGER KAHN Complete text of ''The Hard Hat Who Sued Baseball'' from *The Boys of Summer* by Roger Kahn. Copyright © 1971, 1972 by Roger Kahn. Reprinted by permission of Harper & Row, Publishers, Inc.

ALFRED KAZIN Excerpt from ''From the Subway to the Synagogue'' in *A Walker in the City*, copyright 1951, 1979 by Alfred Kazin. Reprinted by permission of Harcourt Brace Jovanovich, Inc.

ETHERIDGE KNIGHT Poem from *Poems from Prison* reprinted by permission of Broadside Press.

ARTHUR KOESTLER ''Reflections on the Year 15 p.H.'' Copyright © 1960 by The New York Times Company. Reprinted by permission.

JONATHAN KOZOL ''Teaching in an Inner-City School'' from *Death at an Early Age* by Jonathan Kozol. Copyright © 1967 by Jonathan Kozol. Reprinted by arrangement with New American Library, New York, New York.

JOSEPH WOOD KRUTCH ''The New Immorality.'' Copyright © 1960 *Saturday Review* magazine. Reprinted by permission.

LEWIS H. LAPHAM ''Edward Kennedy and the Romance of Death.'' Copyright © 1979 by *Harper's* Magazine. All rights reserved. Reprinted from the December, 1979 issue by special permission.

ROBERT J. LIFTON ''Beyond Atrocity.'' Copyright © 1971 *Saturday Review* magazine. Reprinted by permission.

HAKI MADHUBUTI Poem reprinted by permission of Broadside Press.

N. SCOTT MOMADAY Selection from ''The Night Chanter'' from *House Made of Dawn* by N. Scott Momaday. Copyright © 1966, 1967, 1968 by N. Scott Momaday. Reprinted by permission of Harper & Row, Publishers, Inc.

HONOR MOORE "My Grandmother Who Painted" reprinted by permission of Julian Bach Literary Agency, Inc. Copyright © 1980 by Honor Moore.

JAN MORRIS "Washington, D.C.: The Morning After" from *Destinations: Essays from Rolling Stone* by Jan Morris. Copyright © 1980 by Rolling Stone Press and Jan Morris. Reprinted by permission of Oxford University Press, Inc.

ALLEEN PACE NILSEN "Sexism in English: A Feminist View" is reprinted by permission of the publisher from *Female Studies VI, Closer to the Ground: Women's Classes, Criticism, Programs—1972*, edited by Nancy Hoffman, Cynthia Secor, Adrian Tinsley. Old Westbury, N.Y.: The Feminist Press, 1972.

RUSSELL B. NYE Excerpts from *The Autobiography and Other Writings*, Benjamin Franklin, Russell B. Nye, Ed., reprinted by permission of Houghton Mifflin Company.

GEORGE ORWELL From *Shooting an Elephant and Other Essays* by George Orwell, copyright 1950 by Sonia Brownell Orwell, renewed 1978 by Sonia Pitt-Rivers. Reprinted by permission of Harcourt Brace Jovanovich, Inc., the Estate of the late Sonia Brownell Orwell, and Martin Secker & Warburg Ltd.

WILLIAM OUCHI "Japanese and American Workers: Two Casts of Mind" from *Theory Z*, © 1981, Addison-Wesley, Reading, MA. 6 pages. Reprinted by permission.

DOROTHY PARKER "Arrangement in Black and White" from *The Portable Dorothy Parker*, by Dorothy Parker. Copyright 1933 by Dorothy Parker, renewed © 1955 by Dorothy Parker. Reprinted by permission of Viking Penguin, Inc.

NOEL PERRIN "Country Codes" from *Second Person Rural* by Noel Perrin. Copyright © 1980 by Noel Perrin. Reprinted by permission of David R. Godine, Publisher, Boston.

GERARD PIEL "The Computer as Sorcerer's Apprentice" from *Values in American Culture*, Thomas Eliot Berry, Ed., reprinted by permission of the Author.

MARGE PIERCY "Barbie Doll." Copyright © 1969, 1971, 1973 by Marge Piercy. Reprinted from *Circles on the Water*, by Marge Piercy, by permission of Alfred A. Knopf, Inc.

ISHMAEL REED Excerpt from *19 Necromancers from Now* by Ishmael Reed. Copyright © 1970 by Ishmael Reed. Reprinted by permission of Doubleday & Co., Inc.

RICHARD RHODES "Packaged Sentiment" reprinted by permission of the author.

ADRIENNE RICH "Conditions for Work: The Common World of Women" from *On Lies, Secrets, and Silence, Selected Prose 1966–1978*, by Adrienne Rich, by permission of W. W. Norton & Company, Inc. Copyright © 1979 by W. W. Norton & Company, Inc.

RICHARD RODRIQUEZ "Aria: A Memoir of a Bilingual Childhood," by Richard Rodriguez. Copyright © 1980 by Richard Rodriguez. First published in *The American Scholar*. Reprinted by permission.

SONIA SANCHEZ "We a Baddddd People" reprinted by permission of Broadside Press.

MAY SARTON Selection is reprinted from *Recovering, A Journal*, by May Sarton, by permission of W. W. Norton & Company, Inc. Copyright © 1980 by May Sarton.

ARTHUR SCHLESINGER, JR. "Politics and the American Language" reprinted from *Today's Education* by permission of NEA Communications.

RICHARD SELZER "The Surgeon as Priest." Copyright © 1974, 1975, 1976 by Richard Selzer. Reprinted by permission of Simon & Schuster, Inc.

IRWIN SHAW "The Eighty-Yard Run" excerpted from the book *Short Stories: Five Decades by Irwin Shaw*. Copyright © 1937, 1938, 1939, 1940, 1941, 1942, 1943, 1944, 1945, 1946, 1947, 1949, 1950, 1952, 1953, 1954, 1955, 1956, 1957, 1958, 1961, 1963, 1964, 1967, 1968, 1969, 1971, 1973, 1977, 1978 by Irwin Shaw. Reprinted by permission of Delacorte Press.

GAIL SHEEHY Adapted from *Passages: Predictable Crises of Adult Life* by Gail Sheehy. Copyright © 1974, 1976 by Gail Sheehy. Reprinted by permission of the publisher, E. P. Dutton, a division of New American Library.

JOHN SKOW "Games That Play People." Copyright 1982 Time, Inc. All rights reserved. Reprinted by permission from *Time*.

RED SMITH "On Playing in Ivan's Yard." Copyright © 1980 by Walter W. Smith. Reprinted from *The Red Smith Reader*, edited by Dave Anderson, by permission of Random House, Inc.

GENEVA SMITHERMAN "Where It's At" reprinted from *Talkin and Testifyin* by Geneva Smitherman by permission of the Wayne State University Press. Copyright © 1977 by Geneva Smitherman.

HARVEY SWADOS "Work and the Professions" reprinted by permission of Mrs. Harvey Swados.

SYMPHONY PRESS, INC. "How To Get The Love You Never Thought You Could" reprinted by permission of Symphony Press, Inc.

STUDS TERKEL "Stephen Cruz" from *American Dreams: Lost and Found*, by Studs Terkel. Copyright © 1980 by Studs Terkel. Reprinted by permission of Pantheon Books, a division of Random House, Inc.

LEWIS THOMAS "On Societies as Organisms" from *The Lives of a Cell, Notes of a Biology Watcher*, by Lewis Thomas. Copyright © 1971 by The Massachusetts Medical Society. Originally published in *The New England Journal of Medicine*. Reprinted by permission of Viking Penguin, Inc.

HUNTER S. THOMPSON "Hoodlum Circus, Statutory Rape of Bass Lake" from *Hell's Angels*, by Hunter S. Thompson. Copyright © 1966, 1977 by Hunter S. Thompson. Reprinted by permission of Ballantine Books, a division of Random House, Inc.

JAMES THURBER "University Days" copyright © 1961 James Thurber from *My Life and Hard Times*, published by Harper & Row. Reprinted by permission.

MARK TWAIN "Letter from the Recording Angel." Copyright © 1973 The Mark Twain Company, The Regents of the University of California.

MARGARET WALKER "On Being Female, Black, and Free" by Margaret Walker is reprinted from *The Writer on Her Work*, edited by Janet Sternburg, by permission of W. W. Norton & Company, Inc. Copyright © 1980 by Janet Sternburg.

ROBERT PENN WARREN   "The Patented Gate and the Mean Hamburger." Copyright 1947, 1975 by Robert Penn Warren. Reprinted from his volume *A Circus in the Attic and Other Stories* by permission of Harcourt Brace Jovanovich, Inc.

ROBERT WARSHOW   "The Westerner" from *The Immediate Experience* reprinted by permission of Paul Warshow.

SIMONE WEIL   Reprinted by permission of The University of Massachusetts Press. Copyright © 1968 by Routledge & Kegan Paul.

EUDORA WELTY   "A Worn Path." Copyright 1941, 1969 by Eudora Welty. Reprinted from her volume *A Curtain of Green and Other Stories* by permission of Harcourt Brace Jovanovich.

WALTER WHITE   "The Atlanta Riot" from *A Man Called White*, by Walter White. Copyright Walter Francis White 1948, copyright renewed © 1975 by H. Lee Lurie, the Executor of the Estate of the Deceased Author, Walter White. Reprinted by permission of Viking Penguin, Inc.

TOM WOLFE   "Porno-Violence" reprinted by permission of International Creative Management. Copyright © 1967 by Tom Wolfe. Originally appeared in *Esquire* magazine.

VIRGINIA WOOLF   "How Should One Read a Book?" from *The Second Common Reader* by Virginia Woolf. Copyright 1932 by Harcourt Brace Jovanovich, Inc.; renewed 1960 by Leonard Woolf. Reprinted by permission of the publisher, the Author's Literary Estate, and The Hogarth Press Ltd.

RICHARD WRIGHT   "The Library Card." Complete text of Chapter 13 from *Black Boy* by Richard Wright copyright 1937, 1942, 1944, 1945 by Richard Wright. Reprinted by permission of Harper & Row, Publishers, Inc.

Author/Title Index

▶ ─────────────────